英汉双解
英语短语用法词典

全新版

王俊生 著

四川辞书出版社

图书在版编目(CIP)数据

英汉双解英语短语用法词典 ：全新版 / 王俊生著
.—成都：四川辞书出版社，2023.5
ISBN 978-7-5579-1223-9

Ⅰ.①英… Ⅱ.①王… Ⅲ.①英语—短语—双解词典
—英、汉 Ⅳ.①H314.3-61

中国国家版本馆 CIP 数据核字(2023)第 053042 号

英汉双解英语短语用法词典(全新版)

YINGHAN SHUANGJIE YINGYU DUANYU YONGFA CIDIAN (QUANXINBAN)

王俊生 著

责任编辑 / 干燕飞
封面设计 / 成都编悦文化传播有限公司
责任印制 / 肖　鹏
出版发行 / 四川辞书出版社
地　　址 / 成都市锦江区金石路 238 号
邮政编码 / 610023
印　　刷 / 成都东江印务有限公司
开　　本 / 880 mm×1230 mm　1/32
版　　次 / 2023 年 5 月第 1 版
印　　次 / 2023 年 5 月第 1 次印刷
印　　张 / 28
书　　号 / ISBN 978-7-5579-1223-9
定　　价 / 59.80 元

· 综合办公室电话：(028)86361821

目　录

Table of Contents

前　言

Preface

英语短语是英语在长期发展过程中约定俗成的固定词组。它们在语义上是个不可分割的统一体，往往难以从字面上判定其释义，了解其用法（如 catch/get it“受责骂，受处罚”、down to earth “现实的，实际的”和 under the weather“身体不适”，等等）。英语短语数量众多，运用十分广泛，尤其在国内外各类、各层次的英语教科书中和英语试题中的出现率都很高。

请看这个句子：In response to the US demands related to the nuclear issue, DPRK said it would rather die than submit to conditions that amounted to slavery. 在这个短短的单句中，就出现了 5 个短语。如果不了解它们，就无法正确理解整个句子的意义。因此，要学好、用好英语，提高听、说、读、写、译各方面的能力，提高英语考试的成绩，就必须学习和正确掌握相当数量的英语短语。正因为如此，在当前我国各个层次的英语教学中，短语的学习和使用一直被作为正常教学和应试辅导教学的重点之一。

这部《英汉双解英语短语用法词典》无论在编写的体例上，还是在结构、内容以及文字风格上都有独特、创新之处。它用英汉两种语言、以新颖的文字内容和实用的形式，从各个角度专门讲解英语短语的用法，能够满足当前国内英语教与学的实际需要。它主要有以下几方面的特色：

◆ **短语条目的选定**　本词典中的短语条目主要从目前在全国高校中广泛使用的十几套英语教材中所出现的短语中选定。这些短语（已囊括了国内初、高中英语统编教材中的全部短语）加上一些能反映时代面貌的新短语，完全能够满足大学专科和本科生、硕士和博士研究生以及社会上其他英语学习、使用者学习和使用的需要。

◆ **短语类型的划分**　本词典的作者根据自己 30 多年来在国内外大学中的英语教学实践与研究经验，参考了国内外语言学、词汇学、语法学、语义学有关的理论和参考文献，在和国内外的语言学专家、学者共同研究和探讨的基础上，把英语短语按结构和用法特征划分为 7 种类型：动词性短语、介词性短语、形容词性短语、副词性短语、名词性短语、连词性短语、句子型短语。

本词典中的每一个短语都标注了整体词性。此外，动词性短语还根据用法标示出及物或不及物性，以及及物性动词短语在使用中的可分性或不可分性，旨在帮助使用者全面了解和掌握短语的用法。

◆**英汉双语解释**　本词典中每一短语、每一义项的释义均采用英汉两种语言，目的在于帮助使用者从英语和汉语两个角度加深对短语意义和用法的理解。本书中的英汉释义无论在词语的选择上，还是在文字风格、表达方式上，都体现了"通俗易懂，易记易用，简明地道，英汉对应"的原则。

◆**例句**　本词典所有短语，及其每个义项均按需要选配一个或多个相应例句。本书所选用的例句佐证性强，信息丰富，知识范围宽广，内容涉及政治、经济、历史、文化、科技、教育、体育、卫生、法律、军事、外交、宗教、天文、地理、社会生活，等等，语句新颖、地道，且易懂、易用。此外，本词典还适量选用了时事性例句，不但增强了时代特点和实用性，又适应了大学英语四、六级机考中听力部分时事新闻内容的训练需要。

◆**用法说明**　本词典除了选用不同形式、佐证性强的例句来说明每一短语和义项的用法之外，在短语的义项前或后还提供了用法说明，从不同角度说明某一短语或某一义项的用法。为求简明易懂，用法说明主要使用中文，说明文字力求简单明了。

在本词典编写前和编写过程中，笔者一直得到美国杨伯翰大学语言学 Mark James 教授，加拿大西蒙弗雷泽大学语言学 James Foley 教授，以及广东金融学院英国、美国及新西兰籍教师的指导和帮助。Mark James 教授还审阅了全部书稿，并做了很多修改，提出了很多宝贵的意见和建议，这也保证了本书的权威性和质量的可靠性。

笔者相信，这部词典在面世后能很快成为广大英语学习者和工作者（尤其是英语教师）案头上最实用、最好用、最常用的英语工具书之一。

由于笔者的水平有限，书中错漏之处在所难免，特别是用法说明部分的编撰难度较大，虽经最大努力，仍难至尽善尽美，恳请读者尤其是国内的同行们不吝赐教、指正。

编者

Foreword

The art of dictionary compilation has reached new heights in the last two decades with the advent of electronic desktop publishing, corpus linguistics, and a greater appreciation for the central role that vocabulary plays in second language learning. With greater abilities and greater insights, many individuals and institutions have rushed forward to offer the latest in analyses of the lexicon of English, as well as other languages. Where once dictionaries were a crutch and a barrier to effective second language learning, this newest generation of dictionaries have included a variety of linguistically accurate and pedagogically sound characteristics that serve to elucidate the language and empower the learner.

One of the most common characteristics has been a greater emphasis on collocations and phrases. Recent research in the field of lexicography, corpus linguistics, and second language acquisition has pointed out the importance of knowing when and how words go together. Thus, most modern learner dictionaries include information on usage, collocation, idiomatic combinations, grammatical and stylistic constraints.

What most sets this particular effort apart from the mainstream dictionaries with which we are all familiar (from the great ESL/EFL publishing houses like Oxford, Cambridge, Collins COBUILD, etc) is the fact that this dictionary, *A Practical English-Chinese Dictionary of Phrasal Usage*, comprehensive though it may be, is focused on a specific audience and market. It does not try to be everybody's dictionary. It is the author's goal to be the best phrasal dictionary for Chinese learners of English and does so through a unique cluster of characteristics.

A case in point: the phrases included in this volume were chosen, not because of their general frequency in the English language of native speakers, but by their frequency and usefulness in the texts and materials used to teach in China today. Although one may debate the inclusion or exclusion of some of the entries (as with all phrasal dictionaries), one can not doubt the great assistance this volume will be for Chinese learners. In addition to exhaustive bilingual definitions and discussions of each phrase's meanings and functions, sample sentences from real world, up-to-date sources provide authentic examples of usage in terms of current or recent issues and events.

It has been my pleasure over the years to be associated with Professor Wang Junsheng and to witness the long years of preparation that have led him to this remarkable contribution to our profession. That such a grand project could be carried off by one individual is a testimony to a brand of professional commitment and singularity of purpose which, reminiscent of A. S. Hornby (the father of ESL dictionaries), is rarely seen these days. While this dictionary is not Professor Wang's first attempt (He is the author of numerous titles, including several other dictionaries.), he will certainly be best remembered for this effort.

To all who may be lucky enough to find this dictionary in your hands, I wish you many hours of fruitful use in your language learning journey.

Mark O. James, PhD.
Dean of the Division of Languages and Linguistics
Brigham Young University—Hawaii, USA

序(译文)

随着桌面电子出版系统和语料库语言学的出现,以及人们对词汇在第二语言学习中核心作用的充分认识,词典编纂在过去二十年里已经进入了一个崭新的繁荣时期。许多学者及机构以卓越的才智和见解纷纷对英语及其他语言的词汇进行了“最前卫的”分析。对有效的第二语言学习,词典既是帮助,同时也是障碍。最新一代的词典兼具精确的语言学特征和合理的教学法特征,这有助于阐释语言,也有助于学习者获得语言能力。

词典编纂最为常见的特点之一是重视短语和搭配。近年来词典编纂学、语料库语言学及第二语言习得方面的研究也指出:懂得何时及如何搭配词汇是重要的。因此,现代学习词典大部分包含用法、搭配、成语组合、语法和文体方面的信息。

《英汉双解英语短语用法词典》与我们所熟悉的主流词典(如著名的牛津大学出版社、剑桥大学出版社、柯林斯出版公司等英语二语或英语外语出版社出版的词典)不同。尽管颇具综合性,但本词典并不追求满足所有人的需要,而是针对特定的读者群和市场。作者的目标是,通过一系列独具匠心的特点,为中国的英语学习者编写一部最好的短语词典。

例如,本词典所选短语并非从它们在英语本族语中的出现率考虑,而是从它们在当前中国英语教学材料及课文中的出现率和实用性考虑的。或许有人会对某些条目的取舍另有高见(对所有短语词典都是如此),但是没人能够质疑本词典对中国英语学习者的巨大帮助。除了详尽的双语释义和对每条短语意义及功能的探讨外,取自于现实世界的例句和最新的资料来源也给我们提供了可靠的用法范例。

我很高兴与王俊生教授合作多年,见证了他长年累月的积累,并最终为我们共同所从事的教学事业做出了这一卓越的贡献。独自一人完成如此宏大的工程,这是职业奉献的明证;他对目标的执着实为罕见,这不禁使人想起了英语二语(ESL)词典之父 A. S. 霍恩比(A. S. Hornby)。本词典并非王教授的首作,他是很多著作,包括其他几部辞书的编写者。毫无疑问,人们不会忘记他为此所付出的努力。

祝所有有幸使用本词典的朋友们,在英语学习的征途上硕果累累!

马克・O・詹姆斯 博士

美国杨伯翰大学(夏威夷)语言与语言学系 主任

体例说明

Guide to the Use of the Dictionary

一、条目 (Entries)

1. 本词典中短语条目的排列规则如下：

1)所有条目均按照英语 26 个字母的顺序排列。例如：

have a word with 排在 **have faith in** 之前。

2) 所有条目均按条目中的第一个单词的字母排列顺序，其后的单词依此排序。例如：

a trifle 排在 **abandon to** 之前。

be used to 排在 **bear away** 之前。

3)条目中的斜线后和圆括号中的词语不作为条目的一部分参加顺序排列。例如：

as/so far as ... 排在 **as follows** 之前

call (someone) names 排在 **call off** 之前

2. 两个或多个条目的释义相同或相近、且结构相似者，酌情予以合并立目，中间隔以斜线。例如：

carry about/along/around (均在 C 部中立目)

3. 条目同形，但词性、结构或意义不相同者，分别立目，并在右上角上标示序码。例如：

subject to[1] vt.

subject to[2] *adj.*

4. 参见条目与其他条目按同样顺序排列。

5. 条目均以黑正体出现。

二、词性 (Part-of-Speech Labels)

1. 词性用英语词性缩略语表示。整体词性，即某一类型短语整体体现出的词性，置于各类型短语条目之后。例如：

add up to *vt.*

2. 同一条目整体词性不同且释义也不同者，以黑体罗马数字分列标示。例如：

all over Ⅰ *adv.*

Ⅱ *prep.*

Ⅲ *adj.*

3. 同一条目的整体词性不同，但释义、结构基本相同者，则不以黑体罗马数字分列标示，而并列于条目之后，中间隔以“&”。例如：

in earnest *adj.* &*adv.* serious(ly); not joking(ly) 认真的(地)；郑重的(地)

4. 在动词短语中，同一词性属不同细项者，后者以短中线“—”和词性缩略语标示。例如：

come by *vt.* & *vi.*...

—*vi.*...

—*vt.*...

三、释义、义项、例句与用法说明（Definitions, Senses, Example Sentences & Usage Notes）

1. 释义：

条目中义项的释义用英汉两种文字。英语释义在前，汉语释义在后。

2. 义项：

1)一个条目中义项的多少取决于该条目在日常语言应用中的常用程度。

2)同一条目中多个义项的先后顺序根据这些义项的常用程度安排。每个义项前均标注数字序号。

3. 例句：

1)每一条短语或每个义项均选配一个或多个相应例句，用于体现和佐证该短语或该短语不同义项的不同释义和用法。

2)例句的选配数量根据每一条短语或每个义项中的不同释义和用法形式的需要来决定。

4. 用法说明：

1)较短的用法说明置于被说明的义项之前，放在圆括号内。

2)较长的用法说明则置于整个条目的全部义项之后，以NOTE为起始标志。

四、缩略语和特殊符号（Short Forms & Special Symbols）

1. 缩略语

adj. adjective/phrase adjectival in nature 形容词/形容词性短语

adv. adverb/phrase adverbial in nature 副词/副词性短语

conj. conjunction/phrase conjunctional in nature 连词/连词性短语

etc. et cetera 等等

n. noun/phrase nominal in nature 名词/名词性短语

prep. preposition/phrase prepositional in nature 介词/介词性短语

pron. pronoun 代词

s. phrase as a sentence 句子型短语

v. verb/verb phrase in nature 动词/动词短语

vi. intransitive verb phrase 不能带宾语的不及物性动词短语

vt. transitive verb phrase 能带宾语的及物性动词短语

2. 特殊符号

1)星号(＊)

星号出现于用法说明中所例示的英语错误语句之前。例如：

＊Our new neighbors called at us last week.

2)参见号(⇨)

参见号出现于参见条目中，表示某一条目参见后一条目。

cast light on ⇨ **throw light on**

3)鱼尾号(【　】)

鱼尾号出现于标示及物性动词短语的可分性或不可分性。例如：

call down *vt*.【可分性动词短语】

A a

a bit Ⅰ *adv.* ❶(非正式用语) slightly or a little, to a small extent or degree 有点儿,稍微: I can lend you fifty pounds. That should help *a bit*. 我可以借给你50英镑。那应该对你有点儿帮助。Your article is *a bit* too long for our paper. 你的文章对于我们的报纸来说稍微长了一点儿。If the ball had hit the window *a bit* harder, it would have broken it. 如果球击得再稍微重一点儿的话,就会把窗户打破。Shall I lengthen it *a* little *bit*? 我把它稍微拉长一点儿,好吗? ❷(英国英语用法) very 非常: Tom, it's *a bit* cold outside! 汤姆,外面非常冷啊! And she didn't invite him? That was *a bit* mean! 她竟没有邀请他? 那太刻薄了!

Ⅱ *n.* ❶(非正式用语,常与 of 短语连用,后接不可数名词) a small amount (of something); some 一点儿,一些: There is no sugar in the sugar bowl, but you can find *a bit* in the bag. 糖钵里没有糖了,但你可以在袋子里找到一点儿。With *a bit* of luck we should be able to get there in time. 靠着一点儿运气,我们应该能按时到达那儿。❷(主要用于英国英语中) a short time or distance (指时间)片刻,一小会儿;(指距离)一小段: Tom thought for *a bit* before answering. 汤姆想了片刻之后才作答。I'll do it in *a bit*. I'm busy right now. 我一会儿就做它,我现在很忙。

NOTE **1.** 当本短语用作副词性短语时,一般用来修饰动词、形容词、副词或比较级形式,不能直接修饰名词。若修饰名词,须与 of 连用。例如:

> It is not hard for one to do *a bit of* good.
> 一个人做一点儿好事并不难。

2. 当本短语用作副词性短语时,后常接"too+形容词或副词",作程度状语。例如:

> The price of gas today is *a bit too* high.
> 现在的汽油价格有些太高了。

3. 当本短语用作副词性短语时,与 a little 意义和用法相同,并可互换使用。在英国英语中,主要用本短语,在美国英语中则主要用 a little。但是,a bit 和 a little 前加否定词 not 时,两者意义则大不相同。见 not a bit。

4. 当本短语用作名词性短语作主语时,谓语动词要用单数形式。例如:

> *A bit* is enough.
> 一点儿就够了。

5. 本短语前加副词 quite,即 quite a bit,意为"相当多",而不是"非常少",见 quite a bit。

a bit of *adj.* (主要用于英国英语中,非正式用语) a small amount or piece of (something)一点儿,小(少)量的,些微的:I know *a bit of* Russian. 我懂一点儿俄语。There has been *a bit of* trouble in the office. 办公室里出了一点儿小麻烦。I am going to do *a bit of* Christmas shopping. 我要去买一点儿过圣诞节的东西。It's not *a bit of* use complaining. 抱怨一点儿用也没有。

NOTE 1. 本短语修饰不可数名词。若修饰可数名词，则用 a bit of a 的形式。例如：

> Your friend is *a bit of a* coward to me.
> 对我来说，你的朋友有点儿怯懦。

2. 当本短语与所修饰的名词共同作主语时，谓语动词要用单数形式。

3. 本短语前加副词 quite，即 quite a bit of，意为"相当多的"。例如：

> He's got *quite a bit of* money.
> 他有很多钱。

a case in point *n.* a relevant example of the situation or behavior that you are talking about 显明的例子：As we are talking about education, let me tell you of *a case in point*. 鉴于我们正在谈论教育问题，让我给你们讲一个适当的例子吧。Shoppers tend to think that high prices mean high quality. Electrical goods are *a case in point*. 消费者一般认为，价格高就意味着质量高。电器产品就是一个显明的例子。A person of humble origin may become President. A good *case in point* is Abraham Lincoln, the 16th president of the USA. 出身卑微的人也可能成为总统。一个很好的例证就是美国第十六任总统亚伯拉罕·林肯。

NOTE 本短语的复数形式是 cases in point，而不是 * case in points。本短语的构成形式是"名词+介词+名词"。这类名词性短语复数形式的变化，一般都发生在第一个名词上，例如：brother in law (大/小叔子或大/小舅子)，commander in chief (总司令)，head of state (国家元首)，prisoner of war (战俘)，way of life (生活方式)，等等，-s 均不能加在第二个名词上。

a couple of *adj.* ❶(非正式用语) two (things or people of the same type)(用于说明同类的物或人)两个，一对，一双：Take *a couple of* aspirin — you'll soon feel better. 吃两片阿司匹林，你很快就会感到好一些。A couple of police officers were standing at the door. 有两名警官站在门口。❷(主要用于美国英语中，非正式用语)(used when you are not sure of the exact number of things or people you are referring to) a few; several; a small number of 几个，少数的：I'll be back in *a couple of* minutes. 我几分钟就回来。*A couple of* people objected to the proposal, but the vast majority approved of it. 少数人反对这一提议，而大多数人都赞成。

NOTE 1. 在美国口语中，人们常常把本短语中的介词 of 省略。例如：*a couple* hundred dollars, just *a couple* weeks later, *a couple* books 等。但在正式文体中，这被认为是不正确的。

2. 本短语与 a pair of 都表示"两个，一对，一双"之意。本短语单指两个同类的人或物，两者不一定相互匹配；a pair of 则指两个密不可分、相互匹配的物件。例如：

> Is that *a* new *pair of* gloves/shoes/socks?
> 那是一双新手套/鞋子/袜子吗？
> She's got *a pair of* beautiful blue eyes.
> 她有一双漂亮的蓝眼睛。

试比较：

> I found *a couple of* socks in the bedroom but they didn't make *a pair*.
> 我在卧室里找到两只袜子，但不成一对。

A

a few Ⅰ *n.* (emphasizing that there are indeed some) a small number (of people or things)(强调确有一些)几个,少数: The dry weather killed most of Mother's flowers, but *a few* are left. 干旱的天气使妈妈种的花儿大部分枯死,但还有几株幸存了下来。*A few* of these children have already recovered from measles. 这些患麻疹的孩子,有几个已经复康了。"How many potatoes do you want?" "Oh, just *a few*." "您要买多少马铃薯?""噢,只要几个。" There were only *a few* who failed the test. 考试不及格的人只有几个。

Ⅱ *adj.* (emphasizing that there are indeed some, but not many) a small number of (people or things)(强调确有一些,但不多)几个的,少数的: After the party, *a few* couples stayed to help clean up. 聚会结束后,几对夫妇留下来帮助打扫。The patient is responding quite well to the medicine and will be well in *a few* days. 该患者对药物的反应很好,他几天之内就会痊愈。We need to sketch in *a few* more details before presenting the plan. 我们需要补充几个细节后递交计划。

NOTE 1. 当本短语用作名词性短语作主语时,谓语动词用复数形式。

2. 当本短语用作形容词性短语作定语时,只能用来修饰可数名词的复数形式,谓语动词亦用复数形式。这一点正是它与 a little 的主要区别。作为形容词性短语,无论是本短语还是 a little 都不用作表语。

3. 本短语前加副词 quite,即 quite a few,意为"相当多"而不是"非常少"。见 quite a few。

a good deal ⇨ **a great deal**

a good deal of ⇨ **a great deal of**

a good few Ⅰ *n.* a fairly large number 相当多的人(或物),不少的人(或物): *A good few* attended the mourning meeting. 很多人都参加了追悼会。I think *a good few* of the others were like me, a bit confused. 我认为,还有不少人都和我一样有些迷惑不解。Lots of people at the club are under twenty, but there are *a good few* who aren't. 俱乐部的很多成员都是在 20 岁以下,但也有不少是超过 20 岁的。

Ⅱ *adj.* many; a fairly large number of 相当多的,不少的: You'll have to wait *a good few* weeks before you can get the examination results. 你得等上好几个星期才能得到考试的结果。

NOTE 1. 当本短语用作名词性短语作主语时,谓语动词要用复数形式。

2. 本短语与 quite a few 意义和用法相同,但本短语一般用于英国英语中。

a good many Ⅰ *adj.* quite a large number of; a lot of (people or things)相当多的,许许多多的(人或物): *A good many* people go on holiday in August. 很多人在 8 月份度假。We've lived here for *a good many* years. 我们在这里已住了许多年。We received *a good many* offers of support. 我们得到了许许多多的支持。

Ⅱ *n.* (of people or things) a fairly large number; a lot (指人或物)许多: *A good many* are for our proposal. 许多人支持我们的提议。

NOTE 1. 当本短语作为形容词性短语用作定语时,只能修饰复数名词。

2. 当本短语作为名词性短语用作主语时,谓语动词须用复数形式。

3. 本短语可与 of 短语连用,后接复数名词或代词,谓语动词用复数形式。例如:

> *A good many* of the beggars were blind.
> 乞丐中有很多是盲人。

A

There are *a good many* of them.
那样的人很多。

a great deal Ⅰ *n.* a large quantity or degree 大量,许多:*A great deal* has been accomplished, but more remains to be done. 大量工作已经完成,但仍有更多的事情有待去做。China tomorrow will continue to be a major country that loves peace and has *a great deal* to look forward to. 明天的中国,仍会是一个热爱和平和充满希望的大国。They spent *a great deal* of money. 他们花掉了许多钱。

Ⅱ *adv.* to a very great degree or extent; very much 大量地,许多地: Admittedly, the Chinese government has done *a great deal* in the protection of the Tibetan culture. 无可否认,中国政府在保护西藏文化方面做了大量的工作。If you have a good rest, you will look *a great deal* better; you are so tired. 如果你好好地休息一下,你看上去会好很多。你太累了。

NOTE 1. 当本短语用作名词性短语作主语时,谓语动词须用第三人称单数形式(如第一个例句)。

2. 当本短语用作副词性短语时,用来修饰动词、形容词、副词,以及形容词和副词的比较级。

3. 本短语与 a good deal 用法相同,但本短语的语气稍强。试比较:

There is *a good deal* of starch in bread, and *a great deal* in potatoes.
面包里有许多淀粉,而马铃薯里也有大量的淀粉。

a great deal of *adj.* a large quantity or degree of; a lot of (something) 大量的,许多的:China, as the host nation, has done *a great deal of* work for the talks on the North Korean nuclear issue. 作为东道国,中国为朝核问题会谈做了大量的工作。She seems to have *a great deal of* trouble. 她似乎有许多烦恼。

NOTE 1. 本短语只能用来修饰不可数名词。

2. 当"本短语+名词"作主语时,谓语动词用单数形式。例如:

A great deal of money has been spent on the new hospital.
大量的资金已花在了这所新建的医院上。

3. 本短语与 a good deal of 意义和用法相同,但本短语的语气稍强。

a great many Ⅰ *adj.* very many; a very large number of (people or things) 很多的(人或物):For *a great many* men and women, romance can be a most important part of marriage. 对于很多男人和女人来说,浪漫的情调是婚姻非常重要的部分。There are *a great many* reasons why you shouldn't do it. 你不该做那事的理由有很多很多。I have been there *a great many* times. 我曾去过那里很多次。

Ⅱ *n.* (of people or things) a very large number (指人或物)许多:*A great many* were absent from the meeting today. 许多人都缺席了今天的会议。I can't give you the details of it, but I can say there are *a great many* of them. 我不能将其详情讲给你,但我可以说细节很多。

NOTE 1. 当本短语用作形容词性短语作定语时,只能修饰复数名词。

2. 当本短语用作名词性短语作主语时,谓语动词须用复数形式。

3. 本短语可与 of 短语连用,后接复数名词或代词,谓语动词用复数形式。例如:

A great many of the blind people couldn't find work.
许许多多的盲人找不到工作。

A great many of us dream of living abroad.
我们中有很多很多人都梦想生活在国外。

4. 本短语的同义短语是 a good many,但本短语的语气稍强。

a home (away) from home *n.* a place where you feel relaxed and comfortable as if you were in your own home 像自己家一样的地方;使人感到轻松自在的场所:The guests are made to feel that the hotel is *a home from home*. 客人们都感到这家旅馆就像自己的家一样。Many Americans come to work and stay in South Korea; they regard this country as *a home away from home*. 许多美国人来到韩国工作或逗留;他们把这个国家已视为另一个家了。All the guests found this hotel *a home away from home*. 所有在这家宾馆住宿的客人都有宾至如归的感觉。

NOTE a home from home 是英国英语用法,a home away from home 是美国英语用法。

a little Ⅰ *n.* (常与 of 短语连用,后接不可数名词)a small amount 一点儿,一些:I'll give you just *a little*. 我只会给你一点儿。We thought that the paper was all gone, but *a little* was left. 我们以为纸都没有了,但还剩有一点儿。He knows *a little* of everything. 他什么事都知道一点儿。Bring me *a little* of that wine. 给我来一点儿那种酒。

Ⅱ *adj.* a small amount of (something) 一点儿,一些:With *a little* training she could do very well. 经过一些训练,她就会做得很好。*A little* care would have prevented it. 稍微小心一点儿,就不会发生那事了。She also knows *a little* Arabic. 她还懂一点阿拉伯语。Can I give you *a little* advice? 我能给你提点建议吗?

Ⅲ *adv.* ❶slightly; to a small extent or degree; rather 有点儿,有些,稍微:I found it *a little* difficult to work out this maths problem. 我发现要解出这道数学题还有点儿困难。It makes me *a little* frightened when I think of what might happen. 想到可能要发生的事,我有点儿害怕。On Saturday morning I arrived at the stadium *a little* earlier than my friend for the baseball practice. 星期六上午,我比我的朋友稍早到达体育馆练习棒球。The door was opened *a little*. 房门微开着。❷for a short time or distance (指时间)一小会儿;(指距离)一小段:I stopped and waited for him *a little*. 我停下来,等了他一会儿。We went on *a little*, and then stopped again. 我们往前走了一小段路后,又停了下来。

NOTE 1. 当本短语用作名词性短语时,可作主语和宾语。用作主语时,谓语动词用单数形式。

2. 当本短语用作副词性短语时,与 a bit 意义和用法相同。但本短语主要用于美国英语中,a bit 主要用于英国英语中。

3. 当本短语用作副词性短语时,与 a little bit 意义和用法相同,但 a little bit 为非正式用语。例如:

I'm sorry, Mary. I'm *a little bit* late.
对不起,玛丽。我有点儿晚了。

4. 当本短语用作副词性短语,作"有点儿,有些"解时,用于否定句表示肯定意义。例如:

I was not *a little* annoyed.
(=I was really annoyed.)
我十分气恼。

5. 本短语前加副词 quite,即 quite a little,意为"不少,相当多"。例如:

A

Tasks are not finished; *quite a little* is left to do.
任务还没完成,还有相当多的工作要做。

a little bit ⇨ **a little**

a lot Ⅰ *n.* (非正式用语) a large number, amount, or quantity 很多,大量: There is *a lot* for us to see in London. 在伦敦我们有很多要参观的地方。*A lot* of people don't like the idea very much. 许多人不太喜欢这个主意。You know *a lot* about English names. 你知道许多有关英语姓名的情况。This is *a lot*. 这真不少。

Ⅱ *adv.* (非正式用语) ❶very much; to a great or greater extent or degree 很,非常;……得多: There was a man in the photograph who looked *a lot* like Mr William. 照片中有个人很像威廉先生。He seems to like her *a lot*. 他好像很喜欢她。Women take *a lot* longer in the supermarket than men. 女人在超级市场里花的时间比男人长得多。I can run *a lot* faster than you. 我能比你跑得快得多。❷very often or more often than you would expect 经常: We see her in the mornings quite *a lot*, taking the children off to school. 我们经常看到她早上带孩子去上学。

NOTE 1. 当本短语用作名词性短语,在句中作主语、宾语或表语时,后常有动词不定式短语或介词短语作后置定语。

2. 当本短语用作名词性短语在句中作主语时,谓语动词形式用单数还是用复数,取决于与本短语连用的名词或代词。也就是说,当本短语与复数词连用时,谓语动词的形式是复数;与单数词连用时,谓语动词就用单数形式。请比较下面两个句子:

A lot of us were invited at the last minute.
我们中的许多人都是最后才接到邀请的。
A lot of our land is used to grow crops for export.
我们的土地很多被用来种植出口作物。

3. 本短语与副词 lots 用法相同,但 lots 仅用于口语中,例如:

"Feeling a bit better?" "*Lots* better, Doctor."
"感觉好点儿吗?""好多了,大夫。"

a lot of *adj.* a large number, amount, or quantity of (people or things); many; much 大量的,许多: He used to have *a lot of* friends in New York. 他在纽约曾有许多朋友。There are *a lot of* questions that still remain unanswered. 还有许多问题仍然没有得到回答。A young man died after drinking *a lot of* beer while watching a televised World Cup football match. 一青年男子在观看世界杯足球赛电视直播时喝了大量啤酒后死亡。"This doesn't take *a lot of* technology," he said while walking into a pond, where he raises baby eels. "这不需要很多的技术,"他一边说一边走进他养殖鳗鱼苗的池塘。

NOTE 1. 本短语既可用来修饰可数名词,也可修饰不可数名词。当修饰可数的复数名词时,谓语动词用复数形式;修饰不可数名词时,谓语动词用单数形式。试比较:

There are *a lot of* people in the park on Sunday.
星期天,公园里有很多人。
A lot of time was wasted.
大量的时间给浪费掉了。

A

2. 本短语与形容词 many 和 much 意义相同,在肯定句中常可互换使用。但本短语不能用于否定句和疑问句中。因此,在否定句和疑问句中,一般用 many 或 much。例如:

> I haven't much time for sports. **(否定句)**
> 我没有很多时间运动。
> Were there many people at the meeting? **(疑问句)**
> 有很多人到会吗?

3. 本短语与 lots of 意义相同,用法相近。两者都不能用来修饰表示时间和距离长度的名词。例如,我们不能说: * I stayed in England *a lot of* weeks. 而应说: I stayed in Canada for many/quite a few/four weeks.

a number of *adj.* (used for giving a general idea of how many people or things you are referring to) more than a few, but not many; some 一些(人或物): Quite *a number of* paintings have been sold. 有些画已经售出。We have *a number of* websites to promote our products. 我们拥有一些推销自己产品的网站。

NOTE 1. 本短语只能用来修饰复数名词。当"本短语+复数名词"作主语时,谓语动词须用复数形式。

2. 本短语与 the number of 意义和用法均不同。the number of 指的是"……的数目"或"……的总数",与复数名词连用。当"the number of+复数名词"作主语时,谓语动词用单数形式。例如:

> *The number of* college graduates has sharply increased as a result of a large-scale enrollment expansion scheme.
> 大学毕业生人数剧增,是大规模扩招的结果。

a pair of ⇨ a couple of

a pat on the back ⇨ pat someone on the back

a step at a time ⇨ step by step

a trifle *adv.* (正式用语) slightly; somewhat; to some degree 略微,有些: He felt *a trifle* embarrassed by her rude words. 她的粗鲁言语使他感到有些尴尬。The patient is *a trifle* better today than yesterday. 这个病人今天比昨天略好一些。"Let's go," said Mary, *a trifle* cheerily. "咱们走吧。"玛丽略显爽快地说道。This bag is *a trifle* too heavy. 这背包太重了一点儿。

NOTE 1. 当本短语用作副词性短语时,可以用来修饰形容词、副词及比较级形式,所修饰的形容词或副词前还可使用副词 too(见最后一个例句)。另外,本短语还可用来修饰短语。例如:

> His uniform made him look *a trifle* out of place.
> 他穿的制服使他看上去有点不合时宜。

2. 本短语的同义短语是 a bit 和 a little。

abandon to *vt.*【可分性动词短语】❶give up (someone or something) to (someone or something) 把……遗弃给……: She *abandoned* her daughter *to* her ex-husband when she moved to Thailand. 她移居泰国时,将女儿遗弃给了前夫。They had to *abandon* their dogs *to* the storm. 他们不得不把狗都遗弃在暴风雨中。❷(正式用语,与反身代词连用) allow (yourself) to be completely controlled by (a feeling, desire, etc.); feel an emotion so strongly that you do not think about anything else 沉湎于(某种感情、欲望等);放纵: Many laid-off workers managed to find something they could do well instead of *abandoning* themselves *to* despair. 许多下岗职工都找了些力所能及的事情去做，而不是自暴自弃。All of us should not *abandon* ourselves *to* the pursuit of pleasures. 我们所有的人都不应一味追求享乐。At the harvesting time, most of the villagers would *abandon* themselves *to* wining, eating and even singing folk songs after dark. 在收获季节，大多数村民在天黑后都会大吃大喝，甚至还唱起民歌来。

abide by *vt.*【不可分性动词短语】(常用一般时态) ❶follow or act in accordance with (a law, rule, decision, or agreement)遵守(法律、规章、决定或协议)：Foreign-funded enterprises should *abide by* the laws and regulations of China. 外资企业应遵守中国的法律和法规。I don't think it will be hard for Michael to *abide by* these rules. 我认为让迈克尔遵守这些规章并不会太难。All the competitors must *abide by* the judge's decision. 所有参赛者必须遵从裁判员的裁决。Some people are worried whether they will *abide by* the agreement once it has been signed. 有些人担心签署这个协议后，他们能否遵照执行。❷(无被动语态形式) accept (something) without complaint 接受，承担：You must *abide by* the consequences of your decision. 你必须为你所做出的决定承担后果。

NOTE 本短语中的动词 abide 的过去式和过去分词一般用 abided 的形式，而不用 abode。

able to *adj.* (后接原形动词) having a particular physical or mental skill, power, knowledge, time, or other qualities that are needed in order to do something 有能力做某事，能做某事：He doesn't seem *able to* dance without stamping on his partner's feet. 他在跳舞时似乎无法不踩舞伴的脚。I regret not being *able to* help her. 我很遗憾未能帮助她。She's the person best *able to* cope with such a crisis. 她是最能妥善处理此类危机的人。A 103-year-old man is among those *able to* vote in this district. 在这个地区中，能投票的还有一位 103 岁的老人。

NOTE **1.** 本短语通常与系动词 be 连用。be able to 和情态动词 can 均表示“能”，两者一般可以互换使用。例如：

He will come if he *can*. = He will come if he *is able to*.

I *couldn't* understand him. = I *was not able to* understand him.

但是，can 只有一般现在时和一般过去时两种时态，而 be able to 则有更多的时态：

We will *be able to* see the famous singer soon.

She hasn't *been able to* go to school for one week.

I'm sorry for not *being able to* help you in time.

The magician claims to *be able to* cast out devils.

Any of us should/might *be able to* answer them.

Our going depends upon his *being able to* drive.

2. 本短语后不能用被动语态形式，不能说：* The budget shortfall was able to be solved by selling brownies.

3. 本短语的反义短语是 unable to。

abound in/with *vt.*【不可分性动词短语】(正式用语，无被动语态形式，用一般时态) ❶(of something) exist in large quantity; be rich and abundant in (something) 富于：Natural resources abound in our country. 我国自然资源丰富。The pond near my house *abounds in/with* fish. 我家附近的那个池塘里鱼很多。The district *abounds with* mineral deposits. 这地区的矿藏很丰富。❷(of something or someone) be full of; be filled with (something or someone); have plenty of (something)充满,富有:That book *abounds in* printing mistakes. 那本书充满了印刷错误。The world *abounds with* talented people. 这个世界人才济济。The markets *abound with* imported goods. 这些市场里有很多进口商品。The old man *abounds in* wealth. 这位老人很富有。

NOTE abounds in 的主语可以是人,而 abound with 则不可。

about time ⇨ **high time**

above all (**else**) *adv.* ❶ (used for referring to something that is more important than any of the other things you could mention) most important of all 最重要的是:*Above all* else, the government must keep the promises it has made. 最重要的是,政府必须履行其所作出的承诺。And *above all*, remember to inform us of your e-mail address. 最重要的是,不要忘记把你的电子邮件地址告诉我们。Children need many things, but *above all* they need love. 孩子需要的东西很多,但最重要的是爱。❷especially 尤其是:He did very well in all his subjects in the entrance exam, *above all*, in English. 他在入学考试中各科考得都很好,特别是英语。Never waste anything, but *above all* never waste time. 任何东西都不可浪费,尤其不可浪费时间。

NOTE 1. 本短语与 first of all 意义不同,后者常用来表示次序。见 first of all。

2. 本短语用于表示强调,在大多情况下置于被强调的词、短语或句子之前,但也有置于被强调的成分之后的。例如:

> In choosing the curtains for a room, you should consider the weight, its pattern — but its colour *above all*.
> 在挑选窗帘时,要考虑布料的轻重、图案,但最重要的是颜色。

3. 当本短语作"最重要的是"解时,同义短语是 in the first place 和 first and foremost。

above board Ⅰ *adj.* (用作表语) completely honest and legal 诚实的;守法的;光明正大的:She's been totally open and *above board* about it. 她对此事完全公开,光明磊落。Don't worry. The deal was completely *above board*. 不用担心,这笔买卖做得绝对光明正大。

Ⅱ *adv.* in a legal and honest way; honestly 守法地;诚实地:If you do everything *above board*, you will have to pay tax on your earnings. 如果你凡事守法,那你就得交所得税。

NOTE 1. 本短语的比较级形式是 more above board,最高级形式是 most above board。

2. 本短语可转化为复合词 aboveboard,意为"诚实的(地),光明正大的(地)"。

absent from[1] *vt.* 【可分性动词短语】(正式用语,无被动语态形式,与反身代词连用) ❶ keep (yourself) away from (someone) 避开(某人):I must tell you bluntly that what you have to do is simple: *absent* yourself *from* the person with whom you wish to end the relationship. 我必须直截了当地告诉你,你要做的很简单:不要接近你想与其断绝关系的人。❷ fail to appear in (some place where you should be or are expected to be)不在(某处);缺席(某一场合):If you *absent* yourself *from* a place, you leave it or do not go there. 如果

A

你不在某个地方,那就是说你离开了那里或没去那里。He *absented* himself *from* school on purpose. 他故意没有去上学。

absent from² *adj.* ❶away from or not in (the place where you should be or are expected to be)不在的,缺席的;离开的: The manager of the company is *absent from* London at the moment. 该公司的经理此刻不在伦敦。How many students are *absent from* class today? 今天有多少学生缺课? The figures, therefore, included students in residence, while those temporarily *absent from* the school were excluded. 因此,这些数字包括了那些在校生,而那些暂时离校的却没有包括在内。❷(正式用语) missing from (a place or situation) 没有: Parental affection is *absent from* these children's lives. 在这些孩子的生活中没有父母之爱。The pictures, too, were *absent from* the walls. 墙上的画也都没了。

absolve from/of *vt.*【可分性动词短语】(正式用语,常用一般时态) (especially in religion or law) officially free (someone) from (any guilt, blame or responsibility in a particular matter)(尤指在宗教或法律中)免除(某人的)(罪责、责难、义务等): The priest *absolved* him *of* all his sins. 神父赦免了他的罪过。State education does not *absolve* parents *from* their responsibility to their child. 国家的教育并没有免除家长对其子女的责任。The announcement yesterday *absolved* the police *of* all blame in the incident. 昨天的那份通告免除了警方在事件中的责任。The accused attempted to *absolve* himself *of* the crime. 该被告企图为自己解脱罪责。

absorbed in *adj.* so interested or involved in (something or doing something) that you do not notice anything else 专心于……的,全神贯注于……的: I was *absorbed in* a book and didn't hear your phone call. 当时我正专心看书,没有听到你的电话。I get so *absorbed in* doing something that I am unaware of things happening round me. 我太专注于所做之事,以致意识不到我周围发生的事情。Robert lay on the sofa, totally *absorbed in* a Chinese Kung Fu novel. 罗伯特躺在沙发上,完全沉迷于一部中国功夫小说之中。

NOTE 本短语中的 absorb 是及物动词,意为"使全神贯注"。但它一般以过去分词的形式用于被动语态中,在本短语中用作形容词,与 in 连用形成固定短语。

abstain from *vt.*【不可分性动词短语】(正式用语) ❶ deliberately avoid doing (something that you want to do but may not be healthy or safe)戒除,节制,避免(可能会不利于健康或安全之事): A high percentage of women said they had *abstained from* alcohol during pregnancy. 大部分妇女说她们都在怀孕期间戒了酒。If you *abstain from* eating candy and rich foods, you will not be so fat. 如果你不再吃糖和油腻食物,就不会这样胖了。❷ not do (something that is likely to cause serious problems)不做(可能导致严重问题之事): They agreed to *abstain from* any actions that might endanger the peace process. 他们就停止任何危害和平进程的行动达成了一致。

abstract from *vt.*【可分性动词短语】❶(正式用语,常用被动语态形式) take (important information or essentials) from (a longer document or a piece of complicated writing)从(长篇或复杂的文章中)选摘(重要信息或要点): The *author abstracted* the most important points *from* a new magazine. 该作者从一本新杂志中选摘出了最重要的几点内容。She *abstracted* a few poems *from* some other books. 她从其他书上摘用了几首诗。This information was *abstracted from* newspaper reports. 这条消息摘自于报纸的报道中。❷steal (something) from 把(某物)从……偷走: My ex-wife *abstracted* money *from* her boyfriend and bought a car. 我的前妻从她男友那偷了钱,买了一辆小轿车。The thief abstracted the purse *from* her pocket and disappeared. 小偷从她的衣袋中偷走了钱包便不见了踪影。❸take (something) out of (something) 从……提出,从……提取: We have learned how to *abstract* metal *from* the ore. 我们已学会如何从矿石中提炼金属。Scientists can *abstract* precious medicine *from* ordinary substances. 科学家们能从普通的物质中提取珍贵的药物。

accede to *vt.*【不可分性动词短语】(正式用语,常用一般时态) ❶ give one's agreement to (a suggestion, plan, demand, etc.), often after first disagreeing (常为以前不同意而后来)同意,应允,答应,批准(某一建议、计划、要求等): They were forced to *accede to* all of the hijackers' demands. 他们被迫同意了劫机者的全部要求。The Prime Minister would have to *accede to* any request by the opposition. 首相将不得不答应反对党所提出的任何要求。My application was *acceded to*. 我的申请获得了批准。❷ follow someone and formally take a position of (power or authority, especially as a king or queen) 继承(王位); 继任(某职): Queen Elizabeth II, *acceded to* the throne after her father King George VI died in 1952. 伊丽莎白女王二世是在1952年其父乔治六世国王去世后继位的。When his father died, the prince *acceded to* the position of head of state. 王子在其父王去世后便继任国家元首。Last week she *acceded to* the mayor. 上星期她就任了市长。❸ join (a group of people, countries, etc.), in an agreement 加入: After 15 years' talks, China finally *acceded to* the World Trade Organization on December 11, 2001. 经过15年的谈判后,中国终于在2001年12月11日加入了世界贸易组织。

accept as *vt.*【可分性动词短语】❶believe that(something or someone) is (what they claimed to be) 相信……是……,认可……为……: The people there *accepted* his statement *as* truth. 那里的人们都对他的话信以为真。The emperor finally *accepted* the girl he had never heard or seen *as* his own daughter. 皇上终于把那个从未听说也从未见过面的女孩认作自己的女儿。❷allow (especially someone) to join an organization 接纳(尤指某人)为(某一组织的)成员: They *accepted* me *as* a new member of the club. 他们接纳我为俱乐部新成员。Romania and Bulgaria were formally *accepted as* new members of the European Union. 罗马尼亚和保加利亚被正式接纳为欧洲联盟新成员。

accommodate to *vt.*【可分性动词短语】(正式用语) adapt to; change (especially oneself) in order to fit (new conditions) 使(尤指自己)适应于,改变(尤指自己)以顺应(新环境): Wherever he goes, he readily *accommodates to* new surroundings. 不管走到哪里,他都能很快适应新环境。You have just graduated

from school and entered society, so you have to *accommodate* yourself *to* the new situation. 你刚从学校毕业进入社会,你得使自己顺应新的境况。Our eyes can *accommodate* themselves *to* seeing objects at different distances. 我们的眼睛能自动调节,以看清远近不同的物体。In order to please his girl friend Linda, Jim *accommodated* his plan *to* Linda's. 为了讨好女朋友琳达,吉姆把自己的计划做了调整,以适应琳达的计划。

NOTE 本短语中的 to 是介词,而不是动词不定式符号,故后须接名词、代词和动名词(短语),不能接原形动词。

accommodate with *vt.*【可分性动词短语】❶provide (something special) for (someone)为(某人)提供(某种特殊之物): We will try to *accommodate* you *with* an earlier flight. 我们会尽量为您提供早些的航班。He was *accommodated with* a reserved parking space very close to the building. 给他提供了一个离楼很近的专用停车位。❷(正式用语) provide (a place or room) for (someone) to stay in 向(某人)提供(住所): We can *accommodate* you *with* an apartment with two bedrooms. 我们可以为你提供一套带有两间卧室的公寓。During the three-day meeting in Paris we were *accommodated with* lodgings in a luxury hotel. 在巴黎的三天会议期间,我们被安排住在一家豪华的酒店里。

accord with *vt.*【不可分性动词短语】(正式用语,无被动语态形式,用一般时态,常用于否定句中) agree with or be the same as (something else); consist with or match (something)符合,与……一致: Tom's account does not *accord with* the police evidence. 汤姆的陈述与警方的证据不相符。Your opinion *accords* substantially *with* mine. 你我的意见实际上是一致的。

according as *conj.* (正式用语,后接从句) depending on which or whether 根据……而定,取决于……: You may take an oral or written exam *according as* you prefer. 你可以考口试或笔试,就看你喜欢考哪一门了。You will be praised or blamed *according as* you are diligent or lazy. 是表扬还是责备你,将根据你是勤奋还是懒惰而定。We will play golf or stay at home *according as* the weather is good or bad. 我们是去打高尔夫球还是待在家里取决于天气的好坏。

NOTE 不要将本短语与 according to 混淆。本短语是连词性短语,用来引导方式或条件状语从句,而 according to 则为介词性短语,用作状语。在现代英语中,本短语已不常用。

according to *prep.* ❶ (used for saying where information has come from) as stated, reported or shown by (someone or something) (用于说明信息的来源)据……所说,根据……: *According to* the World Health Organization, in humans the symptoms of A/H1N1 flu are similar to those of ordinary influenza. 据世界卫生组织所述,人患了甲型 H1N1 流感的症状与普通流感的那些症状相类似。Hong Kong's population reached about 7 million 400 thousand at the end of 2018, *according to* Hong Kong's Census and Statistics Department. 根据香港统计处公布的数字显示,2018 年年底的香港人口已达到大约 740 万。❷ following, agreeing with, or depending on (something) 根据,按照: He will be punished *according to* the seriousness of his crime. 他应受的惩处将根据他犯罪的严重程度而定。China's Foreign Ministry spokesman said, the UN Security Council was not "a board of directors" and its composition should not be decided "*according to* the financial contribution of its members". 中国外交部发言人指出,联合国安理会不是"董事会",其构成不应"按照会费交纳的多少"来确定。

NOTE 1. 当本短语作"(用于说明信息的来源)据……所说,根据……"解时,一般不与 opinion(意见)、view (看法)等词连用,也不接第一人称的代词。例如我们不能说:

(1) * *According to* my opinion/view, Obama will win the Democratic presidential nomination.

应改为:In my opinion/view, Obama will win the Democratic presidential nomination.

(2) * *According to* me/ us, the new film *Kung Fu Panda* is wonderful.

应改为:In my/our opinion/view, the new film *Kung Fu Panda* is wonderful.

2. 当本短语作"根据,按照"解时,只能作状语,不能作表语。例如:

(1)这本书是根据一个真实故事写的。

* The book is *according to* a true story.

应改为:The book is *based on* a true story.

(2)在讲话中你应该讲些什么由你自己定。

* What you should say in your speech is entirely *according to* you.

应改为:What you should say in your speech is entirely *up to* you.

❸本短语的同义短语是 in accordance with。两者在含义上有细微的区别:前者强调"根据……所言",而后者则强调"与……要一致"。另外,in accordance with 多用于正式场合,例如表示与一些原则、规律等一致。两者在用法上亦有不同,in accordance with 可用作表语。

account for *vt.*【不可分性动词短语】❶(常用一般时态) be the reason or cause of (something)是……的原因: Melting snow *accounts for* the regular spring floods in this region. 积雪融化是该地区春季定期发生洪灾的原因。The American Lung Association said, smoking during pregnancy *accounts for* about 10 percent of all infant deaths. 美国肺器官协会称,大约10%的婴儿死亡都是女性在孕期吸烟而致。❷give an explanation of (something bad that has happened, especially something you are responsible for)解释,说明……的原因: The former general manager was sentenced to 10 years in prison for taking bribes and possessing a huge amount of money without being able to *account for* its source. 这名原总经理因受贿、巨额财产来源不明被判处十年监禁。How do you *account for* losing five games in a row? 一连输掉五场比赛,你作何解释? The disappearance of the paper has never been *accounted for*. 这份文件丢失的原因从没有被解释清楚过。❸(无被动语态形式) form (the total of an amount of something); make up; constitute (a particular amount or part of something)构成,占: Last year China's imports of soybeans from the US *accounted for* one third of the total US soybean exports. 去年,中国自美国进口的大豆占美国出口总量的1/3。Statistics show that there are more than 600 million disabled persons throughout the world, *accounting for* 10 percent of the total world population, in which 80 percent are in the developing countries. 统计数字表明,全世界共有6亿多残疾人,占世界总人口的10%,其

A

中80%在发展中国家。Students *account for the vast majority of our customers.* 学生占了我们客户的绝大多数。❹(非正式用语) catch, kill, or destroy (animals, people, or fighter aircraft)抓住,杀死,击落: After a long hunt, the tiger was at last *accounted for*. 经过长时间的搜寻,那只老虎终于被捕获。The armed police *accounted for* three terrorists, who had attempted to hijack a plane, at the airport yesterday. 昨天,武装警察在机场打死了三名企图劫机的恐怖分子。

accountable for/to *adj.* responsible for; answerable to 为……负责的: Each person will eventually be *accountable for* his or her own behavior. 每一个人都终将为自己的行为负责。They should be held *accountable for* what they did. 他们应该为其所作所为承担责任。The supervisory board of a listed company shall be *accountable to* all shareholders. 上市公司监事会应向全体股东负责。Should the police be more *accountable to* the public? 警方该不该对公众负有更大的责任?

NOTE 1. accountable for 后接物, accountable to 后接人。

2. 本短语的同义短语是 liable for/to 和 responsible for。

accuse of *vt.*【可分性动词短语】say that (someone) has done (something wrong) or committed (a crime); charge (someone) with (doing wrong or breaking the law) 指责(某人干了什么坏事);指控,控告(某人犯了什么罪): The police *accused* a 75-year-old man *of* selling drugs near a high school. 警方控告一名75岁的老头在一所中学附近贩卖毒品。He was *accused of* abuse of power. 他被指控犯有滥用职权罪。

accustom to *vt.* (常用被动语态形式) make (someone, oneself, or something) used to (something or doing something); get used to (new conditions, different kinds of life, etc.) (使……)适应于;习惯于(新环境、新生活等): It's necessary for an observer to remain in the room 5 minutes to *accustom* himself *to* the darkness. 观察者需要在房间里待上5分钟,使自己适应里面的黑暗。I'm sure you will soon get *accustomed to* the climate here in the south. 我确信,你很快就会习惯南方这儿的气候。He had become *accustomed to* living without electricity. 他已习惯了没有电的生活。

NOTE 1. 本短语中的 to 是介词,而不是动词不定式符号,后接名词或动名词(短语)。

2. 本短语的被动语态形式 be accustomed to 在意义上和用法上都与 be used to 相同。见 used to[2]。

3. 本短语的同义短语是 adapt to, adjust to 和 be used to。

acquaint with *vt.*【可分性动词短语】❶(正式用语,与反身代词连用) make (oneself) become familiar with (something)使(自己)熟悉(某事): They *acquainted* themselves *with* the techniques involved in the production of internal combustion engines. 他们熟悉了有关生产内燃机的技术。❷ make (someone or oneself) learn about (something)使(某人或自己)了解(某事): Travel will *acquaint* you *with* different cultures and customs in other parts of the world. 旅游会使你了解世界其他国家不同的文化和习俗。We aim to *acquaint* policy makers *with* some of these issues. 我们的目的是让决策者了

解这些问题。We must ensure that every Chinese person *acquaints* himself *with* the basic information on what A/H1N1 flu is and how to contain the disease. 我们必须保证使每个国人都了解甲型H1N1流感及其预防的基本知识。

act as *vt.*【不可分性动词短语】(无被动语态形式) ❶do a particular job, especially one that you do not normally do; serve as 充当,当作:You speak Greek? Will you *act as* interpreter when the foreign guests come to visit our college? 你讲希腊语?当外宾来我们学院参观时,你当翻译,好吗? A trained dog can *act as* a guide to a blind person. 经过训练的狗能当盲人的向导。❷have a particular effect or function 有……作用:This kind of tea *acts as* an aid to digestion. 这种茶有助消化的作用。The drugs *act as* a brake on the spread of the disease. 这些药物有抑制这种疾病传播的作用。

NOTE 1. 本短语后可接表示人或物的名词。接表示人的名词时,冠词通常可以省略,但如果该名词前有形容词修饰时,冠词则不能省略。比较下面这个句子与本短语中的第一个例句:

> He *acted as* an excellent interpreter in the negotiation.
> 他在谈判中充当了一名优秀的翻译。

2. 当本短语作"有……作用"解时,在英国英语中还可用act like的形式。例如:

> Some hormones in the brain can *act like* natural painkillers.
> 大脑中的一些荷尔蒙有天然的止痛作用。

但act like还有"行为像……,举动像……"之意。例如:

> That child *acts like* a grown-up.
> 那个孩子的举动像成年人一样。

3. 本短语的同义短语是work as和serve as。

act counter to ⇨ **run counter to**

act for *vt.*【不可分性动词短语】(后接表示人的名词或代词,一般不用被动语态形式) do (something) as (one's representative); perform (duties) in place of (someone) 代表(某人),代理(某人)行职:Lawyers *acting for* Mr Miller will issue a statement this morning. 今天上午,律师将代表米勒先生发表一项声明。As the chairman was ill, I asked Mr Smith to *act for* him. 由于主席病了,我便请史密斯先生代行其职。

NOTE 在英国英语中,本短语常以act on behalf of的形式使用。例如:

> He is *acting on behalf of* my mother.
> 他在代表我母亲行事。

act like ⇨ **act as**

act on/upon *vt.*【不可分性动词短语】❶affect; have an effect on (something) 对……起作用,对……有影响:Does the drug take long to *act on* the nerve center? 这药要很长时间才对神经中枢起作用吗? A body at rest remains at rest unless *acted upon* by an external force. 如果不受外力作用,静止的物体就一直保持静止的状态。As we all know, acid *acts on* metals and alcohol *acts on* the brain. 众所周知,酸对金属起腐蚀作用,而酒精对大脑有影响。❷act in accordance with or take action on (something such as advice, information)按照……去做,根据……采取行动:I'm *acting on* the advice of my lawyers. 我是在按我律师的主意行事。Why didn't you *act upon* his suggestion? 你为什么不按照他的建议行事?

NOTE 本短语中的upon用法比on正式,但不及on常用。

act on behalf of ⇨ **act for**

act out *vt.*【可分性动词短语】❶perform (something), especially in action and behavior rather than in words(尤指以动作而不用语言)表演:The boy tried to *act out* a story that he had read. 那男孩试着表演了他读过的一篇故事中的情节。Would you please *act out* what happened? 请你能把发生的事演示一下,好吗? The scenes that the students *act out* are videotaped. 学生们演出的场景都被拍摄了下来。Which group can *act* the play *out*? 哪一组能表演此剧? ❷express (an emotion, thoughts, etc.) in actions and behavior, rather than in words 把(某种感情,想法等)用行动(而不是语言)表达出来: Children often *act out* their troubled feelings in their games. 孩子们往往在玩游戏中表达他们的焦躁情绪。He *acted out* what he thought. 他以行为来表达心中的想法。It's how people may *act* their feelings *out* in their behaviour. 这就是人们如何以行为方式来表达他们的情感的。

NOTE 当本短语所带的宾语是代词时,该代词须置于本短语的动词和副词中间。

act up *vi.* (常用进行时态) ❶(especially of children) behave badly or in an annoying way (尤指儿童)不守规矩,调皮捣蛋: The kids have been *acting up* again. 孩子们又在调皮捣蛋了。I could hear Tommy *acting up* downstairs. 我能听到汤米在楼下耍闹。The dog *acted up* as the postman came to the door. 当邮递员来到门前时,这条狗又跳又叫。❷(非正式用语) (of a machine, a piece of equipment, etc.) develop problems, or work badly (机器、设备等)出毛病,运转失常:His car *acted up* again because the spark plugs were too dirty. 他的汽车因火花塞过脏又不能正常行驶了。My computer is *acting up*; I think I might have a virus. 我的电脑出现问题。我想,可能有病毒了。❸(非正式用语) (of a part of the body) start to become painful (身体的某一部位)开始疼痛: An old injury to his right foot had begun to *act up* again. 他右脚上的旧伤又开始疼了。My sprained ankle has been *acting up* badly all the week. 我扭伤的脚踝一个星期来一直很痛。I hope my back doesn't start *acting up* again. 我希望我的后背不再疼了。

adapt from *vt.*【可分性动词短语】(常用被动语态形式) change (a book or play) so that it can be made into (a film, TV program, etc.)把(小说或剧本)改编成(电影或电视节目等): He *adapted* his new movie *from* a novel. 他的新影片是根据一本小说改编而成的。The *Harry Potter* films are *adapted from* the books by British writer Rowling.《哈里·波特》系列影片是根据英国作家罗琳的系列小说改编而成的。This play has been skillfully *adapted from* the original. 这出戏是根据原作精巧地改编而成的。

adapt to *vt.*【可分性动词短语】suit to; become used to; make (something, someone, or oneself) fit for; adjust (oneself) to (a new situation)适应,使(自己)适应于(新境况): It took me a long time to *adapt to* the new job. 我用了很长时间才适应了这份新工作。We must *adapt* our thinking and our work *to* the changed circumstances. 我们必须使我们的思想和工作适应已经变化了的情况。But I don't think I shall ever *adapt* myself *to* this hot climate. 但我想我永远也适应不了这种炎热的气候。How can I *adapt to* opening my eyes underwater when swimming? 我怎样才能适应在水下睁着眼睛游泳呢?

NOTE 本短语中的 to 是介词,后接名词或动名词短语,不能接动词。

add fuel to the fire *vi.* (非正式用语) make a bad situation even worse by saying or doing something; worsen a conflict between people 使本来糟糕的情况更坏;火上浇油:The workers were not satisfied with their wages, and when they were asked to work long hours, it *added fuel to the fire*. 工人们本来对工资就不满意,再要求他们延长工作时间,这只能是火上浇油。"The bombings can only *add fuel to the fire* of the conflict," he also said. 他还指出:"轰炸只能是火上浇油,使冲突加剧。"

add on *vt.* 【可分性动词短语】include an extra thing or amount in (something); add (something), usually at the end of a calculation or list; attach (something extra) 加上,补上,附上: Here is your bill. We've *added on* the ten percent service charge. 这是您的账单。我们已把10%的服务费加进去了。She wrote me rather a cold letter; even the inquiry about my health looked as if it had been *added on* as an afterthought. 她给我写了一封十分冷淡的信,甚至询问我身体的话看上去也是经过事后思考才加上去的。You'd better *add* a postscript *on* to the letter inquiring about her health. 你最好在信的末尾附上几句询问她健康状况的话。The referee *added on* eight minutes of injury time. 裁判为伤停补时8分钟。

add to *vt.* ❶ put (numbers or amounts) together to calculate their total; put (something) with (something) so as to increase it 把(数字)加起来,加上: What do you get if you *add* three *to* seven? 3加7等于多少? Would you please *add* a few notes *to* the article? 请您给这篇文章加几条注释,好吗? ❷increase (something) 增加: This trip, I believe, will *add* greatly *to* our knowledge and understanding of your country. 我相信,此行将会大大增加我们对贵国的认识和了解。

add up *vt.* &*vi.* (常用一般时态,不用进行时态) (cause to)make a total of (two or more numbers or amounts); take together 把(数字或数量)加起来,合计: *Add* these figures *up* and see what the total is. 把这些数目加起来,看总数是多少。Now *add up* the number of calories you have eaten. 现在,把你摄入的卡路里的数量加起来。I'm not very good at *adding up* in my head. 我不太擅长做心算加法。

—*vi.* (非正式用语,一般用于否定句中,用一般时态) make sense; form a consistent, reasonable, sensible or believable explanation 有意义,有道理: What he said simply didn't *add up*. 他说的话简直没有什么意义。Police said they arrested Robert because his statements did not *add up*. 警方称,他们拘捕罗伯特是因为他讲话前言不搭后语。

NOTE 当本短语用作及物性动词短语时,所带的宾语必须置于本短语的动词和副词中间。

add up to *vt.* 【不可分性动词短语】❶(不用进行时态)form the total of (a figure); amount to (数目)加起来总计是,共达: How much does that *add up to*? 那些加起来总计是多少? The three angles of a triangle *add up to* 180°. 三角形的三个内

角的总和是180°。According to the charges, the company was involved in 52 instances of tax evasion, and the amount of unpaid tax *added up to* 8.48 million yuan. 根据数项指控,这家公司涉嫌偷税52起,偷税金额共达人民币848万元。❷(无被动语态形式,常用一般现在时) be equal to; mean 等于是,意味着: Your evidence really *adds up to* this — that you were nowhere near the scene of the crime. 你的证据实际上等于说你当时不在犯罪现场附近。What your statement *adds up to* is that you helped to kill the old woman. 你的陈述意味着你是杀害那老妇人的帮凶。❸(无被动语态形式,常用一般现在时) combine to produce (a particular result or effect)归结为……,产生(某种结果或效果): It all *adds up to* this — he is a selfish man. 所有这些归结为一点——他是一个自私自利的人。These new measures do not *add up to* genuine reform. 这些新出台的措施不会导致真正的改革。

NOTE 本短语与 add up 均表示"合计"之意,但 add up 指的是过程,而本短语则指的是结果。

addict to *vt.* (常用被动语态形式) ❶be unable to stop taking (some-thing, especially an illegal or harmful drug)(尤指对毒品或有害药物)上瘾: It doesn't take long to become *addicted to* these drugs. 服用这些毒品用不了多久就会上瘾。He admitted he was *addicted to* heroin by the age of 20. 他承认自己20岁就对海洛因成瘾了。He *addicted* himself *to* drinking. 他喝酒成瘾。❷(非正式用语) like (something or doing something) very much; cannot stop having or doing (something)沉溺于,做(某事)成瘾:"I was very surprised to see my son *addicted* so much *to* the grown-up's activities," the mother said. "看到我儿子那么喜欢成年人的活动我非常吃惊。"这位妈妈说道。"If you are really *addicted to* chatting online, it will be hard for you to concentrate in class," the student said. "如果你真的沉溺于网上聊天,你就很难在课堂上集中精力。"这位大学生说道。

NOTE 本短语中的 to 是介词,而不是动词不定式符号,后接名词、动名词和名词性从句,而不能接动词。

address to *vt.* 【可分性动词短语】❶(常用被动语态形式)send (a letter, parcel, etc.) to (a particular person or organization) by writing the name and address on an envelope, parcel, etc. 把(写上姓名、地址的信、包裹等)寄给(某人或某一机构): I took the liberty of reading the letter, even though it was *addressed to* you. 尽管这封信是写给你的,但是我冒昧地看过了。This letter is *addressed to* the Business Affairs Office. 这封信是寄给商务处的。❷(正式用语) officially tell (either in speech or writing) a particular person or organization (your complaints, questions, or comments, etc.)(以言语或文字形式)把(不满、问题或评论等)正式反映给(某人或某一机构): Please *address* your complaints *to* the manager, not to me. 请你向经理申诉,不要和我说。All enquiries should be *addressed to* head office. 所有情况应向总店咨询。❸(正式用语,常与反身代词连用) speak publicly to (a group of people)向……发表演讲: The president is due to *address to* the conference here this afternoon. 总统将于今天下午在这里向大会发表演讲。It seemed that she was *addressing to* a group of youngsters. 她似乎在向一群

年轻人发表演讲。❹(正式用语) speak directly to (someone who is with you)直接与……谈话:He *addressed* himself *to* me and said that he would no longer remain in his present position. 他向我谈过他将不再担任现职。Throughout the conversation, he addressed his remarks to me. 在整个谈话中都是他在向我讲话。Any questions should be *addressed to* your teacher. 有任何问题都应直接问老师。❺(正式用语,与反身代词连用) turn the attention of (oneself) to (dealing with a task or problem)从事于(某项工作);致力于(解决某一问题等):He made up his mind to *address* himself *to* the most difficult subject of this field. 他决心从事这门学科中最难课题的研究。He ignored the side issues and *addressed* himself *to* the main problem. 他抛开枝节问题,致力于解决主要问题。

adhere to *vt.* 【不可分性动词短语】❶remain attached to; stick fast to (something)黏附于(某物)之上;附着于:Glue and paste are used to make one surface *adhere to* another. 胶水和糨糊是用来黏合两个表面的。It's the sort of surface that paint doesn't *adhere to* very well. 在这种表面上,油漆的附着力是很差的。When a piece of lodestone is dipped into iron filings, they *adhere to* it. 把一块磁铁投入铁屑中时,铁屑就附着在磁铁之上。❷(正式用语,常用一般时态) maintain; steadily follow or be faithful to (an idea, principle, plan, opinion, etc.)坚持(某种思想、原则、计划、意见等):The author points out that to *adhere to* this idea is not easy. 该作者指出,坚持这一思想并非易事。The student *adhered to* her plan to leave early. 这位同学坚持自己的计划要早点动身。I will *adhere to* this opinion until contrary facts appear. 如果没有相反的事实,我将坚持这一意见。He resolutely *adhered to* what he had said at the meeting. 他决意坚持他在会上发表的意见。❸(正式用语,常用一般时态) obey (a rule, law, agreement, etc.)遵守(规则、法律、协议等):We have the right to remove any exhibitor who does not *adhere to* the exhibit hall's rules and regulations. 我们有权取消任何不遵守展厅规章制度的参展商的参展资格。Whether or not we agree with the prevailing wage law, we must *adhere to* the law. 无论我们是否同意现行的工资法,我们都必须遵守这一法律。We must strictly *adhere to* the terms of the contract. 我们必须严格遵守合同中的各项条款。

NOTE 当本短语作"坚持(某种思想、原则、计划、意见等)"解时,同义短语是 insist on, persist in, persevere at/in/with 和 stick to。它们之间的区别见 insist on。

adjacent to *adj.* next to or near (something else)毗邻,靠近:The hotel is *adjacent to* two banks and the largest shopping mall of the city. 那家宾馆毗邻两家银行和全城最大的商场。The site of the new building is *adjacent to* the park. 新楼的地点靠近公园。There is a school *adjacent to* the church. 靠近教堂有一所学校。

NOTE 本短语的同义短语是 close to,但本短语所表示的距离比 close to 更短、更近。另外 close to 后可以接人或物,本短语后不能接人,只能接物。

adjust to *vt.* get used to (something such as a new situation, or someone) by changing your ideas or the way you do things; adapt (oneself) to 适应于;使(自己)适应于:It took her two years to *adjust to* life in England. 她用了两年时间才适应了在英国的生活。His eyes gradually *adjusted to* the darkness in the room. 他的眼睛逐渐地适应了室内的黑暗。We must *adjust* ourselves *to* changing conditions. 我们必须使自己适应千变万化的周围环境。Some animals *adjust* themselves *to* the environment by instinct. 有些动物靠其本能适应环境。

NOTE 本短语的同义短语是 accustom to, adapt to 和 be used to。

admit of *vt.* 【不可分性动词短语】(正式用语,无被动语态形式,用一般时态,常用否定形式) show that something is possible; leave room for (something); allow 有……的可能,留有……的余地,容许: It is, therefore, evident that this plan doesn't *admit of* improvement. 所以,很明显这项计划已无改进的余地。This case did not *admit of* being discussed in public. 本案不能公开审理。The facts *admit of* no other explanation. 这些事实不容有其他解释。The work *admits of* no delay. 此项工作不容拖延。

NOTE 本短语的同义短语是 allow of。

admit to *vt.* ❶allow (someone) to enter (a place, especially a public place such as a theatre or museum) 允许(某人)进入……: You will not be *admitted to* the theatre after the performance has started. 演出开始后就不允许你入场了。A group ticket *admits* six people *to* the zoo and museum. 这张集体入场券允许 6 人进入动物园和博物馆。❷(用被动语态形式) allow (a person or country) to join (an organization or group) 允许(某人或某国)加入(某一机构或组织): In the past only eight hundred students are *admitted* every year *to* our college. 在过去,我们学院每年只招收 800 名学生入学。Albania and Croatia were *admitted to* the North Atlantic Treaty Organization in April 2009. 阿尔巴尼亚和克罗地亚于 2009 年 4 月被接纳为北大西洋公约组织新成员。❸confess (that you have done something wrong or illegal); not deny 供认,承认: The young man *admitted to* his part in the crime. 那个年轻人供认了他在那起罪案中所充当的角色。The nuclear scientist *admitted to* giving away secrets to some other countries. 这位核科学家承认向某些国家泄露了核机密。She *admitted to* having taken the money. 她承认拿走了那笔钱。❹(常用被动语态形式) take (someone) into (hospital) for medical treatment 把(某人)送入(医院)就医: They *admitted* John *to* the psychiatric unit of the Royal Hospital. 他们把约翰送入皇家医院精神病科就医。The man complained of a headache and fever and was *admitted to* the Hospital of the City. 那名男子曾自述头痛、发烧而被市医院收入就医。

NOTE 1. 当本短语作"供认,承认"解时,同义短语是 confess to。

2. 当表示"(某人)被收入医院就医"时,在英国英语中用 be admitted to hospital, 而在美国英语中则用 be admitted to the hospital。

affiliate to/with *vt.* (常用被动语态形式) (of a group or organization) form a close connection with (another larger one) (某一组织)隶属于: We want to *affiliate* our animation institute *to* a foreign university. 我们想要把我们的动画制作研究所归属于一所外国大学。Our club is *affiliated to* a national organization of similar clubs. 我们的俱乐部隶属于一个全国性同类俱乐部的组织。The hospital *affiliated with* our university is one of the first class hospitals in the country. 我们大学的附属医院是全国一流的医院之一。

afraid for *adj.* feeling worried that something unpleasant, dangerous, etc. will happen to a particular person or thing 为……感到担心的：I'm not *afraid for* me, but for the baby. 我担心的不是自己，而是孩子。They had already fired three people and he was *afraid for* his job. 他们已解雇了三个人，所以他很担心自己的工作。Some of their supporters left a protest on Friday evening, *afraid for* their safety, and of course, afraid of being arrested. 他们的一些支持者在星期五晚上因担心自己的安全而不再继续抗议，当然是害怕被捕。

NOTE 不要将本短语与 afraid of 混淆。afraid of 意思侧重于“害怕”。

afraid of *adj.* ❶ fearful of (someone or something), for example because you feel you are in danger 害怕的：Due to the fierce looking of the new teacher, all the pupils of the class are *afraid of* her. 新来的老师样子很凶，班里的学生都怕她。He is the kind of man *afraid of* nothing. 他是那种无所畏惧的人。She is *afraid of* going out alone at night. 她不敢一个人夜里出去。He was *afraid of* what she might say. 他很怕她会说什么。❷ worried or anxious about (something bad that might happen) 担心的：What I am *afraid of* is that we don't have enough time. 我所担心的是我们没有足够的时间。Mary was *afraid of* making a fool of herself. 玛丽担心自己会出丑。

NOTE 本短语中的形容词 afraid 的害怕程度小于 scared, terrified 和 frightened。afraid 后除了接介词 of 外，还常接动词不定式，表示“不敢去做某事，害怕做某事”。例如：

> The girl was *afraid to* open the gate in case the dog attacked her.
> 那女孩不敢开大门，害怕狗咬她。

afraid 后亦常接 that 从句，表示“害怕或担心发生某种情况”。例如：

> I was *afraid* that you'd miss the flight.
> 我担心你误了航班。

after all *adv.* ❶ (used when giving a reason to explain what you have just said) taking everything into consideration; anyway (用于解释刚刚发表的言论)毕竟：Don't be so hard on him. He is only a child of 5 *after all*. 别对他那么严厉，他毕竟是个才 5 岁的孩子。❷ (通常置于句尾) in spite of everything that has/had happened, been said, etc.; in the end 终究，终于，到底：Maybe she was right *after all*. 可能她最终是对的。He failed *after all*. 他终于失败了。I'm sorry, but we've decided not to come *after all*. 对不起，我们最后还是决定不来了。❸ (通常置于句首) (used for reminding someone of a certain fact) it must be remembered (that) (用作提示语)必须记住，别忘了：*After all*, not only does China now accept many international rules; it is also becoming a much more responsible player of the diplomatic game. 请切记，中国不仅现在接受了许多国际准则，她也正在成为一个在外交上十分负责任的国家。And *after all*, though the meeting is important, we should have time to rest. 尽管这会议重要，但别忘了，我们也应该有休息的时间。

NOTE 当本短语作“终究，到底”解时，不同于 finally。所以，我们不能说：* We had a pleasant evening party with drinks 此处 after all and dancing; then, *after all*, we separated. 应改为 finally.

after (a) while *adv.* (非正式用语) later, at some time in the future; after a period of time, that is not short and not long 等一会儿,过一会儿:"Dad, will you help me make this model plane?" "*After while*, son, when I finish reading the newspaper." "爸爸,您能帮我做这个模型飞机吗?""等一会儿,儿子。等我看完报纸。" *After a while* we turned off the television and went out for a walk. 过了一会儿,我们便关掉电视出去散步了。

NOTE 本短语中的 while 是单数名词,意为"一会儿",由其构成的短语还有 all the while, for a while, in a while 和 quite a while 等,具体用法见相关条目。

again and again *adv.* (used for saying that something happens many times) repeatedly 反复地,屡次地,再三地:I read through her letter *again and again*. 我反复地阅读了她的信。The WHO has said *again and again* that people cannot be infected by A/H1N1 virus through consumption of well-cooked pork or exposure to pigs. 世卫组织一再重申,人们不会通过食用煮熟的猪肉或接触猪而感染上甲型 H1N1 病毒。*Again and again*, the policeman asked me the same question. 那警察一遍又一遍地问我同一个问题。

NOTE 本短语与 over and over, over and over again, time and again 均表示"反复地""再三地"。again and again 和 over and over again 常用于英国口语中,over and over 和 time and again 常用于美国口语中。

agree about *vt.* 【不可分性动词短语】(不用进行时态) have the same opinion about (usually something)对(某事)取得一致意见: Have you *agreed about* the price yet? 你们就价格达成一致了吗? The committee members *agreed about* the need for more information. 委员会的成员一致认为还需要更多的信息。They couldn't *agree about* doing the jobs that needed to be done. 他们不能就必须做的事情达成一致意见。

agree on/upon *vt.* 【不可分性动词短语】(不用进行时态) ❶have the same opinion about (usually something)对(某事)取得一致意见:The warring states have *agreed on* an unconditional ceasefire. 交战国各方已就无条件停火达成了一致。They *agreed on* how to evacuate the civilians from the island. 他们就如何撤走岛上的居民取得了一致意见。Do you think they will *agree on* what Dr Smith said in his blog? 你认为他们能同意史密斯博士在其博客上的言论吗? The result *agreed upon* by the two sides shall be considered as part of this treaty. 由双方一致达成的结果将被认为是本条约的一部分。 ❷decide on (something or doing something)商定(某事或做某事):We need to *agree on* a date for our next meeting. 我们需要商定一下下次的开会日期。We *agreed on* leaving there the next day. 我们商定第二天离开那里。But the meeting ended without *agreeing on* when to meet again. 但会谈结束时未能商定何时再次会晤。None of us could *agree on* where to go on vacation, so we went to different places. 我们谁都定不了去哪里度假,于是就各奔东西了。

NOTE 1. 本短语中的 upon 用法比 on 正式,但不及 on 常用。

2. 本短语所表达的意义决定主语必须是复数,而不能是单数。

agree to *vt.* 【不可分性动词短语】(常用一般时态,不用进行时态) accept; approve (something); say that you will do something that someone else wants or suggests 接受,同意,赞同:We have *agreed to* their request for a full investigation. 我们

已接受了他们要进行全面调查的要求。She *agreed to* my leaving early on Friday. 她同意我星期五一早走。Terms for the settlement of the dispute have been *agreed to*. 已达成解决争端的条件。

NOTE 本短语中的 to 是介词,后接名词或动名词短语,不可接动词。但动词 agree 本身可接动词不定式短语。

agree with *vt.*【不可分性动词短语】(不用进行时态) ❶(常用一般时态,后接人) have the same opinion as (someone else)同(某人)意见一致,赞同(某人的意见等):I *agree with* you about his latest book—it's awful. 关于他那本新书我和你的意见一致——很糟糕。In particular, the Prime Minister had been unable to *agree with* the President on some key issues. 该国总理尤其在一些关键问题上与总统意见分歧。❷(常用一般时态,后接事物) accept or approve of (something such as an action or suggestion)接受(某一行为或建议):I don't *agree with* physical punishment in schools. 我不能接受学校中的体罚行为。If you don't *agree with* our suggestions you can object in writing or by email. 如果你们不接受我们的这些建议,你们可以写信或通过电子邮件表示反对。He had to agree to the plan though he didn't *agree with* it. 他虽然不赞成这个计划,但也只好接受了。You should ask them whether they *agree with* what you were doing. 你应问一下他们是否接受你的所作所为。❸(无被动语态形式,用一般时态,后接事物) be consistent with; in accordance with; be the same as (something)与……相一致,符合于……,与……相同:The observations *agree with* the predictions we made earlier. 观测报告与我们先前所做的预测相一致。The witness's statements just don't *agree with* each other. 几个证人的陈述互不相符。❹(无被动语态形式,用一般时态,常用于否定句中,后接人) (of something) suit the health of (someone)利于(某人的)健康:I love the seafood here, but unfortunately it doesn't *agree with* me. 我喜欢这里的海鲜,但遗憾的是海鲜食物不利于我的健康。The humid climate didn't *agree with* her. 潮湿的气候对她的健康不利。Stop taking the medicine if it doesn't *agree with* you. 如果这药不适合你,就不要再服用了。

NOTE 本短语的反义短语是 disagree with 和 disapprove of。

ahead of *prep.* ❶ directly in front of or before (someone or something)在……前面,先于……:At the Beijing Olympics opening ceremony, a 9-year-old boy from Wenchuan walked *ahead of* China's 1099-member delegation, side by side with the 7-foot-6 basketballer Yao Ming. 在北京奥运会开幕式上,一名来自汶川的 9 岁男孩和身高 7.6 英尺的篮球运动员姚明并排走在由 1 099 名成员组成的中国代表团前面。The car *ahead of* us stopped suddenly. 我们前面的那辆汽车突然停了下来。❷in advance of or before (an event or a time) 在(某一事件或时间)之前:He still said he believed in the intelligence material presented to him 他仍坚称,他相信提交给他的情报资料。❸more advanced than or past (someone or something) 领先于:Manchester United striker Cristiano Ronaldo won the FIFA World Footballer with 935 votes, *ahead of* Argentina's Messi (678). 曼联队的前锋 C. 罗纳尔多以 935 票领先于阿根廷球星梅西(678 票),荣膺国际足联世界足球先生。

NOTE 本短语的同义短语是 in advance of。

ahead of schedule *adv.* before the time that was planned 提前于预定时间:The school bus came *ahead of schedule*, and I was not ready. 校车提前到了,可我还没有准备好。The government has fulfilled *ahead of schedule* its debt exemption commitments and cancelled many African countries' debts. 该国政府提前兑现了承诺,减免了许多非洲国家的债务。

NOTE **1.** 本短语中的名词 schedule 之前不能加任何冠词。

2. 如表示提前多少时间,须将具体时间置于本短语之前。例如:

> The plane arrived in Tokyo 5 minutes *ahead of schedule*.
> 飞机提前 5 分钟抵达东京。

3. 本短语的同义短语是 ahead of time 和 in advance;反义短语是 behind schedule 和 behind time。

ahead of one's time *adj.* much more modern, advanced or original for the period one lives in; having new ideas a long time before most other people start to think in the same way 走在时代前面的;思想超前的:She was indeed *ahead of her time* in employing women and the handicapped. 她在雇佣妇女和残疾人方面确实走在了时代的前面。As an artist, he was years *ahead of his time*. 作为一名艺术家,他超前于其所处的时代数年。

NOTE **1.** 本短语中的名词 time 必须用单数形式。

2. 如表示超前多少时间,须将具体时间置于本短语之前。

3. 本短语的同义短语是 before one's time。反义短语是 behind the times。

ahead of time *adv.* (主要用于美国英语中)before the time due; at an earlier time than people expected 在原定时间以前,提前,提早:The plane touched down about half an hour *ahead of time*. 飞机提前大约半个小时着陆了。The new classroom building was completed *ahead of time*. 新教学楼提前竣工了。This has made it possible to fulfill our production half a month *ahead of time*. 这就使我们有可能提早半个月完成生产计划。

NOTE **1.** 本短语中的名词 time 之前不能加任何冠词。

2. 如表示提前多少时间,须将具体时间置于本短语之前。

3. 本短语的同义短语是 ahead of schedule, in advance;反义短语是 behind time 和 behind schedule。

aim at *vt.* ❶point or direct (a weapon or object) towards (someone or something)(用某种武器或物品)对……瞄准,对准……:I didn't mean to hit the cat; I was *aiming at* the tree. 我没想打那只猫,我是在向树瞄准的。The pilot *aimed* his gun *at* the enemy's jet, fired, and hit. 飞行员把机关炮对准了敌机,开火并击中了它。❷make an effort toward (something or doing something); try to achieve (something) 旨在,力求:What are they *aiming at*? 他们的意图何在? The factory must aim at increased production this year. 工厂今年必须力求增产。❸(常用被动语态形式) say or do something that is intended to influence or affect (a particular person or group of people); target 针对(某人或某一群体):My criticism wasn't *aimed at* you. 我的批评并不针对你。The book is *aimed at* very young children. 本书特为幼童撰写。

NOTE 本短语的同义短语是 aim for。

aim for *vt.* ❶have (someone or something) as your target that you want to hit 把……作为目标打击,对……瞄准:The police have *aimed for* the hijackers. 警察已经瞄准了劫持者。❷ strive towards (a particular goal); direct oneself or one's energies towards (something) 争取,力求:

We are *aiming for* success. 我们在争取成功。We should *aim for* a bigger share of the market. 我们应力争占领更大的市场。The factory must *aim for* increased production this year. 工厂今年必须力求增产。❸intend or plan to achieve (something) 旨在: Trade ministers *aim for* agreement as Doha Round begins. 多哈回合谈判开始，贸易部长们旨在达成一致。Activities *aimed for* "living a green life and establishing an ecological civilization" were carried out at the Panda Base. 在熊猫基地开展了旨在"倡导绿色生活，共建生态文明"的活动。

NOTE 本短语的同义短语是 aim at。

alert to[1] *adj.* ❶fully aware of (something, especially a problem or danger) 充分认识到（某一问题或危险）的: The bank was *alert to* the risk. 银行充分地认识到了这一风险。❷watchful and paying attention to what is happening and ready to react quickly if necessary 警惕的，机警的: The province remains *alert to* the influenza spread. 该省对流感的蔓延依然保持着警惕。They warned the public to be *alert to* the sale of fake college entrance exam papers through the Internet and mobile phones. 他们提醒公众警惕通过互联网和手机贩卖假高考试卷的诈骗行为。He is ever *alert to* making money. 在赚钱方面，他一贯是机警的。

alert to[2] *vt.* 【可分性动词短语】（正式用语）warn (someone) about (something such as a danger or threat); make (someone) watchful about and ready for (possible danger) 警告（某人有某种危险）；使（某人对可能的危险）保持警觉: The government *alerted* its people *to* the dangers facing the country. 该国政府向其人民警示了国家所面临的种种危险。We should *alert* the public *to* the dangers of smoking. 我们应该使公众对吸烟的危害性有所警觉。They had been *alerted to* the possibility of further price rises. 他们已被警示价格有进一步上涨的可能性。

align with *vt.* 【可分性动词短语】（常用被动语态形式）❶bring (something) into a straight line with (something else) 使（某物）处于同一条直线上: All letters must be *aligned with* the one on the left-hand side. 所有的字母都必须与左侧的那个字母成一条直线。You have to *align* the picture *with* one directly opposite it. 你得把这幅画和正对着它的另一幅对齐。❷（常与反身代词连用）bring (usually someone or oneself) into agreement with (someone or a particular group) 使（某人或自己）与……一致；与……团结一致: The major unions are *aligned with* the government on this issue. 一些主要的工会在这一问题上的意见与政府一致。We must *align* ourselves *with* other workers in the struggle for better working conditions. 我们必须与其他工人团结一致去争取更好的工作条件。❸（常与反身代词连用）publicly support (an organization, a set of opinions or a person that you agree with) 公开支持: Though not *aligned with* rebels, the opposition had also pushed for the president to resign and leave the country. 虽然该反对派并不支持反政府武装，但也敦促总统辞职并离开祖国。Newspapers traditionally *align* themselves *with* one political party. 传统上来讲，报界通常站在一个政党的立场上。

all alone *adj.* &*adv.* completely by oneself 独自（地），单独（地）: She has been *all alone* since the death of her husband. 丈夫死后，她一直独居。What will you do if the battery on your mobile phone runs out when you are *all alone*? 当只有你孤零零一人

A

时,你的手机又没电了,你该怎么办? She was sitting *all alone* in the hall. 她独自一人坐在大厅里。The house stands on the hillside *all alone*. 这所房子孤零零地坐落在山坡上。He did it *all alone*. 这项工作全是他一个人做的。

all along *adv.* (非正式用语,常用于完成时态) during the whole time; from the beginning; all the time; throughout 始终,从始至终,一直: As a permanent member of the UN Security Council, China has been working *all along* to push forward the Middle East peace process. 作为安理会常任理事国,中国一直致力于推进中东和平进程。I knew *all along* that it wasn't his real name. 我一开始就知道那不是他的真名字。

NOTE 本短语的同义短语为 right along,但本短语更为常用。

all at once *adv.* ❶(of something happening) suddenly, usually when you are not expecting it 突然地(发生): *All at once* a crash of thunder shook the whole house. 忽然间,一声雷响震撼了整所房子。The storm broke out *all at once*. 暴风雨突然来临。❷(of several different things happening) all at the same time; all together (几件不同的事)同时(发生): A number of things happened *all at once*. 几件事同时发生了。You can't be doing two things *all at once*. 你不能同时做两件事情吧。The teacher told the children to talk once a time; if they talked *all at once*, she could not understand them. 老师让孩子们一个一个地讲。如果他们都同时讲,她就不知道他们在讲什么。

NOTE 当本短语作"突然地(发生)"解时,与 all of a sudden 的意义和用法相同,都常用于口语中。本短语的语气较强,故常用于句首。

all but Ⅰ *adv.* almost; very nearly 几乎,差不多: The evening party was *all but* over when we arrived. 我们到的時候,晚会几乎要结束了。The alarm clock *all but* fell down to the ground. 那只闹钟差点掉到地上。It was *all but* impossible to read his writing. 他的字几乎无法看懂。I have known him for *all but* ten years. 我认识他将近 10 年了。

Ⅱ *prep.* everyone or everything except (someone or something) 除了……全都: I know them *all but* two. 他们之中,除了两个人外,我都认识。*All but* the morning star have disappeared. 除了晨星之外,其余的星星都不见了。

NOTE 1. 当本短语用作副词性短语时,all 和 but 都是副词,用来修饰动词、形容词、数词和副词。

2. 当本短语用作介词性短语时,all 是代词,而 but 则是介词,后接数词或名词等。

all day (long) *adv.* for the whole day; throughout the day 整天,一天到晚地: What do you do at home *all day*? 你整天都在家里干些什么? The doctors and nurses in the specialized hospital attended on these special patients by turns *all day long*. 这所专科医院中的医护人员全天候地轮流照看这些特殊患者。She shopped *all day long* looking for a new dress. 为了选购一件新衣服,她逛了一整天的商店。

all in all Ⅰ *adv.* ❶(常用于口语中) (used for showing that you are considering every aspect of something) on the whole; generally 总的说来: *All in all*, I think it has been a very successful conference. 总的来说,我认为这次大会是成功的大会。His reaction to the doctor's treatment is, *all in all*, satisfactory. 他对医生治疗的反应总的说来还是令人满意的。He has his faults, but, *all in all*, he is a good helper. 他虽有缺点,但总的说来,他是一个好帮

手。❷ altogether 总共：In today's class there were seventeen absentees *all in all*. 在今天的课上，总共有 17 人缺席。

Ⅱ *n.*（无复数形式）❶（正式用语）the person or thing that you love most 最心爱的人；最喜欢的东西：She was *all in all* to him. 她是他最心爱的人。Music was his *all in all*. 音乐是他的最爱。❷everything 一切，全部：Painting became his *all in all* after the death of his wife. 他妻子去世后，绘画便成了他的一切。

NOTE 1. 当本短语用作副词性短语时，常位于句首，用以说明全句，间或用作插入语，置于被其说明的词之前(见第二个例句)。

2. 当本短语用作名词性短语时，在句中作表语。

all manner of *adj.*（正式用语）many different types of (people or things)各种各样的(人或物)：He enjoyed interacting with *all manner of* people. 他喜欢与各种不同的人交往。*All manner of* beautiful clothes can be bought in that supermarket. 在那个超级商场，人们可以买到各式各样的漂亮服装。The guests were served with *all manner of* food and drink. 为客人们端上来了各种各样的食物和饮料。

NOTE 1. 本短语可修饰可数名词和不可数名词。

2. 本短语中的名词 manner 必须用单数形式。

all of a sudden *adv.*（of something）happening quickly, and without any sign that it is going to happen; suddenly(指某事)突然地(发生)："*All of a sudden*, I felt my car going up in the air and landing again. Everything turned red and there was a very strong explosion," the driver said. 那位司机讲述道："突然，我感到我的汽车腾空而起，然后落了下来。一切都变成了红色，接着就是十分强烈的爆炸。" We heard a tremendous explosion *all of a sudden*. 我们突然听到了一声剧烈的爆炸。

NOTE 1. 本短语与副词 suddenly 的意义和用法相同，但本短语的语气更强。

2. 本短语多用于句首，间或用于句尾。

all over Ⅰ *adv.* ❶in every part; everywhere 全部；到处：Paint it green *all over*! 把它全部涂成绿色！She is shaking *all over* with cold. 她冻得浑身发抖。I have looked *all over* for my glasses. 我到处寻找我的眼镜。❷from the beginning 重新：He dropped his notebook in the water and had to write the assignment *all over*. 他把笔记本掉到了水里，所以不得不重写作业。

Ⅱ *prep.* in all the parts of; everywhere in 遍及……：Skyscraper homes are being built *all over* the globe, and would you live on the 80th floor? 世界各地都在兴建高层住宅楼，而你愿意居住在 80 层楼上吗？There are reports of people seeing large unidentified flying objects in the skies coming in from *all over* the country. 全国各地纷纷发来人们目击到空中大型不明飞行物的报告。I looked *all over* the house for that letter, and it was in my pocket all the time. 我在屋内到处找那封信，而它竟一直在我的衣袋里。There was mud *all over* the floor. 地板上到处都是泥。

Ⅲ *adj.*（用作表语）(used for saying that a particular event, situation, or period of time has ended) finished; completed（指某一事件、局面或时期）结束的：When the first world war began in August 1914, they said it would be *all over* by Christmas. 当第一次世界大战于 1914 年 8 月份爆发时，人们说它到圣诞节时就会结束。The referee has blown his whistle, and the game is *all over*. 裁判员已经鸣哨，比赛结束了。

all right Ⅰ *adv.* ❶yes; okay 是，好吧："Come to my office at five, ok?" "All right, Mr

Chairman." "5点钟到我办公室来,好吗?" "是,主席先生。" *All right*, class, open your books to page 23. 好,同学们,把书翻到23页。❷(used to emphasize that there is no doubt about something) certainly; without a doubt 当然,肯定: It's cold *all right*. 天气确实很冷。"Are you sure it's her?" "Oh, it's her all right." "你能肯定是她吗?" "哦,肯定是她。" ❸ in proper or working order; in a satisfactory way 运转正常,情况良好: The machine had been running *all right* up till last night. 到昨天晚上为止,这台机器一直运转良好。Did the party go *all right*? 聚会开得好吗? ❹safe and sound 安然无恙地: We hope they have arrived in New York *all right*. 我们希望他们已安然抵达纽约。

Ⅱ *adj*. (用作表语) ❶satisfactory or fairly pleasant, but not excellent; okay 令人满意的,好的,还可以的: Your work is *all right* but I'm sure you could do better. 你的工作令人满意,但我相信你会做得更好。Manchester's *all right*, but I'd rather live in London. 曼彻斯特不错,但我更喜欢住在伦敦。Will it be *all right* with you if I give you that money tomorrow instead of today? 那笔钱我今天不给你,明天再给,可以吗? ❷correct 对的,正确的: Your answers are *all right*. 你答得都对。I thought it was *all right* for her to date him, but it's wrong for her to marry him. 我认为她与他约会没有错,可和他结婚却是错误的。She answered the questions quickly, and she got them *all right*. 她很快地回答了那些问题,并且全答对了。❸(非正式用语) not hurt or ill; fairly healthy; well; okay 身体状况良好: You look terrible, are you *all right*? 你脸色很不好,身体还好吧? I've not been very well, but I'm *all right* now. 我的身体一直不太好,但现在好了。❹(非正式用语) very good or nice 很好的,挺好的: "What's the new boy like?" "He's *all right*." "新来的那个男孩怎么样?" "挺好的。"

NOTE 本短语可转化为复合词all-right,意为"很好的"。例如:

> He is an *all-right* guy.
> 他是个很好的人。

all the more *adv.* even more (or better, harder, etc.) than before (与以前相比)更加,越发: His sincere self-criticism made us respect him *all the more*. 他真诚的自我批评使我们更加尊敬他。I feel *all the more* strongly that your political viewpoints are correct. 我越发感到你的政治观点是正确的。

all the same *adv.* (主要用于口语中,其前常用连词 but) (introducing a statement which indicates that a situation or your opinion has not changed, in spite of what has happened or what has been said) nevertheless; anyhow; still; despite what has been mentioned 仍然,还是,尽管如此: I'm sure I locked the door, but *all the same*, I think I'll go and check. 我确信我把门锁上了,但尽管如此,我想我还要去检查一下。Tom is naughty and stubborn, but you love him *all the same*. 汤姆又淘气又倔强,但你还是爱他。I didn't expect to find anything, but I decided to look around *all the same*. 我不指望发现什么,但我还是决定四处看看。

NOTE **1.** 本短语的另外一种表达形式是 just the same。

2. 本短语与副词 nevertheless, anyhow 和 still 意义相同。但本短语一般置于句尾,而这三个副词则都用于句首或句中。

all the time *adv.* for all of a period of time; throughout the time; during the whole period 一直，总是，始终：When she was sent to the hospital, the schoolgirl was talking to herself *all the time*, unaware of those around her. 当那名女学生被送往医院的时候，她一直自言自语着，没有觉察到四周在场的人。Mary went to college in her hometown, and lived at home *all the while*. 玛丽就在她家所在的城市上大学，所以总是住在家里。He pretended to be asleep, but *all the time* he was watching her. 他假装睡着了，但却始终在盯着她。

NOTE 本短语的同义短语是 all the while，两者都常用于句尾，但本短语比 all the while 更常用。

all (the) year round *adv.* throughout the whole year, without regard to seasons 一年四季，终年：The work at the weather observation station goes on *all the year round* in spite of any weather conditions. 无论天气如何，气象观测站的工作一年四季都在进行。Thanks to the indoor courts we can play tennis *all year round*. 由于有室内球场，我们一年到头都可以打网球。The grasslands beyond this mountain have little rain *all the year round*. 山那边的草原终年少雨。

allow for *vt.*【不可分性动词短语】(常用一般时态) consider or include (something) when making a plan or calculation (在做计划或计算时)考虑到，把……考虑在内：The cost of the new road, *allowing for* inflation, is around $7 million. 考虑到通货膨胀因素，这条新路的成本约为 700 万美元。The research did not *allow for* the fact that some students are doing part-time work. 该项研究没把有些大学生在打零工这一事实纳入考虑之中。We must start early, to *allow for* finding their house. 我们必须早点动身，因为还得花时间去找他们的房子。He missed the target because the wind hadn't been *allowed for*. 由于没考虑到风速，他没有射中靶子。

NOTE 本短语的同义短语是 take account of, take into account 和 take into consideration。

allow of *vt.*【不可分性动词短语】(正式用语，无被动语态形式，用一般时态) give the possibility of (something); make (something) possible 有……可能，使……可能：The facts *allow of* no other explanation. 事实不容有其他解释。The thorough repair of the machine *allows of* no delay. 这台机器非得马上彻底检修不可。This stream is too shallow to *allow of* boating. 这条小河太浅，不能行船。

NOTE 1. 本短语常用于含否定词语的句子中。

2. 本短语的同义短语是 admit of。

allude to *vt.*【不可分性动词短语】(正式用语) mention (someone or something) in an indirect way (间接地)提到……：I did not mean to *allude to* someone you disliked so much. 我并不是有意提起你这么不喜欢的人。In the lecture on Greek philosophy, Professor Smith *alluded to* his earlier essay on the subject. 史密斯教授在希腊哲学讲座中提到他早些时候写的一篇有关该主题的文章。But the new economic strategy, which the President *alluded to* in his Rose Garden news conference, carries some considerable risks. 然而，总统在他的玫瑰园新闻发布会上间接提到的经济新战略具有很大的冒险性。The subject was never *alluded to*. 这一主题从来没有被提及过。

NOTE 本短语的同义短语是 refer to。两者之间的区别见 refer to。

along with *prep.* (used for mentioning additional people or things that are also included or involved in an action or situation) in company with; together with

和……一起,与……一道:At the Beijing Olympics opening ceremony, more than 80 foreign leaders and IOC President Rogge were seated *along with* top Chinese leaders. 在北京奥运会开幕式上,80 多位外国领导人和国际奥委会主席罗格与中国高层领导人坐在一起。Two Chinese scientists received China's annual State Science and Technology Award, *along with* a cash prize of five million yuan. 两位中国科学家获得了一年一度的中国国家科学技术奖,并获得 500 万元的现金奖励。

NOTE 1. 本短语作为介词性短语,在句中是附加成分,因此它不影响句中谓语动词的单复数形式(见第一个例句)。再如:

> The woman, *along with* her three children, has come.
> 那名妇女和她的三个孩子已经来了。

与本短语用法相同的还有 accompanied by, in company with, together with 等。

2. 本短语与 together with 稍有不同。后者只表示"与……一道",而本短语还含有"配合"和"协调"之意。

amount to *vt.*【不可分性动词短语】(无被动语态形式)❶(用一般时态) add up to a particular total; make a total of or add up to (a figure)总计,达到(某一数目):His debts *amount to* over $10,000. 他负债总计超过 10 000美元。Last year, China's import and export volume *amounted to* 2.56 trillion dollars. 去年,中国进出口贸易总额达 2.56 万亿美元。❷(用一般时态) have the same effect as (something else); be the same as or equal to (something else)等同于,相当于:In fact, the President's silence on the matter *amounts to* a refusal. 实际上,总统对此事的沉默就等同于拒绝。His suggestion *amounts to* saying that there is still room for improvement in the work. 他的建议无异于说这件工作仍有改进的余地。❸(常用一般时态,用于否定句中,后接 much 或 a great deal) be very important or successful; make progress 变得重要;取得成功;取得进展:If he goes on like this, he'll never *amount to* much. 如果他这样干下去,他不会取得多大成功的。The results of the research don't really *amount to* a great deal. 研究结果确实没有多大进展。

NOTE 当本短语作"总计,达到(某一数目)"解时,同义短语是 run to。

amuse oneself *v.* (常与 by, with 连用) keep oneself interested or entertained, so that he or she does not get bored 自娱自乐:How do you *amuse yourself* when you have nothing to do? 你无事可做时是怎样自娱自乐的? The child *amused himself* by playing his toy computer. 这孩子以玩玩具计算机取乐。I'm sure we can find *something to amuse ourselves* with. 我确信我们能找到一些事情来自娱自乐。

and so on *adv.* (used at the end of a list to indicate that there are other similar people or things that you could also mention) and others (用于表示还有其他相同的人或物)等等:Economic growth makes us richer, provides more jobs, *and so on*. 经济增长使我们更加富裕,还能提供更多的工作岗位,等等。The assistance they offered valued at 10 million *yuan*, which included food, medicine, tents, *and so on*. 他们所提供的援助价值为1 000万元,这包括食品、药品、帐篷,等等。

NOTE 1. 本短语的同义短语是 and so forth, and the like 和 and what not。在这些短语中,and so on 和 and so forth 较常用,其中,and so on 最为常用。and so forth 较为正式,多用作书面语。and so on 和 and so forth 常可换用。and what not 为非正式用语,与前三个短语不同的是,它仅用来指

事物,常常以 and whatnot 形式使用。

2. 本短语必须用于连接对等的名词,而且在最后一个列举的名词前只能用逗号,不可再加连词 and 或 or 等。

and so forth ⇨ **and so on**

and the like ⇨ **and so on**

and what not ⇨ **and so on**

and yet *conj.* (used for introducing a fact, situation, or quality that is surprising after what has just been mentioned) and despite this; but; nevertheless; however 但是,然而,而:The girl is clever, *and yet* she is not hardworking. 这女孩很聪明,但就是不努力。He felt ill, *and yet* he went to work and tried to concentrate. 他感到身体不适,然而他仍旧去上班,并且竭力集中精神工作。

answer back *v.* ❶(非正式用语) (especially of a child) reply rudely to you when you speak to him or her(尤指孩子)顶嘴,回嘴:I don't like children who *answer back*. 我不喜欢顶嘴的孩子。You should not *answer back* to your mother like that, son. 儿子,你不应该那样和你妈妈顶嘴。Don't you dare *answer* me *back*, young man! 年轻人,你竟敢和我顶嘴! He's a rude boy, always *answering* his mother *back*. 他是个没礼貌的孩子,总和他妈妈顶嘴。❷react to criticism by arguing or explaining 辩解:The company criticized was given the opportunity to *answer back*. 给予被批评的公司辩解的机会。

NOTE 1. 当本短语用作及物性动词短语时,所带的宾语必须置于本短语的动词和副词中间。

2. 当本短语作"顶嘴,回嘴"解时,同义短语是 talk back。两者的区别是:本短语可作为及物性动词短语使用,而 talk back 只能作为不及物性动词短语使用。见 talk back。

answer for *vt.* 【不可分性动词短语】(常用一般时态) ❶ be responsible for (something); take the responsibility for (someone or something)为……负责,对……承担责任:You have to *answer for* any errors in the calculations. 计算中出现任何错误你都得负责。The teacher said that he was ready to *answer for* the students who worked under his direction. 老师说他愿意为在他指导下学习的学生们承担责任。"Many of the reported activities did occur, and I have a lot to *answer for*," he admitted. 他承认说:"许多报道过的活动确实都发生过,我有诸多责任不可推卸。" ❷explain or justify to people in authority (the actions of someone or some act)对……做出解释:Their coach must *answer for* the team's poor performance. 他们的教练必须对其队员的差劲表现做出解释。❸be punished for (something bad or wrong you have done)因(做错事或坏事)而受惩罚:He will be made to *answer for* his crimes one day. 他总有一天会因其种种罪行而受到惩罚。He may not go to jail, but someday he is going to have to *answer for* what he did. 他可能不会坐牢,但总有一天他会为他的所作所为受到惩罚。❹guarantee 担保,保证:I'll *answer for* his loyalty to the country with my life. 我愿以生命担保他对国家是忠诚的。I knew she was innocent. I will *answer for* Linda. 我知道她是无辜的。我为琳达做出担保。He *answered for* it that the results of the experiments were correct. 他保证这些实验结果是正确的。

answer to *vt.* 【不可分性动词短语】❶(常用一般时态) take orders from or obey (someone or something)听命于,服从:The great pleasure about working for yourself is that you don't have to *answer to* anyone. 为自己打工的最大乐趣是不必听命于他人。The Nobel Peace Prize committee is appointed by but does not *answer to* Norway's parliament. 诺贝尔和平奖评审委员会由挪威议会任命,但并不听命于它。❷(无被动语态形式,常用一般现在时,与名词 name 连用) have a particular name; be called by (a name)名字叫,叫作(什么名字):They had a small boy, who *answered to* the name of Andrew. 他们有个小男孩,名字叫安德鲁。No one in this office *answers to* that name. 在这个办公室里没有人叫那个名字。In my class there's a girl *answering to* the name of Elizabeth. 在我的班里,有一个叫伊丽莎白的女生。❸have to explain to (someone) why you did something (就自己的所为之因)向(某人)做出解释:I *answered to* no one except the manager. 除了经理之外,我没向任何人做出解释。❹(无被动语态形式,常用一般时态) match (something, usually a description)与(常指某种描述或说明)相符合:He *answers to* the description given by the police, so he must be the criminal. 他与警方所提供的相貌特征相符,因此他肯定就是那个罪犯。The performance of the antenna does not *answer to* the description of the manual. 这种天线的功能与使用手册中所述不符。

any more *adv.* (仅用于否定句和疑问句中) (used when talking or asking about a situation that has ended, or about something that someone has stopped doing) any longer; again 再,还:He means business when he says he's not going to do it. So there's no use trying to persuade him *any more*. 他说他不干,这不是他随便说说的。所以,再劝他也没用。The Smiths don't live here *any more*. 史密斯一家不再住这里了。

NOTE 本短语与副词 anymore 的意义和用法相同,两者都不能用于句首。

anything but *adv.* (used for emphasizing that a particular word does not describe someone or something, because the opposite is true about them) not at all; far from being; by no means 一点也不,决不:He is *anything but* a scholar. 他决不是个学者。Do *anything but* that. 不管干什么,也决不能干那事。Unfortunately, our hosts were *anything but* friendly. 不幸的是,我们的东道主一点也不友好。He is *anything but* embarrassed. 他毫无局促不安之感。

NOTE 1. 本短语是一种强势否定的用法。短语中的 but 是介词,可接名词、代词和形容词为宾语。此外,本短语可省略宾语,单独使用。

2. 不要将本短语与 anything … but 混淆。anything … but 表示"除……之外"之意。例如:

> I'll do *anything* for you *but* that.
> 除那之外,我什么事都可以为你做。

3. 不要将本短语与 nothing but 混淆。nothing but 表示"只是,只有,只不过"之意。见 nothing but。

apart from *prep.* ❶with the exception of (someone or something)除了……之外:His families *apart from* his grandma attend the wedding ceremony. 除奶奶外,他的家人都出席了这场婚礼。For instance, a teacher at a middle school knew nothing about Lai Ning *apart from* his putting out the fire. 例如,一所中学有一位教师除了知道赖宁救火之外,竟对他一无所知。❷in addition to; as well as; beside or besides 除了……之外,还……:*Apart from* the injuries to her face and hands, she broke one of her legs. 她除了脸部和双手受伤以外,一条腿也断了。*Apart from* being too large, the trousers don't suit me. 这条裤子不但太

大，而且我穿着也不合适。❸not considering 不考虑……，撇开……来说：*Apart from* the salary, it's not a bad job. 不考虑工资的话，这份工作还不坏。Quite *apart from* the cost, we need to think about how much time the job will take. 撇开花多少钱不说，我们得考虑这件工作需要多少时间。

NOTE 1. 本短语用于肯定句时，表示"除了……之外，还……"（＝in addition to）；用于否定句时，表示"除了……之外，无……"（＝except for）。请比较下面两个句子：

> He has a car *apart from* a house.
> 他除了一栋房子之外，还有一辆汽车。（肯定句）
> He has nothing *apart from* a house.
> 他除了一栋房子之外，一无所有。（否定句）

2. 本短语的同义短语是 aside from，aside from 是美国英语用法。

apologize for *vt.*【不可分性动词短语】express (to someone) that you are sorry for (something or doing something wrong or causing a problem) 因……道歉：The vice-chancellor of Cambridge University wrote a letter to the Chinese Premier to *apologize for* the incident disrupting his speech at the university. 剑桥大学副校长致函中国总理，就他在剑桥大学演讲受干扰事件表示道歉。I *apologize for* taking so long to reply. 很抱歉，这么久才给予回复。

NOTE 本短语的另外一种表达形式是 make an apology for。例如：

> The general manager *made an apology for* not being able to carry out his promise for a salary rise this year.
> 总经理因没能履行今年增加工资的承诺而表示歉意。

apologize to *vt.*【不可分性动词短语】（常与 for 连用）say that you are sorry to (someone) 向（某人）道歉：*Apologize to* your teacher for that rude remark. 为你说的那句粗鲁话向你的老师道歉。

NOTE 本短语的另外一种表达形式是 make an apology to。例如：

> I *made an apology to* my friend for not being
> able to write back.
> 我因没能写回信而向我的朋友道歉。

appeal against ⇨ **appeal to**

appeal for *vt.*【不可分性动词短语】earnestly request (someone) for (something or giving you something that you need) 请求，要求；呼吁：The criminal *appealed to* the judge for mercy. 那罪犯请求法官给予宽恕。Somalia's government *appealed for* international help to combat pirates in the Gulf of Aden. 索马里政府呼吁国际社会帮助打击亚丁湾海盗。

NOTE 本短语的另外一种表达形式是 make an appeal for。例如：

> China *made* an urgent *appeal for* millions of tents to shelter survivors of the earthquake.
> 中国紧急要求援助数百万顶帐篷，以安置此次地震中的幸存者。

在这种表达形式中，appeal 之前还可以使用物主代词等来替换不定冠词 an。例如：

> The mother made her last *appeal* to her daughter *for* her early return.
> 那位母亲最后一次请求女儿早日归来。

appeal to *vt.*【不可分性动词短语】❶formally ask (a court of law or similar authority) to change its decision 要求（法院或相同机构）重新裁决，向（法院或同类机构）提出上诉：His lawyer has

appealed to the Supreme Court to stop his extradition. 他的律师已要求最高法院重新裁决,阻止将他引渡回国。Mr Black decided to *appeal to* a higher court. 布莱克先生决定向高一级法院提出上诉。❷make an earnest request to (someone) (to do something or to give you something that you need)向(某人)请求,要求;呼吁:They *appealed to* him to abandon the idea. 他们请求他放弃那个想法。The government *appeals to* the people for support. 政府呼吁人民支持它。❸(无被动语态形式,用一般时态) attract (someone); arouse a favorable response in (someone)对(某人)有感染力,引起(某人)的好感:Does the idea of studying abroad *appeal to* you? 出国留学的主意对你有吸引力吗? These activities were planned to *appeal to* young people thirsting for adventure. 这些活动是为迎合年轻人冒险的欲望而设计的。The dog shows in the Year of the Dog especially *appealed to* children. 狗年办狗展尤其受到了小朋友们的喜欢。❹turn to (something)求助于,诉诸:If you don't obey me, I shall *appeal to* force. 如果你不服从我,我就动武啦。*Appealing to* violence will intensify the crisis in this region. 诉诸暴力将会加剧这一地区的危机。

NOTE **1.** 本短语的第三个义项在运用中易出错。例如,"我喜欢这项工作。"我们不能把它说成:* I appeal to this job. 而应说成:This job appeals to me. 同样,不能把"This job appeals to me."直译为"这项工作喜欢我。"

2. 本短语的另外一种表达形式是 make an appeal to。例如:

> The employee *made an appeal to* his boss for forgiveness.
> 那名雇员恳求老板原谅他。

在这种表达形式中,在 appeal 之前还可以使用物主代词来替换不定冠词 an。例如:

> The mother *made her* last *appeal to* her daughter for her early return.
> 那位母亲最后一次请求女儿早日归来。

3. 本短语与 appeal against 意义和用法相同。本短语为英国英语用法, appeal against 为美国英语用法。

apply for *vt.* 【不可分性动词短语】make a formal request, usually in writing, for (something such as a job or a place in a college or university, or for permission to do or have something)(常指以书面形式)提出申请:Do you know how to *apply for* a job in a foreign enterprise? 你知道如何申请在外企工作吗? In order to *apply for* a US visa and travel to the US, Iraqi citizens must have a "G" series passport. 为了申请到赴美签证,伊拉克公民必须持有 G 系列的护照。Accommodation should be *applied for* as much in advance as possible. 需要膳宿供应的应尽量提前申请。

NOTE 本短语的另外一种表达形式是 make an application for。例如:

> He has *made an application for* membership of the club.
> 他已提出加入该俱乐部的申请。

apply to *vt.* ❶make a formal request to (someone or something such as a school) usually in writing(常指以书面形式)向……提出申请,请求:You have to *apply to* the passport office for a visa. 你得向护照局申请签证。How many universities have you *applied to*? 你向多少所大学提出了申请? All interested in the files must first *apply to* the Foreign Ministry's Archives some 20 workdays in advance.

所有对这些档案感兴趣的人士必须先提前20个工作日向外交部档案馆提出申请。❷(用一般时态,不用进行时态)be fit or suitable for (a particular person or thing)适用于:These textbooks do not *apply to* beginners. 这些教科书不适于初学者使用。The new aircraft lighter ban also *applies to* military passengers. 这项新颁布的禁止携带打火机登机的禁令也适用于军人乘客。These methods also *apply to* learning English. 这些方法也适用于英语学习。❸use (a particular method, process, law, etc.) to help, answer, or work at (something or doing something)运用于:We must pay great attention to *applying* our knowledge of mathematics *to* other techniques. 我们必须注意把我们的数学知识运用于其他技术。A similar technique can be *applied to* the treatment of cancer. 相同的技术亦可运用于癌症的治疗。❹put or spread (a layer of something such as paint) onto (a surface)在(表面)上涂(一层油漆等):*Apply* the paint evenly *to* both sides of the door. 给门的两面都均匀地涂上油漆。This cream is best *applied to* the face at night. 这种乳霜最好在夜里涂抹在面部。❺(无被动语态形式,与反身代词连用) work very hard or with careful attention at (something) for a long time 专注于,全心致力于:*Apply* yourself *to* whatever task you do. 要专心于你所从事的任何工作。If he had *applied* himself *to* his work, he could have finished it in time. 如果他当时全心致力于他的工作,他应该能按时完成任务的。She is determined to *apply* herself *to* education after graduation. 她决心毕业后投身于教育事业。

NOTE 当本短语作"(常指以书面形式)向……提出申请,请求"解时,另外一种表达形式是 make an application to。例如:

> The hospital has made an application to the authorities to build twenty new wards. 该医院已向当局提出新建20间病房的申请。

appoint to *vt.*【可分性动词短语】select (someone) as (the person to occupy a post); choose (someone) for (a particular job or position)指派,任命(某人)担任(工作、职务等):President Barack Obama *appointed* former first lady Hillary Clinton *to* the important position of secretary of state. 巴拉克·奥巴马总统任命前第一夫人希拉里·克林顿担任国务卿这一重要职务。

approve of *vt.*(常用一般时态)【不可分性动词短语】agree to; be in favor of (something or someone)同意,赞成:They don't quite *approve of* him as the captain of their team. 他们不太赞成他当他们的队长。I cannot support a policy *of* which I have never *approved*. 我不会支持我从不赞成的政策。She would never do anything that was not *approved of* by her parents. 她从来不去做她父母不赞成的事情。

NOTE 本短语的同义短语是 agree on/upon, assent to 和 consent to;反义短语是 disapprove of 和 disagree with。

apt at *adj.*(正式用语)(of someone) quick to learn and good at (doing something)敏于,擅长于(做某事):She is *apt at* drawing. 她善于绘画。He is *apt at* picking up a new subject. 他敏于学习新科目。She is *apt at* programming a computer. 她擅长编电脑程序。

apt to *adj.*(后接原形动词)(of someone or something) having a natural or habitual tendency to (do something)惯于(做某事),易于(做某事):Many parents are *apt to* make such mistakes as thinking they're always right in everything they do and their children should always listen to them. 许多家长都惯于犯这样的错误,即他们认为自己做什么都对,孩子就应该听他们的。This kind of shoe is *apt to* slip on wet ground. 这样的鞋子在湿地上容易打滑。My mother is in her eighties now and *apt to* be a bit forgetful. 我母亲现已八十几岁,有点好忘事了。

argue about *vt.* 【不可分性动词短语】discuss or debate about(something or doing something), with each of you giving your difference or opposing opinions 争论,辩论: The young married couples are always *arguing about* money matters. 这些年轻的夫妇总是因钱的事情争论不休。Let us not *argue about* going out tonight. 我们不要再争论今晚出去的事啦。They were *arguing about* how to spend the money. 他们在争辩如何花这笔钱。They were *arguing about* which film to go and see. 他们在争论去看哪一部电影。

NOTE 本短语的同义短语是 argue over。

argue into *vt.* 【可分性动词短语】(英国英语用法,后接动名词或动名词短语) persuade (someone), often with strong feeling, by showing reason for (doing something)(以情、理)说服(某人)做(某事): The children finally succeeded in *arguing* their father *into* taking a vacation with them. 孩子们最终成功地说服了爸爸和他们一起度假。His wife *argued* him *into* leaving his present job. 他妻子极力劝他辞去现在的工作。

NOTE 本短语的同义短语是 persuade into, reason into 和 talk into; 反义短语是 argue out of, persuade out of, reason out of 和 talk out of。

argue out of *vt.* 【可分性动词短语】(英国英语用法,后接动名词或动名词短语) persuade (someone) against (doing something)说服(某人)不做(某事): His parents *argued* him *out of* leaving his present job. 他父母劝他不要辞去现在的工作。I've managed to *argue* her *out of* going to the party. 我已说服她不去参加聚会了。

NOTE 本短语的同义短语是 persuade out of, reason out of 和 talk out of;反义短语是 argue into, persuade into, reason into 和 talk into。

argue over *vt.* 【不可分性动词短语】dispute or quarrel about (something or doing something) with someone 争论,辩论: They are still *arguing over* the details of the contract. 他们还在对合同的细节争论不休。We used to *argue over* who should get up first. 我们过去常常因谁该先起床而发生争论。The two sides are drawing up the contract and *arguing over* what to keep and delete. 双方正在起草合同,并在争论哪些部分该保留,哪些部分该删掉。The two brothers were *arguing over* which TV programme to watch. 两兄弟在争论要看哪个电视节目。

NOTE 本短语的同义短语是 argue about。

argue with *vt.* 【不可分性动词短语】(非正式用语,常用于否定句中) ❶ speak angrily with (someone) about something that you disagree about 与(某人)争论: Don't *argue with* your father — you know he's right. 别和你爸爸争论了,你明知他是对的。You shouldn't *argue with* your girl—friend about this question. 在这个问题上,你不应该和女朋友争论。

❷disagree with (a statement): 不同意(说法); 不承认表述: He's really a successful businessman—you can't *argue with* that. 他确实是一位成功的商人,这一点你就不要否认了。

NOTE 当本短语作"与(某人)争论"解时,另外一种表达形式是 get into (an) argument with。例如:

> Every time we visit my family, my husband *gets into an argument* with my sister.
> 每次回我们家我丈夫都要和我妹妹发生争执。

其中的 argument 还可以用复数形式。例如:

> The department heads *got into* hot *arguments* with the general manager on the issue of whether they should invest in the newly proposed project.
> 各部门的经理与总经理在是否应该投资搞最近提出的工程问题上发生了激烈的争执。

arise from *vt.* 【不可分性动词短语】(正式用语,常用一般时态) exist or start developing because of (something); be caused by (something); result from (something)由……造成,由……引起: His illness *arose from* chronic over-drinking. 他的病是长期酗酒所致。His grandfather died at the age of **97** in Salt Lake City Sunday of complications *arising from* old age. 他的祖父于星期日在盐湖城因衰老引起的并发症逝世,享年 **97** 岁。The dispute *arose from* the lack of communication between the two parties. 这一争执是由于双方缺乏沟通引起的。

NOTE **1.** 不要将本短语的过去时形式 arose from 与 arouse from 混淆。arouse from 意为"(以睡眠中)唤醒激起"。

2. 本短语与 arise out of 意义和用法相同。

arm in arm *adv.* (of two or more persons) with the left arm of one of them bent around the right arm of the other person (指两人或多人)臂挽着臂地: Jim and Mary were laughing and joking together as they walked *arm in arm* down the street. 吉姆和玛丽谈笑风生、臂挽着臂地沿街走着。On their wedding day Prince Charles and Camilla emerged *arm in arm*, smiled and waved to the crowd. 在查尔斯王子和卡米拉举行婚礼那天,他们臂挽着臂地出现了,向人群微笑和招手。I've just seen the three girls going down the road *arm in arm*. 我刚看到三个女孩臂挽着臂地沿着这条路走去。

NOTE 本短语是由"身体某部分的名词+介词+身体某部分的名词"构成的副词性短语。同类的短语还有:hand in hand, shoulder to shoulder, side by side, 等等。

arm with *vt.* 【可分性动词短语】❶(常用被动语态形式) provide (oneself or other people) with (weapons, etc.)用(武器等)把(自己或某人)武装起来: They quickly *armed* themselves *with* sticks. 他们很快都拿起了棍棒作武器。Somali pirates are *armed with* automatic weapons, shoulderfired missiles and various types of grenades. 索马里海盗都配有自动武器、肩扛式火箭弹和各式手榴弹。He *armed* his men *with* any weapons he could find. 他以他能得到的任何武器将他的部下武装了起来。❷provide (oneself or other people) with (useful or impressive equipment, information, etc.)向(某人)提供……: Modern science *arms* men *with* new instruments of mastery over nature. 现代科学给人类提供了征服自然的新工具。I'll need to *arm* myself *with* all the facts before meeting them formally. 我需要掌握全部事实后再与他们正式交锋。

arouse from *vt.*【可分性动词短语】(英国英语用法,正式用语)(of someone or something) wake (someone) from (sleep); excite (someone) from (a dull state of feeling, inactivity, etc.)(从睡眠中)唤醒(某人);激起:We had to *arouse* him *from* his deep sleep. 我们不得不把他从沉睡中唤醒。I was *aroused from* a sound sleep by a knocking at the door. 敲门声把我从酣睡中唤醒。The spread of disease among the refugees at last aroused local people from their indifference towards these unhappy people. 难民群中疾病的流行终于唤醒了本地人民,让他们不再对这些不幸者漠不关心。

arrange for *vt.* ❶ make a plan about (something); plan something for (someone or something); make preparation for (something),为……安排(某事),为……做准备:We will *arrange for* a big celebration at this weekend. 我们将在本周末安排一次大型庆祝活动。We are to *arrange* a reception *for* them. 我们将为他们安排一场欢迎会。The commander has *arranged* his troops *for* battle. 司令员已布置好他的部队准备作战。❷make plans for (someone or something to do something); organize for (something to be done)安排……做(某事),为……做出安排:I have *arranged for* our guests to be driven to the hotel. 我已安排好用车把我们的客人送到宾馆。Please *arrange for* a car to pick me up at six tomorrow morning. 请安排一辆车明早 6 点接我。I shall *arrange for* the job to be done by Friday. 我将安排在星期五前把工作做完。❸change (a piece of music) in a certain way so that it is suitable for (a particular type of voice or instrument)改写(某一乐曲)以适合于(某种类型的发声或乐器):The composer has *arranged* a symphony *for* the piano. 该作曲家将一交响乐曲改编成钢琴演奏曲。

NOTE 当本短语作"为……安排(某事),为……做准备"解时,另外一种表达形式是 make arrangements for。

arrive at *vt.*【不可分性动词短语】❶(无被动语态形式) reach (a place), after having been somewhere else 到达(某处):I *arrived at* the station, exhausted, only to find that the last train had just left. 我精疲力竭地赶到了火车站,结果发现末班车刚刚开走。The 6,800-tonne Fitzgerald, a missile destroyer from the US 7th Fleet, *arrived at* the port of Qingdao for the international fleet review. 美国第七舰队所属的6 800吨的导弹驱逐舰"菲茨杰拉德号"驶抵青岛港来参加这次国际舰队阅兵。❷(常用一般时态) reach (something as a result, conclusion, decision, or solution to a problem), after thinking about it or discussing it (经过思考或讨论而)取得(结果),得出(结论),作出(决定),找到(解决问题的方法):Their efforts to bridge the gap between the two generations *arrived at* no result in the end. 他们为弥合两代人之间的代沟所做的一切努力没有取得任何结果。The two studies *arrive at* very different conclusions. 这两项研究得出了截然不同的结论。After much consideration, we have *arrived at* a decision. 经过反复考虑后,我们作出了决定。

NOTE 本短语与 arrive in 都表示"到达"之意,两者之间的区别见 arrive in。

arrive in *vt.*【不可分性动词短语】(无被动语态形式) reach (a place), after having been somewhere else or at the end of a journey 到达(某处):Next Monday, we'll leave London at 10:00 and *arrive in* Paris at 13:00. 下周一,我们将于上午10点离开伦敦,下午1点到达巴黎。The second fleet of Chinese escort ships *arrived in* the Gulf of Aden on Monday to replace the first fleet sent there earlier on escort missions. 中国第二批护航编队星期一抵达亚丁湾,接替早些时候被派到那里去执行护航任务的第一批编队。Can you imagine the old days before the European settlers *arrived in* the continent? 你能想象得出在欧洲殖民者抵达大陆之前的那些时日吗?

NOTE 本短语中的 arrive 是不及物性动词。若表示"到达某地",后接介词 at 或 in。arrive at 和 arrive in 的英语释义都是 reach (a place)。但在实际使用中,arrive at 之后一般接表示码头、车站、机场、学校等范围较小而具体的地点名词,而当表示到达大洲、国家、大城市等范围较大的地点时,则用 arrive in。另外,说明"到达"经过或短时停留的地点时,常用 arrive at;而说明"抵达"长期停留、居住或工作等的目的地时,则用 arrive in。例如:

> We *arrived at* Paris on the morning of June 19 and finally *arrived in* Berlin 10 days later.
> 我们6月19日上午到达巴黎,10天后才终于抵达柏林。

as a consequence⇨as a result

as a matter of fact *adv.* (used when you are going to give more details about something or disagree with or correct what has just been said) in fact; in reality 事实上,实际上:"*As a matter of fact*, the US trade deficits with China are closely related to the international transfer of industry of economic globalization." he said. "事实上,美国对华贸易逆差与经济全球化背景下的国际产业转移密切相关。"他说道。"You speak English very well." "Yes, well, I am English, *as a matter of fact*." "你的英语说得非常好。""是啊,我本来就是英国人。"

NOTE 1. 本短语主要用于以下两种情况:

(1)用来加强或补充前面所述内容,提供某事的更多细节,例如:

> I haven't been here long. *As a matter of fact*, I just got off the plane yesterday.
> 我到这儿没多久。实际上我昨天才下飞机。

(2)用来表示不同意见或纠正他人所述之言的内容,例如:

> "Has he been in a bad mood?" "No, *as a matter of fact*, he seemed quite cheerful."
> "他的情绪一直不好?""不,实际上他看上去很快乐。"

2. 本短语多置于句首,其后用逗号与句子相分隔。

3. 本短语的复数形式是 as matters of fact,而不是 * as matter of facts。

4. 本短语的同义短语是 in (actual) fact,两者之间的区别见 in (actual) fact。

as a result *adv.* consequently; therefore 结果,因此,所以:He refused to have medical attention in the early stages of his complaint, and *as a result* he became seriously ill. 他在得病初期拒绝接受治疗,结果病情加重。The production has begun, *as a result*, to rise rapidly. 所以生产开始迅速地增长了。*As a result*, the education system needs to change. 因此说,教育体制需要改革。

NOTE 1. 本短语多置于句首,有时也置于句中(如第三个例句)。

2. 本短语与 as a consequence 意义和用法相同,两者可互换使用。

3. 本短语的同义短语是 in consequence,但本短语更为常用。

as a result of *prep.* because of (something)因为,由于:The number of college graduates has sharply increased *as a result of* a large-scale enrollment expansion scheme introduced. 大学毕业生人数剧增是大规模扩招的结果。More than two hundred people lost their jobs *as a result* of the merger of two companies. 由于两家公司的合并,200 多人失去了工作。

NOTE 本短语的同义短语是 because of 和 in consequence of。三者之中,because of 最为常用。

as a (general) rule *adv.* (used for saying what normally happens) usually 通常:*As a rule*, I stay in on Friday nights. 星期五晚上我通常待在家里。What time do you get to the office *as a rule*? 你通常什么时候到办公室? Water consumption, *as a general rule*, increases rapidly with industrial development. 水的消耗通常随着工业的发展迅速增长。

as a whole *adj.* (用作后置定语) considering all the parts of something as one unit and not as separate parts; altogether 总体上的,整个的:We should say that the Chinese people *as a whole* are living a better life. 我们应该说,中国人民的生活总体上有了改善。22 Chinese academicians jointly appealed that the society as a whole support and take part in China's AIDS prevention and control. 22 位中国院士联名呼吁全社会支持并参与中国的艾滋病防控事业。The study suggests vitamin D may help to slow down the ageing process of DNA, and therefore the ageing process *as a whole*. 该项研究表明,维生素 D 有助于延缓 DNA 的衰老过程,从而延缓整个人体衰老的过程。

NOTE 1. 本短语与 on the whole 之间的区别:一是两者的整体词性不同,前者是形容词性短语,而后者是副词性短语;二是意义上的不同,前者指"作为一个整体来看",指百分之百,即从事物的全貌来考虑和分析某一情况,而后者则表示"大体上""基本上",并非包括百分之百。

2. 本短语的同义短语是 at large 和 in general。

as against *prep.* (used for comparing one thing or amount with another) in comparison with (用于比较两个事物或数量)与……相比较:We had 12 hours of sunshine yesterday, *as against* a forecast of continuous rain. 昨天 12 小时都是晴天,而预报却说全天连雨不断。Our profits this year amount to ＄180,000 *as against* ＄140,000 last year. 与去年的(利润)14 万美元相比,我们今年的利润为 18 万美元。My son gets Saturdays and Sundays off in his new job *as against* working alternate weekends in his last one. 我儿子新找的这份工作星期六、星期日休班, 而原来的那份工作周末是隔周休班。

as … as possible *adv.* (在两个 as 之间加入形容词或副词) as … as one can 尽可能地……:We're determined to make sure intelligence is *as* accurate *as possible* for every challenge in the future. 我们决心保证情报尽可能地准确,以应对将来的任何挑战。Please try your best to ship one half of the goods *as* early *as possible*. 请力争尽可能早地先发运一半的货物过来。We have released the schedule of the "golden jubilee" activities now to enable those who plan to come to BYU-Hawaii to plan *as* far in advance *as possible*. 我们现在就公布建校 50 周年大庆活动的安排,目的是让那些计划来杨伯翰大学夏威夷分校的人尽可能提早做出安排。

as best one can *adv.* as well as you are able to 尽最大努力,竭力:The car broke down in the middle of the night, and he had to get home *as best he could*. 汽车在半夜里坏掉了,因此他不得不想尽了办法才回到了家。Do it *as best you can*. 你尽力而为吧。The girl's mother was sick, so the girl prepared dinner *as best she could*. 这女孩的妈妈病了,所以她得尽力把饭做好。

as compared to/with *prep.* (used for talking about the ways in which two things are different, or about the ways in which something has changed) in comparison with 与……相比:25% of school-age children smoke, *as compared to* 21% of adults. 与 21%的成人吸烟相比,学龄少年吸烟者占 25%。German, *as compared with* French, is difficult to learn. 与法语相比,德语是难学的。Pure aluminum is not very strong *as compared with* iron. 与铁相比,纯铝就不算坚硬。

as far as Ⅰ *adv.* to the place or a distance mentioned 一直到,远到:Every morning the old man takes a walk *as far as* the top of the hill. 这位老人每天早晨一直散步到小山顶。She had got *as far as* the museum before he found her. 她都已经到了博物馆他才找到了她。The satellite will fly *as far as* 66,970 kilometers from the Earth, further than any other in China's space history, the China National Space Administration said. 中国国家宇航局称,这颗卫星可飞至离地球 66 970 公里远的地方,这比中国宇航史上任何其他卫星飞得都远。

Ⅱ *conj.* (非正式用语) to the extent, degree or amount that 到……程度:*As far as* I know, he is a good person whom you can trust. 据我所知,他是个好人,你可以相信他。There weren't any buildings there at all, *as far as* I can remember. 就我所能记得的是,过去那里根本没有任何建筑物。*As far as* they could ascertain, only the old and children were left in the village. 据他们能够查明的事实是,只有老年人和孩子们留在了村子里。

NOTE 1. 当本短语作"到……程度"解时,与 so far as 意义和用法相同,两者可互换使用。

2. 不要把本短语误用为介词性短语。

as/so far as … be concerned *adv.* ❶(used when you are giving your opinion about something, especially when this may be different from other people's opinions)in a particular person's opinion 就(某人)而言:*As far as* I am *concerned*, the issue is over and done with. 对我来说,这个问题已经解决完毕。The earlier the better, *as far as* the Committee is *concerned*. 就委员会来说,越早越好。*So far as* we *are concerned* you can go whenever you want. 就我们而言,你想什么时候走就可以什么时候走。❷(used when you want to talk about a particular thing)as for (something)至于,就(某事)而言:*As far as* money is *concerned*, there shouldn't be a problem. 至于资金,不应该有问题。So far as unemployment is concerned, a change of government would be a good idea. 就失业问题而言,更换政府可能是个好主意。

NOTE so far as … be concerned 的语气比 as far as … be concerned 更强。

as follows *adv.* (正式用语,其后常用冒号)(used when you are going to give more details about something) as written or stated in the list below; as comes next 如下,如后: My shopping list is *as follows*: bread, butter, meat, eggs, sugar. 我的购物清单如下:面包、黄油、肉、蛋、糖。Linda planned her day *as follows*: returning all phone calls; a department meeting; lunch with her colleagues; library research. 琳达一天的计划如下:回复所有的电话;开部门会议;与同事共进午餐;作图书馆研究。The standards of specifications for the instruments are defined *as follows*. 这些仪器的技术标准规定如下。

NOTE 1. 本短语被认为是 as it follows 的简略形式。

2. 本短语中的名词 follow 必须用复数形式。

3. 本短语多用作表语。在科技英语中常被用作状语,例如:

> Ohm's Law may now be stated *as follows*.
> 欧姆定律可以表述如下。

4. 本短语后所列示出的一系列名词之间使用逗号或分号。最后一个名词之前不用 and 或 or。

as for *prep.* (用于引起或转变先前所讲的话题)(used when you are starting to talk about someone or something new that is related to what you were talking about before) with regard to; concerning 关于,至于: Much pasture land is under water; *as for* the grain, most of that has been ruined. 大部分的牧场都被淹了;至于谷物,则大部分都被冲毁。*As for* our manager, he can pay for his own dinner. 至于我们经理,他会付自己的餐费的。

NOTE 本短语与 as to 的意义相同,有时可以互换使用。但两者在句中所处的位置和用法上有所不同。见 as to。

as if/though *conj.* as it would be if (something were true); in a way that suggests that (something is true) 似乎,好像,仿佛: He always showed what he thought and felt about me *as if* I were something better than a common flower girl. 他总是表现出他对我的看法和感受,似乎我是一个有身份的女人,而不是一个普通的卖花女。The old man raised his hand *as if/though* to hang the picture on the wall. 老人举起手来,好像是要把这幅画挂到墙上去。The girl listened *as though* turned to stone. 那女孩听得发呆,就像变成了石头一样。She hurriedly left the room *as though* angry. 她匆匆离开了房间,好像生气了。

NOTE 1. 在现代英语中,as if 比 as though 更为常用。

2. 本短语既可用来引出虚拟条件句,又可引出真实条件句。

3. 在美国英语口语中,本短语常常被介词 like 替换。例如:

> She sat there smiling happily *like* it was her birthday.
> 她坐在那里幸福地微笑着,就好像是她过生日似的。

as it is *adv.* ❶ (used when that situation is different from what you expected or need) in reality; in the situation that actually exists 事实上,实际上;照现状看: *As it is*, we can hardly get to the station by 8 o'clock. 实际上,我们很难在8点前赶到车站了。I hope things would

get better, but *as it is* they are getting worse. 我希望情况好转,可实际上情况却越来越糟。We were hoping to have a holiday next week — *as it is*, we may not be able to get away. 我们原来盼着下周放假,但照现状看,可能走不开了。❷already 已经:I don't want to hear any more complaints. I've got enough problems *as it is*. 我不想再听更多的抱怨了。我的问题已经够多的了。Sorry, I can't help — I've got too much to do *as it is*. 对不起,我爱莫能助。我已经有太多的事要做啦。

NOTE 1. 本短语中的第一个义项表示所发生的事情或存在的状态往往与说话人所想象或期望的相反。再如:

> He might have been killed; *as it is* he was severely injured.
> 我们原以为他已经死了,但事实上他并没有死,只是受了重伤而已。

2. 如果表达过去的情况,则要使用本短语的过去形式 as it was。

as it were *adv.* (used when describing someone or something in a way that is not quite exact)as it might be said to be; as if it really were; in a certain way 可以说是,好像是,似乎是:He is my best friend, my second self, *as it were*. 他是我最好的朋友,可以说是第二个我。In many ways children live, *as it were*, in a different world from adults. 在许多方面,儿童宛如生活在一个与成人截然不同的世界里。My friend seemed very relaxed — in his natural setting *as it were*. 我的朋友似乎十分轻松自在——他似乎有着自己随遇而安的天地。They waited, *as it were*, breathless for the result. 他们可以说是屏息以待结果。

NOTE 1. 本短语是 as it were so 的简略形式。

2. 本短语中的 were 为虚拟语气形式,故不能将其说成 as it is 或 as it was。

3. 本短语可用于不同时态的句子中。

4. 本短语的同义短语是 in a way, in a manner of speaking 和 so to speak。

as long as *conj.* ❶(used before saying the conditions that will make something else happen or be true) on condition that; provided that 只要……:My parents don't care what job I do *as long as* I'm happy. 我父母不在乎我做什么工作,只要我开心。*As long as* we persist in so doing, we will surely overcome all difficulties on the road to progress. 只要坚持这样做,我们就一定能够不断克服前进道路上的各种困难。❷ for the period of time that (指时间)达……之久:I'll stay *as long as* you need me. 你需要我住多久我就住多久。❸ because; since 因为,既然:Please buy some milk *as long as* you are going to the store. 既然你要去商店,就请买点牛奶吧。

NOTE 1. 本短语中的第一个 as 为副词,第二个 as 是连词,其后接从句。而在下面的句子中,同样的 as long as,用法和意义则完全不同:

> The world's largest snake, which is about *as long as* a large van and thick as a telephone pole, will be on permanent show at the Columbus Zoo, US media reported Monday.
> 据美国媒体星期一报道,与一辆大型货车长度相当、有电线杆粗细的世界上最大的蛇将在哥伦布动物园永久性展出。

在这个句子中,as long as 的第一个 as 为副词,第二个 as 则是介词,而 as long as 的意思是"和……一样长",用于表示同级的比较。

2. 当本短语作"只要"解时,与 so long as

意义和用法相同,互换使用。

A

3. 当本短语作"只要"解时,后面要使用现在时来表示将来的意义。例如:

> I'll stay with you *as long as* there is a room free.
> 只要有一个空房间,我就和你住在这里。

as many *adj.* the same number of 同数的,其数相同的:I have called on him three times in *as many* days. 我已在 3 天里拜访过他 3 次。He made six mistakes in *as many* lines. 他在 6 行文字中出了 6 处错误。Last season Carlos scored eleven goals in *as many* games. 在上个赛季,卡洛斯在 11 场比赛中踢进了 11 个球。

NOTE **1.** 如果本短语后被修饰的名词与前面出现的名词相同,可省略。例如:

> They say the people of Los Angeles speak 12 languages and teach just *as many* in the schools.
> 他们说洛杉矶人说 12 种语言,在学校也教授 12 种语言。

(as many 后省略了名词 languages)

2. 不要将本短语与 as much 混淆,两者的意义和用法完全不同。

as much *adv.* the same or virtually the same 同样地,相同地:I thought New York was expensive, but it costs just *as much* to live here in Paris. 我曾认为住在纽约花费很大,但实际上住在纽约和住在巴黎的花费一样。Don't thank me; I would do *as much* for anyone. 不用谢我,我对任何人都会这样做的。"Margaret stole the money." "I thought *as much*." "这钱是玛格丽特偷走的。""我也这样认为。"

NOTE 不要将本短语与 as many, much as 和 as much as 混淆。

as much as Ⅰ *conj.* ❶ even though; (al)though 虽然,尽管:*As much as* I hate (to do it), I must stay at home and study tonight. 虽然我不愿意(这样做),但我今晚还得留在家里学习。❷(常与 just 连用) just the same as 正像……一样:We're in the dark just *as much as* you are. 我们和你们一样都被蒙在鼓里。Animals feel pain just *as much as* we do. 动物和我们人一样都有痛觉。

Ⅱ (一般用在动词或动词不定式之前) *adv.* almost; practically 几乎,实际上:By running away he *as much as* admitted that he had taken the money. 他这一跑,就几乎等于他承认偷走了那笔钱。My father nodded his head, *as much as* to say that he would allow me to go abroad. 我父亲点了点头,这等于说他允许我出国了。You *as much as* promised that you would help us. 你实际上已答应要帮助我们。

NOTE **1.** 当本短语作"虽然,尽管"解时,与 much as 意义和用法相同,两者可互换使用。

2. 不要将本短语与下面这个句中的 as much as 的意义混淆:

> She can do *as much as* you can.
> 他能够做得和你一样多。

上句中的 as much as 意为"和……一样多"。也不要将本短语与下面这个句子混淆:

> It was *as much as* I could do not to laugh.
> 我尽了最大的努力才没有笑出来。

句中的 as much as one can do 是"尽某人最大的努力"之意。

as of/from *prep.* (主要用于美国英语中,后接某一具体时间或日期) at, on or until (a given time); starting from (a particular time or date)在……时候,截至,从……时候起:*As of* 11:30 am, no official announcements regarding the two bus explosions have been made by the police. 到今天上午 11 点半，警方还没有对这两起公共汽车爆炸案发表正式声明。What we have learned *as of* now suggests that there has been no progress. 到现在为止我们所了解到的情况表明，还没有任何进展。*As of* next week, all the air fares will be going up. 从下星期起，所有的机票都将涨价。As from today, the bank will be open for business from 9:30 am. 从即日起，银行将从上午 9:30 开门营业。You can use my office *as from* next Monday. 从下星期一起，你可以使用我的办公室了。

as often as not *adv.* on most occasions or in most situations; usually; fairly frequently 常常，往往：*As often as not* she misses the school bus. 她常常赶不上校车。The traffic is so busy there that, *as often as not*, you can not even cross the street. 那儿的交通非常繁忙，你常常连马路都过不去。*As often as not*, the arguments could have been avoided. 这些争论往往本可以避免。

NOTE 1. 本短语一般用于口语中，并可略为 often as not 的形式使用。例如：

> Jean and Chris agree on travel plans, *often as not*.
>
> 简和克尔斯常常在旅行计划上意见一致。

2. 本短语与 more often than not 意义和用法相同，两者可互换使用。

as regards *prep.*（正式用语）(used for introducing the subject that is being talked, discussed, or written about) regarding; concerning; about(something)至于，关于：*As regards* the potential energy crisis — why aren't we putting money into alternative sources of energy? 至于潜在的能源危机，我们为何不把资金投放在替换能源上呢? They said nothing *as regards* wages. 关于工资问题，他们没有说什么。

NOTE 1. 本短语中的 regards 不是名词的复数形式，而是动词的第三人称单数形式，在任何情况下，都要用特定形式 regards。

2. 本短语一般用于书面体，少用于口语中。

3. 本短语的同义短语是 as to, in reference to, with reference to, in regard(s) to, with regard(s) to, in respect to 和 with respect to。

as soon as *conj.* immediately after (something) 一……就：*As soon as* she saw him enter the room she bore down upon him and insisted that he join her for dinner. 她一看见他走进房间就立刻冲到他身边，坚持要他和她一起吃晚饭。They will post me the air tickets *as soon as* they receive my cheque. 他们一收到我的支票就会立刻把机票寄给我。

NOTE 1. 本短语表示主句的动作紧接从句的动作之后发生。表示过去，主句的谓语动词用一般过去时，从句的谓语动词用一般过去时或过去完成时；表示将来，主句的谓语动词用一般将来时，从句的谓语动词用一般现在时或现在完成时。

2. 本短语的同义短语是 no sooner … than 和 scarcely … when。

as such *adv.* ❶as being what is indicated; in that capacity 就以这样的资格(或身份)：He is a guest and should be treated *as such*. 他是一位客人，而且也应该作为客人来款待。❷in itself or themselves 就其本身：The job *as such* was easy, but required a lot of time. 这件工作本身并不难，但用时却不少。Mr Simons said he was not against the schemes *as such*. 西蒙斯先生说，就这些计划本身来说，他并

不反对。❸(用在名词之后,常用于否定句中) properly so named; in the exact meaning of the stated things 按其准确意义来说: It's not an agreement *as such*, but it will have virtually the same effect as one. 就准确意义而言,它算不上是个协议,但其实际上具有与协议相同的作用。I am not a new learner *as such* — I studied English in school years ago. 确切地说,我不是个初学者——我几年前就在学校学过英语。

NOTE 1. 本短语第一个义项中例句完整的形式是: He is a guest and should be treated as a guest. 本短语中的 such 是用于取代被重复使用的名词(如例句中的 a guest)。

2. 不要将本短语与 such as 混淆,两者的意义和用法不同。

as to *prep.* ❶(正式用语,后接名词、代词或由连接代词或副词引导的从句) about; concerning; regarding (someone or something) 关于,对于,至于: *As to* your ability to accomplish the task, I never had the slightest doubt. 对于你完成这项任务的能力,我从来没有丝毫怀疑。He has no idea *as to* what he should do next. 至于下一步该做什么,他全然不知。I'm terribly uncertain *as to* whether Mary is the right person for the job. 我实在不能确定玛丽是不是合适做这项工作。I want to find out *as to* whom this bicycle belongs to. 我要知道这辆自行车是谁的。❷ according to 根据: The candidates were chosen *as to* ability. 根据能力选人。They were asked to sort the costumes *as to* size and color. 要求他们把服装按大小和颜色分类。

NOTE 1. 当本短语用作"关于,对于,至于"解,后接由连接代词或连接副词引导的从句时,往往可以省略。例如:

We inquired (*as to*) whether Fred had called back.
我们询问弗雷德是否回电话了。
(*As to*) why he had not done so, she could not say.
至于他为何没有那样做,她无可奉告。

2. 当本短语用作"关于,对于,至于"解时,与 as for 意义相同,都用于引出一个与前一个话题稍微有些不同的话题,常可互换使用。但两者在位置和用法上有所区别:本短语可置于句首或句中,而 as for 则一般用于句首,不能置于句中;本短语后可接由连接代词或副词引导的从句,而 as for 则不能;另外 as for 在语体上不如 as to 正式。

3. 本短语的同义短语是 as regards,但本短语更为常用。

as usual *adv.* (used for saying what usually happens) as is customary; as always; as one usually did 和往常一样地,照常: After the explosion most people went about their daily activities *as usual*. 爆炸发生后,大多数人还和往常一样地做着每天的事情。*As usual*, at such press conferences, police highlighted several recently solved cases to prove the city is safe. 通常,在这样的新闻发布会上,警方会列举几起最近破获的案件以证明这个城市是安全的。

as well *adv.* in addition; besides; also; too 此外,并且,也: I'd like a cup of coffee, and a glass of water *as well*. 我想要一杯咖啡,此外还要一杯水。Increasing exchanges at all levels have shown not only in our political, economic and trade relations, but in cultural, public health and education fields and among peoples *as well*. 双方多层次的交往不断增加,这不仅表现在政治、经贸关系方面,而且表现在文化、卫生、教育和

民间等方面。

NOTE 本短语作为副词性短语,与副词 too 意义相同,都用于肯定句中,并常用于句尾。但本短语前无须使用逗号。

as well as Ⅰ *conj.* ❶and in addition 和,还有:I have four brothers *as well as* three sisters. 我有四个兄弟,还有三个妹妹。China—US cooperation is conducive to stability in the Asia-Pacific region *as well as* peace and development in the world. 中美合作有利于亚太地区的稳定,以及世界的和平与发展。❷and also 而且,还,也:He publishes *as well as* prints his own books. 他的书是他自己印刷出版的。We sell books *as well as* newspapers and magazines. 我们售书,也售报刊。We are repairing the roof *as well as* painting the walls. 我们在粉刷墙壁同时也在修理屋顶。Television soap operas produced by South Korea are very popular in the Chinese mainland, and Chinese communities in San Francisco, Chicago *as well as* in Malaysia. 韩国拍摄的电视连续剧不仅在中国大陆备受欢迎,就是在旧金山、芝加哥以及马来西亚的华人社团中也很叫座。

Ⅱ *prep.* (后接名词或动名词) in addition to (someone or something); besides 除了……之外(还):Linda and Ammy are coming to the meeting, *as well as* Smith. 除了史密斯以外,琳达和艾米也将与会。*As well as* being the birthplace of Chairman Mao Zedong, Shaoshan is also famous for its natural beauty and scenery. 韶山除了是毛泽东主席的诞生地外,还以其自然美景著称。

NOTE **1.** 不要将本短语与 as well as 混淆,两者的意义和用法不同。例如:

> John plays football *as well as*, if not better than, David.
> 约翰踢足球如果不比大卫强,也和他踢得一样好。

此句中的 as well as 表示比较,意为"和……一样好"。其中第一个 as 是副词,第二个 as 是连词,引导比较状语从句。

2. 当本短语用作连词性短语时,要注意以下几点:

(1)当本短语用来连接句中的两个部分时,这两部分必须是对等的。

(2)当本短语连接两个主语部分时,谓语动词必须与前面的(即第一个)主语保持人称和数的一致。例如:

> Aluminum *as well as* most metals is a good conductor.
> 铝和大多数金属都是良导体。
> I *as well as* they am ready to help you.
> 不仅他们愿意帮助你,我也愿意帮助你。

(3)当本短语连接的是两个简单动词形式时,它和第二个动词实际上起着插入语的作用,与主语保持人称和数的一致。例如:

> He works, *as well as* sleeps, in the room.
> 他既在这间房里睡觉,又在这里工作。

如果第一个动词用于复合谓语(分词或不定式),那么 *as well as* 后的动词应取相应形式,但不定式一般省略 to。例如:

> We are repairing the roof, *as well as* painting the walls.
> 我们既油漆墙壁,又修理屋顶。
> You cannot expect her to do the housework *as well as* look after the children.
> 你不可能叫她既照顾孩子又做家务。

3. 当本短语用作介词性短语,后有动词

出现时,该动词要用-ing 的形式。例如:

As well as breaking his leg, he hurt his arm.
他摔断了腿,还伤了胳膊。
He has his license taken away, *as well as* being fined five pounds.
他不仅被罚了五英镑,还被收缴了执照。

as (of) yet *adv.* (正式用语,用于否定句或含有否定词的句子中) ❶ (used for talking about something that has not happened or been done up to now) up to this moment; so far 到目前为止,迄今为止: Police stated that there have been no arrests made *as yet*. 警方称,到目前为止还没有拘捕任何人。*As yet*, no man has set foot on Mars. 到目前为止,尚无人类踏足于火星之上。The report remains unfinished *as of yet*. 报告至今尚未完成。❷ still 仍然,还是: They hope to raise funds for the project, but the exact plans are *as yet* unclear. 他们希望为此项目筹资,但具体计划还不清楚。

NOTE 本短语与 so far 都表示"到现在为止",但用法有所不同。本短语用于否定句或含有否定词的句子中,而 so far 既可用于否定句中,又可用于肯定句中。见 so far。

ashamed of *adj.* (常用作表语) ❶ feeling guilty or embarrassed because of (something bad you have done) 为……感到羞耻,为……感到惭愧: She was *ashamed of* having lied to him. 她因对他说了谎而感到惭愧。I felt *ashamed of* myself for getting so angry. 我为我如此大动肝火而感到惭愧。❷ feeling foolish or embarrassed because of (something) 为……感到难堪(或难为情): The girl student was *ashamed of* her dirty old clothes. 这位女同学因其又脏又旧的衣服而感到不好意思。Being poor is nothing to be *ashamed of*. 穷没有什么难堪的。

NOTE 1. 本短语后常接反身代词,再如:

You ought to be *ashamed of* yourself, using that kind of language!
你应为使用那样的语言而感到羞耻!

2. 不要将本短语与 ashamed for 混淆。本短语所表达的意义是"为(一般指内在的人或事物,如自己)而感到羞耻",而 ashamed for 所表达的意义则是"为(一般指外在的人或事物,如他人)而感到羞耻"。请比较下面两个句子:

I'm *ashamed of* such behaviors.
我以这样的行为为耻。
I'm *ashamed for* your such behaviors.
我为你这样的行为感到羞耻。

aside from *prep.* (用于美国英语中) except for; beside or besides; not including (someone or something) 除……之外: *Aside from* James, I had no friends on campus. 除了詹姆斯外,我在学校里没有朋友。The factory turns out bicycles *aside from* motorcars. 除了汽车之外,这家工厂还生产自行车。*Aside from* suspending the Olympic torch relay for three days, the Chinese government is ordering all flags be flown at half-staff to mourn earthquake victims. 除了奥运会火炬传递活动中止三天之外,中国政府还下令所有部门下半旗向地震遇难者表示哀悼。

NOTE 本短语与 apart from 的第一个义项意义和用法相同,两者可互换使用。

ask about *vt.* speak or write to (someone) for information concerning (something or someone) (向某人)询问,打听: Were I to meet him tomorrow, I should *ask* him *about* it. 我要是明天见到他,我就会问他这件事。Newspaper

reporters have been *asking about* the missing businessman all day. 记者们整天都在打听有关那名失踪商人的消息。When *asked about* the death of a bicyclist, the defendant laughed. 当被问及一名骑自行车的人之死时，被告人大笑起来。Why don't you telephone the theatre and *ask about* tickets? 你为何不往剧院打个电话询问一下票的事情呢？

NOTE 本短语中的同义短语是 inquire about。inquire about 是英国英语中的正式用语。

ask after *vt.* 【不可分性动词短语】（主要用于英国英语中，无被动语态形式）ask someone about (someone's health, what they are doing, etc.) 向某人询问（某一个人的身体等状况）：I met Bob just now in the street and he *asked after* you. 我刚才在街上碰见了鲍勃，他还向我打听了你的状况。Don't forget to *ask after* her father when you see Helen this afternoon. 你今天下午看见海伦时，别忘了询问一下她父亲的情况。Tom's mother was *asking after* your sister. 汤姆的妈妈在打听你妹妹的情况。

NOTE 本短语的同义短语是 inquire after。inquire after 是英国英语中的正式用语。

ask for *vt.* ❶speak or write to (someone) because you want them to give you (something)（向某人）要，要求（某物）：The children were *asking for* drinks. 孩子们在要饮料喝。They *asked* the waiter *for* a type of wine the restaurant didn't have. 他们向侍者要饭店里没有的那种酒。Tuvalu, a tiny country in the Pacific Ocean, has *asked for* help, as it fears the sea will swallow it up. 太平洋上的小国图瓦卢由于担心将被海洋吞噬，发出了求助讯号。Everything that was *asked for* has now been sent. 所要求的一切物品现均已送出。❷invite (someone) to (something) 邀请（某人）（做客等）：My husband's boss has *asked* us over *for* dinner; what kind of gift should I bring? 我丈夫的老板请我们去吃饭，我应该带什么礼物？We *asked* our neighbours to come *for* tea. 我们邀请邻居们来喝茶。❸say that you want (someone) to come and speak to you 要求找（某人）说话：There's someone in the shop *asking for* the manager. 商店里有个人要求找经理说话。Just now someone telephoned and *asked for* you. 刚才有人打电话，要跟你讲话。❹（无被动语态形式，用进行时态）behave in a way that makes it likely that a particular unpleasant thing will happen to you（以某种行为）招惹（麻烦等）：She's *asking for* trouble speaking to people like that. 她那样与人讲话是在自找麻烦。If you go out without a coat in this weather you're *asking for* cold. 如果你在这样的天气出去而不穿外衣的话，你就是想得感冒。

ask for it *vi.*（非正式用语，常用进行时态）behave in a way that is very likely to result in trouble; risk or invite trouble, danger, punishment, etc., by persisting in some action or manner 自找麻烦，自讨苦吃：Leaving your wallet visible on the car seat is just *asking for it*. 把钱包放在汽车座位显眼的地方，你这是自讨苦吃。Don't be late again, or you'll *ask for it*. 不要再迟到了，要不然你会自找苦吃。

ask for the moon ⇨ cry for the moon

ask of *vt.* 【可分性动词短语】request or demand (something) from (someone, something or a group) 向……要求（某物）：You're *asking* too much *of* them if you expect them to work at the weekend.

如果你想要他们周末也工作的话，那你对他们的要求就太过分了。I would like to *ask* a favor *of* you. 我想求你帮忙。We will *ask* that *of* the board of directors. 我们将向董事会提出那项要求。You should ask the information of your database. 你们应该向数据库要信息。

NOTE 不要因汉语表达方式的影响把本短语中的两个宾语部分安排错位。例如，"你没有权利向我要任何东西。"不能将其说成：* You have no right to *ask* me *of* anything. 而应该是：You have no right to *ask* anything *of* me. 本短语的正确表达形式是 *ask* something *of* someone。

aspire for/to/after *vt.*【不可分性动词短语】(无被动语态形式，常用一般时态) want; seek, or aim for (something)希望得到，追求：China is committed to turning herself into a well-off society in an all-round way and *aspires for* a favorable international climate. 中国致力于全面建设小康社会，希望有一个良好的国际环境。Many unknown writers *aspire to* fame. 许多无名作家都想成名。After he became a millionaire, he *aspired after* a leadership role. 他成了百万富翁后，便想谋个领导岗位。

NOTE **1.** 本短语中的动词 aspire 后还可接动词不定式短语。例如：

> My brother *aspires* to become a doctor, someday.
> 我弟弟希望有朝一日能成为医生。

2. 本短语的同义短语是 aim for, be eager for, hunger after/for, hope for, long for 和 yearn for。

assent to *vt.*【不可分性动词短语】(正式用语，常用一般时态) agree to; give permission for (something such as an idea or suggestion or doing something)同意，批准：The chairman *assented to* the committee's proposals. 主席同意了委员会的建议。Have they *assented to* the terms of the contract? 他们同意合同中的那些条款了吗？My parents will never *assent to* my going abroad to study by myself. 我父母决不会让我独自去国外留学的。

NOTE **1.** 本短语中的 to 是介词，后接名词或动名词(短语)，而不能接原形动词。

2. 本短语的另外一种表达形式是 give one's assent to。例如：

> The manager has *given his assent to* the proposals.
> 经理同意了那些建议。

3. 本短语的同义短语是 approve of, consent to 和 agree to；反义短语是 disapprove of。

assert oneself *vi.* ❶ behave in a way which shows your power, control, importance, etc. and earns you respect from others 显出自己的权力(权威、地位等)：You must *assert yourself* or they will continue to bully you. 你必须显出自己的威力，否则他们还会欺侮你。The laws of historical development will *assert themselves*. 历史发展的规律不可抗拒。❷ put (oneself) forward boldly or forcefully in an effort to make an opinion known(大胆地或有力地)提出(自己的)观点：Don't be so shy; you need to learn to *assert yourself*. 不要这么胆怯，你需要学会大胆地提出自己的观点。

associate with *vt.*【可分性动词短语】❶spend time with (someone); be seen in public often with (someone)与(某人)相处；同(某人)经常来往：He tried to *associate* himself *with* the local people but he found it very hard to adjust himself to their way of life. 他极想和当

地人打成一片,然而他却发现自己很难适应他们的生活方式。They were closely *associated with* each other during the war. 他们在战争期间相互紧密地联合在一起。While she was in Paris, she *associated with* many well-known artists. 她在巴黎期间经常与许多著名的艺术家来往。I don't like your *associating with* such people. 我不喜欢你同这样一些人来往。❷(常用被动语态形式,常用一般时态) form a connection in your mind between (different people or things)把……和……联系在一起;……与……有关:I always *associate* in my mind songs *with* people, situations and places. 我总是在我的心里把一些歌曲与某些人、情境或地方联系起来。The doctor was always *associated* in the child's mind *with* injections and pain. 在那孩子的脑子里,医生总是和打针与疼痛联系在一起。The latest research provides the evidence that a child's sex is *associated with* the mother's diet, and women on low-calorie diets are likely to give birth to a female. 这项最新的研究证明:婴儿的性别与母亲的饮食有关,喜欢低热量饮食的女性易生女孩。

assure of *vt.* 【可分性动词短语】(正式用语,常与代词或反身代词连用) make (someone) certain (that something will definitely happen or is definitely true), especially in order to remove doubt about it 使(某人)确信(某事);向(某人),保证:He *assured* us *of* his ability to do the job well. 他让我们相信他有做好这项工作的能力。The doctor *assured* the young father *of* his baby's safety. 医生向那位年轻的父亲保证他孩子的安全。We booked early to *assure* ourselves *of* getting good seats. 我们提前订了票以保证得到好座位。

astonished at *adj.* feeling very surprised or shocked about (something that was not expected) 对……感到惊诧,对……感到震惊:The doctors were *astonished at* the speed of her recovery. 医生们对她康复得如此之快颇感惊诧。Everybody was *astonished at* the news that the former prime minister was shot in the car. 前总理在汽车里被枪击身亡的消息令所有的人感到震惊。I was *astonished at* the sight of so many elephants having been killed. 看到这么多的大象惨遭杀害,我感到惊诧不已。

NOTE 1. 本短语中的 astonished 可被 astounded 替换,两者的意义和用法相同。

2. 本短语的比较级形式是 more astonished at,最高级形式是 most astonished at。

at a distance *adv.* at a place that is very far from where you are, although you can still see or hear things there 在远处:The policeman followed him *at a distance*. 警察远远地跟踪着他。The railway station is *at a* moderate *distance* from our college. 火车站就在离我们学院不太远的地方。

NOTE 本短语的同义短语是 in the distance.

at a (single) glance *adv.* immediately, as soon as you see someone or something; with one look 立即,一眼就……:He could tell *at a glance* that something was wrong. 他立即看出情况不妙。He saw *at a glance* that she was coming. 他一眼就看到她来了。Believe it or not, I can tell the difference between them *at a glance*. 不管你信不信,我一眼就能看出这两者之间的区别。The technician can see the defects in the machine *at a single glance*.

A

技术人员一眼就能看出这台机器的缺陷。

at a later date *adv.* at some time in the future 在晚些时候：The voting results will be formally announced *at a later date*. 选举结果将在晚些时候正式公布。

at a loss Ⅰ *adv.* below the cost or price of purchase 低于成本地，亏本地：The store was selling merchandise *at a loss*. 这家商店现在是在亏本出售货物。The price was so low that the product was sold *at a loss*. 价格太低，以致产品都在亏本卖出。

Ⅱ *adj.* not sure; uncertain; confused and not knowing what to say or do 茫然，不知所措：I was *at a loss* to understand what had happened. 我茫然不知到底发生了什么事。They felt *at a loss* what to do when the machine was out of order. 当机器出故障时，他们不知所措了。I was *at a loss* for words when she told me the news. 当她告诉我那个消息时，我不知道说什么才好。Excuse me. I'm *at a loss* in recalling your name. 对不起，我想不起你的名字了。

NOTE 当本短语用作形容词性短语时，后常接不同形式的动词不定式短语或介词短语，在句中常用作表语。

at/in a pinch *adv.*（非正式用语）if necessary; in an emergency 必要时，紧急时：*At a pinch*, you can stay here for the night. 如果必要的话，你可以在这里过夜。It's more than I really want to spend, but *at a pinch* I suppose I could manage £100. 这笔钱比我实际想花的要多，但在必要时我想我还能拿得出 100 英镑。Six people, and more *in a pinch*, could be seated comfortably at the table. 这张桌子可以舒舒服服地坐 6 个人，如必要时还可多坐几个。I suppose that, *at a pinch*, we could use my car. 我想，紧急时咱们可以用我的车。

NOTE at a pinch 是英国英语用法，in a pinch 是美国英语用法。

at a run *adv.* at the speed you move when you run; running 奔跑着：The children left the room *at a run*. 孩子们跑着离开了房间。Jack set off *at a run*. 杰克开始跑起来。He started off *at a run* but soon tired and began to walk. 他出发时跑步，但不久就累了，便开始走。

at a time *adv.* ❶(used for saying how many things there are in each group or on each occasion) every time; separately in groups of two, three, etc. 一次，每次：I climb stairs two *at a time*, but I descend stairs one *at a time*. 我上楼时一步两个台阶，但下楼时一步一个台阶。She checked them off, one *at a time*, as they came into the test room. 当他们进入考场时，她逐一地核对。We usually talk to four or five candidates *at a time*. 通常，我们每次找四五名候选人谈话。❷at the same time; simultaneously at each occurrence (of some action) 同时：All the boys jumped into the pool *at a time*. 所有的男孩子都同时跳入水池中。

NOTE 1. 当本短语作“一次，每次”解时，表示事情发生的频率，在使用中其前通常加 one, two, three 等数词。

2. 当本短语作“同时”解时，与 at one time 的第二个义项意义和用法相同，两者可互换使用。

at all *adv.* in any way; to any degree; in the least 丝毫，究竟，根本：She's not *at all* clever. 她一点儿也不聪明。He doesn't know anything *at all* about computers. 他对计算机一点也不懂。Do you agree to the decision *at all*? 你究竟同不同意这个决定？

NOTE 本短语一般用于否定句和疑问句中，有时也用于条件状语从句中。例如：

> If you do the experiment *at all*, do it carefully.
> 如果你非要做这项实验,就要小心地去做。

at all costs *adv.* (used for saying that something must be done, however difficult or dangerous it is) no matter what the cost or outcome may be 不惜任何代价,无论如何:The premier ordered the military forces to open up roads to the epicenter before 12 pm Tuesday *at all costs*. 总理命令部队指战员不惜任何代价,在星期二晚上 12 点钟之前打通通往震中灾区的道路。The bridge must be repaired within three days *at all costs*. 无论如何也要在三天内把桥修好。

NOTE 本短语的同义短语是 at any cost 和 at any price。

at all events *adv.* (主要用于英国英语中) whatever happens or has happened; in spite of everything 无论如何,不管怎样:The main witness was probably lying, but *at all events* the prosecution's case was very weak. 主证人可能是在说谎,但本诉讼案的证据无论如何都是很不充分的。*At all events* I shall telephone before you make a final decision. 无论如何,在你作出最后决定之前我也要给你打电话。She had a terrible accident, but *at all events* she was not killed. 她遭遇了可怕的车祸,但不管怎样她并没有死。

NOTE 本短语的同义短语是 in any event, at any rate 和 in any case。

at all times *adv.* always; constantly; continuously 总是,随时:Please keep your bags with you *at all times*. 请随时把行囊随身保管好。*Geneva Convention* says, prisoners of war must *at all times* be humanely treated.《日内瓦公约》规定:不论任何时候,战俘都必须受到人道的对待。

NOTE 不要将本短语与 at times 混淆, at times 意为"有时"。

at an early date *adv.* at some earlier time 在早些时候:Let us join efforts in seeking feasible solutions to enable the committee to restart its work *at an early date*. 让我们共同努力,继续寻求可行的解决办法,推动委员会早日重新开始工作。China calls for collective efforts to conclude the Doha Round talks *at an early date*. 中国呼吁各方协同努力,早日结束多哈回合谈判。

at any cost *adv.* (used for saying that something must be done, however difficult it is or however much damage it causes) no matter what the cost or outcome may be 不惜任何代价,无论如何:They were determined to win *at any cost*. 他们决心不惜任何代价取胜。We want peace *at any cost*. 求和平,我们不惜任何代价。

NOTE 本短语的同义短语是 at all costs 和 at any price。

at any price ⇨ **at any cost**

at any rate *adv.* ❶ no matter what may happen 无论如何:*At any rate*, we should tell him frankly what we think of his proposal. 无论如何,我们应该直率地告诉他我们对他的建议的看法。I hope to be back by 10 o'clock pm — *at any rate* I'll be back before midnight. 我希望晚上 10 点以前能回来——不管怎样,午夜之前我一定回来。❷(用于口语中) (used for changing a statement, and telling someone that one part of what has been mentioned is true) at least 至少:They both agree with me — well, *at any rate*, Mary does. 他们都同意我的意见,至少玛丽是这样的。Despite his mistakes, he is *at any rate* a kind-hearted man. 尽管他有缺点,但他至少是一个好心肠的人。

NOTE 当本短语表示"无论如何"之意时,与 at all events, in any case 和 in any event 意义和用法相同,并可互换使用。

at(the)best *adv.* under the most favorable conditions; taking the most favorable view 在最好的情况下;持最乐观的看法:He is a fool *at (the) best*, and at(the)worst he is a criminal. 往好里想,他是个傻瓜;往坏里想,他则是个罪犯。His chances of victory are, *at best*, uncertain. 他取胜的机会充其量也是没有把握。

NOTE 1. 不要将本短语与 at one's best 混淆,两者意义和用法均不同。

2. 本短语的反义短语是 at (the) worst。

at (one's) ease Ⅰ *adj.* ❶free from (one's) anxiety or embarrassment; relaxed; not nervous or anxious 安心的;不受拘束的;不紧张的:"We also should create a sound environment for migrant workers to set their minds *at ease* while working in cities," said the expert. 这位专家说:"我们应该为外来工创造一个良好的环境,使他们在城里安心工作。" The mayor tried his best to make everyone feel *at ease* with him. 市长设法让每个人和他在一起时都感到毫无拘束。He was more *at ease* in the classroom than on a political platform. 他在教室里比在政治讲坛上更感轻松。We set little Mary *at her ease* during the thunderstorm by reading her stories. 在雷雨交加时,我们就读故事书给小玛丽听,以使她不感到紧张。❷ in comfort; comfortable 舒服的:After the doctor's visit, the patient felt more *at ease*. 病人在医生来诊后,感觉舒服多了。You can't feel *at ease* with a toothache. 牙疼不会使你好受的。

Ⅱ *adv.* (used as an order for a group of soldiers to stand)in a relaxed position with their feet apart and their hands behind their backs (用于向士兵发出的口令)稍息:Tell your men to be *at ease*, captain. 让你的士兵稍息,上尉。The captain gave his men the command:"*At ease*!" 上尉向他的士兵命令道:"稍息!"

NOTE 1. 当本短语用作形容词性短语时,比较级形式是 more at ease,最高级形式是 most at ease。

2. 当本短语用作形容词性短语时,反义短语是 ill at ease。

at fault *adj.* (用作表语) responsible for a mistake, trouble, or failure 有过错的;有毛病的;有责任的:The traffic accident was investigated by the Police Complaints Commission which concluded the driver of the police vehicle was not *at fault*. 该起交通事故由警务投诉委员会做了调查,得出的结论是警车司机无过错。He kept missing the target and wondered if the sight on his new rifle was *at fault*. 他连续脱靶,因此他怀疑这支新枪的准星是不是有毛病。Her doctor admitted to being *at fault* for not sending her straight to a specialist. 她的医生承认因没有直接把她送交给专家医治而负有责任。

NOTE 本短语的同义短语是 in the wrong;反义短语是 in the right。

at first *adv.* in the beginning (before something changes); at the start 起初,首先:"*At first* I felt huge pressure because all those actresses were more beautiful and more experienced than I," said Nancy. "起初,我感到压力很大,因为所有那些女演员都比我漂亮,又比我有经验。"南希说道。He was violently opposed to our proposal *at first*, but later he agreed to it. 他刚开始强烈地反对我们的提议,但后来又同意了。Since that country became a member of the World Trade Organization,

it should *at first* unify business income tax policies, the expert said. 这位专家称,既然该国已成为世界贸易组织的一个成员,它应该首先统一经营收入所得税的政策。

NOTE 1. 本短语与 in the first place 都有"首先"之意。但本短语强调某一过程或某一段时间的开端,而 in the first place 强调次序,如首先(其次,再次,等等)。

2. 本短语与 first of all 的区别见 first of all。

3. 本短语的反义短语是 at last。

at first glance ⇨ **at first sight**

at first sight *adv.* ❶when you see someone or something for the first time, before you notice any details 初看起来,乍一看:*At first sight* there was nothing especially attractive about her. 初看起来,她并没有什么特别的引人之处。He fell in love with her *at first sight*. 他对她一见钟情。❷when you first begin to consider something 初认为:*At first sight* the difficulty looks greater than it really is. 刚开始认为困难较大,但实际上并没有那么大。*At first sight*, the theory seems to make a lot of sense. 最初认为,这一理论似乎很有道理。

NOTE 本短语的同义短语是 at first glance,但本短语较为常用。

at hand *adj.* (前面多用 close 或 near) ❶very near in place; nearby (指地点)在附近的,在跟前的:To have a few shops and hospitals near *at hand* is an important thing. 附近有几家商店和医院很重要。I want you to be *at hand* during my interview. 在我接受面试时,我需要你在跟前。❷(正式用语) very near in time; likely to happen soon (指时间)临近的,即将发生的:Various flowers are on display throughout Beijing as the Valentine's Day is near *at hand*. 随着情人节的临近,北京到处都在展销各种鲜花。The final examinations are now *at hand*. 期末考试即将来临。The time of his departure is *at hand*. 他出发的时间就要到了。❸(正式用语) quite close to you and within easy reach; available to be used when needed 在手边的,需要时可用的:"We ran to help our neighbor, who was buried in his house, but we could only dig with our own hands since we had no tools *at hand*," he said. "我们跑过去帮助埋在房里的邻居,但我们只能用手挖,因为我们手头没有工具。"他说道。I always keep my dictionary close *at hand*. 我总是随身备有一本词典。❹(正式用语) needing to be discussed, considered or dealt with now 需要现在讨论(考虑或处理)的:What he said is not related to the matter *at hand*. 他所说的与正在讨论的问题无关。They turned their attention to the task *at hand*. 他们把注意力转到了需要现在处理的工作上。

NOTE 1. 与本短语结构和形式相类似的有 in hand 和 on hand。尽管它们的整体词性相同,但它们的意义各不相同。见 in hand 和 on hand。

2. 本短语是"介词+名词"的固定短语,不能在名词 hand 前加任何冠词或物主代词,而且 hand 必须用单数形式。

at heart *adv.* ❶(used for saying what someone's basic character is or what he or she is really like, even though he or she may seem very different) in reality; at bottom 本质上;在心底里:Her manners are cold, but she is *at heart* a very kind person. 她的言谈举止冷淡,但她是一个心地非常善良的人。His manners are rough, but he is a kind man *at heart*. 他虽然举止粗鲁,但是个心地善良的人。❷(常用在动词 have 后) in one's deepest feelings; as a great concern 甚为关心地:Real dog

A

lovers always have the dog's health *at heart*. 真正的爱犬者总是很关心其爱犬的健康。

at home *adj.* & *adv.* ❶ at or in one's own house 在家里:I called you last night, but you were not *at home*. 我昨晚给你打了电话,但你没在家。Some people even make such dangerous products as fireworks *at home* in some places in central China. 在华中的某些地方,有些人甚至在家里制作鞭炮这样的危险品。❷ in the home of one's parents 在父母家:I can't believe it, she's 28 and still lives *at home*. 令我难以置信的是,她都 28 岁了,可还住在父母家里。❸ comfortable and relaxed; at ease (像在家里一般)舒适的,轻松自在的:Try to make the new students feel *at home* in your school. 尽量让新同学们在你们的学校里感到舒适自在。"I like this small town and I am sure I will soon feel *at home* living here," she said smiling. "我喜欢这个小城,我肯定很快就会在这里生活得很舒适。"她微笑着说。Pleased sit down and make yourself *at home* while I get you some coffee. 请坐下,随便些。我去给你拿点咖啡喝。❹(主要用于新闻英语中) at or in one's own country, not in a foreign country 在国内: Despite an ever-changing, complicated international situation, and the occurrence of numerous natural disasters *at home*, China achieved better economic results than forecast. 尽管国际形势复杂多变,国内发生多种自然灾害,中国的经济还是取得了比预期要好的成就。Our goods have enjoyed a good reputation *at home* and abroad. 我们的商品在国内外享有盛誉。❺(常与 with, in 连用) familiar with (something)熟悉:She's completely *at home* with computers. 她对计算机十分内行。He is quite *at home* in modern history. 他精通近代史。❻(in sports) playing on one's own field; at or in the place where a sports team is based (体育比赛) 在本场,在主场:The Houston Rockets are *at home* against the Chicago Bulls. 休斯敦火箭队主场迎战芝加哥公牛队。"Our team played two games well *at home* today," the coach said to the reporters. 教练对记者们说:"我们队今天在主场进行的两场比赛表现不错。"

at intervals *adv.* ❶ sometimes 有时,不时地:It may be necessary to stop *at intervals* and go back over key points in the lesson. 停下来然后回过头去复习课中的重点有时可能是必要的。During the past two weeks it has rained *at intervals*. 在最近的两个星期里,总是不时地下雨。*At intervals*, there were formal receptions at the governor's mansion. 在州长的官邸中不时地举行正式招待会。❷ with spaces of a regular length 每隔一段距离:Trees had been planted *at intervals* along the road. 沿路每隔一定的距离都种植了树木。❸ happening regularly after equal periods of time 每隔一段时间:The workers inspected the new machine *at intervals*. 工人们每隔一段时间就要检查这台新机器。Under the UN Resolution 1483, the United States and Britain were asked to inform the council *at* regular *intervals* of their activities in Iraq. 根据联合国 1483 号决议,美英两国被要求每隔一段时间就要向安理会通报它们在伊拉克的活动。

NOTE 本短语中的名词 interval 必须用复数形式。在 intervals 之前,可以加形容词作定语修饰 intervals,如 brief, long, regular, short, successive, 等等。此外,也可以用表示具体时间的词语作定语。例如:

> Buses are running *at* 10-minute *intervals*.
> 公共汽车每隔 10 分钟开一班。

Further volumes will be issued *at* monthly *intervals*.
后续各卷将每月发行一次。

还可用 at intervals of 的形式来表示间隔时间或距离。例如:

It is repeated *at intervals of* 40 seconds.
40 秒重复一次。
Put the chairs *at intervals of* 5 inches.
每隔 5 英尺放一把椅子。

at large Ⅰ *adj.* ❶(正式用语,用作后置定语)as a whole; in general 全体的;一般的:We have always tried to provide the public *at large* with accurate information. 我们总是尽量为大众提供准确的信息。❷(正式用语,常用作表语)(of a dangerous animal or a criminal)free; having not been captured(指危险的动物或罪犯)不受控制的,在逃的:The big, fierce dog is chained in the day, but *at large* at night. 这条凶猛的大狗白天用链子拴着,晚上撒着。Though millions of dollars were offered on his head, he is still *at large*. 虽然悬赏了数百万美元要他的脑袋,但他仍逍遥法外。The three escaped prisoners remain *at large*. 三名监狱逃犯仍然在逃。Thousands of foreign criminals *at large* in Britain exposes failures in police and customs checks. 有成千上万的外国逃犯在英国,这暴露出了警方和海关检查的失误。

Ⅱ *adv.* in detail; at length 详细地:The question is discussed *at large* in my report. 我在报告中详细地探讨了这个问题。Mary talked *at large* about her plan. 玛丽详尽地谈了她的计划。

NOTE **1.** 当本短语作"全体的,一般的"解时,同义短语是 as a whole 和 in general。
2. 当本短语作"不受控制的;在逃的"解时,同义短语是 at liberty 和 on the loose。

at (long) last *adv.* (used for saying that something you have been waiting for finally happens)in the end; finally 最后,终于:*At last* we defeated them completely. 最后,我们彻底地打败了他们。I'm so glad to meet you *at last*. 我很高兴终于见到了你。We swam two good hours and reached the opposite bank *at last*. 我们足足游了两个小时,终于到达了对岸。Then — *at long last* — their wedding day arrived. 后来,他们结婚的日子终于到来了。

NOTE **1.** at long last 比 at last 的语气更强。
2. 本短语与 at length, in the end 均表示"终于"之意,但它们各自的含义有所不同。本短语指一直期待的事情终于发生,具有较浓的感情色彩,语气强烈,常用于句首,有时用于句尾,也可用作感叹语。at length 是正式用语,强调经历了一段时间或停顿之后,终于做了某件事情。常用于句首或句中。in the end 常指经过长时间的考虑、讨论、探索或一系列的事件或经过许多困难之后,终于出现了某种结果,可指过去,也可预计未来,主要用于口语中,常置于句首或句尾。
3. 本短语的反义短语是 at first。

at (the) least *adv.* ❶ not less than a particular amount or number, and possibly more 至少:*At least* 1.8 million people gathered on the National Mall in Washington DC to watch the new president take the oath of office. 至少有 180 万人集聚在首都华盛顿的国家广场观看新总统宣誓就职的盛况。She smoked *at the least* half a packet of cigarettes a day. 她曾一天至少抽半包烟。❷in any case; whatever happens 不管怎样,无论如何:A two per cent pay rise is not very much, but *at least* it's

better than nothing. 加薪2%虽然不多，但不管怎样，这比不加要好。*At the least*, you should call to tell me that you've arrived there safely. 无论如何，你都应该打个电话告诉我你已平安到达那里。

NOTE 1. 当本短语作"至少"解时，反义短语是 at (the) most。

2. 当本短语作"不管怎样"解时，同义短语是 come what may, in any case 和 in any event。

at leisure Ⅰ *adv.* ❶ free to do what you want 随心所欲地：After a stop for lunch you will be taken to the famous Kenhof Flower Gardens where you can spend the afternoon *at*(your)*leisure*. 停下来用过午餐后，你们将被带到肯霍夫花园。在那里，你们可以随心所欲地度过一个下午。❷ slowly and for as long as you like; without hurrying; at your convenience 不慌不忙地；在方便时：You can take the documents home and study them *at* (your)*leisure*. 你可以把这些文件带回家，慢慢地研究。He walked around the town *at leisure*. 他慢悠悠地在镇子各处走了走。Please drop by *at* (your) *leisure*. 方便时，请来坐坐。

Ⅱ *adj.* (委婉用法) unemployed; idle 失业的；空闲的：Because of this great loss, many employees will be *at leisure*. 由于这次巨大的亏损，许多雇员将要失业。I'm not looking for another job right now; I want to be *at leisure* for a couple of months. 我不想马上再找工作，我想闲几个月。

NOTE 本短语的形容词性用法，现已很少使用。

at length *adv.* ❶ (正式用语) eventually, after a long interval or period of time 终于；过了很长时间后：There was another silence. *At length* Mary said, "You mean you're not going?" 又沉默了片刻后，玛丽终于开口问道："你的意思是说你不去？" After thinking things over she *at length* succeeded in letting reason prevail over her prejudices. 经过仔细考虑之后，她终于以理智战胜了偏见。❷ for a long time and with a lot of detail 长时间而又详细地：Austin was questioned *at length* by detectives. 奥斯汀受到了侦探长时间而又详细的询问。The matter will be discussed *at* greater *length* this evening. 这个问题要更多时间、更详细地讨论一下。

NOTE 当本短语作"终于"解时，length 之前不可加形容词；作"长时间而又详细地"解时，length 之前则可加诸如 great, full, some 等形容词来表示程度。

at liberty *adj.* ❶ (用作表语和补语) free from being kept in prison; not shut in or stopped 不受监禁的，被释放的：Two members of the gang are still *at liberty*. 该团伙的两名成员仍在逍遥法外。The police promised to set the man *at liberty* if he told the names of the other robbers. 警方答应，如果这个人说出其他抢劫犯的名字，就放他走。The thief was set *at liberty*. 那个小偷被释放了。❷ (正式用语，用作表语，后接不定式短语，常用于否定句中) being allowed or having the right (to do something) 获准的；有权的：You are *at liberty* to leave at any time. 允许你在任何时候走都可以。As the investigation is still under way, we are not *at liberty* to release any names. 由于调查仍在进行中，因此我们还无权公布任何人的名字。

NOTE 当本短语作"不受监禁的，被释放的"解时，同义短语是 at large 和 on the loose。

at (the) most *adv.* (used for showing that

you are mentioning the largest possible amount, although the real amount may be less) not more than, taking the greatest estimate 至多：Our teacher of English is *at most* 23 years old. 我们的英语老师至多 23 岁。The whole process will take half an hour *at the most*. 整个过程最多用半个小时。There can be no more than fifty people in the audience *at (the) most*. 观众至多不超过 50 人。A new engine would cost, *at most*, two thousand dollars. 买一台新发动机顶多花 2 000 美元。

NOTE 本短语的反义短语是 at (the) least。

at no time *adv.* (常用于句首) (used for emphasizing that someone did not do something or that it did not happen) never 从来没有；决不：*At no time* in his life has he shown more bravery than in that case. 在他的一生中，他从来没有像那次那样勇敢过。*At no time* and under no circumstance will China be the first to use nuclear weapons. 中国在任何时候和任何情况下都决不会首先使用核武器。*At no time* was the President aware of what was happening. 总统一直未察觉到发生了什么事。

NOTE 当本短语用于句首时，句中的主谓结构一定要构成倒装。当本短语置于句中较后的部分时，句中的主谓结构则不要倒装。我们可以把最后一个例句改为非倒装结构的句子：The President was *at no time* aware of what was happening.

at odds *adj.* (正式用语，常与 with 连用) in disagreement 有分歧，不一致：The European Union and the United States were *at odds* ahead of London G20 summit. 欧盟和美国在伦敦 20 国峰会开幕前就有分歧。Jim found himself *at odds* with his colleagues. 吉姆发现自己的观点与同事们的有分歧。Smith's description of the accident was *at odds* with the police report. 史密斯对该起事故的描述与警方的报告不一致。

NOTE 本短语中的名词 odd 必须用复数形式。

at odds on/over *prep.* in disagreement with (something) 在……上意见不一致，在……上有分歧：The two candidates were *at odds* on the environment. 两位候选人在环境问题上意见不一。It is natural for the young and old to be *at odds* over money matters. 年轻人和老一代在钱的问题上意见不一致是正常的。Biologists have been *at odds* over what's killing these frogs. 生物学家们在究竟是什么致死了这些青蛙的问题上一直各持己见。Democrats are *at odds* over how to advance the President's controversial healthcare reforms. 民主党人在如何推进总统具有争议的医疗保健改革上有分歧。

NOTE 本短语中的名词 odd 必须用复数形式。

at once *adv.* ❶ immediately; without any delay or hesitation 立即，马上：Bake for 35 minutes and then serve *at once*. 烘烤 35 分钟后立即食用。We are willing to stop the war *at once* and leave the remaining questions for later settlement. 我们愿意立即停战，余留的问题待以后解决。The women met at a party and became good friends *at once*. 这些女士们在聚会上见面后很快就成了好朋友。❷(正式用语) (of a number of different things happening) at the same time; simultaneously; together 同时，一起：You can't be doing two things *at once*. 你不能同时做两件事情吧。This

A

book is *at once* interesting and instructive. 这本书既有趣又有益。Tens of thousands of mourners rushed toward the coffin, with feelings of loyalty, pain, sadness and love all *at once*. 数万追悼者怀着忠诚、痛苦、悲伤和热爱交织在一起的心情涌向灵柩。

NOTE 本短语与 before long, right away, right now, straight away 均表示"立即,马上"。at once 广泛用于日常口语,时间概念较强,主要描述毫不犹豫、动作迅速,常用于句尾; before long 常用于日常口语,使用时常置于句尾; right away 原用于美国英语中,现在在英国英语中也普遍使用,常用于句尾;right now 侧重于此时此刻,常用于句尾;straight away 不及其他短语常用。

at one time *adv.* ❶at a particular period or moment in the past, but not now; once; formerly 一度,曾经:*At one time*, that kind of thing would have made me very angry. 在过去,那样的事会使我十分气恼。He was a teacher of English *at one time*, but now he works for foreign trade. 他曾当过英语老师,但现在做外贸工作。❷at the same time; simultaneously 同时:Don't speak *at one time*, children; I cannot hear clearly. 孩子们,大家不要一齐发言。我听不清楚。Several persons were injured when so many tried to get through the door *at one time*. 这么多人都想同时挤过这扇门,结果有几个人受了伤。He can play two chess games *at one time*. 他能同时下两盘棋。

NOTE 当本短语作"同时"解时,与 at a time 的第二个义项意义相同,两者可互换使用。

at one with *prep.* (正式用语,用作表语) in agreement or harmony with (someone or something) 与……一致(或和谐):The Liberals were *at one with* the Tories on this issue. 在这个问题上,自由党人与保守党人的意见一致。We disagree on most things, but on this question we are *at one with* each other. 我们在大多数事情上的意见都不一致,但在这个问题上我们的意见却相互一致。For hundreds of years the Greenland's hunters have been living *at one with* nature. 几百年来,格陵兰的猎人们一直与大自然和谐共存。

at one's best *adj.* (of someone or something) in the best state or condition 处于最佳状态的:Most athletes are *at their best* during their early manhood. 大多数运动员在初成年期间竞技状态最佳。The days when the country was *at her best* are long since gone. 那个国家的全盛时代早已过去了。To see New England *at its best*, you should come in September when the leaves start to change color. 9 月份当树叶开始改变颜色的时候是观赏新英格兰的最佳时期。

NOTE 本短语的反义短语是 at one's worst.

at one's disposal *adj.* (of someone or something) available for you to use whenever you want, and for whatever purpose you want (人或物)供某人随时随意使用的:I put myself *at your disposal* the whole morning. 我整个上午都随时听您的差遣。In our life about fifteen or twenty years are *at our disposal* for active work. 在我们的一生中,能让我们用于有效工作的时间大概是 15 或 20 年。A car and driver were placed *at my disposal*. 汽车和司机都归我随时随意地使用。As the president and commander in chief of the country, he repeatedly vowed that he would use every asset *at his disposal* to defeat the terrorists.

作为国家总统和军队总司令，他一再发誓要使用他所能动用的一切人力和物力战胜恐怖分子。

NOTE 1. 本短语在句子中充当表语、宾语补足语和后置定语。

2. 本短语的另外一种表达形式是 at the disposal of。例如：

> The car of the company was *at the disposal of* the manager.
> 公司的车由经理随时使用。

at one's leisure *adv.* when you have free time and it is convenient for you 当有空时，在方便时：Do it *at your leisure*; it's not urgent. 这事不急，有空时你再做。You can take the books away with you and read them *at your leisure*. 你可以把这几本书带走，在闲时阅读。

at one's mercy ⇨ **at/in the mercy of**

at one's wit's end *adj.* （非正式用语，用作表语）feeling puzzled after having used up all of your ideas or resources; so worried because of your problems or difficulties that you do not know what to do next 智穷计尽的，不知所措的，束手无策的：I have to write a paper and I just can't come up with a topic. I'm *at my wit's end*! 我还要写论文，但连题目都想不出来。我不知如何是好了。He was almost *at his wit's end* what to do. 他几乎不知所措了。She was *at her wit's end* how to pay the bills. 她不知如何付清这些账单。The authorities are *at their wit's end* about juvenile crimes. 当局对青少年犯罪束手无策。

NOTE 1. 本短语的另外一种表达形式是 at one's wits' end，两者可互换使用。

2. 本短语中的 one's 可省略，以 at wit's end 的固定形式使用。

at one's worst *adj.* （of someone or something）in the worst state or condition 处于最坏状态的：Relations between London and Moscow are *at their worst* since the Cold War, the British newspaper said. 这份英国报纸称，伦敦和莫斯科的关系现处于自冷战以来的最低谷。This is an example of prejudice *at its worst*. 这是一例最为严重的歧视事件。

NOTE 本短语的反义短语是 at one's best.

at peace *adj.* ❶not fighting a war 处于和平状态：The two countries are *at peace* after two years of war. 这两个国家在两年的战争之后，现在和平相处了。Everyone wants to live in a world *at peace*. 人人都想生活在一个和平的世界中。❷（常与 with 连用）in a state of quiet or calm; not feeling angry, unhappy, etc. 处于平静状态：The problem was settled and his mind was *at peace*. 问题解决了，他的心情便平静下来。At 50, she was *at peace* with herself and the world. 年至五旬，她心平气和，与世无争。❸（委婉用法）（of someone）dead and therefore having no more worries （某人）故去，安息：The old lady was unhappy when she was alive, but now she is *at peace*. 那老太太活着的时候很不幸，现在安息了。

NOTE 1. 当本短语作"处于平静状态"解时，比较级形式是 more at peace，最高级形式是 most at peace。

2. 当本短语作"处于和平状态"解时，反义短语是 at war。

3. 当本短语作"处于平静状态"和"（某人）故去，安息"解时，同义短语是 at rest。

at present *adv.* currently; right now; at this moment in time 现在，此刻，这会儿：*At present*, there are three thousand employees in the company. 现在，该公司有 3 000 名员工。China is taking a path toward peaceful development and has never threatened any country in the past and *at present*, and will never do so in the future. 中国走的是和平发展的道路。她在过去和现在没有，将来也不会对任何国家构成威胁。Coal and oil are *at present* the chief sources of power. 现在，煤炭和石油是主要的能源。

at random *adv.* without a particular purpose, method, pattern, or system 漫无目的地，随便地，任意地：The policeman fired a shot *at random*. 那名警察漫无目标地放了一枪。These are some of the specimens I have taken *at random* from the shelves. 这些标本是我从架子上随意取下来的。You may choose any number at random. 你可以任意挑选一个数字。

at rest *adj.* ❶(正式用语) free from anxiety or worry 安心的：You can put your mind *at rest*; the train makes only one more stop before our destination. 您可以安心了，火车再停一站咱们就到了。He sat still in his chair, but not *at rest*. 他坐在椅子上一动不动，但心绪不宁。❷not moving 不动的：After having played the toys for two hours, the children were *at rest*. 玩了两个小时的玩具后，孩子们安静了。The markings are white and not visible when the bird is *at rest*. 当这只鸟不动时，其羽毛上的白色斑纹是看不见的。*At rest* the insect looks like a dead leaf. 这种昆虫不动时，就像一片枯叶一样。❸(委婉用法) dead and therefore free from trouble or anxiety 安息，长眠，去世：The heroes were *at rest* at the foot of the hill. 英雄们安息在小山脚下。She now lies *at rest* in the churchyard. 她现在长眠于教堂的墓地。My elder brother is *at rest* after his long illness. 我哥哥长期患病之后，故去了。

NOTE 当本短语作"安心的"和"安息，长眠，去世"解时，同义短语是 at peace。

at risk *adj.* (后常接 of 短语) in a dangerous situation 处于险境中：The disease is spreading, and all children under 6 are *at risk*. 这种疾病正在蔓延，凡 6 岁以下儿童都有被感染的危险。A British government report said a 3 degree increase in global temperature would put between 1.2 billion and 3 billion people *at risk* of water shortages. 英国政府发布的一份报告称，如果全球气温上升 3 度的话，就会有 12 亿到 30 亿人陷入缺水的危险境地。Who are most *at risk* of catching A/H1N1 flu? 谁最有患上甲型 H1N1 流感的危险？

NOTE 1. 本短语的比较级形式是 more at risk，最高级形式是 most at risk。

2. 本短语的同义短语是 at stake, in danger 和 on the line。

at sea Ⅰ *adj.* ❶(especially of a ship or person aboard a ship) travelling in a boat or ship (尤指船只或船上的人)航行，出海：The boat remained *at sea* for 10 days. 这条小船在海上航行 10 天了。He has been *at sea* for four months. 他已经出海四个月了。❷(主要用于新闻英语中) confused and not certain what to do; puzzled or bewildered 茫然，迷惑：We were all *at sea* until instructions arrived. 在接到指示前，我们都茫然不知所措。When it comes to mathematics, I'm completely *at sea*. 谈到数学问题，我完全茫然无知。I'm quite *at sea* in regard to his explanation. 他的解释使我感到迷惘。

Ⅱ *adv.* on the sea, far away from land 在海上：Some 24,000 fishermen die *at sea* each year, making fishing probably the most dangerous occupation in the world, the

UN's Food and Agriculture Organization said in a recent report. 联合国粮农组织在最近的一份报告中称,每年大约有 24 000 名渔民在海上死亡。这使得捕鱼可能成了世界上最为危险的职业。Robbers *at sea* are called pirates; they attack and rob ships *at sea*. 海上的抢劫者叫海盗。他们攻击并抢劫海上的船只。

NOTE 1. 当本短语用作形容词性短语,作"茫然,迷惑"解时,比较级形式是 more at sea,最高级形式是 most at sea。

2. 当本短语用作形容词性短语,作"茫然,迷惑"解时,同义短语是 at a loss。

at/on sight *adv.* as soon as someone or something is seen or shown 一看见就……: The money order was payable *at sight*. 该汇票是见单即付的。The captain ordered us to shoot anyone suspicious *on sight*. 上尉命令我们看到可疑的人就开枪。

at someone's instance ⇨ **at the instance of**

at stake *adj.* likely to be lost or damaged if something fails 濒于(失去……)险境的: The company is on the verge of bankruptcy, and hundreds of jobs are *at stake*. 该公司处于破产的边缘,数百人濒于失业的境地。Thousands of lives will be *at stake* if emergency aid does not arrive in the town soon. 如不迅速到达该镇进行紧急救援,成千上万人的生命就危在旦夕。

NOTE 本短语的同义短语是 at risk 和 in danger。

at the cost of *prep.* at the loss or expense of 以……为代价,牺牲……: *At the cost of* what he had, he went to the seaside for a cure at a famous hospital. 他不惜所有,去了海滨一所著名医院治疗。The driver manages to save the girl from falling, but only *at the cost of* injuring himself. 司机费了好大劲不让那个女孩摔倒,但是自己却受了伤。The young hero saved the girl from the fire *at the cost of* his own life. 年轻的英雄从大火中救出那个女孩,却牺牲了自己的生命。

NOTE 本短语的同义短语是 at the expense of,但 at the expense of 者更为正式。

at the disposal of ⇨ **at one's disposal**

at the earliest *adv.* (used after a date or time to show that something will not happen before then) no earlier than the date or the time mentioned (用于某一日期或时间之后)至早,最早: I think the letter will reach her on Saturday *at the earliest*. 我想,这封信她最早也得星期六才会收到。Basic minimum wage is to remain unchanged at the current level until 2010 *at the earliest*. 最低基本工资将维持目前的水平,最早到 2010 年才会有变动。I can arrive at 3:00 pm *at the earliest*. 我最早下午 3 点钟到达。

NOTE 本短语的反义短语是 at the latest。

at the expense of *prep.* ❶ with money from (someone or something) 由……付费,由……负担: He refused to travel *at the expense of* the company and paid the trip himself. 他不肯由公司出钱供他旅行,而是自己付了旅费。Most of us study at college at the great expenses of our parents. 我们大多数人上大学,都由父母支付巨大的花销。❷ with the sacrifice of (something or someone) 以牺牲……为代价: He finished the book *at the expense of* his health. 他以牺牲健康为代价写完了那本书。It's wrong to aim at sheer quantity *at the expense of* quality. 片面地追求数量而

A

牺牲质量是错误的。I do not understand why our coach will try to keep Cole or Chris *at the expense of* losing a key player like Ryan. 我不明白我们的教练为什么要以失去像瑞安这样的关键球员为代价而竭力要留住科尔或克里斯。

at the instance of *prep.*（英国英语用法，正式用语）at the request or suggestion of (someone)应(某人的)请求(或建议)：*At the instance of* Mr Smith, we decided to stay here for another week for further investigations. 在史密斯先生的建议下，我们决定在这儿再住一个星期，做进一步调查。He wrote two books on popular science *at the instance of* a publishing house. 他应一家出版社之邀，写了两本科普读物。

NOTE 本短语的另外一种表达形式是 at someone's instance。例如：

> The demonstration was organized *at* a cabinet minister's *instance*.
> 这次的示威是在一名内阁成员的建议下组织的。

at the latest *adv.* (used to emphasize that something must happen or be done before a stated time or day) no later than the time or the date mentioned（用于某一时间或日期之后）至迟，最晚：He said he'd arrive by 10:00 *at the latest*. 他说，他最晚10点钟到达。Applications should be in by next Monday *at the latest*. 申请最晚也应该在下星期一之前交上来。

NOTE **1.** 在英国英语中，the latest 之间可加副词 very。

2. 本短语的反义短语是 at the earliest。

at/in the mercy of *prep.* in a situation that is controlled by someone or something with the power to harm you 受……支配，任由……摆布：Workers are entirely *at the mercy of* their employers. 工人们完全受他们雇主的支配。Farmers have to be *at the mercy of* the weather. 农民不得不靠天吃饭。They were lost at sea, *at the mercy of* the wind and waves. 他们在海上迷失了方向，任由风浪摆布。The government should act as consumers are left *at the mercy of* rising food prices. 消费者对食品价格上涨无能为力，政府应该采取行动。

NOTE 本短语的另外一种表达方式是 at one's mercy。例如：

> I was completely *at his mercy*, because the robber had a knife in my back.
> 我完全听任他的摆布，因为这个盗抢者用刀子戳着我的腰部。

at the moment *adv.* at the present time; just now 现在，此刻：They're very sad and don't want to talk *at the moment*. 他们十分悲伤，现在不想讲话。*At the moment*, the only thing left to do is finish mixing the album. 此刻唯一要做的就是把混录唱片的工作完成。

NOTE **1.** 本短语通常与现在时连用。与过去时连用时，意为"当时，那时"。例如：

> She was laid up in bed with a bad cold *at the moment*.
> 当时，她因患重感冒而在卧床。

2. 本短语与 at this moment in time 意义相同，但后者为正式用语，且语气较强。

at the point of *prep.* just before (something is going to happen); very near to 就在……之前，即将，几乎要：*At the point of* losing consciousness, he saw his friends running to his rescue. 就在要失去知觉之前，他看见朋友们跑过来抢救他。The old woman is *at the point of* death. 这位老妇人奄奄一息。

NOTE 本短语的同义短语是 on/upon the

point of。

at the present moment ⇨ **at this moment in time**

at the same time *adv.* ❶(used for saying that two or more things happen together) simultaneously; at the same moment 同时：Your users will do their best to achieve their employer's business goals, while *at the same time* looking after their own personal goals. 你的用户会在实现他们个人目标的同时，尽量实现他们雇主的商业目标。She laughed and cried *at the same time*. 她连哭带笑。❷(used for introducing another fact or opinion that needs to be considered as well as the one that has just been stated) in spite of this; however; nonetheless; yet 尽管如此，然而：The boy can be rude but *at the same time* you can't help liking him. 这男孩可能有些粗野，尽管这样，他还是挺讨人喜欢的。I'll forgive you; *at the same time* you must never do it again. 我将原谅你，然而你决不能再做这事了。

NOTE 当本短语作"同时"解时，同义短语是 at once 和 at one time。

at the sight of *prep.* on seeing (something or someone) 当看到……：I always faint *at the sight* of blood. 我总是一见到血就晕。*At the sight of* her mother, the little girl stopped crying and ran to her. 一看到妈妈，那小女孩儿就止住哭声，跑上前去迎她。

at/behind the wheel *adj.* ❶ driving a motor vehicle 在开车：How many people were in the car and who was *at the wheel* when the car crashed? 撞车时车里有几个人，是谁在开车？I never feel safe with Laura *at/behind the wheel*. 罗拉开车时，我总是没有安全感。I can't wait to get *behind the wheel* again. 我急不可待地要再次驾车。❷in command; in control 掌管，控制：Mary hated being told what to do; she wanted to be *at the wheel* by herself. 玛丽不愿听别人指挥，她想自己做主。You want to know what my career plan is? My ambition is to be *at the wheel* of a big corporation by the time I reach thirty! 你想知道我在事业方面的计划？我的愿望是在我 30 岁的时候能够成为一家大公司的总裁。

NOTE **1.** at the wheel 亦有"在掌舵，在开船"之意。例如：

> The young man was *at the wheel* with the captain close by.
> 小伙子掌着船舵，船长伴在身旁。

2. 当本短语作"在开车"解时，动词形式是 *take the wheel*（开车，开船）。例如：

> Would you like me to *take the wheel* for a while?
> 你让我开一会儿车，好吗？

at this moment in time *adv.*（正式用语）(used for emphasizing that you are talking about the present time or situation) now 现在，此时此刻：There's no problem I have to solve *at this moment in time*. 眼下，我没有什么问题需要解决的。*At this moment in time* it would be inappropriate to comment on the situation. 此时，对局势作出评论还不合适。

NOTE **1.** 本短语的另外一种表达形式是 at the present moment。例如：

> You can choose to do what is necessary *at the present moment*.
> 你可以选择做此刻需要做的事情。

2. 本短语的同义短语是 at the moment。两者间的区别见 at the moment。

at times *adv.* sometimes but not often; occasionally 有时，偶尔，不时地：She was a

fun person to be with *at times*. 与她相处有时很开心。Today television brings into our homes information and entertainment and *at times*, even inspiration. 今天的电视将信息、娱乐,有时甚至灵感都带进家中。*At times* he prepares his lesson well; at other times he does very poor work. 有时他的功课准备得很好;有时则做得非常糟糕。The new computers went out of order *at times*. 这些新电脑也不时地出故障。

NOTE 本短语的同义短语是 every now and then, every so often, from time to time, now and again 和 now and then。在这组短语中, at times 较为正式; every now and then 和 every so often 含有屡次、多次的意味,语气比 now and again 和 now and then 强;now and again 和 now and then 两者无任何区别,可互换使用;from time to time 广泛用于日常口语中,侧重"时常"这一概念。

at war *adj*. (常与 with 连用) (usually of two or more nations) fighting a war (常指国家之间)处于战争状态,打仗:"We are *at war* today because there are still people who want to harm our country and hurt our citizens," the president said in his weekly radio address Saturday. 总统在星期六每周例行的广播讲话中说:"我们今天还处于战争之中,这是因为仍然有人想危害我们的国家和人民。" The two countries have been *at war* with each other for years. 这两个国家已经打了好几年仗。The three brothers are constantly *at war*. 这兄弟三个经常打斗。

NOTE 本短语的反义短语是 at peace。

at will *adv*. (正式用语) as you please or wish 随意地,任意地: With an air conditioner in your room you can enjoy comfortable temperatures *at will*. 房间里有空调,你可以随意地享受舒适的温度。At that time, China implemented a planned economy, which allowed the government to allocate social and natural resources *at will*. 那时,中国实行的是计划经济,该体制允许政府任意调配社会和自然资源。

at work *adj*. ❶at the place where you work 在工作场所,在上班: If he's not at home, he must still be *at work*. 如果他不在家,他就是还在上班。I'm sorry to call you *at work*, but this is urgent. 对不起,在你上班时还打电话给你,但这事紧急。❷(常与 on 连用) in the process of doing one's job or busy doing a particular activity; working 在工作: According to the survey, 93 percent of all employees in the US spend some of their time *at work* surfing the Web. 该项调查表明,全美93%的员工将部分工作时间用来上网。The little boy found it interesting to watch the washing machine *at work*. 那小男孩发现观看洗衣机工作很有趣。❸ having a particular effect or influence; in action or operation 在起作用,在运转中: At last his words were *at work*. 他的话最终起了作用。It is important to understand the powerful economic and social forces *at work* behind their actions. 重要的是要了解在他们的行动背后强大的经济和政治力量所起的作用。In thousands of factories, power plants and mines, machines are busily *at work*. 在成千上万的工厂、发电厂和矿山里,机器都在不停地运转。

at (the) worst *adv*. under the least favorable conditions; taking the least favorable view 在最坏的情况下: She keeps cheerful, even when things are *at the worst*.

即使在最坏的情况下,她也保持心情愉快。Don't worry, you would only lose a couple of dollars. 别担心,最坏你只不过损失几元钱而已。

NOTE 本短语的反义短语是 at (the) best.

attach to *vt.* ❶fasten or join (one thing) to (another)把……系(挂、缚、接)在……上: *Attach* the rope *to* the branch of a tree. 把绳子系到树枝上。*Attach* the labels *to* all the bags. 把所有的包都贴上标签。They *attached* the flag *to* a pole. 他们把旗子挂在了旗杆上。He *attached* a color printer *to* his computer. 他把彩色打印机连接到自己的计算机上。❷(用一般时态) consider as having (a quality or importance, etc.)认为具有(某种性质或重要性等): These girls' parents didn't seem to *attach* any importance *to* their education. 这些女孩子们的家长似乎不重视她们的教育。Pompeo's official visit to China indicates the great importance the new US Secretary of State *attached to* the improvement of relations between the two countries. 蓬佩奥对中国的正式访问表明,美国新任国务卿十分重视改善两国之间的关系。❸(用被动语态形式) (of someone) be sent to work in (a different place, with a different group of people), often only for a short time (指某人)被(常指短期)派往外地工作: Mary is now *attached to* the British Embassy in Beijing. 玛丽现在在英国驻北京大使馆工作。

attached to *adj.* ❶(of an organization or institution) being part of (a larger group or organization)(指某一机构)附属于,隶属于: These clinical hospitals are *attached to* the medical college nearby. 这几所临床医院都附属于附近的那所医学院。World Health Organization (WHO), a specialized agency *attached to* the United Nations, was established in April 1948. 世界卫生组织(简称 WHO)是联合国下属的一个专门机构,始建于 1948 年 4 月。❷(常用作表语) liking or fond of (someone or something) very much or loving them 喜欢,爱慕: She found herself growing deeply *attached to* the new employee. 她发现自己已深深地喜欢上了那名新来的雇员。The two of them are warmly *attached to* each other. 他们两人正在热恋之中。I am deeply *attached to* this car. 我非常喜欢这辆车。

NOTE 当本短语作"附属于,隶属于"解时,同义短语是 affiliated to/with。

attain to *vt.* 【不可分性动词短语】(正式用语,不用被动语态形式,常用一般时态) reach (a desired state or condition); succeed in achieving (something), especially after a lot of effort 取得,达到: He *attained to* great heights in the field of geology. 他在地质科学方面取得了很大的成就。The perfection *to* which the pianist had *attained* was achieved by years of hard work. 那位钢琴家所达到的完美程度是多年苦练得来的成果。

attend on/upon *vt.* 【不可分性动词短语】 look after (someone, especially someone who is ill or someone in an important position)照料(病人);侍奉(重要人物): The report said an 85-year-old mother has been *attending on* her sick daughter who is now 60 for 60 years. 这篇报道说,一位 85 岁的母亲 60 年来一直照料着她那有病的现已 60 岁的女儿。The king has as many as 100 people *attending on* him. 国王有百人侍奉。The

princess was *attended on/upon* by a number of servants. 那位公主有多名用人侍候。

NOTE 1. 本短语中的 upon 用法比 on 正式，但不及 on 常用。

2. 本短语的同义短语是 attend to 和 wait on/upon。

attend to *vt.*【不可分性动词短语】❶(正式用语) pay attention to (something or doing something); deal with (something or someone)专心于;处理:*Attend to* your work and stop talking! 专心工作,不要讲话! We still have a number of other matters to *attend to*. 我们还有一些其他事情要办理。All the most urgent matters have now been *attended to*. 所有最紧急的事务现都已处理完毕。Please take a seat and I'll ask someone to *attend to* you. 请坐下,我就找人处理您的事情。❷give help, especially medical help, to (someone); take care of (someone or something), often in someone's absence 给予(某人)(尤指医疗)护理;照料(某人或某物):The doctors and nurses in the specialized hospital *attended to* the patients by turns all day long. 这所专门医院里的医护人员全天候地轮流护理这些患者。You'd better *attend to* the children first — they need their breakfast. 你最好先去照料孩子们——他们要吃早餐。You'll have to *attend to* the factory while I am abroad. 在我出国期间你得照料工厂了。Has your business been *attended to* by her in your absence? 你不在的时候生意一直由她照料吗? ❸serve (a customer) in a shop, restaurant, etc. (在商店、餐馆等中)接待(顾客):The school trains girls how to *attend to* customers in a special course. 学校在一门特殊的课程中训练女学生如何接待顾客。Are you being *attended to*? 有人照应您吗?

attribute to *vt.*【可分性动词短语】❶(常用一般时态) believe (something) to be the result of (something else)把……认为是……的结果,把……归因于……: The old man *attributed* his longevity *to* his diet based on tomatoes, fish and olive oil 那位老人将其长寿归因于他所吃的食物——西红柿、鱼和橄榄油。The causes of death were mainly *attributed to* multiple organ failure, severe infections and shock. 多脏器衰竭、严重感染和休克是主要致死原因。❷(正式用语,常用被动语态形式) believe or say that something was written, said, painted, etc. by (a particular person)认为(某物为)(某人)所写(或所说、所画等): The play has been *attributed to* Shakespeare. 此剧被认为是莎士比亚所作。

NOTE 1. 当本短语作"把……认为是……的结果,把……归因于……"解时,同义短语是 set down to。

2. 不要将本短语和 contribute to 混淆。contribute to 表示"捐助,贡献,有助于"等意。

avail (oneself) of *vt.* (主要用于英国英语中,正式用语,常用一般时态) use or take advantage of (an opportunity, etc.) 利用(机会等): More and more people have been able to *avail of* high-speed Internet for communication. 越来越多的人能够利用高速的互联网进行交际。I wish to *avail myself of* this opportunity to express sincere gratitude to the

Chinese government that has successfully hosted the meeting. 我愿借此机会对中国政府成功主办本次大会表示衷心感谢。Only a few companies have *availed themselves of* the free training programme. 仅有少数几家公司利用了该项免费培训项目。

NOTE **1.** avail of 主要用于美国英语中。

2. 本短语不能用于被动语态形式。

avenge on/upon *vt.*【可分性动词短语】(正式用语) react to something wrong that has been done to you, your family, or your friends by punishing (the person who did it) 为……报复,为……报仇: They *avenged* themselves *on* their enemy. 他们向敌人进行了报复。Hamlet *avenged* his father's murder *on/upon* his uncle. 哈姆雷特对谋杀他父亲的叔父予以了报复。He swears that he will be *avenged on* you sooner or later. 他发誓说总有一天要向你报仇。

NOTE **1.** 本短语中的 upon 用法比 on 正式,但不及 on 常用。

2. 本短语与 revenge on 意义相同,都表示"为……报仇"。但本短语多指为他人报仇,为某事而复仇,因此,avenge 后接 someone/oneself 或 something; 而 revenge on 则多指为自己报仇,因此,revenge 后与反身代词连用,而不能与 something 连用。

aware of *adj.* (常用于 be, become 之后作表语) knowing about or conscious of (a situation or a fact)知道,意识到,认识到:He was not *aware of* what was going on around him. 他对周围发生的事情茫然不知。She became *aware of* a particular smell. 她意识到有一种奇特的气味。I suddenly became *aware of* him staring at me. 我突然察觉到他在盯着我看。"It's always worthwhile to make others *aware of* their worth," Malcolm Forbes said. 马尔科姆·福布斯说:"让别人认识到自己的价值,总是件值得做的事。"

NOTE **1.** 本短语的比较级形式是 more aware of,最高级形式是 most aware of。

2. 不要将本短语与 beware of 混淆。见 beware of。

B

B b

back and forth *adv.* moving first in one direction and then in the opposite direction many times; to and fro 来回地, 往返地: The female surfing star in Hawaii said the shark pulled her *back and forth*, "but I just held on to my board, and then it let go." 这位夏威夷冲浪女明星讲述说,鲨鱼来回地拖拽着她:"但我紧紧地抓住冲浪板,后来它松口了。" Millions of people traveled *back and forth* across the Taiwan Straits each year 每年都有数百万人. 往返于台湾海峡。Soon after the accident, police barred all visitors from the building of the hospital, as ambulances hurried *back and forth*. 事件发生后不久,警方禁止所有探视者进入医院大楼内,而救护车仍在往返地穿梭着。

NOTE 1. 本短语可转化为复合形容词 back-and-forth, 意为"往复的"。例如:

> Sound is caused by vibration, and is simply a *back-and-forth* movement.
> 声音是由振动引起的,振动只是一种往复运动。

2. 本短语的同义短语是 backwards and forwards 和 to and fro。

back away *vi.* (常与 from 连用) ❶move away or backwards (from someone or something), for example because you are afraid (因恐惧而)后退: The crowd *backed away* in fear when the man pulled out a gun. 人们见那名男子掏出了枪便都吓得往后退去。He *backed away* from the window in great fear when bullets whistled past his ears. 当子弹嗖嗖地从耳边飞过时,他惊恐地从窗边躲开。The dog *backed away* as the man waved his stick. 那人挥起棍子,狗便向后退去。❷refuse to pursue or support (something); gradually become less involved (in something) 放弃,(逐步地)不再参与: I could see she was *backing away* from the idea. 我可以看出她在放弃那种想法。The World Bank is *backing away* from big infrastructure projects. 世界银行不再参与大规模的基础结构性项目。

back chat *n.* (非正式用语) a rude reply that shows you do not respect someone in authority, especially by a younger person or a subordinate (尤指晚辈或下属的)回嘴,顶嘴: Just listen to me! I don't want any *back chat*! 只管听我说! 我不容许有人回嘴! Hill does not tolerate *back chat*; he expects his orders to be obeyed without question. 希尔不容别人对他顶嘴,他希望别人对他唯命是从。

NOTE 1. 本短语为不可数性名词短语,无复数形式。

2. 本短语与 back talk 意义和用法相同。本短语用于英国英语中,可连写成 backchat;而 back talk 则用于美国英语中,可连写成 backtalk。两者都可用作动词。

back down *vi.* ❶(非正式用语) go (down) backwards 退下,退缩:*Back down* carefully, the ladder is not steady. 梯子不稳,下来时要小心。Bill said he could beat Jim, but when Jim put up his fists Bill *backed down*. 比尔说他能打败吉姆,但当吉姆举起拳头时,比尔却退缩了。❷(主要用于英国英语中,常与 from, on 连用) yield in argument, point of view, claim, etc.; stop asking for something, or stop saying that you will do something, because a lot of people oppose you 放弃(主张、观点、要求等),作出让步:The union leader, on the other hand, has shown no signs of *backing down* from his plan. 另一方面,没有迹象表明工会领导人要放弃其计划。They finally *backed down* on their unreasonable demands. 他们终于放弃了不合理的要求。Neither side will *back down* because both believe they are right. 双方都不肯作出让步,因为他们都相信自己是正确的。

NOTE 当本短语作"放弃(主张、观点、要求等),作出让步"解时,与 back off 用法相同,后者为美国英语用法。

back into *vt.* ❶(cause to) go backwards into (a place) (使)退入(某处):We watched the little girl *backing* slowly *into* the room. 我们看着那个小女孩慢慢退入屋内。The young man with a knife *backed* me *into* a dark corner of the street. 那年轻人拿着刀逼我退入街道的一个黑暗的角落里。He *backed* his car *into* the garage. 他把汽车倒入停车房。❷(cause to) hit (something) when driving (a vehicle) backwards, especially because the driver is careless or inexperienced 倒车撞上(某物):I *backed into* another car as I was coming out of the car park. 我从停车场往后倒车时撞上了另外一辆车。Smith bought a new car, and his son backed it into a lamppost the next day. 史密斯买了一部新车,第二天他儿子就在倒车时将其撞在了一根路灯柱上。I really don't enjoy being *backed into* by learner drivers. 我实在不喜欢(我的车)被学开车的人在倒车时撞上。

back of *prep.* ❶(非正式用语) in or at the rear of; at or to the back of; behind (something) 在……后面:Our car was (*in*)*back of* theirs at the traffic light. 红灯亮时,我们的车就在他们的车后面。He led the guests to the hall *back of*/*in back of* the stairs. 他把客人领到楼梯后面的大厅。We may see the hard work *back of* every success. 我们可以看得出每项成就背后的艰辛劳动。❷in support or encouragement of; helping 支持,鼓励,帮助:John will be elected, because many powerful men are *back of* him. 约翰会当选的,因为许多有权势的人物在支持他。Get *back of* your team by cheering them at the game. 在比赛时要向你们队喝彩助威以鼓励他们。❸(非正式用语) being a cause or reason for; causing 是……的原因,导致:The investigators tried to find out what was *back of* the incident. 调查人员力求查明这起事件的原因。Hard work was *back of* his achievements. 勤奋使他取得成功。

NOTE 本短语的另外一种表达形式是 in back of,主要用于美国英语中。

back off *v.* ❶(cause to) move backwards (使)向后退:He *backed off* a few steps and let the old lady go first. 他后退了几步,让老妇人先走。The protesters couldn't help *backing off* as the riot police charged. 当防暴警察冲上来时,抗

议者们不由向后退去。The driver *backed* the car *off*. 司机驾车向后退。Do you mind *backing off* a bit, Sir? 先生,请把车向后倒一倒,您不介意吧? ❷(主要用于美国英语中)(cause to) back down or give up an attempt or claim, etc. (使)放弃(原来的要求、立场等),打退堂鼓:The city council had to *back off* from its criticism of the utility department. 市议会不得不撤回了对公用事业部门的批评。Now the time for action has arrived, it is too late to *back off*. 行动的时间已到,要打退堂鼓已经为时过晚。

NOTE 当本短语作"(使)放弃(原来的要求、立场等)"解时,与 back down 用法相同,back down 为英国英语用法。

back out *vi.* (非正式用语,常与 of 连用) ❶fail to keep a promise; go back on one's word 食言,收回诺言:I promised to help you and I'm not *backing out* now. 我答应过帮助你,我现在就不能食言。If you don't follow my advice, I would *back out* of my words. 如果你不按我的主意去做,我就收回我的诺言。❷decide not to do something you agreed to do or retreat from difficulty; withdraw from undertaking 因难而退;不再干(某事): He agreed to help him with a loan, but *backed out*. 他同意以贷款来帮助他,可后来又不干了。We're hoping that no one will *back out* of the deal. 我们不希望有人在这笔交易上打退堂鼓。The village *backed out* of building a pool when the cost got too high. 由于成本过高,村里就不打算修水塘了。

back talk ⇨ **back chat**

back up *v.* ❶provide moral or physical support to (someone)支持,支援(某人): The candidate claimed the citizens to *back* him *up* by promising better welfare. 候选人承诺给市民提供更好的福利,并呼吁市民支持他。You probably have a lot of detailed information to *back up* your assumptions. 你可能有很多详细的资料来支持你的假设。❷(cause to) move backwards, especially for a vehicle to do so (使)(尤指车辆)后退:You'll have to *back up* your car a bit further. 您得再把车往后倒一点。I advised the middle-aged woman to *back* her BMW car *up* a little to see how serious its mirror was damaged by the quadricycle. 我劝说那名中年妇女稍微向后移动一下她的宝马车,以查看被四轮车所刮的车镜受损情况。The train was *backing up*. 列车在向后退。I need everyone to *back up* about 10 paces. 我需要每人往后退 10 步左右。❸(of traffic) (cause to) hold back; (usually of liquid) block (a narrow place) (使)(交通)阻滞;(常指液体)阻塞:The accident *backed up* the traffic. 事故阻塞了交通。Traffic is backing up for miles. 被堵车辆排了数英里。The floodwater from the storm *backed up* sewer pipes. 暴风雨引起的洪水阻塞了下水管道。❹duplicate (a programme or file stored on the computer), as a security measure 拷贝(计算机上存有的程序或文件):Make sure you *back up* (the information on the disk) before you turn the computer off. 一定要(把磁盘上的信息)拷贝下来再关闭计算机。Business information stored on your computer is important—*back* it *up* or lose it! 在你电脑上储存的业务资料很重要。要拷贝下来,否则会丢失的!

NOTE **1.** 当本短语用作及物性动词短语,所带的宾语为代词时,该代词须置于本短语的动词和副词中间。

2. 本短语可转化为复合词 backup，意为“支持，帮助；后退，退却；倒车，（车辆的）阻塞；（流水受阻后的）积聚；（计算机）备份文件”。

backwards and forwards *adv.* moving first in one direction and then in the opposite direction many times 来回地，往返地：Father began to pace *backwards and forwards*. 爸爸开始来回地踱步。He ran *backwards and forwards* along the cliff. 他沿着悬崖来来回回地跑着。

NOTE 本短语的同义短语是 back and forth 和 to and fro。

badly done-to ⇨ **hard done (-)by**

badly off *adj.*（非正式用语）having little money and few of the things you need to live; poor 不富裕的，贫穷的：They're *badly off*. 他们不富裕。They were so *badly off* that they had to sell whatever was valuable in their possession. 他们穷得不得不变卖所有的值钱之物。His family has been pretty *badly off* since he lost his job. 自从他失去工作以来，他家便一直很困难。

NOTE 1. 本短语中的比较级形式是 worse off 或 more badly off，最高级形式为 worst off 或 most badly off。

2. 本短语的反义短语是 well off。

3. 本短语可转化为复合词 badly-off，意为“不好的，差的；贫穷的，不幸的”。

ban from *vt.*【可分性动词短语】（常用被动语态形式）officially prevent (someone) from (doing something) 禁止（某人）做（某事）：China *banned* shops *from* giving out free plastic bags and called on consumers to use baskets and cloth sacks instead to reduce environmental pollution. 中国禁止商店免费提供塑料袋，并呼吁消费者使用篮子和布袋以减少环境污染。She was *banned from* athletics for two years after failing a drug test. 她没有通过药检，于是被禁赛了两年。

NOTE 本短语的同义短语是 bar from。

bar from *vt.*【可分性动词短语】（常用被动语态形式）❶ officially forbid (someone) from (doing something) 禁止（某人）做（某事）：In Kuwait, a law may be passed which *bars* Kuwaitis *from* enrolling in some private universities located in Egypt and Bahrain. 科威特可能会通过一项禁止科威特人进入某些埃及和巴哈林私立大学学习的法令。He has been *barred from* playing for two months because of his bad behavior. 他因恶劣行为而被禁赛两个月。❷ prevent (someone) from entering; keep out 禁止进入（或加入），排斥于……之外：If I were in charge I would *bar* tourists *from* the wildlife reserve. 如果我说了算的话，我就不允许游客进入野生动物保护区。The club members voted to *bar* women *from* the club. 俱乐部成员表决不准妇女加入该俱乐部。Many years ago, black children were *barred from* the school gates. 很多年前，黑人的孩子都被排斥在学校大门之外。

NOTE 当本短语作“禁止（某人）做（某事）”解时，同义短语是 ban from。

barely … when ⇨ **scarcely … when**

bargain for *vt.*【不可分性动词短语】❶（非正式用语，常用否定形式）expect; anticipate 预料到，想到：I hadn't *bargained for* such heavy rain, and I got very wet. 我没预料到会下这么大雨，所以浑身都浇透了。I didn't *bargain for* Mark arriving so soon. 我没有想到马克会到得这么快。We hadn't *bargain for* finding them here. 我们没有料到会在这

里找到他们。❷(非正式用语) be willing or prepared to accept 期望得到: I just asked for a sandwich but I got more than I'd *bargained for* — they brought me an enormous plate of food! 我只要了一客三明治,但我得到的比我预料的多得多——他们给我送来了一大盘食物。With the good new policies of the government, the Chinese farmers are *bargaining for* a wonderful harvest this year. 有政府新出台的好政策,中国农民期待着今年有个好收成。❸discuss the conditions of a sale, agreement etc., in order to obtain (a lower price or goods at a cheap price) 通过讨价还价得到: In open-air markets it is standard practice to *bargain for* the best price. 在露天市场,争取讨得最低价格是个惯例。That dealer spent hours *bargaining for* the valuable painting. 那个商人花了好几个小时讨价还价,想把这幅珍贵的画廉价弄到手。

NOTE 1. 当本短语作"预料到,想到"和"期望得到"解时,还可用 bargain on 的形式。2. 当本短语作"通过讨价还价得到"解时,还可用 bargain over 的形式。

barge in/into *v.* (非正式用语) ❶(of a person) enter (a room, etc.) suddenly and without invitation, usually interrupting someone in a rude way (指人)闯入(房间等): The kids just *barge in* without knocking first. 这些孩子们也不先敲敲门就闯了进来。Bob doesn't like strangers *barging in*. 鲍勃不喜欢有陌生人闯进来。You can't just *barge in* my room like that. 你不能像那样就闯入我的房间。The boy *barged into* the classroom before everyone else. 那男孩子抢在其他人前面闯进了教室。❷knock against (someone), usually by accident (常指无意地)撞在(某人身上): She ran round the corner and *barged into* one of the teachers. 她跑着绕过拐角,和一位老师撞了个满怀。❸interrupt (usually talk) rudely or clumsily 无礼地打断(常指谈话): Don't *barge in* where you are not wanted. 不需要你的地方就别插嘴。Why must you always come *barging into* the conversation? 你为什么总是打断别人的谈话呢?

NOTE 当本短语作"打断谈话"解时,同义短语有: break in, break into, burst in, cut in, cut into, cut off, cut short, chip in, cut short, get in 和 put in 等。但它们的用法不同,有的是及物性的,有的是不及物性的,有的既有及物性又有不及物性用法。

bark at *vt.* ❶(of a dog) make a short sharp loud sound at (someone or something) (指狗)向……吠,叫: The dog suddenly started *barking at* us. 那条狗突然向我们叫了起来。A small dog *barked at* a seagull it was chasing. 一条小狗向它正在追逐的海鸥叫着。❷say or shout (something) to (someone) in a loud, rough voice 对(某人)大声吼叫: I don't like the way that the teacher *barks at* the children. 我不喜欢老师那样对学生大声吼叫。The officer started *barking* orders *at* me. 那名军官开始对我吼着发出命令。

base on/upon *vt.* 【可分性动词短语】(常用被动语态形式) use (particular ideas or facts) as a basis or foundation for (making a decision, doing a calculation, or developing a theory) 以……为根据,基于: *Base* your composition *on* your experience. 你的作文应根据你的经历写。Many people assert that the central character in the South Korean television soap opera *Dae Jang Geum* is *based on* the real life of the first female royal physician in Korean history. 许多人断言,韩国电视连续剧《大长今》中的主要人物是根据韩国历史上第一位女御医的真实生活塑造的。I *based* my judgment *upon* this fact. 我的判断以本项事实为根据。

NOTE 本短语中的 upon 用法比 on 正式,但不及 on 常用。

battle it out *vi.* (非正式用语) (of two people or groups) compete with each other until there is a definite winner 分出输赢,决一胜负: Twelve football teams will *battle it out* later in the year to see who will become the champion of Europe. 十二支足球队将在年内的晚些时候一决输赢,以确定谁将成为欧洲冠军。The two men decided to *battle it out* since they fell in love with the same girl. 这两名男子爱上了同一个女孩,于是决定一争雌雄。

be able to ⇨ **able to**

be about to *v.* (后接原形动词) be going to happen or do something very soon; be ready to do something new 就要,正要,即将(做某事): I was taken for a thief when I was *about to* break the window to enter my house for my keys I had left inside. 当我要打碎玻璃进屋取我落在里面的钥匙时,人们把我错当成了盗贼。

NOTE 1. 本短语本身就表示某一行为将要发生,因此其后不可加诸如 at once, immediately, in two minutes, soon, tomorrow, next week 之类的时间状语。

2. 本短语与 be going to 意义相近,两者之间的区别在于:前者为书面语,而后者是口语形式;后者在所表示的时间上比前者距现在(讲话时)更远,且常与 tomorrow, next week 之类的时间状语连用。试比较:

> I was just *about to* leave when you telephoned.
> 我正要出去您就来电话了。
> I'm *going to* see my sister tomorrow.
> 我明天要去看我妹妹。

3. 本短语的否定形式是 be not about to。例如:

> I'*m not about to* stop when I'm so close to success.
> 在如此接近成功的时候,我不打算就此罢手。

但在美国英语中,be not about to 又可用来表示"不愿意(做某事)"之意。例如:

> I'*m not about to* pay 150 dollars for a hat like this.
> 我可不愿花 150 元钱买这样一顶帽子。

be accustomed to ⇨ **accustom to**

be caught up in *vt.* ❶ be deeply interested in 对……深感兴趣,着迷于: Most people today *are* not *caught up* in political events, especially those meetings on TV. 如今,大多数人对政治上的事情,尤其是电视上的那些会议不感兴趣。We *were* so *caught up in* the movie that we forgot what time it was. 我们都被那部电影迷住而忘记是什么时间了。❷ be involved in 被卷入……中: The government *was caught up in* a bitter dispute between the miners and their employers. 政府被卷入到矿工和矿主之间的纠纷之中。Today thousands of Indian young people *are caught up in* the wave of going abroad. 当今,成千上万的印度青年都卷入了出国的浪潮中。

NOTE 本短语中的 be 可被 get 替换,两者的意义和用法相同。

be determined to *v.* (后接原形动词)

have a strong will to (do something)有决心(做某事): I *am determined to* break off with those people. 我决心同那些人一刀两断。"We're *determined to* make sure American intelligence is as accurate as possible for every challenge in the future." the US official said. 这位美国官员称:"我们有决心保证美国的情报尽可能准确,以应对将来的任何挑战。"

NOTE 本短语与 make up one's mind 均表示"下定决心做某事",但两者在使用中有区别。make up one's mind to do something 的英语释义是 decide to do something (决定做某事),而本短语的英语释义是 have a strong will to do something (有决心做某事)。

be down on *vt.*【不可分性动词短语】(非正式用语,无被动语态形式) ❶dislike or not approve of (someone or something)不喜欢,看不上(尤指某人): I always get high marks. Why *is* the teacher so *down on* me? 我总是得高分数。老师为什么这样不喜欢我? Don't *be* so *down on* yourself. 不要那样看不起自己。Why are you so *down on* sports? 你为什么这么不喜欢体育运动? ❷quickly note and point out (a mistake)很快地注意到并指出(错误): The teacher *was down on* his mistake in a flash. 老师立刻就发现了他的错误。

be employed in *vt.* (正式用语) ❶(of someone) be paid to work in (a place or trade)受雇于(某处或某一行业): He has *been employed in* the shoe business for twenty-five years. 他已在制鞋业干了 25 年。❷be busy with (something or doing something); spend the time you have available (doing something)忙于(某事),花时间(做某事): The children *were employed in* weeding the garden. 孩子们在忙于为花园锄草。You would *be* better *employed in* writing an apology. 你最好花上点时间写一封道歉信。❸(of something) be used for (a particular purpose)(指某物)用于(某种目的): The electronic computer *is employed in* engineering, in scientific research and in industrial management. 电子计算机被用于工程、科研和工业管理。

be friends with *vt.* be a friend of (someone); form a friendship with (someone)与……做朋友;和……有交情: At first I didn't like John, but now I *am friends with* him. 起初我并不喜欢约翰,但现在我和他做了朋友。He would give anything to *be friends with* Rose. 为了和罗斯好,他什么都愿意付出。I have been *friends with* him for years. 我和他已有多年交情。

NOTE 本短语中的名词 friend 必须用复数形式。

be here to stay ⇨ **come to stay**

be in for *vt.*【不可分性动词短语】(非正式用语,无被动语态形式) ❶enter for (a competition)参加(某种比赛): *Are* you *in for* the basketball match? 你参加篮球比赛吗? I'm *in for* the 100 meters and the high jump. 我参加百米赛跑和跳高。❷be about to experience (something especially something unpleasant as trouble, bad weather, etc.)将经历(麻烦或坏天气等): We *are in for* some trouble if we don't finish quickly. 如果我们不快点做完,就会出麻烦的。I'm afraid we *are in for* a storm. 恐怕我们要遇上暴风雨。❸be an applicant for (a job or position)求(职): How many people *are in for* the job now? 现在有多少人要干这项工作? I know he *is in for* an administrative job in the local government. 我知道他谋求在当地政府做行政工作。

be in on *vt.* 【不可分性动词短语】(非正式用语) ❶be involved in or take part in (something that is being planned or discussed)参与(正在计划或讨论的事情):Most of the staff wanted to *be in on* the new plan. 大多数工作人员都想参与到这一项新的计划中来。I don't know what they agreed to because I wasn't *in on* the deal. 我不知道他们达成了什么协议,因为我没参与这笔交易。❷have knowledge of; be informed of 知道;被告知:Bob *was in on* the family secret. 鲍勃知道家里的秘密。The principal Trade Unions *were in on* the Minister's thinking from the start. 各主要工会一开始就知道这位部长的想法。The other girls didn't like Mary to *be in on* what they know. 其他的女孩都不想让玛丽知道她们所知道的事情。

NOTE 当本短语作"参与"解时,同义短语是get in on。

be it so ⇨ **so be it**

be of age ⇨ **come of age**

be of use *vi.* be helpful or useful 有帮助,有用:After reading the book you'll know that it will *be of* great *use* for your paper. 读了这本书,你会发现它对你的论文很有帮助。This information may *be of use* to him. 这信息可能对他有用。Can I *be of* any *use*(to you)? 我还能(为您)做什么吗?

be on about *vt.* 【不可分性动词短语】(非正式用语,无被动语态形式) keep talking about (someone or something), especially in a dull way for too long, and when other people think it is boring (尤指无聊地)长谈……: I couldn't understand what she *was on about*. 我听不懂她絮叨的是什么。She *is on about* how wonderful her husband and children are. 她絮絮叨叨地讲自己的丈夫和孩子如何如何好。

be on at *vt.* 【不可分性动词短语】(英国英语用法,非正式用语) keep asking (someone to do something), or keep complaining about (his or her behavior), in a way that annoys them 一再要求(某人做某事);不断责备(某人的行为):My wife *was* always *on at* me to get a better job. 我妻子一再要我找一份好一点的工作。She *is* always *on at* the children for one thing or another. 她常常不是因这事就是因那事而责备孩子们。

NOTE 在美国英语中,本短语中的介词 at 可省略。

be over *v.* ❶ (of a particular event, situation, or period of time) have ended 结束:"Now that the election *is over*, the time has come for me to step down." he wrote in his resignation letter. 他在辞呈中写道:"既然大选已经结束,到我该卸任的时候了。" The experiment *being over*, they left the lab. 实验做完后,他们就离开了实验室。❷be more than (a particular amount, number, or age) 多于,超过(某一数量、数目或年龄):The number of students in an English class must not *be over* twenty. 英语班的学生人数一定不能多于 20 人。

be prey to ⇨ **fall prey to**

be ready for ⇨ **get ready for**

be scheduled to *v.* (后接原形动词) be arranged to (do something at a particular time)被安排(做某事),计划(做某事),定于:The delegates *are scheduled to* arrive in Beijing tomorrow for the six-party talks on the North Korean nuclear issue. 出席朝核问题六方会谈的代表定于明天抵京。The high-speed railway *is scheduled to* be opened to traffic by next year. 这条高速铁路计划在明年通车。

be short of ⇨ **short of**

be supposed to *v.* (后接原形动词) ❶(正式用语) believe or have as an opinion to 相信，被认为：She *was* commonly *supposed to* be extremely rich. 大家都相信她是最富有的。He *was* generally *supposed to* have left the country. 一般都认为他已经离开了这个国家。❷have a duty or responsibility to do (something); must do (something)有义务做(某事)，必须做(某事)：Everyone *is supposed to* wear a seat belt in the car. 每个人坐车时都应该系上安全带。*Are* you *supposed to* do homework every day? 你们每天都得做家庭作业吗? Applicants for visas *are supposed to* call the US consulate to set up a face-to-face interview. 申请签证的人必须给美国领事馆打电话提出面试要求。❸ be intended to (do something)打算，旨在：This law *is supposed to* help the poor people in the country. 该法律旨在帮助本国的贫困人口。

NOTE 1. 本短语的否定形式是 be not supposed to，常用于口语中，意为“不被许可；不应当”(= not permitted to)。例如：

> You *are* not *supposed to* smoke in here.
> 你不应该在这里吸烟。

2. 当本短语后面接“have＋过去分词”时，表示本应该做某事而没做。例如：

> He *is supposed to* have arrived an hour ago.
> 他应该一小时前就到了。

be sure to *v.* ❶(后接原形动词) be certain to happen or result 必定会：She's *sure to* win the game. 她一定会赢得比赛。If they persist in their wrongdoing, they *are sure to* lose their credibility among the people of China, other Asian countries and the world as a whole. 如果他们继续坚持其错误做法，必定会失信于中国、其他亚洲国家乃至全世界人民。❷(常用于祈使句中) don't fail to do something 一定要：*Be sure to* switch off the television before you leave. 在离开前，一定要把电视机关掉。Please *be sure to* tell us what you think! 请一定把您的想法告诉我们! He told me to *be sure to* come earlier the next time. 他告诉我下次一定要早点来。

be through with *vt.*【不可分性动词短语】❶(非正式用语) have finished (something) or finished using (something)做完(某事)，用完(某物)：*Are* you *through with* your homework, Tom? 你的作业做完了吗，汤姆? Let me know when you*'re through with* the hairdryer. 你用完吹风机时就告诉我。❷ have ended a relationship with (someone)结束同(某人)的关系：I've told Jim I*'m through with* him, but he keeps bothering me. 我已告诉吉姆我不再和他来往，可他还不断地烦扰我。❸have decided to stop doing (something that you used to do)决定不再做(某事)：*Are* you *through with* politics? 你决定不再从政了吗?

bear away *vt.*【可分性动词短语】(正式用语) ❶carry (someone or something) away 把……带走:It took three cars and a bus to *bear* the guests *away*. 用了三辆小轿车和一辆大巴才送走了宾客。His strength, exhausted by a mind long overwrought, did not suffice to *bear* her *away*, light and delicate though her shape. 他长期以来精神过分疲劳,因而体力消耗极大。尽管她身体很轻,很娇弱,他仍没有足够的力气把她背走。Soldiers are celebrating their *bearing away* so many weapons from enemies. 士兵们在庆祝从敌人手中得到这么多武器。❷win (something such as a prize)赢得(奖品等):Because of his hard work, he *bore away* most of the prizes in the competition. 由于他的努力,他赢得了竞赛的大部分奖项。

NOTE 当本短语所带的宾语是代词时,该代词须置于本短语的动词和副词中间。

bear down *vt.*【可分性动词短语】(正式用语) ❶carry, press or push (usually something) downwards 把……带下去;把……压弯下去:He climbed onto the tree to pick the apples off and then *bore* them *down*. 他爬上树去摘了些苹果,然后把它们送了下来。The branches were *borne down* with the weight of the fruit. 树枝被沉甸甸的果实压弯。❷ defeat; overwhelm; beat 打败,压倒,征服:At last we *bore down* the enemies. 我们最终打败了敌人。His determined efforts finally *bore down* the opposition. 他坚持不懈的努力终于击败了对手。The people in that country were *borne down* by poverty and deprivation. 那个国家的人民被贫穷和困苦压得喘不过气来。

—*vi.* ❶(美国英语用法) try very hard at; use all one's strength and efforts 下苦功,用尽全力:You'll have to *bear down* if you expect to pass the English exam. 如果你想通过英语考试,那就得下苦功。The driver *bore down* with all his strength to control the car when the wheels slipped. 当车轮打滑时,司机使尽全力去控制汽车。❷(of a woman) use effort to give birth to a child (产妇)用力分娩:It's a natural instinct for a woman giving birth to *bear down*. 用力分娩是产妇的一种自然能力。

NOTE 当本短语用作及物性动词短语,所带的宾语为代词时,该代词须置于本短语的动词和副词中间。

bear down on *vt.*【不可分性动词短语】(主要用于英国英语中) ❶(正式用语) move towards (someone or something) forcefully and threateningly, especially at high speed (尤指快速)向……逼近,冲向……:I could see a police car *bearing down on* us. 我可以看到一辆警车朝我们疾驶过来。As soon as she saw him enter the room she *bore down on* him and insisted that he join her for dinner. 她一看见他走进房间就立刻冲到他身边,坚持要他和她一起吃饭。 ❷punish (someone) severely 严惩(某人):We have to continue to *bear down on* those who are continuing to attack our forces. 我们将继续严惩那些仍在袭击我军的人。

bear in mind *vt.*【可分性动词短语】(常用一般时态) remember something, especially something important (when you are thinking about or doing something else)记住(尤指重要的事情):This is a truth we must always *bear in mind*. 这是一条真理,我们必须时刻记住。*Bear in mind* that the train leaves at midnight. 记住,这趟列车是午夜发车。You must *bear in mind* what I'm saying. 你必须记住我说的话。It is important to think long-term and *bear in mind* the larger picture. 立足大局,着眼长远是很重要的。These factors must be *borne in mind*! 这些因素必须予以考虑!

NOTE 1. 本短语中的动词 bear 的过去分词形式用 borne,而不能用另一种过去分词形式 born。

2. 在 in mind 之间有时可加 one's,但这个物主代词必须与主语保持人称和数的一致。例如:

> I'll *bear* your advice *in* my *mind*.
> 我会把你的忠告记在心里。

3. 本短语的宾语为名词、代词和名词性从句。当本短语的宾语为代词时,该代词须置于本短语的动词和介词中间。

4. 当本短语的宾语为从句时,动词 bear 后通常使用形式宾语 it。例如:

> We must *bear* it *in mind* that we are the servants of the people.
> 我们必须牢记:我们是人民的公仆。

bear on/upon *vt.*【不可分性动词短语】(正式用语) ❶(无被动语态形式,用一般时态) show some connection with (something)与……有关系:What he said *bears on* the question we raised. 他所说的与我们提出的问题有关系。How does his story *bear on* what they are investigating? 他的陈述与他们正在进行的调查有什么关系呢? Project Hope of the Chinese government *bears upon* helping the poor children back to school. 中国政府的希望工程是与帮助贫困儿童重返校园有关。❷(常用一般时态) influence (something) in the stated way 对……有影响:This legislation *bears on* the interests of labor. 这条法律影响到劳工的利益。These were vital decisions that *bore upon* the happiness of everybody. 这些决定是十分重要的,对每个人的福祉都有影响。

NOTE 1. 本短语中的 upon 用法比 on 正式,但不及 on 常用。

2. 本短语中的动词 bear 的过去分词形式用 borne,而不能用另一种过去分词形式 born。

bear out *vt.*【可分性动词短语】❶(非正式用语,常与 of 连用) carry (someone or something) out 把……运送出去:The fireman *bore* the fainting girl *out* of the burning house. 消防队员把昏迷不醒的女孩抱出正在燃烧的房子。❷(常用一般时态) show (that something is true or that someone is telling the truth)证实,证明:Scientific evidence *bears out* the claim that stress and disease are linked. 科学证据证实了压力与疾病有关联的说法。If you tell them what happened, I will *bear* you *out*. 如果你把所发生的事情告诉我们,我就为你作证。The prisoner's story was *borne out* by his wife. 该囚犯的供述得到了他妻子的证实。His success *bears out* that where there is a will there is a way. 他的成功证明了"有志者事竟成"。

NOTE 1. 当本短语以人作宾语时,不能用被动语态形式。

2. 当本短语的宾语为代词时,该代词须置于本短语的动词和副词中间。

3. 本短语中的动词 bear 的过去分词形式要用 borne,而不能用其另一种过去分词形式 born。

bear up *v.* ❶ hold up or support (something) without becoming broken 撑住,支撑:The old bridge can hardly *bear up* its own weight any more. 这座旧桥再也支撑不住其自身的重量了。This aid should *bear* them *up* during their difficult times. 这项援助应能使他们在困难时期支撑下来。They were *borne up* by the love of the country in those days. 在那些日子里,他们是靠爱国之心支撑着。Do you think the floor can *bear up* under the weight of these new machines? 你认为这地板能支撑得住这些新机器的重量吗? ❷behave in a brave way in a very sad or difficult situation 承受,经得住,不气馁: Let's see how he *bears up* under pressure. 让我们看看他是如何承受压力的。Old people cannot *bear up* against the midsummer heat this year. 老年人无法忍受今年的仲夏酷暑。A brave child should *bear up* this blow. 勇敢的孩子应该经得住这次打击。She *bore up* bravely under her continued misfortunes. 她连遭不幸,但她毫不气馁。

NOTE **1.** 本短语中的动词 bear 的过去分词形式要用 borne,而不能用另一种过去分词形式 born。

2. 当本短语用作及物性动词短语,所带的宾语为代词时,该代词须置于本短语的动词和副词中间。

beat about/around the bush *vi.* spend a long time getting to the main point of what you are saying, especially because it is embarrassing 拐弯抹角,旁敲侧击: He had been *beating about the bush* for almost half an hour before he came to the point. 他拐弯抹角地扯了差不多半个小时才说到正题。Stop *beating around the bush* and tell me the truth. 别兜圈子了,告诉我实情吧。Let's be frank, don't *beat around the bush*. 咱们打开天窗说亮话,都不要拐弯抹角。

NOTE beat around the bush 用于美国英语中。

because of *prep.* (used for showing the reason something happens or the reason why it is described in a particular way)on account of; by reason of 由于,因为:The companies closed down *because of* the global financial crisis. 由于这场全球性金融危机,这些公司都关闭了。*Because of* this I did not go to the museum. 我因此而没去参观博物馆。He realized that she was crying *because of* what he had said. 他认识到她之所以哭是因为他所说的话而致。

NOTE **1.** 本短语是介词性短语而不是连词性短语,其后不能接原因状语从句,而这正是它与 because 在用法上的区别。

2. 本短语的反义短语是 in spite of。

become of *vt.*【不可分性动词短语】(无被动语态形式,不用进行时态,常用于疑问句中)(used especially for asking what has happened to someone or something, because you are worried about them) happen to (someone or something) often in a bad way; be the end of 发生,遭遇: Whatever *became of* the old men who lived beside our college? 曾经住在我们学院旁的那几位老人发生什么事了? What will *become of* the children, if their father dies? 假如他们的父亲去世,这些孩子的遭遇将会怎样呢? What has *become of* your computer? 你的电脑怎么啦?

NOTE 本短语与 happen to[1] 意义相同,但本短语的主语只能用 what 或 whatever 引出,而 happen to[1] 则不受此限制。

become prey to ⇨ **fall prey to**

before long *adv.* (常用于一般将来时和一般过去时中) soon; in the near future 不久,很快:I shall be seeing you *before long*. 我不久就可以见到你了。The coal resource is going to be used up *before long*. 煤炭资源不久将被用完。She joined the company in 2008, and *before long* she was promoted to sales manager. 她 2008 年进入公司,不久就被提升为销售经理。

NOTE 不要将本短语与 long before 混淆,

long before 意为“很久以前”。例如：

> *Long before* there lived a witch in the forest.
> 很久以前，森林里住着一个女巫。

before one's time *adj.* (主要用于英国英语中) having new or modern ideas or attitudes that are too advanced to be acceptable in the present 思想超前的：His only mistake, he insists, is that he was *before his time*. 他坚持说，他唯一的错误是他的思想超前了。Her ideas were 10 years *before her time*. 她的思想超前了10年。

NOTE **1.** 本短语中的名词 time 必须用单数形式。

2. 若要表示超前的具体时间，须将具体时间置于本短语之前(如第二个例句)。

3. 本短语的同义短语是 ahead of one's time，反义短语是 behind the times。

beg for *vt.* 【可分性动词短语】❶ ask (people) for (money or food), usually because you are very poor 向……乞讨(钱或食物)：The boys went from door to door *begging for* food. 这些男孩子挨家挨户地要饭吃。The old man *begged* me *for* some food. 那老头儿向我要吃的。❷(无被动语态形式) ask for (help, an opportunity, etc.) in a way that shows you want it very much 恳求，乞求：The prisoner *begged* the judge *for* mercy. 那囚犯乞求法官的宽恕。The boy was screaming and *begging for* forgiveness. 那男孩高叫着求饶。We *begged* her *for* another chance. 我们恳求她再给一次机会。

beg of *vt.* (正式用语，无被动语态形式，一般用现在时，主语常为第一人称) ask (someone) very earnestly, especially to do something 请求(某人)(做某事)：I *beg of* you, don't mention her name again. 我求求你，别再提她的名字了。I *begged of* him to stay with me for the night. 我求他留下来与我一同过夜。She *begged of* me not to take any risk. 她请求我不要去冒险。

begin with *vt.* (无被动语态形式，常用一般时态) start (something) with (something) 以……开始，先做……：What shall we *begin with*? 我们先从哪儿入手？When we learn a new language, we usually *begin with* the alphabet. 当我们学习一门语言时，通常是从字母开始学起。The new influenza *begins with* a fever, sore throat, headache, muscular pains, and fatigue. 这种新型流感发病初期先有发热、嗓子疼、头痛、肌肉疼痛和疲倦的症状。We *began* the meeting *with* a discussion about the budget for the next year. 会议开始后我们先讨论了明年的预算。

NOTE 不要将本短语与 to begin with 混淆，两者的意义和用法不同。

behind bars *adv.* (非正式用语) in prison or jail 在狱中：Sooner or later, you will be *behind bars* for your crimes. 或迟或早，你会因你所的犯罪行而坐牢。That boy is always in trouble and will end up *behind bars*. 这个男孩子总闹事，最终会闹进监狱里去。The two hijackers were at last arrested and put *behind bars*. 那两名劫持者终于落网，被投入监狱。

NOTE 本短语中的名词 bar 特指监狱中的铁栏，必须用复数形式，前面不能加任何冠词。

behind schedule *adv.* after the planned or expected time 晚于预定时间，晚点：The plane is two hours *behind schedule*. 飞机比预定时间晚到了两个小时。The train arrived *behind schedule*. 列车晚点到达了。The project is estimated at 33 percent complete, several years *behind schedule*. 据估计,这一项目已完成33%,比原计划拖后了数年。

NOTE 1. 本短语中的名词 schedule 之前不能加任何冠词。

2. 若表示晚点或拖延的具体时间,须将具体时间置于本短语之前。

3. 本短语的同义短语是 behind time;反义短语是 ahead of time 和 ahead of schedule。

behind someone's back *adv.* out of someone's presence or without someone's knowledge 背着某人:You eat her food, enjoy her hospitality and then criticize *behind her back*. 你吃她的、喝她的,享受着她对你的款待,还在背后骂她。He did it *behind their backs*. 这事是他背着他们干的。

behind the scenes *adv.* ❶ secretly rather than publicly 秘密地,私下地: These agreements have been drafted by officials *behind the scenes*. 这些协议都是由官员们秘密起草的。❷ not seen or heard by the audience of a film, play, etc. 在(银幕、舞台等的)幕后: He prefers to work *behind the scenes* as a director. 他宁愿在幕后做一名导演。While enjoying the wonderful performance on the stage, the audience hardly imagine the confusion that was going on *behind the scenes*. 在观看舞台上的精彩演出时,观众们想象不出幕后有多么混乱。

NOTE 1. 本短语中的名词 scene 必须用复数形式。

2. 本短语可转化为复合词 behind-the-scenes,意为"秘密的,私下的,幕后的"。

behind the times *adj.* (of a person or organization) old fashioned in your ideas, methods, etc.; not modern because you have not changed as much or made as much progress as others (指某人或某一机构)(思想或方法等)陈旧的,落后的: My uncle is a little *behind the times*. 我叔叔思想有点陈旧。Old Robert should be made to realize, like it or not, that he is about twenty years *behind the times*. 不管他愿意不愿意,应该让老罗伯特意识到,他已落后于时代 20 年。Oh Jack, your accounting methods are *behind the times*! 杰克,你算账的方法落后了! It was a sleepy little town, about fifty years *behind the times*. 那是一个死气沉沉的小镇,落后于时代约五十年。

NOTE 1. 本短语中的名词 time 必须用复数形式。

2. 若表示落后的具体时间,须将具体时间置于本短语之前。

3. 本短语的反义短语是 ahead of one's time 和 before one's time。

behind time *adv.* after the time due; later than the time when something happens, should be done etc. 迟于原定时间,晚点:This train is running behind time. 本次列车是在晚点运行。The school bus left twenty minutes *behind time*. 校车比原定时间晚发了二十分钟。The flight was an hour *behind time*. 班机晚点了一个小时。

NOTE 1. 本短语中的名词 time 必须用单数形式,前面不能加任何冠词。

2. 表示晚点的具体时间,须将具体时间置于本短语之前。

believe in *vt.* 【不可分性动词短语】 ❶consider (someone or something) to exist 认为,相信……存在:He *believed in* the children being taught through the translation method. 他认为确有孩子在接

受那种翻译法的教学。I don't *believe in* that sort of thing. 我不相信会有那种事情。❷(用一般时态) have faith or trust in (a god, someone or oneself) 信奉,信仰,信任: Some of his supporters have stopped *believing in* him. 他的一些支持者都不再信任他了。In a job interview, you should let the employer know that you *believe in* yourself and that you know your strengths and weaknesses. 在求职面试中,你要让雇主知道你很自信,并确知自己的强项与弱点。❸(一般不用被动语态形式,用一般时态) think that (an idea or a way of doing something) is good, right or true 认为……是好的(正确的或真的): She used to say she didn't believe in marriage. 她过去常说,她不认为结婚是什么好事。Do you *believe in* everything the Bible says? 你相信《圣经》上说的都是真的吗? ❹(用一般时态) favour; support the idea of; consider (something) to be worth 支持,认为应该: He *believes* very strongly *in* female emancipation. 他强烈地支持妇女解放。He *believes in* taking plenty of exercise. 他认为应该多做一些身体锻炼。

NOTE 本短语与动词 believe 的区别是:当本短语表示因可靠、有某种能力、品德高尚等原因而"相信,信任"某人或某种理论等,属总的评价;而动词 believe 只表示相信某人所说的话,并不涉及对其总的评价。试比较:

> I *believe* him. 我相信他。(他说的话)
> I *believe in* him. 我信任他。(不仅是他说的话)

believe it or not *s.* (非正式用语) (used to introduce information that is true but that may surprise people) it is true, whether or not you agree 信不信由你: *Believe it or not*, he asked me to marry him! 不管你信不信,他曾经向我求过婚。I asked my boss for a month's holiday and, *believe it or not*, he agreed! 我向老板请一个月的假,信不信由你,他居然同意了! I'm over eighty years old, *believe it or not*. 我已年过 80,信不信由你。

belong to *vt.*【不可分性动词短语】(无被动语态形式,用一般时态,不用进行时态) ❶ be owned by (someone or something) 属于……所有: Who does this coat *belong to*? 这件上衣是谁的? I don't know *to* whom it *belongs*. 我不知道这东西为谁所有。A passenger plane *belonging to* Air France went missing Monday over the Atlantic Ocean, with 216 passengers and 12 crew members on board. 法国航空公司一架载有 216 名乘客和 12 名机组人员的客机星期一在大西洋上空失踪。❷ be a member of (an organization or a club)……的一员:China is a developing country, *belonging to* the third world. 中国是一个发展中国家,属于第三世界。She *belongs to* the school computer club. 她是学校计算机俱乐部的成员。

NOTE 虽然本短语是及物性动词短语,但不能用被动语态形式,也不能用其过去分词的形式作定语。例如,我们不能说: * China is a country *belonged to* the third world.

bend down *v.* (cause to) fold or lean downwards or move the top part of your body downwards (使)折叠,弯下(腰身): Don't *bend* the corners of pages *down*. 不要折叠页脚。My right hand hurts whenever I *bend* it *down*. Should I go to the doctor? 我的右手弯曲时就会疼,我是否应该去看医生? Helen *bent down* to pick up her pencil. 海伦弯下腰去拾她的

铅笔。

NOTE 当本短语用作及物性动词短语，所带的宾语为代词时，该代词须置于本短语的动词和副词中间。

bend forward(s) *v.* lean forwards or move the top part of your body forwards (身体上部)向前倾：She *bent forwards* and whispered in my ear. 她把上身往前倾了倾，向我耳语了一番。I *bent* my head *forward* to hear what they were saying. 我把头向前探去，好听清她们在说什么。My neck hurts when I *bend* it *forward*. 我的颈部前倾时就疼。

NOTE 当本短语用作及物性动词短语，所带的宾语为代词时，该代词须置于本短语的动词和副词中间。

bend over *v.* (cause to) lean or move the top part of your body downwards to the ground, etc. (使)弯曲，俯身：Then he *bent over* the patient to start the operation. 然后他俯下身子开始给病人做手术。*Bend over* and touch your toes. 弯腰去触摸你的双脚趾尖。

bend to *vt.* 【可分性动词短语】force (someone) to obey (something)迫使(某人)服从：My father was a very powerful man in the family, and used to *bend* us *to* his wishes. 我父亲以前在家里很有权威，总是强迫我们服从他的意愿。

beneficial to *adj.* having a good effect or influence on (someone or something); helpful to; useful to 有利于……的，有用的：The fall in prices will be *beneficial to* small businesses. 价格的下跌有利于小企业。The present government programs *beneficial to* the farmers are highly praised. 现政府制订的一些有益于农民的计划受到了高度的赞扬。The discovery proves *beneficial to* many AIDS patients. 这一发现被证明对许多艾滋病患者有益。

benefit by/from *vt.* 【不可分性动词短语】get help, an advantage or profit from (something)获益于……，从……中得到好处：Who is most likely to *benefit by* the old lady's death? 谁最可能因那位老妇人的过世而获益呢？And merchants *benefit by* receiving protection against fraud. 商家从而避免了受骗而得到保护，也从中获益。I *benefited* a lot *from* talking with other people. 我从同别人的交谈话中获益匪浅。Who was *benefited from* the Hollywood writers' strike? 谁从好莱坞编剧大罢工中受益了？

bent on *adj.* (正式用语) very determined to achieve (something); having one's mind set on (something or doing something)决意要的，决心要的，一心想要的：George used to be *bent on* law as a profession. 乔治曾执意要从事法律职业。He was *bent on* quitting that job even though he was making a lot of money. 尽管他的收入不菲，可他还是决心辞去那份工作。She seemed *bent on* destroying their relationship. 她似乎一心想要毁掉他们的关系。

beside oneself *adj.* (常与 with 连用) unable to think clearly because you are very angry or excited (由于十分气愤或兴奋等而)发狂的，忘形的：I felt *beside myself* with rage when he told me what he had done. 他把他所做的事情告诉了我，我气得发狂。She was *beside herself* (with joy) when the lost ring was found. 当找到了丢失的戒指时她欣喜若狂。

bet on *vt.* 【可分性动词短语】risk (money) on the result of a future event (such as a horse race or the performance of a competitor)对……打赌,下赌注:I *bet* 20 pounds *on* a horse called Silver Star, but it came in last! 我把20英镑的赌注下在了一匹叫作"银星"的马上,可它竟跑了个倒数第一! He told me which horse to *bet on*. 他告诉我该对哪匹赛马下注。I would not *bet on* the result of this election. 我不愿对这次选举的结果打赌。

better off *adj*. ❶in a better condition or situation, especially financially; having more money 情况较好的;收入比较多的:If she is so sick, she would be *better off* in a hospital. 她如果病很重,住院治疗情况会好些。The statistics show that most people in the region are *better off* than they were five years ago. 统计数字显示,该地区的大多数人比5年前过得富裕多了。"As a result of the agricultural tax exemption the average family in the village will be 1,500 yuan a year *better off*," said the village head. 村长说:"由于免除了农业税,村里的普通家庭将每年多收入1 500元。"❷more fortunate, happier 更幸运的;更幸福的:We'd be *better off* without the noise from the neighboring factory. 要是没有附近工厂的噪声,我们会幸运得多了。You'd be *better off* living on your own than quarrelling all the time with your dad. 你单独生活比你总和你爸爸吵嘴更好些。The official said the country was *better off* with the ouster of the former president. 这位官员称,驱逐前总统使这个国家更美好了。

NOTE 1. 本短语是 well off 的比较级形式,见 well off。

2. 本短语的反义短语是 worse off。

beware of *vt*. 【不可分性动词短语】(无被动语态形式,用一般时态,常用于祈使句中,常置于句首) be cautious and watchful about(someone or something); guard against(something or someone)小心,注意:*Beware of* his tricks. 当心他的花招。*Beware of* how you walk on this mountain path. 在走这条山路时,你要小心啊。You'd better *beware of* those who were always wandering on the streets because they might be thieves. 你最好小心街上那些游荡之人,因为他们有可能是小偷。You should *beware of* repeating the same mistakes. 你应该注意不要重犯同样的错误。

beyond compare *adj*. &*adv*. (used for emphasizing the very good qualities of a person or thing) better than anything else of the same kind 无与伦比的(地):Our professional service promises you a wedding *beyond compare*. 我们的专业服务保证为您办一个无与伦比的婚礼。The boy is clever *beyond compare*. 这男孩子聪明绝顶。The view of the mountains is *beyond compare*. 这丛山美景无与伦比。

NOTE 1. 本短语的另外一种表达形式是 beyond comparison,但本短语更为正式。

2. 本短语的同义短语是 without compare,两者可互换使用。

beyond measure *adj*. & *adv*. (正式用语) so much that it can not be measured or figured; without any limits 无可估量,极其:The good they have done for me is *beyond measure*. 他们对我所做的好事简直无可估量。When he died he left a treasure almost *beyond measure*. 他去世的时候留下了一笔几乎无法估量的财富。No one envied her, for she was popular *beyond measure*. 没有人忌妒她,因为她太有名气了。

beyond question *adj*. &*adv*. not in

doubt; without doubt; surely 毋庸置疑,毫无疑问: People always believe anything that Mark says; his honesty is *beyond question*. 马克说的话人们都相信,因为他的诚实是无可置疑的。*Beyond question*, it was the coldest day of this winter. 毫无疑问,这是今年冬季里最冷的一天。He is *beyond question* the brightest student in the class. 他无疑是班中最聪明的学生。

NOTE 1. 本短语中的 question 前不用任何冠词。根据需要,可使用 all。但即使使用 all, question 仍然要用单数形式。例如:

> *Beyond all question*, you are right.
> 毫无疑问,你是正确的。

2. 本短语中的介词 beyond 可被 past, without 替换,构成的短语与本短语意义和用法相同。

3. 本短语的反义短语是 in question。

beyond repair *adj.* so badly damaged that it cannot be repaired or mended 无法维修的,不可修复的:I'm afraid this old radio is *beyond repair*. 恐怕这台旧收音机无法修好了。The old buildings that are *beyond repair* should be destroyed. 这些无法修缮的旧楼都应该被拆毁。Shock reduces the flow of blood to the body's vital organs, often damaging them *beyond repair*. 休克减少了身体内重要器官的血流量,往往使这些器官发生不可修复的损伤。

bid farewell to *vt.* (正式用语) say goodbye to (someone) 与(某人)告别: After the swearing-in ceremony, Obama and his wife Michelle *bade farewell to* Bush and his wife Laura, on the eastern steps of the Capitol. 宣誓就职仪式结束后,奥巴马和夫人米歇尔在国会大厦的东侧台阶上与布什及夫人劳拉告别。Hundreds of people waited silently in a long queue to *bid farewell to* my great father, who passed away Thursday. 数百人默默地排着长队等候向于本周四辞世的我伟大的父亲告别。They *bid* their *farewells to* each other at the café. 他们是在那家小餐馆告别的。

NOTE 1. 本短语的另外一种表达形式是 bid someone farewell。例如:

> Bhutto asked that the sunroof be opened so she could *bid* her supporters *farewell.*
> 布托要求打开汽车天窗好与她的支持者们告别。

2. 本短语中的名词 farewell 既可用作可数名词,又可用作不可数名词。作为告别用词之一,farewell 通常在某人长时间或不会再见到某人时使用,因此,当指与死者或其遗体告别时常用 farewell。例如:

> A *farewell* to Princess Diana!
> 永别了,戴安娜王妃!

3. 本短语与 say farewell to 意义和用法相同,两者可互换使用。

big shot *n.* (美国和澳大利亚英语用法,非正式用语) an important or powerful person in a group or organization; a VIP (某一机构或组织的)重要人物,大腕,大亨:The police stopped all the traffic so some *big shot* and his entourage could pass. 警察挡住所有车辆,让某一位重要人物及其随行人员通过。Mr Madison is a *big shot* in the world of finance. 麦迪逊先生是金融界的一位重要人物。I saw people in front of restaurant act like *big shots*. 我看到酒店前的人举手投足都像大腕。

NOTE 与本短语意义相同的表达形式有 big bug, big dick, big cheese, big Chief, big Daddy, big wheel 等。

B

bill for *vt.*【可分性动词短语】send or give (someone) a written statement of the money they owe 给(某人)送账单,给(某人)开账单:I can't pay now; please *bill* me *for* it later. 我现在无法付款。请稍晚些再给我送这份账单吧。We were *billed for* three nights when we were only there for two. 我们只在那儿住了两个晚上,但给我们开了三个晚上的账单。

bit by bit *adv.* (非正式用语) very gradually; slowly; only a little bit at a time 逐渐地,慢慢地,一点一点地:*Bit by bit* I began to understand what they were doing. 我逐渐开始明白他们在做什么。We eased the lid off *bit by bit*. 我们慢慢地把盖子拧了下来。The large snake moved *bit by bit* toward the sleeping baby. 那条大蛇一点儿一点儿地朝正在熟睡的婴儿爬去。

NOTE 本短语与 little by little 意义和用法相同。

black and blue *adj.* (of someone having the skin) covered in bruises (指某人的皮肤)青一块紫一块的,有瘀痕的:Tom's arm was still *black and blue* from slipping on the ice yesterday. 汤姆昨天在冰面上滑倒,胳膊还是青一块紫一块的。He's been beaten *black and blue* by two young men. 他被两个年轻人打得青一块紫一块。That fall down the stairs left me *black and blue* all over. 那次从楼梯滚下给我留下了一身的瘀痕。

blame for *vt.*【可分性动词短语】say or think that (someone or something) is responsible for (an accident, problem, or bad situation) 谴责,认为……对……负有责任,把……归咎于:Who is to *blame for* this social disorder? Is the government to blame or are the citizens to blame? 谁应该对这种社会混乱现象负责?是应该怨政府还是怪百姓? It's not surprising, therefore, that television is being *blamed for* many of the society's problems. 因此,把许多的社会问题归咎于电视就不足为怪了。

blame on *vt.*【可分性动词短语】fix or place the guilty for (something wrong) on (someone or something) 怪罪于,归咎于,责备:Clumsy workers often *blame* their mistakes *on* their tools. 拙匠常怪工具差。The police department *blamed* the rise of traffic accidents *on* speeding, overloading and illegally overtaking. 公安部门把交通事故的增加归咎于超速、超载和非法超车。

blast forth *vi.* (of sound) come out suddenly (指声音)突然响起:We were watching TV when rock music *blasted forth* from the next door. 我们正在看电视的时候,隔壁突然响起了摇滚乐。

blast off *vt.*【可分性动词短语】raise or remove (something) by an explosion 炸飞,炸掉:The bomb *blasted* the roof *off*. 炸弹把屋顶炸飞了。A group of officials visited the spot where the militants *blasted off* the boat to estimate the damage. 一些官员来到武装分子炸船的现场,对损失进行评估。

—*vi.* (of a missile, rocket, and space vehicle) leave the ground and rise into the air (指导弹、火箭、航天器)发射升空:The newly developed surface-to-surface missile *blasted off* at 10:52 am about 72 km from here. 新近研制的一枚地对地导弹于上午 10:52 分在距离此地大约 72 公里处发射升空。Four seconds after the ignition, the carrier rocket *blasted off*, roaring upward into the sky. 点火后 4 秒

钟，运载火箭呼啸着腾空而起，直指苍穹。

NOTE 本短语可转化为复合词 blast-off，意为"(导弹、火箭、宇宙飞船等的)发射升空"。

blind date *n.* ❶(非正式用语) a meeting arranged for two people who have not met each other before, in order to try to start a romantic relationship (由第三方安排的)从未谋面的男女间的约会：Mary has arranged for me to go on a *blind date* this Saturday with a man that she knows through work. 玛丽安排我与一位她在工作中认识的男士在本周六见面。William was too excited to have dinner. He was having a *blind date* with Mary in the evening. 威廉兴奋得晚饭都吃不下了。晚上他有约与玛丽首次见面。Going out for a *blind date*? Here are six things that you need to be aware of. 要出去与一个从未谋过面的人约会？这是你需要注意的六个事项。He never goes on *blind dates*. 他从不与未谋过面的女士约会。❷either of the people in a blind date 初次约会中的男方(或女方)：He is the first *blind date* of my life. 他是我一生中初次约会的第一位男士。

block off *vt.*【可分性动词短语】prevent (something) from its usual use by closing it 封闭，封锁：The gas pipe has been *blocked off* to prevent escapes. 煤气管道已被封住，以避免泄漏(煤气)。The police *blocked off* the street after the bomb explosion. 炸弹爆炸事件发生后，警察封锁了那条街路。The local government built a road into the area, but environmental activists *blocked* it *off*. 当地政府修了一条通往该地区的公路，但环保人士却将其封闭。

NOTE 当本短语的宾语为代词时，该代词须置于本短语的动词和副词中间。

block out *vt.*【可分性动词短语】❶cover; stop (light or sound) from reaching (something)遮住，隔住(光或声音)：That tree in the neighbor's garden *blocks out* a lot of our light. 邻居家花园里的那棵树很遮挡我们的光线。The black clouds have *blocked* the sun *out*. 乌云遮住了太阳。Let the sun shine in—or *block* it *out*. 要么让阳光照射进来，要么就将它遮挡住。❷stop yourself from thinking about or remembering (something) 不再想，忘记(某事)：She accuses me of having *blocked out* the past. 她指责我忘记了过去。I had to *block* the thought *out* of my mind. 我得把这种想法从头脑中忘掉。

NOTE 当本短语的宾语为代词时，该代词须置于本短语的动词和副词中间。

block up *vt.*【可分性动词短语】close (something); prevent movement through (something) 堵塞，阻挡：A snowstorm *blocked up* railroads. 一场暴风雪阻断了铁路交通。The pipe is *blocked up* again and there's water all over the floor. 水管又堵塞了，水流得满地都是。You'd better *block* the hole in the wall *up*. 你最好把墙上的洞堵上。The toilet gets blocked every now and then. Don't put anything in there that will *block* it *up*. 这个洗手间经常堵塞。不要把任何易堵物品放在那里。

NOTE 当本短语的宾语为代词时，该代词须置于本短语的动词和副词中间。

blog about *vt*【不可分性动词短语】write a blog entry about (something or someone) on the Internet (在互联网上)撰写有关……的博客：This father of nine in Utah *blogged about* his own family and told tales of his ancestors. 犹他州的这位 9 个孩子的父亲在博客上讲述了他的家庭以及其祖先的故事。How do you *blog about* your new boyfriend, Mary? 玛丽,你在博客上怎么写你的新男友呢?

NOTE blog 是 web 和 log 的组合词之缩略形式。log 的原意是"航",后指任何类型的流水记录。Weblog 或 blog(即"博客")作为名词使用得十分流行,也可作为动词使用,并衍生出 blogger, blogging, blogsphere 等新词。

blow away *v.* ❶(常用一般时态)(cause to)go away with or as with the force of wind (使)吹走:She switched on the fan to *blow away* the smoke in the room. 她打开风扇以吹走屋里的烟。His hat *blew away* on the roller coaster in the park. 他的帽子在公园的滑行车上给刮跑了。I am afraid the wind may *blow* the tent *away*. 我担心风会把这帐篷刮走。The wind was so strong that people were nearly *blown away*. 风大得几乎把人都给刮跑了。❷(美国英语用法,非正式用语) kill (someone) by shooting with a gun 枪杀(某人)He *blew* a worker *away*, who was off duty in the midnight. 他枪杀了一名午夜下班的工人。

NOTE 当本短语用作及物性动词短语,所带的宾语为代词时,该代词须置于本短语的动词和副词中间。

blow in *vi.* (非正式用语,用一般时态)(of someone) arrive unexpectedly (指某人)突然到来: Jim *blew in*; we weren't expecting him until Friday. 吉姆突然到了,我们原预计他星期五才会到。He usually *blew in* for a visit to his mother's house to give her a surprise. 他通常突然到妈妈家探望,以给她一个惊喜。

blow off *v.* (常用一般时态) ❶(of the wind) make (something) come off (something)(指风)把……吹离(……): The roof *blew off* in the storm. 屋顶在暴风雨中被掀掉。In the lightning I saw that the roof of the hut had been *blown off*. 在闪电中,我看见棚屋的屋顶被刮掉了。A gust of wind *blew* it *off*. 一阵风把它吹了下来。She picked up a book and *blew* the dust *off* it. 她拾起一本书,把上面的灰尘吹掉。Mission scientists say British Mars lander Beagle 2, which weighs just 75 pounds, might have been *blown off* course by dust storms. 负责该项任务的科学家说重量只有 75 磅的英国"猎兔犬 2 号"火星登陆器可能已经被尘暴吹离了轨道。❷remove and destroy something by shooting it or making it explode; make (something) leave (something) by shooting or exploding (以枪弹)打断;(以爆炸)炸掉: The soldier *blew* the gunman's arm *off*. 士兵把那枪手的胳膊打断了。An explosion blew one of the wings off the plane. 爆炸炸掉了飞机的一侧机翼。In the office there was a mix of blood, body parts and burned clothing, and a clock *blown off* the wall was stopped at 10:30 am. 办公室里到处都是血、肢体和烧焦的衣服。一个从墙上炸下来的时钟停在上午 10 点 30 分。

NOTE 当本短语用作及物性动词短语,所带的宾语为代词时,该代词须置于本短语的动词和副词或介词中间。

blow one's lid *vi.* (非正式用语) lose one's temper; suddenly become very angry; explode with anger 发怒,勃然大怒,大发雷霆: The boss will *blow his lid* when he hears about this. 老板听到这件事后会勃然大怒。Finally she *blew her lid* and kicked him in the stomach. 最后

她火冒三丈,抬脚踢在了他的腹部上。"Was your father upset when you came home at 3:00 am?" "He was more than upset. He *blew his lid*!" "你凌晨3点才回家,你爸爸生气了吗?""他岂止生气,他大发雷霆!"

NOTE 1. 本短语另外的表达形式是 blow one's top 和 blow one's stack。其中,blow one's top 是英国英语用法,blow one's stack 是美国英语用法。

2. 本短语的同义短语是 blow up, flare up, lose one's temper 和 see red;反义短语是 keep one's temper。

blow out *v.* ❶(cause to)stop burning by blowing 吹灭,熄灭:Someone opened the door and the flame *blew out*. 有人开门,火便被吹灭了。He *blew out* all the 25 candles on his birthday cake. 他吹灭了他生日蛋糕上的全部25根蜡烛。All the candles were suddenly *blown out* by a sudden strong wind. 所有的蜡烛都突然被一阵大风吹灭了。❷(常用一般时态)(especially of a tyre)(cause to)burst (尤指轮胎)(使)爆裂: The accident occurred when his front tyre *blew out*. 他汽车的前胎爆裂,于是事故就发生了。❸(常用一般时态)(of a fuse)(cause to) melt;(of electrical machinery)(cause to) stop working(使)(保险丝)熔断;(使)(电器)损坏: The fuse *blew out* and the house was in darkness. 保险丝爆了,房子里一片黑暗。A short circuit will *blow out* the fuse. 短路会烧断保险丝。❹(美国英语用法,非正式用语) defeat (someone) easily 轻易地战胜(某人): They've *blown out* every team they've played this season. 他们轻易地战胜了本赛季的全部对手球队。Sometimes you play really badly and get *blown out*. 有时,你表现得确实差劲,就很容易被人击败。❺(of an oil or gas well) erupt uncontrollably (油井或气井)失控地喷发: Three workers at the gas well that *blew out* in Chongqing were arrested in connection with the accident. 三名油气井工人因涉嫌重庆井喷事故而被逮捕。

NOTE 当本短语用作及物性动词短语,所带的宾语为代词时,该代词须置于本短语的动词和副词或介词中间。

blow up *v.* ❶(of wind) start blowing suddenly (指风)开始刮:The race had to be cancelled when the storm *blew up*. 风暴突起,跑赛只好取消。❷(常用一般时态)inflate; fill (something) with air or gas 充气,给……充气: These plastic balls don't *blow up* easily. 这些塑料球不容易充气。Help me to *blow* my tyres *up*, will you? 帮我给车胎充气,好吗? We *blew up* lots of balloons and hung them around the room. 我们吹起了许多气球,并把它们在房间四处悬挂起来。I've got a flat tyre; I'll have to find a garage and get it mended and *blown up*. 我的车胎瘪了;我得找一家汽修厂去修补和打气。❸(常用一般时态)(cause to) explode; destroy (something or someone) by or as if by explosion (使)爆炸,炸毁: The boiler *blew up*, wrecking the whole house. 锅炉爆炸,摧毁了整栋房子。Twenty-one people have been under arrest in connection with a plot to *blow up* aircraft flying from Britain to the United States, British police said today. 英国警方今天宣布,已逮捕了21名与一起炸毁英国飞往美国班机图谋有关的嫌犯。The former prime minister was shot as she got into her vehicle, then the gunman *blew* himself *up*. 前总理进入自己的汽车时被枪击中。枪击者随后引爆了自己身上的炸弹。❹(非正式用语,

常与 at 连用) suddenly become very angry (with someone)突然(与某人)发脾气: I'm sorry I *blew up* at you this morning. 对不起,我今天上午冲你发脾气了。Father *blew up* when he knew that Tom failed in the final exam. 爸爸知道汤姆期末考试不及格时便大发脾气。❺make (a photograph or picture) bigger 放大(照片或图片): They had *blown up* the picture they took together 10 years ago. 他们把 10 年前他们的一幅合影放大。How big can you *blow* this picture *up*? 您能把这幅照片放大多少? ❻make (something or someone) seem greater than in fact 夸张,吹嘘: It was a small thing to happen but the newspaper had *blown* it *up* until it seemed important. 发生的事情很小,但报纸却把它夸张得似乎很大。The incident has been greatly *blown up* by the local press. 该事件被当地的报纸大肆炒作。

NOTE 1. 当本短语作"突然(与某人)发脾气"解时,同义短语是 blow one's top, flare up, lose one's temper 和 see red;反义短语是 keep one's temper。

2. 当本短语用作及物性动词短语,所带的宾语为代词时,该代词须置于本短语的动词和副词中间。

blurt out *vt.*【可分性动词短语】(常用一般时态) say (something) suddenly and without thinking about the effect it will have, usually because you are nervous or excited (常指因紧张或激动而)脱口说出: She *blurted out* his name. 她脱口说出了他的名字。We expect you to *blurt* it all *out*. 我们期望你能把所有有关情况都讲出来。

NOTE 当本短语的宾语为代词时,该代词须置于本短语的动词和副词中间。

blush for *vt.*【不可分性动词短语】(of your cheeks) become red because (you feel embarrassed or ashamed) 因……而脸红: I *blush for* shame when I remember how I ill-treated you. 每当想起我如何错待你时,我就羞愧得脸红。Jim *blushed for* his not being able to answer the teacher's question. 吉姆因没能回答出老师的问题而脸红。

board of directors *n.* a committee of the directors of a company, which is responsible for the management of the company (公司的)董事会: Linda is the only woman on the *board of directors*. 琳达是董事会中唯一的女性。The spokesman said, the UN Security Council was not a "*board of directors*" and its composition should not be decided "according to the financial contribution of its members". 发言人指出,联合国安理会不是"董事会",其构成不应"按照会费交纳的多少"来确定。

boast about/of *vt.*【不可分性动词短语】proudly tell other people about (you or someone connected with you has done or can do, or about something you own), especially in order to make them admire you 吹嘘,夸耀: Helen's always *boasting about* how clever her children are. 海伦总是吹嘘她的孩子们如何聪明。That boy *boasts of* being the best storyteller in his class. 那男孩自吹是班级里的故事大王。The government *boasted of* its success in helping one million unemployed workers find new jobs last year. 政府夸耀去年成功地帮助 100 万失业工人重新就业。I don't like to *boast of* what I did. 我不喜欢夸耀自己所做的事情。Things may be fitting to be done, which are not fitting to be *boasted of*. 有些事情是只宜于做,而不宜于大肆吹嘘。

bolt out *vi.* (常用一般时态,常与 of 连用) leave in a hurry; run in a sudden way 匆忙离去,突然跑开:The policeman fired at the armed robber as he was *bolting out* of the house. 当那名武装抢劫分子从房中跑出来时,警察朝他开枪了。When I opened the door, a cat *bolted out*. 我开门时,一只猫窜了出来。

book up *v.* keep (seats, rooms in a hotel, service, etc.) for people who have made arrangement in advance 预订(座位、客房、服务等):The play has been very popular; you have to *book up* well ahead. 这出戏非常受欢迎,所以你得提前订座。If you don't *book up* the ticket you'll miss the chance to watch the play. 如果你不预订票,你就会失去看这出戏的机会了。I'm sorry, sir, but the hotel is fully *booked up* tonight. 很抱歉,先生,今晚旅馆的房间全部预订出去了。

born of *adj.* ❶ born in a particular situation, type of family etc. 出身于:China's first astronaut Yang Liwei was *born of* a family of teachers in Suizhong County, northeast China's Liaoning Province. 中国第一位宇航员杨利伟出身于中国东北部辽宁省绥中县的一个教师之家。He was *born of* humble parentage. 他出身卑微。❷owing origin to 源于:Knowledge is born of practice. 知识来源于实践。Love is *born of* the heart but not the mind. 爱产生于心灵而不是头脑。

NOTE 当本短语作"出身于"解时,还可用 born into/to。例如:

> One-third of the children are *born into* single-parent families.
> 在这些孩子中,有三分之一出身于单亲家庭。
>
> He was *born to* a wealthy intellectual family.
> 他出身于一个书香门第、生活优裕的家庭。

both … and … *conj.* (used for emphasizing that each of two things is true) not only … but also … 不但……而且……,既……又……:A new round of talks is just around the corner, *both* words *and* actions of all the parties should serve to realize the common goal. 新的一轮会谈在即,有关各方的言行都应有利于共同目标的实现。These girls can *both* sing *and* dance. 这些女孩儿能歌善舞。The new film is *both* instructive *and* interesting. 这部新影片既有教育意义又有趣。It is believed that water is present *both* on the surface of Mars *and* in its atmosphere. 据信,在火星的表面及其大气中都存在着水。

NOTE 本短语表示全部肯定,可连接主语、谓语、宾语、表语、状语等成分。与本短语意义相反的短语是 neither … nor …,见 neither … nor …。

bound for *adj.* heading for; traveling towards; on the way to (a place) 到……去的,开往……去的:A ship carrying weapons *bound for* Zimbabwe was refused to unload the cargo at the port of Duban. 一艘驶往津巴布韦的军火船被拒绝在德班港卸货。"Then *for* what harbor is the ship *bound*?" "Angola." "那么,船要开往哪个港口?""安哥拉。" ❷ certain or very likely to do (something) in the future 肯定的,很可能的:Steve is doing a Master's at Harvard, and *bound for* a career in finance. 史蒂夫正在哈佛大学攻读硕士,并很有可能将来从事金融业。

bound to *adj.* (后接原形动词) sure to;

obliged to 一定会……的；非……不可的：The new discovery is *bound to* be of great service to mankind. 这项新发现对于人类必定大有用处。If you have problems at home, it's *bound to* affect your work. 如果你在家里有烦心事，那肯定会影响你的工作。We felt *bound to* tell her that her son had been taking drugs. 我们觉得必须告诉她：她儿子一直在吸毒。

bound up in *adj.* ❶very busy with or very interested in 繁忙于……的；对……极有兴趣的：He was so *bound up in* his experiment that he often forgot to have dinner. 他做实验十分繁忙，以至于经常忘记吃饭。We seldom see Mary these days because she's so *bound up in* writing her new book. 最近我们难得看到玛丽，因为她正埋头写新书。Her interests are completely *bound up in* her husband and family. 她的兴趣全都在丈夫和家庭上。❷(前常用副词 closely) connected with or related to (each other) very closely so that it is difficult to think of them separately 与……有紧密关系的：Climate change is closely *bound up in* the issue of energy consumption. 气候的变化与能源消耗问题有密切关系。These girls' lives are completely *bound up in* volleyball. 这些姑娘们的生活完全和排球连在了一起。

NOTE 当本短语作"与……有紧密关系的"解时，与 bound up with 意义和用法相同，两者可互换使用。

bound up with *adj.* (前常用副词 closely) connected with or related to (each other) very closely so that it is difficult to think of them separately 与……有紧密关系的：His future is closely *bound up with* that of the company. 他的前途与公司的前程紧密相关。He admits that it is the children who has had the two of them closely *bound up with* each other. 他承认是孩子们把他们俩相互紧密地联系在一起。The American official pointed out that US security is absolutely *bound up with* the security of Europe. 这位美国官员指出，美国的安全绝对与欧洲的安全息息相关。

brain drain *n.* (非正式用语，常用单数形式) a movement of highly skilled professional people from a region or country to other regions or countries in order to make more money or to improve their living or working conditions 人才流失：Lawmaker Ali Nazari has pointed out that the most critical problem challenging the Iranian society at present is the massive *brain drain*. 立法委员阿里·那扎里指出，伊朗社会目前所面临的最严重的问题是人才的大量流失。For many years, governments of developing countries have been troubled by *brain drains*. 多年来，发展中国家的政府一直受着人才外流的困扰。

break apart *v.* (cause to) break in pieces; come apart (使)折断；(使)裂变：When you try to saw the wood or *break* it *apart*, you will discover the wood is actually pretty brittle. 当你试图锯断或劈裂这木头时，你就会发现其木质实际上非常脆弱。Man has learned to *break apart* the nuclei of billions of atoms and to harness their energy. 人们已经学会使数十亿计的原子核发生裂变，并利用其能量。❷break up or separate 分裂，瓦解：Tribes grow and become powerful under brave and successful leaders, and they *break apart* when their leaders are defeated or killed. 部落在勇敢和成功的

头领的领导下发展和壮大,而当他们的头领被击败或杀死时,部落就会瓦解。

NOTE 当本短语用作及物性动词短语,所带的宾语为代词时,该代词须置于本短语的动词和副词中间。

break away *vi.* (常与 from 连用) ❶escape from a person, place, or situation 逃离: Anna tried to *break away* but the man held her tight. 安娜试图逃脱,但那男人紧紧地抓着她。"Three prisoners *broke away* from a prison in eastern France last night." Reuters said. 据路透社报道:"昨天夜里在法国西部,有三名犯人越狱逃跑。" While the guards were gambling, the prisoner *broke away*. 那名囚犯趁警卫们在赌博时逃跑了。Startled by the sudden whistle of the train, the horse *broke away*. 火车突然鸣笛,那匹马惊跑了。❷ end one's connection with (a group); leave a political party or other group, especially in order to start another one 与(某一组织)断绝关系,脱离(某一党派或组织): Since they couldn't agree with each other, some *broke away* from the team. 由于他们意见分歧,有些队员便脱离了该队。This extremist faction *broke away* from the party in 2006. 这个激进派别于2006 年从该党中分离出去。

NOTE 本短语可转化为复合词 breakaway, 意为"摆脱,脱离;戒除"。

break down *v.* ❶hit (something such as a door or wall) very hard so that it falls down 毁坏(门、墙等物): The firefighters had to *break down* the door to get into the flat. 消防队员不得不破门而进入那套房间。❷(常用一般时态)(of a machine or vehicle) stop working; fail (机器或车辆)出故障: The elevator *broke down*, and we had to walk up to the tenth floor. 电梯出了故障,我们不得不走上 10 楼。The car *broke down* after half an hour's driving. 汽车在行驶了半小时后就出了故障。❸(常用一般时态) suffer poor health; suffer a nervous illness for some time (身体)垮了,(精神)衰弱: Many students have *broken down* from the heavy homework. 许多学生由于作业负担重而身体垮了下来。Since his wife died, he became totally *broken down*. 他妻子去世后,他的精神完全崩溃了。❹(of a relationship or discussion) stop being successful (关系)破裂,(会谈)失败: She passed through a difficult period shortly after her marriage *broke down*, but after a year or so her health and spirits picked up. 婚姻破裂后不久,她经历了一段很困难的时期。但是大约一年后,她的身心就得以康复。The official denied that talks on oil exports between the two governments have *broken down*. 这位官员否认了两国政府就石油出口的会谈已告失败的说法。❺lose control of one's feelings and start crying, especially in public (尤指在众人面前)失声痛哭: On hearing the bad news many people *broke down* and cried. 闻悉噩耗,许多人失声哭了起来。"I heard the explosion of the bomb, saw windows smashing and then I fell," she said before *breaking down* and sobbing. "我听到了炸弹的爆炸声,看到了玻璃在破碎,然后就倒下了。"她说完便失声哭了起来。❻(常与 into 连用) (of a substance) (cause to) separate into the parts that it is made up of (某种物质)(把……)分解: Chemicals in the body will *break* our food *down* into useful substances. 人体内的化学物质会将食物分解为有用的成分。Water is readily *broken down* into

B

hydrogen and oxygen. 水可以很容易地分解为氢和氧。❼remove (a difficulty that prevents something from happening)消除(困难等):The aim of the agreement is to *break down* barriers to trade. 该协定的目的是消除贸易壁垒。

NOTE 1. 当本短语用作及物性动词短语,所带的宾语为代词时,该代词须置于本短语的动词和副词中间。

2. 本短语可转化为复合词 breakdown,意为“故障;破裂;分类;解释”。

break even *vi.* (非正式用语,常用一般时态)(of a person or business) neither make a profit nor lose money 不盈不亏,收支平衡:They made no money on the deal, but they didn't lose either. They just about *broke even*. 他们在这笔交易中没赚钱,但也没亏本,恰好不盈不亏。The airline hopes to *break even* next year and return to profit the following year. 该航空公司希望明年做到收支平衡,后年则要盈利。

break in *v.* ❶break from outside; break and enter 从外部打破(某物),破门(或窗)而入:The firemen *broke in* the door of the burning house. 消防队员打破了正在燃烧着的房子的门。The fire fighters entered the burning house by *breaking in* through the bedroom window. 消防队员打破卧室的窗户进入正在着火的房子中。Why are you *breaking* the door *in*? Here's the key! 你为什么要破门而入呢?钥匙在这里!❷enter (a building) by force, especially in order to steal things (尤指为盗窃而)强行闯入:They *broke in* through an upstairs window and stole some jewelry. 他们从楼上的窗户闯入室内,偷走了一些珠宝。The man was arrested for attempting to *break in*. 那人因企图闯入行窃而被逮捕。Once upon a time, you could leave your doors unlocked at night and not worry about someone *breaking in*. 以前,夜里房门不用上锁都不必担心有人会进来偷东西。❸(用一般时态) interrupt when someone is talking 打断谈话,插嘴:Don't keep *breaking in* with your remarks. 不要老是插嘴说话。“Hillary,” he *broke in* gently, “I'm just trying to help.” “希拉里,我是在尽力帮忙。”他轻声地插言道。❹make (someone) get used to something new, for example a new job 使(某人)熟悉(新工作等):A week in the new office should be enough to *break* you *in*. 在新的办公室工作一个星期应该足够使你适应了。❺train (a horse that is young or wild) 驯服(幼马或野性马):Young horses have to be *broken in*. 幼马必须要经过驯服。In her girlhood she was known for her skill in *breaking in* vicious horses. 她在童年时代就以其驯服烈马的技能而著名。

NOTE 1. 当本短语用作及物性动词短语,所带的宾语为代词时,该代词须置于本短语的动词和副词中间。

2. 当本短语作“打断谈话,插嘴”解时,不用被动语态形式。如我们不能说:* I don't like to be *broken in* when I speak. 而应说:I don't like others to *break in* when I speak.

3. 当本短语作“打断谈话,插嘴”解时,同义短语有:barge in, break into, burst in, cut in, cut into, cut off, cut short, chip in, get in 和 put in。

4. 本短语可转化为复合词 break-in,意为“非法强行进入,闯入”。

break in on/upon *vt.* (常用一般时态) interrupt (something) 打断:It's very impolite of you to *break in on* our conversation. 你打断我们的谈话是很不

礼貌的。I'm terribly sorry to *break in on* you like this. 这样打扰你们的谈话我十分过意不去。I'm sorry to *break in upon* your thought, but I think we should start to work now. 对不起,我打断了你的思绪,可我们现在该开始工作了。

NOTE 本短语中的 upon 用法比 on 正式,但不及 on 常用。

break into *vt.* ❶ divide (something) into (smaller parts); become damaged and separated into (pieces) 把……分成(小块),成为碎片:Mary *broke* the chocolate *into* pieces, one for each person. 玛丽把巧克力分成数块,每人分了一块。The glass slipped from her hand and *broke into* pieces. 玻璃杯从她手中滑落,碎成多片。❷ enter (a building) by force, especially in order to steal things (尤指为盗窃而)强行进入,闯入:The two workers were shot in the head by between three and four armed robbers who *broke into* the factory canteen. 这两名工人是被三四名冲进工厂餐厅里的武装强盗击中头部的。A bank was *broken into* between midnight and 4 am. 在午夜到凌晨 4 点这段时间,有窃贼潜入了这家银行。❸(用一般时态) interrupt (something or someone who is talking or thinking) 打断(谈话或思绪):I'm sorry to *break into* your conversation. 对不起,打断一下你们的谈话。Christopher's voice *broke into* her thoughts. 克里斯托弗的话音打断了她的思绪。❹(无被动语态形式,用一般时态) start doing (something) suddenly 突然开始做(某事):We watched her face *break into* a smile. 我们看着她的脸上突然现出了微笑。All of a sudden he got a terrible pain in his chest and soon *broke into* a cold sweat. 他突然胸部剧痛,接着便冒出了冷汗。The children saw the sea and *broke into* a run. 孩子们一看到大海就跑了起来。As the President's car approached, the waiting crowd *broke into* loud cheers. 当总统专车驶近时,等待着的民众欢呼起来。❺ start to use (an amount of money), usually unwillingly (尤指不情愿地)动用(一笔款项):We had to *break into* our savings to pay the fine. 我们不得不动用存款支付罚金。

break loose *vi.* (常用一般时态) ❶ escape; become free; get away 逃跑:Five prisoners *broke loose* as they were being taken to another prison yesterday. 昨天,五名囚犯在被押往另外一所监狱时逃跑了。The woman managed to *break loose* from her attacker and run for help. 那名妇女逃脱了袭击者之手,跑着呼喊救命。❷(常与 from 连用) become active; out of control 挣脱,摆脱:On the second day, the kidnapped worker managed to *break loose* from his shackles and ran to a safe place. 第二天,这位被绑架的工人挣脱了枷锁,跑到了一个安全的地点。To be efficient in our work, we must *break loose* from the traditional way of doing things. 为提高工作效率,我们必须摆脱传统的工作方法。

break off *v.* ❶ (cause to) come apart (from the main part) (使)(从主体上)脱落,折断:One of the wings of the plane *broke off* in mid-air and the plane crashed. 由于一侧机翼在空中脱落,飞机坠毁了。The chimney *broke off* in the middle during the strong earthquake. 烟囱在大地震中拦腰折断了。I *broke off* a piece of chocolate and gave it to the little boy. 我掰了一块巧克力给了那个小男孩。❷(常用一般时态) (cause to) end (a relationship or a discussion) (使)(关

系)断绝;(使)(会谈)中断:Robert was determined to *break off* with those people. 罗伯特决心同那些人断绝关系。My daughter and Tommy were engaged, but they have just *broken* it *off*. 我女儿和汤米订过婚,但他们刚刚解除了婚约。Talks between the two sides were *broken off* and each side accused the other of refusing to negotiate seriously. 双方之间的会谈被迫中断,各方都谴责对方谈判没有诚意。❸(用一般时态) stop doing something, especially speaking 停止(尤指讲话):Linda *broke off* in the middle of her speech, realizing that she was wrong. 琳达在演讲中间突然停了下来,她意识到自己讲错了。Jim *broke off* telling the story to answer the telephone. 吉姆中断对那件事的讲述去接电话。People would *break off* their conversations when she came into the room. 当她进房间时,人们就会停止谈话。❹(用一般时态) pause in one's work; take a break 暂停(工作),休息:Let's *break off* work and have a cup of tea. 让我们停下工作喝杯茶吧。Let's *break off* for some coffee. 咱们休息一会儿喝点咖啡吧。

NOTE 当本短语用作及物性动词短语,所带的宾语为代词时,该代词须置于本短语的动词和副词中间。

break out *v.* ❶ break (something) in an outward direction 向外捣毁(某物):We had to *break* the door *out* to escape the fire. 我们不得不破门而出,逃出火海。Move to the door and *break* it *out* for escape. 往门口走,然后破门而逃吧。❷(用一般时态) (of war, fire, disease, fighting, or other unpleasant events) start suddenly (指战争、火灾、疾病、打斗等不幸事件)突然发生:A fire *broke out* around 9 pm at a supermarket in the Chinatown of Manhattan, New York City, on May 15. 纽约市曼哈顿唐人街一家超市于5月15日晚9时许发生火灾。A flu never had before *broke out* this April in Mexico, raising fears of a worldwide spread of the virus. 一种前所未有的新型流感于今年4月份在墨西哥爆发。这引起了人们对这种病毒在世界范围流行的担忧。A fight *broke out* among the football fans and soon it went beyond control. 足球迷之间发生了斗殴事件,并且局面迅速失控。The global financial crisis first *broke out* in the United States. 这次的全球性金融危机首先是在美国爆发的。❸(常用一般时态,常与 of 连用) escape (from a place or situation)(从某一地点或状态中)逃出,摆脱:Three prisoners have *broken out* of a top-security jail in eastern France. 三名囚犯从法国西部一座高度戒备的监狱中逃了出去。The horse *broke out* of the stable. 马从马厩里跑出去了。She just couldn't *break out* of her old patterns of behavior. 她就是无法摆脱她旧有的行为模式。❹(无被动语态形式) speak or act suddenly and violently 突然说出,突然做出(某种举动):She *broke out*, "That's not so!" 她突然喊道:"那不是这么回事!" A roar of cheering *broke out* from among the crowd. 人群中爆发出一阵欢呼声。We *broke out* laughing at his joke. 我们听了他这个笑话都放声大笑起来。❺(常与 in, on 连用) (of a rash or sweat) start to appear on the skin (皮肤上)冒出(疹子、汗水等):The skin on my arms was *breaking out* in a rash. 我的胳膊上起了疹子。Sweat was beginning to *break out* on his forehead. 他的额头上开始冒汗了。

NOTE 1. 当本短语用作及物性动词短语，所带的宾语为代词时，该代词须置于本短语的动词和副词中间。

2. 本短语可转化为复合词 breakout，意为“越狱，逃脱，突围”；还有另外一种复合名词形式 outbreak，意为“突然发生，爆发”。

break the ice *vi.* (非正式用语) ❶make a start; pave the way 开创，铺平道路，打破坚冰：Newton's theories *broke the ice* for modern physics. 牛顿的理论为现代物理学开辟了道路。❷do or say something that makes people feel more relaxed and ready to talk, for example at the beginning of a social situation 打破(沉默或拘束的)局面：He *broke the ice* at the meeting by telling an amusing story. 他讲了一个好笑的故事才打破了会议的僵局。Rogers told a few jokes, which helped to *break the ice*. 罗杰斯讲了几个笑话，这才打破了沉默拘谨的局面。

break the news *vi.* (常与 to 连用) tell someone of something, usually a piece of bad news that causes sadness or worry 告诉某人(常指不好的)消息：You'd better *break the news* to her gently that her daughter has left home. 你最好以婉转的方式把她女儿已离家出走的消息告诉她。Then Mary *broke the news* that she was to leave her husband. 接着，玛丽讲了她要离开她丈夫的消息。I'm not looking forward to *breaking the news* to Dad. 我可不想把这消息告诉给爸爸。

break through *v.* ❶ succeed in forcing your way through (something that is stopping you from moving forward) 冲破，突破：The guerrillas soon *broke through* (the enemy encirclement). 游击队很快就突围(突破敌人的重围)了。A group of young demonstrators attempted to *break through* police lines. 一群年轻的示威者试图突破警戒线。❷(常用一般时态，常与 in 连用) make a new advance or discovery, especially after dealing successfully with problems and difficulties (尤指成功地解决了诸多难题之后)取得突破性进展，有新发现：Scientists hope to *break through* soon in their search for a cure for this type of cancer. 科学家希望不久在寻求治愈这种癌症的疗法方面取得突破性进展。Biologists have *broken through* in a number of their areas of research in recent years. 近年来，生物学家们在许多研究领域里都有新发现。❸ overcome; conquer (something in the way) 克服，征服：We'll *break through* all the difficulties with our own hard work. 我们将通过自己艰苦的工作来克服一切困难。No matter how we try, it's almost impossible to *break through* his reserve. 无论我们怎样努力，几乎还是无法打破他的拘谨。❹(常用一般时态) (of the sun or moon) appear (太阳或月亮)出来：At last the sun *broke through*, beginning to dry the dew on the grass. 太阳终于出来了，开始把草地上的露珠晒干。The moon *broke through* the clouds and shed its silvery light all over the land. 月亮从云层中钻了出来，将银光撒满大地。

NOTE 本短语可转化为复合词 breakthrough，意为“突破，重大进展”。

break up *v.* ❶ (cause to) break into smaller pieces 打碎，碎开：The glass fell to the ground and *broke up*. 玻璃杯掉到了地上摔得粉碎。The old woman *broke up* the chocolate and gave each child a small piece. 老妇人把巧克力掰碎，给每个小孩一小块。River ice *breaks up* in the spring. 河冰破在春天时。❷(常用一般时态)(of a meeting or other event) end and people leave (会议等)结束:The meeting *broke up* without reaching any agreement. 会议没有达成任何协议就结束了。The talk didn't *break up* until after midnight. 会谈一直到半夜后才结束。We don't want to *break up* the party so early. 我们不想这么早就结束聚会。❸(especially of the police) stop a fight or gathering (尤指警察)制止(打斗或集会):The police were called in to *break up* the fight. 警察被叫来制止打斗。Police used tear gas to *break up* a gathering of crowd. 警察使用催泪弹阻止了集会。"*Break* it *up*, you two!" the policeman shouted. "你们两个,不要打了!"警察喝道。❹(常用一般时态)(of a group) (cause to) divide; scatter (人群)散开,使分开,驱散,解散:The crowd started to *break up* when the night fell. 天快黑时,人群开始散开了。The big class was *broken up* into several small ones. 这个大班被分成了数个小班。"Come on!" shouted the policeman. "Move along. *Break* it *up*!" 警察喊道:"快,走一走!散开来!"❺(常与 into 连用) decompose 分解,解体:One possible way to *break up* a compound is to raise its temperature. 提高化合物的温度是分解它的一种可能的方法。*Breaking up* water into hydrogen and oxygen is a chemical change. 把水分解为氢和氧是一种化学变化。In the Columbia tragedy, all seven astronauts on board were killed when the space shuttle *broke up* in mid-air. 在"哥伦比亚号"悲剧中,当航天飞机在空中解体时,机上7名宇航员全部遇难。❻(主要用于英国英语中,常用一般时态,常与 for 连用)(of a school, its pupils or teachers) stop working at the end of term (指学校)开始放假:We *break up* on Friday. 我们星期五放假。The school has already *broken up* for the summer holidays. 学校已经放暑假了。❼(非正式用语,常与 with 连用)(of a relationship) (cause to) end or stop (指关系)(使)终止,断绝,绝交,破裂:Her involvement had *broken up* the partnership. 她的参与使合作关系终止。The survey found that only three per cent female said they would consider *breaking up* with someone who did not earn enough. 这项调查发现,只有3%的女性表示,当男友挣得太少时她们可能会考虑与其分手。Mr Smith and Mr Brown had a quarrel and *broke up*. 史密斯先生和布朗先生吵了一架便绝交了。Their marriage *broke up* just a few years later. 他们的婚姻仅几年后就破裂了。❽(of the sound on a radio or mobile phone) no longer being heard (指收音机或手机的声音)中断:I can't hear you, you're *breaking up*. 我听不到你在讲什么,你的声音断了。❾(美国英语用法)(cause to) laugh or cry (使)大笑,大哭:Woody Allen makes me just *break up*. 伍迪·艾伦逗得我捧腹大笑。He was the kind of comedian who *broke up* an audience with extremely funny accents and expressions. 他就是这种能用极其滑稽的腔调和表情使观众捧腹的滑稽演员。"Both of her parents died in the powerful earthquake, and it *breaks* me *up* just to think about it," the old lady said. "她的父母都在那场大地震中遇难。一想起这事,我就哭。"老妇人说道。

NOTE 1. 当本短语用作及物性动词短语,所带的宾语为代词时,该代词须置于本短语的动词和副词中间。

2. 本短语可转化为复合词 break (-) up，意为“(关系或联盟的)终止；解散；别离；崩溃”。

break with *vt.*【不可分性动词短语】(无被动语态形式，常用一般时态) ❶end a friendship or relationship with (someone or something) 与……绝交：When he became rich, he *broke with* his former friends. 他致富后便与他以前的朋友们断绝了关系。❷end a connection with (something such as a tradition or past) and start doing things in a completely new way 与(传统或过去)决裂：The young couple *broke with* tradition and decided to write their own marriage vows. 这对年轻伴侣打破传统，决定自己写婚姻誓言。It's not impossible to *break with* old habits. 与旧习惯决裂不是不可能的。

breeze through *vt.*【不可分性动词短语】(非正式用语，用一般时态) do (something) very easily or confidently; pass (something such as an exam) easily 轻松地做(某事)；轻松地通过(考试等)：She *breezed through* that difficult book with no trouble at all. 她一点儿也不费劲地读完了那本很难读的书。Helen simply *breezed through* her final exams. 海伦轻轻松松地通过了期末考试。

brighten up *v.* ❶make (something) look more brightly coloured and attractive 使……增加鲜艳色彩；使……更加漂亮：You could *brighten up* that skirt with a red blouse. 你穿一件红色的衬衫会使那裙子增彩。Fresh flowers will *brighten up* any room in the house. 鲜花会使任何一个房间更加漂亮。I have dark brown eyes. Do you have any tips to *brighten* them *up*? 我的眼睛是深褐色的。您有什么窍门使它们漂亮些吗？❷start looking or feeling happier 显得高兴，感到欢乐：She *brightened up* when we reached the hotel. 我们到了旅馆，她显得很高兴。Sarah *brightened up* considerably as she thought of Thomas's words. 当想到托马斯的话时，萨拉就感到十分欢乐。❸(of the weather) improve and become brighter (指天气)好转，变得晴朗：According to the forecast, it should *brighten up* later today. 天气预报说，天气在今天晚些时候会好转。I think the sky's *brightening up*. 我想，天会变晴。

NOTE 当本短语用作及物性动词短语，所带的宾语为代词时，该代词须置于本短语的动词和副词中间。

bring about *vt.*【不可分性动词短语】❶make (something) happen, especially to cause changes in a situation 实现；引起；导致：Destruction, slaughter and revenge will never *bring about* peace and prosperity. 摧毁、屠杀和报复永远不会带来和平与繁荣。The reform and opening-up have *brought about* fundamental changes to China. 改革开放使中国发生了根本性的变化。The decrease in business activity was *brought about* by the present financial crisis. 当前的金融危机导致了商务活动的减少。❷cause to move into the opposite direction 使调转方向：They *brought about* the boat when they saw a storm approaching. 看到风暴即将来临，他们便调转了船头。

NOTE 本短语的同义短语是 result in，但两者的用法有所不同。result in 不能用于被动语态形式。见 result in。

bring along *vt.*【可分性动词短语】❶(主要用于英国英语中) take (someone or something) with you when you go somewhere 带上(某人或某物)：If your

sister likes to come to our party, you can *bring* her *along*. 如果你妹妹喜欢来参加我们的聚会，你可以把她带上。They are expected to *bring along* enough schoolwork to keep themselves busy. 他们将带上足够的作业，以使自己有事可忙。I *brought* a notebook *along* to the meeting. 我带了一个笔记本去开会。❷help (someone or something) advance or grow more quickly 帮助(某人)更快进步；促使(作物)更快生长：We're trying to *bring along* one or two promising young swimmers. 我们正在竭力帮助一两名很有前途的游泳运动员，让他们更快地进步。This warm weather we've been having will *bring* the crops *along* very nicely. 我们现有的温暖天气将有助于各种作物更好地生长。

NOTE 当本短语所带的宾语为代词时，该代词须置于本短语的动词和副词中间。

bring around *vt.*【可分性动词短语】(美国英语用法) ❶ bring (someone) to someone's house 把(某人)带到(某人的家)：*Bring* the family *around* one evening; we'd love to meet them. 哪天晚上把你的家人带到我家来。我们都很想见见他们。❷ (cause to) regain health (使)恢复健康：He was quite ill, but good nursing *brought* him *around*. 他的病很重，但良好的护理使他恢复了健康。❸(cause to) return to consciousness (使)恢复知觉：We threw water in his face to try and *bring* him *around*. 我们往他的脸上泼水，试图使他恢复知觉。❹(用一般时态，常与 to 连用) persuade (someone) to change his or her opinion about something and agree with you 说服(某人)同意(自己的观点等)：We must *bring* the rest of the committee *around* to our point of view. 我们必须说服委员会的其他成员同意我们的观点。His letters finally *brought* me *around* to donate money to the school. 他的几封来信终于说服了我捐款给那所学校。

NOTE 1. 当本短语所带的宾语为代词时，该代词须置于本短语的动词和副词中间。

2. 当本短语作"(使)恢复知觉"解时，同义短语是 bring round(第三个义项)和 bring to(第一个义项)。

3. 当本短语作"说服(某人)同意(自己的观点等)"解时，同义短语是 bring round 和 bring over(第二个义项)。

bring back *vt.*【可分性动词短语】❶return (something) 归还(某物)：*Bring* us *back* our books, please. 请把我们的书给我们还回来吧。All library books must be *brought back* before January 31. 所有图书馆的图书都必须在 1 月 31 日前归还。❷ take (something) back; take (something or someone) with you when you come back from a place 退回；带回：If you don't like it when you get home, you can always *bring* it *back*. 假如你回家后不喜欢它了，你可以随时把它退回来。He *brought* some beautiful Persian carpets *back* from Iran. 他从伊朗带回了一些漂亮的波斯地毯。She went to Las Vegas and *brought back* her errant daughter. 她去了拉斯维加斯，把她那步入歧途的女儿带了回来。❸(用一般时态) cause (something of the past) to return to the mind 回忆，想起(往事)：The story *brought back* many beautiful memories. 这个故事唤起了许多美好的回忆。Hearing the English song *brought back* to me my happy life in Hawaii. 听到这首英文歌曲使我回忆起我在夏威夷的快乐生活。I know it happened, but I cannot *bring* it *back* to my mind. 我知道这事发生过，但就是想不起来。❹ start to use (something) again that was used in the past; reintroduce; restore 恢复: He feels that compulsory attendance at chapel should be *brought back*. 他觉得应该恢复强制去教堂做礼拜的规定。Plenty of rest and nutrition *brought* him *back* to health. 充分的休息和营养使他恢复了健康。❺make (a dead person) live again; save (someone's life) when they have almost died 起死回生,挽回生命: He was dead. I couldn't *bring* him *back* to life. 他死了。我无法使他起死回生。Her heart stopped three times, but they *brought* her *back*. 她的心跳停了三次,但他们还是挽回了她的生命。

NOTE 当本短语所带的宾语为代词时,该代词须置于本短语的动词和副词中间。

bring down *vt.* 【可分性动词短语】❶(常用一般时态) make (someone or something) move or fall to the ground 使……倒下,使……落下: Johnson was *brought down* in the penalty area. 约翰逊在罚球区被绊倒。Telephone poles were *brought down* by falling trees. 电话线杆被倒下的树木压倒。Strong winds *brought down* power lines across the region. 大风吹落了该地区的动力电线。The heroic pilot managed to *bring* the plane *down* safely with only one engine. 这位英雄的驾驶员成功地靠唯一的一部发动机使飞机平安降落。❷reduce the rate, level, or amount of (something)减低,下降: *Bringing down* the unemployment rate will take longer than expected, the newspaper said. 该报称,减低失业率还需要比预期更长的时间。We'll give you an injection to *bring down* the temperature. 我们给你打一针,把热度降下来。They have *brought* the death rate *down* to one per cent. 他们使死亡率下降到了1%。❸(常用一般时态) cause (a government or politician) to lose power 使(某一政府或政客)下台: The students were not just asking for reforms, they wanted to *bring down* the government. 学生们不仅仅要求改革,他们想要政府下台。His challenge to Mr Brown *brought* him *down*. 他对布朗先生的挑战使他下了台。❹(常用被动语态形式) give or leave (something) to people who are younger or come later 把(某物)传给(下代人): This ring has been *brought down* in my family. 这枚戒指是我家祖传下来的。

NOTE 1. 当本短语所带的宾语为代词时,该代词须置于本短语的动词和副词中间。
2. 当本短语作"把(某物)传给(下代人)"解时,同义短语是 come down, hand down, hand on 和 pass on。

bring down the house ⇨ **bring the house down**

bring forth *vt.* 【不可分性动词短语】❶produce (something) or cause (a particular reaction)产生,引起(某种反应): These efforts will surely *bring forth* good results. 这些努力必将产生良好的结果。The Macao government has taken active measures in handling issues related to people's livelihood, thus *bringing forth* a good start. 澳门政府采取积极措施,妥善处理民生问题,赢得了良好的开局。Her letter to the paper *brought forth* a flood of supportive comments. 她写给报纸的那封信赢得了广泛的舆论支持。❷(陈旧用法,正式用语) give birth to (a child)生(孩子): She has *brought forth* two children. 她已生了两个孩子。

NOTE 当本短语作"生(孩子)"解时,同义短语是 bring into the world。

bring forward *vt.*【可分性动词短语】❶(正式用语) produce or present (an idea, etc.) for consideration 提出,提议,提供: The various departments have not yet *brought forward* their spending plans. 各部门尚未提出他们的开支计划。You may *bring* the matter *forward* at the next meeting. 你可以在下次会上提出这个问题。A plan was *brought forward* to allow workers to share in the profits. 一项允许工人分享利润的计划被提了出来。Can you *bring forward* any proof of your story? 你能为你所说的情况提供证据吗? ❷(主要用于英国英语中) change (the date or time of an event) so that it happens earlier than had been planned 将(日期或时间)提前: They *brought* the date of the wedding *forward* so her cousins could attend. 他们把婚期提前,这样她的堂姐妹就可以参加婚礼了。The meeting has been *brought forward* from 15 June to 10 June. 会期已由 6 月 15 日提前到 6 月 10 日。In accordance with summer time in England, clocks and watches should be *brought forward* one hour. 按照英国夏令时间,钟表要拨快一小时。

NOTE **1.** 当本短语所带的宾语为代词时,该代词须置于本短语的动词和副词中间。**2.** 当本短语作"将(日期或时间)提前"解时,同义短语是 put forward;反义短语是 put back。

bring home to *vt.*【可分性动词短语】(用一般时态) make (someone) realize (how important, difficult or serious something is)使(某人)认识到(某事的重要、困难或严重): You must *bring* the seriousness of the situation *home to* your friend. 你必须让你的朋友认识到这种局势的严重性。The accident caused a death in his family, and it *brought home to* him the evil of drinking while driving. 那场事故导致他家一人丧生,这使他认识到酒后驾车的危害。

NOTE 本短语中的 home 是副词,而不是名词。

bring in *vt.*【可分性动词短语】❶ bring (something or someone) indoors, etc.; introduce 把(某物)拿进来,把(某人)带进来,引进: *Bring* the washing *in*; it's raining. 下雨了,把洗的东西收进来。The policeman *brought in* two boys he had caught stealing. 警察把他当场抓住的两个偷东西的男孩带到警察局。The change of management is an opportunity to *bring in* new talent. 管理层的变动是一个录用人才的机会。They *brought* some experienced people *in* to help. 他们请了一些有经验的人来帮忙。Many new machines have been *brought in* from abroad after the factory was set up. 这家工厂自建立以来,已经从国外引进了许多新机器。❷produce (a profit); earn (a particular amount of money) 取得(利润),赚得(金钱): Tourism is a big industry of the country, *bringing in* about $7 billion a year. 旅游是该国的一大产业,每年大约赚取 70 亿美元的利润。The students are *bringing in* good wages from their part-time jobs. 这些大学生从临时工作赚取的工资不少。He does odd jobs that *bring* him *in* 50 to 60 pounds a week. 他做零工每星期可赚 50 至 60 英镑。❸ (of a government or organization) introduce (a new law or system into parliament)(指政府或某一机构)(向议会)提出(新议案等): She said the government would *bring in* the necessary legislation to deal with the problem. 她说,政府将提出必要的法令

来应对这样的问题。❹(用一般时态)(of a jury) give (an official decision) in court (指陪审团)在法庭上做出裁决: The jury *brought in* a verdict of guilty. 陪审团正式裁决被告有罪。

NOTE 当本短语所带的宾语为代词时,该代词须置于本短语的动词和副词中间。

bring into *vt.*【可分性动词短语】cause (something or someone) to reach (a state or condition)使(某物或某人)到达(某种状态): The warm spring weather helps to *bring* the fruit trees *into* blossom/flower. 温暖的春季气候有助于果树开花。Her work *brings* her *into* contact with powerful legal and political figures in Washington. 她的工作使她与华盛顿的政法界要人相接触。The tricky behavior of a few individuals has *brought* the whole profession *into* disrepute. 个别人的欺诈行为败坏了整个行业的声誉。When are you going to *bring* the plan *into* operation? 你们打算何时实施这一计划? The farm tool factory was brought into production last year. 这家农具厂是去年投入生产的。

bring into action *vt.*【可分性动词短语】(正式用语,常用被动语态形式) cause (someone or something) to function or start working 使……开始工作;使……运转: The threats *brought* the police *into action*. 这些威胁使警方展开了行动。If necessary, this heavy machine can be *brought into action*. 如有必要,可使这台重型机器投入运转。Because of the state of the ground, the artillery could not be *brought into action* at once. 由于地形的状况,大炮无法立即投入战斗。

bring into being *vt.*【可分性动词短语】(正式用语,常用被动语态形式) create; establish; set up 创造,成立,建立: Modern physicists can *bring* the ultra-high and ultra-low temperature *into being* in their laboratories. 现代物理学家们能在实验室里创造出超高温和超低温。The company was *brought into being* last year. 这家公司是去年成立的。The cost includes attorneys' fees and other outlays necessary to *bring* the corporation *into existence*. 成本包括律师费以及成立公司所必需的其他开支。An information department was *brought into existence* to deal with inquiries. 设立了一个信息部门以处理咨询业务。

NOTE 本短语的名词 being 可被 existence 替换,两者的意义和用法相同。

bring into effect *vt.*【可分性动词短语】(正式用语,常用被动语态形式) cause (something such as a law) to begin to operate 使(法律等)实施,使生效: A new law of taxation will be *brought into effect* next January. 一种新的税法将于明年一月起实施。It is our political will to *bring* this treaty *into effect* as soon as possible. 尽快使该条约生效,是我们的政治意愿。The new law will be *brought into effect* by midnight tomorrow. 这项新法律将于明天午夜开始生效。

NOTE 本短语与 bring into force 意义和用法相同。

bring into fashion *vt.*【可分性动词短语】make (something) fashionable 使……流行起来: The British designers tried to *bring* the miniskirt *into fashion* all over Europe. 英国的服装设计师曾试图使这种短裙在全欧洲流行起来。The leather jacket designed for the Air Force was *brought back into fashion*. 为空军飞行员设计的皮夹克又流行起来。

bring into play *vt.*【可分性动词短语】

(正式用语) cause (something) to be used or have an effect, influence, or force 运用,使起作用,发挥,调动: He had to *bring* all his experience *into play* to beat this difficult opponent. 他不得不运用他的全部经验来击败这个难以对付的对手。*Bring into* full *play* the important role of the private sector in promoting economic growth and creating job opportunities. 要充分发挥个体经济在促进经济发展和创造就业机会上的重要作用。 Anti-terrorism should follow international laws, and the leading role of the UN and its Security Council should be *brought into play*. 反恐应遵循国际法,并发挥联合国和安理会的主导作用。It is imperative to *bring* all positive factors *into play*. 必须调动一切积极因素。

bring into service *vt.*【可分性动词短语】(正式用语,常用被动语态形式) introduce (something) to serve the public; open for use 投入使用: Environmental pressures and restrictions could *bring* more and safer new planes *into service*. 环境方面的压力和限制会使更多更安全的新飞机投入使用。We must do our best to *bring* the river-crossing bridge *into service* prior to the New Year Festival. 我们必须尽最大努力使这座跨江大桥在新年前投入使用。Some additional machine parts can be *brought into service* when required. 必要时可以使用备用的机器部件。

NOTE 本短语的名词 service 可被 use 替换,两者的意义和用法相同。

bring into sight *vt.*【可分性动词短语】cause (something) to be seen 使看到: The clouds suddenly divided, *bringing* the sun *into sight* at last. 乌云突然散开,终于能看到太阳了。A sudden movement of the clouds *brought* the airfield *into sight*. 云朵的突然移动使机场现入眼帘。When we reached the top of the mountain, a large plain was *brought into sight*. 我们登上了山顶,一片辽阔的平原尽收眼底。

NOTE 本短语的名词 sight 可被 view 替换,两者的意义和用法相同。

bring into the world *vt.*【可分性动词短语】❶give birth to (a human being) 生(孩子): She has *brought into the world* a boy. 她生下了一个男孩。You will have to take the responsibility to educate your children as you have *brought* them *into the world*. 你们生下了孩子,就要负起责任来教育他们。The hero of this story was *brought into the world* on the 10th October, 1954. 我们这个故事的主人公是 1954 年 10 月 5 日出生的。❷attend the birth of someone; help a baby to be born 接生: The doctor who *brought* me *into the world* died last week. 为我接生的那位医生上周去世了。I was *brought into the world* by a kindly old doctor. 我是由一位善良的老医生接生的。

NOTE 1. 本短语可根据表达的需要,在名词 world 前加修饰语。例如:

> I wouldn't want to *bring* a child into this cruel *world*.
> 我不愿把孩子生在这个残酷的世界里。

2. 当本短语作"生(孩子)"解时,同义短语是 bring forth。

bring into use ⇨ **bring into service**

bring into view ⇨ **bring into sight**

bring off *vt.*【可分性动词短语】❶take (usually someone) from a dangerous place 把(某人从危险的地方)拯救出来:

The lifeboat *brought off* most of the shipwrecked sailors. 救生艇把失事船只的大多数水手都救了出来。Only some of the passengers and the crewmembers of the Titanic were *brought off*, but most were drowned. 只有部分"泰坦尼克号"的乘客和船员们被救起,而大多都被溺死。❷(非正式用语,常用一般时态) succeed in doing (something difficult); accomplish (something requiring unusual ability) 做成(难做的事),成功: They were about to *bring off* an even bigger deal. 他们就要做成一笔更大的买卖了。It was a difficult deal but we *brought it off*. 这是一笔难做的交易,但我们把它做成了。The concerto is a huge challenge but she *brought* it *off* magnificently. 演奏该协奏曲是一巨大挑战,但她获得了圆满的成功。

NOTE 当本短语所带的宾语为代词时,该代词须置于本短语的动词和副词中间。

bring on *vt.*【可分性动词短语】❶cause (something, usually unpleasant) to happen 引起,导致: Reading in a poor light may *bring on* a headache. 在昏暗的灯光下看书可能会引起头痛。The booming of the country's automobile sales has *brought* heavy pressure *on* oil supplies. 国内汽车销售的迅速增长对燃油供应造成了巨大压力。The cold weather *brought on* many attacks of influenza. 寒冷的天气导致流感多次发作。She nearly died of a heart attack *brought on* by fear. 她几乎死于因恐惧引起的心脏病发作。The crisis in our industry was *brought on* by intense competition from foreign producers. 我们这个行业的危机是由于外国厂商的激烈竞争而致。❷ cause (something or someone) to advance or improve 使……发展,使……前进,使……进步: The fine weather is *bringing* the crops *on* nicely. 好天气使庄稼长势很好。Such a good teacher is sure to *bring* you *on* great success. 这样的好老师肯定会使你有很大的进步。❸(常与反身代词连用,常用一般时态) cause (something bad) to happen to (someone) 给(某人)惹来(坏事): You've *brought* all that trouble *on* yourself. 所有那些麻烦都是你自己惹起来的。

NOTE 当本短语所带的宾语为代词时,该代词须置于本短语的动词和副词或介词中间。

bring out *vt.* ❶ move (something or someone) out of a building or room. 搬出,带出: It is warm enough. *Bring out* the chair for me. 天气够暖和的了,给我把椅子搬出来。"I *brought out* two kids from my house and then ran to help my neighbor, who was buried in his house," he said. "我把家里两个孩子带出来后,又去帮助埋在房里的邻居。"他说道。❷(常用一般时态) make (someone or something) show a quality that they have 使显示出;露出,衬出: The increased responsibility *brought out* her quality. 责任的加重,使她尽显其才能。In an enlargement of a photograph defects are often *brought out* which were not visible in the original. 照片放大后,原来看不出的缺陷往往都显示出来。The investigation is sure to *bring out* some surprising things. 该项调查一定会披露出一些惊人的事来。The new dress *brought out* her hidden beauty. 这件新装衬出了她潜在的美。❸(of someone or a company) produce (a new product) and start to sell it 生产,推出(新产品): The next year they will *bring out* a low-priced car to compete with Ford. 他们明年将推出一款低价轿车与福特汽车相竞争。❹(of a publishing house or someone) publish or produce (a new book or record) 出版(新书或唱片): The publishing house has just *brought out* several selections from English novels. 该出版社刚刚出版了几部英国小说选集。She is *bringing out* a long awaited solo album next month. 她在下个月将推出一张人们期待已久的独唱专辑。❺(常用一般时态) express (something spoken such as a word or statement); help or encourage (someone) to feel less nervous or talk more freely in the company of others 说出;(帮助或鼓励某人在众人面前自如地)讲话: His new opinions were fully *brought out* in his lecture. 他的新观点在他的讲演中得到了充分的阐述。Helen is very shy; try to *bring* her *out* at the gathering. 海伦很腼腆,在聚会上尽量让她多说点话。❻(主要用于英国英语中) cause (workers) to go on strike 使(工人)罢工: They have threatened to *bring* the workers *out* if their demands are not met. 他们威胁说,如果他们的要求得不到满足,他们就发动工人罢工。

NOTE 当本短语所带的宾语为代词时,该代词须置于本短语的动词和副词中间。

bring over *vt.* 【可分性动词短语】❶cause (someone) to come from overseas 从海外把(某人)接过来: Dr Folley has been teaching in China for 3 years. Next summer he hopes to *bring* his family *over*. 弗利博士已在中国任教三年。明年夏季,他希望把他家人接过来。❷(用一般时态,常与 to 连用) persuade (someone) to change his or her opinion and agree with you 说服(某人)改变主意: We must *bring* the rest of the committee *over* to our point of view. 我们必须说服委员会的其他成员改变主意,支持我们的观点。I don't think that many of the people in the center can be *brought over* to the government side. 我认为很多持中间立场的人都不能被说服站到政府这方面来。

NOTE **1.** 当本短语所带的宾语为代词时,该代词须置于本短语的动词和副词中间。

2. 当本短语作"说服(某人)改变主意"解时,同义短语是 bring around 和 bring round (第二个义项)。

bring round *vt.* 【可分性动词短语】(英国英语用法) ❶ take (someone or something) somewhere, especially to someone's house 把……带到(尤指某人的家等): Do *bring* your children *round* to our place this evening. 请今天晚上一定要带你的孩子们到我们家里来。He promised to *bring* the letter *round* in the morning. 他答应上午就把那封信带过来。❷(用一般时态,常与 to 连用) persuade (someone) to change his or her opinion and agree with you 说服(某人)改变主意: Sam was sure he could *bring* the rest of the committee *round* to his point of view. 萨姆确信他能说服委员会的其他成员改变主意,支持他的观点。The manager is not the sort of man who can easily be *brought round*. 经理可不是那种容易被说服的人。❸ make (someone who is unconscious) become conscious 使(某人)苏醒过来,使(某人)恢复知觉: She opened all the windows in the hope of *bringing* him *round*. 她把所有的窗户都打开,希望他能苏醒过来。The little boy was finally *brought round* from high fever. 小男孩终于从高烧中恢复了过来。

B

NOTE 1. 当本短语所带的宾语为代词时，该代词须置于本短语的动词和副词中间。

2. 当本短语作"使（某人）苏醒过来，使（某人）恢复知觉"解时，与 bring around 和 bring to（第一个义项）意义和用法相同，三者可互换使用。

3. 当本短语作"使（某人）苏醒过来，使（某人）恢复知觉"解时，与 come to，come around 和 come round 的意义相近，但用法稍有不同。本短语是及物性动词短语，而 come to，come around 和 come round 都是不及物性动词短语。

bring the house down *vi.*（非正式用语，无被动语态形式）(of a performer or performance) make a group of people or an audience cheer, clap, or laugh very loudly, especially in a theatre（指演出者或演出）博得满场喝彩，使观众（或听众）哄堂大笑：The clown *brought the house down* with a strange song and a ballet dance. 小丑唱了一首怪怪的歌曲并跳了一段芭蕾舞，博得满场喝彩。His amusing performance *brought the house down*. 他那逗趣的表演使观众哄堂大笑。

NOTE 本短语的另外一种表达形式是 bring down the house。例如：

> On the New Year's Eve, my father always tells jokes that *bring down the house*.
> 在除夕夜，爸爸总是讲几个笑话，使家里笑声满堂。

bring through *vt.*【可分性动词短语】（常用一般时态）❶ save the life of (someone very ill) 挽救（病危者）的生命：Can the doctor *bring* the child *through*? 那位医生能挽救这孩子的生命吗？❷ cause to come successfully through (a difficulty or dangerous situation) 使（某人）脱离危险，使（某人）摆脱困境：Mother was very ill but timely treatment and careful nursing *brought* her *through*. 母亲病得很重，但及时的治疗和精心的护理使她脱离了危险。The people's courage *brought* them *through* the war. 民众的勇气使他们摆脱了战争的困境。

NOTE 1. 当本短语所带的宾语为代词时，该代词须置于本短语的动词和副词或介词中间。

2. 本短语与 pull through 的意义相同，但用法不完全相同，后者还有不及物性用法。见 pull through。

bring to *vt.*【可分性动词短语】❶ carry or move (something) or lead (someone) in the direction of (someone or something) 把……带到……：*Bring* your paper *to* me when you have finished it. 你写完论文后就把它带给我。China's economic development will surely *bring* more development opportunities *to* other Asian countries. 中国的经济发展定会给亚洲其他国家带来更多的发展机遇。He was *brought to* court and charged with rape. 他被带到法庭受审并被指控犯有强奸罪。❷ make (something) reach (a certain total or sum) 使……到达（某一总数）：Romania and Bulgaria were formally accepted as new members of the European Union, *bringing* the number of EU countries *to* 27. 罗马尼亚和保加利亚被正式接纳为欧洲联盟新成员，这使欧盟成员国达到了 27 个。❸ cause (something or someone) to reach (a state or condition) 使……到达（某一状态）：The chairman *brought* the meeting *to* an end as it was getting late. 由于时间渐晚，主席便结束了会议。A strike in the factory *brought* production *to* a halt this morning. 工厂工人的罢工使今天上午的生产陷于停顿。His instruction finally *brought* Jack *to* reason. 他的教导终于使杰克醒悟过来了。Let us, under the new circumstances, join hands to *bring* our friendly cooperation *to* a new high. 让我们在新的形势下,携手将我们的友好合作提高到新的水平。❹cause (someone) to regain consciousness 使(某人)恢复知觉: They threw some cold water over her head to *bring* her *to*. 他们往她头上浇了点儿凉水使她苏醒过来。He will soon be *brought to*. 他很快就会苏醒过来。

—*vt.* &*vi.* (常用一般时态) (of a ship or boat)(cause to) stop(使)(船)停下: As the wind dropped the boat *brought to*. 随着风速减低,小船停了下来。Reaching the pier, he *brought* the boat *to*. 到了码头,他便把小船停住。The unidentified ship was *brought to* by the firing of a warning shot. 那艘来历不明的船只受到鸣枪警告才停了下来。

NOTE 1. 当本短语用作及物性动词短语,所带的宾语为代词时,该代词须置于本短语的动词和副词或介词中间。

2. 本短语与 come to 和 come around/round 都有"恢复知觉"之意。但 bring to 是及物性动词短语,而 come to, come around/round 则是不及物性动词短语。

bring to justice *vt.* 【可分性动词短语】(正式用语) make (someone) have a trial in order to find out whether he or she is guilty of a crime 把(某人)送上法庭受审: The police must do all they can to *bring* criminals *to justice*. 警方必须竭尽全力将犯罪分子绳之以法。The girl's killers have never been *brought to justice*. 杀害女孩的凶手从未被送上法庭受审过。

bring to light *vt.* 【可分性动词短语】cause (something such as a fact) to be discovered; become known 发现,为人所知: He succeeded in *bringing to light* some important scientific facts. 他成功地揭示了某些重要的科学事实。Many things left by the ancient Egyptians in tombs have been *brought to light* by scientists and explorers. 科学家和探险家在坟墓中发现了很多古埃及人的遗物。He threatened to *bring* the matter *to light*. 他威胁说要把此事曝光。

NOTE 本短语与 come to light 意义相同,但用法不同。前者为及物性动词短语,而后者是不及物性动词短语。

bring to mind *vt.* 【可分性动词短语】(正式用语) ❶ remind (someone) of (something or someone) 使(某人)想起……: This latest crisis *brings to mind* the events of last year. 最近发生的这一危机使我想起了去年那些事件。The old toy *brought* his childhood *to mind*. 这件旧玩具使他想起了童年时期。His face *brings to mind* an old friend of mine. 他的面孔使我想起了我的一位老友。❷remember; recall (something)记得,回忆起: I cannot *bring to mind* the name of the place where we met first. 我记不得我们初次见面是在什么地方了。She couldn't *bring to mind* where she had seen him before. 她回忆不起来以前在什么地方见过他。

NOTE 本短语与 call to mind 意义相同,但 call to mind 常用于否定句中。见 call to mind。

bring to pass *vt.* 【可分性动词短语】(常用一般时态) cause (something) to happen 使……发生: By much planning, the mother *brought* the marriage *to pass*. 母亲费了好一番筹划,才促成这桩婚事。I doubt if he will ever *bring* his promise *to pass*. 我怀疑他能否实现其诺言。

bring together *vt.* 【可分性动词短语】

❶cause (people or things) to meet or join 使聚在一起:It was their interest in photography that *brought* them *together*. 是对摄影的兴趣把他们聚在了一起。*Bring* the two edges *together* and stick them down. 把这两个边儿对到一块,然后把它们粘上。The event was unique in *bringing together* politicians, business leaders, and academics. 这次的活动很独特,它使政治家、商界领导人士和学者们会聚一堂。❷ cause (two or more parties) to end a disagreement and do something together 使(冲突双方或多方)言归于好:The Minister is trying to *bring* the two sides to the dispute *together*. 部长试图使冲突双方言归于好。I'm not sure that John and Margaret can be *brought together*. 我不敢肯定约翰和玛格丽特能够和解。

NOTE 当本短语所带的宾语为代词时,该代词须置于本短语的动词和副词中间。

bring up *vt.*【可分性动词短语】❶(常用被动语态形式) care for (a child) up to adulthood; educate 养育,教育,培养:He was born and *brought up* in India. 他是在印度出生和长大的。Children who are *brought up* in the country are not necessarily healthier than those *brought up* in towns. 在农村长大的孩子不一定就比在城里长大的孩子更健康。Harvard is a world-famous institution of higher learning, attracting the best minds and *bringing* them *up* generation after generation. 哈佛是世界著名的高等学府,精英荟萃,人才辈出。He set up a school after his retirement and succeeded in *bringing up* a batch of intellectuals. 他退休后创立了一所学校并成功地培养出了一批知识人才。❷raise (an animal) 饲养(动物):We *brought up* the puppies carefully. 我们精心地饲养了这些小狗。We *brought* the dog *up* from a pup. 这条狗是我们从小养到大的。❸(常用一般时态) start discussing (a subject); mention (something or someone) 讨论(某一主题),谈及,提及:Mr Brown said the issue would be *brought up* again at the next meeting. 布朗先生说,那个问题在下次会议上将再次讨论。There's no need to *bring up* his past. 没有必要谈及他的过去。His talk brought up a new idea. 他的讲话提出了一个新观念。I hate to *bring* this *up* but you still owe me $10. 我不愿提起这事,但你还欠我 10 美元。Why did you bring up Jane? I hate talking about her! 你为什么提起简?我不愿谈论她!❹(常用被动语态形式) cause (someone) to appear in court for trial 把(某人)送上法庭受审:They were *brought up* for causing a disturbance and obstructing the police. 他们因扰乱治安和妨碍警务而被送上法庭受审。My friend was *brought up* before the court on a charge of drunken driving. 我的朋友因被指控酒后驾车而被送上法庭受审。❺(主要用于英国英语中,非正式用语) make (food or drink) come back up from your stomach through your mouth; vomit (one's food) 呕吐:This morning I *brought up* most what I had eaten. 我今早把吃下的大部分东西都吐了出来。Once the poison has been *brought up* there is no further danger. 一旦毒药被吐出来就没有什么危险了。

—*vt.* & *vi.* (非正式用语,常用一般时态,常用被动语态形式) (cause to) stop or halt suddenly (使)突然停止:The truck *brought up* suddenly against a building. 卡车突然靠在一幢房子旁边停了下来。He *brought* the car *up* when the light changed to red. 他在交通灯变成红色时把车戛然停住。John was about to enter the room when he was *brought up* by a note on the door. 约翰正要进屋,门上的条子使他停住了脚步。Bill started to complain, but I *brought* him *up*. 比尔开始发起牢骚,但我立刻阻止了他。

NOTE 1. 当本短语用作及物性动词短语,所带的宾语为代词时,该代词须置于本短语的动词和副词中间。

2. 当本短语作"呕吐"解时,同义短语是 throw up。

bring up the rear *vi.* be the last in a line or sequence (在队列中)殿后;(在顺序上)居后:The governor and his staff led the way, with the soldiers on horseback *bringing up the rear* in the procession. 州长和他的幕僚们走在游行队伍的前面,骑兵们殿后。As a slow walker, I'm used to *bringing up the rear*. 我走路慢,惯于殿后。In test results Bill always *brought up the rear*. 比尔的考试成绩总是排在后面。

brush aside *vt.* 【可分性动词短语】❶remove (something) by using a brush or moving your hands quickly over a surface (用刷子)刷去;(用手)拂去:Mother was in the garage, *brushing* the dirt *aside*. 妈妈在停车房中打扫灰尘。Mary *brushed aside* her tears as she listened. 玛丽一边听一边擦拭着泪水。❷ignore; refuse to consider (something) seriously because you feel that it is not important or true 不屑一顾,漠视:He *brushed aside* all objections form his opponents. 他无视反对者的一切异议。You can't *brush* their demand *aside*. 你不能对他们的要求不理不睬。When the employees forwarded their suggestions the boss just *brushed* them *aside*. 当雇员们提出他们的建议时,老板只是将其搁置一旁不屑理睬。Our suggestions were repeatedly *brushed aside*. 我们的建议一再受到漠视。

NOTE 当本短语所带的宾语为代词时,该代词须置于本短语的动词和副词中间。

brush off *v.* ❶(cause to) remove or clean with a brush (用刷子)掸去,刷去,除去:Don't worry about that dust on the car windows; it will *brush off*. 别担心汽车玻璃上的那点灰尘,一掸就掉。Please *brush* the dust on the car windows *off*. 请把汽车玻璃上的灰尘掸去。It was a hard job to *brush off* the stains on his blue jeans. 要刷掉他牛仔裤上的污迹可是件难事。❷(非正式用语,用一般时态) refuse to listen to (what someone says), or refuse to think about (something) seriously 拒绝听取;拒绝考虑:Demonstrators in Tehran *brushed off* a warning from the government and continued protesting the election results. 在德黑兰,示威者拒不听从政府发出的警告,继续抗议选举结果。I felt *brushed off*, ignored, as though I were not important. 我感到没人听我的了,没人理睬我了,仿佛我是一无足轻重之人。We were not prepared to get *brushed off* again. 我们没有想到会被再次拒绝。❸(非正式用语,用一般时态) refuse to have a relationship with (someone) 拒绝与(某人)相处;抛弃(某人):Jack's girlfriend *brushed* him *off* before he met Mary. 杰克的女朋友抛弃了他。后来,他认识了玛丽。

NOTE 1. 当本短语用作及物性动词短语,所带的宾语为代词时,该代词须置于本短语的动词和副词中间。

2. 本短语可转化为复合词 brush-off,意为"不理睬;拒绝;摒弃"。

brush up *v.* (常与 on 连用) quickly improve (your knowledge or skills of something), especially when you have not used it for a time 快速提高(尤指某种生疏了的知识或技艺): I took a class to *brush up* (on) my German before the trip to Munich for the World Cup. 在前往慕尼黑观看世界杯之前,我参加了一个德语提高班。I need to *brush* my French *up* a little bit. 我需要把我的法语水平提高一点。He comes here to *brush up* on his driving. 他到这里来是为了提高驾车技术。

bubble over with *vt.* 【不可分性动词短语】(无被动语态形式,常用进行时态) be full of (a happy or excited feeling) 洋溢着(喜悦或兴奋的感情): She was *bubbling over with* joy and enthusiasm. 她满怀喜悦,充满热情。The audience *bubbled over with* laughter. 听众们开怀大笑。

build in/into *vt.* (常用被动语态形式) ❶make (something such as a piece of furniture) a fix part of a wall or room 把(家具等)装入,嵌入(墙体或房间): These cupboards are *built in*. 这些碗橱都是装在墙体内的。❷make (something) a part of something else 使(某物)成为……的一部分: The difficulties seem to be *built in*. 困难似乎在所难免。The rate of the pay was *built into* his contract. 他的薪金额已写入合同。

build on/upon *vt.* ❶(常用被动语态形式) build a new room or part (onto the outside of a building) 加建,增建: This part of the hospital was *built on* later. 医院的这部分是后来加建的。They've had an extension *built upon* the side of the building. 他们在楼房的一侧加建了一间房子。❷(常用被动语态形式) base (something) on (something else) 基于: These findings *build on* evidence that "positive emotion" can help ward off the common cold and other illnesses. 这些研究结果的主要依据是,"积极的情绪"有助于预防感冒和其他疾病。China holds that the China-US relations should be *built on* the principles specified in the three China-US joint communiqués. 中国主张,中美关系应建立在三个中美联合公报所定的原则基础之上。The insurance business is *built on* trust. 保险业务是建立在信用的基础上的。❸depend on; trust in (someone, something or doing something) 依靠,寄托: The prosperity of a country should *build on* the hard work of its people. 一个国家的繁荣依靠其人民的辛勤劳动。We should not *build* too many hopes *upon* their assistance. 我们不应当把太多的希望寄托在他们的帮助上。

NOTE 本短语中的 upon 用法比 on 正式,但不及 on 常用。

build up *v.* ❶make (something) bigger by building 建起,垒起: They *built* the wall *up* in several stages until it was the height they wanted. 他们一段一段地把墙垒起来,一直达到他们想要的高度。They had to *build up* their fortress to protect against attack. 他们不得不筑起堡垒以防受到攻击。❷(cause to) increase, develop, or form steadily (使)不断增加,形成,树立: These exercises are good for *building up* leg strength. 这些运动对增加腿力有益。Tension is *building up* between the two countries. 两国的紧张局势加剧了。Enemy forces have now *built up* to a dangerous strength. 敌军兵力已形成了一股危险的

势力。He called on the world to *build up* confidence to tide over the current global financial crisis. 他呼吁世界各国树立信心，渡过当前的全球性经济危机。❸form a mass; accumulate so as to form a block 集结，聚集：The clouds are *building up*. We'd better close the windows. 云朵在聚集。我们还是把窗户关上吧。Traffic going out of the city is already *building up*. 出城的车辆都已聚挤在路上。❹accumulate (money, etc.) gradually 逐渐积累(金钱等)：The banks have *built up* sufficient reserves to cope with the crisis. 银行已积累了充足的储备金以应对危机。His books will *build up* into a library. 他的书越积越多，可以开个图书馆了。❺restore (a person's health or strength) after an illness 病后恢复(健康或体力)：You need lots of fresh fruit to help *build* you *up*. 你需要吃大量的新鲜水果以帮助增进健康。He's now trying to *build up* his strength after a serious illness. 重病过后，他现正竭力恢复体力。❻(常用被动语态形式) praise or talk about (someone or something) in a very positive way so that people are impressed with them 赞扬，追捧(某人或某物)：The singer has been *built up* into a great success. 这位歌手已被捧得红得发紫。The play was *built up* to be a masterpiece but I found it very disappointing. 该剧被捧为杰作，但我却觉得它十分令人扫兴。

NOTE **1.** 当本短语用作及物性动词短语，所带的宾语是代词时，该代词须置于本短语的动词和副词中间。

2. 本短语可转化为复合词 build-up，意为"增长；加强；集结；储备"。

bump against ⇨ **bump into**

bump into *vt.*【不可分性动词短语】❶accidentally knock or hit against (something or someone) 偶然撞到……上：As I turned round, I *bumped into* the doorpost. 我转身时撞到了门柱上。The two cars *bumped into* each other. 这两辆汽车撞在了一起。A little boy *bumped into* me. 一个小男孩一头撞在了我的身上。The old man was *bumped into* by a careless boy from behind. 后面来的一个冒失小子撞在了老人的身上。❷(非正式用语，无被动语态形式) happen to meet (someone) 偶然碰见(某人)：Guess who I *bumped into* today? 你猜我今天碰见谁了？I *bumped into* your mother at the supermarket. 我在超级市场碰见了你妈妈。I was surprised to *bump into* Mary at the football game. 在足球赛上碰到玛丽使我感到吃惊。

NOTE **1.** 当本短语作"偶然撞到……上"解时，另外一种表达形式是 bump against。

2. 当本短语作"偶然碰上(某人)"解时，同义短语是 run into 和 chance on/upon。

burn down *vi.* (especially of a fire) burn lower, less brightly or strongly (尤指火)火势减弱，火头变小：Let's leave the fire to *burn down* and go into our tents. 我们就让火慢慢减弱下来，我们进帐篷里去吧。The fire in the grate gradually *burnt down*. 壁炉里的火逐渐变小。

—*vt.* &*vi.* (of a fire) destroy (usually a building); (usually of a building) be destroyed by fire (常指建筑物)(被)烧毁：South Korea's number 1 national treasure Sungnyemun Gate was on fire at a night and the fire *burned down* the wooden structure in about 4 hours. 韩国一号国宝崇礼门在一个晚上燃起大火。在约 4 个小时内大火便烧毁了这一木制结构的建筑。Located in northwest Beijing, Yuan Ming Yuan was *burned* down by British and French troops in 1860. 位于北京西北的圆明园于 1860 年被英法联军焚毁。Her house *burned down*, but she's alive, and her kids didn't die. So it's not the end of the world for her. 她的房子焚毁了,但她还活着,她的孩子们也都没死。因此,对她来说那并不是世界末日。

NOTE 本短语中的动词 burn 的过去式和过去分词形式有两种:burned 和 burnt。这两种形式都用于英国英语中。而在美国英语中,则广泛使用 burned。

burn out *v.* ❶(常用被动语态形式) completely destroy (the inside of something) by fire or electrical burning (火或电)烧毁,烧坏:The ancient palace was *burnt out* during the war. 那座古代宫殿在战争期间被焚毁了。Flames *burnt out* two adjoining houses. 大火把两栋毗邻的房子烧掉了。The electric motor has been *burnt out*. 电动机已被烧坏。We must buy a new bulb; the old one has *burnt out*. 我们得买一个新灯泡,旧的已烧坏了。❷stop (itself) burning because there is nothing left to burn 燃尽,烧完自灭:That small fire can be left to *burn* (itself) *out*. 剩下那点小火就让它烧完自灭吧。The fire *burnt out* for lack of fuel. 由于没有燃料,火便熄灭了。❸burn (someone's home) so that he or she has to leave it (因家遭火灾而)流离失所:The house caught fire, and the family were *burned out*. 房子失火,这家人便流离失所了。They were *burnt out* of their homes, losing everything. 他们因家遭火灾而一无所剩,流离失所。❹(与反身代词连用) ruin (one's health) and stop being active through too much work, pressure, alcohol, etc. (元气)大伤;(精力)耗尽:You'll *burn* yourself *out* if you work so hard. 如果你这样拼命工作,会把身体搞垮的。Bill *burned* himself *out* in the first part of the race and could not finish. 比尔在比赛的第一段路程就已跑得筋疲力尽,因而未能跑到终点。

NOTE **1.** 当本短语用作及物性动词短语,所带的宾语是代词时,该代词须置于本短语的动词和副词中间。

2. 本短语可转化为复合词 burnout,意为"燃尽,熄火"。

burn the candle at both ends *vi.* (非正式用语) work all day and far into the night and so get too little rest; use up all one's strength by trying to do too many different things in too short a period of time 夜以继日地工作,废寝忘食;耗尽体力:Everyone knows that *burning the candle at both ends* is not a healthy life. 人人都知道,夜以继日地工作不是一种健康的生活。"Would you like to go to a party tonight?" "I can't. I'm too tired. I've been *burning the candle at both ends* all week." "你今晚去参加聚会吗?" "我不能去。我太累了。一个星期来我一直夜以继日,没得休息。"

burn the midnight oil *vi.* (非正式用语) study or work all night or until very, very late at night 熬夜(学习或工作),开夜车:My son has been up each night *burning the midnight oil*, working hard to prepare for his final exams. 我儿子每天晚上熬夜学习到深更半夜,用功准备期末考试。I'm not ready for the test tomorrow. I think I'll have to *burn the midnight oil*. 我还没准备好明天的考试。我想我得开夜车了。I could see the light in your window last night. It looks like you have been *burning the midnight oil*. 昨晚,我从你的窗户可以看到你的灯亮着,看来你是在开夜车啦。

NOTE 本短语中的 oil 指的是过去晚上照明用的油灯里的油。半夜还点着油灯，当然是在熬夜做事了。虽然现在油灯已不再使用，但本短语却流传了下来。

burn up *v.* ❶(of a fire, a stove, etc.) flame more brightly or strongly (火、炉火等)烧得旺起来：Put some more wood on the fire to make it *burn up*. 再往火上加些木柴，使它烧得旺起来。❷destroy (something) completely by fire 烧毁，烧光：Mr Smith was *burning up* old letters. 史密斯先生在烧毁旧信件。All the wood has been *burnt up*. 所有的木柴都烧尽了。The house *burned up* before the firemen got there. 在消防队员赶到那里之前，房子就全烧毁了。❸(美国英语用法，非正式用语，用一般时态) cause (someone) to be very angry 使(某人)大怒：The boy's laziness and rudeness *burned up* his teacher. 那男孩的懒惰和无礼使他的老师十分生气。The way he talks to some of his employees *burns* me *up*. 他对他某些雇员讲话的方式令我十分气愤。The manager got *burned up* when he heard that his workers were on strike. 经理听说他的工人在罢工，便大发雷霆。❹(of a satellite or spaceship) catch fire and be destroyed by great heat as it reenters the earth's atmosphere (指卫星或宇宙飞船在返回地球大气层时因强热而)烧毁：The satellite re-entered the atmosphere and *burnt up*. 卫星在重返大气层时被烧毁。The spacecraft has a heat shield to prevent it *burning up* when it re-enters the Earth's atmosphere. 宇宙飞船有一层防热板以保护其在重返地球的大气层时不被烧毁。❺(非正式用语，常用进行时态) have a high temperature 发高烧：You're *burning up* — have you seen a doctor? 你在发高烧。看过医生没有？

NOTE 当本短语用作及物性动词短语，所带的宾语为代词时，该代词须置于本短语的动词和副词中间。

burst in *vi.* ❶(常用一般时态) enter in haste 闯入：A man with a mask *burst in* and told everyone to stand still. 一名蒙面男子突然闯了进来，让所有的人都站着别动。A policeman *burst in* waving a gun. 一名警察挥枪闯了进来。❷(常用一般时态，常与 on 连用) enter suddenly 突然进入：He will be *bursting in* at any moment. 他随时都可能进来。How dare you *burst in* on us without knocking? 你怎么胆敢不敲门就闯进我们的房来？❸(用一般时态) interrupt suddenly 突然打断："I don't see why I should be expected to help," Peter *burst in* angrily. "我不明白为什么非要我去帮忙。"彼得气愤地打断话头说道。

NOTE 当本短语作"突然打断"解时，同义短语有：barge in, break in, break into, burst in on/upon, cut in, cut into, cut off, cut short, chip in, get in 和 put in 等，但它们的用法不同。有的是及物性的，有的是不及物性的，有的既有及物性又有不及物性用法。见相关条目。

burst in on *vt.* (常用一般时态) (of someone) interrupt (someone or something) by entering a place suddenly, often noisily (常指吵吵嚷嚷地)突然进来打断：The headmaster could have *burst in on* them at any moment. 校长随时都会闯进来打断他们的谈话。He burst in on the meeting. 他突然吵吵嚷嚷地闯进来打断了会议。An officer *burst in on* their discussion with the news that the enemy was only two miles away. 一名军官突然打断了他们的讨论，报告了敌人离他们只有 2 英里远的消息。

burst into *vt.* 【不可分性动词短语】(无被动语态形式,常用一般时态) ❶go (somewhere) quickly and suddenly 匆匆闯入(某处): Some security personnel waving rifles *burst into* the news conference and told the journalists to turn off their cameras. 一些保安人员挥舞着枪支闯入记者招待会现场,让记者都把摄像机关掉。A new idea *burst into* my mind, glowing with the heat of creation. 一个新的主意闪烁着创造的光芒猛然间跃入了我的脑海中。❷suddenly change into (a situation or state)突然转入(某种状态):The weekend's fighting *burst into* a full-scale war. 周末的战斗引发了一场全面的战争。The engine burst into life. 发动机突然又能启动了。❸suddenly begin (to cry, laugh or sing)突然开始(哭、笑或唱歌):About 2 million people on the National Mall *burst into* thundering cheers and applause when the new President completed his swearing-in. 当这位新总统宣誓就职的仪式结束时,国家广场上的约 200 万人爆发出雷鸣般的欢呼声和掌声。Having got the bad news, some of Bhutto's supporters at the hospital *burst into* tears. 噩耗传来,一些聚在医院的布托支持者大哭起来。On hearing what he said, the audience *burst into* laughter. 听到他讲的那番话,观众们都放声大笑起来。The students in the next classroom *burst into* song. 隔壁教室里的学生突然唱起歌来。❹(正式用语) (of leaves and flowers of a plant) suddenly open (植物)放叶,开花: The trees in the garden *burst into* flower early in May. 刚进 5 月,园子里的树就都开花了。

NOTE 本短语与 burst out 均有"突然开始(哭、笑)"之意。两者间的区别见 burst out。

burst open *v.* (of a door or container) open quickly and suddenly; make (something) open in this way (使)(门或某种容器)突然打开: The door *burst open* and in came Sam. 门突然打开,山姆走了进来。The envelope *burst open* while circulating through a mail-sorting machine. 这个信封在通过信件分理机时封口破裂了。Firefighters had to *burst* the door *open* and rescued them. 消防队员不得不破门而入,把他们救了出来。

burst out *v.* ❶suddenly start (laughing or crying); or make (a noise)突然开始(笑或哭);突然发出(某种声音): I almost *burst out* laughing when I saw what she was wearing. 当我看到她的穿戴时,我几乎突然大笑出来。On hearing the sad news she *burst out* crying. 听到这悲痛的消息后,她放声大哭。Then the applause *burst out*. 接着便爆发出一片掌声。❷(正式用语,用一般时态) say or shout (something) suddenly and with strong feeling (带着强烈的情感)突然说出,突然喊出: "I hate you!" Julia suddenly *burst out*. "我恨你!"朱丽娅突然喊道。"I don't believe it!" she *burst out* angrily. 她愤愤然脱口而出:"我不信!" ❸ (of a situation or problem) suddenly appear (某种局面或问题)突然出现:Then war burst out. 接着战争就爆发了。Unfortunately malaria is *bursting out* again all over the world. 不幸的是,疟疾又在全球爆发流行了。

NOTE 1. 本短语与 burst into 都有"突然开始(笑或哭)"之意。但本短语后面往往接动名词(短语),而 burst into 后面则往往接名词,例如: burst out laughing = burst into laughter; burst out crying =

burst into tears。另外，burst into 只有及物性用法。

2. 本短语与 cry out 都有"叫喊"之意。两者之间的区别见 cry out。

but for *prep.* ❶except for (something)除了……之外：We all attended the lecture yesterday evening *but for* Dick. 除了迪克之外，我们都出席了昨晚的讲座。The work was now complete, *but for* a final coat of paint. 除了再涂最后一遍油漆外，活儿就都干完了。❷(正式用语)(used for saying that something would have happened if something else or someone had not prevented it) without; if it were not for 要没有，要不是：I'd have been lost *but for* you. 如果没有你，我早就走失了。I would have been in real trouble *but for* your help. 若没有你的帮助，那我真的要有麻烦了。*But for* your coming, I should have been very lonely. 你要是不来，我会十分寂寞的。Smith would certainly have been included in the team, *but for* his recent injury. 要不是史密斯最近受伤，他肯定是队中的一员。

NOTE 在本短语的第二个义项中，本短语连同其后的宾语部分相当于一个虚拟条件句。所以，位于其前或其后的主句中的谓语动词要用虚拟语气形式。例如：

> *But for* the emergency treatment, the patient might/would have lost his life. (= *If it had not been for* the emergency treatment, the patient might/would have lost his life.)
> 要不是紧急治疗，病人可能早就死了。

butt in *vi.* (非正式用语，贬义用法，常与 on 连用) interrupt someone or something, such as a conversation or activity without being asked to; interfere or meddle in other people's affairs 打断，插嘴；插手，干涉：Sorry to *butt in* on you, but there's an important call for you. 对不起，打断您一下。您有一个重要电话。I wish you wouldn't keep *butting in* (on our conversation)! 我希望你(在我们谈话时)不要总是插嘴！John *butted in* on Bill and Tom's fight, and got hurt. 约翰参与了比尔和汤姆之间的打斗，结果受了伤。It was none of his concern, so he didn't *butt in*. 因此事与他无关，所以他没有介入。

NOTE 本短语的反义短语是 butt out。例如：

> No one asked your opinion, so *butt out*.
> 没有人征求你的意见，不要插嘴。
> I want everyone to *butt out* of my life.
> 我希望所有的人都不要干涉我的生活。

butt out ⇨**butt in**

buy in *vt.* (英国英语用法) buy a large quantity of (something) in case of future need or as a precaution in the event of a shortage (以备后用或为防将来紧缺而)大量买进(某种物品)：Supermarkets have been *buying in* champagne for Christmas. 超级市场为圣诞节的需要都购入了大量的香槟酒。People *bought in* stocks of tinned goods in anticipation of food rationing. 人们大量购买罐装食品以备食品的定量配给。

NOTE 当本短语所带的宾语为代词时，该代词须置于本短语的动词和副词中间。

buy into *vt.* 【不可分性动词短语】❶purchase (stocks or shares in a company, or a membership in something) 买入(某一公司的股票)；花钱成为(某一组织的成员)：Investors *buy into* these companies because they want a high income on a regular basis. 投资者购买这些公司的股票,是因为他们希望有稳定的高收入。Mark tried to *buy into* the club but was not accepted. 马克企图花钱而成为俱乐部的会员,但未被接受。❷(非正式用语) believe or accept (something) and allow it to influence you 相信;接受:I'm not the sort of person who will *buy into* everything I am told. I have to prove it myself. 我不是那种别人告诉我什么我就相信什么的人。我要自己去验证它。

buy off *vt.*【可分性动词短语】(非正式用语,常用一般时态) pay (someone) money to persuade him or her to do or say something, or not to do something; bribe (someone)(用钱)收买,买通,贿赂(某人):They tried to *buy off* the witnesses. 他们企图收买证人。Efforts to *buy* her *off* have failed. 贿赂她的企图失败了。

NOTE 当本短语的宾语为代词时,该代词须置于本短语的动词和副词中间。

buy out *vt.* ❶ buy all the goods of (a business)买光(某一商家)所有的商品:Mr Smith *bought out* a nearby hardware store. 史密斯先生把附近那家五金商店的全部商品统统买下。❷(英国英语用法,与反身代词连用,常与 of 连用) pay a sum of money so that you can leave an organization (especially the armed forces), before the time that you had originally agreed 靠给钱来提前解除(尤指某人的兵役):He paid a lot of money to *buy* himself *out* of the army. 他花了很多钱使自己提前解除了兵役。

NOTE 当本短语所带的宾语为代词时,该代词须置于本短语的动词和副词中间。

buy up *vt.*【可分性动词短语】buy the complete stock of (something such as land, or a commodity)把(土地或商品等)全部买下:All the available building land has been *bought up* by property developers. 所有可供建筑的土地统统被房地产开发商买了下来。Housewives, afraid of running short, have *bought up* all the sugar in the shops. 家庭主妇们害怕食糖短缺,便把商店里所有的糖都买光了。The tickets will be on sale somewhere else because the agencies have *bought* them *up*. 票将在别处出售,因为代售点已把票全部买光了。

NOTE 当本短语所带的宾语为代词时,该代词须置于本短语的动词和副词中间。

by accident Ⅰ *adv.* ❶ unexpectedly; as the result of an unrelated series of events 偶然地,碰巧:Occasionally we would meet *by accident* in the corridor. 有时我们在走廊里偶尔相遇。He overheard the information *by accident*. 他碰巧听到了这一信息。❷ accidentally; as the result of an event not expected, aided, or designed by one's will 意外地,无意地:"Evidently the bomb went off *by accident*," the police official added. "This hotel was not the place where the suicide bombers had planned to stage the explosion.""很明显,炸弹被意外地引爆了。"这位警官又说道,"这家宾馆并不是自杀性爆炸者计划搞爆炸的地方。" Sorry. I knocked over the vase *by accident*. 对不起,我不是故意弄倒这个花瓶的。I don't know whether he did it *by accident* or by design. 我不知道他这样做是无意的,还是故意的。

Ⅱ *adj.* as the result of some unforeseen happening or series of events; unexpected 偶然的,碰巧的:The victim's death was *by accident*. 受害者之死是偶然的。

NOTE 1. 当本短语用作副词性短语,作"偶然地,碰巧"解时,与 by chance 意义和用法相同,两者可互换使用。

2. 当本短语用作副词性短语,作"意外地,无意地"解时,同义短语是 by mistake。

3. 当本短语用作副词性短语时,反义短语是 on purpose。

by air *adv.* traveling by or using planes 乘飞机,由空运:It saves a great deal of time to travel *by air*. 乘飞机旅行可节省大量时间。The flowers are sent all over Europe *by air*. 这些鲜花由空运送抵欧洲各地。

NOTE 本短语中的名词 air 可替换成 sea 或 water,构成短语 by sea 或 by water,意为"乘轮船,由海运,由水路",用法与本短语相同。

by all (manner of) means *adv.* ❶(仅用于口语中)(used for politely agreeing with someone, giving permission, or saying "yes") certainly; definitely 当然,必定:"May I invite a few friends?" "*By all means*." "我可以邀请几个朋友吗?" "当然了。" ❷using every possible way; at all costs 竭力,千方百计,不惜一切:The Chinese government has taken a series of measures to further opening up the domestic market and increase export *by all means*. 中国政府采取了一系列措施,以进一步开拓国内市场,同时千方百计增加出口。He even went so far as to set to work, *by all manner of means*, to secure his success. 他为了获得成功甚至不惜一切手段来进行。

NOTE 1. 本短语中的名词 means 必须用复数形式。

2. 本短语的否定形式 not by any manner of means 表示其他意义,即"绝不,绝没有"。见 not by any manner of means。

by all one's might (and main) ⇨ **with all one's might (and main)**

by and by *adv.* ❶(陈旧用法) before long; soon; after a short time 不久,不久以后:You will forget about him *by and by*. 你不久就会把他忘掉的。*By and by* he finished that impossible task. 不久以后,他完成了那件不可能的任务。❷sooner or later 迟早:The mother knew her baby would be a man *by and by* and do a man's work. 这位妈妈知道她的孩子迟早会长大成人,干一份顶天立地的事业。

by and large *adv.* (used for referring to someone or something in a very general way) on the whole; generally speaking; generally 总的说来,大体上:Most people are, *by and large*, aware of the problems faced by a disabled person, but how many are aware of their potentials? 总的说来,大多数人都已意识到残疾人士所面临的诸多问题,但有多少人意识到了他们的潜能? *By and large* I think the emphasis should be on recruiting the right people. 总的说来,我认为重点应放在招收合适的人员上。

NOTE 本短语的同义短语是 in general 和 on the whole。

by any chance *adv.* (非正式用语) ❶if it so happens that 万一:If *by any chance* somebody comes to see me, ask him to leave a message. 万一有人来找我,就请他留个条。If you, *by any chance*, see him, let me know. 你万一看到他的话,告诉我。❷(只用于疑问句中) (used to ask a question in a polite way) perhaps; possibly 可能,也许:Could you lend me a couple of pounds, *by any chance*? 您能借给我几英镑吗? Have you got a spare stamp *by any chance*? 或许你有张多余的邮票吧? Are they *by any chance* related? 它们也许有些关联? Are you Mr Williams, *by any chance*? 请问,您是威廉姆斯先生吗?

NOTE 不要将本短语与 by chance 混淆。

by chance *adv.* accidentally ; without being planned or expected 偶然地,碰巧: It was only *by chance* that I met her in Australia. 我在澳大利亚碰见她纯属偶然。I met one of my former teachers *by chance* on the train. 我在火车上与一位我以前的老师不期而遇。

NOTE 1. 本短语与 by accident 意义和用法相同,两者可互换使用。

2. 本短语的反义短语是 on purpose。

by/in comparison *adv.* (used for talking about the ways in which two things are different) when compared 比较起来,相比之下: *By comparison*, Type A has the advantage of higher cruising speed and Type B has the advantage of great comfort. 比较起来,A 型的优点是航速高,而 B 型的优点是舒适性强。The quality of the new-brand television is good *in comparison*. 相比之下,这种新牌子的电视机质量还是不错的。

NOTE 若表示"与……相比较",则使用 in comparison with 或 in comparison to。见 in comparison with。

by/in contrast *adv.* (used when you are comparing two things or people and saying that the second one is very different from the first) when contrasted 对比之下: The coastal areas have mild winters; *by contrast* the central plains become extremely cold. 沿海地区冬天温暖,可相比之下中部平原却十分寒冷。It is hot in the desert in the day, but *in contrast*, it is very cold at night. 沙漠中白天炎热,晚上却相反,冷得很。

NOTE 本短语与 by/in comparison 意义和用法相近,但本短语更强调前后两种情况之间的悬殊差异。

by day *adv.* during the day 在白天: He worked in the office *by day* and drove a taxi by night. 他白天在办公室上班,夜间开出租车。

NOTE 不要将本短语与 by the day 混淆。它们的形式相似且用法相同,但意义却截然不同。by day 表示"在白天";而 by the day 则表示"以日计算"之意。见 by the day。

by degrees *adv.* slowly and gradually 慢慢地,逐渐地: The angry crowd in front of the Parliament building was thinning, but only *by degrees*. 聚集在议会大厦前的愤怒人群人数在减少。但是,是在慢慢地减少。*By degrees*, their friendship grew into love. 他们之间的友情逐渐地发展成为爱情。

NOTE 本短语中的名词 degree 必须用复数形式。

by far *adv.* (used for saying that something has much more of a particular quality than anything else) much; to a great extent 最……,……得多: This dictionary is *by far* the best. 这词典是最好的一部。She is *by far* the best-looking girl in our school. 她是我们学校最漂亮的女孩。This design is *by far* the better of the two. 在这两种设计中,这种设计要好得多。His work was better *by far* than any other printer in the city. 他的工作比城里其他任何印刷工都好得多。

NOTE 1. 本短语通常用于形容词、副词或形容词最高级所修饰的名词之前,用来加强语气，强调质量、数量、程度等，在句子中作状语。

2. 本短语还可用于修饰比较级，一般置于没有定冠词限定的比较级之后（见最后一个例句）；如用在比较级的前面，比较级前要加上定冠词 the（见倒数第二个例句）。

3. 本短语的同义短语是 far and away。

by force *adv.* by employing violence; by violent means 用强制手段地，用武力地：They left the house by force. 他们被强行搬离这幢房子。The postwar problems can be solved not only *by force*. We also have to engage in dialogue with the people here. 解决战后的问题不能只用武力。我们还得与这里的人民开展对话。

by heart *adv.* by memory 凭记忆，记住地：I've dialed the number so many times I know it *by heart*. 凭记忆我就知道这个电话号码，因为我已经拨过多次。She's learnt the whole speech off *by heart*. 整个发言稿她都记住了。

NOTE 本短语的另外一种表达形式是 off by heart。

by/in leaps and bounds *adv.*（主要用于英国英语中）（used for saying that someone or something improves or increases a lot）very quickly 十分迅速地：His Chinese has improved *by/in leaps and bounds*. 他的中文进步得很快。The profits of our company are increasing *by leaps and bounds*. 我们公司的利润增长迅速。She is gaining *by leaps and bounds*. 她体重增长得很快。

NOTE 1. 本短语中的两个名词都必须用复数形式。

2. by leaps and bounds 比 in leaps and bounds 更常用。

by means of *prep.*（正式用语）by using or with the help of (a particular method, instrument, or process) 用，凭借，靠，通过：We express our thoughts *by means of* words. 我们用言语来表达思想。*By means of* monthly payments, they bought a flat. 他们利用按月分期付款的方式买了一套房子。He will try his utmost to help them *by means of* his conventional medical knowledge. 他会尽全力用他的传统医疗知识帮助他们。He made his fortune *by means of* smuggling. 他靠走私发了家。

NOTE 本短语中的名词 means 必须用复数形式。

by mistake *adv.* ❶ as the result of a mistake; through error 由于失误，错误地：He put salt into his tea *by mistake*. 他错把盐放进了自己的茶水中。*By mistake* she sent the message complaining about the boss's lack of feelings to the boss's daughter! 她误将抱怨老板缺少人情味的信息发给了老板的女儿！❷accidentally; without intending to 意外地；无意地：He locked himself out *by mistake*. 他不小心把自己锁在了门外。I'm sorry; I opened one of your letters *by mistake*. 对不起，我无意中把你的一封信拆开了。

NOTE 1. 当本短语作"由于失误，错误地"解时，与 in error 意义相近，但在用法上有所不同。本短语只在句子中作状语，而 in error 不仅可用作状语，还可用作表语。见 in error。

2. 当本短语作"意外地"解时，同义短语是 by accident。但本短语着重强调由于判断或操作有误而造成意外结果。

3. 本短语的反义短语是 on purpose。

by night *adv.* during the night 在夜间：In the desert we traveled *by night* to avoid the intense heat. 我们在沙漠中都是夜间

旅行以避开酷热。What is done *by night* appears by day. 若要人不知，除非己莫为。

by no means *adv.* (正式用语) (used as a way of emphasizing a negative statement) in no way; not at all; not in the least 决不,一点儿也不: It was *by no means* excellent but still better than last year. 这决谈不上很好,但比去年的好多了。*By no means* should petrol be placed near the fire. 决不要把汽油放在靠近火的地方。I advise him *by no means* to be involved in their trouble. 我劝他决不要卷入他们的纠纷中去。

NOTE **1.** 本短语中的名词 means 必须用复数形式。

2. 当本短语用于句首时,句中的主谓结构一定要倒装。例如:

> *By no means* shall we misunderstand you.
> 我们绝不会误解你的。

但是,当本短语置于句中较后的部分时,句中的主谓结构则不用倒装。

3. 本短语另外的表达形式是 by no manner of means和 not by any means。

4. 本短语与 in no way, not at all, not in the least 和 not by any manner of means 意义相同,常可互换使用。not at all 比较通俗,常用于日常口语中;in no way 在语气上更加郑重一些;not by any manner of means 用于英国英语的口语中,其语气比较正式,但用法已陈旧;not in the least 与本短语一样,语气较强,含有"绝对不""丝毫不"的意味。

(all) by oneself Ⅰ *adv.* & *adj.* (completely) alone; unaccompanied 独自一个地(的),单独地(的),仅仅:She was sitting there *all by herself*. 她孤零零地一个人坐在那里。The house stood *by itself* on a hill. 那所房子独立在小山之上。If you enjoy being *by yourself*, I'll leave you. 如果你喜欢独自一个人待着,那我就走了。She was *all by herself* in that big house when I called. 当我拜访她时,那间大房子里仅有她一个人。He sat *by himself* in the corner, waiting quietly. 他独自坐在角落里静静地等待着。Her story *by itself* is not enough to convict him. 仅靠她的陈述不足以证明他有罪。

Ⅱ *adv.* without being helped by anyone else; unassisted 独立地: He couldn't have planned the whole thing *by himself*. 他无法独立做出全部的安排。You can't carry that big table *all by yourself*. 你自个儿是无法搬动那张大桌子的。We can finish the task *by ourselves*. 我们能独立完成这项任务。

by phone *adv.* using the telephone to talk to someone 用电话,通过打电话: We take orders *by phone* or by email. 我们通过电话或电子邮件接收订货。I spoke to him and talked the matter over *by phone*. 我和他通过电话,谈论了这件事情。

NOTE **1.** 本短语的另外一种表达形式是 by telephone。

2. 本短语的同义短语是 over the phone。

3. 本短语的反义短语是 off the phone. 例如:

> I wish my son would get *off the phone*.
> 但愿我的儿子不用电话了。

by reason of *prep.* (正式用语) because of; on account of; owing to 因为,由于: *By reason of* his illness, he was excused from the meeting. 他因病获准免予参加会议。The scheme failed *by reason of* bad organization. 该计划因组织不善而告失败。*By reason of* a crop failure, the prices of rice and oil are bound to rise. 由于作物歉收,粮油价格肯定要上涨。

NOTE 本短语与 because of 意义相同,在用法上比 because of 正式,也不及 because of 常用。

by right(s) *adv.* if things were done as they should be; in fairness; justly 按理应当,正当地: *By rights*, we should split the profits among the three of us. 按理来说,这利润应当由我们三个人分享。The post of vice-president should, *by rights*, have been given to Mr Johnson. 公正来说,这副校长的职位本应该给约翰逊先生。The property belongs to her *by right*. 这份财产理应归属于她。

by sea ⇨ **by air**

by the by ⇨ **by the way**

by the day *adv.* in the measure of the day; based on a day 按日计算: When I worked there I was paid *by the day*. 我在那里做工时是按日计酬的。He paid the laborer *by the day*. 他按日支付雇工的工资。The boat can be hired *by the day*. 小艇可以按日租用。

NOTE 不要将本短语与 by day 混淆,两者意义不同。by day 意为"在白天"。

by the hour *adv.* in the measure of the hour; based on an hour (of work) 按小时计算: You can hire a bicycle *by the hour* to go around the city. 你可以按小时租一辆自行车在城里观光。Are you paid *by the hour*? 你们是按小时付酬吗?

NOTE 不要将本短语与 on the hour 混淆。on the hour 意为"在整点"。

by the same token *adv.* (前面常用连词 and 或 but) (used to mean that something you are about to say is also true)in a similar manner; for a similar reason 同样地,由于同样原因: *By the same token*, don't stop the proceedings and bother a user with problems that are not serious. 同样地,不要因为一些小问题而停止进程打扰用户。I agreed that he hasn't given us many new ideas, but *by the same token* neither have we given him any. 我承认他没给我们提供很多新主意,但同样我们也没给他提供任何主意。He comes from a poor family, and *by the same token*, he was unable to acquire the education. 他出身贫苦之家,就是由于这个原因,他未能受什么教育。

by the way *adv.* (非正式用语) (used for saying that a remark is not relevant to the main subject of your conversation or to introduce a new subject or one that has not been mentioned earlier) incidentally; in addition (用于在谈话中岔开或重启话题)顺便提(问)一下,还有: *By the way*, I wonder if we could discuss my salary some time. 顺便问一下,我想知道我们能不能找个时间讨论一下我的工资问题。What did you have for your lunch, *by the way*? 顺便问一下,你午餐吃的什么? *By the way*, Mr Smith called this afternoon and he wants you to call him back. 还有,史密斯先生下午打来电话,他让你给他回电话。

NOTE 本短语的同义短语是 by the by,但本短语更为常用。

by turns *adv.* ❶ (of persons, groups, actions, etc.) one after another; first one and then another in a regular order 轮流,依次,交替: The doctors are on duty *by turns*. 医生都轮流值班。On the drive to London, they took the wheel *by turns*. 在驾车去伦敦的旅途中,他们轮流开车。❷changing from one state to another 从一种状态变化到另一种状态;忽而……忽而……: When John had a fever, he felt cold and hot *by turns*. 当约翰发烧时,他感到一阵冷,一阵热。He grew pale and red *by turns*. 他的脸一会儿红一

会儿白。

NOTE 1. 本短语中的名词 turn 必须用复数形式。

2. 本短语与 in turn 都表示“轮流,依次”。但 in turn 又表示“然后”之意,强调“后来”这个时间点,例如:

> I told Frank the news and he *in turn* told Sheila.
> 我把消息告诉了弗兰克,后来弗兰克又告诉给了希拉。

by virtue of *prep.* (正式用语) because of or as a result of 由于,因为:He got the job in the laboratory *by virtue of* his qualification. 他是凭着他的资格获得这个实验室的工作的。He claimed a pension *by virtue of* his long military service. 他以在军中服役多年为由要求发给养老金。Plastic bags are used widely *by virtue of* their transparency, toughness, and low cost. 塑料袋因其透明、结实、成本低而得到广泛的使用。

NOTE 1. 本短语与 because of 和 as a result of 意义相同,但本短语一般只用于书面语中。

2. 本短语的另外一种表达形式是 in virtue of。

by water ⇨ **by air**

by way of *prep.* (正式用语) ❶ by the route of or passing through (something such as a place on your journey); via (something) 经由……,取道……:They went to the school *by way of* the church. 他们去学校的途中经过那座教堂。In 1992, I flew to Hawaii *by way of* Tokyo. 1992 年,我是取道东京飞往夏威夷的。❷ for the sake or purpose of; with the intention of or the purpose of (something or doing something) 为了……:“It's a nice day,” she said, merely *by way of* conversation. “天气不错啊。”她这样说只是为了打开话头而已。They worked so hard *by way of* solving the problems. 他们工作如此努力是为了解决那些问题。❸ as a form of (something) or serving as (something) 以……形式或方式,作为……:He received £5,000 in cash *by way of* compensation from the company. 作为公司的一种赔偿形式,他获得了 5 000 英镑的现金。He sent me some flowers *by way of* apology. 他送我一些花作为道歉。*By way of* examples, he described his own experience. 他描述了自己的经历,以其作为例子。❹ as a method of or by means of 借着……,通过……:To help the small enterprises, the state gives them support *by way of* subsidy. 国家通过补贴的方式来扶助小型企业。

NOTE 本短语中的名词 way 前不能加任何冠词。

C

C c

calculate on/upon *vt.* 【不可分性动词短语】(主要用于美国英语中,正式用语,常用一般时态) depend on (something for your plans to succeed); expect (something to happen)依靠,指望,料想: We *calculate on* your help. 我们就依靠你们的帮助了。We *calculated upon* making an early start. 我们指望一早就出发。Don't *calculate on* him agreeing with you. 不要指望他会同意你的意见。We had not *calculated on* any problem with the application. 我们没料想到在申请上会出问题。

NOTE 本短语中的 upon 用法比 on 正式,但不及 on 常用。

call a spade a spade *vi.* (非正式用语) speak very frankly and directly what you think about someone or something even if it is unpleasant 实话实说,实事求是,直言不讳: Let's *call a spade a spade*. The man is a liar. 咱们就实话实说吧。那个人是个骗子。He believes in *calling a spade a spade* and never tries to conceal his own opinions. 他是个实事求是的人,从不隐瞒自己的观点。*Calling a spade a spade* on foreign affairs sometimes seems difficult for diplomats. 外交官在处理外交事务的时候很难做到直言不讳。

NOTE 本短语一般表示直言不讳地说出令他人窘迫、尴尬或不快的事情,为褒义用法。

call at *vt.* 【不可分性动词短语】❶ (of someone) stop to make a short visit to (a place) on the way to another place (指人)顺路到访(某处): Shall we *call at* Mr Green's while we are in Washington? 我们在华盛顿期间去格林先生家拜访吗? I *called at* the office as I was passing, but you were out. 我路经您的办公室时进去拜访您,但您不在。Can you *call at* the shop on your way home and get some milk? 你能在回家的路上到商店买些牛奶吗? ❷ (英国英语用法) (of a train, bus, or ship) stop at a place for a short time, especially to allow people to get on or off, during its journey (指车、船)途中停靠(某处): This train *calls at* Hagley and all stations to Birmingham. 这趟开往伯明翰的列车在黑格利和所有的沿途车站都停。

NOTE **1.** 当本短语作"(指人)顺路到访(某处)"解时,短语后不能接"某人",而只能接"某一地点"。例如:"我们的新邻居上星期曾来我家拜访。"这个句子,我们不能说: * Our new neighbors *called at* us last week. 应该说: Our new neighbors *called at* our house last week.

2. 当本短语作"(指人)顺路到访(某处)"解时,与 call by 意义相同,但两者的用法不同。本短语为及物性动词短语,而 call by 是不及物性动词短语,见 call by。

call attention to *vt.* make (someone)

notice and think about (someone or something)引起(某人)对……的注意:My friend Mary was too proud of her good looks, and was always trying to *call attention to* herself. 我的朋友玛丽为自己的美貌过于感到自傲,所以总是设法吸引别人对自己的注意。The demonstration was intended to *call attention to* the difficult situation of endangered species. 这次游行的目的是使人们注意到濒危物种所处的困境。I'd like to *call* your *attention to* this problem. 我想提请你对这个问题引起注意。Their *attention* was *called to* substituting plastic for steel. 提请他们注意用塑料来代替钢材。

call away *vt.* (常用被动语态形式) ask (someone) to leave a place, usually by telephoning him or sending him a message (常指通过打电话或捎信的方式)把(某人)叫走:Something urgent has *called* him *away*. 因有要紧的事把他叫走了。He was *called away* unexpectedly today, which is why I came to meet you instead. 他今天突然被请走了,所以我代他来接您。The doctor has been *called away* to deal with an emergency. 医生被请去看急诊了。

call back *vt. &vi.* ❶telephone (someone) for the second time at a later time 给(某人)再次打电话:I'm sorry but Mr Lewis is in a meeting at the moment. Can you *call back* later? 对不起,刘易斯先生现正在开会。您等会儿再打电话来,好吗? She'll *call back* Mark when she's heard something. 她听到消息就会再给马克打电话的。Since she is not there, I'll *call* her *back* in an hour. 既然她现在没在那里,我一个小时后再给她打电话吧。❷return a telephone call to (someone who telephoned you earlier)给(某人)回电话:The note says I am to call back. 那个留言要我回电话。I'll have to *call back* my wife now. 我现在得给我夫人回电话了。By the way, Mr Smith called this afternoon and he wants you to *call* him *back*. 顺便提一下,史密斯先生下午打来电话,他让你给他回电话。

—*vt.* recall (a defective product) for repair 召回(有缺陷的产品):Japan's largest auto maker Toyota plans to *call back* 1,113 Lexus GS 430/300 series in China which reportedly have design defects in front seat safety belt. 日本最大的汽车制造商丰田公司拟召回在中国市场的 1 113 辆雷克萨斯 GS430/300 系列车。据报道,这些车辆上安装的前座椅安全带设计有缺陷。

—*vi.* pay another visit, usually for a short time 再次访问:The salesman will *call back* later. 推销员待会儿会再来。"I'll *call back* later and see how you are," the doctor said. "我待会儿再来,看你的情况怎样。"医生说道。

NOTE 当本短语用作及物性动词短语,所带的宾语为代词时,该代词须置于本短语的动词和副词中间。

call by *vi.* (英国英语用法,非正式用语,常用一般时态) visit for a short time, usually when you are going somewhere else 顺路到访:I'll *call by* at the shop on my way home. 我回家时顺路去商店吧。Do you want me to *call by* tomorrow? 你想让我明天来坐一坐吗?

call down *vt.* 【可分性动词短语】❶ask (someone) to come downstairs 叫(某人)下楼:They *called* him *down* from upstairs to answer the telephone. 他们把他从楼上叫下来接电话。❷(美国英语用法,非正式用语) scold (someone);

speak to (someone) in an angry way 责骂(某人),严厉斥责(某人): His father *called down* Tom in front of his girl friend. 汤姆的爸爸当着汤姆女朋友的面责骂了他。The boy was *called down* by his teacher for coming to class late. 这男孩因上课迟到而受到了老师的训斥。He *called* me *down* for my absence at the important meeting. 他因我没有参加那次重要的会议而严厉地斥责了我。

C

NOTE 当本短语所带的宾语为代词时,该代词须置于本短语的动词和副词中间。

call down on *vt.*【可分性动词短语】(正式用语,无被动语态形式) pray for (something bad) to happen to (someone) 祈求……降祸于(某人): The priest *called down* punishment *on* these people for their misdeeds. 神父祈求上帝因他们的恶行而惩罚这些人。

call for *vt.*【不可分性动词短语】❶require or demand; ask for 要求,呼吁: They *called for* further reform and opening-up in the central regions. 他们要求进一步推进中部地区的改革与开放。President Obama *called for* closing the US prison at Guantanamo Bay, Cuba, within a year. 奥巴马总统要求在一年内关闭美国设在古巴关塔那摩湾的监狱。The minister's resignation was *called for* by several senators. 有几位参议员要求该部长辞职。The opposition party *called for* the government to hold parliamentary elections on schedule. 反对党呼吁政府按原定时间举行议会选举。❷(主要用于英国英语中) come or go somewhere and get (someone or something) in order to take them to another place; collect (something) 接(某人);取回(某物): I'll *call for* you at your house at eleven. 我 11 点钟到你家去接你。Your parcel was at the post office to be *called for*. 你的包裹在邮局里待你取回来。❸ask for (something or someone) 要,叫: He entered the restaurant and *called for* a bottle of beer. 他走进饭馆,要了一瓶啤酒。Henry *called for* the waiter in a loud voice. 亨利大声地叫服务员。❹(用一般时态) need or deserve (a particular action or quality) 需要,应得: This sort of work *calls for* a lot of patience. 这种工作需要极大的耐性。Such a scheme will *call for* a lot of money. 这样一个计划需要很多钱。The quality is variable, so careful selection is *called for*. 质量好坏不同,所以需要仔细挑选一下。You are getting married? This *calls for* a celebration! 你要结婚了?这值得庆贺一番!

call in *v.* ❶(常用一般时态) visit (someone or a place) usually for a short time (常指短时间)拜访(某人),到访(某处): I'll *call in* tomorrow and we can discuss it then. 我明天去拜访你,到时咱们好把这事商量一下。I *called in* to see Jeff yesterday. 我昨天探望了杰夫。I'm wondering whether to *call in* on Mark on the way home. 我在想是否在回家的路上拜访一下马克。Will you *call in* at the bank on your way home? 在你回家的路上能到银行去一下吗?❷call (someone) to come indoors 叫(某人)进来: The manager *called* me *in* and demanded an explanation. 经理叫我进去,并要求我做出解释。I waited for only two minutes before I was *called in*. 我只等了两分钟就被叫了进去。❸ ask (a person or organization that provides a service) to come and deal with something 请(某人或某一机构)前来处理问题: Father is very ill; you have to *call* a heart specialist *in* at once. 爸爸病得很厉害,你得马上请一位心脏病专家过来。The doctor was *called in* to an emergency case last night. 昨晚医生被请来看急诊。The company has *called in* the police to investigate. 该公司已请来警察进行调查。❹request the return of (something)要求收回(或归还):The makers have *called in* some cars with dangerous faults. 制造厂商召回一些有危险性缺陷的汽车。The car company *called* many cars back *in* for repairs. 该汽车公司召回了许多汽车进行修理。The bank is *calling in* all its short-term loans. 银行正在回收其全部短期贷款。Some books are not fit for the children to read, so they have been *called in* by the library. 有些书籍不适于孩子们阅读,所以图书馆已把它们收回。❺telephone (a radio or television program) with a comment or question 给(广播电台或电视台的节目组)打电话提出评论(或问题):It's a hot topic, and people have been *calling in* all morning. 这是个热门话题,整个上午人们打给节目组的电话连续不断。

NOTE 本短语与 call at 和 call by 都表示"到访",但它们在用法上有所不同:call at 为及物性动词短语,后接表示"某处或某地"(但不能接表示"某人")的名词宾语。而本短语用作此意义时,既有及物又有不及物性用法。作为及物性用法,其后可接表示"某处或某地"的名词作宾语,如后接"某人",则其前要加介词 on。而 call by 则是不及物性动词短语,如若表示到访"某处、某地"时,要后加介词 at。

call it a day *vi.* (非正式用语) decide or agree to stop what one has been doing, for the remainder of the day, and leave it to be finished later (决定或同意)停止(正在做的某项工作或活动):I'm tired. Let's *call it a day* and go home. 我累了。咱们停下来回家吧。It's getting pretty late — let's *call it a day* and come back tomorrow. 天很晚了,我们今天就做到这儿,明天再来干吧。At midnight, I *called it a day* and went to bed. 半夜时分,我停下工作上床睡觉了。

NOTE **1.** 本短语实际意义并非表示一天的终结,而是一项工作或活动的中止,而这项工作或活动还有待继续去完成。

2. 本短语的另外一种表达形式是 call it a night。

call (someone) names *v.* use ugly or unkind words when speaking to someone or when talking about someone, (usually used by or to children)(尤指儿童)辱骂(某人),骂人:The other children teased her and *called her names*. 其他的孩子们都取笑她、辱骂她。Tom was punished for *calling* his teacher rude *names*. 汤姆因恶言谩骂老师而受到处分。I object to being *called names*. 我反对别人骂我。

NOTE **1.** 本短语中的名词 name 必须用复数形式。

2. 在 call 和 names 之间只能用人称代词的宾格形式(如 me, us 等),而不能用物主代词(如 my, our 等)。

3. 不要将本短语与 call someone by name 混淆。call someone by name 意为"叫(某人)的名字"。例如:

> If you *call him* just *by* his family *name* he would not answer.
> 如果你只叫他的姓,他是不会应声的。

call off *vt.* 【可分性动词短语】(常用一般时态)❶tell (an animal or person) to stop attacking or chasing someone 叫(人或动物)走开:I yelled to the man to *call off* his dog. 我朝那个人大喊,要他把他的狗叫走。The dog was *called off* when it started to bark at the stranger. 那条狗当刚开始朝陌生人吠叫时，就被叫走了。❷cause (something such as a planned event) not to take place; cancel 取消：She's *called off* the trip. 她取消了旅行。Thousands of people have held demonstrations in Tehran urging authorities to *call off* the election result. 成千上万的人在德黑兰举行示威活动，要求当局取消选举结果。It rained so hard that we had to *call* the appointment *off*. 雨下得太大了，我们只好取消了约会。At first the workers planned to strike, but later they *called* it *off*. 起初，工人们计划要罢工，可后来他们却将其取消。❸ decide to stop (something such as an activity that is already happening); abandon 决定停止(某项已经开始的活动等)；放弃：With the weather worsening, they've *called off* the search for survivors. 由于天气变坏，他们已决定放弃搜寻幸存者。

NOTE 当本短语所带的宾语为代词时，该代词须置于本短语的动词与副词中间。

call on/upon *vt.*【不可分性动词短语】❶visit (someone) formally, either socially or on business; see (someone), usually for a short time 正式拜访(某人)；探望(某人)：We *called on* the dean of the department this morning. 我们今天上午拜访了该系的主任。He had come half a dozen times to *call upon* his sister. 他曾来过五六次看望他的妹妹。❷(正式用语) officially ask (a person or organization) to do something 向(某人或某一组织)正式要求；号召，呼吁(做某事)：China banned shops from giving out free plastic bags and *called on* consumers to use baskets and cloth sacks instead to reduce environmental pollution. 中国禁止商店免费提供塑料袋，并呼吁消费者使用篮子和布袋以减少环境污染。He was *called upon* to give a lecture on the situation in the Middle East. 他被请求作一次有关中东形势的报告。❸(正式用语，后常接介词 for, with 短语或动词不定式短语) invite or choose sb to do something 邀请；挑选：I now *call upon* the chairman to address the meeting. 现在，请主席为大会致辞。I *called on* Robert for his help, but he refused. 我请罗伯特帮忙，但他却拒绝了。The teacher *called on* me with a tough question, and I didn't know the answer. 老师要我回答一道难题，可我不知如何作答。

NOTE 1. 本短语中的 upon 用法比 on 正式，但不及 on 常用。

2. 当本短语作"正式拜访(某人)；探望(某人)"解时，其后的宾语只能是人，而不能是地方。即使其宾语是代词，也只能置于其后，而不可置于中间。例如：我们可以说：We *called on* her this morning. 但不能说：* We *called* her *on* this morning.

call out *v.* ❶shout (something), especially when you are trying to get someone's attention (尤指为引人注意而)叫喊：Hands up! Don't *call out*! 把手举起来！不许叫喊！The driver was *calling out* the names of the stops at which the bus would stop. 司机呼喊着报出汽车要停靠的站名。Each person stepped forward as his name was *called out*. 每个被叫到名字的人都向前跨步。❷(常用被动语态形式) summon away from one's home or place of work (从家或工作岗位)叫走，召走：Only if the case is urgent should you *call out* the doctor. 只有在病情危急时才应请医生出诊。The doctor is not at home; he has been *called out* on an urgent case. 医生不在家，他被叫去看急诊了。❸（常用被动语态形式）order (someone) to do something 命令（某人）做某事：The Government had to *call out* the army to restore order. 政府不得不命令军队来恢复秩序。The opposition party hasn't decided whether to *call* supporters *out* to the streets in protest. 反对党尚未决定是否号召支持者们走上街头进行抗议。All the firemen in the city were *called out* to fight the big fire. 全城的消防队员都奉命来扑救这场大火。❹（非正式用语）cause (workers) to go on strike 发动（工人）罢工：The union leader has *called* all the workers of the factory *out* for more pay. 工会的领导人发动全厂工人罢工，要求增加工资。The miners' leader called out his men. 矿工领袖发动矿工罢工了。

NOTE 当本短语用作及物性动词短语，所带的宾语为代词时，该代词须置于本短语的动词和副词中间。

call (the) roll *vi.* （主要用于美国英语中）read aloud the names of all the people on the list to make certain that they are present 点名：The teacher *called the roll* to see if any students were absent. 老师点名看是否有学生缺席。The only reason I *call the roll* everyday is to force the students to come to class. 我每天点名只有一个原因，就是使学生到课。I will *call roll*, and then we will do arithmetic. 我先点名，然后咱们做算术题。

NOTE **1.** 本短语可转化为名词性短语 roll call，意为"点名"。

2. 本短语与 take roll 意义和用法相同，两者可互换使用。

call to mind *vt.* 【可分性动词短语】（常用一般时态，常用于否定句中）remember; recall 想起……：I cannot *call* his face *to mind* at the moment. 这会儿我想不起他的面容来了。I'm sure I know that man, although I can't *call to mind* where I've met him. 我肯定认识那个人，尽管想不起来在什么地方见过他。

NOTE 本短语与 bring to mind 的第二个义项意义相同。两者在用法上的区别见 bring to mind。

call up *vt.* 【可分性动词短语】❶（主要用于美国英语中，非正式用语，常用一般时态）telephone (someone) 给（某人）打电话：She *called up* a friend just to chat. 她给一位朋友打电话就是为了闲聊。I *called* her *up* and told her the reason why he was so sad. 我给她打电话向她讲了他如此悲伤的原因。I was *called up* on the phone. 有人给我打来电话。❷（常用一般时态）make (someone) remember (something); evoke; recollect 使人想起，回忆起：The sound of seagulls *called up* happy memories of his childhood. 海鸥的叫声勾起了他对童年的美好回忆。Many memories of old times were *called up* by the conversation we had yesterday. 我们昨天的交谈使我回忆起许多往事。❸（英国英语用法，常用被动语态形式）officially make (someone) become a member of the armed forces, especially in a war（尤指在战争期间）征召（某人）服兵役：The government decided to *call up* an adequate number of reserves. 政府决定征召足够数量的预备役人员入伍。He won't be *called up* for military service—he's over age. 他不会被征召服兵役，因为他已经超龄了。❹tell (someone) to come (as before a court) 传唤（某人）（到法庭）：The judge *called up* the three witnesses. 法官传唤三名证人到庭。He was *called up* to give evidence by the investigating committee. 调查委员会传他作证。❺（常用一般时态）use magic to try to make (the spirit of a dead person) appear 用魔法召回（死者的灵

魂):The magician claims to be able to *call up* spirits from the dead. 那魔法师声称他能召回死者的灵魂。

NOTE 本短语与 phone up 和 ring up 都表示"给(某人)打电话"之意。三者所带的宾语如果是代词时,该代词须置于动词 call、phone 或 ring 之后,副词 up 之前。例如:

> I've to call/phone/ring him up before I leave.
> 我临走前,得给他打个电话。

它们三者之间的区别见 ring up。

calm down *v.* make or become more relaxed and less emotional (使)平静下来:*Calm down* and tell us what's going on. 冷静下来,告诉我们发生了什么事。We try to *calm* him *down*, but he kept shouting and swearing. 我们试图使他平静下来,但他仍然不停地叫骂着。Can you *calm down* your yapping dog? 你能不能让你这条狂吠不止的狗安静下来?

NOTE 当本短语用作及物性动词短语,所带的宾语为代词时,该代词须置于本短语的动词和副词中间。

cannot be helped ⇨ **cannot help**

cannot (help) but *v.* (后接原形动词) have no choice except (to do something); can only 无法不(做某事),禁不住(做某事):Since it is raining hard outside, I *cannot but* stay in. 由于外面的雨下得很大,我只好待在家中。I *could not help but* like her. 我禁不住地喜欢上了她。I *couldn't help but* realize that something had gone wrong. 我不禁意识到出事了。

NOTE cannot but 是 cannot do anything but 的省略式,虽与 cannot help but 意义和用法相同,但在使用场合上却有所不同:cannot but 为正式用语,而 cannot help but 则为非正式用语。在英国英语中,这两个条目可视为一条。

cannot help *vt.* (后面不能接动词原形) used for saying that someone cannot stop themselves doing something 忍不住,禁不住(做某事):A migrant worker *could not help* smiling when receiving the National Labor Medal on May Day, the country's highest honor for industrial workers. 一位外来务工人员在接受对产业工人来说是国家最高荣誉的"五一全国劳动奖章"时,不禁笑逐颜开。The boy can be very rude but at the same time you *can't help* liking him. 这男孩可能有些粗野,尽管这样,他还是挺讨人喜欢的。We *cannot help* being impressed by their enthusiasm. 我们不禁为他们的热情所打动。

NOTE 1. 本短语后常接动名词或动名词短语,亦可接人称代词或反身代词作宾语。例如:

> She burst out crying; she *couldn't help* it.
> 她突然大哭起来;她实在忍不住了。(代词 it 用来指前句中的动名词 crying)
> I shouldn't have said it but I *couldn't help* myself.
> 我本不该说那件事,但我无法控制自己。

2. 本短语不用被动语态形式,cannot be helped 的形式仅用于 It cannot be helped. 中,意为"这是无可避免的"。例如:

> We learned about your father's death. But don't be so sad; *it can't be helped*.
> 我们得知您父亲去世了,但不要如此悲伤。这是没办法的事情。
> I'm handicapped, but *it cannot be helped*.
> 我身有残疾,但对此无奈。

3. 不要将本短语与 cannot help but 混淆,两者的意义和用法都不相同。

capable of *adj.* ❶ having the ability, capacity, or potential to do something 有

……能力的,能……的:Air Force One, the special plane of the US President, is *capable of* flying half way around the world without refueling. 美国总统的专机"空军一号"能绕地球飞半圈而不用加油。Show your boss what you are *capable of*. 向你的老板展示你的才能。College graduates *capable of* deep reflection are what our world needs. 我们这个世界还是需要能够深思的大学毕业生。❷(of something) ready for; open to (指物)易于……的,可以……的:That remark is *capable of* being misunderstood. 那样的话易于被人误解。The situation is *capable of* improvement. 这种情况可以改善。

NOTE 1. 本短语的比较级形式是 more capable of,最高级形式是 most capable of。

2. 当本短语作"有……能力的,能……的"解时,反义短语是 incapable of。

capitalize on/upon *vt.*【不可分性动词短语】use (an event or a situation) to help you achieve something or gain some advantage 利用(某一事件或形势)达到目的(或获得益处):She *capitalized on* her opponent's mistake and won the game. 她利用了对手的失误而赢得了那场比赛。I'm *capitalizing on* being in bed sick by reading lots of books. 我在利用卧病在床的机会阅读大量的书籍。He is trying to *capitalize on* popular discontent with the government. 他企图利用人们对政府的普遍不满来达到自己的目的。

NOTE 1. 本短语中的 upon 用法比 on 正式,但不及 on 常用。

2. 本短语的同义短语是 take advantage of。

care about *vt.*【不可分性动词短语】❶have or feel concern for (someone or something) 关心:She's selfish — she doesn't *care about* other people at all. 她自私自利,一点也不关心别人。The only thing our boss *cares about* is money. 我们老板唯一关心的就是钱。❷(无被动语态形式,用一般时态) be interested in (someone or something); be worried by (something) 对……感兴趣,在乎,担心:I don't think she *cares about* him at all. 我认为她对他根本就不感兴趣。No one seemed to care about her feelings. 似乎没人在乎她的感受。He doesn't *care about* whether you air your views or not. 他不在乎你发不发表意见。❸(用一般时态) like or be fond of (someone or something) 喜欢:They really *care about* the new students in their classes. 他们真的很喜欢班里的新同学。I don't *care about* this kind of thing. 我不喜欢这类东西。

NOTE 1. 本短语多用于否定句、疑问句和条件状语从句中。

2. 本短语与 care for 均有"关心""喜欢"之意,但在用法上略有不同。care for 更常用于否定句和疑问句中,在日常生活中,care for 也更常用。

care for *vt.*【不可分性动词短语】❶love (someone), especially in a way that is based on friendship rather than sex 喜欢,喜爱(某人):Do you *care for* the new boy? 你喜欢新来的那个男生吗? He really *cared for* her. 他真的喜爱她。❷(正式用语,不用被动语态形式,用一般时态,一般用于否定句和疑问句中) like or want (something)喜欢,想要(某物):I don't *care* much *for* tea; I like coffee better. 我不太喜欢喝茶,我更喜欢喝咖啡。Would you *care for* a drink? 你喜欢喝点什么饮料吗? Do you *care for* modern music? 你喜欢现代音乐吗? ❸ feel trouble or anxiety about; have regard for or show concern for (someone or something)对……感到担忧,关心……:We have a tradition of *caring for* people's safety. 我们有着关心"人民安

全"的传统。❹attend or take care of (someone especially old or sick people or children, or animals)看护,照料(尤指老人、病人或儿童,以及动物):She *cared for* her mother in her dying months. 她在母亲临终前弥留的几个月里一直看护着她。Children who lost their parents in the massive earthquake must be properly *cared for*. 大地震中丧失父母的孩子们必须得到适当的照顾。Teach your children how to *care for* their pets. 教孩子学会怎样照料他们的宠物。❺treat(something) carefully so that it stays in good condition; look after (something) 保管,照料(某物):Your clothes won't last if you don't *care for* them properly. 如果不适当地保养你的衣物,它们就穿不了多久。Who will *care for* the house while the family is away? 全家人都外出时,由谁照料这所房子呢?

carry about/along/around *vt.*【可分性动词短语】(常与 with 连用) carry (something) with you 随身携带(某物):Be sure to *carry* the library card *about* with you when you go to the library. 去图书馆时一定要带上图书证。The director came to the meeting, *carrying* a portable computer *along* (with him). 董事带了一台手提电脑来开会。I *carry* memories of my homeland *around* with me. 我心中时刻想着我的祖国。

NOTE 当本短语所带的宾语为代词时,该代词须置于本短语的动词和副词中间。

carry away *vt.*【可分性动词短语】❶hold (something or someone) using your hands, arms, or body and take them somewhere 把……拿走,送走,带走:The milkman *carried* the empty milk bottles *away*. 送奶员把空奶瓶拿走了。Ambulances rushed to the site of explosion, and *carried* several wounded people *away* to hospital. 救护车迅速赶到了爆炸地点,把几名受伤的人送往医院。On Sunday morning some of the protesters who refused to leave the presidential building were *carried away* by force. 星期日早晨,一些不肯撤离总统府的抗议者被强行拖走。❷steal (someone or something) 偷走:The middle-aged woman *carried away* the child when no one was looking. 那名中年妇女趁没人看着时把孩子偷走了。Someone *carried* our grass cutter away while we were *away* for holiday. 我们外出度假期间,有人偷走了我们的割草机。❸(常用被动语态形式) (cause to) fill with strong feeling or excitement, especially so as to cause unreasonable behavior 充满激情,兴奋不已:The audience was *carried away* by the young singer's performance. 听众们都为那位年轻歌手的演唱而兴奋不已。Let's not get *carried away*. The deal could still fall through. 咱们不要过于兴奋,这笔买卖还有可能落空。The fervor of his speech *carried away* the whole crowd. 他讲话中的激情使所有的听众兴奋不已。Music has *carried* him *away*. 音乐使他忘乎所以。

NOTE 1. 当本短语作"偷走"解时,同义短语是 carry off。

2. 当本短语所带的宾语为代词时,该代词须置于本短语的动词和副词中间。

carry back *vt.*【可分性动词短语】❶bring back (something or someone)把……拿回,放回,带回:Please *carry* the chair *back* to where it was. 请把椅子放回原处。Sarah *carried* her cup of coffee *back* to her desk. 萨拉把她那杯咖啡放回到了自己的桌子上。❷(用一般时态,常与 to 连用) make (someone) return in thought or memory 使(某人)回想起:That incident *carried* me *back* to my schooldays. 那一偶然事件使我回想起了我的学生时代。

NOTE 当本短语所带的宾语为代词时,该代词须置于本短语的动词和副词中间。

carry forward *vt.*【可分性动词短语】cause (someone or something) to advance 使前进,促进,推进,发扬: The politician's successful speech *carried* him *forward*. 这个政治家成功的演讲使他在仕途上又前进了一步。It would be a wise choice for a country to *carry forward* its fine cultural heritages. 弘扬本民族优秀文化遗产将是一个国家的明智选择。We need to *carry forward* the reform of monopoly industries. 我们需要推进垄断行业的改革。The slogan says, "*Carry* the revolutionary tradition *forward* and gain still greater glory." 标语上写着:"发扬革命传统,争取更大光荣。"

NOTE 当本短语所带的宾语为代词时,该代词须置于本短语的动词和副词中间。

carry into *vt.* take (usually something) into (a place) 把(某物)带入(某处): Please *carry* this chair *into* the classroom for me. 请帮我把这把椅子搬到教室里去。The heroic astronaut *carried* the dreams of our nation *into* the space. 英雄的宇航员把我们民族的梦想带入了太空。

carry off *vt.*【可分性动词短语】❶ take (something or someone) by force 夺走,强行带走: They broke into the armory and *carried off* all the rifles. 他们闯入武器库,拿走了所有的步枪。The soldiers seized the young man and *carried* him *off*. 士兵们抓住那名青年并强行把他带走。❷ steal (someone or something) 偷走: Thieves *carried off* most of our valuables at home last night. 昨天夜里,小偷盗走了我家里大部分值钱的物品。❸(非正式用语,无被动语态形式,常用一般时态) perform or do (a part, action, duty, etc.) successfully (成功地)扮演(角色),完成(任务、职责等): Both actors have the self-confidence needed to *carry off* these roles. 这两名演员都有把角色扮演好所必需的自信心。She *carried off* her part in the plan with no difficulty. 她轻而易举地完成了她在该项计划中所承担的任务。It's a risky venture and I'm not sure they'll be able to *carry* it *off*. 这是一个风险项目,我说不准他们能否将其做好。He *carried* the speech *off* well despite feeling nervous. 尽管感到紧张,他还是很好地完成他的发言。❹ win (a prize, trophy, etc.) 赢得(奖品、奖杯等): Who has *carried off* the first prize in the contest? 是谁赢得了比赛的一等奖? Our team *carried off* most of the medals in the race. 我们队在赛跑项目中赢得了大部分奖牌。❺(非正式用语,用一般时态) cause the death of 造成……死亡: Cholera has *carried off* many people in some countries in Latin America. 在拉丁美洲的一些国家中,霍乱已造成了许多人死亡。She was *carried off* by a heart attack. 她因突发心脏病而故去。Pneumonia *carried* him *off* last winter. 去年冬天,肺炎夺去了他的生命。

NOTE 当本短语所带的宾语为代词时,该代词须置于本短语的动词和副词中间。

carry on *v.* ❶(常用一般时态) (cause to) continue doing (something), especially in spite of an interruption (使)继续进行: They decided to *carry on* in spite of the weather. 不管天气怎样,他们决定继续干下去。Now we can *carry on* with our work. 现在我们可以继续工作了。Even after the music started they *carried on* talking. 甚至在音乐响起之后,他们还继

续说话。The glorious patriotic tradition should be further *carried on*. 光荣的爱国主义传统应该继续得到发扬。❷conduct (a business, conversation, etc.) 经营(生意),进行(谈话或对话等): Bill and his father *carried on* a hardware business here for years. 比尔和他的父亲在这里经营五金生意多年了。We propose to *carry on* extensive inter-civilization dialogue and closer cultural exchanges. 我们主张进行广泛的文明对话和更密切的文化交流。❸(非正式用语,常用进行时态) behave in an angry, excited, or emotional way 发脾气,吵闹,哭叫: "It's no good you *carrying on*, Mother," said Mary. "I'm not going to marry him tomorrow." "您不用这样发脾气,妈妈。我不会很快就嫁给他的。"玛丽说道。I wish you'd stop *carrying on* about it. 我希望你不要再对此事吵闹了。You should have heard her *carrying on* when we told her the news. 你应该听到在我们告诉她这个消息后她的哭闹声。❹(非正式用语,常用进行时态,常与 with 连用) have a sexual relationship (with someone), especially an improper one (与某人)有(尤指不正当的)男女关系: Did you know she's been *carrying on* with her boss? 你知不知道她一直在和她的老板有不正当的男女关系?

NOTE 本短语可转化为复合词 carry-on,意为"大惊小怪,不得体的行为"。

carry out *vt.* 【可分性动词短语】❶lift (something or someone) and take it or him/her out 拿出,搬出,抬出: Mary, could you please *carry* the tea things *out* into the garden? 玛丽,你能把茶具拿出来放到花园里吗? Hours after the assassination, the former prime minster's body was *carried out* of the hospital. 暗杀发生几个小时后,前总理的遗体就被抬出了医院。❷(常用一般时态) do (a particular piece of work); put into practice 做,进行,从事,执行: Qatar's Oil Minister told *TIME* that prices would rise further if the US *carries out* a military strike on Iran. 卡塔尔石油部长对《时代》杂志说,如果美国对伊朗进行军事打击,石油价格还会进一步上涨。All staff *carrying out* healthcare tasks must be appropriately trained. 所有执行医疗保健任务的工作人员都必须得到适当的训练。❸fulfil (a promise, duty, etc.) 履行(诺言、义务等): I expect her to *carry out* her promise. 我希望她能履行自己的诺言。They have failed to *carry out* their obligations. 他们没有履行其义务。

NOTE 当本短语所带的宾语为代词时,该代词须置于本短语的动词和副词中间。

carry over *vi.* (用一般时态,常与 from, to 或 into 连用) be left; continue to exist or apply in the new situation 遗留,延续: The money will *carry over* to his children. 这笔款将遗留给他的孩子们。You are not allowed to *carry over* holiday entitlement from one year into the next. 把你当年应享有的假期留到下一年休是不允许的。This habit *carries over* from my childhood. 这个习惯是从我童年时期延续下来的。What you learn in school should *carry over* into adult life. 你应该把在学校所学的知识沿用到成年生活中。

—*vt.* (常与 to 连用) defer (something) until a particular time 把……推迟(到某一时间): Can we *carry* this discussion *over* until later? 我们能否把这次讨论往后推迟一下? OK, let's *carry over* our discussion to next Monday. 好吧,咱们就

把讨论推迟到下周一。

NOTE 本短语可转化为复合词 carry-over，意为"遗留物，残存物"。

carry the day ⇨ **win the day**

carry through *vt.*【可分性动词短语】❶(常与 into 连用) lift (something or someone) into another space 把(某物)搬到(某处)，把(某人)背(或抱)到(某处)：The waiter collected the dishes from the kitchen and *carried* them *through* into the restaurant. 侍者从厨房收理好盘碟，然后把它们拿进餐厅。In the city center, the union leader was *carried through* the streets on the shoulders of demonstrators, shouting "Unity is power!" 在市中心，示威者们用肩膀抬着工会领导人，高呼"团结就是力量!"的口号走过大街。❷accomplish; bring (something) to a successful end, often in spite of difficulties 完成(某事)，将(某事)进行到底：Despite powerful opposition, they managed to *carry* their reforms *through*. 尽管遇到了强大的阻力，他们还是设法进行了改革。Our fight will be *carried through* to the end. 我们将把斗争进行到底。❸ bring (someone) safely out of trouble, difficulty, etc. 使(某人)脱离麻烦，渡过难关：When the tyre blew out, what Jim had learned in his driving class *carried* him *through* safely. 轮胎爆裂了，吉姆在驾驶课上学过的知识帮他安全解难。His strong determination *carried* him *through* many difficulties. 他坚强的意志使他渡过了许多难关。

carry weight *vi.* (of a person or his or her opinion) be respected and have influence (某人或意见)有影响，受尊重：They knew that Senator Kerry *carries* much/a lot of *weight* in Washington. 他们知道，克里参议员在华盛顿有很大影响。What you say *carries* no *weight* with me. 你说什么对我没有任何影响。Dr James has worked in the university for over 30 years, and his opinions *carry* great *weight*. 詹姆斯博士在这所大学中已工作了 30 多年，他所发表的意见很受尊重。

cash in on *vt.*【不可分性动词短语】(非正式用语) use (an opportunity) to earn money or make a profit, or gain an advantage from (something), often in an unfair or dishonest way (常指不公平或不正当地)利用(某一机会)从……中赚钱(或获益)：These companies are *cashing in on* the gas shortage by raising prices. 这些公司利用汽油短缺之机抬高价格。The opposition was not slow to *cash in on* the unpopularity of the measures announced by the government. 政府宣布的那些措施不得人心，反对党立即利用了这一机会。

cash up *vi.* (英国英语用法) count and check all the money that a shop has received in a day 盘点商店一天的全部进款：When she had *cashed up*, she realized there was £50 missing. 盘点完商店一天的全部进款，她意识到少了 50 英镑。I'm not ready to go home for a few minutes; I'm still *cashing up*. 我等一会儿才能回家。我还在盘点商店全天的进款呢。

cast a glance at *vt.* have a hasty look at (someone or something) 匆忙地瞥一眼……：She *cast a glance at* the letter on the desk. 她瞥了一眼桌子上的信。I *cast a glance at* the headlines in a newspaper. 我匆匆地看了一眼报纸的标题。Let me *cast a glance at* your photo. 让我看一眼你的照片。The other girls *cast* sidelong *glances at* me. 其他的女孩都斜着眼睛看我。

NOTE 本短语中的名词 glance 和另一名词 glimpse 的意义相同。但当它们分别用在动词短语中时,它们前面所用的动词和后面所用的介词都不相同。glance 常与动词 cast, give, take 和 throw 连用,后面与介词 at 连用;而 glimpse 则与动词 catch, get 和 have 连用,后面与介词 of 连用。

cast a shadow on/over *vt.* ❶ cause (something or someone) to be in the shade 使……处于阴影之中: The sun was hot, so I sat under a tree whose branches *cast a shadow on* the ground. 太阳火热,于是我便坐在树荫下乘凉。❷make (a situation) seem less hopeful and more likely to end badly 给(某一局势)罩上阴影: Last night killings *cast a* dark *shadow over* the peace talks. 昨晚的杀戮给和平谈判罩上了阴影。

cast about/around/round for *vt.* (正式用语,无被动语态形式) try hard to find or think of (something, especially when this is difficult)急切寻找,苦思,盘算: They were *casting about* for an experienced teacher to take the retiring principal's place. 他们正在物色一名有经验的教师来接替即将退休的校长。The prisoner *cast about* him *for* a way to escape. 那囚犯扫视了周围的环境,以找到一条逃跑之路。He *cast about/around/round* in his mind *for* some plausible excuse for not turning up at the meeting. 他心里在盘算,想找一个说得过去的理由来解释他为什么没有到会。

NOTE cast about for 和 cast around for 主要用于英国英语中。

cast aside *vt.* 【可分性动词短语】(正式用语,常用一般时态)get rid of (someone or something) because it is no longer interesting, necessary, useful or valuable to you 抛弃(某人或某物): He has *cast* his old friends *aside* after he was promoted. 他被提拔后便抛弃了老朋友。She refused to be *cast aside* in this manner. 她不肯这样被人抛弃。It's a shame to *cast aside* a good book such as this. 放弃这样一本好书不读,真是太可惜了。*Cast* your worry *aside*, and be happy. 抛弃烦恼,快乐些吧。

NOTE 1. 当本短语所带的宾语为代词时,该代词须置于本短语的动词和副词中间。

2. 本短语的同义短语是 cast away 和 cast off 。

cast away *vt.* 【可分性动词短语】❶(正式用语) throw (something) away; get rid of (something or someone)扔掉,处理掉(某物),抛弃(某物或某人): It's time you *cast away* those old clothes and bought some new ones. 你该扔掉这些旧衣服,买一些新衣服了。*Cast* that rubbish *away*. 把那些垃圾处理掉。❷(用被动语态形式) leave somewhere as the result of a shipwrecked (因船只失事而)漂流: We were *cast away* on an island without food and fresh water. 我们因船只失事而漂流到了一个孤岛上,没有食物也没有淡水。

NOTE 1. 当本短语作"抛弃(某物或某人)"解时,同义短语是 cast aside 和 cast off。

2. 当本短语所带的宾语为代词时,该代词须置于本短语的动词和副词中间。

cast down *vt.* (正式用语,用被动语态形式) make (someone) feel sad or disappointed; lower (someone) in spirit 使(某人)感到沮丧,使(某人)情绪低落,使气馁: Since he heard of his failure in the English examination, Jim has been very much *cast down*. 吉姆听说自己英语考试不及格后,情绪一直很低落。

cast light on ⇨ **throw light on**

cast lots *vi.* (常后接介词 for 短语或动词不定式短语) make a decision by choosing one of several pieces of paper with different choices written on them 抓阄,抽签:They *cast lots* to see who would speak first. 他们抓阄决定谁先发言。We *cast lots* for the right to go first. 我们抓阄决定谁有先走的权利。

NOTE 1. 本短语中的名词 lot 必须用复数形式。

2. 本短语本身是动宾结构,动词和名词可分开使用。例如:For the first time in a World Cup final, *lots* had to be *cast* to decide who would finish second and three.

3. 本短语与 draw lots 意义和用法与相同,两者可互换使用。

cast off *vt.* 【可分性动词短语】❶(常用一般时态) stop having anything to do with (someone)与(某人)断绝关系:Mr Jones *cast off* his daughter when she married against his will. 琼斯先生的女儿在婚事上违背了他的意愿,他便与她断绝了关系。He never believed that he would be *cast off* by his closest friend. 他绝不相信他最亲密的朋友会与他绝交。❷(正式用语) discard; remove or get rid of (something because it is no longer necessary or useful to you or because it is harmful to you)放弃,摆脱,戒绝:He had *cast off* his idea of going abroad. 他已放弃了出国的想法。There was a feeling of hope, as if a great burden had been *cast off*. 感到有了希望,就好像摆脱了巨大的负担一样。❸get rid of (something such as a skin)蜕去(皮等):Every year the snake *casts off* its skin. 蛇每年都要蜕皮。

—*vt.* &*vi.* ❶ untie the rope fastening your boat to the land so that you can sail away 给船只解缆出航:We *cast off* at 8 am, heading out to the bay. 我们上午 8 时解缆出航,朝海湾驶去。❷set(a boat or ship)free by untying a rope 解缆放开(船只): Don't *cast off* the boat till everyone is on board. 等所有的人都上船后再解开缆绳。

cast out *vt.* 【可分性动词短语】(正式用语,旧式用法,常用一般时态) force (someone or something) to leave a place because you no longer like or need them 逐出,驱逐:He had abandoned her, and had *cast* her *out*. 他抛弃了她,将她逐出了家门。In former times, criminals were often *cast out* and had to live in the wild. 在过去,罪犯往往都被驱逐到偏远的地区生活。

NOTE 当本短语所带的宾语为代词时,该代词须置于本短语的动词和副词中间。

catch a glimpse of *vt.* get a hurried view of (someone or something)对……匆匆一瞥,望一眼……: The fans waited at the airport, hoping to *catch a glimpse of* their idol as he passed through. 歌迷们守候在机场,盼望着他们崇拜的偶像从那里经过时能看上他一眼。More than 6,000 visitors braved a cold Lunar New Year's Day morning to *catch a glimpse of* the giant pandas, Tuan Tuan and Yuan Yuan, at Taipei City Zoo. 6 000 多名游客不惧寒冷,在农历大年初一上午到台北市动物园看大熊猫"团团"和"圆圆"。He *caught a glimpse of* the morning paper before his breakfast. 他在早餐前匆匆看了一眼晨报。

NOTE 本短语的动词 catch 可被 get, have

C

替换，构成的短语与本短语意义和用法相同。

catch ahold of *vt.*【不可分性动词短语】(美国英语用法，非正式用语) ❶grasp or seize (someone or something) with your hands (用手)抓住：I failed to *catch ahold of* him. 我没能抓住他。See if you can *catch ahold of* the rope. 看你能不能抓住这根绳子。❷ begin to understand (something) 开始懂得，了解：When he *caught ahold of* something, he would tell everyone about it. 当他懂得了什么时，他就会把它讲给所有的人。

NOTE 本短语的同义短语是 catch hold of。

C

catch at *vt.* (常用一般时态) ❶(主要用于英国英语中) reach out and try to get hold of or grasp (something)伸手竭力抓住(某物)：He *caught at* the ball but missed it. 他伸手去接球，但没能接住。The beggar kept *catching at* her sleeve as she tried to move away. 当她试图走开时，那乞丐却抓住她的衣袖不放。A drowning man will *catch at* anything, even a straw. 快淹死的人抓住什么都不放，哪怕是一根稻草。❷ discover (someone) in the act of (something, especially something wrong or shameful) 发现(某人)在做(坏事或可耻之事)：I've *caught* you *at* your tricks again. 我又发现你在耍花招。They have been trying to *catch* her *at* it, but she's too clever. 他们千方百计地要抓她个正着，可她太狡猾了。

NOTE 当本短语作"发现(某人)在做(坏事或可耻之事)"解时，另外一种表达形式是 catch someone doing something。例如：

> Don't let me catch you doing that again!
> 不要让我再抓到你做那件事！

catch fire *vi.* ❶(常用一般时态) start burning 着火：The market *caught fire* at about 11:00 pm Sunday. 这个商场星期天晚上 11 点着火了。As the wood is wet, it won't *catch fire*. 木头是湿的，点不着火。❷ become excited 兴奋：On hearing the news that our team won the gold medal, we all *caught fire*. 听到我们队赢得了金牌的消息，我们都很兴奋。

NOTE **1.** 当本短语作"着火"解时，另外一种表达形式是 catch on fire。例如：

> The driver failed to get the passengers out before it caught on fire.
> 司机未能赶在汽车着火前让乘客们下车。

2. 本短语与 on fire 均有"着火"之意，两者之间的区别见 on fire。

catch hold of *vt.*【不可分性动词短语】❶grasp or seize (something or someone) with your hands (用手)抓住：He *caught hold of* a log and was saved from drowning. 他抓住了一根木头，才没被淹死。The boy almost fell out of the window; luckily his mother *caught hold of* him and pulled him back. 那男孩几乎从窗户跌下去，幸好他妈妈抓住了他，把他拉了回来。❷begin to know (an idea) 开始懂得，了解：I *caught hold of* the idea only after much explanation on his part. 经他再三解释我才懂得这个意思。Are you beginning to *catch hold of* our methods now? 你现在对我们的这些方法有所了解了吧？

NOTE **1.** 当本短语作"抓住"解时，同义短语是 catch ahold of, get hold of, grab hold of, have hold of 和 take hold of。

2. 当本短语作"开始懂得，了解"解时，同义短语是 catch ahold of。

catch in the act *vt.*【可分性动词短语】(非正式用语，常用一般时态，常与 of 短语连用) catch (someone) actually doing something wrong or committing a crime 当场抓获(某人): Tom tried to cheat on the exam, but his teacher walked in and *caught* him *in the act*. 汤姆在考试中试图作弊,但老师走了进来将其当场抓获。I *caught* him *in the act* of stealing money from my drawer. 他正从我的抽屉偷钱,我当场抓获了他。

catch it *vi.* (非正式用语,一般不用过去时) receive a punishment or scolding for doing something wrong (因做错事)受责骂,受处罚: We'll really *catch it* from the boss if we're late again. 如果我们再迟到,可真的要受老板训斥了。You'll *catch it* if our teacher sees you smoking. 如果咱们老师看到你抽烟,你会挨罚的。I'm going to *catch it* when I turn in my paper late. 我的论文晚交了就会受责备。

NOTE 本短语与 get it 意义和用法相同。本短语是英国英语用法,get it 是美国英语用法。

catch on *vi.* (非正式用语) ❶ be fashionable or become popular 流行,受欢迎: It was a popular style in Britain, but it never really *caught on* in Italy. 那在英国是时髦样式,但在意大利就从来没真正流行过。There have been several attempts to introduce new styles in men's clothing, but none of them has *caught on*. 有人曾引进几种新款式男装,但没有一种流行起来。E-books *catch on* with American children, according to *Los Angeles Times*. 据《洛杉矶时报》报道,电子书籍很受美国儿童欢迎。Jazz is *catching on* here. 爵士乐在这儿很受欢迎。❷(常用一般时态,常与 to 连用) understand (something) 理解,明白: I threw out some hints, but unfortunately he failed to *catch on*. 我给他提了一些暗示,可惜他没能领会。Being a foreigner, Smith didn't quite *catch on* to the joke. 史密斯是外国人,所以不太理解那玩笑的含义。It was a long time before the police *caught on* to what he was really doing. 过了很长时间警方才搞清楚他究竟在做什么。You'll *catch on* to the job after you have been here a week or two. 在这儿待上一两个星期后,你就知道如何做这项工作了。

catch on fire ⇨ **catch fire**

catch one's attention *vi.* (of something) happen to be observed by someone (某物)偶然引起某人的注意: Something shiny in the grass caught my attention. 草丛中闪闪发光的东西引起了我的注意。The policeman's attention was *caught* by something protruding from the man's pocket. 这个人口袋里鼓出的东西引起了警察的注意。What first *caught my attention* was his voice. 首先引我注意的是他的嗓音。

NOTE 本短语的名词 attention 还可以与其他的动词连用,构成以下动词短语: arouse someone's attention, attract someone's attention, call someone's attention, capture someone's attention, draw someone's attention (to),这些短语与本短语意义和用法相同。

catch one's breath *vi.* ❶ take time to start to breathe normally again after physical exercise (在体力活动之后)喘口气,休息一下: I had to stop about halfway up the hill and *catch my breath*. 上到半山腰,我不得不停下来喘口气。We have finished our work. Let's sit down and *catch our breath*. 咱们已经完成了工作,坐下来休息休息吧。❷ stop breathing suddenly for a short time because you are surprised or impressed

(常指因吃惊或感叹等而)屏息,暂时停止呼吸: The news was so unexpected that I *caught my breath* from shock. 这个消息太出乎意料了,我惊得一下喘不过气来。They *caught their breath* on seeing the terrible scene. 看到这可怕的场景,他们都屏住了呼吸。The beauty of the scene made us *catch our breath*. 这秀丽的景色使我们屏息。

catch one's eye *vi.* ❶ (of something) happen to be observed by someone (某物)偶然引起某人的注意:There was one painting that *caught my eye*. 有一幅油画引起了我的注意。The new buildings along the street *caught every passer-by's eye*. 沿街这些新建筑物引起每个过路人的注目。❷attract someone's attention to you 引起某人对自己的注意:He tried to *catch the girl's eye* but she was already turning away. 他千方百计地引那女孩注意他,可她却已转过身去了。I'll try to *catch his eye* as he leaves the meeting. 我会在他离开会场时尽量让他注意到我。

NOTE 1. 本短语中的名词 eye 相当于抽象名词 notice 或 attention,因此只能用单数形式。

2. 本短语的同义短语是 catch one's attention。

catch out *vt.* 【可分性动词短语】(主要用于英国英语中,非正式用语,常用一般时态) discover (someone) not telling the truth or making a mistake, especially by asking him or her questions (尤指通过问问题)发现(某人)在说谎(或做错事): The school master *caught out* the student and punished him immediately. 校长发现那名学生在撒谎并当即处罚了他。He asked her casual questions to see if he could *catch* her *out*. 他问了她一些随随便便的问题,以从中发现她是否在撒谎。The prosecuting lawyer tried to *catch* the witness *out* by clever questioning. 原告律师试图以巧妙的发问来找出证人的漏洞。Since the first drugs test was carried out at the 1968 Olympics in Mexico City, many cheats have been *caught out*. 自从1968年墨西哥奥运会上第一次实行药检以来,很多运动员被发现有欺诈行为。

NOTE 当本短语所带的宾语为代词时,该代词须置于本短语的动词和副词中间。

catch red-handed *vt.* 【可分性动词短语】(非正式用语,常用被动语态形式,常用一般时态) discover and catch (someone) while he or she is in the act of doing something bad or illegal 当场发现并抓获(某人): We *caught* him *red-handed* while he was just putting the diamonds in his pocket. 当他正把钻石往口袋里装时,我们当场把他抓住。The pickpocket was *caught red-handed* stealing money on the bus by the police. 那扒手在公共汽车上偷钱时被警察当场抓获。

NOTE 1. 除本短语用于被动语态形式外,宾语只能置于动词 catch 与形容词 red-handed 之间。

2. 本短语的同义短语是 catch in the act。

catch sight of *vt.* 【不可分性动词短语】(一般不用进行时态) see or notice (someone or something), often for a moment 瞥见,看到,注意到: I suddenly *caught sight of* her in the crowd. 我突然在人群中看到了她。The doctor *caught sight of* a young man running towards his clinic. 医生看见一个小伙子正向他的诊所跑来。I only *caught sight of* the report from the newspaper. 我只是从报纸上注意到了这一报道。

NOTE 本短语的同义短语是 catch a glimpse of;反义短语是 lose sight of。

catch someone by surprise ⇨ **take someone by surprise**

catch up *v.* ❶come up from behind and reach (the person or vehicle in front of you)追上,赶上: You may go now, and I'll *catch* you *up* later. 你现在就走,我过一会儿就能追上你。I stopped and waited for her to *catch up*. 我停下来等她赶上来。There was a ten-mile chase before the police car *caught up* the thieves. 追赶了10 英里,警车才追上了那些盗贼。❷reach the same stage, standard, or level someone has reached 赶上(先进阶段、标准或水平): I'm falling behind with my work; I must try to *catch up*. 我的工作落后了,我得设法赶上去。Don't worry, you'll *catch* them *up* when you return to good health. 别担心,等你康复后你会赶上他们的。❸size (something) quickly 很快地抓住(某物): The young man *caught up* the lady's handbag and ran. 那小子抢了那位女士的手包就跑。❹(常用被动语态形式,常与 in 连用) trap or fix (someone) in a time or place 困住(某人): They were *caught up* in the rain and some of them caught cold. 他们都遭雨淋了,有些人因此患了感冒。I was *caught up* in the busy traffic again this morning. 今天上午我又被繁忙的交通堵住了。❺(常与 on 连用) do what needs to be done in order to come up to date 赶做(需及时完成的事情): I have to *catch up* on my work tonight, so I can't come out. 今晚我得赶工作,所以不能出来了。

NOTE 1. 当本短语用作及物性动词短语,所带的宾语为代词时,该代词须置于本短语的动词和副词中间。

2. 当本短语作"追上,赶上"解时,在美国英语中是不可分性动词短语,在英国英语中则是可分性动词短语。

3. 当本短语作"追上,赶上"解时,反义短语是 fall behind 和 lag behind。

catch up with *vt.*【不可分性动词短语】come level with (someone or something) 赶上……: You have to work hard in order to *catch up with* the rest of the class. 你必须用功学习,好赶上班里的其他同学。We must try our best to *catch up with* advanced countries in science and technology. 我们必须尽最大努力在科技上赶上发达国家。

NOTE 1. 本短语与 keep up with 意义相近,用法相同。keep up with 指在同时起步的情况下"跟上","不落后";而 catch up with 指在起步较晚或已经落后的情况下"赶上"。见 keep up with。❷本短语的反义短语是 fall behind 和 lag behind。

cater for【不可分性动词短语】(主要用于英国英语中,用一般时态) ❶provide (everything a particular group of people want or need) 提供(某一人群所需之物): I think he will *cater for* your demands. 我认为他会向你提供你所要的东西。These shops *catered for* the needs of men. 这些商店为男士们提供一切所需之物。❷(非正式用语) provide (what is needed) to fulfill (a demand by someone or something) 提供(所需之物)以满足(某种需求),迎合(……的需要): A large hotel had recently been opened to *cater for* the summer visitors. 一家大型旅馆最近开张,以满足夏季游客的需求。Popular newspapers try to *cater for* all tastes. 通俗性报纸试图迎合各种趣味读者的需要。

cater to *vt.*【不可分性动词短语】(主要用于美国英语中,用一般时态) ❶provide (a particular group of people) with (something they want or need, especially something unusual or special) 为(某一人群)提供(所需的特别之物): Filled with such gifts as chocolate, flowers and wine, the special parcel, *catering to* young couples, sold well on the market before the incoming Valentine's Day. 这种特别的礼包,内装巧克力、鲜花和葡萄酒,满足了年轻情侣的需要,在情人节前的市场上特别畅销。Some TV shows *cater to* young male audiences. 一些电视节目专供年轻的男性观众收看。❷provide (what is needed) to fulfill (a demand)提供(所需之物)以满足(某种需求),迎合……的需要: She refused to *cater to* his ridiculous demands. 她拒绝满足他那些荒唐的要求。He said it was to try to *cater to* the development of the logistics industry and give play to China's advantages in the processing industry. 他说,这是满足现代物流产业发展需要,发挥中国加工业优势的一种新的尝试。

cave in *v.* ❶(of a roof, ceiling or the covering over a hollow place)(cause to) fall in or down inwards(使)(房顶、屋棚或洞顶)向内塌陷: The weight of the snow *caved in* the roof of a stadium in Russia yesterday. 昨天,积雪的重量使俄罗斯的一个体育馆顶棚垮塌。"We were afraid that the roof might *cave in* so we started to run out," the house owner said. "我们怕房顶塌陷,就都跑了出来。"那房主说道。Sadly, the tunnel *caved in* on the train. 不幸的是,隧道塌陷,压住了该次列车。❷(非正式用语,常与 to 连用) give up opposition, especially as a result of pressure or persuasion; give in (to somebody or something)(尤指在压力或劝说下)屈服,(向……)让步: The government refused to *cave in* to the terrorists. 政府拒绝向恐怖分子作出让步。The school committee finally *caved in* to the demands of parents and teachers. 校委会最终对学生家长和老师们的要求作出了让步。The children begged their father to stop his work and take them to the circus until he *caved in*. 孩子们请求爸爸停下工作带他们去看马戏,直到他让了步方才罢休。

center on/upon/round *vt.* (常用一般时态) ❶(无被动语态形式) have (something) as its middle or most important point; surround (something or someone)以……为中心,把……包围起来: The small town *centers on* its market square. 该小镇以市场广场为中心。The children always *center round* the teacher at story time. 在老师讲故事的时候,孩子们总是把老师围起来。❷(常用被动语态形式)focus on (someone or something in particular)集中于: Let us *center* the discussion *on* Brown. 我们还是集中讨论布朗的事吧。The conversation *centered on* the forthcoming election. 话题集中在即将举行的选举上。The armed police force should fulfill various tasks *centered on* handling emergencies and fighting against terrorist activities. 武装警察部队应该执行以处理突发事件和反恐怖活动为中心的各项任务。

chain to *vt.* 【可分性动词短语】❶fasten (something or someone) with chains to (usually something)用锁链把……拴(或锁)在(尤指某物)上: He *chained* his bicycle *to* a lamppost. 他用锁链把自行车锁在了灯柱上。The kidnappers *chained* the hostage *to* a tree. 绑架者用锁链把人质拴在树上。Several protesters were *chained to* the railings. 几名抗议者被锁链锁在围栏上。❷(非正式用语,常用被

动语态形式)(of someone) be forced to stay in (an unpleasant situation)把(某人)束缚在……:Work *chained* him *to* his desk. 工作把他束缚在办公桌旁。With a sick husband, she's *chained to* the house all day. 因丈夫有病,她整天被束缚在家中。With a deadline to meet, Mary had been *chained to* her desk all weekend. 期限将至,玛丽整个周末都不得不伏案工作。

chain up *vt.*【可分性动词短语】(常用被动语态形式) fasten (someone or an animal) in place with a chain or rope 用锁链(或绳子)把(人或动物)拴上(或绑上): They kept the dog *chained up* every night and released it each day. 他们每天夜里用锁链把狗拴起来,白天再放开。I'll lock the door and *chain* you *up*. 我要把门锁上,再用绳子把你绑上。

NOTE 当本短语所带的宾语为代词时,该代词须置于本短语的动词和副词中间。

chance it *vi.* (非正式用语) risk something, even though you know it involves a risk, or failure is possible 冒险,碰运气: It looked like rain so I decided not to *chance it* and brought my umbrella. 看上去天要下雨,所以我决定不冒淋雨之险而带了伞。It may be risky, but we will *chance it* anyhow. 这可能有风险,但我们无论如何也要碰一下运气。

NOTE 本短语的另外一种表达形式是 chance one's luck,两者可互换使用。

chance on/upon *vt.*【不可分性动词短语】(正式用语,用一般时态) find or see (something or someone) when you did not expect to 偶然找到,偶然碰上: She *chanced on* some valuable documents when she was cleaning out the attic. 她在打扫阁楼时偶尔发现了一些有价值的文件。We *chanced on* our former teacher of English in the street. 我们在大街上与以前的英语老师不期而遇。I *chanced upon* her on my way to my work. 在我上班的路上意外地遇到了她。

NOTE **1.** 本短语中的 upon 用法比 on 正式,但不及 on 常用。

2. 本短语的同义短语是 bump into, come across 和 run into。

chance one's luck ⇨ **chance it**

(the) chances are (that)(非正式用语,后接 that 从句,that 可省略)(used for saying that something is likely to happen but is not certain) it is likely that …; it is probably that 可能……: *The chances are that* I will be looking for a new job soon. 我可能要找一份新工作。*Chances are* he has already heard the sad news. 他可能已经听到这个悲惨的消息了。Without clear objectives, *chances are that* a meeting will be unproductive. 没有明确目标的会议多半是徒劳无果的。

change for *vt.*【可分性动词短语】exchange (something) for (something else)用……换……:Her new dress didn't fit so she took it back to the shop and *changed* it *for* another. 她新买的连衣裙不合身,因此她拿回商店去换了另一件。The boy *changed* soiled clothes *for* clean ones. 这男孩把脏衣服换成了干净的。Where can I *change* my pounds *for* US dollars? 我在哪儿能把英镑兑换成美元?

NOTE 本短语强调的是对等的换取,如把一件衣服换成同类的另一件衣服等。

change for the better *vi.* start being better; improve 好转:I hope the weather will soon *change for the better*. 我希望天气会很快好转。The world is *changing for the better* under our endeavour. 在我

们的努力下,世界变得更美好了。

change for the worse *vi.* start being worse; worsen 恶化: The patient's condition *changed for the worse*. 患者的病情恶化了。When it grew dark the weather *changed for the worse*. 天近傍晚时,天气变得更糟了。

change from … to … *vt.* change (something or someone) from (a state) to (another) 从……变为……: In autumn the leaves *change from* green *to* brown. 在秋天,树叶由绿色变成褐色。The town has *changed from* a small fishing port *to* a tourist center. 这个城镇从一个小渔港变成了旅游中心地。One purpose of going to school is to *change* yourself *from* ignorance *to* intelligence. 上学的一个目的就是使你从无知变为有智慧。

change hands *vi.* (of a possession) go from one owner to another, especially by being sold (指所有权)(尤指通过买卖)易手,易主: This house has *changed hands* several times in the past two years. 这所房子在过去的两年里曾几度易手。The food got a lot worse after the restaurant *changed hands*. 这家餐馆易主后,饭菜差了很多。

NOTE 本短语中的名词 hand 必须用复数形式。

change into *vt.* ❶take off the clothes or a piece of clothing you are wearing and put on (different ones)脱下并换上(不同衣物): You must *change into* a clean dress before we go out. 在我们外出前,你必须换上一件干净的衣服。You should *change into* some dry socks. 你们应该换上干袜子。❷make (someone or something) change form or state (使……)变成……: When the prince kissed the cat it *changed into* a beautiful princess. 当王子吻了那只猫后,它竟变成了一位美丽的公主。The ugly old man suddenly *changed* himself *into* a handsome young gentleman. 这个丑老头突然把自己变成了一个年轻英俊的绅士。Several days later, caterpillars *change into* butterflies. 几天后,这些毛毛虫就变成了蝴蝶。

NOTE 本短语和 change to 都表示"变成"之意,但本短语强调的是形式和状态上的改变。

change one's mind *vi.* change your or someone else's decision or opinion 改变(自己或他人的)决定(或意见): There's no point in trying to reason with him he'll never *change his mind*. 你劝他没有意义;他决不会改变他的决定的。I've *changed my mind*. I don't want to go out. 我已改变主意,不想出去了。What made you *change your minds*? 是什么使你们变卦的? Many people wonder if this is a consistent position of your country or did your country *change its mind* before the voting? 很多人都想知道这是贵国的一贯立场还是贵国在投票之前改变了主意?

NOTE 1. 本短语中的名词 mind 的单复数形式随前面人称的单复数形式而改变。例如:

> She always *changes her mind*.
> 她总是见异思迁。
> We have *changed our minds* and are going to New York instead of Washington.
> 我们已改变主意,改去纽约而不去华盛顿了。

2. 本短语中的物主代词往往省略。例如:We cannot *change minds* in Congress without first changing minds in cities and

town's nationwide.

change over *vi.* (常与 from, to 连用) stop doing or using one thing and start doing or using something else 改变,改用,更换: The factory *changed over* to the manufacture of storage batteries last year. 这家工厂去年已转产蓄电池了。Britain *changed over* from pounds, shillings, and pence to the new decimal currency in the year of 1971. 英国于1971年从镑、先令和便士的币制改变为新的十进位币制。

NOTE 本短语可转化为复合词 change-over,意为"转变,更换,改组"。

change to *vt.* (cause to) become (something different) or make a change to (something or someone different)(使)变成,(使)换成,(使)改变: I want to *change* some British pounds *to* US dollars. 我想把一些英镑换成美元。You will have to *change to* the trolley bus at the next stop. 你下一站得换乘无轨电车。Don't move your car until the traffic light *changes to* green. 交通信号灯改变为绿色前不要开动汽车。

charge at *vt.* 【不可分性动词短语】rush towards (someone or something), as to attack 冲向: The security men panicked as angry crowd *charged at* them. 当愤怒的人群朝他们冲过来时,那些保安人员惊慌失措。Suddenly the wild animal *charged at* us. 那头野兽突然向我们冲了过来。

charge for *vt.* 【可分性动词短语】ask (someone) to pay an amount of money for (something bought or received) 向(某人)收取费用: This shop doesn't *charge for* delivery. 这家商店送货不收费用。How much do they *charge for* washing a car? 他们洗一台车要收多少钱? We don't charge anything for that. 我们对此不收任何费用。You will be *charged* a small fee *for* food and lodging. 我们要收您少许的食宿费用。

charge up *vt.* 【可分性动词短语】❶(常用一般时态,常与 to 连用) record (something) to (someone's account) for later payment 把……记在某人的账上: Please *charge* these goods *up* to my husband's account. 请把这笔货款记在我丈夫的账上。Guests can make phone calls and *charge* them *up* to their rooms. 客人们可以打电话,话费记入他们的房费中。❷ put electricity into (a piece of electrical equipment such as a battery) in order to make it more powerful or make it last longer 为(电池等)充电: The man in the garage said he would *charge up* my car battery. 汽车修理厂的那个人说他将给我的汽车电池充电。The mobile phone won't work if it isn't *charged up*. 手机如果不充电,就不能用。

NOTE 当本短语所带的宾语为代词时,该代词须置于本短语的动词和副词中间。

charge with *vt.* ❶(常用一般时态) fill (something) with (electric or explosive powder, etc.) 充(电);装满(炸药);使……充满(或装满)……: If we *charged* it *with* electricity, it will become magnetic. 如果我们把它充上电,它就会带有磁性。The bomb was *charged with* dynamite. 炸弹里装满了炸药。*Charge* your glass *with* wine. 把你们的杯子都倒满酒。❷(常用一般时态) accuse (someone) officially of (committing a crime) 指控(某人犯罪): The police have *charged* him *with* murder. 警方指控他犯有谋杀罪。The US military yesterday *charged* seven soldiers *with* mistreating prisoners at a jail in Iraq. 美国军方昨天指控7名士兵在伊拉克的一座监狱中虐待囚犯。❸(常用被动语态形式)make (someone) officially responsible for (doing something); place upon (someone) as (a duty)使(某人)负责(做某事);使(某人)承担(某种任务或责任等): She *charged* me *with* looking after her baby son. 她要我负责照看她的小儿子。They *charged* him *with* the duty of taking care of the warehouse. 他们把照管仓库的任务交给了他。The young police officer was *charged with* the important task of taking 150 prisoners to a prison in another province. 这位年轻的警官被委以重任,把150名囚犯押送到另一省份的监狱去。The company has been *charged with* maintaining our computer systems. 该公司承担起维护我们计算机系统的责任。

chase after *vt.* ❶ follow (someone or something) quickly in order to catch them; pursue 追捕,追赶: The policeman *chased after* the robber for more than a mile. 警察追捕那名强盗跑了一英里多远。The huntsmen rode fast, *chasing after* the fox. 猎人策马飞奔追赶狐狸。❷(非正式用语) try to get (someone) to have a sexual relationship with you 追求(异性): She has been *chasing after* that man for years. 她已追求那名男子多年。Aren't you getting a bit old to be *chasing after* girls? 你还在追女孩子,你老了点儿吧?

cheat into *vt.* 【可分性动词短语】persuade (someone) by a trick into (something or doing something) 骗(某人)去做(某事): The officer was trying to *cheat* the girl *into* believing that she was the only girl he had loved, but the girl saw through him. 那名军官试图骗姑娘相信她是他唯一所爱的姑娘,但姑娘却把他看穿了。The young man who had said he was an employee in a bank *cheated* the old lady *into* giving him all her money. 那个自称是银行职员的小子骗得老太太把所有的钱都给了他。

cheat on *vt.* 【不可分性动词短语】❶(主要用于美国英语中) cheat by not obeying a set of rules on (something) 作弊;逃避(法律): Yes, it's against the law to cheat on taxes, but regardless of which many people in the country did *cheat on* their taxes. 是的,偷税漏税是违法的,但尽管如此,还是有很多国人偷漏了税款。❷(非正式用语) secretly have a sexual relationship with someone other than your husband, wife, or partner or sexually unfaithful to them (在性关系上)背叛: He discovered his wife had been *cheating on* him and he was mad at it. 发现妻子背叛自己与他人私通,他气得发狂。

check in *vt.* &*vi.* arrive at a hotel where you have arranged to stay and give your personal details to the person working at the reception desk; (of a receptionist) deal with (someone who arrives at the hotel) (在旅馆服务台)办理入住登记手续,(旅馆接待人员)为(某人)办理入住登记手续: Not long after my arrival at the hotel, two men *checked in*. 我到达旅馆不久,就有两个人办理了入住登记手续。The receptionist *checked* us *in*. 接待员给我们办理了入住登记手续。

—*vi.* ❶ (常与 at 连用) arrive at an airport and show your ticket to an official (在机场)办理登机手续: You must *check in* at the airport an hour before your plane leaves. 你必须在飞机起飞一小时

前在机场办理登机手续。❷(非正式用语) report your arrival at work (especially by passing a special card through a piece of equipment to record that you are arriving at work)(尤指打卡)上班报到：Most of the staff workers *checked in* before 8 this morning. 今天上午，大多数工作人员都是 8 点前上班报到。

—*vt.*【可分性动词短语】❶(常与 at 连用) give (your bags and cases) to an official at an airport so that they can be put on a plane (在机场)办理(行李或包裹的)托运：Rogers *checked in* his suitcase. 罗杰斯办理了手提箱托运。You can check your suitcases in at the desk. 你可以在服务台办理手提箱托运。❷(主要用于美国英语中) have the return of (an article recorded)办理(某一记录在案的物品)的归还手续：I'm just going to *check in* these books at the library. 我正要到图书馆去还书。The students put their books on the library desk and the librarian *checked* them *in*. 学生们把书放在图书馆借书台上，图书管理员一一点收。

NOTE 1. 当本短语用作及物性动词短语，所带的宾语为代词时，该代词须置于本短语的动词和副词中间。

2. 本短语的反义短语是 check out。

3. 当本短语作"上班报到"解时，同义短语是 clock in/on；反义短语是 check out 和 clock out/off。

4. 本短语可转化为复合词 check-in，意为"(在旅馆住宿)入住登记手续(处)；(在机场办理的)登机手续(报到处)"。

check off *vt.*【可分性动词短语】(美国英语用法) mark (something such as names or items in a list) as having been dealt with 在(名单或清单上)做记号：Check the names off as the guests arrive. 把到达客人的名字都做上记号。She kept a list of books that had been recommended to her, and *checked off* each one as she read it. 她保存了一张别人向她推荐的书单，每读完一本就用记号勾掉一个。You can *check* them *off*. I've already done these jobs. 这些活儿你可以用记号勾出来，我已经把它们干完了。

NOTE 当本短语所带的宾语为代词时，该代词须置于本短语的动词和副词中间。

check on *vt.*【不可分性动词短语】look at (someone or something) so that you are certain they are safe, satisfactory, etc. 查看，视察：I sent Mary to *check on* the kids. 我派玛丽去看一下孩子们。The boss arrived to *check on* our progress. 老板来视察我们的工作进展情况。

check out *vt.*【可分性动词短语】❶(非正式用语，常用一般时态) find out (whether something is correct or true) by making inquiries 检查，核实：The accountant *checked out* the bills and found them OK. 会计检查了一下账单，发现正确无误。Ask him to *check* the information *out* for us. 请他把这情况给我们核实一下。The police are still *checking out* his story. 警方仍在核实他所说的情况。❷(主要用于美国英语中，常与 of 连用) satisfy all requirements for taking away (something) 办妥手续取走(某物)：He *checked* this book *out* of the library this morning. 他今天上午从图书馆借走了这本书。How much money have you *checked out* at the bank? 你从银行里已经支取了多少钱？They have *checked* their luggage *out*. 他们已取走了行李。❸examine the health of (someone) 检查(某人的)身体状况：Go to the doctor and get yourself *checked out*. 到医生那儿去

检查一下身体。❹(非正式用语,常用一般时态) test (something, like a part of a motor) 检测(汽车的部件等): The mechanic *checked out* the car battery. 机械工检测了汽车的电池。

—*vi.* (非正式用语) leave your work (especially by passing a special card through a piece of equipment to record that you are leaving work)(尤指打卡)下班: Most of the employees *checked out* at 5 pm. 大多数员工都是在下午 5 点下班的。

—*vt.* &*vi.* (常与 of 连用) ❶ leave a hotel, motel, etc. after paying the bill 付账后离开(旅馆等): James had already *checked out* of the hotel. 詹姆斯已结账离开旅馆了。The hotel is full because no one has *checked out* today. 旅馆已满员,因为今天没有人退房。❷(常用一般时态) fulfill requirements, as by passing a test 检查合格: The engine *checked out* and we proceeded on our way. 发电机检查合格后我们又继续赶路了。

NOTE **1.** 当本短语用作及物性动词短语,所带的宾语为代词时,该代词须置于本短语的动词和副词中间。

2. 本短语可转化为复合词 check-out,意为"(超市的)付款台"。

check over *vt.* 【可分性动词短语】❶examine (usually something written) very carefully in order to make sure it is correct 仔细检查,核对(常指文稿): Please check this manuscript over carefully and correct any mistakes. 请把这篇稿子仔细检查一遍,把错误改掉。He *checked over* the names on the list to ensure that everything was correct. 他把名单核对了一遍,以确保一切都准确无误。All written work should be *checked over* for spelling mistakes. 所有的文字作品都要进行校对,检查有无拼写错误。❷examine the general health of (someone) to find out whether there is anything wrong with him or her 检查(某人的)身体状况: The nurse began *checking* him *over*. 护士开始为他检查身体。

NOTE **1.** 当本短语所带的宾语为代词时,该代词须置于本短语的动词和副词中间。

2. 当本短语作"检查,核对"解时,还可用 check through 的形式来表达。例如:

> We *checked through* the photographs to make sure there were none missing. 我们核对了照片,以确信无一缺失。

check up *v.* ❶(常与 on 连用)examine the general health of (someone)检查(某人的)身体状况: The doctors want to *check up* on how things are going with us. 医生要检查一下我们的健康状况如何。I asked the doctor to *check* me *up*. 我请医生为我检查身体。❷make enquiries about(something or someone); examine in order to make sure that everything is correct 调查,检查,核对: "Is the baby asleep?" "I'll just go and *check up*." "宝宝睡了没有?""我这就去看看。" The machines should be *checked up* once in a while. 这些机器应该不时地进行检查。The airhostess is *checking up* the passengers' safety belts. 空姐在检查乘客的安全带。*Check* the facts *up* before writing your report. 在写报告之前,你要把所有的事实都核实一下。She is *checking up* the accounts with a calculator. 她在用计算器核对账目。You'd better *check* it *up* with the original. 你最好拿原文核对一下。The police are *checking up* on what the man told them. 警方正在核实那个男人所告诉给他们的情况。

NOTE **1.** 当本短语用作及物性动词短语,所带的宾语为代词时,该代词须置于本短语的动词和副词中间。

2. 本短语可转化为复合词 check-up，意为“检查，调查，核对”。

check with *vt.* ❶agree with 与……相符：The merchandise does not *check with* the invoice. 这批货物与发票不符。His story *checks with* the facts. 他的陈述与事实相符。The translation *checks with* the original. 译文符合原文。❷consult with (someone)与(某人)协商：I have to *check with* the managing director before I sign the contracts. 我得和总经理商量一下，才能签订这些合同。❸get into communication with 与……联系：I have *checked with* the person in charge and find that the meeting will take place as planned. 我已经和有关负责人进行了联系，得知会议将按原计划举行。For further information, *check with* your local tax department 欲了解更多情况，请与当地的税务部门联系。

cheer up *vt.* &*vi.* (cause to) stop feeling sad or depressed and become more cheerful (使)感到高兴：Workers *cheered up* after they successfully capped the blowout natural gas wells. 工人们在天然气井喷压井成功后欢呼起来。Your visit has *cheered up* the sick man. 您的来访使病人感到非常高兴。He was so depressed that nothing can easily *cheer* him *up*. 他如此的沮丧，没有任何办法能轻易地使他快乐起来。

—*vi.* (仅用于口语中，常用于祈使句中) used for telling someone to try to be happier 振作起来：*Cheer up*! Better times may be ahead. 振作起来吧！好日子可能就在前头。

NOTE 当本短语用作及物性动词短语，所带的宾语为代词时，该代词须置于本短语的动词和副词中间。

chew on/upon *vt.*【不可分性动词短语】❶crush or keep biting (something hard) with the teeth 反复咬嚼(硬物)：He was chewing on his meat as if he found it hard to swallow. 他反复嚼着口中的肉，好像很难下咽一样。The dog was *chewing on* a bone. 那条狗在啃着一根骨头。❷(非正式用语) think about (something) carefully for a long time, before making a decision about it (作出决定之前)长时间地仔细考虑(某事)：The committee want time to *chew on* the question of the new appointment. 委员们需要时间来考虑新的任职人选问题。The investors have several economic reports to *chew on*. 这些投资者手里都有好几份经济报告在研究。

NOTE 1. 本短语中的 upon 用法比 on 正式，但不及 on 常用。

2. 当本短语作“仔细考虑(某事)”解时，与 chew over 意义和用法相同，两者可互换使用。

chew out *vt.*【可分性动词短语】(非正式用语，主要用于美国英语中) speak angrily to (someone) because he or she has done something wrong (因某人做错事而)叱责(某人)：He *chewed out* his secretary for being late to work. 他叱责他的秘书上班迟到。The manager *chewed* Jim *out* for being late again. 经理因吉姆再次迟到而叱责了他。When Tom got back to London, Peter called him over and *chewed* him *out*. 当汤姆回到伦敦后，彼得把他叫过去训斥了一顿。

NOTE 当本短语的宾语为代词时，该代词须置于本短语的动词和副词中间。

chew over *vt.*【可分性动词短语】(非正式用语)keep thinking about(a question, problem, etc.) carefully or discussing it carefully with other people before making a decision about it (在作出决定前)仔细考虑,详细商讨(某一问题等): Officials meet regularly to *chew over* the future of the company. 公司官员定期开会商讨公司的发展问题。I'll *chew* it *over* for a few days and then let you have my answer. 我要把这事仔细考虑几天后再给你答复。This matter has been *chewed over* again and again. 这事已经反复再三地讨论过了。

NOTE 当本短语所带的宾语为代词时,该代词须置于本短语的动词和副词中间。

chew up *vt.*【可分性动词短语】❶chew (something) for a long time, until it is very soft or in very small pieces and easy to swallow 把……嚼烂,嚼碎: I always told my child to *chew* his meat *up* well before swallowing it. 我总是告诉我的孩子要把肉嚼烂再咽。I took one of the pills and *chewed* it *up*. 我拿出一片药将其嚼碎。❷(非正式用语,常用被动语态形式)destroy (something) with, or as if with, the teeth 咬坏,绞碎(某物): The dog has chewed up my shoes! 狗把我的鞋咬坏了! That faulty lawn mower *chewed* some grass *up*. 那台有毛病的割草机把草坪的一些地方啃得乱七八糟。My new trousers got *chewed up* in my bike chain. 我的新裤子被自行车车链绞坏了。The logs were *chewed up* for making paper. 根根圆木被粉碎后用来造纸。

NOTE 当本短语所带的宾语为代词时,该代词须置于本短语的动词和副词中间。

chicken (-) and (-) egg problem *n.* (非正式用语)a difficult problem about the hen and the egg, which of them came first, which gives people much trouble because it is impossible to tell which of two existed first and which caused the other one 难分先后的问题,难分因果关系的问题: This problem is precisely a *chicken and egg problem*, because doctors don't know which one comes first—the diabetes or the depression. 这个问题恰好是个先有鸡还是先有蛋的难题,因为医生们不知道哪种病是先患上的——是糖尿病还是抑郁症。In your business life, you are probably going to suffer from what is commonly known as the *chicken-and-egg problem*. 在你的业务生涯中,你可能会受到通常被称之为难分因果关系的问题所困扰。

NOTE 本短语另外的表达方式是 chicken-or-egg question, chicken-and-egg situation 和 chicken-or-egg paradox。

chip in *v.* (非正式用语,常用一般时态) ❶(of a number of people) give or contribute (some money) so that they can pay for something together 共同出(钱),捐(资): The three of us *chipped in* and bought the boat. 我们三个人共同出钱买了这条船。Would you like to *chip in* with a few bucks on a gift for Mary? 你愿意出几块钱给玛丽买件礼物吗? Both organizations *chipped in* sizeable sums of money to finance the project. 这两个机构捐献了几笔可观的资金来资助该项工程。❷(常与 with 连用) enter a conversation between other people with an opinion 插话,插嘴说……: John *chipped in* with a remark. 约翰插了一句话。You shouldn't *chip in* that way, when your elders are holding a conversation. 当长辈讲话时,你不应该那样插嘴。While we were talking my son *chipped in* that it was time to go home. 我们正在谈话时,我的儿子插嘴说该回家了。

NOTE 当本短语作"插话,插嘴说……"解时,同义短语是 barge in, break in, break into, burst in, cut in, cut into, cut off, cut short, get in 和 put in 等。

choke off *vt.*【可分性动词短语】(非正式用语,常用一般时态) stop or prevent (someone or something) from (developing or being successful) 制止,阻止: He began to tell about his adventures again, but I *choked* him *off*. 他又开始讲起了他的冒险经历,但我阻止了他。They'd ruthlessly *choked off* all opposition to their plans. 他们把反对他们计划的各种意见都无情地压制下去了。If prices are too high, demand is *choked off*. 如果物价过高,就会抑制需求。

NOTE 当本短语所带的宾语为代词时,该代词须置于本短语的动词和副词中间。

choke up *v.* ❶ fill (a place) so that it is difficult to move (某处) 充满,挤满,塞满: The entrance was *choked up* with bricks, and we had difficulty getting in. 入口处堆满了砖,我们难以进入。Cars and trucks are *choking up* our streets. 各种车辆阻塞了街路。Leaves *choked up* the pipe. 树叶堵塞了管道。❷(非正式用语) cannot speak because of the effect of a strong emotion; cause (someone) to feel like starting to cry (由于感情的作用而)说不出话来,使(某人)哽咽: She *choked up* over the flowers Tom gave her. 汤姆送来的鲜花使她感动得说不出话来。On seeing her son the mother *choked up* and was unable to speak. 看到儿子,妈妈哽咽得说不出话来。The movie was sad and it *choked* most of the audience *up*. 这部影片令人伤悲,它使大多数观众哽咽。

NOTE 当本短语所带的宾语为代词时,该代词须置于本短语的动词和副词中间。

choose as *vt.*【可分性动词短语】choose (someone or something) to be (someone or something) 把……选为……: Between Lexus and Infiniti which would you *choose as* your next car and why? 雷克萨斯(凌志)和英菲尼迪两款车你想选择哪一款作为你的新座驾? 为什么? Anyone *choosing* politics *as* a career must face intense competition. 凡是选择从政的人都必须面对激烈的竞争。

chop up *vt.*【可分性动词短语】cut (something such as wood or food) into small pieces (把木头或食物)劈(或切)成小块: He *chopped up* some wood for the fire. 他劈了一些木头烧火。These chunks of meat are rather large — could you *chop* them *up* a bit smaller? 这些肉块有些大,你能把它们切小一点吗? Mary was busy *chopping up* vegetables for the soup. 玛丽在忙着切菜做汤。

NOTE 当本短语所带的宾语为代词时,该代词须置于本短语的动词和副词中间。

chuck out *vt.*【可分性动词短语】(非正式用语) ❶ throw (something) away because you no longer need or want it 把(无用之物)扔掉: I *chucked out* all the newspapers yesterday. 昨天,我把所有的报纸都扔掉了。Instead of *chucking* them *out*, we made do with these old pieces of furniture. 这些家具虽旧,我们还是将就着使用,而没有把它们扔掉。❷(常用一般时态,常与 of 连用) force (a person) to leave a place or a job, usually because he has done something wrong 把(某人)赶走,解雇: The owner threatened to *chuck* us *out* of the restaurant if we didn't stop singing. 餐馆老板威胁说,如果我们不停止唱歌就把我们从餐馆里赶出去。He was *chucked out* of office for taking bribes. 他因受贿而被免职。

NOTE 1. 当本短语所带的宾语为代词时,该代词须置于本短语的动词和副词中间。
2. 当本短语作"把(无用之物)扔掉"解时,同义短语是 throw away 和 throw out。
3. 当本短语作"把(某人)赶走,解雇"解时,同义短语是 throw out。

clam up *vi.* (非正式用语,用一般时态) suddenly stop talking or explaining something, or remain silent, especially because you are unhappy, embarrassed, or want to keep a secret (尤指因不快或困窘而)沉默不语;(为保守秘密而)守口如瓶: Whenever I mentioned her husband she *clammed up*, and I could get no more information out of her. 每当我提到她丈夫时,她就一声不吭,我无法从她那儿得到更多的消息。I told you to *clam up*; we don't want the whole world to know our plans! 我告诉过你要守口如瓶,我们不想让所有的人都知道我们的计划!

NOTE 本短语的同义短语是 zip one's lip(s)。

clap in/into *vt.* 【可分性动词短语】(非正式用语,常用被动语态形式) put (someone) somewhere, usually a prison 把(某人)关进(常指监狱): The judge *clapped* her *in* jail before she had time to explain. 法官不容她辩解就把她投入监牢。The robber was *clapped into* a cell. 那个抢劫犯被关进了监狱的小囚室中。The regime's response was to *clap* people *into* prison. 该政权的反应就是把人们抓进监狱。

clap on *vt.* 【可分性动词短语】(非正式用语,常用一般时态) hit (someone) lightly with your hand in a friendly manner, usually on (the back or shoulder)(友好地)用手掌轻拍(某人的后背或肩膀): His boss *clapped* him *on* the back approvingly. 老板赞许地拍了拍他的后背。Smith *clapped* his friend *on* the shoulder in greeting. 史密斯拍了拍他老朋友的肩头以示致意。

clean down *vt.* 【可分性动词短语】clean (someone or something) by brushing or with flowing water 洗刷: He was covered with mud, and we used the garden hose to *clean* him *down*. 他满身都是泥,我们用花园里的水管把他冲洗干净。I'm going to *clean down* my car this afternoon, as it is getting very dirty. 我的车太脏了,我今天下午要把它洗一下。He *cleaned* the lorry *down* thoroughly last night. 昨天晚上他把卡车彻底地冲刷了一遍。These stables must be thoroughly *cleaned down*. 这些马厩必须彻底洗刷干净。

NOTE 当本短语所带的宾语为代词时,该代词须置于本短语的动词和副词中间。

clean off *v.* (of dirt or unwanted marks) (cause to) be removed (从……)除掉(污物或污迹): I *cleaned* the mud *off* my shoes. 我把泥浆从我的鞋上擦掉了。It's quite certain that the detergent will help *clean off* the stain. 洗涤剂肯定会帮助除掉这点污迹的。I hope these oil stains will *clean off*. 我希望这些油迹能除掉。

clean out *vt.* 【可分性动词短语】❶make (a place or container) clean or tidy by removing objects that are not wanted and getting rid of any dirt or dust in it 把(某物的内部)清洁干净: It's time you *cleaned out* your bedroom. 你该把自己的卧室收拾干净啦。They spent the day *cleaning out* the garage. 他们花了一天的时间把车库内部清扫干净。I really must *clean* the study *out*; there are things all over the floor and piles of paper everywhere. 我真得把书房打扫一番了。地板上满是东西,到处都是一堆堆的纸。❷(非正式用语,常用一般时态)empty (a place of objects or goods), especially by stealing or buying them in large quantities 把(某处)偷窃一空;把(商品)买光: The thieves *cleaned out* the store. 盗贼们把这家商店偷窃一空。The supermarkets were *cleaned out* by panicking shoppers. 超市里的商品都被恐慌的购物者们抢购一空。❸(非正式用语,用一般时态)(cause to) use all of (one's money)(使)花光(钱财): She *cleaned out* her savings in a short time. 她很快就把全部积蓄花光了。Jim's friends *cleaned* him *out* when they were playing cards last night. 昨晚吉姆的朋友和他打牌时,把他所有的钱都赢光了。If we have to get the car repaired, we'll be completely *cleaned out*. 如果我们必须修理这台车的话,就得把钱全部花光。

NOTE 当本短语所带的宾语为代词时,该代词须置于本短语的动词和副词中间。

clean up *v.* ❶make (a place) completely tidy and clean 把(某处)收拾干净整洁;彻底打扫: Be sure to *clean up* the kitchen when you finish cooking. 做完饭后,一定要把厨房收拾干净。You must *clean* your bedroom *up*; it's a disgrace. 你必须把你的卧室收拾一下了。它脏得丢人。It's your turn to *clean up*. 该你们清扫了。❷ remove (objects from a place) in order to make it completely clean and tidy 清除(污物等),清洁:*Clean up* this mess at once before the boss sees it. 快把这些乱七八糟的东西清除掉,别让老板看见。The food companies classified as D-grade will be ordered to suspend operation and *clean up* their facilities within a fixed period of time, or face permanent shutdown. 定为丁级的食品公司将被勒令停业,限期彻底清洁设备,否则面临永久性关闭。❸(非正式用语)make (yourself) clean by washing 洗手,洗脸,洗澡: I *cleaned* myself *up* and got ready for dinner. 我洗了洗就准备吃饭了。I need to *clean up*. 我需要洗一洗。You'd better go into the bathroom and get *cleaned up*. 你最好去洗浴间洗洗澡。❹(非正式用语)(of the police or authorities) stop (bad, unfair, dishonest or criminal behavior) in a place (警方或政府)整治,清理(不良、不公、欺诈或犯罪行为): The new mayor has promised to *clean up* the town by getting rid of all the criminality. 新上任的市长承诺要消除一切犯罪行为,整治好该市。New and remarkable achievements have been made in anti-corruption efforts to improve the Party's style and *clean up* the government in the last few years. 在过去的几年里,反腐败和党风廉政工作取得了新的明显成效。❺(非正式用语)win or make (a lot of money) as profit 赢得,赚得(一笔大钱): He *cleaned up* a fortune playing cards. 他打牌赢了不少的钱。He really *cleaned up* on the stock market. 他在股票市场上还真赚了一大笔钱。

NOTE 1. 当本短语所带的宾语为代词时,该代词须置于本短语的动词和副词中间。
2. 本短语可转化为复合词 clean-up,意为"扫除,清扫"。

clear away *vt.*【可分性动词短语】remove (something) 收拾走,除去(某物);赶走(某人): *Clean away* your toys now, children! 把你们的玩具现在都收拾走,孩子们! When you see cigarette ashes on the desk, *clear* them *away*. 你们看到桌

子上有烟灰时，把它们收拾走。The rubbish must be *cleared away*. 这些垃圾必须清除掉。

—*vi.* (of cloud, fog, etc.) disappear (云、雾等)散去，消失：The dark clouds soon *cleared away*. 乌云很快就消散了。The plane didn't take off until the thick fog *cleared away*. 浓雾消散后，飞机才起飞。When he read the letter, his doubts *cleared away*. 读完那封信后，他的满腹疑云便消散了。

—*vt.* & *vi.* ❶ (cause to) leave a place (使)离开：We were told by the police to *clear away* from the scene of the accident. 警察让我们离开事故现场。Thai Prime Minister threatened Saturday to *clear away* the demonstrators in front of the government building by force. 泰国总理星期六威胁说要以武力驱赶政府大楼前的示威者。❷remove (the plates, knives, etc.) from a table after a meal 从餐桌上收走(餐具)：Help your mother to *clear away*, son. 儿子，帮你妈妈收走餐具。You sit down; I'll *clear away*. 您坐着，我来收拾。She *cleared away* the dishes and the tea-things. 她把盘子和茶具收走了。

NOTE 当本短语用作及物性动词短语，所带的宾语为代词时，该代词须置于本短语的动词和副词中间。

clear of[1] *vt.* 【可分性动词短语】❶ free (usually a place) by removing (unwanted things or people) 清除，消除：The ground should first be *cleared of* weeds. 首先要把地面上的杂草清除干净。*Clear* your mind *of* all negative thoughts. 要把你头脑子中的消极思想统统消除。They tried to *clear* him *of* his suspicion. 他们设法消除了他的疑心。❷(常用被动语态形式，用一般时态) prove or declare officially that someone did not do something wrong 证明(或宣告某人)无过错(或无罪)：The boy was *cleared of* the charge of murder. 那男孩子被证明没犯谋杀罪。An investigation *cleared* me *of* any wrongdoing. 调查表明，我没有任何过错。The two men have been *cleared of* murdering the old man. 这两名男子已被证明与那起谋杀老翁案无关。

clear of[2] *adj.* ❶free from things that are blocking the way or covering the surface of something 无阻碍的，无遮盖的：All exits must be kept *clear of* luggage. 所有的出口处都决不能放行李。Most roads are now *clear of* snow. 大多数路面都没有雪了。❷free from something that is unpleasant 没有的：We're finally *clear of* debt. 我们终于没有了债务。They were still not *clear of* all suspicion. 他们还没完全消除疑虑。❸not touching something; away from someone or something 不接触的，远离的：Our ship was *clear of* the rocks. 我们的船避开了礁石。You'd better keep *clear of* him. 你最好对他敬而远之。Please stand *clear of* the doors while the train is moving. 列车运行时，请勿靠近车门站立。

clear off *v.* ❶(英国英语用法，非正式用语) get rid of or remove (something) (from a place)；把……(从……)清理掉：They wanted to *clear off* all the old stock in the warehouse. 他们想要把仓库里所有积压的存货清理掉。I'll just *clear* all my papers *off* the table. 我正要把我所有的文件从桌子上清理掉。❷(英国英语用法，非正式用语，用一般时态，常用于祈使句中) (cause to) leave somewhere quickly 赶快走开，赶走：We don't give money to beggars. *Clear off*! 我们不会给乞丐钱的，赶快走开！When the man saw the policeman he *cleared off* as quickly as possible. 那名男子一看见警察便溜走了。Seeing some children playing in his orchard, the farmer *cleared* them *off*. 那农夫看到一些孩子在他的果园里玩,便把他们赶走了。❸ pay (a debt) completely 还清(债务):Jim always has some debts to *clear off*. 吉姆总是欠有一些债要还。I'm glad I've *cleared off* the money I owed my friends. 我庆幸还清了欠我朋友们的钱。

NOTE 1. 当本短语用作及物性动词短语,所带的宾语为代词时,该代词须置于本短语的动词和副词中间。

2. 当本短语作"还清(债务)"解时,同义短语是 pay off。

clear out *v.* ❶make a container, room, or house tidy by removing (things that are not wanted) 清除,丢弃(无用之物):Please *clear out* all those old clothes from your drawer. 请你把那些旧衣服从你的抽屉中都清理出去。When are you going to *clear* all that rubbish *out* of the greenhouse? 你什么时候把暖房的垃圾清走? Isn't it about time you *cleared out* some of your junk? 你是不是该把你的一些垃圾丢掉啦? ❷(英国英语用法,非正式用语,常与 of 连用)(cause to)(of someone) leave somewhere often quickly and permanently (使某人)离开;把(某人)赶出去,匆匆离开: The police *cleared* all the people *out* of the hotel. 警察让所有的人都离开了宾馆。You'd better *clear out* quickly; it's dangerous to stay here. 你们最好快点离开这里,待在这里很危险。

NOTE 1. 当本短语用作及物性动词短语,所带的宾语为代词时,该代词须置于本短语的动词和副词中间。

2. 本短语可转化为复合词 clear-out,意为"清除,清理,丢弃"。

clear up *vt.* &*vi.* ❶make (a place) tidy by removing things that you have finished using or no longer want put in order 整理,收拾,打扫(某处):*Clear up* your desk before you leave the office. 在离开办公室前,把办公桌整理一下。Don't expect me to *clear up* after you all the time! 不要总是指望我替你收拾东西! That's twice today that room has been *cleared up*. 那个房间今天已收拾两次了。You may have a party in the room, but *clear* it *up* afterwards. 你们可以在这个房间里搞聚会,但事后必须把它打扫干净。❷cure or get rid of (an infection or disease); (of an infection or disease) become cured 治好(某种感染或疾病);(某种感染或疾病)被治好:Antibiotics should be used to *clear up* the infection. 应该使用抗生素来治疗感染。This medicine should *clear up* your cold. 这种药会治好你的感冒。Most colds *clear up* of its own accord after a few days. 大多数感冒都会在几天后自行痊愈。These pills should *clear* your rash *up*. 这些药丸应该能治好你的皮疹。

—*vt.*【可分性动词短语】make plain or clear; find a satisfactory explanation for (a problem, mystery, or misunderstanding) 澄清(问题),弄清(难解之谜),消除(误会):I'd like to *clear up* two or three points. 我有两三个问题要澄清。The police hope to clear the matter up quickly. 警方希望迅速查清此事。After 5 years, the case has finally been *cleared up*. 五年后,这个案子才终于查清。Obviously the misunderstanding will have to be *cleared up*. 很显然,误会需要消除。

—*vi.* (of the weather) become clear or

fine (天气)晴朗起来：I hope the weather *clears up* before Sunday. 我希望星期日前天气会转晴。I'm sure it will *clear up* this afternoon. 我确信今天下午天会晴朗起来。

C

NOTE 当本短语用作及物性动词短语，所带的宾语为代词时，该代词须置于本短语的动词和副词中间。

cling to *vt.*【不可分性动词短语】❶hold tightly to (someone or something) 紧紧附着，紧紧粘住，紧紧抓住：The little child *clung to* his mother. 那小孩儿紧紧地依偎在妈妈的怀里。His wet shirt *clung to* his body. 他那件湿T恤紧紧地贴在身上。Dewdrops were still *clinging to* the trees. 露珠仍然挂在树上。He *clung to* the rope with both hands. 他双手紧紧地抓住绳子。❷ try to keep (something such as an idea, a position or a possession they have) 坚持(某一思想或立场)；不放弃(所有之物)：I am not a man who *clings to* old ideas. 我不是一个固守旧思想不放的人。How could you set aside all the objections and *cling to* your own course? 你怎么能不顾一切反对意见而一意孤行呢? The president appears determined to *cling to* his power. 总统似乎决意不放弃其权力。The old lady tried to *cling to* her old house, but the builders forced her out. 老妇人执意不肯离开她的旧房，是建筑人员强行使她搬走的。

clock in/on *vi.* (非正式用语) (of workers, especially in a factory or a company) pass a special card through a piece of equipment to record that they have arrived at work (尤指工厂工人或公司职员)上班，打卡上班：Most of the workers *clocked in* before 8: 30 this morning. 今天上午，大多数工人都是8点半上的班。When they arrived to *clock in/on* they found the factory gates locked. 当他们赶到要打卡上班时，却发现工厂大门上了锁。

NOTE 本短语的同义短语是check in；反义短语是clock out/off和check out。

clock off/out *vi.* (非正式用语) (of workers, especially in a factory or a company) pass a special card through a piece of equipment to record that they are leaving work (尤指工厂工人或公司职员)下班，打卡下班：The day shift was *clocking off*. 白班人员正在打卡下班。They *clock off* at this time everyday. 他们每天都是这个时候下班。As a rule David *clocks out* at half past four on Saturdays. 每星期六，戴维通常在4点半下班。

NOTE 本短语的同义短语是check out；反义短语是clock in/on和check in。

close by *adv.* at a short distance 在附近：My friend lives close by. 我的朋友就住在附近。Did a new hairdressing shop open *close by*? 这附近是不是新开了一家理发店?

close down *vt.* &*vi.* ❶ (of a shop, factory, etc.) (cause to) stop doing business or operating permanently (使)(商店，工厂等)永久性关闭，停业：The shop *closed down* when the owner died. 店主死后，店铺就关闭了。They've threatened to close our store down, and I think they mean business. 他们威胁说要关掉我们的商店，我认为他们是动真格的。They have decided to *close* that branch *down*. 他们已决定将该分公司关闭。Poultry markets in bird flu-affected areas have also been *closed down* by local administrations for industry and commerce. 受禽流感影响地区内的禽类市场也被当地的工商行政管理部门关闭。❷(of a computer program)(cause to) stop operating and disappear from your computer screen (使)(计算机程序)关闭:*Close down* all programs that are running before you install the software. 在安装软件之前,要关闭所有正在运行的程序。

—*vi.* (英国英语用法)stop broadcasting at the end of a day's television or radio programmes (电视台或广播电台) 结束全天节目的播出: Television *closed down* for the night after twelve o'clock. 一过 12 点,晚间的电视节目便结束了。It is midnight and we are now *closing down*. 已是午夜,我们今天的播音到此结束。

NOTE **1.** 当本短语作"(使)(商店,工厂等)永久性关闭,停业"解时,同义短语是 shut down。

2. 本短语可转化为复合词 close-down,意为"停工,停业,关闭"。

close in *vi.* ❶(of day) grow shorter (白昼)变短: The days are *closing in* now that autumn is here. 秋天来临,白天逐渐变短。❷(of winter or darkness) arrive (指冬天或黑暗)到来,降临: The cold winter has quite *closed in*. 寒冬已至。Darkness *closed in* on the city. 暮色笼罩着该城。

—*vt.* & *vi.* envelop; surround (a place) 包围,封锁(某处): The heavy fog *closed in* and we couldn't see two yards in front of us. 大雾笼罩,我们往前看不出两码远。Enemy troops began *closing in*; they decided to try to make a break. 敌军开始实施包围。他们决定设法突围。The airport was *closed in*. 机场被封锁了。

close in on *vt.* 【不可分性动词短语】get near (someone or something) intending to surround and attack it or them 包围,逼近: The bandits were trapped when the enemy began to *close in on* them. 当军队将他们包围时,这些土匪就成了瓮中之鳖。Hitler committed suicide as Soviet forces were *closing in on* Berlin. 希特勒在苏联军队逼近柏林时自杀。

close to Ⅰ *adj.* near 靠近,接近: The church is *close to* the Teachers' College. 教堂就在师范学院附近。The moon is much *closer to* us than any other planets. 月球比其他任何行星离我们都近得多。The neutron has a mass very *close to* that of the proton but carries no charge. 中子的质量与质子的质量很接近,但不带电荷。You can't go to the party; it's too *close to* your exams. 你不能去参加聚会,你马上就要考试了。

Ⅱ *adv.* ❶nearly; almost 接近于,几乎: *Close to* 90 percent of those polled online said pornographic and junk emails needed to be controlled. 近 90%接受网上调查的人表示,那些色情和垃圾邮件需要加以控制。The cost was *close to* $1 million. 成本接近于 100 万美元。According to Pentagon officials, the new task force has gotten *close to* finding Laden. 据五角大楼的官员说,新组建的突击队几近找到拉登。❷not far off 在附近: We live *close to* the railway station. 我们住在火车站附近。Don't stand *close to* the machine; it's dangerous. 别在机器跟前站着,有危险。

NOTE 当本短语作为形容词性短语,作"靠近,接近"解时,同义短语是 adjacent to。两者之间的区别见 adjacent to。

close up *vt.* & *vi.* ❶(of someone) lock (a building or business) completely and securely, either for a short time or permanently, often because he or she is going away 关门,闭店,收市: We are *closing up* the house for the summer. 今年夏季,我们要封闭这所房子。As the storm approached, people began *closing up* their businesses. 由于暴风雨就要来临,人们都开始关门停业了。❷(of a wound in the skin)(cause to) join and become healthy again (使)(皮肤上的伤口)愈合: The wound in his arm has begun to *close up*. 他臂上的伤口已开始愈合。The cut has *closed up* without a scar. 这伤口愈合得没留一点疤痕。❸(cause to) move (people or things) closer together (使)相互靠拢,靠近: The sergeant ordered his men to *close up*. 中士命令他的士兵们相互靠拢。Children have to learn to *close up* their letters when writing. 孩子们得学会在书写时把字母写紧凑。

—*vi.* (常用一般时态) refuse to talk about your true feelings or thoughts 闭口不语: Why do you *close up* every time I mention your father? 为什么我一提起你的父亲你就闭口不语?

NOTE 本短语可转化为复合词 close-up,意为"近景,特写照片"。

close with *vt.* 【不可分性动词短语】❶begin to fight with 开始交战,格斗: The two armies *closed with* each other. 双方的军队开始交战。❷(英国英语用法)agree with (someone)or to (a price, terms, conditions, etc.)同意(某人的意见),接受(某一价格、条款、条件等): The businessman quickly *closed with* the inspector. 那位商人很快就同意了稽查员的意见。

coffee break ⇨ **tea break**

coincide with *vt.* 【不可分性动词短语】(常用一般时态) happen in the same time as (something else) by chance 与……同时发生,与……巧合: Her holidays don't *coincide with* mine. 她不和我在同一时间休假。The two countries agreed on a comprehensive ceasefire on Tuesday, *coinciding with* the start of the Eid festival. 两国在星期二同意全面停火,这正巧逢开斋节的开始。

collide with *vt.* 【不可分性动词短语】❶(无被动语态形式,常用一般时态) crash violently into (something) 撞上: He *collided with* a pine tree near the north gate. 他在北门处撞上了一棵松树。Smith *collided with* Marvin, but neither was hurt. 史密斯与马文发生了碰撞,但两人都没有受伤。One passenger train *collided with* another yesterday, killing at least 70 people and injuring more than 400. 昨天,两辆旅客列车相撞,导致至少70人死亡,400多人受伤。❷(用一般时态) disagree violently with (something) 与……相冲突,与……不一致: The President *collided with* Congress over his budget plans. 总统在其预算计划上与国会发生了冲突。The chairman's opinion *collided with* that of the rest of the committee. 主席的意见与委员会其他成员的意见不相一致。

combine with *vt.* (cause to) join with (something else) to form a single unit or whole (使)结合,把……与……相结合: Experts fear that bird flu might *combine with* the human influenza virus to create a new strain that could be easily transmitted to humans. 专家们担心,禽流感病毒可能会与人流感病毒结合成新的变种,那就很容易传染给人了。Low profits, *combined with* high inflation, proved fatal to the company. 低利润加上

高通货膨胀对公司的打击是致命的。Theory must be *combined with* practice in scientific research work. 在科学研究工作中,理论必须与实践相结合。

come about *vi.* (常用一般时态,常与 how, when 连用) ❶ happen, occur or arise, especially in a way that seems impossible to prevent (尤指以难以防止的方式)发生,出现: How did this dangerous situation *come about*? 这种危险的情况是怎么发生的? That *came about* when we went to New York last year. 那是我们去年去纽约时发生的。Many a quarrel has *come about* through a misunderstanding. 许多争吵都是由于误解而发生的。How does it *come about* that he is always so busy? 他怎么总是这么忙? ❷ (of a ship or wind) change direction (船或风)改变方向: The ship *came about* from time and time as the wind changed direction. 这条船随着风向的改变而不时地改变航向。The wind *came about* from south to east. 风向由南转东了。

NOTE 1. 当本短语作"发生,出现"解,用于疑问句中时,常用 it 来引导,后面的 that 从句为 it 的同位语。这种形式是较正式的文体。例如:

> How does it *come about* (that) he is so badly off when he earns a good salary? 他收入不少,怎么还如此贫寒呢?

2. 本短语与 come off 和 come around/round 均表示"发生"之意。它们之间的区别是:本短语一般指某事"在无法预防的情况下发生",而 come off 和 come around/round 则指某事"按计划或按期发生或举行"。

come across *vt.* 【不可分性动词短语】(不用被动语态形式,用一般时态) ❶meet, find, or discover (something or someone) by chance 偶然发现(某物);偶然遇到(某人): She came across some old letters in the course of her search. 她在找东西时偶然发现了一些旧信件。I *came across* a word I'd never seen before. 我遇到了一个我以前从来没见过的单词。Have you ever *come across* such a wonderful person in all your life? 你这辈子遇到过这么好的人吗? ❷(of an idea or thought) arise in (someone's mind) (指主意或想法)出现于(某人的头脑之中): A good idea *came across* my mind. 一个好主意出现在我的脑海之中。It *came across* my mind that he might be interested in the problem we had discussed. 我忽然想到他也许对我们讨论的问题感兴趣。

—*vi.* ❶ (常用一般时态) make (something such as an idea) very clear to people 使人十分明白: The moral of this story doesn't *come across* easily. 这篇故事中的寓意不能很容易为人所理解。He spoke so quickly that his meaning didn't quite *come across*. 他讲得太快,以致人们没太明白他讲的意思。❷ be effective and well received 有效果,受欢迎: Your lecture *came across* very well. 您的讲座非常受欢迎。❸ (常与 as 连用) (of someone) make an impression or convey a cetain perception on people who meet him or her (某人)给人某种印象(或感觉): He *came across* very selfish in yesterday's meeting. 他在昨天的会上给人一种非常自私的印象。David *came across* as shy because he spoke so quietly. 戴维说话轻声轻语,给人一种他很腼腆的感觉。She *comes across* as a very cold person. 她给人的感觉是一个十分冷酷的人。❹agree; yield 同意,让步: How can we get him to *come across*? 我

们怎样才能使他同意呢?

NOTE 当本短语表示“偶然发现(某物);偶然遇到(某人)”之意时,同义短语是 bump into, chance on/upon, meet with, run across, run into 和 stumble across/on/upon。

come after *vt.* 【不可分性动词短语】❶(常用一般时态)follow in time (在时间上)跟在……后面,随至: Spring comes after winter. 冬去春来。*After* the banquet *came* a firework display in the garden. 宴会后,接着就是在花园里放烟火。❷(无被动语态形式) try to find or catch (someone), usually in order to punish or harm him or her 竭力找到或抓住(某人):The man *came after* the boy while waving a big stick. 那名男子挥舞着一根大棒子去追赶那小男孩。

come along *vi.* ❶(常用一般时态)arrive 到达: As the train *came along* we could feel the ground vibrating. 当火车到达的时候,我们会感到大地在颤动。He decided to give the money to the first stranger who *came along*. 他决定把钱给最先到达的陌生人。❷(常与 with 连用) go somewhere with someone else 与(他人)同去: He wants to *come along* with us to the movie. 他想和我们一道去看电影。I've never seen a baseball game; do you mind if I *come along*? 我从来没看过棒球比赛。我和你一起去,行吗? I'm getting up a little group to visit Pearl Harbor; would you like to *come along*? 我在组织一个小组去参观珍珠港。你愿一同前往吗? ❸(常用一般时态)(of something or someone) appear or arrive by chance 偶然出现,到来: Take any opportunity that *comes along*. 要抓住每一个出现的机会。I got the job because I *came along* at the right time. 我得到了这份工作是因为我来得正是时候。“Is she married?” “No, she says she is waiting for the right man to *come along*.” “她结婚了吗?”“没有。她说她正等候那个合适她的男子出现。” ❹follow; go somewhere so that you can be with someone who went there earlier 跟着,随后去:You go now; I'll *come along* later. 你先走,我随后就到。Smith had some work to finish and decided to *come along* later. 史密斯有点工作要赶完,所以决定过会儿再去。❺(常用进行时态) make progress or get better in quality, skill, or health 取得进展,取得进步,身体状况好转: Pentagon spokesman says those talks are *coming along* quite well. 五角大楼的发言人称,那几轮会谈进展相当顺利。How are you *coming along* with your English? 你的英语进展如何? Mother's *coming along* nicely after the operation. 我母亲在手术后身体状况好多了。❻(常用祈使语气) encourage (someone) to hurry up, usually when you are rather annoyed with him or her 赶快: *Come along*, the taxi is coming! 赶快,出租车来了! *Come along* — we're late! 快点! 我们迟到了!

come apart *vi.* (常用一般时态)(of something) break into pieces without force being used, either because it has been made that way or because it is very old or in very bad condition (某物)自行破裂: It *came apart* when I tried to lift it off the floor. 当我试图把它从地板上拿起来时,它竟破裂开来。I was afraid our car would *come apart* on that rough road. 我曾担心咱们的车在那条崎岖不平的路上会颠烂的。

come around/round *vi.* ❶travel a long way round 绕道走: Since there is no shortcut, you'll have to *come round* by the park. 既然没有近路可走,你就得绕过公园。❷(常与 to 连用)make a short informal visit to (someone who lives nearby)顺便走访(住在附近的人): I've been so sorry that you couldn't *come around* this week. 这星期你们没能来访,我一直感到很遗憾。I wish he'd *come round* and see us sometime, if only just to say hello. 我希望他什么时候能过来看看我们,哪怕只打声招呼也好。❸(常用一般时态)(of an event)happen again or as usual (再次或按期)发生: Christmas will soon be *coming round*. 圣诞节很快又要到了。Night duty for each doctor *comes around* every 5 days. 每位医生隔 5 天一个夜班。❹ recover consciousness; get back health 恢复知觉,身体复原: You need no worry; this patient will *come around* very soon. 你不必担心,这位病人很快就会恢复知觉的。Given timely medical treatment, the wounded soldier soon *came round*. 伤员得到了及时的救治,很快就康复了。❺(常与 to 连用) change sides or opinions, often influenced by another person's opinion 改变立场(或观点): She will soon *come around* to our way of thinking. 她很快就会改变主意,支持我们的想法。He has *come round* to our point of view. 他已同意我们的观点。❻become calmer after being in a bad temper 消气,息怒: Leave him alone and he'll soon *come round*. 不要理他,他的气一会儿就会消。

NOTE **1.** come around 主要用于美国英语中,come round 用于英国英语中。

2. 本短语与 come over 都有"顺便走访"之意。但本短语通常指彼此住得比较近,如相隔较远时则用 come over。

3. 本短语与 bring to 和 come to 都有"恢复知觉"之意。bring to 是及物性动词短语,而 come to 和本短语则是不及物性动词短语。

come at *vt.*【不可分性动词短语】(无被动语态形式) ❶(常用一般时态)reach or find (something)够到(某物),找到(某物): I saw the ball on the tree, but it was too high for me to *come at*. 我看到了球在树上,但太高了我够不到。Put the food where the cat can't *come at* it. 把食物放在猫够不到的地方。How did you *come at* that result? 你是怎样得到那个结果的? ❷(of a person or animal)move towards you in a threatening manner and try to attack you (指人或动物)向(某人)扑来: A stranger *came at* him with a knife. 一个陌生人拿着刀朝他扑了过来。The enemy *came at* us from three directions. 敌人从三面向我们扑来。I saw the big dog *coming at* me. 我看到那条大狗朝我扑来。❸(非正式用语,常用一般时态) reach a knowledge or understanding of (something) 知道,了解: It was a long time before we *came at* the truth. 我们过了很久才知道了事实真相。It is difficult to *come at* the exact truth of the matter. 很难了解到此事的确切真相。Her real feelings are not easy to *come at*. 她的真实情感不易琢磨。

come back *vi.* ❶(常与介词 from 或 to 连用)return (to a place)回来,返回: Their son *came back* from Iraq missing a leg. 他们的儿子从伊拉克回来,失去了一条腿。A cargo plane was hit by a SAM-7 surface to air missile, but it turned around and *came back* to the airport where it safely landed. 一架货机被一枚萨姆-7 型地对空导弹击中,但它成功调头返回机场并平安着陆。❷(of something) become fashionable or popular again 重新时兴,再度流行: It takes a long time to prevent old customs and habits from *coming back*. 要很长时间才能防止旧的风俗习惯死灰复燃。Do you think long dresses will ever *come back*? 你认为长连衣裙还能重新流行起来吗? ❸(常与 to 连用)(of something that you had forgotten) return to your memory 想起: Their names are all *coming back* to me now! 他们的名字我现在都想起来了! At first I could not remember why everything seemed so familiar; then it all *came back*. 开始我记不起来为何一切都显得如此熟悉,后来才都想起来了。

NOTE 1. 当本短语作"想起"解时,主语必须是某事,而不能是某人。如"我突然想起我们以前曾见过面。",不能说成: * I suddenly *came back* that we had met before. 而应该说: It suddenly *came back* to me that we had met before.

2. 本短语可转化为复合词 comeback, 意为"恢复;复原;复辟"。

come by *vt.* &*vi.* (常用一般时态) pass 走过去,经过: Mary *came by* just as we were talking about her. 玛丽恰好在我们谈论她的时候走过去了。Did you see anyone *come by* this road? 你见到有人从这条路经过没有?

—*vi.* (常用一般时态) ❶go to the place where someone is for a short and informal visit, often when you are going somewhere else (常指顺路)作非正式拜访,串门: I'll *come by* this afternoon and we can talk about the matter. 我今天下午过来,咱们好谈谈那件事。Next time you are over this way, please *come by*. 你下次再到这边来,请来串门。❷arrive 到达: Just then a bus *came by* so we got on. 正在那时,一辆公共汽车到了,我们便上了车。

—*vt.* 【不可分性动词短语】(用一般时态) ❶get (especially something that is hard to get)得到,获得(尤指难得之物): How did you *come by* such a beautiful house? 你是怎么得到一所这么漂亮的房子的? Such a universal genius is hard to *come by*. 这样的全才是很难得的。❷receive (something like a wound), usually accidentally (常指偶然)受伤: How did you *come by* that wound on your arm? 你胳膊上的伤是怎么弄的? That's a nasty bruise — how did you *come by* it? 那块瘀伤不轻,你是怎么弄伤的?

come down *vi.* ❶move down or fall to the ground 下来,落下,倒下: The boy was sitting in a tree and refused to *come down*. 那男孩坐在树上拒不下来。The heavy rain *came down*, so I decided to stay at home. 大雨倾盆而下,于是我就决定待在家里了。More than 80 percent of the buildings in Beichuan County *came down* during the powerful 8.0-magnitude earthquake. 北川县80%以上的建筑物在8级强烈地震中倒塌。❷(of cost, level, or amount of something) become less than it was before (指成本、水平或重量等)下跌,下落,下降: The price of sugar has *come down* dramatically recently. 最近,糖的价格已大幅度下跌。Interest rates should not come down. 利率不该下调。Her weight is slowly *coming down*. 她的体重在缓慢下降。❸(of an aircraft) land or crash (指飞机)降落,坠落: A Boeing 747 *came down* safely on the M1 runway in spite of the fog. 尽管有雾,一架波音747飞机还是平安地降落在了M1跑道上。Two enemy planes *came down* in the battle. 有两架敌机在战斗中被击落。❹(常用完成时态,常与 to 连用) (of something) be passed on from one period of history to another; be given or left to people who are younger or come later (指某物)从历史上流传下来,遗留(给后人): This story has *come down* to us from ancient times. 这个故事是从古代流传下来的。Mary's necklace had *come down* to her from her grandmother. 玛丽的项链是她祖母遗留给她的。

NOTE **1.** 本短语可转化为复合词 comedown,意为"地位下降;令人失望的事"。

2. 当本短语作"遗留(给后人)"解时,同义短语是 bring down, hand down, hand on 和 pass on。

come down in the world *vi.* (主要用于英国英语中) become less rich, powerful, successful, etc. than you were previously 落魄,衰落,潦倒: He is the son of a rich businessman, but he seems to have *come down* a long way *in the world*. 他是一个富商的子弟,不过看上去他早已家道中落了。Smith has *come down in the world* since he started gambling. 史密斯自从开始赌博以来就变得穷困潦倒了。

NOTE **1.** 本短语的另外一种表达形式是 go down in the world。

2. 本短语的反义短语是 come up in the world。

come down on *vt.* 【不可分性动词短语】(无被动语态形式) ❶(常用一般时态) decide to support(one side of argument), especially after long thought (尤指经过长时间考虑后)决定支持(某一方): They clearly *came down on* the side of the unions. 他们明确地支持工会一方。❷(非正式用语,常用一般时态,常与副词 hard 和介词 for 连用) criticize or punish (a person or activity) with severe disapproval 严厉斥责,惩罚(某人或某一活动): The manager *came down* much too hard *on* him for losing the document. 经理严厉地斥责他丢失了那份文件。She *came down* pretty hard *on* the kids for making much noise. 她因孩子们太吵而狠狠地训斥了他们。The school is going to *come down* more heavily *on* staying away from school without permission. 学校将对逃学施以更加严厉的惩罚。❸(非正式用语,常与 for 连用) make a forceful payment demand on (someone)向(某人)强行要求付款: The bank *came down on* us for immediate payment. 银行强行要求我们立即付款。

come down to *vt.* 【不可分性动词短语】(无被动语态形式) ❶ move towards (something or someone) from a higher level 从高处下到……: *Come down to* the ground, I can't hear you at the top of the ladder. 下到地面上来。你在梯子顶端说话我听不到。❷reach (a point)达到: His hair has come down to his shoulders. 他的头发已长到肩部。Our land *comes down to* the water's edge. 我们那块地一直延伸到水边。❸(of something such as property) be passed to (someone) because the previous owner has died (指财产等)传给(某人): This ring has *come down to* me from my grandmother. 这枚戒指是我祖母传给我的。❹(of a question, problem, or decision) be reduced to its real meaning as (something that is the most important factor involved)(用一般时态) 归结为,实质上是: The question *comes down to* whether we ought to act upon his advice. 问题可归结为我们是否应该按他的主意行事。In the end, it all *comes down to* money. 归根结底,这实质上就是钱的问题。Our choices *come down to* destroying the old building or restoring it. 我们的抉择实质上就是拆掉还是修复这栋旧楼。

come down with *vt.* 【不可分性动词短语】(美国英语用法,非正式用语,无被动语态形式) become ill with (a particular disease, usually one that is not serious) 患病(常指某种不严重的疾病): I think I'm *coming down with* a strange illness. 我觉得我得了一种怪病。Researchers then watched the volunteers to see who *came down with* a cold and waited to see how the unlucky ill manifested their cold symptoms. 然后研究人员观察那些志愿者,看谁先感染上感冒,并等着看那些不幸患病的人表现何种感冒症状。

come for *vt.* 【不可分性动词短语】❶(常用一般时态) come to a place so that you can take (someone or something) away with you 来接(某人),来取(某物): He *comes* to the kindergarten *for* his little son every day. 他每天来幼儿园接他的小儿子。The taxi will *come for* us at around 11 o'clock. 出租车将于 11 点左右来接我们。I've just *come for* the book your brother borrowed from me. 我是来取你弟弟从我借的那本书。❷(无被动语态形式,常用进行时态) move towards (someone) in order to threaten him or her, or attack them physically 向(某人)冲来: A stranger *came for* him with a knife. 一个陌生人拿着刀子向他冲了过来。I saw the big fierce-looking dog *coming for* me. 我看到一条样子凶恶的大狗向我冲来。❸(of soldiers or police) come to a place in order to arrest (someone) 来到(某处)抓捕(某人): The police *came for* him in the middle of the night. 半夜里,警察前来抓捕他。

come forth *vi.* (正式用语) appear or emerge; come out 出现,出来: A new force has *come forth* in the field of China's electronic industry. 在中国电子工业领域中出现了一支新军。I had great hopes of the President's speech, but to my disappointment, nothing very new *came forth*. 我对总统的演讲抱着极大的希望,但令我失望的是,他并没有讲出什么很新的东西。

come forth with *vt.* 【不可分性动词短语】(无被动语态形式) provide (information) 提供(信息或情况): None of the witnesses *came forth* with an accurate description of the accident. 没有一个目击者准确地描述出这起事故的经过。

come forward *vi.* ❶offer oneself to fill a position 主动要求(充任某一职务): Only two people have *come forward* for election to the committee. 只有两个人主动要求参加该委员会的竞选。❷offer to give help to the police 自告奋勇(协助警方): Police said no one has *come forward* with any information about the murder. 警方说,还没有人自告奋勇提供有关谋杀案的情况。❸(常用一般时态) be introduced for discussion, as at a meeting (在会上)提出供讨论: The matter was deferred at last evening's meeting, but will *come forward* at our next session. 这个问题在昨天晚上的会议上搁了下来,但是将在下次的全体会议上提出来讨论。

come from *vt.* 【不可分性动词短语】(无被动语态形式) ❶have been born in (a particular place) 出生在(某地): I *come from* New York but I've spent most of my life in Washington. 我出生在纽约,但我一生中大部分时间都是在华盛顿度过

的。My parents *come from* Italy. 我父母都是意大利人。❷have your home in (a particular place); belong to (a particular type of family or social group)来自(某地);出身于(某类家庭或社会阶层): We *come from* Britain, but Mr Smith *comes from* Canada. 我们都是来自英国,但史密斯先生来自加拿大。The Prince of Tightrope Walking *comes from* a family of tightrope walkers in China's Xinjiang. 这位"走钢丝王子"出身于中国新疆的一个走钢丝的世家。❸(用一般时态)be obtained from, produced by, or found in (a particular place or thing)来源于,产自,来自: The money that the Federal Government uses *comes* mostly *from* taxes. 联邦政府所用的资金大部分来源于税收。Some of the best wines *come from* France. 一些上好的葡萄酒产自法国。Where's that noise *coming from*? 那噪声是从哪儿来的? The serum *comes from* a tropical plant. 这浆液出自一种热带植物。❹have (something) as an origin 源于: This word *comes from* an African language. 这个词来源于一种非洲语言。This kind of accident *comes from* being careless. 这种事故源于粗心。

come in *vi.* ❶enter (a room, building, or other place)进来: *Come in* and sit down. 进来,请坐。He was so intent on his magazine that he didn't notice me *come in*. 他太专注于读他那本杂志,连我进来他都没察觉到。❷arrive (somewhere)到达(某处): The train *came in* at 11 o'clock. 该趟列车是在11点到达的。The plane *came in* at 3 o'clock in the morning. 飞机于凌晨3点到达。❸(of a message or report) be received by someone (信息或报告)被某人收到: Some more letters of complaint have just *came in*. 刚刚又收到了一些投诉信件。Reports are *coming in* of a powerful earthquake in Wenchuan of Sichuan province. 不断收到一些有关四川省汶川大地震的报道。❹(后接序数词)finish a race or competition in a particular position (在比赛或竞赛中)获得……名次: Smith *came in* last in the running race. 史密斯在赛跑中得了最后一名。My horse *came in* first. 我的马获得了第一名。❺(of a new idea, fashion, or product) become fashionable at a particular time (指某种新的思想、时尚或产品)(在某一时期)时髦,流行: When did the short skirt first *come in*? 短裙子是什么时候开始流行的? ❻ appear; happen 出现,发生: Nylon products *came in* after 1940. 尼龙产品出现于1940年以后。This is where the mistakes *come in*. 错误就出在这里。❼(of money) be earned or received regularly by someone 收入,赚得(钱): He has £8,000 *coming in* every year. 他每年收入8 000英镑。There is very little money *coming in* at present. 目前,收进的钱很少。I haven't a lot of money *coming in* just now. 我现在还没赚到很多钱。❽(of the water in the sea) gradually rise so that it covers more of the land (海水)涨潮: The tide is *coming in* so don't stay on the sand too long! 涨潮了,不要在沙滩上逗留得太久啦!

NOTE 当请某人进入自己的家里、办公室或房间内时,常用 come on in 的形式,以表示礼貌或客气。例如:

> Hello, you guys. *Come on in*. We're just about to start dinner.
> 大家好,快进来吧,我们正准备开始晚餐。

come in for *vt.*【不可分性动词短语】(常

用一般时态)(of someone or something) receive (criticism or blame)受到(批评或责备): The use of body scanners has *come in for* some criticism in the West as passengers have complained that it violates their privacy. 在西方,使用人体扫描设备一直受到批评。乘客们抱怨这侵犯了他们的个人隐私。Their industrial plan has *come in for* much blame. 他们的工业计划受到很多责难。

come into *vt.* 【不可分性动词短语】❶enter (a space such as a room or building)进入: When the professor *came into* the classroom the students were talking about him. 当教授走进教室时,学生们正在谈论他。The children *came* running *into* the room. 孩子们跑进了屋里。"Then the emergency lights came on and more and more smoke started *coming into* the tube carriage," a witness of the subway bombing said. 一位地铁爆炸案的目击者陈述道:"后来紧急指示灯亮了,越来越多的烟雾进入了地铁车厢。" ❷(无被动语态形式,常用一般时态) receive (a sum of money) after someone's death; inherit 继承(钱财): Mary *came into* a large fortune when her aunt died. 姑妈去世后,玛丽继承了一大笔钱。He doesn't *come into* his share of the legacy until he is 21. 他要到 21 岁时才能继承他那份遗产。❸(无被动语态形式)begin to be in (a particular state or activity)开始处于(某种状态或活动)之中: Their fruit trees will come into blossom. 他们的果树就要开花了。So they *came into* conflict with the workers. 因此,他们和工人发生了冲突。Your suggestions will come into consideration. 你的建议将会得到考虑。This kind of shoes *came into* fashion a few years ago. 这种鞋前几年才开始流行。

come into action *vi.* begin being used 开始使用: If the pressure rises, an overflow valve *comes into action* and the surplus oil returns to the tank. 如果压力升高,溢流阀就会起作用,于是多余的油就返回到油箱。When the big guns *came into action*, we knew the battle would soon be over. 大炮一投入使用,我们便知道战斗快结束了。

come into being *vi.* begin to exist 开始存在,形成: This practice *came into being* in the late Middle Ages. 这种习俗始于中世纪末期。We wish to extend our warm congratulations on the Convention's *coming into being*. 我们对公约的诞生表示热烈的祝贺。The first electronic computer *came into being* at the end of the 1940s. 第一台电子计算机出现于 20 世纪 40 年代末。We do not know when the universe *came into being*. 我们不知道宇宙是什么时候形成的。

NOTE 本短语的另外一种表达式是 come into existence。

come into contact *vi.* (常与 with 连用) touch or come together (with something or someone) 接触: When we see something about to *come into contact* with the edge of our shadow, brain activity suggests it is as if the object is about to touch us instead. 当我们看到有东西将要接触到我们影子的边缘时,大脑的反应就像有东西要碰到我们的身体一样。You must have *come into contact* with someone suffering from an infectious disease. 你肯定和患有某种传染病的人接触过。

come into effect *vi.* (of something such as a law) start to be used or become

effective (法律等)开始实施,生效:The city government has announced that the new no smoking laws will *come into effect* next month. 市政府宣布,新的禁烟法令将于下个月开始实施。A new-generation Test of English as Foreign Language (TOEFL) *came into effect* for students who want to study in North American universities. 为欲赴北美留学的学生设计的新一代托福考试(TOEFL)已开始实施。

NOTE 1. 本短语另外的表达形式是 come into force 和 come into operation。

2. 本短语的同义短语是 take effect。

come into existence ⇨ **come into being**

come into play *vi.* begin to have an effect, influence, or force 开始发挥作用:His early training *came into play* in the new situation. 他以前所受到的训练在新情况下开始发挥作用了。All kinds of forces *come into play* when a nation's vital interests are threatened. 当一个国家的根本利益受到威胁时,各种各样的势力都会发挥作用。

come into service *vi.* begin to be used; begin to operate and function as designed 投入使用,投入运营:When did this elevator *come into service*? 这台电梯是什么时候投入使用的? Three new subway lines have *come into service* in Beijing to ease traffic during and after the Olympic games. 北京新开通了三条地铁线路以缓解奥运会期间和以后的交通状况。

come into sight *vi.* (of something, especially something large) slowly appear; begin to be able to be seen (尤指巨型物体)慢慢出现,开始被看到:By the time the town *came into sight*, we were too tired to go on. 当可以看到那座城镇时,我们已累得不能往前走了。People of all ages waved Chinese national flags and cheered when the torch runners *came into sight*. 当奔跑着的火炬手进入视线时,人们不分老幼都挥舞着中国国旗,高声欢呼。

NOTE 本短语的另外一种表达形式是 come into view。

come into use *vi.* start being used 开始使用:Attack helicopters have *come into* even more frequent use recently during the attacks on resistance forces in central Iraq. 在最近对伊拉克中部地区的抵抗力量的攻击行动中,攻击性直升机更加频繁地投入了使用。When did this word *come into* common use? 这个单词是什么时候开始普及使用的?

come into vogue *vi.* (of something) become to be popular or fashionable 流行起来:When did pointed shoes *come into vogue*? 尖头鞋是什么时候流行起来?

come of *vt.* 【不可分性动词短语】(无被动语态形式,用一般时态) ❶(正式用语) be descended from (a particular family or type of family)出身于(某类家庭):The prime minister *comes of* a farming family. 首相出身于农民家庭。She *comes of* a good family. 她出身良家。❷be the result of (something) 是……的结果:I doubt if any good will *come of* these peace initiatives. 我怀疑这些和平倡议能否带来什么好的结果。This *comes of* your not listening to us. 这都是你不听我们劝告的结果。That car crashed into the tree — that's what *comes of* buying cheap tyres. 那辆车撞到了一棵树上——这就是买廉价轮胎的后果。

come of age *vi.* ❶(常用一般时态)reach the age when you are legally an adult 达

到法定年龄,成年:In Britain a young person *comes of age* on his or her 18th birthday. 在英国,青年男女足龄 18 岁便达到法定年龄。Miss Davidson, the first person in Britain to survive a heart transplant, will be the guest tomorrow at a ball which is being held to mark her *coming of age*. 英国首例接受心脏移植手术的存活者戴维森小姐明天将作为嘉宾参加一场为庆祝她成年而举行的舞会。❷reach a stage of full development 到达成熟(充分发展)时期:The company has now been successfully established for ten years, and has really *come of age*. 该公司已成功地经营了 10 年,现已到达充分发展时期。

NOTE 本短语的另外一种表达形式是 be of age。

come off *v.* ❶ stop being fixed to (something)(从……)脱落:I pulled at the drawer, and the handle *came off*. 我一拉抽屉,把手掉了下来。A button came off as I was climbing over the wall. 我在爬越这堵墙时,一颗纽扣脱落下来。The hook *came off* the wall when I hung up my coat. 我挂上衣时,挂衣钩竟从墙上脱落下来。❷fall off (something that you are riding) 从……上摔下来:The horse refused at the first fence, and that's when I *came off*. 马到了第一道栅栏就不肯跳了,我就是那时摔下来的。He *came off* his bike when the chain suddenly broke. 自行车的链条突然断了,他从车子上摔了下来。❸(如本短语后有代词时,该代词前常用 of)get down off (something); get off (something)从……下来:*Come off* of that horse immediately! 快从那匹马上下来! They have just *come off* the train, waiting for the bus to go home. 他们刚下火车,在等公共汽车回家。❹leave (something, usually a place)离开:*Come off* with me and have some coffee, I'm tired of listening to this speech. 跟我离开这儿去喝点咖啡,我讨厌听这个演讲。She usually *comes off* her shift at 6 o'clock. 她通常 6 点钟下班。❺(常用一般时态)(of something such as dirt or paint) be able to be removed by washing or rubbing (指污迹或油漆等)可被除掉:We didn't know why the stain wouldn't *come off*. 我们不知道这污渍为什么除不掉。The chewing gum would not easily *come off*. 口香糖不易被除掉。❻(美国英语用法,非正式用语,用一般时态)(of something) happen or take place (as planned)(按计划)发生,举行:The match didn't *come off* because of the terrorists' threats. 由于恐怖分子的威胁,比赛未能按计划进行。The wedding *came off* as planned. 婚礼按计划举行了。❼(非正式用语,用一般时态)(of something) succeed or achieve a particular result in an activity 成功,取得效果:I was surprised when the plan *came off* so easily. 我很惊讶,那项计划这么轻而易举地就成功了。It was a clever joke but it didn't quite *come off*. 那笑话不错,可惜没怎么让人发笑。

come off it *s.* (非正式用语,用于祈使句中)(an expression of disbelief) stop talking nonsense; stop pretending that something is true 别胡说了,别瞎扯,别装了:*Come off it*; tell me the truth for God's sake. 别胡说了。看在上帝的分上,告诉我真相吧。*Come off it* — we know you're as poor as the rest of us. 别装蒜了,我们知道你和我们所有的人一样穷。

come on/upon *vi.* ❶(of a light or other

electrical machines) start working or functioning (电灯或其他电器)亮,开始工作: the emergency lights *came on* and more and more smoke started coming into the tube carriage. 紧急指示灯亮了,越来越多的烟雾进入了地铁车厢。What time does the central heating *come on*? 什么时候开始集中供热? ❷(of an actor/actress or a sports player) appear on a stage or a sports field (演员)登台,(运动员)上场: When the famous actress *came on*, the audience applauded wildly. 当那位著名的女演员上台时,观众都疯狂地鼓起掌来。He *came on* as a substitute. 他作为替补队员上场。❸(of a new season or type of weather) start to arrive or appear (指季节或天气)来临: Winter was *coming on* again. 冬季又到了。It came on to rain heavily towards evening. 黄昏时分,开始下起了大雨。There is a storm *coming on*. 暴风雨要来临了。Night *came on*. 夜幕降临了。❹take place, especially in turn (尤指依次)发生,举行: The election's *coming on* this autumn. 选举于今年秋季举行。❺start to appear (in a television or radio programme) 出现在(电视或广播节目中): Then the president *comes on* and tells everyone to spend more money. 接着总统出现在电视节目中,他让大家多消费。❻(of a cold, headache, or some other medical condition) start (感冒、头痛等症状)开始,出现: Eating 1-2 pieces of raw garlic when you feel a cold *coming on* is a good way to prevent it. 当你感到要感冒的时候,吃1~2瓣生蒜是一个很好的预防措施。❼follow; travel later 跟随,随后去: You go first and I'll *come on* later. 你先去,我随后就到。He went by train to his new job, and the family *came on* by bus. 他乘火车去赴新职,其家属随后乘公共汽车而行。❽(of something or someone) improve or make good progress 有改善,有进步: His French has really *come on* since last year. 自去年以来,他的法语确实有所提高。Bob is *coming on* very well now. 鲍勃现在很有进步。❾(仅用于口语中,常用祈使语气)(used for telling someone to hurry) hurry up 赶快: Do *come on*, or we'll be late again! 快点儿,要不我们又要迟到了! ❿(仅用于口语中,常用祈使语气)(used for encouraging someone to do something) try hard; make a greater effort (用于鼓励某人)加把劲,加油: *Come on*; don't give up now when you are so close to finishing. 加把劲,这时候不能放弃,就要完事大吉了。"*Come on*! *Come on*!" shouted the audience again and again. "加油! 加油!"观众们一遍又一遍地喊道。⓫(used for telling someone that you do not believe what he or she is saying) you know what you just said is not true (用于表示不相信对方刚说的话)得了吧: "But I like digging the garden." "*Come on*, John. Digging a garden is not a job for a college graduate like you!" "但我喜欢在花园里翻土。" "得了吧,约翰。在花园里翻土也不是你这样的大学毕业生干的活!"

—*vt.*【不可分性动词短语】(无被动语态形式,用一般时态) meet (someone) or find (something), usually unexpectedly and by chance 偶然遇到(某人);偶然发现(某物): He *came on* an old friend on his way to the office. 在上班的途中,他偶然遇到了一位老朋友。We *came upon* an injured animal lying at the side of the road. 我们发现有一只受伤的动物躺在路边。

NOTE 当本短语作"偶然遇到(某人);偶然发现(某物)"解时,同义短语是 happen

on/upon。

come out *vi.* ❶(常与 of 连用)move outside a room or building, etc. 出来: *Come out*, will you? I'd like to have a word with you. 你出来一下好吗? 我要和你说句话。In Gaza, Israeli army tanks surrounded a house as troops waited for the militants to *come out*. 在加沙,以色列军队的坦克包围了一所房屋,士兵们等待着武装分子的出现。*Out* of the mouth *comes* evil. (谚语)祸从口出。❷(of the sun, moon, or stars) appear, or start to be able to be seen in the sky (太阳、月亮或群星)出现: It started cloudy, but then the sun *came out* and we all went to the park. 天阴了起来,但后来太阳又出来了,我们便都去了公园。The stars *came out* as soon as it was dark. 天一黑,星星就出来了。❸(of colours, stains, or marks) be able to be removed, especially by washing or rubbing (指颜色、污迹等)能被洗掉: The colour won't *come out* even if the material is washed over and over again. 这块布料就是反复洗也不褪色。I've washed the shirt twice and the ink still hasn't *come out*. 这件衬衣我已经洗过两次了,但上面的墨迹还没洗掉。❹(常用一般时态)(of a fact or secret) become known or be revealed to people (某一事实或秘密)为人所知: We believe the truth will *come out*. 我们相信真相会大白的。It eventually *came out* that she was already married. 她已经结婚这一秘密终于让人们知道了。❺(of a new product such as a book or record) become available to the public to buy or see (书籍或唱片等)面世,出版,刊出: We've recorded a new album, and it's *coming out* in the spring. 我们已录制了新专辑,在春季发行。Our local newspaper *comes out* every Friday. 我们的地方报纸每星期五出报。"*Time*" magazine *comes out* weekly.《时代》杂志每周刊出一期。❻(常用一般时态)(of a photograph) have a particular appearance or be successfully developed (照片)显像,被冲洗出: You have *come out* well in that photograph. 你那张照片照得很好。Our holiday photos haven't *come out*. 我们在假期照的照片还没洗出来。❼(用一般时态) have a particular result or end in a particular way 结果是;结束: The answer to the sum *came out* wrong. 这道算术题的答案结果是错的。It's impossible at this stage to judge how the vote will *come out*. 在此阶段不可能判断出选举的结果如何。How did the story *come out*? 那个故事的结局如何? ❽(常用一般时态,与 at 连用) be a particular number or amount that is the result of a calculation or measurement 合计为: The total cost *comes out* to $750 per kW. 总成本达每千瓦 750 美元。The total *comes out* at well over £50,000. 总数为 5 万英镑还多。❾(用一般时态)(in an examination, etc.) have a certain position (在考试等中)获得名次: John *came out* third in the final examination. 约翰在期末考试中获得了第三名。❿ become loose and fall out of some fixed position 脱落: Another of her baby teeth *came out* yesterday. 她又有一颗乳牙掉了。⓫(英国英语用法)(especially of a group of workers) stop working as a protest; go on strike (尤指工人)停工抗议,罢工: The Post Office workers have *come out*. 邮电工人已经罢工。The teachers all *came out* in support of their pay claim. 教师们都罢教以支持增加工资的要求。⓬(常用一般时态,与 for, in favor of 或 against 连用) state a decision or opinion officially or publicly 公开决定，阐明观点：Most of the speakers *came out* for these proposals. 大多数发言者公开表示赞同这些建议。The committee has *come out* openly against any change in the law. 委员会公开反对对该法律做任何修改。

come out of *vt.*【不可分性动词短语】(无被动语态形式) ❶(of someone or something) leave (a place) 离开(某处)：Heavy smoke *came out of* the windows of a high-rise building after a small aircraft crashed into it. 一架小型飞机撞上了一座高层建筑后，浓烟从楼房的数个窗口冒出。❷(用一般时态) be the result of (something) 有……结果：Nothing at all *came out of* the committee's meeting. 委员会会议没有任何结果。The innovation *came out of* the joint efforts of the workers and technicians of the factory. 这项革新是该厂工人和技术人员共同努力的结果。I hope some good will *come out of* all this. 我希望所有这些都能取得一些好的结果。

come out with *vt.*【不可分性动词短语】(无被动语态形式) ❶ come outdoors together with (someone or something) 与……一起走出来：I saw her *coming out with* a handsome young man, hand in hand. 我看到她和一个英俊的小伙子手拉手地走了出来。❷(非正式用语，常用一般时态) say (something) suddenly, usually something that surprises or shocks people 突然说出(常指令人吃惊或震惊的话)：Tom *came out with* a really stupid remark. 汤姆突然说出了一句傻透了的话。You never expect what the children are going to *come out with*. 你绝对想不到孩子们会突然冒出什么话来。At the meeting last night she *came out with* a very good suggestion. 在昨天晚上的会议上，她提出了一项很好的建议。

come over *vi.* ❶(常用一般时态，常与 to, from 连用) come to a place, especially a long way across water (尤指跨海)来到(某处或某地)：When did you first *come over* to England? 你第一次来英国是什么时候？I *came over* from Hong Kong to Hawaii for further study in 1992. 我是1992年从香港来到夏威夷进修的。❷(常用一般时态) pay a short informal visit to someone in the place where they are, especially their house (尤指到某人的家)短时间地拜访(某人)：Please *come over* to our place one evening. 请在哪一天的晚上来我们家坐坐。*Come over* and see us when you are free. 请有空时来看看我们。Why don't you *come over* for dinner? 顺便来我家吃饭，好吧？❸(用一般时态，常与 to 连用) change your position or opinion and start supporting someone you were arguing or fighting with 改变立场，改变观点：Many members of the opposition are *coming over* to our side. 许多反对派的成员都改变观点站到我们这方面来了。The president announced that there would be no punishment for all those who now *came over* to him. 总统发表声明要对所有倒戈归顺他的人免于处罚。❹ be effective and well received 有效果，被接受：Your talk *came over* very well. 你的讲话很受欢迎。❺(英国英语用法，非正式用语，后接表示感觉意义的形容词)(of someone) suddenly start feeling dizzy or shy (指人)突然感到眩晕；感觉羞怯：I suddenly *came over* dizzy, so I had to lie down. 我突然感到头晕，所以只好躺下。

I took a sleeping pill and soon *came over* drowsy. 我服用了一片安眠药,很快就昏昏欲睡了。She came over faint and weak. 她突然感到眩晕无力。She *comes over* all shy when she has to meet new people. 见生人时,她总感羞怯。

—*vt.*【不可分性动词短语】(无被动语态形式) ❶(of a feeling, especially a strange or surprising one) take hold of (someone) suddenly 突然感到:A strange feeling *came over* me. 我突然有一种奇怪的感觉。A wave of anger *came over* him. 怒气涌上他的心头。❷ be unable to explain why someone is behaving in such a strange way 无法解释(某人的行为):He's not normally so rude; I don't know what's *come over* him. 他平常不这样粗鲁。我不知道他怎么这样了。

NOTE 当本短语作"改变立场,改变观点"解时,与 come around/round 意义和用法与相同。

come through *v.* ❶(常用一般时态) be still alive (after a difficult or dangerous experience); survive (经历某种困难或危险后)仍然活着,幸存下来: The driver had lost so much blood that he was lucky to *come through* (the operation). 那司机失血很多,(手术后)能活下来是很幸运的了。The old man has *come through* two world wars unharmed. 这位老人身经两次世界大战而未受到任何损伤。❷(especially of news, results, etc.) become publicly known(消息、结果等)传出,公布:News has just *come through* on the radio that terrorists were behind the simultaneous crashes of two Russian planes in August. 刚从广播中传来消息:8月份两架俄罗斯客机同时坠毁是恐怖分子所为。Have your examination results *come through* yet? 你的考试结果公布了吗?

NOTE 当本短语作"仍然活着,幸存下来"解时,无被动语态形式。

come to *vt.*【不可分性动词短语】(无被动语态形式) ❶move nearer (something or someone); arrive at (a place); attend (an event)走近(某物或某人);到达(某处);参加(某一活动):All the students *came to* the teacher as soon as she called them. 老师一招呼,所有的学生便都到了她跟前。Writes down the names of the classmates who will *come to* our party. 把要参加我们聚会的那些同班同学的名字都写下了。❷(用一般时态) reach (a particular total) when everything is added together 总计,达到(某一总数): How much does the bill *come to*? 账单上一共是多少钱? The planned volume of production will *come to* one million tons in the coming year. 明年计划总产量将达到百万吨。❸(用一般时态) arrive at (a particular state, condition or position) 达到(某种状态或状况):It has *come to* my attention that some money is missing. 我注意到有些钱不见了。After much talk we *came to* an agreement. 经过好一番口舌,我们才达成了一项协议。❹(用一般时态,常用 it 作主语) enter the mind of (someone), especially suddenly (尤指突然)想起: The good idea *came to* him in his bath. 这个好主意是他洗澡时想起来的。At last the name of the book *came to* my mind. 我终于想起了那本书的名字。It came to her that it was foolish to expect him to help. 她突然意识到,指望他的帮助是太傻了。❺(of something) become someone's property, especially because the previous owner has died 成了某人的财产: The house *came to* my younger brother after my father's death.

我父亲去世后，房子就成了我弟弟的财产。❻(用一般时态)introduce or discuss (a new topic or a new aspect of a topic that you are talking about)谈及，提到(某事)：When it *comes to* music, James is an expert. 谈到音乐，詹姆斯是专家。When it *comes to* repairing cars I know nothing. 说到修汽车，我是一窍不通。❼reach a particular state or point, especially one that is bad or unpleasant 达到(尤指不良状态或地步)：If it *comes to* war, NATO forces will be stronger in the air. 如果到了非得打仗的地步，北约的空中力量是比较强大的。

—*vi.* become conscious again after being unconscious 苏醒过来，恢复知觉：In a few minutes the soldier suddenly *came to*. 过了一会儿，那名士兵突然苏醒了过来。When the policeman *came to*, the doctors in Yarmuk Hospital were to transfer him to a teaching hospital in central Baghdad. 当这位警察恢复知觉时，亚姆克医院的医生正要把他转到巴格达市中心的一家教学医院去。

NOTE 当本短语作"谈及，提到"解时，用在 when it 之后，后多接表示某一学科、领域或技术的名词或动名词。

come to a close *vi.* end; finish 结束：The meeting *came to a close* after the voting. 会议在投票选举之后结束了。The bilateral talks *came to a* successful close. 双边会谈圆满结束了。The 2008 Olympic Games officially *came to a close* in Beijing with a spectacular closing ceremony on August 24. 8 月 24 日，2008 年北京奥运会在盛大的闭幕仪式后正式落下帷幕。

NOTE 本短语另外的表达形式是 come to a conclusion 和 come to an end。

come to a conclusion ⇨ **come to a close**

come to a halt *vi.* (用一般时态) stop, either permanently or temporarily 停下，停止，停顿：After the bus *came to a halt*, more people got on. 公共汽车停下，更多的人上了车。Production *came to a halt* owing to our lack of raw material. 由于我们缺乏原料，生产停顿了下来。The dog's barking finally *came to a halt*. 狗的叫声终于停了下来。

NOTE 本短语另外的表达形式是 come to a standstill 和 come to a stop.

come to an end ⇨ **come to a close**

come to blows *vi.* (常与 over, with 连用) have a fight or a serious argument with someone 与某人发生争斗：We almost *came to blows* over what colour the new carpet should be. 我们因新地毯应该是什么颜色的问题而差一点争执起来。At school that morning he had *come to blows* with someone. 那天上午在学校里他曾与别人打了起来。It sounded as if they were about to *come to blows*. 听起来好像他们要打起来。

NOTE **1.** 本短语中的名词 blow 必须用复数形式。

2. 本短语的同义短语是 fall to blows，fall to blows 是英国英语用法。

come to conclusion *vi.* (后常接同位语从句) have a judgment or decision reached after consideration (经过考虑后)作出判断，得出结论：Thus she *came to* the *conclusion* that Jeff was only interested in himself. 于是，她得出了结论：杰夫只对他自己感兴趣。The scientist *came to conclusion* that the universe was expanding. 这位科学家得出了宇宙一度在扩大的结论。What *conclusions* did you *come to*? 你们得出的是什么结论？

come to grief *vi.* (of someone or something) have an accident 出事故：The first time he went out on his new motorcycle he *came to grief*. 他第一次骑他的新摩托车外出就出了事故。David and his friend almost *came to grief* when they were crossing the English Channel in a hot-air balloon. 戴维和他的朋友乘热气球飞越英吉利海峡时几乎出事。The icy runway caused at least one light plane to *come to grief*. 冰滑的跑道导致至少一架轻型飞机出事。

come to grips with *vt.* deal seriously with (someone or something difficult) 认真应对(某人)；认真解决(困难的事情)：I cannot *come to grips with* Jim and his problems. 我是无法应对吉姆和他的那些问题。The government is still trying to *come to grips with* inflation. 政府仍在努力解决通货膨胀的问题。The speaker talked a lot, but never really *came to grips with* the subject. 演说者讲了很多，但从未真正触及主题。

NOTE 1. 本短语中的名词 grip 必须用复数形式。

2. 本短语的另外一种表达形式是 get to grips with。

come to hand *vi.* be available easily and immediately 随手可得：He grabbed the first thing that *came to hand*, and smashed the window with it. 他随手拾起一件东西，把窗户打得粉碎。Use whatever tools *come to hand*. 使用随手可以得到的工具。

come to heel *vi.* (of a person) agree to obey someone and accept his or her orders (指某人)服从，顺从：You have only to apply a little economic pressure to them, and they will soon *come to heel*. 只要你对他们稍施加一点经济压力，他们很快就会顺从你。He was always a naughty child but he had to learn to *come to heel* when he went to school. 他一向顽皮，可是上学后他只好学会听话。

come to life *vi.* become exciting, interesting and active 变得生动有趣，变得活跃：The dull play really *came to life* in the performance by these young people. 这部无聊的剧本被这些年轻人表演得实在生动有趣。The quiet girl has *come to life* since she worked as a salesgirl. 那个少言寡语的姑娘自从当上了售货员后就变得活跃起来了。

come to light *vi.* (of something, such as a fact) be discovered or revealed; become known (指事实等)被发现，为人所知：Two government officials have faced charges since the scandal *came to light*. 自爆出丑闻以来，已有两名政府官员面临指控。New facts about ancient Egypt have recently *come to light*. 有关古埃及的新的史实最近才被发现。When the old woman died, it *came to light* that she was actually rich. 那老妇人去世后，人们才知道她实际上很有钱。Some new information has *come to light* about the accident. 一些有关这次事故的新情况披露了出来。

NOTE 1. 虽然本短语所表达的意义是被动的，但要用主动形式来表示。另外，本短语是不及物性动词短语，不能用被动语态形式。

2. 本短语的主语不能用人，而是要用表示事物的词语来充当。

3. 本短语与 bring to light 意义相同，但用法不同，见 bring to light。

come to nothing *vi.* fail 失败：Their plan

came to nothing because it was divorced from reality. 他们的计划因脱离实际而失败了。The last round of peace talks *came to nothing*. 最后一轮和平会谈已告失败。

come to one's aid *vi.* come to do something to help someone 来帮助某人: A passer-by heard her screams and *came to her aid*. 一位路人听到她的尖叫声,便赶过来救助。I waited patiently hoping that someone would *come to my aid* 我耐心地等待着,希望有人来帮助我。Nearly the whole village *came to their aid*. 几乎全村的人都来帮助他们。

NOTE 本短语另外的表达形式是 come to one's assistance 和 come to one's help。

come to one's feet ⇨ **get to one's feet**

come to one's senses *vi.* ❶ regain consciousness 恢复知觉: After they made him drink a cup of water, the old man gradually *came to his senses*. 他们给那老人灌了一杯水后,他才渐渐地恢复了知觉。She *came to her senses* before the doctor got to the scene. 在医生赶到现场之前,她恢复了知觉。❷ think clearly; become reasonable 头脑清醒,变得明智: Don't act so foolishly. *Come to your senses*. 别做蠢事了。明智点吧。Portman urged the government to *come to its senses* and stop nuclear testing. 波特曼敦促政府明智起来,停止核试验。

NOTE 无论 one's 是单数还是复数,名词 sense 都必须用复数形式。

come to pass *vi.* (正式用语,旧式用法,常用一般时态) happen; become real 发生,实现: How is it that this has *come to pass*? 这事是怎么发生的? Whatever he proposed *came to pass*. 凡是他所提出的事都发生了。

come to stay *vi.* continue to exist for a long time and become generally accepted by most people 继续长期存在并被接受: Like other things athletics have *come to stay*, and the holding of the Olympic Games serves to spur the enthusiasts forward. 正像其他事物一样,体育运动已深入人心,而举办奥运会则激励热心于体育的人们奋发向前。Do you think colored hair *comes to stay*, or will the fashion change again? 你认为染发会被人们所接受吗,还是这种时尚会改变?

NOTE **1.** 本短语通常用完成时形式,即 has/have come to stay。

2. 本短语的另外一种表达形式是 be here to stay。

come to terms *vi.* ❶ (常与 with 连用) make an agreement or end an argument (with someone) (与某人)达成协议: The management and the labour union *came to terms* after a long bargaining. 资方和工会经过长时间的讨价还价之后达成了协议。After the two countries had negotiated for several months, they finally *came to terms* with each other. 两国经过数月的谈判后,才最终相互达成了协议。❷(与with 连用) learn to accept (something that is difficult or unpleasant) and deal with it 接受并应对(困难或令人不快之事): Some old people still find it difficult to *come to terms* with their new ways of life. 有些老年人仍然感到难以接受和应对新的生活方式。It's hard to *come to terms* with going blind. 接受并应对要失明这一事实是很难的。

NOTE 本短语中的名词 term 必须用复数形式。

come to the point *vi.* ❶ stop talking about unimportant details and say what is most important; make one's meaning clear 谈及正题;讲清要点:We don't have much time, so please *come to the point*. 我们没有更多的时间,所以请直谈正题。I'll *come* straight *to the point* — when do you want the money? 我就直说吧,你什么时候要那笔钱? A good newspaper story must *come* right *to the point*. 一篇好的新闻报道必须直接阐明要点。❷arrive at the important or crucial part 到了重要(或紧要)的关头:I hope it never *comes to the point* that we have to dismiss workers. 我不希望事情达到我们被迫解雇工人的那种地步。When it *came to the point*, he is always ready to help others. 到关键时刻,他总是乐于助人。

NOTE 当本短语作"谈及正题;讲清要点"解时,同义短语是 get to the point。

come to the rescue *vi.* save someone or something from danger , failure, or an unpleasant situation 援助;Ar their request, the helicopter *came to the rescue*. 应他们的请求,直升机前来援救。The failing company is hoping international banks will *come to rescue*. 这家即将倒闭的公司希望国际银行能伸出援救之手。

come true *vi.* (of a wish, dream, or prediction) actually happen (指愿望、梦想或预言)实现:"Our wish has *come true*." the coach said after the Chinese girls won the first volleyball World Cup title in 18 years. 教练在 18 年来中国姑娘首次赢得世界杯冠军称号后说:"我们的愿望实现了。" At the age of 16, I was given the chance to make my sea dream *come true* when my sister invited me to go to Hawaii for a summer holiday. 我 16 岁时,我姐姐邀请我去夏威夷度暑假,我才得到了圆我看海之梦的机会。That prediction from Balogun is *coming true*. 巴拉根的预言即要实现。

NOTE 本短语中的 come 是系动词,可被替换成 become,但 become true 不属于固定短语。

come under *vt.*【不可分性动词短语】(无被动语态形式,常用一般时态) ❶be forced to experience (something unpleasant) 遭受: The department had *come under* criticism for poor performance. 该部门因业绩不佳而受到批评。Airport security in Britain will now *come under* increased scrutiny. 英国机场的安全现在受到更严密地审查。❷belong to (a particular group or class) 属于(某一种类):Libraries and swimming pools *come under* leisure services. 图书馆和游泳池都归属休闲类服务设施。What section does this *come under*? 这属于哪一部分?

come up *vi.* ❶(常与 to 连用)(of someone) approach or move towards (someone or something)(指某人)走近(某人或某物): A man *came up* to me and asked me if I knew the time. 一个男人走过来问我几点了。I could hear footsteps *coming up* behind me. 我能听到背后有脚步接近我。"Please *come up* to the blackboard, Tommy," the teacher said. "汤米,请到黑板这儿来。"老师说道。❷ develop; grow 发展,长出: The United Nations official stated, "Mongolia is poor but they are *coming up* very well." 联合国的这位官员说道:"蒙古虽然贫穷,但现在发展的态势很好。" With the adoption of the new method, the seeds *came up* earlier than usual. 由于采用了新的方法,种子比往常提早发出了芽。❸(用一般时态) happen (in the course of time, especially unexpectedly); appear; arise (尤指意想不到地)发生,出

现：I'll be late home tonight because something's just *come up* at work. 我今晚要晚些时候回家，因刚才在工作上出了点儿事。A mechanism for regular coordination and cooperation between the two countries has been established to solve the problems that might *come up*. 两国建立了一个经常性的协调与合作机制，以应对可能会出现的问题。❹(常用一般时态)(of something) be mentioned or discussed (in a conversation or meeting)(指某事)(在谈话或会议中)被提到，被讨论：The same question *came up* again at the meeting. 会上又一次提到了同一个问题。The important subject kept *coming up* in the talks between the two state leaders. 两国领导人在会谈中反复讨论了这一重要问题。❺travel to a place that is further north or is larger or more important than the place you are leaving, as a capital city or university 北上；去较大(或重要)的地方(如首都或大学)：My mother's *coming up* from England for the weekend. 我妈妈要从英格兰北上到此来度周末。Do *come up* to London and see us. 一定到伦敦来看我们。When do the new students *come up*? 新生什么时候到校？❻(与 to 连用) be tall, deep, or long enough to reach a particular higher point or level (高度、深度或长度)达到：The grass in the garden *came up* to her knees. 园子里的草都长到了她的膝盖那么高。The water *came up* to my chest. 水深达到了我的胸部。❼(of a case) be heard and judged in a court of law (在法庭上)进行裁决：His case *comes up* next week. 他的案子下周裁决。❽(of the sun or moon) rise (太阳或月亮)升起：I'd like to get up early and watch the sun *come up*. 我想要早起观看日出。

come up against *vt.*【不可分性动词短语】(无被动语态形式)(of someone) meet or encounter (usually a problem, difficulty or opposition)(某人)遇到(问题或困难)，遭遇(反对)：He often *came up* against the problem of money. 那时他时常碰到钱的问题。We eventually conquered all the difficulties we had *come up* against. 我们最终克服了我们所遇到的所有困难。We may *come up against* a bit of opposition in dealing with the case. 在处理这一案件中，我们可能会遇到一些反对。

come up in the world *vi.* (主要用于英国英语中) become richer, more powerful, or more successful than before 生活富裕；社会地位提升：She has *come up in the world* since she peddled her own baked goods from a pushcart. 她靠用手推车兜售自己烤制的食品而得以发迹。When they started to *come up in the world*, they moved to a flat in London. 当他们飞黄腾达时，他们搬进了伦敦的一所公寓。

NOTE **1.** 本短语的另外一种表达形式是 go up in the world。

2. 本短语的反义短语是 come down in the world。

come up to *vt.*【不可分性动词短语】(无被动语态形式) ❶(常用一般时态) reach (something) 到，达：The path *comes up to* the top of the cliff. 这条小路一直通到悬崖顶上。The water *came up to* my chest. 水深达到了我的胸部。With so much rain in the last few days, the river has *come up to* the danger mark. 由于连日大雨，河水已到了警戒水位线。❷move near to (someone or something)

走近(某人或某物):Strangers *come up to* him in the street and say how much they enjoy his books. 在马路上,一些陌生人走近他,对他说他们十分喜欢看他写的书。❸(常用一般时态)reach (a certain standard); equal (something)达到(某一标准或水平),与……相当: The quality of this new product *comes up to* the standard. 这种新产品的质量达到了标准。Your recent work hasn't *come up to* your usual high standards. 你最近的作品不及你以往的水平高。

come up with *vt.*【不可分性动词短语】(无被动语态形式) ❶ reach (someone who is ahead)追上,赶上(某人):On our way we *came up with* a party of hikers. 在行进的路上,我们赶上了一队远足者。❷come level with (something)赶上,跟上(某物):We are making our efforts to *come up with* advanced level. 我们正在努力赶上先进水平。We must *come up with* the times. 我们必须跟上时代的发展。❸(常用一般时态)think of and suggest (a new idea, a plan, etc.)提出(新思维、计划等): During his visit, the President *came up with* new ideas for increasing economic and trade cooperation between the two countries. 在访问期间,总统提出了两国之间增加经贸合作的新思路。However, the situation is not yet out of hand, as the government has *come up with* various methods of reducing the rate of brain drain. 但由于政府出台了一些不同的措施来减少人才流失率,这种局面并没有失控。❹manage to produce or provide (something such as a sum of money)when it is needed 拿出,提供(一笔款项):If Rogers can *come up with* the $5, 000, we'll go to Hawaii for the holiday. 如果罗杰斯能拿出5 000美元,我们就去夏威夷度假。We're in big trouble if we don't *come up with* the money by 6 o'clock. 我们要是在 6 点之前拿不出那笔钱,我们可就有大麻烦了。

come what may/will *adv.* (正式用语) no matter what may happen 不管发生什么情况: *Come what may*, the great motherland will always be a strong backing to the maintenance of Hong Kong's prosperity and stability. 不管发生什么情况,伟大的祖国都将是香港保持繁荣稳定的坚强后盾。Charles decided to get a college education, *come what may*. 查尔斯决定,无论发生什么事,他都要接受大学教育。*Come what will*, I'm determined to do it. 无论发生什么情况,我都决心要做这件事。

comment on/upon *vt.*【不可分性动词短语】 express one's opinion about (something or someone)对……进行评论:At the year-end press conference, he refused to *comment on* the presidential elections early next year. 在年底的记者招待会上,他拒绝对明年年初的总统选举进行评论。To *comment upon* this would be to paint the lily. 对此加以评,将是画蛇添足。Managements don't like to be *commented upon* or criticised for their faults by their employees. 资方都不喜欢被其雇员就他们的错误作出评论和批评。

NOTE 本短语中的 upon 用法比 on 正式,但不及 on 常用。

commit to *vt.*【可分性动词短语】(常用一般时态) ❶(常用被动语态形式)send (someone) to (a hospital, prison, or some other institution)for a time because he or she is ill or has done something wrong (把某人)送交给(医院、监狱或其

他机构）：She was *committed to* a nursing home. 她被送进了一家疗养院。The man was found guilty and *committed to* prison. 该名男子被判有罪，于是被打入监牢。❷(常用被动语态形式) spend (one's time or energy) on (something)把(时间或精力)投放在……上：He is very *committed to* the cause of language teaching. 他对语言教学事业十分投入。You should be *committed to* what you talked about. 你应该对你谈过的事情投入精力。The President says he is *committed to* promoting democracy and fighting corruption. 总统表示，他将致力于推进民主和反腐败。❸(常与反身代词连用) promise (especially oneself, one's property, etc.) to a certain cause, position, opinion, or course of action 使(尤指自己)承担义务，作出保证，承诺：He has *committed* himself *to* the support of his brother's children. 他已承担起抚养他弟弟的孩子的责任。A secretary general of the United Nations must *commit* himself *to* working hard for the world peace. 联合国秘书长必须保证为世界的和平而努力工作。

common sense *n.* the practical good sense and judgment gained from experience, rather than special knowledge from school or study 常识，情理；(由经验得来的)判断力：Anybody with *common sense* can see through the attempt of these people. 任何一个有常识的人都会看穿这些人的企图。If your friends think you have no *common sense*, this book you must read. 如果你的朋友都认为你不懂常识，这本书是你必读的。Although she is not very academic she's got plenty of *common sense*. 虽然她没多大学问，但她却很通情达理。

NOTE 1. 本短语为不可数性名词短语，前面不可用不定冠词 a，后面不能加 s。
2. 本短语可转化为复合词 commonsense，“常识性的，常理的”。

communicate with *vt.* speak to or send a message to (someone)与(某人)交谈，与(某人)交流：It is always difficult to *communicate with* someone who speaks a foreign language. 和讲外国话的人交谈往往很困难。It was the first time for a Chinese President to have *communicated with* ordinary Chinese netizens via the Internet. 这是中国国家主席首次通过因特网与普通的中国网民进行交流。

NOTE 本短语与 correspond with 均表示“与(某人)交流”。本短语不仅指通过书信交流，还指当面交谈，通过打电话、发电报或电子邮件等方式交流，常用于书面语；而 correspond with 主要指双向的书信来往。

compare notes *vi.* (常与 about 或 on 连用) (of two or more people) talk about something to find out if they have the same information or opinions about it (两人或多人)商谈，交流(信息或意见)：We'd meet to *compare notes* about different things. 我们打算见面商谈一些不同的事情。The kids were *comparing notes* on their latest CDs. 孩子们在交流对他们最新唱片的看法。We saw the play separately and *compared notes* afterwards. 我们分别看了这出戏后交换了对它的看法。

compare to *vt.*【可分性动词短语】(常用一般时态) ❶ say that one thing or person is similar to (another)把……比做……：He jokingly *compared* his learning of German *to* a circus bear learning to ride a bike. 他开玩笑说，他学德语好比马

戏团里的狗熊学骑车。Hundreds of protesters gathered Tuesday evening in central London. 成百上千的抗议者星期二晚上在伦敦市中心集会。Life is *compared to* a voyage. 人生好比旅程。❷ consider how things or people are different and how they are similar 把……与……相比较: The results are then *compared to* the results of previous studies. 然后把这些结果与上次的研究结果相比较。

NOTE 本短语与 compare with 之间的区别见 compare with。

compare with *vt.*【可分性动词短语】(常用一般时态) examine (one thing, person, or group) together with (another), so as to find things that are the same or different 把……与……相比较: If we *compare* French schools *with* British schools, we find there are many differences. 如果我们把法国的学校与英国的学校相比,就会发现许多不同之处。*Compared with* Germany, the nation of Luxembourg seems quite small. 与德国相比,卢森堡就显得相当小了。*Compare* your translation *with* the model one on the blackboard. 把你们的译文与黑板上的范文比较一下。

NOTE 本短语与 compare to 之间的区别是:在表示两物相似的情况下常使用 compare to。而在比较两物的异同时则常使用 compare with。但在当今,两者在表示"把……与……相比较"之意时,它们之间的区分已不很严格,有时可以互换使用。例如:

> London is large, *compared to/with* Paris.
> 与巴黎相比,伦敦大一些。
>
> Now let's *compare* the properties of steel *to/with* those of pure iron.
> 现在,让我们把钢的性能和纯铁的性能进行比较。

compensate for *vt.*【可分性动词短语】pay (someone) money because he or she has suffered a loss or an injury 补偿,赔偿:Nothing can *compensate for* the loss of one's health. 失去健康是无法补偿的。There is nothing that can *compensate for* losing my husband. 什么都无法补偿我失去丈夫的损失。They were unlikely to be *compensated for* the damage to the house. 他们可能不会得到房屋受损的赔偿。

compete against/with *vt.*【不可分性动词短语】try to be more successful than (other companies or people) in business; try to win something such as a prize, in competition with (others) 与……竞争: They tried to *compete against* other countries in trade. 他们力图在贸易上与其他国家竞争。We're too small to *compete with* a company like that. 我们的公司太小,无法与那样的公司相竞争。The young golfer has often *competed against* famous players, but so far he has always been beaten. 那名年轻的高尔夫球手经常和著名的运动员相竞争,但至今一直没赢过。

compete for *vt.*【不可分性动词短语】try to get (something that other people also want to have) in a competition 在竞争中夺得: China will *compete* at the World Table Tennis Championships *for* the group's top place with South Korea. 中国将在世界乒乓球锦标赛上与韩国争夺小组第一名。Contestants from over 80 countries and regions *competed for* the Miss Universe crown. 来自 80 多个国家和地区的参赛者争夺“环球小姐”的桂冠。

complain about *vt.*【不可分性动词短语】say that you are not satisfied with (something)抱怨……,对……表示不满: I've written to the shop three times to *complain about* the faulty watch, but none of my letters have been replied to. 我已三次写信给那家商店抱怨那块有毛病的手表,但没有一封信得到回复。You've got nothing to *complain about*, so shut up. 你没什么可抱怨的,闭嘴吧。You have to stop *complaining about* the job; plenty of people would be happy to have your job. 你不要再对这份工作表示不满了。许多人都巴不得要干你这份工作呢。

complain of *vt.*【不可分性动词短语】❶(正式用语)say that you are not satisfied with (something or someone)抱怨……: Applicants for visas are supposed to call the US consulate to set up a face-to-face interview, but many *complain of* calling the consulate for days on end and only getting a busy tone. 申请签证的人要给美国领事馆打电话提出面试要求,然而很多人都抱怨连续数日给领事馆打电话,听到的都是忙音。Refugees had *complained of* being robbed and beaten by officials. 难民们控诉官员对他们进行抢劫和殴打。❷(一般不用被动语态形式)say that one has (a pain, illness, etc.)诉说自己有(病痛等): The man *complained of* a headache and fever and was admitted to an isolation room at the hospital. 那名男子曾自述头痛、发烧并因此而被医院收入隔离室。He went to the doctor *complaining of* difficulty in breathing. 他去医生那看病,说自己呼吸有困难。

complete with *prep.* with the things mentioned; including 备有,包括: We recently bought a house *complete with* furniture. 我们近日买了一套备有整套家具的房子。There is a very good hotel not far away from the city, *complete with* swimming pool and garden leading to the beach. 离城不远有一家很好的宾馆,带有游泳池和通向海滩的花园。They want a detailed joint statement, *complete with* a timetable for the establishment of the firm. 他们需要一个详细的联合声明,包括这家公司成立的时间表。

NOTE 本短语中的 complete 不是动词,而是形容词,意为“齐备的”。

comply with *vt.*【不可分性动词短语】(正式用语)obey (a rule or law), or do what someone asks you to do 遵守(规则或法律),按……去做: Wherever we go, we should *comply with* rules there. 无论我们走到哪里,我们都应遵守那里的规章制度。In dealing with the customs house, one has to *comply with* all formalities. 与海关打交道,就一定得按其所规定的全部手续办事。Certain of their conditions are not easily *complied with*. 他们的某些条件很难照办。

composed of *adj.* (正式用语)made up of; formed from (the stated parts)由……组成的,由……构成的: The delegation is *composed of* senior officials from the Party, government and the army. 这个代表团由党、政、军的高级官员所组成。The UN Security Council is *composed of* five permanent members — China, Russia, the United States,

France and Britain. 联合国安理会由五个常任理事国构成,它们是:中国、俄罗斯、美国、法国和英国。

NOTE 本短语与 comprised of 意义相同,它们之间的区别见 comprised of。

C

comprised of *adj.* made up of (two or more things or people)由……组成,由……组合而成:The UK is *comprised of* England, Scotland, Wales and Northern Ireland. 联合王国由英格兰、苏格兰、威尔士和北爱尔兰组合而成的。The committee was *comprised of* representatives from all areas. 该委员会是由各地区的代表组合而成。Japan's Self-Defense Forces, *comprised of* about 550 personnel, arrived in Iraq for reconstruction assistance. 由 550 人组成的日本自卫队已抵达伊拉克,从事援建工作。

NOTE 本短语与 composed of 分别来自动词性短语 comprise of 和 compose of。它们均指一个整体由数个分散的个体构成。使用中,两者常可互换使用。

conceal from *vt.*【可分性动词短语】hide (something, someone, or oneself) from (someone or something) 对……隐瞒……,躲藏……:*Concealing* evidence *from* the police is a serious offence. 对警方隐瞒证据属严重犯罪。The death of the president was *concealed from* the republic for 50 days in order to avoid any social disorder. 为了避免社会秩序混乱,总统去世的消息对公众封锁了 50 天。The small house was *concealed from* the road by a mass of trees. 这所小房子被一片树林所遮掩,从大路上看不见。The child tried to *conceal* himself *from* his teacher. 那孩子千方百计地躲着他的老师。

NOTE 本短语的同义短语是 hide from。

conceive of *vt.*【不可分性动词短语】❶(用一般时态) think of or imagine (something or doing something)想出,想象:How can they even *conceive of* doing such a bad thing? 他们怎么会想出要做这样的坏事呢? The modern children find it difficult to *conceive of* the times when there was no radio or television. 现代儿童很难想象没有收音机和电视机的那个时代。I can't *conceive of* your allowing a child of five to go on such a long journey alone! 我想象不出你竟允许一个五岁的孩子独自走这么远的路程! In ancient times the world was *conceived of* as flat. 在古代,地球被认为是扁平的。

concentrate on/upon *vt.* give all your attention to (the thing you are doing)全神贯注于(自己所做之事):"All the players need to *concentrate on* Olympic preparations right now," said the head coach. 这位主教练说:"所有的队员现在都必须把精力集中在奥运会的训练上。" He *concentrated* his attention *on* his studies. 他把注意力都集中在学习上了。This year the company has *concentrated on* improving its efficiency. 该公司今年已把力量集中在提高效率方面。You'll solve the problem if you *concentrate upon* it. 如果你全神贯注于这一问题,你就会解决它。

NOTE 本短语中的 upon 用法比 on 正式,但不及 on 常用。

concern about/for/over *vt.* (常用被动语态形式)pay attention to (something) because it is important or because it worries you 关心,关注,担心,挂念:He *concerned* himself *about* the health of his aging parents. 他担心他年迈父母的健康。Why are you so *concerned for* her safety? 你为什么这么为她的安全担心? The American people are increasingly *concerned over* the continuing US casualties. 美国人民越来越关注驻伊美军持续伤亡情况。

concern in/with *vt.* (常用被动语态形式,不用进行时态) take (for oneself) an interest or active part in (something) 与……有牵连,积极参与: He was only indirectly *concerned in* what took place yesterday. 他和昨天出的事只有间接的关系。The police are anxious to interview everyone *concerned in* last night's incident. 警方急于要找与昨晚事件有牵连的每一个人谈话。The news release would be mainly *concerned with* criminal cases, public order, road accidents, and disasters. 新闻发布会的内容主要将涉及刑事案件、社会治安问题、道路交通事故,以及灾害事故情况。I'm too busy to *concern* myself *with* your affairs. 我太忙,无法参与你们的事情。

condemn to *vt.* 【可分性动词短语】(常用被动语态形式) ❶(of a court of law) give a punishment to (someone who has committed a crime) (法庭)给(犯罪分子)判刑: The court *condemned* the corrupt official *to* ten years' imprisonment. 法庭判处这名腐败官员 10 年监禁。In this country a murderer who is found guilty will be *condemned to* death. 在这个国家,如果一个杀人犯被定罪,就会被判处死刑。❷(of something) force (someone) into a usually unfortunate state or condition 迫使(某人)陷入不幸的境地: Lack of education *condemned* them *to* extreme poverty. 缺乏教育使他们陷入极其贫穷的境地。Her shyness condemned her to a life of loneliness. 她的腼腆使她生活孤寂。He felt *condemned to* being alone. 他感到自己陷入了孤立的境地。

NOTE 当本短语作"迫使(某人)陷入不幸的境地"解时,主语(即动作的发出者)一般不能是人。

confer on/upon *vt.* (正式用语) ❶(常与 with 连用) discuss (something) with other people, especially in order to reach a decision or an agreement (about a matter) 商谈,商讨: I want to *confer* with some of you *on* how to handle the problem. 我想和你们几个人商讨一下如何处理这一问题。❷(正式用语,常用一般时态) give (something such as an honor, academic degree, a gift, or status) to (someone), usually in a ceremony (通常在一仪式上)把(某种荣誉、学位、礼物或地位等)授予(某人): China on Tuesday held a ceremony to *confer upon* the country's astronaut team the title of "Heroic Astronaut Team". 星期二,中国举行仪式,授予国家航天队"英雄航天队"的称号。The Queen *conferred* a medal *on* the brave sailor. 女王把一枚勋章授给了那位勇敢的水手。

NOTE 本短语中的 upon 用法比 on 正式,但不及 on 常用。

confer with *vt.* (常与 about, on 连用) talk together with (someone); consider something at length with (someone) 与(某人)会谈,同(某人)商议: The Oval Office is the US president's formal workspace, where he *confers with* heads of state, diplomats, and his staff. 椭圆形办公室是美国总统与别国首脑和外交官会谈,以及与其工作人员议事的正式工作场所。I want to *confer with* you on the problem of food. 我想和你们商量一下食品问题。

confess to *vt.* ❶(常用一般时态) admit

(having done something such as a fault or crime)承认,供认,坦白(所犯错误、罪行等): The corrupt official was dictatorial and could not stand anyone questioning him, nor did he ever *confess to* his wrongdoing in public. 这名贪官专横跋扈,不容异议,更不肯当众认错。The 25-year-old man has *confessed to* killing 7 pedestrians with a knife in central Tokyo on Sunday, said the police. 警方称,那名25岁的男子已对在星期日于东京市中心持刀行凶杀死7名路人供认不讳。❷ admit (having done something such as a fault or crime) to (someone)向(某人)承认,坦白(所犯错误、罪行等): Robert had to *confess* his involvement *to* the school master. 罗伯特不得不向校长承认自己参与其中了。Eventually he *confessed to* the police. 他终于向警方坦白了。

NOTE 1. 本短语中的 to 是介词,而不是动词不定式符号,因此其后接名词或动名词,不能接原形动词。

2. 本短语的同义短语是 admit to。

confide to *vt.*【可分性动词短语】(常用一般时态) tell (information, personal matters, etc.) to (someone)把(秘密之事或个人之事)讲给(某人): He *confided* his doubts *to* me. 他把他的一些疑虑告诉给了我。The firm's plans were *confided* only *to* the manager. 公司的这些计划只能讲给经理。He *confided to* me that he had spent five years in prison. 他向我吐露道,他曾坐过五年牢。

confine to *vt.*【可分性动词短语】(常用被动语态形式) limit (someone, something or oneself) to (something such a place or subject)把……限制在……之内: He is *confined to* his bed by illness. 他卧病在床。It's a stupid idea to *confine* yourself *to* your study on holidays. 休假时把自己关在书房里是一个愚蠢的想法。Please *confine* your remarks *to* the subject under discussion. 请把你的发言限制在我们所讨论的题目范围之内。The policewoman's duty was *confined to* taking statements from women and children. 这位女警官的职责仅限于把妇女和儿童的陈述记录下来。

conflict with *vt.*【不可分性动词短语】(用一般时态) not match or disagree with; be in opposition to (something)与……不一致,与……相冲突: The policeman's story *conflicts with* that of the accused. 那名警察的陈述与被告人的不一致。I was unable to study music at school because it *conflicted with* history. 我无法在学校学习音乐,因为它与历史课相冲突。Do British immigration laws *conflict with* any international laws? 英国的移民法与国际法相冲突吗?

conform to/with *vt.* ❶ (cause to) be similar to (an idea or wish)(使)符合,同……一致: Facts have provided eloquent proof that the policy of "one country, two systems" *conforms to* the fundamental interests of the country and those of Hong Kong and Macao. 事实雄辩地证明,"一国两制"的方针符合国家的根本利益,也符合香港和澳门的根本利益。What he does does not *conform to* what he says. 他的言行不一。His ideas do not *conform with* mine. 他的想法跟我的不一致。❷obey (something such as a rule, regulation, or law)遵守(规章或法律): If you are a member of a club, you must *conform with* the rules of that club. 如果你是某一俱乐部的成员,你必须遵守该俱乐部的规章。We should *conform* ourselves *to* the regulations. 我

们应该遵从这些规章制度。

NOTE 本短语中的第一个义项里常用 to,而在第二个义项里常用 with。

confront with *vt.*【可分性动词短语】force to deal with or accept the truth of (something) (with a quality such as courage); make (someone) face (something usually bad)(勇敢)面对,面临:The young official *confronted* his pile of work *with* strong determination. 这位年轻的官员以坚强的决心面对大量的工作。The police *confronted* the prisoner *with* proof of his crime. 警方向该囚犯出示了其犯罪的证据。Entering the 21st century, the world is hardly a tranquil place and mankind is still *confronted with* many serious challenges. 进入 21 世纪,世界还很不安宁,人类仍面临诸多严峻挑战。

NOTE 本短语与 face with 意义相同,但 face with 更为常用。

congratulate on/upon *vt.*【可分性动词短语】❶express one's pleasure to (especially someone) about (a happy event or something successfully done) 向……祝贺……:Many country leaders *congratulated* former US Vice President Al Gore *upon* his winning of the Nobel Peace Prize. 许多国家的领导人纷纷祝贺美国前副总统阿尔·戈尔获得诺贝尔和平奖。❷(与反身代词连用) be proud of (oneself) for (being successful or lucky) 私自庆幸:I was *congratulating* myself *on* my lucky escape from the disaster. 我庆幸自己从灾难里逃生。She *congratulated* herself *on* not having been involved in the case. 她庆幸自己没有卷入该案之中。

NOTE **1.** 本短语中的 upon 用法比 on 正式,但不及 on 常用。**2.** 当本短语用作"向……祝贺……"之意时,其中的介词 on 或 upon 有时被 for 所代替,表达同样的意义。但 on 或 upon 后多接名词,而 for 后则多接动名词(短语)。例如:

> China *congratulated* Ram Yadav *for* winning the election as Nepal's first president.
> 中国祝贺拉姆·亚达夫当选尼泊尔首任总统。

conjure up *vt.*【可分性动词短语】❶make (something) appear using magic powers 用魔法变出:The magician *conjured up* a lovely rabbit out of his hat. 魔术师从他的帽子里变出一只可爱的小兔子来。❷(常用一般时态) create or achieve (something difficult or unexpected) as if by magic (像变戏法似的)做出,取得……:Mary can *conjure up* a good meal in only a few minutes. 玛丽在几分钟内就能像变戏法似的做出一顿可口的饭菜来。They managed to *conjure up* a goal and won the match. 他们像变戏法似的进了一个球,并且赢得了比赛。❸(用一般时态) bring (something such as a feeling or memory) to your mind 使人想起,回忆:This place *conjures up* vivid memories. 这个地方使人想起许多生动的往事。The old man likes *conjuring up* his miserable life in the past. 这位老人喜欢回忆他过去的悲惨生活。

connect to *vt.*【可分性动词短语】❶join (something) to (something else) 把……与……连接,把……与……联系:It has speakers inside, which you can *connect to* your sound card. 它有内置音箱,你可将其连接到声卡上。We *connect* the machine *to* the motor by a drive belt or chain. 我们用传动带或传动链条把机器

C

连接到电动机上。Poyang Lake, China's largest fresh water lake in Jiangxi Province, is *connected to* five major rivers in the province in addition to the Changjiang River. 位于江西省的鄱阳湖是中国最大的淡水湖，它连接着长江和该省的五大河流。❷make it possible for (someone) to communicate with (someone else) using a telephone 给(某人)接通电话: Operator, you've *connected* me *to* the wrong person again! 接线员，你又把我的电话接错了人! The operator *connected* her *to* the police station. 接线员给她接通了警察局的电话。

NOTE 当本短语作"给(某人)接通电话"解时，与 connect with(第四个义项)意义和用法相同，两者可互换使用。

connect with *vt.* 【可分性动词短语】❶(常用被动语态形式，用一般时态) unite (something or someone) with (something or someone else) in relationship 把……与……联系在一起，使有联系: The police *connected* this incident *with* last week's terrorist bombing. 警方把这次事件与上周那起恐怖爆炸事件联系在了一起。Most European royal families are *connected with* each other. 欧洲大部分王室都有姻亲关系。❷(用一般时态，常用被动语态形式) join (two things) together ……与……相连接: Where does the gas-stove *connect with* the gas-pipe? 煤气炉在什么地方与煤气管相连接? A heavy copper cable *connects* the lightning rod *with* a metal plate buried in the ground. 一根粗铜线将避雷针与埋于地下的金属板连接起来。The island is *connected* by a steamer service *with* the mainland. 这个岛由轮渡与大陆连接起来。❸(of a bus, train, or plane) arrive at a time which allows passengers to change to (another form of transport) in order to continue their journey (汽车、火车、飞机等)与……联运: Their train *connects with* a bus service to Worcester. 他们所乘的列车与开往伍斯特的汽车联运。This flight *connects with* a flight for New York. 本次航班与飞往纽约的航班联运。❹make it possible for (someone) to communicate with (someone else) using a telephone 给(某人)接通电话: Operator, can you *connect* me *with* the manager, please? 接线员，请给我接通经理，好吗? The operator *connected* her *with* the manager's office. 接线员给她接通了经理办公室。

conscious of *adj.* noticing that (something exists or is happening and realizing that it is important) 察觉到，意识到: We suddenly became *conscious of* a sharp increase in the temperature. 我们突然意识到温度的急剧上升。He was suddenly *conscious of* everyone looking at him. 他突然察觉到所有的人都在看着他。I was not *conscious of* what I was saying at the time. 我没意识到当时我在讲些什么。Jim was not *conscious of* having offended her. 吉姆没有意识到已经冒犯了她。They were *conscious of* being watched. 他们察觉到被人监视了。

NOTE **1.** 本短语中的 conscious 是表示认知的形容词。在英语中，凡是表示认知的形容词一般都与介词 of 短语相连用，如 aware, forgetful, ignorant, oblivious 等。**2.** 本短语的比较级形式是 more conscious of，最高级形式是 the most conscious of。

consent to *vt.* (正式用语) give approval

for or agreement to (something or a course of action)同意,答应: Her parents finally *consented to* her marriage. 她的父母终于同意了她的婚事。At first her parents didn't *consent to* her marrying a foreigner. 起初,她父母并不同意她嫁给一个外国人。More than 80 applications to be *consented to* by the general manager. 有80多份申请要总经理审批。

NOTE 1. 本短语中的 to 是介词,后接名词或动名词(短语),而不能接原形动词。但具有及物性动词用法的 consent 本身可以后接不定式短语作宾语。例如:

> He *consented to* answer their question.
> 他同意回答他们的问题。

2. 本短语的同义短语是 approve of 和 assent to;反义短语是 disapprove of。

consider as *vt.*【可分性动词短语】(用一般时态)regard or think of (someone or something)as (being or doing something) 把……认为是……: The White House spokesman told reporters that President Obama *considered* Michael Jackson *as* "a spectacular performer and pop musician." 白宫发言人对记者说,奥巴马总统认为,迈克尔·杰克逊是"一名杰出的艺人和流行音乐的标志性人物"。We all *considered* him *as* a hero. 我们都认为他是个英雄。I *consider* him *as* belonging to a group of misguided thinkers. 我认为他属于那些误入歧途的思想家。She *considered* herself *as* being the most qualified for the position. 她认为自己最胜任那一职务。

NOTE 1. 本短语后可接名词、动名词和形容词。

2. 本短语中的介词 as 常可省略,或以 to be 取代。例如:

> We all *considered* him a hero.
> 我们都认为他是个英雄。
>
> Remarks like this are generally *considered to* be unacceptable today.
> 这样的话在现在一般被认为是不可接受的。

3. 本短语的同义短语是 regard as。

considering that *conj.* (用于表达事实的句子之前) if one takes into account the fact that 考虑到: He did very well in the exams *considering that* he had studied so little. 他学的很少,鉴于此,他考得很不错了。*Considering that* it was very difficult, he fulfilled his task very well. 就其任务的艰难而言,他完成得很出色了。

NOTE 本短语中的 that 可以省略。

consist in *vt.*【不可分性动词短语】(正式用语,无被动语态形式,用一般时态,不用进行时态) have (something) as the most important aspect or the only aspect; lie within 在于: The beauty of Venice *consists* largely *in* the style of its ancient buildings. 威尼斯的美主要在于其古代建筑的风格。True wealth does not *consist* only *in* what we have. 真正的财富并不仅仅在于我们所拥有的财产。The scientific approach to a problem *consists* first of all *in* collecting ample materials. 研究问题的科学方法首先在于收集丰富的材料。

NOTE 本短语的主语通常为单数形式。

consist of *vt.*【不可分性动词短语】(无被动语态形式,用一般时态,不用进行时态) be made up of (particular parts or things, or people)由……组成,包括: Air *consists of* oxygen, nitrogen and many other kinds of gases. 空气是由氧、氮和其他多种气体组成的。The Board of Directors *consists of* nine members, and each member serves a four-year term. 董

事会由 9 名成员组成，每位成员任期 4 年。This earth *consist of* 193 sovereign countries, with 192 being members of the United Nations. 这个世界是由 193 个主权国家组成，其中 192 个是联合国成员国。

C

consistent with *adj.* containing statements or ideas that are similar to or have the same aim as 与……相符的，与……一致的：This statement is *consistent with* what they said earlier. 这种说法与他们以前所说的相符。This development is *consistent with* the company's aims of reducing its costs. 这种发展与该公司降低成本的目标是一致的。If you take a careful look at his thesis, you may find many of his arguments are not *consistent with* each other. 如果你仔细地读一下他的论文，你就会发现其中很多论点是相互矛盾的。

consult with *vt.*【不可分性动词短语】❶(主要用于美国英语中，一般不用被动语态形式)ask the advice of (someone)请教(某人)：He had *consulted with* his lawyer before he made the decision. 在作出决定之前，他请教了他的律师。❷(正式用语，无被动语态形式)have a formal meeting and exchange opinions, information, etc. with (someone) in order to reach a decision 与(某人)商讨，磋商：On the subject of funds, you may *consult with* Mr James. 关于资金问题，你可以与詹姆斯先生商量。

contend with *vt.*【不可分性动词短语】(常用一般时态) have to deal with (problems or difficulties), especially in order to achieve something 与……作斗争，应付：We must *contend with* the difficulties. 我们必须与困难作斗争。I've got enough problems to *contend with* without your interference! 我要应付的问题够多的了，你还来打扰我！I've got quite enough to *contend with* bringing up three kids. 养育三个孩子，我要做的事情够多的了。

NOTE 不要将本短语与 content with 混淆。

content with *vt.*【可分性动词短语】(常与反身代词连用) be willing to accept (what you have), although you would prefer to have something else; satisfy (oneself) with (something less than one had hoped)满足于，使(自己)满足于：As he had to drive home after the party, he *contented* himself *with* two glasses of Cola. 他因为聚会后还要开车回家，所以只好喝两杯可乐就算满足了。It was too wet to go outside, so the children had to be *contented with* playing indoors. 外面水太多，不能到户外做游戏，所以孩子们只好在室内玩了。Initially, she *contented* herself *with* simply looking after her family. 起初，她以照顾好自己的家庭而感到满足。

content with *adj.* satisfied or contented with 对……满意的，满足于：Over 90 percent of travelers were *content with* their tours during the golden week of the national holiday. 在国庆黄金周期间，90%以上的游客对他们的出游都感到满意。Are you *content with* your grade? 你对你所得的分数满意吗？She is *content with* what she is today. 她对她现在的成就感到满足。Let us rest *content with* that. 让我们对此心满意足吧。Not *content with* having overthrown the government, the military dictator imprisoned all his opponents. 这个军事独裁者推翻了政府还不满足,又把反对他的人全部关进了监狱。

contrary to *adj.* completely different from or wholly opposed to 与……完全不同的,与……完全相反的: *Contrary to* the popular belief, seismologists can not accurately predict natural disasters, said a scientist at the China Earthquake Networks Center. 中国地震台网中心的一位科学家说,不像人们广泛认为的那样,地震学家并不能准确预报自然灾害。The decision was *contrary to* my wishes. 这一决定与我的愿望完全相反。Things turned out *contrary to* what we had expected. 结果事情与我们所预料的完全相反。

NOTE 本短语中的 contrary 是形容词,还可用作名词,用于 on the contrary 和 to the contrary 短语中。

contribute to/towards *vt.* ❶ (of a person, organization, or country) give (money, goods, or time and other resources) to (something), especially when other people are also helping 捐助,捐献: They *contributed* funds, material, and experimental plots *to* the project. 他们为该项目捐助了资金、物资和实验场地。A large amount of money was *contributed to* the earthquake-hit areas by people from all walks of life. 各行各业的人士给地震灾区捐助了大量的资金。All the children *contributed* their free time *to* the concert. 所有的孩子都把空闲时间献给了那场音乐会。He promised to *contribute* $1,000 *towards* the cost of the lawsuit. 他答应捐资 1 000 美元的诉讼费用。❷(无被动语态形式,用一般时态) give help towards; help to bring about 有助于,促成: The development of Sino-US constructive relationship of cooperation will *contribute to* peace, stability and prosperity in the Asia-Pacific as well as the whole world. 发展中美建设性的合作关系将有助于亚太地区乃至全世界的和平、稳定与繁荣。Excessive drinking *contributed to* his ruin. 过度饮酒毁了他。Your help will *contribute towards* overcoming the difficulties. 你的帮助将有助于克服这些困难。❸write (a written article) and send it to (a magazine, newspaper, etc.) 为(杂志,报纸等)投稿: Our professor *contributed* several articles *to* the weekly. 我们的教授为该周刊投了几篇稿件。She regularly *contributes to* the college magazine. 她定期为院刊投稿。

convert into *vt.* change (someone or something) into (something else) 把……改变成……: Can we *convert* you from a meat eater *into* a vegetarian? 我们能不能把你从肉食者改变成为素食者? He proposed *converting* the state Capitol's interior courtyard *into* a "smoking plaza". 他提议把州议会大厦的内院改成"吸烟广场"。Can you *convert* pounds *into* dollars here? 你们这儿能把英镑兑换成美元吗? The sofa *converts into* a bed. 沙发改成了床。Coal can be *converted into* gas. 煤可以转化为煤气。

NOTE 本短语表示"把某种东西改变成不同种类或形式的东西"。例如:

> Electrical energy can be *converted into* heat energy.
> 电能可转变为热能。

convert to *vt.* ❶ change your religious belief, attitude, etc. to (another), or to persuade someone do this 改变宗教信仰;使皈依;改变态度: Priests *converted* many *people to* Christianity. 神父使许多人改信了基督教。John was *converted to* Buddhism by an Indian priest. 一名印度僧人使约翰皈依了佛门。She managed to *convert* him *to* her opinion. 她终于设法说服了他接受她的意见。My daughter has *converted* me *to* popular music. 我女儿使我喜欢上了流行音乐。❷change from one system, use, or method to (another), or to make something do this 转变,改用: You have to *convert* the temperature readings from Fahrenheit *to* Celsius. 你必须把华氏温度的读数转变为摄氏温度的读数。Does electricity *convert* easily *to* other forms of power? 电容易转为其他形式的能量吗? The dishonest treasurer *converted* the club's money *to* his own use. 这名不诚实的财务人员把俱乐部的公款挪为己用。Problems were caused when Britain *converted to* a decimal money system. 英国的货币改为十进制时还引出了很多问题。

convey to *vt.* 【可分性动词短语】❶(正式用语) take or carry (something or someone) from one place to (another)运送,输送: The train *conveys* passengers *to* London. 列车把旅客运往伦敦。Your luggage will be *conveyed* by a truck from the station *to* your hotel. 你的行李将用卡车由车站送到您下榻的旅馆。❷make (something such as feelings, ideas, or thoughts) known to (someone)向(某人)表达,传达(感情、想法、思想): Our government's anger was *conveyed to* their ambassador. 我国政府已向他们的大使表达了愤慨。How can I *convey* these ideas *to* the children? 我怎么才能让孩子们知道这些想法呢?

convict of *vt.* 【可分性动词短语】(常用被动语态形式) declare (someone) to be guilty of (a crime) in a court of law (在法庭上)宣判(某人)犯有某罪: The jury *convicted* the prisoner *of* murder. 陪审团宣判那囚犯犯有谋杀罪。The farmer was *convicted of* murder and was sentenced to death Tuesday at the first trial. 该农民被宣判犯有杀人罪,并在星期二的一审中被判处死刑。The corrupt official *convicted of* taking bribes and abusing his power was executed, and his illegal income has been turned over to the national treasury. 这个被判有受贿罪和滥用职权罪的贪官被执行死刑,其非法所得上缴国库。

convince of *vt.* 【可分性动词短语】(常用一般时态) make (someone) believe the truth of (something) 使(某人)相信……: He failed to *convince* the jury *of* his innocence. 他没能使陪审团相信他是无辜的。"Indonesia is not yet *convinced of* the effectiveness of slaughtering infected birds in controlling bird flu," said a WHO official. 一位世界卫生组织的官员说:"印度尼西亚还没有相信大量屠宰受感染的家禽对控制禽流感是有效的。"

cook up *vt.* ❶prepare (some food) quickly (很快地)煮好: Mary will *cook up* some eggs before you go. 在你走前,玛丽会煮好一些鸡蛋的。❷(非正式用语) invent (a story, excuse, etc.) falsely 编造(假话、借口等): The two boys *cooked up* some story to tell their parents. 这两个男孩编造了假话讲给他们的父母听。The colonialists *cooked up* ridiculous tales and arguments in defense of their gangster acts. 殖民主义者们编造出可笑的谎言和论据来为自己的强盗行径辩解。I'd like to find out who cooked this story up. 我要查出是谁编造的这番谎言。

cool down/off *vt.* &*vi.* ❶ (cause to) become cooler (使)变凉,降温:Let your tea *cool down* a little before you drink it. 让你的茶稍凉一点再喝。We went for a swim to *cool* ourselves *off*. 为了给身体降降温,我们去游泳了。China raised the average price of electricity this week to *cool down/off* the overheated growth of some industries. 中国本周提高了平均电价以抑制某些产业的过热发展。❷(非正式用语)(cause to) become less angry or excited (使)冷静下来: It took me a long time to *cool down* after the argument. 争论过后,我好长时间才冷静下来。I tried to *cool* her *down* but she was too angry. 我试图使她冷静下来,但她还是非常生气。A heated argument can be settled if both sides *cool down/off* first. 只要双方先冷静下来,激烈的争论就会得以平息。Let him cool off, you can talk about it later. 让他冷静一下,你过会儿再和他谈这事。

—*vi.* become less interested in someone or an idea 对……兴趣减弱: Their initial enthusiasm soon *cooled down/off*. 他们最初的那股热情很快就冷淡了下来。

NOTE 当本短语用作及物性动词短语,所带的宾语为代词时,该代词须置于本短语的动词和副词中间。

cooperate with *vt.*【不可分性动词短语】(无被动语态形式) work with (other people) to achieve a result that is good for everyone involved 与……合作: The Chinese side is willing to *cooperate with* Iran in various fields including the field of energy on the basis of mutual benefit. 中方愿与伊朗在互利基础上发展包括能源在内的各领域的合作。Our two countries must *cooperate with* each other for overcoming the current financial crisis. 我们两国必须相互合作,克服当前这场金融危机。

cope with *vt.*【不可分性动词短语】(非正式用语) deal successfully with (a difficult situation or job)成功应对,处理(某种困难局面或工作): We are sure the Hong Kong Special Administrative Region Government is fully *capable* of coping *with* complex situations. 我们确信香港特区政府完全有能力应对各种复杂局面。The World Health Organization, which shoulders the heavy responsibility of keeping everyone in good health, should play an important role in *coping with* this problem. 肩负着让人人都保持健康之重任的世界卫生组织应该在应对这一问题上发挥重要作用。We can use some software to *cope with* junk mail. 我们可以使用某种软件来处理垃圾邮件。

correspond to *vt.*【不可分性动词短语】(无被动语态形式,用一般时态) be equal to or the same as (something else)相当于……,相似于……;与……符合,与……一致: The American Congress *corresponds to* the British Parliament. 美国的国会相当于英国的议会。The wings of a bird *correspond to* the arms of a man. 鸟的翅膀相当于人的手臂。The contents of the box must *correspond to* the description on the label. 箱内的物品必须与标签上的说明相符。

correspond with *vt.*【不可分性动词短语】❶(正式用语) (of two or more people) regularly write letters to (each other)与(某人)互通信件: Mary and Tom *corresponded with* each other for many years. 玛丽和

C

汤姆相互通信多年了。He *corresponds with* leading European scholars regularly. 他与一些主要的欧洲学者定期通信。❷(无被动语态形式,用一般时态,不用进行时态) be the same as (something else), or very much like it; be in agreement or harmony with (usually something) 和……相同,和……一致,与……符合: The problem is that what she says doesn't *correspond with* what she does. 问题是她言行不一。The copy does not *correspond with* the original. 这个复制件与原件不符。

couldn't agree more *vi.* used to mean you completely agree or support very strongly 完全同意,强烈支持:"The movie is really terrible." "I *couldn't agree more*!" "这部影片真是糟透了。""我完全同意。" I *couldn't agree more* with the opinions stated in your recent editorial. 我完全同意你们最近发表的社论中所表明的那些观点。Lots of people think the use of mobile phones while driving should be outlawed, and lawmakers *couldn't agree more*. 许多人认为,开车打手机应被定为违法。对此,立法者们强烈支持。

NOTE **1.** 本短语中的 couldn't 是用来表示语气,而不表示过去时态。例如:

> Life *couldn't* be better.
> 生活再好不过了。

2. 本短语通常用第一人称作主语。

3. 本短语的反义短语是 couldn't agree less.

count as *vt.* (用一般时态) consider or regard (something or someone) as being (something) 把……认为是……,把……视作……: The city government *counts* its library *as* an important part of public service. 市政府将其图书馆看作是为公众服务的一个重要部分。According to the new Marriage Law the stocks and shares bought in marriage should be *counted as* joint property and subjected to property division in divorces. 根据新《婚姻法》,婚后购买的股票、债券被视为夫妻共同财产,离婚时要进行分割。Any member of the committee is *counted as* (being) fit to take the chairmanship. 委员会的任何一名成员都被认为适合担任主席的职务。

count down *v.* count backwards in seconds to zero, especially before sending a space vehicle into the sky (尤指在火箭发射升空前) 倒数秒数,倒计时: The spaceship is already being *counted down*. 发射宇宙飞船已开始倒计时。As the clock *counts down* the few remaining hours to the New Year, I am very delighted to extend New Year greetings to you. 新年钟声即将敲响,我很高兴地向你们致以新年的祝福!

NOTE 本短语可转化为复合词 countdown, 意为"倒读数,倒计时"。

count for *vt.* 【不可分性动词短语】(常用现在一般时,不用进行时态,常与 much, little 或 nothing 等连用) be of importance or be worth (usually much, little, or nothing) 有……重要性,有……价值: In our work quality counts for as much as quantity. 在我们的工作中,质量和数量同等重要。He seems to *count for* little in his firm. 他在他的商行里似乎是个无足轻重的人物。Such small defects really *count for* nothing. 这种小毛病实在不算什么。In business, a strong personality often *counts for* more than formal training. 在商业界,突出的个性往往比受过的正式训练更有价值。

count in *vt.* 【可分性动词短语】(非正式用语,用一般时态) include (someone) in a particular plan or activity 把(某人)包括在(某项计划或活动)中: Does it *count in* farmers in outer areas when the city declares its population number? 该市宣布其人口数字时包括郊区的农民吗? "There's a party on Saturday." "*Count* me *in*!" "星期六有个聚会。" "算我一个!"

NOTE 1. 当本短语所带的宾语为代词时,该代词须置于本短语的动词和副词中间。

2. 本短语的反义短语是 count out。

count on/upon *vt.* 【不可分性动词短语】 ❶depend on (someone or something) 依靠(某人或某物): Is there anything I can do for you? You can *count on* me. 我能为您做点什么吗? 您可以依靠我。That was the only thing they could *count on*. 那是他们唯一能依靠的东西。The company was *counting on* his making the right decision. 全公司都要靠他的正确决策。❷expect (someone) to help you or do what you want or expect him or her to do for you 指望,期望: We can't *count on* politicians for help. 我们不能指望政客的帮助。You can't *count on* him to lend you any money because he has none. 你不能指靠他借钱给你,因为他没钱。❸expect (something) to happen 期待(某事发生): The tension of the company has lasted for over two years. We can't *count on* one or two discussion to resolve the issue at once. 公司的紧张局势已持续两年多,不能期待一两次讨论就解决问题。Many people *count on* the bus to be on time every day. 许多人都指望公共汽车每天能准点运行。We are *counting on* selling at least 5,000 copies of the book. 我们期望至少可以卖出 5 000 册书。

NOTE 1. 本短语中的 upon 用法比 on 正式,但不及 on 常用。

2. 本短语的同义短语是 depend on/upon, lean on/upon 和 rely on/upon。

count out *vt.* 【可分性动词短语】 ❶count (things or people) one by one 一个一个地数: He *counted out* five $20 notes. 他数出了 5 张 20 美元的钞票。*Count out* the books on the shelves and note down the total number. 把书架上的书数一下,记下共有多少本。The teacher *counted* the students *out* as they passed her. 老师在学生们走过她身旁时查了一下他们的人数。❷(非正式用语,用一般时态) not include (someone) in a particular plan or activity 不把(某人)包括在(某项计划或活动)中: If you're playing football in this weather, then *count* me *out*. 如果你们在这种天气踢足球,那就别把我算在内了。Those who have not yet sent in applications should be *counted out*. 那些还没有提交申请的人不应包括在内。❸(常用被动语态形式) (in a boxing competition) (of the referee) count up to ten seconds, and then say someone who fails to get up from the floor has lost a fight (拳击比赛中裁判员)数 10 秒后宣告(被击倒后仍未能起立的运动员)失败: The young boxer was *counted out* in the second round. 那名年轻的拳击运动员在第二回合中就被宣告失败。

NOTE 1. 当本短语所带的宾语为代词时,该代词须置于本短语的动词和副词中间。

C

2. 当本短语作“不把(某人)包括在(某项计划或活动)中”解时,反义短语是 count in。

count up *vi.* (常与 to 连用) say (numbers) one after another in order 数数: *Count up* to three and then open your eyes. 数到 3,然后睁开眼睛。I can *count up* to ten in German. 我能用德语数 10 个数。

—*vt.*【可分性动词短语】❶count(people or things) to see how many there are 清点(人或物的数目):I *counted* the guests *up*, and there are too many to seat. 我查了一下宾客的人数,人太多,座位不够。Please *count up* all these books and tell me how many there are. 请把所有这些书都清点一下,然后告诉我有多少本。❷find the total of (something); add up (figures)算出……的总数,把(数目)加起来:I must *count up* how much money I've spent today. 我得算一下我今天总共花去了多少钱。Please *count up* all the days that he has been absent. 请算一下他缺勤的总天数。

couple with *vt.* ❶(常用被动语态形式) connect(one thing or set of things) to (another)使……与……联系: The name of Mozart is *coupled with* the city of Salzburg. 莫扎特的名字是与萨尔茨堡联系在一起的。A reputation for quality, *coupled with* very competitive prices, has made these cars very popular. 质量的信誉加上颇具竞争力的价格,使得这些汽车非常走俏。Working too hard, *coupled with* not getting enough sleep, made her ill. 工作过累,加之睡眠不足,她病倒了。❷(委婉用语)have sex with (someone)与(某人)发生性关系。Sir I will not have you *couple with* my daughter! 先生,我不会让你和我女儿乱搞!

cover up *v.* ❶ put one thing (over another), in order to protect or hide it (为了保护或掩饰而)把……盖上:The snow *covered up* the rice field, with a white cloak. 积雪给稻田罩上了一件白色的外衣。He had forgotten to have the machine *covered up*. 他忘了把机器盖起来。❷ put more clothes or covers (on your body), to hide it or keep it warm 多穿衣服(以遮盖身体或保暖):When dad saw my short skirt he told me to *cover* myself *up*. 爸爸看到我穿着短裙便让我多穿衣服遮体。It's cold and you should *cover up* warmly. 天气冷,你应该穿得暖和些。❸prevent(something) from being noticed 掩饰:She tried to *cover up* her nervousness before making her speech. 在发表讲演前,她竭力掩饰住内心的紧张。Mother is worried, but she *covers* it *up* by joking. 虽然妈妈很不安,但她却以开玩笑的方式将其掩饰起来。❹(非正式用语)hide (the truth about something) by not telling what you know or by preventing other people from discovering the truth about something bad 掩盖:He tried to *cover up* his guilt by lying. 他企图靠撒谎来掩盖其罪行。A large number of American people think the truth of starting the war on Iraq has been *covered up* on purpose. 许多美国人认为发动伊拉克战争的真相被故意掩盖了。

NOTE 1. 当本短语所带的宾语为代词时,该代词须置于本短语的动词和副词中间。

2. 本短语可转化为复合词 cover-up,意为“掩饰,掩盖”。

cover with/in *vt.*【可分性动词短语】cause (someone or something) to have a lot of (something or things) on top 以……覆盖(某人或某物): You'd better *cover* the child *with* more bedclothes. 你最好给孩子多盖点被子。Last night's snowstorm *covered* the ground *with* deep snow. 昨晚的暴风雪给地面覆盖上了厚厚的一层雪。His coffin, *covered with* the UN flag, was carried out of the special plane by eight soldiers. 他的灵柩,覆盖着联合国国旗,由 8 名士兵抬下专机。His clothes were *covered in* mud. 他的衣服上都是泥浆。

crack down on *vt.*【不可分性动词短语】(非正式用语) take strong and severe action to deal with (something bad) 严格治理,严厉打击: The bulletin says the government will continue to *crack down on* excessive fee charges by departments in various sectors. 公报指出,政府将继续严格治理各部门乱收费的问题。Drug smuggling must be *cracked down on*. 必须严厉打击毒品走私活动。

crash into *vt.* ❶ (cause to) hit (something) with force, usually accidentally (使)(常指意外地)撞上(某物): The old lady crashed into the door in the dark. 老妇人在黑暗中撞到了门上。Yesterday, an Iveco minibus *crashed into* a dump truck on state highway. 昨天,一辆依维柯面包车在国道与一辆自动卸货卡车相撞。This morning a suicide bomber tried to *crash* his car *into* a police station in Baghdad. 今天上午有一名自杀性爆炸者企图驾车撞巴格达市的一个警察局。❷ (of a plane) fall violently from the sky into (something) (指飞机)从高空坠落入……: An Airbus A-330 of Air France *crashed into* the Atlantic Ocean off Brazil, killing all 228 people on board. 一架法国航空公司空客 A330 客机在巴西附近的大西洋海域坠毁,机上 228 人全部遇难。

credit card *n.* a small plastic card which is used instead of money to pay for goods and services on credit 信用卡: Mr Smith used his *credit card* to buy gasoline. 史密斯先生用信用卡购买了汽油。I'd like to pay by *credit card*. 我想用信用卡支付。

crocodile tears *n.* a false or insincere show of sympathy or sadness 鳄鱼泪,假慈悲: In his speeches the mayor always puts on a big show of *crocodile tears* for poor and homeless people. But I don't see him doing anything to help them. 这位市长在讲话的时候总是装得好像他对穷人和无家可归的人非常同情。但是,我并没有见到他做些什么来帮助他们。"Don't shed any *crocodile tears* for Robert; I know you were responsible for his firing," she said. "别为罗伯特发假慈悲了。我知道,他被解雇你有责任。"她说道。The sight of George weeping *crocodile tears* made me sick. 看到乔治那假慈悲的样子使我恶心。

NOTE **1.** 本短语来自一个古老的神话,据说鳄鱼往往发出一种抽泣的声音来引诱那些它们要吃的猎物,然后一面吞食一面流眼泪。现在这种说法已成为常用短语,并为人们广为使用。

2. 本短语中的名词 tear 必须用复数形式。

crop up *vi.* (非正式用语) (of something difficult or unpleasant) appear or happen, usually suddenly and unexpectedly (指困

难或令人不快之事)(尤指突然意外地)出现，发生：Some difficulties have *cropped up*, so we must work late to deal with them. 因为意外出现了一些困难，所以我们必须加班把它们解决掉。Since the end of the Cold War, ethnic, religious, territorial and resources disputes and regional conflicts keep *cropping up*. 自冷战结束以来，由民族、宗教、领土、资源引发的争端和地区冲突此起彼伏。

cross off *vt.*【可分性动词短语】remove (someone or something, such as a name) from a list, by drawing a line or lines through it (从名单中)画掉：She *crossed* him *off* her Christmas card list after they argued. 他们争吵之后，她便把他从圣诞卡寄送名单中画掉了。Did you *cross* her name *off* the guest list? 你把她的名字从宾客名单上画掉了吗? If you can't come, I'll *cross* your name *off* from the list. 如果你不能来，我就把你的名字从名单上画掉。

NOTE 1. 如本短语后有代词时，该代词前常用 of。例如：

> We will have to *cross* him *off* of our list.
> 我们将不得不把他从我们的名单中画掉。

2. 当本短语所带的宾语为代词时，该代词须置于本短语的动词和介词或副词中间。

cross one's fingers *vi.* put one of your fingers over another one hoping for good luck or things will happen in the way you want them to 两指交叉(以求好运或某事顺心如意)：Linda *crossed her fingers* during the race hoping that Jim would win. 在比赛的过程中，琳达两指交叉以求吉姆取胜。We're *crossing our fingers* and hoping that the weather stays fine. 我们都两指交叉，希望天气持续晴好。

NOTE 1. 以食指与中指交叉的方式祈求或祝福某人好运或某事顺利，是西方人的一种迷信做法，也是本短语的起源。

2. 本短语的同义短语是 keep one's fingers crossed。

cross out *vt.*【可分性动词短语】remove (something such as words), by drawing a line or lines through something you have written, usually because it is wrong 删去，画掉(错误文字)：He *crossed out* the last sentence of the article and put another in instead. 他把文章的最后一句删掉，换上了另一句。If you think it's wrong, *cross* it *out* and write it again. 如果你认为那是错的，就把它删去重写。Two of the words had been *crossed out* by someone. 其中两个字已被人画掉了。

NOTE 当本短语所带的宾语为代词时，该代词须置于本短语的动词和副词中间。

cry (out) for *vt.*【不可分性动词短语】❶make a loud noise because 因……而哭或喊叫：That child is always *crying for* no reason. 那孩子总是无缘无故地哭闹。He heard someone *crying out for* help. 他听到有人在呼救。❷(常用进行时态) express a desire for (something of someone) by weeping 哭着要(某物或某人)：The baby was *crying for* milk. 孩子哭着要吃奶。He could hear his little brother *crying for* his mother. 他能听到他的小弟弟在哭着要妈妈。❸(无被动语态形式，常用进行时态) be in great need of (someone or something) 迫切需要(某人或某物)：This country is *crying* *out for* new leadership. 这个国家迫切需要新的领导人。This room is *crying out for* some new furniture. 这个房间急需添置一些新家具。

cry for the moon *vi.* want something that is impossible to get or achieve 想要不可能得到的东西,提出不可能达到的要求:We can't afford all the things you ask for. Stop *crying for the moon* and be satisfied with what you have. 你要的东西我们都买不起。别再要不可能得到的东西了,知足吧。He asked his father to buy him a car as a birthday present. I think he was *crying for the moon*. 他要他爸爸给他买一辆汽车作为生日礼物。我想他是在做非分之想。I'm not *crying for the moon*. What I'm asking for is to be sent to a better school. 我并没有提不可能达到的要求。我只不过要求把我送到一所较好的学校去而已。

NOTE 本短语的动词 cry 可被 ask, wish 等替换,构成的短语与本短语意义和用法相同。

cry out *vi.* shout loudly because you are hurt, frightened, in pain or in trouble 大叫,大声喊出:John *cried out* as his head struck rock. 当约翰的头磕在石头上时他大叫起来。It's enough to make most people *cry out* in horror. 让大多数人吓得大叫就够了。She was *crying out* in pain on the ground when the ambulance arrived. 当救护车赶到时,她正在地上疼得大叫。He *cried out* for help. 他高声求救。"Help!" she *cried out*. 她高声喊道:"救命啊!"

NOTE 本短语与 burst out 都表示"叫喊,喊出"之意。本短语指因害怕、疼痛、遇到麻烦或需要帮助时而叫喊;而 burst out 的叫喊则带有感情色彩。请比较下面两个句子:

She *cried out* in fear.
她害怕得大叫起来。
"He's a cheater!" the girl *burst out* angrily.
"他是一个骗子!"那姑娘生气地大叫道。

cry over spilt milk *vi.* (非正式用语) waste time feeling upset about something bad that has happened and cannot be changed (事后)做无益的后悔: Our car is ruined and that's really too bad, but there's no use *crying over spilt milk*. We're just going to have to get a new car. 我们的汽车毁掉了,这实在是糟透了。但后悔没有用,咱们再买一台新的嘛。I know that you have lost your purse, but since it had happened, let it go; please don't *cry over spilled milk*. 我知道你丢了钱夹,不过既然这件事已经发生了,就让它过去。请不要做无益的后悔啦。

cudgel one's brains *vi.* think very hard about something, often something you are trying to remember 绞尽脑汁,冥思苦想:Both camps on the island *cudgeled their brains* to think out ways to contain the opposing side. 岛上两大阵营都在绞尽脑汁,各自想方设法地去牵制对方。We *cudgeled our brains* trying to remember the lost address. 我们苦思冥想,试图想起那个丢失了的地址。

NOTE 本短语中的名词 brain 必须要用复数形式。

cure of *vt.* 【可分性动词短语】❶ make (someone) completely better in health or spirits after an attack of (an illness) 使(某人)在病后恢复健康:The new finding may point out a good way to *cure of* AIDS. 这一新发现可能会给治愈艾滋病

指出一条很好的道路。This medicine will *cure* you *of* your cough. 这种药能治好你的咳嗽。NASA said its Mars rover, Spirit, will continue to work once it is *cured of* the software problems that have crippled it for more than a week. 美国国家航空航天局说,瘫痪一周多的"勇气"号火星车的软件故障一旦得以修复就将继续工作。❷control or get rid of (a bad habit, feeling, or attitude)控制,消除(某人的不良习惯、情绪或态度):A year in the army will *cure* the boy *of* his laziness. 在军队里当一年兵就会除掉那男孩的懒惰。Can you *cure* him *of* stealing? 你能除去他偷盗的恶习吗? Some people claim that they have been *cured of* smoking by hypnosis. 有些人声称他们已通过催眠术把烟戒掉了。Nothing seemed to *cure* him *of* his nervousness. 似乎没什么可以消除他的紧张情绪。

cut a long story short *vi.* talk about something with little detail and go directly to the most important point 长话短说:To *cut a long story short*, I'll just tell you that in the end they fell in love and got married. 长话短说,我只告诉你们,最后他们恋爱成婚了。Well, as time is limited, I have to *cut a long story short* and leave out the detail. 好吧! 因为时间有限,我只能长话短说,不详细讲了。Would you please *cut a long story short* and tell me what is the point you really want to make? 你能不能长话短说,告诉我你到底想讲什么?

NOTE 1. 本短语常用于口语中,以不定式短语的形式置于句首作状语。

2. 本短语的另外一种表现形式是 make a long story short。

cut across *vt.* ❶go across (an area of land) instead of going around the edge of it 抄近路穿过:You can save some time if you *cut across* the yard. 如果你从这个院子横穿过去,就可以节省一些时间。They were in a hurry, so they *cut across* the hills instead of going around by the road. 因为他们很匆忙,所以就穿过小山而没绕走大路。❷(无被动语态形式,用一般时态) be opposite to (something)与……相反,与……违背:I don't wish to press my suggestion if it would *cut across* anything you have in mind. 如果我的建议与你所想的相反的话,我不打算强迫你接受。The plan didn't work because it *cut* clean *across* the will of the masses. 那项计划完全违背了大众的意愿,因而行不通。

NOTE 当本短语作"抄近路穿过"解时,同义短语是 cut through.

cut back *v.* (非正式用语,常与 on 连用) reduce (an amount spent, produced, etc.)减少(花费、产量等): We oppose any plans to *cut back* the education budget. 我们反对任何减少教育预算的计划。The factory's production has been *cut back* twenty percent. 该厂的产量已减少 20%。The Chinese government encourages enterprises to increase imports from the United States so as to *cut back* on the trade deficit. 中国政府鼓励国内企业增加从美国的进口,以减少贸易逆差。

NOTE 1. 本短语的同义短语是 cut down (第二个义项)。

2. 本短语可转化为复合词 cutback,意为"削减,裁减"。

cut down *vt.* ❶use a knife or other sharp tool to make (something such as a tree) fall to the ground 把(树等)砍倒:Three more people in the village were arrested for having *cut down* trees unlawfully. 该村又有三人因滥砍盗伐而被捕。Many trees were *cut down* to make room for the new road. 许多树木被砍伐以腾出地方修筑新路。*Cut* the grass *down*. 把草割掉。❷(非正式用语) reduce (an amount of something)减少,削减,降低: These measures will effectively *cut down* AIDS infection rates in the area. 这些措施将有效地减少该地区艾滋病的感染率。I shall *cut* his allowance *down* to ten pounds a month. 我将把他的津贴减少到每月10英镑。The factory's production has been *cut down*. 该厂的产量已被削减。With the coming of the national holiday golden week, most car manufacturers in China have decided to *cut down* prices to boost their sales. 随着国庆黄金周的到来,在中国的大多数汽车制造商都决定降价促销。❸reduce the size of (something such as a garment)改小(衣物等): If you *cut down* these trousers they'll fit your daughter. 如果你把裤子改小,就能适合你女儿穿。❹make (something such as a speech or piece of writing) shorter 缩短(讲稿或文章等): You'd better *cut* the story *down* one third. 你最好把这篇故事压缩1/3。Your article will have to be *cut down* to about 2,000 words. 你的文章得缩短到2 000字左右。❺(正式用语,常用被动语态形式) knock down, wound, or kill (someone) 打倒,打伤,杀死(某人): Several soldiers were *cut down* by the machine-gun fire. 机枪的扫射打倒了几名士兵。Cholera *cut down* many in this village last year. 去年,这个村庄中有许多人被霍乱夺去了生命。He was *cut down* in his prime. 他英年早逝。

NOTE 1. 当本短语所带的宾语为代词时,该代词须置于本短语的动词和副词中间。

2. 当本短语作"减少,消减,降低"解时,同义短语是 cut back。

cut down on *vt.* (非正式用语,无被动语态形式) reduce (something), usually out of necessary (常指出于需要而)减少……: The factory cannot afford to employ any more workers, so it will have to *cut down on* production. 工厂雇佣不起更多的工人,所以不得不减少生产。The doctor advised my father to *cut down on* smoking. 医生劝我父亲少吸烟。

cut in *v.* ❶(非正式用语,常用一般时态,常与 on 连用) interrupt someone who is speaking 打断某人谈话: Don't *cut in* so rudely. 不要那么鲁莽地打断别人的谈话。"That's rubbish," she angrily *cut in*. "那是一派胡言。"她气愤地插嘴说道。I'm sorry to *cut in* on your conversation, but the dinner is ready. 对不起,打断一下你们的谈话。饭已经准备好了。❷(非正式用语,常用一般时态) (of someone) start dancing with the person you were dancing with (某人)截走(他人的)舞伴: I was enjoying the dance until that rude man *cut in*. 当我舞兴正浓时,那个粗鲁之人却截走了我的舞伴。Please don't *cut in*. 请不要截走我的舞伴。❸(常用一般时态,常与 on 连用) (of a driver) drive past a vehicle and move quickly in front of it in a dangerous way 超车: Reckless drivers who always try to *cut in* are bound to cause accidents sooner or later. 那些总是试图超车的鲁莽司机迟早会出事故的。You nearly caused a crash by *cutting in* on me like that. 你那样超我的车,几乎酿成撞车事故。❹cut or divide (something) by (a part) 切成,分成: *Cut* the cake *in* four, and share it equally. 把这蛋糕切成四份,平均分掉。The car was *cut in* half in the crash. 在撞车事故中,这台轿车被断为两截。

NOTE 1. 本短语的前三个义项都是不及物性用法,in是副词;最后一个义项是及物性用法,in是介词。

2. 当本短语作"打断某人谈话"解时,同义短语是: barge in, break in, break into, burst in, cut into, cut off, cut short, chip in, get in 和 put in。

cut in line ⇨ **jump the queue**

cut into *vt.* ❶ use a knife, pair of scissors, or other sharp tool to divide (something) into (two or more pieces)把(某物)分(或剪、切)成(几块): *Cut* the paper *into* small pieces. 把纸剪成小块。The tree was *cut into* several large pieces and taken away in the dark. 那棵树被截成了几大块后,在黑暗中被运走。❷(常用一般时态) interrupt (something such as a talk)打断(谈话等): She *cut into* our conversation several times. 她几次打断我们的谈话。She didn't *cut into* their talk but waited until they had finished. 她没有打断他们的谈话,而是一直等到他们把话讲完。

cut off *vt.*【可分性动词短语】❶remove (something) by cutting it 剪掉,切掉,割掉: Why did you *cut off* all your hair? 你怎么把头发都剪掉啦? After the storm we *cut off* the damaged branches. 暴风雨过后,我们把受损的树枝剪掉。His little finger was *cut off* in an accident at the factory. 在工厂的一次事故中,他的小手指被切断了。❷(常用被动语态形式,常用一般时态) prevent (someone) from continuing what he is saying; interrupt (someone who is speaking on the telephone) by breaking the connection 打断(某人的讲话);切断(某人在电话中的通话): His mother *cut off* Jimmy when he was trying to explain. 当吉米试图做出解释时,他妈妈打断了他。Don't *cut* me *off* when I'm talking. 我在讲话的时候,不要打断我。My explanation was *cut off* by loud protests. 我的解释被高声的抗议所打断。We got *cut off* in the middle of the call 我们正在通话时被切断了。❸(常用被动语态形式,常用一般时态) stop (the supply of something) to someone or stop (something) working 停止(供应等),切断: The whole building was plunged into darkness when the electricity supply was *cut off*. 当电力供应中断时,全楼一片黑暗。They were *cut off* for not paying their phone bill. 他们由于没交电话费而被停机。Should there be any trouble with the boiler, the automatic control unit would *cut off* the fuel supply. 假如锅炉出问题的话,自控装置会自动切断燃油的供给。We had to *cut* their gas *off* because they didn't pay the bill. 由于他们没有交费,我们不得不切断了他们的煤气供应。The President decided to *cut off* foreign aid to these countries. 总统决定停止对那些国家的外援。❹stop having a close or friendly relationship with (someone) 与(某人)断绝关系: Why did all his friends suddenly *cut* him *off*? 他的朋友们为何都突然断绝了与他的来往? ❺(常用被动语态形式,常与 from 连用) make (a place) difficult or impossible to enter, leave, or communicate with 隔断: The flood *cut* the town *off* from the rest of the world. 洪水使该镇与外界隔绝了。Landslide-blocked roads had a handful of villages in the quake-hit area *cut off* from the rest of the country. 由于山体滑坡造成道路阻塞,地震灾区的几个村庄与外界隔断

了。❻ stop (someone) from going somewhere, especially by blocking his or her way 阻断(某人的去路): Three firefighters were killed and a fourth severely burned when their only escape route was *cut off* by a fire run from below. 从下面烧上来的大火阻断了他们唯一的逃路,致使三名消防员殉职,另有一名消防员严重烧伤。❼(常用被动语态形式)(especially of war or disease) kill (someone)(尤指战争或疾病)夺去(某人)的生命: Her elder son was cut off in the war. 她的大儿子在战争中丧生。A sudden attack of the disease *cut* him *off* in the prime of his life. 疾病的突然发作,使他盛年夭折。

NOTE 1. 当本短语所带的宾语为代词时,该代词须置于本短语的动词和副词中间。

2. 本短语可转化为复合词 cutoff,意为“停止,截止”。

cut out *vt.*【可分性动词短语】❶(常与 from 或 of 连用) remove (something) from (a larger piece) by cutting 从……剪下,切掉: The reader *cut out* the piece of news from the newspaper. 那位读者把那条消息从报纸上剪了下来。The doctor *cut* the diseased tissue *out* from the girl's leg. 医生切除了那女孩腿上有病的组织。She *cut* a picture *out* of a sheet of paper. 她从一张纸上剪下一幅画来。❷ remove (parts) from (something such as a piece of writing, a speech, a film, or a broadcast), especially because they are not suitable 从(文章、讲话、影片或广播节目中)剪掉(某些尤指不合适的部分): For the sake of the space the editor had to *cut out* the last paragraph of the article. 因版面原因,编辑不得不删掉文章的最后一段。They've *cut out* several violent scenes from the film. 他们把几个暴力的场面从影片中剪切掉了。❸ shape (something) by cutting 剪成,切成: The tailor *cut out* a coat from the roll of cloth. 裁缝从这卷布中裁出了一件上衣。The shoemaker carefully examined the leather before starting to *cut out* the upper. 做鞋人在剪鞋帮之前,把皮子仔细地审视了一番。❹(非正式用语) stop eating (something or doing something), especially because it is bad for your health 戒食……,戒掉……: I've *cut out* chocolate completely. 我完全戒食巧克力了。I must *cut out* smoking and drinking altogether. 我一定要把烟酒一并戒掉。

—*vi.* ❶(用一般时态)(of an engine or machine) stop working suddenly (发动机或机器)突然停止运转: The helicopter crashed when one of its two engines *cut out*. 由于其两台发动机中的一台突然停止运转,该直升机便坠毁了。We had to walk when the engine *cut out* on the way. 汽车发动机在路上突然熄了火,我们不得不步行了。❷(主要用于美国英语中)(of a vehicle) suddenly leave a line of traffic and join another one (车辆)突然改道行驶: The car in front of us *cut out* and then there was a loud bang. 我们前面的那辆车突然改道,接着就是一声响亮的撞击声。

NOTE 1. 当本短语用作及物性动词短语,所带的宾语为代词时,该代词须置于本短语的动词和副词中间。

2. 当本短语作“(车辆)突然改道行驶”解时,同义短语是 pull out。

3. 本短语可转化为复合词 cutout,意为“剪下的图样”。

cut short *vt.*【可分性动词短语】❶ bring (something) to an end suddenly and before the proper time (在时间上)缩短: The astronaut was forced to *cut short* the space-walk because of the malfunctioning spacesuit. 那名宇航员因宇航服出现问题而被迫缩短了太空行走的时间。The accident forced them to *cut* their holiday *short*. 这次意外事故使他们不得不提前结束了假期。The meeting was *cut short* when the chairman fell ill. 主席突然病倒,会议被缩短了。❷interrupt (someone who is talking) so that he cannot finish what he is saying 打断(某人的讲话):He was about to go on talking when I *cut* him *short*. 当他还要接着往下讲时,我打断了他。While I was making the suggestion they *cut* me *short*. 我正提建议时,他们打断了我。

NOTE 当本短语所带的宾语为代词时,该代词须置于本短语的动词和形容词中间。

cut through *vt.* ❶go through (an area) instead of going around the edge of it 从……穿插过去:He decided to *cut through* the forest. 他决定从森林中穿插过去。❷make a path or passage through (something) by cutting 开辟穿越……的道路:They had to *cut* their way *through* the forest with axes. 他们不得不用斧子开辟穿越森林的道路。

NOTE 当本短语作"从……穿插过去"解时,同义短语是 cut across。

cut up *vt.* 【可分性动词短语】❶cut (something) into several smaller pieces 把(某物)切成小块:At this stage, your child will need someone to *cut up* her food for her. 在此阶段,你的小孩还需要有人为她把食物切碎。Yesterday we bought a machine for *cutting up* vegetables. 我们昨天买了一台切菜机。She *cut* the cake *up* and gave each of us a piece. 她把蛋糕切开,给我们每人一块。❷(非正式用语,常用被动语态形式) hurt the feelings of (someone); make (someone) very sad and upset 伤害(某人的)感情;使(某人)十分悲伤:Mary was really *cut up* when her friend died. 玛丽的朋友去世了,她悲伤极了。I'm afraid the bad news will cut him up. 我怕那坏消息会使他难过。Try again; don't be so *cut up* about your failure. 再试试看,不要因为失败就这样沮丧。❸make (someone) laugh 使(某人)大笑:What she said really *cut* me *up*. 她讲的一番话实在让我忍俊不禁。The strange noise made by Bob *cut* the whole class *up*. 鲍勃弄出来的奇怪动静使全班哄堂大笑。❹(英国英语用法) drive past (a vehicle) and move quickly in front of it in a dangerous way (以危险的方式)急速超越(车辆):Did you see the way he *cut* me *up* there? 你看没看到他在那儿是怎样超我车的? I got *cut up* several times on the expressway this morning. 今天早晨在高速公路上,我几次被人急速超车。

—*vi.* (美国英语用法,非正式用语) behave in a noisy and silly way 胡闹,不守规矩:Children are fond of *cutting up* whenever they have an opportunity. 孩子们一有机会就喜欢胡打乱闹。Tom's father scolded him for the way he *cut up* at the party. 汤姆在聚会上不守规矩,他爸爸为此而责骂了他。

NOTE 当本短语用作及物性动词短语,所带的宾语为代词时,该代词须置于本短语的动词和副词中间。

D d

dark horse *n.* (常用单数形式) ❶(美国英语用法) someone who wins a race, competition, election, etc. that no one expected him or her to win (在竞赛或竞选中)出人意料的获胜者,黑马: Although Jack is thought to be the player most likely to win the gold medal, David and Harry are among the *dark horses* for it. 虽然杰克被认为是最有可能夺得金牌的选手,但戴维和哈里也是夺冠的黑马。Every once in a while a *dark horse* candidate gets elected President. 每隔一段时间就有一位黑马候选人当选为总统。❷(英国英语用法)someone who has some special skill but does not reveal it 怀才不露的人: No one knew you had written a novel. You're a *dark horse*. 谁都不知道你曾写过一部小说。你真是个怀才不露的人。

NOTE **1.** 本短语最初源于赛马场,指那些没有名气、赌客们不甚了解但出人意料获胜的马。后来用于形容在比赛或竞选中出人意料的获胜者和怀才不露之人。
2. 不要把本短语误用为 black horse。在英语中,dark 有"隐藏着的"或"秘密的"的意义。

darn it *s.* (常用于美国英语中,非正式用语) used to show that you are very annoyed about something (用来表达某人烦恼的用语)讨厌,该死: Oh, *darn it*! Why haven't I got a ticket for the new movie! 噢,真讨厌! 我怎么就没有得到新电影的票呢! *Darn it*! I was sure I'd left my keys there. 真该死! 我肯定把钥匙落在那儿了。Darn it! You fooled me again. 该死! 你又愚弄了我。

NOTE 本短语中的动词 darn 是 damn 的委婉用法。

dash off (非正式用语,常用一般时态) *vi.* leave quickly or suddenly because you are in a hurry 匆匆离去: I must *dash off* to catch my train. 我必须火速离开去赶火车。I've got to *dash off* straight after lunch to meet a client. 我吃完午饭就得赶去见一位客户。
—*vt.* 【可分性动词短语】(非正式用语) write or draw (something) quickly and without serious attention 匆忙写出,迅速画出:I sat down and *dashed off* a couple of notes. 我坐下来,匆匆地写了两张条子。Bob had forgotten to write his report and *dashed* it *off* just before class. 鲍勃忘记写报告了,于是在课前匆忙地把它赶写了出来。Ann took out her drawing pad and pencil and *dashed off* a sketch of the ancient building. 安取出画板和铅笔,很快地画出了一幅那座古建筑的素描。

NOTE 当本短语用作及物性动词短语,所带的宾语为代词时,该代词须置于本短语的动词和副词中间。

dash out *vi.* (非正式用语,常用一般时

态) run or go out very quickly because you are in a hurry 冲出: The little girl drew on her new gloves and *dashed out*. 小女孩戴上新手套就跑了出去。I *dashed out* into the street, still in my pajamas. 我身上还穿着睡衣就跑到了大街上。

date back to/from *vt.* 【不可分性动词短语】(无被动语态形式,用一般时态) have lasted or existed since (a particular time)从(某一时期)存在至今,追溯到(某一时期);始于(某一时期): In China needle treatment *dates back to* ancient times. 中国古代就有了针刺疗法。Despite the long distance between the two countries, we enjoy good economic relations, which could *date back to* the early 1960s. 尽管两国相距遥远,我们业已存在的良好经济关系可追溯回 20 世纪 60 年代初期。*From* what period do the ceremonies *date*? 这种仪式开始于什么时代? The custom *dates from* the time when men wore swords. 这一习俗始于人类佩带刀剑的时代。

NOTE 1. 本短语中的 date back to 可省略为 date to, 但这被认为是非正式用法。例如:

> The city is famous for containing the well-known temples *dated to* 1, 000 years ago.
> 该城以其著名的千年古刹而闻名于世。

2. 本短语的同义短语是 trace back to。

day after day *adv.* as days go by; repeatedly for many days 逐日地,日复一日地:We waited *day after day*, but the expected guest never arrived. 我们等了一天又一天,可是要来的客人一直没来。*Day after day* the poor child came back and was given some bread. 这个可怜的小孩天天都回来,每天都得到一些面包。

NOTE 1. 本短语与 day in,(and) day out 意义相同,但两者之间的区别是:本短语强调某动作经过的时间长,并含有不打算再继续下去的意味;而 day in,(and) day out 则指长期不断地做尤指单调或枯燥无味之事。

2. 本短语中的名词 day 可被 week, month, year 等时间名词替换,构成的短语意思分别为"周复一周地","月复一月地","年复一年地"。

day and night *adv.* (非正式用语) for days without stopping; every day and every evening; continually; all the time 夜以继日地,日夜不停地: Electricians have been working *day and night* to restore electricity supplies to the area. 电工一直在夜以继日地工作,以恢复对那一地区的供电。Some gas stations on highways are open *day and night* 365 days a year. 公路旁有些加油站一年 365 天日夜不停地营业。I worry about it *night and day*. 我日夜为这事担心。

NOTE 1. 本短语的另外一种表达形式是 night and day。

2. 本短语的同义短语是 round/around the clock 和 the clock round/around。

day by day *adv.* daily; every day; without intermission of a day 每天;一天比一天地,日益: He collected all the necessary data *day by day*. 他每天都要收集必要的数据。*Day by day* he became weaker. 他一天比一天虚弱。*Day by day* the weather is getting colder. 天气一天比一天地冷起来。

NOTE 1. 本短语与 from day to day 意义相同,两者之间的区别是:本短语指"日益,一天比一天",每天在同一地点,重复同一样的事情,强调不断重复或天天发生;而 from day to day 则指"日复一日",含有某种状态持续变化的意味,有时含有没有长期打算的意味。例如：

> They lived *from day to day*.
> 他们活一天算一天。

2. 本短语中的名词 day 可被 week, month, year 等时间名词替换，构成的短语与本短语意义和用法相同。

day in, (and) day out *adv.* as days go by; every day over a long period, often in a way that is boring or unpleasant 逐日地，日复一日地：It's so boring; I've been eating McDonald's *day in*, day out. 日复一日地吃麦当劳，太单调了。*Day in and day out* the postman is busy delivering mail. 邮递员一天到晚地忙于投递信件。

NOTE 1. 本短语与 day after day 意义相同，两者之间的区别见 day after day。

2. 本短语中的名词 day 可被 week, month, year 等时间名词替换。

deal in *vt.* ❶(无被动语态形式，常用一般时态) buy and sell (a particular type of goods) as a business; trade in (something such as goods)做(某种商品的)买卖，经营(商品等)：The police said she was *dealing in* stolen goods. 警方说，她是在做被盗物品的买卖。We *deal in* hardware products but not software products. 我们只经销硬件产品而不经销软件产品。❷ be interested in (something)对……感兴趣：Lawrence was not a man who *dealt in* rumours. 劳伦斯不是一个对传闻感兴趣的人。❸(主要用于美国英语的口语中，非正式用语) allow someone to take part in (something) with you 让某人参与到……：If you're going hiking this weekend, *deal* me *in*. 如果你们这个周末去远足旅行，也算我一个吧。

NOTE 1. 本短语前两个义项中的 in 是介词。最后一个义项中的 in 是副词，而当该义项的宾语为代词时，该代词须置于动词和副词中间。

2. 当本短语作“经营(商品)”解时，同义短语是 trade in。

deal out *vt.*【可分性动词短语】❶ give (something, especially cards) to several people 给予，分发(纸牌)：He *dealt out* the cards and then they started to play. 他把牌发出去后，他们就开始玩了起来。He *dealt* all the cards *out*. 他把牌都发了出去。The money must be *dealt out* fairly and justly. 这笔款必须公平合理地分配。❷(正式用语，常与 to 连用) give a punishment to (someone)惩罚(某人)：The children felt that the teacher had been unfair in *dealing out* the punishment to the whole class. 孩子们认为老师惩罚全班同学是不公平的。Beatings and other cruelties were *dealt out* to the prisoners. 这些囚犯受到了殴打和其他残酷的虐待。

deal with *vt.*【不可分性动词短语】❶(常用一般时态) take action about (something or someone, usually troublesome), in order to achieve something or in order to solve a problem 处理，对付：How do you intend to *deal with* this problem? 你如何处理这个问题？In recent years, we have *dealt with* a number of law-breaking export cases and administered corresponding punishments to the units and individuals involved according to law. 近年来，我们查处了多起违法出口案件，对涉案单位和个人依法进行了相应惩处。He holds that young offenders should be *dealt with* quickly and harshly. 他主张对年轻的犯罪分子从快从严处理。❷(无被动语态形式，常用一般时态) have business relations with (a particular person or an organization)与……有生意往来：I've always *dealt with* Mr Smith, the dressmaker. 我一直和裁缝史密斯先生有生意来往。I usually *deal with* customers from Japan and South Korea. 我通常与日本和韩国的客户打交道。We have *dealt with* the company for years. 我们已同这家公司做了多年生意。❸(用一般时态)(of a book, speech, etc.) be concerned with (a subject); treat or talk about (a subject)(指书籍、演讲等)涉及，论述：This book *deals with* problems in political economy. 这本书论述政治经济学方面的问题。We'll *deal with* the question of unemployment in a moment. 我们一会儿谈失业的问题。

decide on/upon *vt.* 【不可分性动词短语】(常用一般时态) choose (something) from a number of possible choices 选定，决定：The session will *decide on* the list of premier and vice premiers, as well as ministers for government departments. 全会将决定总理、副总理以及政府各部部长的人选。Have you *decided on* where to spend your holiday this year? 你选定今年到哪里去度假了吗？I can't *decide on* whom to invite. 都邀请谁，我定不下来。The school administration had *decided upon* setting up another classroom building. 校方已决定再建一幢教学楼。

NOTE 1. 本短语中的 upon 用法比 on 正式，但不及 on 常用。

2. 本短语的同义短语是 settle on/upon。

declare war against/on/upon *vt.* ❶formally announce that one's nation is now at war with (another nation)正式对(某国)宣战：It was hardly acceptable that the big country *declared war against* a small island state. 该大国竟对一个小小的岛国宣战，令人难以接受。We declared war on Japan for their bombing of Pearl Harbor. Then Germany declared war on us because we *declared war on* their ally. 我们向日本宣战，是因为他们轰炸了珍珠港。后来德国向我们宣战，是因为我们向他们的盟国宣战了。❷announce a serious campaign against (a type of person or a serious problem)向(某种人或严重问题)宣战：The president *declared war against* crime and criminals. 总统向犯罪行为以及犯罪分子宣战。China *declares war on* "white" pollution: the use of plastic bags have been restricted. 中国向"白色"污染宣战：塑料袋已被限制使用。This isn't the first time I've had a noisy neighbor whom I've had to *declare war upon*. 这不是我第一次不得不向我吵闹的邻居"宣战"了。

NOTE 本短语一般用来表示一国对另一国宣战，第二个义项为比喻用法。

dedicate to *vt.* 【可分性动词短语】❶give (oneself or something) completely to (a particular cause, purpose or action) 致力于，献身于：The former US president said, he will continue to be *dedicated to* enhancing the cooperation between China and the US. 这位美国前总统表示，他会继续致力于推进中美的合作。The doctor *dedicated* all his life *to* the sick people. 这位医生把他的一生都奉献给了病人。❷declare (a book, etc.) to be in honor of (a person)把(著作等)题献给(某人)：Mr Smith *dedicated* his first book *to* his mother, who died last year. 史密斯先生把他的第一本书题献给了他去年故去的母亲。This book is *dedicated to* all those fighters — past, present, and future, who devote their lives to the motherland. 本书献给过去、现在和将来

为祖国献身的战士们。

deduct from *vt.* (常用被动语态形式,常用一般时态)take away (something such as an amount, or a part) from (a total) (从某一总数中)扣除,减去: We request you to *deduct* our commission *from* the invoice. 我们请求你方从发票中扣除我们的佣金。Can I sue my employer for his *deducting from* my wages and donating my earned money on my behalf? 我的雇主扣除了我的工资,代替我捐出了我挣的钱。我能起诉他吗? How much percent is *deducted from* wages as income tax in the UK? 在英国,要扣除工资的百分之几作为收入所得税?

deep down *adv.* in essence; in reality; really 实质上,实际上: *Deep down*, she is a caring person. 她实质上是一个关心他人的人。She seems indifferent, but *deep down* she's very pleased. 她看上去满不在乎,但实际上心里非常满意。*Deep down*, she knew that she had cheated her friend and it was wrong. 她明明知道自己骗了朋友是错误的。

define as *vt.* 【可分性动词短语】explain the meaning of (something such as a word) as being (something) 把……解释为……,对……下的定义是: Manual work is broadly defined as work that you do with your hands. "体力工作"被广义地定义为"手工劳动"。In his paper he *defined* a computer virus *as* "a program that can 'infect' other programs by modifying them to include a version of itself". 他在文章中将计算机病毒定义为"一种具有'感染性'的程序,它可以修改其他程序并在其他程序中自我复制"。

delight in *vt.* 【不可分性动词短语】(无被动语态形式,常用一般时态) get a lot of pleasure or enjoyment from (something or doing something) 喜欢,以……为乐: Generations of adults and children have *delighted in* the story. 一代又一代的成人与儿童都喜欢这个故事。The old professor *delights in* corresponding with his former students. 这位老教授喜欢与他从前的学生书信往来。He seems to *delight in* scandal. 他似乎对丑闻津津乐道。

delighted by/with *adj.* very pleased or satisfied with 对……感到高兴的;对……感到满意的: We are *delighted by* the response to our advertisement. 我们真高兴人们对我们的广告有这么好的反应。The US deputy secretary of state said "the US was absolutely *delighted with* the state of our relations with the country." 美国副国务卿表示:"美国对与贵国的现存关系感到绝对满意。"

NOTE 本短语的比较级形式是 more delighted by, 最高级形式是 the most delighted with。

demand of/from *vt.* 【可分性动词短语】command or expect (something) from (someone or something) 要求: Is it wrong for the police to *demand* help *of* the public in fighting crimes? 警方在打击犯罪中要求公众协助有错吗? Hard work will be *demanded of* students in this course. 这门课程要求学生用功学习。He *demanded* great loyalty *from* his employees. 他要求其雇员绝对忠实于他。

depart from *vt.* ❶(正式用语)leave (a place) and start a journey to another place 离开(某地);自(某地)出发: He *departed* on Thursday *from* London for a three-day visit to China. 他星期四离开伦敦去中国进行为期三天的访问。The first intercity train between Beijing and Tianjin *departed from* Beijing South Railway Station at 9:30 am and arrived at Tianjin half an hour later. 首列京津城际列车于上午9:30从北京南站出发，半个小时后就到达了天津。❷(正式用语) turn away from a previous course of action or way of thinking 背离(先前的行为或思想)：I'd like to *depart from* the main subject of my speech for a few moments. 我想暂时搁置一下我的主要话题。Some schools are now *departing from* the traditional idea of homework. 一些学校正在背弃传统的家庭作业理念。Old people don't like to *depart from* old customs. 老年人不愿意背离旧习俗。❸(主要用于英国英语中，在美国英语中只用 depart) resign from (a job) or leave it 辞去(工作)，离任：The first British female Prime Minister Margaret Thatcher *departed from* office, after over 11 years in power. 英国第一位女首相玛格丽特·撒切尔在执政 11 年后离任。

depend on/upon *vt.* 【不可分性动词短语】(正式用语) ❶(用一般时态，一般不用进行时态，后常接介词 for 短语和动词不定式短语) need (someone or something) in order to survive or be successful 依靠，依赖，指望：The old man *depends on* his son for support. 那老爷子靠他儿子供养。Mr Smith is a man to be *depended on*. 史密斯先生是个可依靠的人。These animals all *depend on* Mr Jackson to feed them. 这些动物都靠杰克逊先生喂养。You can't *depend on/upon* the weather being fine tomorrow. 你就别指望明天的天气会好。❷(无被动语态形式，用一般时态，不用进行时态)(of one thing) be changed or affected by (the other thing) 取决于：Yet it will finally *depend on* further consultation among various parties to get the results written down. 但最终能否通过一个书面的成果还取决于各方的进一步协商。Whether I go or not *depends on* the weather. 我去还是不去取决于天气的好坏。Scientists have predicted global temperature increases of between 2.5 and 10.4 degrees by 2100, *depending on* how much is done to limit greenhouse gas emissions. 科学家们预测，到 2100 年，全球气温的上升幅度将会在 2.5 度到 10.4 度之间，具体数值将取决于人类对温室气体排放的限制力度。Choosing the right bike *depends on* what you want to use it for. 选择哪种自行车合适，取决于你用它做什么。It will *depend on* whether you want to do it or not. 这将取决于你想不想做它。Our going *depends upon/on* his being able to drive. 我们能否去，取决于他能不能驾车。❸ trust or have confidence in (someone or something) 信赖，相信：You can *depend on* Robert — he always keeps his promises. 你可以信赖罗伯特——他总是信守承诺的。You cannot *depend on* Mary — she nearly always arrives late. 你可不能相信玛丽——她几乎总是迟到。

NOTE **1.** 本短语中的 upon 用法比 on 正式，但不及 on 常用。

2. 在非正式用语中，当主语为 it 时，本短语中的 on 或 upon 通常省略。例如：

> It *depends* what you mean.
> 这取决于你所表达的意义。
> It *depends* whether the force is small or large.
> 这取决于力的大小。

但在正式写作中，on 或 upon 则不能省略。例如：

It *depends on/upon* how you define the term "hostile".
这取决于你如何定义"hostile"这个词。

3. 当本短语作"依靠，依赖，指望"解时，同义短语是 count on/upon，lean on/upon 和 rely on/upon。

dependent on/upon *adj.* ❶ relying on or needing the help or support of (someone or something) in order to live or succeed 依靠，依赖：Most young Americans hate being *dependent on* their parents. 美国大多数的年轻人都不愿依赖父母。This country is heavily *dependent upon* foreign aid. 这个国家高度依赖外国的援助。❷ decided by or determined by (something else) 靠……决定，取决于：All effects are *dependent on/upon* their causes. 所有的结果均取决于原因。Good health is largely *dependent on* proper nourishment. 身体健康多半取决于适当的营养。Your pay is *dependent on* your work experience. 你的工资取决于你的工作经验。

NOTE **1.** 本短语中的 upon 用法比 on 正式，但不及 on 常用。

2. 本短语中的形容词 dependent 与介词 on 或 upon 连用，但其反义词 independent 却与介词 of 连用。见 independent of。

deprive of *vt.* 【可分性动词短语】(常用被动语态形式) take (something) away from (someone) or prevent (him or her) from (having it) 剥夺(某人的)……，使(某人)失去……：The lawyers had a discussion on the rationality of *depriving of* right of honor as qualification penalty. 律师们对剥夺荣誉权作为资格刑的合理性进行了探讨。You cannot *deprive* me *of* my rights. 你不能剥夺我的权利。

NOTE 本短语中的介词 of 可被 from 替换，但其后一般接动名词或动名词短语。例如：

Her night shift assignment *deprived* her from seeing much *of* her children.
她的夜班工作使她失去了很多看到孩子的机会。

但是，deprive from 不及本短语常用。

derive from *vt.* ❶ receive or obtain something from (something else, or someone) 从……得到：His income *derived from* several different businesses. 他的收入来源于几种不同的生意。Most products being sold here are *derived from* animals. 这里出售的大多数产品都是动物产品。My parents *derive* great pleasure and pride *from* their grandchildren. 我父母从他们的孙子孙女们身上得到极大的乐趣和自豪。❷ have (something) as an origin; come from 来源于，出自：Their fear *derives* mainly *from* a belief that these people have supernatural powers. 他们的恐惧主要来源于他们相信这些人具有超自然的力量。This word is *derived from* a Greek noun. 这个单词源于希腊语中的一个名词。The name of this small town is *derived from* a funny story. 这个小镇的名字来自一个有趣的传说中。

descend on/upon *vt.* 【不可分性动词短语】❶ (of people) arrive, especially in large numbers, to visit or stay with (someone), often unexpectedly (指人)突然到达：They *descended on* us for Christmas. 他们突然来我们这儿过圣诞节。In early August of 2008, thousands of journalists from different parts of the world *descended on* Beijing for the Olympic Games. 2008 年 8 月初，成千上万名世界各地的记者云集北京报道奥运

会。❷(常用一般时态)(of things or a group of people) attack, especially with violence and suddenness(尤指猛烈、突然地)袭击: Waves of sadness *descended on* him. 阵阵悲伤袭扰着他。Floodwater *descended on* the village. 洪水突然袭击了这个村庄。The robbers *descended upon* the lonely house. 强盗突然洗劫了那所孤零零的房子。

NOTE 本短语中的 upon 用法比 on 正式,但不及 on 常用。

describe as *vt.* 【可分性动词短语】(不用进行时态)say that(someone, oneself, or something) is (something)把……说成是……,把……描述为……: People *describe* her *as* the greatest woman inventor. 人们把她说成是最伟大的女发明家。His employer had *described* him *as* being very clever. 他的雇主说他非常聪明。Santa Claus is *described as* a kind old man driving a sleigh full of toys drawn through the air by eight reindeer. 圣诞老人被描述为一位和善的老人,他驾着装满玩具的爬犁,由八只驯鹿拉着在空中驰骋。

despair of *vt.* 【不可分性动词短语】(用一般时态) (of someone)lose all the hope of or confidence in (something or someone) 丧失对……的希望,对……丧失信心: Mike *despaired of* ever seeing her again. 迈克丧失了以后再能见到她的希望。There are signs that many voters have already *despaired of* these politicians. 有迹象表明,许多选民都已对这些政客丧失了信心。

despite of *prep.* (used for saying that something happens even though something else might have prevented it) despite; in spite of 尽管,任凭: He came to the meeting *despite of* illness. 尽管有病,他还是去参加会议了。*Despite of* wanting to see him again, she refused to reply to his letters. 她尽管很想再见到他,但却不愿意给他回信。

NOTE 1. 本短语中的主词 despite 本身就是一个介词。在使用中,of 往往被省略。例如:

> *Despite* pre-Games fears over security, the 2008 Beijing Olympics were held in peace.
> 尽管在奥运会开幕之前人们担心安全问题,但 2008 年北京奥运会是在和平的气氛中进行的。
> He came to the meeting *despite* his serious illness.
> 尽管重病在身,他还是去参加会议了。

2. 本短语是 in despite of 的简略形式,in despite of 为陈旧用法。如:

> *In despite of* his serious illness, he worked on.
> 他不顾重病,继续工作。

develop into *vt.* 【不可分性动词短语】(cause to) grow into; become (someone or something)(使)长成,发展成为: Helen has *developed into* a fine young lady. 海伦已出落成了一个美貌的少女。However, experts said that there is little chance for the recent friction to *develop into* a full-scale trade war between China and the United States. 然而,专家称,最近在中美之间发生的摩擦不会发展成为全面的贸易战。It was not until World War II that radar was *developed into* a practical and useful instrument. 直到第二次世界大战,雷达才发展成为一种实用的仪器。

devote to *vt.* 【可分性动词短语】❶(常用一般时态) spend (a lot of time or effort) doing something; give (oneself) freely and with care to (something)把(时间或精力)投放在……上;致力于,献身于: He's *devoted* most of his time *to* his painting. 他把他大部分时间都花在了绘画上。The departments concerned of the government have *devoted* a great deal of effort *to* publicizing the relevant policies and regulations. 政府的有关部门在宣传相关政策法规方面做了大量努力。Instead of *devoting* themselves *to* their studies, some boy students spend a lot of time and money running after girls. 一些男同学不专心于读书而是花大量的时间和金钱去追求女孩子。❷(常用一般时态) give (something) completely to (something or doing something)全部献出: He *devoted* all his savings *to* the improvement of the city parks. 他献出了全部积蓄来改善市内的公园。Her whole life is *devoted to* studying the origin of cancer. 她的一生都献给了对癌症起因的研究。

NOTE 本短语中的 to 是介词,而不是动词不定式符号,因此其后接名词或动名词,不能接原形动词。

die away *vi.* (especially of a sound, wind, light, etc.) become quieter or weaker and finally stop or disappear altogether (指声音、风、光等)变弱,逐渐停息: Her footsteps *died away* in the dark. 她的脚步声在黑暗中渐渐地消失了。The sound of the engines *died away* in the distance. 马达的轰鸣声在远处逐渐消失了。The wind finally *died away* at sunset. 风终于在日落时停息了。

NOTE 本短语与 die down 所表达的意义有所不同。本短语侧重"逐渐变弱并终止",而 die down 则表示减弱的趋势,并无终止之意。

die down *vi.* (of physical qualities and feelings) become much less strong, powerful, or active; decrease (物质特性和情绪)逐渐变弱,减低: The southern California wildfire *died down* after two weeks of devastation that claimed 3,335 homes and 20 lives. 加利福尼亚南部的山火在肆虐两周,毁掉 3 335 所住房和 20 条生命后,逐渐减弱了下来。The strong wind died down during the night. 大风在夜间减弱了。After the excitement of the audience *died down*, the speaker restarted his speech. 等听众激动的情绪平息后,演讲人又重新开始演讲。

die for *vt.*【不可分性动词短语】❶ be prepared to die to support (an idea) or save (someone) 为……而献身: Many religious people would *die for* their beliefs. 许多信仰宗教的人都愿为其信仰而献身。They were ready to *die for* their country. 他们准备为祖国而献身。❷(非正式用语,用进行时态) want to have (something) so much that you do not want to wait 迫不及待地想要得到(某物): I'm *dying for* a cup of coffee. 我极想喝杯咖啡。I'm *dying for* a breath of fresh air. 我极想呼吸点新鲜空气。

die from *vt.*【不可分性动词短语】die following (something, except illness or feeling)死于,因……而死: A 45-year-old senior Toyota engineer *died from* overwork in January. 今年一月份,丰田公司的一位 45 岁高级工程师由于过度劳累而死亡。A West Virginia woman claims her 11 goldfish *died from* eating contaminated fish food. 西弗吉尼亚州的一名妇女声称,她的 11 条金鱼因吃了污染的鱼食而死亡。A 16-year-old boy *died from* his fall from the undercarriage of a passenger plane Wednesday. 一名 16

岁的男孩子星期三因从客机的起落架上摔下来而死。In a severe winter, wild animals can *die from* cold and lack of food. 在严冬里,野生动物会因冻饿而死。

NOTE 本短语与 die of 均表示"死于,因……而死"。但传统地讲,本短语一般指由于外界因素(如过劳、事故、灾难等)而并非出自自身原因(如疾病或情感等)而导致的意外死亡,即致死的原因是间接的;而 die of 则常指由于病、伤、情感等较直接的原因而致死。但是,在当今的实际运用中,两者的区别已不很明显。从用法上来说,die of 后通常只接名词,而 die from 后不但可接名词还可接动名词短语。

D

die of *vt.* 【不可分性动词短语】die because of (something such as an illness or feeling)死于,因……而死:She *died of* a high fever, and no one could save her. 她因高烧而死,没有人能救她。He *died of* external head injury after falling down a cliff . 他从山崖上坠落,因头部外伤而身亡。My grandmother *died of* a broken heart soon after her husband's death. 我祖父刚刚去世,我祖母就因悲伤而故去。

die off *vi.* (常用进行时态)(of a group of living things) die one by one until none exist (指生物群体)一个一个地死去:The deer in the forest are all *dying off* from disease. 森林中的鹿都因病而一个一个地死去。The generation that fought in the Second World War are all *dying off*. 在第二次世界大战中鏖战的那一代人在相继故去。Being short of medicine, the four wounded soldiers *died off*. 由于缺乏药品,四名伤员先后死去。

die out *vi.* ❶(of a species or family)(指某一物种或家族)灭绝,不复存在:Those species inadaptable to changing conditions may *die out*. 那些不能适应变化中的环境的物种可能会灭绝。A long, long time ago the dinosaurs died out. 很久很久以前恐龙就灭绝了。He is the last of the family; after his death the family will *die out*. 他是这一家族的唯一后人;他死后这个家族就将不复存在了。❷(of practices, ideas, etc.) fade away through time and eventually disappear completely (指习俗、观念等)(随着时间的流逝)消失:The tribe's traditional way of life is gradually *dying out*. 这个部落的传统生活方式正在逐渐消失。It's time this selfish habit died out. 这种自私习惯该绝迹了。Many old customs have *died out*. 许多旧的风俗已不复存在。

differ from *vt.* 【不可分性动词短语】(无被动语态形式,用一般时态) be different from (someone or something else)有异于,与……不同:Though they are twins, they *differ from* each other greatly in character and interests. 虽然他们是双胞胎,但他们的性格和志趣却大不相同。English *differs from* Spanish in that it is not pronounced as it is written. 英语不同于西班牙语,因为它不按拼写发音。

differ with *vt.* 【不可分性动词短语】(无被动语态形式,用一般时态) disagree with (someone or an opinion)不同意(某人或某一观点):Mr Brown *differed with* Mrs Brown on the issue of unmarried couples sharing bedrooms. 布朗先生在未婚情侣同居的问题上与布朗太太观点不同。The two sides in the dispute still *differ with* each other over the question of pay. 争执的双方在报酬问题上仍各持己见。World Bank officials *differed with* some of the observations in the report. 世界银行的官员不同意该

报告中的某些评述。

different from/to *adj.* not the same as (another person or thing)与……不同：What makes him *different from* the rest of the students? 是什么使他与其他的学生不同？Hand, foot, and mouth disease is quite *different from* foot-and-mouth disease of cattle, sheep, and swine, although the names are similar. 手足口病与牛羊猪所患的口蹄疫大不相同，尽管这两种病名称相似。The campus is quite *different from* how it was 20 years ago. 这校园和 20 年前比大有不同了。His opinion is very little *different to* mine. 他的观点与我的没什么不同。

NOTE **1.** different to 主要用于英国英语中。另外，在美国英语中，还使用 different than 的形式。例如：

> The weather here is a lot *different than* it is at home.
> 这儿的天气与在家大相径庭。

虽然这种用法在英国英语中曾被认为不正确，但在当今用得较为普遍。三者当中，different from 最为常用。

2. 本短语的反义短语是 similar to。

dig in *vt.* &*vi.* (of soldiers) dig a protective place (for oneself) where they can wait for an attack (士兵)挖掩体，挖战壕：The soldiers were ordered to *dig*(themselves) *in*. 士兵们奉命挖掘战壕。

—*vt.* mix (something) into the ground by digging 挖土埋进(某物)：You need to *dig* the fertilizer *in*. 你要翻土把化肥埋进去。

—*vi.* (非正式用语，常用祈使语气) start eating food eagerly 开始尽情地吃：Here is your breakfast, so dig in, everybody! 这是你们的早餐，大家开吃吧！Mother set the food on the table and told the children to *dig in*. 母亲把食物放在桌上让孩子们开始吃。

dig into *vt.* ❶ push or press (one thing) hard into (another) 把……插入，把……嵌入(某物)：He *dug* his fork *into* the meat. 他把叉子插入肉中。The seat belt was *digging into* his shoulder. 安全带就要嵌入他的肩头肉中。❷ mix (something) into the ground by digging 挖土埋进(某物)：To *dig* calcium *into* the soil, he warned, does not help the plant. 他警告说，往土壤里埋含钙物质并无助于植物的生长。❸ (非正式用语) examine (something) thoroughly 细查；钻研：The police are *digging into* all the files connected with this case. 警方正在细查与这一案件有关的所有案卷。When he *digs into* a problem he does not give up until he gets to the bottom. 他要是钻研一个问题，不弄个水落石出就不肯罢休。Soon after she entered college she *dug into* psychology and now she can hardly tear herself away. 进入大学校门不久，她就深入地钻研心理学。现在，她几乎难以舍弃这一研究。❹ put your hand in (your pocket or bag) in order to find something 把手伸进(口袋或包中以翻找某物)：She *dug into* her handbag and pulled out a bunch of keys. 她把手伸进手袋里，拿出一串钥匙来。❺ start using (money that you had been saving) 动用(存款)：I've had to *dig into* my savings this month to pay for my car insurance. 我不得不动用这个月的储蓄金来支付汽车的保费。❻ (非正式用语) start eating (food) eagerly 开始尽情地吃(食物)："Listen," said Mary, *digging into* her oatmeal. "听着，"玛丽边吃着燕麦粥边说道。As soon as supper was served, we *dug into* it hungrily. 晚饭一上来，我们就开始尽情地吃起来。

D

dig out *vt.* 【可分性动词短语】❶ get (someone or something) out of a place or out of the ground by digging 把……(从某处)挖出来:Soldiers have *dug out* a 31-year-old woman who was buried for 124 hours under a collapsed building at a chemical factory. 士兵们挖救出了一名被埋在一化工厂倒塌的厂房下长达 124 小时的 31 岁女工。Rescuers are still *digging* people *out* of the collapsed buildings. 救援人员仍在从倒塌的楼房中挖救受困者。They *dug out* some gold coins at the excavation site. 他们在挖掘现场挖出了一些金币。Many fossils of the same kind of dinosaurs have been *dug out* from one place. 从一个地方就挖出了许多同一种类恐龙的化石。❷ (非正式用语) find (something that you have not used or seen for a long time) 找出(很久没用或没看见的东西):I *dug out* these old trousers to give to the boy. 我找出这些旧裤子给那男孩。I'll try to *dig* the book *out* for you if you really want to read it. 如果你实在想读的话,我就设法把那本书给你找出来。

dig up *vt.* 【可分性动词短语】❶ remove (something planted) from under the ground by digging 挖掉(种植之物):We have to *dig up* all the plants in the garden. 我们得把花园中所有的植物全部挖掉。We will have to *dig* that tree *up* and plant some flowers. 我们得把这棵树挖掉,然后栽些花儿。❷ find (something buried in an area of land) by digging holes 挖掘出土:Some Stone Age weapons were *dug up* in a small village in India. 在印度的一个小村庄里挖掘出土了一些石器时代的武器。❸ (非正式用语) discover (facts or information that has not previously been widely known) by searching carefully 发现(不广为人知的事实或情况):When we investigated his background, we *dug up* some interesting facts. 当我们调查他的经历时,查出了一些有趣的情况。These facts are true; but where did you *dig* them *up*? 这些情况是真实的;可你们是从哪查出来的? His description fits perfectly the evidence *dug up* by the police. 他的描述与警方所掌握的证据十分吻合。

NOTE 当本短语所带的宾语为代词时,该代词须置于本短语的动词和副词中间。

dine out *vi.* (非正式用语) have dinner outside one's home (especially in a restaurant or at someone else's home) 在外面(尤指餐馆或别人家)用餐:Don't prepare anything for me tonight; I shall be *dining out*. 今晚不要为我准备吃的了,我要在外面吃。Chinese people have so many restaurants to choose among and Chinese food is so excellent. That's why they *dine out* more often than us. 中国有很多饭馆可供选择,中国菜又是如此的美味,因此中国人比我们更经常下饭馆。My wife doesn't enjoy parties or *dining out*. 我夫人不喜欢聚会,也不喜欢在外面吃饭。

NOTE **1.** 本短语的同义短语是 eat out。
2. 本短语的反义短语是 dine in,意为"在家里用餐"。

dip into *vt.* ❶ put (something) quickly into (liquid) 浸入:She *dipped* her hand *into* the water and began to wash the dust from his face gently. 她把手浸入水中,然后轻轻地把他脸上的灰尘洗掉。❷ put your hand into a container in order to get (something) 把手伸进……中取(某物):*Dipping* his hand *into* his pocket, he produced the letter I'd sent to him. 他把手伸进口袋里,取出了我寄给他的信。

❸read or study (a part of something such as a piece of writing), for a short time and without much attention 浏览,过目:I haven't read the report properly — I've only *dipped into* it. 我还没有好好地看这份报告——只是浏览了一下而已。My husband likes *dipping into* many books at home. 我丈夫喜欢在家博览群书。❹take(some money from an amount you have saved) to use to buy something or pay for something 动用(存款):You'd better stop *dipping into* your savings. 你最好不要再动用你的存款了。The company had to *dip into* a reserve fund to pay for all the new equipment. 该公司不得不动用储备金来支付全部新设备的费用。

NOTE 1. 当本短语作"浏览,过目"和"动用(存款)"解时,为不可分性动词短语用法。

2. 当本短语作"动用(存款)"解时,同义短语是 dig into。

disagree about/on/over *vt.*【不可分性动词短语】(常用一般时态) have a different opinion about (something or someone) 对……有不同的看法: I *disagree about* the singer's performance. 我对那位歌手的演出有不同的看法。However, given their differences in historical background, cultural heritage, and political system, it is natural that the two sides have different views or even *disagree on* some issues. 然而,由于历史文化传统、政治制度的差异,双方在某些问题上存在不同看法和分歧是正常的。The teachers *disagree over* the boy; some think he cannot be blamed; others want him to be punished. 教师们在对待这个男同学的问题上意见分歧。一些认为他不能受责备,而另一些则要处罚他。

NOTE 本短语的反义短语是 agree about/on/over。

disagree with *vt.*【不可分性动词短语】(常用一般时态) ❶(主要用于英国英语中) have a different opinion from (someone); not approve of (something) because you think that it is dishonest or immoral 不同意(某人)的意见,反对: I *disagree with* you —I think she's done a very good job. 我不同意你的意见——我认为她做的工作已经很不错了。Three of these four men *disagreed with* my decision. 这四个人中有三个不同意我的决定。He strongly *disagreed with* what Anne had said. 他强烈反对安妮所说的那番话。❷(主要用于英国英语口语中,无被动语态形式) (of something one has eaten or drunk, of air, or weather) be unsuitable to (someone); harm the health of (someone); make (someone) feel ill (所吃食物、空气或气候),使(某人)感到不舒服,对(某人)的健康不利:I feel dreadful; the prawns I had for lunch are *disagreeing with* me. 我感到很难受。午餐的虾我吃了很不舒服。City air *disagrees with* her. 城市的空气使她感到不舒服。The wet climate *disagrees with* you. 这潮湿的气候对你的健康不利。

NOTE 本短语的同义短语是 disapprove with 和 frown on/upon; 反义短语是 agree with 和 approve of。

disapprove of *vt.*【不可分性动词短语】(常用一般时态)refuse to agree to; have a poor opinion of (something); dislike (someone)usually for a fault 不同意,反对,不喜欢:Tom's parents *disapproved of* his marriage to the American girl. 汤姆的父母不同意他娶那个美国女孩为妻。Many people *disapprove of* setting up a casino on the island. 许多人反对在

D

岛上设赌场。

NOTE 本短语的同义短语是 disagree with 和 frown on/upon;反义短语是 agree to, approve of, assent to 和 consent to。

discharge from *vt.*【可分性动词短语】❶(常用被动语态形式)send (someone) away from or allow (someone) to leave (something such as a place or work)使(某人)从……离开,退离……: The patients have fully recovered and were *discharged from* hospital after more than 10 days of medical treatment. 这些病人经过10多天的医治后,已完全康复并出院。Although she was still ill, she *discharged* herself *from* the hospital. 她虽然仍在病着,却擅自离开了医院。He was honorably *discharged from* the army with a severe leg wound left in a battle . 他因在作战中腿部受重伤而光荣退役。❷ empty (something) from (something such as a container or vehicle)从……排掉,卸掉(某物): Flood water was *discharged from* the Three Gorges Dam yesterday. 昨天,三峡大坝开始泄洪。The ship's goods are being *discharged from* the hold. 正在从这艘巨轮的船舱卸货。

discriminate against *vt.*【不可分性动词短语】treat (someone) unfairly because of their religion, race, or other personal features 不公平对待,歧视(某人): He was accused of *discriminating against* female employees. 他被指控歧视女雇员。Blacks are still widely *discriminated against* in some parts of the world. 在世界的某些地方,黑人仍然普遍地受到歧视。

disguise as *vt.*【可分性动词短语】(常用被动语态形式) hide (someone, oneself, or something) by pretending that he or it is (someone or something else), often by changing the appearance, clothes, etc. 装扮成,伪装成: He escaped *disguised as* a woman. 他装扮成女人逃跑了。Two men *disguised* themselves *as* reporters and easily got into Buckingham Palace with the help of a royal chauffeur. 两名男子装扮成记者,在一名皇家司机的协助下,轻而易举地进入了白金汉宫。Four people were killed on Wednesday when a van *disguised as* an ambulance blew up in front of a hotel. 一辆被伪装成救护车的篷车星期三在一家宾馆前爆炸,有四人被炸死。

NOTE 本短语的同义短语是 dress up。

dispose of *vt.*【不可分性动词短语】❶(用一般时态) get rid of (something that you no longer need or want)把(不再需要的东西)清除掉;把……销毁: All this rubbish must be *disposed of* properly. 所有这些垃圾都必须彻底清除掉。Japanese experts arrived in northeast China to *dispose of* the chemical weapons left by Japanese troops at the end of World War Ⅱ. 日本专家抵达中国东北,对日本军队在二战结束时遗弃的化学武器进行销毁。❷ remove (something such as a problem) by dealing with it successfully (成功地)处理,办理,解决: We ought to be able to *dispose of* all the business in an hour. 我们应该能在一小时内把所有的事情都办好。Most complaints can be *disposed of* pretty quickly. 大部分投诉都可以很快得到解决。❸(正式用语) kill (a person or an animal); destroy 杀掉(人或动物);击毁: He claimed that they had hired an assassin to *dispose of* him. 他声称他们曾雇佣杀手要杀掉他。Our planes *disposed of* two enemy planes. 我方战机击落了两架敌机。

dissatisfied with *adj.* not pleased or happy with (what has happened or what you have achieved) 对……感到不满: Many of them are *dissatisfied with* the treatment they have received in the hospital. 他们当中有很多人对在医院里接受的治疗感到不满。He felt *dissatisfied with* what he had written. 他对自己刚写完的文章感到不满意。Though *dissatisfied with* the road condition, he seemed to really enjoy cycling. 虽然他对路况感到不满,可他还是很喜欢骑车。

NOTE 本短语的反义短语是 satisfied with。

dissuade from *vt.* 【可分性动词短语】persuade (someone) not to do or doing (something) 劝服(某人)不做(某事): I don't know how to *dissuade* my friend *from* his foolish action. 我不知道如何劝服我的朋友不要做那蠢事。They tried hard to *dissuade* him *from* leaving school. 他们极力劝服他不要辍学。He was easily *dissuaded from* going. 他很容易就被劝住不走了。

NOTE 本短语的反义短语是 persuade into。

distinguish from *vt.* 【可分性动词短语】❶(常用一般时态) recognize (someone or something) apart from (someone or something else) by special qualities 辨别,区分: It is important to *distinguish* right *from* wrong. 辨明是非是重要的。One material can be *distinguished from* another by their physical properties: color, density, and so on. 可以通过其物理性能,如颜色、密度等来区分两种不同的材料。❷(用一般时态) show the difference between (someone or something) and (someone or something else); set (someone or something) apart from (someone or something else) 显示出(某人或某物)不同于,使有别于: "Since taking office, the new Japanese prime minister has quickly *distinguished* himself *from* his predecessor," *Washington Post* commented. "自上任以来,这位新上任的日本首相很快就显示出他与其前任的不同。"《华盛顿邮报》这样评论道。Many things *distinguish* man *from* other animals. 许多东西使人类有别于其他动物。

NOTE 本短语既可表示两个人或事物之间的区别,又可指两者以上的区别。如侧重表示两者间的区别还可使用 distinguish between ... and ... 的形式。例如:

> Many customers are unable to *distinguish between* the genuine *and* the fake.
> 许多消费者都无法辨别商品的真假。

distract from *vt.* 【可分性动词短语】take one's attention away from (usually something or doing something) 分散(某人的)注意力,使(某人)分心: Don't make such noise any more; you're *distracting* me *from* my study! 不要再搞出这样的噪声了,你是在影响我学习! My father burned the cakes while his mind was *distracted from* watching them. 我爸爸的思想溜了号,没照看好那些蛋糕,因而把它们都烤焦了。

divide into *vt.* 【可分性动词短语】❶have (separate parts or form) into (separate groups) (使)分成……: The class *divided into* four groups when we went on an outing. 我们外出郊游时,全

班分成了四个小组。Then we *divided* ourselves *into* small groups to carry out our task. 然后我们分成几个小组来执行任务。The Sino-Indian boundary line extending about 2,000 km is *divided into* three sections, east, middle and west. 绵延约两千公里的中印边境线分为三段：东段、中段和西段。❷do a mathematical calculation to find out how many times a smaller number will fit into a larger number (在数学运算中)除，除以：*Divide* 7 *into* 35. 用 7 除以 35。

NOTE 表达“除，除以”之意时，除用本短语外，还可说：Divide 35 by 7 或 35 divided by 7 is 5.

divorce from *vt.*【可分性动词短语】(常用被动语态形式) ❶end a marriage with (a wife or husband) 与……离婚：This famous singer has been *divorced from* four husbands. 这位著名的歌手已与四位丈夫离了婚。Jill is getting *divorced from* Jim. 吉尔要与吉姆离婚。❷separate from (something) completely 使完全脱离：Some of his ideas are completely *divorced from* reality. 他的一些想法完全脱离现实。A scientific worker can never *divorce* himself *from* experiments. 一个科学工作者决不能脱离实验。Politics should not be *divorced from* the lives of ordinary people. 政治不应脱离普通民众的生活。

do (someone) a favor *vi.* do something kind for (someone) 帮(某人)一个忙：Would you *do me a favor* by turning off that radio? 您能帮帮忙把那台收音机关掉吗？I would like to have you *do me a* small *favor*. 我想请您帮我一个小忙。

NOTE 本短语的另外一种表达方式是 do someone a good turn。例如：

> My friend Mark *did me a good turn* by lending me his car.
> 我的朋友马克把他的车借给了我，可帮了我的忙。

do away with *vt.*【不可分性动词短语】❶ remove completely or get rid of (something) 彻底取消，弃除，废除：The government *did away with* free school meals. 政府取消了学校的免费用餐。Why did the United Kingdom *do away with* the death penalty for murder? 英国为什么废除了对杀人犯的死刑？A lot of the restrictions on imports have been *done away with*. 许多进口限制都已被废除。❷(非正式用语) murder; kill (someone or oneself) 谋杀(某人)；自杀：There were rumors that Bob had *done away with* his wife. 有种种传言说鲍勃谋杀了他的妻子。My neighbor tried to *do away with* herself by taking poison. 我的邻居试图服毒自杀。

NOTE 当本短语作“谋杀(某人)；自杀”解时，与 make away with(第三个义项)的意义和用法相同。见 make away with。

do damage *vi.* (常与 to 连用) cause physical harm (to something) so that it is broken, spoiled, or injured 造成毁坏，损害：The typhoon *did* a lot of *damage* here in this region. 这次的台风在这一地区造成了很大的损害。Hurricane Katrina has *done* greater *damage* to the US cities than any previous one. 卡特里娜飓风对美国城市造成的毁坏比以往任何一次都大。

NOTE 1. 本短语本身是动宾结构，其动词和名词可分开使用。例如：

The *damage* that staying up late can *do* to our health is beyond imagination.
熬夜对我们的健康所造成的损害是超乎想象的。
No *damage* had been *done*, and we pushed the car back onto the road.
这台车没有造成损坏,我们就又把它推上了路。

2. 本短语中的动词 do 可被 cause 所替换。例如:

The earthquake *caused* serious *damage to* the surrounding buildings.
这场地震对周边的建筑物都造成了严重的损坏。

do drugs *vi.* (非正式用语) abuse an illegal drug or drugs, especially as a result of chemical addition 滥用毒品,吸毒:She began to suspect that her son was *doing drugs*. 她开始怀疑她的儿子在吸毒。Bob started *doing drugs* when he was 14. 鲍勃 14 岁时就开始吸毒了。

NOTE 本短语另外的表达形式是 abuse drugs, on drugs, take drugs 和 use drugs。

do good *vt.* & *vi.* (常与 to 连用) make (someone) more healthy or feel better; have advantage or benefit (to someone) 对(某人的)健康有益,对(某人)有利:I think a trip to the beach would *do* us all a lot of *good*. 我认为到海滩去游玩会对我们所有人的健康大有益处。This mineral water will *do* a great deal of *good* to the patients. 这种矿泉水对病人的健康很有益。"Acts of terror, acts of occupation, will not *do* either side any *good*," said he. 他表示:"恐怖行为和占领行动对双方都没有利。"

—*vi.* (常与 for 连用) perform good deeds of kindness 做好事,行好:The company claims it has *done* a lot of *good* for the town by providing employment. 该公司声称,它提供就业机会就已经为这个城镇做了很多好事。The village chief's wife has been *doing good* for the villagers all her life. 村长的夫人一辈子都在为村民做好事。

NOTE **1.** 当本短语作"对(某人的)健康有益,对(某人)有利"解时,在动词 do 和名词 good 之间不但可以加宾语,还可加形容词或形容词短语表示程度。

2. 本短语与其反义短语 do harm 可通过一点变化放在一起使用。例如:

In my opinion, students doing part-time work *does more good than harm*.
我认为,大学生打零工利大于弊。

do harm *v.* (常与 to 连用) cause injury, damage, or problems (to someone or something) by something you do (对……)造成伤害:Smoking and drinking both *do* you *harm* at your age. 在你这样的年纪,抽烟、喝酒都会对你造成伤害。Frequent quarrels between parents could *do* more psychological *harm* to children than divorce, experts warned. 专家们警告说,家长经常吵架比离婚对孩子所造成的心理伤害更大。A little drinking will *do* you no *harm* if you don't drink too much. 如果你不喝过量的酒,一点酒不会对你有害。

NOTE **1.** 本短语本身是动宾结构, do 和 harm 可分开使用。例如:

The knowledge about the *harm* pollution can *do* to human beings points up the need for environmental protection.
人类认识到污染给自己造成的危害,更说明了保护环境的必要。

2. 在动词 do 和名词 harm 之间不但可以加宾语，还可加形容词或形容词短语表示程度。

3. 本短语中的动词 do 可被 cause 替换。例如：

> The radiation may *cause harm* to the cells, tissues and organs of the astronauts.
> 这种辐射可能会损害宇航员的某些细胞、组织和器官。

D

do one's best *vi.* (常接动词不定式短语) try as hard as you can in order to achieve something 竭尽(某人)所能，尽力：At a national meeting on public security, he urged police across the country to *do their best* to serve the general public well. 在全国公安工作会议上，他要求全国干警竭尽全力为人民大众服务。The Anti-Secession Law declares China will *do its best* with maximum sincerity for peaceful reunification.《反分裂法》阐明，中国将以最大的诚意，尽最大的努力，实现和平统一。

NOTE 本短语的同义短语是 do one's utmost 和 try one's best。

do one's bit *vi.* (英国英语用法，非正式用语) do what you can to help, or to do your share of what has to be done 尽自己的职责，尽力而为：No one can say Mary *didn't do her bit*. 没人可以说玛丽没有尽其职责。We felt good knowing that we were *doing our bit*. 我们自知尽了自己的职责而感到心安理得。We're *doing our bit* by recycling everything we can, even plastic bags. 回收利用一切可以回收利用的物品，甚至塑料袋，是我们应尽的职责。

NOTE 1. 本短语中的物主代词无论是单数还是复数形式，bit 只能用单数形式。

2. 本短语中的名词 bit 可被 part 所替换，两者的意义和用法相同。

do someone a good turn ⇨ do (someone) a favor

do the dishes *vi.* wash dishes or plates, glasses, and silverware used at a meal 洗餐具：If you walk the dog, I'll *do the dishes*. 如果你去遛狗，我就洗餐具。I don't see how you can get let off *doing the dishes* this time. 我看你这次可躲不了洗碗碟了。

NOTE 本短语在美国英语和英国英语中通用，但在英国英语中，主要用 wash up 表示"洗餐具"。

do up *vt.* & *vi.* fasten (something) in a particular way 系上，扣上：*Do up* your shoelaces. 把你的鞋带系上。You don't need to *do up* the top button. 你不必扣最上边的纽扣。You must *do up* your safety belt in the back of cars and taxis now. 如今，坐在轿车和出租车的后排座位上也必须系上安全带。This dress *does up* at the back. 这条裙子是在背后系带的。

—*vt.*【可分性动词短语】❶(英国英语用法，常用被动语态形式，常与 in 连用) wrap (something) in paper or cloth in an attractive way for decorative purposes; tie (a package)(为装饰之目的)(用纸或布)包好，捆好：He asked the clerk to *do up* his purchases. 他让店员把他买的东西包扎好。She always *does* her presents *up* beautifully in gold and silver paper. 她总是把她的礼物用金银纸包得很漂亮。He held a small parcel *done up* in coloured paper and ribbon. 他拿着一个用彩纸和彩带装饰起来的小包。❷(主要

用于英国英语中，非正式用语）decorate, repair, paint, and improve (an old building, car, boat etc.) 装修，装饰；修缮（房屋）；修理（车船等）：It took them almost six months to *do up* the house before they moved in. 在入住之前，他们几乎用了半年的时间装修那房子。The room was *done up* for the visitors. 房间已装饰完毕，准备待客。We spent our weekends *doing up* a 1997 Rolls Royce. 我们利用了几个周末的时间把一台1997年产的"劳斯莱斯"维修了一下。❸（非正式用语，常用被动语态形式）dress (someone or oneself) in special clothes or put make-up on them 给……穿上（盛装），打扮：Angie was *done up* in a silky black dress and fishnet stockings. 安吉穿上了一件黑丝连衣裙和一双网眼长筒袜。She had spent hours *doing* herself *up* for the party. 她用了几个小时打扮自己，准备去参加聚会。

NOTE 当本短语用作及物性动词短语，所带的宾语为代词时，该代词须置于本短语的动词和副词中间。

do with *vt.*【不可分性动词短语】（无被动语态形式）❶（用一般时态，常用于疑问句中，与 what 连用）treat; deal with (something or someone) 对待，对付：What did you *do with* the errors you found? 你怎么处理你发现的那些错误？What do you usually *do with* the cat when you're away? 你不在时，这只猫你通常怎么处理？"What shall we *do with* the children?" "Take them out to the park." "这些孩子我们该怎么办呀？""把他们带到公园去。" ❷ be satisfied with (something or someone less than one hoped) 满足于；将就：Can you *do with* some cakes for lunch? 午饭吃点蛋糕，你能将就吗？If you can't afford fish we shall have to *do with* chicken. 如果你买不起鱼，我们只好将就吃鸡了。❸（仅用于口语中，用于 could 之后）want or need (something) 需要：I'm sure James could *do with* some help. 我相信詹姆斯需要一些帮助。The room could *do with* a good cleaning. 这个房间需要好好打扫一下了。❹（英国英语用法，非正式用语，常与否定词连用）allow; accept or experience (something) willingly 容许，容忍：We can't *do with* such extravagance and waste. 我们不能容许这种铺张浪费。I can't *do with* all this loud music. 我无法忍受这么吵闹的音乐。❺ be finished with (something or someone) 完成，结束：Are you *done with* the homework? 你做完作业了吗？He told me that he had *done with* Mary. 他告诉我说，他已与玛丽断绝了关系。

NOTE 当本短语作"需要"解时，反义短语是 do without。

do without *v.* ❶（常与 have to, can, could, be able to 连用）succeed in living or working without (someone or something) 无需……，没有……也行：There's no more milk, so I guess we'll just have to *do without*. 没有牛奶了，所以我想我们只好不吃了。They will limit the production of goods that can be *done without*. 他们要限制非必需品的生产。Now that they have a regular income, they should be able to *do without* any help from us. 既然他们有了固定收入，没有我们的帮助也行了。❷（仅用于口语中，表示不满，多与 can 或 could 连用）used for saying that something is annoying you and causing problems for you 用不着,不需要: I can *do without* that kind of advice, thank you! 我用不着那种劝告,多谢了! I could *do without* all these interruptions. 我不需要总打断我。

NOTE 1. 当本短语用作及物性动词短语时为不可分性动词短语用法。

2. 当本短语作"无需……,没有……也行"解时,同义短语是 go without。

do wonders *vi*. (常用一般时态,常与 for, on, with 连用) produce an extremely good result, often so good that it is surprising 产生神奇的效果,创造奇迹: She looked so tired before, but her holiday has *done wonders* for her. 她原先看上去疲劳不堪,但休假对她产生了神奇的效果。I assure you this medicine will *do wonders* for your cold. 我保证这种药对你的伤风会有神奇的效力。A long hot shower *did wonders* on my tired muscles. 长时间的热水淋浴对我疲劳的肌肉产生了神奇的效果。

NOTE 本短语中的名词 wonder 必须用复数形式。

Don't mention it. *s*. (用于口语中) (used as a polite answer when someone has thanked you for something) no thanks are needed; I was glad to do it 不用谢,别客气,没什么: "I appreciate what you have done for my mother." "*Don't mention it.*" "谢谢您为我母亲所做的一切。""没什么。"

doom to *vt*. (用被动语态形式) be fated to meet (something bad) 注定: Why are my hopes always *doomed to* disappointment? 为什么我的希望总是注定成失望? The Iranian President condemned the new sanctions imposed recently by the United States, saying the measures were *doomed to* failure. 伊朗总统谴责美国最近实施的一系列新的制裁措施,称这些措施注定要失败。

down and out *adj*. (非正式用语) ❶(of someone) without money, a home or a job, and having no real hope of improving his or her situation (指某人)贫穷的,穷困潦倒的: After losing his job, car, and home, he was completely *down and out*. 他失去了工作、汽车和房子后,一贫如洗。❷(in boxing) (of a boxer) knocked down and unable to get to his feet before the umpire has counted to ten; certain to be defeated (指拳击选手)被击倒并不能站起继续比赛的;注定要失败的: The bad-tempered boxer was *down and out* in the first round. 那名脾气暴躁的拳击选手在第一回合中就被击倒并不能站起来继续比赛了。

NOTE 本短语可转化为复合词 down-and-out,意为"贫穷的,穷困潦倒的"。在英国英语中,down-and-out 还可用作名词,意为"贫困;穷困潦倒的人"。

down to earth *adj*. realistic and practical, in a way that is helpful and friendly 现实的,实际的: Their ideas seem to be far more *down to earth* and sensible. 他们的想法似乎特别现实和明智。Mary is probably the most *down to earth* person I've ever met. 玛丽可能是我所遇到的最为实际的人。

NOTE 本短语可转化为复合词 down-to-earth,意为"实际的,现实的"。

down with *prep*. used to say, write or shout to show that you are opposed to a person, or to something, and you want to get rid of them (用于说、写或呼喊的

口号)打倒……:Demonstrators shouted "*Down with* the terrorists!" 示威者们高喊"打倒恐怖主义分子!"

doze off *vi.* fall into a light sleep, especially during the daytime and without intending to (尤指在白天和不想睡觉的时候)睡着,打瞌睡: The lecture was so boring that I *dozed off* in the middle of it. 讲座很枯燥,我听了一半就睡着了。A recently released finding disclosed that nearly half of the drivers said they had *dozed off* while driving. 最近公布的一项调查结果表明,近半数以上的驾驶员说他们曾在驾车时打过盹。

NOTE 本短语的同义短语是 drop off。

dozens of *adj.* (非正式用语,后接复数名词,常用于肯定句中)lots of; very many; a large number of (people or things)好几十,很多(人或物): *Dozens of* couples lined up in heavy rain outside San Francisco City Hall awaiting marriage licenses. 几十对情侣冒着大雨在旧金山市政厅外排队等候领取结婚证。Nowadays, abusing drugs, which vanished *dozens of* years ago as a sort of social filthy phenomenon in China, reappears. 现今,滥用毒品这种在中国销声匿迹数十载的社会丑恶现象又沉渣泛起。

drag in *vt.* ❶ pull or force (someone or something) indoors 把……拉进室内: The children are so busy playing that they do not want their dinner; you'll have to *drag* them *in*. 孩子们都忙着玩耍不想吃饭,你得把他们拽进来。❷ start talking about (a subject that is not connected with what you are discussing and that other people do not want to talk about) 谈论(与讨论无关或其他人不想谈论的话题): He seemed determined to *drag in* irrelevant details about my personal life. 他似乎非要谈论一些与我个人生活无关的细节。He doesn't like my *dragging in* his wealth. 他不喜欢我谈论他有多么富有。❸ make (someone) become involved in some kind of situation, condition, or course of action when he or she does not want to 迫使(某人)卷入……中: I don't know anything about the project, so don't try and *drag* me *in*. 我对这一项目毫不了解,所以别试图硬拉我参与其中。

NOTE 当本短语所带的宾语为代词时,该代词须置于本短语的动词和副词中间。

drag into *vt.*【可分性动词短语】❶ pull or force (someone or something) into (something such as a space) 把……拉进去: She said police officers *dragged* her *into* the hallway, then threw her on the ground and filmed her with a video camera while other guests and hotel staff looked on. 她说,警察把她拽进走廊,然后将她摔在地上,并且还在其他客人和旅馆的工作人员的旁观下用摄像机给她录了像。The farmer had to *drag* the unwilling cow *into* the field. 农夫不得不把那头不情愿的牛拉进了地里。❷ make (someone) become involved in an unpleasant event or difficult situation when he or she does not want to 迫使(某人)卷入……中: Don't try to *drag* me *into* your argument. 别硬拉我参与到你们的争论之中。

drag on/along *vi.* (非正式用语)(of an event or process) continue for an unnecessarily long time, usually unpleasantly 长时间地持续; The bombing *drags on* as thousands of foreigners, flee Lebanon. 轰炸在持续,数千名外国人都在逃离黎巴嫩。The meeting *dragged along* for three and a half hours. 会议一直开了三个半小时。Some cases *drag on* for many years. 有些案件拖时多年。

D

drag out *v.* (非正式用语) (of an event or process) (cause to) continue for an unnecessarily long time, usually unpleasantly (使)长时间地持续,(使)延长,把……拖长: The meeting *dragged out* all afternoon. 会议一直开了一个下午。They *dragged out* the meeting with long speeches. 他们冗长的讲话使会议延长了。I never heard a man *drag* a story *out* to such a length. 我从来没有听到一个人把故事拖得那么长。

drain of *vt.* (常用被动语态形式) ❶empty (something) of (its contents)把……排空: First you have to *drain* the container *of* all the old oil. 首先,你必须把容器中的剩油排净。Tanks must be completely *drained of* fuel before the vehicles are crated. 车辆在装箱前必须把油箱里的燃油完全排干。❷ empty (someone or something) of (something or someone)使耗尽……: The day's activities completely *drained* me *of* all strength. 一天的活动使我的体力消耗殆尽。I felt *drained of* energy. 我觉得自己的精力都枯竭了。The civil war *drained* the country *of* its youth and wealth. 那场内战耗尽了该国的青年和财富。

draw (one's) attention to *vt.* (常用一般时态) make (someone) notice (something, someone, or oneself)使(某人)注意……: I'd like to *draw your attention to* the following matters. 我想请你们注意下面几个问题。A headline on the front page *draws attention to* the story inside. 头版上的大字标题会使读者注意文章的内容。The talk with Linda *drew his attention to* the homely-looking girl. 与琳达的谈话引起他对这位相貌平平的女孩的注意。She likes *drawing attention to* herself. 她喜欢别人注意自己。

draw back *vt.* 【可分性动词短语】pull (something such as a curtain) into an open position 拉开(窗帘等): He *drew* the curtains *back* and looked down into the street. 他拉开窗帘,向下面的街道望去。May I *draw back* the curtains, madam? 太太,我可以拉开窗帘吗? They heard the sound of a bolt being *drawn back*. 他们听到插销正在被人拉开的声音。

—*vi.* (常与 from 连用) ❶retreat; move back (from someone or something), usually because you are surprised or frightened (常指因惊吓而)后退,退走: She *drew back* in horror. 她吓得往后退。The children *drew back* from the dog when it barked at them. 当狗向孩子们狂吠时,他们就退走了。❷be unwilling to consider or agree to something 不愿考虑(某事): The firm *drew back* from making an immediate commitment. 那家商行不愿立即作出承诺。

NOTE 本短语可转化为复合词 drawback, 意为"困难;不利条件;弊端"。

draw close ⇨ **draw near**

draw from *vt.* 【可分性动词短语】obtain (something) from (someone, or something)从……得到: It is important to *draw* the best qualities *from* the entrepreneurs and the professional managers. 重要的是从这些企业家和职业经理人身上学到他们最优良的品质。Japan's neighbors hope that Japan can make earnest efforts to *draw* lessons *from* history and act with caution in military and security fields. 日本的邻国都希望日本认真汲取历史教训，在军事和安全领域审慎行事。In addition to the survey data, Jones *drew* his conclusion *from* observations he made while watching students in college computer labs. 除调查数据之外，琼斯根据他对大学电脑实验室里的学生进行的观察得出了结论。

draw in/into *v.* ❶pull (something) in or into 拉进(……中)：The fishermen *drew in* their nets full of fish. 渔民们把满是鱼的网收进来。The horse *drew* the cart *into* the cave. 马拉着车进入洞中。❷take (something such as air) in or into your body 吸入(空气等)：*Draw in* a deep breath and let it out slowly. 深吸一口气，然后慢慢地呼出来。She *drew* the smoke deep *into* her lungs. 她把烟深深地吸入肺中。The ventilator *drew in* plenty of fresh air. 通风器抽入了大量的新鲜空气。❸(usually of a train or bus) arrive (in a place), slowing down to a stop (常指火车或公共汽车)进站，到站：As he reached the ticket barrier, the train was just *drawing in*. 当他到达检票口时，火车刚好进站。The bus *drew in* at 10:40 — ten minutes late. 公共汽车10点40分才驶进站点，晚点了10分钟。The ship *drew in* Plymouth Port ahead of schedule. 轮船提前到达普利茅斯港。❹(常用一般时态)(of a motor car, etc.) move to one side of the road (汽车等)开到路的一边：The bus *drew in* to the side of the road to let the passengers down. 公共汽车开到路的一边让乘客下车。❺get (someone) involved in (something unpleasant) 使(某人)卷入……中：It won't be easy for you to *draw* him *in*. 想要拉他卷入其中是不容易的。Don't let him *draw* you *into* his strategy. 别让他把你卷入他的计谋之中。We do not want to get *drawn into* a long and expensive conflict. 我们不想被卷入到一场时间长、花费大的冲突中。

NOTE 当本短语用作及物性动词短语，所带的宾语为代词时，该代词须置于本短语的动词和副词或介词中间。

draw lots ⇨ **cast lots**

draw near *v.* ❶move somewhere slowly or smoothly 缓慢走近：As the car of the Queen *drew near*, we waved our hands and cheered to her. 当女王的汽车驶近时，我们向她挥手欢呼。As we *drew nearer*, I noticed that the front door was open. 当我们走近时，我发现前门是开着的。❷(常用进行时态) (of an event or period of time) approach (某一事件或时期)将至，临近：As your birthday is *drawing near*, what would you like for a present? 你的生日就要到了，你想要什么礼物?

NOTE 本短语的另外一种表达形式是 draw close，两者可互换使用。

draw on[1] *vt.* ❶(正式用语) put on (a particular piece of clothing)穿上，戴上：I *drew on* my coat and went out. 我穿上上衣就走了出去。Take off those boots you wear, and *draw on* a pair of slippers. 把靴子脱下来，穿上拖鞋。The girl *drew on* her new gloves and ran out. 女孩戴上新手套跑了出去。❷encourage (someone), as to talk, etc. 鼓励(某人)说出: He *drew* the prisoner *on* to tell his story. 他鼓励囚犯讲出自己的事情。❸inhale (smoke from a cigarette, cigar, etc.)吸入(烟): He *drew on* his cigarette and coughed. 他一边吸烟,一边咳嗽。

—*vi.* (of a period of time) come near gradually (指时间)接近,临近: It grows colder as night is *drawing on*. 夜色降临时,天冷了起来了。As winter *drew on*, they felt the lack of heating equipment in the house. 冬天临近,他们感到还缺乏房屋供暖设备。

draw on² *vt.* ❶make use of (something such as your skills, experience you gained or something you have gradually saved)利用(获得的技能、经验或积蓄之物): As a writer, you have to *draw on* your imagination and life experiences. 作为一名作家,你必须利用自己的想象力和生活经历。We hope to *draw on* the advanced experience of other countries and scale new heights in China's road safety capacity-building endeavors. 我们希望借鉴其他国家的先进经验,把中国的道路交通安全能力建设提高到新的水平。❷(常用被动语态形式,常用一般时态) take (money) from a bank account, usually by writing a cheque(常指以支票方式从银行账户)支取(款项): I'll have to *draw on* my savings to pay for the repairs. 我将不得不取出我的储蓄金来支付修理费。He paid with a cheque *drawn on* his company's account. 他用从公司账户开取的支票付款。

draw out *v.* ❶take (something) out 掏出,拔出: He *drew out* his notebook and began to take notes. 他掏出笔记本,开始做笔记。After several attempts he managed to *draw out* the nail with a pair of pliers. 他用钳子拔了好几下才拔出那颗钉子。❷make (something) continue longer than needed 延长,变长: This action could *draw* the regional dispute *out* for another six months. 这一行动会使地区争端延长半年。The discussion was long *drawn out*. 讨论被拖得很长。People with southern accents tend to *draw out* their vowels. 南方人的口音倾向于把元音拉长。❸move out (of a place)离开(某地):(与 of 连用) Slowly the train *drew out* of the station. 火车慢慢地驶离了车站。The ship slowly drew out from the wharf. 那艘船缓慢地驶离了码头。❹take (money) from a bank account (从银行账户中)支取(款项): Customers can *draw out* to $5,000 a day from most accounts. 储户可以从大多账户中单日提取 5 000 美元。I'll need to *draw out* more cash tomorrow. 明天,我需要再取出些现金。❺ encourage (someone) to talk more by making him feel more relaxed and confident 鼓励(某人)说话: The new boy is very shy and it wasn't easy to *draw* him *out* and get him to participate. 新来的那个男生太腼腆,很难使他多说话并参与活动。

NOTE 当本短语用作及物性动词短语,所带的宾语为代词时,该代词须置于本短语的动词和副词中间。

draw to a close *vi.* (正式用语) (of an event or period of time) come to an end, often gradually (某一事件或时期)结束: The World Economic Forum *drew to a* close on Sunday in the Swiss resort of Davos. 世界经济论坛会于星期日在瑞士游览胜地达沃斯落下帷幕。The summer vacation has *drawn to a close*. 暑假已告结束。

NOTE 本短语的另外一种表达形式是 draw to an end。

draw up *vt.* 【可分性动词短语】❶prepare and write (something such as a document or plan)起草,写出(文件或计划):The two sides are *drawing up* the contract and arguing over what to keep and delete. 双方正在起草合同,并在争论哪些部分该保留,哪些部分该删掉。The president wants his ministers to implement the policy instead of simply *drawing* it *up*. 总统要求他的部长们执行这一政策而不只简单地写出来而已。❷(与反身代词连用)make (your back) very straight so that you look as tall as possible, because you want to impress someone or prepare yourself for a challenge 使(自己)挺直身子:I saw the new chairman *drawing* himself *up* and walking into the meeting room. 我看到新任主席挺直身子,走进了会议室。

—*vt.* & *vi.* (of a vehicle)(cause to)arrive at a place and stop (使)(车辆)停下:A police car *drew up* alongside Tom at the red light and asked him to pull over. 一辆警车在红灯亮时并排停在了汤姆的车旁,并让他把车开到路边停下。The driver *drew* the car *up* just in time to avoid hitting the child. 司机刚好及时地把车停住,才没有撞上那个小孩。

NOTE 当本短语用作及物性动词短语,所带的宾语为代词时,该代词须置于本短语的动词和副词中间。

dream of *vt.* 【不可分性动词短语】(用一般时态)think about (something that you hope to have or achieve, or doing something) 梦想: These are inventions we never even *dreamed of*. 这些发明是我们连做梦也没梦到过的。The Chinese people had *dreamed of* flying to the moon for more than 1,000 years and now it has become a reality. 中国人民一千多年的奔月梦想现已成为现实。

NOTE 本短语中的动词 dream 的过去式和过去分词有两种形式: dreamed 和 dreamt。无论是在英国英语还是在美国英语中,都广泛使用 dreamed。

dress up *v.* ❶(cause to) put on special clothes that are more formal than the clothes you usually wear (使)穿上盛装: Don't bother to *dress up* for this informal party. 不必穿盛装去参加这个非正式的聚会。I *dressed* my children *up* for the party. 我给孩子们穿上盛装去参加聚会。❷make (something) look different or more attractive, acceptable or interesting than it really is 装饰(某物): We shall *dress* the room *up* for Christmas. 我们要把房间装饰一番过圣诞节。A coat of paint will *dress up* the old bicycle very much. 刷一层漆就会使这辆旧自行车焕然一新。You needn't *dress* it *up* with all these beautiful words. 你没有必要用这些漂亮的言辞粉饰这桩事。❸(常用被动语态形式,常与 as 连用) make (someone or something) seem different to disguise them 装扮: *Dressed up* as security men, the terrorists drove their explosive-laden car towards the government building. 恐怖分子装扮成保安人员,驾驶着装满炸药的汽车冲向政

府大楼。Mary was *dressed up* to play Cinderella in her school play. 玛丽在学校的演出中化装扮演灰姑娘。For her birthday party, they had *dressed* her *up* as a fairy. 为了她的生日聚会，他们把她打扮成一个仙女。

D

NOTE 1. 当本短语用作及物性动词短语，所带的宾语为代词时，该代词须置于本短语的动词和副词中间。

2. 当本短语作"穿上"解时，同义短语是 have on, pull on 和 put on。它们之间的区别见 put on。

3. 当本短语作"装扮"解时，同义短语是 disguise as。

drive at *vt.* ❶make (a vehicle) move at (a speed)以(某一速度)驾驶(汽车)：My friend was taken to court for *driving* his car *at* an unlawful speed. 我的朋友因以非法速度驾驶汽车而被送上法庭。In order to throw off the photographers on motorcycles, Diana allowed the driver to *drive at* nearly 200 km per hour thus leading to the deadly accident. 为了摆脱那些骑摩托车的摄影记者，戴安娜允许司机以每小时将近 200 公里的速度行驶，于是导致了致命的车祸。❷(非正式用语，无被动语态形式，用进行时态，与 what 连用) mean; indicate; suggest (something) 意指，暗示：I listened carefully to what he was saying but I couldn't understand what he was *driving at*. 我仔细地听他所说的话，可就搞不懂他在意指什么。I don't know what on earth you are *driving at*. 我不明白你究竟是什么意思。❸(无被动语态形式) make an effort towards (something or doing something)努力去做：The factory must *drive at* increasing production this year. 该厂今年必须努力增产。

drive away *vt.*【可分性动词短语】force (someone or something) to go away or stay away (把……)赶走：Don't *drive* them *away*; they're here to help. 别赶他们走，他们是来帮忙的。We smoked constantly, hoping to *drive away* the mosquitoes. 我们不断地吸烟，以期驱走蚊子。What can I do to *drive away* these feelings of sadness? 我怎么才能驱走这些忧伤的情感呢?

NOTE 当本短语所带的宾语为代词时，该代词须置于本短语的动词和副词中间。

drive home *vt.*【可分性动词短语】(常与 to 连用)tell people about(something)in a way that makes them understand and accept it, especially by repeating it many times (尤指通过反复解释后)使人明白并接受……：I find it difficult to *drive home* my thoughts to some of the readers 我发现很难让某些读者理解我的思想。The accident in the factory really *drove home* to us the point that safety regulations must be observed. 工厂里发生的事故向我们清楚地表明了必须遵守安全规则的重要。You should *drive* the point *home*. 你应该把这一点讲透。

drive into *vt.*【可分性动词短语】❶drive (a vehicle) into (something or someone) 开车撞上：He *drove* his truck *into* a wall. 他开着卡车撞上了一堵墙。It would be my bad luck to *drive into* a police car. 要和警车相撞，我可就倒了霉了。❷force(someone) into (a particular state or situation)迫使(某人)陷入(某种状态或处境)：Hospital bills *drove* them *into* bankruptcy. 医疗费使他们破产了。What he said and did nearly *drove* her *into* madness. 他的所作所为几乎使她发疯。

drive off *vt.* &*vi.* (of a vehicle or driver) start moving and leave from a place (车辆)驶离;把(车辆)开走: Without a word, she closed the door and *drove off*. 她一句话也没说,关上车门就开车走了。

—*vt.*【可分性动词短语】force (someone or something) to go away, especially when they are attacking or threatening you 赶走(尤指具有攻击或威胁性的人或物): They *drove off* their attackers. 他们赶走了袭击他们的人。The police used tear gas to *drive* the angry students *off*. 警察使用催泪瓦斯赶走了愤怒的学生。The man *drove off* the dog with stones. 那个人用石块打跑了狗。

drive out *vt.*【可分性动词短语】(常与from, of 连用) force (someone or something) to leave or disappear 把……赶走: Government forces have *driven out* the rebels from the eastern district. 政府军已把叛乱分子赶出了东部地区。The soldiers *drove* them *out* of their homes. 士兵把他们赶出了家园。We had to use cats to *drive* the rats *out*. 我们不得不用猫把老鼠赶走了。

NOTE 当本短语所带的宾语为代词时,该代词须置于本短语的动词和副词中间。

drive up *vi.* (of a vehicle) move near to a person or place and stop (车辆)开到近前: One of the soldiers said that one vehicle *drove up* and its passengers fired at the soldiers. 一名士兵陈述说,一辆汽车开了过来,然后车里的人就朝他们开了火。Witnesses said the vehicle *drove up* to the checkpoint near a bridge and exploded, killing three soldiers. 目击者们称,那辆汽车驶向大桥附近的那个检查站并发生爆炸,炸死了3名士兵。

—*vt.*【可分性动词短语】make (something such as price) increase 使(价格等)上涨: The market uncertainty has *driven* prices *up*. 市场的不确定性使价格上涨。The world's strong demand for oil has helped *drive up* oil prices. 世界对石油的强大需求已促使石油价格上涨。

drop by/over *vi.* (主要用于美国英语中,非正式用语) make a short informal, and usually unannounced visit somewhere 顺便来访: Why don't you *drop by* for coffee some time? 什么时候顺便来喝咖啡吧。*Drop by* and pick up that book sometime. 什么时候顺便过来把那本书拿走。Do *drop over* and see me sometime next week. 下星期的什么时候一定到我这儿来坐坐。*Drop over* to our house for a visit sometime. 有时间到我们家来玩。

NOTE 本短语的同义短语是 drop in。

drop in *vi.* (非正式用语,常与 at, on 连用) make a short informal visit somewhere, often without an appointment or unexpectedly 顺便来访,突访: *Drop in* to see us when you are free. 有空顺便来看我们。I will *drop in* at the office to see you. 我要顺便到办公室去拜访你。Prince Charles, the heir to the British throne, came to Iran Sunday after *dropping in* on British troops in Basra, Iraq. 英国王位继承人查尔斯王子在突访了驻伊拉克巴士拉市的英军士兵后,于星期日抵达伊朗。

NOTE 1. 当本短语表示访问的对象是地点时,其后与 at 连用(如第二个例句);当对象是人时,则与 on 连用(如第三个例句)。

2. 本短语的同义短语是 drop by 和 drop over。

drop off *vi.* ❶decrease in number, amount, value, etc.; become fewer or less (数目、数量等)减少;(价值等)降低: Attendance in this course has been *dropping off* recently. 这门课程的出勤率近来在不断减少。Their sales start to *drop off* at the beginning of July. 他们的销售额于 7 月初开始下降。Business in the stores *dropped off* after Christmas. 过了圣诞节,商店的生意就萧条了。His interest in the game has *dropped off*. 他对这种比赛的兴趣已经降低。❷(非正式用语,常用一般时态) fall into a light sleep, usually without intending to; doze 打盹儿,打瞌睡: She closed her eyes, and soon *dropped off*. 她合上了眼,很快就打起盹儿来。Just as she was *dropping off*, there was a loud bang at the door. 正当她打瞌睡时,传来了响亮的敲门声。—*vt.* &*vi.* (非正式用语)(allow to) leave (a car or other vehicle)下车,让某人下车: Thanks for the free ride. I'll *drop off* here. 谢谢您让我免费搭车。我要在这儿下车。I can *drop* you *off* at school on my way to work. 我可以在上班的途中把你送到校门口下车。We *dropped* our luggage *off* at the hotel and went sightseeing. 我们把行李从车上卸下来放到旅馆就去观光了。

NOTE 当本短语作"打盹儿,打瞌睡"解时,同义短语是 doze off。

drop out *vi.* (常与 of 连用) ❶no longer take part in or be part of (something such as an activity or competition) before you have finished what you intended to do 退出: He was injured in the first round and had to *drop out*. 他在第一轮中就受了伤,并因此而退出比赛。The former Democratic presidential candidate called for her to *drop out* of the race. 这位前民主党总统候选人呼吁她退出竞选。❷ leave school, college, etc. without finishing your studies 退学: He went to Harvard but he *dropped out* in his junior year because of the need to work. 他上了哈佛大学,但在三年级时却因需要工作而退学了。

NOTE 本短语可转化为复合词 drop-out,意为"退学的人;辍学的"。

drown out *vt.* 【可分性动词短语】(常用被动语态形式) prevent (a sound) from being heard properly by (something such as a louder noise)(嘈杂声)使人听不清(某一声音): The children's shouts *drowned* the music *out*. 孩子们的叫喊声使人听不清音乐。Their cheers *drowned out* the protests of demonstrators. 他们的欢呼声淹没了示威者的抗议声。The actors' words were *drowned out* by applause. 演员们的台词被掌声所淹没。

dry off *v.* (cause to) become dry (使)变得干燥: Wash the towels and leave them to *dry off*. 洗了毛巾后把它们晾干。She hung up the towels in order to *dry* them *off*. 她把毛巾都挂起来晒干。He got out of the shower and *dried* himself *off*. 他洗完淋浴后把身子擦干。

NOTE 1. 当本短语用作及物性动词短语,所带的宾语为代词时,该代词须置于本短语的动词和副词中间。

2. 本短语与 dry out(第一个义项)意义和用法相同,两者可互换使用。见 dry out。

dry out *v.* ❶(cause to) become very dry through a gradual loss of moisture (使)

变得干燥：Don't leave these raisins on the table; they will *dry out*. 别把葡萄干放在桌上，它们会干透的。Water the ground regularly to stop it from *drying out*. 要定期浇地以避免干涸。The cold winds *dry out* your skin very quickly. 冷风很快就会使你的皮肤干燥。❷（非正式用语）give up drinking alcohol, or to help (someone) do this, especially by getting medical treatment 戒酒；通过医疗帮助（某人）戒酒：If he goes on drinking like that, he'll have to spend months *drying out* in a special hospital. 如果他继续那样喝下去，他就得花上几个月的时间在专门医院里戒酒了。The doctor will be able to *dry* him *out*. 医生能帮他把酒戒掉的。I approved the doctor's order to keep him in the room till he was *dried out*. 我接受了医嘱，把他关进屋子里直到他把酒戒掉。

NOTE 当本短语用作及物性动词短语，所带的宾语为代词时，该代词须置于本短语的动词和副词中间。

dry up *vt.* &*vi.* ❶（cause to）lose all the moisture and become completely dry or hard（使）干透：The land had *dried up* and no crops would grow. 大地干涸，作物都不能生长了。Warm breezes from the south *dried up* the muddy road. 温暖的南风把泥泞的道路吹干了。The rain hit the ground and then the hot sun *dried* it *up*. 雨水打湿了地面，而后来烈日又把它晒得透干。❷（英国英语用法）wipe the water off (the plates, cups knives, pans, and other things) when they have been washed, using a cloth; dry dishes with a towel after you have washed them 把（盘碟等）洗后擦干：He stood beside Mary, *drying up* dishes while she washed. 玛丽洗盘碟，而他站在玛丽身旁把它们擦干。I'll wash and you can *dry up*. 我来洗，你擦干。

—*vi.* ❶（of a river, lake, well, etc.）become empty of water, usually because of hot weather and a lack of rain（河水、湖水或井水等）干枯：During the drought the reservoirs all *dried up*. 在干旱期间，水库都干枯了。The fountain is said never to *dry up*. 据说，此喷水池之水永不枯竭。❷（of a supply of something）come to an end（供应来源）枯竭，中断：What will happen to the project when the money *dries up*? 当资金枯竭时，这个项目该怎么办？Our sources of information have *dried up*. 我们的情报来源中断了。❸（非正式用语，用一般时态）stop talking in the middle of what you are saying, because you do not know what to say next; cause (someone) to be silent（因不知再说什么而）停止说话；使（某人）住口：If you ask her what she is good at she will *dry up* after two minutes, but if you ask what she is not good at she will talk for two hours. 如果你问她有什么特长，她说两分钟就会停住讲不下去了。但你要是问她不善于做什么时，她就会讲两个小时。*Dry up*! I've had enough of your complaining talk. 住口吧！你抱怨的话我已经听够了。❹（非正式用语）forget one's words when acting in a play 在演出中忘记台词：He *dried up* three times in the second act. 他在第二幕中曾三度忘记台词。

NOTE 当本短语用作及物性动词短语，所带的宾语为代词时，该代词须置于本短语的动词和副词中间。

due to *prep.* because of; by reason of (something); attributable to (something) 由于……，归于……：The accident was *due* to careless driving. 这次事故是由于驾驶疏忽而造成的。Mistakes *due to* carelessness may have serious consequences. 由于粗心所犯下的错误,后果可能是严重的。

NOTE 1. 本短语后只能接物不接人。例如,我们不能说: * We missed the last bus *due to* her.

D

2. 在个别情况下(主要在从句中),本短语可分离使用,而且 to 位于 due 之前。例如:

> In many waters are found various kinds of minerals, *to* which substances the hardness of water is *due*.
> 在许多水域中都发现有各种矿物质,而水的硬度就是由于这些物质所致。

3. 本短语和 owing to, because of 都是介词性短语,作"由于,因为"解时,三者常可互换使用。但它们在实际使用中还是有区别:本短语所引导的短语通常用作表语或后置定语,偶作状语;owing to 所引导的短语则一般用作状语,偶作表语,用作状语时,一般用逗号与其前或后句隔开,并修饰全句;而 because of 一般只修饰句中的某一部分,且不用逗号分隔。

dwell on/upon *vt.*【不可分性动词短语】❶(陈旧用法) live on (something, such as the earth) as a permanent resident (指永久性)居住在(地球等)上: This is the largest turtle that *dwells on* the earth. 这是地球上最大的龟。No one knows exactly how many wonderful creatures *dwell upon* the ocean floor. 没有人确切地知道在海底世界居住着多少奇妙的海洋生物。❷ spend a lot of time thinking, talking or writing about (something) 细想;详说,详述: He *dwelt on* the negative aspects of his performance. 他仔细考虑了自己在表演中的一些不足方面。Smith and James also *dwelt on* whether the countryside would resist the oncoming tide of progress. 史密斯和詹姆斯还仔细考虑了农村会不会抵制即将到来的这股进步潮流。In his speech, the costs of failure to cooperate and cost of delay of cooperation and interchangeable relationship between them were also *dwelled on*. 他在讲话中还阐述了合作失败成本与合作延误成本,以及两者之间的相互转化关系。The book *dwells* too much *upon* the economic aspects of the problem. 这本书对该问题的经济方面写得太多了。

NOTE 1. 本短语中的 upon 用法比 on 正式,但不及 on 常用。

2. 本短语中的动词 dwell 的过去式和过去分词有两种形式: dwelled 和 dwelt。无论是在英国英语还是在美国英语中,都广泛使用 dwelt。

E e

each and every *adj.* (仅用作定语)(used for emphasizing that you mean every person, thing, etc. in a group) every 每一个: Before delivering his lecture, the professor gave *each and every* student a handout. 教授在演讲前给每一个学生发了一份演讲提纲。*Each and every* one of the flowers has its own colour and smell. 每一种花都有其自己的颜色和味道。The captain wants *each and every* man to be here at eleven. 船长要求每一个人 11 点到达这里。

NOTE **1.** 本短语中的 each 与 every 均指许多人或事物中的一个,但 each 强调个体,而 every 则强调整体。each and every 既强调了个体又强调了整体,所以被用来加强句子的语气。

2. 本短语后接单数名词或代词。如"本短语＋单数名词或代词"作主语时,谓语动词须用单数形式。如果其后出现代词,谓语动词也要选用单数形式。例如:

> *Each and every* driver knows what his or her job is to be.
> 每一个司机都知道他/她的工作将是什么。

each other ⇨ **one after another**

each time Ⅰ *conj.* (非正式用语,常用一般现在时和过去时) whenever (something happens) 每当(某事发生时): *Each time* I ask you to do something, you always say you're too busy. 每次我让你做点事,你都说你太忙。My poor spelling annoys me *each time* I try to write something. 每当我想写些什么的时候,我糟糕的拼写就会使我恼火。

Ⅱ *adv.* always 总是: It brews a perfect blend of coffee *each time*. 它总能煮出上好的咖啡。We played with them twice and were defeated *each time*. 我们和他们赛了两场球,每次都输。

NOTE **1.** 当本短语作"每当"解时,本身就是连词性短语,等同于连词 when 或 whenever。因此,在 *each time* 后不能再用连词 when 或 whenever。例如,我们不能说: * I meet up with Mary *each time* when I go to New York.

2. 本短语的同义短语是 every time。

3. 不要将本短语与 one time 混淆,两者的意义和用法不同。

eager for *adj.* very keen on or enthusiastic about (something that will happen or you want) 极想,盼望,渴望(某事的发生): She is *eager for* you to meet her friends. 她很想让你见见她的朋友们。Many people like them are *eager for* tickets to the Olympic Games. 许多人都像他们那样渴望得到奥运会门票。When my son was five years old, I became *eager for* another baby. 我儿子 5 岁时,我便很想再有一个孩子。They crowded round the spokesperson, *eager for* latest news about the two bus explosions. 他们围着

发言人,渴望得到有关那两起公共汽车爆炸事件的最新消息。

eager to *adj*. (后接原形动词) very keen or anxious to (do something)急于,渴望(做某事): She was back, *eager to* see her friends. 她回来了,急着要看望她的朋友们。A senior Zimbabwean official said on Wednesday that the southern African country is *eager to* strengthen economic ties with China. 津巴布韦一位高级官员星期三表示,这个南非国家渴望加强与中国的经济关系。

early bird *n*. (非正式用语) ❶someone who usually arises early in the morning 通常早起的人: People with young children are usually *early birds*. 有小孩的人往往都起得早。You're an *early bird* this morning! 你今天早晨起得真早哇! The *early birds* went for a walk along the seashore before breakfast. 早起的人在早饭前沿着海岸散步。❷someone who arrives somewhere or does something before other people do 早到者:We were among the *early birds* at the party. 我们是出席聚会的早到者。I always come early. The *early bird* catches up the worm! 我总是早到。赶早的鸟儿有虫吃嘛。

NOTE 当本短语作"通常早起的人"解时,反义短语是 late riser。

ease off/up *vi*. ❶(非正式用语)(of something unpleasant or annoying) become weaker or less severe 减弱,缓解: If the rain *eases off*, we'll leave in the morning. 如果雨势减弱,我们上午就动身。When will the pain *ease off*? 这疼痛什么时候能够缓解? The pain should *ease up* after a couple of hours. 几小时后,疼痛就应该缓解了。❷(非正式用语)go more slowly or work less hard; relax 放慢,放松: *Ease off* a bit as you go round the bend. 在转弯的时候要慢一些。The doctor told me to *ease up* and stop working so hard. 医生让我放松下来,不要工作得太累。

—*vt*. 【不可分性动词短语】reduce (something such as pressure)减轻(压力等): Having a cup of coffee can *ease off* your pressure. 喝杯咖啡可以减轻你的压力。He *eased up* the gas pedal to let the car slow down. 他放松了油门踏板,让车减速慢行。

easier said than done *adj*. (非正式用语,前常用 it's 或 that's) used for saying that something is a good idea but will be difficult to do or achieve 说起来容易做起来难: To win the day in the highly competitive society is *easier said than done*, but she has made it. 在竞争激烈的社会里获得成功说起来容易做起来难,但是她已经做到了。We have been told to increase our output, but that's *easier said than done*. 要求我们增加产量,可是这说起来容易做起来难。

eat away *v*. (常与 at 连用) gradually damage or destroy (something) by, or as if by, eating; erode 咬坏,侵蚀,腐蚀: Woodworms had *eaten away* at the door frame. 蛀虫已把门框蛀坏。The rats have *eaten* the woodwork *away*. 老鼠把木制品都咬坏了。Ocean waves are slowly *eating away* (at) the coastal rocks. 海浪在慢慢地侵蚀着岸边的岩石。The acid *ate away* the metal. 酸腐蚀了金属。Rust was *eating away* the pipe. 铁锈把管子锈蚀了。

NOTE 本短语的同义短语是 eat into。

eat in *vi*. have a meal at home instead of going out to a restaurant 在家中吃饭: Are we *eating in* tonight? 咱们今晚在家里吃吗? We *ate in* last night but tonight we are going to eat out. 昨天晚上我们是在家吃的

饭,但今天晚上我们要到外面去吃。

NOTE 1. 不要将本短语与 eat inside 混淆。eat in side 意为"在室内用餐"。

2. 本短语的同义短语是 dine in;反义短语是 eat out 和 dine out。

eat into *vt.* 【不可分性动词短语】❶gradually destroy (something) by, or as if by, eating 侵蚀,腐蚀: The river had *eaten into* the bank, and part of it had collapsed. 河水已侵蚀了堤岸,部分已经塌陷。The acid *ate into* the metal. 酸腐蚀了金属。❷ spend (more money) than you intended 花掉(更多款项):The costs of the legal action *ate* deep *into* the money they saved. 诉讼费用花掉了他们大笔的存款。All these bills are *eating into* our savings. 所有这些账单要把我们的积蓄花光。

NOTE 当本短语作"侵蚀,腐蚀"解时,同义短语是 eat away。但本短语主要指酸性物质或锈对物体的侵蚀或腐蚀。

eat one's words *vi.* (非正式用语) retract your statement because you admit that what you said before was wrong 食言,收回前言: I'm really embarrassed that I have to *eat my* own *words*. 这回我不得不自食其言了。我真是感到非常难为情。They predicted his failure, but he made them *eat their words*. 他们预言他会失败,但他使他们收回了前言。When we got married my friend predicted it would never last. But he's certainly had to *eat his words* and admit he was wrong. 我们结婚的时候,我朋友预言说我的婚姻不会长久。但是,他现在不得不收回他讲的话,并承认自己说错了。

NOTE 本短语中的名词 word 必须用复数形式。

eat out *vi.* have a meal in a restaurant instead of at home 在外面(指在餐馆里)吃饭: Would you please *eat out* with us tonight?. 你今晚愿意和我们外出吃饭吗?

NOTE 1. 不要将本短语与 eat outside 混淆。eat outside 意为"在室外用餐"。

2. 本短语的同义短语是 dine out;反义短语是 eat in 和 dine in。

eat up *vt.* &*vi.* (主要用于口语中) eat all of (the food)吃光: No television until you *eat up* your lunch. 把你的午饭吃光,才能看电视。You're not going out to play until you've *eaten* all your carrots *up*. 不把那些胡萝卜吃完,你就别想去外面玩。The worms will soon *eat up* all the leaves on the tree if we don't stop them. 如果我们不加以控制,虫子很快就会把树叶吃个精光。Some flower seeds fell along the footpath; some birds came and *ate* them *up*. 一些花籽散落在了小径上。一些鸟儿飞来把它们吃光。*Eat up*, and we'll go for a walk. 吃干净,然后我们去散步。

—*vt.* ❶ use or consume (large amounts of your available time, money or resources) 耗掉(大量的时间、金钱或资源):This big old car *eats up* a lot of petrol. 这台又大又旧的车耗油量很大。Idle talk had *eaten up* the hour before they knew it. 他们不知不觉地把时间闲谈过去了。Having children *eats up* a lot of a family's income. 养孩子要耗掉大部分家庭收入。❷travel (a particular distance) easily and steadily 轻快地走完(一段距离): They drove on, *eating up* the distance between themselves and home. 他们驾车前行,轻快地走完了回家的路程。

NOTE 当本短语用作及物性动词短语,所带的宾语为代词时,该代词须置于本短语的动词和副词中间。

either … or … *conj.* ❶ used for showing two or more possibilities or choices 或者

……或者……,不是……就是……:*Either* he *or* you are right. 不是他对,就是你对。What qualifications do I need to become *either* a primary school teacher *or* an infant school teacher? 我需要具备什么条件才能当一名小学或幼儿学校教师? Study after study has shown that vitamin C did little to reduce *either* the length *or* severity of colds among the general population. 不断的研究表明,维生素C在普通人群中对于缩短感冒的时间或者降低感冒的严重程度几乎没有作用。You can contact us *either* by phone, by email, *or* by letter. 你可以同我们通过电话,或者电子邮件,或者写信联系。Enriched uranium can be used *either* to generate electricity *or* to make nuclear bombs. 浓缩铀既可用来发电,也可用来制造原子弹。❷ used for saying that one of two things has to happen or be true 要么……要么……:We had to *either* fight to the end *or* wait for our death. 我们要么战斗到底,要么坐以待毙。He is *either* drunk *or* mad. 他要么是醉了,要么就是疯了。*Either* you must improve your work *or* I shall dismiss you. 要么你改进你的工作,要么我辞退你。

NOTE **1.** 本短语所连接的两个部分要保持平行一致。因此,不能说:* You may *either* have the ring *or* the bracelet. 应改为:You may have *either* the ring *or* the bracelet.

2. 本短语之后,可以再接 or。例如:

> I expect to meet them *either* in New York *or* in Boston or in Philadelphia this winter.
> 这个冬天,我希望在纽约,或在波士顿,或在费城见到他。

3. 当本短语连接两个名词或代词作并列主语时,其谓语动词用单数形式还是用复数形式,一般要遵循如下四条原则:(1)当本短语连接的两个并列主语均为单数时,其谓语动词用单数形式。例如:*Either* Eve *or* Herb has been invited. 在英国英语中,也可用复数形式,但此属非正式用法。(2)当本短语连接的两个并列主语均为复数时,其谓语动词用复数形式。例如:*Either* the Browns *or* the Smiths have been invited. (3)当本短语连接的两个并列主语单复数形式不同时,则要根据邻近一致的原则,其谓语动词的形式与最靠近的那个主语(即 or 后的名词或代词)保持一致。例如:

> *Either* my dog *or* her cats are to be sold.
> *Either* her cats *or* my dog is to be sold.

(4)在一般疑问句中,助动词形式要与 either 后的主语保持人称和数的一致。例如:

> Is *either* your father *or* your brothers coming?
> Are *either* you *or* I going there tomorrow?

4. 本短语与否定词连用时,意为"既不……又不……"。例如:

> The heat that warms a body doesn't change *either* its weight *or* its inertia.
> 加热物体的热量既不会改变物体的重量,又不会改变其惯性。

5. 本短语的反义短语是 neither … nor …。

elaborate on/upon *vt.* 【不可分性动词短语】speak or write about (someone or something such as a subject) in detail 详述,细讲:I want to know more about my new boss. Could you *elaborate on* him? 我想更多地了解我的新老板。你能详细地讲一讲他吗? What you've told me of your plan sounds most interesting; would you care to *elaborate on* it? 你对我讲的你那计划很有意思,你能否将其详谈一下? The Chairman of China's NPC Standing Committee *elaborated upon* the policy concerning the Taiwan's return to the motherland for the realization of peaceful reunification. 全国人大常委会委员长详细阐述了有关台湾回归祖国、实现和平统一的政策。

NOTE 本短语中的 upon 用法比 on 正式,但不及 on 常用。

electronic mail Ⅰ *n.* (无复数形式)❶a system of electronic communication among users of computer networks 电子通信系统:*Electronic mail* is now widely used in modern business circles. 电通信系统现广泛运用于现代商务领域中。Do you have an *email* address? 你有没有电子邮箱地址? ❷a written message that you sent or the messages that you receive using the email system (收发的)电子邮件信息:She checks her *e-mail* first thing every morning. 每天上午她的第一件事就是查看她的电子邮件。I haven't seen my teacher Professor James for thirteen years but we keep in touch by *e-mail*. 我有13年没见到我的老师詹姆斯教授了,但我们通过电子邮件保持着联系。Send me an *e-mail* with the details. 把详情通过电子邮件发送给我。Be polite and respectful when you write *emails* to your business partners. 在给你的业务合作伙伴写电子邮件时,要礼貌、尊重对方。

Ⅱ *vt.* send a message to (someone) by email 给(某人)发送电子邮件:Professor James *emailed* me yesterday. 詹姆斯教授昨天给我发来了邮件。I'll *email* her the documents. 我将通过电子邮件把文件发送给她。And then she *emails* the reports to Mr Burns, the director. 接着她把几份报告通过电子邮件发给了经理伯恩斯先生。

NOTE 本短语日常使用其简写形式 e-mail 或 email,亦被拼写为 E-mail 或 eMail。与本短语形式相同的短语还有 electronic commerce (e-commerce)电子商务, electronic magazine (e-zine)电子杂志,等等。

eleventh hour Ⅰ *n.* (常用于 at/in the eleventh hour 形式中) the very last possible moment before a deadline or the imminence of a decisive or "final" moment 最后一刻,最后关头: At the *eleventh hour*, an agreement was reached, just in time to avoid a strike. 在最后时刻,一项协议达成了,从而及时地避免了一场罢工。All the 007 stories are more or less the same: Whatever the circumstances are, James Bond always manages to overpower his rival in the *eleventh hour*. 所有的007故事都大同小异:不管在什么情况下,詹姆斯·邦德总能在危急时刻成功地制服他的对手。It's the *eleventh hour* for getting this contract signed! If we don't deliver it to the customer before noon, we'll lose the whole deal. 现在已经到了签订这份合同的最后关头!如果我们不能在午前把合同交给客户的话,这笔生意就全丢了。

Ⅱ *adj.* at the last minute 最后一刻的: Many people believe that they might have staged an *eleventh hour* assassination attempt to get votes. 许多人都相信,他们可能策划了选举前最后时刻的谋杀事件,以图拉票。

embark on/upon *vt.* 【不可分性动词短

语】❶ start (something, especially something new, difficult or exciting) 开始,着手(尤指新、难或令人兴奋的事情):After the monarchy was overthrown Nepal *embarked on* serious political and social changes. 君主制被推翻后,尼泊尔开始了重大的政治和社会变革。We will not *embark upon* moon race with any other country and in any form. 我们不会与任何其他国家搞任何形式的月球竞赛。And now I can *embark on* doing something I've always wanted to do. 现在,我可以着手做我一直想要做的事情了。❷ start (a journey) by ship 开始航行:We *embarked on* a voyage to the Caribbean. 我们开始了加勒比海的航行。They are to *embark upon* a tour around the world. 他们即将开始一次环球旅行。

NOTE 本短语中的 upon 用法比 on 正式,但不及 on 常用。

en route Ⅰ *adv.* along the way, or while traveling from or to a particular place 途径;在途中:The shop is *en route* to my parents' house. 去我父母家,途中要经过那家商店。We can finish our discussion *en route*. 咱们可以在路上把事情商定下来。

Ⅱ *adj.* on the way to destination 在途中的:The plane is *en route* from London to New York. 这架飞机是在从伦敦飞往纽约的途中。He arrived early in spite of *en route* delays. 尽管途中延误,他还是到得很早。

NOTE **1.** 本短语是源自法语的短语。不要错误地将其记忆为 * in route 或 * on route。

2. 本短语在美国英语中常被其连体形式 enroute 所替代。例如:I'm in New York today, *enroute to* Tunis for the World Summit on the Information Society.

3. 本短语在英国英语中常与 for 连用。例如:

I'm *en route* for my office.
我正在去办公室的途中。

end in *vt.*【不可分性动词短语】(无被动语态形式) ❶ have (something) at its end 尽头是,末端为;以……为结尾:The narrow lane *ended in* a farmyard. 这条窄胡同的尽头是个农家院。The glass tube *ends in* a bulb. 这根玻璃管的末端呈球体。Not all English words which *end in* -ly are adverbs. 以-ly 结尾的英语单词并不都是副词。❷ have (something) as a final result 以……为最终结果,以……告终:The game *ended in* a draw. 这场比赛最终打成了平局。All their efforts *ended in* failure. 他们的一切努力均以失败而告终。If he goes on like that he'll *end in* being punished. 他要是再那样下去,最后必遭惩罚。

NOTE 当本短语中作"以……为最终结果,以……告终"解时,主要用于英国英语中。

end up *v.* (非正式用语,用一般时态) ❶(主要用于美国英语中) reach (an unfavorable end)终结,终了,以……为告终:"My fear is that if we continue to confront each other over trade dispute, both sides will *end up* into an abyss," the minister said. 这位部长说:"我担心,如果我们在贸易争端上继续相互对抗下去,我们双方都将走向深渊。"Thanks to his laziness, he *ended up* achieving nothing. 由于懒惰,他最终一事无成。❷(常与 as 连用) finish by becoming (someone or something)终于成为:All those who try to falsify history are bound to *end up* (as) criminals in history. 一切伪造历史的人必定会成为历史的罪人。The failure to pick up a signal from Beagle 2 raised fears that the Mars probe had suffered the same fate as so many craft before it and *ended up* as scrap metal. “猎兔犬 2 号”信号接收的失败使科学家们担心这一火星探测器的命运和此前许多探测器一样，最终变成金属碎片。❸come or bring to an end 结束：He finally *ended up* his speech. 他终于结束了自己的讲话。The party *ended up* with singing and dancing. 聚会在歌舞中结束。❹die; be killed 死，被杀死：The hostage *ended up* with a severed head. 人质被砍头杀害。Had he stayed there a few minutes longer, he might have *ended up* among the twelve people killed in the attack. 如果他在那里多待几分钟的话，他就会成为在那次袭击中丧生的 12 人中的一员。

NOTE 本短语的第一个义项后可接不同介词的短语。再如：

> The game *ended up* in a tie.
> I *ended up* with a black eye.
> We *ended up* at the police station.
> The game's increasingly effective publicity caused it to *end up* on national television.

engage in *vt.* ❶take part in (a particular activity, especially something that takes a lot of time or effort)参加，从事：I have no time to *engage in* the debate. 我没有时间参加辩论。He is *engaged in* writing a novel. 他正在写一部小说。A military transport helicopter *engaging in* quake relief work in Wenchuan County crashed on Saturday afternoon. 星期六下午，一架从事抗震救灾工作的军用运输直升机在汶川县失事。❷make (someone or oneself) busy in (something or doing something)(使)忙于：While one of the robbers *engaged* the guard *in* conversation, the others crept into the factory. 当一名强盗与门卫攀谈时，其余的强盗便溜进了工厂。They *engaged* themselves *in* completing the design of the linkage ahead of time. 他们忙于提前完成联结装置的设计工作。

NOTE 不要将本短语与 engaged in 混淆。作为动词性短语，本短语强调的是动作，engaged in 则强调的是状态。

engaged in/on *adj.* (正式用语) taking part in; busy doing (something, especially something that takes a lot of time or effort)参与……；从事于……；忙于……；致力于……：Don't get *engaged in* their quarrels. 别参与到他们的争吵中去。Professor Smith is *engaged in* writing letters of invitation. 史密斯教授正在忙着写邀请信。He is now *engaged on* his second novel. 他现正在致力于第二部小说的写作。

engaged to *adj.* having formally agreed to marry (someone)与(某人)订婚：She's *engaged to* someone she met at work. 她与一个在工作中相识的人订了婚。Our son got *engaged to* a very beautiful young woman. 我们的儿子已与一位年轻漂亮的女子订了婚。

engaged with *adj.* having one's time filled up; busy with (something)忙于(某事)；从事(某事)：The professor is *engaged with* some of his former students. 教授正忙着接待他以前的一些

学生。Most of his time is *engaged with* the day-to-day work in the office. 他大部分时间都在办公室里从事日常事务。

enjoy oneself *vi.* have a good, pleasurable or satisfactory time; be happy; experience pleasure 享受，愉快，过得快活：She did *enjoy herself* very much in your new house. 她在你的新家里确实很开心。I hope you'll *enjoy yourselves* here. 我希望你们在这儿玩得痛快。Everybody seemed to be *enjoying himself* there. 每个人好像在那儿玩得都很高兴。

NOTE 在使用本短语时要注意正确调整反身代词 oneself 的人称和数的形式，以保持与主语的一致。

enroll in *vt.* (cause to) join (an organization or group)(使)参加，加入：She decided to *enroll in* the history course at the local evening school. 她决定参加当地夜校的历史课程的学习。He *enrolled* (himself) *in* the army. 他参军了。Mary *enrolled* her brother *in* a training programme for engineers. 玛丽让她的弟弟参加了工程师的培训项目。The total number of the students from Taiwan *enrolled in* 110 colleges and universities in China's mainland areas last year reached 6,200. 去年，在中国大陆 110 所高校就学的台湾学生总数达到了6 200人。

enter into *vt.* (正式用语，常用一般时态) ❶start to become involved in (an official discussion, formal activity, or relationship with someone) 开始从事(正式磋商或活动，或与他人的关系)：The two heads of state *entered into* a long talk. 两位国家元首开始了长时间的会谈。The company *entered into* motion picture production in 1954. 这家公司于1954 年就开始摄制影片了。Shortly after graduation from college, he *entered into* business. 大学毕业后不久，他就从商。❷(正式用语) agree to be part of (an official agreement or contract) 同意签署(正式协议或合同)：Before you *enter into* an agreement of this type, you should read the contract very carefully. 在同意签署这类合同之前，你应该非常仔细地阅读它一下。Intermediary services that employ rural women and send them to work as housemaids have to buy insurance for the employees before *entering into* employment contracts. 聘用农村妇女做保姆工作的中介机构必须为其聘用人员购买保险后才能签署用工合同。❸(正式用语，无被动语态形式，常用一般时态) become a component of (a situation) 成为(……的)一部分：Oxygen *enters into* many compound bodies. 氧是许多化合物的组成部分。Financial matters *entered into* the discussion. 财务问题成了讨论的一个内容。❹(正式用语，无被动语态形式，常用一般时态) have any important part in or influence on 参与；影响：The money doesn't *enter into* it; it's the principle of the thing that I object to. 钱在这件事上无关紧要，我所反对的是涉及这件事的原则。❺write (information) into (a computer), by typing it on a keyboard 把(信息)输入(计算机)：To *enter* the data *into* the computer, you type it in then press the "Enter" key. 要把数据输入计算机，你先要在键盘上把它打出来，然后按"输入"键。Postal codes will be *entered into* the statisticians' computers. 邮政编码将被输入到统计学家的电脑中。

NOTE 不要将本短语理解为"进入某具体空间"之意。因此,不能说: * I saw him *entering into* the house. (应将 into 删掉)。

enter on/upon *vt.* 【不可分性动词短语】(正式用语,用一般时态) ❶ begin (something, especially a job, a period of official duty, etc.) or begin to take part in (something)开始(某项工作或履行某一职责的任期等),参与: They *entered on* their work with great enthusiasm. 他们满怀热情地开始了工作。He has just *entered upon* a business career. 他刚刚开始从商。The new manager *entered upon* his duties in the autumn. 那位新经理是秋天开始任职的。❷begin to have or enjoy; take possession of (something)开始拥有,享有: He *entered on* his inheritance when he was 21. 他在 21 岁时便获得了遗产。You will be allowed to *enter upon* this fortune when you come of age. 当你到了法定年龄时就可以享有这笔财产了。

entitle to *vt.* 【可分性动词短语】(常用被动语态形式,用一般时态) give (someone) the right to do (something) or have (something)把(做某事或拥有某物的)权利赋予(某人): This ticket *entitles* you *to* a free seat at the concert. 凭此票你可以免费听音乐会。Children are not only the treasured offspring of their parents, but also the priceless wealth of a country, and they are *entitled to* protection and the right to grow up healthily. 儿童不仅是他们父母的宝贝后代,也是国家的无价之宝。他们有权受到保护,也有权健康地成长。As of 2017, every employee in this company became *entitled to* an annual paid leave from 24 to 30 days. 从 2017 年起,本公司每个职员都有权享受每年的 24 到 30 天的带薪休假。

NOTE 本短语中的 to 是介词,其后接名词。

entrust to *vt.* 【可分性动词短语】give (someone) the responsibility for (someone or an important job)把(某人或某项重要工作)托付给: You may *entrust* your son *to* your friend. 你可以把你的儿子托付给你的朋友照料。He didn't look like the sort of man you should *entrust* your luggage *to*. 他看上去不像那种你应该把行李托付给他的人。We cannot *entrust* the country's telecommunications *to* unqualified people. 我们不能把国家的电信部门交给不称职的人管理。

NOTE 本短语中的 entrust 是及物性动词,经常以被动语态的形式出现,后接动词不定式(短语)。例如:

> They can be *entrusted* to solve the problem.
>
> 可以委托他们去解决那个问题。

envious of *adj.* showing or expressing envy about (something or someone) because you want very much to do something that someone else does or have something that they have 羡慕的: Other girls are *envious of* her beauty. 其他女孩们都羡慕她的美貌。He was *envious of* the local boys who could see her every day. 他很羡慕当地的男孩子每天都能见到她。Mary has got a very nice job — I'm very *envious of* her new job. 玛丽得到了一份很好的工作——我太羡慕她的新工作了。

NOTE 本短语与 jealous of 意义相近,用法相同。两者的区别在于:本短语含褒义,指因"羡慕"而极力想做到或同样拥有;而 jealous of 则含贬义,指的是"嫉妒"他人的优点或拥有的物品等令人不快的情绪。

equal to *adj.* ❶ (of one thing) being the

same as (the other thing) in value, amount or number, or size, etc. (在价值、数量或大小等方面)相等的,等于的,相当于……的:They receive an income *equal to* the value of the goods they produce. 他们所得的收入与他们所生产的产品的价值相等。Prices reach a balance at the level at which quantity demanded is *equal to* quantity supplied. 物价应在供求量相等的水平上达到平衡。❷(正式用语) having the ability and determination needed for doing (something difficult) 有能力的,有决心做(某事)的;胜任的:I thought that he would be *equal to* the task of running a large department. 我曾认为他有能力担起管理一个大部门的重任。Being ill, I am not *equal to* the journey. 我因病不能旅行了。She was not *equal to* receiving guests. 她不能胜任做接待客人的工作。❸able to meet or deal with whatever happens 能应付的,能处理的:She had to give a speech to 3,000 people, but she proved quite *equal to* the situation. 她得给 3 000 人做演说,而事实证明她完全能应付这种场面。

NOTE 1. 本短语中的 to 是介词,而不是动词不定式符号,因此后面不能接原型动词。

2. 本短语中的 equal 用作形容词时,与介词 to 连用,构成形容词性短语,在句中作表语或后置定语。equal 还可以用作及物性动词,表示"等于"或"与……相等"之意,它本身就等于 be equal to。因此,其后无需再加 to 或其他介词便可直接带宾语。所以,这样说是错误的:* This year's sales figures up until October equal to the figures for the whole of last year. (要去掉 to。或者在 equal to 前加 are,此时 equal 已成为形容词)

equip with *vt.* (常用被动语态形式) provide (usually someone) with (things) 以……装备,配备:Drug dealers in Peru are *equipped with* satellite communicating facilities, and even have airports for landing small-sized aircraft hidden in the jungle. 秘鲁的毒品贩子都装备有卫星通信设备,甚至在丛林中还藏有能降落小型飞机的机场。Somali pirates use speedboats *equipped with* satellite phones and global positioning system equipment. 索马里海盗使用配有卫星电话和全球定位系统设备的快艇。Did they *equip* the boys *with* strong boots? 他们有没有给男孩子们配备结实的靴子?

escape from *vt.* 【不可分性动词短语】get free from (someone or something) 从……逃出,逸出:Two criminals *escaped from* the prison last night. 有两名囚犯昨天夜里从监狱里逃跑了。A tiger at the San Francisco Zoo was shot and killed after it *escaped from* its cage and killed one visitor and injured two others. 旧金山动物园的一只老虎在逃出牢笼,咬死 1 名游客,咬伤 2 人之后被击毙。Poisonous gas is *escaping from* the pipes. 有毒气体正在从管子往外泄漏。

et cetera *adv.* (在实际使用中,通常用其缩略形式 etc.) (used in writing after a list to show that there are many other similar things or people that you could have added) and the rest; and others of the same kind 等等:The children use computers in many courses, including math, science, language study, *et cetera*. 孩子们在包括数学、科学、语言等很多课程中都使用计算机。

NOTE 1. 本短语来自拉丁语,但在当代英语中使用相当频繁,尤其在书面英语中。在使用本短语时要注意以下几点:

(1)本短语用来列举逻辑上相关联的事

物,而不能是人。

(2)本短语不能用在 and 之后, 因为短语中的 et 本身在拉丁语中就是“and”之意。因此,这样说是错误的: * Put your things into a bag, box, and *etc.*

(3)本短语一般不用在 for example(或 eg), et al, such as 和 and so on 之后。

(4)在一般情况下,不宜在同句中重复使用本短语。

2. 本短语的同义短语是 and so on, and so forth, and the like 和 and what not。

3. 本短语可转化为复合词 etcetera, 意为“等等”。例如:

> His report was full of *etceteras.*
> 他的报告中有太多的“等等”。

even if/though *conj.* despite the fact or belief that; no matter whether; (al) though 即使,尽管: *Even if* no one in your family has diabetes, you can still get it. Genes don't determine whether you'll get diabetes or not. 即使在你的家人中没有糖尿病患者,可你仍然会得上此病。遗传因子并不是你是否会得糖尿病的决定因素。The Chinese football fans remained loyal to the national team *even though* they lost almost every game. 中国的足球迷们仍然忠实地支持国家队,尽管他们几乎屡战屡败。

NOTE 1. 本短语与引导让步状语从句的连词 though, although 一样,使用时其主句不能用 but,从句中亦不用将来时态。

2. 根据表达需要,本短语引导的从句中的谓语动词可用虚拟语气形式。例如:

> Science requires the effort of a lifetime and *even if* you *had* two lives to give it, it would still not be enough.
> 科学要求毕生的精力,即使你有两倍的寿命,也还是不够的。

3. even if 比 even though 常用,而 even though 比 even if 语气更强。例如,在这样的句子中应选用 even though:

> *Even though* your father comes in person, I will not lend him my car.
> 即使你爸爸亲自来,我也不会把车借给他。

even less ⇨ **still less**

even now *adv.* (used for saying it is surprising that something still continues) in spite of what has or had happened 即使现在: *Even now*, after all these years, he cannot mention her name without crying. 即使现在,过了这么多年,他还是一提起她的名字就哭。I've shown her the photograph but *even now* she won't believe me. 我已给她看了照片,可是她现在还是不肯相信我。

even so *adv.* (used for introducing a statement that seems surprising after what you said before) though that is true; in spite of that 虽然这样,即使如此: There are some spelling mistakes; *even so*, it is quite a good essay. 虽然有一些拼写错误,但它仍不失为一篇相当不错的文章。Crashes are rare, but *even so*, there should be stricter safety regulations. 坠毁事件极少发生,即使如此也应有严格的安全规则。

even then *adv.* (used for saying that something is surprising after what has happened) in spite of what has or had happened 即使那样: I explained everything, but *even then* she didn't understand. 我把一切都作了解释,即使那样她还是不明白。

ever since Ⅰ *conj.* during the whole period of time since something happened 自从: *Ever since* I was born, I have lived here. 我从出生起就住在这儿。He's had a drink problem *ever since* his wife left him. 自从他

妻子离他而去,他就有了酗酒的毛病。

Ⅱ *adv.* from that time onwards 自那以后,从那时以来: Castro, who handed over power to his younger brother Raul Castro on July 31, 2007, has rarely been seen in public *ever since*. 卡斯特罗在 2007 年 7 月 31 日把权力移交给他的弟弟。从那时起,他就很少公开露面了。I first met Harry at high school and we've been good friends *ever since*. 我与哈里最初在中学时相识以来,我们一直是好朋友。

NOTE **1.** 当本短语用作连词性短语时,主句一般用现在完成时,引出的从句谓语动词用过去时。

2. 当本短语用作副词性短语时,常用于完成时的句子中,并常置于句尾。

ever so often ⇨ **every so often**

every now and again *adv.* sometimes but not often; occasionally 时时,有时,偶尔: *Every now and again* the old lady wiped her eyes with a handkerchief. 老妇人不时地用手帕擦着眼睛。*Every now and again* an event occurs that changes public attitudes. 偶尔发生的某一事件就会改变公众的态度。

NOTE **1.** 本短语的另外一种表达形式是 every now and then。

2. 本短语的同义短语是 at times, every so often, from time to time, now and again, now and then 和 once in a while。这些短语之间的区别见 at times。

every other *adj.* ❶(of things which can be counted) every second one in a series 每隔一……的: One train pulls in *every other* minute. 每隔一分钟就有一列火车进站。For business I go to the bank *every other* day. 为办业务,我每隔一天去一次银行。Members of the choir meet *every other* Friday and perform without pay. 合唱团的成员每隔一个周五就会齐聚献唱,分文不取。Don't write on every line; write on *every other* line. 不要每行都写,要隔一行写。❷ all the other 所有其他的: *Every other* girl except me is wearing jeans. 除我以外,所有其他女孩都穿着牛仔裤。Everything in the world, no matter how different it may seem from *every other* thing, is made partly of electrons. 世界上的一切物体,无论他看上去与其他物体有多么不同,总是部分地由电子构成。

NOTE **1.** 本短语在句中用作定语,后面所接或修饰的名词为单数名词。

2. 不要将本短语与 each other 混淆,两者的意义和用法不同。

every so often *adv.* (常用于句首或句尾) occasionally; sometimes, but not frequently 时常,不时地: My parents come to visit us *every so often*. 我父母时常来看我们。During the lecture, *every so often* someone would go out. 讲座期间,不时地有人退场。*Every so often* he would stop work and look towards the gate. 他不时地把活儿停下来朝大门口望去。

NOTE **1.** 不要将本短语与 ever so often 混淆。ever so often 也是副词短语,意为"经常地""多次地",常用于英国、爱尔兰英语中。例如:

> *Ever so often* I get a slight pain on the left part of my chest.
> 我的左胸部经常隐隐作痛。

2. 本短语的同义短语是: at times, every now and then, from time to time, now and again, now and then 和(every) once in a while。

every time Ⅰ *conj.* (非正式用语) whenever (something happens); at each occasion that

每当(某事发生时): The nervous server fled from a table of foreigners *every time* she was asked a question. 一位精神紧张的服务员每当被问到什么问题时,她就会从外国人的餐桌旁溜走。"*Every time* I see the security guards I feel nervous," says a resident of this city. "每当看到那些保安人员,我就感到紧张。" 该城的一名居民说道。

Ⅱ *adv.* always 总是: He beats me in table tennis *every time*. 他和我打乒乓球总是赢。Unfortunately, our national football team loses every time. 不幸的是,我们的国家足球队每战必败。

NOTE 1. 当本短语作"每当"解时,本身就是连词性短语,等同于连词 when 或 whenever。因此,在 every time 后不能再用连词 when 或 whenever。

2. 本短语的同义短语是 each time。

3. 不要将本短语与 one time 混淆,两者的意义和用法不同。

except for *prep.* ❶(used for introducing the only thing, person, or fact that is not included in your main statement) apart from; other than 除……之外: Everything was perfect *except for* the weather. 除了天气不好外,其他一切都很完美。*Except for* one old lady, the bus was empty. 除了有一位老妇人外,这辆公共汽车上空无一人。I knew nothing about him *except for* the fact that he lives next door. 我除了知道他住在隔壁外,对他一无所知。❷were it not for 如果不是,若非: *Except for* you, I would pass the exam. 如果不是你,我就会通过考试。I would go and attend your lecture *except for* my cold. 要不是感冒,我就会去听你的课。

NOTE 1. 当本短语作"除……之外"解时,与介词 except 意义相同,均指在整体中除去某一点,引述一个相反的原因或细节,部分地修正句子的主要意思。except 表示从所提到的人或事物中除去,即从整体中除去一部分,一般用来排除同类的事物或行为。而 except for 表示对整体主要部分的肯定和对局部的否定,其后的宾语则与前面(或后面)的句子里所涉及的内容并非同类事物。请比较下面两个句子:

We have an English lesson every day *except* Sunday. (表示同类事物之间的关系)

Your composition is good *except for* some spelling mistakes. (表示非同类事物之间的关系)

虽然两者有时也可互换使用,但要注意以下两点:

(1) 在一般情况下,except for 可置于句首,而 except 则不可。例如: Everyone is here *except* Mary.

本句可改为: *Except for* Mary everyone is here.

(2) 一般说来,在否定句中用 except,肯定句式可以用 except for 来替换。例如: This article has no blunders *except* a few spelling mistakes.

本句可改为: This article is well written *except for* a few blunders.

2. 当本短语作"除……之外"解时,同义短语是 with the exception of。

exchange with *vt.* 【可分性动词短语】❶take (something) in return for something else, with (someone) 以(某物)与(某人)交换(某物): For our holiday, we *exchanged* houses *with* a friend who lives in the country. 为了度假,我们和一位住在乡村的朋友换了房子住。❷ share (words, ideas, etc.) with (someone), as in a conversation 与(某人)交流(语言);交换

(看法或意见等): I've lived here for 2 years, and still haven't *exchanged* more than a few words *with* my neighbors. 我已在这儿住了两年,但还没和邻居有过多少语言交流。During her visit in China, US Secretary of State Hillary Clinton *exchanged* views *with* Chinese leaders on bilateral relations and issues of common concern. 美国国务卿希拉里·克林顿在中国访问期间,与中国领导人就双边关系以及共同关心的问题交换了意见。

E

excuse oneself *vi.* politely ask for permission to leave a place 请求离开: He had another meeting to attend, so he *excused himself* and left. 由于他还有个会要参加,所以就请求离开了。She *excused herself* from the table and went back to work. 她起身告辞,离开桌子去工作了。

exempt from *vt.* 【可分性动词短语】(常用一般时态) free (someone) from (a duty or doing something)免除,豁免: He is *exempted from* military service because of bad health. 他因身体不好而被免除兵役。The regulation *exempted* excellent students *from* taking some of the examinations. 该规定使优秀学生免于参加某些科目的考试。

exercise over *vt.* 【可分性动词短语】(正式用语) use (your power, rights, or influence) to control (someone or something)运用(权力或影响力)控制……: China started to *exercise* sovereignty *over* Macao on December 20, 1999. 中国于1999年12月20日开始对澳门行使主权。We have persisted in *exercising* strict control *over* nuclear exports and nuclear materials. 我们一贯坚持在核出口与核物质方面实施严格的控制。Can't you *exercise* your influence *over* the boy to get him to behave better? 你就不能给这个男孩子施加点影响使他举止表现好一些?

exist on *vt.* 【不可分性动词短语】(of a person) manage to live by means of (something), especially under difficult conditions (指人)(尤指在困难的条件下)靠……活着: It was impossible for them to *exist on* such a small income. 他们靠这么一点儿收入生活是不可能的。They are paid hardly enough to *exist on*. 他们收入微薄,几乎无法维持生活。The mother of my brother's wife *exists* only *on* bread and fruit. 我弟媳的母亲仅靠吃面包和水果活着。

expand on/upon *vt.* 【不可分性动词短语】 talk or write more about (something), adding more details or information 对……详加描述: I don't quite follow your reasoning. Can you *expand on* it? 我不大理解你的推论。你能详细地加以说明吗? The child wanted his grandmother to *expand on* what she had said about the ancient castle. 那孩子非让他祖母再详细点讲述那座古堡的事。I refuse to *expand* any further *on* my earlier statement. 我拒绝进一步详述我先前所述之言。

expect from/of *vt.* 【可分性动词短语】 hope or think it likely that (someone or something, usually good) will be or do (something)对……寄予期望;指望(某人)做(某事): She realized now she *expected* too much *of* Helen. 她现在认识到,她对海伦寄予太多的期望了。There is no need to give the money; I *don't expect* it *from* you. 你不必给我钱，我不指望你给我钱。Don't *expect* too much *of* his idea. 别对他的主意期望过高。

expel from *vt.*【可分性动词短语】❶send (someone) away by force, especially from a country 把（某人）驱逐出境：The diplomat was *expelled from* the country for spying on their naval bases. 这名外交官因刺探该国海军基地的情报而被驱逐出境。❷（常用被动语态形式）make (someone) leave (a place or an organization), usually with dishonor 把（某人）从（某处或某一组织中）开除：No one knew exactly why they had *expelled* the boy *from* the school. 没有人确切地知道他们为什么把那名男孩开除出校。The most popular Chinese diving prince was *expelled from* the national team on Wednesday for failing to concentrate on training. 星期三，中国最受欢迎的跳水王子因没有专心于训练而被开除出国家队。

experiment on/upon *vt.*【不可分性动词短语】make tests on (a person or animal) in order to make discoveries 在……身上做试验：Why are you *experimenting on* the students in this particular class? 你为什么非用这个班的学生做试验呢？Some people feel *experimenting on* animals for medical research is not morally acceptable. 有些人认为，为了医学研究而用动物做实验从道德上来讲是不可接受的。

NOTE 本短语中的 upon 用法比 on 正式，但不及 on 常用。

experiment with *vt.*【不可分性动词短语】use (usually something) in performing a test to find out what happens to someone or something in particular conditions 用……做试验：They *experimented with* the new materials. 他们用新材料做实验。Many areas in China's northeast have already started to *experiment with* new forms of ownership. 中国东北部的许多地区都已开始试行新的所有制形式。

expert at/in/on *adj.* having a particular skill or knowing a lot about (something or doing something) 善于，擅长于：Over the years we've become quite *expert at* dealing with these sorts of problems. 几年来，我们已很善于处理这类问题了。The British royal family are still less than *expert in* handling the media. 英国的王室成员仍不太善于应付媒体。He's said to be *expert in* English speech. 据说他专长于英语演讲。She's *expert on* teaching small children. 她擅长于儿童教育。

NOTE 本短语中的 expert 是形容词，本身就表示“专家的，内行的”之意。当 expert 用作名词时，也可以与介词 at, in 和 on 短语连用，所表达的意义与形容词短语的相同。例如：

> She's an *expert* at teaching small children.
> 她在教小孩这方面很内行。
> Robert is an *expert* in radio communications.
> 罗伯特是无线电通信的专家。
> Our manager is an *expert* on trade in that area.
> 我们的经理是那一地区的贸易专家。

explain away *vt.*【可分性动词短语】（常用一般时态）tell someone about

something in a way that makes him or her think it is unimportant, so that they do not ask questions about it 为……辩解；把……搪塞过去：She made up stories to *explain away* the missing money. 他编造谎言为那笔失踪的款项辩解。I had asked about the blood on my husband's clothing but he *explained* it *away*. 我问到我丈夫衣服上怎么有血迹，他却将其搪塞了过去。

NOTE 当本短语的宾语为代词时，该代词须置于本短语的动词和副词中间。

expose to *vt.* 【可分性动词短语】❶(常用被动语态形式) leave (something or someone) open to the effect of (something); fail to protect (someone or something) from (something harmful or dangerous) 把……暴露于：Why do we still sunbathe when we know the dangers of *exposing* our skin *to* the sun for a long time? 我们都知道皮肤长时间在太阳下曝晒是危险的，但我们为什么还要沐日光浴呢？The soldiers in the open field were *exposed to* the enemy's gunfire. 在旷野中的士兵们暴露在敌人的炮火之下。❷ make known (a secretly guilty person or action) to (someone) usually publicly (常指公开地)揭露(人或罪行)：I threatened to *expose* his shameful crime *to* the police. 我威胁要向警方揭发他可耻的罪行。

extend to *vt.* ❶(用一般时态)(cause to) reach (something) 伸展，延长：The rainy season *extends* from about the middle of June *to* about the middle of July. 雨季从6月中旬一直延续到7月中旬。The underground railway is being *extended to* the airport. 地下铁道正在被延伸到机场。❷(正式用语，常用一般时态) offer (something such as a welcome, thanks, or sympathy) to (someone) 向(某人)表示(欢迎、感谢或同情等)：I would like to *extend* a warm welcome *to* our guests. 我向我们的客人表示热烈的欢迎。May I *extend* my congratulations *to* the winners? 我谨向获奖者表示祝贺。I am writing to *extend* my deepest sympathies *to* you and your family. 我写信向你和你的家属表示深切的同情。We *extend* our apologies *to* the host for the inconvenience caused. 我们因给他造成的不便而向主人表达了歉意。❸ affect or include (someone or something) 影响；包括；适用于：This law *extends to* children under the age of 14. 这条法律也适用于14岁以下的儿童。The regulations do not *extend to* foreign visitors. 这些规定不适用于外国参观者。

F f

face to face *adv.* (常与 with 连用)in or into the direct presence 面对面地: She once met one of her online friends *face to face.* 她曾经面对面地见过她的一位网友。Turning a corner, he found himself *face to face* with a policeman. 拐了个弯，他与一名警察碰了个正着。The church and the school stand *face to face* across the street. 教堂和学校面对面地矗立在街道的两侧。

NOTE 本短语可转化为复合词 face-to-face，意为“面对面的”。

face up to *vt.* 【不可分性动词短语】be brave enough to accept and try to deal with (something difficult or unpleasant) 敢于承担;勇于面对: You have grown up now and must learn to *face up to* your responsibilities. 你现在已经长大，必须学会承担责任了。*Face up to* the fact that you are no longer young. 你要面对这样一个事实:你已经不年轻了。He was the only one who *faced up to* the problem. 他是唯一能勇于面对这一难题的人。

face with *vt.* 【可分性动词短语】(常用被动语态形式) ❶(常用一般时态) (cause to) confront or meet (something bad or difficult)(使)面对，面临: *Faced with* various challenges at home and abroad, he pledged that his administration would take “bold and swift” action to bring the country out of crisis. 面对国内外的各种挑战，他发誓，他的政府将采取“大胆而迅速”的行动使国家摆脱危机。The police *faced* the suspect *with* a simple choice: he could either give the names of his companions, or go to prison. 警察让嫌疑人作出一个简单的选择:要么说出同伙的名字，要么进监狱。❷cover or partly cover (especially the front part of something) with (a different material) (用不同的材料)镶上(……的正面): The front of the house was *faced with* stone. 那座房子的正面用石头镶面。The bathroom is *faced with* tile. 浴室镶着瓷砖。

NOTE 当本短语作“面对，面临”解时，与 confront with 意义和用法相同，但本短语较为常用。

fade away *vi.* ❶ gradually become weaker; die away or disappear slowly 逐渐减弱，渐渐消失: The sound of the motorboat *faded away* in the distance. 汽船的声音在远处逐渐减弱了。The color of the cloth will *fade away* little by little. 这布的颜色会一点一点地褪掉。The shapes *faded away* into the night. 这些景色的轮廓逐渐消失在夜幕中。Our hopes and expectations *faded away* with time. 随着时间的过去，我们的希望和期待渐灭了。❷lose one’s strength, and become ill or die 失去力量;生病;死去: The old man *faded away* and died.

那老人身体逐渐衰弱而死去了。If you don't start eating properly you're going to *fade away*. 如果你还不好好吃饭,就会生病。

NOTE 本短语可转化为复合词 fade-away,意为“逐渐消失”。

faithful to *adj.* ❶ continuing to support (someone) or be his friend, even in a difficult situation 忠实于(某人)的: The dog remained *faithful to* his master. 这条狗仍然忠实于它的主人。❷ continuing to do (something such as a duty) or believe (something such as a cause or belief), even in a difficult situation 忠于职守的;忠诚于(某一事业或信仰)的: Facts have proved that the Chinese people are *faithful to* their international duties. 事实证明中国人民忠于自己的国际主义义务。Many people, *faithful to* their cause, shed their last drop of blood. 许多忠诚事业的人,流尽了最后一滴血。He remained *faithful to* his beliefs. 他仍然忠诚于其信仰。❸ not having sex with anyone other than one's partner 忠实于(配偶)的,忠贞的: Kent has always been *faithful to* his wife. 肯特一直忠实于他的妻子。His wife was *faithful to* him throughout his years in prison. 在他坐牢的那几年里,他妻子一直守贞于他。

NOTE 本短语的同义短语是 loyal to。

fall apart *vi.* ❶ (常用一般时态) break into pieces because of being old or badly made 破碎,分裂: I've read this book so often it's *falling apart*. 这本书我总看,它都破散了。My bicycle is *falling apart*; it was bought only months ago! 我的自行车快散架了。它是我几个月前才买的! The box *fell apart* when I tried to pick it up. 当我试图把这个箱子搬起来时,它却四分五裂了。❷ have so many problems that it is no longer possible to exist or function 不复存在,破裂: The deal *fell apart* when we failed to agree on a price. 我们没能就价格达成一致,这笔买卖便告吹了。Their marriage finally *fell apart* after about ten years. 大约 10 年后,他们的婚姻终于破裂了。❸ (非正式用语) suffer serious emotional problems or a nervous breakdown 精神崩溃: He *fell apart* after his only son died. 他的独生儿子死后,他精神崩溃了。

fall asleep *vi.* start sleeping; go into a state of sleep 睡着,入睡: Do you find it hard to *fall asleep*? These tips can help you *fall asleep* sooner and stay asleep longer. 你感到睡眠困难吗?这些方法可以帮助你睡得快,睡得久。She was so tired she *fell asleep* sitting in her chair. 她太累了,竟坐在椅子上睡着了。

NOTE 本短语与 go to sleep 的意义和用法相同,两者可互换使用。

fall away *vi.* ❶ (of something) break off from the thing it was fixed to and drop to the ground 脱落: Plaster was *falling away* from the walls. 灰泥一直从墙上脱落。❷ become smaller or lower in amount, level, value, etc. 减少,减弱: Sales have *fallen away* sharply in recent months. 近几个月的销售额骤减。The wind *fell away* and all was calm. 风势减弱,一切都平静了下来。❸ (用一般时态,与 to 连用) (of land) slope down suddenly from a particular point (指地势)倾斜: On the other side of the mountain, the land *falls away* to the east. 在山的另一侧,地势向东倾斜。❹ (英国英语用法,正式用语,常用一般时态) (of something such as a sound or feeling) become weaker and disappear (指声音或

感觉等)变弱,消失: All our doubts *fell away*. 我们的疑虑都消除了。

NOTE 当本短语作"减少,减弱"解时,同义短语是 fall off。

fall back *vi.* ❶(用一般时态,主语常为群体名词)move backwards a short distance away from someone or something 向后退去: The crowd around the wounded boy *fell back* when the doctor arrived . 当医生到达时,围在受伤男孩身边的人群才向后退去。The sea waves *fell back*. 海浪退去了。❷(用一般时态,主语常为群体名词)(of an army)retreat during a battle or war (军队)退却: Badly beaten, the invading forces *fell back* in disorder. 侵略军受到重创,狼狈溃退了。❸become smaller or lower in amount, level, value, etc. 缩小,下降,减低:Profits *fell back* slightly this month. 这个月的利润略有下降。

NOTE 本短语可转化为复合词 fall-back,意为"退却"。

fall back on *vt.* 【不可分性动词短语】(无被动语态形式,常用一般时态) ❶begin to use (something held in reserve)动用(储存之物):I had to *fall back on* my savings when I was unemployed. 失业后,我不得不动用我的储蓄金。We had to *fall back on* our emergency generator. 我们不得不动用了应急发电机。❷rely on (something) or turn to (someone) for help when dealing with a difficult situation, especially after other methods have failed 依靠(某物);求助于(某人):If the first plan fails, we can *fall back on* the second. 如果第一个计划失败了,我们还可以依靠第二个计划。If I can't find a job as a teacher, I can *fall back upon* my skill as a printer. 如果我无法找到一份教师的工作,我还可以利用我的印刷技术维持生计。You may *fall back on* your teachers when you have some trouble in your studies. 在学习遇到困难时,你可以求助于你的老师。

NOTE 本短语常用在情态动词后和不定式中。

fall behind *v.* ❶(常用一般时态)move more slowly than other people so that you are behind them (走或跑)落在(……的)后面:After five miles Tom was tired and started to *fall behind*. 走了 5 英里后,汤姆就累了,开始落后了。The horse *fell behind* halfway through the race. 这匹马在赛程的一半时就落在了后面。On the long walk, the small child *fell behind* her brothers. 这次走远路,这小孩儿落在了她哥哥们的后面。❷make less progress or be less successful (than other people who are doing a similar job or activity) 落后,落在……之后: My daughter was ill and is *falling behind* with her school work. 我女儿因病而在功课上落后了。Your work has *fallen behind* that of the other students. 你的学习已落在了其他同学的后面。We cannot afford to *fall behind* our competitors in using new technology. 我们再也不能在使用新技术方面落在竞争对手的后面了。

NOTE 1. 当本短语用作及物性动词短语时,无被动语态形式。

2. 本短语的同义短语是 lag behind;反义短语是 catch up (with)。

fall behind with/in *vt.* 【不可分性动词短语】(无被动语态形式) fail to do (something) or pay (something) at the time that you should 不能按时做(某事);逾期不交;拖欠(租金等): I was ill for a week and *fell behind with/in* my studies; I must try to catch up. 我病了一

F

个星期,学习落后了,我得设法赶上去。The company has many programs to help people who *fall behind in* their utility bills. 公司有很多项计划向那些欠交各项公用事业费用的人提供帮助。Don't *fall behind with/in* your rent, or you will be asked to leave. 不要拖欠房租,否则就"请"你走人。

NOTE fall behind in 用于美国英语中。

F

fall down *vi.* ❶move quickly down onto the ground from a higher position, or from an upright or standing position 掉下;倒下:The boy *fell down* from the bicycle and hurt his knees. 那男孩儿从自行车上掉了下来,把双膝摔伤。"The American military helicopter exploded in the air and *fell down* to the ground," the witnesses said. 目击者说:"这架美军直升机在空中爆炸,接着就坠落地面。" The old man *fell down* on the ice and couldn't get up. 老人在冰上滑倒,站不起来了。❷(常用进行时态)(of a building) be about to become a ruin (建筑物)倒塌:We got the house at a cheap price because it was almost *falling down*. 我们以便宜的价格买下了这所房子,因为它几乎就要倒塌了。❸ fail; be not successful or not good enough 失败;不够好:Their plan has *fallen down*. 他们的计划失败了。

fall down on *vt.*【不可分性动词短语】(非正式用语,无被动语态形式,用一般时态) not be good at (something) in comparison with another thing 在(某方面)不够好:I'm quite good at speaking English, but I *fall down on* the written work. 我的英语口语很好,但在书写方面不行。She was doing well on the exam until she *fell down on* the last question. 在考试中她一直答得不错,就是最后一道题答得不够好。

fall for *vt.*【不可分性动词短语】(非正式用语,无被动语态形式) ❶fall in love with (someone), especially suddenly (尤指突然)爱上(某人):He *fell for* her the moment their eyes met. 四目相对,他对她一见钟情。They met at a friend's house and *fell for* each other instantly. 他们在朋友家里相见并很快就相爱了。❷like (something or a place) as soon as you see it 喜欢上(某物或某个地方):The whole family *fell for* the new house as soon as they saw it. 全家人一看到那所新房就都喜欢上了。❸ be deceived into believing (a lie, a trick or a piece of deception) 对……误信为真,上……的当,受……的骗:She told me that she owned a large house in New York and I *fell for* it. 她告诉我说,她在纽约有一所大房子。我将其信以为真了。How could you *fall for* his story about his being the son of the governor? 你怎么能听信他说自己是州长儿子的谎言呢? She didn't *fall for* his tricks. 她没有被他的诡计所骗。

fall ill *vi.* (用一般时态) get ill 生病:In an experiment, researchers found that people with a generally sunny disposition were less likely to *fall ill*. 在一项实验中,研究人员发现,性格开朗的人生病的概率较小。The manager *fell ill* last week, and had to be taken to hospital. 经理上星期生病了,所以不得不被送进了医院。

NOTE **1.** 本短语强调"生病"的行为本身,即动作。fall 是终止性动词,均不与延续性时间状语连用。be ill 则表示"生病"的状态,具有延续性,可与延续性时间状语连用。例如:

He's *been ill* for a couple of weeks.
他已病了两个星期。

2. 本短语的另外一种表达形式是 fall sick,主要用于美国英语中。

3. 本短语的同义短语是 take ill,但两者在用法上有所不同。take ill 可用作及物性动词短语,并常用被动语态形式。

fall in *vi.* ❶(of a roof, ceiling or wall) fall to the ground; collapse (房顶、顶棚或墙壁)坍塌:The roof *fell in* hurting a lot of people. 屋顶塌落,砸伤了很多人。Part of my bedroom ceiling has *fallen in*, so I had to sleep downstairs. 我卧室的顶棚有部分塌落,所以我只好睡在楼下。The explosion caused the walls of the house to *fall in*. 爆炸使房壁倒塌。❷(of soldiers) take one's place in formation or in the ranks (士兵)集合,列队:"Company, *fall in*!" shouted the company commander. "全连集合!"连长喊道。The captain ordered his men to *fall in*. 上尉命令他的士兵列队。

NOTE 当本短语作"(士兵)集合,列队"解时,反义短语是 fall out。

fall in love with *vt.*【不可分性动词短语】start to love (someone) or like (something) very much 爱上(某人);喜欢上(某物):While in prison, it is said that Valentine *fell in love with* the daughter of his prison guard. 据说瓦伦丁是在狱中爱上了狱卒的女儿。I just couldn't help *falling in love with* that oil painting. 我不禁喜欢上了那幅油画。When I was a child, I saw the sea on TV and I *fell in love with* it at first sight. 小时候,我在电视上看到了大海。第一眼我就喜欢上了它。

NOTE 如果无需说明客体,本短语可省略为 fall in love 的形式。例如:

They *fell in love* when they were in university.
他们俩是在大学期间相爱的。

fall in with *vt.*【不可分性动词短语】(英国英语用法,非正式用语) ❶(无被动语态形式) accept or agree with (someone else's ideas, plan, way of behaving, etc.) without trying to change it 接受,赞同:I'm quite happy to *fall in with* your suggestion. 我很高兴地接受你的建议。At first my friend refused to *fall in with* the scheme we had suggested, but eventually I managed to talk him round. 开始时我的朋友不同意我们提出的计划,但我终于把他说服了。❷become friends with (someone or a group) and start seeing them a lot 与(某人或一伙人)交上朋友:Tom *fell in with* Bob, who had served time in prison. 汤姆和坐过牢的鲍勃交上了朋友。He *fell in with* a group of troublemakers. 他和一伙捣蛋的人交上了朋友。

fall into *vt.*【不可分性动词短语】❶(常用一般时态) move down into (something) by falling or being dropped 落入,掉进:The car turned over twice before *falling into* the river. 这辆小汽车翻了两翻便落入河中。Unless they leave a lamp beside that hole in the road somebody will *fall into* it. 如果他们不在马路的大坑旁放置一盏灯的话,就会有人掉进去。Stage one of the rocket *fell into* the Sea of Japan, and the remaining stages landed in the Pacific Ocean. 火箭的第一级落入日本海,第二级和第三级坠入了太平洋。He *fell into* a trap. 他落入陷阱。❷(无被动语态形式) start (something); pass into (another state), usually not by plan or purpose 开始……

F

起来;进入(另种状态): I climbed into bed and *fell into* a deep sleep. 我爬上床便大睡起来。I *fell into* conversation with someone who said he knew you. 我和一个说是认识你的人攀谈起来。China gradually *fell into* a semi-colonial and semi-feudal society after 1840 as a result of the invasion of western powers. 1840年以后,由于西方列强的入侵,中国逐渐沦为半殖民地半封建社会。❸(无被动语态形式,用一般时态) be divided into (kinds); belong to (a class)被分成(几种);属于(某一类): All changes of matter *fall into* two broad classes: physical and chemical changes. 所有的物质变化可分为两大类:物理变化和化学变化。This book *falls into* the class of children's stories. 这本书属于童话类。Most honors in Britain *fall into* three types: life peerages, knighthoods, and the Order of the British Empire. 英国的主要荣誉头衔分为三类:终身贵族、骑士和大英帝国勋章。

NOTE 本短语的第三个义项是一个典型语言现象:在英语中,某些动词性短语和某些动词一样,以主动形式表示被动意义。请看下面几个含有这类动词的句子:

> The roses *smell* sweet.
> 这些玫瑰花闻起来很香甜。
> This kind of cloth *washes* well.
> 这种布料很耐洗。
> The meat *is cooking* in the pot.
> 肉正在锅中煮着。

fall off *vt.* &*vi.* (of something) separate from (something to which it was attached) and fall towards the ground (从……)落下,脱落: This bridge is too narrow; people may *fall off*. 这桥太窄了,人们可能会掉下去。The driver had to apply all his strength and skill to control the car after the wheel *fell off*. 那司机在汽车的一个轮子脱落后不得不使出全身的力气和技艺控制住车辆。One of the buttons has *fallen off* my coat. 一个扣子从我的外衣上脱落下去。—*vi.* (of an amount, level, size, or value of something) get smaller or become fewer or less; decrease 减少,减低: The demand for this item has *fallen off*. 这种货品的需求已减少。Attendance at my lectures has *fallen off* considerably recently. 近来,听我讲课的人数锐减。Sales always *fall off* in the winter months. 在冬季的那几个月份里,销售额总是很低。

NOTE **1.** 当本短语作"减少,减低"解时,同义短语是 fall away。

2. 本短语可转化为复合词 falloff,意为"减少,下降"。

fall on/upon *vt.*【不可分性动词短语】❶(常用一般时态) descend on (usually a place)落在……上: His eyes *fell upon* me. 他的目光落在了我的身上。❷(无被动语态形式,用一般时态) happen on (a particular day or date)正当(某日)发生,适逢(某日): World AIDS Day *falls on* December 1. 世界艾滋病日是在 12 月 1 日。The 15th day of the eighth month of the Chinese lunar calendar, which was a time for the Chinese to celebrate the Mid-Autumn festival, *fell on* September 11 this year. 今年的中国农历八月十五中秋节适逢公历 9 月 11 日。❸(主要用于英国英语中,正式用语,无被动语态形式) take hold of (someone) suddenly, either to attack or to hug him or her (为了袭击或拥抱而)突然抱住(某人): The robber jumped from behind trees and *fell on* him. 强盗从树丛后窜出突然抱住了他。She was so grateful that she *fell on* him and kissed him. 她十分感激他，一下把他抱住并亲吻了他。❹(主要用于英国英语中，无被动语态形式) be the responsibility of (someone) (to do something)(责任)落在……身上：Thus the responsibility *falls* entirely *on* their shoulders. 这样，责任就全部落在了他们的肩上。Qatar's Oil Minister said in an interview that the blame for rising prices should not *fall on* petroleum producers. 卡塔尔石油部长在接受采访时说，对于油价上涨的罪责不应落在石油生产国的头上。The burden of caring for elderly parents often *falls on* women. 照顾年迈父母的负担往往都落在妇女的身上。

NOTE 本短语中的 upon 用法比 on 正式，但不及 on 常用。

fall out *v.* ❶(常用一般时态，常与 of 连用) leave something in a downward direction, by falling accidentally 偶然掉出：The boy almost *fell out* of the window; luckily his mother caught hold of him and pulled him back. 那男孩几乎从窗户跌下去，幸好他妈妈抓住了他，把他拉了回来。As he picked up the envelope, a key *fell out* (of it). 当他拾起信封时，一把钥匙(从中)掉了出来。If you do *fall out* of the boat, your lifejacket will help you to stay up until we can fish you out. 如果你从船上掉下去的话，你穿的救生衣会使你浮而不沉，到时我们就会把你打捞上来。❷(of something such as a person's hair or a tooth) separate from the body (头发或牙齿等)脱落：Her hair started to *fall out* as a result of radiation treatment. 由于放射治疗，她的头发开始脱落了。❸(英国英语用法，非正式用语，常与 over, with 连用) quarrel (with someone) because you have had a disagreement with him or her (与某人)争吵：Have you two *fallen out*? 你们俩吵架了吗？The brothers *fell out* over their inheritance. 兄弟几个为了遗产而争吵不休。Paul and Jane have *fallen out* with each other over the education of their children. 保罗和简因孩子们的教育问题而相互争吵。❹(非正式用语，用一般时态) happen; result 发生，结果是：Everything *fell out* as we had planned. 一切都是按照我们的计划发生的。There *fell out* a misunderstanding between the two friends. 两个朋友之间曾发生过误会。Let's wait and see how everything *falls out*. 让我们等一等，看事情发展的结果会怎样。It *fell out* that I could not get to the meeting place in time. 结果是我没能及时赶到会议地点。❺(用一般时态)(cause to) leave one's place in a military formation (使)(士兵)解散：After a long drill he told his men to *fall out*. 长时间的操练后，他让士兵们解散了。The officer *fell* the soldiers *out* when he finished speaking to them. 那位军官训完话后便命令士兵解散了。

NOTE 当本短语作"(使)(士兵)解散"解时，反义短语是 fall in。

fall over *v.* (无被动语态形式，常用一般时态) (of a person or object that is standing) fall accidentally, especially to the ground (指人或物体)跌倒，倒塌，(在……)跌下：If he drinks more than two glasses of wine he will *fall over*. 如果他喝酒超过两杯，就会醉倒。Be careful! Don't let the child *fall over*! 注意！别让孩子跌倒！Hurricane Katrina caused many high walls in New Orleans to *fall over*. 卡特里娜飓风使新奥尔良的许多高墙倒塌。The car *fell over* the cliff and the driver was drowned. 汽车跌下悬崖，司机溺水身亡。

NOTE 当本短语用作及物性动词短语时，无被动语态形式。

fall prey to *vt.* （正式用语）❶（of an animal） to be killed and eaten by （another animal or bird）（指动物）被（其他动物）捕食：Many small birds *fall prey to* the domestic cat. 很多小鸟都被家猫捕食。❷（of a person）to be harmed or affected by （something or someone bad）（指人）受……之害，为……所折磨：We don't want our country to *fall prey to* terrorists. 我们都不想让国家遭受恐怖主义分子危害。Police fear that old people could *fall prey to* the criminal gangs. 警方担心老年人会成为这些犯罪团伙的受害者。Left on her own, she *fell prey to* all sorts of strange fears. 每当一个人独处时，她总是为各式各样莫名的恐惧所折磨。

NOTE 1. 本短语中的名词 prey 作不可数名词使用。因此，当本短语的主语为单数形式时，prey 前也不能加不定冠词 a。

2. 本短语的动词 fall 可被 be，become 等替换，构成的短语与本短语意义和用法相同。

3. 本短语的同义短语是 fall victim to。

fall short *vi.* （用一般时态）be insufficient or inadequate; not reach an amount or standard expected 不足，缺乏；没有达到（预计的数量或标准）：The big problem is that the food supply is *falling short*. 很大的问题是食物供应不足。With the development of agriculture, raw materials for light industry do not *fall short*. 有农业的发展，轻工业就不缺原料。We *fall* far *short* in applying what we know. 我们还远远没能应用我们的知识。

fall short of *vt.* （无被动语态形式）❶（用一般时态） be insufficient of （something, such as money, time, etc.） 缺乏（钱、时间等）：We *fall short* of money at the end of the month. 我们每到月底时就缺钱花。Supply often *falls short* of demand. 经常有供不应求的现象。❷not reach （a particular level）or fail to achieve （something you were trying to do）未达到：The company's profits last year *fell* （far）*short of* our expectations. 这家公司去年的利润额（远）未达到我们的预期值。He shot an arrow, but it *fell short of* the target. 他射了一箭，但没射及靶子。

fall sick ⇨ **fall ill**

fall through *vi.* （非正式用语，用一般时态）（of something such as a deal, plan, or arrangement） fail to happen, or be successfully completed （指买卖、计划或安排等）落空，没能实现：Let's not get carried away. The deal could still *fall through*. 咱们不要过于兴奋，这笔买卖还有可能落空。They're not going to England — the whole thing has *fallen through*. 他们不打算去英格兰，全部计划都已告吹。Our irrigation scheme didn't *fall through* at last. 我们的灌溉计划总算实现了。

fall to *vt.* ❶ be lowered to 下降到：Yesterday the temperature here *fell to* its lowest point this winter. 昨天，这里的气温下降到了今年冬天的最低点。US dollar *fell to* a record low against the euro today, with the euro climbing to ＄1.56 for the first time. 今天，美元对欧元汇率跌至历史新低，欧元首次升至 1 欧元兑换 1.56 美元。The price of crude oil *fell* 44 cents *to* 99.18 US dollars a barrel after hitting a new record high of

100 dollars. 原油价格在创每桶 100 美元新高后，每桶下跌了 44 美分至 99.18 美元。❷（正式用语）become the responsibility or duty of (someone) (to do something)（责任）落在……身上：With his partner away, all the work now *fell to* him. 他的搭档走了，整个工作现在就落在了他一个人的身上。It *fell to* me to explain to the manager what happened. 向经理解释所发生的事情的责任落在了我身上。

—*vt.* & *vi.*（英国英语用法，正式用语，用一般时态）begin, especially to eat, attack, or do anything active 开始（做某事）：The meal is all ready, kids; *fell to*! 饭菜都准备好了，孩子们。开始吃吧！As soon as the work was distributed each man *fell to*. 工作一分配完，每个人就开始干了起来。They *fell to* argument. 他们辩论了起来。He *fell to* talking about the early days and his lost friends. 他开始谈论起往日的时光和他那些失去的朋友。

fall to blows ⇨ **come to blows**

fall victim to *vt.*（正式用语）suffer from; become a victim or sacrifice to 遭受，成为……的受害者（或牺牲品）：My friend *fell victim to* a traffic accident. 我的朋友遭遇了车祸。The world's leading car makers have also *fallen victim to* the global financial crisis. 世界上的主要汽车厂商也都成了全球金融危机的受害者。Gandhi, who had driven the British out of India with nonviolent disobedience, *fell victim to* a Hindu extremist. 通过非暴力抵抗手段将英国人赶出了印度的甘地却死在了一名印度教极端分子的枪口之下。

NOTE 1. 本短语中的名词 victim 指代的名词或代词是复数形式时，victim 后面也不能加-s。

2. 本短语的同义短语是 fall prey to。

familiar to *adj.* well known to or easily recognized by (someone) 为（某人）所熟悉的：The name Harry Potter is *familiar to* many readers. 哈利·波特这个名字是许多读者所熟悉的。Her account of the breakdown of her marriage was *familiar to* the psychiatrist. 她对自己婚姻破裂的叙述对精神科医生来说是司空见惯的。Conservatives only accept thing *familiar to* them and are suspicious of anything that is strange or foreign. 保守的人只接受他们所熟的事物，而对任何外来的或陌生的东西都持怀疑态度。

NOTE 本短语与 familiar with 均有"熟悉"之意，但两者在用法上有不同之处：familiar to 的主语一般是事物，宾语必须是人；而 familiar with 的主语必须是人，宾语一般是事物。例如：

> The name seems *familiar to* me.
> I seem *familiar with* the name.
> 这个名字我好像很熟。

familiar with *adj.* ❶ having a good knowledge of (something) 熟悉，通晓：Are you *familiar with* the software system they use? 你熟悉他们使用的软件系统吗？The company would pay special bonuses to some of its key employees, said people *familiar with* the matter. 一些知情人士说，该公司将向一些重要雇员发放特别奖金。My father is *familiar with* French and Esperanto in addition to English. 我父亲除了英语外，还通晓法语和世界语。Are you *familiar with* changing a flat tire? 你知道怎么换漏了气的车胎吗？❷（正式用语）too friendly with (someone) 对（某人）过分亲密的，亲昵的：You are much too *familiar with* my wife, young man!

F

年轻人,你对我妻子过于亲密了吧!

NOTE 不要将本短语误用为"很熟悉(或了解)某人"。如果要表达"很熟悉(或了解)某人",应该说:know someone quite well。

famous for *adj*. (褒义用法) well known for (a particular quality or ability), and usually admired by many people 因……而著名: As well as being the birthplace of the Chinese leader Mao Zedong, Shaoshan is also *famous for* its natural beauty and scenery. 韶山除了是中国领导人毛泽东的诞生地外,还以其自然美景而著称。Zhang Yimou, who is *famous* around the world *for* his films, is the chief director for both the opening and closing ceremonies of the Beijing Olympic Games. 因其电影而闻名于世界的张艺谋是北京奥运会开幕式和闭幕式的总导演。The Victoria Harbor of Hong Kong, *famous for* its night scenery, will become more attractive with dazzling lights as the Christmas, New Year and traditional Chinese Spring Festival are coming. 香港的维多利亚港以其夜景著称。在圣诞节、新年和传统的春节来临之际,令人眼花缭乱的灯光就更加吸引人。

NOTE 1. 本短语的比较级形式是 more famous for, 最高级形式是 most famous for。

2. 本短语的同义短语是 known for 和 noted for; 反义短语是 infamous for 和 notorious for。

far and away *adv*. (used for comparing something or someone with others of the same kind to emphasize how great the difference is between them) by a large degree; greatly 大大地, 很, 极: This design is *far and away* better than that one. 这个设计比那个好得多。At the moment, he is *far and away* the best table tennis player in the country. 他目前是国内最优秀的乒乓球运动员。This hotel is *far and away* the worst hotel we have ever stayed in and I would never recommend anyone to stay here. 这家旅馆是我们所住过的最差旅馆,我绝不会建议任何人来这里住。

NOTE 1. 本短语用于比较两个同类的人或物,以强调两者之间的不同程度。本短语后接形容词的比较级或最高级形式。

2. 本短语与 by far 意义和用法相同,两者可互换使用。

far and near Ⅰ *n*. (用于介词 from 之后) a very wide area; everywhere 四面八方,到处: Children came from *far and near* to see the Christmas display. 孩子们从四面八方赶来观看圣诞节表演。

Ⅱ *adv*. over great areas or distances; everywhere 从四面八方,到处: The news spread *far and near*. 这消息四处传播。They searched for the child *far and near*. 他们到处寻找孩子。

NOTE 1. 本短语的另外一种表达形式是 near and far,本短语更为常用。

2. 本短语与 far and wide 意义和用法相同,两者可互换使用。

far and wide Ⅰ *n*. (用于介词 from 之后) far places and near places; everywhere 远近,到处: Soon after the earthquake, volunteers came from *far and wide*. 地震发生后不久,志愿者便从四面八方赶来。

Ⅱ *adv*. (正式用语) over a large number of places; nearly everywhere 各地,到处: His heroic deeds are well known *far and wide*. 他的英雄事迹远近皆知。The movie company looked *far and wide* for a boy to play the hero in the new movie.

电影公司到处寻找一个男孩在一部新片中扮演主角。

NOTE 当本短语用作副词性短语时,一般置于动词之后。

far from Ⅰ *prep.* a long way off; remote from 远离: The house isn't big enough for us, and furthermore, it's too *far from* the town. 这栋房子不够我们住,而且,它离市区太远。

Ⅱ *adv.* certainly not; not at all; by no means 根本不,绝不: He made it clear that the electoral crisis was *far from* resolved. 他明确地指出,选举的危机根本没有解决。He is *far from* a coward. 他绝不是个胆小鬼。Peace and development remain the two major themes of the world today, but our world is *far from* peaceful. 和平与发展依然是当今世界的两大主题,但天下还很不太平。*Far from* liking him she hates him. 她不但不喜欢他,反而很恨他。

far gone *adj.* (非正式用语) extremely drunk, ill, or crazy 酩酊大醉;病情严重;发疯: He was too *far gone* to take in what we were saying. 他醉得太厉害,我们说的话他都不能听进去。He was so *far gone* when the ambulance arrived that little help was possible. 救护车赶到时,他已经病情严重,无法医治了。He is *far gone* in love with the actress. 他在狂恋着那名女演员。

NOTE 本短语可转化为复合词 far-gone,意为"烂醉的;极疯狂的;行将结束的"。

fed up *adj.* (非正式用语,常作表语,常与with 连用) unhappy; annoyed or bored (with something or someone that you feel you have accepted for too long); not satisfied with (something) 不高兴的;对……感到厌烦的;对……感到不满的: She was a bit *fed up* because you didn't telephone. 因为你没给她打电话,她有点不高兴了。I don't know why I feel so *fed up* this morning. 我也不知道我为什么今天上午心情这么不好。Mary is *fed up* with her husband; she just wants out of the marriage. 玛丽讨厌她的丈夫,便想与他脱离婚姻关系。"I'm *fed up* with being told what I can do and what I can't do!" said George. 乔治说:"我听够了那些我应该做什么,不该做什么的话了!" The management is pretty *fed up* of the union's lack of cooperation. 资方对工会缺乏合作而深感不满。

NOTE 1. 本短语中的 fed 是动词 feed 的过去式和过去分词形式。但本短语与 feed up 的意义和用法完全不同。见 feed up。

2. 本短语后常接介词 with。在英国英语的口语中亦用 of。

3. 本短语的比较级形式是 more fed up,最高级形式是 most fed up。

4. 本短语的同义短语是 sick (and tired) of;反义短语是 fond of。

feed back *vt.* 【可分性动词短语】(常与 to 连用) return (something such as information or opinions) to someone or something where it started 反馈,返送,反应: We should *feed* the information *back* to the factory. 我们应该把信息反馈给工厂。The computer can *feed back* everything you need to know. 计算机能把你需要知道的全部资料反馈给你。Test results will be *fed back* to schools. 考试结果将返送给学校。The teacher complained that nothing was *feeding back* to him from the classroom. 这位教师抱怨说,课堂上学生对他的讲课毫无反应。

NOTE 本短语可转化为复合词 feedback,意为"反馈"。

feed into *vt.*【可分性动词短语】❶introduce (something or someone) into (something such as a machine or institution)把(某物)输入(某种机器);向(某种机构)输送(人员):The main belt *feeds* raw material *into* the machine. 主传送带把原料输入机器中。He took the compact disc from her, and then *fed* it *into* the player. 他从她手里接过光盘,然后将其放入播放机中。How many provinces *feed* their students *into* your university? 有多少个省份向你们这所大学输送学生? ❷put (information) into (a computer)把(信息)输入(电脑):The information and questions are *fed into* the computer, which then supplies the answer. 把这些信息和题都输入电脑,然后电脑就会提供出答案来。

NOTE 本短语的在使用时的公式是:feed A into B,等于 feed B with A。例如,我们可以把 The main belt *feeds* raw material *into* the machine. 转化成:The main belt *feeds* the machine *with* raw material. 但后者是非正式用法。

feed on/upon *vt.* give food to (a person or an animal); (cause to) eat (certain food)用……喂养(人或动物),以……为食:She *fed* her guests *on* the product of the garden. 她用园子里种的东西招待客人。The dogs were *fed on* raw meat. 这些狗都喂生肉吃。You had better *feed on* coarse cereals for a time. 你最好吃一段时间粗粮。Foxes mainly *feed on* small animals. 狐狸主要以小动物为食。

NOTE 本短语中的 upon 用法比 on 正式,但不及 on 常用。

feed to *vt.*【可分性动词短语】❶give (something such as food) to (someone or an animal)用(某种食物)喂(人或动物):You'd better *feed* this old bread *to* the ducks. 你最好把这剩面包喂鸭子。The leftover *food* is fed *to* the pigs. 这些残汤剩饭都用来喂猪。❷(常用一般时态) supply (something such as information) to (usually someone)向……提供(信息等):Reporters all over the world *feed* the news *to* the radio stations. 世界各地的记者都把这一消息提供给了广播电台。

feed up *vt.*【可分性动词短语】(英国英语用法,非正式用语) give (someone or an animal) more food than usual in order to make them stronger or less thin 给(人或动物)充分的食物(以养肥或养壮):Your son looks rather thin; you'll have to *fed* him *up* well. 你的儿子看上去太瘦了,你得好好地给他补养补养。The boy needs *feeding up* to grow stronger. 这孩子需要多吃些东西才会长得强壮些。The farmer is *feeding up* the chickens. 农夫正在喂鸡。

NOTE 当本短语所带的宾语为代词时,该代词须置于本短语的动词和副词中间。

feel butterflies in one's stomach ⇨ **have butterflies in one's stomach**

feel for *vt.*【不可分性动词短语】❶try to find (something) by moving your hand around or touch 摸索着找(某物):In the heavy fog he *felt for* the kerb with his walking stick. 他在浓雾中用手杖摸索着马路边的镶边石行走。Blinded by the soap, he had to *feel for* his glasses. 他被肥皂沫眯住了眼睛,只好用手摸索着找到他的眼镜。He *felt* in his pocket *for* the keys. 他用手在口袋中摸钥匙。❷(无被动语态形式) feel sympathy for (someone); be sorry for (someone); be unhappy about the suffering of (someone)同情,怜悯(某人):I really *feel for* the parents of that boy who was killed in the crash. 我真的同情在撞车事故中丧生的那个男孩的父母。All of us know she's unhappy, and we *feel for* her. 我们都知道她很不幸,所以都可怜她。

feel like *vt.*【不可分性动词短语】(一般不用进行时态) ❶(无被动语态形式,用一般时态)want (something) or have a desire to do (something)想要(某物);想要做(某事):Do you *feel like* a cup of coffee? 你想来一杯咖啡吗? We'll go for a walk, if you *feel like* it. 如果你想的话,我们去散散步。Neither of them *feel like* going back to sleep. 他们俩都不想回去睡觉。I *felt like* I needed a walk in the open. 我觉得我需要到外面走一走。❷(用一般时态)seem like (something) to the touch 摸起来像:The table *felt like* plastic, not wood. 这张桌子摸着像是塑料的,而不是木头的。What's this in your pocket? It *feels like* a lighter. 你的口袋里是什么东西? 摸起来像一个打火机。❸ feel as if one is (someone or something);(of something) give you a particular feeling as 感觉像是,好像是:We'll make you *feel like* being at home in more than 540 cities in Europe. 我们会让你在欧洲 540 多个城市里有宾至如归的感觉。The clock said it was only eight o'clock but it *felt like* midnight. 看钟表,才 8 点钟,但感觉却像是在半夜。I *feel like* I'm catching cold. 我感觉像是感冒了。

NOTE 1. 本短语中的 like 是介词而不是动词。因此,其后不能接动词不定式短语。2. 当本短语作"感觉像是,好像是"解时,尤其在美国英语中,与 feel as if 意义和用法相同。例如:

It *feels like/as if* there's something sticking out of the mattress.
感觉垫子里像是有什么东西戳出来了。
He *felt like/as if* he'd run a marathon.
他感到好像是跑了一场马拉松。

feel sick *vi.* (主要用于英国英语中)feel as though you will vomit soon 感觉要吐:Every day I *feel sick*. It starts in the morning when I get cramps in my stomach and I have to go to the toilet. 每天我都感觉要吐。从早晨开始,我就胃痉挛,不上厕所不行。I am 22 weeks pregnant and am *feeling* really *sick* to my stomach. Is this normal, doctor? 我怀孕 22 周了,我现在总是感觉要吐。这正常吗,医生?

fend off *vt.* ❶ act to avoid (someone's blows) by using your arms or something such as a stick (用手臂或木棍等)挡开,避开(他人的打击):He had to *fend off* a dangerous blow with his arms. 他不得不用双臂挡开那危险的一击。❷ defend (yourself) against (an attack)抵御:The HKSAR Government will surely be able to take up challenges, in particular, in *fending off* the impact of the global financial crisis. 香港特区政府定能应对各种挑战,特别是抵御住全球金融危机的冲击。These women could not *fend off* their attackers. 这些妇女无法抵御袭击她们的人。❸ stop (someone) from coming too near to you 避开(某人)对自己的接近:She was never very good at *fending off* the boys. 她一点儿也不善于避开男孩子对自己的接近。❹ prevent (something) from happening 避免(某事的)发生:He knows how to *fend off* unfriendly questions from news reporters.

他知道如何避免新闻记者提出不友好的问题。

fight against *vt.*【不可分性动词短语】❶use guns or other weapons in a battle or war against(another army or country) 对……作战：The US *fought against* Britain in their War of Independence two centuries ago. 美国在两个世纪前的独立战争期间与英国作战。Britain's Ministry of Defense confirmed that Prince Harry had been in Afghanistan *fighting against* the Taliban on the front line. 英国国防部证实，哈里王子曾一直在阿富汗的前线与塔利班作战。❷try very hard to prevent (something) from happening or getting worse 与……斗争，打击，抗击：We will improve management of the culture market and steadfastly *fight against* pornography and illegal publications. 我们将改善文化市场管理，坚持开展"扫黄打非"。Asian countries join hands in *fighting against* cross-country drug trafficking. 亚洲各国携手打击跨国走私毒品犯罪。Leaders of the government at all levels should stand in the forefront *fighting against* flood. 各级政府的领导人都应该战斗在抗洪斗争的最前线。❸oppose (something or doing something)反对：As a black worker she *fought against* racism all her life. 作为一名黑人工作者，她一生都反对种族主义。The villagers tried to *fight against* being moved to another village. 村民们竭力反对被迁居到另一村庄。

fight off *vt.*【可分性动词短语】❶defeat(someone) in a fight; repel (an attack from someone or something); make (someone who is trying to attack you)go away by defending yourself (在战斗中)打退，击退(进攻)；(在打斗中)赶跑：They *fought off* the enemy with machine-guns. 他们用机关枪打退了敌人。We *fought* the enemy attack *off*, but they returned almost immediately. 我们击退了敌人的进攻，但他们几乎马上又开始了反攻。The young man managed to *fight off* his attackers. 小伙子打跑了那几个袭击他的人。❷keep (something, for example an illness or unpleasant feeling) away with an effort; struggle to prevent (something unwanted); avoid (someone unwanted)竭力摆脱(疾病或不快的情绪)；避开(讨厌的事或人)：She took various medicines to try to *fight off* her cold. 她吃了好几种药以治愈感冒。I got a cold at the start of the week but I seem to have *fought* it *off*. 本周初我得了感冒，看来现已好了。The pop star had to *fight off* all the screaming fans who were trying to touch him. 这位流行曲歌星不得不竭力躲开那些尖声叫喊着试图接触他的歌迷们。

NOTE 当本短语所带的宾语为代词时，该代词须置于本短语的动词和副词中间。

fight one's way *vi.* move through a group of people by pushing them away 挤开一条出路：Steve *fought his way* to the front of the hall. 史蒂夫推挤着走到大厅的前面。After a powerful explosion, black smoke was seen rising from the hotel as many hotel dwellers *fought their way* out. 发生强烈爆炸后，可以看到那家饭店还冒着浓烟，很多住店客人都拼命地往外跑。The crowd was so thick that I had to *fight my way* out of the theatre. 人太多了，我不得不挤着走出了剧院。One of the dreams of this ambitious young man was to *fight his way* into the fashionable world. 这个有抱负的年轻人的一个梦想是跻身上流

社会。

NOTE 本短语中的名词 way 无论其前的物主代词是单数还是复数形式，都必须用单数形式。

figure out *vt.*【可分性动词短语】(非正式用语) ❶calculate (an amount or the cost of something) 计算出：Can you *figure out* the speed of the earth around the sun exactly? 你能精确地计算出地球绕太阳运转的速度吗？*Figure* it *out* and see what comes. 把它计算出来，看结果是多少。Let's go and *figure out* how much we have to pay for the project. 咱们去算算这项工程我们要花多少钱。All the answers have been *figured out*. 所有的答案都已经计算出来的。❷be able to understand (something or someone) with difficulty or solve a problem 理解，搞清："Can you *figure out* his letter?" "No, I can't *figure* it *out*." "你能理解他信中的意思吗？""不能，我搞不清楚。" We had to *figure out* the connection between the two events. 我们必须搞清这两个事件之间的联系。After carrying out a series of careful searches, the police finally *figured out* where the kidnapped worker was. 在进行了一系列的仔细搜索之后，警方最终弄清了被绑架的工人的所在位置。I can't *figure* him *out* — he's a mystery. 我捉摸不透他——他是个谜。

NOTE 当本短语所带的宾语为代词时，该代词须置于本短语的动词和副词中间。

fill in *vt.*【可分性动词短语】❶ put something into (a crack, hole or gap) so that the hole or gap no longer exists 把……填满，填补，弥补：If any cracks have appeared in the wall, *fill* them *in* with cement. 如果墙体出现裂缝，就用水泥将其填平。The canal is now disused and partly *filled in*. 那条运河已废弃不用，其中一部分已被填平了。The hole has been *filled in*. 洞已被堵上了。Most enterprise employees are satisfied with their current payment, but there remains a big gap to *fill in* for social security coverage among them. 大多数的企业员工对他们目前的工资感到满意，但社会保险的范围还有很大差距需要弥补。

❷(主要用于英国英语中) add (information such as your name or address) in the empty spaces on an official document, either on a computer or on paper; fill out 填写：Please *fill in* your name and address in the space provided. 请在所提供的空格中填写你的姓名和地址。I finished *filling in* the form and clicked "submit". 我填写完这份表后，便点击了"提交"。She had to *fill* the form *in*. 她不得不把表填上。*Fill in* the missing words. 把落掉的词都填上。❸(非正式用语，常与 about，on 连用) give (someone) details about something such as information 向(某人)提供详细消息：Did Sam *fill* you *in* about the new project? 塞姆有没有向您提供这个新项目的详细情况？I've asked Robert to *fill in* the marketing team about plans for the fall. 我已叫罗伯特把今年秋季的计划提供给营销组。My secretary will *fill* you *in* on what happened at the meeting. 我的秘书会向您提供会上发生的情况。

—*vi.* (常与 for 连用) do someone else's job temporarily while they are away 暂时顶替(某人的工作)：Our teacher was ill and Miss Jones *filled in* for her. 我们老师病了，琼斯小姐暂时代她上课。I'm *filling in* for the receptionist at the moment. 眼下我在充任接待员。I'm not her secretary — I'm just *filling in*. 我不是他的秘书，只是在打替班而已。

NOTE 1. 当本短语用作及物性动词短语，所带的宾语为代词时，该代词须置于本短语的动词和副词中间。

2. 本短语与 fill out 和 fill up 均表示“填写”之意。但本短语和 fill up 主要用于英国英语中，而 fill out 则主要用于美国英语中。

3. 本短语可转化为复合词 fill-in，意为“临时填补空缺的人；临时填补物”。

F

fill out *vt.* （主要用于英国英语中）add (information such as your name or address) in the empty spaces on an official document, either on a computer or on paper; fill out 填写：In getting a US visa you have to *fill out* an application form, which is easy enough for most people. 要想拿到美国签证，你必须填写一份申请表格，这对大多数人来说都够容易的。I'm tired of *filling out* forms. 我讨厌填表。Print the document, *fill* it *out*, and bring it with you. 把这份文件打印出来，填写完之后带在身上。You must *fill out* a check before you can cash it. 你得先填写支票，才能将其兑换成现金。

—*vt.* & *vi.* （非正式用语）(cause to) grow fatter （使）长胖：Sam's really *filled out*, hasn't he? 塞姆长胖了许多，是吧？His face is beginning to *fill out* as he puts on weight. 随着他体重的增加，他的脸开始长圆了。Eating that food will certainly *fill* her *out*. 吃那些食物当然会使她长胖。

NOTE 当本短语用作及物性动词短语，所带的宾语为代词时，该代词须置于本短语的动词和副词中间。

fill up *v.* ❶ (cause to) become full to top 充满，加满，倒满：The lake *filled up* after the heavy rain. 大雨过后，湖水满了。There were many cars waiting in line to *fill up* at the gas station. 有许多汽车在加油站旁排队等候加油。Mary kept *filling* my glass *up* with champagne. 玛丽不断把我的杯子倒满香槟酒。❷ take up (a space) completely 挤满：By eight o'clock the restaurant was beginning to *fill up* with people. 到 8 点时，餐馆里开始坐满了人。Nearly 500,000 protesters *filled up* the wide streets in front of the presidential office building. 总统府大楼前面几条宽阔的大街上挤满了近 50 万名示威者。Would you please *fill* the room *up* with chairs? 请你们把房间里面都摆满椅子，好吗？❸（主要用于英国英语中）add (information such as your name or address) in the empty spaces on an official document; fill out 填写：I want you to *fill up* this form first according to the instruction. 我要你先按照说明填写这份表格。

NOTE 当本短语用作及物性动词短语，所带的宾语为代词时，该代词须置于本短语的动词和副词中间。

fill with *vt.* 【可分性动词短语】❶ (cause to) become full of (something, things, or people) （使）充满：Katherine's eyes filled with tears. 凯瑟琳的双眼充满了泪水。*Fill* the bucket *with* water. 把桶装满水。*Filled with* such gifts as chocolate, flowers and wine, the special parcel sells well on the market before the approaching Valentine's Day. 这种装满了巧克力、鲜花和葡萄酒的特殊礼包在情人节前的市场上特别畅销。The hall was *filled with* angry people. 大厅里挤满了愤怒的人们。❷（常用一般时态）fill (someone) with (something such as a feeling) 使（某人）充满（某种感情）：The birth of the boy *filled* the whole family *with* joy. 这个男孩儿的降生使全家人充满了欢乐。What netizens said *filled* him *with* great anger. 网民的评论使他十分生气。I could see that his eyes were *filled with* curiosity. 我可以看出,他的眼神中充满了好奇。

final straw ⇨ **the last straw**

find fault with *vt.* criticize (someone or something), often after deliberately looking for mistakes (常指故意)找……的错,对……吹毛求疵:I don't know why he is constantly *finding fault with* me. 我不知道他为什么老是找我的岔。They *found fault with* every meter that factory made. 他们对那家工厂生产的每块仪表都找毛病。No *fault* could be *found with* it on that side. 在那方面,它是无可挑剔。

NOTE **1.** 本短语中的名词 fault 必须用单数形式。

2. 本短语的另外一种表达形式是 have a fault to find with。例如:

> They *have no fault to find with* what you have done.
> 他们对你的所作所为挑不出任何毛病来。

find one's way *vi.* (常与 to 连用) ❶(of someone) manage to find the way to go to a place (指某人)找到去……的路:She managed to *find her way* home. 她找到了回家的路。Can you *find your way* to the museum? 你能找到去博物馆的路吗? ❷(of something) manage to reach or appear (in a place, but you do not know how it arrived there)(指某物)(莫名地)到达,出现在(某处):Somehow the letter had *found its way* onto my boss's desk. 不知怎么地,那封信竟到了我的老板的办公桌上。"Could you explain how the blueprints of nuclear weapons *found their way* to Libya?" asked a foreign reporter. "您能否解释一下这些核武器图纸是如何辗转到利比亚的?"一名外国记者问道。Cellphone GPS services have *found their way* into the market. 手机全球卫星定位系统已进入市场。This news soon *found its way* to a lot of people. 这消息很快就有许多人知道了。

NOTE 本短语中的名词 way,无论其前的物主代词是单数还是复数形式,都必须用单数形式。

find out *vt.* &*vi.* discover something; obtain information about (something) 发现,找出,查明(情况):I don't want anyone else to *find out* about this. 我不想让任何其他人发现此事。They are sure to *find* it *out* sometimes. 这事他们将来准会发现。An investigation *found out* that since last year the company has evaded taxes worth over 10 million yuan. 一项调查发现,自去年以来,该公司偷漏税款超过一千万元。The police are trying to *find out* the cause of the accident. 警方正在竭力查明这一事故的原因。Please *find out* what time the meeting starts. 请查看一下会议什么时间开始。They have to *find out* how to bring about improvement. 他们得弄清楚应如何改进。

—*vt.* 【可分性动词短语】discover (someone who has been doing something dishonest or deceitful) 查出,揭发:The businessman cheated the tax collectors, but then they *found* him *out* and he was punished. 那商人蒙骗了税收人员,但后来他们把他查出来并惩罚了他。After years of stealing money from the company, he was finally *found out*. 他多年来一直盗用公司的资金,最后被揭露了出来。

NOTE 当本短语用作及物性动词短语,所带

F

的宾语为代词时，该代词须置于本短语的动词和副词中间。

finish off *vt.* 【可分性动词短语】❶finish (something such as a task) completely 彻底完成：They hired a smaller company to *finish off* the job. 他们雇用了一家小公司来完成那件工作。I must *finish off* this sewing while the light is good. 我必须趁光线好时把这针线活干完。❷(非正式用语) kill or destroy (a person or an animal, especially one that is badly injured) 结束……的性命：The captain had to *finish* him *off* with his revolver. 上尉只好用手枪把他打死了。❸(非正式用语，常用一般时态) destroy (something, especially something that is badly damaged) 毁掉，毁坏：A long drive like that could *finish* the car *off*. 像那样的长途驾驶会毁坏这台车的。❹(非正式用语，常用一般时态) make (someone) so tired that he or she cannot do any more 使(某人)感到极度疲劳：That walk round the lake just about *finished* me *off*! 绕湖走了一圈几乎把我累垮。

—*vt.* &*vi.* eat, drink, or use all of something so that there is none left 吃光，喝尽，用完：Do you want to *finish off* these sandwiches? 你想把这些三明治都吃光吗？*Finish off* your drinks, please. 请把你的饮料都喝光。Let's *finish off* with some of the excellent cheese. 咱们把这些绝好的奶酪吃光吧。

NOTE 当本短语用作及物性动词短语，所带的宾语为代词时，该代词须置于本短语的动词和副词中间。

finish up *v.* ❶finish (a task) completely 完成：I finally *finished up* this homework assignment. 我终于完成了作业。If I don't finish this work tonight, I'll surely *finish* it *up* tomorrow. 如果这件工作我今晚做不完，我明天一定把它完成。❷(英国英语用法) finally be in a particular place or situation at the end of a long series of events 结束，(以……)告终：We toured Europe and *finished up* in London. 我们游历了欧洲，最后在伦敦结束了旅程。He's probably going to *finish up* in jail if he goes on like that. 如果他继续那样下去的话，他可能会以坐牢为告终。If you're not careful, you could *finish up* seriously ill. 如果你不加保重，你最终会得大病的。He *finished up* being unemployed and living at home again. 到头来，他又失业待在家里了。❸eat, drink, or use all of something so that there is none left 吃光，喝尽，用完：We might as well *finish up* the cake. 我们最好把这蛋糕吃光。*Finish up* your drinks, please. 请把你的饮料都喝光。

NOTE 当本短语用作及物性动词短语，所带的宾语为代词时，该代词须置于本短语的动词和副词中间。

finish with *vt.* 【不可分性动词短语】❶(英国英语用法，非正式用语) complete; bring (something) to an end with (something or doing something) 把……做完，以……为结束：Tomorrow we shall have *finished with* this work once for all. 明天我们就能一劳永逸地把这件工作做完。That man has *finished with* gadding about. 那人不再游手好闲了。The game *finished with* the score at 1-1. 比赛以1比1平的比分结束。To *finish with*, we'll listen to a few songs. 咱们以听几支歌为结束吧。❷(常用完成时态) stop using and no longer need (something or someone) 用完(某物)；不再需要(某人)：I'll borrow the knife if you've *finished with* it. 如果你用完了刀，我想借用一下。Have you *finished* with the newspaper? 这报纸你看完了吗? When you've *finished with* me, sir, I'll leave. 先生,如果您不再需要我的话,我就走了。❸(英国英语用法,非正式用语,常用完成时态) end a relationship with (someone), so that he or she is no longer your boyfriend or girlfriend 结束与(某人)的朋友关系: My boyfriend was threatening to *finish with* me. 我的男朋友威胁要结束与我的朋友关系。I have *finished with* Smith after the way he's treated me. 史密斯以那种方式对待我,我已不和他处朋友了。

fire at *vt.*【可分性动词短语】❶shoot (a weapon) at (someone or something) 向……射击,向……发射……: One of the soldiers said that one vehicle drove up and its passengers *fired at* them. 一名士兵讲述说,一辆汽车开了过来,接着车里的人就朝他们开了火。The soldier lifted his rifle, aimed and *fired at* the target. 那士兵举起步枪朝目标瞄准并射击。Gunmen *fired* a few shots *at* the Taj Mahal Hotel as police were searching the area for survivors. 当警察正在该区域搜寻幸存者时,武装分子向泰姬玛哈酒店打了数枪。❷ask (someone) a question, especially one that is difficult for him or her to answer 向(某人)提出(难以回答的)问题: Reporters *fired* questions *at* her as she left the court house. 当她离开法院时,记者们向她提出了一连串的问题。

NOTE 当本短语作"向……射击,向……发射……"解时,同义短语是 fire on/upon。

fire away *vi.* ❶begin to shoot 开始射击: The soldiers *fired away* at the enemy. 士兵们开始向敌人射击。❷shoot continuously 连续射击: They *fired away* until no bullets were left. 他们连续地射击,一直把子弹全部打光。❸(非正式用语,用一般时态,常用于祈使句中) begin to speak or ask a question 开始讲话,开始提问题: *Fire away*, we're listening. 说吧,我们都在听着。"I've got a few questions." "OK then, *fire away*." "我有几个问题。""那好,问吧。" When it came time for questions, the reporters began *firing away* at the foreign minister. 提问的时间到了,记者们开始向外长提出问题。

fire on/upon *vt.* shoot at (someone or something) 向……射击: A patrol was sent out to search for the attackers, who fled after *firing on* the American troops from a nearby rooftop. 一支巡逻队奉命去搜寻那些从附近的屋顶上向美军射击后逃走的袭击者。A foreign navy warship *fired on* our fishing vessel, killing one person and wounding two others. 一艘外国军舰向我渔船开炮,打死一人,打伤两人。

NOTE 1. 本短语中的 upon 用法比 on 正式,但不及 on 常用。

2. 本短语中的 on 是介词,后面接宾语。但在下面这个句子里,on 是副词,表示"继续""不断"之意:

> The soldiers *fired on* until no bullets were left.
> 士兵们不断地射击,一直把子弹打光。

3. 本短语的同义短语是 fire at(第一个义项)。

fire up *v.* ❶(cause to) become suddenly angry (使)发火: He *fires up* at the least thing. 一点儿小事就会使他发火。She has a quick temper; such little things will *fire* her *up*. 她脾气急躁,这样一些小事就会使她发起火来。❷(主要用于英国英语中,常与 about 连用) make (someone) feel very enthusiastic 使(某

人)感兴趣：She's all *fired up* about this new course she's taking. 她对所修的这门新课很感兴趣。❸(非正式用语)start (a machine, piece of equipment, computer program, etc.)启动(机器、设备、计算机程序等)：We need to *fire up* one of the generators. 我们需要启动其中一台发电机。Let me *fire up* another window. 让我再打开一个(电脑)窗口。❹ light (a pipe, cigar, or cigarette)点燃(烟斗、雪茄或烟卷)：If you *fire* that pipe *up*, I will leave the room. 如果你点燃那烟斗，我就离开房间。Do you mind if I *fire up*? 我点支烟你介意吗?

NOTE 当本短语用作及物性动词短语，所带的宾语为代词时，该代词须置于本短语的动词和副词中间。

first and foremost *adv.* ❶ most importantly; above all else 最重要地，首要地：He has written many different kinds of books, but he's *first and foremost* a poet. 他写过许多种类的书，但他主要还是个诗人。*First and foremost* the victims of the earthquake needed tents, food and medicine. 震区灾民最需要的是帐篷、食品和药品。❷ to begin with 首先：*First and foremost*, I want to thank our sponsors. 首先，我要感谢我们的主办人。

NOTE 1. 当本短语作"最重要地，首要地"解时，同义短语是 above all, in the first place。

2. 当本短语作"首先"解时，与 first of all 意义和用法相同，两者可互换使用。

first of all *adv.* (用于口语中，常置于句首)(used for introducing the first of several things that you are going to say) before anything else; first 首先：*First of all*, I'd like to introduce myself to you. 首先，我想做一下自我介绍。The scientific approach to a problem consists *first of all* in collecting ample materials. 研究问题的科学方法首先在于收集丰富的材料。

NOTE 1. 本短语用于强调所列举的一系列事物中的首者，但其后不能接 second of all，也不接 secondly，而应接 second 或 then，third，fourth 等。

2. 不要将本短语与 at first 混淆。at first 意为"当初，起初"，与后来发生的事相对照。例如：

> He was violently opposed to my proposal *at first*, but later he agreed to it.
> 他起初强烈地反对我的提议，但后来又同意了。

而本短语则表示"首先"，说明顺序，是时间上或一系列行动的开始。例如：

> *First of all*, open the windows. Then turn off the gas and, if necessary, call an ambulance.
> 首先，打开窗户。然后，关掉煤气。如有必要，再叫救护车。

3. 不要将本短语与 above all 混淆。above all 意为"最重要的是；尤其是"，强调要引起特别注意。

fish out *vt.* 【可分性动词短语】❶(常与 of 连用) bring or pull (someone or something) out from water (从水中)捞出：A tourist jumped into the canal to *fish* the boy *out*. 一名游客跳入运河中，把那男孩儿捞了上来。According to the police, two more bodies have been *fished out* of the pond. 据警方报道，又在池塘里打捞出两具尸体。❷(非正式用语，常与 from 连用)pull (something) out of a bag or other container (从包或其他容器中)拿出，掏出：She reached into her bag and *fished out* a pen. 她把手伸进包里，拿出一支笔来。He *fished out* several coins from his pocket. 他从衣袋中掏出了几枚硬币。Kelly *fished out* another beer from his cooler. 凯利从他的冷却器中又拿出一瓶啤酒来。*Fishing out* an old coat from the suitcase, he put it on and went out. 他从提箱里翻出一件旧上衣,穿在身上就出去了。

NOTE 当本短语所带的宾语为代词时,该代词须置于本短语的动词和副词中间。

fit for[1] *vt.* 【可分性动词短语】(主要用于英国英语中,常用一般时态) make (someone or oneself) suitable for (something) 使(某人或自己)适合于: Everything in his background *fitted* him *for* a diplomatic career. 他的全部经历使他适合于做外交工作。He *fitted* himself *for* the journey. 他做好了旅行的准备。

fit for[2] *adj.* suitable or well suited for 能胜任……,适合于……: The manager is not *fit for* his position. 这位经理不胜任其职务。The weather is just *fit for* cricket. 这种天气正适于打板球。Some books are not *fit for* the children to read, so they have been called in by the library. 有些书籍不适于孩子们阅读,所以图书馆已把它们收回。If we go on polluting the world, it won't be *fit for* us to live in. 如果我们继续污染世界的环境,这个世界就不再适于我们生存了。He seems to think that typing documents is all I'm *fit for*. 他似乎认为我只胜任文件的打字工作。The children seem to think I'm only *fit for* cooking and washing! 好像孩子们认为我只是个做饭洗衣服的料!

NOTE 本短语在句中作表语和定语。作表语用时,主要用于以下四种形式中:(1) fit for something;(2) fit for someone;(3) fit for someone to do something;(4) fit for doing something。

fit in *vt.* 【可分性动词短语】❶ have space for (someone or something) 有地方安置(某人或某物) I'll come in your car, if you can *fit* me *in*. 如果还有我的地方,我就上你的车。Let's fit in the computer desk here. 咱们把电脑桌放在这个地方吧。We can *fit* the bookshelf *in* between the windows. 我们可以把书架放在两个窗户之间。There was so much furniture in this room that it became impossible to *fit* any more *in*. 这屋里的家具太多了,不可能再放更多的家具了。The new Apple notebook, the world's thinnest computer, is small enough to *fit in* a file envelope. 苹果公司新推出的笔记本电脑是全球最薄的电脑,小得能装进一个档案袋里。❷ find a time for (someone or something) 给……安排时间: I hope the dentist can *fit* me *in* on Tuesday afternoon. 我希望牙医能把我安排在星期二下午看病。Mr Smith will have to be *fitted in* next week. 下周得把史密斯先生安排进来。Let's *fit in* a visit to our professor in the hospital. 咱们安排一个时间去看望住院的教授吧。

NOTE 当本短语所带的宾语为代词时,该代词须置于本短语的动词和副词中间。

fit in with *vt.* (一般不用被动语态形式,常用一般时态) (of someone or something) (cause to) be correct or suitable in relation to (something or someone else) 与……符合,(使)一致,相配,适合: His ideas didn't quite *fit in with* our aims. 他那些想法与我们的目标不大相符。His explanation didn't *fit in with* what I saw. 他做的解释与我所见的不甚相符。I'll try to *fit* my arrangement *in with* yours. 我设法使我的安排与你们的相一致。She doesn't *fit in with* the other roommates. 她与其他室友合不来。

fit on *vt.*【可分性动词短语】add (a piece of equipment) to (something else)在……上安装: We're *fitting* new locks *on* all the doors. 我们在为所有的门安装新锁。We're having a new handle *fitted on* the door. 我们正在给这扇门安装一个新把手。

NOTE 当本短语所带的宾语是代词时,该代词须置于本短语的动词和副词或介词中间。

F

fit out/up *vt.*【可分性动词短语】(常与 with 连用) provide (someone or something) with (equipment and other things that they need)为(……)配备,装备……: We helped to *fit* him *out* for a trip to Europe. 我们帮他准备去欧洲旅行的必备物品。They are *fitting out* new labs with up-to-date equipment. 他们正在为新实验室配备最新设备。They *fitted* this room *out* as a sound laboratory. 他们把这个房间装备成一间语音实验室。The sitting room was *fitted out* with a tape recorder. 起居室中装有一台录音机。I suggest we *fit* him *up* with an office suite. 我建议咱们为他提供一套办公室。

NOTE 1. 当本短语的宾语是代词时,该代词须置于本短语的动词和副词中间。
2. fit up 主要用于英国英语中。

fix on/upon *vt.*【可分性动词短语】❶focus your eyes or your attention on (someone or something), so you look straight at them and at nothing else 注视;集中注意力于: He *fixed* his gaze *on* Mary. 他把目光盯在玛丽的身上。I kept my eyes *fixed on* the horizon. 我双目凝视着地平线。They *fix* their attention *on* what they are doing. 他们正专心致志地从事他们的工作。❷(非正式用语) choose (usually a particular thing) after considering the situation 选定(尤指某物): We've *fixed on* the 14th of February, the Valentine's Day, for the wedding. 我们已选定 2 月 14 日情人节那天结婚。Have you *fixed on* where to go for your holiday yet? 你们要去哪儿度假定下来了吗? We've finally *fixed on* the Lake District for our summer holiday. 我们最终选定在湖区度暑假。The date for the negotiation hasn't yet been *fixed on*. 谈判的日期尚未决定。We've *fixed on* starting tomorrow. 我们已决定明天动身。

NOTE 本短语中的 upon 用法比 on 正式,但不及 on 常用。

fix up *vt.* &*vi.* arrange for (something)安排,布置: Have you *fixed up* about the photographs for the wedding? 婚礼上照相的事你安排了吗? Perhaps we can *fix up* a meeting for next week. 我们可能会在下星期安排一次会议。They've *fixed up* a temporary platform at one end of the room. 他们已在房间的一头布置了一个临时的讲台。

—*vt.*【可分性动词短语】❶(非正式用语,常与 with 连用) provide (someone) (with something or someone)为(某人)提供(物或人): If you need more equipment, Linda will *fix* you *up*. 如果你再需要什么设备,琳达会提供给你。I can *fix* you *up* with a place to live. 我可以给你提供住处。❷(非正式用语) repair or decorate something 修理,装修: He *fixed up* the old car and sold it at a profit. 他把那辆旧车修了之后卖掉赚了钱。They take old furniture and *fix* it *up*. 他们接收旧家具修理。I'm going to *fix* the house *up* before my mother-in-law arrives. 我要在岳母到来之前把房子

装修一下。

NOTE 当本短语用作及物性动词短语，宾语为代词时，该代词须置于本短语的动词和副词中间。

flare up *vi.* ❶(of a fire) burn quickly and suddenly, especially after having died down (指火灭之后)复燃：The fire could *flare up* again at any time. 那火随时都会复燃。❷show sudden increased anger, activity, or violence (愤怒、暴力事件等)突然发作，突然爆发：President Obama *flared up* at the Wallstreet's $18.4 billion bonus. 奥巴马总统对华尔街发放184亿美元奖金勃然大怒。Mary's temper *flared up* when Jim angered her. 当吉姆惹怒了她时，玛丽的脾气突然发作了。It looked as if long-feared violence might *flare up*. 长期以来一直担心的暴力活动看来要爆发了。❸(of a disease or injury) suddenly return or become painful again (指疾病或伤痛)突然复发：In moments of stress, his asthma always *flares up*. 心绪紧张时，他的气喘病就经常复发。

NOTE **1.** 当本短语作"突然发怒"解时，同义短语是 blow up, blow one's lid, lose one's temper 和 see red；反义短语是 keep one's temper。

2. 本短语可转化为复合词 flare-up，意为"(愤怒、暴力事件、疾病或伤痛等)突然发作"。

flick away/off *vt.* 【可分性动词短语】make (something unwanted) move quickly and suddenly, especially with a quick movement of the hand, etc. 把……驱走；(从……)弹去，拂去，除去：The horse *flicked* the flies *away* with its tail. 那马甩动尾巴把苍蝇驱走。He *flicked* a speck of cigarette ash *off* his sleeve. 他把一小点烟灰从袖子上掸了下去。

NOTE 当本短语的宾语是代词时，该代词须置于本短语的动词和副词中间。

flick through *vt.* 【不可分性动词短语】❶(无被动语态形式) turn (the pages of a book, magazine, newspaper, etc.) very quickly looking at some of the pages for a very short time 将(书、杂志、报纸等)一翻而过：She was *flicking through* some magazines on a table. 她在翻阅桌上的一些杂志。I've just *flicked through* your article; I'll read it again properly when I have more time. 你的文章我只翻阅了一下，等有更多时间时我再好好看。❷quickly change (television channels), having a very quick look at each to see what program is on, for example using a remote control 很快地变换(电视机的频道)：She *flicked through* the channels but nothing interesting was on. 她很快地变换着电视机的频道，但都没有什么好节目在上演。

flip through *vt.* 【不可分性动词短语】(非正式用语) read or look at (a book, paper, etc.) rapidly or carelessly 草草翻阅：He was *flipping through* a magazine in the living room. 他在起居室里翻阅一本杂志。I haven't read the book properly; I just *flipped through* it to see what it was like. 我没好好读这本书，只是翻翻，看这是一本什么样的书。

NOTE 本短语的同义短语是 glance over/through 和 flick through。

flood in *vi.* (of something) come in or arrive in a large quantity 大量涌入：When I drew the curtains back, the sunlight *flooded in*. 当我打开窗帘时，阳光照了进来。Letters of complaint are still *flooding in*. 投诉信件仍源源不断。Telephone calls came *flooding in* from all over the country. 来自全国各地的电话接连不断。

flood into *vt.*【不可分性动词短语】(无被动语态形式)(of people) go or arrive (in a place) in large numbers (指人)大量涌入(某地): According to the village head, the majority of laborers between 20 and 50 in his village have *flooded into* cities to earn a living for their families. 据村长讲,村里大部分 20 至 50 岁的劳力都纷纷进城打工,为家庭谋取生计。Many refugees are *flooding into* the border area due to the continuous civil war. 由于持续的内战,许多难民纷纷涌入边境地区。

flunk out *v.* (美国英语用法,非正式用语,用一般时态,常与 of 连用)(cause to) have to leave (a school or college) because your work is not satisfactory or for failure in exams (因学习成绩不佳或考试不及格而)(使)退学: After George *flunked out* of the college, he did different kinds of low-skill and low paying jobs. 乔治从大学退学后干过几种没什么技术、报酬很低的工作。Some students have been *flunked out* of the school. 有些学生被勒令退学了。If I were the dean, I'd have *flunked* him *out* of the department. 如果我要是系主任,早就把他开除出系了。

NOTE 当本短语的宾语是代词时,该代词须置于本短语的动词和副词中间。

fly into *vt.* ❶ (cause to) arrive at (a place) by plane (使)乘飞机到达(某地): He *flew into* Baghdad on Tuesday. 他星期二乘飞机抵达巴格达。Helicopters were used to *fly* soldiers *into* the heavily forested area. 动用了直升机才把士兵运到那一密林地区。❷ crash into or hit (something) by flying 飞行撞上(某物): On September 11, 2001, nearly 3,000 people were killed when four planes were hijacked and *flown into* New York's World Trade Center, the Pentagon and a field in Pennsylvania. 2001 年 9 月 11 日,4 架飞机被劫持并分别撞击了纽约的世贸中心、五角大楼和宾夕法尼亚州的一片田地,近 3 000 人死亡。A US passenger plane crashed into the Hudson River after both engines failed when birds apparently *flew into* them. 一架美国客机因其双引擎明显遭到飞鸟的撞击而失灵后坠入哈德逊河中。❸(无被动语态形式,常用一般时态)(of someone) suddenly reach (a state or feeling, usually anger or other negative feeling) 突然到达(某种状态或情绪,尤指愤怒等): He *flew into* a temper when I mentioned her name. 我一提到她的名字,他便勃然大怒。Losing a game would cause him to *fly into* a rage. 输掉一场比赛就会使他暴怒。She *flew into* panic. 她突然陷入一阵惊恐中。

fly open *vi.* (常用一般时态)open freely and suddenly, or in a violent manner 突然打开: The door *flew open* and the head teacher marched in. 门突然打开,校长走了进来。He pressed the knob and the lid *flew open*. 他一按旋钮,盖子便猛然弹开了。

focus on/upon *vt.*【可分性动词短语】❶aim (something such as rays of light) directly onto (a particular thing)把(光线等)集中在(某一物体)上: The beam of light moved across the sky and *focused on* the aircraft. 一道道光柱划破夜空,最后集中在了那架飞机上。If you *focus* sunlight *on* dry wood with a glass, it will start burning. 如果你用一片玻璃把阳光

集中在干燥的木头上,它就会燃烧起来。❷(**cause to**) **look at** (**something or someone**) **carefully until you can start to see it/him or her clearly** (使)视线集中在……上:His eyes slowly began to *focus on* what looked like a small ball. 他的视线开始慢慢地集中在一个看上去像一个小球似的东西上。Kelly *focused* her gaze *on* Nathan. 凯利把目光集中在了内森的身上。❸concentrate on (something) and pay particular attention to it 集中(注意力)于……:It is difficult for children to *focus* their attention *on* what they are doing. 孩子们很难把注意力都集中在其所做之事上。The Chinese government will *focus upon* economic development, advance reforms and open further the country to the outside world. 中国政府将集中发展经济,加快改革步伐,并进一步对外开放。Both sides *focused on* exchanging views on strengthening bilateral exchanges and cooperation. 双方着重就加强两国的交流与合作交换了意见。Talks between the two leaders will *focus on* how to further expand the friendly relations between the two countries. 两国领导人之间会谈的主要议题将集中在如何进一步扩大两国间的友好关系上。

NOTE 本短语中的 upon 用法比 on 正式,但不及 on 常用。

foist (off) on/upon *vt.* 【可分性动词短语】❶force someone to accept (something that they do not want)迫使人接受……,把……强加于:The contract was *foisted upon* him through trickery. 这份合同是通过耍花招迫使他接受的。He *foisted* his work *on* me. 他把他的工作强加给我做。Voters are tired of new regulations *foisted on* them by lawmakers. 选民们讨厌那些由立法者强加给他们的新规定。We are not to *foist* our ideas and views *on* them. 我们不会把自己的思想和观点强加于他们。❷pass or sell (something of poor quality or not genuine) to (someone), especially by deceit (尤指以欺骗手段)把(劣质物品或假货)推销给(某人):Don't trust that shopkeeper, he'll try to *foist* damaged goods *off on* you. 不要相信那个店主,他会把损坏的货品骗卖给你的。The peddler *foisted* this piece of glass *off upon* the old lady, as a valuable diamond. 那小贩把这块玻璃当作珍贵的钻石骗卖给了这老太太。

NOTE 本短语中的 upon 用法比 on 正式,但不及 on 常用。

follow around/about *vt.* 【可分性动词短语】follow (someone) wherever he or she goes, especially in a way that annoys him or her 到处跟随(某人):Henry's been *following* me *around* like a puppy! 亨利像小狗一样老是跟着我。The child *follows* her mother *about* all the day. 这孩子整天跟着妈妈转。

follow suit *vi.* do what someone else has done; follow the example of another 照样做,仿效他人:If one of the major banks lowers its interest rate, other banks are expected to *follow suit*. 如果有一家大银行降低了利率,其他银行就会照样去做。It would be too unfortunate if one country leads in putting weapons into outer space, with other states *following suit*. 如果一国率先将武器引入外空,其他国家纷纷效仿,那就太不幸了。The US dollar fell sharply Wednesday and stocks in New York *followed suit* dropping steeply. 美元在周三大幅下跌,纽约股市也随之急剧下挫。

F

NOTE 本短语中的名词 suit 意为扑克里“同一套花色的牌”。在打扑克的时候，上家出什么花色，下家就都必须出什么花色，这叫作 follow suit(跟牌)。所以，follow suit 便用来喻指“跟着做”,“效仿他人”。

follow through *vi.* continue doing something until it is completed 坚持完成，进行到底:(常与 on 或 with 连用) Professor Brown is always starting projects, but he hasn't *followed through* on one project this year. 布朗教授经常开启一些项目，但今年他一个项目都没有搞完。The government needs to *follow through* with some very necessary reforms. 政府需要把一些十分必要的改革进行到底。

follow up *v.* ❶do (something) in addition to what you have already done, in order to be certain of achieving your aim 继续干下去，再接再厉: The students said they were going to collect more money for the sick child, but they didn't *follow up*. 学生们说，他们要为那患病的儿童筹募更多的钱，可他们却没有继续做下去。They should follow this up. 他们应该将此事做下去。We must *follow up* our victories and wipe out the enemy. 我们必须乘胜追击，全歼敌人。❷try to find out more about (something) or do (something) more to deal with it 追查: The police are now *following up* some new leads. 警方正在追查一些新的线索。They never *followed* my complaint *up*. 他们从未对我所投诉的事件进行过追查。❸check the health of (someone who has received medical treatment), in order to be certain that it was effective 对(曾接受过治疗的患者)进行跟踪调查: The study *followed up* over 200 heart patients. 他们对 200 名心脏病患者进行了跟踪调查。

NOTE 1. 当本短语用作及物性动词短语，宾语为代词时，该代词须置于本短语的动词和副词中间。

2. 本短语可转化复合词 follow-up，意思为“对病人的医疗跟踪调查，对消息的补充报道；补充的，继续的”。

fond of *adj.* (常用在 be, become, get, grow 等系动词后作表语) liking and caring about (someone, something or doing something) very much, especially as a result of knowing them well or for a long time 喜欢，爱: Are you *fond of* children? 你喜欢孩子吗? Mrs Green had become *fond of* her. 格林夫人喜欢起她来了。As an American, he was very *fond of* Chinese history and geography. 作为一个美国人，他酷爱中国历史和地理。We had grown *fond of* the house and didn't want to leave. 我们喜欢上了这所房子，都不想离开了。He was extremely *fond of* pointing out other people's mistakes. 他特别喜欢挑别人的错误。

NOTE 1. 本短语指对某人或某物的“喜爱”，语气比 like 强，比 love 弱。有时跟表示令人不快的事物或行为的词语连用，表达贬义。例如:

> You're rather too *fond of* the sound of your own voice!
> 你讲话太多了吧!
> You're too *fond of* leaving the door open when you go out!
> 你太爱出去不关门了!

2. 当表示“不喜欢”时，不说 be not fond of，而用 do not care to/for。例如:

> She *doesn't care to* take a walk after supper.
> 她不喜欢在晚饭后散步。
> I *don't* much *care for* that color.
> 我不太喜欢那种颜色。

foot the bill *vi.* (非正式用语,常与 for 连用) be responsible for paying all the cost of something 付账,买单: Who will be *footing the bill* for the party? 这聚会的费用由谁来付? Once again it will be the taxpayer who has to *foot the bill*. 还得由纳税人再次买单。

for a change *adv.* instead of what usually happens; for the sake of variety or novelty 为改变一下;为了变换花样: Why don't you let me drive *for a change*? 你何不让我开车来换换你? I usually have breakfast at 7:30, but during the holidays I'm having it at 8:00 *for a change*. 我通常 7 点半吃早饭,但在假日中我要改变一下,8 点钟吃。Why don't we go to a restaurant *for a change*? 咱们改去饭馆用餐吧?

for a moment *adv.* for a very short period of time 一会儿,片刻: May I speak to you *for a moment*? 我可以和你谈一会儿话吗? They rested *for a moment* and then resumed their work. 他们休息了片刻,便又接着干起活儿来。

NOTE **1.** 如在本短语前出现否定词 not 或 never 时,即 not/never for a moment,则表示"决不""从来没有"之意。例如:

> *Not for a moment* did I harbor ill intention against you.
> 我绝没有对你怀有过恶意。
> I have never *for a moment* suggested that you should leave.
> 我从没提出过你应该走。

2. 不要将本短语与 for the moment 混淆。for the moment 表示"暂时,目前"之意。

for a time *adv.* (used for saying what happened or existed during a short period before it changed) temporarily; for a certain period 暂时,一度: He is staying at the seaside *for a time*. 他现暂时住在海滨。We were quite happy *for a time*, until his brother moved in. 在他哥哥搬进来住之前,我们曾十分开心过一段时日。*For a time* the police thought she might be guilty. 警方曾一度认为她可能有罪。

for a while *adv.* for a period of time, especially a short one 一段时间,一会儿: Now that the exams are over, we can all relax *for a while*. 既然考试结束了,我们都可以轻松一段时间了。Just wait *for a while* and then I'll go and help you. 稍等一会儿,我就去帮你。

NOTE 本短语相当于副词 awhile,两者可互换使用。

for ages *adv.* (非正式用语) for a very long time 很长时间,很久: She's lived here *for ages*. 她已在这儿住很长时间了。Where's Mary? I haven't seen her *for ages*. 玛丽在哪儿呢? 我很久没见到她了。

NOTE 本短语中的名词 age 必须用复数形式。

for all *prep.* despite; in spite of (something) 尽管: *For all* its faults, Liverpool is a city that you grow to love. 尽管利物浦有些缺憾之处,但你会慢慢喜欢上这个城市。*For all* his wealth, he is not happy. 尽管他很富有,但他并不幸福。

for all intents and purposes ⇨ **to all intents and purposes**

for better or (for) worse *adv.* under good or bad circumstances; whatever happens; with good or bad effect 不管怎样,不论发生什么,不论好坏: "*For better or worse*, Britain's destiny is closely linked to that of the United States," He said. "不管怎样,英国的命运和美国的命运是紧密相关的。"他说道。He promised to take her *for better or worse*. 他许诺说不管发生什么他都要娶她为妻。He's the partner I chose, *for better or for worse*. 不论好坏,他是我选择的伙伴。

NOTE 本短语源自西方教堂婚礼中的结婚誓言。传统的结婚誓言通常有这样一段话:"I(your full name) take thee (your partner's full name) to be my wedded wife/husband, to have and to hold from this day forward, *for better or for worse*, for richer or for poorer, in sickness and in health, to love and to cherish, until death do us apart."[我(本人姓名),愿娶/嫁你(对方姓名),成为我的妻子/丈夫。从今以后,不论是好是坏,是贫是富,是悲伤是快乐,我会好好爱你,珍惜你,直到死亡将我们分开。]

for certain *adv.* certainly or definitely; without any doubt 确实地,肯定地: "How do you know *for certain* this man is the thief?" the policeman asked. "你怎么会肯定地知道这个人就是小偷呢?"警察问道。I think I met her last year, but I can't say *for certain*. 我想我是在去年见过她,但我说不准。They still don't know where the hostage is being held and will know *for certain* only when they have seen him. 他们尚不知人质现在被押何处,只有见到他后才会确切地知道。"Are you going to the party?" "*For certain* I am." "你去参加聚会吗?""我肯定去。"

NOTE 本短语的主词 certain 可被 definite, sure 替换,构成的短语与本短语意义和用法相同。其中 for sure 是非正式用语,常用于 that's for sure 的形式中。例如:

> They don't want any of us there this weekend, that's *for sure*.
> 他们不希望我们任何人本周末在那里。这点是肯定的。

for ever *adv.* ❶for all time in the future, or for as long as you can imagine 永远地,永久: They promised to love each other *for ever*. 他们相互承诺永远相爱。Gone *for ever* are the days when China had to depend entirely on foreign countries for oil. 中国完全依赖国外供油的日子一去不复返了。❷(非正式用语) for a long time, usually longer than you would like 没完没了: He is *for ever* asking whys. 他问这问那,没完没了。The soap opera seemed to go on *for ever*. 这部电视连续剧好像永远也演不完似的。

NOTE 为加强语气,本短语可被扩展为 for ever and ever。例如:

> I will be your true friend *for ever and ever*.
> 我将永远永远做你真正的朋友。

for example *adv.* (used when mentioning something that shows the type of thing you are talking about and helps to explain what you mean) as an example; as proof; to give an example or illustration 例如,比如说: Smith is rather weak in spelling. *For example*, this composition of his is full of spelling mistakes. 史密斯的拼写很差劲。例如,他这篇作文里就满是拼写错误。You may wear something simple for the meeting; *for example*, a skirt and blouse. 你可以穿简单的衣服赴会;比如说,一条裙子和一件衬衫。

NOTE **1.** 本短语常被 eg (拉丁语 exempli gratia 的缩略式)所替换,但只用于书面语中。

2. 本短语常与动词 take 搭配使用,take … for example 意为"以……为例"。例如:

> *Take* the southern province *for example*. It has around 10,000 primary school-age children who don't go to school at all.
> 以这一南部省份为例,该省约有一1万名学龄儿童根本就不上学。

3. 本短语作为插入成分,在句中作状语。在举例说明某一论点或情况时,本短语与 for instance 常通用。但本短语更侧重说明从诸多的事物中列出一种事物为例,而且比 for instance 常用。

for fear of *prep.* because of fear or anxiety of; in case of 因害怕,担忧,唯恐:Helen understood that Virginia dared not leave the house *for fear of* what Paul might do. 海伦知道弗吉尼亚不敢离开家是怕保罗会干出什么事来。The nurse walked on tiptoe *for fear of* waking the patient. 护士踮着脚走唯恐会吵醒病人。I didn't go there *for fear of* him seeing me. 我没敢到那儿去,是因为怕被他看见。

for fear that *conj.* because of fear or anxiety that(something might happen)生怕,唯恐:I didn't go there *for fear that* he will see me. 我没敢到那儿去,是因为怕他看见我。I daren't tell you what he did *for fear that* he should be angry with me. 我不敢告诉您他所做的事,因为怕他对我发脾气。They wouldn't let their cat outside *for fear that* it would get run over. 他们不让猫往外跑,是因为害怕它被车轧着。

NOTE 1. 在本短语所引导的状语从句中,谓语动词前一般要用 will, should, would, may, might 等。

2. 本短语中的 that 可以省略。

for free *adv.* (主要用于美国英语中,非正式用语)without payment; for no charge; free of any cost 免费地: You may download interesting games totally *for free* at the website. 你可以从这个网址上完全免费地下载有趣的游戏。They got a great lunch, *for free*. 他们没花钱就美美地吃了一顿午餐。

NOTE 本短语的同义短语是 for nothing 和 free of charge。

for good (and all) *adv.* (非正式用语) permanently, without the possibility of change in the future; forever 永久地,永远地: It looks like Jamie has left *for good* this time. 看来这次杰米要一去永不回还了。We thought she'd come for a visit, but it seems she's staying *for good and all*. 我们以为她是来串串门,但看来她要永远住在这里不走了。

NOTE for good and all 是美国英语用法。

for instance *adv.* as an example 例如,譬如说: *For instance*, the moon is the earth's satellite. 举个例子说,月亮是地球的卫星。What would you do if you met a wild animal—a lion, *for instance*? 如果你碰上一只野兽,譬如说,一头狮子,你该怎么办?

for lack of ⇨ **from lack of**

for life *adv.* till the end of one's life; for the remainder of one's life 一辈子,终生: The accident caused me to become blind *for life*. 那场事故使我终生盲目。The high-ranking official was sentenced to death, and was also deprived of his political rights *for life*, for accepting huge bribes. 这名高官因收受巨额贿赂而被判处死刑,并被剥夺政治权利终身。How can I make some friends *for life*? 我怎样才能结交一些终生的挚友呢?

for long *adv.* for a long period of time 很长时间,长久地: Have you been married *for long*? 你们结婚很长时间了吗? I haven't known them *for long*. 我认识他们的时间不长。Developing countries won't put up with the situation *for* much *longer*. 发展中国家不会再长久地容忍这种局面了。

for nothing *adv.* ❶ for no money; without any payment; free of charge 免费地, 无偿地: I got this bicycle *for nothing*; my friend gave me it when he bought a new one. 我没花钱就得到了这部自行车——是我朋友买了新自行车后就把它送给了我。Children under 5 can travel *for nothing*. 五岁以下的儿童可以免费旅行。Some of the men volunteered to work *for nothing*. 一些人自愿无偿地工作。❷without result or reward 无收获地, 无结果地, 无回报地: It was not *for nothing* that he spent three years studying the subject. 他花了 3 年时间研究这个题目并非毫无收获。The president says anti-terrorism is not an easy mission, and will not be accomplished overnight, but he will settle *for nothing* less than victory. 总统说,反恐这项使命并不轻松,不会一蹴而就。但是不获全胜,他决不罢休。❸without a reason or purpose 毫无理由地, 无缘无故地, 无端地: It is not *for nothing* that Paris is called the fashion capital of the world. 巴黎被称作世界时装之都不无理由。These children always quarrel *for nothing*. 这些孩子总是无缘无故地争吵。Why did you call me down here *for nothing*? 你为何无端地把我叫到这儿来?

NOTE 1. 本短语的否定形式是 not for nothing。

2. 当本短语作"免费地, 无偿地"解时, 同义短语是 for free 和 free of charge。

for one thing …(**for another**) *adv.* (used for giving a reason for something) in the first place …(in the second place) 首先……(再者……), 一则……(再则……): The house is poorly built. *For one thing*, the roof leaked. 这房子盖得不好, 首先是房顶漏水。We must learn English well. *For one thing*, we have to pass some exams; *for another*, it is a tool for us to communicate with the outside world. 我们必须学好英语。一则, 我们不得不通过某些考试; 二则它是我们与外界交流的一种工具。Why didn't we visit? Well, *for one thing*, it was too far away. And *for another*, she never invited us. 我们为什么没有去? 一是那儿太远, 二是她从来没邀请过我们。

NOTE 1. 本短语是用来解释或说明前面句子的理由或原因的, 因此, 在本短语前必须要有一个句子。

2. for one thing 经常单独使用, 在使用时可将 thing 省略掉。例如:

> There are a lot of reasons I don't want your old car. *For one*, there are squirrels living in the upholstery.
> 我不想要你那辆旧车有很多原因。一则, 就是车椅里住着松鼠。

for one's part *adv.* (正式用语)(used for emphasizing who you are referring to in a statement about something) as far as one is concerned; from one's point of view 至于某人, 就某人来说: You can go with them if you like, but *for my part* I prefer to stay at home. 假如你喜欢, 你可以和他们去; 至于我, 我宁愿留在家里。Napoleon's army was weakened and the British, *for their part*, were eager to attack. 拿破仑军队的战斗力被削弱了, 而英军方面则急于发动攻势。

NOTE 1. 本短语中的名词 part 无论其前的

物主代词是单数还是复数形式，都必须用单数形式。

2. 本短语与 on one's part 意义和用法相同，两者可互换使用。

for oneself *adv.* without the help of others; independently 独自，独立地：You should work out the problem *for yourself*. 你应该独立解决这个问题。Foreign media have been allowed into the Chinese mainland's first confirmed bird flu site to see *for themselves* the health of the residents. 外国媒体的记者已被允许进入中国大陆首个确诊禽流感的疫点，亲眼看一看那里居民的健康状况。

for sale *adj.* available for people to buy; being sold 供出售：This house near the road is for sale. 路旁的那所房子待售。Have you any discount landscape pictures *for sale*? 你有折价的山水画出售吗? Today, advertisers always play up the good quality of the houses *for sale* and fail to mention their disadvantages. 当今，登广告的人总是夸大他们要出售的房子的优点，而不提其欠缺之处。

NOTE 本短语与 on sale 均表示“供出售”。但 for sale 多指私人拥有的物品要出售(如房子、车等)，而 on sale 则多指商店里的商品供出售。另外，on sale 还有“减价出售”的意义。

for short *adv.* as a shorter way of saying the same name; as an abbreviation (名字的)简称，缩写：My name is Elizabeth, or Liza *for short*. 我的名字叫伊丽莎白，或简称莉莎。Organization of Petroleum Exporting coun-tries is called OPEC for short. 石油输出国组织的简称为 OPEC (欧佩克)。

NOTE 本短语的另外一种表达方式是 short for。例如：

> OPEC, *short for* Organization of Petroleum Exporting Countries, is an intergovernmental organization dedicated to the stability and prosperity of the petroleum market.
> OPEC (Organization of Petroleum Exporting Countries 的简称)是一个旨在稳定和繁荣石油市场的政府间组织。

for (one's) sake *adv.* ❶ for the benefit or good of (someone)为了(某人)的利益：We hope *for her sake* that the wedding goes as planned. 为了她，我们希望婚礼如期举行。She did it *for her brother's sake*. 她是为了她弟弟而做此事的。I'm not just doing this *for my sake*, you know. 你知道，我不是在为自己做这件事。❷ for the purpose of (something)为了……起见：*For clarity's sake*, I'd like to reword my statement. 为了清楚起见，我再把我讲的重复一遍。*For safety's sake*, never stand behind a horse. 为了安全起见，千万不要站在马匹的身后。

NOTE 1. 本短语的另外一种表达形式是 for the sake of 。

2. 本短语还常用于这种形式中：*for* God's/christ's/goodness'/heaven's/pete's *sake* (看在上帝的分上)。例如：

> Oh, *for* God's *sake*, leave me alone!
> 哦，看在上帝的分上，别打扰我啦!

这种形式只用于口语中，用于表达不耐烦的情绪。

for sure ⇨ **for certain**

for the benefit of *prep.* for the profit or advantage of (someone or something)为……的利益：*For the benefit of* those people who arrived late, I'll just go over the plan again. 为了那些迟到的人，我把

计划再讲一遍。The EU Constitution was written *for the benefit of* all the member states. 欧盟宪法是为所有成员国的利益而制定的。Hartman should resign *for the benefit of* the party. 哈特曼应该为党的利益而辞职。

NOTE 本短语与 for the sake of(第一个义项)意义和用法相同。

F

for the moment *adv.* as far as the present time is concerned (although perhaps not later); temporarily; for now 暂时,目前:I want to leave this subject *for the moment* and talk about something else. 我想把这一主题暂时搁置一下,讲一点别的。*For the moment* we are content to watch and wait. 目前,我们只能观察和等待了。

NOTE **1.** 不要将本短语与 at the moment 相混淆,两者虽然都是副词性短语,但意义却不同。at the moment 表示"现在,此刻,当时,那时"之意。

2. 不要将本短语与 for a moment 混淆,两者意义不同。for a moment 表示"片刻,一会儿"之意。例如:

> He paused *for a moment*.
> 他停顿了片刻。

3. 本短语的同义短语是 for the present 和 for the time being。

for the most part *adv.* in most cases; mostly or generally 多半,在大多情况下,一般说来:This orange drink is *for the most part* water. 这种橘子汁饮料多半是水。Professors, *for the most part*, are committed to teaching, not research. 教授要多致力于教学,而不是研究。There were a few complaints, but *for the most part* tourists seemed to enjoy themselves during the 7-day long National Day holiday. 尽管有一些投诉,但大多数游客在国庆节七天长假期间都玩得愉快。

for the present *adv.* now but not necessarily in the future; temporarily 目前,暂时:*For the present* we had better do nothing. 目前我们最好不要做任何事。Let's leave things as they are *for the present*; we can always make changes later on if we have to. 我们就暂时保持现状吧。如果必要,我们以后还是可以改变的。He thought the matter might be left over *for the present*. 他认为这事可以暂时不去处理。

NOTE 本短语与 for the moment 和 for the time being 意义相同,都表示"暂时"之意。它们之间的区别见 for the time being。

for the sake of *prep.* ❶ for the good or benefit of (someone or something) 为了对……有好处,为了……的利益:Some parents claim that the reason why they do not divorce is *for the sake of* their children. 一些做父母的声称,他们不离婚的原因就是为了孩子。We moved to the south *for the sake of* my wife's health. 为了我妻子的身体健康,我们搬到了南方去住。❷ for the purpose of (doing, getting, or achieving something) 为了……起见:He speaks slowly *for the sake of* clarity. 为了清楚起见,他讲得很慢。She changed into old clothes *for the sake of* comfort. 为了舒服起见,她穿上了旧衣服。I hope you're not doing this just *for the sake of* the money. 我希望你做这件事不光是为了钱。*For the sake of* settling the matter they decided to hold a meeting to discuss it in detail. 为了解决这一问题,他们决定召开一次会议详加讨论。

NOTE 本短语的另外一种表达形式是 for one's sake。

for the time being *adv.* (正式用语)for a limited period; temporarily 暂时:He has no plan or timetable for a vacation. 他暂时还没有休假的计划或时间表。*For the time being*, you will have to share this room with another person. 你暂时得和另外一个人合住这个房间。

NOTE 本短语与 for the moment 和 for the present,都表示"暂时"之意。for the time being 是比较正式的用语,而 for the moment 和 for the present 则多用于日常口语中,侧重"就目前来说,就眼下情况而论"。

for want of *prep.* for lack of 因缺乏:*For want of* a screw the wheel came off. 由于缺一颗螺钉,车轮脱落了。The plan failed *for want of* money. 这项计划因缺少资金而告失败。I have been refused admittance *for want of* room. 由于没有空房,我被拒绝入住。Many of them have gone into teaching *for want of* anything better to do. 他们中有许多人都因很少有更好的工作可做而从事了教学。

NOTE 1. 本短语的另外一种表达形式是 from want of。

2. 本短语与 from lack of 意义相同,一般在句中作状语。

forget it *s.* (仅用于口语中,用于祈使句中) ❶(主要用于回答道歉语)overlook it; it's not important; it doesn't matter at all 不必在意,没关系:"I'm sorry, Mr Smith. I think I was a bit rude to you." "*Forget it*, but don't do it again." "对不起,史密斯先生。我想我刚才对你有点无礼了。""没关系。但以后不要再这样了。"❷(主要用于回答致谢语,在 forget 和 it 之间常用 about)don't mention it; you're welcome 没什么,别客气:"Thanks so much for helping me!" "*Forget about it*. It was nothing." "十分感谢你对我的帮助!""别客气。这不算什么。"❸(在 forget 和 it 之间常用 about) do not think or worry about it 不要担心:Their attitude was, if you understood all of it, fine, and if not, *forget* (about) *it*. 他们的态度是,如果你全部看懂了,那很好;但如果没看懂,无所谓。❹it is impossible 不可能:"I'd like to take a week's holiday." "*Forget it*, we're too busy." "我想休一周假。""不可能。我们太忙了。" ❺(在 forget 和 it 之间常用 about) do not even ask about it 就不要问了:I enjoyed the dinner, but as for the party, well, *forget* (about) *it*! 吃的我倒挺喜欢;至于晚会嘛,就不要问了。

free from[1] *vt.* 【可分性动词短语】set (someone or something) free from (someone or something) 把……放走;使……摆脱……:The US Navy succeeded in *freeing* the hostage captain *from* the Somali pirates. 美国海军成功地从索马里海盗手中解救出了被扣为人质的船长。With the introduction of automation man can further *free* himself *from* heavy work. 随着自动化的引用,人们进一步地摆脱了繁重的劳动。The rise in personal income tax collection threshold *freed* 70 percent of income earners *from* paying income tax. 此次个人所得税起征标准的上调,使工薪阶层中 70%的人不再缴纳个人所得税。He has been *freed from* all trouble. 他从所有的困扰中解脱了出来。The mouse tried to *free* itself *from* the catcher. 老鼠竭力要从捕鼠器中挣脱出来。

free from[2] *adj.* not containing or involving (something unpleasant) 无……的,免于……的:This laboratory is *free from* outside sound. 这个实验室不受外界声音的干扰。We want to give all children a world *free from* violence. 我们想为所有的儿童提供一个没有暴力的世界。Keep the wound *free from* dirt. 要保持伤口清洁。

NOTE 1. 本短语可在句中充当表语、后置定

F

语和宾语补足语。

2. 本短语后接的宾语一般为抽象名词。

3. 虽然本短语有"免于……"之意,但若"免除"的客体是与金钱有关的名词时,则要用 free of 来表示。例如:free of charge/debt(免交费用/豁免债务)。

free of[1] *vt.*【可分性动词短语】(常用一般时态)take away from (a person, animal, or place) anything uncomfortable, inconvenience, difficult, unpleasant, etc. 使……摆脱…… She can't *free* herself *of* the idea that someone's watching her all the time. 她自己无法摆脱总有人在盯着她的这一念头。This letter should *free* your mind *of* worry. 这封信应该使你免除思想顾虑了。He opened the door and windows to *free* the room *of* smoke. 他打开门窗,把房间里的烟放了出去。

NOTE 本短语的同义短语是 free from[1]。

free of[2] *adj.* without or free from (something or someone unwanted)无……的,免于……的,摆脱……:Most of the roads are *free of* snow now. 大多数的路面上现在都已无雪了。Not very many imports are *free of* all duty. 并非许多进口货全都免税。She's been nothing but a nuisance; I'll be glad to be *free of* her. 她是个令人讨厌的人,摆脱她我会很高兴。

NOTE 本短语的同义短语是 free from[2]。

free of charge *adv.*(主要用于美国英语中)without payment; without charge; without cost 免费地:If you have problems when installing Windows Vista SP1, you can get technical help from Microsoft *free of charge*. 如果您在安装 Windows Vista SP1 时有什么问题,可以免费得到微软公司的技术帮助。The city gardens should be open to the public *free of charge*. 市内的公园应该对公众免费开放。

NOTE 本短语的同义短语是 for free 和 for nothing。

frighten into *vt.*【可分性动词短语】threaten (someone or an animal) into (doing something)恐吓(人或动物)做(某事):He *frightened* the old lady *into* signing the paper. 他恐吓那位老妇人在文件上签了字。The villagers were *frightened into* surrendering all their grain by the armed bandits. 村民们被武装匪徒吓得把所有的粮食都交了出来。Let's try to *frighten* the dogs *into* running away. 咱们想法把这些狗吓跑吧。

NOTE 本短语的反义短语是 frighten out of。例如:

> The presence of the police *frightened* the criminals *out of* attempting further crimes.
> 警察的出现吓得罪犯们不敢继续实施犯罪。

from bad to worse *adv.*(非正式用语,常与动词 go 连用,常用完成时态)much worse even than before; on a steady downward course 越来越糟,每况愈下:The weather has gone *from bad to worse*. 天气越来越糟糕。Tom's grades have gone *from bad to worse*. 汤姆的成绩每况愈下。

from day to day *adv.* each day; daily; in small slow stages as each day passes 每天,一天天,日益:The weather is unpredictable; it changes *from day to day*. 天气不好预测,天天都在变化。We just made our plans *from day to day*. 我们只是一天一天地订计划。

NOTE 本短语与 day by day 意义相同。两者之间的区别见 day to day。

from lack of *prep.* for want of 因缺乏:*From lack of* raw material we had to step down production. 因缺乏原材料,我们不得

不减少了产量。The case was dismissed *from lack of* evidence. 由于缺乏证据，该案被驳回。The plants died *from lack of* water. 植物因缺水而枯死了。The match had to be cancelled *from lack of* financial support. 因缺少资助，比赛被迫取消了。

NOTE 本短语另外的表达形式是 for lack of 和 through lack of。

from now on *adv.* (一般用于表示将来的句子中) from this time onward; starting from the present time 从现在起，从今以后：*From now on* any violation of the regulation will be severely punished. 今后，任何违反该规定的行为将会受到严厉处罚。We hope *from now on* there will be more exchanges between our two peoples. 我们希望今后两国人民之间有更多的交往。

from the (bottom of one's) heart *adv.* (used for emphasizing that a feeling is very strong) very willingly; with one's whole heart; in earnest; in a sincere manner (用于强调某种强烈的感情) 从心底里，十分愿意地，十分真诚地，诚心诚意地：*From the bottom of our hearts* we hope that the friendship between our two peoples will last forever. 衷心祝愿我们两国人民的友谊万古长青。A mother loves her children *from the heart*. 妈妈是从心底里爱自己的孩子。

NOTE 本短语的同义短语是 with all one's heart(and soul)。

from then on *adv.* from that time onward; starting at that time 从那时起，从那以后：*From then on* he refused to talk about it. 从那以后，他就不肯再谈此事了。We graduated last June and I haven't seen John *from then on*. 我们是去年 6 月份毕业的，从那以后，我就一直没见过约翰。

from time to time *adv.* occasionally; sometimes, but not often 不时地，偶尔，有时：This is the principal reason why China-US relations have suffered setbacks *from time to time*. 这就是中美关系不时地遭受挫折的主要原因。He has come to visit Hong Kong *from time to time* since 1997. 自 1997 年以来，他不时地前来访问香港。*From time to time* he brings me a present. 他偶尔给我带一件礼物来。

NOTE 本短语的同义短语是 at times, every now and then, now and again 和 now and then。它们之间的区别见 at times。

from top to bottom *adv.* (of a place or organization) all through; completely and thoroughly (指某一个地方或机构) 彻底地，整个地：We cleaned the house *from top to bottom* this morning. 我们今天上午把房子彻底地打扫了一番。This company needs reorganizing *from top to bottom*. 该公司需要彻底改组。The mountain was covered with trees *from top to bottom*. 这座山整个都被树木所覆盖。

from want of ⇨ **for want of**

frown on/upon *vt.* (用一般时态) show displeasure or disapproval of (someone or something) 对……表示不悦；不同意，不赞成，反对：The boss *frowns on* those who come to work late. 老板对上班迟到的人蹙眉露出不悦之色。She wanted to go to Hawaii all by herself, but her parents *frowned on* the idea. 她想要自己去夏威夷，但她父母不同意她这一想法。Most doctors *frown on* a diet which has a lot of fat. 大多数医生都不赞成脂肪含量过高的饮食。My mother has always *frowned on* spending money needlessly.

F

我母亲历来反对花不必要花的钱。The study found that activities like skating and skateboarding—which adults sometimes *frown upon*—also bring better self-esteem to children. 这项研究发现，诸如轮滑或滑板等有时会遭成年人反对的活动也可以带给孩子们更多的自尊。

NOTE 1. 本短语中的 upon 用法比 on 正式，但不及 on 常用。

2. 本短语的同义短语是 disagree with 和 disapprove of；反义短语是 agree with 和 approve of。

F

full of *adj.* containing or having plenty of 充满，有许多：As a country with a long civilized history, China is also one big oriental country *full of* modern vitality. 中国是一个历史悠久的文明古国，也是一个充满时代生机的东方大国。The British writers, who thought China was *full of* dark streets and cyclists, are greatly impressed by how the country has developed. 英国作家以为中国到处都是阴暗的街道和骑着自行车的人们，而今日中国的发展给他们留下了深刻印象。

full up *adj.*（主要用于英国英语中）❶not having space left for any more people or things 满员的，装满的：The train's *full up*; there are no seats left at all. 火车已经满员，根本就没座位了。His drawer was *full up* with old clothes. 他的抽屉里塞满了旧衣物。❷（非正式用语）not wanting to eat any more because you have eaten or drunk a lot 吃饱喝足的："Would you like some dessert?" "No thanks, I'm *full up*." "你想吃点甜食吗？""不了，谢谢。我已吃饱喝足了。"

NOTE 在美国英语中，本短语中的 up 常省略。

fuss about/around *vt.*（非正式用语）feel worried and nervous about (someone or something) 忧虑，担心：She *fusses* too much *about* her health. 她过分忧虑自己的健康。I wish you would stop *fussing about* me; I'm quite able to look after myself. 我希望你们不要担心我。我完全能照顾好自己。Stop *fussing around* (that child). She will be happier with Mary than with her own family. 别担心（那个孩子）了。她和玛丽在一起生活比和她家人在一起生活会更幸福。

NOTE 1. fuss about 是英国英语用法，而 fuss around 是美国英语用法。

2. 本短语的另外一种表达形式是 make a fuss about。

fuss over *vt.* give (a person or animal) too much attention, especially to show that you are pleased with them or like them 过分关心，非常喜爱（人或动物）：Everyone in the family was *fussing over* the new baby. 家里的每个人都十分喜爱这个新生的宝宝。The old lady *fusses over* her little dog as if it were a sick child. 老妇人过分呵护她的小狗，就好像那小狗是个生病的孩子似的。

NOTE 本短语的另外一种表达形式是 make a fuss over。

G g

gain access to ⇨ **have access to**

gain ground *vi.* (常用进行时态) become more popular or accepted 更受欢迎;被接受: The Democratic candidate is rapidly *gaining ground* in many states. 这位民主党候选人很快就在很多州取得了支持。The idea of equal pay for women is *gaining ground*. 妇女同工同酬的主张已被接受。As the Internet *gains ground*, search engines have become important tools for people to locate online information. 随着互联网的普及,搜索引擎已经成了人们查找在线信息的重要工具。

NOTE 本短语的反义短语是 lose ground。例如:

> The Democrats were *losing ground* in this district.
> 民主党正在失去这一地区的支持。

gain weight *vi.* (of a person) increase in (body weight) and become fatter (指人) 增加体重,发胖: I *gained* a lot of *weight* after the baby was born. 我生了孩子后,长了许多体重。Studies show homemakers tended to *gain weight* more easily and had the highest rate of obesity at 38 percent. 一些研究表明,家庭主妇更容易发胖,其肥胖率是最高的,为 38%。Researchers at Harvard Medical School said on Monday that new mothers who want to lose the extra *weight gained* in pregnancy should try to get more sleep. 哈佛医学院的研究人员于本周一称,新妈妈们如果想减掉怀孕期间增加的体重,应该尽量多睡觉。

NOTE 本短语的同义短语是 put on weight;反义短语是 lose weight。

gamble on *vt.* ❶ risk (money) on (the result of something such as a horse race or the performance of a competitor) (以钱)赌……的输赢: He *gambles* most of his income *on* horses. 他把大部分收入都花在了赌马上。Are you going to *gamble on* the result of the boxing match? 你要赌这场拳击比赛的输赢吗? ❷ take a chance on; be too sure of (something, someone or doing something) 冒险于;过于相信: They carried out robbery on Christmas Day, *gambling on* no one being in the building. 他们以为圣诞节那天楼内无人,便冒险抢劫。Don't *gamble on* getting the job. 不要过于相信能得到这份工作。

gather in *vt.* 【可分性动词短语】❶ collect (crops from the field when they are ready) 收获(成熟作物): The farmers are *gathering in* the corn. 农民们正在收割玉米。There was a week of rain before all the crops could be safely *gathered in*. 在把所有作物都安全收获前,下了一个星期的雨。❷ receive; collect (something such as money) 收敛(钱财等): The workers think that their bosses don't do any work, but just sit in their offices *gathering in* the profits. 工人们认为，他们的老板不做任何工作，只在办公室里坐收渔利。

gaze at *vt.*【不可分性动词短语】stare at (someone or something), usually because they are attractive or interesting 注视，凝视：We *gazed at* the stranger, wondering who he was. 我们注视着那个陌生人，不知道他是谁。We stood on the top of the mountain, *gazing* in wonder *at* the beautiful scenery before us. 我们站在山顶上惊异地凝望着我们眼前的美丽景象。*Gazing at* the gentle waves of the sea, all sorts of emotions surged within me. 我凝视着微波荡漾的大海，不禁感慨万千。

gear to/towards *vt.*【可分性动词短语】(常用被动语态形式) make (something) suitable for (a particular need or purpose) 使……适合于(某种需要或目的)：Education should be *geared to* the children's needs and abilities. 教育应该适合于儿童们的需要和能力。We must *gear* the amount of products we make *to* the level of public demand. 我们必须使产品数量适合于公众的需求水平。My training is *geared towards* winning gold at the Tokyo Olympic Games in 2020. 我的训练就是为了要在2020年东京奥运会上夺金。

gear up *v.* (非正式用语，常与反身代词连用，后常接介词 for 短语或动词不定式短语) prepare yourself or something for an activity or event 准备好：Most banks have *geared* themselves *up* for reforms. 大多数银行都已准备进行改革。The party is all *geared up* for the forthcoming election campaign. 该党为即将来临的大选完全做好了准备。The tobacco companies are *gearing up* to fight the new tax. 烟草公司都准备好抵制新税。

gee whiz *s.* (美国英语用法，仅用于口语中) used for expressing a reaction such as surprise, admiration, or other strong feelings (用于表达惊讶、羡慕或其他强烈情感)哎呀！哇！：*Gee whiz*, I am late again. 哎呀！我又迟到了。You got a new job? *Gee whiz*, that is great news, Mary. I'm really happy for you. 你得到了一份新工作？哎呀，那可是个极好的消息，玛丽。我真为你高兴。*Gee whiz*, Mr Smith! You certainly look as though you ought to own the company! 哇！史密斯先生！你这派头真像是公司的老板！

NOTE 本短语属旧式美国英语用法，现较少使用。本短语被认为是 Jesus! (天哪!) 的委婉说法。

generally speaking *adv.* used for showing that what you are saying is usually true, but not in every instance 一般说来，大体地说：*Generally speaking*, pet owners are law-abiding citizens. 一般说来，养宠物的人都是些守法的公民。*Generally speaking*, students in China are better at math than those in the US. 大体来说，中国学生的数学都比美国学生的好。

NOTE 本短语须置于句首，后面加逗号与其后的句子相隔。

get a glimpse of ⇨ **catch a glimpse of**

get about/around *vi.* (非正式用语) ❶(常用一般时态)go or travel to different places 到处走动；旅行：Old Tom can't *get about* much since he had that illness. 老汤姆自从得了那场病后便不大走动了。She's *getting about* much more than she used to, working for a foreign company. 她为一家外国公司工作，所以现在比过去旅行的多了很多。At the age of 85 Milly still *gets around* quite well. 米利在 85 岁高龄时走路还很好。❷(of news, etc.) become known; spread (消息等)为人所知,传开:The news of their secret wedding soon *got about*. 他们秘密结婚的消息很快就被人们知道了。Somehow it *got about* that Jenny was having a baby. 不知怎么回事,传言说杰妮要生小孩了。It didn't take long for news of his resignation to *get around*. 他辞职的消息很快就传开了。

NOTE get about 是英国英语用法, get around 是美国英语用法。

get above oneself *vi.* (主要用于英国英语中,贬义用法) show or feel that you are better or more important than others 骄傲自大,自命不凡: When the young man *gets* a bit *above himself*, he inclines to be a nuisance. 当这小伙子有点妄自尊大时,就招人烦了。Don't get *above yourself* for such a small victory. 不要为这小小的胜利就骄傲自大。Ever since they made her assistant manager, she's been *getting above herself*. 自从他们提她当上了副经理后,她就自命不凡了。

get access to ⇨ **have access to**

get across *vt.* &*vi.* (常用一般时态,常与 to 连用) make (a crowd) understand or accept (something)使(众人)理解,领会: I spoke slowly, but my meaning didn't *get across* to the crowd. 我讲得很慢,但我的意思并未被听众所理解。Our teacher is clever, but not very good at *getting* his ideas *across* to us. 我们的老师很聪明,但他不善于把自己的观点向我们表达清楚。

—*vt.* 【不可分性动词短语】(主要用于英国英语中,无被动语态形式) annoy or offend (someone) 使(某人)生气,触犯(某人): They really *got across* me. 他们确实使我生气。Take care not to *get across* the manager; he could have you dismissed. 注意不要触怒经理,他会炒你鱿鱼的。

NOTE 1. 当本短语作"使(众人)理解,领会"解时,常以 get it across 的形式使用。例如:

> He'll have to *get it across* to the others.
> 他得把自己的观点向其他人讲清楚。

2. 当本短语作"使(众人)理解,领会"解时,同义短语是 put across 和 put over。

get ahead *vi.* (常与 of 连用) be more successful or make progress more quickly (than other people)取得成功,取得进步: The best way to *get ahead* is through hard work. 取得成功的最佳途径是刻苦工作。Nowadays, you need IT skills if you want to *get ahead* in your career. 如今,如果你想在事业上取得成功,就需要掌握些信息技术方面的技能。By making more efforts, my son *got ahead* of others in his class. 由于付出了更多的努力,我的儿子比班里的其他同学进步都快。

get along *vi.* ❶(主要用于美国英语中) (of people) like each other and are friendly to each other (指人)和睦相处: Why don't you two *get along* nicely? You're always arguing. 你们俩就不能好好地相处吗? 总是争吵不休。Richard and his sister don't *get along*. 理查德和他的姐姐处不来。❷(主要用于美国英语中,常用进行时态) manage to continue doing something or make progress in the work that you do 进展,进步: How's the work *getting along*? 工作进展得怎样? Everything was *getting along* quite well. 一切进展顺利。❸(of a person) manage

G

to make a living, often in spite of difficulties (指人)设法生活下去：He didn't even offer to help us, but I'm sure we can *get along* quite well without him. 他甚至没提出过向我们提供帮助，不过我确信没有他的帮助我们也能生活得很好。Many of them couldn't *get along* on their wages. 他们中有很多人无法靠工资过活。I couldn't *get along* without your financial support. 没有你的资助，我就无法生活下去。❹(非正式用语，常用进行时态)leave (a place); go away (often to some other place)离开，走开：It's late; you'd better be *getting along* now. 天色晚了，你最好现在就走吧。*Get along*, you boys! I don't want you here! 走开，你们这些孩子！我不要你们在这里！

NOTE 不要将本短语与 go along 混淆，两者的意义和用法不同。

get along with *vt.*【不可分性动词短语】❶form or have a friendly relationship with (someone)与(某人)友好相处：Our boss is a person easy to *get along with*. He never puts on airs, making friends with everyone working in the department. 我们的老板是一个很容易相处的人。他从不摆架子，和部门里工作的每一个人都交朋友。Over 300 Chinese scientists working in US National Aeronautics and Space Administration are *getting along* well *with* scientists from various countries and have made great achievements. 目前有300多华裔科学家在美国国家宇航局工作，他们与各国优秀科学家友好相处，成就显赫。❷(常用进行时态)advance with (something such as a job)在(工作等方面)有进展：How are you *getting along with* your schoolwork? 你在学校的学习进展如何？He's not *getting along* very fast *with* his job. 他的工作进展不是很快。❸continue to live or work 继续生活；继续工作：We can't *get along with* so little money. 依靠这么点钱，我们无法生活下去。I suppose I could *get along with* the ironing while I'm waiting. 我想，我可以一边等待一边继续熨衣服。

NOTE **1.** 本短语主要用于美国英语中，在英国英语中用 get on with。

2. 不要将本短语与 go along with 混淆，两者的意义和用法不同。

get (someone) anywhere *v.* (非正式用语，常用于否定句中)(of a particular action or type of behavior) help (someone) to achieve anything (指某一行动或某种行为)有助于取得(某种)结果：Losing your temper won't *get you anywhere*. 你发火是无济于事的。This argument isn't *getting us anywhere*. 这样争论下去对我们无益。So far, Jack doesn't seem to be *getting anywhere* with his writing career. 杰克在他的写作上似乎至今没有什么成果。

NOTE 与本短语有关的短语有 get (someone) nowhere 和 get somewhere，见相关各条目。

get around/round *v.* ❶(常用一般时态)(cause to) move or travel (around a place) (使)走动，(绕……)旅行：My parents are over 80 but they still *get around* quite well. 我父母都已年过八旬，但他们走路还很好。It's easy in this city to *get around* by bus. 在这个城市里乘公共汽车旅行很方便。The quickest way to *get round* the city is by underground train. 在这个城市旅行，最快捷的方式是乘坐地铁。A taxi will *get* you *round* the city faster. 出租车会拉着你快捷地周游这个城市。❷(常用进行时态)(of news or information) become known; spread (消息或信息)公开,传播开: Bad news *gets around/round* quickly. 恶事传得快。News of her pregnancy soon *got round* (the office). 她怀孕的消息很快就(在办公室)传开了。Stories have been *getting round* concerning the government's cut in the educational budget. 一直在流传着政府削减教育预算的消息。❸ find a way of dealing with or overcome (a problem or difficulty)设法解决(问题);克服(困难):None of these countries has found a way yet to *get around/round* the problem of the polarization of wealth. 迄今为止,这些国家还没有一个找到解决贫富两极分化这个问题的办法。❹(常用一般时态) find a way of avoiding (something such as a law or rule)设法逃避(某项法律或法规): The businessman sometimes *gets around* the tax laws. 这位商人有时逃避税法。❺(常与 to 连用) persuade (someone) to do (something) or change his/her position 说服(某人)做(某事);劝(某人)改变立场: She didn't want to accept my application, but I managed to *get around* her. 她起初不想接受我的申请,但我成功地说服了她。I think I can *get round* my father to lend us the car. 我认为我能够说服我爸爸把车子借给咱们。We'll soon *get* him *round* to our point of view. 我们很快就会使他转而支持我们的观点。

NOTE get around 是美国英语用法, get round 是英国英语用法。

get at *vt.*【不可分性动词短语】(一般不用被动语态形式) ❶ manage to reach or touch (something or someone)触及,接近: I keep the sweets up here where the children can't *get at* them. 我把糖果都放在这儿了,孩子们够不到。They couldn't *get at* her for the crowd. 由于人群拥挤,他们无法接近她。❷(非正式用语,无被动语态形式,用进行时态,常用于疑问句中) try to suggest (something) without saying it directly 意指,暗示: I couldn't see what she was *getting at* exactly. 我搞不明白她到底是什么意思。Who is he *getting at*? 他指的是谁? I'm partly to blame? What exactly are you *getting at*? 我要负部分责任? 你究竟是什么意思? ❸(英国英语用法,非正式用语,常用被动语态形式) try to influence (someone) unfairly as by offers of money (利用不正当手段)企图影响(某人);贿赂(某人): The gangsters *got at* the jury, who found them not guilty of all charges. 这伙歹徒贿赂了陪审团,于是陪审团便判定他们所有的罪名都不成立。Policemen in this country cannot be *got at*. 这个国家的警察不受贿赂。Some of the jurors had been *got at*. 有些陪审员受了贿。❹ succeed in discovering (the truth about something)发现(真情事实):This was an attempt to stop journalists *getting at* the truth. 这一企图旨在阻止记者发现实情。❺(英国英语用法,非正式用语,常用进行时态) keep criticizing (someone) in a way that is unfair (反复地、不公正地)批评(某人): She's always *getting at* the children for nothing. 她总是无缘无故地训斥孩子们。Whenever his mother talked about men who drank too much, he had a feeling he was being *got at*. 每当他母亲谈论酗酒之徒时,他就感到是在数落他。Stop *getting at* me like this! 不要老是这样不公正地批评我!

get away *vi.* ❶(常用一般时态,常与 from 连用) manage to leave a place,

G

especially of your work (尤指从工作地点中)脱身：I'm sorry I'm late; I was in a meeting and couldn't *get away*. 对不起，我迟到了。我刚才在开会，无法脱身。The popular singer held a press conference in Hong Kong announcing that he would *get away* from the Hong Kong entertainment industry for the scandal. 这位当红歌手在香港举行了新闻发布会，宣布他将因丑闻而退出香港娱乐圈。❷(常用一般时态) go somewhere different from where you live in order to go on holiday or a short break 去(某地)休假，休息：I couldn't *get away* at all last year. I was too busy. 由于我太忙，去年根本没能休假。I hope to *get away* next Monday for at least a month. 我希望于下星期一开始休假至少一个月。❸(与 with 连用) manage to do something bad without being punished or criticized for it 逃避(惩罚或批评)：They have repeatedly broken the law and *got away* with it. 他们屡次违法，可都未受到惩处。How can she *get away* with speaking to her boss like that? 她那样与她的老板讲话，怎么没挨批评呢？❹(常用一般时态，常与 from，with 连用) escape (from a person or place), especially the scene of a crime 逃离(某人之手或某处，尤指犯罪现场)：A police officer grabbed him, but he *got away*. 一名警察抓住了他，但又给他逃掉了。The dog got away from me in the park. 狗在公园里从我手中跑掉了。They knocked off the bank and *got away* with ＄2 million. 他们抢劫了银行，随即携 200 万美元逃离现场。❺(用于祈使句中，常与 from，with 连用) (used for telling someone to move away from a person or place) leave 走开，离开：*Get away*, you guys! 你们这些家伙，走开！*Get away* from there! It's hot! 离开那儿！它很烫的！*Get away* with you! 你走开！

—*vt.*【可分性动词短语】(非正式用语) take (something) away (from a person, etc.) 把(某物)拿走：I must *get* that letter *away* from her before she reads what I said about her. 在她看到我写的那些有关她的那些言语之前，我必须把信从她手中夺走。

NOTE **1.** 本短语与 run away 均表示"逃跑"之意，都常用于口语中。run away 强调动作的迅速；而本短语指犯罪分子逃离犯罪现场或拒捕而逃掉。

2. 本短语可转化为复合词 getaway，意为"逃走，逃跑"。

get back *v.* ❶(常用一般时态)(cause to) return, especially to one's home 回来，回家：Will you keep an eye on the baby? I'll *get back* in a minute. 你能看一下孩子吗？我马上就回来。When did your neighbor *get back* from their holiday? 你的邻居是什么时候度假回来的？It's late; we must be *getting back* home. 天太晚了，我们得回家了。"Don't worry, child. I'll *get* you *back* safely," the policeman said. "孩子，不要担心。我会安全地把你送回家的。"那位警察说道。❷(常与 to 连用) start talking again about a subject you were talking about before 重谈(某一话题)：Let's *get back* to what we were saying before we were interrupted. 咱们再回到被打断以前的话题上去吧。❸(常与 to 连用)(cause to) return to (a former state or condition) 回到，恢复：I woke early, but could not *get back* to sleep. 我醒得很早，可又睡不着了。She has *got* her strength *back* after her illness. 她病后体

力已经恢复了。❹(常用一般时态) return or regain (something) after loss or separation 归还;找回;重新得到;回收(某物):I have to *get* these books *back* to the library before it closes. 我得在图书馆闭馆前把这些书还回去。He *got back* the watch he had lost. 他把丢失的表找回来了。He *got* his old job *back*. 他又得到了他以前那份工作。After the successful launch of its first moon orbiter, Chang'e 1, the expert said, China will launch a moon vehicle, and then *get* it *back*. 中国成功发射其首颗探月卫星"嫦娥一号"后,这位专家称,中国将发射月球车,然后将其回收。❺(常用一般时态,常与 at 或 in 连用)(of a political party) return to power, especially after being without it (指某政党)重新掌权:Will the Democratic Party *get back* in the next election? 民主党在下次大选中会重新执政吗? ❻(非正式用语,不用被动语态形式,常与 at 连用) revenge or punish (someone) in return for a wrong done to oneself 报复(某人):He was very rude and embarrassed me, but I'll *get* him *back*. 他十分无礼并使我难堪,但我会报复他的。I'll *get back* at her for insulting me at the party. 她在聚会上侮辱了我,我要报复她。

NOTE 当本短语用作及物性动词短语,所带的宾语为代词时,该代词须置于本短语的动词和副词中间。

get blood from a stone *vi.* (非正式用语,常与 be like 连用) try to get something, especially money, from a person, group, etc. that is unwilling or unable to give it; do something extremely difficult or impossible 做极其困难的事,做不可能的事:Getting money out of him is like *getting blood from a stone*. 想从他手里拿出钱来,就如同要从石头里榨出血来一样难。It's no use asking your father for a loan. You can't *get blood from a stone*. 向你父亲借钱是无用的,那是根本办不到的事。Getting my boss to agree to a pay rise is like *getting blood from a stone*. 要想让我的老板同意加薪,那实属妄想。

NOTE **1.** 本短语的另外一种表达形式是 get blood out of a stone。

2. 本短语的同义短语是 squeeze blood from a turnip。例如:

> Expecting good manners from that orphan is like trying to *squeeze blood from a turnip*!
> 指望那个孤儿举止优雅是办不到的。

get butterflies in one's stomach ⇨ **have butterflies in one's stomach**

get by *v.* (常用一般时态)❶pass; be able to move past (someone or something) 通过,从……走过去:How can I *get by* while you stand in the way? 你挡着路,我怎么过去? Please let me *get by* at once. 请立刻让我过去。I don't think that the ship will *get by* the enemy guns. 我认为,船只无法闯过敌人重重的炮火。❷(常与 on, with 连用) have just enough of something such as money or knowledge so that you can do what you need to do 勉强过得去,勉强应付得过去:I couldn't possibly get by on \$200 a month. 我不可能一个月靠 200 美元维持生计。My arithmetic isn't very good, but I *get by*. 我的算术不是很好,但还过得去。You could probably *get by* with that computer, but a more powerful one would be better. 你用那台计算机可能勉强对付,但用一台功能更强大一些的会

更好。❸succeed in cheating 作弊得逞：Don't try to cheat on your income tax; you'll never *get by*. 不要在所得税上耍花招，你不会得逞的。

get caught up in ⇨ **be caught up in**

get down *vt.* &*vi.* ❶(常与 from 连用) descend or cause (someone or something) to move down to a lower position or place (使)下去，下来：They climbed onto the cliff, but couldn't *get down*. 他们爬上了悬崖，但下不去了。The old man *got down* from the bus. 老人下了公共汽车。Some students escaped from the burning building by *getting down* from a ladder. 一些学生从梯子上下来，逃离了燃烧着的楼房。Firefighters *got* him *down* using a ladder. 消防队员用梯子使他下来了。❷lower your body until you are sitting, kneeling, or lying on the ground 坐下，蹲下，趴下："*Get down*!" she yelled. "Somebody is shooting!" "趴下！"她喊道。"有人在开枪！"❸(非正式用语) start feeling sad or losing hope; make (someone) feel sad or lose hope 感到不快(或失望)；使(某人)感到不快(或失望)：She *gets down* from time to time, but mostly she feels well. 她有时感到忧郁，但大多时间都心情不错。This continual wet weather is *getting* me *down*. 这样的连雨天使我感到郁闷。Don't let it *get* you *down* too much. 别让这事使你太失望。

—*vt.*【可分性动词短语】❶ bring (something) down 拿下，取下：He *got* her picture *down* before she arrived. 他在她到来之前把她的照片取了下来。❷reduce 减少，降低：The doctor says I must *get* my cholesterol levels *down*. 医生叮嘱我必须把胆固醇水平降下来。❸swallow (food or medicine), especially with difficulty (尤指勉强地)吞下，咽下(食物或药物)：He could hardly *get* the last piece of meat *down*. 他几乎没能吞下那最后一块肉。The medicine was so horrible that I could hardly *get* it *down*. 这药那么难吃，我好不容易才咽下去。❹note, write or record (something) somewhere 写下，记录下：I couldn't *get down* all he said. 我无法把他所说的话都记下来。I'll just *get* your address *down*. 我来把你的地址记下来。Someone managed to *get down* the license number of the car. 有人记录下了那辆轿车的车牌号。

NOTE 当本短语用作及物性动词短语，所带的宾语为代词时，该代词须置于本短语的动词和副词中间。

get down to *vt.*【不可分性动词短语】start doing (something) seriously or with a lot of effort (认真努力地)着手做(某事)：I must *get down to* work tonight, as I have got exams next week. 我今晚可要认真做功课了，因为下周就要考试了。After lunch we *got down to* discussing the issue of education. 我们吃完午饭后就开始讨论教育问题。

NOTE 本短语中的 to 是介词，而不是动词不定式符号。因此，后面只能接名词、代词、动名词或由 what 引起的从句，而不能接原形动词。

get even *vi.* (非正式用语) ❶(常与 with 连用) cause someone the same amount of trouble or harm as he or she has caused you 报复：He cheated me, but I'll *get even* with him one day. 他欺骗了我，但有朝一日我会报复他的。Last April First Mr Smith got fooled by Joe, and this year he will *get even*. 史密斯先生在上个

愚人节时被乔愚弄了。今年,他要进行报复。❷no longer owe someone money or a favour 不再欠某人的钱(或情):I have a lot of debts, but in a few years I will *get even*. 我现在负债累累,但几年后就会还清。If I pay for the meals then we *get even*. 如果这几顿饭钱我付了,我们就谁也不欠谁的了。

get hold of *vt.*【不可分性动词短语】❶(常用一般时态) start holding (something or someone) with your hands (用手)握住,抓住:Come here. *Get hold of* this for a minute. 到这儿来。把这个东西在手里握一会儿。*Get hold of* this rope, and we'll put you up. 抓住这根绳子,我们把你拉上来。The police appeared all of a sudden and *got hold of* the attacker. 警察突然出现,抓住了那名袭击者。❷(非正式用语,常用一般时态) obtain (something that you need or want) usually after some difficulty 得到(某物):It is hard to *get hold of* guns in this country. 在这个国家里很难搞到枪支。Then he thought of a way to *get hold of* the document. 后来他想出一个搞到这份文件的办法。I've managed to *get hold of* some rather good wine. 我设法搞到了一些非常好的酒。❸manage to contact(someone)联系上(某人):I've been ringing his office all day, but I can't *get hold of* him. 我给他的办公室打了一天电话,可就是联系不上他。Can you *get hold of* Mike and tell him the meeting's postponed? 你能联系上迈克吗? 告诉他会议延期了。

NOTE 当本短语作“抓住,握住”解时,同义短语是 catch hold of, grab hold of, have hold of 和 take hold of。

get home *vt.* &*vi.* (常用一般时态) (cause to)reach home (使)到家: What time did you *get home* last night? 你昨晚是什么时候到家的? Don't worry, I'll *get* you *home* safely. 别担心,我会送你平安到家的。—*vi.* (非正式用语,常用一般时态) win 获胜:At the Beijing Olympic Games Cuba's Robles *got home* in the men's 110m hurdles in 12.93 seconds. 在北京奥运会上,古巴选手罗伯斯以 12 秒 93 的成绩赢得了男子 110 米栏的冠军。Did your horse *get home*? 你的马获胜了吗?

get in *v.* ❶(cause to) enter (a room, car, etc.)(使)进入:We *got in* the strong room with some armed policemen. 我们同几名武装警察进入了保险库。Dad stopped the car and told me to *get in*. 爸爸把车停住,让我上车。I can *get* one more person *in* my car. 我的车还可以上来一个人。❷(of a person) arrive (especially at home or at work)(指某人)到达(尤指家中或工作岗位):You *got in* very late last night! 你昨晚回来的太晚啦! William never *gets in* before 9:30. 威廉从没在 9 点半之前到过岗。❸(of a train, bus, or plane, etc.) arrive at a particular time (指火车、公共汽车或飞机等)到达:The London train *gets in* at 10:05. 从伦敦开来的列车于 10 点 05 到达。What time is the plane expected to *get in*? 飞机预计什么时间到达? My flight *got in* late. 我乘坐的班机晚点了。❹(英国英语用法,非正式用语) buy or collect (things that you need)买进,征收(所需之物): Jane's friends are coming at the weekend, so *get* lots of chocolate *in*. 简的一些朋友周末要来,所以得多买些巧克力。We'd better *get in* some more coal before the price goes up. 我们最好在涨价之前多买进点煤来。The government will have to *get in* more tax money. 政府将不得不征收更多的税款。❺bring (something) inside a place; gather (crops or the harvest) from the land and take them to a particular place 收进(某物);收获(庄稼):It's raining; you' d better *get* the washing *in*. 快下雨了。你把洗的东西都收进来吧。The farmers were happy to *get* the crops *in* so early this year. 今年这么早就收获了庄稼,农民们很开心。❻(英国英语用法) ask (someone) to come to your house, office, etc. in order to do something for you 请来(某人):They have *got* the doctor *in* to look at the child. 他们请来了医生,给孩子看病。We're *getting* a plumber *in* to fix the leaking pipe. 我们要请一名管子工来修理漏水的管子。❼(常用一般时态) say (something), especially by interrupting someone else 插话:She talks so much that it is impossible to *get in* a word. 她话说个不停,别人休想插上一句。He spoke so fast that I was hard for me to *get* a word *in*. 他讲话太快,我很难插上一句话。❽(非正式用语,常用一般时态)(cause to) become involved in (something that other people are doing)参与,使卷入:It's a good idea to *get in* at the start, whatever you're doing. 不管干什么,都是一开始就参与为好。They have *got* him *in* deep in this matter. 他们使他深深卷入了这件事中。❾(常用一般时态)(of a political party or a politician) be elected for a political job (指某一政党或政客)当选(执政):The British Labour Party *got in* again in 2001. 英国工党在2001年再次当选执政。She's running for Congress but I doubt if she'll *get in*. 她在竞选国会议员,但我怀疑她能否当选。❿be admitted to a university, club, etc. 被(大学、俱乐部等机构)接收:He did badly in the entrance exam and didn't *get in*. 他在入学考试中考得不好,所以没有被录取。⓫send or submit (something) to a person or place so that it arrives by a particular time (在某一时间前)递交,送交:I have to *get* this application form *in* by the end of the week. 我得在这周末之前把申请表交上去。

NOTE **1.** 当本短语用作及物性动词短语,所带的宾语为代词时,该代词须置于本短语的动词和副词中间。

2. 当本短语作"插话"解时,同义短语是 barge in, break in, break into, burst in, cut in, cut into, cut off, cut short, chip in 和 put in 等。但它们的用法不同,有的是及物性的,有的是不及物性的,有的既有及物性又有不及物性用法。见相关各条目。

get in touch with *vt.* speak or write to (someone), especially after you have not spoken to him for a long time 与(某人)取得联系:Jury members must not *get in touch with* the defendants and their families in private. 陪审团的成员一定不要私下与被告及其家人进行联系。I'm so glad we *got in touch with* each other again after all these years. 我真高兴我们在这么多年之后又取得了联系。

NOTE 本短语的反义短语是 lose touch with 和 out of touch with。

get in on *vt.* 【不可分性动词短语】(非正式用语,无被动语态形式) share or take part in (something such as an activity that is already happening), because you will gain an advantage from it 参与(某种活动):I want to *get in on* the discussion, too. 我也想参加讨论。A Japanese company tried to *get in on* the deal. 一家日本公司试图参与到这笔交易之中。

NOTE 本短语的同义短语是 be in on。

get in the way of ⇨ **stand in the way of**

get in with *vt.* 【不可分性动词短语】(非正式用语，无被动语态形式) become friendly with (someone often in a position of power), usually for one's own advantage (常指为了自己的利益而)与(有权位之人)搞好关系：It will be to your advantage to *get in* well *with* the leaders of the city council. 与市政厅的领导人友好相处会对你有好处的。I tried to *get in with* them as I thought it would help me at work. 我尽力和他们搞好关系，因为我认为这有助于我的工作。If you want to be elected, she's the person you need to *get in with*. 如果你想当选，她是你需要搞好关系的人。

get into *vt.* ❶(cause to) enter (a space) 进入；把……放入：She forgot her keys and *got into* the house through the window. 她忘带了钥匙，所以从窗子进入房内。She *got into* her vehicle and drove quickly out of the parking lot without glancing over in the direction of his vehicle. 她进入自己的汽车就很快驶出停车场，根本没有向他车的方向看一眼。Can you *get* all your clothes *into* this small case? 你能把你所有的衣服都塞进这小衣箱里吗？❷(常用一般时态) (cause to) fit (clothes) (使)穿得上(衣物)：I've got so fat that I can't *get into* my jeans. 我发胖了，穿不上这条牛仔裤了。He couldn't *get* his feet *into* his shoes as they had swollen so much. 他的两只脚肿得很厉害，都穿不上鞋了。❸(无被动语态形式，常用一般时态) (cause to) arrive at (a place) (使)到达(某处)：What time does the train *get into* Edinburgh? 列车什么时间到达爱丁堡？In spite of the rough seas the captain *got* his ship *into* the harbor safely. 尽管海面上波涛汹涌，船长还是使船平安抵港了。❹become involved in or put (someone or oneself) into (a bad condition or situation) 卷入……之中，(使某人或自己)陷入(某种不良境况)之中：Tom *got into* an argument with his roommate. 汤姆与他的室友吵了起来。Those kids are always advised not to *get into* trouble. 总是要劝告那些孩子别卷入麻烦之中。If you tell the teacher about it you'll *get* me *into* dreadful trouble. 你要是把那件事告诉老师，我就倒霉了。He *gets into* a terrible temper if you contradict him. 如果你逆着他来，他就会大发脾气。❺(非正式用语，无被动语态形式) learn or start (something), or become involved or enthusiastic about it 学会，开始，热衷于(某事)：You'll soon *get into* the way of doing it. 你很快就能学会怎么做它。I must *get into* training soon; the cricket season starts next month. 我必须立即开始训练了；板球季度赛下月就开始了。She has been *getting into* dance music recently. 她最近一直很热衷于舞曲。He said he had a pretty good live before he *got into* politics. 他说，他在从政之前生活得非常好。❻(无被动语态形式) (cause to) start doing (something) regularly in a particular way; acquire (a habit, etc.) (使)养成，染上(某种习惯等)：Try to *get into* the habit of drinking a glass of water every hour. 尽量养成每小时饮一杯水的习惯。Who or what *got* you *into* the bad habit of smoking? 是谁或是什么使你染上了抽烟的坏习惯？It took me ages to *get into* driving on the left. 我花了很长时间才习惯开车靠左侧行驶。❼ be accepted or admitted as a pupil or student by (a school, college, or university)被录取进入(某一学校): I was working very hard to *get into* Cambridge University. 为了上剑桥大学,我在努力学习。❽criticise (someone)批评(某人): He *got into* me for doing it badly. 他因我没有做好那事而批评了我。

get into (an) argument with ⇨ **argue with**

get into/in on the act *vi.* (非正式用语)take part in an activity that someone else started and is doing now, in order to gain some of the advantages for yourself (为自己得到好处而)参与(他人正在从事的活动): Whatever we're doing, Alice always wants to *get into the act*. 无论我们要做什么,艾丽丝总是想要参与。We did all the hard work of setting up the company, and now everyone wants to *get in on the act*. 我们费了九牛二虎之力才开办了这家公司,现在人们都想凑进来干了。

NOTE 本短语的另外一种表达方式是 get in the act。例如:

> I'm sure he plans to *get in the act* and start negotiations with us.
> 他肯定计划要参与进来并要和我们展开谈判。

get it ⇨ **catch it**

get it across ⇨ **get across**

get nowhere *vi.* fail to achieve any result; fail to be successful 没有取得任何结果,没有成功: Our investigation *got nowhere*. 我们的调查没有任何结果。We're *getting nowhere* with this plan; we'll have to try something else. 采用这个计划我们将一事无成,我们得试试别的办法。Trying to bribe the officials *got us nowhere*. 试图行贿官员也没能使我们成功。

NOTE 1. 在本短语中的动词 get 之后,还可接人称代词,变为 get someone nowhere 的形式(见最后一个例句)。

2. 本短语另外的表达方式是 go nowhere 和 not get (someone) anywhere。例如:

> His career is going nowhere.
> 他的事业不会成功。
> Losing your temper won't get you anywhere.
> 你发脾气是无济于事的。

3. 本短语的反义短语是 get somewhere。

get off *v.* ❶(常用一般时态) remove (usually something); (cause to) be removed from (something)拿去,脱去;(使)从……脱去,(使)从……上除掉: Would you please *get* your feet *off* the table? 把你的脚从桌子上拿下去,好吗? I *got off* my wet clothes. 我把湿衣服脱掉了。My feet are so swollen I can't *get* my boots *off*. 我的双脚肿了,靴子都脱不下来了。Can you *get* that dirty mark *off* the floor? 你能把那污迹从地板上除掉吗? ❷(cause to) leave a train, bus or aircraft (使)下火车,下汽车,下飞机: He's *getting off* the train at the next station. 他在下一站下火车。You'd better *get off* at the next stop. 你最好在下一站下车。The driver had to *get* his passengers *off* the bus. 司机不得不让乘客都下了公共汽车。A British drunk passenger tried to open the door of a Boeing 767 and asked to *get off* the plane while it was more than 35,000 feet up, *London's Daily Telegraph* reported. 据伦敦《每日电讯报》报道,一名喝醉酒的英国乘客试图打开波音 767 的舱门,要求下飞机。而当时那架飞机正在

35 000 多英尺的高空飞行。❸help (someone) be ready to leave a place at the right time; start a journey (使)离开,动身,起程:It's time you *got off* to school. 你该上学去了。I have to *get* the kids *off* to school in the mornings by 7:30. 我得在上午 7 点半之前打发孩子们去上学。I'd better be getting off now. 我最好现在就动身。We *got off* comfortably by the ten o'clock train. 我们乘坐 10 点钟的列车舒舒服服地启程了。The plane for New York will *get off* at 9 o'clock. 到纽约去的飞机将在 9 点钟起飞。❹(非正式用语,用一般时态) leave the place you work at the end of the day 离开工作地点,下班:"What time do you *get off* work?" "I normally *get off* at 5 pm." "你什么时间下班?""我通常 5 点下班。" Could you *get off* early tomorrow? 明天你能提前下班吗? ❺leave (a place) or tell someone to leave (a place of land), because he or she has no right to be there 离开(某处);让某人离开(某处):They will *get off* straight after the meeting. 他们一开完会就将离去。I told you. *Get off* my garden! 我告诉过你们,离开我的花园! She will call you as soon as she's *got* the child *off* to school. 她把孩子打发去上学后就给你打电话。❻have (a particular period of time) as a holiday (在某段时间)休假:I'll try to come, but I'm not sure I'll be able to *get* that week *off*. 我会尽量来,但我没把握能不能在那周休假。Do you *get* much time *off* at Christmas? 你在圣诞节期间休假时间长吗? ❼(非正式用语,常用一般时态) not be punished severely or at all for something you have been accused of in court 未受严厉惩罚: This time you can *get off* with a small fine. 这次你可以交一点罚金而免受处罚。He was charged with manslaughter, but *got off*. 他被指控犯有杀人罪,但他却逃脱了惩罚。❽help (someone) avoid a criminal charge 帮助(某人)免遭刑事指控:You'll need a good lawyer to *get* you *off* (the charge). 你需要找一位好律师帮助你免遭刑事指控。❾send (something such as letters, parcels, or messages), for example in the post (通过邮局)寄出(信件、包裹);发出(信息等):Have you *got* the letters *off* yet? 你把信件都寄走了没有? I've just *got off* a parcel to Russia. 我刚刚往俄罗斯寄出了一个包裹。I *got* three emails *off* before the meeting. 在会前,我发出了三个电子邮件。

NOTE **1.** 当本短语用作及物性动词短语,所带的宾语为代词时,该代词须置于本短语的动词和副词中间。

2. 一般说来,凡表示可以在上面走动的地面交通工具(如 bus, train 等),"下车"用 get off,"上车"则用 get on。但若为无法在上面走动的交通工具(如 car, taxi 等),"下车"则用 get out of,而"上车"用 get into。

get on *v.* ❶ put (something such as clothes) on 穿上,戴上:*Get* your overcoat *on* quickly, please. 请快把大衣穿上。My feet are so swollen I can't *get* my shoes *on*. 我的双脚肿得鞋子都穿不进去了。He's *got on* a new hat these days. 这些天里,他戴了一顶新帽子。❷(cause to) take a place on a horse, bus, train, plane or boat (使)上马,上车,上飞机,上船:I'll hold the horse while you *get on*. 我给你牵着马,你骑上去。Nowadays, many people *get on* mountain bikes and head out for suburban areas outside the city on weekends. 如今,许多人在周末骑上山地自行车到市外去郊游。We can only *get* two more people *on* the bus. 我们只能再让两个人上车了。They're calling us to board the plane, let's *get on*. 他们在叫我们登机呢,我们上去吧。A small bus drove us across to the other side of the island. Next, we *got on* a small boat and took a 45 minute ride to our destination. 一辆小巴把我们拉到海岛的另一端。接着,我们便上了一条小船,用了 45 分钟才到达了我们的目的地。❸(主要用于英国英语中,常用进行时态,常与 with 连用)(used for asking or talking about how well someone has done a particular activity) make progress; advance or develop, especially in the stated way 进步,进展: Young Johnny isn't *getting on* very well at school. 小约翰尼在学校的进步不大。Jim seems to be *getting on* very well with his studies. 看来吉姆在学业上进展非常不错。How did you *get on* in your exams? 你考试考得怎么样? ❹(主要用于英国英语中,常与 with 连用)form or have a harmonious and friendly relationship (with someone)(与某人)和睦相处: My parents and I don't *get on*. 我父母和我合不来。I think you two would *get on* well. 我想,你们俩会和睦相处的。She seems to *get on* with everybody. 看来她和所有的人都能和睦相处。❺(英国英语用法)be successful in life or at work (在生活或工作方面)获得成功: Parents are always keen for their children to *get on* in life. 父母总是热切期望子女在生活中获得成功。❻(英国英语用法,常与 with 连用)continue doing (something), especially with more effort or more quickly than before 继续做(某事): Can we please *get on*? Because there are a lot of things still to discuss. 我们还是继续吧,因为我们还有很多事要讨论。They *got on* with their work after a short rest. 他们休息片后又继续工作了。I need to *get on* and cook this chicken before everyone gets here. 我需要继续干,在大家到之前把鸡做好。❼(主要用于美国英语中,非正式用语) criticize (a person) repeatedly 反复地批评(某人): He keeps *getting on* me and I really don't know what I've done wrong. 他总是批评我。我真不知道我都做错了什么。❽(非正式用语,用进行时态,常与 toward 连用)(of people) grow older; be aged (人)上了年纪: Our doctor is *getting on* a bit now and doesn't work so hard. 我们的医生上了点年纪,所以工作不那么卖力了。He's *getting on* toward 60. 他年近六旬。❾(非正式用语,用进行时态,主语常为 time 或 it)(of time) become late (时间)渐晚: Time is *getting on*, so will you all start getting ready, please? 时间不早了,请大家开始准备吧,好吗? It's *getting on* for midnight, let's go to bed. 时间已近午夜,咱们上床睡觉吧。❿leave a place 离开某处: I must be *getting on*; I have other things to do this evening. 我得走了。我今晚还有些其他事要做。

get on for *vt.*【不可分性动词短语】(主要用于英国英语中,无被动语态形式,用进行时态) get nearer (a time or number) 接近(某一时间、数目或年龄): It's *getting on for* midnight, let's go to bed. 已近半夜,咱们上床睡觉吧。There were *getting on for* three thousand people there. 那里有将近 3 000 人。My parents are *getting on for* 80, but they're very energetic. 我的父母都已年近八旬,但他们都很有精力。

get one's hands on ⇨ **lay one's hands on**

get onto *vt.* ❶(cause to) take a place on (a horse, bicycle, etc.) or in (a vehicle or plane)(使)骑上(马、自行车等);上(车,飞机): It takes skill to *get onto* a nervous horse. 需要有技术才能骑上神经紧张的马匹。We can't *get* more people *onto* this train. 我们不能再让更多的人上这趟列车了。They *got onto* the plane just before it took off. 他们在飞机就要起飞之前上了飞机。❷(英国英语用法,非正式用语,无被动语态形式,常用一般时态) write or speak to (usually someone) in order to ask them to do something for you; get in touch with (usually someone)(尤指为了请求帮助而)与(某人)联系,与(某人)接触: I'll *get onto* the director and see if he can help. 我将同董事联系,看他能否帮忙。I'll *get onto* the shop about the order that we've been waiting for. 我将与店方联系一下有关我们一直在等待着的订货。❸(非正式用语,无被动语态形式,常用一般时态) find (a secret, or someone doing something wrong) 发现(某一秘密或正在做坏事的人): It took the police a long time to *get onto* the wanted man's trail. 警方用了很长时间才发现那名通缉犯的踪迹。He tricked his customers for years until the police *got onto* him. 他多年来一直欺骗他的顾客,最终被警方发现。❹(常用一般时态) begin to talk about or discuss (a different subject or topic) 开始谈论(另一主题或话题): How did we *get onto* this subject? It had no connection with what we were talking about. 我们怎么谈起这一话题呢?它与我们所谈论的内容没有任何关联。Let's *get onto* the next item on our agenda. 让我们开始讨论议程的下一项议题吧。❺(无被动语态形式,常用一般时态)(cause to) be elected or appointed to (a group)(使)当选,被任命为: One of my friends *got onto* the City Council. 我的一位朋友当选了市政会委员。The director's influence *gets* him *onto* the boards of many companies. 董事的影响使他就任许多家公司的董事会成员。❻(美国英语用法,无被动语态形式,常用一般时态) succeed in understanding (usually something) 懂得了(常指某事): The children didn't quite *get onto* what the teacher was saying. 孩子们似乎没有听懂老师所讲的内容。

NOTE 本短语的另外一种表达形式是 get on to,本短语更为常用。

get out *v.* ❶(常与 of 连用)(used for telling someone to leave) move out (of a space, building, etc.)(让某人)(从……)出去: The teacher screamed at him to *get out*. 老师大声叫喊让他出去。*Get out* of my house! 从我的家里滚出去! ❷(cause to) leave; leave the house to visit different places and socialize (使)离开,出门,出去参加社交活动: We have to find some ways of *getting* the nurse *out* so that we can talk freely. 我们必须想些办法让护士离开,才好自由地交谈。We don't *get out* much, as we have a young baby. 由于我们的孩子太小,所以都不太出门。You should often *get out* and make friends. 你应该经常出去结交些朋友。❸(cause to) descend from a vehicle (使)下车: The car drew up at the gate and three men *got out*. 轿车停在了大门口，三名男子下了车。If you haven't paid for your ride, *out* you *get*! 如果你坐车没买票，就下车吧。The taxi driver tried to *get* his passengers *out* before the train hit it. 出租汽车司机在火车撞上其汽车之前设法让他的乘客下了车。❹ bring (something) out from a place where it is stored or hidden 拿出（某物）：I'll *get* some clean shirts *out* for you. 我给你拿出几件干净的衬衫吧。The thief *got out* a gun and forced the old couple to give him the jewels. 那盗贼掏出枪来，逼迫老年夫妇交出珠宝。❺（常用一般时态）remove (something that is inside or mixed with something else) 拔出，去除：The dentist managed to *get* the bad tooth *out*. 牙医设法把那颗坏牙拔了出来。I washed the shirt twice, but I couldn't *get* the stains *out*. 这衬衫我洗了两遍了，可那些污迹还是无法除掉。❻（常与 of 连用）(cause to) leave (a place) in order to escape from it（使）撤离，逃跑：New York Mayor Bloomberg praised the pilot for his wonderful job of landing the passenger plane in the river and then making sure that everybody safely *got out*. 纽约市市长布隆伯格称赞飞机驾驶员表现出色，把客机降落在河面上，此后又确认所有的人都安全撤离机舱。They probably wanted to *get out* of the country. 他们可能想要出逃国外。How did their friends *get* them *out* of the prison? They must have given the guards money. 他们的朋友是怎么使他们逃出监狱的？他们肯定用钱买通了看守。❼ (of a secret, news, or information) become known by a lot of people（秘密，消息等）泄露：If this secret *gets out*, there will be trouble. 如果这一秘密泄露出去，那就麻烦了。There was a huge public outcry when the news *got out*. 那消息泄露后，引起大批公众的强烈抗议。It quickly *got out* that Mary was leaving Jim. 玛丽要弃吉姆而去的消息很快就不胫而走。❽（常用一般时态）make (something such as a new book) available for people to buy; publish 出版，发表：They are *getting out* some new books for children this season. 他们要在这个季度出版一些儿童新书。A new edition of the dictionary has been *got out*. 这部词典的一种新版本已经出版。We hope to *get* the report *out* very soon. 我们希望很快发表这一报告。❾ say (something) with difficulty 艰难地说出：She managed to *get out* a few words. 她吃力地说出了几句话。He tried to protest, but couldn't *get* the words *out*. 他试图提出抗议，却说不出话来。

NOTE 本短语可转化为复合词 get-out，意为"脱身，脱逃"。

get out of *vt.* ❶ (cause to) leave (a space, building, etc.)（使）从……离开："*Get out of* my house!" he shouted at me. "你从我家里滚出去！"他向我喊道。*Get* that man *out of* my bedroom! 让那个人从我的卧室里出去！*Get* the cat *out of* the house before Mother sees it. 在妈妈看到那只猫之前，快把它从屋里弄走。*Get out of* here! 离开这里！❷ descend from (a vehicle) 从（车上）下来：We *got out of* the taxi at a busy street. 我们在一条热闹的街上下了出租车。I couldn't *get out of* the bus, as I was sandwiched between an old lady with stiff legs and a schoolboy. 由于我被挤在了一个腿脚不好使的老妇人和一名小学生中间，我无

法从公共汽车上下来了。❸ take off (clothes) so that you can put on more comfortable clothes 脱下(衣物):*Get out of* those wet clothes or else you'll catch cold. 把湿衣服脱下来,否则你会感冒的。❹(一般不用被动语态形式) escape from (a place)逃出(某处): During the fire, at least 36 were killed and others got injured while trying to *get out of* the burning building. 大火中,至少有36人丧生,还有一些在试图逃离燃烧着的大楼时受伤。The bird has *got out of* its cage. 鸟从笼中逃出去了。❺(cause to) avoid (doing something that you should do or said you would do)(使)逃避(应做或说过要做的事情):Ruth always tries to *get out of* doing the washing up. 鲁思总是千方百计地逃避洗餐具。Can you *get* me *out of* going to this meeting? 你能不能使我逃避参加这次会议? I said I'd meet him, but now I want to *get out of* it. 我说过我要见他,可现在我又想回避与他见面。❻ force or persuade (someone) to give (information or money)迫使(某人)讲出(消息),迫使(某人)付出(金钱): The police finally *got* the truth *out of* her. 警方终于使她道出了实情。❼ get (pleasure or a benefit) from (something)从……中获得(快乐或好处):He *gets* a lot of satisfaction *out of* being a teacher. 他从教师这个职业中获得极大的满足。I don't understand what she *gets out of* her relationship with him. 我不理解她与他交往能得到什么快乐。I don't know why people smoke; what do they *get out of* it? 我不知道人们为什么吸烟。他们从中得到什么益处呢? ❽(常用一般时态) abandon gradually (a habit, etc.)逐渐抛弃(某种习惯等): How can I *get out of* the habit of smoking? 我怎么才能抛弃吸烟的习惯呢? Smoking is a habit he can't *get out of*. 吸烟是他弃不掉的一个习惯。

get over *vt.* ❶(常用一般时态) start to feel happy or well again (after something bad has happened to you)从(发生的不幸)中恢复过来: It can take weeks to *get over* an illness like that. 要经过几周的时间才能从那样一种疾病中恢复过来。Soon the earthquake victims will *get over* the shock. 地震的幸存者们很快就会从震惊中恢复平静的。She had a hard time *getting over* the loss of her son. 她很难从失去儿子的痛苦中恢复过来。❷(常用一般时态) find a way to overcome or deal with (a feeling, problem, difficulty, etc.)克服(某种情感);解决(难题);战胜(困难等): She can't *get over* her shyness. 她无法克服羞怯感。I can't *get over* my dislike of her. 我消除不了对她的厌恶之感。There are still many problems to *get over* before the new restaurant can open. 在新餐馆开张之前,还有很多难题要解决。❸(常用一般时态) do or reach the end of (usually something necessary but unpleasant)完成,结束(不愉快但必须做的事): Mary tried to *get* her report *over*, however difficult it might be. 玛丽试图完成她的报告,不管那有多么难。You'll be glad to *get* your operation *over*. 手术做完了,你会高兴的。❹ start to forget (someone) after a relationship has ended (在关系结束后)忘记(某人):Her affair with Dick ended several months ago, but she hasn't really *got over* him yet. 她与迪克在几个月前就分手了,可她还没真正忘记他。

get ready for *vt.* (cause to) prepare for

(what is going to happen)(使)为……做好准备:She's upstairs *getting ready for* going out. 她在楼上正做出去的准备。It was time to *get* the children *ready for* bed. 该让孩子们准备上床了。Jane promised to *get* the room *ready for* our guests. 简答应为我们的客人准备房间。

NOTE 1. 本短语的动词 get 可被 make, be 等替换,构成的短语与本短语意义和用法相同。

2. 本短语的同义短语是 prepare for。两者之间的区别见 prepare for。

get rid of *vt.*【不可分性动词短语】❶do something so that you stop being affected by (something annoying, unpleasant, or not wanted)摆脱,除去:We are to fully utilize our expertise in this area to help them to *get rid of* their problems as soon as possible. 我们将充分利用我们在这一领域的专长,去帮助他们尽早摆脱困难。I wish I could *get rid of* this cold soon. 我希望很快能摆脱这次感冒。The international community should help the two parties *get rid of* disturbances, abandon violence, continue peace talks and follow the Road Map. 国际社会应帮助双方排除干扰,摒弃暴力,继续和谈,执行"路线图"计划。❷throw away, give away, or sell (a possession that you no longer want or need)处理掉(不再使用或需要之物):We're moving, so we have to *get rid of* a lot of our furniture. 我们要搬家,所以得处理掉很多家具。The owner needed to *get rid of* his car for financial difficulty. 这位车主因用钱困难而要卖掉他的车。❸make (someone) go away because he or she is annoying, unpleasant, or not wanted 赶走(某人):I'm sure he knew we were trying to *get rid of* him! 肯定他知道我们在试图赶他走! The new secretary is useless and must be *got rid of*. 新来的秘书没有用,必须让她走人。❹kill or destroy (someone or something)干掉,消灭:He won't change and will continue playing games. The time has come to *get rid of* him. 他不会有任何改变,而且还会继续耍弄各种花招。除掉他的时候到了。How can we *get rid of* all these flies in the kitchen? 我们怎么才能把厨房里的这些苍蝇统统消灭呢?

get sick *vi.* ❶become ill 生病:It's my luck to *get sick* on vacation. 在假期里生病,我算是侥幸。If you eat any more candy you'll *get sick*. 如果你再多吃糖果,你就会生病的。❷become disgusted 讨厌,生气:I'm *getting sick* of peanut butter sandwiches for lunch. 我讨厌午饭吃花生酱三明治。I *get sick* when I hear about his debts. 我听说他欠了债就感到很生气。❸be sick; become nauseated; vomit 恶心,呕吐:Do you know how to fly without *getting sick*? 你知道怎样才能不晕机吗? If she *gets sick* every morning, she must be pregnant. 如果她每天早晨都恶心的话,那她肯定是怀孕了。

NOTE 本短语的同义短语是 fall ill 和 take ill。

get somewhere *vi.* (常用进行时态) make some progress or achieve some result 取得进展,有结果:At last she is starting to *get somewhere* in her career. 她在事业上终于开始有了进展。I think at last we're *getting somewhere*. 我认为我们终于有所进展。He's finally told us the price — now we're *getting somewhere*! 他终于把价格告诉了我们,

现在我们总算有了点结果。

NOTE 本短语的反义短语是 get nowhere。

get the better of *vt.* defeat (someone or something) or gain an advantage in a game, argument, etc. (在比赛或辩论等中)击败,胜过: Sampras finally *got the better of* Agassi in a hard-fought match. 桑普拉斯终于在比赛中艰难地战胜了阿加西。Who *got the best of* the argument? 这场辩论谁赢了? He was determined to *get the better of* his competitors. 他决心战胜其竞争对手。Try to remain calm — don't let your anger *get the better of* you. 尽量保持冷静,不要发火。

NOTE 本短语的另外一种表达形式是 get the best of。

get the measure of someone *vi.* (正式用语) estimate, judge, or discover what someone is like, so that you are able to decide how to deal with him or her 估量,判断,了解某人(以应对于某人): She seems to have *got the measure of the champion*. 她似乎已判断出了那名冠军的半斤八两。Lily was the only person I knew who *got the measure of her brother*. 莉莉是我所知道的唯一了解她弟弟的人。Has he *got the measure of* us and concluded that we're not willing to help? 莫非他已了解了我们,并得出我们不愿帮忙的结论?

NOTE 本短语的动词 get 可被 have, take 等替换,构成的短语与本短语意义和用法相同。

get through *v.* ❶(cause to) pass or move through (something) (使)穿过,通过: Can a large animal *get through* into such a small cave? 一个大动物能钻进这么小的洞里去吗? We finally *got* the box *through* the hole. 我们终于把箱子从洞口弄了出去。I managed to *get* these watches *through* customs without being questioned. 我未被查问就顺利地带着这些手表通过了海关。❷manage to deal with (a difficult or unpleasant period of time) 度过(某段困难时期): The refugees will need help to get through the cold winter. 需要帮助难民度过寒冷的冬季。If we can *get through* the next few months on your financial help things should be easier. 如果我们靠您的资助度过后几个月,事情就好办多了。❸(英国英语用法,常用一般时态)(cause to) be successful (in an exam or test) (使)通过(考试): In the last exam, Tom failed but his sister *got through*. 在上次的考试中,汤姆没及格,可他妹妹及格了。It was very difficult to *get* my weaker students *through* the national English examination. 我很难使那些成绩较差的学生通过这次全国性英语考试。I *got through* the written papers, but failed in the oral examination. 我笔试及格了,但口试没通过。How did he ever *get through* his driving test? 他是怎么通过驾驶考试的呢? ❹(常用一般时态)(of proposals, bills, or new laws) be passed, or have (proposals, bills, or new laws) approved (使)(提议、法案或新法)获得通过: If the proposal *gets through*, it will make things much better for us. 这项提议如果获得通过,就会使我们的情况更好。He would be very disappointed if the bill failed to *get through*. 如果那项法案不能在议会中通过,他会十分沮丧。Such a radical bill would never *get through* parliament. 这样一项激进的法案决不会在议会中通过。*Getting* a bill *through* Congress is a long process. 使一项法案

在国会中通过是一个很长的过程。❺(主要用于美国英语中，常与 with 连用)finish (an amount of work or a task, especially when it is difficult to complete)完成(难以完成的工作或任务)：They probably won't *get through* by eleven o'clock. 他们的任务可能在 11 点前完不成。It is difficult to *get through* this amount of work in such a short time. 在这么短的时间内完成这么多的工作是有困难的。As soon as I *get through* with my work, I'll ring you up. 我这项工作一做完，就会打电话给你。There was a lot to *get through* in the meeting. 会上有很多议题要议。❻(主要用于英国英语中，常用一般时态)use up or consume (a large amount of something)用完(大量物品)；吃(或喝)完(大量食物)：They won a million dollars but they *got through* the whole lot in less than two years! 他们赢得了 100 万美金，但在不到两年时间的时间里就花光了！We *got through* a whole chicken at one sitting! 我们一顿就吃完了一整只鸡。You would wonder how so much food such a small child could *get through*. 你会感到奇怪，这么小的一个孩子怎么会吃完那么多的东西。How do we *get through* so much milk? 我们怎能喝完这么多牛奶？❼(常用一般时态)succeed in talking to someone on the telephone 打通电话：I tried calling her mobile phone, but couldn't *get through*. 我试着打了她的手机，但没能打通。

get through to *vt.* ❶(常用一般时态，与 to 连用)succeed in making (someone) understand (what you are trying to say) 使(某人)理解(自己所讲的意思)：The teacher feels he is not *getting through to* some of the kids in his class. 这位老师感到他没能使班上的一些孩子理解他所讲的意思。❷(常用一般时态)(cause to) be connected to (someone or a place) by telephone (使)打通(某人或某地的)电话：I finally *got through to* Warren on his mobile phone. 我终于打通了沃伦的手机。The operator finally *got* me *through to* New York. 接线员终于给我接通了纽约的电话。

NOTE 本短语中的第一个义项为不可分性动词短语用法。

get to *vt.* ❶(常用一般时态)(cause to) arrive at (a place)(使)到达(某地)：We got to Paris at 10 o'clock. 我们于 10 点钟到达巴黎。He didn't *get to* the hotel until midnight. 直到半夜他才到达旅馆。The boat will only *get* you *to* the nearest island. 船只能把你送到最近的岛上去。❷(无被动语态形式，常用一般时态)start (something or doing something)开始，着手(某事或做某事)：After a short rest we *got to* work again. 稍作休息后，我们又开始工作了。I finally succeeded in *getting to* sleep at midnight. 我终于在半夜时分睡着了。He *got to* thinking that it was all his fault. 他开始认为那都是自己的错。❸(用一般时态)progress to (a particular point) when you are doing something (所做之事)进展到(某种程度)：Where have you *got to* in the book? 这本书你看到哪儿了？I *got to* page 100 of this book. 这本书我已经看到了 100 页。❹(非正式用语，无被动语态形式，常用一般时态)annoy or upset (someone)使(某人)感到气恼：After a while his teasing started to *get to* me. 过了一会儿，他的冷嘲热讽开始使我感到气恼。

NOTE 本短语中的后三个义项均为不可分性动词短语用法。

get to grips with ⇨ **come to grips with**

get to one's feet *vi.* stand up 站起身来：She *got to her feet* when she heard someone coming to her. 当听到有人向她走过来时，她便站起身来。He was so weak, he could hardly *get to his feet*. 他虚弱得几乎站不起来了。

NOTE 本短语的同义短语是 come to one's feet。与本短语之间的区别是，come to one's feet 侧重指"出于礼貌等而起立"。

get to the point *vi.* stop talking about unimportant details and say what is most important 直接谈及正题：We haven't got more time, so please *get to the point*. 我们没有更多的时间，所以请直谈正题。I'm in a hurry, so *get to the point*. 我赶时间，挑主要的说吧。

NOTE 当本短语作"直接谈及正题"解时，其同义短语是 come to the point。

get together *v.* ❶find or collect(things that you need), so that they are in one place and ready to use 收集(所需某物)：I *got together* a list of all their names and phone numbers. 我把他们所有人的名字和电话号码都收集到了一起。You'd better *get* your things *together* so that we can leave at any time. 你最好把东西收拾好，以便我们随时就能走。❷(常用一般时态，常与 with 连用)(cause to) meet in order to do something or to spend time together 聚会，(使)集拢，(把……)召集在一起：In different countries people have very different ideas about drinking tea. In China, for example, tea is always served when people *get together*. 在不同的国家，人们对喝茶的看法有很大区别。例如，在中国，每当人们聚会时，都要上茶。I am exceptionally pleased to *get together* with so many friends here to discuss our enhanced cooperation with the African nations. 今天，同各位朋友一道探讨我们和广大非洲国家新的合作大计，我感到格外高兴。Immediately after the earthquake, the teachers *got* the children *together* in the schoolyard and count them. 地震刚过，老师便把孩子们都集拢在学校操场上查点人数。❸(非正式用语)reach an agreement on an issue that people have had different opinions about (对有歧见的问题)取得一致意见：I hope the committee can *get together* on this matter. 我希望委员会能对这个问题取得一致意见。

NOTE 本短语可转化为复合词 get-together，意为"聚会，联欢会"。

get up *v.* ❶(cause to)get out of bed after sleeping (使)起床：What time do you get up in the morning? 你早晨几点钟起床？I never *get up* before nine. 我从不在 9 点以前起床。John has a habit of *getting up* early. 约翰有早起的习惯。Will you *get* me *up* at six tomorrow? 明天早晨 6 点钟叫我起床，好吗？❷ rise to one's feet; stand up 起立，站起来：Everyone *got up* when the judge came into the court. 当法官走进法庭时，全场起立。Few men nowadays *get up* to give a lady a seat on a bus. 如今，在公共汽车上很少有男士起身给女士让座。The old man fell down on the ice and couldn't *get up*. 老人在冰上滑倒，站不起来了。❸(英国英语用法，非正式用语，常用一般时态，常与 as 连用) dress (someone or yourself) in a particular or special way 打扮(某人或自

G

己),装扮: I shan't *get up* too much; the party is informal. 我不会过分地打扮,因为聚会是非正式的。She *got* herself *up* as Queen Victoria. 她把自己装扮成维多利亚女王。The girl was *got up* as an Indian princess. 那女孩装扮成印度公主。❹(英国英语用法,非正式用语) organize (a group of people) to do something 组织(人员): I'm *getting up* a little group to visit Pearl Harbor; would you like to come along? 我要组织一个小组去参观珍珠港。你愿一同前往吗? Mr Green wants to *get* a committee *up*. 格林先生想要组织一个委员会。❺(英国英语用法) (of the wind) start blowing strongly (风)开始刮得猛烈起来: The wind was *getting up*. 风越刮越大。

NOTE 1. 当本短语用作及物性动词短语,宾语为代词时,该代词须置于本短语的动词和副词中间。

2. 本短语可转化为复合词 get(-)up,意为"起床;式样,格式;装束,打扮"。

get up to *vt.* 【不可分性动词短语】(英国英语用法,无被动语态形式) ❶(常用一般时态) reach 达到: You need more practice to *get up* to the standard. 你需要多做训练才能达到要求。The temperature in the city center *got up to* 35℃ yesterday. 昨天,市中心的气温达到了摄氏 35 度。Which part of the book have you *got up* to? 那本书你看到第几部分了? ❷(非正式用语) do (especially something wrong or naughty) 做(尤指错事或淘气之事): He is always *getting up to* mischief. 他总是在捣鬼。The children are very quiet; I wonder what they are *getting up to*. 孩子们都很安静,不知道他们要搞什么勾当。

give a glance at ⇨ **catch a glance at**

give a hand *vi.* (常与 to, with 连用) help; assist 帮助,协助,支持: I always make a point of *giving a hand* to others. 我始终认为帮助他人是重要的。Can you *give* me *a hand* with these boxes? 你能帮我拿这些盒子吗? Could you please *give* me *a hand* carrying this mattress? 能请您帮我抬这个床垫子吗?

NOTE 1. 不要将本短语与 give someone one's hand 混淆,后者意为"同意嫁给(某人)"。

2. 本短语的另外一种表达形式是 give a hand to。例如:

> He tries to *give a hand to* those in need of help.
> 他千方百计地帮助那些需要帮助的人们。

3. 本短语的同义短语是 lend a hand。

give a reference to ⇨ **refer to**

give an account of *vt.* make a written or spoken statement about (someone or something that has happened) (以书面或口头的形式)讲述(某人),陈述(所发生的事情): You are going to have to *give an account of* yourself to your parole officer. 你得向假释官交代一下自己的情况。*Give* us *an account of* what happened. 把发生的事讲给我们听。The boy *gave* his father *an account of* the game. 那男孩向他父亲讲述了比赛的情形。The passenger was too shocked to *give a* clear *account of* the bus explosion. 这位乘客惊魂未定,无法清晰地描述公共汽车爆炸的经过。

NOTE 在本短语中的名词 account 之前,可使用不同形容词进行修饰。短语中的原不定冠词 an 可根据所使用的不同形容词而改用 a(如最后一个例句)。

give an ear to *vt.* (常用一般时态) listen carefully to (someone or something) 倾

听，听从：You children, come and *give an ear to* me. 你们这些孩子，都过来听我说。He will *give an ear to* anyone with gossip to pass on. 任何人所散布的闲话他都听。

NOTE 本短语中的动词 give 可被 lend 替换，两者的意义和用法相同。

give an eye to *vt.* (常用一般时态) watch (something or someone) carefully 注意照看：Please *give an eye to* the children while I'm out. 在我外出期间，请你照看孩子。

give away *vt.* 【可分性动词短语】❶(常与 to 连用) give (something that you own) (to someone) free of charge 赠送，捐献(自己所有之物)：She *gave away* all her money to the poor. 她把她所有的钱都捐给了穷人。He *gave* his books *away* to a circulating library. 他把自己的书籍捐献给了一家流通图书馆。Ten thousand copies of books are being *given away*. 一万册图书在馈赠中。❷give someone (something such as a prize) 发放(奖品等)：After the competition the president *gave away* the prizes. 比赛结束后，校长颁发了奖品。The report said in October the US government will *give away* 55,000 green cards! 该报道说，10月份美国政府将发放 55 000 张绿卡！❸(常用一般时态，常与 to 连用) reveal (information or facts that you should keep secret) (to other people) (向……) 泄露(秘密等)：She didn't *give* anything *away* about the meeting. 她没有泄露会议的任何内容。Prince Harry served secretly in Afghanistan with the British Army, and had to be sent home when the secret was *given away* by the press. 哈里王子在驻阿富汗英军中秘密服役，但在该秘密被媒体泄露后不得不被送回国内。❹(常用一般时态，常与 to 连用) inform against (someone) 告发，出卖(某人)：Someone in the gang *gave* him *away* to the police. 犯罪团伙中有人向警方告发了他。He was *given away* by one of his friends. 他是被他的一个朋友出卖的。❺show the true nature or identity of (someone or something) 暴露出：Although he is pretending hard to be young, gray hair *gives* him *away*. 尽管他极力装年轻，但他的白发却暴露出了他的真实年龄。She tried to appear indifferent, but her eyes *gave* her *away*. 她竭力装作满不在乎的样子，但她的眼神使她露出了马脚。

NOTE **1.** 当本短语的宾语为代词时，该代词须置于本短语的动词和副词中间。

2. 本短语可转化为复合词 giveaway，意为"(秘密等的)泄露；(用来吸引顾客的)赠品"。

give back *vt.* 【可分性动词短语】❶(常用一般时态，常与 to 连用) return (something you have borrowed or had before) (to someone) 将……归还给(某人)：The company had to *give back* all the money customers had paid. 公司不得不把客户所付的全部款项归还给他们。I'd like you to change this shirt, or else *give* me my money *back*. 我请你把这件衬衣换了，否则就退款给我。Be sure to *give* the camera *back* to me when you've finished using it. 你用完相机后一定要把它还给我。OK, I'll *give* it *back* to you soon. 好吧，我会尽早还给你。❷(用一般时态，常与 to 连用) throw back (sound or light) (声或光) 返回，反射：The wall of rock *gives back* an echo. 这石壁能反射回声。❸ allow (someone) to enjoy or have (something) again; restore 使(某人)重新拥有,恢复:The man was *given back* his freedom at last. 那个人最终被恢复了自由。Living here has *given* me *back* my health. 在这儿生活使我恢复了健康。A win today could *give* her *back* her confidence. 今天的胜利可以使她恢复信心。

NOTE 当本短语的宾语为代词时,该代词须置于本短语的动词和副词中间。

G

give birth (to) *v.* ❶(of a woman or female animal) produce (a baby) from her body(人)生(孩子),(动物)产(幼子):A 72-year-old Indian woman in April, 2016 gave birth to a baby, which makes her the world's oldest woman to *give birth*. 一位72岁的印度妇女于2016年4月产下一婴儿,这使她成了世界上年龄最大的产妇。The latest research provides the evidence that a child's sex is associated with the mother's diet, and women on low-calorie diets are likely to *give birth to* a female. 这项最新的研究证明:婴儿的性别与母亲的饮食有关,喜欢低热量饮食的女性易生女孩。A dog in Mason City, *gave birth to* 13 puppies in a delivery that started just before sunrise and went on for hours. 梅森市的一条狗产下了13条小狗。产程从日出开始,一直持续了数小时。❷(常用一般时态) produce; cause 产生,引起: Radar *gave birth to* a new system of navigation — radio navigation. 雷达产生了一个新的导航系统——无线电导航。Common struggle and common experience have *given birth to* common views and common language. 共同的斗争和共同的经历产生了共同的观点和共同的语言。Her suggestion *gave birth to* dispute at the meeting. 她的建议在会上引起了争论。

NOTE 当本短语作"产生,引起"解时,同义短语是 give rise to。

give credit *v.* (常用一般时态,后常接 for, to 短语) give the praise or honor (to someone who is good at something or has a particular good quality) (for something) (因……)表扬(某人),给予(某人)荣誉: The manager's art of running his business is to lose no time in *giving* his employees *credit* for their wonderful work. 这位经理的管理艺术就是不失时机地表扬那些工作出色的员工。In the preface, the author *gives credit* to three of his colleagues for efforts they have made in collecting data and materials for him. 在书的前言中,作者对他的三名同事因他们为他搜集数据和资料方面所付出的努力加以赞扬。He was *given* no *credit* for his invention. 他并没有因其发明而得到任何荣誉。

NOTE 本短语的名词 credit 必须用单数形式。

give heed to ⇨ pay heed to

give in *vt.* 【可分性动词短语】(常与 to 连用) ❶(英国英语用法) give (something) to someone who is expecting it 把(某物)提交给(某人): She came to the class with a piece of work she should have *given in* last week. 她去上课时带上了她上周就应该交的作业。*Give* your exam papers *in* to the teacher when you've finished. 做完试卷后,把它们交给老师。The term papers have to be *given in* three weeks before the end of term. 学期论文必须在学期末前三个星期交上来。❷offer or submit (something) to someone in authority for judgement or approval 呈

交，提出：The health minister has threatened to *give in* his resignation unless his proposals are accepted. 卫生部长威胁说，如果不接受他的建议，他就提交辞呈。They *gave in* their complaint to the court. 他们向法庭提出了控诉。

—*vi.*（常用一般时态，常与 to 连用）admit that you are defeated or you cannot do something; surrender; yield 屈服，投降，让步：Vowing not to *give in*, he called on his people to unite in the face of the terrorist threat. 他发誓决不让步，并号召人民团结起来，勇敢面对恐怖分子的威胁。I *gave in* to temptation and had a cigarette. 我抵不住诱惑，抽了一支烟。

give off *vt.*【不可分性动词短语】produce or send out (something such as a gas, smoke, heat, or a smell) into the air 产生，散发（某种气体、烟、热量或气味等）：Scientists believe the rubberized surface found in many school and college playgrounds *gives off* a poisonous gas in strong sunlight that can do people serious harm. 科学家们认为，很多中学和大学操场的塑胶表面会在强烈光照下散发出有毒气体，严重损害人体健康。Boiling, water *gives off* steam. 水沸腾时就散发出蒸汽。The police stopped the truck because it was *giving off* a lot of black smoke. 警察因那辆卡车排放大量的黑烟而将其截停。Substances such as ammonia *give out* heat when they dissolve. 像氨这样的物质在溶解后会产生热。The eggs were *giving off* a bad smell. 这些鸡蛋散发出一股臭味。

—*vi.* expand 扩展：The company is *giving off* all over the country. 该公司正在向全国扩展。

NOTE 本短语与 give out 都有"（散）发出"之意，两者之间的区别见 give out 条目。

give oneself airs (and graces) ⇨ **put on airs (and graces)**

give out *vt.* ❶（正式用语）produce (something such as a sound or light) 发出（声、光等）：The devices *give out* only a low, almost inaudible hum. 这种装置所发出的声音很小，只有很低的几乎听不见的蜂鸣声。The cowboy *gave out* a scream. 牧童大叫了一声。The burning fuel *gave out* heat and light. 燃烧着的燃料发出光和热。I looked out my small window into the night. There was a big bright moon hanging in the sky, *giving out* a magic glow. 我向窗外的夜色望去，只见一轮明月高挂在天空，向大地洒着令人不可思议的清辉。❷ distribute (a number of things) among a group of people 分发，散发：*Give out* the question papers ten minutes before the examination. 考试前 10 分钟发放试卷。The local government *gave* food and clothing and other things for daily use *out* to the earthquake victims. 当地政府把食品、衣物和其他日常生活用品分发给地震灾民。They stood at the main entrance *giving out* leaflets. 他们站在主要入口处散发散页宣传单。These blankets must be cleaned before they are *given out* to the children. 这些毛毯在发放给孩子们之前必须要弄干净。❸（主要用于英国英语中，常用被动语态形式，常用一般时态）make (news or information) known publicly 把（消息或信息）公布于众：He has refused to *give out* any farther information on the matter. 他已拒绝再发表任何有关此事的消息。Details of the assassination were *given out* on the nine o'clock news. 暗杀事件的细节是在 9 点

钟的新闻节目中公布于众的。It was *given out* that the former opposition leader was dead. 前反对党领袖的死讯已公布于众。The Nobel Prize Committee *gave* the names of the winners *out* yesterday, and the prizes will be awarded on December 10, the anniversary of the death of Nobel. 诺贝尔奖委员会昨天公布了获奖者名单,并将于12月10日(诺贝尔逝世周年纪念日)颁奖。

G

—*vi.* ❶be completely used up 耗尽,用光: After long swimming his strength *gave out*. 长时间的游泳之后,他的体力耗尽了。Their water *gave out* after a week in the desert. 他们在沙漠中度过了一个星期后,水就用尽了。The teacher's patience at last *gave out*. 老师终于失去了耐性。Our supply of coal has *given out*. 我们的煤炭已经用光。❷(非正式用语)(of a machine or a part of your body) stop working; break down (机器或人体器官)停止工作,失灵: I'd been having trouble with my laptop and it finally *gave out* at the weekend. 我的笔记本电脑一直有毛病,在周末它终于停止了工作。Halfway up the hill, the engine of the car *gave out*. 在上山的途中,汽车发动机熄火了。His heart finally *gave out* under the strain. 因过劳,他的心脏终于出了毛病。❸become exhausted 精疲力竭,筋疲力尽: Both the man and the horse *gave out* after the long ride. 赶了很长一段路后,人马俱乏。The hunted animal's strength finally *gave out*. 被追猎的动物终于筋疲力尽了。

NOTE 1. 当本短语用作及物性动词短语,所带的宾语为代词时,该代词须置于本短语的动词和副词中间。

2. 本短语与 give off 都有"(散)发出"之意。但 give off 通常用来表示"散发出某种气体、气味等",而本短语则表示"发出某种声、光或热等"。

3. 当本短语作"分发,散发"解时,同义短语是 hand out 和 pass out。

give over *vt.* &*vi.* (英国英语用法,非正式用语) stop (something or doing something, especially something that is annoying other people) 停止: Do *give over*! I'm sick of your complaints! 不要再说了! 我讨厌你的牢骚! Tell him to *give over* beating his wife! 告诉他不要再打他老婆了!

—*vt.* (常与 to 连用)【可分性动词短语】yield or hand over (someone or something) (usually to someone) 把……交给,移交,交托: They *gave* the thief *over* to the police. 他们把那盗贼移交给警方。We've *given* the machines *over* to the factory. 我们已把机器交给了工厂。The keys were *given over* to our neighbor during our absence. 我们不在时就把钥匙交托给邻居。

NOTE 当本短语用作及物性动词短语,所带的宾语为代词时,该代词须置于本短语的动词和副词中间。

give (free) rein to *v.* give freedom to (feelings or desires) 任由(情绪或欲望)自由发展,放任,对……不加约束: When left alone in her room in the evening, she stared out of the window at the starry night sky and *gave free rein to* her imagination. 晚上,当她独自一人留在房间里时,她注视着窗外繁星密布的夜空,听任自己的想象力自由驰骋。She could not resist finally *giving rein to* her anger. 她无法忍耐,终于把怒气发泄了出来。

NOTE 本短语的另外一种表达形式是 give

someone (a) free rein to do something。例如：

> They *gave me* (*a*) *free rein to* reorganize the department.
> 他们任由我重组该部门。

give rise to *vt.* 【不可分性动词短语】(of something) make (especially something unpleasant or unexpected) happen or begin(后接的宾语往往是不好或令人不快的事物) 引起，产生，导致：Low level of choline in the body can *give rise to* high blood pressure. 体内胆碱度低会引起高血压。Landmine is a defensive weapon, but if misused, it also poses a threat to the lives of civilians, thus *giving rise to* humanitarian concerns. 地雷是一种防御性武器，但如被滥用，则会对平民安全构成威胁，引发人道主义问题。These bad conditions have *given rise to* a lot of crimes. 这些恶劣的情况导致了许多犯罪。

NOTE 本短语的同义短语是 give birth to (第二个义项)。

give someone a lift *vi.* (英国英语用法) take someone somewhere in your car 让某人搭便车：I can *give you a lift* home. 我可以让你搭我的车回家。Would you like me to *give you a lift* to school? 你愿意搭我的车上学吗？"*Give you a lift*?" "Sure. Thanks." "你搭我的便车吗？""当然。多谢。"

NOTE **1.** 本短语的另外一种表达形式是 give someone a ride，为美国英语用法。
2. 若请求别人让你免费搭乘他的车时，可以说：Would you please give me a lift (in your car)? Could/Can I have a lift? 或 How about a lift? 当到达目的地下车时，应该说：Thanks for the lift.

give someone a pat on the back ⇨ **pat someone on the back**

give someone a start *vi.* ❶ offer someone (a new opportunity in his or her life)给某人提供(生活的新机会)：The money she lent him would *give him* a fresh *start*. 她借给他的钱将会使他重新创业。❷ cause to make a sudden, involuntary movement of the body, as from surprise, or terror 吓某人一跳：You *gave me* (quite) *a start*! 你吓了我一(大)跳。A noise in the road *gave us all a start*. 马路上的声音把我们都吓了一跳。

give someone one's hand *vi.* (of a woman) agree to marry someone (指女士)同意嫁给(某人)：She *gave him her hand* frankly, and wished him a good journey. 她直率地答应了嫁给他，并祝他一路顺风。

NOTE 不要将本短语与 give a hand 混淆，两者的意义不同。

give up *v.* ❶(无被动语态形式，后接名词、动名词，不能接动词不定式) stop doing or having (something); willingly or unwillingly lose (something or someone)放弃，抛弃：Decide what you want and then don't *give up* until you've achieved it. 一旦决定想要得到什么，就不要放弃，直到你得到它。Nepal's King was forced to *give up* his rule and was given 15 days to leave his palace. 尼泊尔国王被迫放弃其统治并被限期 15 天搬出皇宫。We've *given up* trying to persuade them to change. 我们已不再试图说服他们改变主意了。No mother wants to *give up* her children to someone else's care. 没有做母亲的想抛弃自己的孩子让他人养护。❷(无被动语态形式)

resign from (your job)辞去(工作): He's thinking of *giving up* his present job. 他在考虑放弃他现在的工作。❸(常与 to 连用)devote (something or oneself)(to a cause, etc.)entirely 把……全部献给(某项事业等): He has *given up* his life to this lofty cause. 他把生命献给了这一崇高的事业。The scientist *gave* himself *up* to the study of cancer. 这位科学家献身于癌症的研究工作。❹(常与 to 连用) allow someone else to have (something that you have or that you are entitled to) 让出(属于自己或自己有权拥有之物): We had to *give up* the town to the enemy. 我们不得不把城池拱手让给了敌人。Jimmy *gave* his seat *up* to the old lady. 吉米把座位让给了那位老妇人。They agreed to *give* half their office *up* to the temporary staff. 他们同意把办公室中一半的地方让给临时的工作人员使用。❺(常用一般时态)yield (someone or oneself)(to the police); surrender 把(某人)交给(警方);向(警方)自首;投降: If you catch the thief, will you *give* him *up* to the police? 如果你抓住了那个小偷,你会把他交给警察吗? After a week on the run, the murderer was forced to *give* himself *up*. 外逃一个星期后,该凶犯被迫自首了。When the enemy saw that they were surrounded, they *gave up*. 当敌人发现自己已被包围时,便投降了。❻(主要用于英国英语中,常用一般时态)no longer expect the arrival of (someone); have no further hope (that someone can be saved, especially from death)不再指望(某人)到来;对(某人的存活)不存希望: Just as his friends had *given up*, he appeared. 正当他的朋友们认为他无望前来时,他却出现了。The doctor had almost *given* her *up* when she made a dramatic recovery. 医生几乎已放弃她能活的希望,但她却出人意料地康复了。The men who were still in the boat had *given* him *up* for dead. 仍在船上的人都认为他已经死了。

NOTE 当本短语用作及物性动词短语,所带的宾语为代词时,该代词须置于本短语的动词和副词中间。

give vent to *vt.* 【不可分性动词短语】(正式用语) express (a strong feeling, especially anger)freely 自由抒发(强烈的感情);发泄(怒气): The graduates *gave vent to* cheers. 毕业生们发出阵阵欢呼声。He didn't dare *give vent to* his anger in front of her parents. 他不敢在父母面前发火。

give voice to *vt.* 【不可分性动词短语】(正式用语) say or express (your feelings, worries, etc.)aloud 吐露,表达(情感,担心等): The teachers *gave voice to* their anger over the president's decisions. 教师们对校长的决定表示愤慨。Many workers at the meeting *gave voice to* their fears about job security. 许多工人在会议上表达了他们在工作保障上的担心。

give way *vi.* ❶agree to something that someone else wants instead of what you want; yield 让步,投降: After a long argument he *gave way*. 经过长时间的辩论,他让步了。The captives would rather starve than *give way*. 俘虏们宁愿饿死也不投降。❷collapse; break down and fall down under too much weight or pressure 倒塌,塌陷:The wooden bridge *gave way* under the heavy load. 那木桥因不堪重负而垮掉了。The ice *gave way* and they fell into the water. 冰层塌陷,他们掉进

了水中。❸(英国英语用法)stop to allow other vehicles to pass 给其他车辆让路:You must *give way* at this junction. 在这个交叉口处,你必须给其他车辆让路。

give way to *vt.*【不可分性动词短语】❶(主要用于英国英语中)allow (another vehicle) to go before you when you are driving 给(其他车辆)让路:We had to *give way to* the fire engines. 我们不得不给消防车让路。Drivers must *give way to* cyclists. 司机必须给骑自行车的人让道。❷yield to (someone or something) 向……屈服,向……让步:On this point I think we need to *give way to* them. 在这一点上,我认为我们需要对他们作出让步。We mustn't *give way to* those unreasonable demands. 我们一定不要对那些无理要求让步。❸be replaced by (something, especially something newer, better, cheaper, more modern, etc.)被(尤指更新、更好、更便宜、更现代的东西)所取代:Steam trains *gave way to* electric trains soon after the war. 战后不久,蒸汽机车便被电动机车所取代了。In this city, old homes where coal or wood was burned for heat and cooking have *given way to* 25-story apartment buildings. 在这座城市里,曾以烧煤或木头来取暖和做饭的旧房屋已被一幢幢 25 层的公寓大楼所取代。Radio has *given way to* television and computer in popularity. 收音机的普及性已被电视和电脑所取代。

given that *conj.* If one takes into account the fact that (用于表达事实的句子之前)考虑到……,鉴于: *Given that* they are inexperienced, they have done a good job. 考虑到他们缺乏经验这一点,他们的工作算是做得不错了。The United States should have completely halted its weapons sales to Taiwan after establishing diplomatic relations with China in 1979, *given that* Taiwan is an integral part of China. 鉴于台湾是中国不可分割的一部分,美国于 1979 年和中国建交后就应彻底停止售台武器。

glance at *vt.*【不可分性动词短语】❶(常用一般时态)look (somewhere) quickly and then look away 往(某处)很快地看一眼:She *glanced* shyly *at* the young man's face and then lowered her eyes. 她羞怯地看了一眼那青年人的面容,随即垂下了眼帘。"I must go," Mary said, *glancing at* her watch. 玛丽匆匆地看了一下表说:"我得走了。"❷(常用一般时态) read (something such as a newspaper, report, or book) quickly and not very carefully 匆匆地读(报纸、报告或书籍等):He only *glanced at* the newspaper headlines. 他只是匆匆地看了一下报纸上的大标题。I hadn't even *glanced at* the report. 那份报告我甚至一眼都没看。

NOTE 当本短语表示"匆匆地读"之意时,其与 glance ever/through 相同,两者可互换使用。

glance over/through *vt.*【不可分性动词短语】(常用一般时态) read (something such as a newspaper, report, or book) quickly and not very carefully 匆匆地看,粗略地看(报纸、报告或书籍等):I've only had time to *glance over* your work, but I can already see how much it has improved. 我仅有点时间粗略地看了一下你的作品,但我已经看得出它有了很大的改进。He *glanced through* my play and said that it seemed to be worth acting. 他大概地看了一下我的剧本,说这剧看起来值得上演。I picked up the phone book and *glanced through* it. 我拿起电话簿翻看了一下。

NOTE 本短语的同义短语是 glance at, flick through 和 flip through。

glare at *vt.*【不可分性动词短语】look at (usually someone) with an angry expression on your face 横眉怒视(常指某人): She didn't shout or swear, but just *glared* silently *at* me. 她既不喊也不骂,只是默默地怒视着我。The two men stood there *glaring at* each other. 两名男子站在那里,相互怒视着。

G

go about *v.* ❶(主要用于英国英语中) move here and there, travel from place to place 走来走去;到处旅行: Is it dangerous to *go about* bareheaded on the construction site? 不戴安全帽就在建筑工地上走来走去不危险吗? The tourists *went about* London freely. 游客们尽情地游览了伦敦。❷(常用一般时态) start or continue (something or doing something) 着手做,继续做(某事): Just *go about* your homework and don't keep looking out of the window. 着手做你的作业,别总往窗外张望。He didn't know how to *go about* finding a job in such a big city. 他不知道怎样在这么大个城市里找工作。After the explosion most people *went about* their daily activities as usual. 爆炸发生后,大多数人还和往常一样地做着每天的事情。❸(无被动语态形式,常用进行时态)(of something such as an illness or a piece of news) circulate or spread (around a place)(消息、疾病等)流传,流行: A rumor is *going about* that the price of rice and oil will go up. 粮油价格要上涨的传言在流传。The story may not be true, but it is *going about* the town. 这事未必真实,但在镇子上到处流传着。There are a lot of colds *going about* (the school) just now. 目前,(在学校)感冒正在大流行。

NOTE **1.** 当本短语作"走来走去;到处旅行"和"(消息、疾病等)流传,流行"解时,同义短语是 go around。

2. 当本短语作"着手做(某事)"解时,同义短语是 set about。

go after *vt.*【不可分性动词短语】(无被动语态形式) ❶(非正式用语) try to get (something or someone that other people are also competing for) 设法得到,追求: At the job market about fifty university graduates *went after* a same job. 在求职市场上,大约 50 名大学毕业生都想得到这同一份工作。She's *going after* both fame and wealth. 她追求的是名利双收。My friend is *going after* that pretty girl. 我的朋友正在追求那位美丽的姑娘。❷try to catch, stop or hit (someone or an animal) 追拿,追逐,追打;击中: "The people we've caught have some connection to the bombing attack or we would not have *gone after* them," the police officer said. "我们已经抓到的这些人都与这次的炸弹袭击有某种联系,否则我们不会追拿他们。"这位警官说道。The hunting dogs *went after* the wounded deer. 几条猎狗追逐那只受伤的鹿。He *went after* his disobedient son with a stick. 他手拿棍子追打他那不听话的儿子。We're not *going after* civilian targets. 我们不会打击民用目标。

go against *vt.*【不可分性动词短语】(无被动语态形式) ❶(用一般时态)(of someone) act in oppose to; (of something) be contrary to (something) 违反,违背: Those who follow the Heaven's law will survive; those who *go against* it will perish. 顺天者存，逆天者亡。Don't *go against* your parents' wishes. 不要违背你父母的意愿。❷ (of a decision, vote, or result) be unfavorable to (usually someone)(指决定、选票或结果等)对(常指某人)不利：It appears likely the judge's ruling will *go against* them. 法官的裁决好像对他们不利。The prime minister will resign if the vote *goes against* him. 如果选举失利，总理将辞职。

go ahead *vi.* ❶ go to a place before someone else you are with 先走；走在他人前面：You *go ahead* and I'll wait here for Mary. 你们先走，我在这儿等玛丽。Brown *went ahead* of the others to try to find help. 布朗先行其他人一步，去设法寻求帮助。❷ move steadily forward 稳步地前进：The ship *went ahead* against the strong wind. 船顶着强风向前航行。He said he firmly believed that the new manager was of superb competence and would lead this firm to keep *going ahead*. 他表示，他坚信新任经理极有能力引领该公司继续稳步前进。❸ start or continue to do (something), especially after waiting for permission 开始，着手干；进行，执行；继续："Shall I start?" "Yes, *go ahead*, we're all listening." "我可以开始了吗?" "好，开始吧。我们都在听。" But the police officer emphasized that demonstrations would *go ahead* during the visit of the US president. 但这位警官强调说，在美国总统访问期间，游行将继续进行。We must *go ahead* with our plan quickly. 我们必须尽快执行我们的计划。

NOTE 本短语可转化为复合词 go-ahead，意为"许可；有进取心的；前进着的"。

go ahead with *vt.* 【不可分性动词短语】❶ be allowed to continue with (something) 继续：The council at last gave us the permission to *go ahead with* our building plans. 委员会终于允许我们继续执行我们的建筑计划。Are you *going ahead with* the election and then declare yourself re-elected? 你还要继续搞什么选举，然后宣布自己连任? ❷ (常用于祈使句中) continue to speak (something) 继续说：Please *go ahead with* your story; we're all listening. 请继续讲你的故事，我们都在听。

go along *vi.* ❶ (常与 with 连用) travel somewhere with someone else 与他人同行：He's going to New York tomorrow and I think I might just *go along*, too. 他明天要去纽约，我想也同他一起去。Smith, your wife wants to *go along* with you. 史密斯，你妻子要与你同去。❷ (用一般时态) continue to develop with something 继续，进展："This doesn't take a lot of technology," he said while walking into a pond where he raises baby eels. "You just learn it as you *go along*." "这不需要很多的技术。"他一边说一边走进他养殖鳗鱼苗的池塘。"你养着养着就会了。" Everything was *going along* just fairly well until she turned up! 在他到来之前，一切进展得都相当不错!

NOTE 不要将本短语与 get along 混淆。

go along with *vt.* 【不可分性动词短语】❶ go together with or accompany (someone) to a certain place 与(某人)同行，陪同(某人)去(某处)：Brown's going to London next week and his wife will *go along with* him. 布朗下周要去伦敦，他妻子将偕同前往。May I *go along with* you to your friend's house? 我能陪你去你朋友的家吗? ❷(常用一般时态) accept(a rule, decision, or policy) and obey it 接受并服从(某一规定、决定或政策): The main political parties in Cambodia are likely to *go along with* the plan. 柬埔寨各主要政党可能会接受该项计划。❸(常用一般时态) agree with (someone or an idea) 同意: I can't *go along with* you on this point. 在这一点上我无法同意你的意见。I would tend to *go along with* what Tom was saying. 我倾向于同意汤姆所说的话。I don't *go along with* their views on nuclear disarmament. 我不同意他们在核裁军问题上的意见。

NOTE 不要将本短语与 get along with 混淆。

go around/round *v.* ❶(常与 to 连用) go to someone's house to visit him or her 去某人的家: I asked him to *go around to* the house to see if they were there. 我让他去他们家里看看他们是否在家。John *went round* to see them. 约翰去家里看望他们。❷go from place to place; travel; make a short journey, as on a visit 到处走,环游: I *went around* last night, but no one was seen on the street. 昨晚我到处转了转,街上看不到一个人。You can't *go around* saying things like that! 你不能到处讲那样的话。While you're here, would you like to *go round*? 你在这儿期间要到各处走走吗? ❸(常用进行时态) (of a piece of news, an illness, etc.) spread (round a place or a group in the same period of time) (消息、疾病等)流传,流行: There's a story *going around* the office that you're thinking of leaving. 办公室里传说你在考虑离职。A rumor is *going around* the village that you have a new job. 村子里流传说你又有了新工作。Influenza is a disease that is likely to *go around*. 流感是一种易于传播的疾病。He caught a nasty cold that's been *going around*. 他得了一种一直在流行的重感冒。❹(用一般时态) be enough so that everyone can have one or some 够……用,够分配: There should be enough soup to *go around* the whole family. 汤应该够全家人喝。In some classes, there aren't even enough books to *go around*. 在有些班级甚至课本都不够分。

NOTE 1. go around 主要用于美国英语中, go round 主要用于英国英语中。

2. 当本短语作"到处走,环游"和"(消息、疾病等)流传,流行"解时,同义短语是 go about。

go as far as *v.* (后接动词不定式) make such a strong statement or take such strong action as (to do something) 说(或做)到……程度: I wouldn't *go as far as* to say that he's handsome, but he's certainly quite nice-looking. 我还不能说他很英俊,可他确实很好看。We have *gone as far as* to collect some useful statistics. 我们甚至收集到一些有用的统计资料。

NOTE 本短语的另外一种表达形式是 go so far as。

go at *vt.* 【不可分性动词短语】(非正式用语) ❶ do (something) with a lot of enthusiasm or energy 满怀热情地干,起劲地做(某事): Prince Harry was young and ambitious and *went at* things with a daunting eagerness. 哈里王子年轻有志,干起事来生龙活虎。We are *going at* our work as we never have before. 我们的工作干得比过去任何时候都起劲。He *went* *at* his breakfast as if he hadn't eaten anything for days. 他吃早餐的样子就像好几天没吃东西似的。❷(无被动语态形式) attack (usually someone) violently 猛烈攻击,扑向(尤指某人): The two boys were *going at* each other like mad dogs. 这两个男孩像疯狗一样地在相互打斗。Suddenly, he *went at* me with a stick like a madman. 突然,他像疯子一样挥着棍子向我袭来。The dog *went at* the postman's legs. 那条狗向邮递员的腿咬去。

go back *vi.* (常与 to 连用) ❶return (to a person, place, subject, or activity)返回: We didn't think he'd *go back* to his wife after everything that's happened. 我们没有想到在发生了那一切后他还能回到妻子的身边。I'd left my keys in the office and had to *go back* for them. 我把钥匙落在办公室了,得回去取。When do the children *go back* to school? 孩子们何时返校? I'd like to *go back* to what Abby was saying just a minute ago. 我想回到艾比几分钟前刚刚谈到的话题上。Let's *go back* to the original plan, that is to say you go ahead by plane and I'll follow by car with the equipment. 我们还是回到原来的计划上去,也就是说,你乘飞机先去,我坐汽车带着设备随后就到。Hammill escaped from his captors and is now ready to *go back* to work. 哈米尔从他的绑架者手中逃了出来,现正准备重返工作岗位。❷(用一般时态) have existed since or for a particular time; date back 从某一时期就已存在,追溯(到某一时期): Some of the university buildings *go back* as far as medieval times. 该大学的一些建筑物远在中世纪时期就有了。The friendly contacts between our two nations *go back* to the Tang Dynasty. 我们两国间的友好往来可以追溯到唐朝。

go back on *vt.* 【不可分性动词短语】(一般不用被动语态形式,常用一般时态) fail to fulfill (a promise, agreement, etc.)违背(诺言、协议等),背弃: This person cannot be trusted because he consistently lies and *goes back* on his promise. 这个人不可信,因为他一贯撒谎,违背诺言。Later he *went back on* what he had said. 后来他背弃了他的诺言。

go beyond *vt.* 【不可分性动词短语】(无被动语态形式,用一般时态) be more than (something); exceed 超过,超出: The cost of the new prison should not *go beyond* \$2 million. 建新监狱的花费不应超过 200 万美元。He has *gone* far *beyond* me in learning. 他的学问已远远超过我。Police officers have been urged not to *go beyond* the scope of their normal duties. 警务人员被要求不要超越自己的正常职责范围。

go by *v.* ❶(常用一般时态) move past (a place) or stop there for a short time during a journey 从(……)旁边经过;在……作短暂停留: A Benz *went by* very fast. 一辆奔驰牌轿车疾驶过去。I *went by* the post office on the way home. 我在回家的路上去了邮局。❷(of time) pass (时间的)过去: As time *goes by*, my memory seems to get worse. 随着时间的流逝,我的记忆力似乎越来越差。Five days have *gone by* since the earth shook here, but rescue workers are still searching for survivors in the rubble. 这里的地震已过去 5 天了,但救援人员仍然在瓦砾中搜寻幸存者。❸(无被动语态形式) act according to (what someone or something says) when you are deciding what to do or think 按照……行事: *Going by* what the commander said, we should be there by mid-afternoon. 按指挥员的指示,我们应该在下午的中段时间到达那里。He always *goes by* the rules. 他总是循规蹈矩。Police officers protect themselves from criticism by *going by* the book. 警方以按章办事为由来逃避批评。❹(无被动语态形式,常用一般时态) use (something) as a basis for your judgment or action 利用……做判断(或行事): *Going by* the position of the sun, I should say it is about 10 o'clock. 根据太阳的位置来判断,我想大约是 10 点钟了。*Going by* her clothes, she must be very rich. 从她的衣着来判断,她一定很富有。It's never wise to go by appearances. 以貌取人绝不明智。

go counter to ⇨ **run counter to**

go down *v.* ❶fall to the ground; collapse 倒下,落下;倒塌,垮掉: She hit her foot on something and *went down* with a bump. 她的脚踢在了什么东西上,于是猛地摔倒在地上。The whole house *went down* in flames. 整个房子在大火中倒塌了。"It is very hard to get infected by this disease, bird flu, but once you have it you tend to *go down* very fast," the expert in the hospital in Bangkok added. 这位曼谷医院的专家又说:"禽流感这种疾病很不容易感染上,可一旦染上,你就会很快垮掉。"❷lessen; become less; be reduced; fall 减弱,减少,下降: The wind has *gone down* a little. 风减弱了一点儿。The study shows that once the women have children, they become emotionally and psychologically stronger and the suicide rate *goes down*. 这项研究表明,妇女一旦有了孩子,她们在感情和心理上就变得更坚强些,因此自杀率就随之下降。Body temperature of the flu patient *went down* to 36.5 degrees Celsius Saturday morning. 这位流感患者星期六上午的体温已下降到36.5℃。The prices of homemade cars are expected to *go* further *down* next year. 预计明年国产汽车的价格还会进一步下降。Production goes up when production costs *go down* year by year. 生产上去了,可生产成本却年年在下降。❸(常与 in 连用) be written or recorded in (something) 被记入,被载入: It all *goes down* in her notebook. 一切都记入了她的笔记本中。"Obama's speech of today will *go down* in history as one of the best modern speeches," he said. 他说:"奥巴马今天的讲演将作为当代最佳讲演之一而载入历史史册。"❹(of the sun or moon) move below the horizon so you cannot see it any longer; set (指日、月) 落下: "The enormous structures with strange lights are as exciting as Hong Kong when the sun *goes down*," wrote the British student after visiting Shanghai. "日落后,高层建筑上就会亮起形状奇异的灯,就像在香港一样令人兴奋。"这位英国大学生在参观上海后这样写道。You can watch the sun *go down* either from the beach or up on the cliff. 你可以从海滩或在山崖上观看日落。❺(of a ship, etc.) sink below the surface of the water (指船只等)下沉: Hundreds of people died when the ship struck a hidden rock and *went down*. 轮船撞上了暗礁并沉没,数百人罹难。The ship *went down* off the coast of Africa. 该船在非洲海岸附近沉没。

❻become less swollen (肿)消退: How long will it take for the swelling to *go down*? 需要多久才能消肿?

go down in the world ⇨ **come down in the world**

go Dutch *vi.* (非正式用语,常与 with 连用) share the cost, especially of a meal; (of each person) pay his or her own expenses, rather than one person paying for everyone, when eating at a restaurant or going out for entertainment 平摊(尤指用餐的)费用,(在餐馆吃饭或外出娱乐时)各付各的账: Rogers wanted to *go Dutch* with me at the restaurant last night. 昨晚在餐馆里吃饭,罗杰斯要和我平摊饭钱。Let's *go Dutch* this time. 这次我们各付各的账吧。"Will you let me take you out tonight, Mary?" "As long as we *go Dutch*." "玛丽,今晚让我带你出去,好吗?""只要我们各付各的账。"

NOTE 1. 过去,荷兰商人在相聚用餐时一般都是各付各的账,英荷战争后对荷兰人怀有敌意的英国人鄙视他们如此的吝啬和自私,便把各付各的账说成 go Dutch,这也是本短语的来源。

2. 与本短语相关的一个短语是 Dutch treat,意为"各自付费的聚餐或聚会"。例如:

> Her parents agreed that she might go to the party if it was a *Dutch treat*.
> 如果聚会是各自付费的话,她父母就同意她去参加。

go for *vt.* 【不可分性动词短语】❶go somewhere in order to get (someone or something)去接,去请(某人);去拿,去取(某物): She's just *gone for* the kids; she'll be back any minute. 她刚去接孩子,一会儿就回来。He has *gone for* the lawyer. 他去请律师了。I'm going to *go for* a newspaper. 我去取报纸。❷(非正式用语,用一般时态) attack (someone or something) physically or with words 攻击,抨击,批评: The young man *went for* me, and gripped me by the throat. 那个年轻人朝我袭来,并紧紧地扼住了我的喉咙。Our dog *went for* the postman this morning. 我们家的狗今天早晨朝邮递员扑了上去。My boss really *went for* me when I came in late. 我迟到了,老板狠狠地批评了我一顿。❸(非正式用语,无被动语态形式,用一般时态) like (a particular type of person or thing) very much 十分喜欢(某种类型的人或物): Some women *go for* that type of man. 有些女人就喜欢那种类型的男人。I really don't *go for* horror films. 我真的不喜欢看恐怖影片。❹be sold for (a particular amount of money) (以某一价格)卖出: How much do you think these paintings will *go for*? 你认为这些油画能卖多少钱? We expect the house to *go for* about $100,000. 我们希望这房子能卖 10 万美元左右。❺try to get (something that you have to compete for)试图得到(所争取之物): There were about 100 people *going for* just three jobs. 大约有 100 人竞争这仅有的 3 份工作。Robles is *going for* the gold medal in the men's 110m hurdles competition at the next Olympic Games. 罗伯斯想争夺下一届奥运会男子 110 米栏的金牌。

NOTE 本短语与 send for 均表示"去请(某人)"之意。但本短语指亲自去请,而 send for 则是派他人去请。例如:

> If the child gets any worse, I shall have to *go for* the doctor.
> 如果孩子的病情加重,我就得去请医生了。

G

Send for the doctor, please.
请把医生请来。

go home *vi.* ❶ return to one's home or country 回家,回国:The doctor said the young mother and her newly-born baby could leave the hospital and *go home* in a week. 医生说,这位年轻的母亲和她的新生婴儿一周后便可出院回家。"American and British soldiers *go home*!" some Iraqis shouted in front of a line of tanks. "美英大兵,滚回老家去!"一些伊拉克人在一排坦克前面喊道。❷(常用一般时态)have an effect, usually on someone (尤指对某人)产生某种效果:The chairman's pointed remark *went home*, and the committee's members fell silent. 主席那具有针对性的讲话产生了效果,委员会的成员都不作声了。

go in for *vt.*【不可分性动词短语】❶(英国英语用法)take part in (a competition) or take (an examination) 参加(竞赛、考试等):His school had suggested he *go in for* the Young Musician of the Year competition. 他所在的学校建议他参加年度青年音乐人大赛。Which event is he *going in for* at the Beijing Olympic Games? 他参加北京奥运会的什么项目? Are you *going in for* the civil service examination? 你参加公务员考试吗? ❷ enjoy (a particular thing or activity)喜欢(某物或某项活动):I thought he only *went in for* music and tennis. 我想他只喜欢音乐和网球。I don't *go in for* golf much. 我不太喜欢打高尔夫球。I don't *go in for* collecting stamps. 我不喜欢集邮。❸(英国英语用法)occupy oneself with; be engaged in 致力于,从事于:When she graduated from college she *went in for* teaching. 她大学毕业后就从事教学工作了。

go into *vt.*【不可分性动词短语】❶enter (a building, space, etc.)进入:She *went into* the bathroom and washed her face in cold water. 他走进浴室用凉水洗了脸。She *went into* the garden to pull up a few onions for dinner. 她进园子里拔了几棵洋葱就饭吃。Three Chinese astronauts *went into* space aboard Shenzhou-7 and successfully performed the space walk. 中国三名宇航员乘坐"神舟七号"进入太空,并成功地进行了太空行走。❷ start (an activity), or start (to be in a particular state or condition)开始:Repeated death threats have forced him to *go into* hiding. 反复的死亡危胁迫使他躲了起来。The drug is still being tested and will not *go into* production for at least two years. 这种药物还在试验阶段,至少两年内不会投入生产。❸(无被动语态形式)start working in a particular type of job or business 投身于,从事于(某种事业或职业):Eric *went into* the army right after school. 埃里克毕业后就参军了。His parents want him to *go into* politics. 他的父母要他从政。Alex has decided to *go into* nursing. 埃历克斯已决定从事护理工作。❹ examine or investigate (something) carefully 仔细调查:We must *go into* the matter further before making a decision. 对此事我们必须做进一步调查再作出决定。There's something mysterious about Princess Diana's death; it'll have to be *gone into* by the British police. 戴安娜王妃之死有些神秘,英国警方将缜密调查。❺discuss, mention, or talk about (something) in detail 详细地讨论,提及,谈论:We need to *go into* the question of costs. 我们需要详细地讨论一下费用问

题。We can *go into* that later, can't we? 这问题我们以后再讨论,好吗? That's a good question, but I don't want to *go into* it now. 那是一个很好的问题,但我不想现在详谈。The US national security adviser declined to *go into* details about the information ahead of the war against Iraq. 美国国家安全顾问拒绝谈论有关对伊拉克战争前的情报细节。❻(无被动语态形式)(of money, time, or effort) be used or spent in order to do (something)(资金)用在……上;(时间或气力)花在……上: Over 50% of the budget *went into* the design of the equipment. 50%多的预算资金用在了该设备的设计上。Months of hard work have *gone into* making tonight's ceremony a success. 几个月的艰苦工作都是为了今晚这个仪式的成功。Is there a lot of money and effort *going into* this sort of research? 大量的金钱和气力都投在了这种研究上吗? ❼crash into (something) 撞上(某物): The truck swerved violently and *went into* a wall. 那辆卡车突然转弯,撞上了一堵墙。Heavy smoke came out of the windows of a high-rise building after a small aircraft *went into* it in New York City on October 11. 10 月 11 日,一架小型飞机撞上纽约市的一座高层建筑后,浓烟从楼房的数个窗口冒出。

go off *v.* ❶(常用一般时态) leave (something such as a place), especially for a particular purpose 离开(某处),脱离: He *went off* to have lunch in the canteen at eleven o'clock. 他在 11 点钟就离开去食堂吃午饭了。Dave's *gone off* to the south of France for the summer. 戴维去法国南部度夏。A high-speed passenger train *went off* the rails, colliding with another, leaving at least 72 people killed and more than 400 injured. 一辆高速行驶的旅客列车脱轨并与另一辆旅客列车相撞,导致至少 72 人死亡,400 多人受伤。❷(常用一般时态)(of an explosive device or a gun) explode or fire (爆炸装置)爆炸;(枪)发射: The first bomb *went off* at about 8:30 am in Central city. 第一枚炸弹于上午 8 点 30 分在市区中心爆炸。The gun *went off* while he was cleaning it. 他正擦枪时,那枪突然走火。❸(of an alarm) start making a sudden loud noise (闹铃或警报)突然响起来: I was just lying in bed waiting for the alarm to *go off*. 我躺在床上等待着闹铃响起。Around one o'clock in the morning, the alarm *went off*. 大约在凌晨一点,警报突然响了起来。❹(of an electricity supply or a light) stop being available or working (电力供应)停止,(灯)熄灭: While we were there the electricity *went off*. 我们在那里的时候,突然停了电。Suddenly all the lights in the building *went off*. 全楼的灯都突然熄灭了。The heating suddenly *went off*. 暖气突然中断。❺(英国英语用法,非正式用语) stop liking (someone or something) or lose interest in them 不再喜欢,对……失去兴趣: Why have they *gone off* him now? 他们为什么现在不喜欢他了? Mary and I have *gone off* cooking, so we live only on salads these days. 玛丽和我都不喜欢做饭了,所以这些天来我们只吃色拉。I *went off* the idea of buying a sports car; it's too costly. 我对买跑车的想法已失去兴趣——它太昂贵了。❻stop being felt; disappear 不再感觉到;消失: The pain *went off* after three treatments. 治疗了三次之后疼痛就消失了。The effect of the drug will *go off* after two

hours. 药效两个小时之后就会消失。❼(英国英语用法,非正式用语)(of food or drink) be no longer fresh or become sour, or rotten (食物或饮料)不新鲜,开始变酸,开始腐败: Don't eat that cake! It has *gone off*. 别吃那蛋糕了。它已坏了。❽(英国英语用法,非正式用语) become worse in quality (质量)下降,变差: The lessons have *gone off* since we had a new teacher. 自从换了新老师,课程的质量就下降了。His work has really *gone off* recently. 他的工作最近确实差劲了。❾(英国英语用法,非正式用语) happen, especially in the way that was planned or hoped (尤指按计划或期望)发生,举行,进行: The conference *went off* just as we had planned. 会议按我们的计划召开了。The protest march *went off* peacefully with only two arrests. 抗议游行和平举行,仅有两人被捕。There was a fire *going off* next door. 隔壁发生了火灾。❿(英国英语用法,仅用于口语中) start to sleep 睡着,入睡: As soon as the baby *goes off*, I'll be able to relax and watch TV. 孩子一睡着,我就可以休息,看看电视。The baby's just *gone off* to sleep. 孩子刚刚入睡。⓫(美国英语用法,非正式用语,常与 on 连用) suddenly become angry (with someone) 突然(向某人)发火: He just *went off* on her and started yelling. 他突然向她发火,大叫大嚷起来。

NOTE 本短语可转化为复合词 go-off,意为"开始,着手;出发;爆炸"。

go on *v.* ❶(常用一般时态) continue happening or doing (something) as before 继续,持续,接续: We would rather *go on* with the experiment than give it up. 我们宁愿把这项实验继续做下去,也不愿弃而废之。You shouldn't *go on* living this way. 你不应当继续这样生活下去了。❷(常用进行时态) happen; carry out 发生,举行,进行: I wonder what's *going on* next door; they're making a lot of noise. 我不知道隔壁发生了什么事。他们搞出来的声音太吵闹了。Young people are leaving the country for the cities. There's more *going on* there. 年轻人正在从农村流入城市。这种情况在那里更甚。❸(of time) pass (指时间)过去: As time *went on*, things began to change. 随着时间的消逝,情况开始发生变化。❹(英国英语用法,非正式用语,常与 about, at 连用) talk about (something) for a long time that people become bored or annoyed 絮絮叨叨地讲: He *went on* and on about my being late for work again. 他又在絮絮叨叨地讲我上班迟到的事。I wish you'd stop *going on* at me about my haircut. 我希望你不要再唠唠叨叨地讲我的发型了。❺(常与介词 with 和动词不定式短语连用) continue talking, especially after stopping or in order to pass to a new subject 继续说下去: "But," she *went on*, "we have to deal with the problems we're facing." "但是,"她继续说道,"我们必须应对我们所面临的这些问题。" He paused for a sip of coffee, and then *went on* with his story. 他停了下来喝了一小口咖啡,然后继续讲他的故事。*Go on* and tell us all about it. 说下去,把这件事全部告诉我们吧。

NOTE 当本短语作"继续,持续,接续"解时,后接动名词和后接动词不定式所表达的意义不同。后接动名词,表示继续同一件事,而后接动词不定式则表示接着做另一件事。试比较:

He *went on* talking about the world economy.
他继续谈世界经济。
He *went on* to talk about the world economy.
他接着又谈了世界经济。

go (out) on strike *vi.* (especially of workers) stop working as a protest (尤指工人)罢工:Workers voted by a large majority to *go on strike*. 绝大多数工人投票赞成举行罢工。If the postal workers *go out on strike*, other sectors may well join them. 如果邮电工人罢工,其他行业的工人也会加入他们的行列。

NOTE 本短语的同义短语是 go out(第六个义项)。

go on the stage *vi.* become a professional performer 当职业演员: He'd always wanted to *go on the stage*. 他一直想当职业演员。Do you think your children will *go on the stage*? 你认为你的孩子们都要当职业演员吗?

go one's own way *vi.* behave in an independent manner 独立行事,自行其是: His parents must realize that he will soon *go his own way*. 他的家长必须认识到,他很快就会独立行事了。He didn't listen to your advice, but *went his own way*. 他没有听你的劝告,而是自行其是了。

NOTE 本短语的动词 go 可被 take 替换,两者的意义和用法相同。

go out *vi.* ❶(常与 to 连用) leave (your house) and go somewhere, especially to do something enjoyable (走出家门)出去,外出: I wanted the evenings free for *going out* with friends. 我希望晚上有空和朋友们出去。We haven't *gone out* dancing for a long time. 我们很久没出去跳舞了。Let's *go out* to eat tonight. 咱们今晚出去吃饭吧。She wasn't allowed to *go out* and play with the other kids. 不允许她走出房门和其他小朋友们玩。❷(与 to 连用) go to a distant country, sometimes to stay there 出国: My friend *went out* to Australia to find a job. 我朋友到澳大利亚去找工作了。She wished she had been able to *go out* to South Africa with Nicola. 她希望能与尼古拉去南非。❸(of a fire, light, etc.) stop burning or shining (火、灯光等)熄灭: The fire must have *gone out* during the night. 火肯定是在晚上熄灭的。Don't let the fire *go out*! 别让火熄灭! The lights *went out* one after another. 电灯一个接一个地灭了。Have you got a match? This cigar has *gone out*. 你有火柴吗? 这雪茄灭了。❹stop being fashionable at a particular time 不流行,过时: That hairstyle *went out* about ten years ago. 那种发式在大约 10 年前就不流行了。That expression has *gone out* and nobody uses it today. 那种表达法已经过时,现在没人用了。Classic jewelry like this will never *go out* of fashion. 似这样的传统珠宝饰物永远不会过时。❺(常用进行时态,常与 with 或 together 连用) have a romantic relationship with someone and spend a lot of time with him or her 与(异性)相处: How long have Rob and Susan been *going out*? 罗布和苏珊相处多久了? Linda and I are really good friends, but she's not the sort of girl I want to *go out* with. 我和琳达确实是好朋友,但她并不是我要相处的那种女孩儿。They've been *going out* together/with each other for seven months now. 他们至今已在一起相处了 7 个月。❻(especially of workers) stop working as a protest; go on strike (尤指工

人)罢工:If the postal workers *go out*, other sectors may well join them. 如果邮电工人罢工,其他行业的工人也会加入他们的行列。Are we likely to gain anything by *going out*? 我们罢工能得到什么好处吗? ❼(英国英语用法)(of a television or radio programme) be broadcast (电视或广播节目)播出:The series *goes out* at 11:00 pm, Fridays, on Channel 8. 这部连续剧每星期五晚上 11 点在 8 频道播出。❽(英国英语用法,常用一般时态) not be allowed to take part in the next stage of a competition because you have been defeated (在比赛中)被淘汰出局:Last year's champion *went out* in the second round. 去年的冠军在第二轮就被淘汰出局了。Brazil *went out* of the World Cup amid controversy. 巴西队在争议中被淘汰出世界杯。

go out of use *vi.* stop being used 不再使用:These pesticides are gradually *going out of use*. 这些杀虫剂都逐渐地不再使用了。

go out of vogue *vi.* (of something) cease to be popular or fashionable 不再流行:When did mini-skirts *go out of vogue*? 迷你裙是什么时候过时的?

go over *v.* ❶(常与 to 连用) travel or move over (something) (towards someone or something) 走过,越过,前往:Why don't you *go over* and say hello? 你为什么不过去打声招呼? He *went over* to the window and drew the curtains. 他走到窗前把窗帘拉上。The crowd cheered as the horse *went* safely *over* the last fence. 当那匹马安全地越过最后一道栏时,人们欢呼起来。We had met a year ago, when I *went over* to Paris to see an exhibition. 我们还是在一年前我去巴黎观看展览时见过面。❷(常用一般时态) examine and check (something such as a document) very carefully 认真审查(文件等),仔细查看:Could you *go over* this report and correct any mistakes? 你能认真审查一下这份报告,把错误的地方改正吗? Before *going over* the export list, however, please take note of the following important points. 然而,在审查这一出口商品清单前,请注意如下要点。I'd like to *go over* the house before deciding to buy it. 我想先仔细查看一下房子再决定要不要买下来。❸(常用一般时态) search (a place) thoroughly 彻底搜查(某处):This area is to be *gone over* with the greatest care. 这一地区要彻底地进行搜查。❹ practise and repeat (something) in order to learn it 重复,重温:Let's *go over* this chapter once more. 咱们把这一章再温习一遍。He *went over* the events of the day in his mind. 他反思白天所发生的事情。❺(常与 from, to 连用) join a different group, organization, or political party 加入(不同的组织或政党):What makes them *go over* to a party they once fought against? 是什么使他们加入他们以前与之对抗的政党中的呢? He *went over* from the Democrats to the Republicans. 他退出民主党加入了共和党。

go sour *vi.* become less enjoyable or happy; turn out badly or unpleasant 变得不和谐,令人不快;变坏,变糟:Their relationship soon *went sour*. 他们的关系不久就变坏了。My whole life is *going sour* right now. 我整个生活现在每况愈下。His original enthusiasm has *gone sour*. 他当初的热情已淡下去了。

go through *v.* ❶ pass through (something) 穿过,穿越:The fastest way to get to the library is to *go through* the park. 去图书馆最快的路是穿过公园。This material is so stiff even the needle won't *go through*. 这种料子很硬,连针都扎不透。The bullet *went through* the wall. 子弹穿透了墙壁。Soldiers at the base fired at the vehicle, but failed to stop it from *going through* the entrance point, the report said. 据报道,该基地的士兵朝那辆汽车开了枪,但还是没能阻止它穿越入口处。❷(常与 with 连用) perform or complete (a routine, procedure, etc.)办理,完成(某种手续、日常事务等): When exporting the above-mentioned items and technologies, an exporter must *go through* the Customs formalities. 出口经营者出口上述物项和技术时,必须办理海关手续。I can't believe he *went through* with the divorce. 我无法相信他已办理了离婚手续。After months of efforts the work finally *went through*. 经过几个月努力之后,工作终于完成了。He *went through* with his work ahead of time. 他提前完成了任务。❸suffer or experience (something difficult or unpleasant)遭受(痛苦);经历(困难): The old couple *went through* untold sufferings when they were young. 这对老年夫妇在年轻时都受尽了苦难。Since the lunar orbiter entered the moon's orbit on November 7, it has *gone through* a number of tests. 自 11 月 7 日进入月球轨道以来,绕月卫星已经历了一系列的考验。❹examine or search (something) very carefully 仔细检查,审查,审阅,搜查: The accountant is *going through* the items one by one. 会计正在逐笔检查账目。Professor Smith will *go through* your papers. 史密斯教授将审阅你们的论文。All the rooms of the building have been *gone through* by the police. 那座楼的所有房间都被警察搜查过了。❺practise all of (something such as a speech, song, or play)练习(演讲、唱歌或演戏等): Let's *go through* the lines one more time. 咱们再把台词练一遍吧。*Go through* it again, this time with the music. 再排练一次,这回配上音乐。❻(无被动语态形式)(of something such as a law, request, proposal, or contract) be officially accepted or approved by a parliament or committee (法令、要求、建议或合同等)被采纳,通过: The bill has *gone through* (Parliament) without a vote. 这项法案未经投票就(在国会)通过了。In spite of all, the proposal failed to *go through*. 尽管想尽了一切办法,这项建议还是未被采纳。❼ use, spend, or eat all of (something), especially quickly (尤指很快地)用完,花掉,吃完: He's *gone through* all his money by the end of the first week of his holiday. 他在度假的第一个星期结束时就把所有的钱花掉了。Before I gave up smoking I was *going through* 40 cigarettes a day. 我戒烟之前,每天抽 40 支香烟。

go to extremes *vi.* (常用一般时态) do something much more than is usual or reasonable 走极端,采取极端手段: If he wants something, he'll *go to extremes*. 他如果想要得到什么,他就会采取极端手段去搞到它。

NOTE **1.** 本短语中的名词 extreme 必须用复数形式。

2. 本短语还可扩展成为 go from one extreme to the other,意为"从一个极端走向另一个极端"。例如:

> Sometimes he eats enormous amounts and sometimes nothing. He *goes from one extreme* to the other.
> 他有时吃得太多,有时又什么也不吃。他从一个极端走向另一个极端。

G

go to great pains *vi.* (常用一般时态,后常接动词不定式短语、动名词短语和介词短语)do (something) with a lot of care or effort 花大力气,下功夫(做某事): She *went to great pains* to say that public expenditure had gone as far as it could. 她竭力说明公共开支已达到其最大限度。I had *gone to great pains* to make the evening perfect. 我下了很大功夫以使晚会开得完美。She *went to great pains* with her homework because she wanted to get good grade. 她做家庭作业很下功夫,因为她想得到好成绩。

NOTE 1. 本短语中的名词 pains 并不是表示"疼痛、痛苦"之意,其本身是复数性名词,表示"烦劳""努力""辛苦"之意,用于 go to great pains, take (great) pains 和 be at (great) pains to do something 等短语中。pains 不可用 many 来修饰,而要用 much 或 a lot of 来修饰。

2. 本短语的同义短语是 take great pains, 两者的用法相同。

go to sleep ⇨ fall asleep

go up *vt.* &*vi.* ❶ move in an upward direction 上升: Smoke was *going up* in a straight line, showing that there was no wind. 烟在直线上升,这说明没有风。"All of a sudden, I felt my car *going up* in the air and landing again," the driver said. 那位司机讲述道:"突然,我感到我的车飞上了天空,然后又落了下来。" The elevator *went up* to the eightieth floor. 电梯升到了80楼。❷climb 攀爬,攀登: Don't *go up* the tree! 不要爬树! The hill is too steep; the old car won't *go up*. 山太陡,这台旧车爬不上去。Can you *go up* the stairs two steps at a time? 你能一步登上两个台阶吗?

—*vi.* ❶(of a price, amount, or level) rise; be increased; become higher (指物价、数量或水平)提高,增加,增长,升高: We'd better get in some more coal before the price *goes up*. 我们最好在涨价之前多买点煤。Production *goes up* when production costs go down year by year. 生产上去了,可生产成本却年年在下降。We'd like to see the baby's weight *going* steadily *up*. 我们愿意看到孩子的体重稳步增加。The temperature is *going up*; will the snow melt? 温度在升高;雪会融化吗? ❷(of a building, wall, or other structure) be built or fixed in place (指楼、墙或其他建筑物)被建造起来: He noticed a new building *going up* near the South Lake Park. 他注意到,在南湖公园附近建起了一栋新楼。A new office building is *going up* on Oxford Street. 一幢新的办公大楼正在牛津大街兴建。❸(常用一般时态,与 from 连用)(of a shout or cheer made by a lot of people together) arise (众人的呼喊或欢呼声)响起: A cheer *went up* from the crowd as the Queen stepped into the hall. 当女王步入大厅时,人群中响起了一片欢呼声。❹(英国英语用法,常与 to 连用) travel towards the north, or to a place that is larger or more important than the place you are leaving 去北方,去大或重要城市: Max *goes up* to Scotland to fish every summer. 马克斯每年夏天都北上去苏格兰打鱼。Let's *go up* to London next week. 咱们下星期去伦敦吧。❺(英国英语用法,正式用语,常与 to 连用) go to a university, especially Oxford or Cambridge, at the beginning of a term or in order to begin your studies 上大学(尤指牛津或剑桥大学): When are you *going up* to the university?

你什么时候上大学? ❻(与 to 连用)be long or tall enough to reach a particular higher point or level 到达,延伸: The fire only *went up* to the second floor. 大火仅烧到二楼。The trees *go* right *up* to the riverbank. 树林一直延伸到河堤边。❼(of the curtain on stage)be raised or opened and start the performance 启幕,开演: What does the curtain *go up*? 演出什么时候开始?

NOTE 本短语的反义短语是 go down。

go up in the world ⇨ **come up in the world**

go with *vt.*【不可分性动词短语】❶(无被动语态形式)accompany; exist frequently with (someone or something)陪伴,伴随: It was determined that Brown should *go with* Tom to England. 已决定由布朗陪伴汤姆去英格兰。We got some fish to *go with* our rice. 我们搞了点鱼伴着米饭吃。Happiness doesn't necessarily *go with* money. 有钱不一定幸福。Responsibility *goes with* becoming a father. 做了父亲,责任便随之而来。❷(无被动语态形式,用一般时态)match; seem good, natural, or attractive in combination with (something) 与……相配,协调: Which of the shoes *go* best *with* this dress? 哪个样子的鞋与这件连衣裙相配? I want some shirts to go with this pair of trousers. 我想买几件与这条裤子相配的衬衣。"Any change of the Renminbi exchange rate has to *go with* the advancing process of China's financial reform," the expert said at the Conference. 这位专家在会议上指出:"人民币汇率的任何变化都得与中国金融改革的进程相协调。"❸(非正式用语,常用进行时态)have a romantic or sexual relationship with (someone of the opposite sex)与(某人)有异性交往,与……有两性关系: I heard that Elizabeth is *going with* the guy who works downstairs. 我听说伊丽莎白正和楼下干活的那个小伙子交往。

go without *v.* live without (something that you need or would like to have or do)没有,没有……也行: Power failure started on July 17, and more than one thousand homes in New York City have *gone without* electricity for a week. 停电始于7月17日。纽约市1 000多个家庭已一个星期没有电了。We cannot *go without* water, light and air. 我们不能没有水、阳光和空气。He *went without* sleeping for two days. 他两天没有睡觉了。We can't afford it, so we'll just have to *go without*. 这东西我们买不起,所以只好不用了。

NOTE 本短语的同义短语是 do without。

go wrong *vi.* ❶(used when something stops working) fail to work correctly 出毛病,发生故障: My watch has *gone wrong*. 我的手表有毛病了。If it *goes wrong* again, I shall get rid of it. 如果它再出毛病,我就扔掉它。When anything *went wrong* with the engines they called for me. 每当发动机出了故障时,他们就请我去。❷(of something such as a problem) happen and cause the failure of something 出问题: It's difficult to say when it started to *go wrong*. 很难说什么时候会出问题。They also have some money for an emergency if something should *go wrong*. 如果出了什么问题,他们也有钱应急。Everything has *gone wrong* with me today. 我今天事事都不顺。❸(especially of a girl) fall into error (尤指女孩子)犯错误,走入歧途,失足: She told me how she first *went wrong*. 她

G

向我讲述了她当初是怎样走入歧途的。What's the best way to help young girls who *go wrong*? 有什么最佳的办法来帮助失足的年轻女孩呢?

good at *adj.* skilful in (something or doing something); able to do something successfully 善于……的,擅长于……的: There is no limit to the life of a system that is *good at* self-readjustment and self-improvement. 一个善于自我调整、自我完善的制度,其生机是无限的。Our teacher is clever, but not very *good at* getting his ideas across to us. 我们的老师很聪明,但他不善于把自己的观点向我们表达清楚。When he was a pupil he was not very bright at school, but very *good at* sports. 他在学校读书时,功课不太好,但很擅长体育。

G

good for *adj.* ❶giving benefits to or having a useful or helpful effect on (someone or something)有益于……的,对……有好处的:Exercise is *good for* you. 锻炼有益于你的健康。The recent tax cuts will be *good for* business. 最近的减税对商界有益。Electric cars are *good for* the environment of big cities. 电车有益于大城市的环境。Too much sun isn't *good for* them. 太多的阳光对他们没好处。❷(of someone or something)being likely to live or last in use over (a period of time)(指人)能活(多久)的;(指物)能持续(多久)有效的,能用(多久)的:He is *good for* some years more. 他还能活几年。This ticket is *good for* 6 months. 这票半年有效。My car is *good for* another five years. 我的车还能用5年。❸suitable or appropriate; convenient for (someone)适合于……的;对(某人)方便的:She would be *good for* the job. 她会适合于这项工作的。Can you change our meeting? Thursday is not *good for* me. 您能改一下我们的会期吗? 星期四对我不方便。❹(非正式用语)used to praise sb for doing something well (用于表达对某人的赞扬)真棒,真出色:"I passed College English Test Band 6." "*Good for* you!" "我通过了大学英语六级考试。""你真棒!" *Good for* Bill — he's sold the car! 比尔真行,他把车卖出去了!

grab hold of *vt.* 【不可分性动词短语】(常用一般时态) start holding (something or someone) with your hands (用手)握住,抓住: The police appeared all of a sudden and *grabbed hold of* the attacker. 警察突然出现,抓住了那名袭击者。I was woken up by someone *grabbing hold of* my sleeping bag. 有人抓住了我的睡袋将我惊醒。

NOTE 当本短语作"抓住,握住"解时,同义短语是 catch hold of, get hold of, have hold of 和 take hold of。

grammar school *n.* ❶(英国英语) a secondary school for children of high academic ability 中学: I haven't seen her since we were at *grammar school*. 我们曾在中学一起读书,但此后我就再没有见过她。❷(美国英语) a school for young children, usually the first 6 or 8 grades 小学: After I went through the *grammar school*, I entered the Oakland High School in the State of California. 我小学读完后,就进入了加州的奥克兰中学就读。A Boston *grammar school* teacher has been suspended for a number of weeks for some reasons. 波士顿一名小学教师因某些原因已被停职数周。❸(澳大利亚英语)a private school, usually one controlled by a church (常指教会的)私立学校: Knox *Grammar School*, located in the northern suburb of Sydney, Australia, is an independent Church school for boys. 位于澳大利亚悉尼市北郊的诺克斯学校是一所独立的、只收男生的教会学校。

NOTE 本短语指的是英美等英语国家的不同类型的学校,而不是(专门学习语法的)语法学校。

green card *n.* a long-time residence permit, usually with a green cover, granted by a country to a foreigner 绿卡,外国人居留许可证: Under the US President's proposal, millions of illegal immigrants with jobs in the United States would be permitted to apply for a *green card* granting permanent residency in the United States. 根据美国总统的建议,数百万计的在美非法打工移民将被允许申请绿卡,给予在美永久居留权。According to the Exit-Entry Administration of the Ministry of Public Security, China has officially started to implement its own *green card* system. 据公安部出入境管理局称,中国已正式开始实施自己的绿卡制度。

green light Ⅰ *n.* ❶ a signal that gives traffic permission to move forward 绿灯通行信号: Five thousand Olympic cars and buses benefited from longer *green lights* during the Games. 奥运会期间, 5 000辆奥运车辆受到了长时间绿灯通行的待遇。❷(非正式用语,常与动词 give, get, have 连用) a permission, especially an official permission, to begin an action (尤指官方的)许可: Vietnam and China will join forces to build a highway from Hanoi to Kunming, and the Asian Development Bank has given the *green light* to a loan to Vietnam. 越中两国将联合修建河内至昆明的公路。亚洲发展银行已对向越南提供贷款给予许可。"Have you got the *green light* from the police to post such a notice on the website?" one of the internet surfers asked. "你往网站上挂这样的帖子经过警方许可了吗?"一名网上冲浪者问道。We have a *green light* on the project. Work will start next Monday. 我们的项目获批。下周一就开始工作。

Ⅱ *vt.* (非正式用语) give approval for something 批准,允许: Romania's Senate *green lights* legal actions against a current minister accused of corruption. 罗马尼亚参议院批准对一名因贪腐而被起诉的现任部长采取法律行动。So far three directors have *green lighted* the project. 至此,已有三名董事批准了这一项目。

NOTE 当本短语用作名词性短语,作"绿灯通行信号"解时,反义短语是 red light (红灯禁行信号)。

grind to a halt *vi.* slow down and stop 减速后停止: The bus *ground to a halt* at the stop and someone got off. 公共汽车在停车站停车后有人下了车。The traffic on the streets during the rush hours virtually *ground to a halt*. 高峰期间马路上的交通车辆实际上已处于停滞状态。If trade doesn't improve soon, the industry will *grind to a halt*. 如果商情不迅速改善,该产业就将陷入停顿。

grow into *vt.* 【不可分性动词短语】(无被动语态形式) ❶(of a child) grow tall or big enough to fit (clothes, shoes, etc.) properly 长大得适合穿……: The coat is too long now, but he'll *grow into* it. 这件上衣现在太长,但他再长大些就

可以穿了。❷ develop and become (a particular person or thing)成长为，发展成：She had *grown into* a beautiful woman. 她已长成了一个漂亮的成年女子。Mary is *growing into* a good artist. 玛丽正在成为一名很好的艺术家。This seedling should *grow into* a tall plant. 这棵秧苗会长成一株高大的植物。Shenzhen, a former fishing village, has *grown into* a big modern city. 深圳曾是一个渔村，现已经发展成了一个现代化的大城市。

grow up *vi.* ❶ (especially of someone) change from being a baby or young child to being an older child or adult (主要指人)长大，成长：Children are the priceless wealth of a country, and they are entitled to protection and the right to *grow up* healthily. 儿童是国家的无价之宝。他们有权受到保护，也有权健康地成长。Hua Mei, a giant panda born in the United States in 1999, returned to Sichuan where her parents were born and *grew up*. 1999 年在美国出生的大熊猫“华美”回到了它父母出生和成长之地四川。❷(常用一般时态) become established; start existing or being seen; arise 确立，出现，兴起：A troublesome situation has *grown up*. 使人棘手的局面出现了。A variety of heavy industries *grew up* alongside the port. 沿着港口兴起了多种重型工业。

NOTE 本短语可经略微变动转化成复合词 grown-up，意为“成年人；成年的”。

guard against *vt.* (常用一般时态)(of someone) take care to prevent (something) from happening or to avoid being affected by it 防止，警惕，避免：You should wash your hands when preparing food to *guard against* spreading infection. 做饭前要洗手，以防传染疾病。We must take measures to *guard against* fires. 我们必须采取措施避免火灾的发生。Take this medicine regularly; it will *guard* you *against* a return of the illness. 按时服用此药，会避免你的疾病复发。

guard dog ⇨ **watch dog**

H h

had better *v.* (用于口语中,常略写为 'd better,后接原形动词)(used for saying that someone should do something) should; ought to; need to 应该,需要:You'*d better* leave soon. If you don't, you'll miss your bus. 你应该早动身,否则就赶不上公共汽车了。*Had*n't you *better* take an umbrella? 你不觉得应该带把伞吗? We'*d better* not tell him about the sad news right now. 我们这会儿不应告诉他这不幸的消息。Your article *had better* be rewritten. 你的这篇文章需要重写。

NOTE 1. 尽管本短语中的动词是 had,但本短语并不用来意指过去,而是指现在或将来。

2. 当本短语用于口语中时,其中的动词 had 可省略,仅用 better。例如:

You *better* clean up your room!
Better not say too much aloud.
你最好打扫下你的房间。

但在书面语中 had 则不可省略。

3. 本短语只能接动词原形,而不能接带 to 的动词不定式(短语)。

4. 本短语的否定式是"had better+not+原形动词"。

5. 本短语的另外一种表达形式是 had best,主要用于英国英语中,例如:

We'*d best* be going now.
咱们最好现在就走。

但 had best 不及本短语常用。

6. 不要将本短语与 would be better 混淆。两者之间的区别见 would be better。

had rather ⇨ **would rather**

hammer out *vt.*【可分性动词短语】reach (a decision or agreement) after discussing it or arguing about it for a long time (经长时间讨论或辩论而)作出(决定),达成(协议):We've got to get together and try to *hammer out* a solution. 我们得到一起好好讨论一下,设法找出个解决办法来。A new deal was *hammered out* between the two banks. 两家银行做成了一笔新的交易。If we keep talking all night, we should be able to *hammer* a contract *out*. 如果我们彻夜讨论,就应该能达成一份合同。

hand and foot *adv.* (与 wait on/upon 连用)in every possible way 在各方面:He wants a woman to wait on him *hand and foot*. 他需要一个女人在各方面照顾他。A Japanese wife was formerly expected to wait upon her husband *hand and foot*. 从前,日本太太被要求必须无微不至地伺候丈夫。

hand back *vt.*【可分性动词短语】(常用一般时态,常与 to 连用) give (something) back to (someone) by holding it in your hand and offering it to him or her; return 把(某物)亲手交还给(某人):Jean *handed* the letter *back* to John. 琼把那封

信交还给了约翰。The officer *handed* me my passport *back*. 那位警官把我的护照还给了我。He took a calculator from the library but was caught and *had* to hand it *back*. 他从图书馆拿走一个计算器,但被人抓到,所以不得不将其归还。Examination papers will be *handed back* to you after the marks have been recorded. 考试卷将在成绩登记完毕后发还给大家。

NOTE 当本短语所带的宾语为代词时,该代词须置于本短语的动词和副词中间。

hand down *vt.* ❶(常用被动语态形式,常与 to 连用)give or pass (knowledge or skill)or leave (something) to people who belong to a younger generation 把(知识或技艺)传给(后人): These skills have been *handed down* from generation to generation. 这些技艺是一代代传下来的。In old times, property was usually *handed down* to the oldest son at his father's death. 从前,父亲去世时财产通常传给长子。This custom has been *handed down* since the 15th century. 这个风俗是从 15 世纪流传至今。❷(主要用于新闻英语中,常用一般时态)(of a person or group in a position of power) declare (something such as a decision) publicly and officially 公布,宣布: The board of directors will *hand down* its decision on Friday. 董事会将于星期五公布决定。❸(正式用语,主要用于美国英语中,常用被动语态形式)(of the court) announce officially that someone should receive a particular punishment (法庭)宣判,宣布裁决: Although it was only his first offence, the court *handed down* an eight-year sentence. 尽管这是他初次犯罪,法庭还是判了他 8 年徒刑。A death sentence was *handed down* to two men for the milk powder scandal. 有两人因奶粉事件而被判死刑。They looked very much shocked when the court ruling was *handed down*. 他们听法庭宣布裁决时,看上去甚感震惊。

NOTE 1. 当本短语所带的宾语为代词时,该代词须置于本短语的动词和副词中间。

2. 当本短语作"把(知识或技艺)传给(后人)"解时,同义短语是 bring down, come down, hand on, pass down 和 pass on。

hand in *vt.* 【可分性动词短语】(常用一般时态,后接有呈交对象时用介词 to) give (something) to a person in authority; submit (something)by hand 交上,呈交: Please *hand in* your keys when you leave the hotel. 离开宾馆时请把钥匙交上来。If you *hand in* your homework like that, the teacher will give you a low mark. 如果你把那样的作业交上来,老师会给你打低分的。I think anyone who finds anything on a bus should *hand* it *in* to the police. 我认为,任何人在公共汽车上拾到任何物品都应交给警察。All essays must be *handed in* by Tuesday. 星期二之前必须把所有的短文都交上来。

NOTE 1. 本短语为美国英语用法。在英国英语中,用 give in。见 give in。

2. 当本短语所带的宾语为代词时,该代词须置于本短语的动词和副词中间。

hand in hand *adv.* ❶(of two or more people) holding each other's hand (usually with the left hand of one in the right hand of the other)手挽手地,携手: They walked along the cliff top *hand in hand*. 他们在悬崖顶上手拉手地走着。The women tennis players of the two countries entered the court *hand in* hand. 两国女子网球选手手挽手走进球场。African countries have worked *hand in hand* with the other developing countries, promoting South-South cooperation. 非洲国家同其他发展中国家携手推动南南合作。❷(of two things) happening together and closely connected 同时发生，密切相关：Ignorance and poverty often go *hand in hand*. 无知往往与贫穷形影相随。Industrial progress should go *hand in hand* with the development of agriculture. 工业的发展应与农业的发展并进。For us, research and teaching go *hand in hand*. 对我们来说，教学与研究密切相关。

NOTE 1. 本短语是由"身体某部分的名词+介词+身体某部分的名词"构成的副词性短语。同类的短语还有：arm in arm, face to face, shoulder to shoulder, side by side，等等。见相关各条目。

2. 本短语可转化为复合词 hand-in-hand，意为"手牵手的；亲密的，并进的"。

hand it to someone *vi.* (仅用于口语中，用一般时态，用在 have to，have got to 或 must 之后)(used for saying that you admire someone for something he or she has done) give credit or praise to someone 佩服某人，赞扬某人：I have to *hand it to you* for the way you treated that troublesome young man. 我佩服你对待那个惹事的年轻人的做法。You've got to *hand it to him*; he's a good talker. 你得佩服他，他是个能说会道的人。

hand on *vt.* 【可分性动词短语】(常用一般时态，常与 to 连用) ❶(英国英语用法) give (someone) (something that was given to you) 把……传递(或转交)给(某人)：Please read this leaflet and *hand* it *on*. 请阅读这个小册子并把它传给别人看。In the early days, news was *handed on* from one person to another. 早时，消息是由人们相继传送的。I decided not to *hand* this information *on* to the police. 我决定不把这情报交给警方。❷pass (something such as knowledge or skills) to people who are younger or come later 把(知识、技艺等)传给(后代)：The old man wanted to *hand* his skills *on*(to his grandsons). 这位老人想把自己的技艺传下去(给他的孙子们)。The secrets have been *handed on* from generation to generation. 这些秘方是世代相传下来的。❸ give or leave (something) to someone or a group 把……馈赠(或遗赠)给(某人或某一组织)：My father wants to *hand on* the business/ *hand* the business *on* to a foundation. 我父亲想把这份企业馈赠给一个基金会。

NOTE 1. 当本短语所带的宾语为代词时，该代词须置于本短语的动词和副词中间。

2. 当本短语作"把(知识、技艺等)传给(后代)"解时，同义短语是 bring down, come down, hand down 和 pass on。

hand out *vt.* 【可分性动词短语】(常与 to 连用) ❶(常用一般时态) give (things) to different people in a group 分发，散发，颁发：*Hand out* the pencils to every testee in the test room. 把铅笔分发给考场内的每一位考生。Would you *hand* these papers *out* for me? 你能帮我散发这些文件吗? The Oscar Awards were *handed out* at the Kodak Theater in Hollywood, California, the United States, last Sunday. 奥斯卡奖于上周日在美国加利福尼亚州好莱坞的柯达剧院颁发。❷offer; give (something) freely 提供，免费分发：The government *hands out* payments to people out of work. 政府向

失业者提供补偿金。Ralph was *handing out drinks*. 拉尔夫在分发饮料。In the states of Victoria and South Australia, which were hard hit by the forest fire, soldiers were there to *hand out* food and water to the victims. 在遭受森林大火猛烈袭击的维多利亚省和南澳大利亚省，士兵们在那里向灾民分发食品和水。

NOTE 1. 当本短语所带的宾语为代词时，该代词须置于本短语的动词和副词中间。

2. 当本短语作"分发，散发"解时，同义短语是 hand out 和 pass out。

3. 本短语可转化为复合词 handout，意为"施舍物，救济品"。

hand over *vt.*【可分性动词短语】❶(常用一般时态，常与 to 连用) give (something) to (someone) by holding it in your hand and offering it to him or her 把(某物)亲手交给(某人)，交出：*Hand* your suitcases *over* to the doorman; he will see that they are delivered to your room. 把你的手提箱交给看门人就行了，他会把它们送到你的房间。The robber forced the bank clerk to *hand over* all the money he was carrying. 强盗逼迫银行职员交出他所携带的全部现款。❷(常用一般时态，常与 to 连用) give (someone) to the police or another authority that will become responsible for him or her 把(某人)交给(警方或其他机构)：They *handed* the thief *over* to the police. 他们把小偷移交给了警方。❸(与 to 连用) give (power or control) to someone else 把(权力或控制权)移交给他人：Yesterday he resigned his military post and *handed* the command of the armed forces *over* to the Vice Chief of Army Staff. 他于昨天辞去了军职，并将军队指挥权移交给了陆军副参谋长。British forces *handed over* control of Basra Province to Iraq's government on Sunday. 英国军队于星期日向伊拉克政府移交了对巴士拉省的控制权。It is said that this case has been *handed over* to the local police. 据说，这个案子已经移交给了当地的警方。

NOTE 1. 当本短语所带的宾语为代词时，该代词须置于本短语的动词和副词中间。

2. 本短语可转化为复合词 handover，意为"移交"。

hand to *vt.*【可分性动词短语】(常用一般时态) give or pass (something or someone), especially by hand, to (someone) 把……交给：Would you please *hand* this letter *to* Mr Smith? 请你把这封信交给史密斯先生，好吗？

hands up *s.* (非正式用语) ❶(used for asking a group of people to tell you if they know the answer to a question or if they want something) *hold up* your hand 举手：If you have any questions, please *hands up*. 如果你们有什么问题，请举手。*Hands up*, those who want more. 谁还想要，举手。❷(used by someone who is pointing a gun at people) raise your hands or put your arms above your head 把手举起来："*Hands up* or we'll shoot!" shouted the bank robbers as they pulled out their guns. "都把手举起来，否则我们就开枪！"抢银行的劫匪们掏出枪来大声喊道。

NOTE 本短语中的名词 hand 必须用复数形式。但如果只让某一个人举手提问或回答问题，可用单数形式：put your hand up 或 put up your hand。

hang about/around/round *v.* (非正式用语)(常用进行时态) ❶spend time (in the same place) doing nothing usually because you are waiting for someone (在同一地点)干待,干等(某人): They *hung about/around* the station most of the day. 他们大半天都在火车站干待着。I wish he would stop *hanging about* all day and do something useful. 我希望他别整天闲待,而干点有用的事。I *hung around* outside, waiting for the others. 我待在外面等候其他人。Those people were *hanging round* the streets with nowhere to go. 那些人闲待在大街上无处可去。❷(常与 with 连用)spend a lot of time (in a particular place) with (someone)与(某人)(在某处)待在一起: I don't want you to *hang about* my daughter. 我不要你和我女儿待在一起。They usually *hung around* together most of the time. 他们大多数时间都在一起。Marie always *hung round* with boys. 玛利亚总是和男孩子们混在一起。

NOTE **1.** hang about 和 hang around 为英国英语用法,hang round 是美国英语用法。**2.** 当本短语用作及物性动词短语时,无被动语态形式。

hang back/off *vi.* (常用一般时态,常与 from 连用) be unwilling to do (something) immediately, especially because you are not confident, nervous or you do not feel certain about it; hesitate (由于缺乏信心或感到紧张或犹豫而)踌躇不前: He *hung back* before replying. 他犹豫了一下才作回答。When the officer asked for volunteers, not a single soldier *hung back*. 当那名军官征求志愿人员的时候,没有一个士兵犹豫不前。We didn't know why he was *hanging back/off* from making the final decision. 我们不知道他为什么迟迟不作最终的决定。

NOTE hang back 是英国英语用法。

hang on *vi.* ❶(常与 to 连用)hold tightly to (something)抓住,握紧: He *hung on* until at last the rope broke. 他抓住绳子,一直到绳子最后断掉。*Hang on* to the strap; the bus is about to start. 抓紧吊环,公共汽车就要开动了。❷(非正式用语)ask someone to wait for a short time; continue in spite of difficulties 让某人稍等;坚持下去: Could you *hang on* for a moment till she is free? 你能等一会儿吗? 她等会儿才有空。I know you're tired, but try to *hang on* a bit longer. 我知道你累了,但努力再坚持一会儿吧。❸(非正式用语)(used on the telephone) ask someone who is calling to wait until he or she can talk to the person he or she wants (电话用语)稍等: I'm afraid the telephone line is engaged, would you like to *hang on*? 恐怕电话在占线,您能等一下吗?

—*vt.*【不可分性动词短语】❶(非正式用语,用一般时态)depend on (someone or something) in order to be successful 依赖于,取决于: Robert thinks that young people nowadays *hang* too much *upon* their parents. 罗伯特认为当今的年轻人过分依赖父母。The future of the company *hangs* now *on* the outcome of the meeting. 公司的前途现在就取决于这次会议的结果了。It all *hangs on* whether he is willing to help us. 一切都取决于他是否愿意帮助我们啦。Everything *hangs on* where they will go next. 一切都将取决于他们下次要去哪里。❷(无被动语态形式,常用一般时态)listen very carefully to what someone is saying 注意倾听(某人所言): The students admired Professor Smith and

H

hung on every word of his. 学生都很钦佩史密斯教授,因此注意倾听他的每一句话。

—*vt.* &*vi.* (非正式用语) stick closely to; force one's company on (someone)赖着不走,纠缠(某人): The Israeli troops were accused of having been *hanging on* in the unlawfully occupied area. 以色列军队被指控赖在非法占领区不走。Some of the students are always *hanging on* that particular teacher. 一些学生老是纠缠着那位老师。

hang on to *vt.* ❶ hold (something or someone) tightly 抓紧(某物或某人): In Paris, the 27-year-old Chinese torchbearer struggled to hang on to the Olympic torch while protesters tried to wrest it from her. 在巴黎,这位27岁的中国火炬手在抗议者企图夺走她手中的奥运火炬时,奋力紧紧地抱住了它。*Hang on to* my arm on this icy surface. 在这冰面上,抓紧我的胳膊。❷(非正式用语) keep (something), not sell it or give it away 保留(某物): We should *hang on to* the house and sell it later when prices are higher. 我们应该保留这所房子,等以后价格涨上去时再卖。Let's *hang on to* those old photographs—they may be valuable. 把这些旧照片保留下来,它们也许很有价值。

NOTE 本短语的另外一种表达形式是 hang onto,为英国英语用法。

hang out *vt.*【可分性动词短语】❶hang (clothes you have washed) outside on a clothes line to dry 把(所洗衣物)挂出去晾晒: I'll go and *hang out* the washing. 我去把洗的衣物挂出去。It's such a fine day that I want to *hang* the washing *out* to get it dry in this warm wind. 天气这么好,我想把洗的衣物挂出去在暖风中吹干。I can do my laundry the night before, and *hang* it *out* on the line to dry. 我可以在前一天晚上洗衣服,然后挂出去晾干。❷ fasten or show (something) out of doors 把(某物)悬挂出去: *Hang out* the flag; the victory is ours! 把旗子挂出来吧,我们胜利啦! He ran to the window and *hung* the rope *out*, and escaped from the burning building. 他跑到窗口,把绳子悬挂出去,从燃烧的大楼中逃生了。The young lawyer rented an office, *hung out* a sign, and waited for cases to arrive. 那名年轻的律师租了办公室,挂出招牌,便等着诉讼案上门了。

—*vi.* ❶(常与 of 连用) lean out of a window so that the top part of your body is outside (把上身)探出(窗外): Two students were *hanging out* of the second floor window. 两名学生把身子探出二楼的窗外。❷(非正式用语,用一般时态,常与 with 连用) spend a lot of time (in a particular place or with particular people) doing nothing in particular (与某人在某处)消磨时光: She knew all the clubs where he usually *hung out*. 他常去的所有俱乐部她都知道。During the weekend I like to just *hang out* with my friends. 在周末,我喜欢和朋友们共度时光。

NOTE 1. 当本短语用作及物性动词短语,所带的宾语为代词时,该代词须置于本短语的动词和副词中间。

2. 本短语可转化为复合词 hang-out,意为"常去的地方,聚集地"。

hang over *vt.* ❶ cover; be placed above or on top of (something or someone) 笼罩,悬浮在……之上: Dark clouds are *hanging over* the mountain peaks. 乌云笼罩着山峰。A sense of doom *hung over* the town. 注定要毁灭的意识笼罩着全城。An oil lamp *hung over* the table. 一盏油灯悬挂在桌子上方。❷(无被动语态形式)(especially of an unpleasant event)be about to happen or seem like to happen soon (尤指不愉快的事件)即要发生,逼近: The threat of war *hangs over* thousands of families. 战争的威胁逼近了千千万万个家庭。They felt some kind of disaster was *hanging over* them. 他们感到某种灾难就要降临在他们的头上。

hang together *vi.* (常用一般时态) remain united and work together when things are difficult 保持团结,同心协力: We must indeed all *hang together*, or we shall all be hanged separately, as Benjamin Franklin once said. 正如本杰明·富兰克林曾经说过的那样:我们要么团结一致,要么一个一个地被绞死。We have to *hang together* if we are going to finish this project. 要想完成这个项目,我们必须同心协力。

hang up *v.* ❶hang (a piece of clothing)on something 把(衣物)挂起来:The women *hung up* their coats and sat down. 妇女们把她们的上衣挂上就坐了下来。He told the child to hang the *washing up* in the bedroom. 他叫孩子把洗的衣物挂在了卧室里。Don't throw your coat on the floor. *Hang* it *up*. 别把你的上衣往地板上扔。把它挂起了。❷(非正式用语,常用一般时态) put back the telephone receiver (especially at the end of a conversation)(尤指在通话结束后)挂断电话: A man who *picked up* the phone at the police station refused to discuss the incident and *hung up* without giving his name. 警察局里接电话的那个人拒绝谈论该事件,连名字也没给就挂断了电话。With a last "Fine.", Mr Green *hung up* the phone. 格林先生说了最后一句"好的",便挂断了电话。❸(非正式用语,常用被动语态形式)delay; put aside; stop (something or doing something)推迟,搁置;停止: Even the bad weather did not *hang up* the work on the construction site. 甚至恶劣的气候也没耽误建筑工地的工作。For nearly forty minutes the car was *hung up*. 汽车受阻将近 40 分钟。The negotiations were *hung up* for a time. 谈判暂告中断。The famous footballer announced he will *hang up* his boots at the end of the season. 这位著名的足球运动员宣布,他将在本赛季结束时挂靴。

NOTE 1. 当本短语用作及物性动词短语,所带的宾语为代词时,该代词须置于本短语的动词和副词中间。

2. 当本短语作"(尤指在通话结束后)挂断电话"解时,同义短语是 ring off。

3. 本短语可转化为复合词 hang-up,意为"障碍(物);大难题"。

hang up on *vt.*【不可分性动词短语】end a telephone call with (someone)中断(与某人的)通话:"Yon must be here right away!" she shouted, and *hung up on* me. "你必须马上到这里来!"她大声喊道,然后就中断了与我的通话。He started shouting so I *hung up on* him. 他开始吼了起来,于是我就挂断了电话。

happen on/upon *vt.* (正式用语,无被动语态形式,用一般时态)【不可分性动词短语】 meet (someone) or find (something) without planning to 偶然遇到(某人),偶然发现(某物): Walking into the village, I *happened on* a band of gypsies. 走进村子,我偶然遇到了一群吉卜赛人。I *happened on* an old country inn and stopped to have a meal. 我偶然看到一家古朴的乡下小酒馆,就停下进去吃了一顿饭。

NOTE 本短语的同义短语是 come on/upon。

happen to[1] *vt.*【不可分性动词短语】(无被动语态形式)(of especially something unpleasant) take place and affect (someone or something)(尤指不幸之事)发生在……: If anything *happens to* me, you'll have plenty of money to live on. 如果我发生了什么意外,你会有很多钱生活的。Whatever has *happened to* your arm? It's all swollen! 你的胳膊怎么了?肿得好厉害! Who knows what is *happening to* the economy. 谁晓得经济发生了什么问题。

NOTE 本短语与 become of 意义相同,但用法不同。两者之间的区别见 become of。

happen to[2] *v.*(后接原形动词) do or be (something) by chance 偶然,碰巧,恰好: I *happened to* meet an old friend in town. 我在城里碰巧遇到了一个老朋友。She *happened* not *to* have seen the note. 她碰巧没看到这张条子。I *happened to* be inside Omaha mall, when the shooting took place. 枪击事件发生时,我恰好就在奥马哈的商场里。The door *happened to* be unlocked. 门恰好没上锁。

NOTE 当本短语用于疑问句时,表示委婉语气,用于口语中,在翻译时可不译出。例如:

> Do you *happen to* know his address?
> 你知道他的地址,是吗?

hard at it *adj.*(英国英语用法,非正式用语,常用作表语) doing (something) in a fast busy way; working with all one's force in some activity 忙于做(某事),竭尽全力: I'm glad to see you're still *hard at it*. 我很高兴地看到你们仍在尽心竭力地做事。That's what I like to see — everybody *hard at it*! 那是我喜欢看到的——人人都在竭尽全力!

hard done (-) by *adj.*(主要用于英国和爱尔兰英语中,非正式用语,用在系动词 be 和 feel 之后作表语) be treated in an unfair way, or feel as if you have been treated in an unfair way 受到不公平的对待: The little boy cried bitterly as if he had been *hard done by*. 那男孩仿佛受了委屈,哭得很厉害。I felt very *hard done-by* when I got less money than anybody else, after I had worked twice as hard. 我出的力比别人多一倍,但我得到的钱却比谁都少,我感到受到了非常不公平的对待。Stop feeling so *hard done by*; you've already got a perfectly good one, my child. 别感到这么委屈啦;你已经得到了一个非常棒的了,我的孩子。

NOTE 本短语的另外一种表达形式是 hard done-to,为英国英语用法。在英国北部的一些地区还用 badly done-to。

hard on *adj.*(常用作表语) ❶ treating (someone) severely or unkindly 严厉地对待,粗暴地对待(某人):Don't be so *hard on* him. He is only a child of 5 after all. 别对他那么严厉,他毕竟是个才 5 岁的孩子。She is a very nice teacher. I've never known her to be *hard on* her students. 她是位很好的老师。我从未看到她粗暴地对待学生。❷ unfair or unpleasant to (someone) 对(某人)不公平,令(某人)不愉快: It's *hard on* John, having to work when the others are just sitting. 别人都坐着,而让约翰干活,这对

他太不公平了。It's very *hard on* parents when their children are being bullied at school. 孩子在学校里挨欺负，这对他们的家长来说是非常不快的事情。❸(非正式用语) causing damage to (something)对……有损害：It was said that aerobics is quite *hard on* the knees. 据说，增氧健身法对膝关节相当有损害。You'd better not read in such a poor light; it's *hard on* your eyes. 你最好别在这样昏暗的灯光下看书，这损害你的视力。

hard put (to it) *adj.* (非正式用语，后接动词不定式短语) having great difficulty to do something 很难做某事：I think the Conservatives will be *hard put* to gain support. 我认为保守党将很难取得支持。They were *hard put to it* to solve this problem, but they succeeded at last. 他们起初很难解决这一问题，但最终还是解决了。We were *hard put* to find a replacement for our assistant. 我们很难找到一个人来代替我们的助手。

NOTE 1. 本短语的比较级形式是 harder put，最高级形式是 hardest put。

2. 本短语另外的表达形式是 hard pressed (to it)和 hard pushed (to it)。

hard up *adj.* (主要用于美国英语中，非正式用语) ❶greatly in need of something, especially money 缺钱，手头拮据的：Her husband is continually complaining of being *hard up*. 她丈夫不停地抱怨说缺钱花。She was *hard up* for cash to pay the bills. 她缺少现金支付账单。We were very *hard up* when I lost my job. 我失业后，我们的生活就很困难了。❷(与 for 连用) not having enough (of people or things) 缺乏：Some of the schools are pretty *hard up* for teachers. 一些学校十分缺乏教师。We're a bit *hard up* for new ideas. 我们想不出什么新主意了。I don't think anyone enjoys being *hard up* for time, money, or work. 我认为，缺钱、缺时间、没工作谁都不好受。

NOTE 本短语的比较级形式是 more hard up，最高级形式是 most hard up。

hardly … when ⇨ **scarcely … when**

have a ball *vi.* (非正式用语，常用进行时态) enjoy yourself very much; have a very enjoyable time 过得十分愉快，很开心：Mary *had a ball* at the party. 玛丽在聚会上玩得很愉快。Outside the children were sitting on the ground, talking and laughing; they were *having a ball*. 在外面，孩子们坐在地上又说又笑。他们过得十分愉快。Bob and Tom *had a ball* exploring the cave. 鲍勃和汤姆在洞中探奇，十分开心。

have a bearing on *vt.* (用一般时态) be related to (something) or have an influence on it 与……有联系，对……有影响：Experts generally agree that diet *has an* important *bearing on* your health. 专家们普遍同意这样的观点：饮食与健康有着重要的联系。What bearing does your story have on this case? 你的陈述与这一案件有什么联系? His private life *has no bearing on* his competence as a manager. 他的私生活与其作为经理的能力毫无关系。Being a permanent member of the UN Security Council, China *has an* important *bearing on* issues of international peace and security. 作为联合国安理会的常任理事国，中国对国际和平与安全方面的问题有着重要的影响。

NOTE 1. 本短语中的名词 bearing 前可用

H

some 等形容词修饰,但 bearing 只能用单数形式。

2. 在本短语的否定形式中,否定词语 no, not any 或 not much 置于名词 bearing 的前部,不定冠词省去。

have a break *vi.* stop for a brief rest or intermission 休息一会儿:I'm tired; let's *have a short break*, shall we? 我累了;咱们稍微休息一会儿吧,好吗? 19-year-old Miss Ireland, Rosanna Davison, was crowned Miss World this year. She *had had a break* from college to represent Ireland. 19 岁的爱尔兰小姐罗莎娜·戴维森今年荣获了世界小姐桂冠。她是趁大学放假代表爱尔兰参赛的。He *had a* short *break* in the afternoon. 他下午休息了一会儿。

NOTE **1.** 本短语的另外一种表达形式是 have a rest。

2. 本短语的同义短语是 take a break。

have a good mind to *v.* (非正式用语,后接原形动词)be strongly inclined to do something 很想要做(某事),可能要做(某事): I *have a good mind to* tell your parents what you've done! 我很想把你的所作所为告诉你的家长。Those boys have been stealing my apples again; I *have a good mind to* report them to the police. 那些男孩又在偷我的苹果,我真想去报告警察。I *have a good mind to* suggest reporting them to the humane society! 我真想建议把他们报告给保护动物协会。

NOTE **1.** 本短语的另外一种表达形式是 have half a mind to。

2. 本短语的同义短语是 have a good notion to 和 have half a notion to。

have a good time *vi.* (非正式用语) enjoy yourself thoroughly on a particular occasion 过得非常愉快: They all *had a good time* at the party. 他们在聚会上玩得非常愉快。Did you *have a good time* during your stay in the United States? 你在美国逗留期间过得愉快吗? It's my job to make sure the guests *have a good time*. 我的工作就是保证客人们过得愉快。In Hawaii he *had a good time* swimming and sunbathing on the beautiful beach. 在夏威夷,他又游泳又在美丽的海滩上晒太阳,过得十分愉快。

have a hand in *vt.* (非正式用语,常用一般时态)help make (something) happen; be involved in (something) or influence over (something or doing something) 参与,参加: He denied that he *had a hand in former* Prime Minister Bhutto's assassination. 他否认参与了前总理布托遇刺事件。I *had a hand in* arranging the party. 我参与了这次聚会的组织工作。

NOTE 本短语与 have a part in 意义和用法相同,两者可互换使用。

have a glimpse of ⇨ **catch a glimpse of**

have a good opinion of *vt.* think well of (something, someone or oneself) 对……评价好: Most people *have a good opinion of* this new film. 大多数人对这部新影片的评价都很好。The teacher *has a good opinion of* Peter's daughter. 那位老师对彼得的女儿评价很好。He *has a good opinion of* himself. 他自命不凡。

NOTE 本短语中的名词 opinion 前可根据表达需要用其他形容词来修饰,例如: bad, high, low, favorable, poor, ill 等。

have a part in ⇨ **have a hand in**

have a rest ⇨ **have a break**

have a word with *vt.* (非正式用语)

speak or talk with (someone) for a short time, privately (私下里)同(某人)简短谈话: Come out, will you? I'd like to *have a word with* you. 你出来一下好吗? 我要和你说句话。She finally went and *had a word with* her boss about getting a raise. 她最后还是去和老板谈了加薪的问题。

NOTE 不要将本短语与 have words with 混淆。have words with 意为"和(某人)争吵"。

have access to *vt.* (常用一般时态) be able to reach or use (something)能够得到,使用: Only two men in the company *have access to* the secret records. 公司里只有两个人能得到那些秘密记录。Students in our university *have access to* the library even during the vacation. 我们大学的学生甚至在假期中都能使用图书馆。Most Chinese farmers *have* no *access to* this kind of entertainment. 大多数的中国农民还都享受不到这种娱乐。He *had access to* learning abroad. 他得以出国留学。

NOTE 1. 本短语中的名词 access 是不可数名词,因此其前不能用不定冠词 an,其后也不能加-s。

2. 本短语的动词 have 可被 go 或 get 替换,构成的短语与本短语意义和用法相同。

have all one's eggs in one basket ⇨ **put all one's eggs in one basket**

have an advantage over *vt.* have something that makes one person or thing more advantageous and likely to succeed than (others)比……有优势: The home team always *has an advantage over* their opponents. 主队总是比其对手(客队)占优势。Transistors *have an advantage over* vacuum tubes. 晶体管比真空管更有优越性。

have an affair with *vt.* have a sexual relationship with (especially someone who is married)与(尤指已婚者)有不正当的两性关系: Her husband denied that he was *having an affair with* his secretary. 她丈夫否认与他的秘书有暧昧关系。She's *having an affair with* her husband's best friend. 她在和她丈夫的最好朋友私通。

have an effect on/upon/over *vt.* cause a change in; influence (something or someone)使起变化,对……有影响: Any change in lifestyle will *have an effect on* your health. 生活方式发生任何改变都会对你的健康有影响。The summit meeting between Russia and China *had a* significant and profound *effect on* world peace. 俄中高级会谈对世界和平有重大而深刻的影响。Since its appearance television has *had a* great *effect upon* our life. 自从电视问世以来,它对我们的生活有很大的影响。

NOTE 1. 在实际使用中,根据表达需要,本短语中的不定冠词往往被表示程度的形容词,如 great, considerable, profound, significant, no, little 等替换,有时还会被定冠词所替换。

2. 本短语的名词 effect 可被 impact 或 influence 替换,构成的短语与本短语意义和用法相同。如要表示对人体健康的影响时,一般使用 have an effect on,但指某事对某人情绪上或对其他方面的影响时,三者均可使用。

have an eye for *vt.* ❶ have a natural ability for seeing or finding something 有发现……的能力: Proofreaders need to *have a good eye for* spelling mistakes. 做

文字校对工作的人需要善于发现拼写错误的能力。❷ be able to judge correctly of; have good taste in 对……有鉴赏能力:She *has an eye for* color and style in clothes. 她对服装的颜色和样式有较好的鉴赏能力。

NOTE 本短语的另外一种表达方式是 with an eye for。例如:

> I think he was born *with an eye for* beauty.
> 我认为他有审美的天赋。

have an impact on/upon/over ⇨ **have an effect on/upon/over**

have an influence on/upon/over ⇨ **have an effect on/upon/over**

have butterflies in one's stomach *vi.* (非正式用语) feel very nervous about something that you have to do, especially something important (在做尤其是重要事之前)感到非常紧张: When Bob walked into the factory office to ask for a job, he *had butterflies in his stomach*. 当鲍勃走进工厂办公室去求职时,他感到非常紧张。Before the interview Mary *had butterflies in her stomach*. 在接受面试前,玛丽的心情十分紧张。

NOTE **1.** 本短语中的名词 butterfly 必须用复数形式。

2. 本短语的动词 have 可被 get 和 feel 替换,构成的短语与本短语意义和用法相同。

have faith in *vt.* (常用一般时态) have a strong belief in or trust of (someone or something) 信仰,相信,信任: I'm delighted to know you *have* such *faith in* me. 你这样相信我,我很高兴。I'm sure she'll do as she promised; I *have* great *faith in* her. 我确信她会按她所承诺的去做。我十分相信她。The voters have just shown that they *have* no *faith in* the government. 选民们已表明了他们不再信任本届政府。

NOTE 本短语的反义短语是 lose faith in。例如:

> People have *lost faith* in the British Parliament.
> 人们已丧失了对英国议会的信任。

have got *v.* (主要用于英国英语中,尤其用于口语中,常略写为 've got,不用进行时态) used especially in speech to mean "have" 有: I'*ve got* an extra apple if you want one. 如果你想要苹果,我还有一个。He *has got* two children. One boy and one girl. 他有两个孩子。一个男孩,一个女孩。They'*ve got* a lovely garden, haven't they? 他们有一个美丽的花园,是吗? *Have* you *got* time to finish the report today? 你今天有时间把报告写完吗?

NOTE **1.** 本短语并不是完成时形式,而是 have 的口语形式。虽然有些语法学家反对这种用法,但它在日常英语中的应用已十分广泛。

2. 若表示"你有……吗?",英国英语和美国英语说法不同:

英国英语:Have you got …? (回答: Yes, I have. / No, I haven't.)

美国英语:Do you have …? (回答: Yes, I do. / No, I don't.)

3. 在以下几种情况下不能使用本短语:

(1) 在助动词后不能使用本短语。例如,我们不能说: * She doesn't have got a computer at home. 而应使用单个动词 have 来表示,即 She doesn't have a computer at home.

(2) 在情态动词后不能使用本短语。例如,我们不能说: * She may have got a

computer at home. 而应使用单个动词 have来表示，即 She may have a computer at home.

(3) 在动词不定式后不能使用本短语。例如，我们不能说：* We would like to *have got* a new computer. 而应使用单个动词 have 来表示，即 We would like to have a new computer.

(4) 在过去时或完成时中不能使用本短语。例如，我们不能说：* Last year we had got a house in the city. 而应使用单个动词 had来表示，即 Last year we had a house in the city. 我们也不能说：* We have had got the house in the city for 10 months. 而应使用 have had 来表示，即 We have had the house in the city for 10 months.

have got to *v.* (用于口语中，常略写为 've got to，不用进行时态，后接原形动词)be forced to do something or must do something 不得不，必须(做某事)：I'*ve got to* be at the hospital before five. 我得在 5 点钟之前到医院。Linda is a waitress. She'*s got to* work at weekends. 琳达是餐馆服务员，周末也得上班。*Have you got to* leave now? 你现在必须要走吗?

NOTE **1.** 本短语与 have to 意义和用法相同，但语气比 have to 强。两者与 must 的主要区别是：must 表示主观的义务和必要，意为"必须……，得……，要……"；而 have got to 和 have to 则表示一种客观的需要，意思是"不得不"。

2. 在向别人提出建议时，通常不用本短语。例如：我们不说 * You don't have got to smoke. It is bad for your health. 而应使用 shouldn't，即 You shouldn't smoke. It is bad for your health.

have half a mind to ⇨ **have a good mind to**

have half a notion to ⇨ **have a good mind to**

have hold of ⇨ **get hold of**

have little to do with ⇨ **have nothing to do with**

have mercy on *vt.* 【不可分性动词短语】treat(someone who does wrong, etc.) in a kind way instead of a cruel way 宽恕(某人)："*Have mercy on* me, noble knight!" exclaimed Isaac, "I'm poor and helpless." "宽恕我吧，高贵的骑士!"艾萨克高喊道，"我贫穷又无助啊。"

H

have no business *v.* do (something) you should not do, because it does not affect or involve you at all; have no right or reason (to do/doing something) 不该做(某事)，没有权利做(某事)：You *have no business* to meddle in my affairs. 你不该干预我的事情。You *had no business* going through my private papers. 你无权看我的私人文件。

NOTE 本短语的另外一种表达方式是 none of one's business，后者常用在系动词之后。例如：

> How much I earn a month is *none of your business*.
> 我一个月挣多少钱不关你的事。

have no idea *v.* do not know; do not have enough information to make a definite statement about (something) 不知道，不确切："What time is it?" "I *have no idea*." "几点了?" "我不知道。" We *have no idea* about the matter. 我们对此事一无所知。I can't find my keys. I *have no idea* where I put them. 我找不到我的钥

匙了。我不知道把它们放在哪里了。We *had no idea* what time they were supposed to arrive. 我们不知道他们何时到达。

have nothing to do with *vt.* have not a connection with (someone or something) 与……没有关系：She'll *have nothing to do with* that man. 她不会再与那个男人有任何关系。The change of his decision *has nothing to do with* what I said yesterday. 他改变其决定与我昨天说的那番话没有关系。

NOTE 1. 本短语的另外一种表达形式是 is nothing to do with，为英国英语用法。

2. 本短语与 have little to do with 意义和用法相同，两者可互换使用。

have on *vt.* 【可分性动词短语】❶(不用进行时态，用一般时态) be wearing (particular clothes, shoes, etc.) 穿着，戴着：She *has on* her summer clothes. 她穿着夏装。Melissa *had* her new dress *on*. 梅利莎穿着她的新连衣裙。That is a nice-looking hat you *have on*. 你戴的那顶帽子很漂亮。When he woke up, he found that he still *had* his shoes *on*. 当他醒来时发现自己还穿着鞋子。❷(用一般时态) carry with (one), on one's person at a particular time (某人)随身携带(某物)：I *haven't* any money *on* me, but I can get some from the ATM. 我身上没带钱，但我可以从自动取款机中取出一些来。She *had* all kinds of strange objects *on* her person. 她身上带着各种各样稀奇古怪的玩意儿。❸(用一般时态) have (an electronic or electrical device) switched on and working 使(某种电子或电器装置)处于工作状态：I *have* my computer *on* all the time. 我的电脑总是开着的。❹(不用进行时态，用一般时态) have arranged to do (something) at a particular time, so that you are not available to do anything else (在某段时间里)安排做(某事)：Do you *have* anything *on* for tomorrow afternoon? 你明天下午有什么安排吗？We *have* a lot of work *on* at the moment. 我们目前有很多工作要做。❺(英国英语用法，在美国英语中用 put on，非正式用语，常用进行时态) be trying to make (someone) believe something that is not true, as a joke 欺骗，捉弄：She was *having* you *on* when she said that she was married. 她说她已结婚，她那是在骗你呢。You didn't believe her, did you? She was just *having* you *on*. 你不相信她，是吧？她只是在捉弄你。❻(非正式用语，不用进行时态，用一般时态) have (information about someone that shows he has done something dishonest or illegal) 掌握(某人欺诈或违法的证据)：You can't take me to the police station, you *have* nothing *on* me! 你不能带我去警察局，你没有任何证据！They *have* not got anything *on* Marlowe, so they can't arrest him. 他们对马洛没有任何证据，所以无法逮捕他。

NOTE 1. 当本短语所带的宾语为代词时，该代词须置于本短语的动词和副词中间。

2. 当本短语作"穿着，戴着"解时，同义短语是 dress up, pull on 和 put on。它们之间的区别见 put on。

have one's eye(s) on *vt.* (非正式用语) ❶ watch or monitor (someone or something) closely 密切注意，严密监视，密切关注：The teacher *had her eye on* me because she thought I was cheating. 那老师严密监视着我，因为她认为我在作弊。They try to *have their eyes on* future developments in house prices. 他们极力关注房价的发展趋势。❷look after or take care of (someone or something) and make sure that they are safe 照看,照管: She sat on the sofa, *keeping her eye on* her son as he played. 她坐在沙发上照看着正在玩耍的儿子。Will you please *keep your eye on* our house while we're away on vacation? 在我们出去休假期间请您照管一下我们的房子,好吗?

NOTE 本短语的同义短语是 keep one's eye(s) on 和 keep an eye (open) on。

have one's hands full *vi.* (常与 with 连用) be extremely busy with a difficult job that one cannot undertake anything else 十分繁忙,忙得腾不出手来: Mary already *has her hands full* with two kids and a full-time job. 玛丽有两个孩子,还要成天上班,已经很忙了。I'm afraid I cannot help you this afternoon. I'll *have my hands full* trying to finish my research paper. 恐怕我今天下午不能帮你了,我要忙着把研究论文赶完。I've got my *hands full with* all kinds of work, so I couldn't possibly serve on the Committee. 各种各样的工作使我忙得不可开交,所以我无法在委员会服务了。

have one's fingers crossed ⇨ **keep one's fingers crossed**

have pity on ⇨ **take pity on**

have relevance to ⇨ **relevant to**

have something to do with *vt.* have a connection with (something or someone) 与……有关系: The family thinks his death may *have something to do with* a bar fight two weeks earlier. 他的家人认为,他的死可能与两星期前的一次酒吧中的打斗有关系。What is VSI? *Has* it got *something to do with* my not having insurance? 什么是 VSI? 它与我没有保险有关系吗?

NOTE 本短语的疑问形式也可由 anything 来构成。例如:

> *Has* the dispute *anything to do with* safety regulations?
> 这一争端与安全规章有关系吗?

have the floor ⇨ **take the floor**

have the measure of someone ⇨ **get the measure of someone**

have to ⇨ **have got to**

have (got) to do with *vt.* ❶be about; be on the subject of or connected with (something or somebody) 与……有关: The book *has to do with* airplanes. 这本书是关于飞机的。Most of the articles *have to do with* America's role in the world since the end of the Cold War. 大多数文章都与美国自冷战结束以来在世界上的作用这一主题有关。Yes, I have a car, but what does that *have to do with* whether I am qualified for a desk job? 是的,我有车,可那与我是否有资格做文书工作有什么关系呢? I don't know what it *has got to do with* you. 我不明白这与你有什么关系。❷(常用于否定句中) know or be a friend of; work or have business with (somebody) 与(某人)交朋友,与(某人)打交道: My little son said he didn't want to *have anything to do with* the new boy. 我的小儿子说他不想和那新来的男孩子交朋友。A doctor *has to do with* all sorts of patients. 医生得与各种各样的病人打交道。

have (all) to oneself *vi.* not have to share (a place, time, etc.) with anyone

H

else 独自享用(某物): It's possible for you to *have* the place *to yourself* if it's early. 如果早一点,你就有可能独自使用这个地方。One would rather *have* a bedroom *to oneself*. 最好是每个人都各有自己的卧室。With no other guests around, she *had* the pool *all to herself*. 用于没有其他客人,她独自享用了整个游泳池。

have words with *vt.* have an argument with (someone)与(某人)吵架: Must you always *have words with* me when we meet? 我们一见面你就必须和我吵架吗? Linda *had words with* her boyfriend this morning. 琳达今天上午和她的男朋友发生了口角。

NOTE 1. 本短语中的名词 word 必须用复数形式。

2. 不要将本短语与 have a word with 混淆,两者的意义不同。两者之间的区别见 have a word with。

head for/to/towards *vt.* 【不可分性动词短语】go or travel in a particular direction of (usually a place)走向……,朝……方向前进: With this, he *headed for* the door. 说完这话,他就朝门口走去。Nowadays, many people get on mountain bikes and *head* out *for* suburban areas on weekends. 如今,许多人在周末骑上山地自行车去郊游。Richard came in and *headed for* his bed-ridden father. 理查德进屋后便向卧病在床的父亲走去。I don't think the United States and Russia will be *heading towards* a new cold war. 我认为美国和俄罗斯两国不会再走向新的冷战时期。

NOTE 1. head to 不及 head for 和 head towards 常用。

2. 本短语的同义短语是 make for。

head off *vt.* 【可分性动词短语】❶prevent (people or animals) from going somewhere by getting in front of them 拦截(人或动物): The police *headed off* the fleeing driver. 警察截住了逃逸的司机。Let's try and *head* bandits *off* before they cross the bridge. 让我们设法在匪徒们过桥之前截住他们。The horses broke into a wild gallop, and the father yelled for his son Tom to *head* them *off*. 马匹突然开始狂奔起来,爸爸高喊让他的儿子汤姆把它们截住。❷prevent (something unpleasant) from happening, or (someone) from doing something 避免(某事)发生,阻止(某人)做某事: The United States proposed a compromise to *head off* a trade war with the European Union. 美国提出妥协以避免与欧盟发生贸易战。He'll get into trouble if someone doesn't *head* him *off*. 如果没人阻止他,他会陷入麻烦之中。I *headed* him *off* making a speech. 我没让他发表讲话。

—*vi.* (非正式用语,常与 to 连用)leave somewhere to go to another place 离开(某处去另一处): We should be *heading off* soon. 我们应该尽快离开。After work, we all *headed off* to the pub. 下班后,我们都去了酒吧。

NOTE 当本短语用作及物性动词短语,所带的宾语为代词时,该代词须置于本短语的动词和副词中间。

hear about *vt.* 【不可分性动词短语】receive information about (something or someone) 听说: You must have *heard about* the Microsoft's new search engine Bing, which became available worldwide on June. 你肯定听说了今年 6 月份微软向全球推出的新搜索引擎"必应"了。

Have you *heard about* Tom jumping into the pool with all his clothes on? 你听说过汤姆穿着衣服跳进游泳池的事了吗?

NOTE 本短语与 hear of 意义和用法相同,都表示间接而不是直接或亲耳听到,两者可互换使用。例如:

> We've been *hearing quite a* lot recently *about/of* Yao Ming.
> 我们最近听到许多有关姚明的消息。

hear from *vt.* 【不可分性动词短语】❶(常用一般时态) receive a letter, telephone call, or message from (someone or something)接到……的信,接到……的电话,收到……的消息: I'm looking forward to *hearing from* you soon. 我盼望尽早收到你的来信。He ran away as a boy thirty years ago, and his family has never *heard from* him since. 30 年前他还是个孩子的时候就离家出走了。此后,他的家人始终没有听到他的消息。 ❷receive a scolding from (someone)受到(某人的)责备(或训斥): He'd better apologize to you or he'll be *hearing from* me! 他最好向你道歉,否则我就会训他。

hear of *vt.* 【不可分性动词短语】❶(用一般时态)gain (information that something has happened) 得知(消息): We only *heard of* your intended visit yesterday! 我们昨天才得知您要来访的消息! I was shocked to *hear of* his death. 得知他去世的消息,我颇感震惊。❷(用一般时态,常用一般完成时,常用于疑问句和否定句中)have knowledge of the existence of (something or someone)知晓,听说(某物或某人)的存在: Not much was *heard of* him until his reappearance last night. 在昨晚他再次露面之前,人们对他知之甚少。Have you *heard of* Microsoft's search engine Bing? 你听说过微软的搜索引擎"必应"吗? ❸(常用将来时态,用否定形式,与 will not 或 would not 连用) consider the idea of (something or doing something)考虑……的意见: The firm will not *hear of* such a suggestion from the workers. 公司不会考虑工人们提出的这种意见。I said he could stay with us, but he wouldn't *hear of* it. 我告诉他说,他可以和我们一起住,可他就是不听。At all events my father would not *hear of* my going to south with them. 不管怎样,我爸爸就是不肯让我和他们一起去南方。

NOTE 当本短语作"得知(消息)"解时,与 hear about 意义和用法相同,两者可互换使用。

heart and soul Ⅰ *adv.* with all one's attention and strength; completely 全心全意地,完全地: The Chinese President urged the Chinese police to "enforce law for the people and be loyal to the principle of serving the people *heart and soul*". 中国国家主席敦促中国警察"为民执法,坚守全心全意为人民服务的宗旨"。Mike was *heart and soul* against these new rules. 麦克完全反对这些新的规章。

Ⅱ *n.* the entirety of one's energies or affections 全身心;一心: He put *heart and soul* into his music. 他把全身心都投放在了作曲上。She wished with all her *heart and soul* that he would come. 她一心希望他能来。

help oneself *vi.* (常与 to 连用) ❶(常用一般时态)(used for giving someone permission to do or use something) take (something) for oneself; serve oneself with (something)自取所需,随便取食:"Can I have a drink?" "*Help yourself*!" "我可以喝一杯酒吗?""自便吧!"Please *help yourselves* to more wine. 请你们随意多喝点酒吧。He got up and *helped himself* to more coffee. 他站起身来,又给自己倒了些咖啡。❷(非正式用语) take (something) without permission; steal (something)擅自取用,盗取(某物): Tom *helped himself* to some candy without asking. 汤姆没经请示就擅自拿糖果。My husband has been *helping himself* to money from my purse for months. 几个月来,我丈夫一直从我的钱包里偷钱花。

help out *v.* (主要用于口语中,常与 with 连用)give assistance, especially by doing a particular job, for a short time 帮忙,帮助: Who is to *help out* in the garden this afternoon? 谁今天下午在花园里帮忙? He always *helped out* with the housework. 他过去总是帮助做家务。I'm always happy to *help out* a friend. 我总是乐于帮助朋友。Please *help* me *out* with this math problem. 请帮我解这道数学题吧。

NOTE 当本短语用作及物性动词短语,所带的宾语为代词时,该代词须置于本短语的动词和副词中间。

help with *vt.*【可分性动词短语】assist (someone) in dealing with (someone or something)帮助(某人)做,应对(某人或某事): Go and *help* your mother *with* your little brother. 去帮助你妈妈管管你的小弟弟。You may file your applications to the International Press Centre of the Foreign Ministry, and we will *help* you *with* your interviews. 你们可以向外交部外国记者新闻中心提出要求。我们会协助你们进行采访的。The United Nations launched on Friday a 33.5-million-US-dollar appeal to *help with* China's post-earthquake reconstruction. 星期五,联合国呼吁为中国地震灾后重建援助 3 350 万美元。

here and now *adv.* at this moment 现在,这会儿: I want my money back, and I want it *now and here*. 还我的钱,现在就还。Do I have to make up my mind *here and now*? 我必须这会儿就作决定吗?

NOTE **1.** 本短语的另外一种形式是 now and here。

2. 若表示过去发生的事,则使用 then and there 或 there and then。见 then and there。

here and there *adv.* in or to several different places; from place to place 各处,到处: There were a number of cottages scattered *here and there* across the hillside. 一些别墅散布在山腰的各处。*Here and there* he read a little thing, but remembered nothing. 他这里读一点儿,那里读一点儿,可是什么也没有记住。After the train explosion, near the railway station, broken, twisted rails were lying *here and there*. 火车爆炸事故发生后,火车站的附近到处都是断裂、弯曲的铁轨。

NOTE 本短语中的 here 和 there 虽然都表示地点,但在使用时,它们的先后顺序是不能改变的。例如,我们不能说: * I went there and here looking for my pen.

Here you are. *s.* (仅用于口语中)(used when offering or giving something to someone) I have got, found, etc. what you want, are looking for, etc. (用于把某物给别人时)给你: "Could you pass the salt, please?" "*Here you are.*" "您能把盐递给我吗?" "给你。" *Here you are.* Take two of these tablets three times a day. 给你,这些药片每天吃 3 次,每次 2 片。*Here you are.* This is the book you were looking for. 给你,这是你找的那本书。

NOTE 1. 在日常口语中,本短语中的 you are 往往被省略。例如:

> *Here*, try some of this — it's delicious!
> 给你,尝尝这个。这很好吃的!

2. 本短语的另外一种表达形式是 Here you go.,主要用于英国英语中。例如:

> "*Here you go*," the mother handed his son a glass of beer.
> "给你。"妈妈递给儿子一杯啤酒。

3. 不要将本短语与 Here we are. 混淆。Here we are. 是"我们到达了(某处)。"之意。例如:

> *Here we are*—home at last.
> 我们终于到家了。

hide away *v.* (cause to) be hidden completely from sight or knowledge; conceal (someone or something) somewhere 躲藏,把……隐藏起来,隐瞒: The thief *hid away* in a friend's house for several weeks after the robbery. 那盗贼在抢劫之后在朋友家中躲藏了好几个星期。*Hide* Tommy *away* where no one can find him. 把汤米藏到一个谁也找不到他的地方。We *hid* the toys *away* in the attic, where the children would not find them. 我们把玩具藏在了屋顶室内,孩子们是找不到的。She has some chocolate biscuits *hidden away* in the cupboard. 她把一些巧克力饼干藏在了碗橱中。Why do you *hide* your thoughts *away* from me? 你为什么和我还隐瞒思想呢?

NOTE 本短语可转化为复合词 hideaway,意为"隐藏处"。

hide from *vt.* (cause to) be covered from sight or knowledge of (usually someone) 藏起来不被……看见,把……藏起来,向(某人)隐瞒……: The rabbit was trying to *hide from* the fox. 兔子试图藏起来不被狐狸看见。I wanted to *hide* his present *from* him until his birthday. 我想把送他的礼物藏起来不让他知道,直到他生日那天再拿出来。The house was *hidden from* view by a row of tall trees. 这栋房子隐蔽在一排高大的树木之中。How had he managed to *hide* his drug addiction *from* his family? 他是怎样把他吸毒成瘾的事瞒住他的家人的?

NOTE 本短语的同义短语是 conceal from。

hide out *vi.* (常与 from 连用) hide oneself so that one cannot be found by someone or something 躲藏起来: The police knew that the wanted men were *hiding out* somewhere in the town. 警方知道那几名通缉犯都藏在城里的什么地方。We used to *hide out* from our parents here. 我们曾在这里躲避我们的家长。

NOTE 本短语可转化为复合词 hideout,意为"(尤指盗匪或罪犯的)隐藏处"。

high time *n.* (非正式用语,前用 it is,后接虚拟语气形式的 that 从句,that 常可省略) the proper time (for something that has been delayed too long) 该做(拖延已久的某事)的时候: It's *high time* that you got a job, Tom. 汤姆,你该找一份工作啦。It is about *high time* you had your haircut; it's getting much too long. 你该把头发理一下了,长得太长了。It is *high time* we were going. 我们该马上走了。

H

NOTE 1. 本短语后接 for 复合结构,成为非虚拟陈述句:

> It is *high time* for us to have a good rest.
> 我们该好好地休息休息了。

2. 本短语的另外一种表达形式是 about time,用于口语中。例如:

> It's *about time* you went to bed.
> 你该睡觉了。

hinge on/upon *vt.* (无被动语态形式,不用进行时态) depend on; change according to (something, such as a fact) 取决于: The fate of the project *hinge on* the decision of the council. 这项工程的命运取决于委员会的决定。China stressed that the result of the ongoing nuclear talks *hinged upon* attitudes of the relevant sides. 中方强调指出,正在进行的核会谈的结果取决于有关各方的态度。

NOTE 本短语中的 upon 用法比 on 正式,但不及 on 常用。

hit on/upon *vt.* 【不可分性动词短语】❶suddenly have an idea about (something) or a solution to (a problem)突然想出(主意或办法): They *hit on* the idea of celebrating the occasion with a concert. 他们想出了以音乐会的形式来庆祝那一时刻的主意。How did you *hit upon* such a wonderful solution? 你是怎么想出来这么奇妙的一个好办法的? Many a good idea has been *hit on* by accident. 许多好主意都是偶然想出来的。Thinking very hard the whole night, I finally *hit upon* a solution. 苦思了一个晚上,我终于想出了一个办法。❷(用一般时态) discover (someone or something) by lucky chance 幸运发现(某人或某物): At Linda's birthday party, I can't believe I *hit on* her boyfriend! 在琳达的生日聚会上,我真不敢相信幸会了她男友! By a stroke of good luck I *hit on* this dictionary in a second-hand bookstore. 真幸运,我在一家旧书店里发现了这本词典。❸(美国英语用法)ask for money 向……要钱: A beggar *hit on* me when I left the restaurant. 当我离开饭馆时,一个乞丐向我要钱。

NOTE 1. 本短语中的 upon 用法比 on 正式,但不及 on 常用。

2. 本短语与 occur to 都有"想起(主意或办法)"之意。两者在用法的区别是:本短语要以人作主语,而 occur to 则一般是以某事、某种想法或概念为主语,不能用人作主语。例如:

> An excellent idea *occurred to* me suddenly.
> 我突然想到了一个绝好的主意。

hitch a lift ⇨ **thumb a lift**

hold (it/that) against *vt.* 【可分性动词短语】(常用于否定句中) ❶feel angry with (someone), because of something that he or she has done in the past 生(某人的)气: He knows it was an accident; I don't think he'll *hold it against* her. 他知道那是一场意外,所以我想他不会生她的气的。Even if you said that, I won't *hold that against* you. 即使你说了那话,我也不会生你的气。❷(非正式用语) allow (something) to affect one's judgment of (someone)让(某事)影响对(某人)的评价: I don't *hold it against* him that he's spent three years in jail. 我不会因他曾坐过 3 年牢而影响对他的评价。

hold back *vt.* 【可分性动词短语】❶stop (someone or something) from moving forwards 阻止(某人或某物)前进: Mary had to *hold* Tom *back* to prevent him retaliating. 玛丽不得不拉住汤姆,以阻止他去报复。The men built banks of earth to *hold back* the rising floodwaters. 人们筑起土堤以挡住上涨的洪水。The demonstrators, *held back* by police lines, could not be heard inside the hall where the premier spoke. 示威的人群被挡在重重警戒线以外的地方,所以在总理发表讲话的大厅内是听不到他们的。❷prevent the expression of (a feeling, tears, etc.)抑制住(某种情感,泪水等): He *held back* his anger and avoided a fight. 他抑制住了怒火,从而避免了一场争斗。She could not *hold back* her joyful tears after the Chinese girls won the first volleyball World Cup title in 18 years. 她在18年来中国姑娘首次赢得世界杯冠军称号后抑制不住喜悦的泪水。❸stop (someone) from development as he or she should 阻止(某人)应有的发展: She felt that having children would *hold* her *back*. 她认为有孩子会妨碍她的发展。His parents worried that his classmates were trying to *hold* him *back*. 他的父母曾担心他的同学们在千方百计地阻止他的发展。❹ delay (something of someone)推迟,耽误: I'm sorry I'm late, but the heavy traffic *held* me *back*. 对不起,我迟到了。车太多把我给耽误了。❺not allow someone to have (something, for example money)扣压(某人的钱款等): They *held back* the payment because they weren't satisfied with his work. 因为他们对他所做的工作不满意,所以扣压了他的工钱。❻avoid telling someone (the full details about something)向(某人)隐瞒(某事的全部细节): We could tell from her nervousness that she was *holding back* something. 我们从她那紧张的神情中可以看出,她在隐瞒着什么。You must tell us the whole story; don't *hold* anything *back*. 你必须把全部事情都告诉我们,不要有任何隐瞒。❼(常与from 连用) prevent (someone) (from doing something); prevent (something) (from happening)阻止(某人)(做某事),阻止(某事)发生,抑制: There was heavy traffic in the vicinity, he had to *hold* the children *back* from running out into the streets. 附近来往的车辆很多,他不得不阻止孩子跑到街上去。Stagnation in home sales is *holding back* economic recovery. 国内的销售总量停滞不前抑制了经济的复苏。

—*vi.* ❶(常用一般时态) be slow or unwilling to act 退缩不前,不情愿做: We must not *hold back* when other countries are advancing. 别的国家都在发展,我们绝不能停滞不前。I *held back* from jumping into the icy water. 我不愿跳进那冰冷的水中。Mary is afraid of people; she always *holds back* when we take her to parties. 玛丽怕见人,每当我们带她参加聚会时她总是不情愿去。❷decide not to do or say (something)决定不做(或不说某事): He *held back*, remembering the mistake he had made before. 想起他以前所犯的错误,他决定不做了。Because of the uncertain state of the market, buyers are *holding back*. 由于市场情况不稳定,买主们都决定暂不买入了。

NOTE **1.** 当本短语用作及物性动词短语,所带的宾语为代词时,该代词须置于本短语的动词和副词中间。

2. 当本短语作"向(某人)隐瞒"解时,同义短语是 hold out on 和 keep back。

3. 本短语可转化为复合词 holdback,意为“阻碍物;暂时停顿”。

hold down *vt.*【可分性动词短语】❶hold (someone who is lying down), so that he or she cannot move 把(某人)按倒,把(某人)压在身下:It took four of us to *hold* him *down* and stop the fight. 我们四个人把他按倒在地,才终止了这场打斗。The fighter *held* his opponent *down* until the bell rang. 角斗士把对手压在身下一直到铃响。❷keep (something) stay at a lower level 把……保持在低水平上:We must try to *hold down* the rate of interest. 我们必须设法保持低利率。Family planning is introduced to *hold* the population *down*. 实行计划生育就是为了控制人口。❸make (something) move or stay down; hold (something) so it does not move upwards 把……压住,把……垂下:*Hold* the balloon *down* till we are ready to let it go. 把气球压住,等我们准备好了再放开。You should hold your *head down* with shame. 你应该羞愧地把头低下来。❹(非正式用语,无被动语态形式)succeed in keeping (a job)保住(工作):My brother has not *held down* a job for more than a year. 我弟弟干哪件工作都没有超过一年。She seems to be unable to *hold* any job *down*. 她似乎什么工作都保不住。❺prevent (something) from developing or to prevent (someone) from doing what he or she wants 压制,束缚(某人):You can't *hold* a good man *down*. 你们不能压制好人。She proved that being a woman wouldn't *hold* her *down*. 她证明,女人的身份束缚不住她。❻(美国英语用法,非正式用语,无被动语态形式)limit (something, especially a noise)限制(某物,尤指声音):*Hold* it *down*, will you? I'm trying to sleep! 把声音弄小,好不好? 我要睡觉!

NOTE 当本短语所带的宾语为代词时,该代词须置于本短语的动词和副词中间。

hold in *vt.*【可分性动词短语】not allow yourself to express (something such as an emotion or feeling)控制(情感),自制,忍住:It can be bad for you to *hold in* anger. 抑制怒气可能对你没好处。It was difficult to *hold in* my temper. 很难控制住我的脾气。Go ahead and cry. Don't *hold* it *in*. 你就哭出来吧,别憋在心里了。He tried to *hold* himself *in* for fear of saying something he would regret. 他极力控制住自己,生怕说出自己会后悔的话来。These feelings could be *held in* no longer. 这些情绪再也抑制不住了。

NOTE 当本短语所带的宾语为代词时,该代词须置于本短语的动词和副词中间。

hold off *vt.* & *vi.* ❶(cause to)be delayed; delay (doing something or making a decision)(使)推迟,延迟,拖延:The rainy season *held off* for a month, then the rain fell in torrents. 雨季推迟了一个月后,就大雨倾盆了。The young couple *held off* buying a new car because they had not got enough money. 由于没有足够的钱,这对年轻夫妇只得推迟购买新车。The government officials will *hold off* their decision until Friday. 政府官员要拖到星期五才能作出决定。❷(cause to)remain at a distance (使)保持距离:Mary tends to *hold off* from people who try to be friendly. 玛丽总是跟那些竭力示好的人保持距离。She's been holding *him off* for months, but sooner or later she will give in. 她几个月来一直不与他接近,但她迟早会让步的。

—*vt.*【可分性动词短语】stop (someone) from being attacked 抵挡(某人的攻击):

We must *hold off* the enemy's attack. 我们必须抵挡住敌人的进攻。Although Yao Ming was on super condition, the Houston Rockets couldn't *hold* their opponents *off* and lost the game. 尽管姚明的状态极佳,但休斯敦火箭队还是没能抵挡住对方的进攻,输掉了比赛。

NOTE 当本短语用作及物性动词短语,所带的宾语为代词时,该代词须置于本短语的动词和副词中间。

hold on *v.* ❶(常用一般时态)keep (something) tightly or carefully so that you do not drop it or do not fall 抓紧(某物): *Hold on* tight, everyone; the driver's getting ready to go. 大家都握紧些,司机就要开车了。The girl *held on* her father's hand tightly while they crossed the road. 女孩过马路时紧紧地抓着爸爸的手。Bethany, a surfing star in Hawaii said the shark pulled her back and forth, "but I just *held on* my board, and then it let go." 夏威夷冲浪女明星贝思安妮说,鲨鱼来回地拖拽着她,"但我紧紧地抓住冲浪板,后来它松了口。" ❷ fasten (something) in place 固定(某物): This pin *holds* the wheel *on*. 这个销子固定着轮子。The car door was *held on* with string! 车门竟是用细绳固定上的! ❸(常用一般时态)continue in spite of difficulties or opposition; keep on (不顾困难或反对)继续,坚持: We *held on* in spite of the storm. 我们冒着暴风雨继续前进。The hot weather *holds on*. 酷热的天气在继续着。Try to *hold on* until help arrives. 设法坚持到有人来救助。Voting on the bill to send troops to Iraq was delayed due to strong opposition of some lawmakers who *hold on* anti-war stance. 由于一些坚持反战立场议员的强烈反对,对向伊拉克派兵的议案进行的投票表决被推迟了。

—*vi.* (用于口语中,常用于祈使句中,常用一般时态) wait or tell (someone) to wait for a short time, especially on the telephone 等候,(尤指让某人不挂断电话)等一等,稍候: We'll *hold on* another minute, then we'll have to go. 我们再等一会儿,然后我们得走了。*Hold on*! You forgot your card! 等一等! 你忘记了你的卡! He asked me to *hold on* while he left the telephone to find a pen. 他让我等一等,他要放下话筒去找笔。

hold on to/ onto *vt.* 【不可分性动词短语】❶ hold (something or someone) tightly or carefully 紧紧抓住: *Hold onto* your bag, won't you? 把你的包抓紧点儿,好吧? The boy *held on to* one of the soldiers and begged, "Take me along too!" 男孩子抓住一名士兵,恳求道:"把我也带上吧!" ❷(非正式用语)not lose (something or someone) or not let someone else have them; succeed in keeping (something) for yourself 占住,留住(某物或某人),保住(某物): *Hold on to* the two seats in front when we go around. 占着前面的这两个座位,我们去转一转。*Hold on to* the instructions in case you have any problems. 把说明书留着,有问题时好用。Firms are now trying to *hold on to* the people they recruit. 现在,公司都在竭力留住其所聘用的人才。She managed to *hold on to* her job while several of her colleagues lost theirs. 当她的几名同事已经失去工作时,她却成功地保住了自己那份工作。❸ continue to believe in (something such as your beliefs, ideas, or principles)坚持(信念、思想或原则等): He was imprisoned for

15 years yet *held on to* his own belief. 他坐牢15年，但仍然坚持自己的信念。

hold one's ground *vi.* refuse to be forced back, refuse to yield in an argument, claim, etc. 不退却，不让步：Although many were killed, the soldiers *held their ground*. 尽管很多人已牺牲，但士兵们仍不退却。Although many people criticized his theories, he *held his ground*. 虽然很多人都批评了他的理论，但他仍坚持自己的观点。They tried to induce her to withdraw her objections, but she *held her ground*. 他们试图说服她收回异议，可是她却毫不让步。

NOTE 本短语与 stand one's ground 意义和用法相同，两者可互换使用。

hold out *vt.* ❶ stretch (your hand or something you have in your hand) forward 伸出(手或手中之物)：*Hold out* your hands, children. 孩子们，把你们的手都伸出来。We were ready to hold out a friendly hand. 我们准备伸出友谊之手。"I'm Nancy Drew," she said, *holding out* her hand to him. "我叫南希·德鲁。"她说着把手伸给了他。Tom *held out* his cup, asking for a refill. 汤姆伸出杯子要求再倒满。❷(常用一般时态) offer (something such as hope)提供，提出(希望等)：I don't *hold out* much hope that our traffic will improve. 我对交通问题的改善不抱多大希望。❸(主要用于美国英语中，常与 of 连用) prevent (someone or a group) from participating 不让……参加：His parents *held* him *out* of the race because of his health. 他父母因为他的身体而不让他参加赛跑。They *held out* every player who had an injury. 所有受伤的运动员他们都不让参赛。

—*vi.* ❶(常用一般时态) continue to defend (a place that is being attacked) and refuse to surrender 坚守住(某个地方)：We can only *hold out* for a few more hours. 我们只能再坚守几个小时。The town was surrounded, but the citizens *held out* until help at last came. 这个城市被包围了，但市民们一直坚守到了援军的到来。Our troops cannot *hold out* much longer against the superior force of the enemy. 面对敌人的强大优势，我军无法坚守很久了。❷continue to be enough or continue to exist; last 维持：How much longer will your money *hold out*? 你的钱还够花多久？Our supplies will only *hold out* till the end of the month. 我们的给养只能维持到月底。I'm afraid the patient won't *hold out* through the summer. 我担心病人熬不过今年夏天了。

NOTE 1. 当本短语用作及物性动词短语，所带的宾语为代词时，该代词须置于本短语的动词和副词中间。

2. 本短语可转化为复合词 holdout，意为"坚持，不让步；坚持者，不让步的人"。

hold out for *vt.*【不可分性动词短语】insist on obtaining (something better)坚持要得到(更好的人或物)：We will *hold out for* someone who can do the job better. 我们坚持要得到一个能把这项工作做得更好的人。Washington is *holding out for* a commitment from Pyongyang to completely stop its nuclear program. 华盛顿坚持要求得到平壤完全终止核项目的承诺。

hold out on *vt.* (主要用于美国英语中，非正式用语) refuse to tell (someone) (something such as information he or she wants)不告诉(某人)(某事)，瞒着(某人)：He says he knows nothing about it, but I think he's *holding out on* us. 他说他一点儿也不知道那件事,但我认为他是在隐瞒我们。I'm sure she's *holding out on* them. 她肯定在瞒着他们。Are you *holding* something *out on* me? 你有什么事在瞒我吗?

NOTE 当本短语作"瞒着(某人)"解时,同义短语是 hold back 和 keep back。

hold over *vt.* 【可分性动词短语】❶(常用被动语态形式) do (something) or deal with (something) at a later time or date 推迟,延期: One session was *held over* until this evening. 会议被推迟到今晚召开。They intend to *hold* the article *over* for the next edition. 他们打算把这篇文章推到下一期发表。The last item on the agenda we will *hold over* until the next meeting. 我们将推迟到下次会议上讨论议程上的最后一项。❷ use (something you know about someone) to threaten him or her to do what you want 威胁(他人)做某事: He knows I have been in prison and is *holding it over* me. 他知道我坐过牢,并以此来威胁我。Did Robert know something, and *hold* it *over* James? 是不是罗伯特知道些什么事,并以此来威胁詹姆斯? ❸(常用被动语态形式,常与 for 连用) continue (an event, such as a movie, play, exhibit, or sale) for longer than planned 延长……的时间: The movie will be held over for another week. 这部影片将延长放映一周。The gigantic store sale was *held over* two more days because there were so many people. 由于顾客如潮,该店的大型廉价促销活动延长了两天。They have *held* it *over* for another month. 他们已将其延长了一个月。

—*vt.* &*vi.* stay in office beyond the regular term 任期满后继续留任: The former city treasurer *held over* for 6 months when the new treasurer died suddenly. 新任财政局局长突然死亡后,原市财政局局长继续任职了 6 个月。The new president *held* the members of the Cabinet *over* for some time before appointing new members. 新总统在任命新的内阁成员之前,要原内阁成员继续留任一段时间。

NOTE 1. 当本短语用作及物性动词短语,所带的宾语为代词时,该代词须置于本短语的动词和副词中间。

2. 本短语可转化为复合词 holdover,意为"遗留下来的人(或物);任期满后继任的人员"。

hold (a) prejudice against ⇨ **prejudice against**

hold the line *vi.* wait until you can speak to the person you have telephoned 等一等,别挂电话: "The line's busy. Do you want to *hold the line* for a moment?" the operator asked. "现在线路繁忙,您想等一会儿吗?"接线员问道。*Hold the line*, please — I'm trying to connect you. 请别挂电话,我正在设法给您接通。

hold to *vt.* ❶ do or make (someone) do (what he or she has promised or decided) (使某人)坚守(诺言);按(某人)所决定的办: We *held* him *to* his promise. 我们要使他坚守诺言。We decided to *hold to* our original plan. 我们决定坚持按原来的计划办。❷continue having (particular views, beliefs or standards) 坚持(观点、信念或准则): She still *holds to* the view that violence is never justified. 他仍然坚持这样一个观点,即暴力绝非正义。Anyone appointed to this position should be *held to* the highest ethical standards.

任何一个被任命到这个岗位上的人都应坚持最高的道德准则。

hold up *vt.* 【可分性动词短语】❶ hold (something) in a high position, so that people can see it 举起，抬起：Please *hold up* your hands if you have any questions to ask. 如果你们有问题要问，请举手。*Hold* it *up* so that we can see it. 把它举起来，好让我们看到。She was so ashamed that she could not *hold up* her head. 她羞得抬不起头来。❷ (常用被动语态形式) delay (something or someone) 延迟，耽搁：Disputes between Palestinian leaders *held up* the peace process with Israel. 巴勒斯坦领导人之间的争执延迟了巴以和平的进程。Work on the construction site has been *held up* by bad weather. 建筑工地上的工作由于天气不好而被延迟。The passenger train was *held up* for five hours by the flood caused by the fourth typhoon this year. 今年的第四号台风引起的洪水使该次旅客列车晚点了五个小时。Driving the kids to school *held* me *up*. 开车送孩子们上学耽搁了我的时间。❸ rob (a shop, a bank, a vehicle, or people) with violence or threats 抢劫(商店、银行、车辆或人)：An armed robber *held up* the village store last week. 一名武装劫匪在上星期抢劫了村里的那家商店。Two young men tried to *hold* me *up*. 两个年轻人试图抢劫我。He was *held up* at the point of a gun just as he left the bank. 他刚离开银行就遭到了持枪抢劫。❹ (与 as 连用) make (someone or something) known to other people, so that they can praise or criticize them 作为……的典范；成为……的样板：He had always been *held up* as an example to the younger ones. 他一直被树为青年人学习的楷模。The old man always *holds up* his youngest son as a model of hard work. 那位老人总是标榜自己的小儿子为勤奋工作的典范。She said the picture that had appeared in a Sunday newspaper had *held* her *up* to ridicule. 她说星期日报纸上刊登的照片使她成了人们取笑的样板。❺ support (someone or something) so that they do not fall down 支撑：Her legs were almost too shaky to *hold* her *up*. 她的腿几乎抖得支撑不住自己。The underpinnings are *holding* the house *up*. 房基支撑着房体。The whole weight of the deck is *held up* by the four cables. 整个平台的重量由四根钢索支撑着。

—*vi.* ❶ remain strong or in a fairly good condition 坚持，挺住：There were fears that her ankle might not *hold up* for the competition. 人们担心她的伤踝可能会使她无法坚持比赛。Do you think the patient will *hold up* through the night? 你认为这个病人能挺过晚上吗？❷ (of an argument or theory) stand testing; bear close examination (指某一论点或理论)经得住考验，站得住脚：I'm not sure if the argument *holds up*, but it is stimulating. 我不确信这论点是否站得住脚，但它很有启发性。

NOTE **1.** 当本短语用作及物性动词短语，所带的宾语为代词时，该代词须置于本短语的动词和副词中间。

2. 本短语可转化为复合词 hold-up，意为"停顿，阻碍；抢劫"。

hold water *vi.* (非正式用语，常用于疑问句或否定句中) be or prove true, reasonable, or believable; stand testing; bear examination 有理，可信；经得住考验，站得住脚：Does his excuse *hold* water? 他那个借口可信吗? Tom told the police a story that wouldn't *hold water*. 汤姆给警察讲了一套经不住推敲的假话。The high-ranking official's explanation of where he got the money from just doesn't *hold water*. 这名高官对该款项的来源所作出的解释是站不住脚的。

NOTE 本短语的同义短语是 hold up(最后一个义项)。

hold with *vt.*【不可分性动词短语】(正式用语,无被动语态形式,常用一般时态,通常用于否定句中) agree with or approve of (an activity or action)同意,赞成: She doesn't *hold with* their plans. 她不赞成他们的计划。I don't *hold with* letting people smoke in public places. 我不赞成让人们在公共场所吸烟。Why did you join us if you don't *hold with* our going? 你不赞成我们去,那又为什么要加入我们呢?

honor one's promise(s) ⇨ **keep (one's) promise(s)**

hope for *vt.* want and expect (something good) to happen or be true; hope to gain (something)希望……: They *hoped for* more money for their cancer research. 他们希望有更多的资金供他们进行癌症的研究。Let's *hope for* the best and prepare for the worst. 让我们抱最好的希望,做最坏的准备。It isn't what you *hoped for*, is it? 这不是你所希望的,是吧? We learn from the past, experience the present and *hope for* success in the future. 我们总结过去,体验现在,期望将来取得成功。

NOTE 本短语可转化为复合词 hoped-for,意为"盼望中的,期望中的",主要用于书面语,仅用作定语。

How about …? *s.* (仅用于口语中) ❶ an expression used for suggesting what someone may like to do or choose, or a time or place that may be suitable (提出建议或征求对方意见)……怎么样,……好吗: *How about* a drink? 喝杯酒怎么样? *How about* going to France for our holiday? 我们到法国去度假怎么样? "When shall we meet next time?" "*How about* Thursday afternoon? Would that be convenient?" "我们下次什么时候见面?" "星期四下午怎么样? 对您方便吗?" ❷ an expression used for asking about another person or thing, in addition to the ones that have already been mentioned (询问未谈及的人或事)……怎么样: And *how about* your friend? What happened to him? 那你的朋友怎么样? 他出什么事了吗? ❸ an expression used to make an offer or a suggestion that amounts to a request or invitation (提出要求或邀请性的建议)……好吧: *How about* paying back some of that money you borrowed from me? 从我这儿借的那笔钱你该还一些了吧? *How about* having dinner with us tonight? 今晚和我们一起吃晚饭,好吧?

NOTE 在日常口语中,本短语常以 How about it? 的形式出现。例如:

> *How about* it? Do you want to go with us?
> 怎么样,想和我们一起去吗?

How are you? *s.* (非正式用语) ❶ an expression used to question about someone's health 你身体好吗?: Haven't seen you for a long time. *How are you?* 很久没见你了。你的身体可好? ❷ an expression used when meeting someone you already know (见到熟人时用的致候

语)你好:"Hello, *how are you*?" "Fine, thanks." "喂,你好?""我很好,谢谢。"

NOTE 1. 本短语为问候语,问候者并不期待对方给予确切的回答。回答语通常有:I'm very well, thank you. (正式答语)/ Fine, thanks. (非正式答语)/ Fine, and you? (非正式答语)。

2. 本短语与 How do you do? 的回答语完全不同。当用本短语问候的时候,回答时不能再回问"How are you?"。

How come (…)? *s.* (非正式用语)(used for asking why or how something happened) Why is it that? How can it be that …? 为什么? 怎么能……呢? "He didn't show up at the meeting this morning." "*How come*?" "他在今天上午的会议上没露面。" "为什么?" "*How come* you weren't at the party last night?" He asked. "你为什么没有出席昨晚的聚会呀?"他问道。If she spent 2 years in New York, *how come* she can't speak a word of English? 如果她在纽约住过两年,怎么能连一句英语都不会讲呢?

NOTE 1. 本短语是 How did it come about that? 的缩略形式,主要用于口语中;在正式文体中,用 why。

2. 本短语的另外一种表达形式是 How so? 后者是 How is it so? 的缩略式。例如:

> You say he's changed his mind — how so?
> 你说他改变了主意。为什么呢?

3. 本短语与疑问副词 why 均表示"为什么"之意,都可用来引出疑问句或单独使用。两者在用法上的区别是:本短语一般不用于正式的书面语中。另外,在由本短语引起的疑问句中要用陈述语序;而在 why 引起的疑问句中则须用倒装语序。例如:

> *How come* you are so interested in environment protection? (用陈述语序)
> *Why* are you so interested in environment protection? (用倒装语序)

但当本短语单独使用时,用法则与 why 相同。

How do you do? *s.* (正式用语) an expression used as a polite greeting when you meet someone for the first time, especially when they have introduced themselves or have been introduced (与他人初次见面时用的致候语)您好,你好:"*How do you do*? Mr Smith." "*How do you do*? I'm glad to meet you." "您好吗,史密斯先生?""您好。我很高兴见到您。"

NOTE 本短语与 How are you? 完全不同。与他人初次见面时才说 *How do you do*? 回答语与问候语一样,即 *How do you do*?

hunger for/after *vt.* 【不可分性动词短语】(正式用语,常用一般时态) want (something) very much 渴望得到:She *hungered for* some good news from her daughter. 她渴望得到女儿的好消息。The British champion *hungers after* the US Open title. 这位英国冠军极想赢得美国公开赛的冠军。

hunt down *vt.* 【可分性动词短语】❶try to find (a particular thing or person) 寻找,搜寻:They'll *hunt down* old books for you. 他们会帮你找些旧书。We spent the weekend *hunting down* a new house. 我们把周末的时间都花在了找房子上。Those who protested were *hunted down* and put into prison. 那些抗议者被搜寻出来关入监狱。❷chase (a particular person or an animal) until caught 追捕(某

人),追猎(某种动物):The Philippines official said authorities were *hunting down* 8 military officers linked to the coup plot. 这位菲律宾官员说,当局正在追捕8名与兵变阴谋有关联的军官。It took the police four months to *hunt* him *down*. 警方花了四个月的时间才将他捕获。The lion that has escaped from the city zoo must be *hunted down*. 一定要捕捉到那头从市动物园里跑出去的狮子。

NOTE 当本短语所带的宾语为代词时,该代词须置于本短语的动词和副词中间。

hunt for *vt.* 【不可分性动词短语】❶ try to find (something or someone) 寻找,搜寻:What are you *hunting for* in this drawer? 你翻抽屉在找什么呢? The Brazilian government was "shocked" to learn that London police mistakenly shot dead a Brazilian citizen when *hunting for* subway bombers. 巴西政府对伦敦警方在搜寻地铁爆炸嫌犯时误杀巴西公民感到"震惊"。❷ kill (animals) for food or for their skin or other parts, or for sport 猎杀(动物):We *hunted for* rabbits in the hills. 我们在山中猎兔。The natives live by *hunting for* their food. 当地居民靠猎食生活。White tigers have been *hunted* almost to extinction *for* their prized fur and only about 200 remain worldwide, mostly in zoos. 由于白虎的毛皮非常珍贵,白虎已经被捕杀得濒临灭绝。目前世界上仅存白虎200只左右,绝大多数养在动物园中。

hurry away/off *v.* (cause to) do something or move somewhere more quickly (使)匆匆行事,(使)匆匆走开:She *hurried away/off* in the opposite direction. 她朝相反的方向匆匆走去。Mary took Anna's arm and *hurried* her *away*. 玛丽拉着安娜的胳膊催她快走。The prisoners were *hurried off* before the reporters could have a chance to speak to them. 记者们还没来得及和犯人搭上话,犯人们就被匆匆地押走了。

NOTE 当本短语用作及物性动词短语,所带的宾语为代词时,该代词须置于本短语的动词和副词中间。

hurry up *vi.* ❶ (主要用于口语中)(used for telling someone to do something more quickly) be quick (用于催促某人)快点儿:The mother told her son to *hurry up*; otherwise, they'd miss their train. 妈妈催儿子快点,否则她们就赶不上火车了。*Hurry up* and finish your soup! 快点儿,把你的汤喝完! ❷ do something or move somewhere more quickly 赶快:She wished George would *hurry up* with his cup of tea. 她希望乔治赶快喝他的那杯茶。I wish the bus would *hurry up* and come. 我希望公共汽车赶快来。

—*vt.* 【可分性动词短语】 make (someone) do something more quickly or make (something) happen sooner 催促(某人),赶紧做完(某事):I tried to *hurry* him *up* but he wouldn't walk any faster. 我催他走快点儿,但他就是不快些走。They *hurried up* their work in order to go home. 他们赶快做完工作以便回家。We have to *hurry* this job *up* if we want to go home earlier. 如果我们想早点回家,就得赶紧把这项工作做完。

NOTE 当本短语用作及物性动词短语,所带的宾语是代词时,该代词须置于本短语的动词和副词中间。

H

I i

identical to/with *adj.* similar in every detail; exactly the same as 和……一模一样，与……完全相同：Your voice is *identical to* his. 你的声音和他的一模一样。His behavior is *identical to* betraying the Party. 他的行为等同于叛党。This machine is *identical* in design *with* the other one. 在设计上，这台机器与那台机器是相同的。My opinion is *identical with* yours. 我的意见与你们的完全相同。

ID card *n.* an official card with a person's name, photograph, date of birth, and other information on it 身份证：What you need to do is to fill out a form, show your *ID card*, and pay a flat rate fee. 你只需要填写一份表格，出示你的身份证，并交纳一笔统一价格的费用。The first page of the identity document includes the *ID card* number, the issuing town, and the name and surname. 身份文件的第一页上包括身份证号码、签发地及姓名。

NOTE 本短语在美国英语中的全称是 identification card，在英国英语中的全称是 identity card。

idle away *vt.* ❶spend (time) relaxing and doing nothing; waste (time) lazily 消磨(时光)，浪费(时间)：Morse *idled away* most of Monday in his office. 莫尔斯把星期一的大半天时间都在办公室里消磨掉了。We can't afford to *idle away* a single minute; we should make full use of our time in accomplishing our task. 我们不能浪费时间，而应充分利用我们的时间来完成任务。❷(of an engine) run very slowly because it is not in gear, so that power is not used for useful work (指发动机)空挡低速地运转：The car engine needs to *idle away* for 2 or 3 minutes to get it warm in cold weather. 在冷天，汽车发动机需要空转两三分钟预热。

if anything *adv.* (主要用于口语中)(used for saying how someone or something is different when you are not sure whether there really is any change or difference) more likely 很有可能，如果有……的话：The situation is, *if anything*, worsening rather than improving. 情况很有可能更糟，而没有改善。His family, *if anything*, was richer than mine. 要说有什么不同的话，那就是他家比我家富有。

if it were not for *conj.* (used for saying what prevents the situation from being different) but for; if there were no 如果没有，倘非，若不是：*If it were not for* his wife's money he'd never be a director. 如果没有他妻子的钱，他永远也当不上董事。No animals would have the food they need *if it were not for* green plants. 要不是因为有绿色植物，一切动物都不会获得它们所需要的食物。*If it* *were not for* the fact that he is my father, I'd accuse him in public. 如果他不是我的父亲,我一定会当众控诉他。

NOTE 本短语是一种虚拟语气的形式,过去形式为 if it had not been for。例如:

> *If it had not been for* the help of the man, the boy would have been drowned in the brook.
> 如果没有那个人的援救,孩子就淹死在小河里了。

if necessary *adv.* if it is necessary to do so 如果必要:That country has vowed to prevent anyone from leading the island toward a formal independence by using military force *if necessary*. 那个国家发誓,在必要时将动用武力去阻止任何人把那个小岛引向正式独立。

NOTE 本短语的同义短语是 when necessary。

if not *adv.* (前常用连词 and) if this is not true 如果不是这样的话,如果没有: Has anyone dealt with the technical problems? And *if not*, why not? 有人处理技术问题吗? 如果没有,为什么没有? I'll probably see you on Sunday; *if not*, it'll be Monday. 我可能会在周日见你,如果不行就在周一吧。

NOTE 1. 本短语中的 not 与 if 构成缩略条件句,在句中作状语。
2. 本短语的反义短语是 if so。

if only *conj.* (主要用于口语中) ❶(后常用过去时或过去完成时形式表示虚拟) (often used to express a wish or desire, especially one that cannot be fulfilled) I wish that; supposing it were possible to do, have or make something (常用来表示一种不能实现的愿望)但愿……,要是……就好了,只要: *If only* she could marry me. 但愿她能嫁给我。*If only* I had more money, I could buy some new clothes. 我要是有更多的钱就好了,那我就可以买些新衣服了。*If only* you hadn't told Jim what I said, everything would have been all right. 你要是没把我的话告诉吉姆就好了,那样就不会出什么问题了。*If only* we can get to the next gas station we'll be all right. 只要我们能走到下一个加油站就没问题了。❷used for saying that when something good happens, it may only be for a limited purpose, time, etc. 哪怕只……也好:I wish he'd come round and see us sometime, *if only* just to say hello. 我希望他什么时候能过来看看我们,哪怕只打声招呼也好。Seeing her will give me much pleasure, *if only* for 5 minutes. 见她一面会给我很多的欢乐,哪怕 5 分钟也好。

NOTE 本短语后并非一律用虚拟语气的形式。只有当本短语用来表示强烈愿望或没实现的条件,其后从句中的谓语动词要用虚拟语气形式。其他场合可用陈述语气表达。

if so *adv.* (前常用连词 and) if this is true 如果是这样的话: Are you planning to return to work, and *if so*, who is going to look after the baby? 你打算回去工作? 如果是这样的话,由谁来照顾婴儿? Will you get a free evening next week? *If so*, let's talk about the test. 下周你能有一个晚上抽空出来吗? 如果有,我们谈谈实验的事。

NOTE 1. 本短语中的 so 代替前面所述的句子,与 if 构成缩略条件句,在句中作状语。
2. 本短语的反义短语是 if not。

ignorant of/about *adj.* not knowing (something that you should know or need to know)不知道,不了解(应该或需要知

道的事情）：I was *ignorant of* the terms used in business. 我对商务术语一无所知。Those *ignorant of* facts will continue to make the same mistake. 那些不了解事实的人会继续犯同样的错误。I'm afraid I'm rather *ignorant about* computers. 恐怕我对计算机相当无知。They are *ignorant about* what happened. 他们不了解所发生的事情。

ill at ease *adj.* not feeling confident or relaxed, rather nervous and uncomfortable, especially because of lack of social skill（尤指因缺乏社交能力而感到）局促不安的，不自在的：She felt embarrassed and *ill at ease* with the applause that greeted her. 欢迎她的掌声使她感到困窘不安。She's always *ill at ease* at parties. 她在聚会上总觉得不自在。

NOTE 本短语的反义短语是 at ease。

imbue with *vt.*【可分性动词短语】（正式用语，常用被动语态形式）fill (usually someone) with (something such as an idea or a feeling) 使（尤指某人）充满（某种思想、情感等）：In Tibet, folk songs, dances, dramas, tales and other forms of artistic expression have been *imbued with* new ideas. 在西藏，民歌、舞蹈、歌剧、故事和其他的艺术表达形式都充满了新思想。We should continue to *imbue* people *with* lofty ideals, and inspire them with excellent works of literature and art. 我们应该继续以高尚的理性塑造人，以优秀的文艺作品鼓舞人。

immune to/from/against *adj.* ❶safe from (a disease), because you cannot be infected by it 对（某种疾病）有免疫的：The blood test will show whether or not you're *immune to* the disease. 这项血液化验就会显示你是否对那种疾病有免疫力。This injection can make you *immune to* infection. 此次注射可以使你免受感染。The trials show that the vaccine is safe and it works fast to make the body *immune against* flu. 这些试验表明：这种疫苗安全，并且能快速使身体对流感产生免疫作用。❷not influenced or affected by (something) 不受……影响的，免受……的：The president seems to be *immune to* criticism and opposition. 总统似乎不受批评和反对的影响。Few women were *immune to* his charm. 没有几个女人不为他的魅力所动。Iran's Housing and Urban Development Minister said in Tehran the majority of high-rises in the country are *immune against* earthquake. 伊朗住房和城市发展部部长在德黑兰表示，全国的绝大多数高层建筑都是抗震的。❸not affected by (something such as a law), because of a special arrangement 免除……的：Diplomats are *immune from* prosecution. 外交官都有诉讼豁免权。The suspect was told he would be *immune from* punishment if he helped the police. 该嫌疑人被告知说，如果他协助警方，就可以免受惩罚。

NOTE 一般说来，immune to 后常接 disease, infection 等词，immune from 后常接 prosecution, punishment, taxation 等词，而 immune against 后可接前两者的内容，但不及前两者常用。

impose on/upon *vt.* ❶use your authority to introduce (something such as a new law, rule, tax, or punishment), and force people to accept it（利用权力）把（新法律、规定）强加给（某人）；强制惩罚（某人）；向（某人）征税："Don't *impose* foreign law *on* American citizens," they said. “不要把外国的法律强加给美国公民。”他们这样说道。Iran vowed Friday that its nuclear policy remained unchanged after the United States *imposed* new sanctions *on* Tehran. 在美国对德黑兰采取了新的制裁措施后，伊朗于星期五誓言，其核政策依然不会改变。The central government has abolished almost all the taxes and charges *imposed on* farmers. 中央政府已取消了几乎所有向农民征收的税种和收费。❷force (someone) to have (your opinions, beliefs, etc.) as a rule or as a model to copy 把(自己的观点、信念等)强加给(别人)：I wouldn't want to *impose* my ideas *upon* anyone. 我不想把我自己的思想强加给任何人。All the countries of the world, big or small, should be equal and none should *impose* its own will *on* others. 世界上所有的国家，不管大小，都应平等，谁也不应把自己的意志强加给别国。❸cause extra work for (someone) by asking them to do something that may not be convenient for him or her 给(某人)添麻烦：Thank you, but I don't think I will stay for the night. I don't want to *impose on* you. 谢谢您，今晚我不想住了。我不想给您添麻烦。Please come and stay here. You wouldn't be *imposing on* us at all. 请到这儿来住吧。你们不会给我们添任何麻烦的。

NOTE 本短语中的 upon 用法比 on 正式，但不及 on 常用。

improve on/upon *vt.* 【不可分性动词短语】make (something) better than it was before, or do (something) better than you did before 改进，提高：We hope to *improve on* last year's performance. 我们希望把去年的工作加以改进。I was unable to *improve on* his translation. 我无法再改进他的译文了。This design can hardly be *improved upon*. 这一设计很难再改进了。

NOTE 本短语中的 upon 用法比 on 正式，但不及 on 常用。

in a family way ⇨ **in the family way**

in a hurry Ⅰ *adv.* ❶doing something or going somewhere quickly because you do not have much time 急忙地，匆忙地：Mary's letter looked as though she had written it *in a* great *hurry*. 玛丽的信看上去就像是在万分匆忙中写完似的。We left *in* such *a hurry* that we forgot our tickets. 我们走得太匆忙，以致忘记了带车票。❷(非正式用语，一般用于否定句中)easily; quickly 容易地，很快地：You won't untie this knot *in a hurry*. 你不会轻易地解开这个绳结的。I won't forget her kindness towards me *in a hurry*. 我不会轻易忘掉她对我的好。❸(非正式用语，一般用于否定句中)willingly 情愿地：I won't help her again *in a hurry*—she's been so ungrateful. 我不愿再帮她了。她这个人太忘恩负义。

Ⅱ *adj.* (后常接动词不定式)anxiously eager 急于：She seems to be *in a hurry* to leave. 她似乎急于离开。I am not *in a hurry* to leave this happy world. 我还不急于要离开这幸福的人间。

NOTE **1.** 本短语与 in a rush 和 in haste 都是副词性短语，修饰句中动词，表示“急忙地，匆忙地”之意。三者的区别在于：(1)*in a hurry* 和 in a rush 还可作形容词性短语，而 in haste 不可以。(2) *in a hurry* 和 in a rush 在句中都可以作表语，而 in haste 则无此用法。如可以说：We are in a hurry. 也可说 We are in a rush. 但不能说 * We are in haste.

2. 本短语的否定形式是 in no hurry, not in a/any hurry 和 there is no hurry。例如：

I'm *in no hurry* to go.
我不急于要走。
I'm *not in a/any hurry* to get there.
我不着急到那儿。
I'll need to talk with you, but *there's no hurry*.
我要和你谈谈,但不着急。

3. 虽然本短语没有比较级形式,但可以用表示程度的词语修饰短语中的名词 hurry,如:*in a* great *hurry*, *in* more of *a hurry*,等。

in a minute *adv.* (非正式用语)(used for telling someone that you will do something very soon)in a very short period of time 很快地,立即,马上: I'll come down stairs *in a minute*. 我立刻就下楼去。I'm only going down to post this letter. I'll be back *in a minute*. 我只是下去寄封信,一会儿就回来了。Wait; it'll be done *in a minute*. 等一下,很快就会做好了。

NOTE 本短语的同义短语是 in a moment 和 in a second。三者比较起来,in a second 所表示的时间最短、最快。例如:

I'll be with you *in a second* (= in an extremely short period of time).
我马上就来。

in a row *adv.* ❶in a straight line 成一条直线:The children stood *in a row* against the wall. 孩子们靠墙站成一排。❷(常用于表示数目的复数名词之后) one after another, without anything different happening in between 一个接一个地,连续地: He won the competition three times *in a row*. 他接连三次赢得比赛。We've been in the black for two months *in a row*. 我们已连续两个月盈利了。

NOTE 当本短语作"成一条直线"解时,同义短语是 in line。

in a rush *adj.* &*adv.* in a hurry to do something, especially because you do not have much time 急急忙忙:Sorry, I can't stop. I'm rather *in a rush*. 对不起,我不能停下来,我太忙了。We have to send a person *in a rush*. 我们得赶快派一个人了。

in a second ⇨ **in a minute**

in a sense *adv.* in some ways but not all; partly; somewhat; in some respects 有几分,在某种意义上来说,在某些方面: She's wise *in a sense*. 她有几分聪明。I'm from this area, so *in a sense* it's like coming home. 我就是来自这个地区,所以在某种意义上来说,就像回到家一样。*In a sense* I agree with you, but not entirely. 我在某些方面同意你的意见,但并不完全同意。

NOTE **1.** 本短语中的名词 sense 前可根据表达需要加不同意义的限定性形容词,如: *in an* absolute *sense* (在绝对意义上),*in a* broad/large *sense* (在广义上), *in a* literal *sense* (在字面意义上),等等。

2. 本短语的另外一种表达形式是 in some sense。

3. 本短语的同义短语是 in a way。

in a way *adv.* ❶(非正式用语)somewhat; to some or limited extent 有几分,在某种程度上:*In a way* he is right. 在某种程度上他是对的。These two clocks look like each other *in a way*. 这两座钟看上去有几分相像。He considers his wife clever, and *in a way* he's justified. 他认为他妻子很聪明,在某种意义上来说是正确的。❷in certain respect; from one point of view 在某一方面;从某一方面: *In a way*, I agree with you. 我在某一个方面上同意你的意见。The result was satisfactory *in a way*. 从某一方面来看,结果还令人满意。*In a way*, elementary schooling is more important than secondary schooling. 从某方面来讲,小学教育比中学教育更重要。

in a while *adv.* (非正式用语)soon 马上,一会儿: I'll be back *in a while*. 我马上就回来。The boys gathered some wood, and *in a* little *while*, a hot fire was burning. 男孩们拾了一些木柴,过了一会儿,火就熊熊地燃烧起来。

in a word *adv.* (常用于句首,后接总结性语句)(used for giving the shortest answer possible, without explaining anything)in few words; concisely 总而言之,简言之: *In a word*, only on a just, reasonable and comprehensive basis, can the question of Palestine be properly resolved at the end of the day. 简言之,只有在公正、合理、全面的基础上,才可能最终妥善解决巴勒斯坦问题。"Did you like Mary?" "*In a word*, no." "你喜欢玛丽吗?""简而言之一个字,不。"

NOTE 本短语的同义短语是 in brief 和 in short。

in accord with *prep.* (正式用语) in agreement with 与……一致,符合……: The two sides are completely *in accord with* each other on this matter. 双方在这个问题上意见完全一致。This was *in* full *accord with* the common desire of our two peoples. 这是完全符合我们两国人民的共同愿望的。

NOTE 本短语的同义短语是 in accordance with, in agreement with, in harmony with, in line with 和 in step with。

in accordance with *prep.* (正式用语) ❶in a way that follows a particular rule, system, or someone's wishes; according to 根据,依照,按照: *In accordance with* the ruling, two principal criminals were sentenced to death, and the former boss was given life imprisonment. 根据裁决,两名主犯被判处死刑,而原总裁则被判处无期徒刑。The scheme has been revised *in accordance with* the opinions of the masses. 该方案已依照群众的意见做了修改。He acted *in accordance with* his beliefs. 他按照自己的信念行事。❷in agreement with (something) 与……一致,符合……: This is not *in accordance with* facts. 这与事实不相符。His words are not *in accordance with* common sense. 他的话不合常识。

NOTE 1. 不要将本短语与 according to 混淆。

2. 本短语的同义短语是 in accord with, 但本短语更为常用。

3. 当本短语作"与……一致,符合……"解时,其同义短语是 in agreement with, in harmony with, in line with 和 in step with。

in action *adj.* & *adv.* in a condition of working or fighting 在工作中;在战斗中: I've heard he's a good player, but I've never seen him *in action*. 我听说他是个不错的运动员,但我从未见过他在比赛。How long before we can see the new lift *in action*? 新电梯还要多久才能使用? The soldiers are *in action*. 士兵们在战斗。Within days, three of Ryan's brothers were killed *in action*. 几天内,瑞恩就有三个弟兄在战斗中阵亡。

NOTE 本短语的反义短语是 out of action。

in addition *adv.* (used for adding an extra piece of information to what has already been said or written) as well; also 除此之外,而且,还: The boy has collected many American stamps and some foreign stamps *in addition*. 这男孩已收集了很

多美国邮票,此外还有一些外国邮票。New types of computers are smaller in size and *in addition* they are simpler in operation. 新型计算机体积较小,而且操作也比较简单。

NOTE 本短语可被副词 plus 替换,但 plus 为非正式用法。例如:

> They've got a strong army. *Plus*, it is highly trained.
> 他们有一支强大的军队。而且这支军队受过良好的训练。

in addition to *prep.* besides; as well as 除了……之外,还……: *In addition to* TOEFL, the International English Language Testing System (IELTS) is also accepted by more and more Chinese students. 除了"托福"考试外,"雅思"考试也为越来越多的中国学生所接受。As an English-major, *in addition to* English, he has to study an additional foreign language. 作为一名英语专业的学生,他除英语外,还须学第二外语。*In addition to* being used as a building material, wood is also manufactured into paper. 木头除了用作建筑材料,还用来造纸。

in advance *adv.* beforehand; ahead of time 事先,提前:The raid on the border police was a terrorist attack and had been carefully planned *in advance*. 对边防警察的袭击案件是一次事先精心策划的恐怖袭击活动。All interested in the files must first apply to the Foreign Ministry's Archives some 20 workdays *in advance*. 所有对这些档案感兴趣的人必须先提前20个工作日向外交部档案馆提出申请。Accommodation should be applied for as much *in advance* as possible. 需要提供食宿的应尽量提前申请。

NOTE **1.** 本短语的比较级形式是 more in advance,最高级形式是 most in advance。**2.** 本短语的同义短语是 ahead of schedule 和 ahead of time。

in advance of *prep.* ❶ before (a particular date or event); ahead of 在(某一日期或事件)之前:Galileo's ideas were well *in advance of* the age in which he lived. 伽利略的思想远远超越了他所生活的时代。Environmental groups strongly attacked the government policies *in advance of* US President's visit to Canada. 环保组织在美国总统访问加拿大前夕猛烈抨击政府的政策。❷in front of (another person or thing) 在……前面:In the parade, the band will march *in advance of* the football team. 在行进式上,乐队将走在足球队的前面。

NOTE 本短语的同义短语是 ahead of。

in agreement with *prep.* (正式用语)(of someone or something such as a fact, an opinion, or purpose) in harmony with (another) 与……一致,符合……: I found myself *in* complete *agreement with* John. 我发现我(的观点)与约翰(的观点)完全一致。These findings are *in agreement with* our previous conclusions. 这些调查结果与我们以前所作出的结论相符。

NOTE 本短语的同义短语是 in accord with, in accordance with, in harmony with, in line with 和 in step with。

in all *adv.* ❶as the total, when the whole of an amount or number is included 总计,总共:The repairs come to \$500 in all. 修理费总计达 500 美元。"How much are they *in all*?" I asked the salesman. "总计多少钱?"我问售货员。"*In all*, the force of people operating against us does not exceed 5,000," the American general in Baghdad said at a news conference. "与我们相对抗的武装力量总共也不超过5 000人。"美军将领在巴格达举行的一次记者招待会上这样说道。❷considering everything 总体上，总之：We won ten games and lost two, doing very well *in all*. 我们十胜二负。总之，干得很不错。

in all conscience *adv.* (英国英语用法，正式用语，常用于否定句中)(used for talking about what you believe to be fair or right) being fair or reasonable 凭良心；有理由地，公平地：I cannot *in all conscience* cast my vote against the defendant. 凭良心，我不能投票反对被告人。I couldn't *in all conscience* shut him out on such a wet night. 在这样的雨夜，把他关在外面，我于心不忍。

NOTE 本短语的另外一种表达形式是 in (all) good conscience。

in answer to *prep.* in response to; as a reply to 回答，响应，答复：The doctor came at once *in answer to* my telephone call. 医生一接到我电话就立即赶来了。*In answer to* his request, I gave him two hundred dollars. 应他的请求，我给了他200美元。The editorial was *in answer to* the readers' angry letters. 这篇社论是对读者愤怒的来信的答复。

in any case *adv.* anyhow; anyway; whatever the situation is or will be; no matter what happens 无论如何，在任何情况下，不管发生什么：The cost may be lower than we first thought, but *in any case* it will still be quite substantial. 成本也许会比我们原想的低一些，但还是相当高的。*In any case*, you should hear what he says. 在任何情况下，你都应该听取他的意见。But I will try to come *in any case*. 但不管发生什么事，我也会尽力前来的。Traffic may be bad, but *in any case* we'll be there in time for lunch. 交通状况可能不好，但不管怎样，我们都要及时赶到那里吃午饭。

NOTE 本短语与 at any rate, at all events 和 in any event 意义和用法相同，三者可互换使用。

in any event *adv.* (常用于英国英语中) whatever happens or may happen in the future, or has happened 无论发生什么，不管怎样：*In any event*, you ought to attend the meeting on time. 无论如何，你都该按时到会。I may not go to Europe, but *in any event* I'll visit you during the summer. 我可能不去欧洲，但无论如何我也会在夏天去拜访你的。This problem must be solved *in any event*. 不管怎样这个问题也必须得到解决。She had a terrible accident, but *in any event* she was not killed. 她遭遇到可怕的车祸，但不管怎样她并没有死。

in any way *adv.* ❶in any manner 以任何方式：China further declared that it had no intention to assist any country *in any way* in the development of missiles that can be used to deliver nuclear weapons. 中国进一步表明，无意以任何方式帮助任何国家发展可被用于运载核武器的导弹。He is not *in any way* trying to escape his responsibility. 他没有以任何方式试图逃避责任。❷(常用于否定句中) no matter what happens 无论如何：The composition of water is not changed *in any way*. 水的成分无论如何也不会变化。

in as far as ⇨ **in so far as**

in back of ⇨ **back of**

in (full) bloom *adj.* &*adv.* (of a tree or

I

plant) covered with flowers (树或植物)盛开着鲜花的(地): I have seen it *in (full) bloom* once. 我曾经看见过它开花。Flowers spread over the growing grass *in* delicate *bloom* and filled the air with their fragrance. 青葱的草地上,百花盛开,阵阵花香洋溢在空中。By April the flowers in the garden are *in bloom*. 到四月份,花园里的鲜花就都开了。

NOTE 本短语的另外一种表达形式是 in (full) blossom。

in brief *adv.* using as few words as possible, and without many details; in short; briefly 简而言之: The plan is to change the radio station's style: *in brief*, less talk and more music. 该计划旨在改变广播电台的特点,简而言之,减少谈话内容,增加音乐节目。*In brief*, the story is about a man's adventures on a deserted island. 简而言之,那是一个人在荒岛上的历险故事。This, *in brief*, is the view of the trade union. 简而言之,这就是工会的观点。

NOTE **1.** 本短语除了用作状语外,还可以用作后置定语。如:

> I only heard the news *in brief*.
> 我只是听到了简要的新闻。

2. 本短语的同义短语是 in a word 和 in short。

in broad daylight *adv.* ❶ in the full light of day; during the day 大白天地: The official was shot to death *in broad daylight* in front of his house. 那名官员在大白天于自家门口被枪杀。Robert stood there *in broad daylight*, but we never saw him! 罗伯特白天就站在那里,可我们却从来没看见过他! ❷ when anyone can see what is happening 在光天化日之下: These robberies took place *in broad daylight*. 这些抢劫案都发生在光天化日之下。How can a thief run away with a safe *in broad daylight*? 小偷怎么能够在光天化日之下把保险箱偷走呢?

in bulk *adv.* ❶ (bought or sold) in large quantities 大批地(买进卖出): Large companies buy and sell *in bulk*. 大公司都是大批地买进或卖出。Buying *in bulk* is more economical than shopping for small quantities. 批量购买比小量零购便宜得多。❷(正式用语,常用于句首) in large amounts or volume 大量地: The ship was carrying wheat *in bulk*. 这艘船装载了大量的小麦。

in case Ⅰ *conj.* ❶ (后接从句) for fear that; because … might 万一,要是……就: It's a good idea to keep in with the police *in case* you need their help one day. 和警察保持友好的关系是个好主意,说不上哪一天你会需要他们的帮助。❷(主要用于美国英语中) if 如果: *In case* you can't come, give me a call before I leave for work. 如果你不能来,在我去上班前给我打个电话。He will resign *in case* you drive him too hard. 如果你逼他太甚,他会辞职不干的。

Ⅱ *adv.* (非正式用语,前常用 just,置于句尾) in order to be prepared; as a precaution 以防万一: The bus is usually on time, but you should start early, just *in case*. 公共汽车一般都会正点,但你还应早些动身,以防误车。The big dog was tied up, but I carried a stick, just *in case*. 那条大狗是拴着的,但为防万一,我还是拿了一根木棍。

NOTE **1.** 作为连词性短语,本短语用来引导条件状语从句。当表示"万一"之意时,在本短语引导的从句中,不用 will 或 would 表将来,而是用一般时或用

"should 十原形动词"来表示。例如:

> *In case* he comes, let me know.
> 万一他来的话,告诉我。

2. 当本短语作"如果"解时,相当于 if。但用 in case 和 if,事情发生的先后顺序是不一样的。试比较:

> You should insure your house *in case* there is a fire.
> 你应在失火之前给房子上保险。
> In the United States, you should telephone 911 if there is a fire.
> 在美国,发生火灾应拨打 911。

从例句中可以看出,in case 表示预防措施,if 则指的是结局或后果。

in case of *prep.* (后接名词或动名词) if there should happen to be; in the event of 如果……,万一……: *In case of* differences and contradictions, both sides should keep cool and be sensible, try to increase communications, reduce mistrust and seek common ground. 如遇分歧和矛盾,我们双方应保持冷静和理智,加强沟通、减少猜疑,求同存异。*In case of* poisoning, immediately give large quantities of salty water in order to induce vomiting. 如遇食物中毒,马上灌以大量的盐水用以催吐。

NOTE 本短语与 in the event of 意义和用法相同,两者可互换使用。

in cash *adv.* & *adj.* with or of the money in the form of coins and notes, rather than checks, credit cards, etc. 以现金方式(的): In this store you have to pay *in cash*; not by credit card. 在本店,您必须以现金支付,而不能使用信用卡。China decided to offer an urgent aid of 1 million US dollars *in cash* for storm-hit Myanmar. 中国决定向缅甸风暴灾区紧急提供 100 万美元现汇援助。

in charge *adv.* & *adj.* having the care or management; in authority or control over someone or something and are responsible for them 负责,照顾,主管: I have checked with the person *in charge* and find that the meeting will take place as planned. 我已经和有关负责人进行了核实,得知会议将按原计划举行。The sick man was taken *in charge* by the doctor. 该病人在医生的监护之下。Jones was *in* complete *charge* while the manager was on holiday. 琼斯在经理度假期间全面主管工作。

NOTE 本短语中的介词和名词之间往往使用一个物主代词来说明"由谁负责",例如:

> She always worried a lot about the young children *in* her *charge*.
> 她总是很担心由她负责的那些小孩儿。

in charge of *prep.* having control over or responsibility for (someone or something) 掌管,照管,负责: In his new role, Mr Black will be *in charge of* sales for the company. 布莱克先生的新角色将是掌管公司的销售业务。The nurse is *in charge of* these children. 这位保育员负责照管这些孩子。These are the telephone and fax numbers of the departments *in charge of* foreign experts affairs. 这些是负责外国专家事务部门的电话和传真号码。Philip is *in charge of* collecting payments. 菲利普负责收费工作。

NOTE 不要将本短语与 in the charge of 混淆。in the charge of 是"在某人的看管(或监督)下"之意。若表达"史密斯医生负责医院的这一病房",我们除了使用本短语外,还可以使用 in the charge of 来

表示,但主客体语序不同。试比较:

> Doctor Smith is *in charge of* this ward of the hospital. (主动)
> This ward of the hospital is *in the charge of* Doctor Smith. (被动)

in chorus *adv.* (of a group of people speaking or singing) all together (指众人)齐声地(说话或唱歌):"Good morning, Miss Smith," the children answered *in chorus*. "早上好,史密斯小姐。"孩子们齐声回答道。The students were singing *in chorus*. 学生们在合唱。

in/into circulation *adj.* (非正式用语) ❶(of a newspaper, book or magazine) being sold (报纸、图书或杂志)发售:The book is no longer *in circulation*. 那本书已不再发售了。❷(of money, etc.) being used by the public (货币等)在流通,在使用:The government has reduced the number of ＄2 notes *in circulation*. 政府已减少了2元钞票的流通数量。A new law was made to reduce the number of guns *in circulation*. 新制定了一项旨在减少流散枪支数量的法令。Some new coins have been put *into circulation*. 又发行了一些新硬币。❸(of news) going around from place to place or from person to person (消息)在传播:The gossip *in circulation* is vicious. 正在传播中的谣言是很恶毒的。❹(常与back连用) participating actively in public or social activities; going around and doing things as usual 积极参加(公共或社会)活动,恢复以往的活动:She's been in hospital but she's back *into circulation*. 虽然她一直住在医院里,可她又积极参加起社会活动了。Tom broke his leg and was out of school for several weeks, but now he is back *in circulation* again. 汤姆摔断了腿,休学了数周,但现在他又上学了。

NOTE 本短语的反义短语是 out of circulation。

in cold blood *adv.* (常用来指杀戮或谋杀,常与动词kill, murder或shoot连用) in a cruel calm way, without showing any emotion 冷酷地,残忍地:The 26-year-old man killed his parents *in cold blood* and was sentenced to 100 years in prison. 这名26岁的男子残忍地杀害了自己的父母,并因此被判处了100年监禁。Thousands of innocent victims were massacred *in cold blood* by the foreign invaders. 成千上万的无辜受害者惨遭外国侵略者的杀戮。Unarmed civilians were shot *in cold blood*. 手无寸铁的平民被残忍地枪杀了。

NOTE 本短语与副词cold-bloodedly意义和用法相同,两者可互换使用。

in common *adv.* ❶ shared with one or more others 与他人共有,共用:Mr Brown and his brother own the store *in common*. 布朗先生和他的弟弟共同拥有此店。This swimming pool is used *in common* by all the children in the neighborhood. 这个游泳池为附近所有儿童所共用。❷(与have连用)(of two or more things) having the same characteristic or feature (指事物)(在特性或特征方面)有共同之处:Hip-hop and rap have much *in common* with blues and rock, but they also have their own characteristics. 街舞音乐和说唱乐与布鲁斯和摇滚有许多共同之处,但它们也各有自己的特点。Physical changes have nothing *in common* with chemical changes. 物理变化与化学变化毫无共同之处。❸(与have连用)(of two or more people) having or sharing the same interests or experiences (指人在兴趣或经历方面)有共同之处: Although they are twins, the two sisters have few interests *in common*. 虽然她们是一对双胞胎,但姊妹俩在兴趣方面几乎没什么共同之处。The only experience we have *in common* is that we've both been to the United States and stayed there for a year. 我们俩唯一的相同经历是,我们都去过美国,并都在那里住了一年。

in company *adv.* ❶(英国英语用法) when other people, especially visitors or guests are present 在众人(尤指客人)面前: You should never swear *in company*. 你决不能在众人面前骂人。You must behave yourself well *in company*. 在众人面前,你得规矩一点。❷(正式用语,常与 with 连用) together (with someone or something else)一起,一致: I went on a tour in company with my friends. 我和朋友们一起去游玩。Plague, *in company* with famine, killed almost half the population. 瘟疫与饥荒几乎毁灭了一半的人口。Germany, *in company* with France, refused to lift the ban. 德国与法国一致拒绝解禁。

in comparison with/to *prep.* (正式用语)(used for talking about the ways in which two things are different) when compared with 与……相比: The driver's injuries were trivial *in comparison with* those suffered by his passengers. 司机受的伤与其乘客的相比就微不足道了。Why are things cheaper *in comparison to* last year? 东西为什么比去年的便宜了呢?

in concert *adv.* (正式用语,常与 with 连用) (of two or more people doing something) together; jointly; in agreement 一齐,一致: They laughed *in concert* at the joke. 他们听了这个笑话都不约而同地大笑起来。The president wanted to act *in concert* with other nations. 总统想要与其他国家一致行动。

in conclusion *adv.* (used in writing or formal speech for showing that the next thing you say will be the last thing you say) finally; lastly; to conclude 最后,在结束时: *In conclusion*, I would like to thank everyone who helped to make this conference a success. 最后,我要感谢有助于使这次大会成功的每一个人。*In conclusion*, it must be said that nuclear energy is presently one of the cheapest forms of energy in the market. 最后,必须说明的是:核能是目前市场上最便宜的能源形式之一。

in condition *adj.* thoroughly healthy or fit 健康状况好的;状态良好的: After the three astronauts exited from the capsule, physicians immediately conducted a physical check-up of them, and found them *in* good *condition*. 三名宇航员走出返回舱后,医生立刻对他们进行了身体检查,结果表明他们的健康状况良好。Walk to work every day and you'll soon be back *in condition*. 每天步行去上班,你的健康状况就会很快恢复。All the systems of China's first lunar probe are *in* good *condition* after its four orbit transfers. 中国首颗月球探测卫星在经过四次变轨后,各系统状态良好。

NOTE 1. 本短语中的名词 condition 前可加形容词修饰,但不能加不定冠词。也不可加定冠词。

2. 本短语的比较级形式是 more in condition,最高级形式是 most in

condition。

3. 本短语的同义短语是 in shape；反义短语是 out of condition 和 out of shape。此外，还可以使用 in no condition 和 in bad shape 来表达与 in condition 相反的意义。例如：

> He was certainly *in no condition* to be driving a car.
> 他的身体状况不好，肯定不能驾车。
> He's been working too hard and he's *in* pretty *bad shape*.
> 他一直工作太累，以致他现在的身体状况很不好。

I

in confidence *adv.* as a secret 作为秘密："I'm telling you this *in confidence*," she whispered. 她小声说："我告诉你的这事要保密。" Any information given during the interview will be treated *in* the strictest *confidence*. 此次采访期间的任何消息都将绝对保密。

NOTE 不要将本短语与 with confidence 混淆。with confidence 意为"有信心地"。本短语中的名词 confidence 意为"秘密"，而不是"信心"。

in connection with *prep.* (正式用语) in relation with or relating to (something) 与(某事)有关联，关于：Police want to talk to him *in connection with* his wife's disappearance. 警察想就他妻子失踪一事与他谈话。

in consequence *adv.* (正式用语，其前常用连词 and) (used for saying that one thing is the result of another) as a result; therefore; so 结果，因此：Tom got up late, and *in consequence* he missed the school bus. 汤姆起床晚了，结果没赶上校车。You studied hard, and *in consequence* you passed the English test. 你学习努力了，因此你通过了英语考试。She has lived in France, and *in consequence* speaks French fluently. 她一直住在法国，因此她法语讲得很流利。

NOTE 本短语的同义短语是 as a consequence 和 as a result。三者之中，as a result 最为常用。

in consequence of *prep.* (正式用语，常用于句首) as a result of; because of 由于……的结果，因为：*In consequence of* your laziness and rudeness, I have to kick you out. 由于你的懒惰和粗鲁，我不得不辞退你。The child was born deformed *in consequence of* an injury of its mother. 由于母亲受过伤，孩子生下来有些畸形。

NOTE 本短语的同义短语是 as a result of 和 because of。三者之中，because of 最为常用。

in consideration of *prep.* (正式用语) ❶ because of; taking into account 因为，考虑到：They didn't give him a lot of work *in consideration of* his poor health. 因为他的身体不好，所以他们没给他许多工作。*In consideration of* what you say, I'll put off my departure till tomorrow. 考虑到你所说的这些话，我将把出发的时间推迟到明天。❷ in return for (something) or as a payment for (something) 作为对……的报酬：I gave him a small payment *in consideration of* his service. 我给了他一点儿报酬以酬谢他的服务。The lady gave the boy tickets to the ballgame *in consideration of* his helpfulness. 那位太太给了那男孩几张球赛入场券以酬谢他的帮助。

NOTE **1.** 当本短语作"因为，考虑到"解时，同义短语是 in view of 和 on account of。
2. 当本短语作"作为对……的酬报"解时，另外一种表达形式是 in consideration for。

in contact with *prep.* ❶ (of people) in communication with (someone), either by seeing, talking or writing 与(某人)联系,与(某人)接触: Do you keep *in contact with* your old school friends? 你同老校友们还保持联系吗? I asked her if she could put me *in contact with* a good piano teacher. 我问她能否让我和一位好的钢琴教师接触上。❷ (of people or things) touching with (each other) (指人或物体)与……相互接触: The number of people who were *in* close *contact with* the A/H1N1 flu patient has reached 30. 与这位甲型 H1N1 流感患者密切接触过的人员数字已达 30 人。Everyone comes *in contact with* metal through their many everyday uses. 每个人都在诸多的日用品中接触到金属。

NOTE 1. 当本短语作"与(某人)联系,和(某人)接触"解时,同义短语是 in touch with。

2. 本短语的反义短语是 out of contact with 和 lose contact with。

in contrast to/with *prep.* ❶ in comparison with (someone or something) 与……相比: "*In contrast to* Mr. Smith, he had never formally apologized for his crimes committed during the Second World War." 与史密斯先生相比,他从来没有为他在二战期间所犯下的罪行正式道歉过 *In contrast with* electrons, protons appear very large. 与电子相比,质子就显得很大了。❷ different from or contrary to (someone or something) 与……不同,与……相反: *In contrast to* his predecessor, George Bush, President Obama was willing to engage in dialogue with Tehran. 与其前任乔治·布什不同,奥巴马总统愿意同德黑兰进行对话。*In contrast with* your belief that we shall fail, I know we shall succeed. 你认为我们会失败;与此相反,我却知道我们会成功。

in course of *prep.* (正式用语) going through a particular process 在……的过程中: The world's largest ship is *in course of* construction. 世界上最大的轮船正在建造的过程中。The new textbook is *in course of* preparation. 新教科书正在准备之中。

NOTE 不要将本短语与 in the course of 混淆,两者的意义和用法不同。见 in/during/over the course of。

I

in danger *adv.* & *adj.* in a situation in which harm, death, damage, or destruction is possible 处于危险之中: You must leave immediately. You're *in* great *danger* here. 你必须马上离开这里。你在这儿十分危险。We should always be ready to help those *in danger*. 我们应随时准备帮助那些身处险境的人们。Everyone finds himself *in danger*. 人人自危。

NOTE 1. 本短语的否定形式是 in no danger。例如:

> Make sure that the President is *in no danger* at any time.
> 要保证总统在任何时候都不会出危险。

2. 本短语的同义短语是 at risk 和 at stake;反义短语是 out of danger。

in danger of *prep.* likely to incur risks, etc. from 有……的危险: Although these chemical weapons were sealed off, they were *in danger of* leakage because of eroded containers. 虽然这些化学武器已被封存,但是由于容器腐蚀仍有泄露的危险。She is *in* great *danger of* losing her job. 她大有失去这份工作的危险。

in debt *adj.* ❶(常与 to 连用)the state in which you owe money to other people 负债:I don't like being *in debt* to anyone. 我不喜欢欠任何人的债。Now the old man is *in debt* for over 5,000 dollars. 现在这位老人负债5 000多美元。Right now he is *in debt* to me for more than 1,500 dollars. 现在他还欠我1500 多美元。He and Republican leaders argued that Iraq was already too deeply *in debt* to borrow more money. 他和一些共和党的领导人争辩说,伊拉克已经负债太多,难以借到更多的钱了。❷(正式用语,常与 to 连用) under an obligation to be grateful to someone because they have done something for you, etc. 感激(某人),欠(某人)的情: I'll always be *in debt* to you for your help. 我对你的帮助永远感激不尽。I know I shall feel for ever *in* her *debt*. 我知道我永远会感到欠她的情。

NOTE 1. 本短语中的 debt 是不可数名词,所以不能用其复数形式。

2. 当要表示"欠某人的债或情"时,一般用 in debt to someone 的形式;当要表示"还清债或情"时,则用 out of debt。

in defense of *prep.* in the process of defending or supporting someone or something that is being attacked or criticized 保卫,辩护:It's a monument of enormous significance recording the history of struggle waged by China's sons and daughters *in defense of* national unification and territorial integrity. 这是一座记载中华儿女维护国家统一、领土完整的奋斗历史的丰碑。The minister has been fierce *in defense of* the present system. 这位部长一直强烈地为现有体制辩护。

in demand *adj.* (of someone or something) very popular and wanted by a lot of people (指人)受欢迎的,(指物)有需求的,销路好的:He was much *in demand* as a lecture in the US, as well as at universities all over Europe. 作为一名讲演者,他在美国以及全欧的大学中都很受欢迎。Oil is *in* great *demand* these days. 现在,石油的需求量巨大。Our software is *in demand* all over the world. 我们的软件在全球销路都很好。

NOTE 本短语的比较级形式是 more in demand,最高级形式是 most in demand。

in depth Ⅰ *adj.* ❶ having a specified depth 有……深:In winter the snow there in the north is three feet *in depth*. 在冬季,北方的雪有 3 英尺深。The rail tracks were seriously damaged in the train explosion, which produced two huge pits 8 to 10 meters *in depth*. 铁轨在火车爆炸中严重损坏,爆炸造成了两个深 8 米至 10 米的大坑。❷comprehensive; thorough; detailed 全面的,彻底的,详尽的:The following is an *in depth* analysis of income and taxes in the United States over the past 20 years. 如下是对过去 20 年来美国收入与税收的全面分析。

Ⅱ *adv.* in a very detailed way and giving a lot of information; thoroughly; deeply; fully or completely 详尽地,彻底地,深入地,全面地: We discussed the issue *in* some *depth*. 我们比较详细地讨论了那个问题。

NOTE 1. 本短语可转化为复合词 in-depth,意为"全面的,详尽的,彻底的,深入的"。

2. 本短语的比较级形式是 more in depth,最高级形式是 most in depth。

in (one's) despair *adv.* in a situation

that is so bad that nothing you can do will change it; without hope 在恶劣情况下;绝望地: *In* (*his*) *despair* he phoned the embassy. 绝望之中,他给大使馆打了电话。She cried loudly *in despair*. 她绝望地放声大哭。*In despair* she jumped from the top of the burning building to the street below. 绝望之中,她从着火的楼房顶部朝下面的街道上跳了下去。

NOTE 本短语的另外一种表达形式是 in desperation。

in despite of ⇨ **despite of**

in detail *adv.* including many facts or aspects of a situation 详细地:We suggested that his project be discussed *in* all *detail*. 我们建议全面地讨论他的计划。

NOTE 虽然本短语没有比较级形式,但可以用表示程度的修饰词语修饰短语中的名词 detail,例如:in more/greater/greatest detail。

in disfavor of ⇨ **in favor of**

in disguise *adv.* & *adj.* in changed fashion of dress and personal appearance in order to conceal your identity; looking like something else 化装,伪装,假扮:The movie star often went out *in disguise* to avoid journalists and her fans. 这位影星为了避开记者和她的影迷们经常化装出门。I didn't recognize him; he was *in disguise*. 我没认出他来,他化装了。

in doubt *adj.* undecided; being in the state of uncertainty 未确定的,怀疑的:The result of the election is still *in doubt*. 选举结果尚未见分晓。I am *in doubt* as to what to do. 要做什么,我无法确定。The life of the present cabinet hangs *in doubt*. 现内阁的前程未卜。When *in doubt* about the meaning of a word, consult a dictionary. 如果拿不准某一单词的意义,就查一查词典。

NOTE 当本短语的使用形式为 be in doubt 时,主语是"人"和"物"的含义不同。前者有主动的意味,而后者则有被动的意味。试比较:

> I am *in doubt* about her age.
> 我怀疑她的年龄。(主动)
> Her age is *in doubt*.
> 她的年龄令人怀疑。(被动)

in due course (**of time**) *adv.* (正式用语,常用于表示将来时的句子中)at the right time later, and not before 在稍后的适当时候:You will receive notification of the examination results *in due course*. 你会在适当的时候收到考试成绩通知书。We will announce the results of our investigation *in due course of time*. 我们将适时公布调查的结果。*In due course*, we'll discuss the details of this arrangement. 我们将稍后讨论这项安排的细节。

NOTE 本短语的另外一种表达形式是 in due time。

in earnest Ⅰ *adj.* serious and meaning what you say 认真的,郑重的:When I said I wanted to help you, I was *in earnest*. 我说过我要帮助你,我是认真的。Are you *in earnest* about resigning? 你当真要辞职? I'm sure he was *in earnest* when he said he wanted to marry her. 我确信,他说要娶她为妻是郑重其事的。

Ⅱ *adv.* in a serious manner 认真地,郑重地:She was crying *in earnest* now. 这回她是真的哭了。"If Palestine asks China for further assistance in the future, we will consider *in* real *earnest*," said the Chinese official. 这位中国官员表示:"今后,如果巴勒斯坦方面向中国提出进一

步援助的要求,我们将十分认真地给予考虑。”

NOTE 当本短语用作形容词性短语时,常以 in dead earnest 的形式使用。其中的 dead 用于加重语气。例如:

> I'm in dead earnest about selling my house.
> 我要卖掉我的房子,我绝对是认真的。

in effect Ⅰ *adv.* (used for giving a summary of what you think the situation really is) in fact; in reality; in practice; effectively 事实上,实际上:They have no formal contract, but he is, *in effect*, her sales manager. 他们没有正式合同,但事实上他是她的销售部经理。Their response was *in effect* a refusal. 他们的答复实际上是拒绝了。*In effect*, this means we'll all have to work longer hours for the same pay. 这实际上意味着我们都得加班加点地干活但还不加工钱。

Ⅱ *adj.* (of a law or rule) in or into operation; active (法规等)实施,有效:The new laws will be *in effect* from next Monday on. 一些新的法律将从下星期一起开始实施。There's still a flood warning system *in effect* across much of southwestern Ohio. 在俄亥俄州西南的大部分地区,水灾警报系统仍然有效。

NOTE 当本短语作“(法规等)实施,有效”解时,同义短语是 in force。

in error *adv.* (正式用语) by mistake, especially in your judgment; not deliberately (尤指因判断失误而)错误地: It was said that the passenger plane was shot down *in error* by a NATO missile. 据说,是北约的一枚导弹误将那架客机击落。You will be *in error* if you assume that there is only one way to solve this mathematical equation. 假如你认为解这个数学方程只有一种方法,那就错了。

NOTE 本短语与 by mistake 在用法上的区别是:by mistake 只在句中作状语,而本短语不仅可用作状语,还可用作表语。

in essence *adv.* (正式用语) in one's nature; essentially 本质上,实质上: *In essence*, the problem is a simple one. 从本质上看,这个问题是很简单的。The two things are the same in outward form but different *in essence*. 那两样东西在外表上相同,但在本质上不同。The two arguments are *in essence* the same. 这两个论点实质上相同。

in excess of *prep.* (正式用语,后接表示数量的词或数目)more than (a particular amount or number) 多于,超出: The deficit had grown to a number *in excess of* a hundred million dollars. 赤字已增至多于 1 亿美元。Investigators said that the passenger train was traveling at 131 kilometers per hour before the accident, far *in excess of* the speed limit of 80 km/h. 调查人员指出,该旅客列车在出事前的运行速度是 131 公里每小时,这大大超过 80 公里每小时的速度限制。Luggage *in excess of* 40kg will be charged extra. 超过 40 公斤的行李要额外收费。

in exchange for *prep.* (相同类型或价值相等之物) exchanging for (something else of a similar type or equal value)交换,互换: What would you give me *in exchange for* my recorder? 我给你我的录音机,那你给我什么作为交换呢? They said they were willing to freeze its nuclear reactors *in exchange for* the US compensation for the move. 他们表示愿

以冻结其核反应堆来换取美国因此行动而给予的补偿。

NOTE 本短语也常用来表示人与人的"交换"。例如:

The government of Pakistan released 25 militants today *in exchange for* 213 soldiers captured by militants in August.
巴基斯坦政府今天释放了 25 名武装分子,以交换于 8 月份被武装分子俘虏的 213 名士兵。

in (actual) fact *adv.* (used for saying what is really true, when this is surprising or different from what people think) actually or really 事实上,实际上:I did well in school. *In fact*, in a number of courses I received the highest exam scores in the class. 我在学校表现得不错。事实上,有好几门功课我的考分都居全班第一。But *in actual fact*, sportsmen have been using drugs to cheat their way to victory since the Olympic Games first began. 但事实上,从奥运会一开始,就有运动员使用药物去骗取胜利。

NOTE 1. 本短语的另外一种表达形式是 in point of fact。

2. 本短语与 as a matter of fact, in effect, in practice, in reality, in truth 都是副词性短语,都表示"事实上"之意。其中,in fact 和 as a matter of fact 最为常用。

in fashion *adj.* (of something such as a style of dress or an activity) being popular and approved of at a particular time 流行,时髦,时兴:This kind of dress is quite *in fashion* . 这种服装现在很流行。That sort of house is back *in fashion*. 那种房子的样式又流行起来了。These songs are *in fashion* in both the United States and Britain. 这些歌曲在美国和英国都很流行。

NOTE 本短语的同义短语是 in style 和 in vogue;反义短语是 out of date, out of fashion 和 out of style。

in favor of *prep.* ❶ (of people) supporting (an idea, proposal, etc. that you believe is right)支持,赞成:Those *in favor of* the motion, please raise your hands now. 支持这项动议的现在请举手。He voted *in favor of* the Iraq war and several months later said the Iraq war as the"wrong war in the wrong place at the wrong time". 他投票支持对伊开战,可几个月后又转而说伊拉克战争是"在错误的地点、错误的时间发动的一场错误的战争"。❷(of a thing or action) to the advantage of (someone or something) (某一事物或行动)有利于,有益于:The verdict of the jury was *in favor of* the accused. 陪审团的判决有利于被告。The pressure of unemployment demands a change of the current business registry system *in favor of* young people who are going to start their own business, experts say. 专家们表示,失业的压力要求对现行的企业登记制度进行改革,以有益于创业的年轻人。❸(of a cheque) payable to (支票)支付给:This check is made out in favor of the Animal Protection Society. 这张支票是开付给动物保护协会的。

NOTE 1. 当本短语作"支持,赞成"解时,反义短语是 in disfavor of。

2. 本短语的另外一种表达方式是 in one's favor。

in flames *adj.* burning 在燃烧的,在着火的:The whole building was soon *in flames*. 整个楼房很快就都烧了起来。A hotel employee in Mosul said he saw one low-flying Black Hawk helicopter *in flames* before it hit the other. 一名在摩苏尔酒店工作的雇员说，他看到一架低空飞行的黑鹰直升机着火后撞上了另一架飞机。

NOTE 本短语中的名词 flame 必须用复数形式。

in force Ⅰ *adj.* (of a law, rule, order, etc.) being applied and people must obey it(法律、法规、命令等)在实施中：After Hong Kong returned to the motherland, the overwhelming majority of its laws previously *in force* have been maintained. 香港回归祖国后，其以前实施的法律绝大多数都予以了保留。This traffic regulation has been *in force* for many years. 这部交通法规已实施多年。

Ⅱ *adv.* in large numbers; on a large scale 大批地，大规模地：Thousands of spectators came *in force* to see the Olympic torch pass through San Francisco. 成千上万的观众赶去观看奥运火炬通过旧金山。The enemy attacked *in force*. 敌军发起了大规模的进攻。

NOTE 当本短语作"(法律、法规、命令等)在实施中"解时，同义短语是 in effect。

in front of *prep.* ❶close to the front part of (something, someone or a group)在……的前面：Overjoyed Chinese cheered and applauded *in front of* their TVs at home as the long-anticipated Olympic Games opened in Beijing on Friday night. 当期盼已久的奥运会于星期五晚上在北京开幕时，极度欢喜的中国人在他们家里的电视机前欢呼喝彩。I couldn't see anything because of the big man *in front of* me. He blocked my view completely. 因为在我前面有一个高大男人，所以我什么都看不见。他完全挡住了我的视线。❷in the presence of (someone)当着(某人)的面：Let's not fight *in front of* the children. 咱们别当着孩子们的面打架。The mere mention of his cousin's name was like waving a red flag *in front of* him. 只要当着他的面一提起他表兄的名字，他就生气。

NOTE 1. 当本短语作"在……的前面"解时，多用于表示"物"的名词之前，而 before 或 facing 则常用在表示"人"的名词之前。例如：

> I stood there before/facing the teacher, not knowing what to say.
> 我站在那里，面对着老师，不知道说什么才好。

2. 本短语与 in the front of 所表达的意义有所不同。本短语表示"在……的前面"，相当于介词 before；而 in the front of 则表示"在……的前面那一部分"。例如：

> She sat in the front of the bus.
> 她坐在公共汽车的前排座位。

in full *adv.* completely, including the whole of something 完整地，全面地，全部：*The Regulations on Disciplinary Penalties* will be published *in full* on Wednesday.《纪律处分条例》将于星期三全文发表。Fines must be paid *in full* within 30 days. 罚金必须在 30 日内全部交齐。

in full swing *adj.* (常用作表语)(of something) active; at the most effective of highest level of operation or activity 活跃的，在全力进行中的：The city's free market is *in full swing*. 该市的自由市场十分活跃。The evening party was *in full swing* when the police burst in. 晚会

正进行得热闹的时候，警察闯了进来。We arrived an hour late and found the work already *in full swing*. 我们迟到了一个小时，发现工作已经全面展开。

in (the) future *adv.* (用于句首或句尾) from the present time continuing forwards in time 将来，未来，今后：*In the future* people may live on the moon. 将来人们可能会住在月球上。The two leaders said in London that the joint declaration will play an important role in boosting Sino-British ties *in the future*. 两国领导人在伦敦表示，联合声明将对增进未来的中英关系起重要作用。The new social security plan will be released "*in the* near *future*". 新的社保方案不久就将公布于众。Could you be more careful *in future*? 你以后就不能多注意点吗？

NOTE **1.** in future 主要用于英国英语中，in the future 主要用于美国英语中。

2. in future 常用于警告语，且置于句首。例如：

> In future, make sure you get there on time!
> 今后，你一定要准时到那儿！
> In future I'm going to check every single piece of work that you do!
> 以后，你所做的每件工作我都要检查！

in general Ⅰ *adv.* on the whole, without giving details; in most situations 总体来说，一般说来，大体上：*In general*, women live five to ten years longer than men. 总体来说，女性的寿命比男性长 5 至 10 年。The speaker talked about sports *in general* and about football in particular. 讲演者总体地谈了谈体育运动，接着详细地讲了足球。Those who make their dress a principal part of themselves, will, *in general*, become of no more value than their dress. 一般说来，那些只注意衣着打扮的人就不会比他们的衣服多值几文钱。

Ⅱ *adj.* (用于复数名词之后，作后置定语) most of (the people or things in a particular group) 大多数(人或物)：Boys *in general* like sports more than girls do. 大部分男孩子比女孩子喜欢体育运动。Ms Zhang, the first Chinese to take up a WTO post, enjoys a good reputation among the Asian international law circles *in general*. 张女士是在世界贸易组织中任职的第一位中国人，她在亚洲国际法学界享有盛名。I like sports *in general*, and especially football. 大多数体育运动我都喜欢，尤其是足球。

NOTE **1.** 当本短语用作副词性短语时，另外一种表达形式是 as a general rule。例如：

> *As a general rule*, we don't allow children in the bar.
> 一般来说，我们不允许孩童泡吧。

2. 当本短语用作形容词性短语时，同义短语是 as a whole 和 at large。

in half *adv.* in (to) two (approximately) equal parts 成两半：Peel the potatoes and cut them *in half*. 先把这些土豆的皮削掉，然后把它们切成两半。I once saw a man tear a telephone directory *in half*. 我有一次看见一个人把电话簿撕成了两半。

in hand Ⅰ *adj.* ❶(常用于英国英语中) (of time) able to be used; (of something) in one's possession (指时间)可支配的，手头有(某物)：Don't worry; we've still got two days *in hand* before the work is due. 不要担心，离这件工作规定完成的日期还有两天时间呢。I still have some cash *in hand*. 我手头还有些现金。A bird

I

in hand is worth two in the bush.（谚语）一鸟在手胜于两鸟在林。❷(of a job, problem, etc.) being dealt with; being done, etc.（指问题、工作等）正在处理中，正在做的：The investigation is now *in hand*, but not finished. 这项调查现正在进行之中，尚未完成。They should finish the work they have *in hand* as soon as possible. 他们应该尽快完成正在做的工作。

Ⅱ *adv.* (of a particular situation) under control（指局势）在控制中，在掌握中：The police now have the situation well *in hand*, and no further outbreaks are expected. 警方现已完全控制了局势，不会再有暴乱发生。

NOTE 1. 当本短语作"(指局势)在控制中，在掌握中"解时，同义短语是 under control；反义短语是 out of hand 和 out of control。

2. 不要将本短语与 at hand 和 on hand 混淆，三者意义各不相同。

in harmony with *prep.* ❶in a situation in which people live and work well with (other people or things around them)与……和谐共存：These tribes are living *in* perfect *harmony with* nature. 这些部落与大自然十分和谐地共存着。The people living in the village were organized to transform the environment and created a rural society which was *in harmony with* nature. 村民们组织起来，改造环境，创造了一个人与自然和谐相处的乡村社会。❷in agreement with (someone or something)与……一致：What you have said is not *in harmony with* Mark. 你所说的与马克说的不一致。Her ideas are no longer *in harmony with mine*. 她的想法不再与我的一致了。

NOTE 当本短语作"与……一致"解时，同义短语是 in accord with, in accordance with, in agreement with, in keeping with, in line with 和 in step with。

in haste *adv.* quickly or hurriedly, without careful planning or thought 匆忙地，不经仔细考虑地，草率地：He packed his bags *in haste* when he heard the police were looking for him. 当听说警察正在搜寻他时，他便匆匆忙忙地收拾起行装。*In* her *haste*, she forgot to bring her umbrella. 匆忙之中，她忘记了带伞。Marry *in haste*, and repent at leisure.（谚语）草率结婚，后悔莫及。It is very important that decisions should not be made *in haste*. 不应草率作出决定，这一点是很重要的。

in honor of *prep.* ❶in order to show respect and admiration for (someone)为了对（某人）表示敬意：We celebrate Mother's Day *in honor of* our mothers. 我们庆祝母亲节是为了对母亲们表示敬意。The Chinese President hosted a grand banquet at the Great Hall of People *in honor of* foreign leaders who are in Beijing to attend the Olympic opening ceremony. 中国国家主席在人民大会堂举行了盛大宴会，款待在北京出席奥运会开幕式的外国领导人。❷in memory of (someone or something)为了纪念……：The Freedom Tower is being built at the World Trade Center site *in honor of* the people who lost their lives in the terrorist attack on the twin towers on September 11, 2001. "自由之塔"正在世贸中心原址兴建，以纪念 2001 年 9 月 11 日在世贸中心双子塔遭受恐怖袭击中丧生的遇难者。❸in celebration of (a particular event)为了庆贺……：The special ceremony was held *in honor of* Queen Elizabeth's 80th birthday. 这一特殊仪式是为了庆贺伊丽莎白女王 80 岁生日而举行的。

NOTE 本短语的另外一种表达形式是 in one's honor。例如:

> The former President will attend an outdoor concert *in his honor* in the Center of Arts.
> 这位前总统将出席在艺术中心为他举办的户外音乐会。

in (and of) itself *adv.* with respect to its inherent nature; without considering the rest 就其本质而言,就其本身而论: The problem is unimportant *in itself*, but its long-term effects could be very serious. 这个问题就其本质而言并不重要,但其长远影响可能会十分严重。*In and of itself* the plan might be practical, but I doubt that it will be approved. 这项计划本身可能很实用,但未必能获得批准。

in keeping with *prep.* in harmony or agreement with (something else) 符合……,与……一致: Whatever we do should be *in keeping with* the objective law. 我们所做的都要符合客观规律。Don't trust him, his acts are not *in keeping with* his promises. 别相信他;他的行动与其诺言总是两码事。We should deepen regional cooperation *in keeping with* such principles as mutual benefit, and gradual progress. 我们应该遵循互利和渐进的原则深化区域合作。

NOTE 本短语的同义短语是 in accord with, in accordance with, in agreement with, in harmony with, in line with 和 in step with;反义短语是 out of keeping with 和 out of step with。

in less than no time ⇨ **in no time (at all)**

in (the) light of *prep.* ❶ because of; taking into account; considering 由于,鉴于,考虑到: *In (the) light of* the muddy field, the football team wore their old uniforms. 由于场地泥泞,足球队员们都穿上了旧球衣。*In (the) light of* all these facts, what he did was completely right. 鉴于所有这些事实,他的所作所为是完全正确的。I'm sure that you can sell more this year *in (the) light of* the market conditions at your end. 考虑到你们地区的市场情况,我方确信今年可以销得更多。❷according to 根据,依照: He acted *in (the) light of* the regulations. 他按规章办事。He takes medicine and rest *in (the) light of* the doctor's advice. 他遵照医生的意见服药和休息。❸ from the standpoint of 从……的观点: He views progress *in (the) light of* scientific achievement. 他从科学成就的角度来看待进步。

NOTE in the light of 主要用于英国英语中, in light of 主要用于英国美语中。

in limited supply ⇨ **in short supply**

in line *adv.* (of the people) in a row, side by side or one behind the other (指人)排成一队: I had to stand *in line* for seven hours for the two tickets. 为买这两张门票,我不得不排了 7 个小时的队。Eager iPhone buyers are trying to break a world record for most time spent waiting *in line* to buy something. 争购苹果公司手机的人们试图打破排队购物等候时间最长的世界纪录。

NOTE 1. 本短语中的介词也可被 on 替换。例如:

> The recruits are waiting *on line* to be examined.
> 新兵们正排成一队接受体检。

但 on line 只用于美国英语中，尤其用在纽约及美国东北部地区。

2. 本短语的同义短语是 in a row。

in line for *prep.* (用作表语) about to or likely to obtain (something, especially something good) 即将得到，可能得到：Tom has been doing very well; he is *in line for* a promotion soon. 汤姆一直干得很不错，因此他很快就会得到提升。Mr Smith is *in line for* the presidency of the association next month. 史密斯先生下个月有望成为该协会主席。

in line with *prep.* ❶ straight or level compared with 和……在一条直线上：The North Star is almost exactly *in line with* the North Pole. 北极星几乎恰好与北极成一条直线。The wheel at the back isn't *in line with* the one at the front. 后轮和前轮没有保持在一条直线上。❷ in accordance with; in agreement or harmony with 按照，根据；与……一致，符合……：*In line with* international law and practice, any part of one nation has no legal right to secede from that nation through self-determination or referendum. 按照国际法律与惯例，一个国家的任何一部分都无权通过自决或公决从这个国家分离出去。The company's profits were *in line with* what was expected. 公司的利润与所预期的相一致。It should be stressed that, any measures in this regard should be *in line with* the national conditions. 应该强调的是，任何这方面的措施都应符合国情。

NOTE 当本短语作"与……一致，符合……"解时，同义短语是 in accord with, in accordance with, in agreement with, in harmony with 和 in step with。

in love with *prep.* ❶ feeling love and desire for (someone) 和(某人)恋爱；爱上了(某人)：She's madly *in love with* the black football player she met in Munich during the World Cup in Germany. 她狂恋着她在德国世界杯期间在慕尼黑相识的那名黑人球员。They met and fell *in love with* each other at college. 他们在大学相识并相爱。❷ very fond of (something) 热爱，迷恋于：He fell *in love with* the house. 他喜欢上了这所房子。He never married because he is *in love with* his work. 他从未结过婚，因为他太迷恋于自己的工作了。

NOTE 1. 本短语只表示状态。若表示动作，则用 fall in love with。见 fall in love with 条目。

2. 如果无需说明客体，本短语只用 in love 就可以。例如：

> They were madly *in love* for about half a year.
> 他们俩狂恋了大约半年。

in memory of *prep.* in honour of (someone who has died), so that people will remember him or her 纪念(某人)：Chinese top leaders attended a grand concert Friday evening *in memory of* Chairman Mao Zedong. 中国高层领导人星期五晚上出席了纪念毛泽东主席的大型音乐会。On May 12, 2018 a ceremony marking the ten-year anniversary of Wenchuan earthquake was held in the town of Yingxiu *in memory of* the earthquake victims. 2018 年 5 月 12 日，在映秀镇举行了纪念汶川地震十周年的仪式，以缅怀地震中的死难者。

in motion *adj.* moving or working 在运

动,在运转:Matter is *in* constant *motion* and in constant change. 物质处于不断运动和不断变化中。When we talk about electric current, we refer to electrons *in motion*. 当我们谈论电流时,我们指的是运动中的电子。When the bus is still *in motion*, it is dangerous to try to get off. 公共汽车还在运行时就试图下车,这是很危险的。They put the plan *in motion*. 他们启动了该计划。

in need *adj.* (正式用语,常用作后置定语和表语)not having enough food, money, clothing, or other things that are necessary for life 贫穷的,困难的: We're collecting money to help those families (most)*in need*. 我们正在为那些(最)困难的家庭搞募捐。A friend *in need* is a friend indeed. 患难与共的朋友才是真正的朋友。Remember that when both of you were *in need*, I was the one who loaned you the money. 记住,当你们两个困难的时候,是我借给了你们钱。

in need of *prep.* (常用作表语和后置定语)needing (especially something)需要: The educational system of our country is *in* urgent *need of* reform. 我国的教育体制亟须改革。He makes sure that his wife is *in need of* nothing. 他确保他的妻子应有尽有。China's IT and telecommunications sectors, high-tech and financial industries are particularly *in need of* foreign talents, the official said. 这位官员表示,中国的信息技术和电信部门、高科技和金融业尤其需要外来人才。Prices start at $20,000 for a small house *in need of* some repair. 一所需要做些修缮的小房子起价是2万美元。

in next to no time ⇨ **in no time (at all)**

in no case *adv.* under no circumstances; by no means; never 在任何情况下都不,决不: *In no case* should we prevent the students from exploring new ideas. 在任何情况下,我们都不应阻止学生对新思想的探索。I will *in no case* reveal your secret. 我决不会泄露你的秘密。

NOTE 当本短语用于句首时,句中的主谓结构一定要构成倒装。但是,当本短语置于句中较后的部分时,句中的主谓结构则不倒装。与本短语意义相近,用法相同的短语包括 at no time, by no means, in no way, in/under no circumstances,等等。

in no circumstances ⇨ **under no circumstances**

in no condition ⇨ **in condition**

in no mood *adj.* (后常接 for,亦可接用动词不定式)not prepared; not feeling like doing something at all 没有准备好的,没有情绪的: The management is *in no mood* for compromise over this issue. 资方无意在这个问题上妥协。Dad was *in no mood* for joking. 爸爸没有情绪开玩笑。She says she feels bad and is *in no mood* for doing anything. 她说她心情不好,没有情绪做任何事情。I am *in no mood* to listen to pop music now. 我现在没有情绪听流行音乐。

NOTE **1.** 本短语的另外一种表达形式是 not in the mood。

2. 与本短语相关的表达方式有:in a good mood (情绪好), in a bad mood(情绪不好), in a bit of mood (心情有点儿不好)。

3. 本短语的反义短语是 in the mood。

in no time (at all) *adv.* in a very short time; very quickly; before long; immediately 很快,立即,马上:We called the fire-brigade, which arrived *in no time* at all. 我们给消防队打了电话，他们很快就赶到了。He helped her when she needed someone, and *in no time* they fell in love. 他在她需要人帮助时帮助了她，并且他们很快就相爱了。With a pair of scissors, she can turn out a beautiful design *in no time*. 她用一把剪刀能立即剪出一个美丽的图形来。

NOTE 1. 本短语与 at no time 的区别是：at no time 表示否定意义，用于句首时，句中的主谓结构一定要构成倒装。例如：

> At no time was the President aware of what was happening.
> 总统一直未察觉到发生了什么事。

而本短语即使用于句首时，句中的主谓结构也不可倒装(见第二个例句)。

2. 本短语另外的表达形式是 in less than no time 和 in next to no time。

in no way *adv.* (used for emphasizing that something is not true or possible) by no means; in no respect; not at all 决不，一点也不：*In no way* should the Labor Party be held responsible for the problem. 工党决不应该对此问题承担责任。The British Prime Minister said that the discussions he is having with other European countries would *in no way* undermine NATO. 英国首相称，他与其他欧洲国家开展的一些讨论绝无损于北约组织。His words are *in no way* true. 他的话没有一句是真的。

NOTE 1. 当本短语用于句首时，句中的主谓结构一定要构成倒装。例如：

> *In no way* will I work for this company any more.
> 我决不会再为这家公司工作了。

但是，当本短语置于句中较后的部分时，句中的主谓结构则不倒装。

2. 本短语与 by no means, in no way, not at all, not in the least 等意义相同，有时可以互换使用。

in number *adv.* in sum total; altogether; forming a group of (a certain number of people, things, etc.) 总计，总共，在数目上：Although small *in number*, our troops defeated the enemy. 虽然敌众我寡，我军却打败了敌人。The company was more than 500 *in number*. 该公司总共有 500 多人。

NOTE 本短语中的名词 number 要用单数形式。如用其复数形式，则构成 in numbers，意为"分册地出版"。例如：

> This book will be published *in numbers*.
> 这本书将分册出版。

in numbers 与形容词 great, large, considerable 等连用时，则表示"大量的，许多的"。例如：

> People came from all the directions *in large numbers*.
> 人们从四面八方涌来。

in office ⇨ in power

in one's absence ⇨ in the absence of

in one's behalf ⇨ on behalf of

in one's eyes ⇨ in someone's eyes

in one's favor *adj.* &*adv.* to one's benefit or advantage or giving one an advantage 对某人有利：The judgment given was *in your favor*. 作出的判决对你有利。Prices are *in buyers' favor*. 价格对买主有利。This candidate has a lot *in her favor*, especially her experience of teaching. 这位候选人有很多优势，尤其是她的教学经验。The delay might actually work *in our favor*. 这种延误实际上对我们有利。

NOTE 本短语的另外一种表达方式是 in

favor of。

in one's hands *adj.* being taken care of or controlled by someone 在某人的掌控中：Though the President has given up his army post, when the emergency rule will be lifted remains *in his hands*. 虽然总统已辞去了军职，但紧急状态法何时解除仍掌控在他的手中。At that time, the city was *in enemy's hands*. 当时，该城还在敌人的手中。Let's put this part of the project *in Richard's hands*. 咱们把项目的这一部分就交给理查德搞吧。

NOTE 1. 本短语中的名词 hand 必须用复数形式。

2. 本短语的另外一种表达形式是 in the hands of。

in one's heart of hearts *adv.* in one's most secret and true feelings; in reality 在内心深处，实际上：I said I love her, but *in my heart of hearts* I knew it wasn't true. 我说过我爱她，但在内心深处我知道那并不是真的。She knew *in her heart of hearts* that it was a lie from the very beginning. 实际上，她一开始就知道那是谎话。

in one's honor ⇨ in honor of

in one's (own) interest(s) ⇨ in the interest(s) of

in one's mind's eye *adv.* in one's memory or imagination 在某人的记忆中，在某人的想象中：*In his mind's eye* he saw again the house he had lived in when he was a child. 在他的记忆中，他又看到了他小时候住过的房子。*In our mind's eye* she is forever young. 在我们的想象中，她永远是年轻的。

NOTE 本短语中的名词 eye，无论其前的物主代词是单数还是复数形式，都必须用单数形式。

in one's name ⇨ in the name of

in one's opinion *adv.* (used for saying what someone believes) according to what one thinks; to one's way of thinking; as one judges 据某人看来，按某人的意见：*In my opinion*, taekwondo practice offers benefits for a lifetime. 依我看来，练跆拳道对一生都有益。*In your opinion*, should the United States withdraw troops from Iraq right away? 你们认为美国应该立即从伊拉克撤军吗？The prisoner was released, which *in the court's opinion* was wrong. 该囚犯被释放了，法庭认为这是错误的做法。

NOTE 1. 本短语中的名词 opinion，无论其前的物主代词是单数还是复数形式，都必须用单数形式。

2. 本短语的另外一种表达形式是 in the opinion of someone。例如：

> *In the opinion of* other people, the plan is not acceptable.
> 其他一些人认为，该计划不可接受。

3. 本短语与 to one's mind 的意义和用法相同，两者可互换使用。

in one's own right *adv.* through your own skills, achievements, qualifications, etc. and not because of anyone else 靠自己的技能（或成就、条件等）：Her father is a well-known author, but she is an excellent writer *in her own right*. 她父亲是一位知名的作家，但她靠自己取得的成就也成了一名优秀作家。Bill Gates is one of the world's richest men *in his own right*, rather than by inheritance. 比尔·盖茨是世界上最富有的人之一，但他的财富不是继承而来的。This wine is becoming more and more popular *in its own right*. 这种酒以其本身的质量正日益受到欢迎。

I

in one's place *adj.* &*adv.* ❶ used for talking about what you would do if you were in the same situation as someone else 处在……的位置上：Wouldn't you do the same if you were *in Bill's place*? 如果你处在比尔的位置上，你就不会那样做吗？❷ instead of (other person or thing) 代替(某人)，替换(某物)：John was ill, so I went *in his place*. 约翰病了，所以我代替他去了。The manager is away; I am acting *in his place*. 经理不在，我在代他行事。They are nice pictures and we have nothing to put *in their place*. 这些图画很美，我们没有什么其他的能替换它们。

NOTE 1. 本短语中的名词 place，无论其前的物主代词是单数还是复数形式，都必须用单数形式。

2. 当本短语作"处在……的位置上"解时，同义短语是 in one's shoes。

3. 当本短语作"代替(某人)，替换(某物)"解时，另外一种表达形式是 in place of。例如：

> Joe had to work as blacksmith in place of his lazy father.
> 乔只好代替他懒惰的父亲去当铁匠。

in one's possession *adj.* (正式用语，常与 have 连用) kept or controlled by someone 为某人所有，由某人掌握：This property is *in his possession*. 这份财产为他所有。The information *in our possession* is strictly confidential. 我们手中掌握的这些资料都是绝密的。In the struggle, the strap broke and, with her bag *in their possession*, both men started running through the trees. 在争抢中，手提包的带断了，她的包便落入这两名男子手里，他们拔腿跑进了树林。

NOTE 本短语另外的表达形式是 in possession of 和 in the possession of。

in one's presence ⇨ **in the presence of**

in one's right mind *adj.* (非正式用语，常用否定形式) thinking clearly, and in a healthy mental state 思维清晰，头脑正常：Linda is not *in her right mind*; she's gone out of her mind. 琳达思维混乱；她已经疯了。Who *in their right mind* would pay all their income for housing? 头脑正常的人谁会用他们所有的收入去购房呢？

NOTE 1. 本短语中的名词 mind，无论其前的物主代词是单数还是复数形式，都必须用单数形式。例如：

> Anyone *in their right mind* would not starve themselves.
> 任何头脑正常的人都不会让自己挨饿。

2. 本短语的反义短语是 out of one's mind。

in one's shoes *adv.* (非正式用语，常用于 if 条件句中) in the position or situation that someone else is in 站在他人的立场上，处于他人的境地：What would you do if you were *in my shoes*? 如果你处于我的境地，你怎么办？If I put myself *in their shoes*, I think I would have done what they did. 如果我身处他们的境地，我想我也会干他们所干的事情。I'm glad I'm not *in his shoes*, with all those debts to pay. 我很高兴自己没有处于他那种境地，要偿还那么多的债务。

NOTE 本短语的同义短语是 in one's place (第一个义项)。

in one's way *adj.* ❶ in the pathway of someone 挡住了某人的去路：Don't get *in Mary's way*. 不要挡住玛丽的去路。I couldn't get through the gate because your car is *in my way*. 我无法走过大门，

因为你的车挡住了我的去路。❷ in a position that prevents someone from making progress 阻碍，妨碍：Fresh graduates dreaming of starting their own businesses listed lack of business experience and social networks, and objections from family members as major factors that stood *in their way*. 做起了创业梦的大学应届毕业生们把从业经验不足，缺乏社会关系以及家人反对列为阻碍创业的主要因素。

NOTE 本短语中的名词 way，无论其前的物主代词是单数还是复数形式，都必须用单数形式。

in operation *adj.* ❶ (of a machine or device) running; working; in action（指机器或装置）在运转中，在操作中：The new power station has been completed and will soon be *in operation*. 新发电站已经建成，并将很快运营发电。The two leaders agreed to set up a military hotline between Beijing and Washington, without saying when the line might be *in operation*. 两位领导人同意在北京和华盛顿之间设立一条军事热线，但并没有说明这条热线何时开通。❷ (of a plan or system) in effect or in use（指计划或制度）生效，在实施中：These regulations are still *in operation*. 这些法规依然有效。Similar schemes were *in operation* in other countries. 同样的计划也在其他国家中实施。

in opposition to *prep.* being opposed to or fighting against (someone or something) 反对，敌对：I was *in opposition to* my teacher on this question. 在这一问题上，我与我老师的意见相对立。He acted *in opposition to* his father's wishes. 他的所作所为与他父亲的意愿背道而驰。

in order *adj.* &*adv.* ❶（常与动词 be, get, have, keep, put 连用）in the correct arrangement or proper order; in a situation in which everything is well organized or arranged 整齐，秩序井然：My younger sister always keeps her room *in order*. 我妹妹总是把她的房间整理得井井有条。Let's put things *in order* and sweep the room clean. 咱们把东西整理好，把房间打扫干净。Can you get your bed *in order*? 你能把你的床铺整理好吗？The travel market throughout the country was *in* good *order* and over 90 percent of travelers were contented with their tours during the golden week of the National Day holiday. 在国庆黄金周期间，全国的旅游市场秩序井然，90%以上的游客对他们的出游都感到满意。❷ in good condition; working or functioning properly 状况良好，工作情况良好：This car is *in* good running *order*. 这部汽车运转良好。The fishing vessel's safety equipment was not *in* good *order*. 这艘渔船的安全设备状况不佳。❸ right for the occasion 恰当的(地)，合适的(地)：Is it *in order* to call him right now? 现在就给他打电话合适吗？It is *in order* for me to speak now, but I'm not sure what I should say. 现在该我发言了，但我还不知道该说些什么。

NOTE 本短语的反义短语是 out of order。

in order that *conj.*（正式用语，后接从句）so that something can happen; for the purpose of allowing or causing something to happen 为了，以便，目的在于：I get up early *in order that* I can catch up the early bus. 我早起是为了能赶上早班车。*In order that* everybody may understand it, I write it in simple language. 为了使人人都能看懂起见，我便以简单的语言写出。I came *in order that* I could see

Mary. 我来是为了能见到玛丽。

NOTE 本短语的否定形式并不体现在短语自身而是体现在后面的从句中。例如：

> Before he left, he turned off all the lights *in order that* electricity should not be wasted.
> 在离开之前，他关闭了所有的灯，以免费电。
> You must take measures *in order that* such mistakes may never be made again.
> 为了不致重犯这类错误，你必须采取点儿措施。

in order to *conj.* (后接原形动词) with the purpose or intention of; so that someone can do something or something can happen 为了，以便：*In order to* improve the US image in the world, US Secretary of State Hilary Clinton pursued the so-called smart power diplomacy. 为改善美国在世界上的形象，美国国务卿希拉里·克林顿奉行的是所谓的"巧实力"外交。We started early *in order to* arrive before dark. 我们动身很早，以便在天黑前到达。*In order* to be profitable for the company , the sales volume would need to rise by at least 60%. 为了使公司赢利，需要把销售量至少提高60%。

NOTE 1. 本短语与单纯地用不定式表示目的的用法比起来，更具有强调性。如本短语带逻辑主语，则采用"in order (for+名词或代词) to (do something)"的形式(如最后一个例句)。再如：

> *In order* for water *to* flow through a pipe, it must have some pressure behind it.
> 为了让水通过管道，其后必须有一定压力。

2. 本短语的否定形式是 in order not to。例如：

> I'll have everything ready in order not to keep you waiting.
> 为了不让你等待，我会把一切都准备好。

3. 在使用本短语时，in order 有时可以省略，只用 to。例如：

> (In order) To understand the true China—a changing society full of promises—it is necessary to get to know her yesterday, her today, and her tomorrow.
> 要了解一个真实的、发展变化着的、充满希望的中国，就有必要了解中国的昨天、今天和明天。

4. 本短语与 so as to 意义相同，用法上有下面几点区别：

(1) *in order to* 常含有能动的意味，常与表示意志的动词搭配使用；而 so as to 则常含有被动的意味，一般不和表示意志的动词搭配使用。请比较这两个句子：

> I got up early in order to catch the first bus.
> I got up early so as to be in time for the first bus.
> 我起了个早以便赶上第一趟公共汽车。

(2) *in order to* 可以用于句首，而 so as to 则不可以。

(3) *in order to* 语气比 so as to 强，常用于口语中；而 so as to 则少用于口语中。

in other words *adv.* (used for introducing another way of saying or explaining something) in another way, especially a more simple way 换句话说，也就是说：Literal translation, *in other words*, word-for-word translation, is not to be encouraged. 直译，换句话说，逐字地翻译，不应提倡。*In other words*, while opening still wider to the outside world, we must more fully depend on our own efforts to solve the problems of resources and the environment. 换言之,我们要在进一步扩大对外开放的同时,更加充分地依靠自己的力量来解决资源和环境问题。

NOTE 本短语的同义短语是 that is。

in pairs *adv.* in groups of two people or things 成双,成对: The children were asked to cross the street *in pairs* hand in hand. 孩子们都被要求两人手拉手地过马路。The third law of motion tells us that all forces occur *in pairs*. 运动第三定律告诉我们,所有的力都是成对出现。

NOTE 本短语中的名词 pair 必须用复数形式。

in part *adv.* (正式用语)(often used when you are discussing the causes of something or reasons for something) partly but not completely; to some degree or extent (常用于说明原因或理由)部分地,在某种程度上: I was not there, *in part* due to my disagreement about the purpose of the meeting. 我没有出席会议,部分原因是我不赞成开会的目的。The green color of the ocean comes, *in part*, from tiny creatures that live in it. 海水呈现的绿颜色部分地来自生活在其中的微小生物。The pedestrian was responsible for the traffic accident *in part*. 该行人对这起交通事故也负有一定的责任。

NOTE 本短语中的名词 part 必须用单数形式。

in particular Ⅰ *adv.* ❶ particularly; especially; in a way apart from others; more than others 尤其,特别: A Japanese senior official said Sunday that Japan attaches importance on its relations with Asian countries, China *in particular*. 日本一名高级官员星期日表示,日本重视其与亚洲国家,尤其是中国的关系。The engineer *in particular* must be able to communicate his ideas to others rapidly and accurately. 工程技术人员尤其必须能够迅速而准确地将自己的想法传达给别人。❷individually; in detail 个别地,详细地: Please write to me *in particular*. 请单独写信告诉我。The speaker talked about sports in general and about football *in particular*. 演讲者总体地谈了谈体育运动,接着详细地讲了足球运动。

Ⅱ *adj.* (用作后置定语,常与 anyone, no one, nobody, anything, nothing, anywhere, nowhere 等词连用) special, specific or important 特别的,明确的,重要的: Is there anything *in particular* you'd like to eat? 有没有你特别喜欢吃的东西? She directed the question at no one *in particular*. 她并没针对某一个人提出那一问题。I have nothing *in particular* to talk about. 我没有什么重要的事要说。

NOTE 作为副词性短语,本短语与副词 particularly 和 especially 同义,但本短语通常用于名词之后,而 particularly 和 especially 则用于名词之前。请比较下面这两个句子:

> I like everyone here, Tom *in particular*.
> I like everyone here, *particularly*/*especially* Tom.

in parts *adv.* in some parts only but not all of something 部分地,不完全地: The novel is funny *in parts*. 这本小说有些部分滑稽好笑。The set of the equipment was shipped here *in parts*. 这套设备是分

几部分运抵这里的。This play was good *in parts*. 这出戏的有些部分不错。

NOTE 本短语后同义短语是 in patches。

in peace *adv.* in a state of quiet or calm; being free from disturbance 安宁地,和平地,和睦地:Now the children have gone, perhaps I can get on with my work *in peace*. 孩子们离开了,也许我可以安静地继续工作了。May he rest *in peace*! 愿他安息! Let's settle it *in peace*. 让我们和平解决这个问题吧。You must live *in peace* with your neighbors. 你必须要和邻居们和睦相处。

NOTE 本短语的比较级形式是 more in peace,最高级形式是 most in peace。

in person *adv.* in your physical presence, rather than by writing, telephoning, or sending someone else 本人,亲自地:I've talked to him on the telephone and *in person*. 我已与他通过电话,也面谈过。Although we chatted online very often, we'd never met *in person*. 虽然我们经常在网上聊天,却从来不曾谋面。"I wish we would thank him *in person*," Mr Brown said fervently. "我希望我们能当面向他致谢。"布朗先生热情地说道。

NOTE 1. 本短语中的名词 person 必须用单数形式。

2. 本短语的同义短语是 in the flesh。

3. 本短语可转化为复合词 in-person,意为"亲自的"。

in place Ⅰ *adj.* ❶(of something) in the correct or usual position 在正确的位置,在平时的位置:I like to have everything *in place* in my room. 我喜欢我房间里的每件东西都放在适当的位置上。The chairs were not yet *in place* for the concert. 音乐会用的椅子还都没有摆放好。Nothing was *in place* after the powerful 8.0-magnitude earthquake. Even trees were turned over. 那场8级强烈地震过后,一切都移了位,就连树都翻转了。When trees are cut down, there is nothing to hold the soil *in place* on the hillside. 树木被砍伐后,山坡上就没有什么能阻挡土壤流失了。❷in existence and ready to be used 准备好投入使用的:The new regulations are now *in place*. 新的条例已制定完毕,只待实施。All concerned parties agreed that conditions for the opening of the new round of Middle East talks have been *in place*. 有关各方都认为召开新一轮中东会谈的条件已经具备。❸suitable; proper 适当的,恰当的:It was not *in place* to raise the issue at the time. 当时提出这个问题是不合适的。I don't think your suggestion is quite *in place*. 我认为你的建议不太恰当。

Ⅱ *adv.* (美国英语用法,在英国英语中用 on the spot) without leaving the position you are in; in the original or natural place or site 在原处,在原地:The gym teacher made us run *in place* for ten minutes. 教体操的老师让我们在原地跑步10分钟。While marching *in place*, the band played six more numbers. 乐队原地踏步,又演奏了6支曲子。

NOTE 1. 当本短语用作形容词性短语,作"在正确的位置,在平时的位置"和"适当的,恰当的"解时,反义短语是 out of place。

2. 不要将本短语与 in places 混淆,两者意义和用法不同。

in place of *prep.* (正式用语) instead of (something or someone); as a substitute for (someone or something) 代替,取代:Nylon is widely used *in place of* cotton today. 如今,尼龙被广泛地用来代替棉花。*In place of* our advertised program we will be showing a film. 我们将放映一部影片来取代广告节目。The Chinese use chopsticks *in place of* knives and forks. 中国人使用筷子而不用刀叉。James came to see us *in place of* Laurence who was unfortunately ill. 詹姆斯代替不幸生病的劳伦斯来看望我们。

NOTE 1. 本短语与 instead of 均表示"代替",但本短语强调用 A 代替 B,并没有否定 B 的意味;而 instead of 则强调用 A,含有否定 B 的意味。例如:

> Mark will be playing instead of me on Saturday.
> 马克将在星期六代替我比赛。(我根本不能上场比赛了)

另外,本短语后只可接名词和代词;而 instead of 后可接名词、代词、数词、副词、介词短语、动名词和复合宾语。

2. 当本短语后接某人,表示"代替某人"时,另外一种表达形式是 in one's place。

in places *adv.* at several points within an area (在同一区域中)有些地方,部分地:Even now the snow along the roadside is five or six feet deep *in places*. 甚至现在沿路还有些地方的积雪有五六英尺深。The wall was damaged *in places*. 部分墙体已被毁坏。

in point *adj.* appropriate; which proves or is an example of the subject under consideration; exactly fitting the case 适当的,切题的:What you said is not *in point*. 你说的不切题。Shoppers tend to think that high prices mean high quality. Electrical goods are a case *in point*. 消费者一般认为,价格高就意味着质量高。电器产品就是一个恰当的例子。

in point of fact ⇨ **in fact**

in possession of *prep.* (正式用语) having, holding, or occupying (something)具有,拥有,占有(某物):I am *in possession of* some information that I think will interest you. 我有一些我认为令你感兴趣的消息。She was found *in possession of* dangerous drugs. 她被发现拥有危险药品。I don't think anyone *in possession of* his or her senses would agree with you. 我认为明智的人都不会同意你的意见。

NOTE 1. 本短语与 in the possession of 的区别是:本短语意为"(常指某人)占有(某物)",含有主动意义;而 in the possession of 则意为"(指某物)为(某人)所占有",含有被动意义。试比较下面两个句子:

> Our president is in possession of the large house. (人作主语,表主动意义)
> The large house is in the possession of our president. (物作主语,表被动意义)

2. 本短语的另外一种表达形式是 in one's possession。

in power *adj.* (of a group of people) having political control of a country or government 掌握政权,执政:Putin said he is satisfied with his eight years *in power*. 普京说,他对自己执政 8 年的表现感到满意。The Social Democratic Party has been *in power* for ten years. 社会民主党已执政 10 年。

NOTE 本短语与 in office 在大多情况下可以互换使用。但就两者的中心词来讲,前者侧重"权力",而后者侧重"职位"。例如:

> He is *in office* but not *in power*.
> 他虽然在位,但不掌权。(即有职无权)

in practice I *adv.* (used for talking about what really happens as opposed to what you think will or should happen) actually; practically; in reality; in fact 实际上,事实上:Drivers say we need speed limits but, *in practice*, they don't respect them. 驾驶员都说需要制定速度限制,但实际上他们并不遵守它们。They said they are ready to abandon *in practice* their nuclear program under certain conditions. 他们表示,他们实际上已准备好在一定条件下放弃其核项目。

Ⅱ *adj*. ❶ (of a doctor or lawyer) practising (医生或律师)执业:The doctor is no longer *in practice*. 那医生已不再执业了。❷in proper condition to do something well through practice (通过练习)保持良好状态:A pianist gets his finger *in practice* by running over scales on the piano. 钢琴家通过在钢琴上练指法来使自己的手指保持良好的状态。An ice-skater keeps *in practice* by skating every day. 滑冰运动员通过每天进行滑冰练习来保持良好状态。

NOTE 1. 当本短语用作副词性短语,作"实际上,事实上"解时,反义短语是 in principle。

2. 当本短语用作形容词性短语,作"(通过练习)保持良好状态"解时,反义短语是 out of practice。

in preparation (for) *adj*. & *prep*. being prepared (for)(为……)做准备:Plans for the new school are now *in preparation*. 建造新学校的计划正在准备之中。The flowers were ordered *in preparation for* the wedding. 为准备婚礼而订购了这些鲜花。*In preparation for* grinding into Adirondack, US Mars rover Spirit cleaned off a portion of the rock's surface with a stainless steel brush. 美国"勇气"号火星车在准备钻探一块名为"阿迪朗达克"的岩石时,用一把不锈钢刷将石面部位清理干净。

NOTE 本短语的动词形式是 make preparations (for)。

in principle *adv*. (used for saying that something is possible in theory, although it has not yet been tried) in regard to the main idea; in general, as opposed to in detail 原则上,大体上:China's State Council on Friday approved *in principle* a draft plan on adjusting its national holidays. 中国国务院星期五原则上通过了调整全国节假日的草案。

NOTE 1. 不要将本短语与 on principle 混淆。on principle 也是副词性短语,意为"按照或根据原则"。

2. 本短语的反义短语是 in practice。

in private *adv*. in a place or situation where other people cannot watch or listen; privately; not publicly; secretly 私下地,秘密地:I'd like to talk with you *in private*, if you don't mind. 如果你不介意的话,我想和你私下里谈谈。The president is very much concerned about Cuba and he says the same things *in private* that he says in public. 总统十分关心古巴,他私下里所说的话与其在公开场合中的言论是一致的。The rebel leaders met *in private* to plot against the government. 叛乱头目们秘密集会,谋划反政府事宜。

NOTE 1. 本短语的比较级形式是 more in private,最高级形式是 most in private。

2. 本短语的反义短语是 in public。

in progress *adj*. going on; happening or being done 正在进行中,正在发生中:Harwich Road will be closed while the maintenance work is *in progress*. 哈维治路将在维护工程进行期间关闭。There is a meeting *in progress*. 会议正在举行。

in proportion Ⅰ *adj.* balanced; in symmetry 均衡的，相称的：This drawing isn't *in proportion*; the man is larger than the house. 这幅图画的比例不相称，人比房子还大。Everything in the room is *in* perfect *proportion*. 室内的一切都十分协调。

Ⅱ *adv.* according to real importance; sensibly 相称地，合情理地：When you are angry you don't always see things *in proportion*. 人生气时往往不能理性地看待事物。

NOTE 本短语的反义短语是 out of proportion。

in proportion to *prep.* ❶according to; at the rate of 根据，按……的比例：All the ethnic elements will be represented in the new Iraqi government *in proportion to* their populations, he said. 他表示，在新的伊拉克政府中，各民族都会按人口比例拥有自己的代表。Are you paid *in proportion to* the number of hours you work? 你是按工作的时数领取报酬吗？❷when compared with (two things) in size, amount, etc.; in relation to (the degree)与……相比，与……成比例：His head is large *in proportion to* his small frame. 与他瘦小的身架相比，他的头太大了。The tax increases *in proportion to* the amount you earn. 所得税随着你的收入额按比例增加。His expenditure is not *in proportion to* his income. 他的支出与收入不成比例。

NOTE 1. 本短语在表示比例关系时，其中的名词 proportion 前可加 direct, inverse 等形容词，来表示"正比"或"反比"等。例如：

> The camel possesses strength *in* direct *proportion to* its size.
> 骆驼的力气与其身体的大小成正比。

2. 本短语的反义短语是 out of (all) proportion to。

in public *adv.* in the sight or hearing of many people; openly; publicly 当众，公开地：The corrupt official was dictatorial and could not stand anyone questioning him, nor did he ever confess to his wrongdoing *in public*. 这个贪官专横跋扈，不容异议，更不肯当众认错。Castro, who handed over power to his younger brother Raul Castro in 2007, had rarely been seen *in public* ever since. 卡斯特罗在 2007 年把权力交给了他的弟弟。从此，他就很少公开露面了。

NOTE 本短语的反义短语是 in private。

in quantity *adv.* in large amounts 大量地：It is often less expensive to buy goods *in quantity*. 购买大量货物往往便宜些。These goods are greater *in quantity* than in quality. 这些货物量较大但质量较差。

NOTE 本短语中的主词 quantity 还可使用复数形式，即 in quantities，意义与本短语相同。

in question *adj.* ❶(正式用语，常用作后置定语) under consideration; being talked about 在考虑之中的，所论及的：*In question* here is his carelessness, not his qualification. 这儿所考虑的问题是他的粗心，而不是他的资格。That is not the point *in question*. 那不是谈论的要点。He always visited the factory *in question* to learn about its production process. 他经常去所谈论的那家工厂，以了解其生产过程。❷not very certain 存有疑问的：Are you saying that the usefulness of this test is *in question*? 你

I

是说这种考试的有效性还存有疑问? Her fitness to operate on a patient is *in question*. 她是否适宜为患者动手术还是个问题。

NOTE 1. 当本短语作"在考虑之中的,所论及的"解时,同义短语是 in hand 和 under consideration。

2. 当本短语作"存有疑问的"解时,反义短语是 beyond question, past question 和 without question。

in/into raptures *adj. &adv.* (主要用于英国英语中,正式用语,前常用动词 be 和 go,后常用介词 about, at 和 over) feeling extremely happy or excited; into an extremely happy and excited state 狂喜,进入狂喜状态: She was *in raptures* at the news. 她听到那消息高兴极了。The little boy went *into raptures* about his new toys. 小男孩对这些新玩具高兴万分。The fans went *into raptures* over the news that Germany whitewashed Ecuador 3-0 to top Group A at the World Cup on Tuesday. 在星期二的世界杯足球赛上,德国队以 3 比 0 狂扫厄瓜多尔队,夺得 A 组头名的消息使球迷们欣喜若狂。

NOTE 本短语中的名词 rapture 必须用复数形式。

in reality *adv.* (used for saying that the true situation is different from what has been said or thought) really; actually; in actual fact 实际上,事实上: *In reality*, there are three routes of HIV infection, that is, blood, sex and mother to child transmission. 实际上,艾滋病病毒有三条感染途径,即血液、性交和母婴传染。Reports put the death toll at 50, but *in reality* it was closer to 200. 报道把死亡人数说成是 50 人,但事实上是近乎 200 人。

in/with reference to *prep.* (正式用语) (used to indicate what something relates to) in relation to; in connection with 关于,涉及: *In reference to* the question you asked, I haven't written anything about the trip to Vietnam but I'll, once I find the time. 关于你问的问题,我还没写过任何有关越南之行的东西。但一旦找到时间,我一定要写的。*With reference to* your recent complaint about the quality of the mobile phone, we decided to exchange one for you. 关于您最近对那部手机质量问题的投诉,我们决定给您换一部。I would like to draw some conclusion *with reference to* what was said yesterday. 我想就昨天所说的内容作几点结论。

NOTE 本短语的同义短语是 as regards, as to, in regard(s) to, in respect to, in relation to, with relation to, in respect of, with respect to 和 with regard(s) to。

in regard(s) to *prep.* (正式用语)(used to indicate the subject that is being talked or written about) regarding; concerning (what has been mentioned)对于,关于(某一问题): *In regard to* his work, we have nothing to complain. 对于他的工作,我们没有什么可埋怨的。What is your comment *in regard to* his remarks on the recent turbulences in global financial markets? 对于他有关最近全球金融市场动荡不安的一些说法,您作何评论? What advice do you have *in regard to* setting up an e-mail server? 对于如何建立电子邮件服务器,你有什么高见? *In regards to* military clashes between Israel and Lebanon, the UN head said the international community has to find the way to stabilize the situation in the Middle East. 关于以色列和黎巴嫩之间的军事冲突,联合国秘书长指出,国际社会要设法稳定中东局势。

NOTE in regard to 为标准用法,更为常用;而 in regards to 则为非标准用法,一般不用于书面体中。

in/with relation to *prep.* ❶(正式用语) in connection with; concerning (something) 与……有关,关于: Police said they had arrested one man *in relation to* the terrorist attack. 警方称,他们已逮捕了一名与那起恐怖袭击有关联的男子。*In relation to* the complaint you have made our reply is we can do nothing to improve the quality of these goods. 关于您所提出的意见,我们的答复是:我们无法再提高这些商品的质量。❷(used to compare the size, condition, or position of the two things) in comparison to (something) 与……相比: Unemployment here is high *in relation to* national levels. 与全国的水平相比,这儿的失业率高。

in respect of *prep.* (英国英语用法,正式用语) relating to; concerning 关于,涉及,至于:There is no objection *in respect of* the location of the proposed museum. 没有人对于那个拟建的博物馆馆址提出任何异议。Bilateral exchanges will be deepened and broadened *in respect of* policies of inland river transport and navigation safety. 要深化和扩大双方在内河航运政策、航运安全等方面的交流。

NOTE 本短语与 with respect to 意义和用法相同,两者均用于引入先前提到过的,或者一个新的话题。但本短语比 with respect to 更为正式。

in reply to *prep.* as a verbal answer, or reaction to (something); in answer to 作为对……的答复,作为对……的反应,响应: *In reply to* your letter dated June 4, I regret to tell you that the trade is dismissed. 作为对你 6 月 4 日来信的答复,我很遗憾地告诉您这项交易取消了。Improvements were done *in response to* our customer's demands. 应客户要求,我们的改进工作已全部完成。He proposed to establish a strategic dialogue mechanism between the two countries *in response to* economic and financial eventualities. 他建议两国建立一个应对经济和金融突发事件的战略对话机制。

NOTE 本短语的同义短语是 in response to。

in return *adv.* (常与 for 连用) in exchange or in repayment (for) (something received, or done to or for one) 作为……的交换,作为对……的回报,作为对……的报答: He got extra pay *in return* for his industry. 由于工作勤奋,他得到了额外报酬。The most common gifts from men on Valentine's Day are roses for their sweethearts, and most women give chocolates *in return*. 男士在情人节送给他们心上人的最常见礼物是玫瑰花。而女士们则大多以送巧克力作为酬答。

in search of/for *prep.* looking for or trying to find (something or someone) 寻找,搜寻:Many people in the countryside had left their homes to go to cities *in search of* jobs. 许多农村人口都已离开家园进城寻找工作。Families *in search of* a housemaid should check beforehand whether she has bought personal insurance. 寻求保姆的家庭应该事先检查她是否买了个人保险。The helicopters flew across the area, *in search for* suspects. 直升机飞过这一地区,搜寻可疑分子。

I

in season Ⅰ *adj.* ❶ (of fruit and vegetables) at the time when they are usually ready for eating and are widely available (水果或蔬菜)当令的,应时的: Fruit and vegetables are cheaper when they are *in season*. 水果和蔬菜在当令时价格就比较便宜。This region provides a lot of fruits *in season*. 该地区供应许多时令水果。❷(especially of holiday business) at the busiest time of year (尤指节日期间的生意)处于旺季: Hotel rooms are more expensive *in season*. 旅馆的房间价格在旺季时就比较高。*In season*, the rooms with an ocean view are more than 200 US dollars a night. 旺季时,住海景房一个晚上要 200 多美金。

Ⅱ *adv.* at the proper or best time 在最佳的时机,及时: They arrived *in season* for the meeting. 他们及时赶来开会。He gave me a word in season. 他及时地给了我劝告。Applicants will be notified of our decision *in* good *season*. 我们将在适当的时候把我们的决定通知申请人。

NOTE 本短语的反义短语是 out of season。

in secret *adv.* without anyone else knowing; in a private way; not openly; secretly 秘密地,私下地: The negotiations were conducted *in secret*. 谈判是秘密进行的。For years, Washington has accused Tehran of trying to develop nuclear weapons *in secret*. 多年来,华盛顿一直指控德黑兰在试图秘密研制核武器。I have said nothing *in secret* that I would not say openly. 我没有什么在公开场合不能说而非要在私下说的话。

NOTE 本短语中的名词 secret 前不能加任何冠词。in the secret 表示“知道内情”“参与秘密”。例如:

Is your friend *in the secret*?
你的朋友知道内情吗?

in session *adj.* (of a congress, parliament, court or other official group) operating or functioning; meeting to deal with business (国会,议会,法庭或其他团体)开会,开庭: Parliament is not *in session* during August. 国会在八月期间休会。Please be seated! This court is now *in session*. 请坐!本法庭现在开庭。The teachers were *in session* all Tuesday afternoon. 教师们在星期二开了一下午的会。

in shape *adj.* (非正式用语) ❶ (of someone) in a good state of health (指人)身体状况良好: He's been working too hard and he's *in* pretty bad *shape*. 他一直工作太累,以致他现在的身体状况很不好。The football team will be *in* good *shape* for the first game of the season. 该足球队将以良好的身体状态参加本季度的第一场比赛。❷(of something) in good condition (指物)状况良好: China's economy last year was *in* good *shape* and characterized by fast growth, improved economic returns and stable prices. 去年中国的经济呈现增长较快、效益较好、价格较稳的良好局面。I think I'd better get my room *in shape* if I have guests. 我想,如果我有客人来,我还是把我的房间整理好。

NOTE 1. 本短语中的名词 shape 前可加形容词修饰,但不能加不定冠词和定冠词。2. 本短语的同义短语是 in condition; 反义短语是 out of shape 和 out of condition。此外,还可以使用 in bad shape 和 in no condition 来表达与本短语相反的意义。

in short *adv.* (用于句首)(used for introducing a summary of something you have just said) to put it into as few words as possible; briefly; by way of summary 简言之,总之: *In short*, I am going to live there myself. 简而言之,我要一个人住在那里。*In short*, opening-up is so much better than closing-up, and a nation or a country can advance and develop only when it opens up to the outside world. 总之,要开放,不要封闭。一个民族、一个国家,只有开放,才能进步和发展。

NOTE 1. 本短语的比较级形式是 more in short,最高级形式是 most in short。

2. 本短语的同义短语是 in a word 和 in brief。三者之间的区别见 in brief。

in short order *adv.* (主要用于美国英语中) very quickly; without delay 迅速地,不耽搁地: I managed to get her out of the room *in short order*. 我很快就把他赶出了房间。He'll be here *in short order*. 他马上就到。

NOTE 本短语的比较级形式是 in shorter order,最高级形式是 in shortest order。

in short supply *adj.* available only in small quantities, so that there is not enough; lacking 供应不足的,短缺的: Food is likely to be *in short supply* until the strike is over. 在罢工结束之前,可能要出现食品供应不足的现象。Qualified English teachers are *in short supply* in the broad areas of the countryside. 广大的农村地区缺乏合格的英语教师。Electricity is *in shot supply* on the island. 岛上的电力短缺。

NOTE 1. 本短语的比较级形式是 more in short supply, 最高级形式是 most in short supply。

2. 本短语中的形容词 short 可被 limited 替换,两者意义和用法相同。

in/within sight *adj.* &*adv.* ❶visible; in any place that you can see from where you are 看得见的,在看得见的地方: The old man walked so slowly that an hour later he was still *in sight*. 那位老人走得很慢,一个小时后还能看得见他。There was nobody *in sight*. 一个人也看不见。The bus came *in sight* at last after we waited at the bus stop for nearly twenty minutes. 我们在汽车站等了将近 20 分钟才终于看见了车的影子。Every home should have the emergency telephone number 911 posted *in* plain *sight*, the police said. 警方告诫每个家庭都应把紧急电话号码 911 贴在显眼的地方。❷(used about something that is going to happen soon) near 临近: The next presidential election in the island country is already *in sight*. 该岛国下一届总统的选举已经临近。Political independence seemed to be *within sight*. 政治独立似乎就在眼前。

NOTE 1. 本短语中的名词 sight 可以有前置定语。如:

> I had the deer *in* my *sight*, but it ran away before I could fire.
> 我已瞄准了那只鹿,但还没来得及开枪,它就跑掉了。

2. in sight 的比较级形式是 more in sight,最高级形式是 most in sight。

3. 本短语的同义短语是 in/into view;反义短语是 out of sight 和 out of view。

in silence *adv.* in a state of complete quiet 沉默地,默不作声地: She is listening to the radio *in silence*. 她在默默地听着收音机。At the meeting he simply sat there *in silence*. 在会上,他只是默不作声地坐在

I

那里。

in so far as *conj.* (正式用语)(used for talking about the degree to which something happens, or the situation in which something happens) to the extent that 到……程度: I'll help you *in so far as* I can. 我会尽可能地帮助你。She cites other scholars' work only *in so far as* it supports her own theories. 她引用了一些其他学者作品的内容只是用于佐证自己的理论而已。

NOTE 1. 本短语的另外一种表达形式是 in as far as。

2. 本短语的同义短语是 so far as。

in some sense ⇨ in a sense

in someone's eyes *adv.* in one's view or opinion 在(某人)的心目中: *In his parents' eyes*, the boy can do no wrong. 在他父母看来,这孩子不会做错事。You're only a child *in his eyes*. 在他的心目中,你只是个孩子。Tom was, *in their eyes*, a very honest and reliable person. 在他们的心目中,汤姆是一个非常诚实又可靠的人。

NOTE 1. 本短语中的名词 eye 必须用复数形式。

2. 本短语的另外一种表达方式是 in the eyes of。

in someone's hands ⇨ in the hands of

in spite of *prep.* (used for referring to a fact that makes the rest of the statement seem surprising) despite; against the influence or effect of; taking no notice of, or not prevented by 不顾,尽管: The children went to school *in spite of* the storm. 孩子们不顾风暴,都去上学了。*In spite of* feeling very tired, we decided to go ahead. 尽管感到非常疲劳,我们还是决定继续干下去。

NOTE 1. 本短语与介词 despite 意义和用法相同,但 despite 是正式用词,而本短语为一般用语。在语气上,本短语比 despite 强。

2. 本短语的同义短语是 despite of 和 in despite of。

3. 本短语的反义短语是 because of。试比较:

> He married her *because of* her looks.
> 他因她的相貌好而娶了她。
> He married her *in spite of* her looks.
> 尽管她的相貌差,他还是娶了她。

in/into step *adj.* &*adv.* (especially of soldiers) putting the right feet to the ground at exactly the same time as others (in marching, walking, etc.) (尤指士兵)(在行军、走路等中)步伐一致的(地): The soldiers marched *in step* from beginning to the end. 士兵们行军的步伐自始至终都很整齐。Those soldiers should not be *in step* when they cross the bridge. 那些士兵在过桥时不该齐步走。He had difficulty keeping *in step* with the rest of the marchers. 他很难与其他行进者保持同一步伐。She slipped her hand into his and fell *into step* beside him. 她悄悄地拉住他的手并与他同步而行。

NOTE 1. in step 的比较级形式是 more in step,最高级形式是 most in step。

2. 本短语的反义短语是 out of step。

in step with *prep.* (of a person or behavior) in harmony or agreement with (others)(指人或行为)与……一致: If he expects to be able to continue in office, a politician must keep *in step with* his backers. 一位政治家要想继续执政的话,就必须与其支持者保持一致。These old people are not *in step with* the times. 这

些老年人跟不上时代的步伐。The British Government is always anxious to stay *in step with* Washington. 英国政府总是急于与华盛顿保持一致。

NOTE 本短语的同义短语是 in accord with, in accordance with, in agreement with, in harmony with 和 in line with; 反义短语是 out of step with。

in stock *adj.* having (goods) available to sell (in a shop) (商店里)有现货的: Do you have any of these batteries *in stock* at the moment? 你们现在有这些电池的现货吗? I intend to dispose of the whole of goods *in stock*. 我计划将全部存货都处理掉。The book is *in stock*. 此书有现货。

NOTE 本短语的反义短语是 out of stock。

in store *adj.* ❶(英国英语用法) save up in case of need; ready for use or for some purpose 储存着,备有: My furniture was *in store* while I was abroad. 我在国外期间,我的家具都存放起来了。These small animals have a lot of nuts *in store* for the winter. 这些小动物储有大量的坚果供冬天食用。❷(与 for 连用) (of something) about to happen at some time in the future; awaiting (someone) in the future 即将发生的,将要到来的;等待: There's trouble *in store* for her. 她要有麻烦。None of us knows what lies *in store* for us tomorrow. 我们谁都不知道自己将来会怎么样。Work hard, children. There is a bright future *in store* for you! 努力吧,孩子们。你们的前途是光明的!

in style Ⅰ *adj.* in fashion; fashionable 入时的,时兴的,时髦的: This black dress isn't *in style* any more, my friend. 我的朋友,这件黑色连衣裙已不再时兴了。I don't care whether it's *in style* or not. 它时不时兴我不在乎。Long skirts are back *in style*. 长裙子又时髦起来了。

Ⅱ *adv.* in a very comfortable, impressive, or expensive way, so as to cause admiration by being fashionable 讲排场地,赶时髦地: Let's rent a big car and go there *in style*. 咱们租一辆大型轿车,风风光光地到那里去。When my friend got married he decided to do it *in style*, and gave a big party. 我的朋友结婚时决定赶时髦,于是搞了一个大型宴会。

NOTE 本短语的同义短语是 in fashion; 反义短语是 out of date, out of fashion 和 out of style。

in succession *adv.* (of things of the same kind) in a series; one after another in order, sequence, or in the course of events; successively 连续地,相继地,一连串地: In China's agriculture, bumper harvest has been reaped for ten years *in succession*. 在中国,农业连续 10 年获得了丰收。High-level officials of US Department of Commerce visited China *in succession* to discuss the problem of the trade imbalance between the two countries. 美国商务部的高级官员相继访华,商讨两国间的贸易逆差问题。The reporters had questions fired at them *in* quick *succession*. 记者们像发连珠炮似的向他们提问。

in sum *adv.* (正式用语) (used for giving a summary of what you have said) considered as a whole; in simple words 总之,简而言之: The teacher, *in sum*, is doing a good job. 总之,这位教师的工作干得不错。*In sum*, theory must be combined with practice. 简而言之,理论必须与实践相结合。

NOTE 本短语与 in summary 的意义和用法相同,两者可互换使用。

I

in summary *adv.* (正式用语)(used at the end of a talk or piece of writing for introducing a short statement that gives the main information about something, without giving all the details) to sum up 总之,概括论之: *In summary*, nobody knows where the disease originated. 总之,无人知晓此种疾病源于何方。*In summary*, it is my opinion that this complete treatment process was very successful. 概括论之,我认为这整个治疗过程都是非常成功的。

in support of *prep.* giving support or help to (someone or their ideas or aims) because you want them to succeed 支持: Thousands of people marched in Caracas on Wednesday *in support of* their state leader. 成千上万的人星期三在加拉加斯游行,支持其国家领导人。The government of Turkey told the United States that it would not send troops across the border *in support of* the American military action in Iraq. 土耳其政府通知美国,其不会派兵越境去支持美国在伊拉克的军事行动。

in tears *adv.* & *adj.* crying; weeping 流着泪,哭泣着: She answered the questions *in tears*. 她是流着眼泪回答这些问题的。I saw her standing there *in tears*. 我看到她站在那里哭泣。He broke down *in tears* when he learned that his father had died. 听说父亲已经去世的消息,他哭了起来。She was *in tears* over the broken doll. 她因玩具娃娃坏了而哭泣着。

NOTE 本短语中的名词 tear 必须用复数形式。在一些与 tear 有关的短语中,tear 都用复数形式,例如: burst into *tears*, close to tears, on the verge of tears, fight back (the) *tears*, reduce someone to *tears* 等。但有时只能用单数形式,例如: bring a *tear* to someone's eye。

in terms of *prep.* on the subject of (something); regarding (something); concerning (something); with regard to (something) 就……而论,至于: The book has been well reviewed, but *in terms of* actual sale it hasn't been very successful. 这本书获得了好评,但从实际销售情况来看,它并不太成功。*In terms of* money we are rich, but not in terms of happiness. 就钱而论,我们很富有,但就幸福而言就不然了。Presently, China ranks among the top destinations in the world *in terms of* both tourist arrivals and foreign currency receipts. 目前,中国入境旅游人数和旅游外汇收入均位居世界前列。

NOTE 1. 本短语中的名词 term 必须用复数形式。在一些与 term 有关的短语中,term 都用复数形式,例如: come to *terms* (with), on good *terms* 等。

2. 本短语在使用中经常为单个介词所取代,以避免烦琐和对本短语的过度使用。例如:

> We have to plan soon what to do for Thanksgiving. (用 for 取代本短语)
> What are we going to do about paying these bills? (用 about 取代本短语)
> A little chili powder goes a long way towards spicing up any dish. (用 toward 取代本短语)

in that *conj.* (正式用语) (used for introducing an explanation of what you have just said, showing in what way it is true) for the reason that; because 因为,由于: Human beings are superior to animals *in that* they can use language as a tool to communicate. 人类比其他动物

高级,因为他们能用语言做交际工具。The new system is better *in that* it provides faster access to the Internet. 这种新系统比较好,因为它所提供的入网速度更快。*In that* you will be busy for the next few weeks, let's go over your paper now. 由于你后几周要忙,那咱们现在就把你的论文研究一下吧。

NOTE 本短语与 because 相同,都用来表示原因。但本短语所说明的、位于其前的主句多为"主语+系动词+形容词"结构,如:She is amazing *in that* she knows 5 different languages. 而 because 则不受此限制。

in that case ⇨ **in this case**

in that event *adv.* if that happens 如果那样的话:There's a possibility of my flight being delayed. *In that event* I'll phone to let you know. 我所乘坐的航班有可能晚点。要是那样的话,我会打电话告诉你。

in that regard ⇨ **in this regard**

in the absence of *prep.* (of someone or something) not existing or being present; without (someone or something) 没有,不在:*In the absence of* any further evidence the police were unable to solve the murder. 由于没有任何进一步的证据,警方无法侦破这起谋杀案。I don't think it will get us anywhere to discuss the problem *in the absence of* exact data. 我认为,在我们手头没有准确资料的情况下来讨论这个问题,是不会有什么结果的。*In the absence of* the teacher, the students study quietly in their classroom. 老师不在时,学生们安静地在教室里学习。

NOTE 1. 本短语的另外一种表达形式是 in one's absence。例如:

Mark will be in charge *in Steve's absence*.
史蒂夫不在时便由马克来负责。

2. 本短语的反义短语是 in the presence of。

in the abstract *adv.* thinking about something only as a general idea without referring to real situations or practical experience 就一般而言,抽象地:Language, *in the abstract*, is our facility to talk to each other. 抽象地讲,语言就是指人们交际的能力。We cannot consider this mater *in the abstract*. 我们不能抽象地考虑这个问题。

in the air Ⅰ *adj.* (非正式用语) ❶ (of stories, talk, rumors, etc.) being passed on from one person to another (故事、话语、谣言等)在流传:The idea of a co-production of the film has been *in the air* since 2007. 自 2007 年以来一直流传着联合摄制该影片的说法。There's a rumour *in the air* that Diana had been pregnant before she was killed in a traffic accident in Paris. 传言说戴安娜在巴黎遭遇车祸身亡之前就已有身孕。❷ uncertain; not yet decided 未定的,悬而未决的:We may be going skiing at Christmas, but it's still all up *in the air*. 我们可能在圣诞节时去滑雪,但还都没最后定下来。The location of the new library is *in the air*. 新图书馆的馆址尚未确定。

Ⅱ *adv.* everywhere 到处:There is such a feeling of victorious joy *in the air*. 到处都洋溢着这种胜利的喜悦。

NOTE 不要将本短语与 on the air 混淆。on the air 意为"在广播"。

in the background *adj.* ❶ behind the main person or thing you are looking at 在背后:She showed me a picture of palm trees with mountains *in the background*. 她给我展示了一幅以丛山为背景的棕榈树林图片。❷in a place or situation in which people do not notice you 在看不见(或看不清)的地方，在幕后：The shy girl kept *in the background* when there were visitors at home. 当家里有客人时，这位腼腆的姑娘便一直待在不让人看见她的地方。She has a lot of power, but likes to remain *in the background*. 她掌握很大的权力，但喜欢身居幕后。He is a learned man, but he always keeps his knowledge *in the background*. 他是个有学问的人，但他的学问总是深藏不露。

in the balance *adj.* (常用在动词 be 或 hang 之后) (of something) in a state of uncertainty; (of the future or fate) in doubt; (of life) at risk 悬而未决的，(前途或命运)未定的，(生命等)在危急状态中的：Jack's career is hanging in the balance. 杰克的工作还悬而未决。The future of the nation is *in the balance*. 该国的前途未卜。The fate of the refugees continues to hang *in the balance*. 这些难民的命运仍未确定。She was very sick and her life hung *in the balance*. 她病情严重，生死未卜。

in the black *adj.* &*adv.* (非正式用语) in a situation in which you are earning more money than you are spending; not in debt 有盈余，不亏欠：We've managed to stay *in the black* for over a year. 一年多来，我们一直保持有盈余。We've been *in the black* for six months in a row. 我们已连续六个月盈利了。His store is running *in the black*. 他的商店营业有盈余。

NOTE 1. 不要将本短语与 in the dark 混淆。
2. 本短语的反义短语是 in the red。
3. 本短语和 in the red 用颜色分别表示"盈或余"或"亏或欠"。这是因为传统的财务记账方式用黑色数字表示余款，而用红色数字表示欠款(亦称"赤字")。

in the charge of ⇨ **in charge of**

in/during/over the course of *prep.* (后接表示某段时间的名词) during; while something is happening or continuing; in the process of 在……期间：He has seen many changes *in the course of* his long life. 在他长期的生命旅程中，他见证了许许多多的变化。*During the course of* the morning I learned a lot about the project. 我在上午期间了解到了很多有关该项目的情况。The company faces major challenges *over the course of* the next few years. 公司在今后的几年里面临着巨大的挑战。

in the dark *adv.* & *adj.* ❶ without any light 在黑暗中(的)：Unlike the cat I can see nothing *in the dark*. 我和猫不一样，在黑暗中我什么都看不见。Thousands of people in New York City are left *in the dark* as blackout problem enters fifth day. 停电已进入了第五天，纽约市仍有成千上万的人生活在黑暗中。❷ in secrecy 秘密地(的)：It is not necessary to keep it *in the dark*. 没有必要对此事保密。That deal must have been carried on *in the dark*; there's been something strange going on. 那笔交易肯定是秘密进行的，其中有些蹊跷。❸(常用在动词 be 或 keep 之后，后用介词 about) in a state of ignorance; not knowing very much about something, because other people are keeping it secret from you 不知道，蒙在鼓里，全然不知：The two boys decided to keep their parents *in the dark* about where they got the money. 这两个男孩决定不让他们的家长知道他们

是从哪儿搞到的这笔钱。I'm *in the dark* about who is in charge around here. 我不知道谁是这里管事的。We are still *in the dark* about how the money was lost. 那笔款是怎么丢的,我们仍然蒙在鼓里。We were totally kept *in the dark* about what happened that night. 我们对那天晚上发生的事情全然不知。

NOTE 当本短语作"不知道,蒙在鼓里,全然不知"解时,反义短语是 in the know。

in the distance ⇨ **at a distance**

in the end *adv.* (主要用于口语中)❶ at last; finally, after a period of time or thought 最终,最后: We are convinced that *in the end* we will win. 我们相信,我们最终一定会取得胜利。*In the end*, we decided not to buy it. 最后,我们还是决定不买它。❷ when everything is considered 到头来,归根结底: *In the end*, I think one must blame these children's parents. 我认为,到头来人们要责怪的还是这些孩子的家长。*In the end*, it comes down to money. 归根结底,这实质上就是钱的问题。

NOTE 本短语与 at(long) last 和 at length 均表示"最后""终于"之意。它们之间的区别见 at (long) last。

in the event of *prep.* (used for saying what will happen in a particular situation) if (something) happens 如果(某事)发生,万一: But *in the event of* further conflict in the region, such as a threatened US attack on Iran's nuclear installations, there will be a big jump in oil prices. 但是,如果这一地区发生进一步冲突,比如像美国所威胁的那样对伊朗的核设施进行打击的话,石油价格会大幅上升。*In the event of* his not coming, what shall we do? 万一他不来,我们怎么办?

NOTE 1. 本短语与 in case of 意义和用法相同,两者可互换使用。

2. 本短语中的介词 of 可被关系代词 that (亦可省略)替换,后接从句。例如:

> In the event (that) the attacks continue, we will retaliate.
> 如果袭击再不停下来,我们就将反击。

in the extreme *adv.* (正式用语,用以加强语气,用于形容词之后) extremely 极端地,极度地,非常: It is unlikely *in the extreme* that she will change her mind. 她绝不可能改变其主意。He has been generous *in the extreme*. 他一直非常慷慨。

in the eyes of *prep.* in the view or opinion of (someone) 在(某人)看来: The baby is beautiful *in the eyes of* its mother. 在这个婴儿的母亲看来,这个婴儿是漂亮的。*In the eyes of* the public the mayor was guilty of serious neglect of duty. 公众都认为市长有严重的玩忽职守行为。

NOTE 1. 本短语中的名词 eye 必须用复数形式。

2. 本短语的另外一种表达形式是 in someone's eyes。

in the face of *prep.* in spite of; against (something difficult or unpleasant) 面对……而不顾: *In the face of* great hardship, she managed to keep her sense of humor. 面对极大的困苦,她仍然保持着幽默感。In her letter, the vice-chancellor of Cambridge University also showed her admiration to Premier Wen's composure *in the face of* the disruption. 剑桥大学副校长在她的信中还对温总理面对干扰从容应对表示敬佩。

I

in the family way *adj.* (非正式用语,委婉用法)pregnant 怀孕: Have you heard that our teacher is *in the family way*? 你有没有听说咱们老师怀孕了? Tommy's mother is *in the family way* again. 汤米的妈妈又怀孕了。They decided to get married now that he's put her *in the family way*. 男方已致使女方怀孕,因此他们决定结婚。

NOTE 1. 本短语的另外一种表达形式是 in a family way。

2. 人们用本短语来取代 pregnant 一词,是因为直用 pregnant 不够礼貌,而本短语更委婉。

in the final analysis *adv.* when everything is known and considered 归根结底:China owes all this progress to the policy of reform and opening-up and, *in the final analysis*, to the freedom-inspired creativity of the Chinese people. 中国所有这些进步,都得益于改革开放,归根结底来自中国人民基于自由的创造。*In the final analysis*, their society still lacks a deep cultural root. 追根究底,他们的社会仍缺乏深厚的文化底蕴。

NOTE 本短语的另外一种表达形式是 in the last analysis。

in the first place *adv.* ❶used for stating the most basic reason for something 作为根本原因:There were several reasons he couldn't sleep. *In the first place*, Peg snored. 他不能入睡有几个原因。首因是佩格打呼噜。Why do strikes occur so frequently in coalmines, *in the first place*? 罢工如此频繁地在煤矿发生,根本原因是什么? ❷(用于句尾)to begin with; in or at the beginning (of a situation)一开始,起初: I don't think we should have been there *in the first place*. 我认为,我们一开始就不该在那儿。If you don't like her, why did you invite her *in the first place*? 如果你不喜欢她,你为什么起初要约人家? I didn't want to come here *in the first place*. 我起初并不想来这里。

in the first place, (and) in the second place *adv.* (用于句首) an expression used to introduce the first and second, etc. in a series of points or reasons in an argument, explanation, etc. (用于表示论点、原因等中的系列顺序)首先,其次,……: We decided not to buy the house, because *in the first place* it was too expensive, and *in the second place* it was too far from our offices. 我们决定不买这所房子,因为首先它价格太贵,其次它离我们上班的地点又太远。*In the first place* you are not old, Norman, *and in the second place*, you are very strong. 首先,你还不老,诺曼;其次,你还很健壮。

NOTE 若仅列示其中的一个论点或原因,本短语中的后部分则无需使用。例如:

> *In the first place*, inflationary pressures in the United States and the euro zone have been easing over the recent years.
>
> 首先,在近年来,美国和欧元区国家通货膨胀的压力缓解了。

同样,如有必要,还可在本短语后使用(and) in the third place。但一般不用 in the fourth place, the fifth place, etc. 。

in the flesh *adv.* present here and now, instead of by television, telephone, radio etc. 本人: It was a pleasure to finally meet him *in the flesh*. 很高兴终于见到了他本人。She looks more beautiful on television than *in the flesh*. 她在电视上

比本人更好看。

NOTE 本短语的同义短语是 in person。

in the form of *prep.* having the particular shape, character, style, etc. of 以……形式,以……形状: His opening remark was *in the form of* a question. 他以提问的方式开始发言。You can get the medicine *in the form of* a liquid or as a tablet in that drug store. 你可以在那家药店买到这种药,有液体的也有片剂的。

in the front of ⇨ **in front of**

in the habit of *prep.* (后接动名词,用在系动词后作表语) having the habit of (doing something) 习惯于(做某事),有(做某事)的习惯: They were *in the habit of* going for long walks. 他们习惯于长途散步。I'm not *in the habit of* lending money, but I'll make an exception in this case. 我没有借钱给人的习惯,但这一回我要破一次例。

in the hands of *prep.* possessed by (someone); under the authority of (someone); being dealt with, done, etc. by (someone) 掌握在(某人)手中,在(某人)手中得以处理: This town is still *in the hands of* the enemy. 该城仍然掌握在敌人的手中。In spite of the damaged wheel, the plane touched down safely *in the hands of* her skilled pilot. 尽管飞机的轮子损坏,但它还是在其技艺高超的驾驶员的控制下平安着陆。I left the matter *in the* capable *hands of* our deputy manager. 我把那件事交给了我们很有能力的副经理处理。

NOTE 1. 本短语中的名词 hand 必须用复数形式。

2. 本短语的另外一种表达形式是 in someone's hands。

in the hope(s) of *prep.* (后常接动名词或动名词短语) wanting (something to happen) 希望,期待着(某事发生): Police are carrying out house-to-house enquiries *in the hope of* finding the missing girl. 警察在挨家挨户地进行查询,希望找到那个失踪的女孩。China is making serious preparations with other parties *in the hopes of* conducting substantial discussions during the nuclear talks. 中国正与其他各方一起认真准备,希望此次核会谈能够开展实质性的讨论。I underwent an operation *in the hopes of* an early recovery. 我怀着早日痊愈的希望接收了手术。

NOTE 1. 本短语中的介词 in 可被 with 替换。例如:

> She tried again, *with the hope of* persuading them.
> 她再次进行了尝试,以期成功地说服他们。

2. 本短语中的介词 of 可被关系代词 that 所替换,即 in (the) hope(s) that,后接从句。例如:

> She did it *in (the) hope that* she'd succeed.
> 她抱着成功的希望做的这件事。

3. 本短语中的定冠词 the 可省略。

in the interest(s) of *prep.* ❶in order to preserve, develop, or achieve (something) 为了……: In this dictionary the entries are arranged alphabetically *in the interest of* ready reference. 为查索方便起见,本词典的短语条目都是按字母顺序排列的。The political march was banned *in the interests of* the public safety. 为了公共安全,这次政治性游行被禁止了。❷for the benefit of or to the advantage or advancement of (a particular person or group)为了……的利益: In a telephone conversation with the Chinese president, President Obama said enhancing Sino-US cooperation is *in the interest of* not only the two countries, but the world at large. 在与中国国家主席的电话交谈中,奥巴马总统表示:推进中美两国的合作不仅有利于两国,而且有利于全世界。Did they act *in the interests of* their club? 他们的所作所为是不是为了他们俱乐部的利益?

NOTE 当本短语作"为了……的利益"解时,另外一种表达形式是 in one's (own) interest(s)。例如:

> I think it's *in your own interest to* quit the job now.
> 我认为,你现在放弃那件工作对你自己有利。

in the know *adj.* (非正式用语) having more information (about something that is secret and not many people know about it) than other people 知情的,熟知内幕的: He makes crucial decisions without consulting people *in the know*. 他也不与熟知内情的人商量一下就作出重大决定。It was gratifying to be *in the know* about this important meeting. 了解这次重要会议的内幕是件趣事。I heard this from someone who is *in the know*. 我是从熟知内幕的人士那里得知此事的。

NOTE **1.** 本短语的比较级形式是 more in the know, 最高级形式是 most in the know。

2. 本短语的反义短语是 in the dark(第三个义项)。

in the least *adv.* (用于强调否定句或疑问句) (used for emphasizing a negative statement or question) even a little; at all; in the smallest degree or amount 一点儿: This book is not *in the least* difficult. 这本书一点儿也不难。I'm not *in the least* surprised that she's leaving. 她要走人,我对此一点儿也不感到奇怪。Are you *in the least* interested in skiing? 你对滑雪有没有点儿兴趣?

NOTE **1.** 本短语除了常用于否定句、疑问句中外,还用于条件句中。例如:

> If you are *in the least* doubtful about it, don't do it.
> 如果你对那事有丝毫的怀疑,就不要去做了。

2. 本短语的另外一种表达形式是 the least bit。例如:

> Alice wasn't *the least bit* frightened。
> 艾丽丝一点儿也没害怕。

in the long run *adv.* not immediately but at a time in the future; in the end; in the final result 从长远来看,最后,终究: It'll be cheaper *in the long run* to use real leather because it will last longer. 从长远来看,使用真皮制品还是便宜的,因为它比较经久耐用。The actions we have taken will make the world more secure and the world more peaceful *in the long run*. 我们所采取的行动最终会使这个世界更安全、更安宁。Such addiction would *in the long* run undermine the 'Internet syndrome' sufferers' mental and physical health. 这种上网成瘾将最终会损害这些"因特网综合征"患者的身心健康。

NOTE 本短语的反义短语是 in the short run。

in the main *adv.* (正式用语) mostly; in most cases; for the most part; usually; generally 大体上,大部分,基本上,一般

说来：The students of our university are industrious *in the main*. 总体来说，我们大学的学生是勤奋的。The response, *in the main*, has been quite positive. 反应基本上是很积极的。*In the main*, small boys and dogs are good friends. 一般说来，小男孩和狗是好朋友。

in the meantime/meanwhile *adv.* during the time between two events or between the present time and a future event; at the same time 在此期间，同时：The new secretary won't come until next week; *in the meantime*, we've arranged for a temporary one. 新任秘书下星期才能到，在此期间，我们已安排了一位临时秘书。*In the meantime*, the local government released a notice, asking construction firms not to delay payments for migrant laborers they hired. 当地政府也同时发出了通知，要求建筑公司不要拖欠所雇用的农民工的工资。I hope to go to medical school eventually. *In the meantime*, I am going to study chemistry. 我想最终读医科学校。同时，我还要学习化学。

NOTE 本短语的另外一种表达形式是 in the meanwhile。

in the middle of *prep.* (后接名词或动名词) during; while; in the process of 在……的时候，在……中间，在……的过程中：He fell asleep *in the middle of* the film. 他在看电影时睡着了。I was *in the middle of* cooking dinner when she phoned. 她打来电话时，我正在做饭。The bomb exploded *in the middle of* rush hour traffic, turned cars into fires and sent metal flying hundreds of yards away. 炸弹正值交通高峰时爆炸，多辆汽车起火，金属部件飞出数百码远。

NOTE 本短语的另外一种表达形式是 in the midst of。in the midst of 是正式用语。

in the mood *adj.* (后常接 for 或动词不定式短语) feeling like doing something 有心情的：Are you *in the mood* for a movie? 你想看电影吗？I'm not really *in the mood* for dancing. 我没有心情跳舞。I am not *in the mood* to listen to pop music now. 我现在没有情绪听流行音乐。I don't want to go out — I'm not *in the mood*. 我不想出去——没有心情。

NOTE 本短语的反义短语是 in no mood 和 not in the mood。

in the name of *prep.* ❶ showing that something officially belongs to (someone) 在(某人)的名下：We opened this account *in the name of* Brown. 我们是以布朗的名字开的这个账户。This house is *in the name of* my wife. 这所房子在我夫人的名下。❷using the authority of (someone or something) 凭……的权威，以……的名义：I arrest you *in the name of* the law. 我依法逮捕你。❸ used to give a reason or excuse for (doing something), often when what you are doing is wrong 以……为名(常指做不良之事)：Some performance groups have been organizing body painting shows *in the name of* art, which harmed social ethics and disrupted social order. 一些演出团体以艺术为名组织人体画展，损害了社会道德，扰乱了社会治安。No one should interfere in a country's internal affairs *in the name of* religion. 任何人都不应以宗教为名干涉他国内政。❹ as a representative of (a group) 代表……：In that country the Labour Party governs *in the name of* the people. 在那个国家,工党代表人民执政。She accepted the gift *in the name of* the Save the Children Fund. 她代表"救助儿童基金会"接受了捐赠。

NOTE 本短语的另外一种表达形式是 in one's name。例如:

> The car is registered *in my name*.
> 这部车是以我的名字注册的。

in the open Ⅰ *adv.* in any place that is out of doors rather than in a house or other building 在户外,在露天:Will the meeting be held *in the open*? 会议在户外开吗? It's cold out here *in the open*. 在这里,户外是很冷的。Many ores near the surface can be mined *in the open*. 许多接近地表的矿石都可以露天开采。

Ⅱ *adj.* (前常用 out) (of an attitude, situation, etc.)no longer kept secret (态度或状况等)不再保密的,公开的: The doctors had advised us to keep it a secret, but we wanted it *in the open*. 医生建议我们把病情保密,但我们却想将其公开。The names of the ministers who voted against the government are now out *in the open*. 投票反对政府的那几位部长的名字现已公开。

in the possession of ⇨ **in possession of**

in the presence of *prep.* in the existence of (someone or something)in a particular place 在……面前,有……参加: The document is valid only if it is signed *in the presence of* a witness. 这份文件只有当证人在场时签字才有效。The concert will be performed *in the presence of* the Queen. 女王将出席音乐会。The reaction takes place only *in the presence of* a catalyst. 这种反应只有使用催化剂时才会发生。

NOTE 1. 本短语的另外一种表达形式是 in one's presence。例如:

> She never seemed at ease *in my presence*.
> 有我在时,她总是显得不自在。

2. 本短语的反义短语是 in the absence of 和 in one's absence。

in the public eye *adj.* ❶ (of a person) often seen in public or on television, or mentioned in newspapers (指人)常在公开场合露面的:The new premier is very much *in the public eye* these days. 新任总理近来在传媒上频频出现。❷ well known to people in general 广为人知的,著名的:Her job keeps her *in the public eye*. 她的工作使她广为人知。The former senator remained *in the public eye* even after retirement. 这位前参议员就是在退休后依旧那么有名气。

NOTE 1. 不要将本短语与 in the eyes of the public 混淆,in the eyes of the public 意为"公众认为……"。例如:

> *In the eyes of the public* the mayor was guilty of serious neglect of duty.
> 公众都认为市长有严重的玩忽职守行为。

2. 本短语的反义短语是 out of the public eye。

in the raw Ⅰ *adj.* in an original natural state; without civilization 处于原始状态的,未开化的: He spent a couple of months there to experience life *in the raw*. 为体验原始生活,他在那里度过了几个月。

Ⅱ *adv.* (主要用于美国英语中,非正式用语) without clothes; completely unclothed; naked 赤身裸体地,一丝不挂地:She likes to sleep *in the raw*. 她喜欢

一丝不挂地睡觉。

in/into the red *adj.* &*adv.* (非正式用语) with more money being spent than there is available; in/into debt 亏欠,亏损,负债: Their bank account was in the red again. 他们的银行账户上又有亏欠了。A large number of American radio stations operate *in the red*. 美国有许多广播电台都负债经营。This company has gone thousands of dollars *into the red*. 这家公司已亏损了上万美元。His wild extravagance is running his family *into the red*. 他挥霍无度使其家庭负债累累。

NOTE 本短语的反义短语是 out of the red 和 in the black。

in the right *adj.* (of someone) having justice on one's side; not deserving blame (指某人)有理,没错: In many disputes, it is hard to say who is *in the right*. 在许多争吵中,很难说谁有理。He was *in the right* when he said that. 他那样说是没错的。We stood up for her, as she was entirely *in the right*. 我们支持她,因为她是完全正确的。

NOTE 本短语的反义短语是 in the wrong 和 at fault。

in the sale ⇨ **on sale**

in the short run *adv.* for a short period of time from now; in the immediate present; for the moment 在短期内,暂时,目前: Of course plastic's cheaper than leather *in the short run*, but it won't last as long. 从短期来看,塑料制品当然比皮革制品便宜,但塑料制品并不那么经久耐用。Most diets produce weight loss only *in the short run*. 大多的特种饮食所产生的减肥效果都只是暂时性的。*In the short run*, the mood of the investors counts. 目前,投资者的情绪如何是很重要的。

NOTE 本短语的反义短语是 in the long run。

in the twinkling of an eye *adv.* in an instant; very quickly 一眨眼的工夫,转瞬间,一刹那: The mood of the crowd can change *in the twinkling of an eye*. 群众情绪转眼就能发生变化。*In the twinkling of an eye*, the conjuror pulled a bird out of a cup. 刹那间魔术师从杯中取出一只鸟来。

NOTE 本短语的另外一种表达形式是 in the wink of an eye。例如:

> *In the wink of an eye* the plane was so far away that it could hardly be seen. 转瞬间,飞机就飞远了,几乎看不见了。

in the vicinity of *prep.* ❶near; around; in the neighborhood of (a particular place)在……附近: There were a hundred or so hotels *in the vicinity of* the railway station. 在火车站附近,大约有 100 家旅馆。All the ships *in the vicinity of* the crash joined in the search for survivors. 撞船现场附近的船只都参加了搜寻幸存者的工作。❷(used before a number to show that it is not exact) about; close to 大约,接近,……左右:(正式用语,用于数字之前,表示该数字不是精确数字) Its present value is *in the vicinity of* $20,000. 其现值约为两万美金。The new manager is *in the vicinity of* thirty. 新任经理大约 30 岁左右。This is a boat costing *in the vicinity of* $800. 这条小船的成本大约是 800 美元。

in the view of ⇨ **in view of**

in the wake of *prep.* as a result of;

coming after or following 作为……的结果，随着……而来：Airport security in Manila was extra tight *in the wake of* yesterday's bomb attack. 在昨天发生炸弹爆炸后，马尼拉机场的保安格外地加强了。Hunger and disease followed *in the wake of* the war. 紧随战争而来的便是饥饿和疾病。

in the way *adj.* (常与 of 连用) in your path as a hindrance; placed so as to prevent progress or make it difficult for someone to do things 阻碍，妨碍：I couldn't get through the door because there was a big box *in the way*. 一个大箱子挡住了去路，我过不去了。Don't leave your bicycle where it will get *in the way* of pedestrians. 不要把你的自行车放在阻碍行人通行的地方。The Philippines President said that she would no longer stand *in the way* of the death penalty starting from the beginning of the next year. 菲律宾总统说，她不再阻止将从明年初开始执行的死刑。

NOTE 1. 不要将本短语和 in a way 混淆，两者的意义和用法均不同。见 in a way。

2. 本短语的比较级形式是 more in the way，最高级形式是 most in the way。

3. 本短语的另外一种表达方式是 in one's way。

in the way of *prep.* in the matter of, as regards or relating to (something) 在……方面，关于：He doesn't have much *in the way of* education. 他没受过多少教育。The government has done much *in the way of* improving living conditions for the farmers. 政府在改善农民的生活条件方面做了大量工作。

in the wind *adj.* likely to happen soon, although you do not know exactly how or when 即将发生的：Once again, changes in top management of the company are *in the wind*. 公司的高级管理层即将再次发生变动。The boss is behaving very strangely; I don't know what it is, but there's something *in the wind*. 老板的举动很古怪，我不知道是怎么回事。不过好像有什么事要发生。

in the wink of an eye ⇨ **in the twinkling of an eye**

in the world *adv.* (非正式用语，用于强调疑问句中所述内容，与 what, how, where, who 等疑问词连用，表示惊讶或气愤) (used for adding emphasis to a question, especially because you are surprised or angry) on earth 到底，究竟：What *in the world* do you mean? 你到底是什么意思？How *in the world* did they make a mistake like that? 他们怎么竟犯下了那样的错误？Where *in the world* did you go last night? 你昨晚究竟去哪儿了？Who *in the world* told you that? 那事究竟是谁告诉你的？

NOTE 本短语与 on earth(第二个义项)相同，两者可互换使用。除这两者之外，还可用 the hell 来表达相同的意义。例如：

> What *the hell* do you mean?
> 你到底是什么意思？

但这种用法被认为比较粗俗，故较少用。

in the wrong *adj.* ❶mistaken or wrong; morally or legally incorrect 有过错的，犯错误的：Even though he is *in the wrong*, he won't admit it. 即使他有过错，他也不会承认。He acknowledged himself *in the wrong*. 他承认自己不对。❷responsible for (something wrong, a quarrel, etc.); deserving blame 为(某一过错，争吵等)

负责,该受责备:Your mother always puts herself *in the wrong* whenever something goes wrong at home. 不管什么时候家里出岔子,你妈妈总是把不是揽到自己身上。She was the one *in the wrong*. 她是该受责备的人。

NOTE 本短语的同义短语是 at fault;反义短语是 in the right。

in this case *adv.* (indicating that what you are going to say is true)if this is so; if this should have happened 如果是这样的话,假使这发生的话:*In this case* you will expect liquids to expand more when they are heated than solids do. 在这种情况下,你可以料到液体受热后膨胀得要比固体大得多。They may not offer me much money. *In this case* I won't take the job. 他们给我的工资可能不多。要是这样的话,我就不接受那份工作。

NOTE 本短语的另外一种表达形式是 in that case。

in this regard *adv.* (正式用语)concerning what has just been said 在这方面:"Now we need more than 3 million tents for quake homeless. We hope and welcome international assistance *in this regard*," he told reporters. 他向记者表示,"我们目前需要300多万顶帐篷来安置地震后无家可归的人。我们希望也欢迎国际社会在这方面给予援助。" The company is owned by its staff, and *in this regard* it is rather unusual. 这家公司为其职员所有,这是非常特别的现象。

NOTE 本短语的另外一种表达形式是 in that regard。

in this way *adv.* ❶ thus; in so doing 这样:*In this way*, the cooperation between the two countries will grow from strength to strength and deliver greater benefits to both sides. 这样,两国间的合作就会不断加强,这对双方都大有裨益。Only *in this way*, can the world maintain peace and stability, and a more brilliant future be created for mankind. 只有这样,世界才能保持和平与安宁,人类文明才能走向更加辉煌的未来。❷ in such method 以这种方法:To solve the problem *in this way* is thought most convenient. 用这种方法解题被认为是最简便的。

in time *adv.* & *adj.* ❶(本短语之前常用副词 just,之后常接用 to、for 短语)early enough; not too late 及时地,及早地:We got to the station just *in time* to check in. 我们到达车站正及时赶上检票。Will you be *in time* for the plane? 你还来得及赶上这班飞机吗? I want to be home *in time* for lunch. 我想及时赶到家里吃午饭。❷ after a certain period of time, especially after a gradual process of change and development 过一会儿,过一段时间:I think that *in time* we may win. 我想我们过一会儿可能会赢。*In time* you will forget him. 过一段时间你就会把他忘掉的。I am sure he will see changes in the company, *in time*. 他肯定能在一段时间后看到公司的变化。❸ sooner or later; eventually when a lot of time has passed 迟早,最终:It'll be crystal clear to you *in time*. 你迟早会一清二楚的。You'll learn how to do it *in time*. 你早晚能学会如何做此事的。Any scientific discovery will have its use *in time*, even if at present no use can be foreseen. 任何科学发现迟早会有用,即使现在尚无法预见其用处。❹(常与 to, with 短语连用)(of musicians, dancers, etc.)all playing or acting at the same rhythm or speed 和着节奏,同步: It is important to dance *in time* to the music. 跳舞要跟上音乐的节奏,这一点是重要的。They danced *in time* with the band. 他们和着乐队演奏的节拍翩翩起舞。

in total *adv.* counting everyone or everything; when all have been added up 总计,合计: *In total*, China's first lunar probe experienced four orbital transfers, one orbital correction and three brakings. 中国首颗月球探测卫星总共经历了四次变轨、一次轨道矫正和三次制动。These products, *in total*, account for about 80% of all our sales. 这些产品总共占我们全部销售额的大约80%。

in touch with *prep.* ❶in contact with or in communication with (someone) by telephoning, or writing to him or her (通过电话或写信)与(某人)接触,和(某人)联系: The president will be *in touch with* the prime minister via hotline during his 3-day stay in Japan. 总统在日本停留三天期间将通过热线与总理联系。I'm trying to get *in touch with* my friend; he emigrated to Canada, and I lost touch with him. 我正设法与我的朋友取得联系。他移居加拿大了,我和他失去了联系。Though we live in different cities, we still keep *in touch with* each other. 虽然我们生活在不同的城市,但我们一直保持着联系。I can put you *in touch with* a very good eye doctor, if you would like him to examine you. 我能给你联系一位很好的眼科医生,如果你愿意让他给你诊治的话。❷understand and know about(a situation or subject)了解,熟知(某一状况或主题): To be successful in business, you must keep *in touch with* the market. 要想在生意上获得成功,就必须不断了解市场行情。Newspapers keep one *in touch with* the world. 报纸使人们了解世界。

NOTE **1.** 当本短语作(通过电话或写信)"与(某人)接触,和(某人)联系"解时,同义短语是 in contact with。

2. 本短语的反义短语是 out of touch with 和 lose touch with。

in trouble *adj.* ❶ in a difficult or dangerous position or situation 在困境中,在险境中:The company is *in trouble* because of poor management. 由于管理不善,公司陷入困境之中。When one is *in trouble*, help comes from all directions. 一方有难,八方支援。Let's pray for those *in trouble*, or hopelessness. 让我们为那些身处困境或感到绝望的人祈祷。❷in a situation for which you are likely to be blamed, criticized, or punished 遭遇麻烦(如受责备、挨批评或受惩罚等): If he hears about this, you'll be *in* big *trouble*. 如果他听说这事,你可就要有大麻烦啦。I hear the mini-bus driver is *in trouble* with the police again. 我听说那辆面包车司机又遇到警察的麻烦了。❸(委婉用法) pregnant and unmarried 未婚怀孕: They had to get married. She was *in trouble*. 他们不得不结婚,因为她怀孕了。

in truth *adv.* (正式用语,用于肯定句中加强语气)(used when saying what something is really like, or what you really think about a situation) in fact; really 事实上,的确: *In truth*, the situation could have been much worse for them. 事实上，情势对他们可能更糟。This is *in truth* an ideal site for a power plant for it's close to the source of coal supply. 这里的确是一个很理想的发电厂厂址，因为它离煤炭供应地很近。

in tune with *prep.* in agreement with (someone or something); having the same opinions, feelings, interests, etc. as (someone or something) 与……协调，与……一致：In her new job, Mary felt *in tune with* her associates. 在她的新工作中，玛丽觉得自己与同事们很协调。These proposals are perfectly *in tune with* our own thoughts on the subject. 这些建议与我们对这个项目的一些想法完全一致。

NOTE 本短语的反义短语是 out of tune with，两者的用法相同。

in turn *adv.* ❶ (of more than two persons, groups, etc.) one after the other 一个接一个地，逐一：The students were summoned *in turn* for the oral test. 学生们一个接一个地被叫进去进行口试。The students called out their names *in turn*. 学生们逐一报出自己的名字。❷in the proper order or in sequence; when one's turn comes 依次地，轮流地：We look at each step of the process *in turn*. 我们依次地观看该过程的每一个步骤。The annual meeting of the Asia-Pacific Parliamentary Forum is held *in turn* by APPF members on both sides of the Pacific Ocean. 亚太议会论坛年会轮流在太平洋两岸的成员国举行。Someone must be awake at all times, so let's sleep *in turns*. 因为必须有人总是醒着，所以我们要轮流睡觉。❸afterwards 然后：I told Frank the news and he *in turn* told Sheila. 我把消息告诉了弗兰克，后来弗兰克又告诉给了希拉。Her mother taught her, and she *in turn* taught her own daughter. 她妈妈教会了她，然后她又教会了她自己的女儿。❹inevitably 必然地：Man is destroying nature, and nature *in turn* is punishing man. 人类在毁坏自然，而自然也必然惩罚人类。

NOTE 本短语与 by turns 都表示“轮流、依次”。两者之间的区别见 by turns。

in use *adj.* being used regularly 在使用着：Black Hawk Helicopters are *in* wide *use* in Iraq both for transport and to carry out raids on suspected guerrilla hideouts. 黑鹰直升机在伊拉克被广泛用于运输和向可疑的游击队藏匿点实施空袭。This is the dictionary mostly *in use* among our students of English. 这是我们学习英语的学生最常用的一部词典。I'll be glad to see the building *in use* again. 我会很高兴看到这幢楼房重新启用。

NOTE 本短语的反义短语是 out of use。

in vain Ⅰ *adj.* &*adv.* without success in achieving what you intend; without effect 徒劳，白费，无效：All his efforts to the study were *in vain*. 他对这项研究所做的努力都白费了。We walked a couple of blocks, looking *in vain* for a cab. 我们走了两个街区都没有找到一辆出租车。We tried *in vain* to make him change his mind. 我们试图使他改变主意，结果无效。

Ⅱ *adv.* in a way that has no purpose or meaning 毫无意义地，白白地：Did all these young men die *in vain*? 这些年轻人都死得毫无意义吗？Yassin's supporters said that Yassin's blood would not be spilt *in vain* and vowed to avenge him. 亚辛的支持者说亚辛的鲜血不会白流并发誓要为他报仇。An old dog barks not *in vain*. (谚语)老狗不乱吠。

NOTE 当本短语作“徒劳，白费，无效”解时，比较级形式是 more in the way，最高级形式

I

是 most in the way。

in/into view *adv.* & *adj.* ❶in sight; visible 看得见,在望:We came around a bend and there was the ocean *in view.* 我们走过弯路就看见了大海。Stand here, and you can have everything *in view.* 你站在这儿,一切就能一览无遗。When we reached the top of the mountain, we came *in view* of a wide plain below. 当我们登上山顶时,下方辽阔的平原便尽收眼底。When I opened my eyes a wide plain came *into view.* 当我睁开眼时,一片辽阔的平原纳入了眼帘。❷(正式用语)already planned or suggested 计划好的(地),已提出的(地):Do they have a plan *in view*? 他们有制订好的计划吗? What plan have you got *in view* now? 你现在考虑好什么计划没有? ❸as a purpose, hope, or expectation 作为目的,作为希望:He bought the land with expansion of the business *in view.* 他买下这块土地,目的在于扩大经营。The lawyer's son has his father's profession *in view.* 这位律师的儿子希望从事他父亲那一行。

NOTE 当本短语作"看得见,在望"解时,同义短语是 in/within sight;反义短语是 out of view 和 out of sight。

in view of *prep.* taking in consideration (facts that have just been mentioned or are just about to be mentioned) 考虑到,鉴于:*In view of* our long-standing relationship, we agree to allow you a discount. 考虑到我们长期的关系,我们同意给你折扣。There is a possibility a new round talk on the nuclear issue could be convened next month *in view of* various political situations. 鉴于一些不同的政治形势,新一轮核问题会谈可能下月举行。

NOTE 本短语中的名词 view 必须用单数形式,而且在前面不能加任何冠词。如加定冠词,即 in the view of,意为"在……看来"。例如:

> *In the view* of these theorists, the people are the makers of history.
> 以这些理论家们看来,人民是历史的创造者。

in virtue of ⇨ **by virtue of**

in vogue *adj.* in the state of being popular or fashionable 流行的,时髦的:Traditional Chinese New Year pictures are now *in vogue* again, and have become a hot collectors' item for both Chinese and foreigners. 传统的中国年画现又开始流行,并已成为中外人士的热门珍藏品。Short skirts are no longer *in vogue* in Britain. 短裙在英国已不再时髦。

NOTE 1. 本短语的同义短语是 in fashion。

2. 本短语的动词形式是 come into vogue。

in want of *prep.* (正式用语) in need of (something)需要(某物):Our house is *in want of* repair. 我家的房子需要修缮了。Are you *in want of* more money? 你还需要些钱吗? We are so well provided that we are not *in want of* anything. 我们应有尽有,什么也不缺。

incapable of *adj.* not having the ability, capacity, or potential to do something 没有……的能力的,不能……的:He is a man *incapable of* violence. 他是一个没有施行暴力能力的人。These children seem to be *incapable of* understanding simple instructions. 这些孩子似乎连最简单的指令都不懂。

NOTE 本短语的反义短语是 capable of。

inclined to *adj.* (后接原形动词) ❶having a tendency to behave in a particular way, or to be interested in a particular thing 易于……的,有……倾向(做某事)的:I'm *inclined to* get tired very easily. 我很容易疲倦。Younger people here seem more *inclined to* save money than their parents. 这里的年轻人似乎比他们的父母更节省钱。Most animals are *inclined to* run when they feel threatened or frightened. 大多数动物在受到威胁或惊吓时就会奔跑。❷(只用作表语) feeling that you want to do something 想要(做某事)的: I'm *inclined to* forgive him because of his youth. 因为他年轻,所以我想要原谅他。Karen didn't feel *inclined to* help. 卡伦不想帮忙。He did not seem *inclined to* do work. 他不像想要干活的样子。

independent of *adj.* not governed by (another country); not depending on (other people for money) (脱离其他国家)独立的;(在经济上)不依赖于(他人)的: India became *independent of* Britain in 1947. 印度于 1947 年脱离英国而独立。In the United States most young people want to be *independent of* their parents. 在美国,大多数年轻人都想离开父母而自立。His wages enabled him to become economically *independent of* his family. 他的工资使他在经济上不再依赖家里。

NOTE 本短语中的形容词 independent 与介词 of 连用,但其反义词 dependent 与介词 on 或 upon 连用。

indifferent to *adj.* (of someone) lacking interest in (something); not caring about or noticing (对某事)不感兴趣的,冷漠的,不关心的: I was *indifferent to* the whole subject. 我对整个论题都不感兴趣。I was so excited to see snow that I was *indifferent to* the cold. 我看到雪激动得连寒冷都不在乎了。

indispensable to *adj.* (of someone or something) absolutely necessary or essential to (other people or things or doing something)对……是绝对必要的,对……是不可缺少的: The young man has become quite *indispensable to* the company. 这个年轻人已成了公司不可或缺的人物。Mathematics is *indispensable to* progress in physics and chemistry and astronomy. 数学对物理学、化学和天文学方面的发展都是十分重要的。International cooperation is *indispensable to* resolving the problem of the drug trade. 解决毒品贸易问题必须依靠国际间的合作。

indulge in *vt.* 【不可分性动词短语】(非正式用语) allow yourself to have or do something that you enjoy, especially something that is considered rather bad or harmful and people do not approve of (让自己)纵情享受,沉溺于(尤指有害或为人们所唾弃的事物): No, I don't *indulge in* contact sports anymore. 不,我不再热衷于接触性运动了。To *indulge in* excessive drinking or smoking is harmful to health. 纵情于过度的饮酒或吸烟是有损健康的。He confessed that he had *indulged in* affairs with several women. 他承认自己曾沉溺于与数个女人鬼混。

infamous for *adj.* (贬义用法) famous or widely known for something bad 以……臭名昭著: These boy students are *infamous for* their practical jokes on any new teachers. 这些男生以他们对所有新任老师搞恶作剧而声名狼藉。Some industries are *infamous for* their inefficiency and consumption of more energy sources to produce less amount of output. 有些行业以其效率差、消耗能源多但产量低而臭名远扬。

NOTE 本短语的同义短语是 notorious for; 反义短语是 famous for。

I

infect with *vt.*【可分性动词短语】(常用被动语态形式) cause (someone or oneself) to catch (a disease, that can be spread from one person to another); transmit disease-causing organisms to (someone)使(某人或自己)感染(某种疾病或病毒): Go away, I don't want to *infect* you *with* my cold. 快走开,我不想把感冒传染给你。Unfortunately, they *infected* themselves *with* the SARS virus they were studying. 不幸的是,他们都感染上了他们正在研究的SARS病毒。

NOTE 本短语现已不限于表示"(人)感染(某种疾病或病毒)"之意,也用来表示"(物)感染(某种病毒等)"。例如:

> This is how to check if your computer system *is infected with* the new "Trojan Horse" virus.
>
> 这就是如何检查你的计算机系统是否感染了这种新"木马"病毒的方法。

inferior to *adj.* (正式用语) ❶ lower in ability, status or rank than (someone else) (能力、地位或官阶)低于(他人): Women are, in many respects, not *inferior to* men. 妇女在很多方面并不比男人差。He preferred the company of those who were intellectually *inferior to* himself. 他喜欢与那些智力比自己低的人为伴。A corporal is *inferior to* a sergeant, the fact of which is known even to a small child. 下士的级别低于上士。这是个连小孩儿都知道的事实。❷not as good as (something else) in quality, value, etc.; worse than (在质量、价值等方面)差于,低劣于,次于: These oranges are *inferior to* those I bought last week. 这些橘子比我上周买的要差。This design is *inferior to* the one the German company proposed. 这种设计方案不如德国公司所提出的那种方案。

NOTE 1. 不要将本短语误用为 inferior than。

2. 本短语的反义短语为 superior to。

inform of/about/on *vt.*【可分性动词短语】(正式用语) officially tell (someone something) or give (someone) information about (something)把……正式告诉给(某人),把……报告给(某人),把……通知给(某人): Why wasn't I *informed of* her arrival? 她来了为什么没通知我? The American residents are being kept *informed about* security issues through messages from the diplomatic institution. 当地的美国居民正通过来自外交机构的信息了解有关安全方面的问题。You ought to *inform* the police *about* that man who has been hiding in the bushes outside your gate. 你应当把你们大门外灌木丛中藏着的那个男子报告给警察。We will keep you *informed on* anything that happened and will happen. 我们会把任何发生或将要发生的情况报告给你。

inject into *vt.*【可分性动词短语】❶force or drive (usually a fluid) to enter (a body part or something)把……注(射)入: They will *inject* the vaccine *into* the muscle of your upper arm: the vaccine should not be given into your bottom. 他们会把疫苗注射入你的上臂肌肉中,因为这种疫苗不应往臀部注射。This drug works best if it is *injected* directly *into* the bloodstream. 如果把这种药物直接注射入血管中,那么其效果最佳。Mosquitoes not only suck our blood but also *inject* poison *into* our bodies. 蚊子不仅仅吸我们的血,还把毒注入我们的体内。This is a more efficient way of *injecting* fuel *into* the engine. 这是一种往发动机中注油的更有效方式。❷ add (something needed) to (something)给……增加……: We hope to *inject* new life *into* our business. 我们希望给

我们的业务工作注入新的活力。

inquire about ⇨ **ask about**

inquire after ⇨ **ask after**

inquire into *vt.* make a search or inquiry into (something), in order to discover information or find out the truth about something; examine (something)查究,调查:The court ordered the council to *inquire into* the conduct of the two officials. 法庭责令该委员会对那两名官员的品行进行调查。The police are still *inquiring into* the case. 警方仍在调查此案。The matter is now being *inquired into*. 此事现正在调查之中。

NOTE 本短语的另外一种表达形式是 enquire into。

inside out *adv.* ❶with the usual inside parts on the outside 内外翻转,里朝外:Mary's umbrella blew *inside out*. 玛丽的伞被吹得翻转过来。Robert mistakenly wore his raincoat *inside out*. 罗伯特错把雨衣里朝外地反穿了。She turned all her drawers *inside out* looking for her ring. 为了找戒指,她把所有的抽屉都翻了个底朝上。❷(非正式用语,用于动词 know 之后) with complete knowledge; very thoroughly 一清二楚;极彻底地:Why don't you go and ask James? He knows this subject *inside out*. 你为何不去问詹姆斯?他对这一科目了如指掌。

NOTE 本短语的第二个义项为 inside and out 的缩略形式。

insist on/upon *vt.* 【不可分性动词短语】❶keep firmly to (some demand, or some position)坚持(某种要求或立场):I *insisted on* a contract that gave me some sort of security. 我坚持要一份给我提供某种保障的合同。Many graduates *insist on* getting into foreign-owned or large State-owned companies in cities that pay good salaries. 许多毕业生都坚持要进入城市中工资较高的外资或国有大公司工作。The doctor *insisted upon* the patient staying in the hospital for two more weeks. 医生坚持让病人在医院再住两个星期。❷keep doing (something that annoys people)不断地做(令人讨厌之事):Why do you *insist on* leaving your dirty clothes all over the floor? 你为什么总把你的脏衣服扔的满地板都是?

NOTE **1.** 本短语中的 upon 用法比 on 正式,但不及 on 常用。

2. 本短语后接名词、动名词短语和代词,但不能接"代词的宾格＋不定式"结构。例如,"他坚持要我与他同去。",不能说:* He *insists on* me to go with him. 应该说:He *insists on* my going with him.

3. 当本短语作"坚持"解时,同义短语是 adhere to, persist in, persevere at/in/with 和 stick to。它们之间的区别是:本短语指坚持某种主张、要求或立场,persist in/with 指坚持所说或所做的事(可能是错误的),有"固执己见,偏执"之意;persevere at/in/with 指坚持某种努力、克服困难而达到某一目的;stick to 指坚持不改变、不停止、不放弃地做所决定或承诺之事;adhere to 指坚持或遵守(某种思想、意见、原则、计划、信念等)。

instead of *prep.* in place of; as substitute for; rather than 代替,而不:Welson will be playing *instead of* me on Saturday. 威尔逊将在星期六代替我比赛。The production in the plant has been increased very quickly *instead of* very slowly. 该厂的生产增加得很快,而不是很慢。We went there by train *instead of* by bus. 我们是乘火车而不是坐公共汽车去那里的。It's our teacher who should ask you *instead of* you asking him. 是我们老师应该问你,而不是你问他。

I

instruct in *vt.*【可分性动词短语】teach (someone)(a subject or skill)教(某人)(某一科目或某种技能)：All children should be *instructed in* the use of the library. 应教会所有的孩子使用图书馆。Girls as well as boys should be *instructed in* woodwork. 女孩子和男孩子一样都应教做一些木工活。Richard *instructed* my secretary *in* the best method *of* entering data into the computer. 理查德教了我的秘书往电脑里输入数据的最佳方法。The sergeant was *instructing* the soldiers *in* how to do the drill. 那位中士在教士兵们如何操练。

I

integrate into *vt.*【可分性动词短语】❶(常用被动语态形式) make (someone) become a full member of a group or society and be involved completely in its activities 使(某人)融入(某一社会)：It's necessary to *integrate* released prisoners back *into* society. 使刑满释放人员重新融入社会是必须的。How would such culturally different people be *integrated into* our society? 在文化上(与我们)如此不同的人们怎样融入我们的社会呢? ❷(正式用语) join (one thing) to (something else) so as to form a whole 使成为一体：I am trying to *integrate* the different sections of my work *into* a single report. 我力图把我工作的不同方面汇总成一份报告。Many schools are now *integrating* computer programs *into* the curriculum. 目前，许多学校都在把计算机程序纳入学校课程。

integrate with *vt.*【可分性动词短语】(常用一般时态) combine (something) with (something else); join or cause (a member of a social group) to join in society as a whole 把……与……相结合，把……与……融为一体：We should, most of all, *integrate* theory *with* practice. 我们尤其应该把理论与实践结合起来。To grow and prosper, we must stay open and *integrate* ourselves *with* the global economy. 为了发展与繁荣，我们必须继续开放，使自己融入全球经济。Not all foreign immigrants want to *integrate with* us. 并非所有的外国移民都愿意与我们同化。

intend to *v.* (后接原形动词) wish or mean to (do something) 打算(做某事)：The President announced on Thursday that he *intended to* lift the state of emergency on December 16. 总统星期四宣布，他打算在12月16日解除紧急状态。An NASA's satellite *intended to* study global warming crashed into the sea near Antarctica just minutes after blast-off. 美国宇航局一颗旨在研究全球变暖的卫星在发射升空几分钟后就坠入南极洲附近的海域。I don't think she *intended* me *to* hear the remark. 我认为她不想让我听到那番话。

intent on *adj.* ❶ concentrating hard on (something or doing something) 专心于，专注于：He was so *intent on* his gardening magazine that he didn't notice me come in. 他太专注于读他那本园艺杂志，连我进来他都没察觉到。❷(后接动名词短语) having a determined intention in (doing something) 一心想要(做某事)：She seemed *intent on* making me miserable. 她好像一心想让我痛苦。He's *intent on* going to the United States to continue his studies. 他一心想要去美国深造。

interested in *adj.* feeling or showing interest in (something or someone) 对……感兴趣：I am very *interested in* what he said. 我对他所讲的很感兴趣。If you didn't run after her so much, she might be more *interested in* you.

如果你不是拼命追求她的话,她也许会对你更感兴趣。

interfere in/between *vt.* 【不可分性动词短语】(贬义用法) deliberately become involved in (a situation) and try to influence the way that it develops, although it does not concern you, and your involvement is not wanted 干涉,干预,介入:I don't *interfere in* what others do. 别人做什么,我不干预。I never *interfere between* husband and wife. 我从不介入夫妻之间的事。

NOTE 1. interfere between 是英国英语用法。
2. 本短语的同义短语是 interfere with, intervene in 和 step in。三者之间的区别是:本短语指蓄意参与与你无关的、你没有权利做的事情,从而干涉他人的事务;interfere with 则指阻止或妨碍某事的发生或发展而干预;intervene in 通常表示主动出面干预一项争端或争论,以达到调停之目的;step in 则表示出于帮助之目的而出面干涉或 介入。

interfere with *vt.* 【不可分性动词短语】❶get in the way of; prevent something from (happening or developing) in the correct way 妨碍,干扰,干预:I wish you would stop *interfering with* my work. 我希望你不要再妨碍我的工作。Even a low level of noise *interferes with* my concentration. 哪怕一点点声音都会干扰我的注意力。According to the report, Japan had moved 125 billion US dollars to *interfere with* the foreign exchange market to prevent yen from devaluating. 据报道,日本已动用了 5 亿美元来干预外汇市场,以阻止日元贬值。❷use, handle, or change (something), although you have no right to do this, especially so that you damage or spoil it 擅用,(私自)乱动(某物):I saw him *interfering with* the new computer. 我看到他在乱动那台新电脑。Who's been *interfering with* my books? 是谁一直在乱动我的书?❸(英国英语,委婉用法,常用被动语态形式)(euphemism) attack (a child) by touching her or him sexually 对(儿童)进行性侵犯:The police doctor says that the dead girl had been *interfered with* before her death. 法医说,那死去的女孩在死前曾被性侵犯过。

intervene in *vt.* 【不可分性动词短语】(常用一般时态)intentionally become involved in (a difficult situation) in order to improve it or prevent it from getting worse 介入,干预:The Central Bank *intervened in* the currency markets today to try to stabilize the exchange rate. 中央银行今天介入货币市场,试图稳定汇率。The chairman thought that it was necessary to *intervene* personally *in* the quarrel between two of his committee members. 主席认为有必要亲自干预其委员会中两名成员之间的争吵。

NOTE 本短语通常表示主动出面介入困难局面或干预一项争端或争论,以达到改善或调停之目的。

introduce into *vt.* 【可分性动词短语】cause (something) enter or exist in (a place such as a country) for the first time 传入,引进:(常用被动语态形式) Buddhism was *introduced into* China from India more than 2,000 years ago. 佛教是在2 000多年前由印度传入中国的。It was said that they have agreed to *introduce* their advanced missile technology *into* the country. 据说,他们已同意将其先进的导弹技术引入该国。

invest in *vt.* ❶(常用一般时态)give, lend, or spend money on (something) in order to improve it or make it more successful 投资于:He *invested* ten thousand pounds *in* a building firm. 他为一家建筑公司投资10 000英镑。Investors should understand that stock markets are risky and they must be cautious in entering the market, especially those who use all their savings to *invest in* stocks, the expert said. 这位专家提示,投资者,尤其是那些用掉全部存款投资股市的人,应该懂得:股市有风险,入市须谨慎。❷(非正式用语,常用一般时态) buy (something, especially something that you need and will use a lot)买(所需和常用之物): I think it's time I *invested in* a new computer. 我想,我该买一台新电脑了。❸use(something such as time or effort) for a particular purpose (为某一目的而)花(时间或气力)于……: You have to be willing to *invest* a lot of time *in* taking care of elderly parents. 你得愿意花很多时间来照料年迈的父母。

involve in *vt.* (常用一般时态) get (someone) to take part in (something); be deeply concerned in (something or doing something)使(某人)参与(某事),卷入,陷入: The goal is to *involve* workers *in* the decision-making process. 其目的是让工人们也参与到决策的过程中来。It's best not to *involve* yourself *in* other people's private affairs. 你最好不要介入到他人的私事中去。An informer supplied the police with the names of those *involved in* the crime. 告密者向警方提供了涉及该罪案的人名。How many of the children are *involved in* preparing for the concert? 有多少孩子参与这场音乐会的准备工作?

involved with *adj.* closely related or connected with (someone or something) 与(某人)有关系,与(某事)有关联: How long has Mary been *involved with* that boy? 玛丽和那个男孩子的关系有多久了? I don't want my son to get *involved with* any criminals. 我不想让我的儿子与任何犯罪分子有瓜葛。He denied that he was *involved with* the crime. 他否认与那宗罪案有关联。

iron out *vt.* 【可分性动词短语】❶make (clothes or folds in clothes) smooth with an iron 熨平(衣物): She *ironed out* the folds in her skirt. 她把裙子上的皱褶熨平了。Would you mind *ironing* the collar of this shirt *out* for me? 请你替我把这衬衣的领子熨平,好吗? ❷(非正式用语) remove or resolve (something such as a difficulty or problem)消除,解决(困难、问题等): It did not take long to *iron out* the difficulties. 没用多久,困难就解决了。These problems should have been *ironed out* months ago. 这些问题本应在几个月前就得到解决。

irrelevant to *adj.* not directly connected with (a subject; what you are discussing or doing)与……无直接关系的: I think his remarks are *irrelevant to* the subject. 我认为他的话与这一主题无关。I think they are clinging to an issue *irrelevant to* our debate. 我认为,他们所抓住不放的问题与我们辩论的主题无关。Of the companies not holding patents, most consider them *irrelevant to* their business. 那些不具专利权的公司,大多数认为专利权与他们的生意无关。But this film is *irrelevant to* what we discussed in class. 但这部影片与我们在课堂上讨论的内容无关。

NOTE 1. 本短语的另外一种表达形式是

have no relevance to。例如：

> Politicians' private lives have no relevance to their public roles.
> 政治家们的私生活与他们在社会中的角色没有直接关系。

2. 本短语的反义短语是 relevant to。

irrespective of *prep.* (正式用语) without regard to; regardless of 不管，不论，不顾：Personal liberty will be given *irrespective of* social status. 个人自由，不分社会阶层，人人都应享有。He is going to buy a new car *irrespective of* what his wife says. 不管他妻子说什么，他都要买一部新车。They send information to us every week, *irrespective of* whether it is useful or not. 不论有没有用，他们每周都要给我们发送信息。

NOTE 本短语的同义短语是 in spite of 和 regardless of。

it (all) depends *s.* (主要用于口语中) (used to indicate that you cannot give a clear answer to a question because the answer will be affected or determined by other factors) it/that has not yet been decided 那得看情况而定："Are you going to Mary's party?" "I don't know, *it depends*." "你去参加玛丽的聚会吗?" "我不知道。看情况定吧。" "But how long can you stay there?" "*It all depends*." "你要在那儿住多久?" "那得看情况而定。"

NOTE 本短语的另外一种表达形式是 that (all) depends。

it goes without saying *s.* (非正式用语，后接 that 从句) it is clear without needing to be stated 不必说：*It goes without saying* that consumers would be happier if prices were lower. 不必说，物价低，消费者自然会高兴。*It goes without saying* hard work is the key to success. 不用说，刻苦工作乃成功之关键。

NOTE 本短语的另外一种表达形式是 that goes without saying。

it's a wonder ⇨ **no wonder**

ivory tower *n.* a place where you are separated from the practical or unpleasant things that exist in most people's lives 象牙塔(脱离现实生活的小天地)：This research report was produced by some academic experts in their *ivory towers*, far away from the reality of the society. 这份研究报告是由一些学术专家远离社会实际在他们的象牙塔中炮制而成的。

NOTE 本短语为贬义用语，现多用来指高等院校等学术机构。

I

J j

jealous of *adj.* ❶ feeling slightly angry or bitter because someone else has something you would like, or can do something you would like to do 嫉妒的：Other girls have been *jealous of* her good looks. 其他的女孩都嫉妒她的美貌。He is *jealous of* his brother's success and wealth. 他嫉妒他弟弟的成功与财富。Don't be *jealous of* what your friends have. 不要嫉妒你朋友所拥有的东西。❷（正式用语）wanting very much to protect or keep (something) 极欲守护的，唯恐失去的：She became increasingly isolated and *jealous of* her privacy. 她变得越来越孤独，并极欲保持自己独处的状态。He is *jealous of* good name. 他唯恐失去良好的声誉。

NOTE 当本短语作"嫉妒"解时，同义短语是 envious of，两者之间的区别见 envious of。

join forces with *vt.*【不可分性动词短语】start to work together with (other people) in order to achieve a shared goal or common purpose 与（他人）联合（以达到共同的目标或目的）：We're *joining forces with* some friends to hire a hall for a party. 我们正联合一些朋友租用一个大厅举行聚会。The two countries *joined forces with* each other to fight their common enemy. 这两个国家联合起来抗击他们共同的敌人。Jordan and Palestine *joined forces with* Israel to save the Dead Sea. 约旦和巴勒斯坦与以色列联手拯救死海。

join hands *vi.* ❶ (of two or more people) hold each other's hands (for example for dancing) 拉起手（跳舞等）：They *joined hands* and danced on the floor. 他们拉起手来，在地板上翩翩起舞。Let us *join hands* and pray together. 咱们拉起手来，一起祈祷吧。❷ work together in doing something 携手合作：We must *join hands* in meeting the challenges to human survival and development. 我们必须携手合作，共同应对人类生存与发展所面临的挑战。Many people are ready to *join hands* to improve health care around the world. 许许多多的人都准备携手合作，共同改善全球医疗保健水平。

join hands with *vt.*【不可分性动词短语】❶ hold (someone else's hand) in your hand (for example for dancing) 与……携起手（跳舞等）：We all *joined hands with* our partners and danced round in a circle. 我们都和各自的舞伴拉起手来，围成一个圆圈跳舞。❷ work together with (other people or groups) to help and support each other 同……携手联合（相互帮助和支持）：We must *join hands with* our friends in Europe. 我们必须同欧洲的朋友携手合作。We will also share information with those countries and *join hands with* them in fighting against transnational drug trafficking. 我们还将与那些国家互通信息，联合打击跨国走私毒品犯罪。

NOTE 本短语中的名词 hand 必须用复数形式。

join in *v.* (常用一般时态) take part; take part in (something such as an activity or doing something); do an activity with (people who are already doing it) 参加, 参与, 加入: She laughed and Tom *joined in.* 她大笑起来, 于是汤姆也跟着大笑起来。While *joining in* the international campaign against terrorism, we will contribute to resolving the drug problems in the region. 在参与国际反恐的同时, 我们还将协助解决该地区的毒品问题。The whole crowd *joined in* singing the popular song. 人群中所有的人都跟着唱起了这首流行歌曲。

NOTE **1.** 本短语特指参加某一活动、运动或加入已在从事某种活动的人群中, 动词 join 是指参加到一群人中(或和另一个人一起)进行活动, 也指"成为某一组织的一名成员", 如: join the Party(入党), join the army(参军), 等等。

2. 本短语与 take part in 和 participate in 的意义相同, 用法相近。take part in 和 participate in 都强调参加某项活动, 并在其中发挥一定作用, 其后常接表示集体活动的宾语。另外, take part in 和 participate in 都比本短语更正式。

joke about *vt.* 【不可分性动词短语】 say (something) not seriously so as to make people laugh; treat (something) not seriously enough 把……当笑话说, 把……当儿戏: Do you know that they often *joked about* it? 你知道吗? 他们还经常把那当笑话说呢。You shouldn't *joke about* such a serious thing. 你不应该把这样严肃的事情当儿戏! For Robert to lose his job is nothing to *joke about*. 对罗伯特来说, 失业可不是闹着玩儿的。

joke with *vt.* 【不可分性动词短语】 make a joke about (someone); have fun with (someone) 开(某人)的玩笑, 与(某人)开玩笑: You mustn't *joke with* him in religion. 你千万不要在宗教的问题上开他的玩笑。I *joked with* my friends that we should pretend to be from Canada while we were in Europe, to avoid confrontations with anyone who was not happy with Americans. 我和我的朋友们开玩笑说, 我们在欧洲期间应该装作是加拿大人, 以避免与任何一个不喜欢美国人的人发生冲突。

judge by/from *vt.* (常用一般时态) (used for giving the reason why you think something is true) base your opinion of (something) on (something); form an opinion based on (something) 用……来判断……, 根据……来判断……: Schools tend to be *judged by* the performance of their students in exams. 人们常以其学生的考试成绩来判断学校的好坏。Don't *judge* a person *by* his appearance. 不要以貌取人。I don't think this is a proper standard *by* which to *judge* people. 我认为这不是一个判断人的合适标准。*Judging from* what he said, I think it is unlikely that he'll support your application. 根据他所说的话, 我认为他不会支持你的申请。

NOTE 在 judge by 中, judge 是用作及物动词, 因此 judge by 是可分性动词短语; 而在 judge from 中, judge 是用作不及物动词, 因此 judge from 是不可分性动词短语。

jump at *vt.* 【不可分性动词短语】 (非正式用语, 常用一般时态) take or accept (usually an opportunity, or chance, or an offer, etc.) quickly and eagerly 急切地接受(某一机会等): He told the budding actors to *jump at* every opportunity they can to perform Shakespeare. 他让初露头角的演

J

员抓住一切可以抓住的机会去演莎士比亚剧。You must *jump at* the chance to go abroad with him. 你必须抓住这个机会，和他一起出国。He *jumped at* every invitation he got to speak about his discovery. 他不放过任何一次被邀请的机会去宣讲他的发明。

NOTE 本短语常以 jump at the chance 的形式使用。

jump on *vt.*【不可分性动词短语】(非正式用语) ❶ attack (someone) physically 袭击(某人)：The man with a knife *jumped on* my friend. 那个人拿着刀朝我的朋友袭来。❷ attack (someone) verbally, or criticize (someone), as soon as he or she has done something wrong or said something that you disagree with 训斥，批评(某人)：He *jumps on* me every time I get something wrong. 每当我做错了事时，他都会训斥我一顿。I hate the way she's always *jumping on* me for the slightest little mistake. 我不喜欢她总是因我一点点小错就批评我。I don't enjoy this class; I'm always afraid of being *jumped on*. 我不喜欢这个班级，我总是担心挨批评。

jump out of *vt.*【不可分性动词短语】(常用一般时态) leave (a place) suddenly; with a springing movement 从……突然跳出：During the fire, a number of people broke their limbs or suffered injuries when they *jumped out of* windows. 在发生火灾期间，一些人在从窗户往外跳时而摔断肢体或受伤。Have you *jumped out of* an aircraft with a parachute? 你有没有从飞机上跳过伞？

jump the queue *vi.* (主要用于英国和澳大利亚英语中) move into a queue ahead of other people who have been waiting longer 不按次序排队，插队：If you try to *jump the queue* at a bus stop you'll get shouted at by old ladies. 如果你在汽车站试图插队，年龄大的女士们就会向你喊叫。It makes me mad when someone *jumps the queue*. 有人插队时，我就气得不行。You will have to wait your turn; we can't allow anyone to *jump the queue*. 你得等着轮到你。我们不容许任何人插队。

NOTE **1.** 本短语中的名词 queue 意为"队，行列"，主要用于英国和澳大利亚英语中，在美国英语中用 line，表达"插队"则为 cut in line。例如：

> Wal-Mart outed a former American senator for trying to *cut in* line to get a Sony's PlayStation3.
> 沃尔玛因一位美国前参议员试图插队购买索尼产的 PS3 游戏机而将其逐出了商店。

2. 本短语的复合动词形式是 queue-jump，复合名词形式是 queue-jumping。

jump to a conclusion *vi.* decide something too quickly and without thinking about it or considering all the facts; be too quick to make a judgment based on too few facts 匆忙地决断，草率地下结论：Wait till you have the facts; don't *jump to a conclusion*. 不要急于下结论；等你掌握了事实以后再说。Be careful not to *jump to a conclusion*. 注意不要匆忙下结论。

NOTE 本短语的动词 jump 可被 leap 替换，两者的意义和用法相同。例如：

> It serves no purpose to *leap to conclusions* for none of us really know the cause of his death.
> 草率地下结论毫无意义，因为我们谁都不确知他的死因。

just about *adv.* (非正式用语) almost; very nearly 几乎，差不多：We were *just about* ready to leave when it started to rain. 我们

就要准备出发时，天下起了雨。*Just about* everyone in town came to hear the mayor speak. 几乎镇上每个人都来听了市长的演讲。This job is *just about* done. 这项工作差不多做完了。

NOTE 本短语有时可单独使用。例如：

> "Have you finished your work?" "*Just about*."
> "你的活儿干完了吗?""差不多了。"

just as *conj.* ❶at the very moment when 正当……的时候：He arrived *just as* I was leaving. 我正要走时，他到了。The earth started to tremble *just as* students were having their classes in their classrooms. 正当学生们在教室里上课时，大地开始颤抖。❷(used for emphasizing that something is equally good, bad, etc.)in exactly the same state as 正如……一样：*Just as* a jet fighter needs an ejector seat lever, complex desktop applications need configuration facilities. 就像一架喷气式战斗机需要一个弹射座椅操作杆一样，复杂的桌面应用需要一些配置设施。Animals feel pain just as much as we do. 动物和我们人一样都有痛觉。

just as well *s.* it is fortunate or convenient in the situation that exists; it is a good thing; there is no harm done 幸亏，幸好，没关系，无妨：It's *just as well* I brought my overcoat—it's freezing in here. 我幸亏带了大衣。这儿太冷了。It's *just as* well we have neighbors who don't mind noise. 幸好我们的邻居对噪声都不介意。"We were too late to see the film." "*Just as well*; I hear it isn't very good." "我们太迟了，没看上那部电影。""没什么，我听说那电影不怎么好看。" You may *just as well* go. 你尽管走好了。

NOTE 1. 本短语经常以 it's just as well 的形式使用。其后的从句前往往省略 that。

2. 不要将本短语与 as well 混淆，两者的意义和用法完全不同。

3. 不要将本短语与 may just as well 混淆，两者的意义和用法完全不同。

just now *adv.* ❶(与一般过去时连用) only a short time ago 刚才：Who spoke *just now*? 刚才谁讲话了? I felt a sudden pain in my chest *just now*. 我刚才感到胸部有一阵突然的疼痛。"When did you see him?" "*Just now*, at the house." "你是什么时候见到他的?""刚才，在房里。" ❷(英国英语用法，用一般现在时或现在进行时态)at the present time; exactly at this moment 目前，此刻：Japan would be very pleased to offer relative information if it had it. But such information is not available *just now*, the Japanese expert said. 日方专家说，如果日本有相关的资料，十分愿意提供出来，但这种资料目前是没有的。Mrs Collins is busy *just now*, so you'll have to wait. 克林斯太太此刻正忙，所以您得等一下。

just the same ⇨ **all the same**

K k

keen on/about *adj.* (非正式用语) ❶interested in and enthusiastic about (something or doing) 对……感兴趣,对……有热情: They must be very *keen on* that, I guess. 我猜测他们一定对它很感兴趣。My son is mad *keen on* playing *table* tennis. 我儿子对打乒乓球极感兴趣。Environmentalists are *keen on* degradable materials. 环保主义者特别推崇可降解材料。Robert is fairly *keen about* doing physical exercises. 罗伯特对体育锻炼一向很积极。❷like (someone) or think that she or he is attractive 喜欢(某人): He seems rather *keen on* her. 看上去他非常喜欢她。

keep a cool head ⇨ **kept one's head**

keep abreast of/with *vt.* ❶(无被动语态形式) stay level or in line with (someone or something ahead) 不落后于,紧跟上,保持与……并进: You will have to run fast to *keep abreast of* our best runner and prevent him from winning. 你得快跑才能不落后于我们那名最佳赛跑运动员并使他不能取胜。We must *keep abreast with* the times and press ahead with continued reforms. 我们要与时俱进,继续把改革不断推向前进。❷(一般不用被动语态形式,常用一般时态) make sure that you know all the most recent facts or information about (something) 了解最新情况: How can anyone *keep abreast of* all this new technology? 一个人怎样才能及时了解所有最新的技术呢? Please *keep* me *abreast of* any change in his condition. 他的情况有任何变化请及时告诉我。To survive in a world full of intense competition, an enterprise must *keep abreast with* the most advanced development in its field. 一个企业要想在这个充满激烈竞争的社会中生存下去,就必须掌握其所在行业的最新发展。

NOTE 本短语的动词 keep 可被 stay 替换,两者的意义和用法相同。

keep all your eggs in one basket ⇨ **put all one's eggs in one basket**

keep an eye (open) on *vt.* (非正式用语) ❶keep a close watch on (someone or something) 密切注意,注视: Be careful what you do today. I'll be *keeping an eye on* you. 你今天做事要小心点儿。我要盯着你的。You'd better *keep an eye open on* that fellow in a blue cap; he's a pickpocket. 你最好注意那个戴蓝帽子的家伙。他是个扒手。The farmer can easily *keep an eye on* what is happening in the cornfield. 那个农夫可以很容易地注意到玉米地里的动静。❷look after or take care of (someone or something) and make sure that they are safe 照看,照管: Will you *keep an eye on* the baby? I'll get back in a minute. 你能看一下孩子吗? 我

马上就回来。I have to go to the bathroom. Can you *keep an eye on* my suitcase while I am away? 我要去盥洗室。你能在我去的时候照看一下我的手提箱吗?

NOTE 本短语的同义短语是 have one's eye(s) on。

keep at *vt.* (无被动语态形式,常用一般时态) ❶have (something) present in (a place)把(某物)置于(某处): I *keep* a warm coat *at* my work place in case it suddenly turns cold. 我在工作的地点放一件保暖的上衣,以备天气突然转冷时用。❷(非正式用语)(cause to) continue working at(something difficult)(使)继续干下去: If you *keep* hard *at* the job, you'll soon have it finished. 如果你继续努力地干下去,工作很快就会做完。The work is tiring, but he'll *keep at* it until he's finished. 这项工作很累,但他会继续把它干完。The teacher *kept* us *at* it all afternoon. 老师让我们整个下午都在学习。

NOTE 当本短语作"(使)继续干下去"解时,常以 keep at it 的形式使用。

keep away *v.* (常用一般时态)(cause to) avoid (someone or something)(使)避开,(使)不接近: I've told him to *keep away*, but he won't listen. 我让他避开,可他就是不听。She *kept* her children *away* until he had left. 她让孩子们避开,一直等到他离去。There is a common saying "An apple a day *keeps* the doctor *away*." 常言道:"一天吃一个苹果,不用看医生。" A heavy police presence, ensured that demonstrators and the visiting US President and his party were *kept* far *away*. 大批的警力保证了示威者远离来访的美国总统及其随行人员。

keep away from *vt.* (常用一般时态) (cause to) remain at a distance from (someone or something)(使)离开……,(使)不接近……: *Keep away from* me; I've got a bad cold. 离开我,我得重感冒了。*Keep away from* the edge of the cliff. 切勿靠近悬崖边。Children should be *kept away from* the river. 不应该让儿童靠近河边。

keep back *vi.* (用一般时态,常与 from 连用) remain in a safe distance; move backwards 保持一段安全距离,留在远处,不靠近: *Keep back*, children; the wall is falling! 孩子们,离远点。墙快倒了! The police told the crowd to *keep back* from the fire. 警察让人们不要靠近大火。

—*vt.*【可分性动词短语】❶(常用一般时态) keep (something or someone) in place; prevent (something or someone) from coming forward 挡住: The dikes *kept back* the flood waters. 堤坝挡住了洪水。I would have been here earlier, but the rainstorm *kept* me *back*. 要不是下暴雨,我早就来了。❷(常与 from 连用) not tell someone (something) or not show how you feel; keep silent about 隐瞒: He said he was fine, but I knew he was *keeping* something *back* from me. 他说他很好,但我知道他是有些事情在瞒着我。The doctor recommended that the exact nature of the woman's illness should be *kept back* from her. 医生建议不要让那女患者知道她的真实病情。❸(常用一般时态) control (something such as a feeling) 控制(感情等): She couldn't *keep back* her anger and fought with the middle-aged lady. 她抑制不住怒火,与那中年妇女打了起来。She struggled to *keep back* her tears. 她极力控制住自

己的泪水。❹keep (part of an amount of money that belongs to someone or is owed to him or her)扣留(某人的部分款项):His employers *kept back* some of his wages to pay for the damage he'd done. 他的雇主扣下了他的部分工资以偿付他造成的损失。The payroll office *kept* twenty dollars *back* for my income tax. 财务室扣了我 20 美元的收入所得税。❺keep (part of something) so that you can use it later 留下(一部分物品以备后用): *Keep back* some strawberries for decoration. 留下一些草莓做装饰用。I *kept* a few books *back* for myself to read and gave him the rest. 这些书我留了几本自己看,其余的都给了他。

NOTE 1. 当本短语的宾语为代词时,该代词须置于本短语的动词和副词中间。

2. 当本短语作“隐瞒”解时,同义短语是 hold back 和 hold out on。

keep body and soul together *vi.* (英国英语用法)have just enough money to pay for the things that you need in order to live 勉强维持生计: With this sum of money the family could hardly *keep body and soul together*. 靠这么一点儿钱,一家人几乎无法维持生计。In these days of rising prices, it is difficult for many people to *keep body and soul together*. 在这些物价上涨的日子里,许多人都勉强维持生活。

keep clear of *vt.* (非正式用语,常用一般时态)(cause to) avoid (someone or something unpleasant or dangerous)(使)回避,躲避(某人或令人不快、危险之事物): When you are in a tropical country, *keep clear of* insects which may be carrying dangerous diseases. 在热带国家里,要避免接触昆虫,因为它们可能携带有各种危险的疾病。The police were on the road with signals to *keep* the traffic *clear of* the accident. 警察站在马路上打着手势让车辆驶离事故现场。

NOTE 本短语的动词 keep 可被 remain, stay 或 steer 等动词替换,构成的短语与本短语意义和用法相同。

keep contact with *vt.* 【不可分性动词短语】have a connection or exchange information or ideas with (someone else) 与(他人)保持联系: It's hard to *keep contact with* all your old school friends. 与所有的老校友都保持联系是很困难的。Our company will continue *keep* close *contact with* most of large-scale petrochemical industry and fertilizer enterprise at home and abroad. 我公司将与国内外多家大型石油化工和化肥企业保持着密切的关系。

NOTE 本短语的同义短语是 get in contact/touch with, keep in touch (with) 和 in contact with; 反义短语是 lose contact with。

keep something dark ⇨ **keep (someone) in the dark about**

keep down *vt.* 【可分性动词短语】❶(用一般时态) control (something) and prevent it from increasing in size, number or amount 使下降,减低,减少: This medicine will *keep* your blood pressure *down*. 这种药会使你的血压降下来。I hope the wind *keeps down*. 我希望风力能减低下来。We have to try and *keep* costs *down*. 我们得设法降低成本。Some people have more difficulty than others in *keeping* their weight *down*. 有些人比另一些人在减少体重这方面困难多一些。❷(常用一般时态) control (a feeling such as anger)控制(某种感情):

She couldn't *keep down* her anger and fought with the young lady. 她抑制不住怒火，与那位年轻的女士打了起来。I couldn't *keep* my temper *down* when I saw the picture. 当我看到那张图片时，我按捺不住自己的脾气了。❸(常用一般时态) hold in subjection or under control; stop (a group of people) from achieving what they are capable of achieving; repress 控制，压制，压迫，镇压：The government is trying to *keep down* inflation. 政府正设法控制通货膨胀。Even if you're intelligent, they still try to *keep* you *down*. 即使你再有才智，他们也会千方百计地压制你。The minister said the government would take a strong force to *keep down* the riot. 那位部长表示政府将大力镇压骚乱。❹(常用一般时态) succeed in keeping (food in your stomach) although you feel as if you want to vomit 使(胃中食物)不吐出来：I'd eat something if I thought I could *keep* it *down*. 如果我认为我能不吐的话，我会吃东西的。I can't *keep* this terrible medicine *down*. 吃这难吃的药，没法不吐出来。

NOTE 当本短语的宾语为代词时，该代词须置于本短语的动词和副词中间。

keep fit *v.* (cause to) become or remain healthy, strong, as through physical exercise (通过身体锻炼等)(使)保持身体健康：In order to *keep fit*, Mary does morning exercises every day. 为了保持身体健康，玛丽每天进行晨练。Running around after the kids *keeps* me *fit*. 跟着孩子们跑一跑能使我保持身体健康。*Keeping fit* doesn't necessarily mean you have to reduce your diet. 保持身体健康不一定意味着你必须减少饮食。

keep from *vt.* ❶(正式用语) prevent (someone) from (doing something) or prevent(something) from (happening) 阻止，防止，阻碍：These worries *kept* her *from* sleeping properly. 这些愁事使她睡不好觉。Over 10 Asian countries and region were affected by the bird flu virus, with millions of chickens being killed to *keep* the disease *from* spreading. 十几个亚洲国家和地区感染上了禽流感病毒，有数百万鸡只被宰杀，以防止疫情的蔓延。I know you're busy; I won't *keep* you *from* your work. 我知道你忙，我不会妨碍你工作的。❷(用一般时态，后接动名词或动名词短语) avoid; try to stop yourself from (doing something) 避免，克制(自己)：The troops withheld fire to *keep* the situation *from* escalating. 军队实行停火是为了避免局势恶化。She tried to *keep from* arguing with him. 她竭力克制住自己，没有和他吵。❸not tell (someone)(something)，把(消息等)瞒着(某人)：*Keep* the news *from* her. She'll tell everyone about it. 不要把这消息告诉她。她会见人就讲的。He *keeps* nothing *from* his friends. 他什么都不瞒他的朋友们。

keep guard over *vt.* 【不可分性动词短语】 watch or protect (something or someone) 看守，守卫：The police are *keeping guard over* the house. 警察把守着这所房子。Armed personnel *kept guard over* the palace. 武装人员守卫着皇宫。

NOTE 本短语的动词 keep 可被 mount, stand 等动词替换，构成的短语与本短语意义和用法相同。

keep hold of *vt.* 【不可分性动词短语】 ❶(常用一般时态) not take your hands away from (something that you are holding)握住，抓住：She *kept hold of* his arm. 她抓住他的胳膊不放。*Keep hold of* the rope, and we'll pull you up. 抓住绳子，我们把你拉上来。❷not lose (something) or not let someone else get it 掌握，控制住(某物)：They managed to *keep hold of* the ball in the second half. 他们在下半场控制住了球。

keep house *vi.* (常与 for 连用) be responsible for cooking meals, washing clothes, cleaning the house and doing other similar jobs for someone in a home 料理家务：He lives with a relative who *keeps house* for him. 他和一个亲戚住在一起。他的亲戚为他料理家务。My grandmother *kept house* for nearly fifty years. 我祖母做了近 50 年的家务。

keep in *v.* (主要用于英国英语中，常用一般时态) make (someone) stay in a place, especially in school as a punishment, or make (someone) stay in hospital 罚(学生)留校；把(某人)留住院：The teacher *kept* the students *in* after school because they had misbehaved. 由于这些学生表现不好，老师把他们留校了。They were *kept in* after school for bad behavior. 他们因表现不好而被罚留校了。If he takes her to hospital they might *keep* her *in* for observation. 如果他带她去医院，他们可能会留她住院观察。

NOTE 1. 当本短语用作及物性动词短语，所带的宾语为代词时，该代词须置于本短语的动词和副词中间。

2. 当本短语作"罚(学生)留校"解时，同义短语是 stay in。

keep in touch (with) *v.* remain informed (about someone); contact (someone) by writing, calling, sending e-mail, etc. on a regular basis (通过定期通信、通话、发电子邮件等)(与……)保持联系：Now that we've met again after all these years, let's *keep in touch*. 既然我们在这么多年以后又见面了，咱们可要保持联系喽。I haven't seen my friend P. J. Rogers for more than 10 years but we *keep in touch* by e-mail. 我有 10 多年没见到我的朋友 P. J. 罗杰斯了，但我们通过电子邮件保持着联系。

NOTE 1. 本短语强调的是"与(某人)保持联系"，get in touch with 则强调的是"与(某人)取得联系"这一过程，in touch with 则表示"与(某人)联系"的状态。

2. 本短语的动词 keep 可被 stay 替换，两者的意义和用法相同。

keep in mind *vt.* 【可分性动词短语】(用一般时态) remember (something), especially something that will be important in the future; consider (something or someone) 记住，考虑：All of us must *keep* these lessons of history firmly *in mind*. 我们大家都必须牢记这些历史教训。We must always *keep in mind* the fact that our Party is in power. 我们必须考虑到这样一个事实，我们党是执政党。It must be *kept in mind* that we shall have to be present before eight tomorrow. 一定记住，我们要在明天 8 点以前到场。Don't give your secret to others regarding the plan you *keep in mind*. 不要把你考虑的计划向别人泄露。

NOTE 当本短语的宾语为代词时，该代词须置于本短语的动词和介词中间。

keep (someone) in the dark about *vt.* not tell (someone) about (something) because you want to keep it secret from them 不让(某人)知道有关……的事情，不把(某事)告诉(某人)：The two boys decided to *keep* their parents *in the dark about* where they got the money. 这两个男孩决定不让他们的家长知道他们是从哪儿搞到的这笔钱。We were totally *kept in the dark about* what happened that night. 我们对那天晚上发生的事情全然不知。We'd better *keep her in the dark about* the death of her mother before she gets home. 我们最好在她回到家之前不让她知道她母亲去世的事。

NOTE 在英国英语中，还可用 keep something dark 的形式，主要用于口语中。例如：

> He's got two children, but he's *kept that/it dark*.
> 他已经有两个孩子了，但他却对此一直保密。

keep in with *vt.*【不可分性动词短语】(主要用于英国英语中，非正式用语)(try to) stay friendly with (someone), often in order to gain some advantage for yourself (常指为自己得到好处而)与(某人)友好相处，讨好(某人)，不得罪(某人)：In order to get promoted he had to *keep in with* the people who were important. 为了得到提拔，他不得不巴结重要人物。It'll pay you to *keep in with* the director, as his influence could get you a better position in the company. 讨好董事是划算的，他的影响能使你在公司内得到一个更好的职位。

keep off *vt.* &*vi.* ❶not touch (something or someone) or prevent (something or someone) from touching (something or someone)(使)不接触(某物或某人)：*Keep* the flies *off* the food. 不要让苍蝇接触食物。Children must be *kept off*; it's dangerous to get shocked! 别让孩子们靠近，有触电的危险！*Keep* your hands *off* me! 你的手别碰我！❷not go onto (a particular area of land)不踏入(某一地域)：Don't walk across the lawn; *keep off* the grass. 不要穿越草坪，不准践踏草地。Dogs must be *kept off* the beach. 不得将狗带入海滩。

—*vt.* ❶ ward off, avert 挡住，防止：In the past, umbrellas were only used to *keep off* the rain. 在过去，伞只是用来挡雨。We should take environmental health measures to *keep off* infectious diseases. 我们应该采取一些环境卫生措施以防止传染病的发生。They made a big fire to *keep* wild animals *off*. 他们生起大火以防止野兽接近。❷ avoid (a particular food, habit, etc.)戒食，戒绝(某种习惯等) I'm trying to *keep off* fatty foods. 我尽量不吃高脂食品。After his illness the old man *kept off* liquor for a whole year. 这位老人在病后整整一年没有饮酒。❸(cause to) avoid (a subject of conversation)(使)避开(某一话题)不谈：This is a delicate subject; we'd better *keep off* it. 那是个微妙的话题，我们最好避开它不谈。*Keep* him *off* politics, for goodness sake. 看在老天的分上，让他莫谈政治。

keep on *v.* ❶(常用一般时态) continue (doing something) or do (something) repeatedly 继续，反复(做某事)：They've failed several times, but they still *keep on* (with it). 他们已经失败了好几次，但他们仍继续做下去。Prices *keep on* rising although the government has taken some measures to control them. 尽管政府已采取了一些控制措施，但物价仍在继续上涨。❷ keep (something such as electricity) switched on (电灯等)一直开着：Spared the blackouts are key government offices, hospitals, schools and military installations. For others, *keeping* the lights *on* can be a matter of luck. 免受断电影响的有重要的政府部门、医院、学校和驻军单位。对于其他单位,不停电是一件幸运的事。❸continue to employ (someone), for example after he or she is old enough to retire or after other employees have lost their jobs 继续雇用(某人):Will you be able to *keep* your secretary *on*? 你能够继续留用你的秘书吗? With the worsening economic situation, the company could no longer *keep on* so many workers. 由于经济状况不断恶化,公司再也不能雇用这么多工人了。Only highly skilled people were *kept on* after the merger. 只有那些高技能的人员在企业合并后被继续雇用了。❹continue to have (something)继续保有(某物):I'll *keep* the flat *on* through the summer. 我整个夏天都要租用这套房子。

keep on about *vt.*【不可分性动词短语】(英国英语用法,非正式用语,无被动语态形式,常用一般时态) continue talking about (a subject) in a way that annoys people 唠唠叨叨地说(某一话题):I don't know why you *keep on about* this. 我不知道你为什么老是絮叨这事。She *kept on* at me *about* the money, even though I told her I hadn't got it. 她絮絮叨叨地和我说钱的事,尽管我已告诉她那钱我已得到了。The teacher *kept on about* good behavior. 老师反复再三地讲有关良好行为的话题。

keep on at *vt.*【不可分性动词短语】(英国英语用法,非正式用语,无被动语态形式,常用一般时态,常与 about 连用) repeatedly ask (someone) something or tell (him or her) something or to do something in a way that annoys him or her 不断要求(某人做某事):He has *kept on at* people about that. 他一直在向人们打听那事。His wife *kept on at* him to buy her some new clothes. 他的妻子不断地唠叨要他给她买一些新衣服。

keep one's eye(s) on ⇨ **have one's eye(s) on**

keep one's eyes (and ears) open *vi.* (非正式用语,与 for 连用) pay attention to what is happening, especially in order to find out something 留神,注意: Journeying with their kidnappers in the jungles in western Sudan, the two kidnapped workers continually *kept their eyes open* for a chance to escape. 跟着绑架者在苏丹西部的丛林里行走期间,两名被绑架的工人一直在留意逃跑的机会。Any businessman has to *keep his eyes and ears open* for a chance of making a profit. 任何商人都得留心能赚到钱的机会。

keep one's fingers crossed *vi.* (非正式用语) put one of your fingers over another one hoping for good luck or things will happen in the way you want them to 两指交叉(以求好运或某事顺心如意):Many people have been *keeping their fingers crossed* that we can live in a peaceful world. 许多人都在祈求好运,盼能在和平的世界里生活。We'll just keep to *keep our fingers crossed* that the weather will stay fine for our picnic tomorrow. 我们只能为明天的野餐乞求天气保持晴朗。

NOTE 1. 以食指与中指交叉的方式祈求或祝福某人好运或某事顺利,是西方人的一种迷信做法。

2. 本短语的另外一种表达形式是 have

one's fingers crossed,后者不及本短语常用。

3. 本短语的同义短语是 cross one's fingers。

keep one's head *vi.* stay calm and sensible, for example in a crisis or sudden difficulty (在危机中或突然出现的困难时)保持理智: It is imperative to *keep your head* in a time of crisis. 在危急关头保持镇静是十分重要的。It seemed that a crash was inevitable, but luckily the pilot *kept his head* and landed the plane in the Hudson River safely. 当时看来飞机坠毁已不可避免,但幸而飞行员镇定自若,使飞机安全降落在了哈德逊河河面上。

NOTE 1. 本短语的另外一表达形式是 keep a cool head。例如:

> She *kept a cool head* under pressure and won the race.
> 她在压力之下保持冷静,并赢得了比赛。

2. 本短语的反义短语是 lose one's head。

keep one's mind on *vt.* give your thoughts or pay attention to (something) 专注于: Can you say that again? My *mind* was *kept on* something else. 您能再把那讲一遍吗? 我刚才在想其他事了。She could hardly *keep her mind on* what he said. 她很难用心听他讲话。I can't *keep my mind on* work when it's so sunny outside. 当外面的阳光灿烂时,我就无法专注于工作。

keep one's mouth shut *vi.* (非正式用语) ❶not tell anyone about(something) 不把……讲给别人: If I tell you the story, will you promise to *keep your mouth shut* about it? 如果我把事情告诉你,你能保证不把此事讲给别人吗? You can tell him a secret; he knows how to *keep his mouth shut*. 你可以把秘密告诉给他,他知道怎样守口如瓶。❷not say anything; keep silent 默不作声,保持沉默: When she starts talking about marriage, I just *keep my mouth shut*. 当她开始谈论婚姻的事情时,我就默不作声。

keep one's temper *vi.* stay calm and not get angry 捺住性子,不发火: It's important to *keep your temper* with the children. 对孩子要有耐性,这一点很重要。He was behaving so foolishly that I found it hard to *keep my temper*. 他的行为太愚蠢了,我觉得我很难捺住性子了。Only a saint could *keep his temper* under such irritating circumstances. 在这种令人气愤的情况下,只有圣人才不会发火。

NOTE 本短语的反义短语是 lose one's temper。

keep one's word *vi.* uphold one's promise; do what you promised to do 坚守诺言,履行诺言: You can count on Mary; she always *keeps her word*. 你可以依靠玛丽;她总是很守信用。Musharraf promised he would take off his uniform, and he *kept his word*. 穆沙拉夫承诺他将脱去军服。他履行了诺言。

NOTE 1. 本短语中的名词 word,无论其前的物主代词是单数形式还是复数形式,都必须用单数形式。

2. 本短语的同义短语是 keep (one's) promise(s)。

keep out *vt.* 【可分性动词短语】❶(cause to) stay outside or prevent (someone or something) from entering a place 不让……入内: They've shut the door and mean to *keep* us *out*. 他们把门

关上,意味着不让我们进去。Please close the window and *keep* the cold *out*. 请把窗子关上,不要让寒气进来。Cars should be *kept out* of the city centre. 汽车不应进入市中心。❷provide insulation against 隔离,遮挡:This is used to *keep* the rain *out*. 这是用来挡雨的。Trees around the house can *keep out* wind and dust. 房屋周围的树木能遮挡风尘。

—*vi.* used on signs to tell people not to go into a place (用在警示牌上)禁止入内: Can't you boys read? The notice says "*Keep out*!" 你们这些孩子不识字吗? 这个牌子上写着"禁止入内!" On the sign are the words: Danger! *Keep out*! 牌子上写着:危险! 禁入!

NOTE 当本短语用作及物性动词短语,所带的宾语为代词时,该代词须置于本短语的动词和副词中间。

keep out of *vt.* 【可分性动词短语】❶(常用一般时态)(cause to) stay outside or not enter (something)(使)不进入: In Baghdad many fearful parents *kept* their children *out of* schools after the suicide attacks. 在巴格达市,许多胆怯的家长在多起自杀性袭击发生后,不再让孩子上学。Most teachers advocate *keeping* religion *out of* the biology classroom. 大多数教师拥护禁止宗教进入生物学课堂。❷(无被动语态形式) not become involved with (something); (cause to) stay away from (something such as trouble)不卷入(某事),(使)避开(麻烦等):You *keep out of* this. It's none of your concern. 你避开这事儿。这不关你的事。I tried to *keep out of* their family quarrels. 我设法不卷入他们的家庭争吵之中。I hope you'll *keep* him *out of* trouble while I'm away. 我希望我不在期间,你不要让他卷入麻烦中去。

keep pace with *vt.* 【不可分性动词短语】❶(常用一般时态)move at the same speed as (someone or something else)与……齐头并进: Ron had to run to *keep pace with* Smith. 罗恩得跑着才能跟上史密斯。He *kept pace with* the car on his motorbike. 他骑着摩托车与汽车并驾齐驱。❷develop or progress at the same rate as (someone or something)与……步调一致,跟上: She works so fast that I can't *keep pace with* her. 她的活儿干得太快,我赶不上她。His mental development *kept pace with* the growth of his body. 他的智力发展与他的身体发育保持了同步。Price increase failed to *keep pace with* rising cost. 价格的提高跟不上成本的增长。

keep (one's) promise(s) *vi.* keep one's word or statement that one will or will not do something, give something, etc. 遵守诺言,守约:"China has made great efforts to *keep promises*," said the Chinese ambassador to the World Trade Organization. 中国驻世界贸易组织大使说:"中国已尽了很大的努力去履行其各项承诺。" He didn't *keep his promise*, so I got angry. 他没有守约,所以我发火了。We hope they would *keep their promise* on the Taiwan issue and handle the issue cautiously. 我们希望他们遵守其在台湾问题上的承诺,谨慎处理台湾问题。

NOTE 本短语的同义短语是 keep one's word 和 honor one's promise(s)。

keep to *vt.* ❶follow (a plan, an agreement, a promise or a rule), by doing what you should do or what you said you would do; abide by; stick close to 遵守,坚守,坚持:You must *keep to* the timetable of waking and sleeping. 你必须遵守起床和就寝时间表。I know you don't like the agreement but we have to *keep to* it. 我知道你不喜欢这个协议，但我们得遵守它。As a driver, you must always *keep to* the traffic regulations. 作为驾驶员，必须一贯遵守交通规则。Once you've made a promise, you should *keep to* it. 一旦许下诺言，你就要坚守不渝。❷(用一般时态) remain in (a stated position or place); stay on (a path, road, etc.) when you are going somewhere 留在(某一位置或地方)；沿(某一路线)行驶(或行走)：He *kept to* his room for the first few days of this term. 这个学期的最初几天他一直待在自己的房间里。Traffic in Britain as well as in Hong Kong *keeps to* the left. 在英国，香港也是如此，车辆都是靠左侧通行。If you *keep to* the main road, you won't get lost. 如果你沿这条主干道走，就不会迷路的。❸(无被动语态形式，常用一般时态) write or talk about (the subject you have started to talk about, and not any other) (写作或谈话中)谈论(某一主题)，不偏离(某一主题)：Don't raise irrelevant matters; we must try and *keep to* the subject. 不要提不相关的问题，我们要尽量围绕这个主题谈。The writer *kept to* the question of environment pollution in his article. 作者在文章中谈了环境污染问题。I must *keep to* saying what I've seen with my own eyes. 我必须谈谈我亲眼所见的情况。❹ cause (something) to remain known only to (yourself) 限于使(自己)知道(某事)：I'm resigning — but *keep* it *to* yourself. 我要辞职了，但你自己知道就行了，不要告诉别人。

keep track of *vt.*【不可分性动词短语】❶(非正式用语) remain aware or in touch about (someone or something) 使了解，使熟知(某人或某事)：It's hard to *keep track of* all one's old school friends. 要了解所有老校友的情况是很困难的。He reads newspapers everyday to *keep track of* events of the Olympic Games. 他每天看报纸以了解奥运会的赛况。My sister has had so many different jobs; I find it hard to *keep track of* what she's doing. 我姐姐有好几份工作。我发现很难知道她现正在做什么。❷keep or maintain a record of (something) 记录：We need a system to *keep track of* all our expenses. 我们需要一个系统来记录我们所有的开支。*Keep track of* the time you actually travel. 把你旅行的实际时间记录下来。I have the habit of *keeping track of* my activities with pen and paper. 我有用笔纸记录自己活动内容的习惯。

NOTE 当本短语作"使了解，使熟知(某人或某事)"解时，反义短语是 lose track of。

keep up *v.* ❶(cause to) remain high (使)居高不下，提高，上涨：The shortage of fresh vegetables *kept* the prices *up*. 新鲜蔬菜的短缺使价格居高不下。The shops are trying to *keep* quality *up* but prices steady. 这些商店都在努力提高质量，但又保持价格稳定。They *kept up* their spirits by singing. 他们以唱歌来保持高昂的情绪。❷(常与 with 连用) move at the same speed or remain level (as or with someone or something) 跟上，不落后：You're going too fast; I can't *keep up*! 你走得太快了，我跟不上。I can't *keep up* with these changes in fashion. 我无法赶上这些时装的变化。By studying hard she managed to *keep up*. 通过刻苦学习，她没有落后于他人。❸(cause to) continue to do (something) (使)继续，持续：*Keep up* the good work! 继续把工作做好！The treatment should be *kept up* after the patient leaves hospital. 该患者出院后

K

还应继续治疗。He works far too hard; he'll never be able to *keep* it *up*. 他工作过于努力,他再也无法继续这么工作下去了。We've *kept up* our friendship for over 20 years. 我们的友谊已持续了 20 多年。❹(非正式用语,常用一般时态) prevent (someone) from going to bed 不让(某人)睡觉: It's late, I'd better not *keep* you *up* any longer. 时间很晚了,我还是别再打扰你上床睡觉了。We often *keep up* very late. 我们常常很晚才睡。❺(常用一般时态) look after and keep in good condition 把……照料好: How do you *keep up* such a large house? 你是如何照料好这么大的房子的? The municipal authorities have *kept* the roads *up* well. 市政当局把道路保养得不错。❻(常用一般时态) (usually of weather) remain the same; last (常指天气)持续不变,继续: Will the fine weather *keep up*? 好天气会持续下去吗? The rain *kept up* for three days and the roads were all flooded. 雨持续下了三天,所有的道路都被淹没了。

NOTE 当本短语用作及物性动词短语,所带的宾语为代词时,该代词须置于本短语的动词和副词中间。

keep up at *vt.*【不可分性动词短语】continue; not quit 继续,不放弃: Learning a foreign language is difficult, but if you *keep up at* it, you'll succeed in the end. 学习一门外语是不容易的,但如果你锲而不舍就终会成功。

keep up with *vt.*【不可分性动词短语】❶move at the same speed as (someone) 跟上(某人): She had to run to *keep up with* her brother. 她必须跑才能跟上她哥哥。I had to work hard to *keep up with* the other students. 我不得不努力学习以跟上其他同学。❷remain level with or keep in advance of (an idea, fashion, etc.) 跟上(某种思想、时尚等)的发展: Today science, moving rapidly, has so many ideas that it is difficult to *keep up with* them. 当今,要跟上迅速发展着的科学所产生的形色众多的思想是很难的。❸continue to learn or be informed about (something) 不断了解: Anybody who wants to *keep up with* the development of science has to read scientific journals. 任何想要不断地了解科学发展的人都得读一些科学类杂志。❹stay contact with (someone) (especially by writing, telephoning, or visiting him or her regularly) (尤指通过定期通信、通话或走访)与(某人)保持接触: We have *kept up with* each other ever since we left school. 自从离校以来,我们一直保持相互联系。

NOTE 本短语与 catch up with 均表示"跟上"之意。本短语指在同时起步的情况下"跟上";而 catch up with 却指在起步较晚或已经落后的情况下"赶上""追上"。

keep (a) watch *vi.* ❶(of someone) look around all the time, usually when other people are asleep, so that he or she can warn others of danger or an attack 观察,放哨: Officers can *keep watch* from far away using binoculars. 军官们可以从远处用望远镜进行观察。Joe, as usual, had climbed a tree to *keep watch*. 乔和往常一样,爬上了树去放哨。❷(常与 on 或 over 连用) watch someone carefully to make sure that they are safe 看护,监护(某人): We sat by his bed and *kept watch* over him. 我们坐在他的床旁看护着他。*Keep a* close *watch* on him in case he gets worse. 如果他的病情恶化,对他实施严密监护。

key in *vt.*【可分性动词短语】put (data or information) into a computer or other electronic machine using a keyboard 用键盘

输入(数据或信息)：It took her a lot of time to *key in* all the new data. 她花了很长时间用键盘输入了所有的新数据。The new data will need to be *keyed in* immediately. 需要立即把这些新数据都输进去。I don't have time to *key* them all *in*. 我没有时间把它们都输进去。

kick in *vt.*【可分性动词短语】damage or destroy (something) by kicking 踢坏(某物)：The old woman said two young men *kicked in* her door and robbed her this morning. 老妇人述说道，今天上午有两个年轻人踢坏她家房门抢劫了她。The firemen had to *kick* the door *in* to get into the burning house. 消防队员不得不踢开门进入着火的房子。

—*vi.* (非正式用语) ❶begin to operate; start to have an effect; begin to take effect 开始运转，开始发生作用，生效：Finally the motor *kicked in* and we could get started. 发动机终于运转了，我们可以启程了。If the pain *kicks in* again, call me. 如果再疼，就喊我。The medicine took some time to *kick in*. 这药过了一会儿才发生作用。The new rules *kicked in* last year. 这些新规则都是去年生效的。❷die 死，去世：No one knows when he'll *kick in*. 没人知道他什么时候会死去。

—*vt.* &*vi.* (美国英语用法，非正式用语) give or add (one's share of something, especially money) 捐献(尤指钱款)：He *kicked in* another $1 million to the Washington, DC-based Enterprise Fund. 他又向总部设在华盛顿特区的企业基金会捐献了100万美元。Everyone *kicked in* for the Christmas party. 每个人都为圣诞节晚会捐了款。

NOTE 当本短语作"死，去世"解时，同义短语是 kick off。

kick off *vt.*【可分性动词短语】❶(常用一般时态) remove (something) by shaking the foot 用脚踢走：Don't *kick* your shoes *off* into the corner as you usually do. Leave them neatly. 你别像往常那样把鞋子往角落里踢。把它们摆好。The big dog attacked me, but I *kicked* him *off*. 那条大狗向我扑来，但我用脚把它踢开了。❷(非正式用语，常用一般时态) force (someone) to leave (a group) 把(某人)从(某一组织)开除：Robert was difficult to work with and finally we *kicked* him *off* the planning committee. 由于很难和罗伯特共事，我们最终把他从计划委员会辞退。He was *kicked off* the team for being lazy. 他因懒惰而被开除出队。

—*vi.* ❶(用一般时态) (of a game of football) start; start play in a football game by kicking the ball (足球比赛)开始，开球：What time does this afternoon's game *kick off*? 今天下午的足球比赛什么时候开始？Johnson *kicked off* in the last game. 最后一场比赛由约翰逊开球。❷(美国英语用法，非正式用语) die 死，去世：The old lady might *kick off* any minute. 这老太太随时都可能死去。It's a wonder that old cow hasn't kicked off yet. 真奇怪，这头老牛还没有死。

—*vt.* &*vi.* (非正式用语，常用一般时态) start (something); begin 开始：The world eye-catching project of water diversion from south to north along the middle of China is to *kick off* in full in October. 举世瞩目、横贯华中的南水北调工程将于10月份全面开工。Have you got any suggestions? Jim, you *kick off*. 你们有什么建议吗？吉姆，你开个头。

NOTE **1.** 当本短语用作及物性动词短语，所带的宾语为代词时，该代词须置于本短语的动词和副词中间。

2. 当本短语作“把(某人)从(某一组织)开除”解时,同义短语是 kick out, lay off, pay off, send away, stand off 和 turn off。

3. 当本短语作“开始”解时,同义短语是 start off。

4. 本短语可转化为复合词 kickoff,意为“开始;(足球等)开球”。

kick out *vt.*【可分性动词短语】❶(常用一般时态) push (something or someone) outside with the foot or feet 把……踢出去: Don't *kick* the cat *out* like that; it's cruel. 别那样把猫往外踢,那太残忍了。❷(非正式用语,常用被动语态形式,常与 of, for 连用) remove or dismiss (someone); force (someone) to leave a place or organization, often for a fault 开除(某人),把(某人)辞退,解雇: The student was *kicked out* of college for cheating in exams. 那名学生因考试作弊而被学校开除。In the team's history, a former world women's doubles champion was once sent home after she was 90 minutes late for a training session and a former world top player had been *kicked out* for smoking. 在该队历史中,一位原世界女子双打冠军曾因在一次训练中迟到 90 分钟而被打发回家;另一位原世界头号选手因吸烟而被开除。

—*vi.* kick the foot in an outward direction or suddenly (突然)向外侧踢去: Don't walk behind a horse in case it *kicks out* at you. 不要在马的身后走,以防它踢了你。

NOTE 1. 当本短语用作及物性动词短语,所带的宾语为代词时,该代词须置于本短语的动词和副词中间。

2. 当本短语作“开除(某人),把(某人)辞退,解雇”解时,同义短语是 kick off, lay off, pay off, send away, stand off 和 turn off。

3. 本短语可转化为复合词 kick (-) out, 意为“(足球中的)踢球出界;撵走,解雇”。

kill two birds with one stone *vi.* (非正式用语) achieve two aims with one action; manage to do two things at the same time instead of just one, because it is convenient to do both 一举两得: Since Mary lives near my mother, I'll call in on her as well and *kill two birds with one stone*. 既然玛丽住在我母亲家附近,我也去看看她,这样就可以一举两得。If you bike to work, you will get some exercise as well as saving money travelling, so you'll *kill two birds with one stone*. 如果你骑自行车上班,不但能得到一些锻炼,还能省下车钱,所以,你这是一举两得。

NOTE 本短语常可省略成 kill two birds 的形式使用。

kind of *adv.* (仅用于口语中)(used when you are trying to explain or describe something, but you cannot be exact) in a certain way; rather; to some extent 有点,相当,有几分: I am feeling *kind of tired*. 我感到有点儿累。“I am *kind of* disappointed on hearing what he said,” Mary said. 玛丽说:“我听了他的话后,有点失望。” They *kind of* laughed at me. 他们有些嘲笑我的味道。This small animal looks *kind of* like a rabbit, but it has short ears. 这种小动物有点儿像兔子,只是耳朵短。He seems like *kind of* a big shot. 他有几分大人物的派头。“Do you like what you're doing in school, Tom?” “*Kind of*.” “你喜欢在学校里做的事情吗,汤姆?”“还可以。”

NOTE 1. 不要将本短语与 a kind of 混淆。a kind of 意为“一种”“某种”,后面常接不可数名词或抽象化的单数可数名词。

2. 不要将本短语与 of a kind 混淆。of a

kind 有“同类的”之意，用作后置定语。

3. 本短语与 sort of 意义和用法相同，两者可互换使用。

knock around/about *v.*（非正式用语）❶treat(someone) roughly, especially by hitting him or her a lot 虐待，经常殴打（某人）：Her husband had been *knocking* her *around*. 她丈夫过去一直虐待她。He *knocked* his brother *about* after they argued. 吵架之后，他把弟弟打了。The prisoner seemed to have been *knocked about* a bit. 这名犯人似乎刚被打过。❷be in a place or in various places especially over a long period of time 游历，漫游：I *knocked around* the Mediterranean for a few months after leaving school. 毕业后，我在地中海国家游历了几个月。He's *knocked about* in Africa for years. 他在非洲已游历了好几年。He used to *knock about* the job market, trying to find a job. 他常常漫游在劳务市场，力图找到一份工作。❸（与 with 或 together 连用）spend a lot of time (with someone), often sexually 与（某人）厮混：Who was that lad you used to *knock around* with? 总和你厮混在一起的那个小伙子是谁？

NOTE knock around 是美国英语用法，knock about 则是英国英语用法。

knock at/on *vt.*【不可分性动词短语】hit (something such as a door or window) with your hand so that the people inside know you are there 敲（门或窗）：They walked up to the door and *knocked at* it loudly. 他们走近门口，大声地敲起门来。*Knock at* my window at eight o'clock and I'll be out. 你 8 点钟敲我的窗子，我就出来。I went directly to Jim's room and *knocked on* his door but got no reply. 我直接走到吉姆的房间去敲门，但无人应答。

knock down *vt.*【可分性动词短语】❶（常用一般时态）hit (someone) very hard, so that he or she falls to the ground or becomes unconscious, as with a blow 把（某人）击倒：He *knocked* his opponent *down* three times in the first round. 他在第一回合中就三次把对手击倒。❷（常用一般时态）(of a car or other vehicle) hit (someone) so that he or she fall to the ground and may be injured or killed（车辆）把（某人）撞倒：The car *knocked* a child *down* at the bend in the road. 小汽车在弯道处撞倒了一个孩子。The car *knocked* her *down* and she broke her arm. 车把她撞倒，她摔断了手臂。The old lady died in hospital after being *knocked down* by a taxi. 老妇人被一辆出租车撞倒后，死在了医院中。❸（常用被动语态形式）destroy or demolish (a building or part of a building) 拆毁，毁坏（建筑物）：The whole block will be *knocked down* to make room for new buildings. 整个街区将被拆除，以腾出地方建造新楼房。The typhoon *knocked down* quite a number of houses and left more than 100 people dead or missing. 台风毁坏了许多房屋，并致 100 多人死亡或失踪。Why did they just *knock* the wall *down*? 他们为什么只把墙推倒了？❹（常用被动语态形式，与 to 或 at 连用）sell (goods) at an auction, especially at a low price（尤指以低价）拍卖（商品）：The article is *knocked down* to the highest bidder. 这件物品被出价最高者买了去。The wine was *knocked down* at $50. 这葡萄酒以 50 美元的低价拍卖出去了。❺（非正式用语，常用一般时态，与

K

to 连用) reduce (the price of something or the amount you want for something) 减低(价格或数量): The price was *knocked down* to £3. 价格减低到了 3 英镑。He *knocked* the price of the hat *down* to $4 from $8. 他把这顶帽子的价格从 8 美元降到了 4 美元。❻(非正式用语) persuade (a seller) to reduce the price of something they are selling 说服(卖主)降价: He wanted $30, but I managed to *knock* him *down* to $20. 他要价 30 美元,但我设法使他把价格降到了 20 美元。

NOTE 1. 当本短语的宾语为代词时,该代词须置于本短语的动词和副词中间。

2. 当本短语作"(车辆)把(某人)撞倒"解时,与 knock over (第二个义项)意义和用法相同,两者可互换使用。

knock off *vt.* ❶(非正式用语,常用一般时态)(of a seller) reduce (a price or an amount); take (part) from (a price)(卖主)减低(价格),(给价格)打折扣: If you *knock off* five dollars, I'd consider buying it. 如果你减价 5 美元,我就考虑把它买下了。I *knocked* you fifteen pounds *off* the price if you buy five. 如果你买 5 件,我就给你 15 英镑的折扣。❷(非正式用语,常用一般时态) write (words or music) quickly or (too) easily (匆忙或轻易地)写出: She *knocked* that article *off* in no time. 她很快就把那篇文章写了出来。He can *knock off* an article in an afternoon. 他在一个下午就能写出一篇文章来。❸(英国英语用法,非正式用语,常用一般时态) steal (something) 偷窃(某物): He was planning to *knock off* a colour TV set. 他计划偷一台彩色电视机。He *knocked* it *off* and sold it. 他将其偷到手后便卖掉了。❹(英国英语用法,非正式用语,常用一般时态) rob (a place) 抢劫(某处): They *knocked off* the bank and got away with £5 million. 他们抢劫了银行,随即携 500 万英镑逃之夭夭。❺(非正式用语) consume (something) 把……吃(或喝)掉: The little boy has *knocked off* the whole cake! 这小孩儿把整个蛋糕都吃掉了! After work we *knocked off* a few beers before going home. 干完活,我们喝了几瓶啤酒才回家。

—*vt.* & *vi.* (非正式用语,无被动语态形式) stop working or finish work at the end of the day 停工,下班: What time do you *knock off*? 你什么时候下班? Do you want to *knock off* early tonight? 你今晚想早下班吗? Let's *knock off* our work early and go to watch the football game. 让我们早下班去看足球赛吧。

NOTE 1. 当本短语用作及物性动词短语,所带的宾语是代词时,该代词须置于本短语的动词和副词/介词中间。

2. 本短语可转化为复合词 knocked-off, 意为"偷窃的"。

knock out *vt.*【可分性动词短语】❶(常用一般时态) cause (someone) to become unconscious 使(某人)失去知觉: The ceiling fell on her and *knocked* her *out*. 天花板塌落在她身上,把她砸昏了。The explosion hurt no one, except that it *knocked out* a little girl. 除了一名小女孩被炸昏外,爆炸中无人受伤。She hit her head on the ceiling and *knocked* herself *out*. 她的头撞在了天花板上,随即昏了过去。❷(常用一般时态)(in boxing) make (your opponent) unable to get up before a count of 10 seconds (拳击中)击倒(对手): A boxer was *knocked out* by his opponent. 一名拳击运动员被其对手击

昏。The champion boxer *knocked out* the challenger in the second round of the fight. 这位拳击冠军在第二轮比赛中就将挑战者击倒。❸(常用一般时态)(of a drug or alcohol) make (someone) go to sleep (药物或酒精)使(人)入睡: A few sleeping pills will really *knock* you *out*. 几粒安眠药片真的会使你昏昏入睡的。One cup of wine *knocked* him *out*. 一杯白酒便使他倒头睡了过去。❹(常用被动语态形式) make (someone or a team) leave a competition by defeating them 将(某人或某队)击败: They *knocked out* our other team as well. 他们把我们另外一个队也击败了。England football team lost to Portugal 1-3 Saturday and was *knocked out* of the World Cup quarterfinals. 英格兰足球队在星期六的世界杯足球赛上以1比3输给了葡萄牙,被淘汰出四分之一决赛。❺(常用被动语态形式) cause to suddenly fail to work or stop functioning, usually by bad weather; make useless (常指由于恶劣天气)使不能工作,使无用: Telephone communications in these areas were *knocked out* by the worst snow storm in 50 years. 50年不遇的特大暴风雪使这些地区的电话通信中断。A strong earthquake struck the area, *knocking out* power, causing great damage to buildings, and killing many people. 一场强烈地震袭击了该地区,使电力中断,建筑物严重受损和许多人死亡。❻(非正式用语,常用一般时态) make (someone) feel very shocked or amazed 使(某人)感到吃惊: I was almost *knocked out* by the news. 我几乎被这消息所惊呆。The great success of the performance by the disabled girls *knocked* me *out*! 那些残疾女孩们的表演获得的极大成功令我吃惊! ❼(非正式用语,常用一般时态) make (someone) very tired 使(某人)疲劳不堪: My friend *knocked* herself *out* cooking this dinner for ten of us. 为我们10个人做的这顿饭使我的朋友疲劳不堪。Hours of shopping has *knocked* me *out*! 好几个小时的购物都要累死我了。

NOTE **1.** 当本短语的宾语为代词时,该代词须置于本短语的动词和副词中间。

2. 当本短语作"使(某人)失去知觉"解时,该代词同义短语是 pass out 和 put out。这三者中,只有 pass out 是不及物性动词短语。

3. 本短语可转化为复合词 knockout,意为"(在拳击中)把对手打倒在地的一击;击倒的;引人注目的,使昏迷的"。

knock over *vt.*【可分性动词短语】(常用一般时态) ❶ make (something) fall by pushing or hitting, often accidentally (常指意外地)把(某物)打翻: The cow *knocked* the milk bucket *over*. 奶牛把奶桶弄倒了。Who *knocked* the bottle *over*? It couldn't have tipped over by itself. 是谁把瓶子弄倒了? 它不会自己翻倒的。❷(英国英语用法) hit (someone) very hard, so that he or she falls to the ground or becomes unconscious, as with a vehicle or its driver (车辆)撞倒(某人): A car *knocked* him *over* as he ran for the bus. 当他跑着赶公共汽车时,一辆轿车把他撞倒了。Over 100 people are *knocked over* on Britain's roads every day. 在英国的路面上,每天被车撞的人过百。Driving too fast, I *knocked over* a child on a bicycle. 由于行驶速度太快,我撞倒了一个骑自行车的孩子。❸(美国英

K

语用法)steal or rob (something)偷窃,抢劫(某物): They are *knocking over* banks to get money. 他们为得到钱而抢劫银行。

NOTE 当本短语的宾语为代词时,该代词须置于本短语的动词和副词中间。

knock together *vt.*【可分性动词短语】(英国英语用法,非正式用语,常用一般时态)make or build (something) quickly and roughly, using whatever materials are available (仓促而粗糙地)做成(某物): We *knocked together* the bookcases in about half an hour. 我们用大约半个小时的工夫就做成了这些书橱。I'm no woodworker, but I can *knock* a bookshelf *together* when necessary. 我不是木匠,当必要的时候我也能做出个书架来。The shelter was *knocked together* using wooden doors and doorframes. 这个棚屋是用木门和门框搭凑而成的。

NOTE 1. 当本短语的宾语为代词时,该代词须置于本短语的动词和副词中间。

2. 本短语与 knock up(第二个义项)意义和用法相同,两者可互换使用。

knock up *vt.*【可分性动词短语】❶(主要用于英国英语中,非正式用语)wake or call (someone) by knocking on the door (以敲门来)唤醒(某人): Will you *knock* me *up* at 6:00 tomorrow morning? 你明天早上 6 点能敲门叫醒我吗? ❷(常用一般时态)create or produce (something) quickly and roughly, using whatever materials are available (仓促而粗糙地)做成(某物): Any snow-skiing enthusiast can *knock up* a pair of skis in a few hours. 任何一名滑雪爱好者都能在几个小时里赶做出一副滑橇来。They *knocked* a model *up* overnight. 他们一夜之间就做出了一个模型。❸(主要用于英国英语中,常用一般时态)tire (someone or oneself) very much, as by overwork 使……筋疲力尽: Hours of gardening in the sun have quite *knocked* me *up*. 在太阳底下从事园艺数小时把我累得筋疲力尽了。Don't *knock* yourself *up* trying to finish the job. 别为了赶完工作而累坏自己。❹(主要用于美国英语中,非正式用语)make (a woman, especially one who is not married) pregnant 使(尤指未婚女子)怀孕: The soldier *knocked up* the village girl and had to be transferred. 该士兵因致使那村姑怀孕而不得不被调走。

NOTE 当本短语的宾语为代词时,该代词须置于本短语的动词和副词中间。

know about/of *vt.* (用一般时态) have knowledge or information about or have heard of (someone or something)知道,听说(某人或某事): But I *know* nothing whatever *about* you. 但我对你一无所知。His remarks showed how little he *knows of* the matter. 从他所说的话中可以看出,他对此事知之甚少。

NOTE 1. know of 主要用于英国英语中。

2. know about 为可分性动词短语,know of 则是不可分性动词短语。

3. know of 的口语否定形式是 not that I know of (=I do not know)。例如:

> "Is he home yet?"
> "他到家了没有?"
> "*Not that I know of.*"
> "我不知道。"

know better than *v.* (常用一般时态,后接动词不定式短语)be wise, sensible or experienced enough not to do something wrong or impossible 懂得,明事理(而不

至于)：She *knew better than* to spend all her money on clothes. 她还不至于无知到把她所有的钱都花在穿着上。She should *know better than* to go there alone on such a night. 她应该懂得在这样的夜晚不宜单独去那里。

known as *adj*. ❶ generally recognized as 被公认为……：Thomas Alva Edison was *known as* one of the greatest inventors of his time. 托马斯·阿尔瓦·爱迪生被公认是他那时代最伟大的发明家之一。The Golden Rooster Awards and the Hundred Flowers Awards were combined into the Golden Rooster and Hundred Flowers Film Festival, *known as* China's Oscars. 金鸡奖和百花奖合并成为"金鸡百花电影节",被公认为"中国的奥斯卡"。❷ publicly called; named 被称为……,被叫作：Both parts wanted to restart the Mideast peace plan, *known as* the road map. 双方都想重启"中东和平计划",亦称作"路线图"。The National Aquatics Centre in Beijing, also *known as* the Water Cube, was built for swimming competitions of the 2008 Summer Olympics. 位于北京的国家游泳中心,又被叫作"水立方",是为 2008 年夏季奥运会的游泳比赛而建造的。

NOTE 本短语的比较级形式是 more known as,最高级形式是 best known as。

known for *adj*. (of someone or something) famous for (a particular quality or ability), and usually admired 以……著称：Madame Curie is well *known for* her discovery of radium. 居里夫人因为发现镭而著称于世。The Nobel Prize for Literature was won by a 88-year-old British woman writer, Doris Lessing, who is also *known for* having strong political views. 88 岁的英国女作家多丽丝·莱辛赢得了诺贝尔文学奖。她还以其持有强硬的政治观点而著称。The Su embroidery is *known for* its delicacy and elegance. 苏绣以精细、素雅著称。

NOTE 1. 本短语的比较级形式是 more known for,最高级形式是 best known for。

2. 本短语的同义短语是 famous for 和 noted for。

known to *adj*. known by 为……所熟知的,被……所知道：As is *known to* all, having a good knowledge of vocabulary is basic to language learning. 众所周知,具有很好的词汇知识是学习一门语言的基础。The Mayor of Sanya City hoped Sanya's reputation could be made *known to* the world via hosting more international events such as Miss World beauty competition. 三亚市市长希望通过主办更多像"世界小姐"选美大赛这样的国际性活动使三亚为世界所知。

NOTE 本短语的比较级形式是 more known to,最高级形式是 best known to。

L l

labor along *v.* 【不可分性动词短语】(of someone or something) move along slowly and with difficulty (指人或物)缓慢而费力地前进,费力地沿……前进: The rescuers were *laboring along* towards the flooded village. 救援队员们费力地朝着受水灾的村庄走去。He *labored along* with his bag of groceries. 他扛着一袋子杂货吃力地前行。The damaged car was *laboring along* the muddy road. 那辆受损的汽车沿着泥泞的道路吃力地向前行驶着。

labor at/over *vt.* (of someone) put a lot of effort into (achieving something) (指人)下大力地做: If you *labor at* perfecting your style, make sure that it doesn't sound false and stiff. 如果你要下力改善你的写作风格,就要保证其听起来真实而流畅。I *labored over* the report, trying to get it exactly right. 我下大力气写这份报告,力求准确无误。At midnight she was still *laboring over* the accounts. 半夜了,她还在埋头理账。

lack for *vt.* 【不可分性动词短语】(正式用语,无被动语态形式,常用于否定句中,用一般时态) not have any or enough of (something you need or want) 缺乏(某物): Teachers never *lack for* new ideas and have made good use of the Internet for their courses. 教师们从不缺乏新思想,并已充分利用互联网授课。Because the number of private cars is increasing and many people *lack for* awareness of the importance of obeying the traffic regulations, the city is facing serious traffic problems. 由于私家车数量增多,加之很多人对遵守交通规则的重要性缺乏认识,该市正面临着严重的交通问题。We *lack for* nothing, thank you. 我们什么东西都不缺。谢谢。

NOTE **1.** 本短语中的动词 lack 本身就是及物性动词,因此,介词 for 往往省略。例如:

> As the only child of wealthy parents, he *lacked* (*for*) nothing.
>
> 作为富有家庭的独生子,他应有尽有。

2. 本短语的同义短语是 lack in 和 be short of。

lack in *vt.* 【不可分性动词短语】(正式用语,无被动语态形式,常用进行时态) not have any or enough of (a particular quality) 缺乏(某种品质或特点): She felt nervous, increasingly *lacking in* confidence about herself. 她感到紧张,对自己越来越缺乏信心。You will not be *lacking in* support from me. 你将得到我的支持。The head coach said his team *lacks in* playoff experience. 这位主教练称,他的队缺乏夺标决赛的经验。

lag behind *v.* ❶ not be as successful or advanced (as another person, or thing) 落后: Modesty helps one to go forward, whereas conceit makes one *lag behind*. 虚心使人进步，骄傲使人落后。They now *lag* 10 points *behind*. 他们现在还落后10分。❷walk more slowly than (the people you are with) 走在(别人)后面：Come on, you two, stop *lagging behind*! 你们两个快点儿，别再落在后面了！She *lagged behind* the rest of the children because she kept stopping to look in shop windows. 她不断地停下来看商店橱窗，所以就落在了其他孩子的后面。

NOTE 本短语的同义短语是 fall behind；反义短语是 catch up (with)。

land on/upon *vt.* ❶(cause to) come to rest on (a surface), especially after flying or sailing; fall on (something) (使)降落在……上，落在……上：The big bird *landed* safely *on* the branch near our window. 那只大鸟儿安全地落在了我们窗边的树枝上。It seemed that a crash was inevitable, but luckily the pilot *landed* the plane *on* the Hudson River safely. 当时看来飞机坠毁已不可避免，但幸好飞行员使飞机安全降落在了哈德逊河河面上。A drop of rain *landed on* my head. 一滴雨点落在了我的头上。❷(美国英语用法，非正式用语) criticize (someone) severely 严厉斥责(某人)：He really *landed on* me for being late. 他因我迟到而对我大加斥责。❸arrive somewhere, especially unexpectedly or in a way that causes problems (意外地)到达：The whole family *landed on* my doorstep for the weekend. 他们一家人突然来到我家度周末。Thousands of letters a week were *landing on* his desk. 一星期上千封来信堆到了他的办公桌上。❹(非正式用语) make (a blow) hit (part of the body) (一拳)打在(身体的某一部位)：I was so angry that I *landed* him a punch *on* the nose. 我太气愤了，一拳打在了他的鼻子上。

NOTE 本短语中的 upon 用法比 on 正式，但不及 on 常用。

lap up *vt.* 【可分性动词短语】❶(usually of an animal) drink (liquid) gently with its tongue (常指动物)舔食(液体或流质食物)：The dog was *lapping up* its milk eagerly. 狗在贪婪地舔食着牛奶。The milk you put out in the saucer was *lapped up* by the cat. 你放在碟子里的牛奶被猫舔光了。Don't *lap up* your soup, children. It's not polite. 孩子们，不要舔食你们的汤。这样不礼貌。❷accept eagerly or enjoy (what someone says) without thought (欣然)接受，享受：You could see she was very pleased; she *lapped up* their praise. 你可以看得出，她十分高兴。她欣然接受了他们的赞扬。The jokes were crude but the audience were *lapping* them *up*. 这些笑话都很粗俗，但听众们还都喜欢听。

lash out *vi.* ❶(常与 at 连用) try to hit or attack suddenly and violently 猛然袭击：Occasionally the patients will *lash out* at the nurses. 有时，这些患者还会袭击护士。Riot police fired into the sky and *lashed out* with clubs at the demonstrators. 防暴警察朝天上开枪并用警棍猛击示威者。The horse *lashed out* at me with its hind legs. 那马抬起后腿猛然向我踢来。❷(非正式用语，常与 at, against 连用) attack (someone or something) violently with words; criticize 猛烈抨击，批评：President Obama *lashed out* at the Wall Street companies for giving out $18.4 billion as bonuses to their top executives.

L

奥巴马总统抨击华尔街公司给其高层管理人员发放了184亿美元奖金。The young writer *lashed out* against the government's policies against ethnic minorities. 这位年轻的作家猛烈抨击了政府歧视少数民族的政策。

—*vt.* &*vi.*（英国和澳大利亚英语用法，非正式用语，常与on连用）spend a lot of money (on something, especially luxuries)（尤指为奢侈品而）大量花钱：We *lashed out* \$50 each on the best seats. 我们每人花了50美元买了最好的座位。He *lashed out* on a new car. 他花一大笔钱买了一辆新车。

last but not least *adv.* (used for introducing the last person or thing on a list) last in sequence but not least in importance; equally important, despite being mentioned at the end 最后但同样重要：This is Jeremy, this is Kathy, and, *last but not least*, this is Elizabeth. 这是杰里米，这是凯西，最后这位也是个重要人物：伊丽莎白。*Last but not least*, I'd like to thank all the people who work behind the scenes. 最后也同样重要的一点是，我要对所有幕后的工作人员表示感谢。I've brought with me the money, the sunglasses, swimsuit, and, *last but not least*, my lipstick. 我随身带上了钱、太阳镜、游泳衣，还有一件同样重要的东西：我的口红。

NOTE 1. 本短语后一般要用逗号，与后面的部分相隔。

2. 在介绍数个人中的最后一位时，除了像第一个例句所表达的那样外，更正式的说法是：*Last but not least*, let me introduce Elizabeth, our new secretary.

later on *adv.* happening in the future or after the time that you have already mentioned; afterwards 后来，过一会儿，以后：*Later on* in the hearings, Mary told an entirely different story. 后来，在听证会上玛丽讲的一套与之前完全不同。At first things went quite well, but *later on* we ran into trouble. 起初事情进展得十分顺利，但后来我们就遇到了麻烦。I'll come and see you *later on*. 我过一会儿来看你。This is only going to cause me more problems *later on*. 这只会在以后给我造成更多的麻烦。

NOTE 1. 本短语可用于过去时态和将来时态。用于过去时态时，意为"后来"；用于将来时态时，意为"以后"。

2. 本短语有时可单独使用。例如：

"When can I use the sewing machine?"
"*Later on*."
"我什么时候可以用这台缝纫机？"
"待会儿吧。"

laugh at *vt.*【不可分性动词短语】❶ be amused by (something or someone funny) 因……而发笑：The audience didn't *laugh at* his jokes. 观众听了他的这些笑话并没发笑。She *laughs at* everything you say. Do you know why? She has fine teeth! 你说什么她都笑。你知道为什么吗？因为她有一口靓丽的牙齿！❷ make fun of or make jokes about (someone or something); mock 嘲笑：If you're fond of *laughing at* other people, you'll certainly be *laughed at* by others. 如果你喜欢嘲笑别人，你一定会被别人嘲笑。It's not polite to *laugh at* a blind person. 嘲笑一个盲人是不礼貌的。They both *laughed at* the idea. 他们两个都嘲笑这个想法。❸（常用一般时态）behave in a way that shows you are not worried or frightened by (something); be careless of 藐视，不怕，不以为然：She *laughed at* the difficulties. 她藐视一切困难。He's always been able to *laugh at* danger. 他历来不怕危险。I advise you not to *laugh at* the official warnings. 我劝你不要对官方的警告不以为然。

laugh in one's face *vi.* ❶ laugh in derision directly to someone's face 当面嘲笑(某人): It is very impolite to *laugh in someone's face*! 当面嘲笑别人是很不礼貌的。❷(非正式用语)refuse to listen; openly show disrespect or disobedience (toward someone)拒而不听,(公开表示)不服从: If someone had told me this was going to happen, I would have *laughed in their face*. 如果有人告诉我这事就要发生,我会拒而不听的。I suggested that he should work late and he *laughed in my face*. 我建议他晚些下班,而他没有听从。He asked them to put out their cigarettes but they just *laughed in his face*. 他让他们把烟掐灭,但他们拒不服从。

NOTE 本短语中的名词 face 无论修饰词是单数还是复数形式,都必须用单数形式。

laugh off/away *vt.* 【可分性动词短语】joke about (something) to show that you think it is not important or serious 对……一笑置之: They just *laughed off* the rumours that they are getting married. 他们对那些他们要结婚的传言只是一笑置之。I know you are very brave, but you can't just *laugh* a toothache *away*. You'll have to see a dentist. 我知道你很勇敢,但你不能忽视牙疼。你得去看牙医。

NOTE 当本短语所带的宾语为代词时,该代词须置于本短语的动词和副词中间。

laugh one's head off *vi.* (非正式用语) laugh very loudly 大笑: We *laughed our heads off* as the old man began to dance. 当那老头儿开始跳舞时,我们都大笑不止。When the joke was over, all the people *laughed their heads off*. 笑话一讲完,大家都捧腹大笑。

lay a finger/on *vt.* ❶(非正式用语,常用一般时态,常用于否定句、疑问句或条件从句中) hit or harm (someone) in any way 打,伤害(某人): He swears he'll never *lay a finger on* the child. 他发誓说绝不打那孩子。Do you dare to *lay a finger on* her? 你敢碰她一根毫毛吗? Nobody *laid a finger on* me, Mother. 妈妈,并没人伤害我。❷touch (someone or something), even slightly, as with only a finger (用手指)触摸: If you *lay a finger on* me, I'll scream. 如果你碰我一根手指头,我就大喊。You'd better not *lay a finger on* those documents! 你最好不要动那些文件!

NOTE 1. 本短语的另外一种表达形式是 lay a hand on。

2. 不要将本短语与 lay one's finger(s) on 和 lay one's hands on 混淆。

lay all one's eggs in one basket ⇨ **put all one's eggs in one basket**

lay aside *vt.* 【可分性动词短语】❶(正式用语) put (something) down or on one side, especially for a short time 把……放在一边: I *laid aside* my book and turned on the radio to listen to the Special English program on VOA. 我把书本放在一边,打开收音机收听"美国之音"的"特别英语"节目。She finished the tea and *laid* the cup *aside*. 她喝完茶,便把杯子放在了一旁。"What do you want?" He asked, *laying aside* his pen. 他把笔放下,问道:"你想要什么?" ❷(正式用语,常与 for 连用) save (something, especially money), so that you can use it in the future; keep (money or time) for a particular purpose 积蓄(钱或时间): For years my mother *laid aside* a small amount out of her wages each week. 几年来,我妈妈都要从每星期发的工资中留出一点钱储蓄起来。Half the prize money he spent, and the rest was *laid aside* for a rainy day. 他花掉一半奖金,其余留作应急之用。I've *laid aside* the whole weekend for house-hunting. 我已把整个周末的时间都留出来找房子。❸give up; abandon (something as a belief or habit)抛弃,放弃(某种习惯等): You should look to the future and *lay aside* all these thoughts. 你应该抛弃这些思想向前看。He has *laid aside* the habit of smoking. 他已放弃了吸烟的习惯。❹stop using, doing, or preparing, especially for a short time (尤指暂时)停止使用,把……(暂时)搁置起来: The freighter was *laid aside* for repair. 该货船需要修理,暂时停止使用。They agreed to *lay aside* their differences for the good of their families. 他们同意为了各自家庭的利益,把分歧搁置起来。Facing the new challenge from the present financial crisis, party differences should be *laid aside*. 面对目前金融危机的新挑战,各党派之间的分歧应弃之一旁。Why don't you *lay* that problem *aside* for a while? 你为何不把那个问题暂时搁置起来呢?

NOTE 本短语的同义短语是 put aside 和 set aside。

lay bare *vt.* (常用一般时态) ❶take the clothes or cover off (something such as part of the body), to show it (把衣物等脱去以)显露(身体的某一部位): The doctor *laid* her leg *bare*, ready for a minor operation. 医生把她的腿部暴露出来,准备进行一个小手术。❷(非正式用语) show clearly; make known (something formerly hidden)表明,揭露,披露: The major problem has been *laid bare* of its various guises. 去掉了种种假象,主要问题就暴露了出来。She never *lays* her private thoughts *bare*. 她从不把自己的个人看法表露出来。The old man *laid bare* the whole story of his life. 这位老人袒露了他整个人生的故事。

lay down *vt.* ❶put (something) down, usually because you have finished using it 把(某物)放下: Please stop writing and *lay down* your pencils. 请不要再写了,把铅笔都放下。When the fire alarm sounded, the mechanic *laid down* his tools and rushed to the warehouse. 一听到火警报警器响,这位机械师便放下手中的工具,向仓库跑去。❷(常用一般时态)place (someone or oneself) down, as on the ground, furniture, etc. (使)躺下: The young mother *laid* the baby *down* gently. 那位年轻的妈妈轻轻地把婴儿放了下来。She *laid* herself *down* in the grass and fell fast asleep. 她躺在草地上并很快就睡着了。❸(常用被动语态形式)(of rules or people in authority) state officially (what someone must do or how he or she must do it)规定,制定,提出: The rules *laid down* that he could not directly intervene. 这些规章规定他不得直接介入其中。These price limits are *laid down* by the government. 这些价格限制都是政府制定的。It was *laid down* that all applicants should sit a written examination. 根据规定,所有申请人均应参加笔试。❹start the building or making of (a house, ship, railway, etc.) 建造(房屋);造(船);铺设(铁路): The foundation of the building were *laid down* in 1954. 这座建筑物于 1954 年奠基。A new ocean-going freighter is being *laid down* at that shipyard. 那家船厂正在建造一艘新的远洋货轮。The workers were busy *laying down* the railway. 工人们正忙于铺设铁路。❺(正式用语)give up (an idea, attitude, rank, etc.) willingly 放弃,辞去,自愿献出: They were forced to *lay down* their plans. 他们被迫放弃了自己的计划。After losing the battle the general *laid down* his command. 战斗失败后,这位将军辞去了指挥官的职务。Thousands of young men *laid down* their lives for the cause of peace. 成千上万的年轻人为了和平事业献出了自己的生命。

lay emphasis on *vt.* 【不可分性动词短语】(常用一般时态) emphasize the importance of (something or doing something)强调,把重点放在……上,重视:The minister *laid* special *emphasis on* the importance of agricultural mechanization. 这位部长特别强调了农业机械化的重要性。*Emphasis* must be *laid on* practice, both written and oral. 必须把重点放在写作以及口语的实践上。The country has also been *laying emphasis on* growing edible oil-bearing crops in order to meet domestic consumption. 该国还一贯重视种植食用油料作物,以满足国内消费的需要。

NOTE 本短语的动词 lay 可被 place, put 替换,构成的短语与本短语意义和用法相同。

lay (someone) low *vt.* ❶(常用被动语态形式)(of a disease or an illness) make (someone) ill or weak and unable to do the things they usually do 使(某人)病倒,虚弱: I've been *laid low* by the flu for a weak. 我患流感,病倒了一个星期。The illness *aid* him *low*. 疾病使他十分虚弱。❷(of bad news) make (someone) extremely sad (坏消息)使(某人)极为悲伤:The death of her father really *laid her low*. 父亲去世的消息使她极度悲伤。

NOTE 本短语的动词 lay 可被 leave 替换,两者的意义和用法相同。

lay off *vt.* 【可分性动词短语】(非正式用语,常用被动语态形式) force (a worker) to give up a job, especially temporarily, because there is not enough work for him or her or for other business reasons (尤指暂时)解雇(员工): Because of the economic recession, the company *laid off* one-third of its staff. 由于经济衰退,该公司解雇了三分之一的员工。The factory had to *lay* some workers *off* when its orders decreased. 当订货量减少时,工厂不得不将一些工人解雇。People *laid off* from work will be helped until they find new jobs. 下岗人员在找到工作之前,都会得到帮助。

—*vi.* (非正式用语,常用一般时态) rest 休息: The doctor advised me to *lay off* more. 医生建议我多休息。

—*vt.* & *vi.* (非正式用语,常用一般时态) stop (something or doing something) especially for a short period of time (暂时)停止: She usually runs several miles every day but *lays off* in the hot weather. 她通常每天都跑几英里,但天热时就不跑。He went on hitting his wife until two of his friends arrived and told him to *lay off*. 他一直在殴打他的妻子,直到他的两个朋友到了让他停下来方才

罢休。You'd better *lay off* alcohol for a while. 你最好戒酒一段时间。

NOTE 1. 当本短语用作及物性动词短语，所带的宾语为代词时，该代词须置于本短语的动词和副词中间。

2. 当本短语作"(暂时)停止"解，用作及物性动词短语时，不用被动语态形式。

3. 当本短语作"解雇"解时，同义短语是 kick off, kick out, pay off, send away, stand off 和 turn off。

4. 本短语可转化成复合词 laid-off，意为"临时解雇(期)；停止活动(或比赛)的时期"。

lay on *vt.* ❶(常用被动语态形式)provide for the supply of (water, gas, electricity, etc.)安装(水、煤气、电等设施)：We are waiting for them to *lay* the water *on*. 我们正在等他们来安装自来水。You can't move into the house until gas, water and electricity are *laid on*. 在安装好煤气、水电之前，你们不能搬进这房子里。❷put(something or someone) down on (a surface, etc.)把……放在……上：Obama *laid* his left hand *on* the Bible, which Lincoln used for his inauguration in 1861, and took the oath. 奥巴马把左手放在林肯 1861 年宣誓就职时使用过的那本《圣经》上进行宣誓。Nurses helped to *lay* the unconscious woman *on* the operating table. 护士们帮助把那名不省人事的妇女放在了手术台上。❸(主要用于英国英语中，非正式用语) provide (something such as food, entertainment, or a service) for a group of people, especially without charging for it (尤指免费)提供(食物、娱乐或某种服务)：The organizers *laid on* a free lunch for us. 组织者为我们提供了免费午餐。They *lay on* free entertainment at the club. 他们免费提供在俱乐部的娱乐活动。❹(非正式用语) cause to have (something such as a duty, responsibility, or blame)on (someone)把(义务、责任或罪责等)加诸，归咎于(某人)：When parents grow older, they *lay* a special duty *on* their children. 当父母上了年纪时，他们就赋予子女们一种特殊的义务。That's rather unfair to *lay* the entire blame *on* one person. 把全部罪责都归咎于一人未免太不公平了。Don't *lay* that *on* me! I wasn't even there when it happened. 不要把那栽赃给我。事情发生时我根本就没在场。❺apply a coat of (paint, etc.)to or spread on (a surface)(在表面上)涂抹(油漆等)：He *laid on* the paint thickly against the weather. 他把漆刷得很厚，以防风吹雨淋。*Lay* the butter *on* thick, please. 请厚厚地涂抹一层奶油。

lay one's finger(s) on *vt.* show exactly (the cause, fault, etc. of something)明确指出(原因、错误等)：(常用于否定形式中) The experienced doctor *laid* his finger *on* the source of the disease. 这位经验丰富的医生明确地指出了病因之所在。The engineers couldn't *lay their fingers on* the reason for the rocket's failure to enter orbit. 工程师们无法找出火箭没能进入空间轨道的具体原因。I know there's something wrong, but I can't *lay my finger on* what it is. 我知道出了差错，但我无法明确指出毛病出在哪里。

NOTE 1. 本短语中的名词 finger 的单复数形式要根据前面动词的主语和修饰它的物主代词的单复数形式而作相应变化。

2. 本短语的动词 lay 可被 put 替换，两者的意义和用法相同。

3. 不要将本短语与 lay a finger on 混淆。

lay one's hands on *vt.* (非正式用语,常用一般时态)manage to obtain (something) or seize (someone)得到(某物),抓住(某人): I'll show you the letter if I can *lay my hands on* it. 如果我能搞到这封信,我一定给你看。I couldn't *lay my hands on* the book you suggested. 我无法搞到你推荐的那本书。This lady wants to *lay her hands on* all the money left by her husband. 这位女士想得到她丈夫遗留下来的所有钱财。

NOTE 1. 本短语的动词 lay 可被 get, put 等替换,构成的短语与本短语意义和用法相同。

2. 不要将本短语与 lay a hand on 混淆。

lay out *vt.* ❶(常用被动语态形式)spread (something) out or arrange (things) so you can see them easily 摆开,陈列: She *laid out* her best dress to wear at the party. 她把最好的衣服摆出来,准备在聚会时穿。My daughter *laid* all her new dresses *out* on the bed. 我的女儿把她所有的新衣服都摆在了床上。A giant Brazilian national soccer jersey was *laid out* on the field of Rio de Janeiro's Maracana Stadium, soon after FIFA announced that Brazil will host the 2014 World Cup. 国际足联宣布巴西将主办 2014 年世界杯后没多久,一件巨大的巴西国足球衫便展现在里约热内卢的马拉卡纳体育场的球场上。❷arrange (something); plan (something) in detail 安排,制订(计划): The government has *laid out* its plans to ban junk food ads during TV shows watched by under-16s. 政府已制订计划,禁止在播放 16 岁以下的少年儿童电视节目期间插播垃圾食品广告。Our plan must be well *laid out* before we begin to work. 我们在开始工作之前,必须制订好计划。❸(常用被动语态形式) design or plan (how something should look and arrange it in this way)设计: The hill has been *laid out* as a park. 这座小山已被设计成公园。❹ explain (something) carefully and clearly (仔细或清楚地)解释: The documents *lay out* the principles clearly enough. 文件对这些原则作了足够仔细、清楚的解释。Let's review the points one more time before we *lay* them *out* for the media. 咱们把这几点再审查一遍,再向媒体做出解释。❺(非正式用语,常用一般时态,常与 for, on 连用) spend (money, especially a large amount)花掉(尤指一大笔钱): They had already *laid out* a substantial sum for the wedding. 他们已经为办婚礼而花掉了一大笔钱。He *laid out* $800 on a new carpet. 他花了 800 美元买了一块新地毯。❻hit (someone) so hard that he or she falls to the ground and become unconscious 将(某人)打昏:(非正式用语,常用一般时态) The thieves *laid out* two of guards during the armed robbery. 在武装抢劫时,盗贼们打昏了两名守卫人员。Joe *laid* Ken *out* with one punch. 乔一拳就把肯打昏在地。Tyson was *laid out* for several minutes by a blow to the head. 泰森被拳击中头部,昏倒在地数分钟。❼prepare (a dead person's body) so that people can come to see it before it is buried 为(尸体)做殡葬准备: Two of the women came to *lay out* the body. 两个女人来为尸体做殡葬准备。

NOTE 1. 当本短语的宾语为代词时,该代词须置于本短语的动词和副词中间。

2. 当本短语作"摆开,陈列"解时,同义短语是 set out。

3. 本短语可转化为复合词 layout，意为“布局，陈设，安排，设计”。

lay siege to *vt.*【不可分性动词短语】surround (a place), either to prevent the people inside from receiving food and water or to protest about something or to force the people inside to come out 围困，包围(某一地点)：The army *laid siege to* the town until the hungry citizens were forced to yield. 军队围困此城一直到饥饿的市民被迫投降为止。Hundreds of students *laid siege to* the American embassy. 成百上千的学生包围了美国大使馆。

lay up *vt.*【可分性动词短语】❶get and keep a supply of (something such as food) to use in the future 贮存(食物等)：They have *laid up* large supplies of food. 他们贮存了大量的食物。He *laid up* some money against a rainy day. 他积蓄了一些钱以备不时之需。Try to *lay* as much of it *up* as you can. 这东西你尽量多贮存一些。❷(常用被动语态形式) not use (a vehicle or ship) for a period of time, especially because it needs to be repaired (尤指因需要修理而)暂停使用(汽车或船只)：If you *lay up* a car for the winter, you should take out its battery. 你要是冬天把车闲置起来，就应该把电瓶取出来。This ship was *laid up* for repairs. 这条船已停用待修。Bill had to *lay up* his boat when school started. 开学后，比尔只得把他的小船闲置起来。A wreck *laid* the bus *up* for months. 一次损毁使这辆公共汽车几个月不能上路营运。❸(非正式用语，常用被动语态形式，常与 with 连用) force (someone) to stay in bed as a result of being ill or injured (因病或伤)使(某人)卧床：I have been *laid up* for a week with a serious disease. 我因重病已卧床了一个星期。The traffic accident *laid* him *up* with a broken leg. 交通事故使他断了腿而卧床不起。You'll *lay* yourself *up* if you go on working like this. 如果你继续这样工作下去的话，你就会累得爬不起来。He's still *laid up* with a bad back. 他因腰病还在卧床。

NOTE 当本短语的宾语为代词时，该代词须置于本短语的动词和副词中间。

lead a life *vi.* live your life in a particular way 过着……的生活：He had always *led* a quiet *life* until he met Mary. 在与玛丽相识之前，他一直过着安静的生活。When a boy leaves college and begins to earn money he can *lead a life* of independence. 男孩子大学毕业后开始赚钱时，便可独立生活了。Thanks to the reforms and opening-up we're now *leading a* better *life*. 由于改革开放，我们现在都过着更美好的生活。

NOTE 本短语的动词 lead 可被 live 替换，两者的意义和用法相同。

lead to *vt.* ❶guide (someone, something, or an animal) to (a place) 把……带到……，把……引到……，把……牵到……：The girl *led* her little brother *to* school. 那女孩带着小弟弟上学去了。Developing the use of tools *led* man *to* a new kind of life. 工具的使用和改进把人类引向一种崭新的生活。He was *leading* the horse *to* the stable when she arrived. 当她到达时，他正把马牵往马厩。❷(of a road, etc.) provide a way (for someone) to reach a place (道路等)通向：This road *leads to* the new airport. 这条路通往新机场。And as the saying goes, all roads *lead to* Rome. 正如常言

所说，条条道路通罗马。Take the left path; it will *lead* you *to* the house. 走左边那条小路，你就会走到那所房子的。There is a very good hotel not far away from the city, complete with swimming pool and garden *leading to* the beach. 离城不远有一家很好的宾馆，带有游泳池和通向海滩的花园。❸ be (partly) the cause of (something or doing something); begin a process that causes (something) to happen or exist 引起，造成，导致：It's sleeping late in the morning that *leads to* his being late for work. 早上睡过了头是他上班迟到的原因。There was a fear among the government officials that interference in the market would *lead to* a collapse. 一些政府官员担心干预市场可能会引起崩盘。

lead up to *vt.* ❶(of a road, etc.)go up to (a place)(道路等)通向(某处)：This staircase *leads up to* the roof. 这楼梯通向屋顶。A little path *led up to* the garden gate. 有一条小路通往花园大门。Which path will *lead* us *up to* the top of the hill? 走哪条道我们能到山顶？❷ come before (an event); cause (something) 导致，引起：These circumstances will *lead up to* war. 这些情况会导致战争。We studied the events *leading up to* the Gulf War. 我们对引起海湾战争的那些事件进行了研究。❸introduce; prepare to say; make a gradual or indirect approach to (a main topic)介绍；准备讲；引到(主要话题)：The speaker took far too long *leading up to* his main point. 演讲人用了过长的时间来介绍其讲演的要点。I wondered what he was *leading up to*. 我不知道他要讲些什么。He *led up to* our favorite topic. 他把话头引到我们最感兴趣的话题上去。

leak out *v.* ❶(of liquid, gas, etc.)(cause to)escape through an accidental hole (使)(液体、气体等)泄漏：The oil has *leaked out* into the surrounding soil. 油泄漏出来并渗入周围的土壤中。There's a hole in the bucket and the water is *leaking out*. 桶上有一个洞，水正往外渗漏。This pipe seems to be *leaking out* gas. 这管子好像漏煤气。❷(of a piece of news or information, a secret, etc.)(cause to) become known to the public (使)(消息、秘密等)泄露出去：I knew how the secret had *leaked out*. 我知道这秘密是怎么泄露出去的。They have *leaked* the information *out* to the press. 他们已把消息泄露给了报界。

lean on/upon *vt.* ❶ stand or be set at an angle against(something)for support instead of being upright 靠在，倚在：*Leaning* her head *on* my shoulder, she began to cry. 她把头靠在我的肩上便哭了起来。He *leaned on* the back of the chair. 他斜靠在椅背上。He walked in, *leaning on* a cane. 他拄着手杖走了进来。❷depend on (someone) for support and encouragement 依靠，依赖(某人)：Everybody needs someone to *lean on* in times of trouble. 每个人在身处困境时都需要依靠别人的帮助。When I grew up I came to realize he was the one I could *lean on* whenever I had difficulties. 我长大以后才意识到，他是我有困难时随时都可以依靠的人。The minister *leans on* his advisers to help him to solve his problems. 这位部长靠他的顾问他解决问题。It was reassuring to have someone *upon* whom he could *lean*. 令人欣慰的是，他有人可以依靠了。❸(非正式用语) put pressure on or threaten (someone) to make him or her do or say (something)向(某人)施加压力：The Prime Minister's been *leaning* pretty heavily

on her to resign. 首相一直向她施以重压，迫使她辞职。I'm being *leant on* to pay up straightaway. 我正受到威胁，要我立刻付清全部欠款。

NOTE **1.** 本短语中的 upon 用法比 on 正式，但不及 on 常用。

2. 本短语中的动词 lean 的过去式或过去分词形式有两种：leaned 和 leant，这两种形式都用于英国英语中；而在美国英语中，主要用 leaned。

3. 当本短语作"依靠，依赖(某人)"解时，同义短语是 depend on/upon 和 rely on/upon。

leap to conclusions ⇨ **jump to a conclusion**

learn about *vt.*【不可分性动词短语】❶gain new information about (a situation, event, or person) 了解，初晓：Examinees worldwide can visit its official website to *learn about* the new-generation TOEFL, the US Educational Testing Service said. 美国教育考试服务中心说，全球的考生可访问其官方网站来了解新一代托福考试。I think that children should start to *learn about* sex whenever you notice them becoming curious about it. 我认为，孩子们应该在你注意到他们对性感到好奇时开始了解性知识。❷(常用一般时态) come to hear about (something or someone) 听说，知道：We *learned about* the project from the chairman. 我们是从主席那里听说那个项目的。We only *learnt about* the collision of British and French nuclear submarines deep in the Atlantic Ocean from media reports on Monday. 我们只是通过星期一的媒体报道得知英法两国的核潜艇在大西洋深处相撞的消息。

learn by heart *vt.*【可分性动词短语】fix (something, especially a piece of writing) in the memory; memorize 记住，背熟：She is *learning by heart* the traffic regulations. 她在熟记交通法规。Our teacher told us to *learn* the poem *by heart*. 我们的老师要我们背熟这首诗。Once the lines have been *learnt by heart*, the students are divided into smaller groups and helped to devise their own performance. 学生们一旦记住了这些台词，就把他们分成若干小组，并帮助他们设计自己的表演。

learn from *vt.* ❶gain (knowledge, skills or experience of something) from (someone or something) 从……学到(知识、技能或经验)，向……学习：You were lucky to *learn* English *from* such a good teacher. 你和这样一位好老师学习英语太幸运了。To *learn from* other Games hosts, London sent some staff members to Beijing to see the opening and closing ceremonies of the 2008 Summer Olympics. 为向其他奥运会主办城市学习，伦敦曾派出了一些工作人员奔赴北京观摩了 2008 年夏季奥运会的开幕式和闭幕式。❷come to know (something) from (someone or something) 从……得知(某事)：I *learnt* this *from* someone else. 这事是我从别人那儿知道的。As we *learn from* what is said above, the tides can be very useful. 综上所述，我们知道了潮汐是非常有用的。❸become wiser because of (something such as an unpleasant experience); study (one's mistakes, etc., and those of others) to ensure that they are not repeated 从(自己或他人的错误等)中汲取教训：One important lesson we have *learnt from* the ice disaster is that we have to emphasize coordinated development. 我们从这一冰雪灾害中所汲取的一个重要教训就是，必须强调协调发展。We hope he'll *learn from* his mistakes. 我们希望他从错误中汲取教训。All of us should *learn* lessons *from* the past failures and mistakes. 我们所有的人都应从过去的失败与错误中汲取教训。

learn of *vt.* (正式用语,常用一般时态) become informed of (something or someone)(自他人处)听说,得知,获悉: She only *learnt of* her son's marriage long after the event. 她在很久以后才听说儿子结婚的事。I'm not in the telephone book. How did you *learn of* me? 电话号码簿上并没有我的电话号码呀,你是怎么知道我的电话号码的?

least of all *adv.* (通常用于否定句之后)(used after a negative statement for showing that it applies to a particular person, thing, or group more than any other) especially not 尤其不: None of you should complain, Jim *least of all*. 你们都不该抱怨,吉姆尤不应该。No one believed her, *least of all* me. 没有人相信她,尤其是我。There is not much there to attract tourists, *least of all* the weather. 那里没有多少吸引游客的东西,天气就更糟糕了。

NOTE 如本短语置于句首,后面的句子结构则要倒装。例如:

> *Least of all* would I lie to you.
> 尤其是我不会对你撒谎了。

leave alone *vt.*【可分性动词短语】❶let (someone) remain on his or her own 让(某人)独自待着: I wish you just go away and *leave* me *alone*. 我希望你走开,让我一个人待着。They *left* the child *alone* in the house all night. 他们把那孩子整夜独自留在家中。Now she was *left alone*. 这回只剩她一个人待着了。❷(常用一般时态) stop behaving annoyingly in someone's presence; stop bothering (someone) or touching (something)别打扰(某人),别碰(某物): The principal is busy at his desk; you'd better *leave* him *alone*. 校长正忙着办公,你最好别去打扰他。*Leave* that ornament *alone*; you might break it. 别碰那件装饰品,你会弄坏它的。❸stop trying to deal with (something) 不处理(某事): It's none of your business, so why don't you just *leave* it *alone*? 这不干你的事,你干吗要管它? I should *leave* that question *alone*, if I were you. 我要是你,这问题我就不管。

NOTE **1.** 当本短语的宾语为代词时,该代词须置于本短语的动词和形容词中间。

2. 当本短语用作及物性动词短语时,与 let alone 意义和用法相同,两者可互换使用。但 let alone 还用作连词性短语,而本短语则不能。

leave behind *vt.*【可分性动词短语】❶(常用被动语态形式) cause (a person, country, or organization) to lag behind 把(某人、国家或组织)落在后面: The best runner was rapidly *left* the others far *behind*. 那位跑得最快的运动员很快就把其他运动员远远地甩在了后面。The other climbers were more experienced and I was worried I'd get *left behind*. 其他的登山者经验多一些,所以我担心我会被他们落在后面。I didn't want to be *left behind*. 我不想被落在后面。❷forget to take (something); go away without taking (someone or something); abandon 遗落,留下,遗弃: When she was halfway home she realized that she'd *left* her purse *behind*. 她在回家的半路上才意识到把钱包忘带了。He had to *leave* his wife and two children *behind* in Chile. 他只好把妻子和两个孩子留在了智利。The diary *left behind* by the brave soldier has been kept in the museum. 那名勇敢的士兵遗留下来的日记一直保存在博物馆里。❸(常用一般时态) cause to remain afterwards or after (something or someone)遗留：The last government has *left behind* a terrible debt. 上届政府遗留下了一笔巨额债务。The terrorist network has to be pulled up by its roots and examined to make sure we have *left* nothing *behind*. 对这一恐怖组织必须要加以彻底根除，经查后保证绝除后患。

leave for *vt.* ❶go away from (a place) and travel to (another)离开(某处)去(某处)，动身去(某处)：He *left* his office *for* the airport an hour ago. 他在一个小时之前离开办公室去机场了。In case you can't come, give me a call before I *leave for* work. 如果你不能来，在我去上班前给我打个电话。❷ cause (something) to remain or wait for (someone)使(某物)留下，将(某物)留给(某人)：Has anyone *left* a message *for* me? 有人给我留过条子吗？*Leave* some cake *for* the rest of us! 把蛋糕留给我们其他人一些！

leave it at that *vi.* (非正式用语)not say anything more or not argue any further about a matter; (对某事)别再说什么了，别再争论下去了：I've decided to quit; so I think we'll *leave it at that*. 我已经决定辞职。所以，我想咱就别再多说了。Let's *leave it at that*. You go ahead and I'll follow you. 咱们别再争论下去了。你先走，我跟在后面。

leave (someone) low ⇨ **lay (someone) low**

leave off *vt.* &*vi.* (英国英语用法，非正式用语) (of someone) stop (something or doing something); cease 停止：He sat at the piano again and started playing from where he *left off*. 他又坐回到钢琴旁，从停下来的地方继续弹奏。She was so ill she had to *leave off* work. 她病得很重，只好停止工作了。*Leave off* that noise, will you? 别再吵嚷了，行吗？I wish he'd *leave off* moaning about everything! 我希望他不要再抱怨一切了。

—*vt.*【可分性动词短语】❶(常用被动语态形式) not include (someone or something) (on a list) (在名单中)不把……包括其中，把……排除在外：The judge *left* Tom's name *off* the list of those who he wanted to arrest. 法官没有把汤姆的名字列入他要逮捕的那些人的名单之中。She has been deliberately *left off* the guest list. 她被有意地排除在宾客名单之外。❷no longer put on or wear (clothes)不再穿(某种衣物)，脱下：They *left* their woolen underwear *off* when the weather got warm. 天暖了，他们都脱掉了羊毛内衣。I *left off* my shoes when I entered the room. 我进屋后便脱了鞋子。

leave out *vt.*【可分性动词短语】❶(常与of连用) not include (something or someone)把……排除掉，没把……包括，漏掉……：We decided to *leave* the chapter *out* of the book altogether. 我们决定把整章内容都从书中删掉。England has *left* him *out* of their football team. 英格兰队没有把他包括在队中。You've *left out* the most important word in this sentence. 你在这个句子中漏掉了最重要的一个词。When you're giving out the invitations don't *leave* Rogers *out*. 你在发请帖时，别把罗杰斯漏掉。❷fail to consider (something) 没有考虑到(某事)：You *left out* the possibility that the train might be late. 你没有考虑到火车会

晚点的可能性。We should not *leave* these factors *out* of account. 我们不应该不考虑这些因素。❸(常用被动语态形式)pay no attention to or exclude (someone)忽视,冷落(某人): She feels *left out* because the other children don't play with her. 她感觉受到了冷落,因为别的孩子都不和她玩。No one spoke to him; he was *left out* at the party. 在聚会上没有人和他说话,他受到了冷落。The older brothers *left* their young sister *out* of most of their games. 在大多数游戏中哥哥们都冷落着他们的小妹妹。

NOTE 当本短语的宾语为代词时,该代词须置于本短语的动词和副词中间。

leave over *vt.* 【可分性动词短语】❶delay (something) or leave (a matter) to be dealt with at another time 推迟,延期: Don't *leave over* the work that can be done right away. 马上可以办好的事情就不要往后拖。We'd better *leave* the matter *over* until tomorrow. 这件事我们最好明天再说吧。I regret that these matters will have to be *left over* until our next meeting. 很抱歉,这些问题只得留待我们下次开会解决了。❷(常用被动语态形式)remain after the rest has been used or divided 留下,剩下: We'll *leave* the meat *over* for tomorrow. 我们将把这肉剩下明天吃。I gave the children two copies each and I had three copies *left over*. 我给每个孩子发了两册,我还剩下三册。These sweets were *left over* from last night's party. 这些糖果是昨晚聚会剩下来的。

NOTE 当本短语的宾语为代词时,该代词须置于本短语的动词和副词中间。

leave room for ⇨ **make room for**

lend a (helping) hand *vi.* (常与 to, with 连用) give (someone) support or help (with something or doing something)支持,帮助(某人): Davis is someone who is always ready to *lend a helping hand*. 戴维斯是一个随时都肯帮忙的人。We *lent a* sincere *helping hand* to African countries' endeavor at national economic development. 我们真诚地援助非洲各国发展民族经济。Could you *lend* me *a hand* with this heavy table, please? 请你帮我抬一下这张沉重的桌子,好吗?

NOTE 本短语的同义短语是 give a hand,两者可互换使用。

lend an ear to ⇨ **give an ear to**

lend itself to *vt.* (正式用语,用一般时态)(of something)be good or suitable for (something or doing something)(指某物)适合于: This topic *lends itself to* class discussion. 这个题目适合于课堂讨论。This play *lends itself to* being performed in an open-air theatre. 这出剧适合于在露天剧场演出。

less and less *adv.* gradually getting smaller (in amount or degree)越来越少,越来越小,越来越不: Because of his illness he eats *less and less*. 由于有病,他吃的越来越少。Though the public cares about the story *less and less*, the papers continue to report it. 尽管公众对此事已越来越不关心了,可报界仍在连篇累牍地报道。Nowadays, farming is growing *less and less* profitable. 现在种田越来越无利可图了。

NOTE 本短语的反义短语是 more and more。

less than Ⅰ *prep.* to a smaller degree than 少于,小于,低于: Nothing in this store is *less than* 20 US dollars. 该商店中的商品没有低于 20 美元的。A new

L

Gallup poll released today shows *less than* 50 percent of Americans trust the mass media. 根据今天发布的一项盖洛普民意调查表明，不足半数的美国人相信大众传媒的报道。

Ⅱ *adv.* not 不：We were busy and *less than* delighted to have company that day. 那天我们很忙，不高兴有客人来。It was obviously a *less than* perfect marriage. 很显然，这是一桩不完美的婚姻。

NOTE **1.** 当本短语前加否定词 no 和 not 时，两者含义不同：

> No less than 500 students attended my lecture!
> 听我讲座的竟有 500 名学生！
> There were not *less than* 500 students attending my lecture.
> 至少有 500 名学生听了讲座。

2. 当本短语作为介词性短语，表示"少于，小于，低于"之意时，反义短语是 more than。

let alone Ⅰ *vt.* 【可分性动词短语】(常用于祈使句中，通常不用被动语态形式，常用一般时态) not do anything to or not disturb or touch (someone or something) 不管，不理，不干扰，不碰：When Mary gets mad, just *let* her *alone*. 当玛丽生气时，你就别理她。He is busy at his desk; you'd better *let* him *alone*. 他正在伏案忙着工作，你最好别干扰他。Please *let* that new computer *alone*. 请不要动那台新电脑。

Ⅱ *conj.* (一般用于否定句后) (used for saying that the thing mentioned next is even less likely to happen than the one mentioned before) to say nothing of; not to mention 更不用说，更谈不上：He will not help his own brother, *let alone* a stranger. 他连自己的弟弟都不会帮助，更谈不上陌生人了。She doesn't like singing, *let alone* dancing. 她不喜欢唱歌，更不用说跳舞了。He hardly wrote to me, *let alone* sent me any gifts. 他没给我写过信，更不用说送过物给我了。I haven't decided where to go, *let alone* when to leave. 我还没有决定去哪儿，更谈不上什么时候动身了。I never thought of it, *let alone* did I do it. 我想都没有想到它，更谈不上去做了。

NOTE **1.** 当本短语作为动词性短语，所带的宾语为代词时，该代词须置于本短语的动词和形容词中间。

2. 当本短语用作动词性短语时，与 leave alone 意义和用法相同，两者可互换使用。

3. 当本短语作为连词性短语，从句动词与主句动词不同时，如果主句有助动词，则从句用不带 to 的动词不定式；如果主句中动词是现在时，则从句中动词亦用现在时；如果主句中动词是过去时，则从句中动词亦用过去时。

4. 当本短语作为连词性短语时，同义短语是 not to mention, not to speak of, to say nothing of。

let down *vt.* 【可分性动词短语】❶cause or allow (something or someone) to go down; lower 放低，放下：*Let down* a rope so that I can climb up. 放下一根绳子来，我好爬上去。*Let* the bucket *down* carefully into the well. 小心地把桶向下放入井内。The prisoner *let* himself *down* slowly from the window by means of a rope. 囚犯是借助一根绳子从窗子慢慢荡下来的。The rescue party was *let down* into the mine by a rope. 救护队是用一根绳子被放下矿井的。❷make (someone) disappointed by not doing something he or she is expecting you to do; fail to keep a promise to (someone) 使(某人)失望,失约于(某人): The families of the victims feel that the justice system has *let* them *down*. 遇难者家属感到司法制度使他们失望。I felt *let down* when he didn't phone me. 他没给我打电话,我感到很失望。The singer we had engaged *let* us *down* at the last moment, so we had to find a quick replacement. 我们雇用的歌手在最后时刻失约了,因此我们只好急忙找人打替场。❸make (clothes) longer by using the extra cloth in the bottom fold of a piece of clothing (利用放下衣物底边的余出部分)把(衣物)加长: I'm going to *let down* this old dress for my daughter. 我要把这件旧衣服加长给我女儿穿。Margaret is growing so fast that I have had to *let* all her skirts *down* again. 玛格丽特长得太快了,所以我不得不再次把她所有的裙子加长。❹(英国英语用法)allow the air to go out of (something such as a car tyre)放掉(车胎等)的气: Someone has *let down* the back tyre of my bike. 有人把我自行车的后胎放了气。I *let* the tyres *down* on his car. 我把他汽车的轮胎给放了气。

NOTE 1. 当本短语的宾语为代词时,该代词须置于本短语的动词和副词中间。

2. 当本短语作"把(衣物)加长"解时,反义短语是 turn up。

let go (of) *v.* ❶stop holding, release or set free (someone or something)松开,放开;放弃,释放: *Let go*! That hurts. 松开!太疼了。Bethany, a surfing star in Hawaii said the shark pulled her back and forth, "but I just held onto my board, and then it *let go*."夏威夷冲浪女明星贝思安妮说,鲨鱼来回地拖拽着她,"但我紧紧地抓住冲浪板,后来它松口放开了我。" He wouldn't *let go of* me. 他不肯放开我。*Let go of* my hand, you're hurting me! 放开我的手,你都把我弄疼了! ❷shoot or throw (something)发射,投掷: He pulled back the bow-string and *let go* an arrow. 他拉满弓弦,射出了一箭。We waited until the enemy was close enough and then *let go*. 我们等敌人足够接近时便投了出去。❸ignore or forget about (something said or done)别理会,忘掉: "Did you hear what that rude storekeeper said to me?" Jack asked. "*Let* it *go*, Jack," I replied. "你听没听到那个粗鲁的店主和我说的话?"杰克问道。"不要去理会它,杰克。"我回答道。❹end (someone's employment); dismiss (someone)解雇(某人): It was too bad that we had to *let* him *go*. 很遗憾,我们不得不把他解雇。The factory has *let go* about 70 workers. 该厂已经解雇约 70 名工人。

let in *vt.*【可分性动词短语】❶ allow (someone or something) to enter (a house, room, etc.) 准许……进入(某处): Lock the door and don't *let* anybody *in*; I'll be back in 15 minutes. 把门锁上,别让任何人进来。我过一刻钟就回来。I'll give you a key so that you can *let* yourself *in*. 我给你一把钥匙,这样你就可以进去了。❷allow; admit 容许,许可: This new evidence *lets in* the possibility of doubt. 这一新的证据有可能受到质疑。❸(非正式用语) talk to (someone) about (your problems, etc.) 把(自己的问题等)讲给(某人): You've got to learn to *let* me *in*, my dear. 我的宝贝儿,你得学会把你的问题讲给我听。—*vt.* &. *vi.* allow (water, mud, air, etc.) to enter (something), usually because there is a hole or crack 进水；漏气：My old boots had been *letting in* water on damp ground. 在湿地面上行走时，我的旧靴子就进水。My old boots are *letting in* badly. 我的旧靴子严重渗水。Make some holes in this paper box to *let* air *in* if you are to put the bird in. 如果你要把鸟儿放在这个纸盒箱子里的话，要扎些孔来透气。

NOTE 当本短语用作及物性动词短语，所带的宾语为代词时，该代词须置于本短语的动词和副词中间。

let in on *vt.* 【可分性动词短语】（非正式用语）tell (someone)(a plan, an activity, a secret, etc.)把（计划、活动、秘密等）告诉给（某人）：They were planning something, but they wouldn't *let* me *in on* it. 他们在计划着什么，但他们不会让我知道的。If you promise not to tell, I'll *let* you *in on* a secret. 如果你保证不往外说，我就会把一个秘密告诉你。He has not yet been *let in on* the bad news. 那坏消息还没告诉他。

let loose *vt.* 【可分性动词短语】free, loosen or give up what you hold on (someone, an animal, etc.)释放，放走，放开：The farmer opened the gate and *let* the bulls *loose*. 那农人打开大门把牛放了出来。At two o'clock in the afternoon, all the children were *let loose*. 下午两点钟，所有的孩子都放学回家了。Someone *let* the lion *loose* from its cage, and it has been wandering all over the town, terrifying people. 有人把狮子从笼子里放了出来，它一直在城中到处游荡，吓煞人们。The children *let* the balloons *loose* to let them rise in the air. 孩子们撒手放飞气球，让它们飞上天空。

NOTE 本短语的动词 let 可被 set，turn 等替换，构成的短语与本短语意义和用法相同。

let off *vt.* 【可分性动词短语】❶allow (a passenger) to leave (a vehicle, ship, etc.)让（乘客）下（车、船等）：The conductor wouldn't *let* me *off* (the bus) until I'd paid the fare. 直到我买了票，乘务员才让我下了（公共汽车）。You can't *let* me *off* at the dark corner. 你不能让我在黑暗的角落处下车呀。I asked the captain to *let* me *off* at the next port of call. 我要求船长让我在下一个停靠港下船。❷ fire (a gun or bullet); make (something such as a bomb, firework) explode 开枪（或炮）；使（炸弹等）爆炸；放（烟花、爆竹等）：He *let* the revolver *off* at the crowd. 他向人群开枪了。The warship *let off* its guns at the boat moving near the island. 军舰向驶近该岛的船只开了炮。A bomb was *let off* in an underground train in London yesterday. 昨天，一枚炸弹在伦敦的地铁列车上被引爆。Several years ago, in some places of China, it's quite common that firecrackers are *let off* at weddings and other celebrations. 数年前，在中国有些地方，在婚礼上和其他庆典燃放鞭炮是很普遍的。❸ release; give (someone) lighter or no punishment at all (for something he or she did wrong)释放，宽恕（某人）；（对某人）从轻处罚：They *let* the boy *off* because he's only sixteen. 他们释放了那个男孩子，因为他才 16 岁。If you promise not to do it again, I'll *let* you *off*. 如果你保证不再这样做了，我就饶恕你。They *let* the man *off* with a fine instead of sending him to prison. 他们没让那个人坐牢，而只是罚款了事。❹（主要用于英国英语中）allow (someone) not to do (something he or she was expecting to have to do)免除(某人的工作): When we were in port, he *let* me *off* work and allowed me to go ashore. 我们进港后,他没让我工作,而是让我上岸了。Girls always get *let off* the heavy work because they're weaker. 女孩子总是因为体力较弱而被免做重活。She *let* the boy *off* doing his music practice. 她免除了那男孩的音乐练习作业。❺permit the renting of (a building) in separate parts 准许租用(房屋): These old-style houses are being *let off* as separate flats. 这些旧式房屋都在分为套间出租。

NOTE 当本短语的宾语为代词时,该代词须置于本短语的动词和副词或介词中间。

let on *vt.* &*vi.* (非正式用语,常用一般时态) ❶tell a secret 泄露秘密;流露真情: She knew where the children were hiding, but she didn't *let on*. 她知道孩子们藏在哪儿,但是不肯讲出实情。Don't *let on*(to others)about the meeting. 不要(向其他人)泄漏会议的秘密。You mustn't *let on* where the money is hidden. 你一定不要泄露藏钱的地方。She never *let on* that she was married. 她从不透露自己是个已婚之人。❷pretend 假装: He's not as knowledgeable as he *lets on*. 他并不像他装的那样有学问。He got the job by *letting on* that he had a lot of experience. 他装作很有经验的样子而得到了那份工作。

—*vt.* allow (someone or something) to get on (a vehicle)允许……上(车): The driver wouldn't *let* the man *on* (the bus) with that big box. 司机不肯让那名男子带那个大箱子上车。

let out *vt.* 【可分性动词短语】❶allow (a person or animal) to leave a place 让……出去: Mother won't *let* us *out* when it rains. 妈妈不让我们在下雨时出去。The farmer *let out* the cow after milking. 农夫挤完奶后,就把奶牛放了出去。❷(常与 of 连用) set (usually someone) free (from somewhere) 把……放走: The doctors are *letting* Mother *out* of hospital next week. 医生下星期就会让妈妈出院的。He was *let out* of prison after serving five years of an eight-year sentence because he's been a model prisoner. 他被判8年徒刑,但因他一直是模范囚犯,服刑5年便被释放出狱。❸ allow (something such as water, air or breath) to flow out or escape 放出(水或气体);呼出(气息): There's a hole in the bottom of the bucket that *lets* the water *out*. 水桶底部有个孔,水是从那儿流出来的。Someone has *let* the air *out* of the back tyre of my bicycle. 有人把我自行车后车胎的气给放了。The old man *let out* his breath in a long sigh. 那老人长叹了一口气。❹(正式用语,常用一般时态) make (a particular sound, such as a cry, scream, yell, or sigh) 发出(某种声音等): He *let out* a cry as the dentist touched his bad tooth. 当牙医触到他那颗坏牙时,他大叫了一声。As he walked away, he *let out* a sigh of relief. 他走开时,轻松地叹了一口气。❺(常用一般时态)allow (something such as a secret) to become known 泄露(秘密),透露(消息): I'll never tell you another secret if you *let* this one *out*. 如果你把这个秘密泄露出去,我再也不告诉你别的了。He accidentally *let out* that he hadn't been home for 10 days. 他无意中透露出他已10天没回家了。❻ make (a piece of clothing, such as a dress, skirt, or

trousers) wider, looser, larger, etc. 把(衣物等)加大: I'm going to have my trousers *let out* around the waist. 我要把我的裤腰部位加肥。Since she started putting on weight her skirts had to be *let out*. 自从她开始发胖以后,她的裙子都得放大一些了。She has to *let* all her dresses *out* because she is getting so fat. 因日渐长胖,她不得不把连衣裙全部放大。❼(主要用于英国英语中,常与 to 连用)allow (someone) to use (especially a room or house, a vehicle or equipment) in exchange for money 出租(尤指房屋、车辆或设备): We could always *let out* the spare room. 当时我们总有空房出租。The top floor of the house is *let out* to a young couple. 房子的顶层租给了一对年轻的夫妇。They *let out* cars by the day. 他们按日出租汽车。

—*vi.* (美国英语用法,常用一般时态) (a school, film or a show) end and people leave (学校)放学;(电影或演出)散场: When does school *let out*? 学校什么时候放学? The movie *lets out* at 11 o'clock. 电影 11 点钟散场。

NOTE 1. 当本短语用作及物性动词短语,所带的宾语为代词时,该代词须置于本短语的动词和副词中间。

2. 当本短语作"把(衣物等)加大"解时,反义短语是 take in。

let up *vt.*【可分性动词短语】(常用一般时态) allow (someone) to come upstairs or to a higher level 让(某人)上楼,让(某人)上来: The doctor is here; shall I *let* him *up*? 医生到了。请他上楼吗?

—*vi.* (非正式用语) ❶(of something bad or unpleasant) slow down or gradually stop 减缓,减弱,逐渐停止: The pain finally *let up*. 疼痛终于减轻了。It's raining hard. You'd better wait till it *lets up* a little. 雨下得很大。你最好等雨小一点再走。The icy wind never *let up* for a moment. 寒风刮得一直也没停。❷(常用一般时态) work less hard; put less effort into something, especially criticizing someone or making them work harder (工作)松劲: Boys, don't *let up*; the job is nearly finished. 小伙子们,不要松劲呀,活儿快干完了。

level off/out *vt.* &. *vi.* make or become level or flat 把(表面)弄平,变平: They *leveled off* the wet concrete with a piece of wood. 他们用一根木头把未干的混凝土整平。The gardener has *leveled* the ground *off*. 园丁已将地面弄平。The ground will have to be *leveled off* before we can start building. 在我们开工建筑之前,要先把地面弄平。The road *levels out* as you get close to the village. 当你快到村口时,路就变得平坦起来。❷abolish (distinctions, differences, etc.)消除(差别、分歧等):We expect the differences in their educational attainment to gradually *level out*. 我们期望他们在教育目的上的分歧能逐渐消除。The reforms of the tax system in China are intended to *level out* the big differences between rich and poor. 中国税收制度的改革旨在消除贫富之间的巨大差别。

—*vi.* ❶(of an aircraft) stop sloping or moving up or down; travel horizontally after having been traveling in an upwards or downwards direction (飞机)停止升降运动,水平飞行:The plane will *level off* at around 35,000 feet. 飞机到 35 000 英尺左右的高度时就会水平飞行。❷(of something that is progressing or developing) stop growing or diminishing at such a fast speed; remain steady 停止波动，保持稳定：After going up for several months, prices of goods *leveled off* in September. 物价上涨了数月之后，9 月份开始稳定了。Oil prices should *level out* now that the war is over. 既然战争已经结束，石油价格应该稳定了。

liable for/to *adj.* having (legal) responsibility for (something or someone)对……负(法律)责任：They are arguing about who should be *liable for* the traffic accident. 他们在争论谁该对这起交通事故负责任。Men between the ages of 18 and 35 were *liable for* military service. 18 至 35 岁的男性都有服兵役的义务。Is a wife *liable for* her husband's debts? 妻子对丈夫的债务负法律责任吗? The airline is *liable to* you for any damage to your luggage. 航空公司对你的行李受损负有责任。

NOTE 本短语的同义短语是 accountable for/to 和 responsible for。

lie behind *vt.* (无被动语态形式，用一般时态) be the real reason for (a decision or action)是……的原因：We'd like to know what *lay behind* her decision to change her will. 我们想知道是什么原因使她决定改变意愿的。Do you know what *lies behind* her reluctance to speak? 你知道她吞吞吐吐地不愿说是什么原因吗?

lie down *vi.* ❶lie at full length, as when resting or sleeping 躺下，休息：I *lay down* for a while and felt better. 我躺了一会儿，才感到好一些。Why don't you go upstairs and *lie down* a bit? 你何不上楼去休息一会儿呢? ❷(非正式用语，后与 on the job 连用)not work as hard at something as you should do; put no effort into your work (工作)不卖力：Why are the workers *lying down* on the job? 工人们为什么又在消极怠工?

NOTE 本短语可转化为复合词 lie-down，意为“小睡，小憩”。

lie in *vi.* (英国英语用法，非正式用语) stay in bed in the morning for longer than usual (晚起床)睡懒觉：We usually *lie in* on Sundays. 我们通常在星期日晚起床睡懒觉。

—*vt.*【不可分性动词短语】❶(用一般时态) exist in; be found in 在于：The advantage of railways *lies in* their large capacity over long distances. 铁路的优点在于其巨大的远距离运输能力。His worst mistake *lay in* thinking that all his workers were trustworthy. 他最严重的错误在于他认为他的工人都可靠。A man's worth *lies* not so much *in* what he has as *in* what he is. 一个人的价值与其说在于他的财富，倒不如说在于他是什么样的人。❷be placed in (somewhere) 置于(某处)，位于(某处)：You'd better not keep your money *lying in* the bank; since the deposit rate is so low nowadays. 如今的储蓄利率太低，所以你最好别把钱存在银行里。The village *lay in* ruins after the war. 战争过后，那个村庄已成了一片废墟。

NOTE 1. 当本短语作“(晚起床)睡懒觉”解时，在美国英语中的表达形式为 sleep in。例如：

> It's a holiday tomorrow, so you can *sleep in*.
>
> 明天是假日，你可以晚起睡懒觉了。

2. 本短语可转化为复合词 lie-in，意为“睡懒觉；(在大街等处)卧地抗议示威”。

light on/upon *vt.*【不可分性动词短语】

❶(of a bird, insect, etc.)stop flying and land on (something or someone)(指鸟、昆虫等)落在……上:A big bird *lighted on* the branch. 一只大鸟落在了树枝上。Two butterflies *lighted on* the baby, causing her to shriek with delight. 有两只蝴蝶落在了宝宝身上,这使她高兴得尖叫起来。A drop of rain *lit on* my hand. 一滴雨点落在了我的手上。Her glance *lit upon* the toys in the store window. 她的目光落在了商店橱窗里的玩具上。❷(正式用语,用一般时态) suddenly find (something, usually good) or think of (something)突然发现(往往是好的东西);突然想到: If you look hard in this field, you could *light on* some valuable ancient coins. 如果你在这片地里仔细寻找,就会找到一些很值钱的古币。Suddenly she *lit upon* a new way of solving the problem. 她突然想出了一个解决这个问题的新方法。

NOTE 1. 本短语中的 upon 用法比 on 正式,但不及 on 常用。

2. 本短语中的动词 light 的过去式和过去分词有两种形式:lighted 和 lit。在英国英语中,多用 lit。

light up *vt.* (常用被动语态形式) make (something)brighter by giving it light 使……发亮: They could see the airport *lit up* far below them. 他们可以看到远在他们下方的灯火闪烁的机场。The house was all *lit up* as though a big celebration was going on. 满屋灯火通明,就好像隆重的庆典正在进行。When the Beijing Olympic Games were declared open, splendid fireworks *lighted up* the night sky of Beijing. 当宣布北京奥运会开幕时,斑斓绚丽的焰火照亮了北京的夜空。—*vi.* ❶(of a light)start to shine (灯)开始闪亮: A warning signal lit up on the dashboard. 仪表板上的警示信号灯开始闪亮。❷ become clear 晴朗起来: The sky *lighted up* after the storm. 风暴过后,天空晴朗。❸(常用一般时态)(of your face or eyes)look very happy (使)笑逐颜开: A smile of happiness *lit up* the soldier's face. 那名士兵的脸上露出了幸福的笑容。When I said I'd like to help her eyes *lit up*. 当我表示愿意提供帮助时,她笑逐颜开。

—*vt.* &*vi.* (非正式用语) make (a cigarette, cigar, or pipe) start burning; start smoking a cigarette, cigar, or pipe 点燃(香烟或烟斗),吸烟: Whenever he becomes nervous he *lights up* a cigarette. 每当他神经紧张时,他总是点支烟抽。I had difficulty *lighting* my cigar *up* in the strong wind. 大风中我好不容易才点燃了雪茄烟。Studies show non-smokers are apparently affected by the smoke from their friends, family members and strangers who *light up* in their presence. 研究表明,非吸烟者显然会受到他们吸烟的朋友、家人以及在他们面前吸烟的陌生人的伤害。

NOTE 不要将本短语与 lighten up 混淆,两者意义不同。

lighten up *vt.* &*vi.* ❶(cause to) become lighter or brighter in colour (使)变得更亮:I think some white paint will *lighten* this room *up* a lot. 我认为,涂些白色油漆会使这个房间亮堂很多。❷(of a situation or someone's mood) (cause to) become more relaxed or cheerful (使)缓和,放松,愉悦:What can we do to *lighten* things *up*? 我们做些什么才能使状况缓和些呢? After a glass of wine, he *lightened up* a bit. 一杯酒下肚,他的情

绪好了一点。The conversation *lightened* me *up* a bit. 这次谈话使我愉快了一些。—*vi.* (非正式用语，常用于祈使句中) used for telling someone to be less serious and make an effort to be more relaxed (用以告诉某人)放松，不要紧张：This is only a party. *Lighten up*. 这只是聚会，放松些。*Lighten up*! It's not a matter of life or death. 不要紧张，这又不是生死攸关的事。

like a shot *adv.* ❶ (非正式用语) immediately and very quickly 立即，飞快地：He heard a noise downstairs and was out of bed *like a shot*. 他听到楼下有动静便立即下了床。The hunting dog was after the rabbit *like a shot*. 猎狗飞快地追赶兔子。❷very willingly and eagerly 非常乐意地，急切地：If I had a chance to go to Great Britain I'd take it *like a shot*. 如果我有去英国的机会，我会非常乐于接受的。He accepted the offer *like a shot*. 他迫不及待地接受了这一提议。

line up *v.* ❶(主要用于美国英语中) form a row or arrange (people or things) in a row or stand in a row (使)排队，排列：Before the Spring Festival people *lined up* in long queues in the cold winter waiting for their turns to get the home-bound tickets. 春节前，人们在寒冬中排长队等候购买返乡车票。The general *lined up* his troops. 将军命其部队列队。*Line* the bottles *up* and I'll fill them. 把瓶子都摆好，我把它们都装满。The books are *lined up* on a shelf above the desk. 那些书都排列在办公桌上方的架子上。❷(非正式用语) organize or arrange (an event or activity)组织，安排(某种活动)：We've *lined up* a great competition to celebrate the centenary with some of the best runners in the world taking part. 我们组织了一个有一些世界上最优秀的运动员参加的隆重赛事以庆祝 100 周年纪念日。We have a series of activities *lined up* to keep you entertained. 我们安排了一系列能使你们娱乐的活动。

NOTE 1. 当本短语作"(使)排队"解时，英国英语中的表达形式为 queue up。

2. 当本短语用作及物性动词短语，所带的宾语为代词时，该代词须置于本短语的动词和副词中间。

3. 本短语可转化为复合词 lineup，意为"一排人，(比赛的)阵容；一批东西"。

line with *vt.* ❶(常用被动语态形式) form rows along the sides of (something) 沿……排成行：The streets were *lined with* crowds watching the Olympic torch relay. 沿街路两侧排满了观看奥运火炬传递的人群。❷(用被动语态形式) (usually of skin) have lines caused by (something such as a feeling or age) 因(某种情绪或年龄)布满皱纹：The face of the mother is *lined with* signs of worry. 那位母亲的脸上布满了愁容。His skin was *lined with* age. 由于上了年纪，他的皮肤上满是皱纹。

link to *vt.* 【可分性动词短语】❶(常用一般时态) join (something or someone) to (something or someone) with or as with a chain 把……连接到……：The new bridge will *link* the island *to* the mainland. 那座新桥将把小岛与大陆连接起来。More and more companies began selling products with the aid of the computer *linked to* the Internet. 越来越多的公司开始借助互联网电脑销售产品。The prisoners were *linked to* each other by irons. 囚犯们被铁索链连在了一

L

起。❷(of people, things, or events) relate to (each other) in some way 与……有联系：Police have evidence *linking* Bates *to* a drug-importation operation. 警方拥有贝茨与一次毒品输入活动有关联的证据。A lot of studies have *linked* cigarette smoke *to* increased risk of other cancers, including throat, breast and bowel cancer. 很多研究把吸烟同患上其他癌症，包括喉癌、乳腺癌和肠癌的危险增加联系到了一起。Twenty-one people *linked to* a plot to blow up aircraft flying from Britain to the United States have been under arrest, British police said on Thursday. 英国警方星期四宣布，已逮捕了21名与一起炸毁英国飞往美国航班图谋有关联的嫌犯。

link up *v.* (常与 by 连用) make a connection (between two or more things)连接：The two highways *link up* here. 两条公路在这里相连接。The train *links up* the cities. 火车把这些城市连接起来。Engineers can *link up* distant countries by radio or telephone. 工程师们能用无线电或电话把相距遥远的国家连接起来。*Link up* these rings as fast as possible. 尽快把这些环都串联起来。

NOTE 本短语可转化为复合词 link (-)up，意为"连接，联系，连接物"。

link up with *vt.* make a connection with (something)与……相连接，与……相联系：The space shuttle will *link up with* the space station this afternoon. 航天飞机将于今天下午与宇宙空间站对接。My own work *links up with* the research you are doing. 我自己的工作就和你所从事的研究有联系。

link with *vt.* 【可分性动词短语】❶(常用一般时态)connect(one thing of a group of things) to (another)把……与……连接起来：China plans to build 12 international highways *linked with* the Central Asian region. 中国计划修建12条连接中亚地区的国际公路。❷(常用被动语态形式) connect the idea of (one person or thing) with (someone or something else)把……与……相联系：The police said that the explosion was possibly caused by a suicide bomber *linked with* a terrorist group. 警方说，爆炸可能是由一名与一个恐怖主义组织有关联的自杀性爆炸者制造的。French wine has always been *linked with* riches, romance and nobleness. 人们往往把法国红酒与财富、浪漫和高贵联系在一起。

listen to *vt.* 【不可分性动词短语】❶pay attention to (a sound), or to try to hear (a sound) intentionally 留心听：Come off with me and have some coffee; I'm tired of *listening to* this speech. 跟我走去喝点咖啡，我讨厌听这个讲演。Be quiet! Will you *listen to* me, children? 静一静！孩子们，你们听我讲话，好吗？❷pay attention to (what someone tells you) and do (what he or she suggests)倾听；听信，听从：We must *listen* patiently *to* views which differ from our own. 我们必须耐心地倾听与自己不同的意见。Don't *listen to* him; he doesn't know anything about it. 别听信他的，他根本不了解这事。I've tried to give Jim advice, but he just won't *listen to* me. 我设法给吉姆出主意，可他就是不听。

little by little *adv.* (非正式用语) very gradually; slowly; only a small amount at a time 逐渐地，慢慢地，一点一点地：*Little by little* his eyes adjusted to the light. 他的眼睛逐渐地适应了光。If you study regularly each day, *little by little* your vocabulary of English will increase. 如果你每天有规律地学习,你的英文词汇将逐渐增加。His health seems to be improving *little by little*. 他的健康似乎慢慢地好转了。*Little by little* rust ate the iron bar. 铁条一点点地被锈蚀了。

NOTE 本短语与 bit by bit 的意义和用法相同。

little wonder (that) ⇨ **no wonder (that)**

live a life ⇨ **lead a life**

live in *vt.*【不可分性动词短语】have one's home in (a particular place)居住在:They *live in* a basement flat in South London. 他们住在伦敦南区的一所地下室套房里。Canada is one of the most desirable country to *live in*, according to a survey by the UN. 据一项由联合国进行的调查表明,加拿大是最适于居住的国家之一。

—*vi.* live at the place where you work or study 住在(某人工作或学习的地方): Household servants used to *live in*, and have their own rooms in their master's house. 过去,用人都住在他们干活的地方,在其雇主家中都有自己的房间。Will you *live in* when you go to college or will you get a room in town? 你上大学后是住在学校里还是在市区里找房子住?

NOTE 当本短语作"住在(某人工作或学习的地方)"解时,反义短语是 live out。

live off *vt.*【不可分性动词短语】❶(of someone) depend on (someone or something) for the money or food that you need 依靠……过活: He's 25 and still *living off* his parents. 他 25 岁了,可还在依靠父母过活。They find it hard to live off the money they make. 他们发现仅靠自己挣的钱很难生活。How can you *live off* the land without experience in farming? 你靠土地为生,而又不懂做农活怎么能行? ❷(非正式用语)(of someone or an animal) eat (a particular kind of food)以吃(某种食物)为生: We *lived off* fruit for a week. 我们靠吃水果活了一个星期。Do these animals *live off* raw fish? 这些动物是以吃生鱼为生吗? Giraffes *live off* the leaves of tall trees. 长颈鹿以高大树木的叶子为食。

live on *vi.* (常用一般时态) ❶continue to be alive after a particular point in time or after a particular event 继续活着: As a member of the Red Detachment of Women in Hainan island she *lived on* until 2004, when she died at the age of 95. 作为海南岛红色娘子军连的一员,她一直活到 2004 年,享年 95 岁。The baby *lived on* for a week after its mother died. 那婴儿在其母亲死后又活了一个星期。❷continue to exist, often for a long time; not be forgotten (常指长期地)继续存在: Though he is dead, his memory *lives on*. 虽然他已去世,但人们将永远怀念他。The scientist's name will *live on* from generation to generation. 这位科学家的名字将流芳百世。

—*vt.*【不可分性动词短语】❶(of someone or an animal) keep alive by eating (a particular kind of food)靠吃(某种食物)而活着,以(某种食物)为食: Mary and I have gone off cooking, so we *live* only *on* salads these days. 玛丽和我都不喜欢做饭了,所以这些天来我们只靠吃沙拉活着。These children seem to *live on* nothing but chips and chocolate. 这些孩子似乎仅以炸土豆条和巧克力为食,其他什么都不吃。Cattle *live* mainly *on* grass. 牛主要以草为食。❷depend upon (someone or something such

L

as a particular amount of money) to buy the things that you need to live 依靠……生活：He refuses to find a job, and *lives on* his parents. 他拒绝去找工作，而靠父母生活。They have to *live on* a pension of $500 a month. 他们只得靠每月 500 美元的养老金生活。I don't know what he *lives on*. 我不知道他靠什么生活。

NOTE 当本短语用作及物性动词短语时，与 live off 相同，两者可互换使用。

live out *vi.* live in a place away from one's work or study 住在(某人工作或学习之地以外的地方)：In Addis Ababa, most household servants *live out*, but many houses have rooms for those who choose to live in. 在亚的斯亚贝巴，大多数用人都不住在雇主家里，尽管很多家庭都为那些选择住在雇主家里的用人备有房间。Chinese students in colleges and universities were recently asked not to *live out* for their safety's sake. 最近，为安全起见，中国在校大学生被要求不要在校外居住。

—*vt.* ❶(常用一般时态) live to the end of (a period of time) 活过(某一段时间)："Will the old man *live out* the winter?" "Hardly. I doubt if he can *live out* the month." "这位老人能活过今年冬天吗?" "够呛。我怀疑他能否活过这个月。" ❷fulfill (an ambition or fantasy) 实现(某种理想、抱负或梦想)：I suppose some people create an idea of who they want to be, and then they *live* it *out*. 我以为，有些人是先想象自己是什么人，然后实现这一理想。His success enabled him to *live out* his dreams. 他的成功使他实现了自己的梦想。

live through *vt.*【不可分性动词短语】(常用一般时态) ❶remain alive during (a time) 活过(某一时间)：I don't know whether Grandpa will *live through* the night. 我不知道爷爷是否能活过今天晚上。❷experience; remain alive during and in spite of (an unpleasant event or dangerous period) 经历(困难、危险之后仍旧活着)：The old man had *lived through* two world wars unharmed. 这位老人身经两次世界大战而未受到任何损伤。She had *lived through* the terrible years of the depression. 她曾经历过大萧条时期的可怕岁月。

live up to *vt.*【不可分性动词短语】❶be as good as (what was expected); fulfill (something such as an expectation placed upon) 不辜负(所寄予的期望等)：Did the film you saw last night *live up to* your expectation? 你昨晚看的那部电影如你所望吗? New York Governor apologized to New Yorkers for his scandal, saying "I did not *live up to* what was expected of me." 纽约州州长因其丑闻向纽约州人民致歉说："我辜负了人们对我的期望。" ❷put (your faith, principle, promise, etc.) into practice 实践(信仰、原则、诺言等)：It's difficult to *live up to* the principles of a religion like Christianity. 实践诸如基督教的宗教信条并非易事。We urge the new mayor to *live up to* his election promises. 我们敦促新任市长实践其在选举时做出的各项承诺。

live with *vt.*【不可分性动词短语】❶share a living place with (someone) 与(某人)住在一起：By the way, do you *live with* your parents or have a house of your own? 顺便问一句，你是和父母住在一起还是自己有房? ❷live in the same house and have a sexual relationship with (someone you are not married to) 与……未婚同居：Did Jane *live with* Bob before they were married? 简

在结婚之前就和鲍勃同居了吗？❸exist at the same place with 与……共存：All the countries, big or small, should *live with* each other in peace. 所有国家，无论大小，应和平共存。It is said that dogs and cats cannot *live with* each other in the same house. 据说猫狗不能同室而居。❹（非正式用语，常与 have to, must, can 连用）accept or put up with (something unpleasant that you cannot change) 接受，忍受：Whether you like it or not, we'll have to *live with* the new regulation. 不管我们喜欢与否，我们都得接受这一新的规则。That is not acceptable. I can't *live with* that. Please change it. 那是不可接受的。我无法容忍。请将其改掉。

load with *vt.*【可分性动词短语】❶（常用被动语态形式）make (something) full or heavy with (a weight) 放满，装满，载满：She *loaded* my plate *with* grapes and plums. 她在我的盘子里放满了葡萄和李子。The ancient merchant boat, named Nanhai Number 1, *loaded with* fine porcelain, which sank into the South China Sea 800 years ago, was raised from the sea on Friday. 一艘被命名为"南海一号"的满载精美瓷器的古代商船在星期五被打捞出水。这艘船是在 800 多年前沉没于南中国海的。❷put (something) into a piece of equipment so that it is ready to use; supply (a gun) with (something such as a kind of bullet)（往某种装置里）装（某物）：He *loaded* the camera *with* film. 他往相机里装了胶卷。He stopped to *load* his rifle *with* bullets. 他停下来开始往枪里装子弹。

lock in *vt.*【可分性动词短语】put (something, someone or oneself) inside (a place or container) and lock the door so they cannot get out 把……锁在里面：She *locked* the documents *in* the safe. 她把文件锁进保险箱里。They *locked* him *in* the room until he had calmed down. 他们把他锁在房间里，直到他冷静下来。Help me, somebody — I'm *locked in*! 谁来帮帮我，我被锁在里面啦！She went to her hotel room and *locked* herself *in*. 她进了所住旅馆的客房后便把自己锁在里面。

NOTE 1. 当本短语的宾语是代词时，该代词须置于本短语的动词和副词或介词中间。
2. 本短语的反义短语是 lock out。

lock out *vt.*【可分性动词短语】❶（常与 of 连用）prevent (someone or oneself) from coming into a room or building by locking the door 把……锁在外面：She *locked* her husband *out* of the house after an argument. 争吵之后，她把丈夫锁在了房外。I've *locked* myself *out* again; could I use your phone? 我又把自己锁在了外面，我能用一下您的电话吗？❷(of a factory or company) prevent (its workers or employees) from entering to work（工厂或公司）阻止（其工人或雇员）进入工作：Although the workers agreed to go on working while their pay claim was being considered, the employers *locked* them *out* in an attempt to force them to give up their demand. 虽然工人们同意在他们的加薪要求被考虑期间继续工作，但厂方却关闭了工厂，以迫使他们放弃其要求。The company *locked out* the workers, and then the rest of the workers went on strike. 公司不让这些雇员进入公司工作，于是其他雇员便举行了罢工。

NOTE 1. 当本短语的宾语是代词时，该代词须置于本短语的动词和副词中间。
2. 本短语可转化为复合词 lockout，意为"封闭（工厂或公司）"。

lock up *vt.* &*vi.* lock (all the doors and

windows of a building or a car) so that no one can get in 把(房屋和汽车的全部门窗)锁好：I *locked up* and went to bed. 我把门窗锁好后便上床睡觉了。The last person to leave *locks up* the shop. 最后走的人把商店的门窗都锁好。Leave your car here and *lock* it *up*. 把你的车放在这里，把门窗都锁好。

—*vt.*【可分性动词短语】❶ put (something) in a safe place and fasten the lock 把(某物)锁起来：*Lock* the money *up* in the drawer. 把钱锁在抽屉里。The documents were *locked up* in a safe. 文件锁在保险箱里。❷(非正式用语) put (someone) in prison or a special hospital for mad people 把(某人)监禁(在监狱或精神病院中)：She kept asking me not to *lock up* her husband. 她不断地要求我不要把她丈夫关进监狱。They *locked* him *up* for burglary. 他们因他偷窃而把他关了起来。She's mad and ought to be *locked up*. 她疯了，应该把她关进精神病院里去。❸(常用被动语态形式) put (one's money) where it cannot be easily moved or changed into cash 把(资本)固定：They had most of the money *locked up* in the building and expansion program. 他们把大部分钱都投放在了基建和扩展项目上了。

NOTE 1. 当本短语用作及物性动词短语，所带的宾语为代词时，该代词须置于本短语的动词和副词中间。

2. 本短语可转化为复合词 lock-up，意为“拘留所；(短期)不能获益的资金”。

log in/on *vi.* (常与 to 连用) enter a computer system, for example by typing your username and password (通过输入用户名和密码)登录进入(计算机系统)：In order to *log in* to the system you have to type in a special password. 为了登录进入该系统，必须键入一个特殊的密码。I would like to *log in* to check my email , but I can't remember my password. 我想登陆进去查一下我的邮件，可我想不起自己的密码了。Customers have to pay to *log on* and chat with other users. 用机者必须付费入网与其他用户聊天。Logon failure: user not allowed to *log on* to this computer. 登录失败：不允许用户登录进入本系统。

—*vt.*【可分性动词短语】allow (someone) to enter a computer system 允许(某人)进入(某一计算机系统)：The user gives his password and the machine *logs* him *in*. 用户给出了密码，便允许使用该机了。The system is unable to *log* you *on*. 你无法进入本系统。

NOTE 1. 本短语还可以用另外一种形式 log onto 来表达。例如：

> Users may *log onto* the anonymous account using any password.
> 用户可以使用任意密码通过匿名账户登录。

2. 当本短语用作及物性动词短语，所带的宾语为代词时，该代词须置于本短语的动词和副词中间。

3. 本短语可转化为复合词 login 或 logon，意为“登陆，进入(计算机系统)”。

log off/out *vi.* finish using or exit a computer system 退出(计算机系统)：Before you *log off*, close any programs and documents you have open, ensuring that you save any changes you make. 在退出系统前，要关掉你打开的所有程序和文件，并保证把你所做的任何修改都保存起来。There was a problem and everyone had to *log out* of the system. 因为出了问题，请大家退出系统。You have been successfully *logged out*. 你已经成功地退出了系统。

—*vt.*【可分性动词短语】cause (someone)

to finish using a computer system 使(某人)退出(某一计算机系统): The system will automatically *log* you *off* after 30 minutes. 30 分钟后,本系统将自动使你退出。*Log off* the system and then shut down. 退出系统后再关机。

NOTE 1. log out 常与 of 连用。

2. 本短语可转化为复合词 logoff 或 logout,意为"注销,退出(计算机系统)"。

log onto ⇨ **log in/on**

long for/after *vt.* 【不可分性动词短语】wish or want very much for (something or someone)渴望,极想得到: We have been *longing for* seeing the movie stars, and now the chance has come. 我们一直渴望见到这些电影明星。现在,机会来了。I was tired and was *longing for* her to leave. 我很疲倦,所以极希望她离去。It was freezing outside, and Maria *longed for* a hot drink. 外面冷极了,玛利亚极想喝一杯热饮料。Is this the house *for* which you *longed* so much? 这就是那所你曾极想得到的房子吗?

NOTE 本短语的同义短语是 yearn for。两者之间的区别见 yearn for。

Long time no see. *s.* (非正式用语)used to say hello to someone who you have not seen for a long period of time 长时间不见了,久违了: Hello, Bob. *Long time no see.* How have you been? 你好,鲍勃。很久不见了。你近来可好?

NOTE 1. 本短语是一句 Chinglish (Chinese English,中国式英语),在语法上来说应该是错误的。但是,这一中国式的英语短语,在英美英语口语中早已流行并被广为使用。

2. 与本短语形式相同的一个短语是 Long time no hear. (= I haven't heard from you for a long time.)。例如:

Glad to see you, James! Long time no hear! How have you been doing?
见到你真高兴,詹姆斯!很久没有你的消息了!你近来好吗?

look about/around [1] *v.* look in different directions (about a place)四处观看,环视(某处): *Looking about*, I saw no one on the street. 我四处看了看,大街上看不到一个人。I *looked around* the station but couldn't see my wife anywhere. 我环视火车站,到处看也不见我的妻子。

look about/around [2] *vt.* walk around (a room, building, or place) and see what is there 环游,参观: I *looked around* the city with my friends last night. 昨晚我和朋友们环游了该市。Do you want to *look around* our school? 你想参观一下我们的学校吗?

look about/around/round for *vt.* 【不可分性动词短语】(无被动语态形式,常用进行时态) search in order to find (someone or something that you want or need)寻找(所需要的人或物): As soon as we got there, we began to *look about for* a place to pitch our tent. 我们一到那儿就开始找能支帐篷的地方。We've started *looking around for* a house in London. 我们开始在伦敦寻找住房。He's been *looking round for* a new partner in the business. 他一直在寻找一位新的生意伙伴。

look after *vt.* 【不可分性动词短语】❶take care of (someone, oneself or something) and make certain that they have everything they need 照顾,照料: It's hard work *looking after* three children all day. 整天照顾三个孩子是很繁重的工作。I can *look after* myself. 我能照顾我自己。You could see that the car had been well *looked after*. 你可以看出这台车保养得不错。❷take care of (something that belongs to someone else) and make certain it is not damaged or stolen 照看，看管：Who is *looking after* the luggage? 谁在照看行李？A fisherman was *looking after* the ship for him. 当时是一个渔夫在替他照看着那只船。❸be in charge of (something)负责：They've an organization that *looks after* the interests of artists. 他们有一个负责保护艺术家利益的组织。Who's *looking after* the department while you're away? 你不在时，由谁负责这个部门？

NOTE 本短语与 take care of 和 care for 都表示照顾某人，尤其是老人、病人和孩子，也都有"悉心照料某物"之意。三者之中，care for 的用法最正式。

look ahead *vi.* ❶try to see a long way in front of one 向前看：*Look ahead*. What can you see on the top of the mountain? 向前看。你看见山顶上有什么东西？If you *look ahead* in the distance, you can see the lights of the village. 如果你向前远望，就可以看到那个村庄的灯火。❷think about what is likely to happen, or plan what you are going to do in the future(常与 to 连用)考虑到将来，展望未来：*Looking ahead*, I think the company needs to develop some new services. 考虑到将来，我认为公司需要开发一些新的服务项目。Have you *looked ahead* to what you'll be doing in five years' time? 你是否考虑过五年后你要做些什么？*Looking ahead* to the coming year, the global economic growth will accelerate at a higher rate than this year. 展望明年，全球经济的增长速度将比今年的更快。

look alike *vi.* (用一般时态)(of two or more things or people) have the same or nearly the same appearance 看上去相像：All the houses in this street *look alike*; it's very dull. 这条街上所有的房子看上去都一样，太单调乏味了。The two sisters don't really *look alike*. 这对姐妹看上去并不相像。

NOTE 1. 本短语与 look like 都有"看上去相像"之意，但两者在用法上不同：本短语是不及物性动词短语，而 look like 是及物性动词短语。

2. 本短语可转化为复合词 look (-) alike，意为"看上去像的人(或物)"。

look at *vt.*【不可分性动词短语】❶direct your eyes towards (someone, yourself or something) so that you can see them; watch 看，注视，观看：He turned and *looked at* her. 他转过头来看着她。Susannah *looked at* herself in the mirror. 苏珊娜照了照镜子。They *looked at* the children skating. 他们观看孩子们滑冰。The children spend too much time *looking at* television. 孩子们看电视花的时间太多了。Please don't wear that terrible skirt; you'll get *looked at*. 请你不要穿那条难看的裙子。你会招人观瞧的。❷read (something) quickly 迅速阅读，浏览：Would you like me to *look at* your essay before you hand it in? 你愿意在把作文交上去之前让我帮你看一下吗？❸ regard; judge by the appearance of someone or something 看待，对待；根据外表来判断(某人或某物)：John thinks that success is being rich, but I don't *look at* it like that. 约翰认为致富就是成功，但我却不那样看。Whether he's a good boy or a bad one depends on how you *look at* his action. 他是个好孩子还是坏孩子，这取决于你如何看待他的行为。To *look at* him you'd never think he was near fifty. 从他的外貌上看，你根本就不会想到他已是个快50岁的人了。❹(常用于否定句中)think about (a situation or subject) carefully, especially in order to make a decision 仔细考虑: I wouldn't *look at* such a small offer! 那么少的报酬我是不会考虑的! They refused to *look at* my proposal. 他们拒不考虑我的建议。❺examine (something) and decide what to do 检查,查看,研究:I'd like a skin specialist to *look at* that rash of yours. 我要请一位皮肤科专家检查一下你的疹子。Will you please *look at* the battery of his car? 请你检查一下他车子的电池,好吗? We're *looking at* the message and we hope they will return to the talk. 我们正在研究这一信息。我们希望他们会回到会谈中来。❻(仅用于口语中,一般用于祈使句中)(used for giving an example that proves what you are saying is true)notice 你看……,瞧瞧……: *Look at* Helen. She's much happier now because she's changed jobs. 瞧瞧海伦。因为换了新工作,她有多高兴。

look back *vi.* ❶direct one's eyes behind one 回头看: She *looked back* and waved her hand to us. 她回过头来,朝我们挥了挥手。Don't *look back* or I'll fire! 不准回头看,否则我就开枪。❷(常与 on 或 upon 连用) think about a time or event in the past; remember 回想,回顾,回忆: *Looking back* now, it's easy to see where they went wrong. 现在回想起来,就很容易明白他们错在何处了。We *look back* on the past with pride and look to the future with full confidence. 回顾过去,我们充满自豪;展望未来,我们信心满怀。I *look back* upon those days as the happiest time of my life. 回忆起那些日子,我把它看作我生活中最幸福的一段时间。

look down on/upon *vt.* 【不可分性动词短语】(常用一般时态) think that you are better or more important than (someone else), or think that something is not good enough for you 看不起,蔑视: They think the long tradition of *looking down on* workers is still affecting career choices. 他们认为:看不起工人的长期传统观念依然在影响着职业的选择。At first, Mary's parents *looked down up on* her marrying Jim. 起初,玛丽的父母很看不上她和吉姆的婚姻。

NOTE 1. 本短语中的 upon 用法比 on 正式,但不及 on 常用。

2. 本短语的反义短语是 look up to。

look for *vt.* 【不可分性动词短语】(一般不用被动语态形式) ❶try to find or search for (someone or something) 寻找: I'm *looking for* Jim. Have you seen him? 我在找吉姆。你看见他了吗? The Mars probe, Phoenix, was sent to Mars to *look for* organic material and other signs of life on the planet, 63 million miles from Earth. "凤凰"号火星探测器被送上火星去寻找远离地球 6 300 万英里的行星上的有机物质和其他生命迹象。❷(常用进行时态)hope to get (something that you want or need)希望得到: He was *looking for* work as a builder. 他希望得到一份建筑工的工作。He is always *looking for* praise. 他总是希望受到表扬。❸(非正式用语)behave in a way that is likely to cause (something bad) 招来,惹来: If you say the opposite of everything that others say, you are *looking for* a quarrel. 如果你尽跟别人唱反调,那你是在招引争吵。Tom often goes into fights because he's always *looking for* trouble. 汤姆常常跟人打架,因为他是个好惹是生非的人。

NOTE 本短语与 search for 均表示"寻找"之意,两者常可互换使用,但 search for 侧重

指"寻找所失之人或物",例如:

> He's *searching for* the missing child.
> 他在搜寻走失的孩子。

look forward to *vt.*【不可分性动词短语】expect, anticipate or wait for (something pleasant to happen)期待,盼望: We *look forward to* serving you. 我们期待着为您服务。Iraqi President Ghazi al-Yawar said at the power handover ceremony, "the day was a happy day that all Iraqis have been *looking forward to*." 伊拉克总统亚瓦尔在政权交接仪式上说:"这一天是全体伊拉克人一直盼望着的大喜日子。"

NOTE 1. 本短语中的 to 是介词,而不是动词不定式符号。因此,后面不能接原形动词。例如,我们不能说: * We are looking forward to hear from you soon.

2. 修饰本短语的状语通常置于 forward 和 to 之间。例如:

> We have been *looking forward* more and more eagerly *to* seeing you.
> 我们越来越急于见到您。

look in *v.* ❶ direct one's eyes into (something such as a building); look at the inside of (something)朝(……)里看: When I draw back the curtains, there outside the window stood a crowd of people *looking in*. 当我拉开窗帘时,一群人正站在窗外那儿朝里看。She lagged behind the rest of the children because she kept stopping to *look in* shop windows. 她不断地停下来往商店橱窗里看,所以就落在了其他孩子的后面。❷(非正式用语,常用一般时态,常与 on 连用) make a short visit to (someone), especially in his or her house, on your way to another place, when he or she is ill or needs help 顺便看望(某人): "I'm glad to see you so much better; I'll *look in* again," the doctor said to me. "看到你好多了,我很高兴。我会再来看你的。"医生向我说道。Paul decided to *look in* on his uncle on his way downtown. 保罗决定在去市区的途中顺便看望他的叔叔。

NOTE 本短语可转化为复合词 look-in,意为"观察;(顺便)拜访"。

look into *vt.*【不可分性动词短语】❶direct one's eyes inside; try to see in (something) 朝……里看: We cannot see the minerals by *looking into* the water. 用眼睛往水里看是看不见这些矿物质的。I got such a shock when I *looked into* the mirror and saw the color of my hair. 当我照镜子看到自己头发的颜色时,我大惊失色。I *looked into* his eyes and found them stony. 我看着他的眼睛,发觉他的眼光冷酷无情。❷(of a person or organization) try to find out and examine the facts about (something such as a problem or crime); investigate 调查: I wrote a letter of complaint, and the airline company has promised to *look into* the matter. 我写了一封投诉信,航空公司已答应对此事进行调查。They insisted on *looking into* the cause of the accident. 他们坚持调查事故发生的原因。❸(常用一般时态)dip into (a book, etc.)浏览(书等): I have *looked into* the book you mentioned the day before yesterday. 你前天提到的那本书我已翻过了。I've just *looked into* the scientific article. 我刚刚浏览了那篇科技文章。

look like *vt.*【不可分性动词短语】(一般不用进行时态) ❶have a similar appearance to (someone or something else); resemble (someone or something)看上去像……,与……相像: The girl *looks* exactly *like* her twin sister. 这个女孩长得和她的孪生妹妹一模一样。"What does your brother *look like*?" "He's tall and thin, with brown hair." "你弟弟长得什么样?""他细高挑个头,一头棕色的头发。" The shape of that mountain *looks like* a dragon. 那座山的形状看上去像一条龙。❷(常用 it 为主语,无被动语态形式) give the appearance that suggests (that something is true or will happen)好像要,看起来要:"The sky *looks like* rain." "No, it *looks like* snow." "天好像要下雨。""不,好像要下雪。" Our football team never *looked like* winning the game. 我们的足球队好像永远也不会赢得比赛。"It *looks like* these women are relatively healthy as a result of combining work and family life," said the expert. "看起来,这些妇女身体相对健康是她们的工作与家庭生活相结合的结果。"这位专家说。

NOTE 当本短语作"好像要,看起来要"解时,尤其在美国英语口语中,常常用来代替 look as if/though。但是,在英国英语的正式文体中,这种用法被认为是不正确的。

look on *vi.* watch an activity or event without taking part in it 旁观,观望:His parents *looked on* with a smile as he collected his prize. 在他领奖时,他的父母面带微笑在旁边看着。About 100 local people *looked on* in silence as the two coffins were taken into the church. 当那两口棺材抬进教堂时,大约有 100 个当地人在默默地旁观。

—*vt.*【不可分性动词短语】(常用一般时态,常与 as, with 连用) think of (someone or something) in a particular way; regard; consider 看待,视作,认为:We're not related but I *look on* him as a brother. 我们非亲非故,但我把他视为我的兄弟。I *look on* it as a challenge. 我将其视为一种挑战。Ten years ago, young people *looked on* such music with contempt. 10 年前,年轻人还都看不上这种音乐。

NOTE 1. 本短语与 sit back, sit by, stand aside 和 stand by 都表示"旁观"之意。它们之间的区别见 sit by。

2. 本短语可转化为名词 onlooker,意为"(袖手)旁观者"。

look out *v.* ❶(常与 of 连用) direct one's eyes outside 向外看:*Look out* and see if the rain has stopped yet. 向外看看,雨是不是已经停了。I *looked out* of my small window into the night. There was a big bright moon hanging in the sky, giving off a magic glow. 我向窗外的夜色望去,只见一轮明月高挂在天空,向大地撒着令人不可思议的清辉。❷(非正式用语,常用于祈使句中)(used for warning someone to be careful, especially because he or she is likely to have an accident) take care; be on the watch; be careful 当心,留神,警惕,注意:If you don't *look out*, you may fall on the ice. 如果你不当心,就会在冰上摔倒。*Look out*! Don't let the fire get near the gasoline! 当心! 别让大火接近汽油! *Look out* when you're crossing the street. 过马路时要当心。*Look out* that you don't catch cold. 你注意别感冒了。❸(英国英语用法) search for and find something 找出(某物):I'll *look out* that book I told you about and send it to you. 我把我给你讲过的那本书找到,然后寄给你。

NOTE 当本短语作"当心,留神,警惕,注意"解时,与 watch out 意义和用法相同,两者可互换使用。

look out for *vt.*【不可分性动词短语】❶try to find (a particular person or thing around you) 寻找,搜寻(某人或某物):The police are *looking out for* the murderer. 警察在搜寻凶手。We were ordered to *look*

L

out for a blue van. 我们奉命查找一辆蓝色的带篷小货车。❷ keep a watch for (something)注意,提防,留神,小心:What are the symptoms to *look out for*? 要注意的症状都是什么? The weather is changeable. We must *look out for* catching colds. 天气变化无常,我们必须注意预防感冒。"*Look out for* the train!" the warning sign at the railway crossing says. 铁道路口的警示牌上写道:"小心火车!" ❸take care of (someone or oneself)照顾(某人或自己):I'm the oldest, and I always *look out for* my younger sisters. 我是最大的孩子,所以我总要好好地照顾我的妹妹们。I felt that I had to *look out for* myself, because I didn't see that anyone else was going to. 我感到我得很好地照顾自己了,因为没有任何其他人会照顾我。

look over *vt.* 【可分性动词短语】❶examine (someone or something) quite quickly in order to get a general idea of what they are like (尤指迅速)过目,浏览:He *looked over* the leaflets he'd picked up earlier. 他看了看他早些时候拾起来的那些传单。Here is the report. Please *look* it *over* and let me know what you think. 这是报告。请过目并把你的想法告诉我。I had a few minutes before the meeting to *look over* what he'd written. 我在会前的几分钟时间里浏览了一下他写的东西。Mrs Smith spent the evening *looking over* the month's accounts. 史密斯太太花了一个晚上的时间把这个月的账目都看了一遍。❷visit (a place) in order to examine it; inspect 检查,核查(某一地点):The government sends officials to *look over* each factory, to see that it keeps to the safety regulations. 政府派出官员去检查每个工厂,以使其切实遵守安全规则。They came to *look* the house *over* with a view to buying it. 他们过来查看房子,想把它买下来。

NOTE 1. 当本短语的宾语为代词时,该代词须置于本短语的动词和副词中间。

2. 本短语可转化为复合词 look-over,意为"查看,察看"。

look round *v.* ❶(英国英语用法)look in various directions (about a place)四下环顾,向……周围看:Don't *look round*; a police car is following us. 别东张西望的,有辆警车在跟踪我们。I *looked round* the station but couldn't see my friend anywhere. 我向车站四周看去,但到处也看不见我的朋友。❷walk around (a place or a large building), and look at the different parts of it; visit 参观,游览(某处):I don't want to buy anything; I'm just *looking round*. 我不想买什么东西,只是参观一下。Do you have to pay to *look round* the castle? 你们参观这座城堡要付费吗? ❸inspect; examine (something such as a house)检查,查看(房子等):The door was half open and I *looked* carefully *round* it before I decided to enter the house. 房门是半开着的,我仔细地查看了一番才决定进去。

NOTE 1. 当本短语作"四下环顾,向……周围看"解时,同义短语是 look about/around[1]。

2. 当本短语作"参观,游览(某处)"解时,同义短语是 look about/around[2]。

3. 当本短语用作及物性动词短语时,为不可分性动词短语。

look someone in the face *vi.* (非正式用语,常用否定形式,用一般时态) look directly at someone's face when you are talking to him or her, without fear or shame 敢于正视某人:I felt so embarrassed — I just couldn't *look him in the face*. 我感到

如此尴尬，我都不敢正眼看他了。*Look me in the face* and tell me you didn't do it. 正眼看着我，告诉我那不是你干的。Can you *look me in the face* and say that you really love him? 你能当着我的面说你真的爱他吗？

NOTE 本短语的另外一种表达形式是 look someone in the eye(s)，但本短语更为常用。

look someone up and down *vi.* (常用一般时态) look carefully at someone from their head to their feet as if you are trying to make a judgment about him or her 上下打量(某人)：The guard *looked us up and down* and then let us in. 卫兵把我们上上下下地打量了一番后才让我们进去。She *looked me up and down*, but I couldn't tell whether she approved of my appearance or not. 她上上下下地打量了我一番，但我不知道她有没有相中我的长相。

look through *vt.* ❶ examine or study carefully (especially something written or printed) to check that there are no mistakes in it 仔细审查(尤指文稿或印刷品)：I always *looked through* my work carefully before I handed it in. 我总是认真地把我的作业检查好后再交上去。❷ read (something written or printed) quickly, especially to find the information you need 浏览(尤指文稿或印刷品)：He *looked through* the catalogue, but didn't find the articles he wanted. 他把目录从头到尾地看了一遍，但没找到他所需要的文章。❸(常用一般时态) not recognize or pretend not to recognize (someone you know); ignore 故意不理睬，视而不见：I saw Mary this morning, but she *looked straight* through me. 我今早见到了玛丽，可她干脆没理睬我。

look to¹ *vt.* ❶(用一般时态，无被动语态形式) face (something) 面朝，面向：The front of the house *looks to* the sea. 这所房子的正面朝向大海。He said that he respected the views of those who plan to protest, but asked them to *look to* the future rather than the past. 他说，他尊重那些计划搞抗议活动的人们的意见，但要求他们不要纠缠旧账而要面向未来。❷(正式用语，常用一般时态) pay attention to, especially in order to improve 注意：Try to *look to* your own shortcomings. 尽量注意你自己的缺点。*Look to* it so that this doesn't happen again. 注意今后不要再发生类似事件。❸ depend on (someone) (to do something) 依靠，依赖：The nation *looks to* its army as its chief means of defense. 国家依靠其军队作为国防的主要工具。As young children, we *looked to* our parents for guidance. 因为我们还小，我们还要依靠父母的引导。❹ hope or expect to get (help, advice, etc.) from someone 指望，期待(某人的帮助或主意等)：The city government is *looking to* drivers for traffic solution. 市政府欲期待驾驶员来帮助解决交通问题。The terrorist group leader told reporters that his group would *look to* women to step up suicide attacks. 该恐怖组织的领导人告诉记者说，他的组织将指望妇女加紧制造自杀袭击事件。

look to² *v.* (后接用动词不定式短语) ❶ try to find ways of doing something 设法做某事：The government is *looking to* reduce the price of oil. 政府在设法减低油价。❷ expect or plan to do something 希望；计划：I'm *looking to* sell my car in

L

July. 我希望 7 月份能把我的车卖掉。North Carolina lawmakers *look to* legalize online scalping. 北卡罗来纳州的立法者计划把网上高价倒卖高价票合法化。

look up *v.* ❶direct one's eyes upwards 向上看："When I *looked up*, I saw the helicopter in flames, and I watched it go down," the farmer said. "当我往上看时，我看到那架直升机着了火，并且我眼看着它掉了下来。"这位农民说道。❷try to find (a particular word, number or a specific piece of information) by consulting a reference book or on a list, or by using a computer (在参考书、名单或电脑中)查找，查阅：He consulted his dictionary to *look up* the meaning of the word "abacus". 他查阅词典找"abacus"这个单词的意思。If you do not know his number, *look* it *up* in the telephone directory. 如果你不知道他的电话号码，查一下电话号码簿。Will you *look up* the train in the timetable? 你能否在列车时刻表上查一下这趟车？❸(非正式用语，常用一般时态，不用被动语态形式) go and see (someone you know and have not seen for a long time) when you are visiting the place where he or she lives (到某人的居住地)拜访：*Look* me *up* next time you come to Sydney. 下次你再来悉尼时可要来看我。He *looked up* some of his old friends while in London. 他在伦敦期间拜访了几位老朋友。❹(非正式用语，常用进行时态) (of a situation) become or get better; improve (情势) 好转，有起色："How is business?" "Oh, things are *looking up*. I just got a lot of new orders." "生意好吗？""喔，情况正在好转，我刚收到一大批订单。" The weather is *looking up*. 天气在好转。Oil shares are *looking up* these days. 石油股票近些天来呈现起色。

NOTE 1. 当本短语用作及物性动词短语，所带的宾语是代词时，该代词须置于本短语的动词和副词中间。

2. 当本短语表示"查找，查阅"之意时，对象一般是"单词""电话号码"或"时刻表"。若查阅的对象是"工具书"，要用 refer to。见 refer to。

3. 本短语可转化为复合词 look-up，意为"查找，检查"。

look up to *vt.* 【不可分性动词短语】(常用一般时态) admire and respect (someone) 羡慕，崇拜，尊敬(某人)：He is a great football star and is *looked up to* by all his fans. 他是一个了不起的足球明星，因此他受到他所有球迷的崇拜。Professor James is a wonderful teacher, and we always *look up to* him. 詹姆斯教授是个非常好的教师。我们一直都很尊敬他。His students *look up to* him as a walking dictionary. 他的学生都尊称他为"活字典"。

NOTE 本短语的反义短语是 look down on/upon。

lose touch with *vt.* no longer be able to contact or communicate with (someone) 与(某人)失去联系：The plane's radio equipment failed and the crew *lost touch with* air traffic controllers at the base. 飞机的无线电系统出现故障，机组便与基地的飞行控制人员失去了联系。You can find old friends you've *lost touch with*, get back in touch, and organise reunions. 你可以找到已失去联系的老朋友，重新建立联系，并组织重聚活动。

lose ground ⇨ **gain ground**

lose heart *vi.* lose one's courage or

confidence and try less hard because something is not progressing as you would like 丧失勇气，失去信心，气馁：I think he *lost heart* after losing the first game. 我想，他输掉首场比赛后就丧失信心了。She failed again to pass the TOEFL test, but she never *lost heart*. 她又没通过托福考试，但她并没有泄气。

NOTE 1. 本短语的反义短语是 take heart。

2. 不要将本短语与 lose one's heart to 混淆。lose one's heart to 为及物性动词短语，意为"爱上（某人），倾心于（某事物）"。

lose one's head *vi.* （非正式用语）fail to stay calm and sensible, for example in a crisis or sudden difficulty 惊慌失措，失去理智：When the fire broke out in the cinema, the people *lost their heads* and ran in all directions. 当电影院里突然起火时，人们都惊慌失措，四处乱窜。It is a difficult situation — try not to *lose your head*. 这是一个困难的局面，要努力保持理智。

NOTE 1. 本短语的反义短语是 keep one's head。

2. 不要将本短语与 out of one's head 混淆，两者的意义不同。out of one's head 意为"（尤指因滥用毒品而致的）思维不正常"。

lose one's heart to *vt.* （正式用语）start to love (someone) or like (something) very much 爱上（某人），倾心于（某事物）：She *lost her heart to* the boy who had always helped her in her studies. 她爱上了那个总是帮助她学习的男生。I *lost my heart to* airplanes when I was a child, and I've wanted to be a pilot ever since. 我在孩童时就喜欢上了飞机。从那时起，我就一直想当一名飞行员。My son who studied laws in college has *lost his heart to* writing. 我的儿子在大学里学的是法律，现已倾心于写作了。

lose one's temper *vi.* suddenly become very angry and fly into rage, especially after you have been trying not to 发脾气，勃然大怒：The nurses in the kindergarten never *lose their temper* even if the children are very naughty. 即使孩子们非常淘气，幼儿园的阿姨们也从不发脾气。It's understandable, but not helpful, to *lose your temper* with small children. 和小孩子们发脾气可以理解，但无济于事。

NOTE 本短语的同义短语是 blow up, blow one's top, flare up 和 see red；反义短语是 keep one's temper。

lose one's tongue *vi.* （非正式用语）be so embarrassed or surprised that you can't talk（由于窘迫或惊奇而）说不出话来，开不了口：Mary is very shy and she always *loses her tongue* before strangers. 玛丽很腼腆，在生人面前总是窘迫得说不出话来。Tom was so surprised by his teacher's question that he *lost his tongue* and could not answer. 老师的提问使汤姆措手不及，他支支吾吾，无以作答。

NOTE 不要将本短语与 loosen one's tongue 混淆。loosen one's tongue 意为"信口开河"。例如：

> A couple of glasses of champagne had *loosened my tongue* and I said things that I shouldn't have.
> 几杯香槟酒下肚，我便信口开河，说了些本不该说的话。

lose one's way *vi.* （不用进行时态）❶not know where you are or how to get to where you want to go 迷路：He *lost his way*, which delayed him considerably. 他

迷了路，这使他耽搁了很久。I have *lost my way*. Can you help me? 我迷路了。您能帮忙指路吗？We *lost our way* and had to ask a policeman. 我们迷了路，不得不向一名警察打听。❷no longer know what your aim or purpose is or what to do next 迷惘：The company has *lost its way* in recent years. 该公司近几年前途迷茫。

lose sight of *vt.*【不可分性动词短语】（不用进行时态）❶be no longer to see (someone or something) 看不见：The policeman *lost sight of* the thieves when they ran into a shopping centre. 当小偷跑进一家购物中心时，警察便找不见他们了。We soon *lost sight of* the boat in the dense fog. 浓雾之中，那条船很快就看不见了。The escaped prisoner was *lost sight of* in the crowd. 那名逃犯在人群中不见了踪影。❷forget (an important fact or what your main aim is), because you are thinking too much about other things 忘掉(某一重要事实或主要目的等)：I think he has *lost sight of* the regulation of the company. 我想他已经忘记了公司的那条规定。Under no circumstance should we *lose sight of* our purpose in life. 在任何情况，我们都不能忘掉我们的人生目标。

NOTE 当本短语作“看不见”解时，反义短语是 catch sight of。

lose trace of *vt.*【不可分性动词短语】（不用进行时态）no longer know (where someone or something is)失去……的踪迹(或下落)：The police *lost trace of* the murderer in the woods. 警察在树林中失去了凶手的踪迹。All *trace of* the missing child has been *lost*. 那名失踪儿童已下落不明。Three days past, we *lost trace of* the tiger in the forest. 三天过去了，我们在森林中还没有找到老虎的踪迹。

NOTE 不要将本短语与 lose track of 混淆，两者意义不同。

lose track of *vt.*【不可分性动词短语】（不用进行时态）❶forget(something) or forget(where something is)忘记，记不得：I *lose* all *track of* time when I listen to this music. 我一听到这段音乐就会全然忘记时间。He soon *lost track of* how much money he had spent. 他很快就忘记了自己花了多少钱。I've *lost track of* how many times he called last week. 我已记不得他上星期打了多少次电话。Mother has *lost track of* her glasses again. 妈妈又忘记眼镜在什么地方了。❷lose contact with (someone)失去和(某人)的联系：Bob *lost track of* his friends at camp after the summer was over. 鲍勃在夏季过后就失去了和她那些营友的联系。The plane was *lost track of* about two hours out from London. 那架飞机在飞离伦敦约两小时后便失去了联系。

NOTE 本短语的反义短语是 keep track of。

lose weight *vi.* (the amount that your body weighs) become less 体重减轻，变瘦：Have you *lost weight*? 你的体重减轻了吗？If you want to *lose weight*, here are some do's and don'ts. 如果你想要减轻体重，这是一些注意事项。She's *lost* a bit of *weight* since I saw her last. 自上次我见到她以来，她瘦了点儿。

NOTE 本短语的反义短语是 gain weight 和 put on weight。

loosen one's tongue ⇨ **lose one's tongue**

lots (and lots) of *adj.*（非正式用语）a

large number, amount, or quantity of; many; much 大量的,很多的: We have *lots of* work to do in the coming holiday. 在即将到来的假期里,我们有大量的工作要做。There are *lots of* students, not necessarily organized by their schools, visiting the Chairman Mao's Memorial Hall in Beijing to show their respect to the great leader. 许许多多的学生,不一定是由学校组织,来到北京毛主席纪念堂表达他们对伟大领袖的敬爱。There were *lots and lots of* posters to choose from. 有许许多多的招贴画供你挑选。

NOTE **1.** 本短语既可修饰可数名词,也可修饰不可数名词。当修饰可数名词的复数时,动词形式就用复数形式;而当修饰不可数名词时,动词形式就用单数形式。试比较:

> There are *lots of* people in the park on Sunday.
> 星期天,公园里有很多人。
> There is still *lots of* snow in the garden.
> 花园里仍然有许多雪。
> *Lots of* work is to be done this week.
> 本星期将有许多工作要做。

2. lots and lots of 是 lots of 的强调形式,通常用于肯定句中;有时还会重复使用多次:There you can make *lots and lots and lots and lots of* money this way.

3. 本短语与 a lot of 意义相同,但在用法上有区别见 a lot of。

loyal to *adj.* faithful to (someone or something such as a country, party, or principle)忠实于:The Chinese President urged the Chinese police to "enforce law for the people and be *loyal to* the principle of serving the people heart and soul". 中国国家主席敦促中国警察"为民执法,忠实于全心全意为人民服务的原则"。Dozens of militants *loyal to* al Qaeda attacked a village north of Baghdad around dawn Sunday, killing more than a dozen people. 几十名忠实于基地组织的武装分子在星期日黎明时分袭击了巴格达北部的一个村庄,致十几人丧生。The Chinese football fans remained *loyal to* the national team even though they lost almost every major game. 中国的足球迷们仍然忠实地支持国家队,尽管他们在大赛中几乎屡战屡败。

NOTE 本短语的同义短语是 faithful to。

M m

mad about/at/on/with *adj.* (非正式用语,在句中一般作表语) ❶(常用于动词 be, get, make 后)angry with 为……发火,生……的气: What is he *mad about*? 他因何发火? He was *mad about/at* missing the bus. 他因没赶上公共汽车而恼火。The director got *mad at* me because I forgot my lines. 导演因我忘记了台词而很生我的气。If she gets *mad with* me she will not speak to me for days. 如果她和我生气,就会好几天不和我说话。❷ very much in love with (someone); very enthusiastic about (something)迷恋于,热衷于: She's *mad about* my brother, but is too shy to tell him. 她在迷恋着我的弟弟,却羞于告诉他。I was *mad about* pets and ignored everything else until I was about twelve. 我迷恋宠物,无视其他,一直到 12 岁左右。He's not as *mad about* sports as I am. 他没有我那么热衷于体育运动。My brother is *mad on* swimming. 我弟弟热衷于游泳。

NOTE 当作"为……发火,生……的气"解时,mad about/at 主要用于美国英语中,mad with 主要用于英国英语中。

maintain contact with ⇨ **keep contact with**

major in *vt.* 【不可分性动词短语】(主要用于美国英语中,一般不用被动语态形式) study (something) as your main subject at college or university (在高校中)主修,专修: Australia's Prime Minister Kevin Rudd, who *majored in* Chinese language and history at Australian National University, was the first Mandarin speaker among Western leaders. 曾在澳大利亚国立大学主修中国语言和历史的澳大利亚总理陆克文是第一位讲汉语的西方领导人。He studied at Claremont College in California *majoring in* finance. 他在加利福尼亚州克莱尔蒙特学院专修金融学。

make a difference *vi.* have an important effect on something, especially a good effect 对……有重要(尤指良好的)影响: The UN Secretary-General said that the deployment of a peacekeeping force in Sudan's Darfur region will *make a* great *difference*. 联合国秘书长表示,在苏丹的达尔富尔地区部署维和部队十分重要。This scheme will certainly *make a difference* to the way I do my job. 这一方案对我工作的方式将产生重要影响。A big/great *difference* was *made* to our trading position. 这对我们的贸易地位有很大影响。

NOTE 1. 本短语中的不定冠词 a 可根据意义表达的需要被其他修饰词,如 big, great, a great deal of, not much 等替换,但名词 difference 的单数形式不变。例如:It *makes* a great deal of bit *difference* to me which side may win.

2. 当本短语用在以疑问代词为首的疑问句中,不定冠词 a 则不再使用。例如:

> Many would ask, "What *difference* does it *make* to the dead, the orphans and the homeless?"
> 很多人会问:"这对死者、孤儿和无家可归者有什么重要影响呢?"

3. 本短语的反义短语是 make no difference。

make a face *vi.* (常与 at 连用)put a silly or rude expression on your face, or an expression that shows you dislike someone or something 做鬼脸,做出不满(或厌恶)的表情:"I hate pizza!" He said, *making a face*. "我不喜欢比萨饼!"他做出一副厌恶的表情。At the mere mention of his name she *made a face*, which I took for as sign of disapproval. 一提到他的名字,她就做了个怪相;我认为,这是她对他厌恶的表示。

NOTE **1.** 本短语可根据意义表达的需要变为复数形式使用。例如:

> The children sat at the window *making faces* at the passers-by。
> 孩子们坐在窗台上,朝过路的人做着鬼脸。

2. 本短语的动词 make 可被 pull 替换,两者的意义和用法相同。

make a fire *vi.* put a small pile of wood, coal, etc. ready and then light them in order to produce heat 生火:They *made a fire* to cook their evening meal. 他们生起火来做晚饭。We went off to collect wood to *make a fire*. 我们都出去拾木柴好生火。

make a fool (out)of *vt.*【不可分性动词短语】deliberately make (someone or oneself) seem stupid, for example by tricking them; deceive (someone)捉弄,愚弄,欺骗:What a fool you *made out of* him, letting everyone read his letter! 你真能捉弄他,把他的信让每个人都看了。I felt that Sally had *made a* complete *fool* of me. 我感到萨利完全欺骗了我。He *made a fool of* himself by turning up drunk to a TV chat show. 他醉醺醺地出现在电视的访谈节目中,使自己出了丑。

NOTE 本短语可根据意义表达的需要变为复数形式使用。例如:

> We were all *made fools of* by the door-to-door salesman.
> 我们都被那个挨门挨户搞推销的人欺骗了。

make a fortune *vi.* gain a very large amount of money; become rich 发财,致富:He dreamed of *making a fortune*. 他连做梦都想发财。He had *made a* great *fortune* from mining. 他通过采矿发了大财。The answer is yes; you're about to *make a fortune* off us. 答案是肯定的。你要在我们身上赚一笔。

NOTE 本短语的另外一种表达形式是 make one's fortune。例如:

> She *made her fortune* in lottery.
> 她中彩票发了财。

make a fuss *vi.* ❶(非正式用语,常与 about 连用)become angry or excited (about something)and complain 发牢骚,抱怨:I have to *make a fuss* about the service in this restaurant. 我不得不对这家餐馆的服务进行投诉。❷(常与 about, over 连用)express a lot of unnecessary worry or excitement (about someone, something, or doing something)无事自扰,小题大做,大惊小怪:Don't *make a fuss* about nothing. 你不要无事

自扰。She's always *making a fuss over* such a small matter. 她总是对这样的小事小题大做。Why are you *making* such *a fuss* over losing a watch? 丢了一块表用得着这样大惊小怪的? ❸(与 of 连用) give a person or animal a lot of attention to show that you love them 过分关心,宠爱: When the dog came out of the hospital his master *made a* great *fuss* of him. 那条狗出院后,它的主人对它倍加呵护。

NOTE 本短语中的不定冠词 a 可根据意义表达的需要被其他修饰词语所替换, 也可因名词 fuss 受定语的修饰而不用。例如:

> Don't make so *much fuss* of the children.
> 不要过分宠爱孩子。

make a long story short ⇨ **cut a long story short**

make a mess of *vt.*【不可分性动词短语】❶make (a place) look dirty or untidy, especially you don't put things away after using it 把(某处)弄得脏乱: You can play upstairs with your friends if you promise not to *make a mess of* it. 你可以和你的朋友在楼上玩,如果你答应不把它弄得又脏又乱。Violent storms are *making a mess of* the small town. 猛烈的暴风雨把这个小镇搞得又脏又乱。❷(非正式用语) spoil or ruin (something), especially because people have done it badly or made mistakes 毁掉,弄乱,弄糟: The illness *makes a mess of* my holiday plan. 这场病毁掉了我的度假计划。We must handle this with great care; otherwise we may *make a mess of* it. 我们要慎重处理这件事,否则就会把事情搞糟。They *made a mess of* this international organization. 他们把这个国际组织搞得乱七八糟。

NOTE 当本短语中的第一个义项无需说明宾语时,可只用 make a mess 的形式。例如:

> You can play upstairs with your friends if you promise not to *make a mess*.
> 如果你答应不搞得乱七八糟,你可以和你的朋友在楼上玩。

make a move *vi.* ❶ change position or move in a particular way or direction 动,移动: Don't *make a move*; they'll see you. 你别动,他们会看到你。He *made a* quick *move* for his gun. 他动作迅速地去掏枪。❷(非正式用语,后常接用动词不定式短语) start doing something to achieve an aim or solve a problem (为达到某种目的或解决某一问题而)开始行动: The government is *making a move* to reduce international tension. 该政府正在采取行动来缓和国际紧张局势。No one *made a move* to help us. 没人采取任何行动来帮助我们。❸(英国英语,非正式用语) prepare or begin to leave one place and go somewhere else 离开某地,出发: We should *make a move* to leave here before it gets any later. 我们应该尽早离开这里。Shall we *make a move* now? 我们现在就出发吗?

NOTE 1. 本短语中的不定冠词 a 可根据意义表达的需要,被其他词语所替换。例如:

> Who will *make* the first *move* towards resolving the dispute?
> 谁将为解决争端能开始行动呢?

2. 本短语的反义短语是 make no move。

make a name for oneself *vi.* become famous or well-known; get a (usually good) reputation, etc. 成名，出名：Schwarzenegger first *made a name for himself* as an action star; then he became a famous politician. 施瓦辛格最初是作为动作片明星而成名，后来成了著名的政治家。She has *made a name for herself* by her broadcast talks. 她所作的广播谈话使她出了名。

NOTE 本短语的另外一种表达形式是 make one's name。例如：

> The Chinese director *made his name* in the 1990s with off-beat movies.
> 这位中国导演以其非常规的影片于 20 世纪 90 年代成名。

make a note *vi*. (后常接 of 短语和动词不定式短语) write something down or remember it carefully 写下，记下：Please *make a note* of my telephone number. 请记住我的电话号码。*Make a note* to phone again next Monday. 记住下星期一再打电话。

NOTE 本短语的同义短语是 take a note 和 take notes。

make a note of *vt*. write down (something that reminds you of something)把……记下来(以备忘)：I will *make a note of* that lady's name. 我会记下那位女士的名字。I *made a* careful *note of* where I had left the bag, so as to be sure to find it on my return. 我仔细地记下了我放包的位置，好在回来时肯定能找到它。I've *made a note of* what needs to be repaired. 我已把需要修理的东西都记了下来。*Make a note of* how much money you spend. 你花了多少钱，要记下来。

make a nuisance of oneself *vi*. do something that causes difficulty or trouble for other people; annoy other people 惹人讨厌，让人厌烦：Sit down, and stop *making a nuisance of yourself*. 坐下，别再惹人讨厌。The children are *making a nuisance of themselves*. 这些孩子让人讨厌。I hope the kids didn't *make* too much of *a nuisance of themselves*. 我希望这些孩子别太让人厌烦。

make a point of *vt*. (后常接动名词短语) show clearly that you do something that you think is important 清楚地表明：From then on he *made a point of* avoiding her. 从那时起，他就刻意地回避她。Why do you *make* such *a point of* rising early? 你为什么要起这么早呢?

make a reference to ⇨ **refer to**

make a study of *vt*. 【不可分性动词短语】make (anything) a special study 研究，考察：She's *made a study of* the language of Shakespeare's plays. 她对莎士比亚戏剧的语言作了研究。The joint experts' team visited the restaurant where the patient had been working as a waitress, and *made a* thorough *study of* its environment. 联合专家组探访了该患者曾当过服务员的餐厅，并对其环境进行了全面考察。

NOTE 本短语实际等同于动词 study。在日常英语中，这样的短语往往被用来替换与其意义相同的动词，例如：make mention of = mention, make use of = use, pay a visit to = visit, have a rest = rest, have a try = try, have a look = look，等等。

make an apology for ⇨ **apologize for**

make an apology to ⇨ **apologize to**

make an appeal for ⇨ **appeal for**

make an appeal to ⇨ **appeal to**

make an application for ⇨ **apply for**

make an application to ⇨ **apply to**

make arrangements for *vt*. 【不可分性

M

动词短语】organize (something)安排,组织:Have you *made arrangements for* a photographer to attend the wedding? 你有没有安排一名摄影师来参加婚礼? I'll *make arrangements for* a car to meet you at the airport. 我会安排一辆车去机场接您。Who is *making arrangements for* the next meeting? 谁组织下次的会议?

NOTE 1. 本短语中的名词 arrangement 必须用复数形式。

2. 本短语的另外一种表达形式是 arrange for。

make away with *vt.* 【不可分性动词短语】❶escape with (something that you have stolen) 盗走,带走(某物):The burglars *made away with* all the store's silverware. 盗贼们把店内所有的银制器皿都偷走了。The former head of the bank and two of his predecessors *made away with* US $482 million and fled to the US. 该银行原行长和他的两位前任把4.82亿美元卷走逃往美国。❷get rid of (something)除掉(某物):It took her several hours to *make away with* the rust on the pan. 除掉锅上的锈迹花掉了她好几个小时的时间。❸(非正式用语,常用一般时态) murder (someone) secretly; kill (oneself) 秘密杀害(某人);自杀:They *made away with* their opponents. 他们秘密杀害了自己的对手。The despondent girl *made away with* herself at last. 那个绝望的姑娘最后自杀了。

NOTE 1. 当本短语作"盗走(某物)"解时,同义短语是 run away with, walk away with 和 walk off with。

2. 当本短语作"秘密杀害(某人);自杀"解时,与 do away with(第二个义项)意义和用法相同。

make believe *vt.* pretend (that something is real), especially in a game (尤指在游戏中)假装,装扮,装作:The children like to *make believe* that they live in a castle. 孩子们喜欢装作住在城堡中。The boys *made believe* they were astronauts. 男孩们都装扮成宇航员。The thief tried to *make believe* that he was innocent. 那小偷极力装出一副无辜的样子。

NOTE 1. 本短语是由两个动词结合而成的。第二个动词是第一个动词的宾语补足语。按常规,宾语应置于及物动词与宾语补足语之间,但由于本短语的宾语常为 that 从句(无需先行词 it),所以一般置于这两个动词之后。

2. 本短语可转化为复合词 make-believe,意为"假装;妄想"。例如:

> She lives in a world of *make-believe* if she thinks she can get to college without working hard.
> 她若认为不努力就能上大学,那只是妄想。

make both ends meet ⇨ **make ends meet**

make certain *v.* ❶take action in order to be sure (that something happens) or be sure (that it is true); make sure 保证,确保:We went to the theatre very early and *made certain* of getting better seats. 为了保证都能得到较好的座位,我们很早就到了剧场。You should call the office to *make* absolutely *certain* everything is in order. 你应该给办事处打电话,要绝对保证一切顺利。They will repeat their experiment several times to *make certain* that their results are correct. 他们要反复做几次实验以确保结果正确。❷(常用一般时态) feel sure 有把握:They could not *make certain* whether I was safe or not. 我是否安全,他们也没有把握。You must *make certain* that you know what time the train leaves. 你一定要确知火车发车的时间。

NOTE 本短语的同义短语是 make sure。

make clear *vt.* show; explain (something) clearly 明确地表示,解释: Some examples will *make* the point *clear*. 几个例证会说清楚这点。The government has *made clear* that it welcomes other countries' assistance for the victims of the tropical storm. 政府明确表示,欢迎其他国家为热带风暴的灾民所提供的援助。

NOTE 本短语可用于多种结构形式: make clear(+名词), make(+名词) clear, make clear(+that 从句)。

make do (with) *v.* (非正式用语) accept or use what is available, although less satisfactory, because there is no alternative 凑合着用,勉强应付: Can't you *make* that shirt *do* for another day? 这件衬衫你就不能再凑合着穿一天吗? I don't know how they *make do* on so small an income. 我不知道他们靠这么一点收入日子是怎么将就过的。The new teachers have to *make do with* the old computers until the new ones arrive. 在新电脑到之前,新来的老师得凑合着用那些旧电脑。

make ends meet *vi.* (非正式用语) have just enough money for all you need 使收支相抵,勉强维持生计: Even though the government has raised their salaries, the Iraqi police officers say they still cannot *make ends meet*. 尽管政府提高了他们的工资,但伊拉克的警官们说,他们还是难使收支相抵。Born in Hong Kong, she started singing at five to help *make ends meet* for her family. 她出生于香港,五岁就开始唱歌,帮助维持全家人的生活。To *make ends meet*, he had to take a second job. 为维持生计,他不得不打第二份工。

NOTE 本短语中的名词 end 必须用复数形式。有时,ends 前可用代词 both,但短语意义不变。例如:

> She scarcely earns enough money to *make* both *ends meet*.
> 她几乎挣不到足够的钱来维持生计。

make fast *vt.* 【可分性动词短语】 fix (something) tightly and firmly somewhere so that it cannot move 把……拴紧,把……系牢: He *made* the rope *fast* to the metal ring. 他把绳子在金属环上拴紧。She tied the rope round a post and *made* it *fast*. 她把绳子绕在柱子上系牢。

NOTE 当本短语的宾语为代词时,该代词须置于本短语的动词和形容词中间。

make for *vt.* 【不可分性动词短语】(无被动语态形式) ❶move towards (a place); go in the direction of (something), usually in a hurry (常指匆匆地)向……走去,驶去: He *made for* the toilet as soon as we got home. 我们一到家,他就匆匆朝洗手间奔去。While all the other passengers *made for* the exit, he alone remained in his seat, as if unwilling to leave the plane. 当所有乘客都向舱口走去时,他却独自留在座位上,好像不愿意离开这架飞机似的。The American aircraft carrier Kitty Hawk left Hong Kong and *made for* the open sea. 美国航空母舰"小鹰号"离开香港,向公海驶去。❷ move towards (usually someone) violently and threateningly 冲向,向……猛扑: Our troops *made* straight *for* the enemy positions. 我们的部队直向敌人的阵地冲去。Our dog *made for* the boy

M

and he cried in fear. 我们的狗向那男孩扑了过去,把他吓哭了。❸(非正式用语,常用一般时态)help to cause (something) to happen or exist; favor (something)有助于,有利于;致使: The application of new computers will *make for* much greater productivity. 新型计算机的应用将有助于更大幅度地提高生产力。The large print *makes for* easier reading. 大号的印刷字体使读起来更容易。Money does not always *make for* happiness. 金钱不一定总是能带来幸福。Physical exercises *make for* good health. 体育锻炼对健康有益。

NOTE 当本短语作"向……走去,驶去"解时,同义短语是 head for/to/towards。

make free with *vt.* 【不可分性动词短语】(主要用于英国英语中) use (something, even when it does not belong to you) as though it does belong to you 随意使用(某物),擅用(他人之物): You can *make free with* the hot water. We have a huge tank. 你可以随意使用热水。我们有一大罐呢。He's *made free with* my cigarettes during my absence. 我不在时他就随意抽我的烟。You had no right to *make free with* my name in your report. 你无权在你的报告中擅用我的名字。

make friends (with) *v.* ❶become friends (with)(与……)成为朋友: Jim and Mary have only just met, but they've *made friends* already. 吉姆和玛丽刚刚认识,但他们已成为朋友。They *made friends with* the children next door. 他们和隔壁的孩子们成了朋友。❷form friendships (with) (与……)建立友谊,结交朋友: You'll *make* a lot of new *friends* at college. 你会在大学里结交很多朋友。Life has changed for millions of teenagers across the world who *make friends* online. 对于全世界许许多多的青少年来说,网上交友改变了他们的生活。Even though she likes chatting, she is careful about *making friends* with strangers online. 尽管喜欢聊天,但她还是对在网上与陌生人交友十分慎重。

NOTE 本短语中的名词 friend 必须用复数形式。即使句子的主语是单数,如表示"与……为友",名词 friend 也要用复数形式。例如:

> I made friends with him several years ago.
> 我几年前就和他成了朋友。

make from *vt.* 【可分性动词短语】(常用被动语态形式) produce; form; cause (something) to exist by using (an existing object as material) 由……制造,由……形成,用……为原料制取: They *make* paper *from* old rags. 他们用破旧碎布造纸。Coal is *made from* trees and other plants that grew on the earth millions of years ago. 煤是由数百万年前地球上生长的树木和其他植物形成的。This kind of wine is *made from* rice. 这种酒是用稻米酿造的。

NOTE 本短语与 make of 之间的区别是: make from 后通常跟的是制成某物的原料,而 make of 后通常跟的是构成某物的材料。be made from 表示通过一种化学变化而形成某物,制成的物品改变了本质,往往已看不出其原料的模样;而 be made of 则表示通过一种物理变化而制成其物,制成物不改变本质,可以直接看出制造用的原材料的模样。

make fun of *vt.* 【不可分性动词短语】 make a joke about (someone or something) in an unkind way 取笑,捉弄: The other children *made fun of* him because he was always so serious. 别的孩子们取笑他,是因为他总是那么一本正经。Please *stop making fun of* his English; he's just a beginner. 请不要嘲笑他的英语。他仅仅是个初学者。I felt embarrassed whenever I was *made fun of* for my strong southern accent. 每当别人取笑我浓重的南方口音时，我都感到很尴尬。

NOTE 本短语的同义短语是 poke fun at。

make good *v.* ❶(常用一般时态) fix, replace, or pay for (something you have done wrong, damaged etc.) 修理，更换，补偿(被损坏之物)：They spent nearly half a year *making good* the run-down train. 他们用了近半年的时间才把破损的列车修好。We intend to *make good* any damage we may have caused. 我们准备对我们可能造成的任何损失给予补偿。The loss to the company was *made good* by the contributions from its subsidiaries. 该公司的亏损靠其子公司的捐助得到了补偿。❷(美国和澳大利亚英语，非正式用语，用一般时态) (of someone) become successful; succeed in doing (something difficult) (指某人)取得成功，做成功：We've drawn a lesson from the failure, so we'll *make good*. 我们从失败中汲取了教训，因此我们将会取得成功。He's always *made good* in everything he has done. 他总能把他所做的每件事情做成功。The prisoners slipped over the wall and *made good* their escape. 囚犯们翻过围墙，成功地逃跑了。❸(常用一般时态) prove (something) 证实，证明：The hypothesis has been *made good* after many times of experiments. 经过多次的实验，假说已得到证实。Can you *make good* your charge against him? 你能为你对他的指控提出证据吗？

make good on *vt.* 【不可分性动词短语】(美国和澳大利亚英语，常用一般时态) ❶do what you have threatened or promised to do 实践(所发出的威胁或做出的承诺)：Venezuela's president threatened to cut off oil supplies to the US, but market analysts said it is unlikely that he would *make good on* such threats. 委内瑞拉总统曾威胁说要切断对美国的石油供应，但市场分析家们表示，他不太可能去实践这种威胁。Our manager refused to *make good on* his promise to donate \$5,000. 我们经理拒绝履行其捐款5 000美元的承诺。❷(非正式用语) give back or repay (money that you owe someone) 偿还(借款)：I want to *make good on* that loan I got from Johnson. 我要偿还从约翰逊那儿借来的钱。

make into *vt.* 【可分性动词短语】❶(常用被动语态形式) shape (material) into (a finished object) 把(某种材料)制成(某种成品)：I'm going to *make* this material *into* a skirt. 我要把这块布料做成一条裙子。Waste products from factories can be *made into* road building material. 工厂的废品可以制成筑路材料。❷ change (someone or something) so that they become something else 把……改变成……：It is the 1984 sci-fi action movie *The Terminator* that *made* Schwarzenegger *into* a superstar. 是 1984 年的科幻动作影片《终结者》使施瓦辛格一跃成为超级影星。The story was *made into* a film two years ago. 这个故事在两年前就被拍成了影片。

NOTE 当本短语作"把……改变成……"解时，同义短语是 turn into。

make it *vi.* (非正式用语，常用一般时态) ❶succeed in a particular activity; achieve a goal 办成功，做到：She *made it* in films when she was still a teenager. 当她还是个十几岁的孩子时，她就在影坛取得了成功。He's never really *made it* as an actor. 他当演员从未有所成就。To win the day in the highly competitive society is easier said than done. But she has *made it*. 要在竞争激烈的社会里获得成功说起来容易做起来难，但是她做到了。❷manage to arrive at a place or go to an event 赶到，赶上：The plane won't leave for another forty minutes, so I think we can *make it*. 飞机还有 40 分钟才起飞，我想我们能赶得上。We just *made it* in time for the wedding. 我们及时地赶上了婚礼。❸(常用于否定句中) be able to attend a particular event that you have been invited to (应邀)出席：We *made it* to the meeting. 我们都应邀出席了会议。She was to show up at the meeting, but she didn't *make it*. 她原来要出席会议，但却没来。Sorry, I can't *make it* to your dinner on Friday. 对不起，我无法出席你们星期五的宴会。❹stay alive 活下来：The girl was losing so much blood; I really thought she wasn't going to *make it*. 这女孩失血太多，我真的以为她活不成了。

make it clear (that) *vt.* declare clearly and firmly (that)清楚而坚决地宣布，阐明：But scientists *make it clear that* the center of the earth is definitely fiery hot, in fact over 2,000 degrees! 但科学家们清楚地表明，地心无疑是炽热的，实际上超过 2000 度！

NOTE 本短语是 make clear 的另外一种表达形式。本短语中的代词 it 为形式宾语，实际宾语是 that 从句。

make no bones about *vt.* talk about or do (something) in a very open way although you may embarrass or offend someone 毫无顾忌地说(或做)：He *makes no bones about* the fact that he wants my job. 他竟毫无顾忌地说出他想要干我这份工作。Mary *makes no bones about* wanting Johnson to leave. 玛丽直言让约翰逊离开。I'll *make no bones about* it—I don't think you did a good job of painting my house. 我直言不讳地说吧，我觉得我的房子你们粉刷得很糟糕。

NOTE 本短语中的名词 bone 必须用复数形式。

make no difference *vi.* be not important or not have any effect on what you are doing 不重要，没影响，无所谓：It *makes no difference* if you are coming or not. 你来与不来都没关系。It *makes no difference* which road you take; both lead to the city and they are equally long. 你走哪条路都一样；这两条路都通城里，而且都一样远。It *makes no difference* to us whether the baby is a boy or a girl. 这婴儿是男还是女对我们来说都无所谓。

NOTE 1. 本短语特指两件不同的事或物，常用在"It makes no difference＋疑问词引导的名词性从句"的句型中。

2. 本短语的另外一种表达形式是 does not make any difference。例如：

> It *doesn't make any difference* now what he says—it's too late for apologies.
> 现在他说什么都不重要了。道歉已太晚了。

3. 本短语的反义短语是 make a difference。

make no move *vi.* do nothing 无动于衷，不采取行动：They *made no move* to help her. 他们无动于衷，不出手帮助她。

Although suspicion for the killing fell on the group, the police *made no move* against it. 尽管那个组织有凶杀的嫌疑，但警方却不对其采取任何行动。

NOTE 本短语的反义短语是 make a move。

make of *vt.* 【可分性动词短语】❶(常用被动语态形式)produce (something) from (a material)用(某种材料)做成：The children like *making* houses *of* sticks and clay. 孩子们喜欢用木棍和泥土搭房子。In the poor and remote mountain villages in China, folks still use manual labor and animals to farm and live in houses *made of* sun-dried mud bricks. 在中国贫穷、偏僻的山村，人们还在使用人力和畜力耕作，居住的是土坯房。Her necklace is *made of* glass. 她的项链是用玻璃制成的。❷(用一般时态，常用于否定句和疑问句中) understand (someone or the meaning of something) in a particular way 明白，理解：I don't know what to *make of* him. 我弄不明白他是怎样一个人。What do you *make of* this news? 你是怎样理解这条新闻的? I could *make* nothing *of* what she said. 我理解不了她所说的那番话。I apologize for the untidiness of my letter, but I hope you can *make* something *of* it. 我的信写得不工整，为此我表示道歉，但我希望你能看得懂。❸ train (someone) as; cause (someone) to develop into (a kind of person)把(某人)训练(或培养)成……；使(某人)发展成为……：The Navy has *made* a real man *of* him. 海军生涯把他训练成了一名真正的男子汉。Can't you *make* a musician *of* your son? 你就不能把你的儿子培养成一个音乐家吗?

NOTE 1. 当本短语作“明白，理解”解时，宾语多为代词。除上述例句中的 little, nothing, something 外，还可用 anything, much 等。

2. 在第三个义项中，不要受汉语表达方式的影响把两个宾语安排错位。例如，“他爸爸想把他培养成一名律师。”我们不能说成：* His father wanted to *make* him *of* a lawyer. 而应说成：His father wanted to *make* a lawyer *of* him.

make off *vi.* (非正式用语) leave somewhere in haste, usually in order to escape 匆忙离开，仓皇逃走，溜走：This morning I wanted to speak to him, but he *made off* in a hurry. 今天上午，我想要和他说话，可他却匆匆离去。The thieves *made off* in a stolen car before the police arrived. 在警察到达之前，盗贼们开着偷来的汽车逃掉了。After the child had broken the glass, he *made off* for fear of being beaten. 那个孩子把玻璃杯打碎了之后，因怕挨打便溜之大吉。

make off with *vt.* 【不可分性动词短语】❶steal and carry away (something) 携(所窃之物)逃走：The police said they chased a thief, but he *made off with* more than $50,000 worth of jewelry. 警方称，他们追踪一窃贼，但那窃贼还是携价值 5 万多美元的珠宝逃之夭夭。❷(非正式用语) rob or steal (something) 抢劫，偷窃(某物)：Two robbers stopped John on a dark street and *made off with* his wallet and mobile phone. 两名抢劫分子在昏暗的街道上截住约翰，抢劫了他的钱包和手机。Thieves *made off with* twenty boxes of watches from the warehouse of the supermarket last night. 昨天夜里，盗贼从超市仓库中偷走了 20 箱手表。

make one's fortune ⇨ **make a fortune**

make one's name ⇨ **make a name for oneself**

make one's peace (with) ⇨ **make peace**

make one's way *vi.* ❶(常为正式用语，后接介词短语或副词) walk or travel (in a particular direction or towards a place)(朝某一方向或某处)走去：We *made our way* to the front of the crowd. 我们往人群的前面走去。"In 30 minutes or so," a witness of the subway bombings said, "people overcame their fear and *made their way* out of the tube carriage." 一位地铁爆炸案的目击者陈述道："大约半个小时后，人们才克服了恐惧，从地铁车厢中走了出来。" He *made his way* up the stairs. 他朝楼上走去。❷(后接介词短语) reach (a place or condition) 到达(某处)；达到(某种状态)：Radar has *made its way* into other fields of engineering. 雷达已经进入其他工程领域。Mary's poems finally *made their way* into print. 玛丽的诗歌终于付印了。❸(后常接介词短语) start to make progress in a career or activity (在某项事业或活动上)取得进步：Edward was just beginning to *make his way* in life. 爱德华刚刚在生活的道路上取得进步。That young man will *make his way* in the world. 那个年轻人将成就一番事业。

make out *vt.* 【可分性动词短语】❶(用一般时态) see, hear, or identify (someone or something), especially with difficulty (尤指困难地)看到，看出，听出，辨认出：From the moon, astronauts cannot *make out* any man-made structures on earth and the continents are very hard to see. 从月球上宇航员无法看见任何人造物体，也难以看见各大洲。The numbers are too small — I can't *make* them *out* at all. 这些数字太小，我根本看不清。The outline of the house could just be *made out*. 那房子的轮廓勉强可以看出。I couldn't *make out* what he was saying. 我听不出来他在说什么。I cannot *make out* whether this figure is a 3 or an 8. 我辨认不出这个数字是 3 还是 8。❷(英国英语用法) write (all the necessary information on an official document such as a cheque, receipt, or order form) 写出，开出(支票、收据、订单等)：She *made* a check *out* and handed it to me. 她开出一张支票递给了我。After he paid for the books, the cashier *made out* a receipt for him. 他为书付了款后，收款员给他开了一张发票。The teacher *made out* the report cards and gave them to the students to take home. 老师写出了成绩单交给学生带回家。❸(非正式用语，常用于否定句中，用一般时态) try to understand (something, someone's character or someone) 理解，懂得：I didn't quite *make out* what she said. 我没怎么理解她所说的话。To the present day I can't *make out* why she did it. 时至今日，我仍不理解她为什么做了那件事。I can't *make out* the meaning of this poem. 我不懂这首诗的意义。He's an odd character; I can't quite *make* him *out*. 他是个古怪的人，我搞不太懂他。❹(非正式用语，常用一般时态) claim; describe (someone or something) 声称，描绘：He *made out* that he had never been to the place before. 他声称他从未去过那个地方。He *made* me *out* to be a liar. 他把我描绘成了一个骗子。The British weather is not always as bad as it is *made out* (to be). 英国的天气并不总是像被描绘的那样坏。❺(非正式用语,常与不定式和 that 从句连用)pretend (that something is true); try to prove 假装,企图证明: He *made* himself *out* to be very important. 他装出一副自己是重要人物的样子。He *made out* that he had forgotten all about that. 他假装对那件事什么都记不得了。The man tried to *make out* that that boy hadn't stolen the lady's purse. 那个人企图证明那男孩并没有偷那位女士的钱包。

—*vi.* (美国英语用法,非正式用语,常用进行时态) succeed or advance, especially in your work (尤指在工作中)取得成功,取得进展: The company isn't *making out* as well as was hoped. 公司的生意不像所期望的那样成功。Their business *made out* better than expected and profits were slightly up. 他们的生意比预想的好,利润略有增加了。How is Frank *making out* in his new job? 弗兰克的那件新工作干得怎样?

NOTE 1. 当本短语用作及物性动词短语,所带的宾语为代词时,该代词须置于本短语的动词和副词中间。

2. 当本短语作"写出,开出(支票、收据、订单等)"解时,同义短语是 write out。

make out of *vt.* 【可分性动词短语】(常用被动语态形式) produce (something) from (a material or existing object)用(某种原料或现有的东西)制造出(某物): This evening dress is *made out of* pure silk. 这件睡衣是用真丝做的。There are many ways to *make* steel *out of* pig-iron. 用生铁炼钢有许多方法。I'm going to *make* a skirt *out of* this material. 我要用这块布料做一条裙子。

make over *vt.* 【可分性动词短语】❶(主要用于美国英语中) make (something) anew; remake 更新,重做: She *made over* her mother's dress for herself. 她把妈妈的衣服改做了一下给自己穿。The father's jacket was *made over* for his son. 父亲的上衣重做了一下给儿子穿。They're going to *make* the whole thing *over*. 他们准备把整个事情重做一遍。❷(常与 into 连用) change or improve the appearance of (someone or something)改变,改善……的外形: The old house was *made over* into a garage. 那旧房子改成车库了。

make over to *vt.* 【可分性动词短语】pass over (especially the possession or ownership) to (someone else), especially legally (尤指合法地)(向某人)转让,移交(财产或所有权): One of my friends *made over* his motorcycle *to* me. 我的一个朋友把他的摩托车转让给了我。Before his death, he made all his *money over to* his wife. 在去世之前,他把所有的钱都给了妻子。They moved to the larger farm and in time *made* it *over to* Francis. 他们搬进了较大的那个农场,并在一段时间后就将其移交给了弗朗西斯。The property was *made over to* the son before his father died. 在父亲去世之前,其财产转让给了儿子。

NOTE 当本短语的宾语为代词时,该代词须置于本短语的动词和副词中间。

make peace *vi.* (of two people, countries, etc.) agree to end an argument, quarrel or hostilities 言归于好,和解: The brothers who had been fighting over their inheritance finally *made peace*. 一直在遗产继承问题上打闹不休的兄弟几个终于言归于好了。Have you *made peace* with your wife yet? 你与你妻子言归于好了吗? The UN Secretary General urged the

M

two countries to *make peace*. 联合国秘书长敦促两国和解。

NOTE 1. 本短语的另外一种表达形式是 make one's peace (with)。例如:

> Mary knew she had to go back into the house and *make her peace with* her parents.
> 玛丽知道她得回到屋里,和爸爸妈妈和解。

2. 本短语可转化为两个复合词: peace-maker,意为"调解人,和事佬"; peace-making,意为"调解的,调和的"。

make preparations for *vt.* 【不可分性动词短语】make all the arrangements for (a future event) 为……做准备: She's been working in the kitchen the whole day to *make preparations for* the party in the evening. 为准备晚上的聚会,她已在厨房里干了一整天。The developing countries should *make* good *preparations for* dealing with economic globalization. 发展中国家要为应对经济全球化做好准备。Before the week-long National Day holiday arrived, Hong Kong shops, big or small, had already *made preparations for* tourists flooding into the region. 在国庆黄金周到来之前,香港的大小商店都已做好了准备迎接涌入该地区的游客。

NOTE 1. 本短语中的名词 preparations 必须用复数形式。

2. 本短语的另外一种表达形式是 prepare for。

make progress *vi.* improve; develop or move forward 进步,取得进展,前进: She's not *making much progress* with her English. 她的英语进步不大。The UN International Atomic Energy Agency chief ElBaradei said Saturday that the IAEA has been *making* good *progress* to solve Iran's nuclear crisis. 联合国国际原子能机构总干事巴拉迪星期六表示,该机构在解决伊朗核危机上取得了不错的进展。The ship *made* slow *progress* through the rough sea. 船在汹涌的海浪中行驶得很慢。

NOTE 本短语中的名词 progress 前可用修饰性形容词,表示取得怎样的进步、进展或进程。

make public *vt.* (of a fact) make known to all or to many rather than being kept secret 公开,公布: Supreme Court judges should *make* their assets *public* like any other public servants. 最高法院的法官们应像任何其他公职人员一样公开他们的资产。The Commission issued a bulletin on its just-concluded meeting, *making public* its major anti-corruption tasks for the next year. 该委员会发布了其刚刚结束的会议公报,公布了其下一年的主要反腐任务。The talk between the two parties will take place next Monday, but the exact location hasn't been *made public*. 双方的会谈将于下周一举行,但确切地点还没有公布。

NOTE 本短语中的 public 是形容词,意为"公开的,当众的",在短语中充当宾语补足语。

make ready for ⇨ **get ready for**

make room for *vt.* 【不可分性动词短语】create space or find time to be given to (something or someone) 给……腾出地方;给……让出时间: We need to *make room* in here *for* the new computer. 我们要在这儿给新计算机腾出个地方来。I don't know how we can *make room* on the timetable *for* any more courses. 我不知道我们怎样才能在时间表上腾出些时

间多上几门课程。More *room* will have to be *made* on the program *for* these performers. 节目单上一定要给这些演员多留出些时间。

NOTE 1. 本短语中的名词 room 是不可数名词,必须用单数形式,而且前面也不能加不定冠词。

2. 本短语的同义短语是 leave room for,两者的用法相同。例如:

> *Leave* enough *room* between each plant *for* the roots to grow.
> 在每株秧苗之间要留出足够的株距以利于根部生长。

make sense *vi.* ❶(常用于否定句和疑问句中,常用一般时态)(of something or a course of action) be sensible or reasonable 有意义,有道理,讲得通: Your proposal doesn't *make* any *sense.* 你的建议无任何意义。It made good sense to continue with the reforms. 继续改革是大有道理的。Does it *make sense* what he says? 他所说的话有道理吗? Your argument *makes* no *sense.* 你的论点讲不通。❷(of something) be easy to understand 容易理解: Her argument *makes* considerable *sense* to me. 他的论点很容易为我所理解。

NOTE 本短语中的名词 sense 前可用表示程度的形容词或短语,诸如 some, more, much, any, (almost) no, little, a lot of 等。

make sense (out) of *vt.* 【不可分性动词短语】(常用于疑问句和否定句中,常用一般时态) succeed in understanding (someone or something that is complicated or unusual) 理解,弄懂,明白: I can't *make sense out of* Frank and what he has done! 我无法理解弗兰克以及他所做出来的事情。Can you *make* any *sense of* what this writer is saying? 你能理解这位作者在说什么吗? I've read it many times, but can *make* no *sense of* it. 我已读了多遍,但还不明白它说些什么。We've been trying to *make sense of* our dreams. 我们一直在千方百计地想搞明白我们所做的梦。

make sure *vt.* &*vi.* ❶check (something) so that you can be sure about it 弄清,查明: I just wanted to *make sure* whether you know where to go. 我只想弄清楚你是否知道去哪儿。They test the car to *make sure* if all parts work correctly. 他们检验这台车,以查明所有的部件是否运转正常。Before we leave the station we'd better *make sure* about the train for the return journey. 在我们离开车站之前,我们最好查明回程的火车。❷(常用一般时态) become sure or make certain 确信,肯定: I think I locked it but we'd better *make sure*. 我认为我把它锁上了,但我们最好再确认一下。Before he left the room, he *made sure* that all the lights were turned off. 他确信所有的灯都关掉了才离开房间。

—*vt.* 【不可分性动词短语】take the action necessary to be sure (that something will happen or be done)(采取必要行动以)保证……: We're determined to *make sure* our intelligence is as accurate as possible for every challenge in the future. 我们决心保证情报尽可能地准确,以应对将来的任何挑战。

NOTE 1. 当本短语后接 that 从句时,从句中的时态应使用一般现在时或现在完成时。

2. 本短语的同义短语是 make certain。

make sure of *vt.* 【不可分性动词短语】❶(无被动语态形式) know (something) without doubt 确信：I think I locked the door but I'd better go back and *make sure of* it. 我想我是把门锁上了，但我最好还是回去确认一下。❷find out for certain 弄清楚，查明：We'd better make some experiments to *make sure of* the problem. 我们最好做一些实验以弄清楚这个问题。❸take action so as to succeed in having (something)(采取行动以)保证得到(某物)：Always *make sure of* your facts before accusing anyone. 一定要保证在掌握事实以后再起诉他人。There aren't many copies of the book left; you'd better *make sure of* a copy quickly. 这书没剩下多少册，你最好赶快弄一本。They *made sure of* winning by scoring two goals in the last ten minutes. 他们在最后10分钟进了两个球，确保了夺取这场比赛的胜利。

make the best of *vt.*【不可分性动词短语】try to make full use of (something) as well as you can, despite a bad situation (在不利的情况下)(尽量地)充分利用：It rained all day, but we *made the best of* it. 下了一天的雨，但我们却尽量地利用了这个雨天。You have only a short holiday, so *make the best of* it. 你只有很短的假期，所以要尽量地利用好这段时间。

NOTE 本短语的同义短语是 make the most of。两者之间的区别见 make the most of。

make the most of *vt.*【不可分性动词短语】use (a good situation) to get the best possible result; take full advantage of (an opportunity, etc.), because it may not last long 充分利用(某种有利因素)：It's a beautiful day today. Let's *make the most of* it. 今天天气不错，咱们充分利用这个好天气吧。He *makes the most of* his opportunities to learn English. 他利用一切机会学习英语。Let's *make the most of* having the car for the day, and go for a long drive. 让我们充分利用今天有车的机会，来一次长途旅行吧。

NOTE 本短语与 make the best of 都表示"充分利用……"，但 make the best of 指"在不利的条件下，尽量地利用好……"，而本短语则指"在有利的条件下，充分利用好……"。

make up *vt.* ❶repay a loss of (money or time) 补偿，弥补：When the money was stolen, his father offered to *make up* the loss. 那笔钱被盗之后，他父亲答应补偿这一损失。Our economic losses have to be *made up* with more loans. 我们的经济损失必须靠更多的贷款来弥补。Sorry I'm late; I'll *make up* the time lost this evening. 对不起，我迟到了，我会在晚上把这耽搁的时间弥补上。If you miss a lesson, you can *make* it *up* later. 如果你缺一次课，可以以后补上。❷invent (an excuse for something or a story), often in order to deceive (常指为欺骗而)编造，捏造：He *made up* some excuse about the dog eating his homework. 他编造理由说他做的作业被狗吃掉了。I'm not *making* it *up*. The character exists in real life. 这个人物不是我编造出来的，他就存在于实际生活中。His story was *made up* though it seemed true. 尽管他的故事显得真实，但它是编造的。❸(常用被动语态形式，常与 of 连用) form; compose or be part(s) of 组成，构成，占：Three women and twelve men *make up* the committee. 3位女士和12位男士组成了该委员会。Our Members of Parliament *make up* 55 percent of the House of

Commons. 我们的议员占下院 55%的席位。❹(常用一般时态)make (an amount or a number) complete as it should be 凑足(某一数量或数目): We still need $500 to *make up* the required sum. 我们还需要 500 美元才能凑足所需的款额。The football team had six professionals and *made* the number *up* with five amateurs. 6 名专业球员,外加 5 名业余球员,凑成了这个足球队。These three articles *make up* the whole book. 这 3 篇文章凑成了一本书。❺prepare (a medicine) by mixing or putting different things together 配制(药品): The chemist *made up* a bottle of medicine for the patient. 药剂师为那病人配制了一瓶药。I'll get the chemist to *make* this prescription *up* for you. 我会请药剂师为你按此方配药。❻get ready (a bed) by putting sheets and blankets onto it so that someone can sleep there 准备(床铺): You should stay the night here — I'll *make up* a bed for you. 你应该在这里过夜,我给你准备一张床铺。Many more wounded people are arriving at the hospital, but the beds are not *made up* for them yet. 更多的伤员到了医院,但他们的床铺还没准备好。❼ produce (something) from (material) by cutting and sewing 剪裁出,缝制成: You could *make up* some new curtains from that material. 你可以用那块布料剪裁出一些新的窗帘来。She *made* the material *up* into a dress. 她用这块料子做了一件连衣裙。❽ repay or give (an amount) in return 偿还: You must *make up* what you owe before the end of the month. 你必须在月底之前还清欠款。

—*vt.* & *vi.* ❶put make-up on someone's face to change his or her appearance 化妆,化装,打扮: Do you like to see women *make up* in public? 你喜欢看女人在众人面前涂脂抹粉吗? It took two hours every morning to *make up* the film actor for his character part. 每天上午都要花两个小时给这位电影演员化妆以让他进入角色。For the film, they *made* him *up* as an Indian. 为演电影,他们把他装扮成一个印第安人。❷(of two people) become friendly with (someone) again after a quarrel or disagreement 重新和好,和解: The new couple usually *made up* their quarrel the same day. 这对新婚夫妇常常在吵架的当天就能重新和好。Why don't you two forget your differences and *make up*? 你们俩为何不忘掉分歧而重新和好呢? It's time you *made* it *up* with your sister. 是和你妹妹和解的时候了。

NOTE **1.** 当本短语用作及物性动词短语,所带的宾语为代词时,该代词须置于本短语的动词和副词中间。

2. 当本短语作"重新和好,和解"解时,在英国英语中常用 make it up 的形式。

3. 本短语可转化为复合词 makeup,意为"组成,构造;虚构,捏造;补给,补充;(演员的)化装用具,(妇女用的)化妆品"。

make up for *vt.* 【不可分性动词短语】(一般不用被动语态形式) replace or compensate for (something that has been lost or damaged, or what is bad before) 弥补,补偿: We're working fast to try to *make up for* the lost time. 我们在加速工作,尽量把失去的时间弥补上。You must *make up for* the lessons you missed yesterday. 你必须补上昨天所缺的课。Nothing can *make up for* missing such a good opportunity. 错失这样好的一次机会,是无法弥补的。

make up one's mind *v.* decide; reach, make, or come to a decision about something 决定,拿定主意:I can't *make up my mind* whether to go or not. 我无法决定去还是不去。He had not *made up his mind* yet what he should do. 他还没有决定到底怎么办。It's still early to *make up your mind* about your future career. 现在决定自己的未来职业还为时尚早。*My mind* is *made up*. I'm handing in my resignation tomorrow. 我主意已定,明天就递交辞职报告。

make use of *vt.*【不可分性动词短语】use (something) for a particular purpose, especially one that brings a benefit to you 使用,利用:Could you tell me how to *make use of* a photo editing software? 您能否给我讲一讲怎么使用照片编辑软件? I hope you've *made* full *use of* your time. 我希望你充分地利用了你的时间。The result depends on the *use* we *make of* the energy. 结果取决于我们对能源的利用。These data are *made* full *use of*. 这些数据得到了充分的利用。

NOTE 1. 本短语根据意义表达的需要,可以在 make 和 use of 之间使用形容词或其比较级及最高级形式。例如:

> We should learn to *make* good/better/best *use of* computers in our work.
> 我们都应学会在工作中很好/较好/最佳地使用计算机。

2. 本短语的被动形式除了 be made use of 形式外,还有另外一种形式,即 use be made of。例如:

> Full *use* is *made of* these data.
> 这些数据得到了充分的利用。

make way for *vt.*【不可分性动词短语】❶(常用一般时态) move away so that someone or something can get past you 给……让路:We were asked to *make way for* the bride and groom. 有人让我们给新娘和新郎让开路。All traffic has to stop and *make way for* an ambulance. 所有的车辆都得停下,给救护车让路。❷be replaced by (someone or something) (给某人)让位,(给某物)腾出地方:After the general election, George Bush *made way for* Barack Obama, who became the 44th US President. 大选后,乔治·布什让位于巴拉克·奥巴马。于是巴拉克·奥巴马就成了美国第 44 任总统。Most of the old houses have been knocked down to *made way for* new hotels and offices. 大多数的旧房子都已被拆除以腾出地方建造新的宾馆和办公大楼。

make yourself at home *vi.* (常用于祈使句中) (saying to a guest) feel free, relaxed and behave in the same way as you do in your own home 随便,不拘礼节:Sit where you like and help yourselves to coffee. *Make yourselves at home*. 你们喜欢坐在哪里就坐在哪里,随便喝点咖啡吧。*Make yourself at home* while I go and find those photographs. 你就随便点儿,我去找那些照片。

many a *adj.* (正式用语,语气比 many 强,后接单数名词) more than a few; a large number of (people or things involved in something) 许多:*Many a* good climber has met his death on this mountain. 许多优秀的登山者都在这座山上身亡了。For *many a* day it rained. 雨一连下了很多天。*Many a* business deal has been brought off over a bottle of wine. 许多生意都是在酒桌上谈成的。No doubt she had *many a* tale to tell of the old days. 毫无疑问,她有许多过去的故事可讲。

NOTE 1. 当"many a+单数名词"作主语时,

虽然表达复数意义,但谓语动词必须用单数形式。

2. 当本短语所修饰的名词之首字母为元音字母时,则用 many an 的形式。例如:

> I have visited your site on *many an* occasion, and I think it is one of the best web sites on the Internet today.
> 我多次访问过贵网站。我认为,它是当今因特网上最佳网站之一。

many a time *adv.* often; frequently; many times 经常,多次:I recalled *many a time* that we traveled this road together. 我时常想起我们曾在这条路上同行。That's happened *many a time* to me. 那事在我身上发生过多次。*Many a time* have I told the children to behave themselves. 我多次告诫孩子们要规矩点。

NOTE **1.** 本短语相当于 many times,但不及 many times 常用。

2. 当本短语用于句首时,该句的主谓要构成倒装(如最后一个例句)。再如:

> *Many a time* had she stood there waiting for a bus.
> 她过去经常站在那里等候公共汽车。

map out *vt.* plan or design (something) in detail (详细)规划,设计:Many young parents begin to *map out* a plan for their children's life as soon as they are born. 很多年轻的家长在孩子一出生后就开始为他们规划人生。We are *mapping out* where to go for our holiday. 我们正计划去哪里度假。When we *mapped* it *out* before we began this project, we thought we would be finished by now. 我们在这个项目开始前的规划中曾以为现在就能完工。The plan has been *mapped out* for some time. 计划早已安排就绪。

NOTE 当本短语的宾语为代词时,该代词须置于本短语的动词和副词中间。

mark down *vt.* 【可分性动词短语】❶write (something) down in order to have a record of it 记下,写下:*Mark* these points *down* in your notebook. They're very important. 把这几点记在笔记本上,它们都很重要。Use this pen to *mark down* how much each item costs. 用这支钢笔把每件物品的花费都写下来。❷(常用被动语态形式)reduce the price of (goods) 减低(商品的)价格:This bookstore has *marked down* prices sharply. 这家书店大幅度地减低了书价。All our stock has been *marked down* for the sales. 我们所有的存货都减低了价格。These winter coats have been *marked down* from $50 to $35. 这些冬天穿的上衣已从 50 美元减价到 35 美元。❸(of a teacher) give (a student) a lower mark for his or her work for a particular reason 指教师(因某种原因给学生)打低分:This teacher tends to *mark* students *down* even when they deserve a better result for their work. 这位老师惯于给学生打低分,尽管他们的功课应该得到比较好的分数。They'll *mark* you *down* for poor spelling. 他们会因你差劲的拼写而给你打低分的。

NOTE **1.** 当本短语的宾语为代词时,该代词须置于本短语的动词和副词中间。

2. 本短语的第二、三个义项的反义短语是 mark up。

mark off *vt.*【可分性动词短语】❶mark (the limits of an area) using a line, fence, rope, etc. 标出(界线、范围等):We *marked off* the limits of our lots with stakes. 我们用木桩为我们的地标出界线。The crime scene was *marked off* with police tape. 犯罪现场用警戒带标示

出来。They *marked off* the experimental corn plot from the rest of the field. 他们把玉米试验田同其他田地分开来。❷mark (something) with a word, letter, or symbol in order to show that you have dealt with it (用字、字母或符号)标画出: He *marked off* the names of all the suitable candidates. 他把所有合适的人选都标画了出来。The teacher called out our names and *marked* them *off*. 老师点叫我们的名字,并把叫到的名字画了标记。

NOTE 1. 当本短语作"标出(界线、范围等)"解时,同义短语是 mark out(第一个义项)。

2. 当本短语的宾语为代词时,该代词须置于本短语的动词和副词中间。

mark out *vt.*【可分性动词短语】❶draw (an area) with lines, often of paint 画标出(某一区域): They *marked out* the tennis court with white paint. 他们用白色油漆画标出网球场。Now that it's spring, we must *mark* the tennis court *out* ready for play. 现已是春季了,我们得给网球场画线,好准备玩球了。The site of the new chemical fertilizer plant has been *marked out*. 新化肥厂的厂址已经划定。❷(常用被动语态形式,常与as, for 连用) assign; select (someone or something that is unusual or special and different from others) 指定,选定: The directors have had you *marked out* as a best candidate for a higher position in the company. 董事们都指定你为担任公司较高职位的最佳人选。One tenth of them are *marked out* for special training. 他们中有十分之一被指定接受特殊训练。Three of his paintings have been *marked out* for exhibition. 他的三幅画已被选定参展。

NOTE 当本短语的宾语为代词时,该代词须置于本短语的动词和副词中间。

mark up *vt.*【可分性动词短语】❶charge (something) to someone's account 把……记在某人的账上: He bought some spare parts for his car and asked us to *mark* them *up*. 他买了些汽车零件,但让我们先记上账。❷make changes, correct or write notes or instructions on (a piece of writing), especially before it is published (尤指在出版前)修改,校正,批注(文稿): Could you tell me what changes have been made so I can *mark up* my copy? 请告诉我都做了哪些更改,我好把我这份稿子改一下,好吗? He read through the manuscript and *marked* it *up*. 他把稿子通读了一遍,并作了校注。❸increase the price of (goods) so as to make a profit 提高(商品)的价格: The shops often *mark up* the goods unfairly. 商店常常无理地提高商品价格。They *mark* the goods *up* by 25% before they sell them. 他们在出售这些商品之前将其价格都提高了 25%。Foreign cars are often *marked up* by 40 per cent in the British market. 进口车在英国市场上都常常被提价 40%。❹(of a teacher) raise the marks of (a student) for his or her work for a particular reason (指教师)提高(学生)的分数: If we *mark* her *up* a bit she'll just scrape a pass. 我们只要给她稍提一点儿分,她就会勉强及格。

NOTE 1. 当本短语的宾语为代词时,该代词须置于本短语的动词和副词中间。

2. 本短语中的第三、四个义项的反义短语是 mark down。

may (just) as well *v.* (非正式用语,后接原形动词) (used to suggest doing something because you cannot think of anything better to do) have no good reason for not to (do something) 不妨……,还是以……为好: It's no use carrying the debt forward; we *may as well* write it off. 这笔欠账不必再往下转了,我们不妨把它一笔勾销。We *might as* well sit down while we're waiting. 我们还是坐下来等吧。You *may just as well* tell me the truth. 你还不如告诉我真相。

NOTE 本短语的另外一种表达形式是 might (just) as well。might (just) as well 语气比本短语更委婉,所表示的可能性也较小。例如:

> You *might as well* stay here tonight.
> 你不如今晚住在这里。(对方很可能不会留下来)

mean business *vi.* (非正式用语) seriously intend to do what you say you will do 当真,说到做到,不是随便说说: They've threatened to close our store down, and I think they *mean business*. 他们威胁说要关掉我们的商店,我认为他们是真格的。Don't laugh. I *mean business*. 你别笑。我说到做到。He *means business* when he says he's not going to do it. So there's no use trying to persuade him any more. 他说他不干,这不是他随便说说的,所以再劝他也没用。

mean well *vi.* (用一般时态) do or say what is intended to be helpful, but often does not 怀有善意: He's a good person, and I know he *means well*. 他是个好人。我知道他是出于善意的。Maybe they *meant well*. 或许他们用心是好的。

NOTE 本短语常与 by sb 连用,表示"对某人怀有好意"。例如:

> I wasn't hungry; I only ate that big meal because your mother *meant well* by us.
> 我并不饿,我吃那顿丰盛的大餐只是因为你母亲对我们一片善意。

measure up *vt.* 【可分性动词短语】(常用一般时态) measure (something) in preparation for making, building, or fitting something else 测量……: He *measured up* the wood before he started. 在动工之前,他先量了一下木料。*Measure* the wall *up* carefully; we don't want to buy too much wallpaper. 仔细地把墙量一下,我们可不想多买壁纸。

—*vi.* (常用一般时态,常与 to 连用) be good enough to achieve a standard or fulfill someone's expectations 够得上,合格,胜任: He is a good worker, but as a manager he doesn't quite *measure up*. 他工作干得很好,但当经理还够不上。The machines are being tested to see how they *measure up*. 这些机器正在试机以检验其质量如何。These products did not *measure up* to the set standards. 这些产品没达到所规定的标准。It's a tough one, but I'm sure you'll *measure up* to the job. 这是个艰巨的工作,但我相信你能胜任它。

NOTE 当本短语用作及物性动词短语,所带的宾语为代词时,该代词须置于本短语的动词和副词中间。

meddle in *vt.* 【不可分性动词短语】(贬义用法) take unwanted action about (other people's private affairs or business)干预(他人的私事): You have no business *meddling in* my affairs. 你没有权利干预我的事情。Our affairs are constantly being *meddled in* by

M

outsiders. 我们的事务不断地受到外部人的干预。

NOTE 本短语的同义短语是 interfere in, interfere between, interfere with, intervene in 和 step in。

meddle with *vt.* 【不可分性动词短语】touch or cause damage to (something that is not your concern)摆弄,摸弄(他人之物): Somebody has been *meddling with* my papers again. 又有人乱动我的文件了。Who has *meddled with* my floppy disks? I do wish everyone would leave them alone! 是谁擅自动我的软盘了? 我不希望任何人动它们!

meditate on/upon *vt.* 【不可分性动词短语】think deeply and sincerely about (something)深刻思考: After all the consoling people were gone, she spent hours *meditating on* her future. 当前来慰问的人都走了以后,她用了几个小时考虑自己的未来。While all others were mad with joy, he was *meditating upon* his plans for revenge. 其他所有人都欣喜若狂,而他却在思考着复仇计划。

NOTE 1. 本短语中的 upon 用法比 on 正式,但不及 on 常用。

2. 本短语的同义短语是 reflect on/upon。

meet one's Waterloo *vi.* suffer a decisive defeat at something that you have always been successful at until now (在连续的胜利后)遭遇决定性的惨败: After winning 5 games in a succession, the team *met its Waterloo* and was knocked out of the quarterfinals. 该球队在连胜五场之后惨遭失败,被淘汰出四分之一决赛。As the small boys were fearless and united as one, the bully *met his Waterloo*. 由于那些小孩子们毫不畏惧,团结一致,那个恃强凌弱的家伙败下阵来。

NOTE 本短语中的 Waterloo(滑铁卢)是比利时一个小镇的名字。1815 年,攻克了欧洲多国的拿破仑率领其不可一世的法国军队在此小镇被英军打得大败。

meet up *vi.* (非正式用语,常与 with 连用) ❶ come together with (someone), either unexpectedly or as planned 与(某人)相遇: We usually *meet up* for a quick coffee in the morning. 我们通常在早晨碰到一起喝几口咖啡。Let's *meet up* after the play. 咱们看完戏后再碰头。I *met up* with him as I left the building. 我离开那栋楼时遇到了他。❷(of roads, streets, etc.)join or cross each other (道路等)相交: The streets *meet up* at the next intersection. 这几条路在下一个道路交叉点相汇。The path *meets up* with the main road ahead. 这条小路与前面的大路相交。

meet with *vt.* 【不可分性动词短语】❶(常用一般时态) find or meet (something or someone), especially by chance (尤指偶然)发现(某物),遇到(某人): The botanist *met with* many rare plants. 这位植物学家偶然发现了许多稀有植物。He *met with* a stranger with a gun in the woods this morning. 今天早上他在树林里碰见一个拿枪的陌生人。❷(主要用于美国英语中) have a formal meeting with (someone or a group of people)正式会见(某人或某一团体): Russian President *met* in the Kremlin *with* Chinese children from the quake-hit Sichuan Province, who came on holiday in Russia at his invitation. 俄罗斯总统在克里姆林宫会见了应他邀请来俄度假的中国四川省地震灾区的孩子们。❸(无

被动语态形式，用一般时态）receive (something)受到：They *met with* warm welcome yesterday. 他们昨天受到了热烈的欢迎。They finally came to a decision that has *met with* general approval. 他们最终做出了一项受到普遍赞成的决定。❹(无被动语态形式，用一般时态) encounter or experience (something, especially something unpleasant such as a trouble, danger, difficulty)遭遇(尤指麻烦、危险、困难等)：The farmers in this area *met with* misfortune: their crops were destroyed by a storm. 这个地区的农民遭遇了不幸：暴风雨毁了他们的庄稼。This scheme of theirs *met with* the same failure. 他们的这一图谋也遭到了同样的失败。She *met with* an accident on her way home yesterday. 她昨天在回家的途中遭遇了车祸。We *met with* some unexpected difficulties when we tried to enter the country. 我们在入境时遇到了一些没有预料到的困难。

NOTE 1. 当本短语表示"(尤指偶然)发现(某物)，遇到(某人)"之意时，同义短语是 bump into, chance on/upon, come across, run across, run into 和 stumble across/on/upon。

2. 当本短语作"遭遇"解时，后面一般接 something unpleasant。但在美国英语中，有时也可接 something pleasant。例如：The International Space Station project has met with great success. 句中的 met with 不能译为"遭遇了"，而应译为"获得了(极大的成功)"。

melt down *vt.* 【可分性动词短语】heat (a metal) until it becomes liquid, especially in order to make something new from it 熔化(金属)：He *melted down* the lead and poured it into the moulds. 他把铅熔化掉，然后倒进模具中。They offer fair prices for scrap-iron to be *melted down* for reuse. 他们以合理的价格收购废铁以熔掉后重新利用。

NOTE 当本短语的宾语为代词时，该代词须置于本短语的动词和副词中间。

mend one's ways *vi.* improve your behaviour after you have been behaving badly for a long time 改进(行为)：Threatened with suspension, Henry promised to *mend his ways*. 因害怕被停职，亨利承诺改进自己的行为。If he wants to continue living here, he's going to have to *mend his ways*. 如果他想继续住在这里，他就得改善他的行为。

NOTE 1. 本短语中的名词 way 必须用复数形式。

2. 本短语中的名词 ways 可被 manners 替换，两者的意义和用法相同。

mess about/around *vi.* (非正式用语) ❶ spend time lazily or doing things without any particular purpose or plan 无所事事，闲度时光：We spent the whole morning just *messing around* at the mall. 我们整个上午都在商场里闲逛。We spent the weekend *messing about* on John's boat. 这个周末我们是在约翰的小船上轻闲度过的。❷(贬义用法，与 with 连用) interfere or play with (something), especially when this is unnecessary 摸弄，摆弄，玩弄(某物)：Who's been *messing about* with my paper? 是谁摸弄我的文件了？He'll spend hours *messing about* with that motorbike. 他一摆弄起那台摩托车就是几个小时。He's always enjoyed *messing around* with boats. 他总是喜欢玩弄小船。❸behave in a joking or silly

M

way 开玩笑,胡闹:Don't take it seriously. I was only *messing around*. 这事儿可别当真。我只是开个玩笑。Stop *messing about*! I'm serious about this! 别再胡闹了! 这事我是认真的。

—*vt*. (主要用于英国英语中,非正式用语,常与 with 连用) treat (someone) badly or carelessly, especially by changing your mind or not doing what you promised 虐待(某人);(尤指以变卦或爽约的方式)轻率地对待(某人): He was always *messing around* with her, and she was right to leave him. 他总是虐待她。所以,她离开他是对的。Don't *mess* me *about*/*around*; I want the money you promised me. 别对付我了。我要那笔你答应过给我的钱。I think they've been *messed around* far too much. 我认为他们被过分地亏待了。

M

NOTE 1. 当本短语用作及物性动词短语,宾语为代词时,该代词须置于本短语的动词和副词中间。

2. mess about 用于英国英语中, mess around 多用于美国英语中。

mess up *vt*. 【可分性动词短语】(非正式用语) ❶make (something) dirty or untidy 把……弄脏,弄乱: They *messed up* my room and left stuff all over the place. 他们把我的房间搞得又脏又乱,东西扔得到处都是。The wind had *messed* his hair *up*. 风刮乱了她的头发。❷ disorder or spoil (something) 打乱,破坏: I'm not going to let him *mess up* my life. 我不会让他打乱我的生活。Her late arrival messed up our plans. 她的迟到把我们的计划破坏了。Our travel arrangements have been *messed up* by the ticket office. 我们的旅行计划被售票处破坏了。

NOTE 当本短语的宾语为代词时,该代词须置于本短语的动词和副词中间。

might (just) as well ⇨ **may (just) as well**

mind one's own business *vi*. (仅用于口语中) a rude way of telling someone not to ask questions about something that you do not want him or her to know about, or not to pay attention to things that do not concern them 不要多问,不要多管闲事: "Where are you going?" "*Mind your own business*!" "你要去哪儿?""你不要多问!" I asked Smith what was wrong and he told me to *mind my own business*. 我问史密斯出了什么事,可他要我别多管闲事。

NOTE 本短语一般用来责备或教训某人,表达方式较粗鲁,在使用时要注意场合和对象。本短语还可用另一种较为委婉的表达方式来代替: It's none of your business. 例如:

> "What are you doing?"
> "*It's none of your business*!"
> "你在做什么?"
> "你不要多管闲事!"

mind you *s*. (非正式用语) (used for making something that you have already said less strong or less general) please note; take this fact into account 请注意,你要考虑到: You need a bit of cold water. Not too cold, *mind you*. 你需要一点凉水,但注意,不要太凉。They provide a good service. *Mind you*, they charge enough for it. 他们提供的服务不错。但你要知道,他们为此要价也够高的。He spent a lot of time in bed now; *mind you*, he is over 90! 他现在大部分时间都

在床上度过。可你要知道,他已经 90 多岁了。

NOTE 在日常使用中,本短语中的 you 常被省略。例如:

> Mary might be there, *mind*.
> 注意,玛丽可能会在那里。

mingle with *vt.* (正式用语) ❶(cause to)mix with (something)(使)同(某物)混合: The fresh water of the Amazon *mingles with* the salt water of the South Atlantic. 亚马孙河的淡水和南大西洋的咸水混合在一起。Shall I *mingle* some of these blue flowers *with* the pink ones? 我把一些蓝色花同粉色花混放在一起,好吗? He gave a speech that contained praise *mingled with* blame. 在他所作的报告中有赞扬,也有责备之辞。❷(无被动语态形式)join or mix with (a group of people)混入(人群)中: He rushed out into the busy street and *mingled with* the crowd, hoping that that way the police wouldn't spot him. 他冲了出去,跑入繁闹的街上混入人群之中,希望那样一来警察就找不见他了。In the city of Basra, Prince Charles *mingled with* about 200 British soldiers, shaking hands with them. 在巴士拉市,查尔斯王子置身于200多名英军士兵当中,同他们一一握手。

NOTE 本短语的同义短语是 mix with。

miss out *vi.* (非正式用语,常用进行时态,常与 on 连用) lose an opportunity to do or have something 失去(做某事或拥有某物的)机会: We will be repeating the questions later, so you won't *miss out*. 我们稍后会把这些问题重复一遍,不会让你失去机会的。I *missed out* on a chance to visit Vancouver during my one-month stay in Canada. 在加拿大逗留一个月期间,我失去了游览温哥华的机会。You'll be *missing out* on a lot of fun if you don't come to the party. 如果你不来参加聚会,就会失去很多欢乐的机会。

—*vt.* 【可分性动词短语】(英国英语用法,常与 of 连用)fail to include (someone or something)没把……包括其中,遗漏掉: The organizer *missed* Jim *out* of the team. 组织者没把吉姆包括在队中。I notice that the advertisement *misses out* the price of the product. 我注意到这则广告漏掉了该产品的价格。Don't *miss* my name *out* of your list. 别在你的名单上把我的名字漏掉。An important fact had been *missed out*. 一项重要的事实被漏掉了。

mistake for *vt.* 【可分性动词短语】 wrongly think that (a person or thing) is (the other person or thing)把……错认为……: The policeman had *mistaken* him *for* a drug dealer. 警察误认为他是个毒品贩子。I had *mistaken* friendship *for* love. 我错把友情当成爱情。I *mistook* that rope *for* a snake. 我把那条绳子误当成了一条蛇。

NOTE 本短语与 take for(第二个义项)的意义和用法相同。

mix up *vt.* 【可分性动词短语】❶confuse (things or people)把……搞混: I'm sorry I *mix up* your names; you're so much alike. 对不起,我把你们的名字搞混了,你们长得太像了。They look so alike that it's easy to *mix* the two sisters *up*. 她们长得太像了,很容易把她们姐妹两个搞混。Little Tommy doesn't know colors yet; he *mixes up* purple with blue. 小汤米还不能分辨颜色,他把紫色

M

和蓝色混淆。I got *mixed up* with the dates and went there on the wrong day. 我把日期搞混了,于是在一个错误的日子去了那里。❷put (things) together without any order; disorder 搞乱:If you *mix up* those papers we won't be able to find the one we need quickly enough. 如果你把那些文件搞乱,我们就不能很快地找到所需要的那一份了。They got all my books *mixed up*. 他们把我所有的书搞得乱七八糟。I sorted all the papers and you've *mixed* them *up* again. 我把所有的文件都分类理好了,可你又把他们搞乱了。

NOTE 1. 当本短语的宾语为代词时,该代词须置于本短语的动词和副词中间。

2. 本短语可转化为复合词 mix-up,意为"混乱,迷惑;混合物"。

M

mix with *vt.* (常用一般时态)(cause to) be combined with (something or someone)(使)……与……相混合: You can't *mix* oil *with* water, however much you may stir the two together. 不管你怎样搅拌,你也不可能使油和水两者相混合。Maria's parents didn't approve of the people she was *mixing with*. 玛利亚的父母不赞成她和那些人混在一起。The party gave me a chance to *mix with* the new students. 这次聚会给我提供了一个与新生打成一片的机会。

NOTE 本短语的同义短语是 mingle with。

mop (up) the floor with *vt.*【不可分性动词短语】(非正式用语,无被动语态形式) ❶ defeat (someone) very easily or quickly in a game or an argument (在竞赛或争论中)轻易而迅速地击败(对手): Our team *mopped* (*up*) *the floor with* the visiting team. 我们队轻松而迅速地战胜了客队。Smith was a skilled debater, and *mopped the floor with* his opponent. 史密斯是个善辩的能手,他轻而易举地驳倒了对手。❷ scold (someone) severely 痛斥(某人): I could hear the manager *mopping the floor with* Tom for being late every morning this week. 我能听到经理因汤姆本周每天早晨都迟到而在训斥他。

NOTE 本短语的另外一种表达形式是 wipe (up) the floor with,常用于英国、美国和澳大利亚英语中,而本短语则仅用于美国英语中。

more and more Ⅰ *adv.* increasingly; to an increasing degree 越来越……:As the situation grew worse, he became *more and more* depressed. 随着情况变得越来越糟,他也变得越来越沮丧。Water evaporated *more and more* quickly as the temperature grew. 随着温度的升高,水蒸发得越来越快。The State Forestry Administration said that public attention paid to the wild South China tigers shows Chinese people care *more and more* about protecting wild animals. 国家林业局表示,公众对野生华南虎的重视说明国人越来越关注对野生动物的保护。

Ⅱ *adj.* (used for saying that something is increasing in number or degree all the time) increasingly more (people or things)越来越多的:In China, *more and more* people take short messages as a means of greeting and communication. 在中国,越来越多的人把短信作为致贺和交流的方式。I seem to spend *more and more* money on food every week. 我每星期在饮食上花的钱似乎越来越多了。

NOTE 1. 当本短语用作副词性短语时,可用来修饰形容词、副词和动词。

2. 当本短语用作形容词性短语时，可用来修饰可数名词和不可数名词。

3. 本短语的反义短语是 less and less。

more often than not *adv.* on most occasions or in most situations; usually; very often 通常，常常，经常：*More often than not*, the arguments could have been avoided. 这些争论通常是可以避免的。When it's foggy the trains are late *more often than not*. 雾大时，火车常常会误点。In winter the days are very short, and *more often than not* you're driving with your headlights on. 冬季里白天很短，所以你要经常开着车头灯开车。

NOTE 本短语与 as often as not 意义和用法相同，两者可互换使用。

more or less *adv.* ❶ almost; nearly 几乎，差不多，将近：The team is *more or less* the same as it was last season. 该队几乎与上个赛季相差无几。As his parents died early, his elder sister has been *more or less* a mother to him. 由于父母早亡，他的姐姐对他来说差不多就像妈妈一样。The job is *more or less* finished. 那项工作已接近完成。❷ approximately; somewhat 大约，或多或少，有点：A sum of $5,000, *more or less*, will be needed to carry out repairs. 要进行修理将需要一笔约 5 000 美元的款项。Each of the calls was *more or less* 10 minutes long. 每次通话时间的长度大约都是 10 分钟。The distance is ten kilometers, *more or less*. 其距离大约是 10 公里。"Are you happy with your new job?" "*More or less*." "你喜欢你的新工作吗?""有点儿吧。"

NOTE 当本短语与数词或与表示数量的短语连用时，可置于其前，也可置于其后。例如：

> The table weighs 30 pounds *more or less*.
> 这张桌子重约 30 磅。
> There were *more or less* 300 people attending the conference.
> 大约有 300 人与会。

more than Ⅰ *prep.* (用于数词之前) (used before a number or amount) over; above 多于，在……以上，不止：The grand opening ceremony of the Beijing Olympic Games was witnessed by 91,000 people in the National Stadium and a global television audience of *more than* 4 billion. 在国家体育场内的 9.1 万人和全球 40 多亿电视观众目睹了北京奥运会的盛大开幕式。*More than* 71 percent of Mexican women and 66 percent of Mexican men are overweight, according to the latest national surveys. 据墨西哥全国性的最新调查结果显示，超过 71% 的女性和 66% 的男性体重超标。

Ⅱ *adv.* (正式用语) very 极其，非常，十分：We were *more than* glad/happy to hear of your success. 听说你成功的消息，我们极其高兴。It's *more than* likely that there's oil here under the ground. 这里的地下很可能有石油。That lady was dressed *more than* simply. 那位女士穿着太朴素了。

NOTE **1.** 当本短语用作介词性短语，后接"one+单数名词"时，意为"不止一个"或"多个……"。在使用这一结构时，注意以下两点：

(1) 当"more than one 以单数名词"作主语时，句中的谓语动词要用单数形式。例如：

M

> *More than one* student in our class has passed the Cambridge International Examination.
> 我们班不止一名同学通过了剑桥国际考试。

(2)当 more than one 单独作主语时,其谓语动词常用单数形式,也可用复数形式。例如:

> The operating rooms are all in good order. *More than one* is/are equipped with the latest imaging technology.
> 所有手术室的状况俱佳,多间手术室都装有最新的影像技术设备。

2. 本短语前可用 not 或 no 加以否定,但两者的意义有所不同。not more than 和 no more than 的区别见 no more than。

3. 当本短语用作介词性短语,表示"多于,在……以上,不止"之意时,反义短语是 less than。

more than once *adv.* on more than one occasion; several times 不止一次,数次: I've warned him *more than once* not to interfere. 我已不止一次地警告过他不要插手。I met the girl in the same Internet cafe *more than once*. 我曾数次在那同一家网吧里见过这女孩儿。

mount guard over ⇨ **keep guard over**

move about/around/round *v.* (cause to)move or go from one place to another 运动;到处走动;搬家;移动: Sometimes molecules *move about* very fast. 有时分子运动得很快。It's love that makes the world *move round*! We all need love. 是爱使这个世界运转! 我们都需要爱。I can hear someone *moving about* upstairs. 我听到有人在楼上走动。Stay where you are. Don't *move around*! 待在原处,不要到处走动! We'll be *moving around* a lot, and you may be unable to reach us. 我们经常搬家,因此你可能找不到我们。Why do you *move* the table *around* again? 你为什么又移动那张桌子?

NOTE move about/around 主要用于英国英语中。

move along *vi.* (常用于祈使句中) leave a place and move farther in the direction indicated when a police officer or someone in authority tells you to (沿着所指示的方向)往前走: The police were telling us to *move along*. 警察让我们往前走。"*Move along*," said the usher, "You may go as far as the barrier."引座员说:"您往前走,一直走到栏杆处。"

—*vt.*【可分性动词短语】(of a police officer or someone in authority) tell (someone) to move away from a place and go somewhere else 让(某人)离开(某一地点): The police were *moving* us *along* and not allowing us to stand there watching. 警察让我们走开,不要站在那里观瞧。A guy in a uniform was *moving* some kids *along*. 一个身穿制服的人正在让一些孩子离开。

—*vt.* &*vi.* (cause to) progress or develop (使)进展,发展: The general manager told us that things keep *moving along* in an upward direction for his company since last June. 总经理告诉我们说,从去年六月份起他的公司一直在蓬勃向上地发展着。It's up to the committee to *move* the process *along*. 该由委员会负责推动进程的发展。

NOTE 当本短语用作及物性动词短语,所带的宾语为代词时,该代词须置于本短语的动词和副词中间。

move forward *vt.* &*vi.* (cause to) go

ahead or in front (使)向前移动: Finally the long line of people waiting to buy tickets began to *move forward*. 等候买票的长队终于向前移动了。We shall have to *move* some more of our men *forward* if the enemy keeps attacking. 如果敌人继续发动进攻,我们得派更多的士兵到前沿阵地去。Please *move* the chair *forward*. 请把椅子往前移动一下。—*vi*. advance; improve 进步,改进: More and more newly independent nations are *moving forward* into a better life. 越来越多的新独立的国家正在向着更美好的生活迈进。

move in *v*. ❶(cause to) live in (a new or different house or flat)(使)搬入(新居): We have bought our new house, but we can't *move in* till the end of the next month. 我们已买了新房,但要到下月底才能搬进去。If the house stands empty for too long, the council will *move* a homeless family *in*. 如果这所房子空闲的时间过长,委员会就将让一个无房户搬进来。❷(cause to) take control or attack (使)控制,进攻: The US special forces had located the Al-Qaeda leader in a mountainous area near the Afghanistan border, and they were waiting for orders to *move in*. 美国特种部队已在阿富汗边境附近的山区锁定了"基地"组织领导人,并在等待进攻的命令。When is the best time to *move* the troops *in* to catch the terrorist group leader? 什么时候是部队进攻捉住这个恐怖组织头目的最佳时间?

NOTE 1. 当本短语作"(使)搬入(新居)"解时,反义短语是 move out。

2. 本短语可转化为复合词 move-in,意为"移入,搬入"。

move in on *vt*.【不可分性动词短语】❶(非正式用语) try to control (something that someone else controlled before), often illegally (常指非法地)控制: Criminals have been *moving in on* the city's taxi business for some years. 这些年来,该市出租汽车的生意一直由一些犯罪分子控制着。❷get closer to (a person or place), especially to arrest or attack them 向(某人或某处)逼近: The police are beginning to *move in on* their principal suspects. 警察开始向数名主要嫌犯逼近。Government troops are *moving in on* the rebel stronghold. 政府军向叛军据点逼近。

move on *vt*. &*vi*. (cause to) leave one place where you have been staying or waiting and go or travel to another (使)走开,离开: They'll stay for only a few days before *moving on*. 他们只住几天就离开。Don't halt here. *Move on*, *move on*! 不要停在这里。往前走,往前走! I've been in New York long enough — it's time to *move on*. 我在纽约住的时间够长的了,该搬走了。The drunk was annoying people, so the policeman *moved* him *on*. 那个醉汉令人们讨厌,于是警察便把他赶走了。

—*vi*. (常与 to 连用) stop discussing or doing (something) and begin discussing or doing (something different)改变话题;改做别事: Let's *move on* to your next proposal. 让我们来讨论你的下一个建议吧。We talked about the plans for a while and then *moved on* to another house. 我们把一些计划讨论了一会儿后就到另一家去了。He wrote popular songs in the

M

1980s but *moved on* to become a producer of musicals in the 1990s. 他在20世纪80年代写流行歌曲，但在90年代却改做音乐剧制作人了。

NOTE 当本短语用作及物性动词短语，所带的宾语为代词时，该代词须置于本短语的动词和副词中间。

move out *v.* （常与 of 连用）❶ leave a place; begin to depart 撤离，撤出：The protestors started to *move out* of the area about midnight. 抗议者在半夜时分开始撤离该区域。The International Committee of the Red Cross *moved* most of its international staff *out* of Iraq following the October 27 bomb attack on its Baghdad headquarters. 国际红十字会在10月27日其驻巴格达总部遭炸弹袭击后就将其大部分工作人员撤出了伊拉克。❷ (cause to) leave the house or flat where you live （使）搬出，搬走：We *moved out* because we were unhappy here. 我们搬走是因为我们在这里住得不开心。No sooner had our family *moved out* of the house than all the windows of it were broken. 我们家刚刚从那房子里搬出来，房子的所有玻璃就被打碎了。You will be *moved out* by force if you don't pay the rent. 如果你不交房租的话，就会被强行搬出去。

NOTE 1. 当本短语作"撤离，撤出"解时，主语通常为数量众多的人或物。

2. 本短语的反义短语是 move in。

move up *vi.* （英国英语用法，非正式用语）change your position to make space for someone or something （为腾出地方而）挪动位置：Could you *move up* a bit, please? You're taking up all the space. 请你们让出点地方，好吗？你们把整个地方都占了。

—*vt.* & *vi.* (cause to) move to a better position or to a better job; go to a higher level, etc. （使）提升，提高：We are ready to *move* you *up*. You have been doing quite well. 我们准备提拔你。你干得一直非常出色。He's been *moved up* to the position of manager. 他被提升到了经理的位置。Interest rates are beginning to *move up*. 利率开始提高了。

NOTE 1. 当本短语用作及物性动词短语，所带的宾语为代词时，该代词须置于本短语的动词和副词中间。

2. 当本短语作"挪动位置"解时，在英国英语中还可用 move along 和 move over 的形式。例如：

> If you *move along/over* a bit, Mary can sit next to me.
> 如果你稍挪动一下位置，玛丽就能挨着我坐了。

much ado about nothing *n.* （常用于动词 be, make 之后）a lot of trouble and excitement over something that was really not serious or important 无事自扰，小题大做：As a matter of fact, that was *much ado about nothing*. 其实这完全是庸人自扰。When it comes to my business my mother always makes *much ado about nothing*. 一谈到我的事时，我妈总是小题大做。

NOTE 本短语出自莎士比亚一部著名戏剧的名字：*Much Ado about Nothing*（《无事生非》，又译为《小题大做》）。

much as *conj.* although 虽然，尽管：*Much as* I like him, I wouldn't like to be married to him. 虽然我很喜欢他，但我并不愿意嫁给他。*Much as* I would like to stay here, I really must go home. 虽然我

很愿意住在这里，但我真的必须回家。*Much as* I want to, I can't come. 尽管我很想来，可我又来不了。

NOTE 1. 由本短语引出的从句通常置于主句之前。

2. 不要将本短语与 as much 混淆。

3. 本短语与 as much as(第一个义项)意义和用法相同，两者可互换使用。

much less *conj*. (正式用语)let alone; and even less so (to); and certainly not 更不用说，何况，肯定不：I never think of it, *much less* say it. 我想都没想到它，更不用说讲到它。Happiness is an emotion not often spoken of at the magazine, *much less* experienced. 幸福不是经常在杂志上提到的感情，更不用说是能够时常体验得到的。They are short of water to drink, *much less* to bathe in. 他们连喝的水都不够，更谈不上有水洗澡了。I am no-one's spokesman, *much less* his. 我不是任何人的代言人，更不是他的。

NOTE 1. 本短语常用于否定句之后，其后所接的结构要与前面的一致。

2. 本短语的同义短语是 even less, still less 和 let alone。

much of a *adj*. ❶(非正式用语，一般用于否定句中)(of someone or something) being a very good example of something 够好的，够得上的：He is very good at football, but he is not *much of a* swimmer. 他足球踢得很好，但游泳却不好。He'd never take part in a fight; he's too *much of a* coward for that. 他从不参与打架，在这点上他确实够得上是个胆小鬼。❷very similar to each other 相同的，相近的：He and his brother are *much of a* size. 他和他的弟弟身材近乎相同。We found it hard to choose a carpet; they were all *much of a* muchness. 我们发觉要挑选一块地毯很难：它们全都差不多。

much of a muchness *adj*. (英国英语用法，非正式用语，用作表语)(of two or more things) very similar or not different from one another, in standard, quality, etc. (在标准、质量等方面)十分相同的，大同小异的：Pop music these days is all *much of a muchness* as far as I'm concerned. 依我看来，当今的流行音乐都大同小异。I don't know which car to buy—they are all *much of a muchness*. 我不知道要买哪辆车——它们都没什么两样。

much too *adv*. (用于修饰形容词、副词或其比较级形式，以加强语气) used for emphasizing that there is a lot more of a particular quality than you want or than is right 太，过于：The system is *much too* complicated. 这套系统太复杂。You're driving *much too* fast. 你的车开得太快啦。I'm very much afraid that you have given *much too* little care to you work. 我很担心，你工作太不细心了。

N n

name after【可分性动词短语】give (something or someone) the same name as (something or someone else), especially as an honor 以……的名字命名或取名: Champagne, a drink used in celebrations, is *named after* the Champagne region of France. 常常用于庆祝场合的香槟酒是以法国的香槟地区而命名的。Valentine's Day was *named after* Valentine who was a priest in the third century Rome. 瓦伦丁节(即情人节)是以公元 3 世纪一名罗马牧师瓦伦丁的名字命名的。She *named* her baby girl *after* her grandmother. 她用祖母的名字来给自己的小女儿取名。

near and far ⇨ **far and near**

needless to say *adv.* (used for saying that something is already known or understood) of course; obviously; as was to be expressed 当然;明显地: We have, *needless to say*, turned the matter over pretty carefully. 我们当然已仔细地盘算过这桩事。*Needless to say*, it rained when I left my windows open. 很明显,在我走后把窗户都开着期间下过雨。

neither here nor there *adj.* (非正式用语,用作表语) (used for saying that something is not important because it is not relevant) irrelevant; off the subject; not important 不相关的,无关紧要的: What you have just said is *neither here nor there*. Try to keep to the topic. 你刚才所讲的与主题无关,要紧扣主题。Whether they go or not is *neither here nor there* as far as I'm concerned. 对我来说,他们去不去无关紧要。

NOTE 不要将本短语误用为 * neither there nor here 或 * either here or there。

neither … nor … *conj.* (used for showing that something is not true of two or more people, things, actions, qualities, or ideas) not … and not 两者都不……,既不……也不: *Neither* the teachers *nor* the headmaster knows anything about it. 老师们和校长都不知此事。*Neither* you *nor* I nor anybody else knows the answer. 无论你和我,或其他任何人都不知道这个答案。I *neither* know *nor* care what happened to her. 我不知道也不关心她出了什么事。She came at just the right time, *neither* too early *nor* too late. 她来得正好,既不太早,也不过晚。

NOTE 1. 本短语可连接主语、谓语、宾语、表语和状语等结构。连接的部分可有多种成分,如名词、代词、动词、形容词、副词、介词(短语)、动名词(短语)等。

2. 本短语所连接的两个部分结构必须是平行一致的。

3. 当本短语连接的两个并列主语单复数形式不同时,要根据邻近一致的原则,谓语动词的形式与最靠近的主语(即 nor 后的名词或代词)保持一致。但当本短语连接的两个主语都是单数名词时，在英国英语中，谓语动词的形式则既可用单数形式也可用复数形式，用复数动词形式则是非正式用法。例如：

> *Neither* the TV *nor* the video actually works/work.
> 电视录像带都不能用。

4. 本短语中的 neither 后可以接用不止一个 nor。例如：

> *Neither* rain, *nor* snow, nor sleet can stop the milkman.
> 雨、雪、冰雹都不能阻挡送奶员送奶。

5. 本短语表示全部否定，与本短语意义相反的短语是 both … and …。见 both … and …。

never mind Ⅰ *s.*（用于口语中，用祈使句形式）(used for telling someone not to feel upset about something) it does not matter; don't trouble yourself（用于劝慰别人）不要紧，没有关系："We've missed the show!" "*Never mind*, we can go next week."“我们错过了看这次的演出。”“不要紧，我们可以下星期去看。” *Never mind*, next time I'm sure you can do better. 没有关系，我相信你下次一定能做得好些。

Ⅱ *vt.*（用于祈使句中）(used for emphasizing that something is less important) do not worry about or pay attention to (someone or something) 不必担心，别介意（某人或某事）：*Never mind* them, you look after yourself. 不必担心他们，你管好自己。Do what your doctor advices you; *never mind* what other people say. 你就按医嘱去做，不要介意别人说什么。*Never mind* that we didn't sell anything; we got lots of publicity. 我们不必理会没卖出去多少东西，我们毕竟做了许多宣传。

news conference *n.* a meeting or an interview held for news reporters by a political figure or famous person 记者招待会，新闻发布会：Some security personnel waving rifles burst into the *news conference* and told the 30 or so journalists to turn off their cameras. 一些保安人员挥舞着枪支闯入新闻发布会现场，让大约30个记者关掉摄像机。The following is a partial *news conference* transcript. 下面是新闻发布会文稿的一部分。

NOTE **1.** 当表示“在记者招待会或新闻发布会上”时，news conference 前可用介词 at 或 in。

2. 本短语与 press conference 意义和用法相同，两者可互换使用。

next to Ⅰ *prep.* ❶ beside or very near to (someone or something) 挨着，接近：We were informed that an additional explosive device was placed in the post office *next to* the hospital. 有人通知我们说，还有一爆炸装置被安放在了邻近医院的那家邮局里。❷ following in order, degree, importance, etc. after (something or someone) 仅次于：*Next to* the Changjiang River, the Huanghe River is the second longest river in China. 在中国，黄河是仅次于长江的第二大河流。*Next to* skiing, I like swimming best. 除滑雪外，我最喜欢游泳。*Next to* John, Jamie is my best friend. 杰米，仅次于约翰，是我最好的朋友。

Ⅱ *adv.*（用于表示否定意义的词语前）almost but not completely; nearly 几乎，差不多：Even if we practice all week, it will be *next to* impossible to win. 尽管我们一个星期都在练习，但几乎没有取胜的可能。A modern refinery is *next to* noiseless. 一个现代化的精炼厂几乎是没噪声的。It was *next to* unthinkable that the boy would steal. 那孩子竟会偷东西,这几乎是不可想象的事。

nibble at/on *vt.*【不可分性动词短语】❶(of someone) eat (something) slowly by taking a lot of small bites (指人)小口地咬吃(食物):Tom was *nibbling at* a chocolate biscuit. 汤姆在小口地啃着一块巧克力饼干。The baby is *nibbling on* a bit of bread. 婴儿在咬着一小块面包。❷(of a mouse or other small animals) take small bites out of (something) quickly and repeatedly (指老鼠或其他小动物)反复地小口啃咬(某物): Mice have been *nibbling at* the doorpost again. 老鼠又在咬门柱了。You can see this kind of tiny "doctor fish" *nibbling at* the dead skin of the customers' feet in the water. 你可以看到这种小小的"鱼医生"在水中慢慢啃掉足疗者脚上的死皮。

nibble away at *vt.*【不可分性动词短语】❶eat at (something) in tiny bits; erode away (tiny bits of something)小口地咬吃;侵蚀:The mouse *nibbled away at* the huge cheese on the table. 那只老鼠在咬吃桌子上的大奶酪。The sea waves *nibble away at* the base of the cliff year after year. 海浪年复一年地侵蚀着崖基。❷reduce (the total amount of something) by gradually using small amounts of it 一点点地耗减(某物的总量): Beware of hidden costs that can *nibble away at* your family income. 注意隐性花费,它会逐渐耗掉你的家庭收入。

night and day ⇨ **day and night**

no doubt *adv.* ❶ undoubtedly; without question 必定,无疑地: These agreements will *no doubt* have a significant impact on our relationship. 这些协议对我们的关系必定产生重要影响。*No doubt* you have already heard about the terrible forest fire we just had. 你们肯定已经听说了我们刚刚经历过的那场可怕的森林大火。❷probably; most likely 可能,很可能:*No doubt* you've heard the news about Mother. 你可能听到妈妈的消息了。You're tired, *no doubt*. Let me do it for you. 你可能累了。我来替你干吧。

NOTE 当本短语作"必定,无疑地"解时,与 without doubt 意义相近,用法相同,但本短语不及 without doubt 的语气强烈。

no end *adv.* ❶(非正式用语) very much 非常,极其: Her English has improved *no end*. 她的英语提高了很多。That beef and pickles was *no end* good. 那牛肉和腌菜太好吃了。Your latest book amused me *no end*. 你最近这本书我觉得非常有趣。❷on and on for a long time; endlessly 长时间不停地,没完没了地:The child cried *no end*. 这孩子不停地哭。

no end of *adj.* (非正式用语,用作定语) a lot of (problems, trouble, worry, etc.); very great deal of (something) 很多的(问题、麻烦、烦恼等),大量的: We've had *no end of* problems with this washing machine. 这台洗衣机给我们带来的问题不断。This will cause *no end of* trouble. 这会引起很多麻烦。It caused me *no end of* worry. 这给我造成了无穷的烦恼。There are *no end of* books in this house. 这房子里有大量的藏书。

NOTE 本短语一般用来修饰物,但有时也可用来修饰人。例如:

> He has *no end of* handsome dining rooms, tables and tableware, and *no end of* cooks and waiters.
> 他拥有很多漂亮的餐室、餐桌和餐具,还有众多的厨师和侍者。

no good *adj*. (非正式用语) ❶not useful; worthless 没有用的,没有价值的: It is considered *no good* reciting without understanding. 只会背而不理解被认为是没有用的。All his riches are of *no good* to him if he is so ill. 如果他身体这么糟,那么他的所有财富对他毫无用处。A car is *no good* to me, I can't drive. 汽车对我来说没什么用,我不会开车。❷of a low standard or level of ability; bad 水准或水平低的,能力差的;不好的: My son was *no good* at chemistry. 我儿子的化学曾经很差。The pictures I took in the park were *no good*. 我在公园里照的照片都不好。Stay away from Bob—he's *no good*. 离鲍勃远点儿,他很坏。

NOTE 1. 本短语中的 no good 还有"不合适,不方便"之意。例如:

> Monday is *no good*—I'm busy.
> 星期一不合适,我忙。

2. 本短语另外的表达形式是 not much good 和 not any good。

no longer *adv*. (used when something happened or was true in the past but is not true now) formerly but not now; not any more 已不,不再: He is *no longer* what he used to be. 他已不再是从前的他。*No longer* is television just a laboratory marvel. 电视已不再仅仅是实验室的奇迹了。*No longer* does Tom live here. 汤姆不再住这里了。

NOTE 1. 本短语可置于句中、句首或句尾。当其用于句首时,句中的主谓一定要构成倒装结构。

2. 本短语的另外一种表达形式是 not any longer。

3. 本短语与 no more(第一个义项)意义和用法相同,两者可互换使用。

no matter *conj*. (used for saying that something is not important or will not have an effect) however, whatever, … the conditions are 无论: *No matter* how the invaders come, they will be wiped out clean. 无论侵略者怎样来,他们必将被消灭得一干二净。He can't buy everything, *no matter* how rich he is. 不管他怎么富有,他也不能把所有东西都买下来。Don't trust him, *no matter* what he says. 无论他说什么,都别相信他。*No matter* when you come, you'll always be welcome. 无论你什么时候来,都欢迎你。*No matter* where I am, I'm always thinking of you. 无论我到哪里,我总会想着你的。*No matter* whether it will rain or not, we have decided to leave at six in the morning. 不管是否下雨,我们都已决定于清晨 6 点出发。Don't believe in rumors *no matter* who says them. 谣言不管是谁说的,都不要相信。

NOTE 1. 当 no matter 位于句尾时,其后某些与主句相同的部分往往省略。例如:

> Anyone can point out our shortcomings in our work, *no matter* who.
> 不管是什么人,谁都可以指出我们工作中的缺点。

2. 本短语后一般与 how、what、where 等疑问词连用,表达"无论怎样""无论什么""无论哪里"等意思。

3. 有时,在 no matter what 引出的从句中省略谓语动词。例如:

> *No matter what* the provocation (is), she would be calm.
> 无论受到什么样的挑衅,她都会镇定自若。

no more *adv*. ❶(used for saying that the future will be different from the past

N

because something has stopped happening) no longer; never again 不再：Time lost will return *no more*. 时光一去不复返。I fear I shall see my grandfather *no more*. 恐怕我永远不能再见到我的祖父了。*No more* will prisoners have to suffer the misery of being locked in their cells for 23 hours a day. 囚犯将不再遭受一天23小时都被锁在牢房中之苦。❷neither 也不，也没有：She can't afford a car, and *no more* can I. 她买不起汽车，我也如此。Glass cannot conduct electricity, *no more* can rubber. 玻璃不能导电，橡胶也不能导电。

NOTE 1. 本短语只可用于句首或句尾，不可置于句中。这样的说法是错误的：* Tom *no more* lives here. 而应说：Tom lives here *no more*. 或 *No more* does Tom live here.

2. 如本短语置于句首，句中的主谓结构要构成倒装。

3. 当本短语作"不再"解时，同义短语是 no longer 和 not any more。

no more than *adv.* (used for saying that a particular situation or result seems suitable or normal) only 只不过，仅有：I'm glad he was put into prison, it's *no more than* he deserved. 他进了监狱我很高兴，这只不过是他罪有应得。Computers do *no more than* you tell them to do. 计算机只能做你指令它们去做的事情。

NOTE 1. 本短语与 not more than 意义和用法基本相同。但本短语比 not more than 常用，两者的侧重点也不完全一样。no more than 等于 only，而 not more than 则等于 probably less than。试比较：

> *No more than* five people applied for the job.
> 仅有五人申请了这份工作。
>
> There were *not more than* fifty people at the meeting.
> 大概不到50人与会。

2. 不要将本短语与 no more ... than 混淆。

no more ... than *conj.* (used to emphasize that someone or something does not have a particular quality or would not do something) in no greater degree ... than 与……一样都不：He is *no more* a god *than* we are. 他和我们一样都不是神。He's *no more* able to read French *than* I am. 他和我一样都看不懂法文。The whole atom is *no more* positive *than* it is negative. 整个原子不带正电，也不带负电。

no news is good news *s.* (用于口语中) having no information means that bad developments are unlikely 没有消息就是好消息：I haven't heard from them for over a month, but I suppose *no news is good news*. 我已有一个多月没听到他们的消息了。但是，我想没有消息就是好消息。

no other than ⇨ **none other than**

no problem *s.* (用于口语中) ❶(used to show that you are happy to help someone) there's no difficulty about this 没问题：Of course I can change the tire for you. *No problem*. 我当然会为你换车胎。没问题。"Can I pay by credit card?" "Yes, *no problem*.""我可以用信用卡付账吗？""可以，没问题。"❷(used after someone has thanked you) you're welcome; don't mention it 不用谢，别客气，没什么："Thanks for the ride, Dad." "*No problem*!" "谢谢您用车送我，爸爸。""没什么！"

no question of ⇨ **out of the question**

no sooner … than *conj.* (used for saying that something happens immediately after something else) as soon as; when … at once 一……就……,刚一……就: She was *no sooner* graduated *than* she was on her way to London. 她一毕业就去了伦敦。We had *no sooner* reached the railway station *than* the train left. 我们刚到火车站,列车就开了。

NOTE 1. 本短语所连接的是主从结构。这种主从复合句不用现在时或将来时。如主句动作发生在时间状语之前,用过去完成时,从句用一般过去时。但也有主句和从句都用一般过去时的现象(如第一个例句)。

2. 如果 no sooner 位于句首,其后的主谓要采用倒装语序。

3. 本短语中的 no sooner 不可与 when 相连用。这一点一定要与 barely … when, hardly … when 和 scarcely … when 相区别,不可混淆。

4. 本短语与 as soon as 意义相同,都表示"一……就",在句中起连接作用。作为固定搭配的短语,as soon as 这三个单词必须连用,而 no sooner … than 这三个词则不能连用。如连写,则表示"不早于(某一时间)"之意。另外,两者的用法亦有不同。见 as soon as。

no thanks to *prep.* (用于口语中) without the benefit of help from 并非由于: We've finished the task, *no thanks to* Robert, who suddenly decided to leave for his holiday! 罗伯特突然决定离去度假! 没有他的帮助,我们也完成了任务。It's *no thanks to* you that I arrived on time. 没有你,我也准时到达了。We finally found your house, *no thanks to* the confusing map you drew. 我们没有用上你画的那张混乱不清的地图,最终还是找到了你的家。

NOTE 本短语是 thanks to 的否定形式,见 thanks to。

no way *adv.* (非正式用语) ❶ (used for saying that you will definitely not do something or that something will definitely not happen) certainly not; never (用来表示拒绝或否定)不,不会: "Are you inviting Paul to your party?" "*No way*!" "你邀请保罗参加聚会吗?""不!" *No way* am I going to refuse an offer like that! 那样的提议我是不会拒绝的。❷ something that you say when someone says something that is very surprising (用来表示对某一令人惊奇之事难以置信)不会吧: "Hey, I saw Mary out with Andrew last night." "*No way*!" "嘿,我看到玛丽昨晚和安德鲁一起出去了。""不会吧。"❸ not possibly (用来表示拒绝或否定)不可能: Now he's asking me to lend him my car. *No way*! 现在他求我借给他车,没门儿!

NOTE 1. 本短语在第三个义项中常以 there's no way 的形式出现。例如:

> *There's no way* I could have paid for it.
> 我绝不可能花钱买它。

2. 本短语可转化成复合词 noway,意为"一点也不,决不"。

no wonder (that) *adj.* (主要用于口语中) (used to say that you are not surprised by a particular situation or event) not surprising (that) 不足为奇,怪不得: He resigned, and (it's) *no wonder*. 他辞职了,此事不足为奇。The book is very interesting. *No wonder* (*that*) the children like it very much. 这本书很有趣,怪不得孩子们都很喜欢看它。It's *no wonder* the children are bored. 怪不得孩子们都感到无聊了。*No*

N

wonder that he decided to take no part in the debate. 难怪他决定不参与辩论了。

NOTE **1.** 本短语的 no 可被 little, small 替换,构成的短语与本短语意义和用法相同。

2. 本短语的反义短语是 it's a wonder。

none but *adv.* (正式用语,后常接人)only 只有: *None but* a wise man can employ leisure well. 唯智者善于利用闲暇时间。*None but* a coward dares to boast that he has never known fear. 只有胆小鬼才敢吹嘘说他从来不知道什么是害怕。*None but* fools have ever believed it. 只有傻瓜才相信那事。*None but* the best ingredients are used in our products. 我们的产品只用最好的配料。

NOTE **1.** 本短语和 no one but 意义相近,但本短语用于实义结构,而 no one but 用于虚拟结构。例如:

> *None but* a fool is always right.
> 只有傻瓜才是一贯正确。
> *No one but* a fool would be always right.
> 除了傻瓜也许没有人是一贯正确的。

2. 当"本短语+单数名词"作主语时,谓语动词用单数形式。例如:

> *None but* him knows this plant.
> 只有他认识这植物。

但是,当"本短语+复数名词"作主语时,谓语动词则用复数形式。例如:

> *None but* his most loyal supporters believe his story.
> 只有他最忠实的支持者们才相信他的话。

none of *adj.* not one of (a group of people or things); not any (在一些人或物中)没有一个: *None of* my friends ever comes/come to see me. 我的朋友中没有一个来看过我。He told me all the news but *none of* it was exciting. 全部消息他都告诉了我,但没有一条令人兴奋的。

NOTE **1.** 作为形容词性短语,本短语既可修饰可数名词,又可修饰不可数名词。需要注意的是:

(1)当"本短语+复数名词或代词"作主语时,谓语动词既可用单数形式也可用复数形式。例如:

> *None of* the trains is/are going to London.
> 没有一趟列车是开往伦敦的。(复数名词)
> We have three sons but *none of* them lives/live nearby.
> 我们有三个儿子,但没有一个住在跟前。(复数代词)
> *None of* her family has/have been to college.
> 他们家没有一个人上过大学。(群体名词的单数形式)

在英国英语的正式文体中,则都用单数形式。

(2)当"本短语+不可数名词"作主语时,谓语动词用单数形式。例如:

> *None of* the work was/has been done.
> 一点儿工作也没干。

2. 在 none 的前面,不能再使用否定词,不能说 * I didn't want none of them. 而应改为: I want none of them. 或 I didn't want any of them.

none of one's business ⇨ **have no business**

none other than *conj.* (used for expressing surprise that a particular person or thing has done something or is connected with something) the very same person as; no one else (but)(不是别人或他物)正是,

恰恰是：The thief was *none other than* the host himself. 偷东西的不是别人，正是房主人自己。The biggest surprise was that the false report was written by *none other than* the company's personnel department. 最令人吃惊的是，这份虚假报告恰恰出自公司的人事部。He was talking to *none other than* the schoolmaster himself. 与他说话的竟是校长本人。

NOTE 本短语的另外一种表达形式是 no other than，但本短语更常用。

none the less *adv.*（英国英语用法，正式用语）despite what has just been said; nevertheless; but all the same 尽管如此，仍然，还是：I can't swim. *None the less*, I'll try to cross the river. 我不会游泳，尽管如此我还是要试着渡过河去。It's a difficult race. *None the less*, about 1,000 runners participate every year. 这是一项很难跑的比赛，但每年还是有大约1 000名参赛者。For all his years, he's *none the less* vigorous and active. 这么多年来他依然精力旺盛，生气勃勃。

NOTE 本短语可缩合成副词 nonetheless，与本短语的意义和用法大致相同。另一同义词 nevertheless 比 nonetheless 常用。

none too *adv.*（正式用语，用于形容词或副词之前）not very; not at all 不太，一点也不：Other tobacco companies are clearly *none too* keen on the suit; for them, nicotine remains what they call a harmless flavor enhancement. 很显然，其他烟草公司对那起诉讼案并不太感兴趣。对他们来说，尼古丁仍然是他们所称的无害的提味剂。The service in this restaurant is *none too* fast and the food is none too good, either. 这家餐馆中的服务不太快捷，饭菜也不太好。He did *none too* well. 他干得一点儿也不好。

NOTE 本短语的另外一种表达形式是 not too。例如：

> I'm afraid this secretary is *not too* smart.
> 恐怕这个秘书不太精明。

not a bit *adv.* not at all; not in any way 一点儿也不：I'm *not a bit* hungry tonight. 我今晚一点儿也不饿。I don't want any mashed potatoes. *Not a bit*! 我不想要土豆泥。一点儿也不要！

NOTE 虽然 a bit 和 a little 两个短语的意义和用法基本相同，但两者前加否定词 not 时，它们的意义则大不相同：not a bit 意为“一点也不”，而 not a little 意为“十分，非常，相当”。例如：

> He is *not a bit* tired. (=He is not tired at all.)
> 他一点也不累。
> He is *not a little* tired. (=He is very tired.)
> 他非常累。

not a little ⇨ **not a bit**

not any good ⇨ **no good**

not any longer ⇨ **not any more**

not any more *adv.* (used for saying that a situation has ended or someone has stopped doing something) formerly but not at the present time 已不，不再：The Whites do*n't* live here *any more*. 怀特一家已不住这里了。I used to smoke 20 cigarettes a day, but *not any more*! 我以前每天吸 20 支烟，但现在再也不那么吸了！

NOTE 本短语的另外一种表达形式是 not any longer。

not at all Ⅰ *adv.* (used for emphasizing a negative statement) not any; none; not in the least (用于强调否定语句)一点儿也不,决不: My parents were *not at all* satisfied with my exam results. 我父母对我的考试成绩一点儿都不满意。He is *not at all* stupid.. 他一点儿也不傻。Some diseases are *not at all* dangerous if treated in time. 如能得到及时的治疗,有些疾病绝无危险。

Ⅱ *s.* (used as a polite reply when someone has thanked you for something) it was nothing; it is not important, etc. (用于回答致谢的语句)没什么,不用谢: "Thanks for having come to our evening party." "*Not at all*. I enjoyed it." "感谢你光临了我们的晚会。""不必客气。我很开心。""Thank you for all your help." "*Not at all*." "感谢你所有的帮助。""不用谢。"

NOTE 当本短语作"一点也不,决不"解时,同义短语是 by no means, in no way 和 not in the least。

not by any manner of means *adv.* (英国英语用法,正式用语)(used as a way of emphasizing a negative statement) not at all; not in any way 决不,一点儿也不:I have *not* given up hope *by any manner of means*. 我绝没有放弃希望。I haven't lost my interest in politics by any manner of means. 我对政治一点儿也没有失去兴趣。I'm not satisfied with his excuse—*not by any manner of means*! 我不满意他说的理由—— 一点儿也不!

NOTE 1. 本短语中的名词 means 必须用复数形式。

2. 本短语的同义短语有 by no means, by no manner of means, in no way, not at all, not by any means, not in the least。它们常可互换使用。

not by any means ⇨ by no means

not in the mood *adj.* (后常接介词 for 或动词不定式短语) not feeling like doing something at all 没有情绪(做某事):She says she feels bad and is *not in the mood* for doing anything. 她说她心情不好,没有情绪做任何事情。I am *not in the mood* to listen to pop music now. 我现在没有情绪听流行音乐。

NOTE 本短语的同义短语是 in no mood,两者可互换使用。

not more than ⇨ no more than

not much good ⇨ no good

not necessarily *adv.* not in a way that must be so 不一定如此: It's financial contribution to the United Nations does *not necessarily* ensure that the country will take a permanent seat on the UN Security Council. 一个国家对联合国在财政上所做出的贡献不一定保证它就能成为联合国安理会的常任理事国。There are lots of students, *not necessarily* organized by their schools, visiting the Chairman Mao's Memorial Hall in Beijing to show their respect to the great leader. 许许多多的学生,不一定是由学校组织,来到北京毛主席纪念堂表达他们对伟大领袖的敬爱。"He was lying, and we're trapped." "*Not necessarily*." "他在撒谎。我们入了圈套。""不一定。"

not on any account *adv.* (正式用语) absolutely not; under no circumstances 决不,无论如何也不:A doctor should *not on any account* accept bribes from drug companies. 医生决不应该收受医药公司的贿赂。Will I say I'm sorry? *Not on any account*. 由我来道歉? 没门儿!

NOTE 本短语的同义短语是 on no account

和 under/in no circumstances。

not on speaking terms *adj.* (常与 with 连用) (of two people) very angry with each other and not talking to each other (指两人因彼此怄气而相互)不讲话: Jim and Tom are *not on speaking terms* now after a quarrel last month. What can we do to bring about a reconciliation? 吉姆和汤姆自从上个月吵架后现在还不讲话。我们怎么才能让他们和解呢? We have heard from various people that the coach is *not on speaking terms* with his best player. 我们从不同的人口中听说,教练与他的最佳运动员彼此怄气而相互不讲话。

NOTE 1. 本短语中的名词 term 必须用复数形式。

2. 本短语与 on speaking terms 的否定形式所表达的意义并不完全相同。见 on speaking terms。

not only … but (also) *conj.* (used for emphasizing that, although something is true, something else is also true or is more important) not merely … but likewise 不但……而且: Mr Li is *not only* a foreign minister *but also* a poet. 李先生不仅是一位外交部长,而且还是个诗人。She is *not only* beautiful *but also* clever. 她不但长得漂亮而且还很聪明。*Not only* the children *but also* their father is coming tomorrow. 明天要来的不仅仅有那几个孩子,还有他们的爸爸。

NOTE 1. 本短语连接句中的两个部分必须是对等的句子成分。不能这样用: * Last night, Jim *not only* read the assignment *but also* many poems. (第一部分连接的是动词,而第二部分连接的却是名词。)应改为: Last night, Jim read *not only* the assignment *but also* many poems.

2. 由本短语连接的复合主语,其谓语动词的单复数形式要根据毗邻一致的原则,与最近的主语的数相一致。例如:

> *Not only* my father, *but also* all of us, are looking forward to seeing you.
> 不仅我爸爸,我们所有的人都盼望着见到您。

3. 当 not only 用于句首表示强调时,句中的主谓结构要构成倒装。例如:

> *Not only* did we enjoy the film, *but* we *also* had a wonderful time.
> 我们不仅看了电影,还度过了一段美好的时光。

4. 本短语与 as well as 意义相同,用法相近。两者之间的区别见 as well as。

not that I know of ⇨ **know about/of**

not to mention *conj.* (used for adding a comment that emphasizes the main idea of what you have already said or explained) and also (something or someone else) (用于强调所述内容)此外,还: The weather here is wonderful, *not to mention* the good food. 这里的气候很好,此外东西也好吃。He is handsome and smart, *not to mention* being a good athlete. 他英俊又聪明,还是个优秀的运动员。They don't have any of the players from that championship team, *not to mention* its coach. 他们没有一个那支冠军队的球员,更不用说该队教练了。

NOTE 本短语的同义短语是 let alone, not to speak of 和 to say nothing of。

not to speak of *prep.* (正式用语) (used for adding extra information to what you have just said) in addition to; besides; without ever needing to say about 此外,

除了……以外，更不必说：They have two handsome sons, *not to speak of* their two beautiful daughters. 他们有两个漂亮的儿子，此外还有两个美丽的女儿。Pollution affects the soil, *not to speak of* its impact on wildlife. 污染影响土地，对野生动物的影响就不言而喻了。

not too ⇨ **none too**

note down *vt.*【可分性动词短语】record (something short like a phone number) in writing for future reference 记下，写下：*Note down* her telephone number in case you forget it. 把她的电话号码记下来以防忘记。If you find the names that are on the list that I've given you, *note* them *down*. 如果你在我给你的名单上找到那些名字，就把它们记下来。Please *note down* what I am about to say. 请把我要说的都写下来。

NOTE 1. 当本短语的宾语为代词时，该代词须置于本短语的动词和副词中间。

2. 本短语的同义短语是 put down, take down 和 write down。

N

noted for *adj.* famous or well known for (a particular quality or ability), and usually admired for it 以……而出名的：What is this painter most *noted for*? 这位画家以什么画最为闻名？He is particularly *noted for* his watercolors. 他尤其以他的水色画而闻名。Kuwait used to be *noted for* its rich oil deposits, but now experts predict that the reserve will not last as long as most people would think. 科威特曾以其丰富的石油储量而著称。然而，现在专家们却预言其储量可供开采的年限并非像大多数人所想象的那样长。Our company is *noted for* providing quality services throughout Asia. 我们公司以向整个亚洲提供优质服务而著称。

NOTE 1. 本短语的比较级形式是 more noted for，最高级形式是 most noted for。

2. 本短语的同义短语是 famous for 和 known for。

nothing but *adv.*（用于名词、动词不定式和动名词之前）only; just 只是，只有，只不过：She's been *nothing but* a nuisance; I'll be glad to be free of her. 她是个令人讨厌的人，我会很高兴能摆脱她。*Nothing but* a miracle can save the seriously wounded man. 只有出现奇迹才能挽救那个受重伤的人。We could see *nothing but* fog. 我们所能看到的只有雾。The doctor told him *nothing but* to stop smoking. 医生除了让他戒烟，其他什么都没有说。

NOTE 1. 本短语中的 but 不是连词，而是介词。

2. 本短语后可接用动词不定式，但须要意以下两点：

（1）在“谓语动词 do 的某种形式＋nothing but”的结构后，接不带 to 的动词不定式。例如：

> I can do *nothing but* let him know.
> 我只好告诉他。
> Last night I did *nothing but* watch TV.
> 昨天晚上，我除了看电视别的什么也没有干。

(2)如果谓语动词不是 do，而是“其他动词＋nothing but”的结构，则接带 to 的动词不定式。例如：

> He wanted *nothing but* to stay here for another day.
> 他只是想在这再待一天。

3. 当本短语后接复数名词作主语时，谓语动词常用单数形式。例如：

> *Nothing but* roses delights my eyes.
> 只有玫瑰花悦我之目。

notify of *vt.*【可分性动词短语】(正式用语,常用被动语态形式) give notice to or inform (someone or a body) officially about(something)向(某人或机构)通报,报告:Soon afterwards, they *notified* the World Health Organization *of* the first case of new flu in the country. 他们很快就把国内发生的第一起新型流感病例通报给了世界卫生组织。Have the police been *notified of* your neighbor's death? 你的邻居死亡,警方接到报案了没有?

notorious for ⇨ **infamous for**

now and again ⇨ **now and then**

now and here ⇨ **here and now**

now and then *adv.* sometimes, but not regularly or often; at times; occasionally 偶尔,时常,不时地:*Now and then* we meet each other although we don't live in the same apartment. 尽管我们不住在同一公寓,可我们相互时常见面。She comes to London *now and then*. 她时常来伦敦。I like to visit art galleries *now and then*. 我喜欢不时地去美术馆参观。

NOTE 本短语的同义短语是 at times now and again, every now and then 和 from time to time。它们之间的区别见 at times。

now that *conj.* seeing that; since; because (the thing mentioned is happening or has just happened)既然,因为:*Now that* the exams are over, we can all relax for a while. 既然考试结束了,我们都可以轻松一段时间了。You ought to have a good rest *now that* you've finished the work. 既然你已完成了这项工作,就应该好好地休息一下了。*Now that* prices are rising so fast, all my money is draining away. 由于价格上涨太快,我的钱都快花光了。

NOTE **1.** 由本短语引导的从句,谓语动词一般要用现在时、过去时或完成时,而不用将来时态。

2. 有时,尤其在口语中,本短语中的 that 往往省略,此时的 now 作连词使用。例如:

> *Now* (that) John has arrived, we can begin.
> 既然约翰已到,我们可以开始了。

3. 不要将本短语与 that 引导的宾语从句混淆。

O o

object against *vt.*【不可分性动词短语】(正式用语,常用一般时态,常与 for 或 that 从句连用) be opposed to or express your disapproval to (usually someone) in words (以言辞)反对(常指某人): Some committee members *objected against* Mr Smith for the chairmanship. 有些委员会成员反对史密斯先生担任主席一职。I *object against* him that he is too young and lacks experience for that job. 我反对他做那项工作,因为他太年轻又缺乏经验。

NOTE 本短语与 object to 均表示"反对"之意。但本短语反对的对象通常是人,而后者反对的对象是物或所做之事。

object to *vt.*【不可分性动词短语】be opposed to (something) or to express your dislike or disapproval of (something or something being done) in words (以言辞)反对(某事/物),不赞成(所做之事):I strongly *object to* the plan on the grounds that it is too expensive. 我强烈反对该项计划,理由是其花费太大。He wanted us to go on foot but I *objected to* that. 他想让我们走着去,但我对此表示反对。I strongly *object to* being treated like a prisoner. 我强烈反对被人当作囚犯一样对待。Some readers may *object to* what I wrote about the Iraq war. 一些读者可能会反对我所写的有关伊拉克战争的内容。

NOTE 本短语中的 to 是介词,而不是动词不定式符号,其后只能接名词、代词、动名词短语和名词性从句,不能接原形动词。这样说是错误的: * I strongly *object to* be treated like a child.

obliged to *adj.* (正式用语) ❶(后接代词或名词,常与 for 连用)(used for thanking someone politely) very grateful to (someone) 非常感激(某人): Thank you very much indeed, Doctor, I am extremely *obliged to* you. 真的非常感谢您,医生。我万分感激您。I'm much *obliged to* your friend for telling me how to operate the computer. 我非常感谢你那位朋友告诉我如何使用这台计算机。❷(后接原形动词) forced to do something because it is the law, a rule, expectation, or a duty 被迫(做某事): Employers are legally *obliged to* pay the minimum wage. 雇主或用人单位必须按照法律支付最低工资。I felt *obliged to* leave after such an unpleasant quarrel. 在这样一次不愉快的争吵之后,我觉得必须离开了。

NOTE 本短语中的 to 在第一个义项中是介词,其后不能接原形动词。而在第二个义项中的 to 则是动词不定式符号,其后只能接原形动词。

occupy in/with *vt.*【可分性动词短语】(常用被动语态形式) keep (oneself or someone) busy at (an activity) 忙于(做)某

事,专注于:I have *occupied* myself *in* compiling this dictionary for more than three years. 三年多来,我一直忙于编写这部词典。You need to find something to *occupy* yourself *with* when you retire. 你退休后得找点事情做。Don't interrupt father when he is *occupied with* his work. 当爸爸忙于工作时不要去打扰他。He's still fully *occupied with* writing his new book. 他还在全身心地忙于写他的新书。

occur to *vt.* 【不可分性动词短语】(无被动语态形式,用一般时态,常用于否定句和疑问句中)(of a thought or idea) come to the mind of (someone)(某种想法或主意)浮现在(某人)脑海中,想到: The possibility that she might be wrong never even *occurred to* her. 她从未想到过自己可能会错。It never *occurred to* me that they were playing a trick on me. 我从未想到他们是在和我耍花招。Didn't it *occur to* you that he might be late? 你当时就没有想到他会迟到吗? It didn't *occur to* her to ask how he'd found her. 她没想到问他是怎样找到她的。

NOTE 本短语与 hit on/upon 都有"想起"之意,两者在用法上的区别是:hit on/upon 要以人作主语,而本短语的主语则是某种想法、主意或概念,而不能是人。

odd jobs *n.* small pieces of work of various types, needing to be done as they occur but not providing a steady, continuous pattern of work, often done for other people in their homes (常指为他人在其家中所做的)零活,杂务: Brown works on and off doing *odd jobs*. He has no steady work. 布朗时而做点零活,因为他没有固定的工作。The landlord often gave him some *odd jobs* to do, in the way of small repairs. 房东经常给他找些杂活干,像各种小修理什么的。

NOTE 1. 本短语都以复数形式使用。当本短语用作主语时,谓语动词用复数形式。

2. 本短语可转化为复合词 odd-job,意为"做零活的,干杂务的"。

odds and ends *n.* (非正式用语,多用于英国英语和澳大利亚英语中) a group of small objects of different kinds without much value or importance 各种(不值钱或不重要的)小物件:There were various *odds and ends* lying about on the table. 桌子上放着一些零碎的东西。In the small room he has only a bed and a desk with a drawer full of *odds and ends*. 在这个小房间里,他仅有一张床和一张桌子,桌子的抽屉里装满了零碎东西。

NOTE 1. 本短语中的两个名词都必须用复数形式。当本短语用作主语时,谓语动词用复数形式。

2. 本短语的另外一种表达形式是 odds and sods,是英国俚语。例如:

> I finally found my keys beneath the *odds and sods* in the bottom of my bag.
> 我最终在我提包底部的零碎物件下面找到了钥匙。

of a kind *adj.* (常用作后置定语) ❶ of the same kind 同一类的: Things *of a kind* come together. 物以类聚。They look alike, talk alike, even think alike, they're very much *of a kind*. 他们长得很像,说话很像,连想法都很像,完全是一个类型。❷ (used for saying that something is not as good as it should be) of a not very good sort; of an inferior kind 不大好的: It was advice *of a kind*, but it wasn't very helpful. 这算得上是一个主意,但没什么大用。

NOTE 1. 不要将本短语与 a kind of 混淆。a

kind of 意为“一种”“某种”,后面常接不可数名词或抽象化的单数可数名词。例如:

> He had *a kind of* feeling that she would phone him.
> 他有一种感觉,她会打电话给他。

2. 不要将本短语与 kind of 混淆。kind of 是副词性短语,意为“有点儿,有几分”。

3. 不要将本短语与 of a sort 混淆。of a sort 也是形容词性短语,意为“勉强称得上的;较差的”。

4. 当本短语作“同一类的”解时,另外一种表达形式是 two of a kind。例如:

> Father and son are two *of a kind*, they're both very generous.
> 父子两个是同一类人,他们都十分慷慨。

of a sort ⇨ **of sorts**

of course *adv.* ❶ used for saying "yes, very definitely", in answer to a question (用于答复某一问题,表示肯定)是的:"Do you know what I mean?" "*Of course.*" “你明白我的意思吗?”“是的,明白。” ❷ used for giving someone permission in a polite way (用于表示允许)当然可以:"May I come in?" "*Of course* you may." “我可以进来吗?”“当然可以。” ❸ used for agreeing or disagreeing with someone (用于表示同意或反对)当然是;当然不:"I'm sure everything's going to be OK." "*Of course* it is." “我确信一切都会顺利。”“当然会。” *Of course* these figures may not be completely accurate. 当然这些数字可能不完全准确。 ❹ naturally or obviously; certainly or surely 自然,当然:*Of course* I'll give you your money back. 我自然要还你的钱了。Soon after the fire started the firemen came, *of course*, complete with rescuer equipment, first aid kit, etc. 火灾发生不久,消防员就赶到了,当然他们都带着救援设备和急救箱等等。

NOTE 本短语的否定形式是 of course not。例如:

> "Is she really going to leave without being paid?" "*Of course* not!"
> “她真的工钱都没收就要走吗?”“当然不会!”

of late *adv.* (正式用语) recently; lately; not long ago 近来,最近:*Of late*, Professor Wang has been busy in compiling an English dictionary. 近来,王教授一直忙于编写一部英语词典。He has been behaving very strangely *of late*. 最近以来他的行为非常古怪。She doesn't seem to be very happy *of late*. 她最近看上去不太开心。

NOTE **1.** 本短语中的 late 不是形容词或副词,而是名词。

2. 本短语常用于现在完成时态,偶尔与一般时连用。

of necessity *adv.* (正式用语) (used for saying that something must be done, designed, etc. in the way it is and cannot be different) necessarily; unavoidably or inevitably 必然地,不可避免地:Being a professional actor *of necessity* means working nights and Sundays. 当职业演员,势必晚上和星期天都要工作。Negotiations between the enemies are *of necessity* indirect. 敌对双方之间的谈判必然要间接地进行。

of no use *adj.* (正式用语,常用在系动词 be 后,常与介词 to 连用) (of something or someone) unhelpful or useless 没有帮助的,没用的:This book is *of no use* whatever. 这本书没有什么帮助。I think you'll find this book of *no use* to you. 我想你会发现这本书对你没有用。I'm sorry, I'll be of *no use* to you. 对不起，我不会对你有什么用。

NOTE 1. 本短语可在句中充当表语、(后置)定语和宾语补足语。

2. 本短语中的介词 of 可以省略。

3. 本短语的反义短语是 of use。

of one's own *adj.* (用作后置定语) belonging to a particular person or thing and not to any other 属于自己的：Japan has no energy resources *of its own* and is heavily reliant on imported produce. 日本资源匮乏，大量产品依靠进口。Former US President Bush is considering writing a memoir *of his own*. 美国前总统布什正考虑写一本自己的回忆录。Besides two adopted children Mary has two small children *of her own*. 除了两个领养的孩子外，玛丽还有两个亲生的小孩。

NOTE 1. 本短语中的代词 one's 并不仅仅用来指人，还可指物。

2. 不要将本短语与 on one's own 混淆。

of/on one's own accord *adv.* ❶ (of someone doing something) without being asked or forced; willingly (指某人做某事)主动地，自愿地：When you start learning English *of your own accord*, instead of being forced, you'll enjoy learning it. 当你主动地而不是被迫地学习英语时，你就会喜欢学它。The children went to bed *of their own accord*, because they were so tired. 孩子们都主动去上床睡觉了，因为他们都太疲劳了。❷ (of something) happening automatically, without anybody making it happen (指某事物的发生)自动地：Most colds clear up *of their own accord* after a few days. 大多数感冒都会在几天后自行痊愈的。

NOTE 当本短语作"主动地，自愿地"解时，另一种表达方式是 of one's own free will。例如：

> No, I'm climbing this mountain *of my own free will*.
> 不，爬这座山是我自愿的。

of service *adj.* (用在系动词 be 后，常与 to someone 连用)(of something or someone) useful; helpful 有用的，有帮助的：Computers are *of* great *service* to us. 计算机对我们很有帮助。A good jack-knife is often *of service* to a camper. 一把好的折刀往往对露营者很有用。Can I be *of* any *service* to you? 我能帮您什么忙吗？If we can be *of service*, do not hesitate to call. 如果我们能帮得上忙，尽管招呼一声。

of sorts *adj.* (非正式用语，用在指物的名词之后作后置定语) of a kind that is not exactly the same as the actual thing, or not as good as the actual thing 勉强称得上的，较差的：It's a painting *of sorts*, but hard to describe. 这东西难以名状，勉强算是一幅画吧。He managed to make a curtain *of sorts* out of an old sheet. 他用旧被单勉强做成了一幅窗帘。

NOTE 本短语的另外一种表达形式是 of a sort。

of the opinion *adj.* (正式用语，后接 that 从句)(of someone) thinking or believing (that …)认为，相信：My wife and I are *of the* same *opinion* that smoking is harmful. 我和我妻子都同样认为吸烟有害。The mayor is *of the opinion* that the factory causing too much pollution should be closed. 市长认为那家制造严重污染的工厂应该关闭。The doctor was *of the opinion* that surgery was unnecessary. 医

生认为不必要做手术。

of use *adj.*（正式用语，常用在系动词 be 后，常与介词 to 连用）(of something or someone) helpful or useful 有帮助的，有用的：This information may be *of use* to him. 这信息可能对你有用。After the train explosion at the railway station, some people who live nearby were cleaning up the scene and trying to collect from the debris things still *of use*. 火车站发生的火车爆炸后，有些在附近居住的人们在打扫现场，并从废墟中拣回还能用的物件。I think you'll find this book *of* great *use* to you. 我想你会发现这本书对你非常有用。Can I be *of* any *use* to you? 我能为您效劳吗？

NOTE 本短语可在句中充当表语、(后置)定语和宾语补足语。

off and on *adv.*（常用来修饰动词或整个句子）sometimes but not regularly; not regularly or continuously; from time to time; 有时，不时地，断断续续地：I wrote to her *off and on* over the past few years. 在过去的几年里，我不时地给她写过一些信。It rained *off and on* last week. 上星期，天断断续续地下雨。She's written to a pen pal in English *off and on* for several years. 几年来，她一直断断续续地用英文给笔友写信。

NOTE 本短语的另外一种表达形式是 on and off。但不要把此处的 on and off 与下面这个句子中的 on and off 混淆：

> You must keep these standards *on and off* campus.
> 你们在校园内外都要遵守这些准则。

此处的 on 和 off 是两个并列副词，单独在句中作状语，而上面这个句子中的 on 和 off 则是两个并列介词，后接它们的共同宾语 campus。

off balance *adj.* ❶ unsteady; not in balance; not able to stand up straight and not fall; not able to keep from turning over or falling 不平稳的，失去平衡的：He kept pulling my arm, so I was *off balance*. 他不断地拉我的胳臂，我便失去了平衡。A hole in the road threw/caught him *off balance* and he fell over. 路面上的一个坑使他失去平衡而摔倒了。❷(of a person) extremely surprised or confused by something 冷不防的，不知所措的：The teacher's surprise test caught the class *off balance*, and nearly everyone got a poor mark. 老师趁学生没有准备而进行了一次突然的考查，结果几乎每个学生得的分数都很差。I was thrown completely *off balance* by Anna's reply. 安娜的回答使我不知所措。

NOTE 本短语可转化为复合词 off-balance，意为“不平衡的(地)”。

off by heart ⇨ by heart

off duty *adj. & adv.* not supposed to be at work at that moment; having free time; (while) not working 不在工作，下班(时)：Come and see us when you're *off duty*. 下班后来看我们吧。A policeman does not have to wear his uniform while *off duty*. 警察在不值勤的时候，不必穿制服。He goes on duty at 9:00 am and gets off duty at 5:00 pm. 他上午 9 点上班，下午 5 点下班。Some police officers were punished for gambling, drinking on duty, drunk driving, and carrying guns *off duty*. 有些警官因赌博、值勤中饮酒、醉酒驾车和非执行警务时佩带枪支而受到处罚。

NOTE 1. 本短语可转化为复合词 off-duty，意为“不在工作的，下班的”。

2. 本短语的反义短语是 on duty。

off hand *adv.* at once; without time to consider; without previous thought or preparation 马上,立即,事先无准备地:I can't give you the exact figures *off hand*. 我无法立刻给出确切的数字。He composed a song *off hand*. 他即兴作了一首歌曲。

NOTE 1. 不要将本短语与 off one's hand 混淆。off one's hands 意为"不由某人控制"。

2. 本短语可转化为复合词 off-hand,用作形容词,意为"即席的,临时的,简慢的",还可用作副词,意为"立即,当下;事先无准备地"。

off limits *adj.* ❶(主要用于美国英语中,常与 to 连用)(of a place or area) not allowed to go or enter; out of bounds (某一地点或区域)禁止进入的: Certain places of the town have been declared *off limits* to military personnel. 该城镇的某些地点已宣布禁止军人进入。The entire control area will remain *off limits* until official notices are published lifting restrictions. 整个控制区在正式取消限制之前将一直禁入。Don't let the dog go into the kitchen. It's *off limits* to him. 不要让狗进厨房。那是它不能进的地方。❷ not allowed 禁止(某事或做某事): Guns are *off limits* within New York City. 在纽约市内枪支是违禁物品。

NOTE 本短语中的名词 limit 必须用复数形式。

off one's head *adj.* ❶ insane; mad; crazy 精神错乱的,疯的:You're *off your head* if you think I'll pay you. 如果你认为我会给你工钱,那你是疯了。❷(英国英语用法,非正式用语)(of someone's ideas or behaviors) very strange, foolish, or dangerous (指某人的思想或行为)十分怪异的,愚蠢的,危险的: He must be *off his head* to go jogging in this weather! 他一定是疯了,这样的天气还出去慢跑!

NOTE 本短语的同义短语是 out of one's head。

off the hook *adj.* (非正式用语) having avoided a difficult situation, or a punishment 摆脱困境或惩罚: As soon as he saw her smile he knew he was *off the hook*. 他看到她的笑脸,就知道自己脱离了困境。Rogers might get *off the hook* by putting the blame to others. 罗杰斯也许会把罪责推到别人身上从而摆脱困境。I don't believe his boss has let him *off the hook* again. 我不相信他的老板会再次放过他。

off the phone ⇨ **by phone**

off the record *adj.* & *adv.* (非正式用语)(of a remark or comment) not official (ly) or not intended to be known publicly or recorded officially; not for quotation or publication 非正式的(地);私下说说的(地),不供引用(或发表)的(地): The senator told the reporters that his remarks were strictly *off the record*. 那位参议员告诫记者们,他的话决不可以被刊登出来。*Off the record*, many Conservatives admit they cannot win the election. 许多保守党人都私下里承认不会赢得大选。He spoke to the reporter *off the record*. 他对记者的讲话不供引述。

NOTE 1. 本短语的反义短语是 on (the) record。

2. 本短语可转化为复合词 off-the-record,意为"不准公开发表的(地);不供引用的(地);私下的(地)"。

on a diet *adj.* living on a limited list of

food and drink that a person is allowed, especially when this is controlled for medical reasons (尤指因医疗原因)吃限定饮食:I mustn't have chocolates — I'm *on a diet*. 我不能吃巧克力——我在节制饮食。The doctor ordered her to go *on a diet* to lose weight. 医生命她吃限定饮食以减肥。The doctor put him *on a diet*. 医生给他限定了饮食。

on a rampage ⇨ **on the rampage**

on account of *prep*. (正式用语)(used to introduce the reason or explanation for something) owing to; because of 由于,因为: He drove very slowly *on account of* the heavy fog. 由于雾大,他车开得很慢。He is unlikely to take part in the construction of the bridge *on account of* his being busy at present. 他大概不能参加这座桥梁的修建工作了,因为他现在很忙。Why did you do it? Was it *on account of* what I said yesterday? 你为什么干那件事? 是因为我昨天说的那些话吗?

O

NOTE 本短语的同义短语是 due to, owing to 和 because of。用作状语时,四者可互换使用.

on (the) alert *adj*. in a state of being ready to deal with danger, especially after a warning (对……)保持着戒备状态,警惕着:The army was put *on alert* as the peace talks failed. 由于和平谈判失败,军队处于戒备状态之中。We have to keep being *on the alert* against the occurrence of a flu pandemic. 我们必须对流感全球大流行保持警惕。All the countries in the region are *on* high *alert* for a potential outbreak of influenza A (H1N1). 该地区的所有国家都对甲型 H1N1 流感的可能爆发保持着高度的警惕。

on and off ⇨ **off and on**

on and on *adv*. (非正式用语) continuing for a long time; without stopping 继续不断地,不停地: The patient kept moaning *on and on*. 那病人不停地呻吟着。*On and on* we climbed up, until there was only one peak left. 我们不停地往上爬,直到只剩下一座山峰。

NOTE 本短语可在同一句中重复使用多次,表示强调。例如:

> The opera was a very long one, it seemed to go *on and on* and *on and on*.
> 这部剧很长,似乎要没完没了、无休无止地演下去。

on approval *adv*. (非正式用语)(of goods you bought) being allowed to be sent back within a particular time if you are not satisfied with it (对所购商品)可以退还地: I bought this camera *on approval*, for a month. 我买的这部相机一月内可以退换。Goods sent *on approval* must be paid for at the time of ordering, but if goods are returned within 7 days customers will get their money back in full. 商店送出可退还的货物在订购时必须付款,但顾客如在七天之内退货,可将原款全部收回。

on at ⇨ **be on at**

on (an/the) average *adv*. ❶ considered on the basis of the average 平均说来,平均:*On average*, women live between five and seven years longer than men. 平均说来,女性比男性长寿 5 至 7 年。*On the average*, Mr Smith trades in his car for a new one every five years. 史密斯先生平均每 5 年换一辆新车。❷ in most cases; usually; as a rule 在大多数情况下,通常: Their health conditions were *on the* *average* pretty good. 他们的健康状况在大多数情况下都很好。Women *on average* tend to be more interested in shopping than men are. 女士们通常比男士们对购物更感兴趣。

on/in behalf of *prep.* & *adv.* (正式用语) ❶instead of (someone), or as a representative of (someone)代表(某人), 做(某人)的代表: The president can't be here today, so I'm going to speak *on behalf of* him. 今天校长不能光临,所以我将代表他发言。❷ in order to help (someone); for the benefit of (someone) 为了帮助(某人),为了(某人的利益): The school children donated clothing *in behalf of* the families whose homes were destroyed by the flood. 小学生们都捐献了衣物以帮助那些房屋被洪水冲毁的家庭。I thank you for all the trouble you have taken *on behalf of me*. 我感谢您为了我而费了这么多的事。

NOTE 1. 本短语的另外一种表达形式是 on/in one's behalf.

2. on behalf of 多用于英国英语中, in behalf of 多用于美国英语中。

on board Ⅰ *adj.* & *adv.* in or on a ship, train, bus, plane or other vehicles 在轮船上,在火车上,在汽车上,在飞机上: As soon as I'm *on board* I always feel sick. 我总是一上车就想吐。This morning a high-ranking officer went *on board* for an inspection of our ship. 今天上午,一位高级军官来我舰上视察。Shenzhou-7, China's third manned spacecraft, carried three astronauts *on board* for a three day space mission which included a spacewalk. 中国第三艘载人宇宙飞船"神舟七号"上搭载了三名宇航员,执行了三天的航天使命,其中包括太空行走。

Ⅱ *prep.* on or in (a ship, plane, train, or other vehicles)在(轮船、飞机、火车或其他运载工具)上: Let's get *on board* the train right now. 我们马上上火车吧。NASA astronauts answered questions from people on Earth from *on board* the International Space Station via YouTube. 美国国家航空航天局的宇航员通过 YouTube 网站从国际空间站上回答了人们从地球上提出的问题。

on business *adj.* & *adv.* in the process of doing business or something official 因公,因事: Johnson was away *on business*. 约翰逊因公出差了。He went to New York *on business*. 他因公去纽约了。No admittance except *on business*. 非公莫入。

NOTE 不要将本短语与 in business 混淆。in business 意为"经商",例如:

> He is no longer *in business*.
> 他不再经商了。

on/upon completion *adv.* when it is finished 结束时,竣工后: The Three Gorges Project is designed to have 26 generators, and will be able to generate 84.7 billion kilowatt hours a year *on completion*. 三峡工程设计有26个发电机组,到建成时年发电847亿千瓦时。We can only be paid *upon completion* of the project. 我们在项目完工后才能得到报酬。

on (the) condition that *conj.* (正式用语) (used for saying that one thing will happen only if another thing also happens) providing that; only if 只要,如果,在……条件下: Iron will not rust *on (the) condition that* it be kept dry. 铁只要保持干燥,就不会生锈。I'll do it *on the condition that* you pay for everything. 我

可以做此事,条件是你得支付一切费用。

NOTE 本短语有推测之意,其引出的从句中的谓语动词可用虚拟语气形式(如第一个例句)。但在一般情况下,其后的从句往往为真实条件句。如:

> I'll come *on condition that* Mary is invited, too.
> 只要玛丽也被邀请,我就会来。

on display *adj.* (of things) being shown in an exhibition, showroom, etc., so that they are able to be seen by many people (指物品)被展出的: Various flowers are *on display* throughout Beijing as Valentine's Day is near at hand. 随着情人节的临近,北京到处都在展销各种鲜花。The costumes were placed *on display* at the museum. 这些戏装都放在了博物馆中展出。There are over five hundred paintings *on display* here. 这里共展出了500多幅油画。

on duty *adj.* & *adv.* working at that moment; (while) doing one's job during a certain period 上班,值班(时),值勤(中): At the road crossing in the town, policemen are *on duty* for possible emergency. 在该镇的十字路口处有警察值勤,以防备可能的紧急情况发生。The policeman *on duty* has caught a pickpocket. 值勤的警察捉到一个扒手。

O

on earth *adv.* ❶(用于加强语气,常用于含有最高级形式的句子中) in the world 在世界上: He wanted to be the fastest man *on earth*. 他想成为世界上跑得最快的人。In the 19th century, Britain was the most powerful nation *on earth*. 英国在19世纪时曾是世界上最强大的国家。About two thirds of all elements found *on earth* are metals, but not all metals can be used in industry. 在地球上所发现的元素中,三分之二是金属,但并不是所有的金属都能应用在工业上。❷(仅用于口语中,用于疑问句中表示惊讶) (used for adding emphasis to questions to convey surprise) ever 究竟,到底: Take your money away from me. What *on earth* do you take me for? 你把钱拿走。你究竟把我当成什么人了? How *on earth* did the mouse get out of the cage? 这老鼠到底是怎么从笼子里跑出来的? Where *on earth* could Tommy have learned such behavior? 汤米究竟从哪儿学来的这种行为? Who on earth is he? 他到底是谁?

NOTE 当本短语作"到底,究竟"解时,用于加强语气,与 in the world 的意义和用法相同,两者可互换使用。

on edge *adj.* excited; nervous and unable to relax because you are worried 兴奋的,紧张不安的: The magician kept the children *on edge* all through his show. 魔术师的表演使孩子们自始至终感到十分兴奋。We were all *on edge* as we waited for the surgeon's report. 我们都紧张不安地等待着医生的报告。Knowing that I might be called on to answer a question always puts me *on edge*. 得知我可能被叫起来回答问题,这使我一直紧张不安。The accident set us *on edge* for several days. 这起事故使我们焦急不安了好几天。

NOTE 本短语的比较级形式是 more on edge,最高级形式是 most on edge。

on end *adv.* ❶(与表示时间的,复数名词连用) (of time) without a break; seeming endless; continuously (指时间)连续,不断地: The children sat watching television for hours *on end*. 孩子们连续坐了好几个小时看电视。It snowed for days *on end*, we thought it would never stop! 雪一连下了多日。我们认为它会下个没完! Last month he shut himself in for 3 weeks *on end*. 上个月他一连三周没有出门。For months *on end*, her face was splashed across television screens around the country. 她的面容连续几个月出现在全国的电视屏幕上。❷(of something) in a straight upright position instead of in its normal or natural position (指某物)直立着,竖着:They had to stand the desk *on end* to get it through the door. 他们只能把桌子立起来,才把它搬过门去。Some of those ghost stories make my hair stand *on end*, even though I don't believe in ghosts. 虽然我不相信鬼,但有些鬼故事还是使我毛骨悚然。

on file *adj*. stored in a file so it can be found easily 存档,入卷:The fingerprints *on file* with the police matched those taken from the body. 警方所存档的指纹与从尸体上所取的指纹均相配。I'll keep your report *on file*. 我将把你的报告存档。These documents should be kept *on file* for future reference. 这些文件应存档以供将来参考。The EU decided to place a case *on file* for anti-dumping investigation into the wooden bedroom furniture imported from that country. 欧盟决定对从该国进口的木制卧室家具立案进行反倾销调查。

on fire *adj*. (of something not meant to burn) burning (意外)着火,在燃烧:They could not but abandon the ship *on fire*. 他们只好放弃了已经着火的船。The bombing destroyed a three-story concrete building, setting cars *on fire*, and badly damaged nearby houses. 炸弹爆炸摧毁了一栋三层的混凝土大楼,并使汽车着火,附近的房屋严重受损。

NOTE 本短语与 catch fire 均有"着火,燃烧"之意。但 catch fire 表示动作,不能与表示延续性的时间状语连用;而 on fire 则表示状态,在句中作表语(后置)定语和宾语补足语。

on foot *adv*. & *adj*. ❶(by) walking rather than using any form of transport 步行:It takes longer to travel *on foot* than by bus. 步行去比乘公共汽车去用的时间长。Did you come *on foot* or by bus? 你是走来的还是乘公共汽车来的? Relief troops are approaching Wenchuan County *on foot* in the rain, the epicenter of a powerful earthquake measured at 8.0 on the Richter scale. 多路救灾部队正冒雨徒步挺进里氏 8.0 级强烈地震的震中汶川县。❷(英国英语用法)(of work, plan, etc.) in progress; in a state of being used, made, prepared, etc. (指工作、计划等)在进行中,在使用,制造,准备当中:I hear that plans are *on foot* to build a new school. 我听说创办一所新学校的诸项计划正在制定中。There's a scheme *on foot* to build another big department store in this area. 有计划要在本地区再建一个大型百货商店。

NOTE 不要将本短语与 on one's feet 相混淆,两者的意义不同。见 on one's feet。

on good terms *adj*. (用作表语,常与 with 连用) having a good relationship (with someone) (与某人)关系良好:Even after their divorce, they remained *on good terms*. 甚至在离婚后,他们仍保持着良好的关系。The states of Central Asia are eager to remain *on good terms* with the United States and European powers. 中亚国家都极想与美国和欧洲强国保持良好关系。I'm *on good terms* with my ex-wife. 我与前妻的关系很好。

NOTE 1. 本短语的比较级形式是 on better terms,最高级形式是 on the best terms。
2. 本短语中的名词 term 必须用复数形式。
3. 本短语中的形容词 good 可被 friendly, bad 等替代,构成的短语用法和本短语相同。

on (the) grounds of/that *prep.* by reason of/that 由于……的原因,以……为理由: Employers cannot discriminate *on grounds of* age. 雇主不可以年龄之由歧视人。He left *on the grounds of* ill-health. 他以身体不好为由而告辞了。British potato farmers wanted the expression "couch potato" to be removed from the *Oxford English Dictionary on the grounds that* it harms the vegetable's image. 英国种植土豆的农民们要求把短语"couch potato (终日懒散之人)"从《牛津英语词典》中删除,理由是这一短语有损这种蔬菜的形象。

NOTE 本短语中的名词 ground 必须用复数形式。

on guard *adj.* ❶very careful, aware and watchful because a situation might be dangerous 注意,警惕,警戒: The police warned people to be against pickpockets *on guard* the buses. 警方警示人们在乘坐公共汽车时要谨防扒手。The speed of climate change has put scientists *on guard*. 气候变化的速度已引起科学家们的警觉。❷at one's post; on duty 站岗,值勤: Two soldiers are *on guard* at the door, to prevent anyone getting in or out. 有两名士兵在门口站岗,禁止任何人出入。There are two soldiers *on guard* at the gate of the building. 楼房的大门处有两个士兵在站岗。

NOTE 本短语的第一个义项与 on one's guard 意义和用法相同。

on hand *adv.* & *adj.* ❶(of something) in your possession; ready for use or immediately available when needed 在手头(的),现有(的): He has a lot of work *on hand*. 他手头有许多工作要做。Jim had no cash *on hand* to pay for the gas. 吉姆手头没有现金支付汽油钱。You should always have what your customers want *on hand*. 你们应该总是有顾客所需要的现货。❷about to happen; coming near; soon 即将发生(的),即将到来(的),临近(的): What is *on hand* for this evening? 今天晚上有什么事? It was reported that there was trouble *on hand*. 报道说,麻烦即将临头。❸present; in attendance 到场地(的),出席地(的),参加地(的): He was always *on hand* when they needed him. 他们需要他时,他总是到场。Please be *on hand* at 8 o'clock sharp. 请您于 8 点整准时出席。Are there enough people *on hand* to hold a meeting? 要开会,与会的人员够吗? ❹within reach; nearby; close 在近处(的): Outside the Buckingham Palace, some 5,000 British police officers are *on hand* to protect the visiting US president. 在白金汉宫外的附近区域,大约有 5 000 名英国警察在保护着到访的美国总统。

NOTE 与本短语结构相同的有 at hand 和 in hand,三者意义各不相同,见相关条目。

on (an) impulse *adv.* (of someone) suddenly feeling that you want to do something; without taking time to plan or think carefully about(something)一时冲动之下,未经计划地,未经考虑地: Now psychologists know more about why men act *on impulse*. 现在,心理学家对为

什么男性易冲动行事有了更多的了解。He saw them get into the car and *on an impulse* he followed them. 他看到他们上了车,冲动之下他跟踪而上。

NOTE 本短语的同义短语是 on the spur of the moment。

on leave *adj.* not working at your job, because you are on holiday or for some other reason 休假:I'm in command of the regiment while the colonel is *on leave*. 上校休假期间,由我指挥这个团。He is *on leave* from his newspaper for the campaign. 他为了参加竞选运动而休假不去报社上班。The helicopter was carrying US soldiers home *on leave* when Iraqi guerrillas shot it down with a surface-to-air missile. 这架直升机是在运送美国士兵回国休假时被伊拉克游击队的一枚地对空导弹击落的。

on line Ⅰ *adj.* ❶connected to, or able to be connected to, a computer network or the Internet (与计算机网络或因特网)联网的:We need every household to be *on line* within 5 years. 我们要让每户家庭在五年内都能联网。❷(美国英语用法)on a queue, waiting one's turn for something 排成一队: I'm waiting *on line* at the bakery. 我正在面包店排队等候。

Ⅱ *adv.* (doing something) by using a computer or a computer network 在网上,在线(做某事):Life has changed for millions of teenagers across the world who make friends *on line*. 对于全世界许许多多的青少年来说,网上交友改变了他们的生活。

NOTE 1. 不要将本短语与 on the line 混淆,两者意义不同。

2. 当本短语作"排成一队"解时,与 in line 意义和用法相同。

3. 本短语可转化为复合词 on (-) line,也意为"网上的(地),在网上的"。

on no account *adv.* (正式用语)(used to say in a strong and definite way that something must not happen or be done) absolutely not; not for any reason 决不,无论如何也不: *On no account* are visitors allowed to feed the animals in this park. 本公园内,游人一律不准喂食动物。My name must *on no account* be mentioned to anyone. 无论如何也不要向任何人提起我的名字。

NOTE 当本短语用于句首时,句中的主谓结构一定要构成倒装。

on occasion *adv.* (正式用语) sometimes but not often; occasionally 有时,不时地: He continues to work with us *on occasion*. 他有时还继续和我们一起工作。*On occasion* we feel like celebrating and have a party. 我们有时喜欢搞一次聚会庆祝一番。I meet the girl *on occasion* at the same Internet cafe. 我有时在同一家网吧里见到那女孩。

NOTE 1. 不要将本短语与 on the occasion of 混淆。on the occasion of 意为"值……之际",例如:

> There was a celebration *on the occasion of* the school's anniversary.
> 在学校的周年纪念日之际还庆祝了一番。

2. 本短语的同义短语是 from time to time 和 now and then。

on/in one's behalf ⇨ **on/in behalf of**

on one's feet *adj.* & *adv.* ❶standing up; not sitting or lying down 站立着: I'm exhausted, I've been *on my feet* all afternoon! 我太累了。我已经站了一个下午! In a busy gas station, the attendant is *on his feet* all the day. 在繁忙的加油站

里,加油员要整天地站着工作。❷(常与 again 连用)(of someone or something) fully recovered; getting better or back to normal from illness or difficult period (从病后或困难时期)完全恢复过来: This medicine will soon have the patient back *on her feet* again. 这药很快就会使那病人恢复健康。He said they all needed to work together to put the country *on its feet* again. 他说,他们所有的人都要同心协力使国家复兴。❸being independent, especially in money matters(尤指在经济上)独立,自立:His son is *on his feet* now and does not need any more financial help. 他的儿子现在在经济上已能自立而不再需要任何资助了。

on one's guard *adj.* (常与 against 连用) thinking or behaving carefully, so that you do not say or do something you did not intend to; vigilant 小心的,谨慎的,警惕的: I should be *on my guard* if I were you. He's not the sort of man I would trust. 如果我要是你,我就要提高警惕。他可不是我应该相信的那种人。

on/upon one's honor *adj.* & *adv.* (正式用语)(used for making a serious promise to do something) on trust; being trusted to behave rightly 以名誉(或人格)保证: You are *on your honor* not to cheat during the examination. 你们要保证在考试中不作弊。He was put *on his honor* not to tell the secret. 他要以名誉担保不泄露秘密。I swear, *on my honor*, to keep your secret. 我以我的名誉保证,为你保守秘密。We were *upon our honor* to help them. 我们以人格担保给予他们帮助。

NOTE 不要将本短语与 in one's honor 混淆。见 in one's honor。

on one's own *adv.* ❶alone 单独地:It's a lonely life for him, living there all *on his own*. 他只一个人单独住在那里,过着孤独的生活。You'd be better living out *on your own* than quarrelling all the time with your dad. 你单独住在外面比你总和你爸爸吵嘴更好些。It would be dangerous to go after the killer all *on your own*. 你单枪匹马地去捉拿凶犯是很危险的。❷dependent upon your own resources for support; without any help from other people 靠自己的力量,独立地:No country can develop solely *on its own* in isolation of the world economy. 任何国家都难以完全脱离世界经济而独立发展。

on one's part *adv.* done or experienced by someone; as far as one is concerned 就某人而言,在某人那方面: It was a mistake *on Johnson's part* to sign the contract without reading it. 没看合同就签了字,那是约翰逊的错误。The agreement has been kept *on our part*, but not on his part. 我方遵守了合同,可他那方却没有。

NOTE 1. 本短语的另外一种表达形式是 on the part of someone。

2. 本短语与 for one's part 意义和用法相同,两者可互换使用。

on/about one's person *adv.* (正式用语)(of something) carried about with you, as in your pocket in the clothes you are wearing 随身带着(某物): My father never carried money *on his person* as he didn't need it. 我爸爸口袋里从来不带钱,因为他不需要钱花。She always carried a small pair of scissors *about her person*. 她总是随身带着一把小剪子。

NOTE about one's person 不及 on one's

person 常用,尤其在美国英语中罕用。

on one's side *adj.* giving one an advantage and increasing one's chances of success 对某人有利的:Don't hug yourself for joy when things are *on your side*; and similarly, don't give yourself up for lost when everything is not *on your side*. 一帆风顺时,不可沾沾自喜;同样,事事不如意时,也不要自暴自弃。Next year, the weather may not be *on their side*. 明年,天气可能对他们不利。The champion is a more experienced fighter, but the challenger has got youth *on his side*. 这位冠军是一名经验较丰富的拳击手,而那位挑战者则有年轻的优势。

on one's way to *prep.* traveling towards or en route to (a place)在去往……的途中:I met him *on my way to* the school library this morning. 我是在今早去校图书馆的路上碰到他的。The President and eight other officials were *on their way to* London for an international economic conference. 总统和另外八位官员在去伦敦出席国际经济会议的途中。

on principle *adv.* according to a fixed rule or practice 按照已定原则,按惯例:*On principle* she would not stay in a place more than six months. 按其原则,她不会在一个地方住半年以上。The police were locking up the demonstrators *on principle*. 警察按惯例把示威者都关了起来。

on purpose *adv.* (常置于句尾)deliberately; intentionally; purposely; by intention 故意地: She left the letter here *on purpose* for you to read. 她是故意把信落在这儿让你看的。A large number of British people think the truth has been covered up by the government *on purpose*. 许多英国人都认为真相被政府蓄意掩盖了。

NOTE 本短语的反义短语是 by accident 和 by chance。

on (the) record *adj.* &*adv.* ❶(of a fact or event) written down in a record (事实或事件)记录在案的(地),在记录中的(地):The judge's opinion is *on record*. 法官的意见是记录在案的。The police had kept his name *on record*. 警方已将他的名字记录在案。This is the coldest winter *on record*. 这是有史以来最冷的冬天。❷(常与动词 be 和 go 连用,后常接介词 as 短语) used for stating that you are saying something officially or publicly 公开宣布的(地): The governor is *on the record* as favoring the highway. 州长支持修建这条公路是公开宣布过的。The minister has gone *on (the) record* as saying the law should be changed. 部长曾公开说过,该项法律应该改变。

NOTE 本短语可转化成复合词 on-the-record,意为"记录在案的;公开宣布的"。

on sale *adj.* ❶offered to be sold; available for people to buy, especially in a shop 出售的,供出售的:Olympic tickets are now *on sale* through a booking website and a hotline. 奥运会门票现正在通过一家票务网站和一条热线电话销售。An inspection yesterday by some reporters of two busy small-commodity markets in the city, found *no such* products on sale. 一些记者昨天调查了市内两家小商品市场,并没发现这些产品有售。The relics, a bronze rat head and a bronze rabbit head, which went *on sale* in Paris, were stolen from China by French and British troops in 1860. 在巴黎出售的鼠首、兔首铜像两件文物,是1860年英法联军从中国盗走的。❷(美国英语用法) available for sale at a reduced price; selling things at lower prices than usual 减价出售的，贱卖的：I got this pair of shoes *on sale*, it was very cheap. 我买的这双鞋是减价的，很便宜。This kind of watch is now *on sale* for 20 dollars. 这种手表正在减价卖20美元。

NOTE 1. 当本短语作"出售的，供出售的"解时，与 for sale 意义和用法相同。

2. 当本短语作"减价出售的，贱卖的"解时，另外一种表达形式是 in the sale，这种形式常在英国英语中使用。例如：

> Can you tell me if this dress is *in the sale*?
> 请问，这件连衣裙减价卖吗？

on schedule *adv.* happening or done at the planned or expected time 按预定时间，在正点：The opposition parties called for the government to hold parliamentary elections *on schedule*. 反对党呼吁政府按原定时间举行议会选举。They finished their work *on schedule*. 他们按期完成了工作。The train is sure to arrive *on schedule*. 列车肯定会正点到达。

NOTE 1. 本短语的名词 schedule 前不能加任何冠词。

2. 与本短语相关的短语有 ahead of schedule（提前于预定时间）和 behind schedule（落后于预定时间，晚点）。

on/upon second thought(s) *adv.*（主要用于口语中）(used when you change your mind about something you are saying or something that you have decided to do) after having thought about something again; after further consideration 经再三考虑后（改变与之前所说或所决定要做的事）："You wait here!" Linda rose. "No, *on second thought*, follow me." "你在这里等着！"琳达站起身来说道。"不，我想你还是跟我走。" *On second thought(s)* I decided to accept the job. 经过再三考虑，我决定接受这项工作。He had planned to go at once, but *upon second thoughts* he decided to wait for a few days. 他本打算马上就去，但经再三考虑后，决定再等几天。

NOTE on/upon second thoughts 用于英国英语和澳大利亚英语中；在美国英语中，只用单数形式，即 on/upon second thought。

on speaking terms *adj.*（常用于否定句中，常与 with 连用）on friendly terms with someone; feeling friendly towards someone, not angry with him or her, often after having been unfriendly previously 关系友好的；（常指在争吵后）和好的；合得来：They have been *on speaking terms* with the new neighbors. 他们和邻居们的关系一直很好。We are *on speaking terms* again after the quarrel. 我们在争吵后又合好了。For a long time my mother and my grandmother had hardly been *on speaking terms*. 长期以来，我母亲和我祖母一直合不来。He is barely *on speaking terms* with half of the family. 他几乎和家里一半的人合不来。

NOTE 本短语中的名词 term 必须用复数形式。

on strike *adj.* (especially of workers) stopping work as a protest, because of disagreement, for example over work or working conditions（尤指工人）在罢工的：Workers have been out *on strike* since Friday. 工人自周五以来一直在罢工。If the postal workers are *on strike*, other sectors may well join them. 如果邮电工人罢工，其他行业的工人也会随之加入。

NOTE 1. 本短语中的两个词之间有时插入

某种意义的形容词,短语意义上会略微变化。如:

> US military said on Sunday that the former president was not *on* a hunger *strike*.
> 美国军方于星期日表示,这位前总统并没有进行绝食抗议。

2. 本短语的动词形式是 go on strike。见 go on strike。

on the air *adj.* & *adv.* (of radio or television) broadcasting(广播或电视)在广播:It is New Year's Day and the prime minister will be *on the air* in a few seconds. 今天是元旦,首相马上就要发表广播讲话了。The programme first went *on the air* 15 years ago. 这个节目是 15 年前首次开播的。The football game is *on the air* now on Channel 40. 足球赛正在 40 频道播出。

NOTE **1.** 在英国英语中,本短语中的定冠词 the 可以省略。

2. 不要将本短语与 in the air 混淆。in the air 的意为"(故事、话语、谣言等)在流传的;未定的,悬而未决的"。

3. 本短语的反义短语是 off the air。如:

> Most radio stations are *off the air* from midnight to six in the morning.
> 大多数广播电台从午夜到次日清晨 6 时不广播。

on the basis of *prep.* (used for giving the reason why something is done) according to; on the foundation of 根据,在……基础上:Don't make your decision *on the basis of* cost alone. 不要只根据成本做决定。China and Japan will further discuss the issue of gas and oil exploration in fields in the East China Sea *on the basis of* peace, cooperation and joint benefits. 中国和日本将在和平、合作与互利的基础上,进一步讨论在中国东海开发油气田的问题。

on the brink of *prep.* (后常接动名词短语) almost in a (crucial or critical) condition or situation of 濒临……边缘:This kind of rare animal is *on the brink of* extinction. 这类珍稀动物已濒临灭绝。He said his country is *on the brink of* a civil war. 他说,他的国家正濒临内战的边缘。The situation may go in a direction that is bad for various sides, and it is *on the brink of* going out of control. 局势可能会朝着对各方都不利的方向发展,并且濒临失控。

NOTE 本短语的同义短语是 on the edge of, on the point of 和 on the verge of。

on the contrary *adv.* (used for expressing strong opposition or disagreement with what has just been said, suggested, etc.) exactly the opposite; rather; instead (用于反驳他人之言)正相反,反之:"Does it rain a lot in the desert?" "No, *on the contrary*, it hardly ever rains." "沙漠里雨多吗?""不,正相反,几乎不下雨。" I'm not sick; *on the contrary*, I'm in the peak of health. 我没病。正相反,我现在的身体状况最佳。The evidence of history, *on the contrary*, shows that these ancient people had a very advanced culture. 恰恰相反的是,历史证据表明,这些古人有着十分先进的文化。

NOTE 本短语与 to the contrary 都可用作副词性短语,表示"相反"。两者的区别是:(1)两者所指不同。本短语指"强烈反对或不赞成别人刚说过的话",而 to the contrary 则指"与某一意义或事实相反"。(2)两者在句中的位置和修饰对象不同。本短语常置于句首,之后用逗号,用来修饰全句,而 to the contrary 则常置于句尾,修饰句中动词。(3)本短语只用作副词性短语,而 to the contrary 还可用作形容词性短语。

on the decline *adj.* getting lower (in the amount or quality of something)在下降的: The birth rate of this country is *on the decline*. 该国的人口出生率在下降。In our city, interest in sports is *on the decline*. 在我们市,人们对体育运动的兴趣每况愈下。

NOTE 本短语的反义短语是 on the rise。

on the edge of *prep.* ❶on the border of (something)在……的边缘: Victoria was sitting *on the edge of* the bed. 维多利亚正在床边上坐着。They live *on the edge of* the forest. 他们居住在森林的边上。If you don't want it, leave it *on the edge of* your plate. 如果你不想吃,就把它放在你的盘子边上。Many railway stations are built *on the edge of* town. 许多火车站都建在城镇边上。❷on the point of (doing something) 即将(做某事): Walt Disney Company is *on the edge of* reaching an agreement with the government over a plan for a Disneyland theme park in Shanghai. 沃尔特·迪斯尼公司就建造迪斯尼乐园主题公园的计划即将与该政府达成协议。He is now *on the edge of* losing his office. 他现在即将丢掉官职了。❸nearly in (a particular state or condition)接近(某种状态),快要,濒临: My father is *on the edge of* 80. 我父亲已年近八旬了。She felt she was *on the edge of* madness. 她觉得自己快要疯了。The company is *on the edge of* bankruptcy. 这家公司现在濒临破产。

on the eve of *prep.* just before (something), possibly the evening before (something); on the day before; during the period of time just before (an important event)在……的前夜,在……的前一天,在……前夕: I came back home *on the eve of* the Christmas. 我在圣诞节前夜才回到家。China Mobile alone sent 4.6 billion messages *on the eve of* the Spring Festival. 仅中国移动在大年除夕就发送了46亿条短信。I am always in a state of nerves *on the eve of* an examination. 临考的前夕我总是非常紧张。

on the go *adj.* (英国英语用法,非正式用语)(of a person) very busy and active (指人)十分忙碌的,活跃的: I'm exhausted — I've been always *on the go* since six o'clock this morning. 我筋疲力尽了。从今早6点开始,我就一直在忙。Healthy, happy people are usually *on the go*. 健康、愉快的人一般都很活跃。

NOTE 本短语的比较级形式是 more on the go,最高级形式是 most on the go。

on the hour *adv.* at or on the time that is exactly one o'clock, two o'clock, three o'clock, etc. 在整钟点(如一点、两点、三点等): The doctor told his patient to take the medicine *on the hour*. 医生嘱咐他的患者每小时按时服药。The radio station broadcasts news *on the hour*. 广播电台于整点播报新闻。Trains for Edinburgh leave every hour *on the hour*. 开往爱丁堡的列车每小时整点发车。

NOTE 不要将本短语与 by the hour 混淆,后者意为"按小时计算"。

on the line *adj.* ❶at risk; in danger of being harmed 处于危险中的,冒着危险的: He was warned that his job was *on the line* because of his lack of sense of duties. 他受到警告,因他缺乏责任感而有失去其工作的危险。Firefighters lay their lives *on the line* every working day. 消防队员每天都冒着生命危险工作。

John puts his reputation *on the line* and publicly asks the state to let Massachusetts physicians advise patients on birth control. 约翰不惜以自己的声誉为代价公开促请马萨诸塞州允许医生建议患者实行节育。❷on the phone 打电话：Mike is *on the line* from New York. 麦克从纽约打来了电话。I've got Mary *on the line* for you. Do you want to take it now or call her back later? 我已为你接通玛丽的电话。你想现在就接还是稍后再打过去？I got *on the line* to the hospital as soon as I heard about the accident. 我一听说出了事就给医院打了电话。

NOTE 1. 当本短语作"处于危险中的，冒着危险的"解时，同义短语是 at risk。

2. 当本短语作"打电话"解时，同义短语是 on the phone。

on the lookout for *prep.* watching carefully in order to find, obtain, or avoid (someone or something) searching for 密切监视，寻找：Police in Paris are *on the lookout for* a gang of car thieves. 巴黎警方正在密切监视着一个盗窃汽车的团伙。The public was always *on the lookout for* a beautiful new face in the movies. 公众总是不断地寻觅电影中漂亮的新面孔。We are *on the lookout for* new computer programmers. 我们一直在寻求新的计算机程序设计员。

on the loose *adj.* (of a person or animal) free to move about, especially having escaped from prison (指人或动物)无束缚的；逍遥法外的：Some of the terrorists are still *on the loose*. 一些恐怖分子仍逍遥法外。There's a serial killer *on the loose*, this time terrorizing Portland, Oregon. 有一个连环杀手仍然在逃，这次可使俄勒冈州的波特兰市充满了恐怖。That dog of theirs is *on the loose* all the time. 他们的那条狗总是没被栓着的。

NOTE 本短语的同义短语是 at large 和 at liberty。

on the move *adj.* ❶traveling from place to place; very active 在行走的，在迁移的，在频繁活动的：Don't jump off the bus when it's *on the move*. 汽车未停稳时切勿跳下。I don't know where Tom is this week, he is always *on the move*. 我不知道汤姆本周在什么地方，他总是漂泊不定。❷(非正式用语)very busy all the time 一直很忙：He's always *on the move* and never has time to talk. 他总是很忙，从来没有时间说话。❸(非正式用语) developing or progressing quickly 迅速发展的，快速进步的：It's a new industry *on the move*. 这是一个迅速发展的新兴行业。It is said that civilization is always on the move. 人们说文明总是在进步。

NOTE 本短语的比较级形式是 more on the move，最高级形式是 most on the move。

on the occasion of ⇨ **on occasion**

on the one hand … on the other (hand) *adv.* (an expression used for giving two different opinions about an argument, etc.) from one point of view … from another point of view 一方面……，另一方面：*On the one hand* I know this job of mine isn't well paid, but *on the other hand* I don't have to work long hours. 一方面我知道我这份工作报酬不高，可从另一方面来说，我不必工作太长时间。When handling the nuclear issue, *on the one hand*, the issue of nuclear dismantlement should be solved and *on the other (hand)*, reasonable concern of related countries should also be addressed. 在解决核问题的过程中，一方面要解决弃核

O

的问题,另一方面也要解决有关国家的合理关切。

NOTE **1.** 本短语中的两个部分可以分开单独使用。例如:

> *On the one hand*, I'd like more money, but I don't want to work extra hours.
> 一方面,我想多赚点钱,但我又不想加班加点地工作。
> Father and Mother wanted to go for a ride, the children, *on the other hand*, wanted to stay at home and play with their friends.
> 爸爸和妈妈想驾车出游,但孩子们却想留在家里和小朋友们玩。

2. 当本短语的两个部分连用时,第二个部分中的名词 hand 可以省略,但当第二个部分单独使用时则不可省略。

3. 本短语中的两个部分常用连词 but 或 and 相连接,即使是第二部分单独使用时也如此。例如:

> I like classical music, but *on the other hand*, my husband loves jazz.
> 我喜欢古典音乐,但我丈夫却钟爱爵士乐。

4. 本短语第一部分中的定冠词在美国英语中可省略,但在英国英语中则不可。

on the part of *prep.* for the part of; on the side of 在……方面: He expressed appreciation on the part of himself and his colleagues. 他代表自己和他的同事们表达感激之情。The other team blamed their defeat on unfairness *on the part of* the referee. 另一队将其失败归罪于裁判方面的不公正。

on the phone *adv.* & *adj.* ❶ talking to someone by means of the telephone 打电话: Get *on the phone* and call Robert back immediately! 打电话,让罗伯特马上回来! My son spends hours *on the phone* every day. 我儿子每天都要花几个小时打电话。Your mother was *on the phone* when they came in. 他们进来的时候,你母亲正在打电话。You're wanted *on the phone*, Linda. 琳达,有人打电话找你。❷(英国英语用法) provided with a telephone in your home, office, etc. 装有电话的: Are the Browns *on the phone*, do you know? 你可知道布朗家有电话吗? I can't believe you're not *on the phone*. 我无法相信你没有电话。

NOTE **1.** 本短语和 on the telephone 的意义用法相同,两者可互换使用。

2. not on the phone 没有"不使用或不打电话"之意,而是"没有安装电话(而不能与他人通话)"之意。

on/upon the point of *prep.* (后常接动名词短语) ready to start doing (something) or about to do (something) 就要,正要,几乎要: She seemed to be *on the point of* tears. 她看上去就要哭了。The baby was *on the point of* crying when her mother came home. 婴儿刚要哭时,她的妈妈恰好到家了。As we were *on the point of* giving up hope, the telephone rang. 正当我们几乎绝望时,电话铃响了。The old building seemed to be *on the point of* collapse. 这座旧楼看上去几乎就要倒了。

on/under the pretext of *prep.* giving a false reason or excuse for (doing something) 以……为由,以……为借口: It is not allowed to fire women *on the pretext of* marriage, pregnancy, maternity leave or baby nursing. 不允许以结婚、怀孕、产假、哺乳等为由,辞退女职工。He came to the house *on the pretext of* seeing Mr Smith, but he really wanted to see his beautiful daughter. 他以到家看望史密斯先生为由,其实想看的是史密斯先生漂亮的女儿。

on the rampage *adj.* (of people, animals or something) behaving in a violent or wild way, especially causing damage or destruction to property over a wide area (指人、动物或某物)暴怒的,狂跳猛冲的:Football fans went *on the rampage* through the town, breaking shop windows and damaging cars. 暴怒的足球迷横冲直撞地穿过市镇,一路上砸碎商店橱窗,捣毁汽车。The escaped elephant was *on the rampage* for two days. 这头逃出来的大象狂跳猛冲了两天。The river has gone *on the rampage* and flooded all the country roads. 河水暴涨,淹没了所有的乡村公路。

NOTE 本短语的另外一种表达形式是 on a rampage。

on the rise *adj.* rising or increasing 上升的,增加的,增长的:"They chose a good opportunity to raise the interest rates because the US dollar was *on the rise* these days," the expert said. 这位专家称,"他们选择了一个很好的机会提高利率,因为近日来美元在升值。" However, the world is still not tranquil, with uncertainties affecting peace and development *on the rise*. 但天下仍不太平,影响和平与发展的不确定因素在增加。

NOTE 本短语的反义短语是 on the decline。

on the road *adj.* ❶traveling in a car, bus, or truck, especially for a long distance or a long period of time, especially for one's work 乘汽车旅行的,上路(去上班)的:We've been *on the road* now for five hours. 我们现已乘车旅行了 5 个小时。I was *on the road* very early this morning and I'm really tired now. 我今天很早就上路了,现在实在累了。❷(of entertainers or sales representatives) traveling to many different places to perform (专业演员)巡回演出的;(推销员)到处搞推销的:The band was *on the road* for seven months last year. 该乐团在去年巡回演出了七个月。Mr Simpson is *on the road* for his insurance company. 辛普森先生为其保险公司到处搞推销。❸going from one place to another because you do not have a permanent home 居无定所的:250,000 teenagers in this country decided to live a life *on the road*. 这个国家有 25 万少年决定过流浪生活。❹(常与 to 连用)moving towards (a desirable result) 朝着(预期的结果)进展的: After two weeks' treatment he was out of danger and well *on the road* to recovery. 经过两个星期的治疗,他脱离了危险而且在很快复原。Scientists have not yet found a cure for the disease, but they believe they are *on the road*. 虽然科学家们至今未发现治愈这种疾病的方法,但他们相信他们已取得了一些进展。

on the run Ⅰ *adj.* ❶(of someone) trying to escape or hide from someone, especially the police or an enemy 在逃的:The United Nations Anti-Corruption Agreement is sure to make life harder for corrupt officials *on the run* and make would-be criminals think twice before they act.《联合国反腐败公约》不仅让外逃的贪官日子没那么好过,还会让试图犯罪的官员们三思而后行。Criminals who robbed a bank and escaped with up to $300,000 last month are still *on the run*. 上个月抢劫银行并携带多达 30 万

美元巨款逃跑的几名罪犯现仍逍遥法外。Andrew is put behind bars after eighteen months *on the run*. 安德鲁在逃18个月后,被捕入狱。❷(非正式用语) busy or in a hurry 忙碌着的,匆匆忙忙的: As the manager of the company, he is *on the run* from morning till night. 作为该公司的经理,他从早到晚地忙碌着。With three young children to take care of, she is kept *on the run* every minute of the day. 由于要照料三个小孩,她每天时时刻刻都在忙碌着。

Ⅱ *adv.* while you are busy or hurrying 匆忙地:I had to eat lunch *on the run* today. 我今天不得不匆忙地用了午餐。

NOTE **1.** 本短语的比较级形式是 more on the run,最高级形式是 most on the run。

2. 当本短语作"在逃的"解时,同义短语是 at large。

3. 当本短语作"忙碌着的,匆匆忙忙的"解时,同义短语是 on the go。

on the scene *adv.* in the place where something is happening or has just happened 在出事现场:Reporters arrived *on the scene* within minutes of the explosion. 爆炸刚发生几分钟,记者们就赶到了出事现场。The police were called and they were *on the scene* within three minutes. 报警后,警察在3分钟内就到了出事现场。The police officer *on the scene* has requested 20 more men. 在出事现场的警官要求增加20名警力。

NOTE 本短语的同义短语是 on the spot。

on the side *adv.* (非正式用语)(of someone doing something) as a sideline (in addition to his or her main work)(在主要工作之外)作为兼职(或副业): Besides his weekly wage, he makes some money working *on the side*. 除了每周的工资外,他还从兼职中赚些钱。Her job at the hospital did not pay much, so she found another *on the side*. 她在医院工作的工资较低,所以她又找了份兼职工作。He is a teacher, but he makes some money *on the side* by repairing cars in his free time. 他是一名教师,但他在业余时间兼职修理汽车挣一些钱。

on the spot *adv.* & *adj.* ❶(非正式用语) in the exact place where something is happening 当场(的),到场(的),在现场(的):Whenever I need help, my mother is always *on the spot*. 每当我需要帮助时,我妈妈总是到场。We'll have a police officer *on the spot* immediately. 我们得赶快叫警察到现场。❷immediate(ly); at once; without delay 马上(的),立即(的): She liked it so much that she bought it *on the spot*. 她非常喜欢它,所以马上就把它买下了。Anyone disobeying the order will be shot *on the spot*. 任何违抗命令的人都要被立即枪毙。❸(英国英语用法)without moving away from the place where you are 不离原地(的):The gym teacher made us run *on the spot* for ten minutes. 教体操的老师让我们在原地跑步十分钟。

NOTE 本短语可转化成复合词 on-the-spot,意为"现场的,当场的"。

on the spur of the moment *adv.* (of someone doing something) on a sudden impulse; without taking time to plan or think carefully about (something)一时冲动地,未经计划地,未经考虑地:John had not planned to take the trip, he just left *on the spur of the moment*. 约翰并没计划去旅行,他只凭一时冲动就动身了。She bought this dress *on the spur of the moment* and afterwards she found she did not really like it. 她一时冲动买了这条连衣裙,事后才发现自己并不是很喜欢它。

on the stroke *adv.* at the exact time; punctually 准时: We agreed to meet to lunch, and she arrived *on the stroke*. 我们约定一起吃午饭,她准时到达了。The band began to play *on the stroke* of three. 乐团于3点准时开始演出。

on the surface *adv.* when not observed, thought about deeply 表面上,外表上,从表面上看: *On the surface*, they looked like a happily married couple. 他们表面上像一对幸福的夫妻。The plan seems *on the surface* to be quite practical. 从表面看来这个计划切实可行。She seems rather shy *on the surface*, but she is quite different when you get to know her. 从外表上看,她似乎很腼腆,但你了解她之后就知道她完全不是这样。

on the telephone ⇨ **on the phone**

on the threshold of *prep.* at or near the beginning of (a new experience, etc.)在……就要开始的时候: I congratulate the graduates for they are *on the threshold of* a career. 我祝贺毕业生们,因为他们就要开始做一番事业了。Tyler is *on the threshold of* becoming a very successful singer. 泰勒即要成为一名非常成功的歌手。Scientists are now *on the threshold of* a better understanding of how the human brain works. 科学家现在对人脑如何工作开始有了更多的了解。

on the tip of one's tongue *adv.* (非正式用语) not quite able to be remembered; on the verge of being said 差一点说出,话到嘴边: Now what's her name? It's right *on the tip of my tongue*. 她叫什么名字来着? 就在嘴边,但想不起来了。It was *on the tip of Mary's tongue* to tell them her secret, but she was too frightened. 玛丽刚要告诉他们她的秘密,但是她太害怕没敢说出口。I have his name *on the tip of my tongue*. 他的名字就在我的嘴边。

on the way *adv.* & *adj.* ❶ on the route of a journey 在路上,在途中: *On the way* home we saw a terrible car accident. 在回家的路上,我们目睹了一场重大的车祸。If the man-made satellite returns to earth too fast, it burns up *on the way*. 如果人造地球卫星返回地球太快,它在归途中就会烧毁。❷ (of something or someone) happening or arriving soon 即将来临(的),即将到来(的): The weather forecast said a storm was *on the way*. 暴风雨就要来临了。Economists fear a recession is *on the way*. 经济学家担心经济将衰退。They have three kids, and another *on the way*. 他们已有三个孩子,而第四个孩子又即将出世。

NOTE 不要将本短语与 on one's way to 混淆,on one's way to 意为"去往……"。

on the whole *adv.* with everything considered; in most ways; generally; mostly 总体上,总的看来,大体上: *On the whole*, the article is very well written, but the last part needs touching up. 总体来说,这篇文章写得不错,只是最后一部分需要再改进一下。The two buildings are similar *on the whole*. 从整体来看,这两幢楼大同小异。My opinion, *on the whole*, is the same as yours. 我的意见大体上和你的相同。

NOTE 本短语与 as a whole 之间的区别见 as a whole。

on time *adv.* & *adj.* ❶ according to schedule; punctual or punctually 按时

O

(的),准时(的):The president promised that the general elections would be held *on time* and would be free and fair. 总统承诺,大选将按时,并且自由、公正地举行。The plane was *on time*. 飞机准时到达了。She's always *on time* for her appointment. 她总是准时赴约。❷ by paying in installments; on credit; with time in which to pay 以分期付款方式的:Many young people are never out of debt because they buy everything *on time*. 许多年轻人永远有还不完的债,因为他们每件东西都是以分期付款的方式购买。The young couple bought a flat *on time*. 那对年轻夫妇以分期付款的方式买了一套公寓。

on top *adj.* & *adv.* ❶on the highest point or surface 在最上面(的),在顶部(的):The green book is at the bottom of the pile and the red one is *on top*. 绿皮书在那一堆书的底下,红皮书在最上面。Stand *on top* and look down. 站在最上面往下看。Do you know what building it is? The one with a red flag *on top*. 你知道那是什么大楼吗?就是楼顶上有红旗的那栋。He's going bald *on top*. 他秃顶了。❷(非正式用语)in a leading or successful position; successful 领先的(地),成功的(地):She remained *on top* in the race. 她在赛跑中一直领先。The company will have to expand if it wants to stay *on top*. 如果公司想保持领先地位,就得进一步扩展。Tom had been afraid that he was not prepared for the exam, but he came out *on top*! 汤姆一直担心考试没准备好,但他的成绩竟名列前茅! ❸ in addition 此外:Here's 30 dollars for you, and I'll buy you lunch *on top*. 给你 30 美元,此外我再给你买顿午餐。

on top of the world *adj.* (非正式用语) extremely delighted or satisfied 极其高兴;非常满意:Her youngest son just got married and all her children are doing well. She tells me she's *on top of the world* now. 她最小的儿子刚结婚,所有的孩子都很发达。她对我说,现在她真是感到非常高兴。He felt *on top of the world* after she agreed to marry him. 她同意嫁给他后,他感到极其高兴。

once again *adv.* (used when something has happened before) now again as before; one more time (像以前那样)再一次地:If you've been watching the news lately, you must've noticed that the Israeli-Palestinian conflict has flared up *once again*. 如果你最近一直在看新闻的话,你就会注意到以巴冲突又爆发了。He was forced to publicly apologize *once again* for his wrong action. 他不得不再次为自己的错误行为而公开道歉。

NOTE 本短语的另外一种表达形式是 once more。

once (and) for all *adv.* for the last time; finally and permanently 最后一次地,一劳永逸地:*Once and for all*, I tell you I will not do it. 我最后一次告诉你,我不做这种事。The Supreme Court's ruling has decided this matter *once and for all*. 最高法院的裁决最终判决了此案。This is not something that can be completed *once for all*. 这不是件一劳永逸的事。The candidate for presidency says he'll put an end to corruption *once (and) for all*. 这位总统候选人宣称,他将永久消除腐败。

once in a while *adv.* sometimes but not very often; not regularly; occasionally 偶尔,有时,间或:It's a good idea to eat out *once in a while*, a change of scenery and cooking is good for you. 偶尔在外面吃点饭倒是个好主意,因为换一换景色和烹调口味对你有好处。*Once in a while* clouds are dark because the wind has blown dust up into them. 有的时候云是黑的,因为风把灰尘吹到云里去了。The machines should be checked on *once in a while*. 这些机器应该不时地检查一下。

NOTE 本短语的同义短语是 at times, every so often, from time to time, now and again 和 now and then。它们之间的区别见 at times。

once more ⇨ **once again**

once upon a time *adv.* ❶(used at the beginning of children's stories about events that happened in the past) formerly; a long long time ago (用于给小孩讲故事的开头语)从前,很久很久以前:*Once upon a time*, in a faraway kingdom, there lived a clever prince. 从前,在很远的一个王国里有一个聪明的王子。"*Once upon a time*," he began, "there was a rich man who had everything." "很久很久以前,"他开始讲道,"有一个无所不有的富人。"❷(仅用于口语中)(used for talking about a situation that existed in the past but no longer exists, especially when it was better than the situation now and you wish that it still happened now) some time ago 以前:*Once upon a time*, you could leave your doors unlocked at night and not worry about someone breaking in. 以前,你的房门夜里不用上锁都不必担心有人会进来偷东西。

one after another *adv.* (used for saying that actions are done or things happen with very little time between them) successively; one by one; first one person or thing and then the next, followed by more 相继,一个接一个地,连续地:They got married young and had four children *one after another*. 他们很年轻时就结了婚,并相继生了四个孩子。They use their creativity to make miracles *one after another*. 他们运用自己的创造力创造出了一个又一个的奇迹。Two happy events came *one after another*. 两桩喜事接踵而至。

NOTE 1. 本短语与 one after the other 意义和用法基本相同,它们之间的区别是:本短语常用于三者或三者以上的场合,而 one after the other 则常用于两者的场合。

2. 本短语常以"one + 名词 + after another"的形式使用。例如:

> The mountaineers overcame *one* difficulty *after another* and finally took the Olympic flame to the top of the 8844.43-meter summit of Mount Qomolangma.
> 登山队员们克服了重重困难,终于把奥林匹克圣火送上了 8844.43 米高的珠穆朗玛峰峰顶。

3. 不要将本短语与 one another 混淆,one another 意为"彼此,相互"。

one after the other ⇨ **one after another**

one another ⇨ **one after another**

one by one *adv.* first one, then the next, then the next etc., separately and in order 一个一个地,逐一:Add the eggs *one by one*, and stir as you do so. 把鸡蛋一个一个地加进去,然后像你这样搅拌它们。As the teacher called out our names, we stepped up *one by one* to receive our report cards. 随着老师叫我们的名字,我们一个一个走上前去拿成绩报告单。We'll overcome the difficulties

before us *one by one*. 我们将逐一地克服面前的困难。

NOTE 本短语与 one after another 意义和用法相同。

one day *adv.* ❶(常用将来时态) some time in the future; some day 将来总有一天,有朝一日: He hopes to go to Hawaii to enjoy the sunlight, the air, and the beaches there *one day*. 他希望将来能有一天去夏威夷享受那里的阳光、空气和沙滩。I will take you there *one day*, if you like. 如果你愿意,有朝一日我带你去那里。❷(用过去时态)on an unspecified day in the past 在过去的某一天: *One day* he just walked out and never came back. 一天他走了出去就再也没有回来。*One day* the temperature in the city was 40℃. 有一天市区的温度竟达到了 40 摄氏度。

NOTE 当本短语作"将来总有一天,有朝一日"解时,同义短语是 one of these days 和 some day。

one of these days *adv.* (非正式用语,常用将来时态)on some day in the future; some day 将来总有一天,有朝一日: If you don't take better care of your purse, someone is going to steal it *one of these days*. 如果你不放好你的钱包,总有一天会有人偷走它。*One of these days* we will get lucky. 我们总有一天会有好运的。

NOTE 不要将本短语误用为 one of those days。后者是一个名词性短语,意为"不顺心或倒霉的日子"。如:

> The car wouldn't start, I lost my glasses—it was just *one of those days*!
> 汽车打不着火,眼镜又丢了——这可真是个倒霉的日子。

one time *adv.* once 曾经: *One time* I went to a second-hand book market and bought ten books. 我曾去过旧书市场,并买了 10 本书。

NOTE 不要将本短语与 each time 和 every time 混淆,三者的意义和用法均不同。

only just *adv.* ❶(of something happening) a very short time ago; very recently 刚刚: I'm not hungry. I've *only just* had lunch! 我不饿。我刚刚吃过午饭。The film's *only just* started, so you haven't missed much. 电影刚刚开演,所以你们没少看多少。❷barely; almost not 勉勉强强;几乎不: At present we are *only just* managing to satisfy the demands of our customers. 目前,我们只是勉强满足顾客的需求。He *only just* missed the train. 他几乎没赶上火车。I've got *only just* enough money to last me the month. 我的钱几乎不够这个月花。We arrived in time for our flight, but *only just*. 我们及时到达赶上了飞机,但好险没误机。

only too *adv.* (used to emphasize that something is true or exists to a much greater extent than you would expect or like) very; completely 非常,很,完全,极其: We are *only too* willing to accept your offer. 我们非常愿意接受您的建议。We were *only too* glad to hear the news that China won the Asian Women's Cup. 听到中国队夺得了女足亚洲杯的消息,我们都高兴极了。They discovered that, unfortunately, the rumor was *only too* true. 他们不幸地发现,那传言极其真实。She remembered that happy night *only too* clearly. 她极其清楚地记得那个幸福的夜晚。

NOTE 不要将本短语第二个例句中在 only too 后出现的不定式与单个副词 too 后接

的不定式混淆。单个副词 too 后接的不定式表示“(太……)以至于不能”。如:

She was *only too* glad to help you.
她非常高兴帮助你。
She was *too* busy to help you.
她太忙以至于不能帮助你。

open fire *vi.* (常与 at, on 连用) start shooting a gun (at or on someone or something) 开火,开枪(炮):“*Open fire*!” the officer gave his men the order. 那军官向他的士兵们发出了命令:“开火!” When the policeman called the robber to stop, the latter returned and suddenly *opened fire* at him. 当警察命令那劫匪站住时,那劫匪却转过身来突然向他开了枪。The trainees *opened fire* on the target. 受训人员向靶子开火。

NOTE 1. 本短语的反义短语是 stop fire。
2. 不要将本短语与下句中的 open fire 混淆:

On a footstool near the *open fire* sat Rebecca, silent and shy.
丽贝卡安静羞怯地坐在露天篝火旁的脚凳上。

open to[1] *v.* ❶cause (something such as a door or gate) to be open so as to allow (something or someone) to enter 给……开门:Don't *open* the door *to* strangers, it's not safe. 不要给陌生人开门,那不安全。The farmer *opens* his gates *to* visitors during the lambing season. 这位农民在羊产羔季节开门迎客。❷allow (something) to be entered, visited, seen, etc., by (someone) 对……开放:The city government plans to *open* the gardens *to* the public. 市政府计划把这些花园向公众开放。The newly renovated Qianmen Street in Beijing *opened to* the public one day ahead of the start of the Olympic Games. 新近改造完成的北京前门大街在奥运会开幕前一天向公众开放了。

open to[2] *adj.* ❶ available for anyone to take part in or see 对公众开放的:The China National Space Administration announced that data obtained by the lunar probe Chang'e-1 will be *open to* scientists all over the world for their study. 中国国家航天局宣布,月球探测卫星嫦娥一号所获取的数据将完全公开,供全世界的科学家研究。Most government files from the period are now *open to* scrutiny. 大多数那个时期以来的政府档案现在都供公众查阅。❷not safe from (criticism, question, etc.) 容易遭受到(批评、质疑等)的:The new tax law is *open to* criticism. 这部新税法容易受到批评。His truthfulness is *open to* doubt. 他讲话的真实性让人怀疑。What he said is *open to* being misunderstood. 他的话易于被人误解。❸(of someone) willing to consider or receive (suggestions or ideas) 愿意考虑,愿意接受(建议或主意)的:I have some ideas about what to do, but I'm always *open to* suggestions. 我对要做什么已有些想法,但我一贯愿意听取各种建议。The manager is very modest and *open to* new ideas from his employees. 经理很谦虚,乐于接受其雇员的新想法。❹possible for you to do it 可行的:It's the only course of action *open to* you. 这是你唯一可采取的行动步骤。Taking him to court was the only option left *open to* me. 把他送上法庭是我唯一可做的选择。

open up *v.* ❶(非正式用语,常用于祈使句) open a locked door or building so that people can get in 开门:“Police! *Open up* or we'll break the door down!”

shouted the policeman. “警察！开门，否则我们就要破门了！”警察喊道。We don't *open up* the shop till 9:30. 我们9点半以后才开店门营业。❷ open (something) completely, especially, if it has been closed for a long time 打开：The police had to get special permission to *open up* the grave. 警察不得不经过特别许可才打开了墓穴。He couldn't wait to *open* the parcel *up*. 他急不可待地要打开包裹。❸ (of a place, economy, etc.) (cause to) become accessible to more people (使)(某地或经济等)开放：In short, opening-up is so much better than closing-up, and a nation or a country can advance and develop only when it *opens up* to the outside world. 总之，要开放，不要封闭。一个民族、一个国家，只要开放，才能进步和发展。If this agreement's going to succeed, the European Union will *open up* more of its markets. 如果此项协议成功实施，欧盟会开放更多的市场。❹open (a shop) for business (商店)开业，开(商店)：New cinemas are starting to *open up*. 新建的电影院在先后开业。Donald wants to retire and *open up* a bookshop. 唐纳德想要退休，开一个书店。❺ cut (something) open, as to provide a way through to make it easier to travel 开通，开掘，开辟：The premier stressed the military forces should try their best to *open up* roads to the epicenter and at the same time to air-drop food and medicine to the areas. 总理强调，部队指战员要全力以赴打通通往震中灾区的道路，同时要将食品和药品空投到灾区。The building of canals *opened up* the interior of the country. 筑造运河开通了该国的内陆地区。Another new canal has been *opened up*. 又有一条新运河已经开通。❻(非正式用语) cut into (someone's body) for medical reasons, as in a hospital 手术切开，割开：When the surgeons *opened* her *up* they found a huge tumor. 当外科医生给她开刀时，发现了一巨大肿瘤。The surgeon *opened up* the man's stomach to get at the source of the trouble. 外科医生切开这个病人的胃以便诊察病源。❼ make possible the development of 开发，开拓：The work of *opening up* the oilfield met with difficulties from the very beginning. 开发油田的工作一开始就遇到了许多困难。The sales manager wants to *open up* new markets in the Far East. 销售经理想在远东开辟新市场。Biophysics *opened up* a new field in science. 生物物理学开拓了科学的一个新领域。❽(of a gun) begin firing; (of a person) start shooting a gun (枪，炮)开始射击；(人)开火：A machine gun *opened up* from a concealed position. 机关枪在一个隐蔽的位置开火了。He *opened up* on the crowd with an automatic rifle. 他用一支自动步枪向人群开火。❾(非正式用语) (of someone) start to talk in a free, honest or frank way about your personal feelings or thoughts 畅谈，(坦率地)倾吐心事：When she felt she could trust me, she began to *open up*. 当她觉得可以信赖我时，便开始向我倾吐心事。After a few months, Mary is finally starting to *open up* to me. 几个月后，玛丽终于开始向我坦率地倾吐她的心事。❿(常用一般时态) (of a vehicle) (cause to) go fast (使)(车辆)加速：When we got out on the highway, the driver *opened up* and drove at 80 miles per hour. 我们一驶上公路，司

机便加快车速，以每小时 80 英里的速度行驶。He *opened up* his car and drove straight towards the stadium. 他加快了车速，直向体育场驶去。We took the new car on the highway and *opened* it *up*. 我们把新车开到公路上并使其加速行驶。

NOTE 当本短语用作及物性动词短语，所带的宾语为代词时，该代词须置于本短语的动词和副词中间。

operate on *vt.*【不可分性动词短语】（常与 for 连用）(of a doctor) perform surgery on (a patient's body) in order to remove, replace, or repair a diseased or damaged part, usually in an operating room in a hospital（医生）给……做手术：The surgeons at a hospital in New York City *operated on* former US president Bill Clinton for his heart disease. 纽约市一家医院的外科医生给美国前总统比尔·克林顿做了心脏手术。How many wounded are left out there who haven't been *operated on* yet? 那儿还有多少伤员没有做手术？

opposed to *adj.* disapproving of (something or doing something) 反对的：The Chinese Ambassador to the UN told reporters after the vote that Beijing was firmly *opposed to* North Korea's nuclear test and wants to see a denuclearized Korean peninsula. 中国驻联合国大使在投票后对记者说，北京坚决反对朝鲜进行核试验，并希望看到一个无核化的朝鲜半岛。Many people were *opposed to* imposing a death penalty on the former President. 许多人反对判前总统死刑。

or else *conj.* ❶used for stating the second of two possibilities（用于说明两种可能性中的第二种）要么：You could drive across France, *or else* fly to Geneva and hire a car. 你可以驾车穿越法国，要么就飞到日内瓦后租一辆车。Either he's asleep, *or else* he's just ignoring me. 他要么已经睡着，要么就是故意不理睬我。❷(used for saying that there will be a bad result if something does not happen) or otherwise（用于说明如果不做某事将面临某种严重后果）否则：We must hurry *or else* we will not be able to catch the school bus. 我们得快点，否则就赶不上校车了。Employees must accept these new terms of employment *or else* face dismissal. 员工们必须接受这些新的雇佣条款，否则面临解雇。❸（主要用于口语中，其后的从句往往省略）(used for expressing a threat) if not; or suffer the consequences（用于表示威胁或恐吓）要不然：Give me back those letters *or else* I'll scream. 把那些信还给我，要不然我就喊啦。Pay up, *or else*! 把款付清，要不然让你好瞧！

or so *adv.*（非正式用语，置于所修饰的名词或数词之后）(used for showing that a number or amount is not exact) approximately; roughly; about 大约，左右：The job won't take long, about twenty minutes *or so*. 这件工作不会用多长时间，大约 20 分钟。

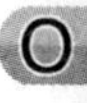

or something (like that) *adv.*（非正式用语）(used for referring to any of a group of things or possibilities without being specific) or some similar thing, person, condition, activity, etc. 或是什么的，大概是……之类的：Would you like a sandwich *or something*? 你想要三明治，还是要别的什么东西？She said she was going shopping *or something*. 她说她要去买东西或是什么的。Her name is Mary or Margaret *or something*. 她的

名字叫玛丽或玛格丽特什么的。What's up with David? Is he drunk *or something*? 戴维怎么了？他是喝醉了酒，还是怎么回事？

NOTE 本短语在说话人对某事不能肯定时才使用。

other than *prep.* ❶（常用于否定句中）with the except of; apart from; besides; in addition to (something or someone)除……以外：I had no ambitions *other than* to have a happy life and be free. 除了要生活幸福、自由自在外，我无所奢求。There was nothing we could do *other than* wait. 除了等待以外，我们无事可为。All parts of the house *other than* the windows are in good condition. 除了窗户外，屋子的其他部分状况都不错。*Other than* one sister, she has no close relatives. 除了一个妹妹外，她没别的近亲。❷different from 与……不同，不同于：The truth is quite *other than* what you think. 事实与你所想的完全不同。His tastes are quite *other than* mine. 他的口味与我的十分不同。

NOTE 当本短语作"除……以外"解时，后面还可接 that 从句。如：

> *Other than* that the nearest store was five miles away, it was a perfect location.
> 除了最近的商店在 5 英里以外，那是个十分理想的位置。

out of *prep.* ❶from the inside of (a place) 从（某一场所）出来：Frank was just coming *out of* the library. 弗兰克刚刚从图书馆出来。I followed him *out of* the house and down the stairs. 我跟随他出了房门，朝楼下走去。Several minutes later, people overcame their fear and made their way *out of* the tube carriage. 几分钟后，人们才克服了恐惧，从地铁车厢中走了出来。❷away from 离开，不在：I'll be *out of* town for two or three weeks. 我要离开镇子两三个星期。He's *out of* hospital, but he can't go back to work. 他虽已出院，但还不能去工作。Dr. Scott Taylor, an American scientist, said he found a type of tropical fish that can survive for up to 66 days *out of* water. 美国科学家斯科特 · 泰勒博士称，他发现了一种离水时间长达 66 天还能存活的热带鱼。❸(of someone or something) no longer in (a situation, especially an unpleasant one)脱离(尤指某种不佳境遇)：We are *out of* danger now. 我们现已脱离了危险。The economy is starting to climb *out of* recession. 经济开始摆脱衰退的困境。❹from among (a group) 从……之中：Our team won eight *out of* ten games last season. 我们队在上个赛季中，十战八胜。*Out of* the money donated by Party members all over the country, 100 million yuan was allocated to the quake-hit areas. 从收到的全国各地党员所捐款中，一亿捐往了地震受灾区。❺in or into (a state of loss) or not having; without; lacking 失去，没有，缺乏：She's been *out of* work for several months. 她已失业好几个月了。We are nearly *out of* petrol. 我们的汽油快用光了。I'm running *out of* ideas, can you suggest anything? 我没有主意了，你能出一点儿吗？I was out of money then. 我当时正缺钱花。❻used to show what something is made from 用……（制成）：Would you advise people to make a building *out of* wood or stone? 你会建议人们用木头或石头建房子吗？He carved a figure *out of* a piece of wood. 他用一块木头雕刻了一个木人。Her clothes are made *out of* cotton. 她的衣服都是用棉布料做的。❼because of, as a result of; by reason of 因为,由于,出于:Some members of high-risk groups refuse to take AIDS tests *out of* fear of discrimination. 一些高危人群的成员拒绝接受艾滋病检测是因为怕受歧视。I took the job *out of* necessity because I had no money left. 我接受这件工作是出于需要,因为我没有钱了。❽from 从……,自……:He woke up *out of* a deep sleep. 他从沉睡中醒来了。As a store owner you must know how to get more money *out of* consumers' pockets. 作为店主,你必须知道如何从顾客的口袋中赚到更多的钱。Relevant parties should work together to obtain real progress *out of* the talks on the Korean nuclear issue. 有关各方应该同力协作,使朝核问题的会谈取得实际进展。❾beyond the limits or range of (something)超出,在……范围之外:The plane flew *out of* sight soon. 飞机很快就飞得看不见了。The airport is forty miles *out of* the city. 机场在该城40英里之外。

out of action *adj*. (of someone or something such as a machine or gun) unable to move, operating, etc., especially due to injury or damage (指人因伤而)失去活动能力的;(指武器或机器因损毁而)失去战斗力的,发生故障的: He's been *out of action* for 10 months with a serious knee injury. 他因膝部严重受伤而10个月没能活动。That accident forced my boss *out of action* for almost a month. 那场事故使我的老板几乎一个月不能活动。Something has put this washing machine *out of action* again. 又有什么故障使这台洗衣机不能工作了。Accurate gunnery had already put three of the leading tanks *out of action*. 准确的炮火使领头的三辆坦克瘫痪。

NOTE 本短语的反义短语是 in action。

out of breath *adj*. breathing fast and with difficulty, for example because you have been running 气喘吁吁的,上气不接下气的:The boy ran so much that he got *out of breath*. 这男孩儿跑得太多,都上气不接下气了。She is weak and is *out of breath* from climbing the stairs. 她身体虚弱,上楼梯都气喘吁吁。The long run left Bill *out of breath*. 长跑使比尔上气不接下气。

NOTE 本短语的比较级形式是 more out of breath, 最高级形式是 most out of breath。

out of circulation *adj*. ❶(of something such as money) no longer available for use by the public (指货币等)不再流通的,不再使用的:Gold coins were taken *out of circulation* many years ago. 金币在很多年前就不再流通了。You cannot use the money *out of circulation*. 不再流通的钱你不能用。The faulty and potentially dangerous electric blankets were driven *out of circulation*. 质量低劣且有潜在危险的电热毯都被取缔使用。❷(非正式用语)(of someone) no longer taking part in his or her usual public or social activities (指某人)不再参加(以往的)社会活动: She is *out of circulation* at the moment because she is studying for her exams. 目前,她因准备考试而不参加公共活动了。Work on my latest book has kept me *out of circulation* for the past few months. 新书的写作使我在

过去的几个月里一直没能参加以往的社会活动。

NOTE 本短语的反义短语为 in circulation。

out of condition *adj.* (of someone or something) not healthy or unfit (指人)健康状况不好的;(指物)保存得不好的,不合用的: He knew that he was *out of condition* from sitting for so long in the office without exercise. 他知道自己在办公室坐得很久不运动而健康状况不好。You must not sell the grain *out of condition*. 保存不好的粮食绝不能出售。

NOTE 1. 本短语中的名词 condition 前不能加任何冠词。

2. 本短语的比较级形式是 more out of condition, 最高级形式是 most out of condition。

3. 本短语的反义短语是 in condition。

out of contact with *adj.* no longer in communication with (someone) 与(某人)失去联系: If I'm *out of contact with* Robert, I'll still be in contact with his younger brother. 如果我和罗伯特失去联系,我还会和他的弟弟联系。She moved to France three years ago and we have been *out of contact with* each other ever since. 她三年前移居法国,从那以后我们相互就失去了联系。

out of control *adj.* (常用在动词 be, get, go 之后) ❶ (of a person) not under the authority or power of someone (指人)失去管束的: Those children have been completely *out of control* since their mother died. 那些孩子自从母亲去世后便完全失去了管束。The kids got *out of control* again. 孩子们又失去了管束。❷ (of a situation or a machine) not under control (指形势或机器)失去控制的: In less than 30 seconds a small flame can get *out of control* and turn into a major fire. 在不到 30 秒钟内,较小的火势就会失控并发展成为大火。The computer is *out of control* and making strange-looking characters all over the screen. 电脑不听使唤,满屏幕都是些奇怪的字符。The car went *out of control* and crashed over the cliff. 汽车失去控制,从悬崖上坠毁。

NOTE 1. 本短语的比较级形式是 more out of control, 最高级形式是 most out of control。

2. 本短语的同义短语是 out of hand; 反义短语是 under control 和 in hand (第二个义项)。

out of danger *adj.* safe; not in danger or expected to die 安全的,脱离生命危险的: The bus blast that occurred yesterday killed 11 people and injured 7 others who have been *out of danger* and are hospitalized locally. 昨天发生的公共汽车爆炸致使 11 人死亡,7 人受伤。伤者已脱离危险,住进了当地医院。She helped him *out of danger* by stealing food and medicine from her own home. 她从自己家中偷偷拿来食物和药品,帮他脱离了危险。

NOTE 本短语的反义短语是 in danger。

out of date *adj.* ❶ no longer useful; past the point of expiration 废弃不用的,过期的: A lot of new words go *out of date* very quickly. 许多新词很快就废弃不用了。The monthly bus pass is not valid if it is *out of date*. 如果公共汽车月票过期就无效了。❷ not modern; not fashionable 过时的,不时兴的: Almost nobody likes wearing the clothes *out of date*. 几乎没有人喜欢穿过时的衣服。Cassette tape recorders are *out of date* now. 现在，盒式磁带录音机过时了。I just cleaned out my wardrobe and it feels so good to be rid of all the old clothes that don't fit or are *out of date*. 我刚刚清理了我的衣柜。把那些穿起来不合适或不时兴的旧衣服统统扔掉，感觉真好。

NOTE 1. 本短语的比较级形式是 more out of date，最高级形式是 most out of date。

2. 当本短语作“过时的，不时兴的”解时，同义短语是 out of fashion 和 out of style；反义短语是 up to date，in fashion 和 in style。

3. 本短语可转化为复合词 out-of-date，意为“过时的”。

out of doors *adv.* in the open air; outside a building rather inside it 在露天，在户外：We often have our food *out of doors* in summer. 在夏季，我们经常在露天吃饭。He spends a lot of time *out of doors*. 他的很多时间都在户外度过。We couldn't wait to get *out of doors* again after the long rain. 漫长的雨天过后，我们都迫不及待地想要重到户外去活动。

NOTE 1. 本短语中的名词 door 必须用复数形式。

2. 本短语可以转化为复合词 out-of-doors，用作：副词，意为“在露天，在室外”；用作形容词，意为“露天的，室外的”；用作名词，意为“露天，室外”。

3. 本短语与副词 outdoors 意义和用法相同。例如：

> Their cat lives mainly *outdoors*.
> 他们家的猫一般住在户外。
> We have an *outdoor* swimming pool at our university.
> 我们学校里有一个室外游泳池。

out of fashion *adj.* (of something such as a style of dress or an activity) not fashionable or popular, and not approved of at a particular time 不流行的，不时髦的，不时兴的：And though some consider this *out of fashion*, many parents are saving on their children's clothing. 尽管有些人认为这已过时，但许多父母还是在孩子的穿戴上节省花钱。These shoes have gone *out of fashion*, but I like them. 虽然这些鞋子已不时兴，但我还是喜欢它们。

NOTE 本短语的 fashion 可被 style 替换，两者的意义和用法相同。

out of hand *adv.* ❶ (of a person or situation) out of control (指人或局面)失去控制：The angry crowd was getting *out of hand*. 愤怒的人群已失去了控制。We decided to leave before things got *out of hand*. 我们决定在情势失控之前撤离。However the situation is not yet *out of hand*, as the government has come up with various methods of reducing the rate of brain drain. 但由于政府出台了一些不同的措施来减少人才流失率，这种局面并没有失控。❷ (especially of decisions not to do something) at once and without any further thought 立即，不假思索地(尤指拒绝做某事)：The proposals were rejected *out of hand*. 这些建议都当即遭到了拒绝。Moving to New York is not a good choice, so I dismissed the idea *out of hand*. 搬到纽约去住不是一个好的选择，因此我不假思索地拒绝考虑那主意。

NOTE 1. 本短语的比较级形式是 more out of hand，最高级形式是 most out of hand。

2. 不要将本短语与 out of one's hands 混淆。

out of keeping with *prep.* (of something said or some behavior) not in harmony or agreement with (something) (指某种言

论或行为)不符合……,与……不一致: That is quite *out of keeping with* your statement of yesterday. 这和你昨天说的那番话大相径庭。The funeral arrangements seemed *out of keeping with* the family's wishes. 葬礼的一些安排似乎不符合家属的愿望。What he has done is completely *out of keeping with* our standards of behavior. 他的所作所为完全违背了我们的行为准则。

NOTE 本短语的同义短语是 out of step with; 反义短语是 in keeping with, in accord with, in accordance with, in agreement with, in harmony with 和 in line with。

out of one's hands *adj.* no longer your responsibility; no longer in someone's control 不再由某人负责的,不再由某人掌控的: I'm afraid the matter is now *out of my hands*. 恐怕这件事不再由我负责了。The committee decided to take the project *out of his hands*. 委员会决定不再让他负责该项目。The project had to be gotten *out of Robert's hands* because he said that he was leaving. 该项目不再由罗伯特负责了,因为他说要离职。

NOTE 本短语中的名词 hand 必须用复数形式。

out of one's head *adj.* (非正式用语) crazy; insane; unable to think clearly 发疯的,精神错乱的,思维不正常的: You're *out of your head* if you accept those terms. 如果你接受那些条款,你就是疯了。The man who committed that crime must have been *out of his mind*. 犯下那种罪行的人肯定是精神错乱了。Why did you do that? You must be *out of your head*! 你为什么做那样的事? 你肯定精神不正常!

NOTE 本短语的名词 head 可被 mind, sense 等替换,构成的短语意义和用法与本短语相同。

out of one's wits *adj.* feeling very much afraid and extremely frightened (吓得)惊慌失措的,魂不附体的: We were scared *out of our wits* by a loud bang at the door. 我们被很响的敲门声吓得惊慌失措。The explosion in the building near my house frightened me *out of my wits*. 我家附近那栋楼内的爆炸吓得我魂不附体。

NOTE 本短语中的名词 wit 必须用复数形式。

out of order *adj.* &*v. adv.* ❶(of a machine or device)not working properly; not in good condition (指机器或装置)有毛病的(地),出故障的(地): I have never found the machine *out of order*. 我从来没发现过这机器有毛病。The telephone is *out of order* and needs repairing. 电话机出了故障,需要修理了。According to the report of *Science & Space*, Hubble telescope instrument went *out of order* not long ago. 根据《科学与太空》杂志报道,哈勃望远镜设备前不久出了故障。❷in the wrong order or not properly arranged; in confusion 颠三倒四的(地),乱七八糟的(地): Some of the names on the list are *out of order*. 名单上的一些名字顺序搞乱了。Peter wrote the words of the sentence *out of order*. 彼得把这个句子中的单词写得颠三倒四。He can't stand to see the workshop *out of order*. 他无法容忍看到车间里乱七八糟。❸(正式用语)(of remarks or actions) not following the formal rules of a court of law, a parliament etc. (指言论或行为)不符(法庭或议会等的)规程的(地): The last speaker was *out of order* in saying that. 最后发言的人那样说是违背会议规程的。The witness's comment was ruled *out of* order by the judge. 证人的那番评论被法官裁定有违法庭规程。

NOTE 1. 当本短语作“有毛病,出故障”解时,通常指小物件的毛病或故障。如果是大东西(如汽车、机械等)出现故障或毛病,则用 break down。如:

> The car *broke down* just outside Hanoi.
> 汽车刚驶出河内就出了故障。

2. 本短语的比较级形式是 more out of order,最高级形式是 most out of order。

3. 本短语的反义短语是 in order。

out of place *adj.* ❶ inappropriate or unsuitable (to the occasion or situation) 不适宜的,不恰当的:It was *out of place* for Mary to wear a T-shirt at the press conference. 玛丽在记者招待会上穿 T 恤衫是不适宜的。His statement was entirely *out of place* on such an occasion. 他的话在这种场合说是很不合适的。One word *out of place* would make the manager angry. 一句话说得不合适,就会使经理发起火来。The luxurious furnishings would not have been *out of place* in a palace. 这些豪华富丽的家具就是放在宫殿里也很适宜。❷(of someone) feeling uncomfortable in a particular situation or place, or he or she does not belong there (指人在某种场合中)感到不自在的:Mary felt very *out of place* among Helen's friends. 玛丽和海伦的朋友们在一起时感到很不自在。❸(of something) not in the proper place or usual position 不在适当地方的,不在原来位置的:I saw at once that someone had been in my study, because some of my books were *out of place*. 我一眼就看出有人来过我的书房,因为我的一些书放得都不是地方。It's a lovely table but it would look *out of place* with all our antique furniture. 这张桌子是很漂亮,但和我们所有这些古董家具放在一起就显得不相称了。

NOTE 当本短语作“不适宜的,不恰当的”和“不在适当地方的,不在原来位置的”解时,反义短语是 in place。

out of practice *adj.* bad in skill at doing something because you have not been doing it regularly (由于久不练习而)技艺生疏的:The basketball team got *out of practice* during the Christmas holidays. 篮球队在圣诞节休假期间球艺生疏了。I haven't played tennis for years, so I'm really *out of practice*. 我已多年不打网球,技术已完全生疏了。

NOTE 1. 本短语的比较级形式是 more out of practice,最高级形式是 most out of practice。

2. 本短语的反义短语是 in practice。

out of proportion *adj.* & *adv.* not balanced; not in symmetry; more important or worrying than something is really is 不均衡的(地),不相称的(地);过分的(地):As the speed of a plane approaches 750 miles an hour, the amount of power needed increases *out of proportion*. 当飞机的速度接近每小时 750 英里时,所需的动力就会不成比例地增加。Jessica Lynch said the story of her rescue in Iraq was exaggerated *out of* all *proportion*. 杰西卡·林奇说她在伊拉克被营救的事被夸张得离谱了。Haven't you got things just a little *out of proportion*? 你是不是把事情搞得有点过分了?

NOTE 1. 本短语的比较级形式是 more out of proportion,最高级形式是 most out of proportion。

2. 本短语的反义短语是 in proportion。

out of (all)proportion to/with *prep.* (much) too great as compared with 同……(很)不成比例: My friend was caught spitting in Hong Kong and was fined 1,500 HK dollars, but I think the fine was *out of all proportion to* the seriousness of her fault. 我的朋友因在香港吐痰被抓,罚款1500元港币。但我认为这罚金与她所犯过错的严重程度很不成比例。The figures in the painting are completely *out of proportion with* their surroundings. 油画中的人与其周围的环境完全不成比例。

NOTE 本短语的反义短语是 in proportion to。

out of question *adv.* without doubt; beyond question 无疑问地: His honesty is *out of question*. 他的诚实是毋庸置疑的。Computer science will *out of question* develop at a high speed. 毫无疑问,计算机科学将以高速度发展。*Out of question*, he ought to have the position. 他无疑应当得到这个职位。

NOTE 不要将本短语与 out of the question 相混淆。out of the question 意为"不可能"。

out of (one's) reach *adj.* ❶ not able to touch by stretching 伸手不可及的: Put the bottle of weed killer *out of the children's reach*. 把那瓶除草剂放在孩子们拿不到的地方。The book is on the top shelf, *out of (my) reach*. 这本书在顶架上,(我)够不着。❷ not able to have or do something because of not having enough money or skill 买不起的,做不到的: Such a luxury is *out of our reach*. 这样的奢侈品我们可买不起。I wanted to be a manager, but I'm afraid that such a goal is *out of reach*. 我想当经理,可我又怕这样一个目标达不到。

NOTE 1. 本短语与 beyond (one's) reach 意义和用法相同,两者可互换使用。
2. 本短语的反义短语是 within (one's) reach。

out of season Ⅰ *adj.* (of fruit and vegetables) not grown at the normal time or under normal conditions; not available fresh locally (水果或蔬菜)不当令的,不应时的: I don't like to eat fruit that is *out of season*. 我不喜欢吃不当令的水果。Cucumber is *out of season* now and really expensive. 黄瓜现在不是应时蔬菜,所以很贵。

Ⅱ *adv.* not at the proper or best time 不在适当时候的,不在最佳时机的: Their importations frequently arrived *out of season*. 他们的进口货物经常不适时而到。Hotel charges are lower *out of season*. 旅馆在淡季收费较低。

NOTE 本短语的反义短语是 in season。

out of shape *adj.* ❶ (非正式用语) (of something) no longer in its proper or original form, for example because it has been damaged or wrongly handled (指物)变形的,走样的: Don't ride on that bicycle, its wheels are *out of shape*. 别骑那辆自行车了,它的轮子都变形了。The children have been playing with my hat, they've knocked it *out of shape*. 孩子们一直玩着我的帽子,都把它弄得不成样子了。❷ (of someone) unhealthy or in bad physical condition (指人)身体状况不佳的: He has been working too hard, and is *out of shape*. 他工作一直太累,以至于身体状况欠佳。I can't believe how *out of shape* I am. 我无法相信我的身体状况有多么糟。

NOTE 本短语的反义短语是 in (good) shape。

out of sight *adj.* &*adv.* ❶ unable to be seen; beyond one's range of vision 看不见的(地),超出视力范围的(地): In a few seconds, the rocket was *out of sight* in the sky. 几秒钟

后，火箭就在空中不见了。Before the hunter could take aim, the deer ran *out of sight*. 猎人还没来得及瞄准，那只鹿便跑得不见了踪影。Put that book *out of sight*. 把那本书放在看不见的地方。Don't let the kids *out of* your *sight* for a second. 一刻也不要让孩子们离开你的视线。❷(非正式用语)very high in price; very expensive 价格很高的(地)，十分昂贵的(地)：The prices are *out of sight* in this department store. 这家百货商店的价格很高。They have realized their cost of medical care has gone *out of sight*. 他们已经认识到他们的医疗费用太高了。❸in hiding 躲藏起来的(地)：You better stay *out of sight* for a few days. 你最好躲几天。Get *out of sight*, or they'll see you! 藏起来，要不他们就会看见你！❹(仅用于口语中) fantastic; marvelous; excellent 极好，好极了的(地)："How was the evening party?" "*Out of sight*!" "晚会开得怎么样？" "极好！" The opening ceremony was *out of sight*. 开幕式棒极了。

NOTE 1. 当本短语作"看不见的(地)，超出视力范围的(地)"解时，其中的名词 sight 前可加定语。例如：

> Get *out of* my *sight*!
> 别让我再看见你！

sight 也可有后置定语。如：

> We were soon *out of sight* of the plane.
> 很快，我们就看不见那架飞机了。

2. 当本短语作"看不见的(地)，超出视力范围的(地)"解时，同义短语是 *out of view*；反义短语是 in/within sight 和 in/into view。

out of step *adj. &adv.* ❶(especially of soldiers) marching in such a way that each person's right foot and left foot move forward at a different time (尤指士兵)在行进中步调不一致的(地)：Bob was *out of step* during most of the march. 鲍勃在行进中大多时与别人的步调不一致。One of the soldiers marched *out of step* with others at the very beginning. 有一名士兵一开始行进时步伐就与其他士兵的不一致。❷(常与 with 连用)(of people, their ideas or opinions) different or not agreeing (with each other) 不一致的(地)，不和谐的(地)：Because of his different cultural background, he often finds himself *out of step* with his classmates on many issues. 由于他的文化背景不同，他在许多问题上常常与他的同班同学不相一致。The British Government is once again *out of step* with world opinion. 英国政府再一次与世界舆论相背。

NOTE 本短语的反义短语是 in/into step。

out of step with *prep.* (of a person or behavior) not in harmony or in accordance with (others)(指人或行为)与……不和谐，同……不合拍：Just because you smoke, it doesn't mean you are *out of step with* rest of us. 不能只因你抽烟就说你同我们大家不和谐。He has frequently been *out of step with* society because of his radical opinions. 由于他的激进观点，他常常同社会不合拍。

NOTE 本短语的反义短语是 in step with。

out of stock *adj.* having none for sale, usually only temporarily; sold out (常指暂时性地)无现货的，已售完的："Have you any blue shirts in stock?" "No, I am afraid they're *out of stock*, but we shall be having some more in next month." "你们这儿有蓝色衬衫吗？" "恐怕没有现货了，但我们下个月会进一些的。" So many children have bought the balloons that the store is now *out of stock*. 买气球的孩子太多了，以至于这家商店的气球都卖光了。

NOTE 本短语的反义短语是 in stock。

out of style ⇨ **out of fashion**

out of the public eye ⇨ **in the public eye**

out of the question *adj.* (用作表语) completely impossible or unacceptable 完全不可能的；不可接受的：Taking a holiday then is *out of the question*, you'll have to arrange it for some other time. 在那个时间休假是不可能的，所以你得把它安排在其他时间。The boys had no money, so it was *out of the question* for them to go to the movies. 孩子们没有钱，所以不可能去看电影。The union thought the management's offer was *out of the question*, so the workers went on strike. 工会认为资方的提议不可接受，所以工人们罢工了。

NOTE 本短语的同义短语是 no question of，但两者的用法有些不同。no question of 后常接动名词或动名词短语。例如：

> There's *no question of* accepting these terms.
> 接受这些条款是不可能的。

out of the red ⇨ **in/into the red**

out of the way *adj.* ❶ remote from populous or much-traveled regions 偏僻的，偏远的：It's a very nice store, but it's a little *out of the way*. 那是个很不错的店铺，可就是偏远了一点儿。We have bought a little cottage, quite *out of the way*. 我们在十分偏远的地方买了一套小别墅。❷unusual or uncommon; out of the ordinary 不平常的，特殊的：The boy's behavior was quite *out of the way*. 这男孩的行为很特别。The house wasn't anything *out of the way*. 这栋房子没什么特殊之处。❸ off the right path; improper; wrong 脱离正轨的，不适当的，错误的：He has done nothing *out of the way* yet. 他还没干过什么不轨之事。To leave before the guest of honor would be *out of the way*. 在主宾之前退席是不合适的。I'm sorry if I said something *out of the way*. 如果我说错了什么，我很抱歉。❹completed 完成的，结束的：I'm very glad my final exams are *out of the way*. 期末考试考完了，我真高兴。

NOTE 1. 本短语前三个义项的比较级形式是 more out of the way，最高级形式是 most out of the way。

2. 本短语可转化为复合词 out-of-the-way，意为"偏僻的；罕见的，少有的；破例的"。

out of touch *adj.* (常与 with 连用) ❶(of people) no longer in communication (with each other) (相互)失去联系的：We have been *out of touch* with each other for five years. 我们相互之间已有 5 年没联系了。The presidential candidate failed to appear the next day at his own scheduled news conference, and remained *out of touch* over the weekend. 该总统选候选人没有在第二天他自己安排的记者招待会上露面，而且整个周末都失去联系。❷(of someone) no longer having recent knowledge or information (about something) 不了解(某事)的：It is obvious that he is *out of touch* with the latest innovations in his field. 显然他不了解其领域的最新革新成果。The church has become so *out of touch* with the modern world. 该教会已变得与现代世界格格不入。

NOTE 本短语的比较级形式是 more out of touch，最高级形式是 most out of touch。

out of tune with ⇨ in tune with

out of use *adj.* not being used any longer 不再使用的:Such coins have been *out of use* for several years. 这样的硬币几年前就已不再使用了。This custom has fallen *out of use*. 这种风俗已不时兴了。The present telephone boxes will go *out of use* next year. 现在的这些公用电话亭明年就不再使用了。

NOTE 1. 不要将本短语与 of no use 混淆,of no use 意为"没有帮助的,没用的"。

2. 本短语的反义短语是 in use。

out of view ⇨ in/into view

ou of wedlock *adv.* (常用在 born 之后) outside marriage 婚外地,非婚地: Some children were born *out of wedlock*. 一些孩子是非婚生的。As the married couple can't have children, they have adopted a child born *out of wedlock*. 由于这对已婚夫妇不能生育,所以他们领养了一个私生子。

NOTE 本短语可转化为复合词 out-of-wedlock,意为"非婚的"。

out of work *adj.* not having a paid job; unemployed 没有工作的,失业的: We have all been *out of work*, and we've all got tired of having to visit endless sites everyday and trying to find the newly posted jobs. 我们都已没有工作可做了。但我们又厌倦每天访问一个又一个的网站,去找新招贴出来的工作岗位。The number of people *out of work* now is greater than it was last year at this time. 目前的失业人数比去年同期的要多。The depression threw millions of people *out of work*. 经济萧条致使数百万人失业。

over age *adj.* too old according to law or to particular regulations to do something 超过法定年龄的,超龄的: He won't be called up for military service — he's *over age*. 他不会被征召入伍,因为他已经超龄了。His application was rejected because they said he was *over age*. 他的申请被拒绝。因为他们说,他已超过了年龄。

NOTE 1. 本短语的反义短语是 under age。

2. 本短语可转化为复合词 overage,意为"超龄的;太旧而不中用的"。

over and over (again) *adv.* repeatedly; once again; once more; many times 反复地,一再地,多次: That was the problem they talked about *over and over*. 那就是他们反复谈论的问题。Jackie Chan and Jet Li had said *over and over again* that they were waiting for the right opportunity to cooperate —*The Forbidden Kingdom* finally brought them together. 成龙和李连杰曾多次表示过他们在等待合适的机会合作。最终,《功夫之王》把他们结合到了一起。

NOTE 本短语与 again and again, time and again 均表示"反复""再三"。但 over and over、time and again 常用于美国口语中, over and over again、again and again 常用于英国口语中。

over the phone ⇨by phone

owe to *vt.* 【可分性动词短语】❶(常用一般时态)have a duty to repay (money) to (someone or a group)欠……的债: The companies *owe* as much as 200 million dollars *to* foreign lenders. 这些公司欠的外贷有两亿美元之多。❷(用一般时态) feel grateful to (someone) because of the way they have helped you 感激,多亏了(某人): I *owe* it *to* you that I am still alive, doctor. 大夫，我还能活着，这得感谢您。I *owe* the fulfillment of the task *to* you. 多亏了您我才完成了这项任务。She *owes* her life *to* you. 她能活下来都亏了您。At last it's coming to me how much I *owe to* my parents. 我终于懂得父母给我的恩惠是多么多。❸（用一般时态）believe (something) to be the result of (someone or something) 把……归功于，归因于：The company *owes* its success *to* its excellent leaders. 公司将成功归功于其卓越的领导人。She owed her success to hard work. 她把她的成功归因于辛勤工作。We *owe* all our achievements most fundamentally *to* our hard work. 这一切成就的取得，最根本的原因是我们勤奋的工作。

owing to *prep.* (used for introducing the reason for something) because of; on account of (something) 由于，因为：Flights from London Airport were cancelled, *owing to* bad weather. 由于恶劣的天气，由伦敦机场起飞的航班都被取消了。*Owing to* global warming the average global temperature will increase by 1.4 to 5.8 degrees Celsius by 2100. 由于全球变暖，全世界的平均气温到2100年将增加1.4至5.8摄氏度。It was *owing to* this difficulty that the plan did not succeed. 正是由于这种困难，才使得计划失败。

NOTE **1.** 本短语后只能接物，不能接人。**2.** 本短语和 because of, due to 和 on account of 都是介词性短语，表示“由于，因为”。because of 强调因果关系，在句中仅作状语，修饰句中的某一部分，与他成分不用逗号隔开。即可置于句首，也可置于句尾；due to 所引导的短语一般用作表语或后置定语，偶作状语，但作状语时一般不可置于句首；on account of 用作状语，可与另外三个短语互换使用；owing to 所引导的短语一般用作状语，用于修饰整个句子，即可置于句首，也可置于句尾，偶也作表语。

P p

pace about/around/round *v.* walk with regular steps around (a small area), because you are anxious, worried, nervous, or impatient (由于焦急、忧虑、紧张或不安而)踱步(于某处): I had a bad toothache, so I couldn't sleep and *paced about* most of the night. 我牙疼得很厉害,所以睡不着觉,大半夜都来回踱着步子。She found John *pacing* restlessly *around* his room, unable to sleep. 她发现约翰没能睡觉,在他房间里不安地踱着步子。The lion *paced* restlessly *round* its cage. 狮子在笼子里烦躁不安地走来走去。

pace off/out *vt.* 【可分性动词短语】 measure (a distance or place) by counting the number of steps that you need to walk from one end of something to the other 步测,用步子量出(一段距离或地方的长度): He *paced off* the wooden bridge and found it was 150 feet long. 他步测出那座木桥长约 150 英尺。If you want to know how far it is from the school to the post office, just *pace* it *off*. 你要想知道从学校到邮局有多远,用步子量一下就行了。I had already *paced out* the dimensions of my new home. 我早已经量出了我新房的面积。I think the hall is 80 meters long. I'll *pace* it *out* to be sure. 我想,这走廊有 80 米长;为把握起见,我来步测一下吧。

NOTE 当本短语的宾语为代词时,该代词须置于本短语的动词和副词中间。

pack away *vt.* 【可分性动词短语】 ❶put(something)back into the container where it is stored, after you have finished using it 把……用完后收起来: We *packed away* the picnic things and started up the engine. 我们把野餐用的东西都收拾放好后便启动了发动机。She *packed away* the winter clothes when they were not needed. 她把不再穿的冬装都收藏了起来。I'll try to find that old book, but it's been *packed away* for years. 我会尽力找到那本旧书,不过它已被收起来多年了。❷(非正式用语)eat(a large quantity of food)吃掉(大量食物): She can really *pack* it *away*. 她真的能把那些东西全部吃光。

NOTE 当本短语的宾语为代词时,该代词须置于本短语的动词和副词中间。

pack in *vt.* 【可分性动词短语】 ❶(cause to)be pressed together, as in a container or space 把……塞入: Don't forget to *pack* your toothbrush and paste *in*. 别忘了把你的牙刷和牙膏装进包里。❷fill (a limited space) with a lot of people or things 往(有限的空间)里塞满(人或物): The bus is already overcrowded but they are still *packing* people *in*. 公共汽车已经拥挤不堪了,可他们还在往里塞人。The more people they can *pack in*, the more money they can make. 往里塞的人越多,他们就能赚越多的钱。❸(非正式用语,无被动语态形式)(of films, plays, performers, etc.) attract (very large audiences) to see them (电影、戏剧、表演者等)吸引(大批观众或听众): The new action film *Spider-Man* Ⅱ is really *packing in* the crowds. 新拍的动作影片《蜘蛛侠 2》确实吸引了大批的观众。The play was still *packing* them *in* after several weeks. 这出戏在上演数周后仍吸引着大批的观众。Her Friday night appearances at the club have been *packing* them *in*. 她星期五晚上在俱乐部的演出一直吸引着他们。❹(主要用于英国英语中,非正式用语) stop doing (an activity or a job) 停止(某种活动),放弃(工作等): I'm trying to *pack in* drinking. 我正在试图戒酒。Smoking is bad for you, you ought to *pack* it *in*. 吸烟对你没好处,你应该戒掉它。I decided to *pack in* my university studies and get a job. 我决定放弃大学的学习,找一份工作做。A year ago, she *packed in* her job to join the band. 一年前,她放弃工作,加入了乐团。❺(英国英语用法,非正式用语) end (a relationship) with someone, or to stop (meeting or spending time) with them 中断(与某人的关系): She *packed* her boyfriend *in* lately. 她最近中断了和男朋友的关系。"Is Linda still seeing Bob?" "No, she's *packed* him *in*." "琳达还在和鲍勃约会吗?""不了,她已经不再和他相处了。"

NOTE 1. 当本短语的宾语为代词时,该代词须置于本短语的动词和副词中间。

2. 当本短语作"停止(某种活动),放弃(工作等)"解时,同义短语是 give up。

pack off *vt.* 【可分性动词短语】(常与 to 连用) ❶(非正式用语) send (someone) away somewhere to stay for a period of time, especially to avoid trouble; dismiss (someone) (尤指为了避免麻烦)把(某人)打发走,解雇(某人): We *packed* our kids *off* to their grandparents for the weekend. 我们把孩子们打发到他们的爷爷奶奶那儿过周末。I finally succeeded in *packing* her *off* to bed. 我终于成功地打发她上床睡觉了。To avoid family disgrace, Frank was *packed off* to India. 为避免给家庭带来耻辱,弗兰克被打发到印度去了。He *packed off* his servant. 他辞退了他的用人。❷send (something) in a parcel 把(某物)寄走: He has *packed* the books *off* to his friend. 他已把书寄给了他的朋友。

NOTE 当本短语的宾语为代词时,该代词须置于本短语的动词和副词中间。

pack up *vt.* &*vi.* ❶put your things (into a bag, case, or box, etc.) before you are leaving; do one's luggage 把……打包,收拾行李: We'll *pack up* all the contents in the house before we move. 我们在搬家前要把房子里的东西全部打包。Have you *packed* your things *up*? 你把你的东西都收拾好了吗? They *packed up* the children and sent them to their native home. 他们给孩子们打好行装,把他们送回老家。Once the term finished we all *packed up* and went home. 学期一结束,我们就都打好行装回家了。❷(英国英语用法,非正式用语) finish working for the day by putting work or equipment away 完成工作,停工,收工: We have already *packed up* the job. 我们已经完成了工作。As business was not good, she *packed up* early. 由于生意不好,她早早地收工了。The workmen have already *packed up* and left. 工人们都已收工走了。❸(主要用于英国英语中,非正式用

语)stop (something you are doing) and not try to start again; give up 不再做,停止: If I can't find a job soon, I might as well *pack up*. 如果我不能很快地找到一份工作,我就不找了。He *packed up* his job after three months. 三个月后他就不再干那份工作了。She's *packed up* smoking at long last. 她终于戒烟了。You're making too much noise, *pack it up*, will you? 你们太吵闹了,能不能静下来?

—*vi.* (主要用于英国英语中,非正式用语)(of a machine or piece of equipment) stop working or operating because they have broken or gone wrong (指机械或装置因故障而)停止工作或运转: One of the aircraft's engines *packed up*. 飞机的一个引擎停止了运转。My watch has just *packed up*. 我的表刚停。The camera had *packed up*. 照相机早就不好使了。

NOTE 当本短语用作及物性动词短语,所带的宾语为代词时,该代词须置于本短语的动词和副词中间。

pair up *v.* (常用一般时态,常与 with 连用)(of people) form a pair or make (two people) form a pair, especially in order to do something together (指人)(尤指为做某事)(使)结成一对: Two students from each class *pair up* to produce a short play. 每班出两名学生结成对子编演短剧。Smokers and nonsmokers are *paired up* as roommates. 吸烟的和不吸烟的结对成为室友。He was *paired up* with my sister in the tennis tournament. 他在网球比赛中与我妹妹搭档。

part with *vt.* 【不可分性动词短语】❶sell (something), especially at a very low price (尤指廉价)出售(某物): He has *parted with* his house. 他已廉价卖掉了自己的房子。No, I don't want to *part with* my bike! 不,我不想卖掉我的自行车。❷give (something) to (someone) although you would prefer to keep it 舍弃: I don't want to *part with* any of my favorite possessions. 我不愿舍弃自己所喜爱的任何物品。In order to raise money she had to *part with* some of her most treasured possessions. 为了筹款,她不得不舍弃自己的一些最珍贵的物品。

participate in *vt.* 【不可分性动词短语】take part in (something such as an activity) 参加,参与(某项活动): More than 10,000 athletes from 204 countries and regions *participated in* the 29th Olympic Games of Beijing. 有来自 204 个国家和地区的 10 000 多名运动员参加了第 29 届北京奥运会。Beside the five research institutes the Library of National History also *participated in* developing the database of Ching Dynasty. 除了那五个研究所以外,国史馆也参与了清史资料库的开发。

NOTE 1. 当本短语作"参加,参与"解时,与 take part in 意义和用法相同。但本短语多用于书面语,在日常会话中不及 take part in 常用。

2. 本短语与 join in 的区别见 join in。

pass away *vt.* 【可分性动词短语】spend (time, especially an evening) in a pleasant, easy way 愉快地度过(尤指晚上的)时光: He *passed* the evening *away* looking at his collection of stamps. 他翻看自己的集邮册,愉快地度过了晚上的时光。Magazine reading helped us to *pass away* the time in the train. 在火车上,看杂志有助于我们消磨时间。

—*vi.* ❶(of time) go by (指时间)过去: Thirty years had *passed away* since they had met. 自他们见面以来,30 年已经过去了。The evening *passed away* pleasantly as they sat together talking about their good old days. 他们坐在一起谈论着他们过去的好时光,那个晚上就这样愉快地度过去了。❷(of something) cease to exist; come to an end or disappear; vanish 不复存在,消失:The doctor assured him the dizziness would soon *pass away*. 医生让他放心,他的眩晕症很快就会消失。The storm soon *passed away*. 暴风雨不久就过去了。❸(委婉用法)die 去世,逝世:I'm sorry to hear that your grandmother has *passed away*. 听说你的祖母去世,我很难过。Chairman Mao Zedong was born on December 26, 1893 and *passed away* on September 9, 1976. 毛泽东主席诞生于1893年12月26日,逝世于1976年9月9日。People were deeply grieved when they heard the news of the former prime minister's *passing away*. 听到前总理逝世的消息,人民都悲痛万分。

NOTE 当本短语作"去世,逝世"解时,与pass on, pass over 的意义和用法相同。三者中,本短语最为常用。

pass by *vt.* & *vi.* go past or near (someone or something) on your way to another place without stopping 从旁边经过,经过……旁边:Just now he *passed by* (me) without saying anything. 他刚才从(我)旁边经过时,没说话。Despite the spread of bird flu I saw big crowds when I *passed by* KFC stores on the busy streets in the city. 尽管禽流感在流行,但当我路过位于市内繁忙街道上的肯德基店时,仍看到有大群的顾客。A cork, bobbing on water as waves *pass by*, is not swept along with the water. 当水波经过时,在水面上下浮动的软木不会随水漂走。

—*vi.* (of time) elapse without notice (指时间)不知不觉地过去:Time quickly *passed by* without our knowing it. 时间不知不觉地很快过去了。A year *passed by*, and still she had not found a suitable job. 一年过去了,可她还没有找到一份合适的工作。

—*vt.*【可分性动词短语】not consider; take no notice of; pay no attention to; overlook (someone or something) 不理,不考虑;不注意,忽略:We cannot *pass* the matter *by*. 我们对此事不能置之不理。The voters *passed* him *by* and elected his opponent. 选民们没有选他,却选了他的对手。I inadvertently *passed* this essay *by*. 我漫不经心地把这篇散文忽略过去了。Don't let the opportunity *pass by*. 不要错过机会。

NOTE 1. 当本短语用作及物性动词短语,所带的宾语为代词时,该代词须置于本短语的动词和副词中间。

2. 当本短语作"不理,不考虑;不注意,忽略"解时,同义短语是 *pass over*。

pass down *vt.*【可分性动词短语】(常与to 连用) ❶ send (something such as information) from person to person 传递(消息等):*Pass* the message *down* to the people at the end of the table. 把这个消息传给桌子那端的人。❷(常用被动语态形式) give or leave (something) to people who are younger or live later 遗留给,传给:The skill has been *passed down* from father to son. 这手艺是父亲传给儿子的。

NOTE 当本短语作"遗留给,传给"解时,同义短语是 bring down, come down, hand down, hand on 和 pass on。

pass for/as *vt.*【不可分性动词短语】(无被动语态,常用一般时态)(of someone or something) be mistakenly accepted as or believe to be (a particular type of person or thing)(错误地)被看作,误认为是:Do you think he will *pass for* a cook wearing that hat? 你认为他戴着那顶帽子会不会被人误认为是个厨师? Seen at a distance, she might have *passed for* a woman of thirty. 从远处看,她会被认为是 30 岁的女人。His English is so good that he could *pass as* a native speaker. 他的英语那么好,以至于有人会误认为英语是他的本族语。That fake painting would *pass for* an original. 那幅赝品油画会被误认为是原作品。

NOTE 本短语以主动形式表示被动意义。因此,不要把"她被认为很富有。"说成: * She is *passed for* rich. 谓语动词须用主动形式来表示:She *passes for* rich. 见 fall into。

pass into *vt.*【不可分性动词短语】❶enter(something)进入:He *passed into* the house without my noticing him. 他进了这所房子,而我没有注意到他。❷change gradually into (something else)逐渐变成,转入:When water boils, it *passes into* steam. 水沸腾时变成蒸汽。His disease has *passed into* a chronic state. 他的病已逐渐转入了慢性阶段。On his death, the farm *passed into* the hands of the state. 在他死后,农场转为了国有。❸(无被动语态,常用一般时态)become a part of (something such as history)成为……的一部分,载入(史册): Some foreign words have *passed into* the English language. 一些外来语已成为英语的一部分。His heroic exploits have *passed into* folklore. 他的英雄事迹已成为民间传说的一部分。

pass off *vi.* ❶(of something such as a feeling or condition) gradually disappear (某种感觉或状态等)逐渐消失:An hour after he took the medicine, the pain *passed off*. 服药一小时后,他的疼痛就逐渐消失了。A few minutes after we started, the fog began to *pass off*. 我们动身后几分钟,雾就开始消散了。❷(英国英语用法,常用一般时态)(of an event) take place and end without any trouble (某项活动)顺利进行并结束: The demonstration *passed off* peacefully. 游行在和平的气氛中进行并结束。A disturbance was expected at the meeting, but it *passed off* without any incident. 原预料会议上会出乱子,但会议开得圆满无事。The transaction *passed off* without a hitch. 这笔交易顺利地做成了。—*vt.* ❶make someone accept (something) by deceit 以赝品行骗: The police caught him for *passing off* fake money. 因使用假币行骗,他被警方逮捕。The watches are fakes, but they tried to *pass* them *off* as genuine Rolexes. 这些手表都是假货,但他们却千方百计地把它们当作劳力士牌真表来行骗。Don't try to *pass* that fake *off* on the clever jeweler. 不要试图用那件赝品来蒙骗聪明的珠宝商。❷(常与 as 连用) make people believe that (a person or thing) is (someone or something else)冒充,假冒: He has been *passing* himself *off* as a deaf mute. 他一直冒充为一个聋哑人。They tried to *pass off* that piece of glass as a gemstone. 他们企图用那块玻璃假冒宝石制品。

NOTE 当本短语用作及物性动词短语,所带的宾语为代词时,该代词须置于本短语的动词和副词中间。

pass on *vt.*【可分性动词短语】(常与 to 连用) ❶hand or give (something) (to another person)把……交给(某人),把……传给(某人): Please *pass on* this book to the next person on the list. 请把这本书传给名单上的下一位看。Please read the note then *pass* it *on* (to the others). 请你看完后,传阅此便条。❷send or spread (something such as information, news or gossip) from person to person 传递,传播(信息、消息或流言蜚语等): Could you please *pass* this message *on* to your manager? 请你把这个信息转达给你的经理,好吗? You should report China's earthquake relief work in an objective and comprehensive manner instead of making things up or writing irresponsible reports by *passing on* wrong information. 你们应客观、全面地报道中国抗震救灾的情况,而不是做出一些无中生有、以讹传讹的不负责任的报道。❸give (someone) an infectious illness 把疾病传染给(某人): I took the day off work because I didn't want to *pass on* my flu to everyone in the office. 我休了一天的班,因为我不想把我患的流感传染给办公室里所有的人。❹leave (something) to people who are younger or come later 遗留给,传给: The late Earl *passed on* most of his fortune to his only daughter. 刚刚故去的伯爵把他大部分钱财都遗留给了他唯一的女儿。It's wonderful that you have *passed* your interest in music *on* to your children. 你把你对音乐的兴趣传给了你的孩子们,这太好了。This ring has been *passed on* in my family from mother to daughter. 在我家,这个戒指已由母亲传给女儿。Different cultures often share the same rational core elements that can always be *passed on* by people. 不同的文化,其合理内核往往是相同的,总能为人类所传承。

—*vi.* ❶ move further on from one activity, or stage, to another; get on to 继续(某一活动等),往下进行: If there's no further discussion, perhaps we can *pass on*. 如果没什么再讨论的,那我们就往下进行吧。Let's now *pass on* to the next subject. 现在,咱们接着谈下一个问题吧。❷(委婉用法) die 去世,逝世: All the people were very sad to hear that their great leader had *passed on*. 所有的人听到他们的伟大领袖逝世的消息都非常悲痛。The old professor *passed on* with a heart attack at his home last night, at the age of 73. 老教授因心脏病复发昨晚在家中故去,享年73岁。

NOTE 当本短语用作及物性动词短语,所带的宾语为代词时,该代词须置于本短语的动词和副词中间。

pass out *vt.* ❶(美国英语用法) give (something) to each member of a group; give out; distribute 发给,分发: The teacher *passed out* the textbooks to the students. 老师把课本分发给学生。Please *pass* these *out* to everyone. 请把这些发给大家。The room was silent as the examination papers were *passed out*. 发放考卷时,室内一片寂静。❷give things (generously or freely, as a gift) (作为礼物)免费赠送给: The Olympic sponsors, including Coca-Cola, Lenovo and Samsung, *passed out* flags and T-shirts with their logos for the torch relay. 奥运会赞助商(包括可口可乐、联想和三星公司)都为火炬传递活动免费派送了旗帜和带有它们公司标志的T恤衫。He is a generous person, when he wins money at the races, he starts *passing out* the beer and cigarettes. 他是个慷慨之人:每当他在赌马中赢了钱,他就送别人啤酒和香烟。

—*vi.* ❶(非正式用语,常与from连用) suddenly become unconscious, for example because you are too hot; faint or collapse 失去知觉,昏过去: People everywhere were *passing out* from the heat. 到处都有人因中暑而晕倒的。He had a bad fall and *passed out*. 他摔得很厉害,失去了知觉。If I only point a gun at him and say bang, bang, and he would *pass out* from fright. 如果我只是用枪指着他,口中发出"砰、砰"两声响,他就会被吓昏。He *passed out* drunk. 他醉得不省人事。❷(英国英语用法) officially complete a course at a military or a police college (在军校或警校) 完成学业,毕业: How many of the young men *passed out* this year? 今年有多少年轻人毕业? He *passed out* in November and was posted to the 4th Infantry Division. 他于9月份毕业后被分配到第四步兵师任职。

NOTE 1. 当本短语用作及物性动词短语,所带的宾语为代词时,该代词须置于本短语的动词和副词中间。

2. 当本短语作"发给,分发"解时,同义短语是 give out 和 hand out。

3. 当本短语作"失去知觉,昏过去"解时,同义短语是 knock out 和 put out。三者中,knock out 和 put out 都是及物性用法。

pass over *vt.* 【可分性动词短语】❶ignore or not mention (a statement or subject); fail to include; try not to notice 忽略,漏掉;(对某问题)暂不考虑,对……置之不理: That was a serious problem so we could not *pass* it *over*. 那是一个严重的问题,我们不能轻易放过。We will *pass over* the details of the campaign, and go on to consider its outcome. 我们暂且不考虑(竞选)运动的细节而考虑其结局。I mentioned that you were unhappy with your salary, but it was *passed over*. 我提到你对你的工资不满,但却没人理会。❷(常用被动语态形式,常与 for 连用) fail to choose (someone), usually for promotion or appointment (在提职或任命中)没有选中(某人): In filling up the post, the boss *passed* Lewis *over* in favor of Smith. 在填补职位空缺时,老板没有选择刘易斯而选中了史密斯。She was *passed over* for promotion because she was pregnant. 她因怀孕而未获提升。Bill was upset about being *passed over* for the marketing job. 比尔因未被选中做销售工作而心烦意乱。

—*vi.* (常用一般时态) (euphemism) die (委婉用法)去世,逝世: I'm sorry to hear that your father *passed over* last week. 听说你父亲上星期去世了我很难过。

NOTE 当本短语用作及物性动词短语,所带的宾语为代词时,该代词须置于本短语的动词和副词中间。

pass through *vt.* & *vi.* go through (a place), especially perhaps making a brief halt before continuing a journey (在行程中)通过,经过,路过: The crowd backed away to let the ambulance carrying the wounded firemen *pass through*. 人群向后退去以便让载着受伤消防员的救护车通过。The T27 train departing from Beijing's West Railway Station to Lhasa *passes through* six cities. 从北京西站发车,开往拉萨的 T28 次列车途经 6 个城市。Much of the energy is absorbed as the sun's rays *pass through* the atmosphere. 阳光穿过大气层时,许多能量被吸收了。

—*vt.*【不可分性动词短语】❶(常用一般时态) undergo, and complete, a course of training in or at (a college, university, etc.) 在(大学等)中修完课程: After *passing through* college, he started working in a research institute. 读完大学后,他就开始在一个研究所工作。❷experience; suffer (something) 经历,

P

遭受：She *passed through* a difficult period shortly after her marriage broke down, but after a year or so her health and spirits picked up. 婚姻破裂后不久，她经历了一段很困难的时期。大约一年后，她的身心才得以康复。He *passed through* considerable hardship when he was working on the farm. 他在农场干活时受了很多的苦。

pat someone on the back *vi.* (非正式用语，常与 for 连用) encourage or praise someone (or oneself) for doing well 鼓励，赞扬(某人)：Sometimes it is a good thing to *pat children on the back* for their achievement. 有时，因孩子们取得成绩而表扬他们是件益事。All the members of the team gathered round him, *patting him on the back*. 全体队员将他围拢起来对他加以称赞。I *patted myself on the back* for managing to keep my cool. 我称赞自己保持了冷静。

NOTE 1. 本短语的另外一种表达形式是 give someone a pat on the back。例如：

> If you do something well, *give yourself a pat on the back*.
> 如果你事做得很好，不妨自我表扬一下。

2. 本短语的名词性短语是 a pat on the back。例如：

> She deserves *a pat on the back* for doing the right thing.
> 她事做得正确，值得表扬。

patch up *vt.* 【可分性动词短语】❶ mend or repair quickly or roughly, especially with a patch 匆忙地缝补：Mother is busy *patching up* my worn-out clothes. 妈妈正忙于缝补我穿破的衣服。His trousers were *patched up*, and he was ashamed of them. 他的裤子上缝了补丁，他为此而感到难堪。❷ (非正式用语) settle (a quarrel or disagreement) 平息(争吵)，解决(争端或分歧)：We managed to *patched up* their quarrel. 我们平息了他们之间的争吵。The matter was *patched up* without resorting to the police. 这件事情没用警察就解决了。Is there any way we can *patch* things *up*? 我们就没有什么办法解决分歧吗？❸ give basic medical treatment to (someone who is injured) 给(受伤者)包扎：The doctors *patched up* the wounded soldiers and sent them back to the front again. 医生们给伤兵做了包扎后，又把他们送回了前线。The first aider managed to *patch* her *up* temporarily. 急救人员给她做了临时性的包扎。

NOTE 当本短语的宾语为代词时，该代词须置于本短语的动词和副词中间。

pave the way for *vt.* create a situation which will make it possible for something to happen in the future 为……创造条件，为……铺平道路：This decision *paved the way for* changes in employment rights for women. 这一决定为妇女就业权益方面的变革创造了条件。Their findings *paved the way for* developing a new vaccine. 他们的发现为研制一种新疫苗创造了条件。The successful launch of Chang'e-1 and the clear images of the lunar surface it has sent back have *paved the way for* the future human exploration of the moon. 嫦娥一号的成功发射和它所发回的清晰的月球表面图像为将来人类探索月球铺平了道路。

NOTE 1. 本短语的主语和宾语通常为事物，但也可为人。例如：

> Has TV *paved the way* for a female American president? (宾语为人)
> 电视为一位女性美国总统创造了条件吗？

> Bush somehow *paved the way for* Obama to the White House. (主语、宾语均为人)
> 布什以某种方式为奥巴马入主白宫铺平了道路。

2. 本短语中的介词 for 有时可以被 to 代替。例如:

> I believe this treaty will *pave the way to* a lasting peace in Europe.
> 我相信,该条约将为欧洲的持久和平铺平道路。

pay attention to *vt*【不可分性动词短语】listen to, watch, or consider (someone or something) very carefully; attend to (something)留心听,注意看,重视: *Pay* particular *attention to* the warnings printed on the label. 要特别注意看标签上的警示语。Special *attention* should be *paid to* the development of light industry. 对轻工业的发展要给予特别的重视。This issue has never been *paid attention to*. 这个问题从未被重视过。

NOTE 本短语有两种被动语态形式:(1)以 attention 作主语;(2)以介词 to 后面的宾语作主语(见最后一个例句)。

pay back *vt.*【可分性动词短语】❶give (someone) the same amount of money that you borrowed from him or her; repay 向(某人)偿还借款: He said he would *pay back* every cent he borrowed from us. 他说,他将偿还和我们借的全部款项。I don't think we can afford to *pay* the full amount *back* now. 我想我们现在还无力全额偿还。I'll be able to *pay* you *back* next week. 下星期我就能还你的钱了。The sum was *paid back* to the bank with interest. 这笔款连本带息地还给了银行。❷do something bad to (someone) because he or she has done something bad to you; take your revenge on (someone who has done something wrong to you)报复(某人),向(某人)报复: We'll *pay* them *back* one day for the trick they played on us. 他们捉弄了我们,我们早晚要报复他们。He is a kind-hearted person and will probably not try to *pay* anybody *back* for the insult. 他是个心地善良之人,可能不会因受到侮辱而试图报复任何人。

NOTE 1. 当本短语的宾语为代词时,该代词须置于本短语的动词和副词中间。

2. 当本短语作"报复"解时,与 pay out(第二个义项)意义和用法相同,但现多用 pay back。

3. 不要将本短语与 pay off 混淆。本短语只表示"偿还(借款)",并无是否还清之意。而 pay off 则是"还清(债务)"。见 pay off。

pay for *vt.* ❶give (money) in order to buy (something); give (someone) money as the cost of (something)为买……而付钱,支付: She tried to leave the shop without *paying for* the dress. 她企图买了衣服不付款就离开商店。I *paid* good money *for* that bicycle, now take care of it. 那台自行车是我花了很多钱买的,你要小心地用它。I *paid* him £5,000 *for* this Toyota. 我付给了他5 000英镑买下这台丰田车。How soon can you *pay* me *for* the work? 你要多久才能付给我工钱? ❷ receive punishment or suffering because of (something you have done)因……受到惩罚,为……得到报应,因……付出代价:These terrorists must be made to *pay for* their crimes. 这些恐怖主义分子必为其所犯罪行受到惩罚。The evildoers will have to *pay for* what they have done. 作恶之人将会因他们的所作所为而得到报应。Sometimes you have had to *pay* dearly *for* your mistakes. 有

P

时你不得不为你所犯下的错误付出高昂的代价。

pay heed to *vt.*【不可分性动词短语】(正式用语) pay careful attention to or consider carefully (what one says or something which is important and not to be ignored)注意,留意,关注: For the first time he had to *pay heed to* his appearance, and in fact he became very well dressed from then on. 他第一次注意了自己的外表,并且从那时起他变得衣着非常讲究。You should *pay heed to* what they are saying instead of dismissing their comments. 你应该听他们说些什么,而不要对他们的意见置之不理。The new prime minister appeared to be *paying* little *heed to* the welfare of the soldiers in foreign countries. 新上任的首相似乎不怎么关心驻外官兵的福利。

NOTE 本短语与 take heed of 的意义和用法相同。

pay off *vt.* ❶finish paying the money you owe for something 还清(欠款): You'll have to *pay off* your old loan before being allowed a new one. 你得还清以前的贷款才允许你借贷新款。I can ask for a loan to buy a new car, but it's not easy to *pay* it *off*. 我可以贷款买新车,但还清这笔贷款就不容易了。Only another six months and the house will be *paid off*. 只要再过半年,房款就还清了。❷pay the full amount on wages and discharge (someone) from his or her service 付清(某人)工资后解雇: When the building was completed he *paid off* the workers. 楼房建好后,他付清了工人们的工钱。His work was most unsatisfactory, so we *paid* him *off* at the end of the week. 他的工作非常差劲,因此我们在周末给他结清工资后将其解雇了。The crew of the merchant ship was *paid off* at the end of the trip. 该商船的船员在航行结束结清了工资后便被解雇。❸(非正式用语)give (someone) money so that he or she will do something bad or dishonest for you 用钱贿赂,收买(某人): We had to *pay off* the official in charge in order to get the contract. 我们为了得到那份合同而不得不贿赂那名主管领导。There were suspicions that officials had been *paid off*. 人们怀疑那些官员都被收买了。

—*vi.* (非正式用语)(of an action) bring you some good result; prove profitable or successful after a period of time (指所做的事情)带来好的效果,获益,成功: All those weeks of studying will *pay off* when you take the exam. 这几个星期的学习会使你在考试时取得好的效果。It is a risk and it may *pay off*. 这是件冒险的事,但有利可图。That gamble did not *pay off*. 那次下赌没有赢钱。The anti-drug campaign is *paying off*. 反毒品运动显现成效。

NOTE 1. 当本短语用作及物性动词短语,所带的宾语为代词时,该代词须置于本短语的动词和副词中间。

2. 当本短语作"付清某人工资后解雇"解时,其同义短语是 kick off, kick out, lay off, send away, stand off 和 turn off。

3. 本短语可转化为复合词 payoff,意为"发工资;分配盈利;分赃;报应;决定性的事"。

pay out *vt.*【可分性动词短语】(非正式用语) ❶spend or pay (money), especially a large amount of money 花费,支出(尤指大笔款项): We've *paid out* thousands of pounds in health insurance over the years. 这些年来,我们在健康保险上花了上万英镑。The federal government *paid* several billion dollars *out* in emergency aid this year. 联邦政府今年在紧急援助上支出了数十亿美元。❷ return bad treatment, rudeness, etc., (to someone who has done something wrong to you) 报复(某人),为……而得到报应: He'll *pay* you *out* for this. 他将因此而报复你。Wrongdoers are usually *paid out* in the end. 干坏事的人最终一般都会得到报应。

NOTE 1. 当本短语的宾语为代词时,该代词须置于本短语的动词和副词中间。

2. 本短语可转化为复合词 payout,意为"(大笔)花费,支出"。

pay (a) tribute to *vt.* express one's praise and thanks for (someone or something) publicly 向……公开表示赞扬,向……公开表示感谢: I'd like to *pay tribute to* the office staff for all the hard work they've put in on this project. 我谨对在这一工程中努力工作的工作人员表示感谢。I want to take this opportunity to *pay a tribute to* him. 我愿借此机会公开表扬他。The chairman of the Association *paid tribute to* the team's contribution to professional baseball. 该协会主席称赞那个球队对职业棒球运动所做出的贡献。

pay up *v.* (非正式用语)pay (all the money that you owe to someone), especially unwillingly or late (尤指不情愿或拖延地)还清(欠款): When I see Tom, I'll ask him to *pay up*. He owes me $200. 当我看到汤姆时,我要让他还钱。他欠我 200 元钱。*Pay up*! If you don't *pay up*, I'll take you to court! 还钱! 你要是不还,我就拉你上法庭! *Pay up* what you owe before you leave town. 在你离城之前,把你欠的债款要还清。The monthly installments on the house were finally *paid up*. 住房的每月分期付款终于全部付清。

peel off *v.* ❶remove an out layer of skin or covering, etc. from (a fruit, vegetable, etc.)剥去(水果、蔬菜等的)皮: She's *peeling off* the thick skin of the orange. 她在把厚厚的橘子皮剥掉。Yesterday we bought a machine that *peels* the skin *off* the potato. 昨天,我们买了一台削马铃薯皮的机器。One of the kids was *peeling* plaster *off* the wall. 一个孩子在往下剥墙皮。*Peeling off* birch bark can kill the tree. 剥掉桦树皮可致桦树死亡。❷(of an outer covering) come off (a surface), especially in small pieces (外皮)(尤指小块地)脱落: The bark of these trees *peels off* regularly. 这些树的树皮定期脱落。The paint was *peeling off* the damp walls. 油漆从潮湿的墙上一块块地脱落。❸(of a plane) turn and move away quickly from other aircraft in the air in order to land or make a dive (指飞机在飞行中为了降落或俯冲而)迅速脱离编队,飞离机群: One by one the aircraft started to *peel off*. 飞机一个个地开始脱离编队。❹remove (especially a tight or wet piece of clothing)脱掉(紧或湿的衣物),脱衣服: Helen *peeled off* her gloves and started to work. 海伦摘下手套便开始干活。The kids *peeled off* their wet clothes. 孩子们都脱去了湿衣服。The boys *peeled off* their clothes and jumped into the water. 男孩子们脱光衣服跳入水中。It's too hot in here, I think I'll *peel off* (my clothes). 这里太热了,我想我得脱掉衣服了。

peep out *vi.* (of something) appear slightly from behind or under something, or through a narrow opening (指某物)(从某物的后面或下面,或从缝隙中)显

P

露出来：His head *peeped out* from under the blanket. 他的头从毯子下面露了出来。The sun *peeped out* through a gap in the clouds. 太阳从云朵的缝隙中展露出来。Some strands of hair *peeped out* from under her hat. 几绺发丝从她的帽子下方微微露出。

per capita *adj.* & *adv.* (正式用语)for or by each person in a country or area 每人的(地)，人均的(地)：Gross national product (GNP) *per capita* reflects the average income of a country's citizens. 人均国民生产总值反映一个国家公民的平均收入。

per cent Ⅰ *n.* (单复数同形，常与 of 连用) one part in every hundred 百分之一：It is often said that we use only 10 *per cent* of our brain. 人们常说，我们仅仅利用了大脑的 10%。There are 700 workers in the factory, more than 70 *per cent* of whom are women. 该厂有 700 名工人，其中 70%多是女工。

Ⅱ *adj* & *adv.* (calculated) in or for every hundred 百分之……的(地)：This restaurant has a 10 *percent* service charge. 这家饭馆收取 10%的服务费。I agree with you a hundred *per cent*. 我完全地同意你的意见。

NOTE 1. 本短语主要用于英国英语中，在美国英语中则通常使用其连用形式 percent。

2. 本短语与数词相连用；但无论表示百分之多少，per cent 后都不能加-s。

3. 当"本短语＋of＋单数名词或不可数名词"作主语时，谓语动词用单数形式。例如：

> Eighty *per cent* of the land is cultivated.
> 80%的土地已被耕种。
>
> In the end 10 *per cent* of the wool was rejected by the buyer.
> 最后，10%的羊毛被收购者拒收。

当"本短语＋of＋复数名词"作主语时，谓语动词用复数形式。如：

> 65 *percent* of children play computer games.
> 65%的儿童玩电脑游戏。

当"本短语＋of＋单数群体名词"作主语时，谓语动词可用单数形式，也可用复数形式。例如：

> Seventy *per cent* of the work force is/are against the strike.
> 70%的职工反对罢工。

当本短语与前面的数字单独作主语时，谓语动词单复数形式主要由其所代替的名词决定。如果代替的是单数名词或不可数名词，谓语动词用单数；如果代替的是复数名词，则谓语动词也用复数形式。例如：

> Of the students who came, 20 *percent* were unprepared.
> 在来的学生当中，20%都没有做任何准备。

不要将本短语与 percentage 混淆。percentage 意为"百分比""百分率"，是可数名词，但在使用中一般用其单数形式，并与 of 短语连用。下面两个句子只能用 percentage：A high /large /small *percentage* of people have come 以及 What *percentage* of babies die of scarlet fever every year?

persevere at/in/with *vt.*【不可分性动词短语】continue steadily trying to achieve (something or doing something) with determination in spite of difficulties 坚持：If you *persevere at* your work, you'll succeed in the end. 如果你坚持工作，最终会取得成功的。She *persevered in* her ideas despite obvious objections raised by friends. 她不顾朋友们明确提出的反对仍然坚持自己的想法。If you *persevere in* studying hard, you're sure to learn the skill well. 如果你坚持努力学习,你一定会学好这门技术的。Police negotiators will *persevere with* their efforts to free the hostages. 警方的谈判人员将坚持努力使人质获释。

NOTE 本短语的同义短语是 adhere to, insist on, persist in 和 stick to。它们之间的区别见 insist on 的用法说明。

persist in/with *vt.* 【不可分性动词短语】(正式用语) continue (to do or doing something) in a course of action or way of behaving, firmly and perhaps unreasonably, often in spite of difficulties, opposition, or warning 坚持继续做(某事),执意做(某事): He *persisted in* his own belief and would never listen to other people's opinions. 他固执己见,从不听别人的意见。Why do you *persist in* denying that it was your fault? 你为什么坚持否认那是你的错? If this behavior is *persisted in* it could lead to serious trouble. 如果这种行为继续下去的话,会导致严重问题的。They are determined to *persist with* their campaign. 他们决意将运动坚持下去。

persuade into *vt.* 【可分性动词短语】 make (someone) willing to follow (a course of action or doing something) by repeatedly talking to him or her or encouraging him or her, etc. 劝服(某人)做(某事): We *persuaded* her *into* going to the party with us. 我们说服了她和我们一同去参加聚会。The young man claims that he was *persuaded into* (committing) the crime. 那年轻人声称他是被别人唆使犯罪的。

NOTE 本短语的同义短语是 argue into, reason into 和 talk into; 反义短语是 persuade out of, argue out of, reason out of 和 talk out of。

persuade out of *vt.* 【可分性动词短语】 prevent (someone) from (a course of action or doing something) by repeatedly talking to him or her 劝服(某人)不做(某事): Can't the boy be *persuaded out of* such behavior? 就不能说说让这个男孩子放弃这种行为? His parents *persuaded* him *out of* leaving his present job. 他父母劝他不要辞去现在的工作。

phone up *vt.* 【可分性动词短语】(英国英语用法) speak to (someone) by telephone 给(某人)打电话: I must *phone* her *up* tonight. 我今晚必须给她打电话。Have you *phoned up* all your friends to tell them the change of date yet? 你有没有给你的朋友们打电话,告诉他们改变日期的事?

NOTE **1.** 本短语中的 up 可以省略。

2. 当本短语的宾语为代词时,该代词须置于本短语的动词和副词中间。

pick off *vt.* 【可分性动词短语】 ❶ pull or break off (part of a plant) from a tree or plant 从(树或某种植物上)摘下,摘掉: She *picked off* some ripe apples from the tree. 她从树上摘下一些熟了的苹果。All the best apples have been *picked off* by the children. 所有最好的苹果都让孩子们摘掉了。❷ (of someone) shoot at (a particular person, animal, vehicle, or an aircraft) from a distance one by one or selectively (指某人)(从远处)逐个地射击,有选择地射击;击落(飞机等):(非正式用语) Our snipers *picked* the enemy soldiers *off* one by one as they emerged from the dugout. 我军的狙击手把从掩体中出现的敌兵逐一地消灭了。The army patrol was *picked off* by snipers. 这队巡

P

逻兵被狙击手一一打死。The man *picked off* a wild duck rising from the thick grass. 那名男子射下了一只从茂密的草丛里飞起的野鸭。Five enemy bombers were *picked up* by our fighters. 敌军有五架轰炸机被我军战机击落。

NOTE 当本短语的宾语为代词时,该代词须置于本短语的动词和副词中间。

pick on *vt.* 【不可分性动词短语】❶(常用一般时态,一般不用被动语态形式) choose (something) 选择(某物): We've *picked on* a beautiful place for our holiday. 我们已选择了一个很美的地方去度假。❷ choose (someone) for an unpleasant job 选中(某人)(去做某项不愉快的工作): Why do you always *pick on* me for the unpleasant jobs? 你为什么总是选我去干一些令人讨厌的工作? The examiners can *pick on* anyone to answer the questions. 主考人可以挑选任何人来回答问题。❸(非正式用语) choose (someone) for criticism, blame or punishment, especially repeatedly or unfairly(尤指屡次、不公正地)选出(某人)(作为批评、责备或惩罚的对象): Why are you always *picking on* me? 你为什么老是责备我? I'm tired of being *picked on* by the manager. 我讨厌经理总批评我。My younger brother was always *picked on* at school. 我弟弟在学校里总是挨罚。

pick out *vt.* ❶(常用一般时态) choose (something or someone) specially or carefully from among others 精心挑选: She *picked out* a red scarf to wear with her dress. 她选了一条红色围巾以与她所穿的连衣裙相配。I'll buy you a tie, but you will have to *pick* it *out*. 我要给你买一条领带,可是你得自己挑选。❷(常用一般时态) recognize (someone or something) clearly from a group of similar people or things, especially with difficulty (尤指较难地)认出,辨别出: Can you *pick out* your friend whom you haven't seen for years from the crowd? 你能在人群中认出你那位多年没见的朋友吗? Can't you *pick* me *out* in this old school photograph? 你就不能在这张学校的旧照片里辨认出哪一个是我吗? His house is easily *picked out* from the rest, it has a large blue door. 他家的房子很容易从其他房子中辨别出来,因为它有一扇蓝色的门。❸(常用被动语态形式) make (something) clear to see 使显眼: The houses in the painting were *picked out* in white. 这幅画中的房子在白色的衬托下很显眼。❹shine a light on (someone or something) so that they are easy to see 用光圈罩住: A woman in the crowd was *picked out* by a spotlight. 聚光灯罩住了人群中的一个女人。❺ understand (something) by careful study 明白,领会,理解: Can you *pick out* his words? 你明白他话中的意思吗? It's usually easier to *pick out* the meaning of a sentence in a given context. 在特定的上下文当中理解一个句子的含义往往更容易些。

NOTE **1.** 当本短语的宾语为代词时,该代词须置于本短语的动词和副词中间。

2. 当本短语作"精心挑选"解时,同义短语是 single out 和 sort out。

pick up *vt.* ❶ lift up and take hold of (something small or light, or someone, especially a little child) and lift it up from a surface 捡起,拾起,拿起,抱起: As he *picked up* the envelope, a key fell out. 当他捡起信封时,一把钥匙掉了出来。Don't scatter your clothes, *pick* them *up*, my son. 我的儿子,不要把你的衣服

乱丢，把它们拾起来。A man who *picked up* the phone at the police station refused to discuss the incident and hung up without giving his name. 警察局里接电话的那个人拒绝谈论该事件，连名字也没给就挂断了电话。❷(主要用于美国英语中，非正式用语) put (things) away and make (a room) neat, especially for someone else (尤指为别人)把……收拾起来，收拾(房间)：I am constantly *picking up* the things the children leave lying around. 我总得把孩子们到处乱放的东西收拾起来。I've already asked them to *pick* their toys *up*. 我已经让他们把玩具都收拾起来了。*Pick up* the room for the guest, Jane. 简，为客人收拾房间。❸go and meet (someone or something that you have arranged to take somewhere) (often in a vehicle) (常指用车辆)接走(某人)，拉走(某物)：We drove to the airport to *pick up* Mary. 我们驱车去机场接玛丽。You have to give a little extra to the cab driver for being there to *pick* you *up*. 对于去那里接你的出租车司机，你得额外地给一点小费。I'll *pick up* my luggage in the morning. 我要在早晨把我的行李拉走。❹take (someone who is waiting by the road) into your vehicle and take him or her somewhere 让(某人)中途搭车：We *picked up* a hitchhiker on the way. 我们在中途搭载了一个坐便车旅行的人。We *picked up* two students on our way to the town. 在去往城里的途中，我们让两个学生搭了车。❺(非正式用语，常用被动语态形式) (of the police) catch or arrest (someone) and take him or her away in a car to a police station(警方)捉住，逮捕(某人)：The police *picked* him *up* (for theft), but the judges just let him go. 警方(以盗窃罪)把他抓了起来，但法官却把他放了。He was *picked up* on Sunday night for drunken driving. 他是在星期天的晚上因醉酒驾车而被逮捕。❻(of a person or animal) become aware of (a faint smell or a quiet sound) (指人或动物)嗅到(淡薄的气味)，听到(微弱的声音)：The dog must have *picked up* his scent. 这条狗肯定嗅到了他的气味。His ears are so sensitive that they can *pick up* very faint sounds from a long way away. 他的耳朵很灵敏，能从很远的地方听到非常微弱的声音。❼(非正式用语) receive (an electronic signal, sound waves, etc.) on a radio or similar piece of equipment (无线电等设备)接收到(电子信号、声波等)：I don't believe this thing can *pick up* foreign stations. 我不相信这玩意儿能收到外国电台。The failure to *pick up* a signal from Beagle 2 raised fears that the probe had suffered the same fate as so many craft before it. "猎兔犬2号"火星探测器信号接收的失败使科学家们担心它也遭遇了此前许多航空器同样的厄运。I could hear a voice, but my cell phone couldn't *pick* it *up* well enough for me to know who it was. 我能听到有声音，但我的手机接收不太好，我不知道打电话的人是谁。❽(与反身代词连用) raise (yourself) slowly after you have fallen or been knocked down (跌倒或被打倒后)慢慢地爬起来：The boy *picked* himself *up* and started running again. 那男孩跌倒后爬了起来，又开始跑了。❾(非正式用语) learn (a new skill) quickly or start (a habit), usually without intending to 很快地学会(某种新的技艺)；(常指不经意地)染上(某种习惯)：The young workers are *picking up* skills quickly. 这

些青年工人正在迅速掌握技术。She *picked* some German *phrases up* while staying in Berlin. 她在柏林逗留期间学会了一些德语短语。I don't want to *pick up* any bad habits from those people. 我不想从这些人身上染上任何不良习惯。⑩(非正式用语)get or catch (an illness) from somewhere or something 染上(某种疾病): They have *picked up* a nasty stomach bug from something they have eaten. 他们因所吃的食物而染上了一种严重的胃病。He *picked up* an illness while he was abroad. 他在国外期间染上了病。⑪(非正式用语)buy (something), usually cheaply (常指便宜地)买到(某物): There you can *pick up* some amazing bargains. 在那里,你能买到非常便宜的东西。We need some milk, so I'll *pick* some *up* on the way home. 我们需要些牛奶,所以我就在回家的路上买了一些。

—*vt.* & *vi.* ❶ put (a room) in good order; tidy (a room); clear 整理(房间),收拾(房间): *Pick up* your room before you go out, please. 在你出去之前,请把你的房间收拾一下。I'm fed up at having to *pick up* after you and your friends. 我讨厌总得在你和你的朋友们走后收拾房间。❷(of a vehicle)(cause to)gain speed or move more quickly (使)(车辆)加速: The train *picked up* quickly. 火车很快地加快了速度。With just a slight touch of the accelerator, the car *picked up* the speed. 轻轻一踩加速器,车子的速度就加快了。❸ start (something) again; continue from the point where you stopped 重新开始,继续: He seems to think that we can get back together and just *pick up* where we left off. 他似乎认为我们能再重聚到一起,从我们停顿下来的地方重新开始。The Korean TV series is over for this year, but the station plans to *pick* it *up* again next year. 这部韩国电视连续剧今年已经播完,但电视台计划明年重播。We'll *pick up* this conversation when I come back. 等我回来咱们再继续谈这个话题吧。

—*vi.* ❶ (of trade or the economy of a country) improve; return to a former good state (一国之贸易或经济)改善,好转: The government official hopes that trade will *pick up*. 这位政府官员希望该国贸易会有改善。❷ (of someone) get better in his or her health (某人的身体)好转: They won't let him out of hospital until his health has *picked up* quite a lot. 如果他的身体没有很大好转,他们是不会让他出院的。Mother is *picking up* wonderfully since she came out of hospital. 自出院以来,妈妈的身体有了很大的好转。

NOTE **1.** 当本短语用作及物性动词短语,所带的宾语为代词时,该代词须置于本短语的动词和副词中间。

2. 本短语可转化为复合词 pickup,意为"拾起;加速(能力);偶然结识(的人);(商业等的)好转;兴奋剂,刺激(品)",还可用作形容词,意义是"临时拼凑成的"。

piece of cake *n.* (非正式用语,仅用单数形式,作表语) a job, task or other activity that is very easy or simple to do 轻而易举的事,简单的事: He thought his first solo flight was a *piece of cake*. 他原以为他的首次单独飞行是件轻而易举的事。I've always had a hard time studying English, but math is a *piece of cake*. 我学习英语总感到很难,但数学却很容易学。Persuading him to give us the day off won't be a *piece of cake*. 要说服他放我们一天假可不是一件容易的事。How was the interview? "*Piece of* cake. ""面试怎么样?""很容易。"

NOTE 本短语常用于英国英语、美国英语和澳大利亚英语中。它的另外一种表达形式是 piece of piss,这是英国英语中的非正式用语用法。例如:

> "How do you do that?" "It's a *piece of piss*! Watch!"
> "那你是怎么做的?""很简单!你瞧吧!"

pile up *v.* ❶(cause to) gradually form a pile; collect or gather 把……堆成一堆,堆积起来,积累:*Pile up* the books on the table. 把书堆在桌子上吧。Newspapers and magazines were *piled up* on the floor. 报纸和杂志都堆积在了地板上。The clouds are *piling up* thick. 云层积得很厚。Don't let your work *pile up*, never leave till tomorrow what you can finish today. 不要积压工作,今天能做完的决不要拖到明天去。He *piled up* a huge fortune. 他积累了一大笔财富。❷(of a number of vehicles traveling close behind each other) crash into each other (若干前后紧随行驶的车辆)相互撞在一起:Several cars *piled up* in the dense fog the other day. 那天,大雾弥漫,有好几辆汽车撞到了一起。

NOTE 1. 当本短语用作及物性动词短语,所带的宾语为代词时,该代词须置于本短语的动词和副词中间。

2. 本短语可转化为复合词 pile (-)up,意为"(繁重任务等的)堆积;(若干车辆或数名球员等的)同时碰撞事件"。

place all your eggs in one basket ⇨ **put all one's eggs in one basket**

place emphasis on ⇨ **lay emphasis on**

plan on *vt.* intend (doing something); make a plan for (something); expect 准备(做某事),计划(做某事);预料到:Do you *plan on* staying here another year? 你准备在这儿再住一年吗? I'd *planned on* doing some work this afternoon. 我原计划今天下午要做些工作。They hadn't *planned on* my whole family coming. 他们没有想到我们全家人都来了。I had not *planned on* their early arrival, and the meal was not ready. 我没预料到他们到得这么早,饭还没准备好。

play a joke on *vt.* do (something) to trick (someone) for fun (与某人)开玩笑,捉弄(某人):The farmers liked *playing jokes on* us when we were together. 农民们和我们在一起时喜欢同我们开一些玩笑。Robert decided to *play a joke on* his teacher. 罗伯特决定捉弄他的老师。Children like to *play a joke on* on people. 孩子们喜欢捉弄人。

play a part (in) *v.* ❶act a character (in a play or film, etc.) (在戏剧、电影等中)扮演角色:I hate to *play the part* of Cinderella. 我不愿扮演灰姑娘。I *played* only *a* small *part* in the play. 我在剧中只扮演了一个小角色。Tobey Maguire *played the* leading *part in* *Spider-Man II*. 托比·麦奎尔在《蜘蛛侠 2》中扮演主要角色。British soccer superstar David Beckham *played a part* as a soccer player *in* the Hollywood movie *The Pink Panther*. 英国超级足球明星戴维·贝克汉姆在好莱坞影片《粉红豹》中饰演了一名足球运动员。❷ be involved (in something), especially in a way that is important (在……中)起(重要)作用:They have worked very hard, but luck has *played a part* too. 他们工作得很努力,运气也起了作用。As a permanent member of the UN Security Council, China has *played an* important *part in*

P

international affairs in a responsible manner. 作为联合国安理会的常任理事国,中国本着负责任的态度在国际事务中发挥了重要作用。The club has *played a* unique and important *part in* the life of the people there. 该俱乐部在那里的人民生活中起到了独特而重要的作用。

NOTE **1.** 当本短语用作及物性动词短语时,不用被动语态形式。

2. 本短语的不定冠词 a 可根据表达需要替换成 the 或者在后面加形容词。

3. 本短语可以以下面这种形式分开使用:

> He had an important *part* to *play in* ensuring the success of the scheme.
> 他为确保计划的成功起过重要的作用。

play a trick on *vt.* ❶do (something) in order to annoy (someone) or make people laugh at him or her 捉弄(某人): We *played a trick on* Liza. We sent her picture to a beauty contest. 我们捉弄了莉莎。我们把她的照片寄给了选美大赛。We'll pay them back one day for *a trick* they *played on* us. 他们捉弄了我们,我们早晚要报复他们。❷deceive (someone) for one's advantage or profit 与(某人)耍花招: I thought he was *playing a trick on* me. 我认为他是在和我耍花招。The firm won the contract unfairly by *playing a trick on* its competitors. 这家公司与竞争者耍了花招,不公平地赢取了这项合同。

NOTE **1.** 本短语后通常接人称代词,表示对象。trick 也可用复数形式。例如:

> The children loved *playing tricks on* their teacher.
> 孩子们喜欢捉弄他们的老师。

2. 本短语与 play a joke on 意义相近,但 play a joke on 多用于善意的行为。

play back *vt.* 【可分性动词短语】play (a message, music, film, etc. that has been recorded on a tape, video, etc.) in order to listen to or watch it; replay 重新播放(录音或录像带等): *Play back* the phone message to me. 把电话录音重新给我放一遍。He *played* the videotape *back*. 他又把录像带放了一遍。You can edit the song on your computer and *play* it *back*. 你可以在你的电脑上编辑这首歌,然后再播放。

NOTE **1.** 当本短语所带的宾语为代词时,该代词须置于本短语的动词和副词中间。

2. 本短语可转化为复合词 playback,意为"(录音或录像带等的)重新播放,回放"。

play down *vt.* (非正式用语) try to make (something) seem less important or serious than it is 减低……的重要性;贬低: He *played down* the seriousness of his condition because he didn't want anyone to worry. 他把自己的病情说得很轻,因为他不想让任何人担心。It's a sensitive issue, and they want to *play* it *down* until after the elections. 这是一个敏感的问题,所以他们想在大选前降低这个问题的重要性。

NOTE **1.** 当本短语所带的宾语为代词时,该代词须置于本短语的动词和副词中间。

2. 本短语的反义短语是 play up。

3. 本短语可转化为复合词 downplay,意为"贬低,轻视"。

play off *v.* (in sport) play (a game or an additional game) to decide which side will win (在体育竞赛中)进行决赛,打加赛决胜负: Each team had won three games so they had to *play off* to decide the championship. 每个队都赢了三场,所以

他们必须以决赛定冠军。The losing semifinalists will *play off* for the third place. 在半决赛中失利的选手将打加赛以争夺第三名。They decided not to *play* the tie *off* because it had grown so late. 由于天色太晚,他们决定不再打平局后的决赛。The two equal winners had to *play off* an additional game to decide the winner of the whole competition. 两个比分相同的胜队还得打一场加赛来决定整个比赛的获胜者。

NOTE 本短语可转化为复合词 play-off,意为"决赛,加赛"。

play off against *vt.*【可分性动词短语】(英国英语用法,非正式用语) oppose (someone) against (someone else) for your own advantage 使(他人)相互对立,挑拨矛盾: She *played* her two rivals *off against* each other and got the job herself. 她挑拨她的两个竞争者相互对立,从而自己得到了那件工作。Have you ever heard of a parent who *played off* one child *against* another? 你有没有听说过挑动一个孩子与另一个孩子搞对立的家长? Are you *playing* us *off against* each other? 你是在挑拨我们相互对着干吗?

play on/upon *vt.* ❶ perform (music or a play) on (an instrument, stage, etc.) 在(乐器)上演奏乐曲,在(舞台)上演出(戏剧等): He'd written a tune, and *played* it for us *on* the piano. 他写了一首曲子,并在钢琴上弹给我们听。Over there you can see a young man *playing* beautiful tunes *on* the flute. 在那里,你可以看到一个年轻人用笛子演奏着动听的曲子。Some school children were standing at the school gate, *playing on* drums. 一些学生站在校门口打着鼓。This piece of music can be *played on* almost any musical instrument. 这支曲子几乎在任何乐器上都能演奏。❷ try to use (especially the feelings or attitudes of others) for one's own advantage 利用(尤指他人的情绪或态度): The speaker knew how to *play on* the audience's feelings. 这位演讲者懂得怎样利用听众的情绪。It *played upon* its neighbors' fears to obtain trade concessions from them. 它利用邻国的恐惧心理,获得了它们在贸易上的让步。She *plays on* the fact that people feel sorry for her. 她利用了人们对她感到同情。

NOTE 本短语中的 upon 用法比 on 正式,但不及 on 常用。

play up *vt.* (非正式用语) try to make (something) seem more important than it is; emphasize; stress 夸大……的重要性,渲染,强调: Advertisers always *play up* the good quality of the houses for sale and fail to mention their disadvantages. 登广告的人总是夸大他们要出售的房子的优点,而不提其缺憾之处。In the job interview you should *play up* your work experience abroad. 在求职面试时,你应强调你在国外的工作经验。

play with *vt.*【不可分性动词短语】❶ amuse oneself (with a game) with (something or someone) 以……自娱,和……玩: You should give the boy credit for his young age. Other boys at his age are still *playing with* toys. 就凭这男孩儿这么小的年龄就应该表扬他。其他与他同龄的男孩儿们还在玩玩具呢。The new girl seemed to enjoy *playing with* other children. 看来新来的女孩儿和其他的小朋友们玩得很开心。❷ keep touching (something) with your hands without thinking about what you are doing, especially because you are bored or nervous (由于无聊或紧张而无意识地)摆弄(某物): Stop *playing with* your hair! 别再摆弄你的头发了! He stood silent, *playing with* a button on his coat. 他默默地站着,摆弄着上衣的一颗纽扣。❸ treat (something such as an idea, someone or someone's feelings) in a casual, absent-minded, or insincere way; toy with 轻率地对待(某一想法),玩弄(某人或某人的感情): She's been *playing with* the idea of starting her own business. 她一直没太认真对待自己创业的问题。Do you mean to say he's been *playing with* me all the time? But I'm not one to be *played with*. 你是说他一直在玩弄我? 我可不是一个可以被玩弄的人。

NOTE 1. 不要将本短语的意义误解为"(在体育竞赛中)某队对某队或某人对某人比赛"。

2. 本短语的同义短语是 toy with。

play with fire *vi.* (非正式用语,常用进行时态) do something dangerous or risky that could cause lots of problems 干危险的事,玩火,冒险: He knew quite well that he was *playing with fire* by having an affair with a married woman. 他明明知道与已婚女子鬼混是在干危险的事。He who *plays with fire* gets burnt. (谚语)玩火者必自焚。The chairperson of the opposition party called upon the government to stop *playing with fire*. 反对党主席呼吁政府不要再玩火了。

plead for *vt.* 【不可分性动词短语】(正式用语) ask for (something) in an urgent, emotional and begging way 恳求,乞求: When the rent was due he *pleaded for* more time to pay. 当房租到期时,他恳求再宽限一下他的付款日期。He knelt in front of the king, *pleading for* mercy. 他跪在国王面前,恳求宽恕。I don't want to *plead for* what's already mine. 我不想乞求已属于我的东西。

NOTE 本短语中的动词 plead 的过去式和过去分词的形式有两种:pleaded 和 pled。后者常用于美国和苏格兰英语中。

plenty of *adj.* (非正式用语) a large amount of (something), or a large number of (things or people), usually more than enough 大量的,许多的: I had *plenty of* time to think over what I was going to do. 我有大量的时间来考虑我该做些什么。You're always complaining. *Plenty of* people would be happy to have your job. 你总是发牢骚。许多人都巴不得要干你这份工作呢。

NOTE 1. 本短语用于肯定句中,只作定语。

2. 本短语可用来修饰不可数名词和可数名词。既可用来修饰物,又可修饰人。

3. 当"本短语+不可数名词"作主语时,谓语动词用单数形式。如:

> There is *plenty of* water in the pail.
> 桶里还有好多水。

当"本短语+可数名词"作主语时,谓语动词形式视可数名词的单复数而定。如:

> There are *plenty of* eggs in the box.
> 箱子里有好多鸡蛋。

4. 当本短语与 more 连用时,可省去 of。如:

> We have *plenty* more time to spend in scientific research than before.
> 我们比以前有更多用于搞科研的时间。

plunge into *vt.* ❶ jump or dive into (water) 跳入,扎入(水中): Two police officers *plunged into* freezing water to rescue a man yesterday. 昨天,两名警官跳进冰冷的水中去救一名男子。❷move quickly into (something) 迅速冲入: Firemen *plunged into* the burning building to rescue the child. 消防队员冲进燃烧着的大楼去营救那名儿童。The train *plunged into* the tunnel. 列车疾速驶入隧道。❸quickly push (something) a long way into (something else)(迅速地)把(某物)伸入,插入: He *plunged* his arm *into* the sack once more. 他再次把胳臂伸入大口袋中。❹(常用被动语态形式) (of something) suddenly put (someone or something) in (a particular state or situation); suddenly get into (a particular state or situation)(使……)突然陷入(某种状态): The death of the great leader *plunged* the whole nation *into* great sadness. 伟大领袖的逝世使全体国民陷入极度的悲痛之中。The whole community was *plunged into* deep sorrow with the news of the passing of a great friend and servant Philip. 当听到他们伟大的朋友和公仆菲利普逝世的噩耗时,整个社区都陷入深切的悲痛之中。The company *plunged into* difficulty. 该公司陷入困境之中。❺ suddenly start doing (something) with energy and enthusiasm, but sometimes without thinking about it first 突然做(某事)仓促地开始做(某事): She *plunged into* a description of her latest illness. 她突然描述起她最近患病的情况。This was not the time to be *plunging into* some new business venture. 现在不是仓促地进行新的商业冒险的时候。

point at *vt.* ❶ show (something) by holding out your finger (用手)指着(某物): The girl *pointed at* the kind of ice cream that she wanted. 女孩用手指着她想要的那种冰激凌。❷aim or direct (an object, usually a weapon) at(someone or something)(用某物,尤指武器)瞄准,对准,指着: When the pilot landed, every gun was *pointed at* him. 当飞机驾驶员着陆时,所有的枪口都对准了他。Using a stick, the teacher *pointed at* the words on the blackboard and asked me to read them. 老师用教鞭指着黑板上的字让我读。When we answered incorrectly, the teacher *pointed* his long stick *at* us and shouted, "No!" 每当我们回答错误时,老师就用他长长的教鞭指着我们喊道:"不对!"

NOTE 本短语与 point to 均有"指"之意。但本短语侧重表示"指着"具体的东西,且距离在视线之内;而 point to 则表示"指向",侧重指示方向或位置,且距离可以在视线之外。

point of view *n.* a way of judging a situation based on a particular aspect 观点,看法,见解: We need someone with a fresh *point of view*, who can suggest changes. 我们需要的是有新观点、能提出改革建议的人。I want next to hear your *point of view* about me. 下面,我想听一听你对我的看法。This is my *point of view*: Religion is a private matter. 宗教信仰是个人的事情——这是我的见解。That's very handy from our *point of view*, isn't it? 据我们看来,那是非常方便的,是吗?

NOTE 1. 本短语的构成形式是"名词+介词+名词"。它的复数形式的变化,发生在第一个名词上。如:

> There is a significant difference between the two *points of view*.
> 这两种观点有着很大的不同。

2. 本短语可转化为复合词 viewpoint,意为"观点,看法,见解;观察点;视点"。但 viewpoint 的复数形式是 viewpoints。

P

point out *vt.* ❶ show (who or what a particular person or thing is), especially by pointing 把(某人或某物)指出来: You've never met her before? I'll *point* her *out* to you if I see her. 你从没见过她? 如果我看见她,就把她指给你看。I *pointed out* to him where I used to live. 我把我过去住的地方指给他看。He *pointed out* the best beaches on the map. 他在地图上指出了几个最好的海滩。❷ tell someone about(a fact or mistake)and draw his or her attention to them (为引起某人的注意而)说明指出(某种事实或错误):It was *pointed out* to us that the office was closed. 有人向我们说明办公室关门了。If I made some mistakes, please have them *pointed out*. 如果我犯了错误,请指出。

NOTE 当本短语的宾语为代词时,该代词须置于本短语的动词和副词中间。

point to/towards *vt.* ❶direct; show the direction or position of, with or as with a finger or a long thin object (用手或细长之物)指向,指示(方向或位置):She *pointed to* the house on the corner and said, "That's where I live." 她用手指向拐角处的房子说:"那就是我住的地方。" The hands of the clock *pointed to* twelve. 钟表的指针指向 12 点。A compass needle always *points to* the north. 罗盘的指针总是指向北的。US rover Spirit's first job on Mars surface was to locate the sun with its camera and calculate from the sun's position how to *point* its main antenna *to* Earth. 美国"勇气"号火星车在火星表面上首先做的工作是利用照相机确定太阳方位,并据此计算如何使其主天线朝向地球。❷aim or direct (an object, usually a weapon) at (someone or something)把(尤指武器)对准,指向 …:We demanded that all guns be *pointed to* foreign invaders. 我们要求枪口一致对外。A loaded gun was *pointed towards* me. 子弹上了膛的枪对准了我。❸(常用一般时态) show the truth or importance of (something) 表明: The evidence clearly *points* to her guilt. 证据清楚地表明她有罪。All the evidence *points towards* George as the murderer. 所有的证据都表明乔治就是杀人凶犯。All the facts *pointed to* the same conclusion. 所有的事实都说明了同样的结论。

point up *vt.* (正式用语) emphasize (something); add more force to; show clearly (the qualities of something)强调,清楚说明: Both articles mentioned the event, one of them does not *point* it *up* enough. 虽然两篇文章都谈到了这件事,但其中一篇却强调得不够。The increasing number of accidents *points up* the need for stricter road-safety measures. 越来越多的交通事故清楚地说明,需要采取更加严厉的道路安全措施。

NOTE 当本短语的宾语为代词时,该代词须置于本短语的动词和副词中间。

poke fun at *vt.* (非正式用语) make unkind jokes about (someone or something)嘲弄,取笑: The other children in the class *poked fun at* him because of his accent. 班里的其他同学都因他带有的口音而嘲笑他。All the kids *poked fun at* Tom's new haircut. 所有的孩子们都取笑汤姆的新发型。

NOTE 本短语的同义短语是 make fun of。

pop up *vi.* ❶(非正式用语,常用一般时态) happen; arrive suddenly or unexpectedly 意外地发生,突然地到来: Some difficulties have just *popped up*, so we have to work late to deal with them. 刚刚出了一些问题,我们得加班把它们处理

掉。He always *pops up* when he's least expected. 他总是不期而至。❷ (of windows or dialogue boxes on a computer screen) appear (计算机屏幕上的窗口或对话框)出现: The dialogue box *popped up* when I pressed Enter. 当我按下"确定"键时,对话框就出现了。The menu *pops up* when you click twice on the mouse. 你双击鼠标,菜单就会弹出。

portray as *vt.* 【可分性动词短语】give (usually someone or oneself) the character of (a kind of person), as in a book, play, film, or picture 把(某人或自己)描述为: The play *portrays* the people of the small town *as* ignorant and rude to strangers. 该剧把小城里的人描绘成无知并对外地人粗鲁的人。By *portraying* himself *as* a strong leader in the global war on terrorism, he won the second term of presidency. 他把自己标榜为全球反恐战争的坚强领袖,而赢得了总统连任。

pose for *vt.* (cause to) sit or stand in a particular position for (an artist) or for (a painting, photograph, etc.) (使)为(画像或拍照)摆好姿势: At the local market I *posed for* a photograph with a boy in Highland dress. 在当地的市场上,我和一名身着(苏格兰)高地服装的男孩合了影。The photographer *posed* the children *for* their pictures in the best position. 摄影师让孩子们摆出最佳姿势拍照。The beautiful girl makes a living by *posing for* art students in drawing classes. 这个漂亮的女孩靠给学美术的学生做绘画课模特为生。

post code ⇨ **zip code**

postal code ⇨ **zip code**

pounce on/upon *vt.* 【不可分性动词短语】❶ (常用一般时态) (of someone) quickly jump on or take hold of (someone) (指人)向(某人)猛扑,突然袭击(某人): They *pounced on* their suspect. 他们向犯罪嫌疑人猛扑了过去。He was *pounced on* by a young man last night. 昨天夜里他遭到了一名青年男子的突然袭击。❷ (of an animal or bird) leap on and grab (their prey), in order to kill it (指动物或鸟类)扑向(捕猎物): The cat *pounced on* the unsuspecting mouse as it came out of the hole. 那猫猛然扑向一只刚出洞而毫无戒备的老鼠。This morning I watched a hawk *pounce on* a baby rabbit. 今天上午,我看到一只老鹰朝一只幼兔扑去。❸ (of someone) be eager to discover (someone's fault); seize (a chance, etc.); accept eagerly (指某人)急于发现(某人的错误),抓住(机会等),急切地接受: White House aides *pounced on* his remarks. 白宫的助手们抓住了他话中的错处不放。If you make a single mistake, she'll *pounce on* it. 你要是出一点差错,她就会抓住它不放。Jane *pounced on* the offer to let her play the piano at the school concert. 简没有放过让她在学校音乐会上演奏钢琴的机会。

NOTE 本短语中的 upon 用法比 on 正式,但不及 on 常用。

pour cold water on/over *vt.* (非正式用语) speak discouragingly about (a plan, idea, suggestion, etc.), to spoil someone's enthusiasm 对(某一计划、想法、建议等)泼冷水: Her parents *poured cold water on* her plan to move into her own flat. 她的父母对她搬进自己公寓的计划泼了冷水。His suggestion seemed quite reasonable, but his boss *poured cold water on* it. 他的建议似乎很有道理,但他的老板却给泼了冷水。

P

pour into *vt.* ❶(cause to) arrive in large numbers in (something)(使)涌入: Hundreds of demonstrators *poured into* the streets demanding the execution of a female foreign teacher who was accused of insulting Islam. 数百名示威者涌上街头,要求处死被指控侮辱伊斯兰教的一名外国女教师。Letters have been *pouring into* the office complaining about the new computers. 办事处不断收到对新电脑投诉的信件。❷(非正式用语) put a lot of (money) into (something or doing something) 大量投入(资金)于: With the stock having taken a continuous bullish view of the prospects, more and more people *pour* their savings deposits *into* the stock markets. 随着股市行情不断地看涨,越来越多的人把存款投入股市。Although billions of yuan annually have been *poured into* building more roads over the past few years, it is still hard to balance supply and demand for traffic facilities. 尽管在过去的几年里每年都投放数十亿元的资金建筑公路,但仍难以平衡交通设施的供与求。

P

pour oil on (the) fire *vi.* (非正式用语) make matters worse 火上浇油,使事情更糟: By brutally suppressing the strikers they simply *poured oil on the fire*. 他们残酷地镇压罢工群众只能是火上浇油。His criticism seemed to *pour oil on the fire* of her anger. 他的批评似乎是给她的愤怒火上加油。

NOTE 本短语 pour oil on (the) flame(s)与意义和用法相同,两者可互换使用。

pour oil on (the) flame(s) ⇨ **pour oil on (the) fire**

pour oil on troubled water(s) *vi.* (非正式用语) try to stop trouble, a quarrel, etc. by making the people who are causing it calmer 平息风波,息事宁人: My friend Mary is very good at *pouring oil on troubled water*. 我的朋友玛丽很善于平息事态。The two groups were nearing a bitter quarrel until the leader *poured oil on troubled waters*. 双方就要发生一场恶吵,领导人出面才平息了风波。To *pour oil on troubled waters*, I pretended to agree with what Mother had said. 为息事宁人,我假装同意了妈妈的话。

NOTE 本短语源于在起波浪的水面上泼洒一层油就能有效平息波浪这一常识。

pour out *v.* (usually of liquid)(cause to) flow out freely; put (some drink) into a glass or cup from another container (常指液体)(使)流出,把(某种饮料)倒入杯中: When the pipe was unblocked, the dirty water *poured out*. 当管子打通时,脏水流了出来。The chimney was *pouring out* black smoke. 烟囱往外冒着滚滚黑烟。Would you *pour* some water *out* for me, please? 请给我倒点儿水,好吗? ❷(常与 to 连用) tell someone (everything that you are feeling)向某人诉说,倾吐(心事): She began *pouring out* her fears about the future to her friend. 她开始向朋友诉说她对将来的担心。The young woman *poured out* her worries to the doctor. 那名少妇向医生倾诉了自己的忧愁。She wrote him a long letter, *pouring* her heart *out*. 她给他写了一封长信诉说衷肠。❸come out in large numbers or quantities 大量地涌出: At five o'clock workers *poured out* of the factory. 5 点钟时,工人们从工厂蜂拥而出。

practice on/upon *vt.* 【可分性动词短语】 ❶perform (something) on (something or someone) in preparation for a real activity 在……上练习,把……用作实习对象:She's been *practicing* the tune *on* the piano for two hours. 她一直在钢琴上练习那支曲子有两个小时了。But the boy was always unwilling to *practice on* the piano regularly. 但这个男孩却总是不愿意按时练习弹钢琴。Can I *practice* my French *on* you? 我能把你作为我练习法语的对象吗? ❷ do (something bad or unpleasant) to (someone) by taking advantage of (his or her feeling) 利用(某人的心理)做(坏事等): By *practicing on* her fear, the criminals made the old lady give them all her money. 犯罪分子利用了老妇人的恐惧心理,使她把所有的钱都给了他们。We can't let him *practice* this emotional blackmail *upon* us. 我们不能让他对我们进行感情敲诈。

NOTE 本短语中的 upon 用法比 on 正式,但不及 on 常用。

prefer to *vt.* 【可分性动词短语】(不用进行时态) like (someone, something, or doing something) more than (another), and so you more likely to choose them if there is a choice 喜欢……,而不喜欢……;宁愿……,而不愿……: Even today, most Americans *prefer* coffee *to* tea. 甚至现在大多数的美国人仍喜欢喝咖啡而不喜欢喝茶。I became a teacher because I *preferred* books and people *to* politics. 我当了老师,因为我喜欢教书育人,不喜欢从政。I *prefer* her plan *to* yours, in that I think it is more practical. 我喜欢她的计划而不喜欢你的,因为我想她的计划更实际些。I *preferred* reading *to* sitting idle. 我宁愿看书,也不愿闲坐着。

NOTE 与本短语相近的一个句型是"prefer to+rather than"。但在此句型中,prefer to 和 rather than 后均须接原形动词。例如:

> They *prefer to* go with us *rather than* stay at home.
> 他们愿意和我们一起去,而不愿待在家里。

prejudice against *vt.* 【可分性动词短语】(常用被动语态形式) cause (someone) to form an opinion about and dislike (usually a kind of thing or a particular group of people, or doing something) before they have enough information 使(某人)对……有偏见,歧视: His testimony might *prejudice* jurors *against* him. 他的证词可能会使陪审员对他产生偏见。They accused him of being/having *prejudiced against* his female employees. 他们指责他歧视其女雇员。She is *prejudiced against* French wine because she's Italian. 她对法国酒抱有偏见,因为她是意大利人。

NOTE 本短语的另外一种表达形式是 have (a) prejudice against。如:

> I'm sure the judge *had a prejudice against* us.
> 那名法官肯定对我们有偏见。

prepare for *vt.* (cause to) make plans and get ready for (someone or a future event) 为……制订计划,(使)做好准备,为……做好准备: We're *preparing* a special reception *for* him when he returns. 我们正在制订计划等他归来时为他举行一个特别的欢迎会。The doctor *prepared* Mother *for* her operation. 医生为妈妈做好了手术准备。He *prepared* himself *for* the examination for Harvard at one of the large private schools. 他在一所大的私立学校里准备参加哈佛大学的入学考试。

P

The World Health Organization urged world governments to take adequate precautionary measures against the newly found A/H1N1 virus and to *prepare for* the case of a pandemic. 世卫组织敦促世界各国政府对新发现的 A/H1N1 病毒采取充分的预防措施，并为疫情大流行做好准备。

NOTE 本短语与 be ready for, get ready for, 都表示“为……做好准备”之意，但 be ready for 强调准备就绪，而 prepare for 和 get ready for 则指准备的动作或过程。如：

> Has everything *been ready for* the party?
> 聚会的一切都准备就绪了吗？
> Not yet, but we're busy *preparing for*/ *getting ready for* it.
> 还没有，但我们正忙着准备呢。

present with *vt.* (常用被动语态形式) formally give (someone) (something such as a present or reward), especially at a ceremonial occasion (尤指在仪式上)给(某人)颁发(礼物或奖品)；向(某人)赠送(某物)：When my uncle left the company, the director *presented* him *with* a gold medal. 当我叔叔离开公司时，董事给他颁发了一枚金质奖章。I am happy to *present* the hospital *with* this gift of money. 我很高兴把这笔赠款赠给医院。Medal winners at the Olympic Games were *presented with* flowers when they entered the hall. 当奥运会奖牌获得者们进入大厅时，人们向他们献了鲜花。

preside over *vt.* 【不可分性动词短语】❶act as the chairperson at (a ceremony or meeting) 主持(仪式或会议)：The minister of commerce *presided over* the ceremonial signing of the three contracts. 商务部长主持了三个协议书的签字仪式。A church wedding is a ceremony *presided over* by a priest. 教堂婚礼是由神父主持的一种仪式。❷ witness (usually bad events) from an important position of power in which one has little control (指某人在担任要职时)目击(无能为力的事件)：As prime minister he *presided over* the biggest ever rise in unemployment. 作为首相，他对前所未有的高失业率无能为力。The directors were not content to *preside* inertly *over* the liquidation of their subsidiary. 董事们不甘心袖手旁观地让他们的子公司被清理掉。

press ahead *vi.* ❶(非正式用语，常与 with 连用) continue with a task or activity in a determined way, despite difficulties, opposition, or interruptions 坚定地继续进行：They *pressed ahead* regardless of objections. 他们不顾反对，坚定地继续做了下去。Mr Scott ignored the comment and *pressed on* with his original plan. 斯克特先生对意见不理不睬，执意继续执行其原定的计划。The president of China's Supreme People's Court said he would *press ahead* with judicial reform, and improve the proficiency of judges. 中国最高人民法院院长表示，他将继续推进司法改革，提高法官的水平。❷continue with a journey, even though it is becoming more difficult or more dangerous 继续向前行进：I considered turning back, but it was getting late, so I *pressed ahead*. 我想原路返回，但天太晚了，所以只好继续前行了。

NOTE 本短语的同义短语是 push ahead 和 push forward。

press conference ⇨ **news conference**

press for *vt.* ❶(无被动语态形式) urge;

make repeated and urgent request for (something) from someone 催促,敦促,一再要求: I don't know whether to accept this new job, and the firm is *pressing* me *for* a decision. 我不知是否该接受这份新工作,而那公司一直在催促我做出决定。The miners keep *pressing for* higher wages. 矿工们一直在要求提高工资。They had *pressed for* their children to be taught English. 他们曾一再要求给他们的孩子讲授英语。❷(非正式用语,用被动语态形式) have hardly enough (money, time, etc.)缺乏(资金),(时间)紧迫: At that time we were *pressed for* money, and could not employ any more people. 当时我们缺少资金,无力再雇用新人。I'm *pressed for* time, so I can't see any one else today. 我今天时间很紧,不能再见任何人了。

press into *vt.* 【可分性动词短语】❶use force or weight to push (things or people) in a mass into (something such as a container) 把……用力塞入: The minister *pressed* a *Bible into* his hand. 牧师把一本《圣经》塞入他的手中。She filled a bowl and *pressed* it *into* my hands. 她盛满了一碗,塞到我手里。Too many people were *pressed into* the room, and we could hardly breathe. 屋子里塞进来的人太多,我们几乎透不过气来了。❷ use force or weight to make (something) become (something else) 用力把……挤压成……: To make wine, you have to *press* grapes *into* liquid. 要制葡萄酒,就必须把葡萄挤压成液体。Before cooking, the pastry must be *pressed into* flat and thin pieces. 糕饼在烘烤之前,要擀平压薄。❸(常用被动语态形式) force (someone) to do (something)强迫(某人)做(某事): She was *pressed into* marriage by her parents. 是她父母迫使她成婚的。Because of the renewed fighting near the border, every young man in the village between the age of 18—28 was *pressed into* service. 由于边境的战事不断,村里所有18至28岁的青年男子都被迫从军。Don't be *pressed into* making any decision. 不要被迫做出任何决定。

press on/upon *vt.* ❶try in a determined way to give (someone) (something, especially something that they do not really want) 逼迫(某人)接受……;将……强加给(某人): He wanted to *press* another drink *upon* me. 他想逼我再喝一杯酒。Teachers are not allowed to *press* their political views *on* their students. 不允许教师把他们自己的政治观点强加给学生们。It's not sensible to keep *pressing* chocolates *on* her when she's trying to diet. 她正在吃规定的饮食,强迫她吃巧克力是没道理的。❷(无被动语态形式)(of something unpleasant such as sadness, anxiety, or a problem) cause worry to (someone) and he or she is always thinking about it 使(某人)感到担心: I've got another problem that is *pressing on* me. 还有一个问题让我感到担心。

NOTE 本短语中的 upon 用法比 on 正式,但不及 on 常用。

presume on/upon *vt.* 【不可分性动词短语】(正式用语) take unfair advantage of (someone's kindness or your relationships with other people) 滥用,不正当地利用: I think she has *presumed* too much *on* your generosity. 我认为,她过分地利用了你的慷慨。Take care that you don't *presume on* our short friendship. 你得注意,不要滥用咱们这份短暂的友谊。

P

NOTE 本短语中的 upon 用法比 on 正式，但不及 on 常用。

pretend to *vt.* 【不可分性动词短语】(正式用语，常用于否定句中) claim to possess (something such as a quality) without good cause 自称拥有：He's never *pretended to* any great knowledge of art. 他从未自称过拥有广博的艺术知识。I don't *pretend to* much expertise in these matters. 在这些问题上，我不敢说自己有太多的专门知识。

NOTE 不要将本短语误用为 pretend to do something。本短语中的 to 是介词，后不能接原形动词。pretend to do something 意为"假装做某事"。例如：

> We mustn't *pretend to* know what we don't know.
> 我们一定不要不懂装懂。

prevail against/over *vt.* 【不可分性动词短语】(正式用语) defeat(someone)in a game, competition, argument, etc.; gain control or victory over (someone or usually something)战胜，胜过，压倒：At last we *prevailed against* our rivals. 我们最终战胜了对手。*Good will prevail against* evil in the end. 正义终究将战胜邪恶。After thinking things over she at length succeeded in letting reason *prevail over* her prejudices. 经过仔细考虑之后，她终于以理智战胜了偏见。

prevail on/upon *vt.* 【不可分性动词短语】(正式用语) ask or persuade (someone)to do (something)请求，劝说(某人)(做某事)：I'll be late for my train — could I *prevail on* you to drive me to the station? 我快赶不上火车了，我可不可以请您开车把我送到车站去？He *prevailed upon* me to believe in his innocence. 他劝我相信他是无辜的。They might be *prevailed upon* to come with us. 他们也许会被说服跟我们一起来。

NOTE 1. 本短语中的 upon 用法比 on 正式，但不及 on 常用。

2. 本短语一般以"动词＋介词＋宾语(通常是人称代词的宾格)＋动词不定式(短语)"的结构使用。

prevent from *vt.* 【可分性动词短语】(后接动名词短语) stop (someone or something) from (doing something) or stop (something) from happening 阻止(某人)做(某事)，防止(某事)发生：They have taken measures to *prevent* the relics *from* being damaged. 他们采取措施以避免文物受损。All the government officials must be *prevented from* abusing their power and enjoying special privileges. 必须防止所有政府官员滥用职权和享受特权。

NOTE 本短语中的介词 from 常可省略。如：His disability *prevents* him (*from*) driving. 但当本短语用在被动语态形式中时，from 则不能省略。例如：He was *prevented from* going to work because of his illness.

previous to *prep.* (正式用语) in the period before (something existed)在……之前：*Previous to* his present employment he was a bus driver. 在他做这份工作之前，他是个公共汽车司机。They told their families about their engagement *previous to* publishing it in the newspaper. 他们把订婚的事情告诉了他们的家庭，然后才登在报纸上。Women are now in a majority on the committee, although *previous to* 2008 there were no female members at all. 现在，妇女在该委员会里已占多数，但在 2008 年以前连一名委员也没有。

P

NOTE 本短语与 prior to 均表示"在……之前"。本短语指事物在发生、发展的次序上是"在前的";prior to 也为正式用语,除在时间上,还常指在顺序、重要性等方面占先,含有优先、更重要的意味。

pride oneself on *vt.* (常用一般时态)feel proud about or take satisfaction in (an achievement, skill, or special quality that you have)以……自豪,以……感到自鸣得意: We *pride ourselves on* the quality of our work. 我们以我们的工作质量而自豪。On her ability to learn new languages my friend always *prided herself*. 我的朋友总是为其学习新语言的能力而自豪。He *prides himself* on his skill in negotiation. 他为自己的谈判技术而自鸣得意。Jane *prided herself on* being fair and honest with all of her students. 简因其对她所有的学生都公平正直而感自豪。

NOTE 本短语的同义短语是 take pride in。

prime of life *n.* the best years of one's life, when one is at the peak of one's powers 壮年时期: He was in the *prime of life* when he began to lose his sight. 他正值壮年时期失明。He was cut down in the *prime of life*. 他英年早逝。The *prime of life* will not come back again. 盛年不再来。

NOTE 本短语中的名词 life 前可加物主代词。例如:

> He was barely 30 and in the *prime of* his *life*.
> 他将近三十,正值壮年。

prior to *prep.* (正式用语) before (something happened or existed); preceding 在……之前,先于……: *Prior to* her marriage my mother was a nurse in a large hospital. 在我妈妈结婚之前,她在一家大医院里当护士。The plane seemed to catch fire a few seconds *prior to* taking off. 这架飞机似乎在起飞的几秒钟之前就起火了。

probe into *vt.* 【不可分性动词短语】(主要用于新闻英语中) make (enquiries) or examine (an activity that appears wrong) in order to discover facts; investigate 调查: China on Monday asked the World Trade Organization to establish an expert panel to *probe into* the US anti-dumping measures on Chinese products. 星期一,中国要求世界贸易组织建立一个专家组,就美国对中国产品实施的反倾销措施进行调查。The mystery of the missing woman has been *probed into* by the police, but without result. 警方一直在调查那名妇女失踪的谜案,但仍无结果。

proceed against *vt.* 【不可分性动词短语】(正式用语,无被动语态形式) begin a case against (someone) in a court of law 对(某人)提出诉讼,起诉(某人): Are you sure that you are to *proceed against* your neighbor over such a small matter? 你一定要因为这样一件小事而对你的邻居提出诉讼? He threatened to *proceed against* me for the recovery of a debt. 为了索取债款,他威胁说要起诉我。

proceed from *vt.* (正式用语,无被动语态形式) ❶arise from; happen or exist as a result as; come forth from 来自;从……发出: Clouds of smoke *proceed from* that chimney. 这团团的烟雾都来自那座烟囱。We will, *proceeding from* the fundamental interests of the Chinese people and the people of the world, determine our stand and policy. 我们将从

P

中国人民和世界人民的根本利益出发，决定自己的立场和政策。To *proceed from* reality and seek truth from facts is our fundamental stand as materialists. 从实际出发和实事求是，是我们唯物主义者的根本立场。❷have a cause or beginning in (something); result from 因……而产生，产生于：Fear often *proceeds from* ignorance. 恐惧往往出于无知。These are diseases that *proceed from* negligence of hygiene. 这些疾病都是由于不讲卫生而引起的。*From* this small error many unfortunate misunderstandings have *proceeded*. 由这个小小的失误，产生了许多不幸的误会。

prohibit from *vt.*【可分性动词短语】❶(正式用语，常用被动语态形式) prevent (someone) from (doing something) 阻止(某人)做(某事)：He stood in front of the door and *prohibited* us *from* leaving. 他站在门前，不让我们离开。Single women are *prohibited from* getting pregnant through "test-tube baby" technology, according to a newly-revised regulation. 根据一项新修订的规定，禁止单身妇女通过"试管婴儿"技术怀孕。❷prevent (something) from (happening) or from (doing something) 阻止(某事的发生)；禁止(某物的行动)：The pesticide products listed below are *prohibited from* use in schools. 下面所列出的农药产品不允许在学校内使用。Why do you want to *prohibit* the cars *from* traveling on this street during rush hour? 你们为什么在交通高峰期间禁止小轿车在此路通行？

project on/onto/upon *vt.*【可分性动词短语】❶cause (a picture, film or image) to appear on a screen or other surface 投影于(屏幕或其他表面之上)：Images of the bacterial structures were *projected onto* a screen. 细菌结构的影像投射在了屏幕上。You can *project* the slides *upon* an empty white wall. 你可以把幻灯片投射在一片白墙壁上。❷imagine (one's own feelings, especially one's guilt or anger) as being experienced by (someone else) 想象(他人)具有(自己的感情的经历)：You shouldn't *project* your guilt feelings *onto* me. 不应该把你自己的内疚心情往我身上套。

prone to *adj.* likely to suffer from (something) or to do something or be affected by (something, especially something bad) 易于(做某事或受不良影响)的：People who work with computers for long hours are *prone to* headaches. 长时间使用电脑的人易患头痛病。She's *prone to* gaining weight. 她很容易发胖。Doctors believe that people who do little physical labor are more *prone to* catch cold than physical laborers. 医生们认为，很少干体力活的人比体力劳动者更易于患感冒。People are *prone to* make mistakes when they are tired. 人们在疲劳时就容易出差错。

NOTE 本短语中的 to 既可作为介词，后接名词或动名词(如前两个例句)，也可作为动词不等式符号，后接原形动词(如后两个例句)。介词后的词语虽表达的不是动作，但在翻译时，可转换为动词意义译出。例如：

> Working without a break makes you more *prone to* error.
> 如果你只工作不休息就更容易出差错。

pros and cons *n.* the advantages and disadvantages or the good and bad aspects (of something) (事物的) 正反两个方面，利弊两个方面：We need to look at the *pros and cons* of each system. 我们需要仔细考量每一种制度的正反两个方面。Weighing up the *pros and cons*, we think the Renminbi's exchange rate should remain basically stable. 权衡利弊,我们认为人民币的汇率应保持基本稳定。He stresses that the government must fully consider the *pros and cons* of the Internet on the national economy and social order. 他强调说,政府必须全面考虑因特网对国民经济和社会秩序的利与弊。

NOTE 1. 本短语源自拉丁语短语 pro et contra。其中的 pro 意为 for, et 意为 and,而 contra 意为 against,整个短语等于 arguments for and against。自 16 世纪以来,pros and cons 一直作为标准用语使用。

2. 本短语的副词性形式为 pro and con,意为"正反两方面地"。例如:

> We must be fair and consider their argument *pro and con*.
> 我们必须公正,从正反两个方面考虑他们之间的争论。

protect against/from *vt.* 【可分性动词短语】keep (someone or something) safe from (harm, injury, damage, or loss)保护……免受,使……免于,防止: An armored shield will protect the driver *against* a direct hit. 装甲会保护驾驶员免受直接火力的打击。The fence along the middle of the road is intended to *protect* vehicles *against* crashing into each other. 沿马路中间所设的隔离栏是为了防止车辆相撞的。Vitamin D is produced naturally by the skin in response to sunlight and may help to slow the ageing process and *protect against* heart disease, according to the study. 该项研究称,皮肤受到阳光照射后而自然产生维生素 D。而维生素 D 会有助于延缓衰老,防止心脏疾病。It's important to *protect* your skin *from* the harmful radiation of the sun. 重要的是,要防止你的皮肤受到阳光中的有害辐射。

NOTE protect against 还有"(以保险来)保护(某人的财产)"之意。例如:

> Many of the homes were *protected against* flood damage.
> 许多家庭都办了保险以保护水灾给他们的财产造成的损失。

protest against *vt.* 【不可分性动词短语】complain or disagree strongly with (someone or something), often by making a formal statement or in the form of an organized demonstration 反对,抗议: He filed a complaint that *protested against* his supervisor. 他提出申诉,表示对其监督人的反对。Workers are protesting against high unemployment and inflation. 工人们反对高失业率和通货膨胀。Thousands of German demonstrators *protested against* the US policy toward Iraq and demanded immediate withdrawal of American troops from Iraq. 成千上万的德国抗议者们抗议美国对伊拉克的政策并要求美军立即从伊拉克撤走。

proud of *adj.* feeling happy about (your achievements, your possessions, or people you are connected with)为……自豪,为……骄傲: You will not continue to make progress if you are *proud of* what you have achieved. 如果你因已取得的成绩而骄傲,你就不会继续进步。My friend Mary was too *proud of* her good looks, and was always trying to call attention to herself. 我的朋友玛丽为自己的美貌过于感到自傲,所以总是设法吸引别人对自己注意。She feels *proud* of having such an intelligent and pretty daughter. 她为有这样一个聪慧又美丽的女儿而感到骄傲。

provide for *vt.* ❶ supply (something or someone) for the needs of (someone or something)为……提供: China *provided* 25 million US dollars to Iraq *for* its reconstruction at the donors' conference in Madrid, Spain. 中国在西班牙马德里召开的伊拉克重建捐助国大会上,向伊拉克提供了2 500万美元的援助。There is no possibility that we can *provide* another teacher *for* that class. 我们不可能为那个班再配备一名教师。❷ support (someone) financially and make sure that he or she has the things that he or she needs 供养(某人),为(某人)提供生计: She has always *provided for* her children. 她一直在供养着她的几个孩子。Her father ensured she was well *provided for*. 她父亲保证很好地为她提供生计。❸ make the necessary future arrangements for (something)为……做好准备: We have provided for every eventuality. 我们已为一切可能发生的事做好了准备。The plans *provide for* road traffic increasing to twice its present volume. 这些计划为应付道路的交通流量比目前增加一倍做好了准备。❹(正式用语)(of a law, treaty, contract, etc.) contain (statements or plans that set conditions for dealing with a particular issue)(法律、条约、合同等)规定: The regulations also *provide for* strict procedures for the examination and approval of exports. 这些法规还规定了严格的出口审批程序。As a special administrative region of China, Hong Kong enjoys a high degree of autonomy as *provided for* by the Basic Law. 香港作为中国的特别行政区,享有基本法所规定的高度自治权。The possibility of the book being translated is *provided for* in your contract. 在你们的合同中已确定有可能要翻译这本书。

provide with *vt.*【可分性动词短语】supply (someone or something) with (necessary things or people)为……提供(必要的物品或人员): After the ice storm disaster the government *provided* the victims *with* food, medicine and clothes in addition to power generators. 冰雪灾害发生后,政府向灾区群众提供了食品、药品和衣物,此外还有发电机。Hong Kong and Macao's return to China has *provided* the international community *with* a successful example of peaceful settlement of historical issues between states. 香港和澳门回归中国,为国际社会提供了一个以和平方式解决国家间历史遗留问题的成功范例。Senior members of the government are *provided with* research assistants. 政府的高级官员都配备有研究助手。The pirate ship is *provided with* modern radar equipment. 那艘海盗船装有先进的雷达设备。

provided that *conj.* ❶ if (a particular thing happens or is done)如果,只要: You can go out to play *provided that* you finish your homework first. 如果你先完成作业,你就可以出去玩。*Provided that* you pay me back by Friday, I'll lend you the money. 只要你在星期五之前把钱还我,我就把钱借给你。❷ and only if; on (the) condition that 只有……才,以……为条件: They are prepared to be generous, *provided that* it is not their own money they are spending. 只要花的不是他们自己的钱,他们就会出手大方。I'll go, *provided* (*that*) you go too. 只有

你去,我才会去。

NOTE 本短语的另外一种表达形式是 providing that。本短语是正式用语,引导的从句多位于主句之后; providing that 是一般用语,平时少用,有时用于口语或商务英语中,引导的从句多位于主句之前。

pull a face ⇨ **make a face**

pull apart *vt.* & *vi.* (常用一般时态) (cause to) separate, usually with force, into pieces (使)分开,拆开,撕碎: This toy is made to *pull apart* easily. 这种玩具做得就是易于拆卸的。He *pulled* the fence *apart* with his bare hands. 他用双手把篱笆拆掉。The cat has *pulled* the newspaper *apart* once again! 猫又把报纸扯烂了。

—*vt.* 【可分性动词短语】❶ separate (people or animals that are fighting) 把(正在打斗的人或动物)拉开: He rushed in and *pulled apart* the boys who were fighting. 他冲了进来,把正在打架的男孩子们拉开。A fight broke out in the pub and it was hard to *pull* the people involved *apart*. 酒吧里发生了打斗,很难把参与打斗的人拉开。They went for each other with their fists and had to be *pulled apart*. 他们挥拳打在了一起,必须把他们拉开。❷ (非正式用语) find severe fault with (usually someone's work) 对(尤指某人的作品)百般挑剔: Don't *pull* her performance *apart* even if it was bad, it could destroy her. 即使她的演出不好,你也不要对她百般挑剔,这样会毁掉她的。Our teacher's latest book has been *pulled apart* by many of his colleagues. 我们老师最近出的那本书受到他许多同事的挑剔。

NOTE 当本短语用作及物性动词短语,所带的宾语为代词时,该代词须置于本短语的动词和副词中间。

pull away *v.* (常与 from 连用) ❶ use force to move (something or someone) away (especially from danger) by pulling 拖走,拉掉(某物);拉走(某人): Help me *pull* the sofa *away* from the wall. 帮我把这沙发从墙边拉走。*Pull away* the wrapper, and you will see what the periodical is. 拽去包装纸,你就会知道里面是什么刊物了。*Pull* the child *away* from the edge of the well! 把那孩子从井边拉走! ❷ (of a vehicle or its driver) start to move away (from a place) (指车辆或司机)(从某处)驶离: I saw her back the car out of the garage and pull away. 我看到她把车从车库退出来就开走了。The car *pulled away* from the lights at high speed. 小汽车以高速驶离交通灯。The thieves steadily *pulled away* from the police car. 窃贼们稳稳当当地从警车旁驾车离去。❸ (常用一般时态) cause (someone or oneself) to move away (from someone who is trying to hold you or touch you) (使某人或自己)挣脱(某人之手): She tried to *pull away* from the man who was holding her. 她竭力挣脱了抓住她的那名男子。

NOTE 当本短语用作及物性动词短语,所带的宾语为代词时,该代词须置于本短语的动词和副词中间。

pull back *vt.* 【可分性动词短语】move (something or someone) back by pulling 拉回: He *pulled* the curtain *back* and looked down into the street. 他拉开窗帘,朝下面的街道望去。The boy almost fell out of the window, luckily his mother caught hold of him and *pulled* him *back*. 那男孩几乎从窗户跌下去,幸好他妈妈抓住了他,把他拉了回来。

—*vt.* & *vi.* (of troops) retreat or

P

withdraw; move (the troops) back from a battle towards their own land (军队)撤退,撤离,撤回(军队): The enemy were forced to *pull back*. 敌人被迫撤退了。Other countries are considering *pulling back* their troops from Iraq. 其他国家也在考虑从伊拉克撤军。

NOTE 1. 当本短语用作及物性动词短语,所带的宾语为代词时,该代词须置于本短语的动词和副词中间。

2. 本短语可转化为复合词 pull-back,意为“阻力;逆境;撤回”。

pull down *vt.* ❶ lower (something) by pulling; make (someone or something) fall 拉下(某物),拉倒(某人或某物): The shopkeeper *pulled down* the blinds. 店主拉下了百叶窗。Try to *pull* your opponent *down* and get the ball from him. 设法把你的对手拉倒,好从他的手中抢到球。❷break in pieces and destroy (something such as a building) 拆毁(建筑物等): Before we build the new house we have to *pull* the old one *down*. 在建新房前,我们不得不把旧房拆掉。❸(英国英语用法,非正式用语)(of something such as an illness) make you physically weaker than usual (指疾病等)使(某人)身体虚弱: It is high fever that has been *pulling* him *down*, he still hasn't fully recovered. 高烧一直使他身体很虚弱,他还没有完全复原。He's pretty much *pulled down* by his illness. 疾病使他的身体很虚弱。❹(美国英语用法) make (someone) depressed 使(某人)感到沮丧: Losing her job *pulled* her *down*. 失业使她感到沮丧。❺(主要用于美国英语中,非正式用语) earn (an amount of money) 赚(钱): He *pulled down* a big fortune there. 他在那里赚了大钱。They must be *pulling down* over $100,000 a year. 他们一年肯定能赚 10 多万美元。You can *pull down* good wages in this company. 在这家公司里你能拿到不错的工资。

NOTE 1. 当本短语的宾语为代词时,该代词须置于本短语的动词和副词中间。

2. 当本短语作“拆毁(建筑物等)”解时,同义短语是 tear down。

pull in *v.* ❶bring in by pulling 把……拉入: Throw me a rope and pull me in! 扔过一条绳子来,把我拉进去! On the boats men were *pulling* nets *in*. 船上的人正在收网。❷(of a train) arrive at a station (火车)进站: One train *pulls in* every other minute. 每隔一分钟就有一列火车进站。The express from New York *pulled in* on time. 从纽约开来的快车正点到站了。❸(英国英语用法)(of a vehicle or its driver) move to the side of the road and stop there (车辆或司机)驶向路边停车: The bus *pulled in* and waited. 公共汽车驶向路边停车等候。The driver *pulled in* at a roadside store. 司机把车停靠在路边的一家商店门前。❹(of a boat or ship) move towards the side of the bank (船只)靠岸: The ship *pulled in* to the shore at dawn. 那艘船在拂晓时靠了岸。❺(主要用于英国英语中,非正式用语,常用被动语态形式) take (a possible criminal) to a police station (for questioning)(把犯罪嫌疑人)带往警察局(讯问): The police have *pulled* him *in* for questioning. 警察把他带到警察局盘问。Two youths wandering around the bank were *pulled in* on suspicion. 两个在银行周围游荡的青年因有作案嫌疑而被带往警察局。❻(美国英语用法,非正式用语) earn or collect (a particular amount of money) 赚取(一定数量的钱): I only *pull in* £15,000 a year as a teacher. 作

P

为一名教师，我一年仅赚 15 000 英镑。The show *pulled* millions *in*, and still lost money. 演出赚了几百万，但还是赔钱。❼(of a performer or a performance, or a match) attract (a large number of people to come to watch them)(演员、演出或比赛等)吸引(大批观众)：The program *pulled in* 2.5 million viewers. 这个节目吸引了 250 万观众观看。Each World Cup match *pulled in* an enormous crowd. 每场世界杯比赛都吸引了大批观众。She is still beautiful, and still *pulling* them *in* at sixty. 她仍然很漂亮，在 60 岁时还在吸引着他们。

NOTE 1. 当本短语用作及物性动词短语，所带的宾语为代词时，该代词须置于本短语的动词和副词中间。

2. 当本短语作"(车辆或司机)驶向路边停车"解时，同义短语是 pull over 和 pull up。pull over 和 pull up 还都可用作及物性动词短语。

3. 当本短语作"(船只)靠岸"解时，同义短语是 put in；反义短语是 pull out 和 put out。

4. 本短语可转化为复合词 pull-in，意为"路边休息处，咖啡馆"。

pull into *vt.* (of a vehicle or its driver, or a ship) (cause to) arrive or stop at (a place)(使)(车辆或其司机、船只)到达，停在(某处)：The first intercity train between Beijing and Tianjin *pulled into* Tianjin Railway Station at 11:10 am on time. 首列京津城际列车于上午 11:10 准时到达了天津站。Find a good place to *pull into* for some tea. 找个好地方停一下车，喝点茶吧。He *pulled* the car *into* the car park. 他把汽车停在了停车场。

pull off *v.* ❶take off (clothes), especially quickly (from a part of body)(尤指迅速地)(从……)脱掉(衣物)：He *pulled off* his coat and joined us in the work. 他脱掉上衣便和我们一道干起活儿来。Please help me *pull* the shoes *off* (my feet). 请帮我把鞋(从脚上)脱下来。❷(常用一般时态)(of a vehicle) be driven or moved away or onto the side of the road; (of a boat) be moved away from the shore 把车开走，把船驶离岸边：When the lights turned green, the car *pulled off*. 绿灯亮时，车才开走。He *pulled* his car *off* the road at a small inn. 他把车停靠在了路边的一家小酒店旁。The boat *pulled off* from the shore this morning. 小船今早离岸起航了。❸(非正式用语，一般不用被动语态形式，常用一般时态) succeed in (doing something that is difficult)成功，做成(难事等)：He *pulled* that deal *off* skillfully. 他巧妙地做成了那笔生意。They nearly managed to get the loan but just failed to *pull* it *off*. 他们几乎就得到了那笔贷款，可就是没有拿到手。

NOTE 当本短语用作及物性动词短语，所带的宾语为代词时，该代词须置于本短语的动词和副词中间。

P

pull on *vt.* ❶put on (clothes), especially quickly (尤指迅速地)穿戴上(衣物)：The boy *pulled on* his coat and ran out to play. 那男孩穿上外衣就跑出去玩了。Emily *pulled on* her gloves as she walked. 埃米莉一边走，一边戴上了手套。She *pulled on* her new hat. 她戴上了她的新帽子。❷suck smoke from (a cigarette, pipe, etc.) into your mouth or lungs 吸烟，抽(香烟、烟斗等)：Mr Harris stood at the door *pulling on* his pipe. 哈里斯先生站在门口抽着烟斗。Some interviewees who were waiting outside were *pulling* nervously *on* cigarettes. 一些等候在外面的面试者紧张地抽

着烟。

NOTE 1. 当本短语的宾语为代词时,该代词须置于本短语的动词和副词中间。

2. 本短语可转化为复合词 pull-on,意为"套穿上去的衣物;套穿的"。

pull out *vt.*【可分性动词短语】❶(常与 from 和 of 连用) produce; take or draw (something or someone) out (从……)掏出,取出,拉出: She *pulled out* a handgun from inside her jacket. 她从夹克衫内掏出了一把手枪。In the twinkling of an eye, the conjuror *pulled* a bird *out* of a cup. 刹那间魔术师从杯中取出一只鸟来。Rescuers from Japan, Russia, and the Republic of Korea were still struggling to *pull* quake survivors *out* from debris of collapsed buildings. 来自日本、俄罗斯和韩国的救援队员仍在奋力把地震幸存者从倒塌建筑物的瓦砾中救出。A 46-year-old man was *pulled out* alive, after being buried for 129 hours in the rubble of a collapsed residential building. 一名 46 岁的男子在被埋于一座倒塌住宅楼的瓦砾中 129 个小时后被活着救了出来。❷(常与 of 连用)(cause to) be removed, often by force (把……)拔出: The decayed tooth should be *pulled out*. 那颗坏牙应该拔掉。He *pulled* the arrow *out* of his arm with his other hand. 他用另一只手从胳膊上拔出了那支箭。

—*vi.* (常与 of 连用)❶(of a train) leave a station; (of a boat) leave the shore (火车)驶离车站,(船只)离岸: The train was *pulling out* of the platform as I ran into the station. 当我跑进火车站时,列车正驶离月台。The steamer is *pulling out* of the harbor. 轮船正在驶出港口。❷(of a vehicle or its driver) start moving out (of something, such as a driveway, parking space, garage, or stream of traffic)(车辆)驶离……: The car *pulled out* of the driveway and nearly hit a truck. 那台轿车驶离私人车道后,几乎撞上一辆卡车。She just *pulled out* in front of me without indicating! 她没给任何信号就在我车的前方驶离车流。❸ stop being involved in (an activity, event, or situation) 不再参与: The firm is to *pull out* of the personal computer business. 该公司将不再经营个人电脑业务。The other side got impatient with the negotiations and *pulled out*. 对方对谈判失去了耐性便退出了。

—*vt.* & *vi.* (非正式用语,常与 from 连用)(of soldiers)(cause to) leave (军队)撤离,撤走(军队): The Spanish troops *pulled out* from Iraq for home. 西班牙军队已撤离伊拉克回国了。They demanded that all the foreign troops be *pulled out* from the country. 他们要求把外国军队从这个国家撤出来。

NOTE 1. 当本短语用作及物性动词短语,所带的宾语为代词时,该代词须置于本短语的动词和副词中间。

2. 当本短语作"(车辆)驶离……"解时,同义短语是 cut out。

3. 本短语可转化为复合词 pull-out,意为"拔,拉;撤军,撤出"。

pull out of *vt.* ❶produce or move (something or someone) from (something such as a place) using your hands (用手)把……从……取出,拔出,拉出: Putting his hand in his pocket, he *pulled* some money *out of* it. 他把手伸进衣袋,从中掏出了一些钱。She nearly lost a shoe *pulling* her foot *out of* the hole. 她把一只脚从洞里拔出来时,鞋子几乎丢在里面。Swimming against the current, he was able to *pull* her *out of* the river. 他逆流

游去,把她从江水中救了出来。❷(of a train, boat, or a vehicle or its driver) move away from (a station, shore, or stream of traffic)(火车)驶离车站,(船只)驶离岸边,(车辆)驶离车流:Dear passengers, the train will *pull out of* the station in five minutes. 旅客们,本次列车再过5分钟就要从本站发车了。My train was *pulling out of* Platform Three as I ran into the station. 当我跑进火车站时,我要乘坐的那列火车正驶离第三站台。The large ship is *pulling out of* the harbor. 那艘巨轮正在驶出港口。He suddenly *pulled out of* the main stream of traffic to overtake the car in front of him. 他突然驶离车流,去超其前面那辆小车。❸ withdraw from (an agreement, a contest, or an organization)退出(某一协议、某项竞赛或某一组织):The team threatened to *pull out of* the final if the authorities fail to take measures to ensure the safety of their supporters. 该球队威胁说,如果当局不采取措施保证其支持者们的安全,他们就要退出决赛。As an American, I say we *pull out of* NATO, and pull back from Iraq. 作为美国人,我认为我们应退出北大西洋公约组织,并撤离伊拉克。❹(of troops) (cause to) leave (a place of trouble); withdraw (使)撤离(是非之地),撤走:The Palestinian leader demanded that Israel troops *pull out of* Palestinian towns and cities. 这位巴勒斯坦领导人要求以色列军队撤离巴勒斯坦城镇。The general has decided to *pull* his troops *out of* the area. 将军已决定把他的部队从该地区撤离。

NOTE 当本短语的宾语为代词时,该代词须置于本短语的动词和副词中间。

pull over *vi.* (of a vehicle or its driver) move closer to the side of the road and stop there(把车辆)开到路旁停下:All the cars *pulled over* to let the fire engines pass. 所有的车辆都开到路旁停下,让消防车通过。The policeman signaled to him to *pull over*. 警察示意他把车开到路边停下。

—*vt.*【可分性动词短语】(of the police) order (a vehicle or its driver) to move closer to the side of the road and stop there (警察)命令(车辆或其司机)靠路边停下:Police *pulled over* his Mercedes-Benz near a crossroad. 在一个十字路口附近警察令他把奔驰车开到路边停下。The policeman *pulled* the car *over* and tested the driver for alcohol. 警察令那辆轿车靠路边停下并对司机进行酒精测试。They *pulled over* several drivers who went through the red light. 他们令几名闯红灯的司机把车开到路边停下。

NOTE 当本短语用作及物性动词短语,所带的宾语为代词时,该代词须置于本短语的动词和副词中间。

pull through *v.* (非正式用语) ❶(cause to) stay alive or regain health (after a serious illness or bad injury)(使)(在重病或重伤后)活下来,恢复健康:Don't worry, your dad's going to *pull through*. 不要担心,你爸爸会活下来的。The patient is very ill, but with proper treatment and careful nursing he'll *pull through*. 那病人病得很重,但通过适当的治疗和精心的护理,他会康复的。We prayed that she would *pull through* the operation. 我们祈祷她能够经得住手术,恢复健康。Good nursing will *pull* him *through*. 良好的护理会使他术后康复的。❷(cause to) succeed in (surviving a period of danger or crisis)(使)渡过(一段危险期或危机):He succeeded in pulling

P

through the difficulty. 他顺利地渡过了难关。The singer said the support of his fans had *pulled* him *through*. 那位歌手说，是他歌迷们的支持使他渡过了难关。She said her religious faith *pulled* her *through* this illness. 她说，她的宗教信仰使她闯过了疾病关。The company was in great difficulties this year until a gift of money from the government *pulled* it *through*. 这家公司今年遇到了很大的困难，直到政府赠送了一笔款才使它渡过了难关。

NOTE 1. 当本短语用作及物性动词短语，所带的宾语为代词时，该代词须置于本短语的动词和副词中间。

2. 本短语与 bring through 的意义相同，但用法不完全相同，bring through 只有及物性用法。见 bring through。

pull up *vt.* 【可分性动词短语】❶ lift; raise (something or someone) by pulling 拔起，往上拉：She was *pulling up* the weeds. 她当时正在拔草。Keep hold of the rope, and we'll *pull* you *up*. 抓住这根绳索，我们把你拉上来。❷ get information (from a computer) (从电脑中)调出信息：Police can now *pull up* your driving record on the computer in their car. 如今，警察能从他们的车载电脑中调出你的驾驶记录。They asked me for those files and I still haven't *pulled* them *up*. 他们向我要那些文件，但我还没有把它们从电脑中调出来呢。

—*vt.* & *vi.* ❶ (of a vehicle or its driver) (cause to) stop moving forward; halt (使)(车辆或其驾驶员)停下：A white Toyota sedan with no license plates *pulled up* in front of the Education Ministry building. 一辆无牌照的白色丰田轿车停在了教育部大楼前。He *pulled* his car *up* within a few yards of the wreckage. 他在离残骸几码远的地方把车停住了。The police *pulled* the driver *up* for breaking the speed limit. 警察因其违章超速行车而拦住了那名司机。❷ (of someone) suddenly stop (what he or she is doing); (of something) unexpectedly stop (someone or what he or she is doing) (指某人)突然停止(正在做的事情)；(指某物)出乎意料地使(某人或其正在做的事情)停下来：Suddenly, he *pulled up* in his stride, and fell to the ground. 他突然停止大步前行，倒在地上。She was pulled up for her error. 她因出错而被叫停。His unexpected criticism *pulled* me *up*. 他那出乎意料的批评使我停下手来。

NOTE 1. 当本短语用作及物性动词短语，所带的宾语为代词时，该代词须置于本短语的动词和副词中间。

2. 本短语可转化为复合词 pull-up，意为“路边休息处，咖啡馆”。

pull up stakes *vi.* (美国和澳大利亚英语用法，非正式用语) leave the place where you have been living or working; move away 迁离，搬家：We've lived here for years, but now it's time to *pull up stakes*. 我们在这里住了多年，现在该迁离了。They lived in Los Angeles for several years before *pulling up stakes* for Hawaii. 他们在洛杉矶居住了几年后就搬家到夏威夷去住了。

push ahead *vi.* (非正式用语) ❶ (常与 with 连用) continue with a plan or activity despite opposition or difficulties (不顾反对或困难)继续推进(某项计划或活动等)：Despite opposition, they're *pushing ahead* with their scheme for a new airport. 尽管有人反对，他们仍在推进建新机场的计划。The government intends to *push ahead* with its reform programme. 政府准备继续推进其改革计划。❷ continue one's journey or march 继续行进：If we *push ahead*, we can get home before dark. 如果我们继续往前走，在天黑前我们就会赶到家。

push along *vi.* (非正式用语)(of a guest) leave one's host (指客人)离开(主人家)：I'm afraid it's time for me to *push along* now. 恐怕我现在该告辞了。It's getting late, we must be *pushing along* now. 天色已晚，我们现在得走了。

push aside *vt.* 【可分性动词短语】❶push (someone or something) firmly or roughly to one side (用力或粗野地)把……推到一旁：Two young men *pushed* all the others *aside* and got on the bus first. 两个年轻人把所有的人都推到一旁，最先上了公共汽车。People standing at the gate were roughly *pushed aside* by the police. 站在大门口的人们被警察粗暴地推到了一旁。She *pushed aside* the papers and put her books on the desk. 她把文件都推到一旁，把自己的几本书放在了桌子上。❷ refuse to think about (something unpleasant); ignore 不去考虑(不快之事)，忽视：She *pushed* her doubts *aside* and carried on. 她放弃疑虑，继续干了下去。

NOTE 当本短语的宾语为代词时，该代词须置于本短语的动词和副词中间。

push for *vt.* (一般不用被动语态形式) urge; demand urgently and forcefully; repeatedly request (something) (from someone or to do something) 敦促，一再要求：The opposition party had also *pushed for* the President to leave the country. 反对党还敦促总统离开国家。People living near the airport are *pushing for* new regulations on night flights. 住在飞机场附近的人们一再要求制定限制夜航班机的新规定。The newspaper reporters have been *pushing* the government *for* details. 该报记者一直在要求政府交代细节。Many parents are *pushing for* the local school to be reopened. 许多家长都在要求重开当地的学校。

push forward *vt.* cause to advance, often with efforts (努力)推进：We shall continue making efforts to *push forward* the building of a well-off society in an all-round way. 我们将继续努力推进全面建设小康社会。Bilateral cooperation between agricultural research institutes, universities and colleges as well as enterprises should be *pushed forward*. 应推动双方农业科研机构、大专院校和企业间的合作。

—*vi.* (非正式用语) continue (with something); move forward 继续，向前进：They are *pushing forward* with their work, hoping to finish it soon. 他们继续工作，以期尽快做完。If we *push forward*, we can get the destination before dark. 如果我们继续向前走，天黑前我们就能到达目的地。

push over *vt.* 【可分性动词短语】make (someone or something) fall over by pushing 把……推倒：She nearly *pushed* me *over* in the playground. 她在操场上几乎把我推倒了。The wall is leaning at such a dangerous angle that it wouldn't take much effort to *push* it *over*. 这堵墙倾斜到了如此危险的角度，不用费劲就能把它推倒。He *pushed over* the table lamp. 他把台灯弄翻了。

NOTE 当本短语的宾语为代词时，该代词须置于本短语的动词和副词中间。

push through *vt.* & *vi.* make a passage through (something such as a group, mass or space) 走过，在……中间挤过去：The snow was very deep, but I *pushed through*. 雪很深，但我还是走过去了。He tried in vain to *push through* the crowd. 他怎么也没能从人群中间挤过去。I had to *push* my way *through* the crowd. 我不得不从人群中挤了过去。

—*vt.* (非正式用语) (of someone) succeed in getting (a law, agreement, etc.) accepted quickly although a lot of people oppose it 使(法律、协定等)迅速获得通过：They're trying to *push* the patients' rights legislation *through* before the Christmas recess. 他们试图在圣诞节休会之前力促患者权益法通过。He is determined to *push* the bill *through* Parliament. 他决心使该议案在国会迅速获得通过。Thousands of people demonstrated to protest the impeachment *pushed through* by the parliament of the President on Friday. 成千上万的人举行示威，抗议国会在星期五通过的对总统进行弹劾的议案。

NOTE 当本短语的宾语为代词时，该代词须置于本短语的动词和副词或介词中间。

push up *vt.* ❶raise or lift (someone) 使(某人)站起：Bill is sliding down again. *Push* him *up*. 比尔又滑倒了，把他扶起来。❷(主要用于英国英语中) cause (something such as prices) to increase at a steady rate 使(价格)上涨，提高(价格)：Any war in the gulf will *push up* the price of oil. 任何一场海湾战争都会使石油价格上涨。Shops are no longer allowed to *push up* their prices whenever they want. 已不允许商家随时随意地涨价。

NOTE 当本短语的宾语为代词时，该代词须置于本短语的动词和副词或介词中间。

put a stop to ⇨ **put an end to**

put across *vt.*【可分性动词短语】(非正式用语) ❶(常用一般时态，常与 to 连用) succeed in explaining (something) (to someone) in a way that is easy to understand (以易懂的方式)把……解释清楚：This young teacher doesn't know how to *put* his ideas *across* very well. 这名年轻教师不知道如何把自己的思想表达得很清楚。He could not *put across* his point of view to the audience. 他没能向听众阐明他的观点。He found it difficult to *put across* what he wanted to say at the meeting. 他发现难以将自己想要在会上讲的内容讲清楚。❷(非正式用语，与 it, that 连用) deceive (someone) into believing or accepting (something) 骗得(某人)相信，骗(某人)接受……：You can't *put* that old excuse *across* your boss. 你无法骗得你的老板相信你那老掉牙的借口。The woman in the free market *put* it *across* me by selling me some bad eggs. 自由市场上的那个老妇人使我上当买了她的臭鸡蛋。

NOTE **1.** 当本短语的宾语为代词时，该代词须置于本短语的动词和副词或介词中间。

2. 当本短语作"(以易懂的方法)把……解释清楚"解时，同义短语是 get across 和 put over。

put all one's eggs in one basket *vi.* (非正式用语，常用于否定句中) ❶depend completely on one particular course of action for success 孤注一掷，在

一棵树上吊死：I've applied for several jobs. I don't want to *put all my eggs in one basket*. 我申请了几份工作，我可不想在一棵树上吊死。"Go out with several friends, don't *put all your eggs in one basket*," he advised. "多交几个朋友，不要把自己局限在一个人身上。"他建议道。❷invest all your money in just one area 把所有资金都投放在一个项目上：My father is a very careful investor, he never *puts all of his eggs in one basket*. 我父亲是一个非常谨慎的投资者，他从不把财力集中投资在一个项目上。If you want to play the stock market, it's smarter to divide your money and buy three or four different stocks instead of *putting all your eggs in one basket*. 要是你想玩股票，最好把你的钱分开来买三四种不同的股票，这是比较聪明的做法。不要把所有的钱都用来买一种股票。

NOTE 1. 本短语的字面意义是"把所有的鸡蛋都放在同一个篮子里"，与其相似的还有 trust all one's goods to one ship，均指一个人把财力都集中投放在一个项目上，而这样做所要冒的风险是极大的。

2. 本短语中的动词 put 还可被 have, keep, lay 或 place 替换，构成的短语意义和用法与本短语相同，但本短语最为常用。

put an end to *vt.* ❶cause (something) to cease 使停止，消除，结束，制止：the students quarreled with one another, the teacher *put an end to* it. 学生们互相争吵起来，老师给予了制止。The candidate for presidency says he'll *put an end to* corruption once and for all. 这位总统候选人宣称，他将永久消除腐败。They must *put an* immediate *end to* their provocations. 他们必须立即停止挑衅活动。We ought to find some way of *putting an end to* that noise. 我们应该找个方法消除那种噪声。❷destroy or kill 毁掉，杀死：The new highway took most of the traffic from the old road and *put an end to* Mr Hanson's motel business. 新建的公路使大多数车辆不再走旧路，这就毁了汉森先生的汽车旅馆生意。He *put an end to* his own life. 他自杀了。本短语的另外一种表达形式是 put a stop to.

put aside *vt.*【可分性动词短语】❶place (something) to one side, especially for a short time 把……放在一边：My son *put aside* his textbooks immediately after the vacation started, and never reopened them again. 我的儿子一放假后就把课本丢到一边，并从没再翻过它们。He *put* the newspaper he was reading *aside* and went to answer the door. 他放下正在看的报纸，去开房门。She took up a slice of bread nervously, but then *put* it *aside*. 她紧张地拿起一片面包，但后来又把它放在了一边。❷save (something, especially money or time); reserve for later or special use 积蓄(钱)，节省(时间)，留下……供专用：Each month I *put* some money *aside* just in case I need it later. 我每个月积蓄一些钱以备后用。We have a sum of money *put aside* for a rainy day. 我们积蓄了一笔钱，以备不时之需。I have *put* some time *aside* to talk to you. 我留出一点时间跟你谈话。They *put aside* some grain every year for future use. 他们每年都存储一些粮食以备后用。❸ disregard; choose not to consider or deal with (something) 不顾，

P

不考虑，搁置起来：All the countries in the world should strive for common development through seeking common ground while *putting aside* differences. 世界各国应在求同存异中共同发展。For issues we cannot settle for the time being, let us *put* them *aside* and consider them later. 对于一时解决不了的问题，我们可以从长计议。

NOTE 当本短语的宾语为代词时，该代词须置于本短语的动词和副词中间。

put at *vt.*【可分性动词短语】(用一般时态)guess, judge or estimate (the nature, value, size, amount, etc.) to be 推测，判断，估计(……为……)：We'd *put* our new teacher's age *at* 21. 我们猜我们的新老师有 21 岁。Official estimates *put* the damage done by the southern California fire *at* over 2 billion dollars. 据官方估计，加利福尼亚州南部大火造成了 20 多亿美元的损失。

NOTE 当用本短语表示"猜测某人的年龄"时，还可以用以下形式表示：

I'd *put* her *at* about 30.
我猜她大约有 30 岁。

put away *vt.*【可分性动词短语】❶ put (something) in the place where you usually keep it when you are not using it 把(某物品)用完后放回原处：*Put away* the tea things in the cupboard. 把茶具都放回到橱柜里。He *put* the notebook *away* in his desk and stood up. 他把笔记本放在书桌里便站起身来。The letters were *put away* in numbered files. 信件都收存在编号的文件夹里了。❷ save (an amount of money) so that you can buy or pay for something in the future 储存(钱)：Try and *put away* a little each month. 试着每个月存点儿钱。Each month she *puts* some money *aside* for her retirement. 她每个月都攒一点钱以备退休时用。❸ forget or cease to consider (something such as a feeling or difference) so that you can achieve something more important 不再考虑，放弃(某种情感或分歧)：He *put* his worries *away* for an easy weekend. 他不再想他的愁事，以便度一个轻松的周末。Laura *put aside* those ideas and went on with her job. 劳拉放弃了那些想法，继续她的工作。Both sides need to *put aside* their differences and continue the peace talks. 双方需要扬弃歧见，继续和谈。❹ keep (something) so it can be used or taken away later 保留(某物以备后用或取走)：The shop offered to *put* the dress *aside* while I went to the bank. 商店提出在我去银行这段时间为我保留那件连衣裙。❺(委婉用法，非正式用语，常用被动语态形式) put (a criminal or mentally ill person) in a prison or a mental hospital 把(犯罪分子)送进监狱，把(精神病患者)送进精神病院：He's an animal! He ought to be *put away* for a long time. 他是个畜生！应该把他长期地关押起来。He had to *put* his wife *away* when she became mentally ill. 他的妻子得了精神病，他只好把她送进精神病院。The woman was *put away* for attacking young children. 那女人因袭击儿童而被送进了精神病院。

NOTE 当本短语的宾语为代词时，该代词须置于本短语的动词和副词中间。

put back *vt.*【可分性动词短语】❶ put (something) in the place where it was before it was moved 把(某物)放回原处：

Can you *put* the book *back* when you've finished with it? 你看完这本书后能把它放回原处吗? When you have finished using the pen, please *put* it *back* where it was. 用完笔后,请将其放回原处。❷(常用一般时态) make (something) happen later than it should happen 拖延: The fire has *put back* the opening of the theatre by several months. 那场火灾拖延了该剧院的开业长达数月。❸ change (the time or date of an event) so that it happens later than originally planned; delay 延期,推迟: They tried to *put back* the reform for another decade or two. 他们企图把改革推迟一二十年。We've *put* the trip *back* until June. 我们已经把旅行日期推迟到了 6 月份。The meeting has been *put back* to next week. 会议已延期到了下星期举行。❹move the hands of (a clock or watch) to an earlier time 把(钟表的指针)向回拨,拨回: He *put* the clock *back* an hour. 他把钟往回拨了一个小时。My watch is 2 minutes fast, so I've to *put* it *back*. 我的表快了 2 分钟,我得把它拨回去。"There was no *putting back* the clock," said he. "时钟不能倒拨。"他说道。❺(用一般时态) cost (someone) (a certain amount of money) 花掉(某人)(一定数额的钱): My daughter's wedding *put* me *back* $20,000. 我女儿的婚礼花掉了我 2 万美元。—*vt.* & *vi.* (of a boat or ship) (cause to) return on its course (使)(船只)返回: The captain *put* the ship *back* to port for repairs. 船长使船返港待修。The ship was *put back* owing to bad weather. 因天气恶劣,这艘船又返回了港口。

NOTE 当本短语用作及物性动词短语,所带的宾语为代词时,该代词须置于本短语的动词和副词中间。

put down *vt.* ❶stop holding (someone or something) and place him or it on a surface 把……放下: "*Put* me *down*!" the small boy yelled on my back. "把我放下来!"小男孩在我的背上喊道。*Put down* the knife before you hurt somebody! 把刀放下,别伤着人! She *put* the sewing needle *down* on the chair by the window. 她把缝衣针放在了靠窗子的椅子上。❷(of a plane, etc.) (cause to) land or settle (使)(飞机等)降落: The helicopter circled over us, looking for a place to *put down*. 直升机在我们的头上盘旋,寻找着降落的地点。The pilot couldn't *put down* the plane in the heavy fog. 驾驶员无法在大雾中降落飞机。❸(英国英语用法) stop a car, bus, etc. and let (someone) get out of it 停车让(某人)下车: The bus stopped to *put down* some passengers. 公共汽车停下来让一些乘客下车。He told the driver to *put* him *down* at the gate. 他告诉司机让他在大门口处下车。❹write or type (words, sentences, etc.) somewhere 把……写下来: *Put* the date *down* on a piece of paper so that you don't forget it. 把这日期写在一张纸上,免得把它忘掉。Make sure that you *put down* every word he said. 你务必把他所说的话都记下来。Can you *put* your phone number *down* in the book? 你能把你的电话号码写在这个本子上吗? *Put down* what we've just said. 把我们刚刚说的内容都写下来。❺(of soldiers, police, or government) use force to stop (a protest or an attempt by people to take power away from a government or leader)(指军队、警察或政府)用武力镇压(抗议或叛乱等): The king *put down* the rebellion and killed all those involved. 国王镇压了那次反叛,杀死了所有那些参与者。The government sent the police to *put* the protest *down*. 政府派警察镇压了抗议活动。The armed uprising was soon *put down* by the government troops. 武装起义很快就被政府军镇压下去了。❻(英国英语用法) reduce (a price or a charge)减低(价格或费用): Shops are being forced to *put* their prices *down* in order to attract more customers. 为吸引更多的顾客,商店都被迫减低了价格。It's time that the government *put down* interest rates. 到政府降低利率的时候了。❼(非正式用语)criticize (someone), especially when other people are present, in a way that makes them appear stupid (尤指当众)批评(某人)并使其难堪: He's always trying to *put* me *down*. 他总是千方百计地要当众批评我,让我难堪。❽pay (an amount as part of the cost of something), with a promise to pay the rest later 支付(部分款项),付(定金): I think I'll *put down* part of the money now and pay the rest next month. 我想先付一部分款,其余的下个月付清。

NOTE **1.** 当本短语的宾语为代词时,该代词须置于本短语的动词和副词中间。

2. 当本短语作"(使)(飞机等)降落"和"停车让(某人)下车"解时,同义短语是 set down。

3. 本短语可转化为复合词 put-down,意为"平定;(飞机的)降落;贬低(的话)"。

put down as *vt.*【可分性动词短语】(常用一般时态) consider (someone or something) to be (a particular type of person or thing)认为……是……: They *put* her *down as* being one of their best Prime Ministers. 他们认为她是最佳首相之一。I *put* her rudeness *down as* accidental. 我认为她的粗鲁是偶然的。

NOTE 当本短语的宾语为代词时,该代词须置于本短语的动词和副词中间。

put down to *vt.*【可分性动词短语】(常用一般时态) consider (something) to be the result of (something)认为(某事)是由(另一事)引起,把(某事)归因于……: I *put* his irritability *down to* tiredness. 我认为他的烦躁是疲劳所致。My brother *put* his success *down to* hard work. 我弟弟把他的成功归因于勤奋工作。

put emphasis on ⇨ **lay emphasis on**

put forth *vt.* ❶stretch (something) out 伸出: She warmly *put forth* both hands towards us. 她热情地向我们伸出双手。❷(正式用语)(of a plant or tree)start to grow (leaves, roots, etc.)(植物)开始发出(芽),长出(叶),生出(根): The bushes *put forth* new branches after being cut. 这些矮树在修剪后都长出了新枝。In spring the bushes *put forth* new leaves. 灌木在春天长出新叶。❸(正式用语)state or suggest (an idea, opinion, proposal, plan etc.) for consideration 提出(思想、意见、建议、计划等): The Chinese nation has rich cultural reserves. "Harmony without uniformity" is a great idea *put forth* by ancient Chinese thinkers. 中华民族具有丰富的文化底蕴。"和而不同"就是中国古代思想家提出的一个伟大思想。You'd better *put forth* your reasons right now. 你最好把你的理由马上提出来。The government has *put forth* a modest plan to streamline the whole system. 政府提出了一个适度的计划以简化整个体系。

put forward *vt.* 【可分性动词短语】❶advance, propose or suggest (something) or offer (an idea, opinion, reason, proposal, etc.), especially so that people can discuss it and make a decision 提出(某种思想、意见、理由、建议等): In 1982 Deng Xiaoping *put forward* the concept of "one country, two systems" for the first time. 1982 年，邓小平首次提出了"一国两制"的理念。If you want us to consider your suggestions *put* them *forward* at the next meeting. 如果你想让我们考虑你的建议，那你就在下次会议上把它们提出来。We wish to express our support for the proposal *put forward* by the committee. 我们愿意表达我们对委员会那项提议的支持。❷(常用被动语态形式，常与 as, for 和 to 连用) officially suggest or recommend (someone or oneself), for a particular job or position or to do something 推荐(某人)，自荐: Your name was *put forward* as a possible team leader. 你已被作为组长的推荐人选。Mr Smith *put* his name *forward* for the presidency. 史密斯先生自荐任会长职务。I've thought about *putting* myself *forward* to chair the meeting. 我曾考虑过要毛遂自荐，主持这次会议。❸(常与 by, to 连用) change (the time or date of an event) so that it happens earlier than originally planned; advance 提前: The warm weather has *put* the crops *forward* by a month. 温暖的天气使作物提前成熟了一个月。The meeting has been *put forward* to this week. 会议已提前到了这个星期。❹change (the time of a clock or watch) to a later time, by moving the hands of them 把(钟表的时间)拨快，把(钟或表的指针)向前拨: Clocks should be *put forward* one hour tonight at the beginning of Summer Time. 今晚在夏令时开始时，要把钟拨快一小时。*Put* your watch *forward* three minutes. 把你的手表向前拨 3 分钟。

NOTE **1.** 当本短语的宾语为代词时，该代词须置于本短语的动词和副词中间。

2. 当本短语作"提前"解时，同义短语是 bring forward 和 set forward; 反义短语是 put back。

3. 当本短语作"把(钟表的时间)拨快，把(钟或表的指针)向前拨"解时，同义短语是 set forward，反义短语是 put back。

put in *v.* ❶place (something or someone) inside (something such as a container)把……放入……: You find the tea too strong? Just *put in* more water. 你觉得茶太浓吗？多加些水就行了。*Put* your hand *in* and see what's in the box. 把手伸进去，看盒子里面装的是什么。Did I *put* my wallet in your bag? 我是不是把我的钱包放在你的包里了？We've had to *put* my mother *in* a nursing home. 我们不得不把我母亲送入一家养老院。❷add (something such as in writing); add to what has been said; say (something) in addition to what others say 添写，加进(字句，话语): Don't forget to *put in* your full name and address. 别忘记写上您的姓名和地址。Please *put in* the proper punctuation marks. 请加进适当的标点符号。My father *put in* a word for me and I got the job. 我父亲为我多说了一句话，

P

我就得到了这份工作。The important thought was *put in* the Party charter in the 16th CPC national congress. 这一重要思想在中共十六大上写入了党章。❸(常用一般过去时)interrupt by saying (something that interrupts someone who is speaking), usually to give some extra information about the subject (常指为补充话题内容而)打断谈话，插话：While the boys were discussing the car accident, Ben *put in* that the road was icy. 当男孩子们在谈论那场车祸时，本插话说，当时的路面很滑。"Why don't you ask them?" he suddenly *put in*. "你为什么不问他们呢？"他突然插话问道。"Helen had something to eat before she left," *put in* Mary. "海伦在离开前吃了东西。"玛丽插话道。❹use (a particular amount of effort) in order to do something 花费(气力) If we *put in* more efforts this year, we may be able to reach that mark. 如果我们今年多花些气力，我们就有可能达到那个指标。They must have *put in* a lot of work to achieve such an interesting exhibition. 展览会办得这么有趣有味，他们肯定花费了很多工夫。❺spend (a particular amount of time) doing something 花费(时间)：Wendy has been *putting in* more hours at the office recently. 最近，温迪在办公室里花的时间比较多了。She *put in* a year's work on her project. 她花了一年时间干自己那个项目。It all depends on how much time you'd like to *put in*. 这完全取决于你要用多少时间。❻(与 for 连用) make or submit (a formal request, claim, offer, etc.)提出(正式的请求、要求等)：He has *put in* repeated requests for permission to do the job. 他反复提出申请要求批准他做那份工作。If the goods were damaged in the post, you can *put in* a claim for compensation to the post office. 如果物品在邮寄过程中损坏，可向邮局提出赔偿要求。The sailor *put in* for leave to visit his family before the ship went to sea. 这名水手在出海前提出了请假探家的要求。❼fix (something such as a large piece of equipment or system) in the place where it will be used and make it ready to use 安装(某种设备等)：How much does it cost to *put in* central heating? 安装中央供暖设备要花多少钱？We're having a burglar alarm *put in*. 我们要安装一个防盗警报器。❽invest (money) in a business or an account 往……投入(资金)：To start up the business, they each *put in* $50,000. 为开办这个企业，他们每人投入资金 5 万美元。❾(of voters) elect (a politician) to a parliament or (a political party) to govern a country 选举(某人)进入国会，选举(某一政党)执政：We only need three more votes to *put* our man *in*. 我们需要再有三票就能把我们的人选入国会。The Labor Party was *put in* once again at the last election and Gordon Brown became UK's Prime Minister. 工党在上次的大选中再次赢得选举继续执政，戈登·布朗成为英国首相。❿appoint (someone) to (an important position of responsibility)任命：They *put in* a new manager to improve sales. 他们任命了一名新经理以改善销售状况。The captain hopes to be *put in* command of a bigger ship. 船长希望被任命为一艘大船的指挥者。⓫(与 at, to 短语连用)

(of a ship or boat) go into a port or harbour for a short stop (船只)进港停泊: Our ship *put in* at Singapore and remained there for a day. 我们的船在新加坡港停泊,并在那里停留了一天。We'll *put in* at the next port for repairs. 我们将在下一个港口停泊维修。The boats *put in* to shelter from the storm. 小船都已进港躲避风暴。

NOTE 1. 当本短语用作及物性动词短语,所带的宾语为代词时,该代词须置于本短语的动词和副词中间。

2. 本短语与 pull in, pull into 和 put into 均有"(船只)进港停泊"之意;但前两者是不及物性用法,后两者是及物性用法。

put in for *vt.* ❶(主要用于英国英语中) officially ask for (something)正式提出申请,请求: She *put in for* a transfer to another office. 她申请调到另一个办事处去。They have *put in for* a government grant. 他们已申请政府补助。I decided to *put in for* a job as secretary. 我决定提出当秘书的申请。A claim has been *put in for* higher wages. 已正式提出了增加工资的要求。❷(非正式用语) arrange for (someone, oneself or something) to take part in a competition or examination 使……参加比赛或考试: We are thinking of *putting* young Peter *in for* the 100 meters. 我们正考虑让年轻的彼得参加 100 米跑赛。Have you *put* yourself *in for* the competition? 你参加比赛了吗? I'm *putting* some of my best roses *in for* the flower show. 我要把我的一些最好的玫瑰花拿到花展去参赛。❸recommend or propose (someone) as deserving, as being a suitable applicant for (a reward or a position)推荐(某人)获得(某种奖励),推荐(某人)担任(某职): His commanding officer is *putting* him *in for* the Victoria Cross. 他的指挥官推荐他为维多利亚十字勋章的获得者。He is being *put* in *for* something in an administrative department. 他被推荐到一个行政部门任职。

NOTE 当本短语的宾语为代词时,该代词须置于本短语的动词和副词中间。

put in/into use *vt.*【可分性动词短语】put(something) to application 应用,把……投入使用: He will be able to *put in use* everything he learned at the university. 他在大学里学到的一切都将能派上用场。Although Windows 2,000 and windows XP have been *put in use*, Windows 98 is still being widely used. 虽然 Windows 2000 和 Windows XP 已经投入使用,但 Windows 98 仍被广泛地使用。Beijing *put* 264 new subway cars *into use* on two key metro lines to modernize the capital's subway system. 北京在两条主要的地铁线路上投入了 264 辆新车以更新首都的地铁运输系统。The model has been *put into* practical use. 该模型已得到实际应用。

put into *vt.* ❶ place (something or someone) in position inside (something) 把……放入,把……送入: Jones *put* the ball *into* the net after only 2 minutes of play. 琼斯在开场仅 2 分钟时就投球入网了。After *putting* three astronauts *into* orbit, top Chinese space officials set out new targets, including a space station within 10 years. 又把 3 名宇航员送入太空轨道后,中国负责太空项目的高级官员制订了新的目标,其中包括在 10 年内建立太空站。❷ spend (a particular amount of time doing something); make (a particular amount of effort in order to do something)花费(时间),花费(气力): They should *put* more effort and time *into* the new policies. 他们应在新出台的政策上投入更多的精力和时间。I *put* a lot of work *into* the speech. 我在这篇演讲稿上花费了很多工夫。❸improve (something) by adding a particular quality to it (为改进……而)增加: Try and *put* some enthusiasm *into* your work. 尽量在工作上再多些热情。I'm glad she's coming, she'll *put* life *into* this party. 她来了,我很高兴,她会给这次聚会增添活力的。I want to *put* some excitement *into* my life. 我想给自己的生活增加一些刺激。❹(无被动语态形式) (of a ship or boat) arrive and stay at (a port)(船只)抵港停泊: The big ship *put into* the port of Monaco for fuel. 这艘巨轮抵达摩纳哥港进行燃料补充。❺(常用一般时态) express (a thought) in (words); translate (something) into (a language)用(文字)表达(思想),把……翻译成(某种语言): I can't *put* my feelings *into* words. 我的心情无法用语言来表达。Try to *put* your ideas *into* simpler sentences. 设法用比较简练的句子把你的思想表达出来。Please *put* this article from English *into* French. 把这篇文章从英语译成法语。❻invest (your money) in (something such as a business or project)投资于(某一企业或项目等);把(钱)花在……上: How much are you prepared to *put into* the business? 你准备向该企业投资多少? He's *put* all his savings *into* buying that house. 他花掉了全部的积蓄买那所房子。

put into action *vt.*【可分性动词短语】perform or fulfill (something planned); cause (something such as a law) to be active, and have to be obeyed 执行,实行,实施(法律等);把……付诸实施: It's time I *put* my intention of hard work *into action*. 我该把努力工作的意愿付诸行动了。They have already begun to *put* the plans *into action*. 他们已经开始执行这些计划了。Some new laws will be *put into action* next Monday. 一些新法将于下星期一生效。We have decided to *put* the plan *into action*. 我们已决定将该计划付诸实施。

NOTE 本短语的名词 action 可被 effect、execution、force、operation 或 practic 等替换,构成的短语与本短语意义和用法相同。

put off *vt.*【可分性动词短语】❶change (the time or date of something) so that it happens later than originally planned, especially because of a problem; delay doing (something)推迟,延期: Never *put off* till tomorrow what you can do today. (谚语)今日事,今日毕。Many European Union women are *putting off* having their first child to concentrate on their career. 许多欧盟国家的妇女为集中精力干事业而推迟生育。Because of the riots, the parliamentary elections were *put off* to February. 由于骚乱,议会选举被延期到了2月举行。❷(主要用于英国英语中) switch off (a light, a machine or a piece of equipment) by pressing or turning a button or switch (把电灯、机器或某一设备)关掉,闭上: Be sure to *put off* the light before you leave. 在走前一定要把灯关掉。Don't forget to *put off* the radio. 别忘了把收音机关掉。Under the official regulations the central heating was *put off* on the first of May each year. 根据官方规定，每年5月1日这一天停止集中供热。Please *put off* the television and do your homework. 把电视机闭了，做你的作业。❸(英国英语用法)stop a car, bus, boat, etc. and let (someone) get out of it (停车)让(某人)下车，(停船)让(某人)下船：She asked the driver to *put* her *off* in front of the school gate. 她叫司机让她在校门口下车。Where do you want to be *put off*, sir? 先生，您想在哪儿下车？If you don't behave yourselves, I'll have you *put off* the ship! 你们如果再不规矩点儿，我就把你们赶下船去。❹delay (doing something), especially because you do not want to do it 推脱，搪塞(做某事)：You can't *put* the decision *off* any longer. 快做决定吧，你不能再推脱了。Don't try to *put* me *off* this time. I don't want to talk round the subject, I want to talk about it. 这次可不要搪塞我了。我不希望拐弯抹角，要直谈问题。He was glad to have an excuse to *put off* telling her the news. 我很高兴找到了推脱不告诉她那消息的理由。I won't be *put off* with such vague promises. 这种含混的诺言是敷衍不了我的。❺(非正式用语，常用一般时态)make (someone) not want to do (something), or make (someone) not like (someone or something)使(某人)气馁；使(某人)不喜欢：Lack of parking space was *putting* potential customers *off*. 停车场的车位不足使一些潜在的顾客不来此购物。The smell *puts* me *off* eating for a week. 那味道使我一个星期都吃不下东西。We wanted very much to visit the palace but were *put off* by the long queues. 我们很想参观那座宫殿，但排得长长的队伍使我们打消了那一念头。Robert's attitude towards women really *puts* me *off* (him). 罗伯特对妇女的态度的确使我(对他)很反感。❻get rid of; cease to have or consider (something such as a feeling or duty)摆脱，抛弃，不再考虑：How can I *put off* these fearful doubts? 我怎么才能消除这些可怕的怀疑呢？He decided to *put off* all his personal considerations and accept the task assigned to him. 他决定抛弃一切个人得失，接受交给他的任务。❼(非正式用语) (of someone or something) prevent (someone) from concentrating on something so that he or she has difficulty doing it 使(某人)分心，分散(某人的)注意力：Stop laughing, you'll *put* him *off*. 别笑了，你会使他分心的。Don't talk, it *puts* her *off* (her game). 别说话，这会影响她的(比赛)。

NOTE **1.** 当本短语的宾语为代词时，该代词须置于本短语的动词和副词或介词中间。

2. 当本短语作"推迟，延期"解时，同义短语是 put back 和 put over。

3. 当本短语作"(把电灯、机器或某一设备)关掉，闭上"解时，同义短语是 turn off 和 switch off；反义短语是 put on, switch on 和 turn on。

4. 当本短语作"(停车)让(某人)下车，(停船)让(某人)下船"解时，同义短语是 put down。

5. 本短语可转化为复合词 put-off，意为"推迟；搪塞"。

put on *vt.* ❶ place (usually something) on (something)把……放(到……)上去：She *put* her hand *on* Jim's arm. 她把手放在了吉姆的胳膊上。Please *put* the plates *on*. 请把这些盘子放上去。The talks would be broad and open, even the sensitive political issues could be *put on* the table for full discussion. 谈判的空间是广阔而开放的，即使是敏感的政治问题也可以摆到桌面上充分讨论。❷ place (clothing, etc.) on one's body in order to wear it; cover (part of the body) with (something, especially clothing) (给……)披上，穿上，戴上(衣物等)：The mother *put* a coat *on* her son. 妈妈给儿子披上了一件上衣。The astronauts aboard the spacecraft entered the orbital capsule from the return capsule after taking off space suits and *putting on* blue work clothes. 飞船上的航天员脱下宇航服，穿上了蓝色工作服从返回舱进入了轨道舱。He *put* his hat *on* hurriedly and ran out of the house. 他匆忙地戴上帽子跑出房门。He *put on* his glasses and began to read the new book. 他戴上眼镜，开始读那本新书。❸ (主要用于英国英语中) cause (a light, an electrical apparatus, etc.) to operate by pressing or turning a button, switch, etc. 打开(电灯、电器等)：I *put on* the light by the bed. 我打开了床头灯。Can you *put* the light *on*, please? 你能把灯打开吗？*Put* the radio *on*, please. I want to listen to the news. 请把收音机打开，我想听新闻。Have you *put* the heating *on*? 你开暖气了吗？❹ (英国英语用法，常用一般时态) add (a particular amount of money) to the cost or value of (something) 增加，提高(费用或价钱)：The bill came to two pounds but the waiter *put on* a few extra pence. 账单上是两英镑，但侍者又给加上了几个便士。The government shall *put* one dollar *on* the price of petrol. 政府将提高汽油价格一美元。❺ (of a person) increase (body weight) and become heavier(指人)增加(体重)：She's *put on* a lot of weight since she gave up smoking. 她戒烟后，体重增加了许多。She said she *put on* 10 pounds while she was on holiday. 她说她在休假期间体重长了10磅。If I *put* another inch *on* my waist, I won't be able to wear this dress. 如果我的腰再长肥一寸的话，我就穿不了这件连衣裙了。❻ (主要用于美国英语中，非正式用语) pretend to have (a particular feeling or a particular way of speaking or behaving which is not real or natural to you); deceive (someone into believing something that is not true) 假装，装出(某种样子)，欺骗：She's not really ill, she *puts* it *on* to get people's sympathy. 她其实没什么病，她是为了博得他人的同情而装病的。Stop *putting on* that funny voice! 别再装出那种滑稽的腔调！Her modesty is all *put on*. 她的谦虚全是假装的。I am not *putting* you *on*. 我没骗你。❼ organize (an event, show, performance, etc.) 组织(活动)；演出；展出：We're *putting on* a concert to raise money for AIDS patients. 我们将为艾滋病患者募集资金而组织一场音乐会。We are *putting* the play *on* again next week owing to its success. 由于那部话剧演得成功，我们在下星期还要重演。He *put on* the shooting the day before the election to win sympathy votes. 他上演的

选举前一天的枪击闹剧，是为了赢得同情选票。Six cubs from a rare white tiger have been *put on* display in an Argentine zoo for the first time. 六只稀有的白虎幼崽首次在阿根廷的一家动物园展出。❽ put(a particular amount of money)on the result of (a race or competition) to make a bet about it 在(竞赛结果上)下赌注，打赌：Many people are *putting* their money *on* Matthew scoring the first goal. 很多人都把钱赌在马修能进第一个球上。I *put* \$5 *on* No. 4 horse to win the race. 我出5美元打赌，4号马能赢得比赛。❾ force acceptance of (something such as a responsibility) on (someone or something)把……强加于：I feel that too much responsibility is *put on* teachers. 我感到强加给教师的责任太重了。Advertising aimed at children *puts* a lot of pressure *on* parents. 针对儿童做的广告给家长施加了很大的压力。Why are you trying to *put* the blame *on* me? 你为什么非把罪责强加在我的头上？❿ record (something) in (an account) so that someone can pay for it later 把……记在(账上)：Can you *put* the drinks *on* my bill, please? 请把这些饮料都记在我的账单上，好吗？⓫ provide (a bus, train, etc.) for people to use 提供(车辆)：They're going to *put on* extra buses to take fans to the concert. 他们将额外提供大客车送歌迷们去听音乐会。So many people wanted to go to the match that another train had to be *put on*. 有那么多人都想去看比赛，所以不得不加开一班火车。⓬ pass (the telephone) to (someone) so he or she can speak to the person you have been talking to 把(电话)交给(某人)接听：Wait a minute, Mum, I'll *put* Joe *on*. 等一下，妈妈，我让乔来接听。

NOTE **1.** 当本短语的宾语为代词时，该代词须置于本短语的动词和副词或介词中间。

2. 本短语作"穿上，戴上"解时，与 dress up, have on 和 pull on 均有"穿，戴"之意。本短语表示"穿，戴"的短暂动作，而且其宾语一般都是衣物，而不是饰物等。dress up 指"给(某人)穿上盛装"，表示动作。例如：

> I *dressed* my children *up* for the party.
> 我给孩子们穿上盛装去参加聚会。

have on 则强调"穿，戴"的状态。例如：

> When I went into his room, he *had* nothing *on* but his shorts.
> 当我进到他的房间时，他只穿着裤衩。

pull on 指"匆忙穿上衣物"的动作。例如：

> He *pulled* them *on* hurriedly.
> 他匆忙地把它们穿在身上。

另外，wear 表示"穿，戴"的状态，宾语既可以是衣物，也可以是戒指等首饰、眼镜、手表等。

3. 本短语转化为复合词 put-on，意为"假装，欺骗，模仿剧(或作品)；假装的"。

put on airs (and graces) *vi.* (非正式用语) pretend to be very important or superior, in order to impress people 摆架子：I don't have to *put on airs* with my friends. 我用不着和我的朋友们摆架子。Our boss is a person easy to get along with. He never *puts on airs and graces*, making friends with everyone working in the department. 我们的老板是一个很容易相处的人。他不摆架子，和部门里工作的每一个人都交朋友。

P

NOTE 1. 本短语的名词 air 必须用复数形式。

2. 本短语的另外一种表达形式是 give oneself airs(and graces)。例如:

> Don't *give yourself airs*, my sister, simply because you can sing well.
> 我的妹妹,你不要因为你歌唱得好就摆架子。

put on to *vt.*【可分性动词短语】❶(常用一般时态) help (someone) to meet or speak to (someone); put (someone) in touch with (someone)帮助(某人)同(某人)面谈;使(某人)同(某人)相接触: He insisted on being *put on to* the man in charge. 他坚持要与负责人面谈。I'll *put* you *on to* the director, he may be able to help. 我将安排您与董事长接触一下,他也许能帮忙。❷(非正式用语) introduce (someone) to (someone or something that he or she wants or needs)把(某人)介绍给……: I can't help you myself, but I can *put* you *on to* a good lawyer. 我本人爱莫能助,但我可以向你介绍一位好律师。It was Roy who had *put* Tom *on to* this club. 是罗伊把汤姆介绍到这个俱乐部的。I was *put on to* this wonderful thing by a friend of mine. 这件奇妙的玩意儿是我的一个朋友介绍给我的。This elastic is a very useful thing, which a friend in clothing trade *put* me *on to*. 这种松紧带是很有用的东西,它是我服装业的一位朋友介绍给我的。

NOTE 1. 本短语与 put onto 意义和用法相同,put onto 主要用于英国英语中。

2. 当本短语的宾语为代词时,该代词须置于本短语的动词和介词中间。

put on flesh ⇨ **put on weight**

put on weight *vi.* (of a person) increase (body weight) and become fatter (指人)增加体重,发胖: She *put on* a lot of *weight* after the baby was born. 她生了孩子后,体重增加了许多。Since she started *putting on* weight her skirts have to be let out. 自从她开始发胖以后,她的裙子都得放大一些了。Too many sweets and not enough exercise will make you *put on* weight. 吃过多的糖果,加上运动量不足就会使你长胖。

NOTE 本短语的同义短语是 gain weight;反义短语是 lose weight。

put one's finger(s) on ⇨ **lay one's finger(s) on**

put one's hands on ⇨ **lay one's hands on**

put one's heads together *vi.* (of two or more people) talk together about a problem they have and try to solve it 共同讨论(以解决某一问题),集思广益: The maths problem is extremely difficult. The teacher says we can *put our heads together* and find the solution. 这道数学题极难。老师说,我们可以一起思考,找出答案。They *put their heads together* and decided on all the details of the project. 他们集思广益,把整个项目的所有细节都定了下来。

put out *vt.* ❶ place (something) outside your house 把……放在户外: I *put* the washing *out* when the sun shone, but I soon took it in again. 我趁阳光灿烂时把洗的东西放在外面晾上,但很快我又把它们收了进来。I *put out* food for the birds in cold weather. 在冷天,我把给鸟吃的食物放在外面。❷ stretch (something) out or forward 把……伸出来: The doctor told him to *put out* his tongue. 医生让他把舌头伸出来。He *put* his hand *out* to shake hands with her. 他把手伸出来去和她握手。❸ make (something such as a fire or cigarette) stop burning 把(火、香烟等)熄灭: The eight-floor building suddenly collapsed when local firemen were trying to *put out* the fire, leaving 20 firemen dead. 当地消防队员正在奋力救火时,那栋 8 层大楼突然倒塌,致使 20 名消防队员牺牲。The fire had already been *put out* by the people on the spot before the firemen arrived. 在消防队员到达之前,火已被在场的人们扑灭了。He *put out* his cigarette before entering the building. 在进楼之前,他把烟熄灭了。❹ turn or switch off (an electric light)(把电灯)关掉: The nurse drew the curtain and *put out* the lights. 护士拉上了窗帘,关闭了电灯。Mary *put* the light *out* and went to sleep. 玛丽把灯关掉就睡觉了。❺ force (someone) to leave, usually a building 迫使……离开,赶出: The next time he brings his noisy friends to the club we'll have them *put out*. 下次他要是再带他那些吵闹的朋友来俱乐部的话,我们就把他们赶出去。If you keep talking in class, I'll have to *put* you *out*. 如果你在课堂上再讲话,我就把你赶出去。He was *put out* of the room for being rude. 他因粗野而被逐出屋外。❻ make (a statement, story, or information) known to many people 公布,发布,发出: The organization *put out* a statement denying rumors of a split. 该组织发表了一项声明,否认了其要分化的说法。The Chinese Government has officially banned research on human cloning and has *put out* written policy on human cloning. 中国政府已正式禁止克隆人的研究并公布了有关克隆人的文字政令。A report has been *put out* from the government information office about the worsening unemployment figures. 政府的信息机构发布了一项有关日趋严重的失业数字的报告。Police have *put out* a warning to people living in the area. 警方已向那一地区的居民发出了警告。❼print (material such as a book) 印刷(书刊等): They also *put out* pamphlets in English of this statement. 他们还印刷了这份声明的英文小册子。❽publish (a book, magazine, or newspaper), or produce (a video or CD) for sale 出版,发行: The company has *put out* several new English dictionaries this year. 该公司今年已出版了几部新的英语辞书。This press *puts out* books on various subjects in various languages. 这家出版社出版各种题材和语言的书籍。❾ broadcast (a programme) on television or radio (电视或广播)播出(节目): Most of the stuff they *put out* isn't worth watching. 他们播出的大部分节目都不值一看。Can the new singers have their songs *put out* on the radio? 这些新歌手能使他们的歌在电台播出吗? ❿ produce (something such as goods or power) in large quantities 大量生产(某种产品);发电: Last year the factory *put out* over 5 million records. 去年,这家工厂生产了 500 万张唱片。This engine *puts out* more electric current than the other one. 这台电机比那台发电多。⓫(常用被动语态形式) upset or annoy (someone) 使(某人)感到不快;使(某人)恼怒: Don't

put yourself *out* for my not having come to your birthday party. 不要因为我没来参加你的生日聚会而不高兴。She was so *put out* by his rudeness that she didn't know what to say. 他的粗鲁使她气得不知道说什么好。His father was very much *put out* about the matter. 他父亲对此事感到非常恼火。⓬(非正式用语,一般用于疑问句或否定句中) cause problems or inconvenience to (someone) by making him or her do something for you 给(某人)制造麻烦,给(某人)带来不便: Will it *put* you *out* if I bring another guest? 我要是再带一位客人来会不会给您添麻烦? I hope it hasn't *put* your housekeeper *out*. 我希望这没给你的管家添麻烦。It would be lovely to stay with you, but I don't want to *put* you *out*. 和您住在一起固然很好,但我不想给您带来不便。⓭(非正式用语,用一般时态) put(a part of body such as a joint)out of place; dislocate 弄脱(关节),使脱臼:I can't play tennis today, I've *put* my ankle *out*. 我今天不能打网球了,我的踝关节脱臼了。She fell down and *put* her shoulder *out*. 她跌了一跤,使肩关节脱臼了。⓮(in a sporting competition) defeat (a player or team) and eliminate them from the competition (在体育比赛中)击败并淘汰(某选手或某队): The champion boxer *put* his opponent *out* in the second round. 那名拳击冠军在第二轮比赛中就把对手淘汰了。Our team was *put out* from the competition in the first round. 我们队在第一轮比赛中就被淘汰出局。⓯(常用一般时态) make (someone) unconscious 使(某人)失去知觉: This gas will *put* you *out* during your operation, you won't feel a thing. 这种气体会使你在手术过程中失去知觉,你什么感觉也不会有的。I didn't mean to *put* him *out*. It was a careless blow. 我没想把他打昏。那一拳没小心。

—*vi*. (常与 to 连用)(of a ship or boat) begin sailing to the open sea; sail away from a port, the shore or coast (船只)出航,离港,离岸: The ship will *put out* to sea on this evening's high tide. 船将趁今晚涨潮时出航。A Coast Guard boat *put out* through the waves. 一艘海岸巡逻艇破浪出航。

NOTE 当本短语用作及物性动词短语,所带的宾语为代词时,该代词须置于本短语的动词和副词中间。

put over *vt*. 【可分性动词短语】(非正式用语) ❶describe or explain (something such as an idea) clearly (to someone)把(某一想法等)(向某人)讲清楚: He knows how to *put over* his ideas clearly. 他懂得如何把他的想法讲清楚。I don't think I *put* my point of view *over* very clearly. 我认为我没有把我的观点讲清楚。She's not very good at *putting over* her ideas. 她不太善于把自己的想法讲清楚。❷ delay (something such as an event) till a later time or date; postpone 推迟,延期: The discussion of this problem will be *put over* till the next week. 这个问题将推迟到下个星期讨论。They *put over* the meeting to the following Thursday. 他们把会议推迟到下周四召开。❸carry out successfully; complete 做成,完成: The experienced businessman *put over* a complex and difficult business deal. 那位经验丰富的商人做成了一笔复杂而困难的交易。

This is a very hard thing to explain to a large audience. I hope I can *put* it *over*. 向大批听众做解释是件很难的事,我希望我能把它做好。

NOTE 当本短语的宾语为代词时,该代词须置于本短语的动词和副词中间。

put over on *vt.*【可分性动词短语】(非正式用语) deceive (someone) into believing or accepting (something that is not true); trick 蒙蔽,欺骗(某人): Don't believe him, he's just trying to *put* something *over on* us. 不要相信他,他是在试图要我们上当。Can you *put* it *over on* the teacher, so that he doesn't discover our secret plan? 你能蒙过老师,不让他发现我们的秘密计划吗? He tried to *put over on* me by selling me a car that didn't work. 他想骗我,要把一辆开不动的汽车卖给我。

NOTE 当本短语的宾语为代词时,该代词须置于本短语的动词和副词中间。

put pressure on *vt.*【不可分性动词短语】❶apply weight or pressure to (something) 压住(某物): *Put pressure on* the artery that carries blood to the wound to stop the bleeding. 压住通往伤口的血管以止血。❷try to force (someone or something) (to do something) by argument, threats, etc. 向……施加压力: The labour unions have been *putting pressure on* the government to reduce its limits on wage increases. 工会一直向政府施加压力,使其减少对增加工资的限制。Former BBC Director General released a letter which demonstrated the "intense pressure" 10 Downing Street was *putting on* the BBC. 英国广播公司前总经理公布了一封信件,证明唐宁街10号对英国广播公司所施加的"强大压力"。

put right *vt.*【可分性动词短语】❶repair, fix or mend (something) 修理: The washing machine broke down again, so I called the repairman to see if he could *put* it *right*. 洗衣机又坏了,所以我叫来了修理工看他是否能修好它。The short circuits, having been located, can be *put right*. 查出短路的位置后,就能把它修好。❷correct (something that was wrong) 纠正(错误): Minor mistakes can be quickly *put right*. 小错误可以很快得到纠正。I'm sorry about all the trouble I've made, I'll do my best to *put* things *right*. 我很抱歉制造了所有这些麻烦,我将尽最大努力矫枉过正。❸(英国英语用法,常用一般时态) explain (the real facts about a situation) to (someone who does not understand it correctly) 向(有误解的人)解释(实际情况): I think I ought to *put* you *right*, John is just my business partner. 我想我应该向你解释一下,约翰只是我的生意伙伴。❹(英国英语用法,非正式用语) make (someone) feel better 使(某人)感到好转: A week by the sea will soon *put* you *right* again. 到海边休息一个星期,你很快就会好转的。Try taking extra vitamins, that'll *put* you *right*. 试着多吃点维生素,就会使你感到好些。

NOTE **1.** 当本短语的宾语为代词时,该代词须置于本短语的动词和形容词中间。

2. 当本短语作"修理"和"纠正错误"解时,同义短语是 set right。

put someone in mind of *vt.* (常用一般时态) remind someone of (someone or something) 使(某人)想起……,提醒(某人)……: This *puts me in mind of* a similar situation we had last year. 这使我

想起了我们去年所遇到的相同境况。You *put me in mind of* my dead brother. 你使我想起了我去世的哥哥。I must *put you in mind of* the promise you made not long ago. 我必须向你提醒你前不久所许下的诺言。

put the cart before the horse *vi.* (非正式用语)do or put things in the wrong order or sequence 本末倒置,倒果为因: Don't you think you will be *putting the cart before the horse* if you get married before you get yourself properly established in society? 你不认为先成家后立业是本末倒置了吗? Why are you buying paint for your flat when you don't yet have a flat? Aren't you *putting the cart before the horse*? 你为什么现在还没有房子就买了涂房子的油漆,你这不是本末倒置了吗?

put through *vt.* ❶complete (a piece of work or business) successfully 成功地做成: We can *put* this task *through* tomorrow. 我们明天就能完成这项工作。Production will start up again when these changes have been *put through*. 当这些改革完成以后,生产就将恢复。The experienced businessman has recently *put through* a difficult business deal. 那位经验丰富的商人最近成功地做成了一笔难做的买卖。❷(常与to连用)connect (a caller or telephone call) to allow the caller to speak to the person he or she is phoning 给……接通电话,打通(电话): If he is not in, can you *put* me *through* to his secretary? 如果他不在,请给我接通他秘书的电话,可以吗? If this man rings up for me again, please *put* him *through* to 3721-6267. 要是这个人再给我打电话,请给他接通37216267。The switchboard operator refused to *put* the call *through*. 交换台的话务员拒绝接通那一电话。I spent all evening trying to *put through* a call to my friend in London. 我整个晚上都在试图打通伦敦朋友的电话。❸(常用一般时态) force (someone or something) to undergo (a test or trial) in order to make sure everything is working correctly 使……经过(化验、检验等): He was *put through* a series of tests to discover what was wrong with him. 对他进行了一系列的化验以发现他到底有什么毛病。The drug has been *put through* several trials. 这种药物已经过数次检验。❹cause (something such as a law) to be passed, as by Parliament or other law-making bodies 使(法律等)(在议会或其他立法机构中)获得通过: Their huge majority in the Congress means they can *put through* any legislation they want. 他们在国会占有绝大多数的席位,这意味着他们可以使任何他们想要通过的法律获得通过。A string of similar measures had already been *put through* Parliament. 一系列的相似措施都已在议会获得通过。❺(常用一般时态)make (someone) do or experience (something difficult or unpleasant)使(某人)做(困难的事情),使(某人)经历(令人不快的事情): The team are *put through* a daily fitness programme. 队员每天都要进行体能训练。He's *put* me *through* absolute hell during the last year. 在过去的一年里,他使我遭受了极大的痛苦。

NOTE 当本短语的宾语为代词时,该代词须置于本短语的动词和副词或介词中间。

put to death *vt.* 【可分性动词短语】(常用被动语态形式) kill or execute (someone), especially with official permission as a means of punishment (尤指经官方允许作为一种惩罚手段而)处死(某人): Soldiers were given the order to *put to death* anyone appearing in the streets after curfew. 士兵们奉命把宵禁以后在街上出现的任何人打死。Valentine continued to perform marriage ceremonies for young lovers in secret. When his actions were discovered, the Roman emperor had him *put to death*. 瓦伦丁继续秘密地为年轻的恋人们举行结婚仪式。当他的行为被发现后,罗马皇帝便将他处死。

put to use *vt.* 【可分性动词短语】employ or use (something that you have) for a sensible purpose that brings a benefit to you 使用,利用: Here he could *put to use* everything he had learned in the army. 他在军队里学到的东西在这里全都能派上用场。Do you promise to *put* the money *to* good *use*? 你答不答应很好地使用这笔钱? The new space launch center in Hainan was completed in 2012 and formally *put to use* in 2013. 海南新航天发射中心预计于 2012 年竣工,2013 年正式投入使用。

put up *vt.* ❶ build (something such as a building, wall, fence or other structure)建造,支起,搭起: They are *putting up* several new office buildings on our street. 他们正在我们这条街上建造几幢新办公楼。A chemical plant will be *put up* near our school. 一座化工厂即将建在我们的学校附近。John is in the garden *putting* a fence *up*. 约翰正在园子里筑篱笆。People have *put up* tents outside to sleep in, fearing buildings would collapse in the aftershock. 人们都在外面支起帐篷睡觉,很怕楼房在余震中倒塌。❷ fix (something such as a picture or notice) onto an upright structure such as a wall, notice board, or in a public place where people can see it 贴(图画);张贴(布告);公布: I *put* a few pictures *up* to make the room look less bare. 我贴上了几张画,使房间看上去不那么空无装饰了。We'd better *put up* a notice about the game. 我们最好贴出一张关于这场比赛的通知。She *put up* the examination results. 她贴出了这次考试结果的布告。The names of the candidates will be *put up* on the college notice board. 候选人的名字将在学院的广告板上公布。❸ increase (the value or price of something)提高(某物的价值或价格): Their friends suggested that they should *put up* their prices. 朋友们都建议他们提高价格。The grocer's *put* the price of coffee *up* again. 这家食品店再次提高了咖啡的价格。The government has promised that taxes will not be *put up* again this year. 政府许诺说今年不再增加税收。Several of the banks have decided to *put up* their interest rates. 几家银行已决定提高利率。❹ provide (a large amount of money) for (something)为……提供(大量资金): The rich man *put up* a lot of money to start making the movie. 这位富翁提供了大笔的金钱用来开拍那部影片。The money for the new hospital was *put up* by an anonymous donor. 建新医院的资金是由一位匿名人士捐献的。❺(常与 for 连用) place (something) on sale; offer (something) for sale 拿出……供出售: The next thing I shall *put up* is a fine, old picture. 我要拿出来出售的下一件物品是一幅精美的老画。She is to *put* her house *up* for sale. 她要出售自己的房子。The old house has been *put up* for sale. 这所旧房子

P

已供出售。❻offer (opposition) in order to prevent something 提出(反对),进行(抵抗):Residents have *put up* a fight against plans to build a new road. 居民们奋起斗争,反对建筑新公路的计划。In the end the Kurds surrendered without *putting up* any resistance. 最后,库尔德族人没有进行任何抵抗便投降了。❼ keep or store (something such as food or fruit), especially for later use 储藏(食物或水果等):The farmer *put up* three tons of hay for his cows for the winter. 那农夫储藏了三吨干草供他的奶牛冬天食用。Each winter my mother used to *put up* great quantities of fruits and vegetables. 每年冬天,我母亲总要贮藏大量的水果和蔬菜。❽pack (goods such as food or a parcel)把……打成包:Every morning Mother *puts up* lunches for the three children. 每天早晨妈妈都要为三个孩子装午餐饭盒。Please *put up* two pounds of tea for me. 请给我包两磅茶叶。The druggist *put up* the medicine that the doctor had prescribed. 药剂师把医生开的药打成了包。

—*vt.* &*vi.* ❶(非正式用语,常与 for 连用) (of a person or hotel)let(someone)stay in the house or hotel for one or more nights 向(某人)提供食宿:I'm afraid I can't *put* you *up*; you'll have to go to a hotel. 恐怕我不能为你提供食宿,你得去住旅馆了。Could you *put* me *up* for a few days when I come to London? 我来伦敦时您能让我住几天吗? ❷(especially of a political party) suggest(that someone should be elected to a particular position); (of someone) offer (oneself)as a candidate (for election)(尤指某政党)提出(某职务的候选人);(某人)自荐(作候选人): In all, 60 political parties *put up* candidates. 总共有 60 个党派提出了候选人。They'd like to *put* him *up* for the chairmanship, but he won't accept the nomination. 他们愿意提名他为主席的人选,可他却不肯接受提名。He was *put up* for the president of the club. 他被提名为俱乐部的主席。John is *putting* himself *up* for election to the committee. 约翰推荐自己入选委员会成员。He *put up* as a candidate. 他自荐作候选人。

—*vi.* (主要用于英国英语中,常与 at 连用) stay or get food and lodging (at a person's house or at a hotel)投宿: We'll *put up* for the night at a small hotel in the center of the city. 我们将在市中心的一家小旅馆投宿过夜。

NOTE 1. 当本短语用作及物性动词短语,所带的宾语为代词时,该代词须置于本短语的动词和副词中间。

2. 本短语可转化为复合词 put-up,意为"用不正当手段安排好的;预先确定的"。

put up to *vt.* 【可分性动词短语】(非正式用语) encourage; give (someone) the idea of (something they wouldn't normally do or doing something usually stupid or wrong)唆使(某人)做(蠢事或坏事): How do you know he beat me? You *put* him *up to* it. 你怎么知道是他打的我? 是你唆使他干的。I think I know who *put* him *up to* cheating. 我想,我知道是谁唆使他作弊。

put up with *vt.* 【不可分性动词短语】(非正式用语,一般不用被动语态形式) tolerate or accept(something unpleasant or someone)in a patient way 容忍,忍受: The patient cried that she could not *put up with* the pain any longer. 那病人叫喊道,她再也忍受不住疼痛了。Because of his work, he had to *put up with* meeting many cold

P

eyes. 他的工作使他不得不忍受着冷眼相对。Such conditions would never be *put up with* nowadays. 如今，这样的条件不会再有人忍受了。How has Jane *put up with* him for so long? 简怎么忍受了他这么久？

NOTE 本短语与动词 tolerate 的意义相同，但 tolerate 更多用于口语中。

puzzle out *vt.*【不可分性动词短语】find the solution or answer to (a confusing or complicated problem or question) by thinking hard about it 经过冥思苦想而得出(难解、复杂问题的答案)：We finally *puzzled out* how to open the box. 我们终于想出了打开这个匣子的方法。He went back to his room to *puzzle out* what he might try to do next. 他回到自己的房间揣摩下一步该做什么。She seemed to be trying to *puzzle out* who the caller might be. 她似乎在极力揣摩着打电话的人是谁。I've been trying to *puzzle out* which piece of work is most urgent. 我一直在琢磨哪件工作是最急做的。

NOTE 1. 当本短语所带的宾语为代词时，该代词须置于本短语的动词和副词中间。

2. 本短语的同义短语是 figure out 和 work out。

puzzle over *vt.*【不可分性动词短语】think hard and carefully about (someone or something) in an attempt to find the answer to it or to understand it 苦思冥想，苦思以求得(对……的答案或理解)：Williams is a bit strange. I've spent some time *puzzling over* him. 威廉姆斯这个人有点怪，我一直在琢磨他。He *puzzled over* it for weeks before he realized what it means. 他对那件事苦思数周后才领会到其意义。Why waste effort *puzzling over* his intention? 为何浪费精力去揣摩他的意图呢？Medical experts are *puzzling over* what may be the biggest problem in stopping the spread of the new flu. 医学专家们苦苦思量在阻止这种新型流感蔓延方面的最大问题是什么。

Q q

qualify as *vt.* (cause to) win recognition, usually official, as by passing examinations, as being (usually a professional person) (使)取得……专业资格: Have you *qualified as* a teacher yet? 你取得了教师的资格了吗? He *qualified as* a lawyer a few years ago. 他几年前就取得了律师的资格。Spending a month in Russia doesn't *qualify* you to talk about it *as* an expert. 在俄罗斯住了一个月并不能使你有资格像个专家一样地谈论它。What makes you think you're *qualified as* a judge? 是什么使你认为你有当裁判的资格?

qualify for *vt.* (常用一般时态) have the right qualities or be in the right situation to be considered as (something) or to receive (something) 具有资格,获得……的资格,符合……的条件: His teaching experience *qualified* him *for* the job. 他的教学经验使他具有担任这项工作的资格。He's not *qualified for* doing the research. 他没有资格做这项研究工作。

quarrel about/over *vt.* 【不可分性动词短语】 have an argument, especially between people who know each other well, on the subject of (something unimportant) (尤指在熟人之间)因(琐事)争吵: We often *quarrel about* who should take the dog out. 我们经常因谁应该带狗出去而争吵。They were *quarrelling* furiously with each other *about* whose turn it was to cook the dinner. 他们正为该轮到谁做晚饭而激烈地争吵着。Let us not *quarrel over* going out tonight. 我们不要为今晚出去的事而争吵了。We'd better not *quarrel about* whether she should go or not. 我们最好别为她该不该去而争吵了。

quarrel with *vt.* 【不可分性动词短语】 ❶argue angrily (with someone) (about something) 与(某人)争吵: Meanwhile, the president *quarreled with* the new prime minister over control of security forces. 在此同时,总统在保安部队控制权的问题上与新任总理发生了争吵。There are few people *with* whom she hasn't *quarreled*. 没有几个人她没与之争吵过。I hate *quarrelling with* you. 我不愿与你争吵。❷think (someone or something) is wrong; disagree with (an idea); refuse to believe or accept (something) 认为……不对,不同意,反对: I would *quarrel with* you on that figure. 我认为你那数字不对。Few people would *quarrel with* the aims of these proposals. 这些提议的目的不会有人认为不对。I won't *quarrel with* your estimate of costs, it seems reasonable enough. 我不反对你对成本的估算,它很有道理。

NOTE 本短语和动词 quarrel 在意义上的区别见下面两个句子:

> Tom is always *quarrelling with* his wife. 汤姆总是和他的妻子吵。(这并不指他妻子也和他吵)
>
> Tom and his wife are always *quarrelling*. 汤姆和他的妻子总是吵。(指两个人相互吵)

queue up *vi.* (后常接动词不定式短语)(of people)stand in a row waiting for (something such as an opportunity to do or have something)(指人)排队,排队等候:I hate *queuing up* in the cold to get into a cinema. 我不愿在寒冷的天气里排队入场看电影。Visitors wishing to see the pandas, Tuan Tuan and Yuan Yuan, have to *queue up* to obtain numbered tickets, and then wait for their turn to get into the enclosure. 想要看熊猫“团团”和“圆圆”的游客必须先排队抽得号码牌,然后再等候入馆。

NOTE 本短语的同义短语是 line up。本短语用于英国英语中,line up 用于美国英语用中。两者在用法上的区别是:本短语是不及物性动词短语,而 line up 还可用作及物性动词短语。见 line up。

quiet down *vt.* 【可分性动词短语】make (especially someone) become less noisy or active 使(尤指某人)安静下来:*Quiet* those children *down*, I can't hear myself talk. 让那些孩子们安静了下来,我连自己说话的声音都听不见了。He waved his arms to *quiet* them *down*. 他挥舞双臂,让他们安静下来。

—*vi.* (of someone or something) become less noisy or active 安静下来,平静下来:The room *quieted down*. 房间里安静了下来。The meeting *quieted down* after repeated warnings from the chairman. 经过主席反复的警告,会场才安静下来。The father yelled up the stairs, "Hey kids, *quiet down*! I can't sleep." 爸爸在楼上喊道:“喂,孩子们,安静点儿! 我都无法睡觉了!”

NOTE **1.** 本短语仅用于美国英语中,英国英语则使用 quieten down。

2. 当本短语用作及物性动词短语,所带的宾语为代词时,该代词须置于本短语的动词和副词中间。

quite a bit *adv.* quite a lot; a large number or amount 相当多地:She will have *quite a bit* to say to him when he comes. 他来后,她会有很多很多话对他讲。"The Pakistani government has done *quite a bit* now to roll up the terrorist network," he said in Washington. 他昨天在华盛顿说:“巴基斯坦政府在打击恐怖主义组织方面现已做了很多。”

quite a few Ⅰ *n.* a fairly large number 相当多,不少:*Quite a few* went to watch the World Cup match on TV. 很多人去观看电视转播的世界杯赛。*Quite a few* of them have been elected leaders in the factory. 他们中有不少的人已被选为工厂的领导人。Do you need one? I have *quite a few*. 你需要一个吗? 我还有不少。

Ⅱ *adj.* many; a fairly large number of (people or things)相当多的,不少的:I know *quite a few* people who've had the same problem. 我认识好多有同样问题的人。I've been married for *quite a few* years. 我结婚已经有好几年了。There were *quite a few* rotten apples in the basket. 这筐子里有不少烂苹果。

NOTE **1.** 当本短语用作名词性短语,作主语时,谓语动词要用复数形式。

2. 当本短语用作形容词性短语,作“相当多的,不少的”解时,所表示的数量比 a few 多,但比 a lot 少。

3. 本短语与 a good few 意义和用法相同,但 a good few 主要用于英国英语中。

quite a while *adv.* a fairly long time or period 很久,相当长的一段时间:She's been away *quite a while*. 他已经走了相当长一段时间了。It is *quite a while* since I was back from Hawaii. 我从夏威夷回来已经有很长一段时间了。

Q

R r

race through *vt.* ❶(cause to) complete (something) in a hurry (使)匆匆做完(某事):My son *raced through* his homework in order to watch the football match on TV. 我儿子为了看电视转播的足球赛而匆匆赶完了他的作业。The government *raced* the new law *through* all its stages, so as to complete it before the election. 政府匆匆完成了该项新法的各个阶段,以便在选举之前完成立法。❷ think very fast about (something)闪念:Bits and pieces of the past *raced through* her mind. 过去的点滴往事在她的头脑中闪过。

rain cats and dogs *vi.* (非正式用语)a lot of rain is falling; rain very heavily 下倾盆大雨,大雨滂沱:You can't leave just now! It's *raining cats and dogs* and you don't have an umbrella or raincoat! 你现在不能走! 正下着倾盆大雨,你还没有雨伞或雨衣。It was *raining cats and dogs* by the time I got home. 我到家时,雨下得正大。It could be *raining cats and dogs* but she'd still do the washing. 天要下大雨,可她还洗衣服。

NOTE 1. 本短语的另外一种表达形式是 rain dogs and cats,但已很少使用。

2. 本短语的同义短语是 rain buckets 和 rain pitchforks。如:

> It's been *raining buckets*/ *pitchforks* all day.
> 倾盆大雨整整下了一天。

rainy day *n.* ❶a day on which it rains for its duration 下雨天: Today is a *rainy day*. It is not downpour but it is not convenient to go out. 今天是个下雨天。虽然雨下得不大,但也不方便外出。*Rainy days* and Mondays always get me down. 下雨天和星期一总是让我感到郁闷。❷(比喻用法)a time (in the future) when something, especially money, may be needed (将来)需用某物(尤指钱)之时: My wife never spends all the money I bring home every month. She insists on saving for a *rainy day*. 我妻子从来不会把我每个月带回家的钱花光,她坚持存钱以备不时之需。We have a sum of money put aside for a *rainy day*. 我们积蓄了一笔钱,以备不时之需。He laid up some money against a *rainy day*. 他积蓄下了一些钱以未雨绸缪、有备无患。

NOTE 1. 当本短语作"(将来)需用某物(尤指钱)之时"解时,只用单数形式。

2. 本短语可用作定语,修饰另一名词。例如:

> I'm hoping that I can pay for my holiday without using my *rainy day* fund.
> 我希望不用我的积蓄,就能支付假期。

ramble on *vi.* (非正式用语,贬义用法) talk or write at length (about someone or something) for a long time in a way that is boring or annoying 讲个不停没完没了,写下去: We didn't think of asking

Peter to make the speech of welcome, but he did *ramble on*. 我们并没想让彼得致欢迎辞,可他却讲了个不停。He stood in my kitchen drinking beer, *rambling on* about Mary. 他站在我的厨房里喝着啤酒,唠唠叨叨地谈论着玛丽。Her letter doesn't contain any news, but it *rambles on* for 5 pages. 她的信虽然没什么新内容,但还是写了5页。

range from … to … *vt.* (用一般时时态) vary from (something smaller or less) to (something bigger or more); cover the range from (one point) to (another) 从……到……不等,自……至……的范围:The court sentenced the employees to jail sentences *ranging from* three years *to* seven years, along with fines ranging from \$2,000 to \$10,000. 法庭判处这些雇员 3 年至 7 年不等的徒刑,并处以 2 000 至 10 000 美元不等的罚金。Temperatures here *range from* the low 30's *to* the upper 80's Fahrenheit. 这里的温度从低至 30 华氏度到高至 80 华氏度不等。

NOTE 1. 本短语所连接的两个部分,无论是数字还是程度等,都是按第一部分小或轻,第二部分大或重来排列。如:

> The prices of colour TV sets in this store *range from* \$400 *to* \$1,000.
> 本店的彩电价格从 400 美元到 1 000 美元不等。

2. 本短语的同义短语是 vary from … to …。

rather than *conj.* & *prep.* (used for saying that one thing is preferred to another or happens instead of another) more willingly … than; instead of 宁愿……,而不愿……; 是……, 而不是……: The brave soldiers chose to die *rather than* surrender to their enemy. 这些勇敢的士兵宁死也不向敌人投降。These shoes are comfortable *rather than* pretty. 这双鞋与其说漂亮,不如说穿起来舒适。He *rather than* you should be responsible for doing such a silly thing. 做出这样的蠢事该由他负责任,而不是你。You should help them *rather than* they should help you. 你们应当帮助他们,而不是他们来帮助你们。

NOTE 1. 当本短语用来连接两个主语时,谓语动词随第一个主语而变化。例如:

> He *rather than* I is wrong.
> 是他,而不是我错了。

2. 本短语还有另外一种形式,即把它们拆开来使用,即 rather A than B。如:

> This is *rather* for Father to decide *than* for you(to decide).
> 此事由爸爸决定而不是由你(决定)。

reach for *vt.* move (your arm, hand, etc.) so as to touch or pick up (something)(伸手)去抓,去拿(某物):There was no time for me to *reach for* my gun. 我没有时间去掏枪。He turned round and *reached for* the phone. 他转过身去抓电话。Don't you dare *reach* your hand *for* that cake! 你胆敢伸手去拿那块蛋糕!

reach into *vt.* (cause to) stretch your arm, hand, etc. towards (something that you are trying to touch or pick up)(把手、胳臂等)伸入……中:Smith *reached into* his pocket and took out his car keys. 史密斯把手伸进口袋里拿出了车钥匙。I saw you *reaching* your hand *into* the cake tin. 我看见你把手伸进了饼干桶! Tearing the cover away, the child *reached into* the box to see what his birthday present was. 那孩子把封套扯掉后,把手伸进盒子想知道他那件生日礼物是

什么。

reach out *v.* ❶ extend one's hand, etc. (to touch or hold something)把(手等)伸出去(触摸,抓或拿取某物): She *reached out* to touch his face. 她伸出手去抚摸他的脸。*Reaching out*, he took a firm hold of the rope. 他把手伸出去,紧紧抓住了绳索。The monkey *reached out* a hand for the banana. 猴子伸出手去拿香蕉。Would you mind *reaching* an arm *out* for the tobacco pouch? 你能不能伸出一只胳臂来拿烟袋? ❷(主要用于美国英语中,常与 to 连用)attempt to communicate (with a person or a group of people)试图(与……)联系: I try to *reach out* to one of my former classmates, who is a mayor, but he doesn't want to have anything to do with me. 我试图和我一位当市长的老同学联系,可他却不想和我有任何关系。

NOTE 当本短语用作及物性动词短语时,无被动语态形式。

reach out to *vt.* 【不可分性动词短语】❶offer help to (someone)帮助(某人): We are *reaching out to* the most vulnerable members of the community. 我们在帮助社会中最弱势的群体成员。I went through a hard time, and my friend James *reached out to* me during that period. 我经历了一段艰难的时期,在那期间是我的朋友詹姆斯伸出援手帮助了我。❷ask (someone) for help and support 要求(某人)帮助和支持: I *reached out to* you when I was in trouble and you were a great help. 每当我处于困境时,我就请求您的帮助。您对我的帮助太大了。She urged him to *reach out to* his family. 她敦促他求助于其家人。

react on/upon *vt.* 【不可分性动词短语】(常用一般时态) have an effect on (something); influence (someone)对(某物)起作用,对(某人)有影响: Certain acids *react on* metals to cause chemical changes. 某些酸性物质对金属产生作用,引起化学变化。Only strong leaders can *react on* this angry crowd. 只有强有力的领导才能对这愤怒的人群有所影响。

NOTE 本短语中的 upon 用法比 on 正式,但不及 on 常用。

react to *vt.* 【不可分性动词短语】❶feel and express the effect of (something that has happened) 对……做出反应: The government has *reacted to* the outbreak of violence by sending army patrols to police the area. 政府对发生暴力事件所做出的反应是派出武装巡逻队维持该地区的治安。The students *react* very well *to* an active teaching style. 学生们对活跃的教学方式反应很好。❷(of someone) be affected unpleasantly or mad ill by (a substance such as a drug)对(药物等)有不良反应: We were alarmed at the way in which Kate *reacted to* the drug. 凯特对这药有如此不良的反应令我们吃惊。The patient *reacted* badly *to* the acupuncture treatment. 该病人对针刺疗法有不良反应。Someone allergic to milk is likely to *react to* cheese. 对奶过敏的人很可能对乳酪有不良反应。

read between the lines *vi.* find meanings from a text that are not openly stated but implied 看出字里行间的意义,了解言外之意: If you *read between the lines*, this letter is really a request for money. 如果你能看出言外之意的话,这封信其实是在要钱。*Reading between the lines*, she sensed the strong affection the writer of the letter had for her. 她从字里行间里感到了写信人对她强烈的爱慕之

情。I'm *reading between the lines*, but I can see they're both unhappy. 我在体会这字里行间的意义,但我可以看出他们都不幸福。

read one's mind *vi.* be able to know what someone is thinking 能知道别人的心思:We've been close friends ever since our childhood. We know each other so well that we can *read each other's mind*. 我们从童年开始就是密友,相互非常了解,对方心里想什么彼此都一清二楚。I've known John so long that I can *read his mind*. 我认识约翰这么久了,我都能读懂他的心思。Her comment surprised me. It was as if she had *read my mind*. 她的一番评论令我吃惊,好像她已知道了我的心思。

NOTE 1. 本短语可转化为复合词 mind-reader,意为"看透别人心思的人"。

2. 本短语与 read one's thoughts 意义和用法相同,read one's thoughts 主要用于英国英语中。

read out *vt.* 【可分性动词短语】❶ say (the words you are reading) aloud (to audience) so that they can hear them 大声读出,朗读,宣读:He *read* the list of names *out*. 他把名单大声地读了出来。After morning exercises, important notices were *read out* to the assembled students. 早操做完后,向集合在操场上的学生宣读了重要通知。Shall I *read* them *out*? 我把它们读出来吗? ❷(常用被动语态形式,常与 of 连用)make (someone) leave an organization, usually for a fault 开除(某人):The former governor was *read out* of the Party and arrested after he was proved guilty. 这位原省长因被证明有罪而被开除出党并予以逮捕。

NOTE 1. 当本短语的宾语为代词时,该代词须置于本短语的动词和副词中间。

2. 本短语可转化为复合词 readout,意为"读出,宣读;宣告开除"。

read over/through *vt.* 【可分性动词短语】read all of (a document, book, etc.) in order to check or correct it 通读(文件、图书等):He had to *read* the passage *over* several times before he could understand it. 他把这段文章从头至尾地读了好几遍之后才理解了它。*Read* the contract *through* carefully before you sign. 在签署合同之前,一定要把它仔细地通读一遍。I *read through* her letter again and again. 我反复地阅读了她的信。

NOTE 当本短语的宾语为代词时,该代词须置于本短语的动词和副词中间。

read up *vt.* 【不可分性动词短语】(非正式用语) study (something such as a particular subject), as by reading a lot about it 研读(某一科目等):*Read up* these rule and you will see that I am right. 好好看看这些规则,你就会知道我是对的。I need to *read up* on some British history as I'm going to live there next year. 我需要读点英国历史,因为我明年就要去那里生活了。It's a good idea to *read up* about a company before going for an interview. 在去面试前,把有关那家公司的情况看一看,是个好主意。

ready for *adj.* (of a person or thing) prepared and fit for (what is going to happen) 为……做好准备:The new railway station is *ready for* operation on July 1. 新火车站已准备好于7月1日运营。It was time to get the children *ready for* bed. 该让孩子们准备上床了。Jane promised to make the room *ready for*

R

our guests. 简答应为我们的客人准备房间。The clothes are all *ready for* wearing. 衣服都已准备好就等穿用了。

ready to *adj*. (后接原形动词) ❶willing to (do something)愿意(做某事): He is satisfied with the military relationship between the two countries, and is *ready to* work with China to continue the existing momentum. 他对两国的军事关系感到满意,并愿与中方共同努力,将这一良好的发展势头继续下去。You're too *ready to* criticize. 你太喜欢批评人了。❷prepared to (do something)准备好(做某事): We'd better get ready to leave. 我们最好准备离开吧。The World Health Organization was *ready to* declare a flu pandemic and to raise the alert level to Phase 6 from the current Phase 5. 世界卫生组织已准备宣布流感大流行并将目前的警戒级别五级提升到六级。❸likely to (do something)就要(做某事): She felt *ready to* cry with frustration. 受了挫折,她都要哭了。Not far from here there's a tree *ready to* fall. 离这儿不远,有一棵树要倒了。The engine looked *ready to* explode at any minute. 这发动机好像随时就会爆炸。

R

reason into *vt*.【可分性动词短语】persuade (someone) to do (something) by reasoned argument (以理)说服(某人)做(某事): Let me try to *reason* the members *into* joining us. 让我来劝服这些委员们加入我们中来。This is something he can be *reasoned into*, given time. 如果有时间,这件事是可以劝他做的。

NOTE 当本短语的宾语为代词时,该代词须置于本短语的动词和副词中间。

reason out *vt*. 【可分性动词短语】(常用一般时态) arrive at (an answer) to (something) through careful reasoning 通过推理得出,推断出: They have presented the facts, and *reasoned* the things *out* instead of quarrelling. 他们没有争吵,而是摆事实,讲道理。He tried hard to *reason out* the answer to the mystery. 他努力想通过推理来揭开这个秘密。Let's try and *reason* this *out*. 咱们试着把这事分析出个头绪来。The police *reasoned out* that the men had left the town by the midday train. 警方推断那些人已乘午间列车离开了镇子。It's easy to *reason out* what the consequences of the experiment will be. 那个实验的结果是容易推断出来的。

NOTE 当本短语的宾语为代词时,该代词须置于本短语的动词和副词中间。

reason out of *vt*. 【可分性动词短语】persuade (someone) not to do (something) by reasoned argument (以理)说服(某人)不要做(某事): Try to *reason* him *out of* his fear. 尽量说服他消除恐惧。Father must be *reasoned out of* driving home in such dangerous conditions. 必须劝爸爸不要在这样危险的情况下驾车回家。

NOTE 当本短语的宾语为代词时,该代词须置于本短语的动词和副词中间。

reason with *vt*. 【不可分性动词短语】talk or argue with (a person) reasonably in the hope of convincing him to act in a wise way or to change his or her behaviour or a decision 说服,规劝(某人): There's no point in trying to *reason with* her, she'll never change her mind. 你劝她没有意义;她决不会改变主意。The police *reasoned with* the hijackers to let the children go free. 警方规劝劫持者释放儿童。Don't think that they won't be *reasoned with*. 不

要以为他们不听劝导。

reckon in *vt.*【可分性动词短语】(非正式用语) include (people or things) as part of a total; take (an amount) into account in a sum 把……包括在内,把……计算在内: When the city declares its population numbers, does it *reckon in* the farmers in outer areas? 该市所宣布的人口数字把郊区的农民包括在内了吗? Don't bother to tip, the service charge has already been *reckoned in*. 不用再付小费了,服务费已包括在内了。Have you *reckoned in* the power consumption? 你把耗电量计算在内了吗?

NOTE 当本短语的宾语为代词时,该代词须置于本短语的动词和副词中间。

reckon on/upon *vt.*【不可分性动词短语】(非正式用语) expect (something) to happen and plan for it 希望,指望,期待: We hope we can *reckon on* your support in our experiment. 我们希望在我们的实验中能得到你们的支持。Don't *reckon on* going abroad this summer, we may not have the money for it. 不要指望今年夏天出国了,我们可能没有那笔钱。Jenny hadn't *reckoned on* having twins! 詹尼没想到会生双胞胎。

NOTE 本短语中的 upon 用法比 on 正式,但不及 on 常用。

reckon up *vt.*【可分性动词短语】(主要用于英国英语中,非正式用语) find the sum, total or amount of (something, things, or people)计算出……的总数: A mechanic *reckoned up* the cost of repairing the damage to my car. 修理工计算了一下修理我那部被撞坏的车的总花费。It's difficult to *reckon* the members of the class *up* when so many are absent. 有这么多人缺席,很难了解全班人员的总数。Heroes in World War Ⅱ still living in our town today can be *reckoned up* on the fingers of one hand. 如今我们城里仍然在世的二战英雄屈指可数。

NOTE 当本短语的宾语为代词时,该代词须置于本短语的动词和副词中间。

reckon with *vt.*【不可分性动词短语】❶(用一般时态) take into account; anticipate 考虑到,估计到;预料到: They had many difficulties to *reckon with*. 他们有许多困难要考虑。They hadn't *reckoned with* so many obstacles. 他们没有预料到会有如此多的障碍。My wife didn't *reckon with* having to cook dinner for 8 unexpected guests. 我夫人没有料到得为八位不速之客做饭。❷(非正式用语) deal with (a difficult or powerful person or thing)对付;应对;处理: I know how to *reckon with* the troublesome Bill this afternoon. 我知道今天下午如何对付捣蛋的比尔。Barcelona will be a strong team to be *reckoned with* this season. 巴塞罗那队将是本赛季要应对的一支强队。We have to *reckon with* many problems every day. 我们每天都得处理许多问题。All these problems had to be *reckoned with* as they arose. 所有这些问题一经出现,都必须得以处理。

reckon without *vt.*【不可分性动词短语】(主要用于英国英语中,非正式用语,用一般时态) fail to think about (something or someone) when you are making plans and therefore not be prepared to deal with it; ignore 未考虑到,忽视: They made careful plans for an outing but they *reckoned without* a sudden change in the weather. 他们精心计划了一次郊游,但是他们却没有考虑到天气的突然变化。He thought he'd get away with his crime, but he *reckoned without* the FBI agents. 他认为他能逃脱罪

行,但他却忽视了联邦调查局的侦探们。He's not the sort of man you can afford to *reckon without*. 他不是那种你可以置之不理的人。

recognize as *vt.*【可分性动词短语】(常用被动语态形式) ❶accept (that someone or something is legal or real); admit (someone or something) formally as having the right to claim (a position, rank, authority, etc.) 认定……为……,承认……是……: It is not certain that the court will *recognize* him *as* his father's lawful successor. 法庭能否认定他为其父的合法继承人,还无法确定。He is *recognized as* the new champion. 他被认定为新一届冠军。❷ regard; consider (someone or something) to be (something such as a quality, usually good) 认为……是……: It didn't take long for him to be *recognized as* the natural leader of his society. 没用多久人们就都认为他是其社团理所当然的领导人了。He is *recognized* internationally *as* an authority in this field. 国际上公认他是这一领域中的权威。Mark's first book was soon *recognized as* the most informative on the subject. 马克出的第一本书就被认为是那一学科资料最丰富的书。

R

reconcile with *vt.*【可分性动词短语】❶(常用被动语态形式) cause (someone) to become friendly again with (someone) after a disagreement or quarrel 使(某人)与(另某人)和解: My attempt to *reconcile* Tony *with* Bill failed once again. 我劝托尼与比尔和解的努力再次失败。He was *reconciled with* his brothers not long after a fierce family quarrel. 他在一次激烈的家庭争吵后不久,便与其兄弟们和解了。It was his father's wish that he become *reconciled with* his family. 他父亲希望他能与家人和解。❷(用一般时态) make (one fact, etc.) match or be consistent with (another) 使……与……相符,使……与……相一致: I can't *reconcile* these figures *with* the bill you prepared. 我这些数字和你所开的账单对不上。How can their aggressive actions be *reconciled with* their talk of peace and brotherhood? 他们的侵略行径与他们所谈的和平与友谊怎能一致呢?

recover from *vt.* ❶ get back (something lost or stolen) from (usually someone); regain 重获,要回: Several of the missing gold coins were *recovered from* the bed of the river. 几枚丢失的金币从河床处被捡了回来。Don't lend books to your friends, it's difficult to *recover* them *from* them when you want them. 不要把书借给你的朋友们,当你需要它们的时候你就很难要回来了。❷ (of someone or something) return to the proper state of health, strength, after (illness or failure, etc.) (指身体、力量、能力等)从……恢复到正常状态: A healthy child quickly *recovers from* a high fever. 健康的孩子在高烧后身体很快就能复原。She has not yet *recovered from* the shock. 她受了惊吓还没有完全恢复过来。How long will it be before the nation *recovers from* its present crisis? 这个国家要从当前的危机中恢复过来需要多长时间? The country had not *recovered from* the effects of the war yet. 这个国家还没从战争的创伤中恢复过来。

red letter day *n.* (非正式用语) a special happy day that will always be remembered 纪念日,大喜日子,节日: We take the day of Hong Kong's return to the motherland as a *red letter day* for the Chinese people and the entire Chinese nation. 我们认为香港回归祖国这一天是全体中国人民和中华民

族的盛大节日。It was a real *red letter day for* me when my son came home from Iraq. 我儿子从伊拉克回到家的那天对我来说真是一个大喜日子。On *red letter days*, judges of the English High Court wear their scarlet robes. 每逢节日，英国高等法院的法官都身穿鲜红色法衣。

red light ⇨ **green light**

reduce to *vt.*【可分性动词短语】❶(常用被动语态形式，常用一般时态) make (something) smaller or less in size, amount, importance, etc. 把……减少到……，把……降低到……：The company has *reduced* its size from about 15,000 employees *to* 10,000 due to the financial crisis. 由于金融危机，该公司已将其雇员的规模从 15 000 人减到了 10 000 人。The book will be *reduced to* 200 pages, as printing costs have risen so much. 由于印刷费用大幅上涨，这本书将删减至 200 页。Risks must be *reduced to* the minimum. 必须把风险降低到最小。❷(常用被动语态形式，常用一般时态) bring (something such as a price) down to (a lower level) 把(价格等)降低到……：I bought this shirt because it was *reduced* from $20 *to* $10. 我买了这件衬衣是因为它的价格从 20 美元降到了 10 美元。All children's shoes are now *reduced to* $15 a pair. 所有童鞋的价格都降到了每双 15 美元。❸(常用一般时态) cause (something) to reach (a certain condition) 使陷入……状态：The bombing *reduced* the city *to* ruins. 轰炸使这座城市成了一片废墟。This group is still the great threat to global security, though its training camps have been *reduced to* dust. 尽管其训练营地已化为灰尘，但这一组织仍是世界安全的巨大威胁。❹(常用一般时态) separate (something such as a mixture or combination) into (its parts) 把……分解为：We can *reduce* a compound *to* its elements. 我们可以把化合物分解为元素。Water can be *reduced to* oxygen and hydrogen. 水可以被分解为氧和氢。❺(常用被动语态形式) consider (separate things) together as (a unity) 把……归纳为：I think we can *reduce* his rather lengthy conclusions *to* one or two essential points. 我认为，我们可以把他这些冗长的结论归纳为一两个要点。These examples can be *reduced to* three categories. 这些例子可以归纳为三类。❻ change (something) to (a less complicated form) 把……简化为：It is necessary to *reduce* an equation *to* its simple form. 有必要把方程式化成简单的形式。❼(常用被动语态形式) bring or force (someone) to (especially a weaker, unpleasant or less favorable state) 使(某人)沦为，使(某人)陷于：She was *reduced to* begging for a life. 她沦落到以乞讨为生。Hunger had *reduced* the poor children *to* skin and bones. 饥饿使这些可怜的儿童骨瘦如柴。The old lady was *reduced to* a skeleton by the illness. 这老妇人被病折磨得只剩下一把骨头了。His extravagances *reduced* him *to* poverty. 他的奢侈生活使他陷于贫困。❽(of someone or something) make (someone) feel so helpless that he or she cannot speak 使(某人)哑口无言：His remarks *reduced* them *to* silence. 他的一番话使他们哑口无言。❾(与复数名词 tears 连用) (of someone or something) make (someone) feel so sad that he or she cries 使(某人)哭泣：The attentions of the

media reduced her *to* tears. 媒体的关注使她潸然泪下。The child was *reduced to* tears. 这孩子被弄哭了。

refer to *vt.* ❶(正式用语) mention (someone or something) when you are speaking or writing 提到,谈到: Jack was careful not to *refer to* the woman by name. 杰克留心没提那名妇女的名字。In his speech made at the welcome ceremony, the Professor did not *refer to* his new book. 教授在欢迎仪式上所发表的讲话中,没有提及他的新书。❷(cause to) look at (something) for information; consult (something) to refresh one's memory (使)查阅,参考,查看: Please *refer to* our catalogue for details of all our products. 欲了解我们产品的详情,请查阅我们的目录册。We can *refer to* an encyclopedia for information about this subject. 我们可以在百科全书中查阅这论题的有关资料。As he cannot answer my question, he *refers* me *to* this dictionary. 由于他回答不出我的问题,他便让我查阅这本词典。He carried a bundle of notes, *to* which he frequently *referred* during the course of the talk. 他随身带了一大叠纸条,在讲话的过程中他不断地去翻看它们。❸(无被动语态形式,用一般时态) concern; be directed towards (something or someone)涉及,指的是: The new law does not *refer to* land used for farming. 那条新法律不涉及农用土地。"What we are doing here is important," the army officer said, *referring to* the war against terrorism. "我们在这里做的事情很重要。"这位军官说道。他指的是反恐战争。I did not know what she *referred to*. 我不明白她指的是什么。What I have to say *refers to* all of you. 我要讲的话关系到你们所有的人。❹hand or pass (something or someone) to (another person or place) for help, decision or action 把……提交给……: The members *referred* the question *to* the committee, as they were unable to reach a decision. 由于委员们对这个问题做不了决定,所以将其提交给了委员会。The proposal will have to be *referred to* the European Union. 这一提案将提交给欧盟处理。If he gives you any more trouble, *refer* him *to* me. 如果他再给你找麻烦,你就把他交给我处理。❺send (someone who is ill) by a doctor to (another hospital or specialist) in order to be treated 把(病人)转至(其他医院或专家)治疗: Patients who have a high fever are *referred to* a larger hospital nearby. 发高烧的患者都被转到附近一所大一些的医院诊治。The doctor *referred* me *to* a skin specialist. 医生把我转诊给一位皮肤科专家。❻(常与 as 连用) use a particular word, expression, or a name to mention or describe something or someone 把……称为: The scientists *referred to* the discovery as the most exciting new development in this field. 科学家们把这一发现称为这一领域中最令人兴奋的新进展。The professor *referred to* him as a graduate student with a bright future. 教授称他为很有前途的研究生。❼(常用一般时态)(cause to) ask (someone) for information or opinions concerning the ability or character of someone else (使)向(某人)打听(他人的能力,品行等情况): She *referred to* John's former employer for his character. 她向约翰过去的雇主打听他的品行。For remarks on my recent

teaching experience, please *refer to* Mrs Grey at Lowlands School. 要了解有关对我最近教学情况的意见,请向洛兰兹学校的格雷夫人询问。❽(用一般时态) believe (something) to be the result of (something) 把……归因于: They *referred* this phenomenon *to* electrical disturbances. 他们把这种现象归因于电的干扰。The discovery of gunpowder is usually *referred to* China. 通常把火药的发明归功于中国。

NOTE 1. 当本短语作"提到,谈到"解时,另外一种表达形式是 give a reference to。例如:

> In his new book, he *gave a reference to* his journey to Tibet.
> 在他的这本新书中,他提到了他的西藏之行。

2. 当本短语作"提到,谈到"解时,同义短语是 allude to。allude to 指以间接或含蓄的方式"提到"某人或某事。另外,本短语复为正式。

3. 当本短语作"查阅,参考,查看"解时,另外一种表达形式是 make a reference to。例如:

> You should *make a reference to* the dictionary for the exact meaning of these words.
> 你应该查一下词典,搞清这些词的确切意义。

4. 本短语和 look up 都表示"查阅"之意,但当要表"查阅词典"时,只能用本短语,而"查单词"则用 look up。换言之,本短语后的宾语为"词典",而 look up 后的宾语为"单词"。请比较下面这两个句子:

If you don't know the word, please *refer to* the dictionary.

If you don't know the word, please *look* it *up* in the dictionary.

reflect on/upon *vt.*【不可分性动词短语】❶consider or think about (something) carefully and seriously 仔细地考虑,认真地思考: I *reflected on* the child's future. 我仔细地考虑了孩子的前途。He *reflected upon* the likely consequences of the action. 他仔细地考虑了这项行动可能会产生的后果。She's been *reflecting on* how to solve the problem. 她一直在仔细地考虑怎样解决那个问题。I have been *reflecting on* what you said. 我一直在仔细地考虑你所说的那些话。❷(无被动语态形式,用一般时态)(of an event or action) give people a good or bad opinion of (someone, a group, or something)(某一事件或行为)给……带来影响: The affair *reflected* very badly *on* the government. 这件事给政府带来了非常坏的影响。As a teacher your personal behavior outside school *reflects upon* the school. 作为一名教师,你在校外的个人行为会影响到学校的声誉。Be careful to do nothing that *reflects upon* the reputation of the department. 注意不要做有损于本部门声誉的事。

NOTE 1. 本短语中的 upon 用法比 on 正式,但不及 on 常用。

2. 当本短语作"仔细地考虑,认真地思考"解时,同义短语是 meditate on/upon。

refrain from *vt.*【不可分性动词短语】❶hold oneself back from (something or doing something unpleasant); deliberately not do (something) 忍住,抑制,不做: How will I *refrain from* tears when we part? 当我们分别的时候,我怎么能忍住不流眼泪呢? I'm trying to *refrain from* drowsing at work. 我尽量做到在工作时不打瞌睡。❷stop oneself from (doing something) 禁止,戒除: We urge you to *refrain from* smoking. 我们敦促您把烟戒掉。You must *refrain from* spitting in the street, or you'll be fined. 你千万不要在街上随地吐痰，否则会被罚款的。

regard as *vt.*【可分性动词短语】(常用被动语态形式，用一般时态) consider (someone, oneself or something) to be (something, or doing something) 把……看作是……，认为……是……: Only then can we *regard* ourselves *as* having done our duty. 只有那时，我们才能认为自己尽到了责任。*Regarded as* one of the most important Chinese traditional festivals, Qingming Festival usually occurs on April 4 or 5 each year. 清明节被认为是中国最重要的传统节日之一，通常是在每年的4月4日或5日。We shouldn't *regard* what is possible *as* impossible. 我们不应当把可能的事看作是不可能的。

NOTE 1. 本短语中的as表示"当作"之意，后面不仅能接名词、动名词，还可接形容词。如：

> All of us *regarded* such contacts and communications *as* beneficial.
> 我们所有的人都认为这样的接触和沟通是有益的。

2. 本短语的同义短语是consider as。但consider as中的介词as常可省略，或以to be取而代之。

regardless of *prep.* paying no attention to or without caring about (something); in spite of (something) 不管，不顾，不论: *Regardless of* what you say, I am going. 不论你说什么，我都要走。A researcher at the University of Massachusetts found that the more money a married woman earns, the less housework she will do *regardless of* how much her spouse earns. 马萨诸塞大学的一名研究人员发现，已婚女性挣钱越多，她做的家务活越少，而这与她们的丈夫挣多少钱无关。*Regardless of* whether he was right or wrong, we had to obey his order. 不论他是对还是错，我们都得服从他的命令。They will support whichever candidate they choose, *regardless of* who wins the primary election. 不论谁赢得初选，他们都会支持他们所选择的任何一位候选人。The Red Cross helped all the wounded people *regardless of* which side they were fighting for. 红十字会帮助所有的伤员，不管他们是为哪一方作战。

NOTE 本短语的同义短语是in spite of和irrespective of。

rejoice at/over *vt.*【不可分性动词短语】(正式用语，无被动语态形式) take pride and pleasure in; be glad about (something) 为……感到自豪和高兴，为……欢欣鼓舞: We *rejoiced at* the news of his success. 我们听到他成功的消息感到自豪和高兴。We *rejoiced at* every victory won by our national team. 我们为国家队的每一场胜利而感到欢欣鼓舞。The team are still in their dressing room, *rejoicing over* their victory. 队员们还都在更衣室里，沉浸在胜利的喜悦之中。

rejoice in *vt.*【不可分性动词短语】(正式用语，无被动语态形式) take great pride and pleasure in; find joy in; be glad about (something, or doing something) 为……感到自豪和高兴，在……中寻求欢乐，为……欢欣鼓舞: The whole family *rejoiced in* the birth of a boy. 全家人都为生了个男孩而欢天喜地。The young teacher *rejoices in* making his students feel greatly embarrassed. 那位年轻教师以把学生搞得狼狈不堪为乐。The young singer *rejoiced in* her unexpected success. 那位年轻的歌手为自己意想不到的成功感到欢欣鼓舞。

relate to *vt.* ❶(正式用语)tell (a story) to (someone)给(某人)讲述(故事或事情): He *related to* us the story of his escape. 他向我们讲述了他逃生的经过。The children enjoyed *relating* their imaginary adventures *to* the visitors. 孩子们喜欢给来访者讲述他们想象出来的冒险故事。He had as yet no opportunity of *relating* the incident *to* them. 他还一直没有机会把这个事件讲给他们听。❷ show a link or connection with (something or someone); establish a connection between (something such as an event) and (something else)与……有关,把……与……联系起来: These trade deficits are closely *related to* the international transfer of industry of economic globalization. 这些贸易逆差与经济全球化背景下的国际产业转移密切相关。The report seeks to *relate* the rise in crime *to* the increase in unemployment. 这份报告试图将犯罪率上升与失业率上升联系起来。❸(无被动语态形式,用一般时态)(of something) concern (a particular subject); be directed towards (something or someone)涉及,指的是,针对: The new tax law does not *relate to* land used for farming. 新颁布的税法不是针对农用土地的。These regulations *relate* only *to* people under the age of twenty-one. 这些规则仅针对21岁以下的人。❹(常用一般时态) have or form a friendly, understanding relationship with (someone)与(某人)友好相处: She finds it difficult to *relate to* her fellow-students. 她发现自己很难和同学们友好相处。My son is not good at his work, but he's best at *relating to* people. 我儿子在工作上不行,但很善于与人交往。❺understand and accept 理解并接受: I can't *relate to* his ideas at all. 我根本无法理解并接受他的想法。

release from *vt.* 【可分性动词短语】set (someone or something) free from (something usually bad or unpleasant) 把……从……中释放出来,把……从……中解放出来: He was rearrested on a fresh charge two days after being *released from* prison. 他刚从监狱里放出来两天,就又因一项新的指控而再次被捕。We've now learned how to *release* energy *from* the nucleus of the atom. 我们现在知道如何从原子核中释放能量。She *released* the rabbit *from* the trap. 她把兔子从捕捉器上放走。Death *released* her *from* her pain. 死亡使她不再遭受疼痛之苦。

relevant to *adj.* directly connected with (a subject; what you are discussing or doing) 与……有直接关系的: I don't think his *remarks* are *relevant to* the subject. 我认为他的话与这一主题无关。How is that *relevant to* this discussion? 那与这次的讨论有什么直接关系呢? His nationality isn't *relevant to* whether he's a good lawyer. 他的国籍与他是不是一位好律师无关。We can collect some information *relevant to* your concerns for you. 我们可以为您搜集一些与您所关注的问题有关的信息。

NOTE 1. 本短语的另外一种表达形式是 have relevance to。如:

> What you say *has* no *relevance to* the subject.
> 你所说的与此主题无关。

2. 本短语的反义短语是 irrelevant to。

relieve of *vt.* 【可分性动词短语】❶cause (an unpleasant feeling or situation) to disappear completely 彻底消除(某种不愉快的感觉或状况): Can traditional Chinese medicine and acupuncture help *relieve*

R

clinical symptoms *of* patients with Parkinson's disease? 传统中药和针灸能否有助于消除帕金森氏病患者的临床症状? ❷(正式用语)take away (something heavy to carry or hard to do) from (someone) to help him lighten his burden, etc. 解除,减轻(某人的负担等): Let me *relieve* you *of* that parcel, it looks terribly heavy. 让我帮你拿这包袱吧,它看上去太沉重了。The rise in personal income tax collection threshold aims to *relieve* medium-and-lower income earners *of* their economic burden. 个人所得税起征标准上调的目的是减轻中低收入者的经济负担。❸(正式用语,常用被动语态形式) dismiss or remove (someone) from (a position), usually because he or she has done something wrong 解除(某人的)职务: The foreign minister of that country was *relieved of* his duties last month. 该国的外交部长在上月被解除了职务。The two high-ranking provincial officials have been *relieved of* their leading positions. 这两位省级高层领导因被免职。❹(幽默用语) steal (something) from (someone)偷走(某人之物): It did not take the thieves long to *relieve* the passengers *of* their money. 这些盗贼没用多长时间就把乘客们的钱偷走了。The pickpocket *relieved* her *of* her handbag in which there were bankcards, some cash, and her mobile phone. 扒手偷走了她的手包,里面装有银行卡、一些现金和手机。

reluctant to *adj.* (后接原形动词) not willing to (do something)不愿(做某事): Political tension and economic problems in that country have caused foreign investors to become *reluctant to* invest in it. 该国国内紧张的政治局势和经济问题已使外国投资者不愿投资于这个国家。How will you deal with those *reluctant to* go back to their homes in the remote earthquake-hit areas? 对那些不愿回到位于偏远的地震灾区的家园的人,你们怎么看待他们?

NOTE 1. 本短语的比较级形式是 more reluctant to,最高级形式是 most reluctant to。

2. 本短语的反义短语是 willing to。

rely on/upon *vt.* 【不可分性动词短语】❶need or depend on (someone or something)依靠,依赖: Don't *rely on* him doing that for you. 你就别指靠他为你做那事。We know such people are not to be *relied upon*. 我们知道这种人是依靠不上的。For a fairly long time in the past, China practiced a planned economy, and the state *relied* mainly *on* administrative measures for import and export control. 在过去相当长的时期中,中国实行的是计划经济体制,国家主要依靠行政手段对进出口进行管理。❷ trust or have faith in (someone, something, or doing something)相信,信赖: You should *rely on* your own judgment. 你应该相信自己的判断。You can *rely on* me to keep your secret. 你可以相信我能保守你的秘密。She had proved that she could be *relied on* in a crisis. 她已表明,在紧要关头,她是可以信赖的。

NOTE 1. 本短语中的 upon 用法比 on 正式,但不及 on 常用。

2. 当本短语作"依靠,依赖"解时,同义短语是 depend on/upon 和 lean on/upon。

remain clear of *vt.* 【不可分性动词短语】(非正式用语,无被动语态形式,常用一般时态) (continue to) avoid (someone or something unpleasant, risky or dangerous) (保持)回避,远离,躲避(某人或令人不快、危险的事物): At busy hours, it's best

R

to *remain clear of* the main roads until the worst of the traffic is over. 在交通繁忙时刻,最好避开主要街路,等到交通高峰过后再走。No one mentioned the divorce, so Lisa decided to *remain clear of* that subject. 没有人提到离婚的事,所以利萨也决定对那一话题避而不谈。Tourists are advised to *remain clear of* the area until further notice. 在另行通知前,建议游客不要去那一地区。

NOTE 1. 本短语的动词 remain 可被 stay, steer 等替换,构成的短语与本短语意义和用法相同。

2. 本短语的同义短语是 keep clear of。

remember to *vt.* 【可分性动词短语】(非正式用语,常用于祈使句中,常用被动语态形式) give one's greetings, best wishes, etc. to (someone) by means of someone else (通过他人代自己)向(某人)问好: Be sure to *remember* me *to* Dr Smith and his family if you happen to see him at the University of London. 如果你能在伦敦大学看到史密斯博士的话,一定代我向他及其家人问好。She asked to be *remembered to* you. 她要我代她向您问好。

remind of *vt.* 【可分性动词短语】❶tell or cause (someone) to remember or not to forget(something)提醒: I've forgotten his name, will you *remind* me *of* it? 我忘了他的名字,你提醒我一下好吗? ❷(用一般时态)make (someone) remember (someone or something that happened in the past)使(某人)想起(某人或某件往事): Sometimes his eyes *remind* me *of* his father. 有的时候他的眼睛使我想起了他的爸爸。He was often *reminded of* the days when he worked at a fast food restaurant while studying in the United States. 他常常想起在美国求学时在一家快餐店打工的那些日子。

remit to *vt.* 【可分性动词短语】(正式用语,常用一般时态) ❶ send (money) to (someone in a distant place), usually by arrangement with a bank, post office, etc. 汇(款)给……: Migrant workers regularly *remit* part of their pay *to* their wives and families. 在外务工人员定期给他们的妻子或家人汇去自己的部分薪金。Most college students have to live on money *remitted to* them by their parents back at home. 大多数大学生都靠家里的父母寄给他们的钱生活。❷ send (a matter) to (someone in a higher position) for consideration 将(某种事务)上交给……: All questions of cost will be *remitted to* the officer in charge of the accounts. 所有的费用问题都将上交给负责账目的官员处理。The proposal has been *remitted to* the executive committee. 该提案已提交给执行委员会处理。

remove from *vt.* ❶ take (something) away from (something or someone) 把……从……移走,拿走,带走: Please *remove* your belongings *from* my office. 请把你的东西从我的办公室里拿走。He removed the child from the class. 他把孩子从班上带走了。A passenger who ignored flight attendants' orders was *removed from* the flight by airport security guards. 一名不听机上乘务员命令的乘客被机场保安人员从飞机上带走。❷take out; get rid of (something unwanted) from (something) 把……从……中除去,把……从……中排除;解除: Three power company workers, who were *removing* ice *from* a 50-meter tall

R

tower, died when the equipment collapsed. 三名正从 50 米高的电力塔上除冰的电力公司员工,因设备倒塌而殉职。The flu patient was discharged from hospital today and all the people in contact with her have been *removed from* medical observation. 该流感患者已于今天出院,所有与她接触过的人也全部解除了医疗观察。❸(常用被动语态形式) dismiss (someone) from (a position, usually of responsibility)把(某人)免职,解聘: That officer responsible for the abuse of prisoners was *removed from* his position. 那名军官因负有虐待囚犯的责任而被解除了职务。When he was found guilty of cheating, Mr Smith was *removed from* the chairmanship. 当史密斯先生被发现有欺骗行为后,他就被免去了主席的职务。❹(正式用语) move one's home from (a place) and go to live or work in (another place)从(某地)搬走,移居: The couple don't live here any more, I think they *removed from* the city last year. 这对夫妇已不住这里了。我想,他们是去年从这个城市搬走的。Our office has *removed to* Harlow from London. 我们的办事处已从伦敦迁至哈洛。

R

render into *vt.* 【可分性动词短语】(正式用语,常用被动语态形式) put or translate (something in a particular language) into (another language)把……翻译成……: There are some English idioms and American idioms that are very hard to be *rendered into* other languages. 有些英美习语很难翻成其他语言。It was a collection of short stories, badly *rendered into* English. 这部短篇故事集英语译得很糟糕。*Into* how many languages have the plays of Shakespeare been *rendered*? 莎士比亚的戏剧已翻译成了多少种语言?

NOTE 本短语的同义短语是 translate into。

reply to *vt.* 【不可分性动词短语】❶say or write (something) to (someone) as an answer; answer (something) by saying or writing (something)(以言语或书面形式)回答,答复: At the end of his talk the speaker spent ten minutes *replying to* questions put to him by the audience. 在演讲结束时,演讲者用 10 分钟回答了听众向他提出的问题。Have you *replied to* the applicant's letter? 你回复那位求职者的信了吗? I've written to the shop three times to complain about the faulty watch, but none of them have been *replied to*. 我已三次写信给那家商店投诉那块有毛病的手表,但没有一封信得到答复。❷return; give back (something similar or suitable) as a way of returning (something such as gunfire, an attack, or an argument) in response (以行动)答复,还击,反驳: The ship *replied to* the flagship's signal. 那艘舰艇应答了旗舰的信号。We *replied to* the enemy's attack and completely wiped them out. 我们对敌人的进攻进行了还击,并把他们全部歼灭了。The next speaker will *reply to* the argument that you have just heard. 下一位发言者将对您刚刚听到的那个论点给予反驳。❸defend oneself in answer to (a charge)对(某项指控)答辩: How shall I *reply to* the charge? 我对那项指控怎样答辩呢?

NOTE 当本短语作"(以言语或书面形式)回答,答复"解时,同义短语是 respond to。但 respond to 主要指以书面形式来"回答"或"答复"。见 respond to。

report to *vt.* ❶ give information about (something) to (someone in charge) 报告,告发,举报: *Report* any changes in his temperature *to* the head nurse. 把他所有的体温变化都报告给护士长。Any case of stealing should be *reported* immediately *to* the proper authorities. 任何盗窃案件均应立即向有关当局报告。The investigation began early this year when people *reported* his corruption *to* the central government. 今年初,有人向中央政府举报他的腐败问题后,调查就展开了。❷ give an account (of something) to (someone in a position of power) 向……汇报: The Chinese President met respectively with chief executives of Hong Kong and Macao, who are in Beijing *reporting to* the central government on their work. 中国国家主席先后会见了在京向中央政府汇报工作的香港和澳门特别行政区行政长官。❸ declare one's arrival to (someone or a place) 向……报到: While she is out on bail she has to *report to* the police every day. 在她保释期间,她必须每天向警方报到。All visitors to the hospital must *report to* the service desk in the hall. 所有来医院的探视者都必须在大厅中的服务台报到。

representative of *adj.* typical of (people or things in a particular group) 代表……的: Are your opinions *representative of* those of the other workers in the plant? 你们的意见代表厂内其他的工人吗? If this is *representative of* the quality of your work, I'm not very happy about it. 如果这就代表你的工作质量,那我对此并不满意。

research into *vt.* 【不可分性动词短语】study or analyze (something such as a subject or area of difficulty) carefully and thoroughly, in order to discover answers to problems, gain information, or extend knowledge 研究,探讨: The scientists are *researching into* the effects of cigarette smoking on lungs and other organs. 科学家们正在研究吸烟对肺和其他器官的影响。This is an important problem *into* which few social scientists have *researched*. 这是一个没有几位社会学家着手研究的重要问题。She is *researching into* the reading problems of young school children. 她在探讨学龄儿童在阅读中出现的一些问题。

reserve for *vt.* 【可分性动词短语】❶ keep (something) for (a particular purpose, or situation); keep in store for later use; put aside (something) for (someone) 为……保留,把……留给(某人): Don't forget to *reserve* some of your money *for* your holiday. 别忘了节省一些钱在假日用。*Reserve* some energy *for* the last lap of the course. 保留点儿体力跑最后一圈。He *reserved* his rudest comments *for* the manager. 他把最粗鲁的话留着讲给经理听。❷ make an arrangement so that something such as a place or a seat is being kept free (for someone), especially on public transport, or in a theatre, stadium or restaurant 预定(位置),保留(座位): "Do you mind if I sit here?" "I'm sorry, I'm *reserving* the place *for* a friend." "我可以坐在这儿吗?""对不起,这是我给一位朋友留的位置。" The front seats on the bus are *reserved for* old and sick people. 公共汽车上的前排座位都是留给老人和病人坐的。

resign from *vt.* 【不可分性动词短语】

R

(formally) give up or cease working at (a job or position)(正式)辞去(工作或职务):Several young teachers *resign from* teaching when they discover how tiring it is. 有些年轻教师发现教学太辛苦,便纷纷辞去了教学工作。Japan's finance minister who appeared drunk at a G7 press conference *resigned from* his post. 在"七国集团"会议的一场新闻发布会上,疑似醉酒的日本财务大臣辞职。

resolved to *adj.* (后接原形动词) having firm determination to (do something) 决心(做某事): My son is *resolved to* do well in the coming school examinations. 我的儿子决心在即将到来的学校考试中考出好成绩。The new premier was *resolved to* crack down on all forms of corruptions. 新任总理决心打击各种腐败行为。

NOTE 本短语的同义短语是 determined to。

resort to *vt.* 【不可分性动词短语】❶(正式用语) visit (a pleasant place), especially often, usually for a purpose 常去(令人愉快的地方): The dealer used to *resort to* the Club for his luncheon. 那位商人经常到这家俱乐部用午餐。Would you like to go to the beach *to* which our teachers *resort* in the summer? 你想去我们老师夏天常去的那个海滩玩吗? ❷ use or do (something, often extreme or unpleasant) in order to solve a problem 使用,采取,诉诸: You must never *resort to* violence. 你们一定不要使用暴力。She *resorted to* stealing when she had no more money. 她没有钱时就去偷窃。

respond to *vt.* 【不可分性动词短语】❶ reply, especially in writing (尤指以书面形式)回答,答复: Thousands of readers *responded to* our questionnaire. 成千上万的读者回答了我们的调查问卷。They still haven't *responded to* my letter. 他们还没有答复我的信件。❷ react to (something) by taking a particular course of action in a favorable way 对……做出(积极的)反应: Colleges *responded* swiftly *to* the demand for new courses. 一些院校对开设新课程的要求很快就做出了反应。The government has *responded to* the pressure from the public and dropped the proposal. 政府对公众的压力做出了反应,取消了那项提案。❸(常用进行时态)(of a patient or his disease or a part of his body that is hurt) get better as a result of treatment; react favorably to (treatment)(病人或其疾病、身体的受伤部分)对医疗有良好反应: The patient is *responding* quite well *to* the medicine and will be well in a few days. 该患者对药物的反应很好,几天之内就会痊愈。The disease failed to *respond to* the drugs. 这些药对该病未能奏效。Is her leg *responding to* treatment? 她的腿治疗有效果吗?

NOTE 1. 当本短语作"对……做出(积极的)的反应"和"对医疗有良好反应"解时,同义短语是 react to。但,react to 所表示的"反应"并不一定是"积极"或"良好"的。见 react to。

responsible for *adj.* ❶(of something or someone) being the cause of (especially something bad); deserving to be blamed for (especially something bad that has happen) 是造成(尤指某种不良事件)的原因;为所发生的(尤指某种不良事件)负责: The storm is *responsible for* the extensive damage to the crops. 这场暴风雨是造成庄稼大范围毁坏的原因。Who is *responsible for* breaking the window?

这窗子是谁打碎的? ❷having the duty to deal with (something), and making decisions relating to it 负责……,对……负责: He will be *responsible for* buying the properties for the television series. 他将负责采购电视系列片所用的道具。We shall hold you *responsible for* any loss which occurs through this delay. 由于这一延误而带来的任何损失我们将要求你方负责。

NOTE 本短语的同义短语是 accountable for。

rest on/upon *vt.* ❶(of someone)(cause to) lie or lean on (something); (of an object) (cause to) be supported by (something)(指某人)(使)躺在(某物)上,把(某物)放置在……上,(指某物体)放置在……,由……支撑着: We like to *rest on* the green grass on summer afternoons. 我们喜欢在夏天的下午躺卧在青草地上。He *rested* his arms *on* the back of the chair. 他把双臂放在了椅背上。The heavy machine *rested upon* the firm foundation. 重型机器安放在了坚实的基础上。The bridge *rests on* stone arches. 这座桥靠石拱支撑着。❷(正式用语,无被动语态形式,常用一般时态)(of one's eyes) be fixed or directed towards (someone or something)(目光等)凝视,注视……: She let her gaze *rest on* his face for a long time. 她用目光许久地凝视着他的脸。His eyes *rested on* the wallet lying on the table. 他的目光落在桌上的钱包上。It's good to *rest* one's eyes *on* such a beautiful view. 看着这样美丽的景象真是好极了。❸(正式用语) depend or rely on (someone or something)依靠: The Chinese president said in his speech at Waseda University in Tokyo that the future of the Sino-Japanese friendship *rests on* the youths of the two countries. 中国国家主席在东京早稻田大学发表的演讲中指出,中日友好的未来靠两国青年开创。All our hopes *rested upon* this venture. 我们的一切希望都寄托在这次冒险上了。❹(正式用语,用一般时态)(especially of an argument, theory, etc.)(cause to) be based on (something)(尤指论点、理论等)以……为基础: Your argument *rests on* a statement that can't be proved. 你的论点是建立在一项无法得到证明的陈述的基础上的。The theory *rests on* the assumption that there are enough jobs for everyone. 该理论是建立在有足够的工作提供给每个人这一假设的基础之上的。

NOTE 本短语中的 upon 用法比 on 正式,但不及 on 常用。

restrain from *vt.*【可分性动词短语】❶prevent (someone or oneself) from something or doing something 使(某人或自己)不……,阻止,抑制: Please *restrain* yourself *from* coughing during the performance. 在演出时请控制自己不要咳嗽。The police had difficulty in *restraining* the crowd *from* rushing onto the football pitch. 警察很难阻止人群冲入足球场。The man lost his temper, and had to be *restrained from* violence by neighbors who held his arms. 那男子大发脾气,邻居们抓住他的胳膊才使他没能动武。❷physically control (the movements of a person or animal)约束,管住(人或动物的行动): It's difficult to *restrain* oneself *from* eating too much. 约束自己不要吃得过多是件难事。If you can't *restrain* your dog *from* biting people you must lock it up. 如果你无法

管住你的狗让它不咬人,那你就把它锁起来。

restrict to *vt.* ❶(常用被动语态形式) control; keep (something, someone or oneself) down to a (place, level, etc.); limit(someone or oneself) to (something) 控制,抑制,限制:I *restrict* myself *to* two cigarettes a day. 我控制自己每天只抽两支烟。Speed is *restricted to* 30 miles an hour in this part of the road. 在此路段的车速限于 30 英里每小时。❷ensure that only specified people can see (certain materials)仅限某些人员看(某些材料): The information in that booklet is *restricted to* military personnel. 那小册子中的资料仅限于军事人员参阅。

result from *vt.* 【不可分性动词短语】(无被动语态形式,常用一般时态) be the result of (a particular event or action); happen or arise as a consequence of 是……的结果,由于……而发生,因……而致:The nation's troubles result from the government's stupidity. 国家出现麻烦是政府昏庸无能的结果。The tsunami *resulted from* the strong earthquake in the Indian Ocean and it killed over 60, 000 people in Southeast Asia. 印度洋的强烈地震引发了海啸,致使东南亚 6 万多人丧生。His illness *resulted from* eating bad food. 他的病是因为吃了变质的食物引起的。Many hair problems *result from* what you eat. 头发出问题,多因所吃的食物而致。

result in *vt.* 【不可分性动词短语】(无被动语态形式,常用一般时态) cause or produce (something); have (something) as an outcome or result; end in (something)导致,引起,造成,结果是,以……而告终:Mary's carelessness *resulted in* a terrible traffic accident. 玛丽的粗心大意导致了一场可怕的事故。The traffic accident *resulted in* three passengers dying. 那次交通事故导致了 3 名乘客死亡。A government official earlier said the military operation had *resulted in* catching a "big fish". 一位政府官员曾说过此次军事行动钓到了"一条大鱼"。

NOTE 1. 不要将本短语与 result from 相互混淆。result from 是指某种结果由某种原因所引起,而本短语则指某种原因引起某种结果。

2. 本短语的同义短语是 bring about。

retire from *vt.* 【不可分性动词短语】❶(of older people) leave (one's job, position) at the end of one's life's work, or because of one's age (指老年人)退休,离休:My father *retired from* his job as a teacher when he reached the age of sixty. 我父亲到 60 岁时就从教师的岗位上退休了。The general *retired from* the army at the age of 65. 这位将军在 65 岁时退役了。❷(of a sports player) stop competing in (a race, a match, etc.)(指体育选手)退出(某种比赛):I've decided to *retire from* Formula One racing at the end of this season. 我已决定在本赛季结束时退出一级方程式汽车大奖赛。He was forced to *retire from* the match with the leg injury. 由于腿部受伤,他不得不退出比赛。❸(of soldiers) move back from (a position) (usually in an orderly manner); retreat from (指士兵)撤离(阵地),从……撤退:The soldiers received orders to *retire from* the positions that they had just won. 士兵们奉命撤离了他们刚刚夺取的阵地。The enemy destroyed the fortifications *from* which they were *retiring*. 敌人摧毁了他们从中撤离的防御工事。

return to *vt.* ❶go back to (a place where you were earlier), or come back from (a place where you have just been)回到(原处): The former Prime Minister reaffirmed he would quit politics after *returning to* his country. 这位前总理再次表示,他返回祖国后将不再从政。In the third phase of China's three-stage moon mission, a moon rover will land on the moon and *return to* Earth with soil and stone samples for scientific research. 中国探月任务三步走的第三步则是月球车登陆月球,并将带着用于科学研究的土壤和岩石标本返回地球。❷give or send (something) back to (someone)退还,寄还,归还: The local education department has so far tracked down nearly 4 million yuan overcharged, most of which has been *returned to* the students. 当地的教育部门迄今已查处多收费款近 400 万元,其中大部分已退还给学生。Please complete the questionnaire and *return* it *to* the personnel department. 请将此调查表填完后交还给人事部。Parcels which cannot be delivered will be *returned to* the sender. 无法投递的包裹将退还给寄件人。❸cause (someone or a group) to have (power, office) again 使……恢复(权力,职务): He *returned to* power after he lost control of the firm for eight years. 在失去对公司控制的 8 年后,他重掌政权。The exiled president told *The Washington Times* that he still considered himself the rightful president of the country and that he wanted to *return to* his duties as soon as possible. 这位流亡总统对《华盛顿时报》说,他仍然认为自己是其国家的合法总统,他打算尽早返回重新执政。❹(常用一般时态)go back to (a subject that has already been mentioned)重讲(某一主题): He will *return to* this subject later. 他以后还要讲到这个主题。I'd like to *return to* what David was saying earlier. 我想重述一下戴维先前讲的那番话。❺resume; go back to (a former state or condition)继续,恢复(原有状态): She looked up momentarily and then *returned to* her reading. 她往上看了看便又继续读了下去。He gave up drinking for a while, but soon *returned to* his old ways. 他戒了一阵酒,但很快又故态复萌。More state leaders have sent their messages of sympathy to Chinese leaders hoping people's life in the earthquake hit areas would soon *return to* normal. 又有一些国家领导人给中国领导人发来慰问电,希望地震灾区的人民生活尽快恢复正常。Bush *returned to* being a private citizen after seeing President Obama sworn in at the Capitol on Tuesday. 星期二在国会大厦观看了奥巴马总统的宣誓就职仪式后,布什就重新做回了普通公民。

NOTE 当本短语作"重讲(某一主题)"和"继续,恢复(原有状态)"解时,同义短语是 revert to。

reveal to *vt.* 【可分性动词短语】❶(常用一般时态)let(something) become known to (someone), for example a secret or information that was previously not known 把……透露给(某人): The doctor didn't *reveal to* him his hopeless condition. 医生没有向他透露他不治的病情。She *revealed* the fact *to* us without realizing its importance. 她向我们透露了

这个事实,却没意识到它的重要性。He is not the sort of person *to* whom such important policy decisions should be *revealed*. 像这样重要的决策,不应该透露给他那样的人。❷uncover (something or someone that has been out of sight or hidden) to (someone) 把……展现给(某人): Drawing back the curtain, she *revealed* the sleeping criminal *to* the police. 她拉开帘子,把那个正在睡觉的罪犯展现给警察。

revenge on/upon *vt.*【可分性动词短语】(正式用语,常用被动语态形式,常用一般时态,常与反身代词连用) do something to hurt or punish (someone who has hurt you or someone else); repay (a crime) by punishing (the criminal) 向……进行报复,向……报仇: In some places it is an honor to *revenge* oneself *on* somebody who has insulted a member of one's family. 在某些地方,因家人受辱而向他人进行报复是一件光荣的事。I'll be *revenged upon* the whole lot of you for this. 我要为此事向你们这帮人进行报复。He swore to *revenge* himself *on* his enemy. 他发誓要向敌人报仇。

NOTE 1. 本短语中的 upon 用法比 on 正式,但不及 on 常用。

2. 本短语一般以 revenge oneself on/upon someone (for something) 或 be revenged on/upon someone (for something) 的形式使用。动词 revenge 后不能接 something。

3. 本短语的另外一种表达形式是 take revenge on。例如:

> Nature will *take* terrible *revenge* on man if he keeps on destroying the balance of nature.
> 如果人类继续破坏自然界的平衡,大自然就会对其进行可怕的报复。

revert to *vt.*【不可分性动词短语】❶(法律用语,无被动语态形式,常用一般时态) (of land or possession) be returned to (a former owner), after someone else has had it for a period of time (土地或财产)复归(原主): When he dies his land will *revert to* the state. 他死后,其土地将重新归属国家。Possession of the house *reverts to* the original landowner when the contract comes to an end. 这所房子的所有权将在合同期满时复归原地之主。❷(正式用语) start talking about (something that you were talking about earlier) 重讲(原来的话题): The Minister *reverted to* the point several times in the course of his speech. 部长在他讲话的过程中反复几次地讲到那一点。I'd like to *revert to* your earlier point about our export trade. 我想回过头来谈一谈你们先前提出来的关于我们出口贸易方面的问题。❸(正式用语,无被动语态形式) (of things or people) return to (a previous state, or way of behaving), often one that is not good or less satisfactory 恢复到(尤指原有不良的状况或行为方式): After the settlers left, the fields soon *reverted to* moorland. 早期移民离开之后,这些田地很快又重新变成一片荒地。If you *revert to* your old eating habits, you'll gain weight again. 如果你恢复你以前的饮食习惯,那你还会长胖的。

revolve about/around/round *vt.* ❶(of one object) have (something) as the middle point of its movement (指某一物体)围绕着(某物)运动: Traffic is kept *revolving about* an island in the middle of the area. 车辆都绕着那个区域的中心岛行驶。The satellite *revolves around* the

Earth once every hundred minutes. 这颗卫星每100分钟绕地球一周。The moon *revolves round* the earth. 月亮围绕着地球旋转。❷(无被动语态形式，用一般时态，不用进行时态)(in a conversation or discussion)(of one thing) have (another thing) as the main subject or focus (在谈话或讨论中)以……为主题，以……为焦点：The conversation *revolved around* the terrible condition of the road. 谈话的主题集中在了恶劣的路况上。The dispute at the moment *revolves around* whether other delegates should attend. 目前争端的焦点是其他代表是否也应出席。❸(正式用语) consider (something) or be considered carefully 仔细考虑：All sorts of mad ideas *revolved around* my mind. 各种疯狂的想法在我的脑海中翻腾。He *revolved* the matter *round* in his mind but could decide upon nothing. 他反复地考虑了这件事，但还是无法做出任何决定。

NOTE revolve about 和 revolve around 常用于英国英语中，revolve round 则常用于美国英语中。

rich in *adj.* having or containing a lot of the stated thing 富有……的，富含……的：Africa is *rich in* natural and human resources and China has applicable know-how and experience. 非洲有丰富的自然和人力资源，中国有适用的技术和经验。Rome is a city *rich in* ancient buildings. 罗马是一个古建筑众多的城市。The liver of fish is *rich in* Vitamins A and D. 鱼肝富含维生素A和维生素D。Chinese food is *rich in* fiber and low in sugar and fat. 中国人的饮食中富含纤维素，而且低糖低脂。

ride on/upon *vt.*【不可分性动词短语】❶ sit on (something such as an animal or vehicle), control it and travel along on it 骑在……上：Have you ever ridden on a camel? 你骑过骆驼吗？They still *ride* around *on* horses. 他们还在骑马到处转着。He *rides* to school *on* his bicycle. 他骑自行车上学。❷(非正式用语，无被动语态形式，用一般时态)(of one thing) depend on (the other thing), especially for success 取决于，依……而定：It's vital that we win this contract, the whole future of the company is *riding on* it. 我们赢得这份合同是至关重要的，公司的整个前途都依此而定了。The committee's decision often *rides on* the chairman's vote. 该委员会的决定一般取决于其主席的表决。

NOTE 本短语中的 upon 用法比 on 正式，但不及 on 常用。

ride roughshod over *vt.*【不可分性动词短语】(非正式用语) behave in a way that shows you have no respect for (someone or something); do as you wish without consideration for (the feeling or wishes of another person); show no sympathy for (someone) 专横地对待(某人或某事)；对(某人的感情或愿望)置之不理；对(某人)毫不同情：The boss *rode roughshod over* the men when they asked for high wages. 老板对那些要求增加工资的人置之不理。You can't just *ride roughshod over* people's feelings like that. 你们不能那样不顾人民的感情。The city officials *rode roughshod over* the people who didn't want their homes torn down for a new office building. 市政官员根本不同情那些不想拆毁住房建新办公大楼的人们。

NOTE 本短语与 run roughshod over 意义和用法相同，但不及本短语更为常用。

rig out *vt.*【可分性动词短语】(非正式用语) ❶provide or supply (someone) with clothes and other equipment 置备衣物：As

R

winter gets near, we have to *rig* the whole family *out* with warm clothing. 随着冬季日近,我们得给全家人置备保暖的服装了。Each September the children were *rigged out* with clothes for coming winter. 每年9月,都要为孩子们置备服装,准备过冬。❷(常用被动语态形式)dress (someone or oneself) for a special occasion in special or unusual clothes 以盛装打扮(某人或自己): They were *rigged out* in new silk dresses for the occasion. 他们身着丝绸新装去应酬场面。They *rigged* their son *out* as a sailor. 他们把儿子打扮成水手的样子。She *rigged* herself *out* in a bright red uniform. 她穿了一套鲜艳的红色制服。Some of them were very oddly *rigged out*. 他们中有些人打扮得很奇特。

NOTE 当本短语的宾语为代词时,该代词须置于本短语的动词和副词中间。

rig up *vt.* 【可分性动词短语】❶(非正式用语)make (something) for a short time out of materials easily found (利用简易材料)临时赶造: The first thing to do when you're shipwrecked is to *rig up* some kind of a shelter, and only afterwards look for food. 当你所乘坐的船失事后,你要做的第一件事是找些简易材料搭一个栖身之处,然后再寻找食物。A makeshift bed was *rigged up* for the sick person. 为病人就地搭了一张临时床铺。❷ put together the parts, especially ropes of (a boat or ship); put together the parts of (something) 把(船只各部分)装配起来,安装(某物): Has the boat been properly *rigged up* with suitable ropes and sails? 小船都装上合适的绳索和帆了吗? Then we got the recording machine and *rigged* it *up* near the cave. 然后我们拿了录音机,把它安装在了洞穴附近。

NOTE 当本短语的宾语为代词时,该代词须置于本短语的动词和副词中间。

right away/off *adv.* (主要用于美国英语口语中) immediately; at once; without delay 立即,马上: Don't leave over the work that can be done *right away*. 马上可以办好的事情就不要往后拖。The teacher said he could not remember the name of the book *right off*. 老师说他不能马上想起那本书的名字。

NOTE 本短语与 at once, by and by, right now, straight away/off 均表示"立即,马上"。它们之间的区别见 at once。

right now *adv.* (主要用于口语中) ❶immediately; at once 立刻,马上: Go to bed *right now*! 立刻上床睡觉! We're to work on it *right now*, so it should be ready soon. 我们马上就做这件事,应该很快就做好。❷ at the present time; exactly now 现在,目前,此刻: I'll do it in a bit. I'm busy *right now*. 我一会儿做它,我现在很忙。Over 180 thousand overseas students of China's mainland have worked or studied in the US, with 60 thousand still studying *right now*. 在美国工作或学习过的中国内地留学人员已超过18万,目前仍然在读的有6万余人。They are doing the experiment *right now*. 他们此刻正在做实验。

ring in *vi.* ❶(主要用于英国英语中) make a telephone call to (someone at your place of work, or a radio station) 给(办公室或广播电台)打电话: Tom has *rung in* to say that he'll be late today. 汤姆打来电话说他今天要晚一会儿到。❷ mark the time of your arrival at work 计时上班: We have to *ring in* at the shop before eight o'clock in the morning. 我们必须在早上 8 点之前到店上班。

—*vt.*【不可分性动词短语】mark the beginning of (the New Year) by ringing bells 鸣钟迎来(新年):The ringers rang out the old year before *ringing in* the new. 敲钟人鸣钟辞旧岁,迎新年。

NOTE 当本短语作"计时上班"和"鸣钟迎来(新年)"解时,反义短语是 ring out。

ring off *vi.* (英国英语用法) put down the receiver at the end of a telephone conversation (通完话后)挂断电话: The girl laughed and *rang off*. 那女孩大声笑着挂断了电话。I'll have to *ring off* now, I have a train to catch. 我现在得挂断电话了,我要去赶火车。He *rang off* before she had a chance to reply. 她还没来得及回答,他就挂断了电话。

NOTE 本短语的同义短语是 hang up。

ring out *vi.* ❶(常用一般时态)produce a loud clear sound, usually suddenly (常指突然地)发出响亮的声音: Bob's laughter *rang out* from the back of the church, interrupting the wedding. 鲍勃从教堂后面突然发出了响亮的笑声,打断了正在进行的婚礼。Several gunshots *rang out* from the military camp, and one woman fell to the ground. 从军营传出了几声枪响,一名妇女应声倒在了地上。❷(主要用于美国英语中)mark the time of your leaving work 计时下班: John can't leave early in his new job, he has to *ring out*. 约翰在他新的工作岗位上无法早退,他得计时下班。

—*vt.*【不可分性动词短语】usher out(the old year) by or as if by ringing bells 送走,鸣钟送走(旧岁): At this moment of *ringing out* the old year and ringing in the new, I am very happy to extend New Year greetings to you all. 在这辞旧迎新的时刻,我很高兴地向你们大家致以新年的祝贺!

ring up *v.* (主要用于英国英语中,非正式用语) phone (someone) (给某人)打电话: I'll *ring up* the theatre and see when the show finishes. 我来给剧院打个电话,问演出什么时候结束。I'll *ring* you *up* sometime during the week. 我将在本周内的什么时候给你打电话。

—*vt.*【可分性动词短语】record (the amounts being paid for goods) by pressing keys or buttons on a cash register, especially one with a bell 把(购物所付款额)记入(尤指带铃的)现金收入记录机: The cashier *rang up* $50 instead of 50 cents by mistake. 收款员在现金收入记录机上将 50 美分误记成了 50 美元。If a sales clerk forgets to *ring* something *up* do you call it to her attention? 如果售货员忘记打现金出纳机,你会提示她吗?

NOTE 1. 当本短语用作及物性动词短语,所带的宾语为代词时,该代词须置于本短语的动词和副词中间。

2. 本短语与 call up 和 phone up 均表示"(给……)打电话"。它们之间的区别是:本短语既有及物性又有不及物性用法,而 call up 和 phone up 都只有及物性用法。另外,本短语和 phone up 都用于英国英语中,而 call up 则用于美国英语中。

3. 在英语中,表示"给……打电话"的表达方式有多种: call someone, give someone a (phone) call, give someone a ring, ring someone, phone someone, telephone someone, call someone by phone, call someone up, phone someone up, ring someone up 等。"接电话"通常用 answer/receive/take a (phone) call。

"回电话"一般说 return a (telephone) call 或 call/ring back 等。

rise from *vt.* 【不可分性动词短语】❶(正式用语)(of someone) stand up from (something)从……站起身来: Mary *rose* slowly *from* the chair to greet me. 玛丽慢吞吞地从椅子上站起身来迎接我。❷(of something) move upwards or to a higher level out of (something)从……升起: Heavy smoke could be seen *rising from* the helicopter crash site in Tikrit, 175 km north of Baghdad. 可以看到从位于巴格达北部175公里的提克里特直升机坠毁处冒出的浓烟。❸(常与 to 连用)(of someone) reach a higher position or social level than (something)从(某一职位或社会地位)高升(至……): He *rose from* captain to the rank of general in seven years. 他七年内就从上尉官衔高升到了将军。He *rose from* humble origins to become prime minister. 他出身卑微,后来当了首相。❶(无被动语态形式,常用一般时态,不用进行时态)be caused by (something); have its origin in 起因为,起源于: The quarrel *rose from* a misunderstanding. 这场争吵是由一场误会引起来的。

rise to *vt.* 【不可分性动词短语】reach (a high level, position, etc.)达到(高水平),升任(高一级职务等): Temperature *rose to* highest point. 温度达到了最高点。She eventually *rose to* an important position in the company. 她终于升任该公司要职。He *rose* from captain *to* colonel in five years. 他在五年内就从上尉升到了上校。

rise to one's feet *vi.* stand up (usually to make a speech, propose a toast, etc.) 起立,站起身来(发言或祝酒等): A reporter from Russia *rose to his feet* to ask the spokesman two questions at the press conference. 在新闻发布会上,一位俄罗斯记者站起身来向发言人提出了两个问题。Pushing back her chair, she *rose to her feet* to propose a toast. 她把椅子向后推了推,站起身来祝酒。The nearly 10,000 people in the stadium *rose to their feet*, applauding, cheering and whistling. 体育场内的近万人站起身来,鼓掌、欢呼、吹口哨。

rob of *vt.* 【可分性动词短语】❶ take (money or property) illegally from (a person or place), often using threats or violence 抢去,夺去(某人或某处的钱或财物): The man who had *robbed* the old lady *of* her gold ring was arrested. 那个抢走老妇人金戒指的人被抓住了。A famous academician was *robbed of* his laptop computer by two men riding on a motorcycle on the street. 一位著名的院士在大街上被两个骑摩托车的人抢走了手提电脑。❷take (something such as an opportunity, or skill) from (usually someone), often in an unfair way 剥夺(某人的机会或技艺等),丧失……: I can't forgive him for *robbing* me *of* an Olympic gold. 他使我失去了奥运会夺金的机会,我不能宽恕他。"For some people, forgiving themselves is the biggest challenge," Frederic says. "But it can *rob* you *of* your self-confidence if you don't do it."弗雷德里克说:"对于有些人来说,宽恕自己才是最大的挑战。但是如果你不宽恕自己,你就会失去自信。" Television has *robbed* the cinema *of* its former popularity. 电视使电影失去了其原有的广大观众。❸steal (something) from (someone)偷走: The thieves *robbed* the newly married couple *of* all their valuables. 盗贼们把这对新婚夫妇所有值钱的东西都偷走了。Daniel was *robbed of* his month's wages by a pickpocket. 丹尼尔一个月的工资被扒手偷走了。

roll back *v.* ❶(cause to)move backwards or away by rolling (使)滚回,把……卷起来:The colored Easter egg *rolled back* from the higher point of the lawn. 那只复活节彩蛋从草坪的高处滚了回来。Let's *roll* the carpet *back* and have a dance. 让我们把地毯卷起来跳舞吧。The car has a soft hood, which can be *rolled back* in fine weather. 这部车的车篷是软性的,天气好时可以卷起来。❷(of a time in the past) return steadily to someone's consciousness; recall (a time in the past) steadily to someone's consciousness (使)(过去的某一时期)渐渐回到某人的记忆中:The pictures *rolled back* the days of childhood to me. 这些照片使我回忆起童年时代。❸retreat; force (opponents) to move back; push back 退却,击退,使退却,使倒退:The army *rolled back* when they came under attack. 该部队受到攻击后便退却了。We *rolled back* the enemy forces on all fronts. 我们全线击退了敌军。We can't *roll back* the reforms of the last thirty years. 我们不能让过去 30 年的改革倒退。❹(美国英语用法)reduce (something such as a price or cost)减少,降低(价格或成本等): The authorities took measures to *roll* commodity prices *back*. 当局采取了一些降低商品价格的措施。No one believed that the current high prices will be *rolled back*. 没有人相信现行的高昂价格会降下来。The official said the government will decide in a "short period of time" whether or not to *roll back* disputed steel tariffs. 这位官员表示,政府将在"近期"内决定是否降低有争议的钢铁关税。

NOTE 本短语可转化为复合词 rollback,意为"击退;(政府将价格)压低到标准水平"。

roll on *v.* ❶(主要用于英国英语中,仅用于口语,用于祈使句中来表达良好的愿望)(used to express a wish of something nice in the future) may that day, etc. come quickly 但愿(那一天等)早日到来:I really need a break. *Roll on*, Christmas! 我真的需要休息一下了。圣诞节,快来吧! *Roll on* the summer holidays! 但愿暑假早日到来! ❷put (clothing) on by rolling (卷着)穿上(衣物):*Roll* your stockings *on*, to avoid damaging them. 长筒袜要卷着往上穿,以免拉坏。No sooner had she *rolled on* her stockings than she ran out of the room. 她穿上长筒袜就跑出了房间。

roll out *v.* ❶make (a substance) flat by pushing something heavy (such as a rolling pin) across it 把……擀平:*Roll out* the pizza dough on a well-floured surface. 把做比萨的生面饼放在撒好面粉的表面上擀平。❷spread (something) by unrolling it 把……铺开:We *rolled out* the red carpet for the distinguished guests from Russia. 我们铺开红地毯欢迎来自俄罗斯的贵宾。*Roll out* the map so that we can all see it. 把地图铺展开来,好让我们都能看到它。She *rolled out* the document on the table. 她把文件展开放在了桌面上。❸introduce (a new product or service); produce (a new product, etc.) in large quantity 推介(新产品或服务),批量生产(新产品等):Microsoft started to *roll out* Bing at the beginning of June and the new search

service was fully deployed worldwide on June 3. 微软公司于 6 月初开始推出其新搜索引擎"必应",这项新的搜索服务在 6 月 3 日就遍布了全球。They've experimented with the system, and will *roll* it *out* nationally this fall. 他们已对这套系统进行了试验,并于今年秋季在全国推出。The company keeps *rolling out* these new types of camera. 该公司在不断地大量生产这些新型照相机。This new model of car is to be *rolled out* in October. 这种新车型将在 10 月份批量生产。

roll over *vt.* & *vi* (cause to) change the position of your body when you are lying down by turning over (使)翻身,打滚: Every time Tom *rolled over*, he pulled more of the bedclothes to his side. 每当汤姆翻一次身,他都会把被子往他那侧拉过去一些。A motorcycle hit me and *rolled* me *over*. 一辆摩托车撞上了我,使我在地上打了个滚。

—*vt.* 【不可分性动词短语】move steadily and smoothly along (something) (as if) on wheels (似车轮)沿……平稳地滚动前进,(车轮)滚动压过(某物): The waves *rolled over* the sand. 波浪滚滚,涌上沙滩。The explosive devices like landmines are sometimes set off when American military vehicles *roll over* them. 像地雷这样的爆炸装置有时在美国军车压过时便引起爆炸。

NOTE 当本短语用作及物性动词短语,所带的宾语为代词时,该代词须置于本短语的动词和副词中间或介词之后。

roll up *v.* ❶(cause to) form (something) into a ball or cylinder by wrapping it several times; wrap (something or someone) 卷起,缠绕,裹起: She *rolled* her scarf *up* and put it into her bag. 她把围巾卷起来放进包里。The paintings were taken from their frames and *rolled up* for storage. 把这些油画从画框中取下并卷起来以便收藏。She *rolled up* her umbrella. 她收拢了雨伞。I kept myself warm by *rolling* myself *up* in a thick blanket. 我用一条厚厚的毛毯把自己裹了起来以保暖。❷fold (the ends of your sleeves or trousers legs) several times until they are shorter 挽起(衣袖或裤腿): The sleeves of his shirt were *rolled up* to the elbow. 他把衬衣袖子挽到了肘部。*Roll up* your trousers before putting your legs in the water. 先把你的裤腿挽起来,再把腿伸入水中。*Roll* your sleeves and the legs of your trousers *up* before you start to do this job. 在开始干这活儿前,先把衣袖和裤腿都挽起来。❸(usually of smoke) rise in rolling masses (常指烟)袅袅上升: Smoke could be seen *rolling up* from the chimneys in the village. 可以看到村庄里炊烟袅袅升起。❹(非正式用语,常用一般时态) (of people) arrive somewhere, especially late or in some unacceptable way, especially in a vehicle (指人)(尤指乘车)姗姗来迟,(以某种不合适的方式)到达: They eventually *rolled up* at lunchtime. 他们终于在午餐时间乘车到达了。I might have known you wouldn't *roll up* until the meeting had nearly finished. 我本应估计到你可能在会议快结束时才会到。❺force (an enemy) to move back or away 击退,赶走(敌人): The government has done quite a bit now to *roll up* the terrorist network. 政府在打击恐怖主义组织方面现已做了很多。

NOTE 当本短语用作及物性动词短语,所带的宾语为代词时,该代词须置于本短语的动词和副词中间。

round/around the clock *adv.* all day and all night, without stopping for rest; for or during all 24 hours 昼夜不停地,连续 24 小时,全天候地: The schoolboy had shown symptoms of mental disorder after staying on the Internet *around the clock* for days. 这名男同学在连续数日昼夜不停地上网后,出现了精神分裂的症状。The hotel in the city center, which is used by Westerners and journalists, is guarded *round the clock*. 位于市中心的那家饭店是专供西方人和记者使用的。它一天 24 小时有人守卫。He was so tired that he slept *round the clock*. 他太累了,所以连续睡了 24 个小时。

NOTE **1.** 本短语的另外一种表达形式是 the clock round/around, 本短语更为常用。

2. 本短语可转化为复合形容词(a) round-the-clock, 意为"连续 24 小时的"。

3. 本短语的同义短语是 day and night 和 night and day。

round/around the corner *adv.* & *adj.* (常与 just 连用) ❶(非正式用语)(of something) very near; not far away 在附近: They live just *round the corner*. 他们就住在附近。The kids go to school just *around the corner*. 孩子们就在附近上学。❷(of something) coming or about to happen very soon 临近: As the Chinese Lunar New Year is *round the corner*, we particularly have Taiwan compatriots in our minds. 随着中国农历新年的临近,我们更加挂念台湾同胞。As the new round of nuclear talks is just *around the corner*, both words and actions of all the parties should serve to realize the common goal. 新一轮核问题会谈召开在即,有关各方的言行都应有利于共同目标的实现。

round up *vt.* 【可分性动词短语】❶bring (animals or people) together in one place for a particular purpose 把(动物或人)聚拢在一起: I used to help *round up* the cows at milking time. 过去,在挤奶的时间我也帮忙圈牛。The shepherd's dog *rounded up* some stray sheep. 牧羊犬把离群的羊赶到了一起。The guide *rounded up* the tourists and led them back to the coach. 导游把游客集拢到一起,带他们回到大巴上。❷ collect or gather 搜集: John *rounded up* many names for his petition. 约翰为他那份请愿书征集到了许多人的签名。❸(of police or army) find and capture (a number of people, especially criminals) (指警方或军队)发现并抓获(尤指罪犯): The police have *rounded up* more than 20 suspected militants linked to the bombings. 警方已逮捕了 20 多名被怀疑与系列爆炸案有关联的武装分子。Two of the robbers were arrested outside the bank, and the rest of the gang was *rounded up* later. 两名劫匪在银行外被捕,其余的团伙成员后来也被抓获。❹increase (an exact figure) to the next highest whole number, or the nearest number ending in zero 把(数字)(按四舍五入法)调高为整数: I'll *round* the cheque *up* to ＄10, and you can keep the change. 我把这份支票调到 10 元这个整数,零头您就留下吧。All measurements have been *rounded up* and are not exact. 所有的测量数字都调到了整数,所以不精确。

NOTE **1.** 当本短语用作及物性动词短语,所带的宾语为代词时,该代词须置于本短语的动词和副词中间。

2. 本短语可转化为复合词 roundup, 意为

"聚拢;围捕;综述,摘要"。

rub down *vt.*【可分性动词短语】❶make (a rough surface) smooth by rubbing it (with something such as sandpaper)(用砂纸)把(某物的粗糙表面)磨平:They started to work, *rubbing down* the top of the desk with sandpaper. 他们开始干活,用砂纸把桌面磨平。*Rub* the door *down* before you paint it. 先把门打磨光滑再涂油漆。❷rub and press with the fingers on the body of (a person) to loosen muscles or prevent stiffness; massage 按摩:Trainers *rub down* an athlete after hard exercise. 每次在强度大的训练之后,教练员都会给运动员按摩。The trainer *rubbed* her legs *down* after the race. 赛后,教练给她的双腿做了按摩。❸dry (someone or oneself, or an animal) with something such as a towel or cloth 擦干(某人、自己或动物的)身体:He set the baby on the bed and *rubbed* him *down* with a dry towel. 他把婴儿放在床上,用一条干毛巾把他身子擦干。*Rub* yourself *down* after your swim, I won't have you catching cold. 游完泳后,把身子擦干。我不想让你感冒。Stablemen *rub down* a horse after a race. 赛马会结束后,马夫把马身上的汗擦干。She *rubbed* her horse *down* with a towel after her ride. 她骑过马后用毛巾把马周身擦净。

NOTE 1. 当本短语的宾语为代词时,该代词须置于本短语的动词和副词中间。

2. 本短语可转化为复合词 rubdown,意为"擦,摩擦"。

rub off *v.* (cause to) be removed (from something such as a surface) by rubbing; erase (把……从……)擦掉,磨去:*Rub* these rude words on the wall *off* at once! 立即把墙上写的这些粗俗语擦掉! Don't worry, the dirty marks will *rub off* quite easily. 别担心,这些污迹很容易擦掉。The writing on the blackboard had been *rubbed off* before the teacher came in. 黑板上的字在老师进来之前就被擦掉了。These new boots are so stiff that they *rub* the skin *off* my ankles. 这双新靴子太硬了,把我脚踝的皮都磨掉了。

rub out *v.* (常用一般时态) ❶(主要用于英国英语中)(cause to) remove with a rubber (something that you have written or drawn in pencil), especially because you have made a mistake; erase 用橡皮(把……)擦掉:These marks won't *rub out* properly. 这些痕迹用橡皮擦不干净。Will this rubber *rub out* ink marks? 这橡皮能擦掉墨迹吗? Write your answer in pencil so that you can *rub* it *out* if you change your mind. 用铅笔来写答案,在你改变主意时好用橡皮把它擦掉。❷(美国英语用法,非正式用语)kill (someone)杀掉(某人):Nobody else believed that they had tried to *rub out* the pope. 没谁会相信他们曾企图杀掉教皇。The gangsters *rubbed* him *out*. 那伙歹徒杀害了他。Anyone who opposes our organization will get *rubbed out*. 任何与我们组织作对的人都会被干掉。

NOTE 当本短语用作及物性动词短语,所带的宾语为代词时,该代词须置于本短语的动词和副词中间。

rub up *vt.*【可分性动词短语】❶make (something) shine by rubbing 把(某物)擦亮:He asked me to *rub up* the silver plate. 他要我把银盘子擦亮。Please *rub* it *up* with a clean dry cloth. 请用一块干净的干抹布把它擦亮。Those chairs will look better once they've been well *rubbed* *up*. 这些椅子一旦擦得很亮就好看多了。The silver needs *rubbing up*. 这银器需要擦亮。❷(非正式用语) improve (one's knowledge of a subject that has been neglected for some time)改进,提高(某人生疏了的知识): Your English grammar needs to be *rubbed up*. 你的英语语法需要进一步改进。If I'm to spend two weeks in Italy, I'd better *rub up* my knowledge of the language. 如果我要在意大利住两周的话,我还是提高一下我那门语言的知识为好。

NOTE 当本短语的宾语为代词时,该代词须置于本短语的动词和副词中间。

rule out *vt.* 【可分性动词短语】(常用一般时态) ❶exclude (a possibility); make it unnecessary to think about (something or someone)排除(某种可能性);不予考虑(某事或某人): He did not *rule out* changing his mind. 他没有排除改变主意的可能性。The spokesman said human infection of bird flu could not be *ruled out*. 发言人表示,人感染禽流感的可能性不能排除。We have to find a baby-sitter for tonight, Betty has a date, so that *rules* her *out*. 我们今晚得找一个人看小孩,贝蒂有约会,就不要考虑她了。❷make it impossible for (something) to happen; say that (something) must not be done; not allow (someone) to do (something)使(某事)不能发生,禁止(某人)做(某事): Heavy rain *ruled out* the match for that day. 大雨使那天的比赛没能进行。Father's death seems to *rule out* college for Jane. 看来父亲一去世,简就上不成大学了。The principal *ruled out* dances in schoolrooms at night. 校长禁止晚上在教室内跳舞。

NOTE 当本短语的宾语为代词时,该代词须置于本短语的动词和副词中间。

rule out of *vt.* 【可分性动词短语】make it impossible for a player to take part in (a game or competition)使(运动员)不能参加(比赛): A shoulder injury *ruled* the world-famous footballer *out of* the World Cup. 肩部的伤情使这位世界闻名的足球运动员不能参加世界杯大赛。An ankle injury *ruled* her *out of* the big match against the women's volleyball team of Cuba. 脚踝受伤使她不能参加这场对阵古巴女排的大赛。

NOTE 当本短语的宾语为代词时,该代词须置于本短语的动词和副词中间。

rule over *vt.* 【不可分性动词短语】(of a person, group, or something) have and use the power to control (the affairs of a country or a group of people) 统治: Queen Elizabeth Ⅱ has *ruled over* the United Kingdom for 67 years and worked with 10 prime ministers. 女王伊丽莎白二世已统治英国 67 年,先后同超过 10 位首相共过事。He turned his attention to the Netherlands, a rich and prosperous country that was *ruled over* by Spain. 他把注意力转向了一个曾被西班牙统治过的富裕而繁荣的国家——荷兰。

run across *vt.* 【不可分性动词短语】(用一般时态)(of someone) find (something) or meet (someone) unexpectedly (指某人)偶然发现(某物),偶然遇到(某人): I *ran across* the letter while I was tidying the drawers. 当我收拾抽屉时,我偶然看到了这封信。She *ran across* her old friend Jane in the street in London last week. 上周她在伦敦的大街上与她的老朋友简不期而遇。

NOTE 本短语的同义短语是 bump into, chance on/upon, come across, meet with, run into 和 stumble across/on/upon。

run after *vt.* 【不可分性动词短语】 ❶chase (something or someone), as by running, in order to catch them or stop them (跑着)追赶：Quick, *run after* him. He's left his wallet on the counter. 快，追上他。他把钱包落在柜台上了。Bob *ran after* the car waving his fists. 鲍勃挥舞着拳头追赶那辆小轿车。I like to watch my dog *running after* a rabbit. 我喜欢看我的狗追逐兔子。❷(非正式用语，贬义用法，常用进行时态) try to start a relationship with (someone of the opposite sex)追求(异性)：If you didn't *run after* her so much, she might be more interested in you. 如果你不是拼命追求她的话，她也许会对你更感兴趣。Instead of devoting themselves to their studies, some boy students spend a lot of time and money *running after* girls. 一些男同学不专心于读书，而是花大量的时间和金钱去追求女孩子。I hate to feel that I'm being *run after*. 我不喜欢有被别人追求的感觉。❸(非正式用语) perform the duties of a servant for (someone) (像仆人一样地)伺候，服侍(某人)：I can't keep *running after* you all day, my son! 我不能整天像仆人一样地伺候你，我的儿子!

run against *vt.* 【不可分性动词短语】 ❶compete with (someone) in an election 在选举中与(某人)竞选：Barack Obama *ran against* Republican candidate John McCain in the last presidential election. 巴拉克·奥巴马在上次的总统选举中与共和党候选人约翰·麦凯恩角逐。There were two candidates *running against* her. 曾有两名候选人与她竞选。❷turn out badly or unfavorably for (someone or something); disfavor 不利于，违背："We are to send troops to Iraq on condition that it does not *run against* our national interests," the Foreign Minister said. 这位外交部长表示："我们向伊拉克派兵的条件是，它不能违背我们的国家利益。" Time is now *running against* us in this affair. 如今在这件事上时间对我们不利。Roach also criticized severely their doings that *run against* market economy. 罗奇还严厉地批评了他们违反市场经济的一些做法。

run along *vi.* (非正式用语，常用于祈使句中) (a command used especially to a child, junior or familiar) go away; be off with you (尤用于命令儿童、下级或熟人)走开：Be a good girl. *Run along* now and play for a bit, Daddy's busy. 做个乖女儿。你玩一会儿去，爸爸在忙着。For God's sake, *run along*. 看在上帝的分上，你快走开吧。*Run along* to bed, Tom. 汤姆，去上床睡觉。

run at *vt.* 【不可分性动词短语】(无被动语态形式) run towards (someone), in order to attack him or her, or towards (something) with the aim of jumping over it 向(某人)冲过去(以袭击某人)；向(某物)冲过去(以从上跳过)：The big fellow *ran at* me with a knife in hand. 那高大的家伙手拿刀子向我冲了过来。The dog *ran at* the visitor and bit him. 这条狗朝客人扑了过去并咬了他。If you *run at* the fence fast enough, you should be able to jump over it. 如果你用足够快的速度朝栅栏冲去，你就会跳过去。

run away *vi.* ❶(常与 from 连用) leave (a person or a place) suddenly and secretly, often because you are not happy 突然(秘密地)离开，(离……)出走：Why did you *run away* from me? 你为什么离我而去? After he was given a severe beating by his father, Tom *ran away* and hasn't been heard of ever since. 被爸爸痛打了一顿之后,汤姆便离家出走并一直没有音讯。I *ran away* from home when I was fourteen. 我 14 岁时就离家出走了。❷(常与 with 连用) secretly go away (with some one of the opposite sex) in order to live with or marry him or her (与异性者)私奔: They *ran away* and got married. 他们私奔后结了婚。She deserted her family and *ran away* with him. 她抛弃了自己的家庭与他私奔了。❸(常与 from 连用) go away quickly; escape (from a place)跑掉,(从……)逃走: The horse became frightened and *ran away*. 马受惊跑了。Don't let the fox *run away*. 不要让那只狐狸跑掉。The strong earthquake made a wall of the prison fall down, and many prisoners *ran away*. 强烈的地震使监狱的一面墙壁倒塌,许多囚犯趁机逃走了。

NOTE **1.** 本短语与 get away 均表示"逃跑"之意,常用于口语中。get away 尤指犯罪分子逃离犯罪现场或拒捕而逃跑;而本短语用的范围较广,可与动词 escape 互换使用,强调动作的迅速。

2. 本短语可转化为复合词 runaway,意为"逃跑,逃亡;逃跑者,脱缰的马;脱离控制;压倒性的优胜"。

run away from *vt.*【不可分性动词短语】❶escape from (something or someone) usually because the life is unpleasant (常指因生活不愉快而)逃离: He was so unhappy that he tried to *run away from* school. 他的心情不愉快,所以就设法逃学。Because of his stepfather's ill treatment, the little boy *ran away from* home to return to live with his uncle in Baghdad at the age of ten. 由于受继父虐待,这个小男孩十岁时就离家出走,回到巴格达与叔叔一起生活。Please don't *run away from* me. I mean you no harm. 请不要从我这儿跑掉,我无意伤害你。❷(常用一般时态)try to avoid (someone or something unpleasant) because you are shy, frightened, lacking confidence, etc. 躲避,回避: It is a disease and there is no cure, but you must not *run away from*, people with AIDS. 这是一种疾病,而且无药可医,但你大可不必见到艾滋病患者就躲。You can't keep *running away from* the problem. 你不能总是回避这个问题。Difficulties should not be *run away from*; they should be faced resolutely. 不应当逃避困难,而应当坚决地去应对它。

run away with *vt.*【不可分性动词短语】❶(无被动语态形式)get out of control of (someone or something such as a strong feeling)对……失去控制: I'm sorry I let my tongue *run away with* me, please forgive me for my accidental rudeness. 对不起,我话出失口。请原谅我意外的失礼。Don't let your enthusiasm *ran away with* you. 不要热心得过了头。❷(especially of a thief) steal (something)(尤指小偷)偷走(某物): Someone's *run away with* all my valuables. 有人偷走了我所有值钱的物品。A thief *ran away with* my grandma's silver teapot. 小偷偷走了祖母的银制茶壶。Someone in the office *ran away with* the plans of the new engine. 办公室有人盗走了新发动机的方案。❸secretly go away with (someone of the opposite sex, in the hope of marrying without someone's consent)与(异性者)

私奔:Mary said if her father wouldn't let her marry the young man, she would *run away with* him. 玛丽说,如果父亲不准她嫁给那年轻人,她就与他私奔。Tom has *run away with* his boss's daughter. 汤姆与他老板的女儿私奔了。She is not a girl who would be quite willing to be *run away with* by any attractive young man. 她不是一个很愿随任何一个有吸引力的小伙子私奔的姑娘。❹(常用一般时态) consume (something such as money) freely 大量花掉,消耗(金钱等): The project will *run away with* a lot of the tax-payers' money. 这个项目将花掉纳税人大量的金钱。Those new heaters *run away with* a lot of electricity. 那些新取暖器耗电量很大。❺(非正式用语,常用一般时态) win (a competition, game, or prize) very easily 轻而易举地赢得(比赛或奖品): The Brazilian football team *ran away with* the first match in the series. 巴西足球队轻而易举地赢得了系列赛中的第一场比赛。Theresa *ran away with* the women's gold medal. 特里萨轻而易举地夺取了女子金牌。

run counter to *vt.* 【不可分性动词短语】(无被动语态形式,用一般时态) (of one thing) be opposite to (another thing); contradict; not match; conflict with 违背,与……背道而驰,与……相反: But his views apparently *ran counter to* those of ours. 但是他的这些观点明显与我们的背道而驰。The article presented facts that *run counter to* what many of us believed had happened. 该文所提出的一些情况与我们很多人所相信已发生的情况相反。

NOTE 本短语中的动词 run 可被 act, go 替换,构成的短语与本短语意义和用法相同。例如:

> He acted counter to all advice.
> 他逆所有忠告而行之。
> Things always go counter to one's will.
> 情况往往事与愿违。

但这两者均不及本短语常用。

run down *v.* ❶ move quickly downhill or to a distance, as by running 往下跑,在……上跑下: Walk down the stairs, don't *run down*. 下楼梯时走着下,别往下跑。After the explosion, groups of young girls *ran down* the street in their navy blue school uniforms, screaming in terror. 爆炸发生后,一群群身穿海军蓝校服的女孩沿街奔跑,惊恐地尖叫着。❷(常用一般时态) (of a vehicle or its driver) knock to the ground and hurt (a person or animal) or damage (something) with a motor vehicle or ship (指车辆,船只)把……撞倒,撞坏,撞伤: Jack rode his bicycle too fast and almost *ran down* his little brother. 杰克的自行车骑得太快,几乎撞上了他的小弟弟。She claimed that the motorcycle driver was trying to *run* her *down*. 她声称,那个骑摩托车的人企图要撞她。She got *run down* just outside school. 她在校门外被车撞倒了。It was so foggy that the steam-ship almost *ran down* a small boat leaving port. 由于雾太大,汽船几乎撞上了一艘正在离港的小船。❸ (especially of a clock or an electric battery) (cause to) gradually lose its power and stop working (使)(钟表)停止工作,(使)(电池)用完: The kitchen clock *ran down* because we forgot to wind it. 厨房里的钟停了,因为我们忘记给它上发条了。The batteries in your radio are *running down*, so you have to recharge them. 收音机电池中的

电都要用完了,你得给它们充电了。Switch your headlights off, or you'll *run* the battery *down*. 把你的车头灯关掉,否则就会把电瓶里的电耗尽的。❹(主要用于英国英语中)deliberately reduce (the size or activity of an industry a company, etc.)刻意减小(工业、公司等的规模或活动):More and more disasters forced the government to *run down* the coal industry. 越来越多的矿难迫使政府缩小了煤炭工业的规模。The air force had been *run down*. 已裁减了空军的规模。They wanted to *run* our supplies *down* some more. 他们想要进一步减少我们的供应品。❺(常用一般时态)find (something) eventually after a long search, usually after a lot of difficulty (经过长期艰难地寻找)终于找到(某物):At last I *ran down* the article that I had been looking for in the university library. 我终于在校图书馆里找到了我曾一直在找的那篇文章。See if you can *run down* that book in the library for me. 看你能不能给我在图书馆里找到那本书。❻(常用一般时态)chase and catch (someone or an animal)追捕(某人或动物):The policemen *ran down* the escaped prisoner at the far end of the wood. 警察在密林尽头追捕到了那名逃犯。The Border guards are *running* those illegals *down* and will take them back. 边防兵在追捕那些非法越境者并将把他们押回境内。The suspect was finally *run down* at the home of one of his associates. 那名嫌犯终于在他一个同伙的家里被抓获。The dogs *ran down* the wounded deer. 这群狗追猎到那只受伤的鹿。❼(非正式用语)express a low opinion of (something or someone)说……的坏话,贬低,诽谤:You're always *running me down*! 你总是说我的坏话!I don't understand why she's always *running* her husband and his family *down* in public. 我不明白她为什么总是当众说她丈夫及其家人的坏话。I am not going to risk being *run down* before my friends by a fellow I despise. 我不愿意冒险让一个我所蔑视的人在我的朋友面前诽谤我。Mary *ran down* the club because its members wouldn't let her join. 玛丽对该俱乐部进行诽谤,是因为俱乐部的成员不让她加入进去。❽(常用被动语态形式)be tired and in poor condition, because of overwork, lack of sleep, etc.; use the strength off (因过劳或缺乏睡眠而)身体衰弱,精疲力竭:After having had four periods of class in the morning, I felt *run down*. 上完一上午的四节课后,我感到精疲力竭了。The doctor said he was *running down* and should rest for a few days. 医生说他身体虚弱,应休息几天。❾quickly read (everything on a list)浏览,扫视(名单中的内容):I'll just *run down* the list and see if we've forgotten anything. 我只看一眼名单中的内容,看看我们是否忘掉了什么。*Running* her eye *down* the page, she caught sight of another mistake. 她用眼睛扫了一下那一页,便看到了另外一处错误。

NOTE **1.** 当本短语用作及物性动词短语,所带的宾语为代词时,该代词须置于本短语的动词和副词中间。

2. 本短语可转化为复合词 run-down,意为"(军备等)裁减;简要的总结,纲要;(钟表等)停了的;精疲力竭的"。

run for *vt.* 【不可分性动词短语】(主要用于美国英语中,无被动语态形式) offer oneself for election to (a group) or for (a position)参加竞选:Three US senators were *running for* president in 2008: two

Democrats and a Republican. 当时有三位美国参议员参加2008年的总统竞选：两位民主党人和一位共和党人。So no one is permitted under the present Constitution of Russian Federation to *run for* a third successive term. 因此，按现有的俄罗斯联邦宪法，任何人都不允许参加竞选三连任。

run in *vt.* & *vi.* make a brief, informal visit(to a place)短暂过访(某处)：*Run in* and see me this evening. 今晚顺便来看我吧。The neighbor boy *ran in* our house for a minute to see Bob's new model plane. 邻居家的男孩到我家来看了一眼鲍勃的新模型飞机。

—*vt.*【可分性动词短语】❶(英国英语用法，常用进行时态) drive (a new vehicle) slowly and carefully so that you do not damage the engine 对(新车辆)进行磨合试车：Don't expect me to get you home quickly — I'm *running* my car *in*. 别指望我很快就把你送到家，我正在对我这辆车进行试车。We had better allow plenty of time, as I can't drive fast, the car isn't *run in* yet. 我们的时间最好充裕些，因为我不能开快车；这辆车子还没有磨合好呢。❷(非正式用语，常用被动语态形式)(of the police) find (a criminal) and take (him or her) to a police station; arrest (指警方)发现并拘留(犯罪分子)：The police *ran* him *in* for driving without a license. 警察因他无照驾车而拘留了他。My friend was *run in* for dangerous driving on Saturday night. 我的朋友因在星期六晚上危险驾车而被拘留。If you throw eggs at the speaker, you are liable to get *run in* for causing a breach of peace. 如果你朝讲演者投掷鸡蛋，你就会因扰乱治安的行为而被拘留。

NOTE **1.** 当本短语用作及物性动词短语，所带的宾语为代词时，该代词须置于本短语的动词和副词中间。

2. 本短语可转化为复合词 run-in，意为"口角，争吵；(发动机)试车"。

run into *vt.* ❶(非正式用语，常用一般时态) meet (someone) when you did not expect to 意外地遇到(某人)：Do you know whom I *ran into* while I was on holiday in Scotland? 你知道我在苏格兰休假期间遇到谁了？I *ran into* Mary in the bookshop yesterday morning. 我昨天上午在书店与玛丽不期而遇。❷(cause to) strike forcefully (usually something) with one's vehicle, etc. (使)(车辆等)撞上(某物)：Two trains *ran into* one another. 有两列火车相撞。He *ran into* a taxi at the zebra crossing. 他驾车在斑马线人行横道处撞上了一辆出租汽车。Joe lost control of his car and *ran* it *into* a tree. 乔失去了对汽车的控制，使其撞在了一棵树上。The front part of the boat *ran into* the bank. 小船的船头撞上了河堤。❸unexpectedly begin to experience (problems or difficulties); get into (a difficult or unpleasant situation); (cause to) meet (debt, etc.)意外地遇到(问题或困难)；陷于(困境)；(使)负债：The store agreed to sell their computers after it *ran into* financial problems. 该店遭遇了经济困难后才同意出售他们的电脑产品。In that way the company will only *run into* trouble. 那样的话，该公司只会陷入麻烦之中。The new project of the government has *run into* strong resistance from the country's youth. 政府的这项新项目遭到国内年轻人的强烈反对。His wild extravagance is *running* his family *into* the red. 他挥霍无度使其家庭负债累累。❹(无被动语态形式，常用一般时态) reach (a particular number or amount of money)(数量)达到;(款额)总计:The number of people killed on the highways during holidays *runs into* hundreds. 假日期间,在公路交通事故中丧生的人数达几百人之多。His latest novel has *run into* three editions within the year. 他那部新小说在年内已经出了三版。They had debts *running into* thousands of pounds. 他们所负的债务达到数千英镑。

run off *v.* ❶(cause to) go away or leave (a place) quickly, as by running 跑开,迅速脱离,(使)匆匆离去:On hearing the gunshot, the man jumped to his feet and *ran off*. 那名男子听到枪声后撒腿便跑。A high-speed passenger train *ran off* the rails, colliding with another, leaving many people killed and injured. 一辆高速行驶的旅客列车脱轨并与另一辆旅客列车相撞,致多人伤亡。Dad tried to *run off* some people who were camping behind our house, but they wouldn't leave. 爸爸试图赶走在我们房后宿营的那些人,但他们却不肯离去。If you don't quiet down, he'll *run* you *off* the office. 如果你不安静下来,他就会把你赶出办公室。❷(英国英语用法)(of a liquid)(cause to) flow away freely (使)(液体)流出:Melted snow *ran off* the mountain every spring, flooding the rivers. 每年春季,融化了的雪水从山上流下来,使河水泛滥。When the temperature reaches melting point, the metal *runs off* as a liquid and flows into special moulds. 当温度到达熔点时,金属就成为液体而流出并进入特制的模具中。The oil in your engine looks very dirty, get the garage to *run* it *off*. 你的发动机里的油看上去很脏,到修车厂去把它引流出来。❸(非正式用语) produce (copies of a piece of writing) by using a machine 复印:He has *run off* 200 copies of the test paper on the duplicating machine. 他已在复印机上复印了200份试卷。Could you *run* me *off* five copies of this article, please? 请把这篇文章给我复印五份,好吗?❹recite or write (words) quickly and easily from memory (流利而轻易地)背出,写出:Can you *run off* a good article within half an hour? 你能在半小时内写出一篇好文章来吗?❺get rid of (unwanted weight) by running (用跑步)减少(体重):You're too fat, try and *run off* all those excess pounds. 你太胖了,试一试跑步减肥吧。

NOTE 1. 当本短语用作及物性动词短语,所带的宾语为代词时,该代词须置于本短语的动词和副词中间。

2. 本短语可转化为复合词 runoff, 意为"(雨水、融雪等的)径流量;决赛;决定性竞选"。

run off with *vt.* ❶secretly go away (with someone of the opposite sex), in order to live with or marry him or her 与(异性者)私奔:Mary has *run off with* her music teacher. 玛丽和她的音乐教师私奔了。He has *run off with* a woman he met at the office. 他和他在办公室认识的一个女人私奔了。❷steal and carry away (something) 偷走,带走(某物):Someone has *run off with* the keys to my safe. 有人偷走了我保险柜的钥匙。The so-called warm-hearted woman *ran off with* her bag. 那个所谓的好心肠女人拿着她的包跑了。The dog *ran off with* my shoe. 狗把我的一只鞋叼走了。

run on *vi.* (主要用于美国英语中,非正式用语) ❶talk for a long time about something in a way that is boring 喋喋不休地讲,滔滔不绝地说:She is very talkative, and will *run on* for hours about

R

her trip to Canada if permitted. 她十分健谈，如果得到允许，她会连续几个小时喋喋不休地讲她的加拿大之行。He kept *running on* and on, telling me the same story repeatedly. 他继续反复地向我讲那同样的故事。*On* he *ran*, until most of his audience was restless with impatience. 他滔滔不绝地往下讲，直到大多数听众感到厌烦方才住口。❷continue for longer than expected or planned 持续，继续下去：This disease can *run on* for months. 这种疾病能持续几个月之久。The concert *ran on* until eleven o'clock. 音乐会一直持续到 11 点才结束。I hope this meeting doesn't *run on* too long. 我希望会别开得太久。

run out *vi.* ❶go outside by running 跑出去：We were afraid that the house might cave in so we started to *run out*. 我们怕屋顶塌陷，就都跑了出来。When the loud bang was heard, lots of people *ran out* of their houses to see what had happened. 听到响亮的爆炸声后，许多人都跑出家门去看发生了什么。❷（of an official agreement or document）stop being legal at a certain date; expire 到期，不再有效：My passport is going to *run out* in a few weeks. 我的护照再有几个星期就要到期了。The policeman told the driver that his license had *run out*. 警察告诉驾车司机，他的执照已经过期。His term of office has *run out*. 他的任期已满。❸be completely used up; use all one's supplies; have no more （of something） left 耗完供应，用完，没有了：Our food soon *ran out*. 我们的食品很快就吃完了。What will you do if the battery on your mobile phone *runs out* when you are all alone? 如果只有你孤零零一人，而且你的手机又没电了，那你该怎么办？He has lived through countless dangers but time may be *running out* for him. 尽管曾经躲过了无数劫难，但是他弥留在世上的时间也许不多了。There's been tremendous demand for that brand. We've *run out*. 那一品牌需求量特大。我们已经没货了。My patience *ran out* on him a long time ago. 我早就对他失去了耐性。❹project 伸出，突伸：That is a pier *running out* into the sea. 那是一个突伸到海中的码头。

NOTE 本短语可转化为复合词 run-out，意为"逃开，避开"。

run out of *vt.* ❶（非正式用语，常用一般时态） force or compel （someone） to leave （a place）把（某人）赶出（某地）：The government had wanted to *run* him *out of* the country. 政府曾想要把他驱逐出境。The mayor has warned that all vagrants will be *run out of* the city. 市长警告说，所有的流浪者都将被驱逐出城。❷（of someone） have no more of （something） left; lack （something）用完，缺乏（某物）：We *ran out of* gas right in the middle of the main street and blocked traffic. 我们的汽车正好在主要大街的中央没油了，这堵塞了交通。We're *running out of* time. 我们的时间不多了。He has *run out of* his inspiration. 他的灵感匮乏了。The Turkish President said that Ankara is *running out of* patience and will not tolerate any terrorist activities against Turkey. 土耳其总统称，安卡拉已经失去耐性，不能再容忍任何针对土耳其的恐怖活动。

run over *v.* ❶（of a liquid or its container） flow over （something）; overflow （某种液体）溢出，（容器）满出：The river is *running over* its banks and we shall be flooded. 河水正在漫过堤岸，我们要遭受水灾了。Billy forgot he had left the water on, and the bath *ran over*. 比利忘

记了水龙头还开着，于是浴缸中的水满出来了。❷(常用被动语态形式，常用一般时态)(of a vehicle or its driver) knock down (a person or animal) or roll over them (车辆)撞倒……，轧过……：He *ran over* a five-year-old boy as he was driving back home. 他在开车回家的路上撞倒了一个五岁的小男孩。A man tried to *run* him *over*, but Fred luckily escaped. 一名男子企图轧死他，但弗雷德幸运地逃过了这一难。Tom was *run over* by a car outside his house. 汤姆在他家外面被小汽车撞了。They wouldn't let their cat outside for fearing that it would get *run over*. 他们不让猫往外跑，是因为害怕它被车轧着。❸practise or rehearse (what you are going to say in a speech, performance, etc.) 温习(演讲稿)；演练(节目)：Mary *ran over* in her mind what she was going to say at the meeting. 玛丽把她在会上要说的话在脑中又重温了一下。Let's *run over* the second act again. 让我们再把第二幕演练一遍。❹(causeto) pass over (something) in order to check through it (使)浏览，审视：Could you *run* your eyes *over* this list? 你能浏览一遍这份名单吗？Let's *run* quickly *over* the procedure of the experiment so as to do it better. 咱们再把实验的程序看一遍，以便做得更好。Just *run over* these proofs for me as I'm in a hurry. 替我看一下这些校样，我急着要。

NOTE 当本短语用作及物性动词短语，所带的宾语为代词时，该代词须置于本短语的动词和副词中间。

run roughshod over ⇨ **ride roughshod over**

run short *vi.* (used for saying that you have used almost all of a particular thing and there is not much left) be in short supply 几乎用完，缺乏：(常与 of 连用) The party had just begun and we were already *running short* of beer. 聚会刚刚开始，我们的啤酒就已快喝完了。The ship *ran short* of fresh water. 这艘船缺淡水。Supplies were *running short* as winter came on. 随着冬天的来临，我们的供应品紧缺了。

run the risk ⇨ **take a (the) risk**

run through *vt.* ❶(常用一般时态，常与 with 连用) push (a sword) through (someone's body)(用剑)刺穿(某人的身体)：I *ran* my sword *through* his body. 我用剑刺穿了他的身体。He attacked the post with grenades and *ran* the survivors *through* with the bayonet. 他用手榴弹袭击了哨所，并用刺刀刺死了没炸死的人。The man's chest was *run through* and soon died. 那名男子的胸部被刺穿，很快就死了。❷(无被动语态形式)(of an idea, piece of news, or emotion) pass quickly through (something or a group of people)(某种想法)闪过……，(某一消息)迅速传遍……，(某种情绪)感染……：An alarming thought kept *running through* my mind. 一个令人惊恐的念头一直在我脑海里闪现。The news *ran through* the village. 这个消息传遍了全村。Excitement *ran through* the audience. 听众都兴奋了起来。❸(无被动语态形式，用一般时态)spread through (something) 贯穿：A keen humor *runs through* his writings. 在他的文章中贯穿着一种辛辣的幽默。This is a deep-rooted prejudice that *runs through* our society. 这是普遍存在于我们社会中的一种根深蒂固的偏见。❹read (something) quickly 匆匆阅读，把……粗略过目：I'll just *run through* the names and make sure everyone's here. 我只匆匆地看一下名单，确认是不是人人都到

了。*Run through* your notes the night before the examination. 在考试的前一天晚上把你做的笔记过目一下。❺(cause to) act, perform (especially at rehearsal); practise (something such as words or music) from beginning to end without stop (使)从头至尾地排练,练习(歌词或曲子): You'll have to *run through* the whole play at seven o'clock. 你们得在七点钟把全场戏排练一遍。I'd like to *run* you *through* that scene you have with Mary. 我想让你们把和玛丽合演的那场戏排练一下。The school band will have to stay late to *run through* the pieces for the concert. 校乐队的得晚走一会儿,练习一下将在音乐会上演奏的几支曲子。❻spend (all one's money) quickly and especially wastefully 迅速花掉,挥霍掉(某人所有的钱): How can you have *run through* so much money so quickly? 你怎么能这么快就把那么多钱花掉了呢? He soon *ran through* the money he had won at poker. 他不久就把玩扑克赢来的钱挥霍一空。The money inherited from his father was quickly *run through*. 从他父亲那里继承下来的钱很快就挥霍掉了。

R

NOTE 1. 当本短语的宾语为代词时,该代词须置于本短语的动词和副词中间。

2. 本短语可转化为复合词 run-through, 意为"浏览;概要;从头至尾的排练"。

run to *vt.*【不可分性动词短语】(无被动语态形式) ❶(用一般时态)(of something) reach (a particular amount or size)达到(某一数目或规模): It is said that the cost of developing the new project will *run to* two billion dollars. 据说开发那个新项目的成本将高达 20 亿美元。The transcript *runs to* 1,500 pages. 这份文字记录长达 1 500 页。❷(主要用于英国英语中,常用于否定句中,用一般时态,不用进行时态) afford to buy; have enough money to cover or pay for (a particular thing) 买得起,(钱)足够买……之用: I don't think we can *run to* a new computer at the moment. 我认为咱们眼下还买不起一台新电脑。My income won't *run to* buying a second car. 凭我的收入,还买不起第二辆车。With all this money left, I'm afraid we can't *run to* central heating in all rooms. 我们剩余的这些钱恐怕不足以把所有房间都装上中央空调了。❸ go to ask (someone) for help, especially when you should not need their help (尤指在无须求助的情况下)跑向(某人)求助: She *runs to* the doctor with every little pain. 她有一点点疼痛便往医生那里跑。Aren't you a little old to *run* home *to* your mother? 总往家跑要你妈妈帮助,你还没长大吗?

NOTE 当本短语作"达到(某一数目或规模)"解时,同义短语是 amount to。

run up *v.* ❶raise (a flag) to the top of a pole 升起(旗帜): They *ran up* the Union Jack. 他们升起了英国的国旗。They *ran* the national flag *up* on the Queen's birthday. 他们在女王生日那天升起了国旗。Then the white flag was *run up*, the enemy had surrendered. 紧接着,白旗就挂了出来,敌人投降了。❷ increase sharply; cause (an amount) to rise quickly 迅速上升,迅速提高(数量): The price of gas is *running up* all over the world. 全世界的汽油价格都在上涨。The sales of the book *ran up*. 这本书的销售量激增。After having bought these books, Karl *ran up* a big bill at the bookstore. 买了这些书后,卡尔在书店账单上的金额迅速上升。They *run up* costs unnecessarily.

他们不必要地提高了成本。❸allow (something such as a debt) to increase or accumulate (债务)上升,积债:His debts *ran up* alarmingly. 他的债务惊人地上升。His wife *ran up* a large bill in the beauty parlor. 他的妻子积欠了美容院一大笔账。❹ put together or make (something) hastily; sew (something such as a dress or a skirt) quickly together 迅速地造好;(指缝纫)赶做:We *ran* that shed *up* in two days, but it soon collapsed. 我们在两天内就把那棚屋赶造起来了。但它很快就倒掉了。Mary *ran up* a dress for the party on her sewing machine. 玛丽用缝纫机赶做出了一件参加聚会穿的连衣裙。

NOTE 本短语可转化为复合词 run-up,意为"激增,猛涨;(事情的)序幕;(跳远等的)助跑"。

run up against *vt.*【不可分性动词短语】❶hit (something) by running 撞上(某物):The car *ran up against* the tree. 那辆汽车撞到了树上。❷(非正式用语,常用一般时态) encounter or come face to face with (something such as a problem or difficulty) 遇到(问题或困难):We *ran up against* a few problems collecting the money. 我们在筹措这笔款的过程中遇到了一些问题。Whenever he *ran up against* difficulties, they all gave him encouragement. 每当他遇到困难的时候,他们都给予他鼓励。The same opposition had been *run up against* when we tried to introduce the measures. 当我们要推行那些措施时,遭遇到了同样的反对。❸(非正式用语,常用一般时态) meet (someone who is difficult to deal with) 遇到(难以对付的人):England *ran up against* and lost to Portugal 1∶3 Saturday and was knocked out of the World Cup quarterfinals. 英格兰在星期六的世界杯足球赛上遭遇并以 1∶3 输给了葡萄牙,被淘汰出四分之一决赛。He's the cleverest speaker I've ever *run up against*. 他是我所遇到的最为聪明的讲演者。

rush at *vt.*【不可分性动词短语】❶move quickly towards (someone), especially in order to attack him or her (尤指为袭击而)向(某人)冲去:We *rushed at* the guard and captured his gun. 我们突然冲向那名卫兵并缴下了他的枪。Two dogs *rushed at* me, growling and baring their teeth, and scared me to death. 两条狗龇着牙哼叫着向我冲了过来,吓得我要死。❷do (something) in a hurry, often too quickly or without enough care 仓促地做(某事):You tend to *rush at* things. 你总是仓促行事。

rush hour *n.*(常用单数形式) the time of day when there are a lot of cars on the road because most people are traveling to or from work (上、下班时)交通拥挤的时间,交通高峰时段:The bomb exploded in the middle of *rush hour* traffic, turned cars into fires and sent metal flying hundreds of yards away. 炸弹正值交通拥挤的时间爆炸,多辆汽车起火,金属部件飞出数百码远。Statistics shows the city's traffic pressure during the *rush hour* has been relatively reduced. 统计数字表明,市区交通高峰时段的交通压力已相对减轻。They left work early for home to avoid the *rush hour*. 他们提前下班回家,以避开交通拥挤时间。

rush into *vt.* ❶(of someone or something such as liquid) enter (a space) hastily (指人)跑进,冲入;(指水等)流入:A schoolboy *rushed into* a burning house to save a little boy's life. 一名男同学冲进正在燃烧的房子去抢救一个小男孩。Two persons were detained for organizing dozens of people to try to *rush into* and protest in the government building. 有两人因纠集几十人试图冲入政府大楼搞抗议而被拘留。You turn the switch and the water *rushed into* the fields by itself. 你扭动开关,水就会流入田地之中。❷(cause to) do (something) too quickly without thinking about it carefully (未经仔细考虑地)匆忙行事、催促: Don't *rush into* marriage, you might regret it later. 不要草率结婚,不然你以后会后悔的。Don't let anybody *rush* you *into* joining; think it over. 不要别人一催促你就加入,再考虑考虑。I was *rushed into* buying these fur boots. 我被催促着买下了这皮靴。

rush out *vi.* ❶hurry outside 匆匆跑出: On hearing the explosion a lot of people inside the building *rushed out*. 听到爆炸声,楼里的很多人都跑了出去。❷(常与 from 连用)jump out(from a hiding place) (从隐蔽处)突然跃出: The attackers *rushed out* from the bushes. 几名袭击者突然从灌木丛中跃出。

—*vt.* quickly produce (a document or something for people to buy)赶写(文件);赶制(商品): A statement was *rushed out*. 匆匆起草了一份声明。The publishers *rushed out* a paperback edition of the book. 出版社赶印出了这部书的平装版本。They *rushed out* 1,000 cheap copies of the princess's wedding dress. 他们照着王妃的结婚礼服赶制了 1 000 件廉价仿制品。These bicycles have been *rushed out* and are not up to our usual standard. 这些自行车是粗制滥造的,达不到我们一般的标准。

rush through *vt.* 【可分性动词短语】❶pass (something such as a law) through hastily 匆匆通过(法律等): The bill was *rushed through* with no further discussion by the end of the session. 该项法案在会议结束前没有经过进一步讨论就匆匆通过了。Government members are trying to *rush* the tax cuts *through* before the next election. 政府成员企图在下次选举之前仓促通过减税法。❷complete (a job) in a shorter time than usual 匆匆赶完(某项工作): We'll try to *rush* the contract *through* before Saturday. 我们要争取在星期六之前完成这项合同。The farmers had *rushed through* the harvest before the rain came. 农民们赶在下雨之前匆匆收完了庄稼。

NOTE 当本短语的宾语为代词时,该代词须置于本短语的动词和副词中间。

rush to *vt.* (cause to) hurry towards (someone or something) (使)急忙赶往,送往: Hours after the powerful earthquake occurred on Monday, the Chinese Premier *rushed to* Sichuan to direct the disaster relief work. 星期一的强烈地震发生后几小时,中国总理便赶赴四川指挥救灾工作。American pop star Michael Jackson was announced dead by doctors Thursday afternoon after being *rushed to* a Los Angeles hospital. 星期四下午,美国流行歌星迈克尔·杰克逊在紧急送往洛杉矶的一家医院后被医生宣布死亡。Ambulances *rushed to* the site of explosion, and carried several people away to hospital. 救护车迅速赶到了爆炸地点,把几个人送往医院。Several other countries were expected to *rush* troops *to* the island nation after the emergency meeting of the UN Security Council. 在联合国安理会的紧急会议后,有几个国家将向该岛国急速派遣军队。

S s

safe and sound *adj.* & *adv.* (of someone) not hurt or harmed at all after being in danger; (of something) completely undamaged (指人)平安无事,安然无恙,(指物)安全无损:The next morning, the kidnapped Chinese worker returned *safe and sound*. 次日上午,那名被绑架的中国工人平安返回。We are very glad to see them *safe and sound* after their dangerous adventure. 我们非常高兴地看到他们历险之后安然无恙。The travelers were found *safe and sound*. 旅行者们都安全无恙。The fragile china survived the bumpy journey *safe and sound*. 那批易碎的瓷器经过颠簸的旅程仍安然无损。

safeguard against/from *vt.* 【可分性动词短语】(常用一般时态) prevent or protect (something or someone) from (being harmed or having problems)防止,避免,保护……不受……:We have to *safeguard against* friction leading to an immediate equipment failure. 我们要防止由于摩擦而发生的瞬间设备故障。Take this medicine regularly, it will *safeguard* you *against* catching cold. 按时服用此药,就会避免感冒。This agreement will *safeguard* the newspapers *from* government interference. 这项协议将保护各家报纸免遭政府干预。

sandwich between *vt.* (非正式用语,用被动语态形式) ❶be in a small or tight space between (two things that are larger or two people)把……紧紧挤在中间:Our car was *sandwiched between* two big trucks, almost touching them. 我们的小汽车被夹在了两辆大卡车中间,几乎与它们擦肩而过。The tiny kingdom was *sandwiched between* Austria and Czech Republic. 这个小王国位于奥地利和捷克共和国之间。She was *sandwiched* in her airplane seat *between* two fat men. 她在飞机上坐在了两名肥胖男子的中间。❷face a difficult choice between (two duties or responsibilities)面临(两种责任或义务)之间的艰难选择:Many women are *sandwiched between* the needs of children and parents. 许多妇女都面临着抚养子女和赡养老人两种需要的选择。

satisfied with *adj.* being pleased or happy with (what has happened or what you have achieved)对……满意的:The manager, said he is *satisfied with* his eight years in office. 经理说他对自己任职八年的表现感到满意。The Chinese people are far wealthier than they were a decade ago, but some of them are not very *satisfied with* their quality of life. 中国人比十年前富裕多了,但有些人对生活质量却不是很满意。

NOTE 本短语的反义短语是 dissatisfied with。

S

save for *vt.* 【可分性动词短语】put (something such as money or a supply) away until (a certain time or occasion) or for (a purpose)保留(或节省)……以备后用: We must *save* the rest of the milk *for* tomorrow. 我们得把其余的牛奶留待明天喝。*Save* your strength *for* hard work you'll have to do later. 你要保存体力以应付将要做的繁重工作。I'm trying to *save* as much of my income as I can *for* my old age. 我在尽量地把我的收入积攒下来,留待养老。We're *saving for* a new car. 我们在攒钱好买新车。

save from *vt.* 【可分性动词短语】❶make (someone or something) safe from (danger, harm, or destruction)救出,抢救,挽救: A policeman friend of mine *saved* a young man *from* drowning, and he felt it was part of his job. 我的一位警察朋友救了一个溺水的年轻人,而他认为这是他分内的工作。Houston Rockets center Yao Ming failed to *save* the Rockets *from* the Minnesota Timberwolves in yesterday's game. 在昨天的比赛中,休斯敦火箭队的中锋姚明没能从明尼苏达森林狼队口中救出火箭队。Luckily our precious records were *saved from* the fire. 幸运的是,我们的珍贵记录从大火中抢救了出来。❷(常用一般时态)prevent (something or someone) from (having or doing something bad)使免于,避免: They hoped to *save* their marriage *from* failure by having another baby. 他们希望通过再生一个孩子来避免婚姻的破裂。A brush with a long handle will *save* you *from* having to bend down to clean the floor. 长柄的扫帚可以免去你弯腰扫地之苦。

save up *v.* ❶regularly put (money) in a bank or invest it so that you can use it later 储蓄,攒(钱): She's *saving up* for a new bike. 她在攒钱买自行车。They are *saving up* to buy the plane tickets for their holiday abroad. 他们在攒钱好买去国外度假的机票。Wise people *save* some money *up*, instead of spending it all. 聪明人储存一些钱,而不是把它全部花光。He had some money *saved up*. 他攒了一些钱。❷collect (a set of things) and keep them for a particular purpose 收集(一套物品): You can *save up* the tokens to get a prize. 你可以把这套代价券收集起来好得奖。

NOTE 本短语的同义短语是 lay aside。

savings account *n.* an account with a bank that you can deposit money in and withdraw money from 银行账户: Now there are many different types of *savings accounts*, but not all will be the right type for you. 现在有多种类别的银行账户,但并不是所有的种类都适合于您。Some banks deploy tricks, which you need to look at when applying and opening a *savings account*. 有些银行设置圈套,你在申请开户之前需要做些考虑。

NOTE 本短语中的复数性名词 savings 作"储蓄金"解,用作定语时,仍须用复数形式。例如: savings bank 储蓄银行, savings bank book 储蓄存折, savings bonds 储蓄公债, savings certificate 储蓄存单, savings deposits 储蓄存款。

say about/on *vt.* 【可分性动词短语】(常用一般时态) express (something) in words about (something or someone) 对……说些什么: Did she *say* anything *about* your new book? 对这本新书她说什么了吗? What today's college students *say about* conducting research in the digital age? 当今的大学生对在数字时代

里如何做研究有何评论？Did your mother have much to *say about* your being so late home last night? 你昨晚很晚才回家，你妈妈对此没少絮叨吧？I think that Mary must have *said* something *about* me to you. 我想玛丽肯定和你说了一些有关我的事情。

say farewell to ⇨ bid farewell to

scarcely … when *conj.* (used for emphasizing that the first event was followed immediately by the second) as soon as 刚一……就……：*Scarcely* had his car drawn to a halt *when* armed police surrounded it. 他的车刚一停下，武警就将其团团围住。We had *scarcely* dropped off to sleep *when* the doorbell began to ring. 我们刚要合眼入睡时，门铃就响了起来。*Scarcely* had he begun to speak *when* the audience interrupted him. 他刚一说话，就被听众打断了。

NOTE 1. 当 scarcely 用于句首时，主句中的主谓结构要构成倒装。例如：

> *Scarcely* had I arrived *when* I had a new problem to cope with.
> 我刚刚到达就有了一个新的问题需要处理。

2. 本短语所在的主句的动作发生在 when 所引导的从句动作之前，主句的谓语动词用过去完成时，从句的谓语动词用一般过去时。

3. 本短语与 as soon as 意义相同，都表示"一……就"，在句中起连接作用。在使用中，as soon as 这三个词不可分开，而本短语则不能连在一起使用。另外，as soon as 更为常用。

4. 本短语中的 scarcely 可被 barely, hardly 替换，构成的短语与本短语意义和用法相同。

scare away/off *vt.*【可分性动词短语】❶(非正式用语) make (a person or animal) so frightened that they run away 把……吓跑：Having been caught in Hangzhou, the man said he was a HIV carrier in order to *scare away* the police. 在杭州被抓后，为了吓走警察，这名男子自称是个艾滋病病毒携带者。Not many people come to my house. I think our bulldog *scares* them *off*. 没多少人来我家做客。我想，是我们那条斗牛犬把他们吓住了。The attacker was *scared away* when the woman started to scream. 袭击者被那名妇女的叫喊声吓跑了。If you make a noise you'll easily *scare off* the birds. 如果你弄出一点声响，就会很容易把鸟吓跑。❷make (someone) feel so frightened or worried that he or she does not do (something they had planned to do) 使(某人)不敢做(计划要做的事情)：The city's high murder rate has *scared away* tourists. 该市的杀人案发案率高，使人们不敢到那里去旅游。The high price is *scaring away* possible buyers. 高昂的价格使有意购物的顾客望而生畏。I don't think that revealing your past to your boyfriend will *scare* him *off*. 我认为把你过去的事情透露给你的男友不会使他离你而去。

NOTE 当本短语的宾语为代词时，该代词须置于本短语的动词和副词中间。

scoop up *vt.*【可分性动词短语】take up or gather (something) or pick it up using something such as a spoon or your curved hand 舀起，铲起，拿起：You may use these small buckets to *scoop up* the water. 你可以用这些小桶舀水。The machine *scoops up* the earth and dumps it over there. 铲土机将土铲起，然后将其倒在了那边。He *scooped* the books *up* off

S

the floor. 他一下就把书从地板上捡了起来。

NOTE 当本短语的宾语为代词时,该代词须置于本短语的动词和副词中间。

scores of *adj.* a large number of (people or things)许多的:The fire was put out and *scores of* fire fighters are continuing to work at the site. 大火已被扑灭,但仍有许多消防队员在火场工作着。In the last few months, terrorists carried out *scores of* shootings and suicide bombings, killing and wounding hundreds of people. 在过去的几个月中,恐怖分子制造了多次枪击和自杀性爆炸事件,致使数百人死伤。

NOTE 本短语中的名词 score 必须用复数形式。scores 本身就表示"很多",后接 of 短语,表示具体说明的对象。在英语中,许多复数名词加 of 都有与 scores of 同样的用法。例如:

> We received *dozens/hundreds of* applications for the job.
> 我们收到了好几十/好几百份要求做这份工作的申请。
> After *days/weeks/months/years of* hard work he succeeded.
> 经过好几天/好几个星期/好几个月/好几年的艰苦工作,他成功了。

S

scramble for *vt.* 【不可分性动词短语】hurry or try very hard to get(something or someone), often competing with other people 争抢,争夺:I saw young people *scrambling for* pamphlets on AIDS prevention in front of an office building on December 1, the World AIDS Day. 我看到年轻人在 12 月 1 日"世界艾滋病日"那天在一座办公楼前争抢防治艾滋病的宣传册。Many companies today are *scrambling for* skilled workers. 当前,各公司都在争夺技术工作人员。

screw up *vt.* 【可分性动词短语】❶fasten or tighten with a screw or screws 用螺丝拧住:They have *screwed up* the door so that it cannot be opened. 他们用螺丝把门钉住,使它不能打开。*Screw* the board *up* firmly to the window frame. 把这块板子用螺丝牢牢地拧在窗户框上。❷make (a piece of paper) into a smaller shape by squeezing or twisting it, usually when you are throwing it away 把(纸)揉成一团:Peter *screwed up* the letter into a ball and threw it onto the floor. 彼得把信揉成一团扔在了地板上。Several pages had been *screwed up* and tossed in the wastepaper basket. 好几页纸被揉成了团扔进了废纸篓中。❸(非正式用语)cause (something) to be spoiled; make (something) fail or get it badly wrong and cause disorder 把(某物)弄坏;把(事情)搞糟:You can't open the window because it *screws up* the air conditioning. 你不能开窗子,那会损坏空调的。It was such a simple plan, how could you have *screwed* it *up*? 这是一个很简单的计划,你怎么会把它搞得一团糟呢? Don't ask them to organize the trip, they'll only *screw* everything *up*. 别让他们组织这次旅行,他们只会把一切搞乱。❹(of something) cause (someone) to become confused, nervous, unhappy, etc. 使(某人)不知所措;使(某人)紧张;使(某人)不幸福:(非正式用语) He's divorced, and he is really *screwed up* about his relationships with women. 他离过婚,所以他对自己如何同女士相处确实感到不知所措。Waiting for an operation tends to *screw* you *up*. 等着做手术往往会使你感到紧张。Divorce doesn't necessarily *screw* your kids *up*. 离婚不一定就会使你的孩子不幸福。❺force (oneself) to be brave; gather up (one's courage, etc.) for doing something difficult 迫使(自己)勇敢,鼓起(勇气等): The small boy *screwed up* his courage and went upstairs in the dark. 那小男孩鼓足了勇气,摸黑走上了楼。Don't stand there, *screw up* your courage and jump! 别呆立在那里。鼓起你的勇气来,跳! *Screw* your nerve *up*, and tell your boss what you think of him. 鼓起你的勇气来,告诉你的上司你对他有什么看法。❻tighten (the muscles of your face or eyes) to form wrinkles, because you are in pain or because the light is too bright 皱紧(脸),眯起(眼): His face *screwed up* in agony. 他疼得皱起脸皮。Janet *screwed* her face *up* into an expression of the utmost seriousness. 珍妮特绷起脸,神情极为严肃。His face was *screwed up* in a funny fashion. 他的脸扭成了一副滑稽的模样。She *screwed up* her eyes in the bright sunlight. 在强烈的阳光下,她眯起了双眼。

NOTE 1. 当本短语的宾语为代词时,该代词须置于本短语的动词和副词中间。

2. 本短语可转化为复合词 screw-up, 意为"弄糟事情的人;弄糟的事,混乱局面"。

scrub out *vt. & vi.* remove (a mark, etc. which is lodged in a fabric, etc.) by rubbing it hard using a stiff brush, soap and water 擦掉,擦净: Remove the split ink at once, or else you won't be able to *scrub* it *out* later. 马上把撒上的墨水擦掉,否则待一会儿就擦不掉了。As soon as they moved in, they started to *scrub out* the rooms. 他们一搬进去就开始把各个房间擦干净。—*vt.* (非正式用语) cancel (a future event, or something which affects it); remove (something) from consideration or from a list 取消,作废: The match had to be *scrubbed out* because of the heavy rain. 比赛因大雨而被迫取消。The researchers had to *scrub out* the first set of results and started again. 研究人员不得不把初得的结果作废,并重新开始。

NOTE 当本短语用作及物性动词短语,所带的宾语为代词时,该代词须置于本短语的动词和副词中间。

seal off *vt.*【可分性动词短语】❶prevent (an opening, object or area) from having its usual use by closing it 封闭(通道);封存(某物): The gas pipe has been *sealed off* to prevent escapes. 为防止泄漏,煤气管道已封闭。Although these chemical weapons were *sealed off* in a warehouse, they were in danger of leakage because of eroded containers. 虽然这些化学武器已封存在一个仓库中,但是由于容器腐蚀仍有泄漏的危险。❷prevent (people) from entering an area or building, often because it is dangerous 封锁(某一区域或建筑物): A column of smoke rose from the crash site in Tikrit, 175 km north of Baghdad, and US troops *sealed off* the area. 烟柱从巴格达以北175公里处提克里特的坠机现场滚滚升起。美军已把该地区封锁了起来。The whole area has been *sealed off* and demining experts have arrived at the scene. 整个地区已被封锁,排雷专家已到达现场。Soldiers there are going to *seal* the airport *off*. 那里的士兵将封锁机场。

NOTE 1. 当本短语的宾语为代词时,该代词须置于本短语的动词和副词中间。

2. 本短语的同义短语是 seal up。

seal up *vt.*【可分性动词短语】close (something) completely by sealing, so that nothing can get in or out 把(某物)密封,封闭,封存:Please read the letter over again before you *seal* it *up*. 请把信再看一遍之后再封上。US soldiers *sealed up* the underground hole where former Iraqi President Saddam was captured to prevent it from becoming a tourist attraction. 美军士兵把伊拉克前总统萨达姆被捕前藏身的地洞封死,以避免该洞成为名胜景点。Scientists put the virus into the box, safely *sealed up* in tubes. 科学家们把病毒安全地封存在管内,放在了箱子里。

NOTE 当本短语的宾语为代词时,该代词须置于本短语的动词和副词中间。

search after *vt.*【不可分性动词短语】try to gain (something that one desires such as a quality), as by inner enquiry 寻求:Many people have been *searching after* peace of mind, often with little success. 许多人一直在寻求一个安宁的心境,但往往都不成功。Scientists throughout the world are *searching after* a cure that will wipe out cancer. 全世界的科学家们都在寻求能根除癌症的疗法。

search for *vt.*(一般不用被动语态形式)try to find (something or someone) by looking carefully and thoroughly 找,寻找,搜寻:From January, policemen from Beijing Public Security Bureau started patrolling with police dogs at Tiananmen Square to *search for* dangerous goods. 北京市公安局的民警从 1 月份开始带警犬在天安门广场巡逻以搜寻危险品。Ten days have gone by since the earth shook here, but rescue workers are still *searching for* survivors in the rubble. 这里的地震已过去十天了,但救援人员仍然在瓦砾中搜寻幸存者。All his friends are helping him to *search* the woods *for* his little son. 他所有的朋友都在帮他搜索树林,寻找他的小儿子。

NOTE 本短语与 look for 均表示"寻找"之意。两者之间的区别见 look for。

Search me! *s.*(非正式用语)(used to emphasize that you do not know the answer to someone's question) I don't know 我不知道:"Why didn't she say anything?" "*Search me*!""她为什么一言不发?""我哪里知道?" "Where's John?" "*Search me*! I haven't seen him for weeks." "约翰在什么地方?""我哪里知道? 我都好几周没看到他了。"

NOTE 本短语用在回答别人提出的问题时强调不知道某事。比 "I don't know."有更深的内涵。

search out *vt.*【可分性动词短语】work hard in order to find (something or someone) by searching (竭力)找到,查出:It took me several weeks to *search out* the books that I wanted. 我花了好几周的时间去找我需要的那些书。With clever questioning the lawyer *searched out* the weaknesses in the witness's statement. 律师以巧妙的提问找到了证人证词中的弱点。Many people want jobs. They try to *search* them *out* every day. 许多人都想要工作,所以他们每天都在千方百计地寻找工作。How can we *search out* the right man for the job? 我们怎么才能找到适合做这项工作的人呢?

NOTE 当本短语的宾语为代词时,该代词须置于本短语的动词和副词中间。

search through *vt.*【不可分性动词短语】look in (a space) or among (things) to find something or someone 翻找,查找,

搜寻：I spent more than 10 minutes *searching through* the drawers for the key, and it was in my bag all the time. 我用了十多分钟翻抽屉找钥匙，可它却一直在我的包里。Police with dogs are *searching through* the woods for the missing child. 警察带着警犬搜索树林寻找失踪的儿童。My drawers were *searched through* thoroughly. 我的抽屉都翻遍了。

secede from *vt.*【不可分性动词短语】(正式用语，常用一般时态)(especially of part of a country) officially leave (the nation or large organization to which it belongs)(尤指国家的一部分)正式脱离，退出：There is likely to be civil war if the region tries to *secede from* the country. 如果该地区试图脱离国家，就可能有一场内战。We do not want to *secede from* the organization, but we will if we must. 我们并不想退出组织，但必要时我们也会退出。

second to none *adj.* the best; superior to anything or anyone else 最好的，一流的：As a footballer he is *second to none*. 作为一名足球运动员，他是最棒的。We provide a service that is *second to none*. 我们提供一流的服务。

see about *vt.*【不可分性动词短语】❶take care of; attend to (someone or something)照料，负责：I'll *see about* that boy as soon as I get back. 我一回来就去照料那男孩儿。The security guards *see about* locking up the building after office hours. 保安人员负责下班后把大楼锁好。❷inquire about (something or someone)打听，探询，调查：We must *see about* where we change trains. 我们得打听一下在哪里换车。I'll *see about* movie times and call you back. 我查询一下电影上映的时间，然后给你回电话。As for the second applicant, we will have to *see about* him, we'll check his past experience. 至于第二个申请人，我们有必要对他进行调查，弄清他过去的经历。❸(非正式用语) prepare or make arrangement for (something)准备，安排：It's time for me to *see about* lunch. 我该准备午饭去了。My secretary *sees about* my appointments. 我的秘书给我安排这些约会。Who is going to *see about* getting us a larger room for this big class? 这个大班应有一个大教室。这由谁来安排？❹deal with or make arrangements for (something)处理，安排：I must go and *see about* this job. 我得去把这工作处理一下。There are many things that have to be *seen about*. 这里有许多的事情需要处理。❺(仅用于口语中) consider (something) further; think over 进一步考虑，仔细思量：We can't give you an answer now, but we'll *see about* it. 我们现在不能给你答复，不过我们会考虑的。

see around/round *vt.* (cause to) visit (a place) by walking around it; tour; be shown (a place)(使)参观，游览，观看(某处)：What a beautiful house! I'd love to *see around* it. 多么漂亮的一所房子！我很想参观一下。Would you like to *see round* the old castle? 你想不想参观那座古堡？Mr Freeman will *see* the visitors *round* the imperial palace. 弗里曼先生将带领参观者游览皇宫。

NOTE see around 常用于美国国英语中，see round 常用于英国英语中。

see as *vt.*【可分性动词短语】(常用被动语态形式，用一般时态，不用进行时态) consider (something or someone) to be 认

为(某人或某物)为……: Americans *see* international terrorism *as* the most critical threat to the United States, according to a new poll. 根据一项新的民意调查显示,美国人把国际恐怖主义视为对美国最大的威胁。Olympic Games are *seen as* the most important sports meeting in the world. They are held every 4 years. 奥运会被看作是世界上最重要的体育运动会。其每隔四年举办一次。Parental divorce, drugs and alcohol, and youth unemployment were all *seen as* threatening adolescents well being. 父母离婚,吸毒和酗酒,以及青年失业都被认为是威胁青少年福祉的问题。

see into *vt.*【不可分性动词短语】❶examine or enquire into (something)调查,了解(某事): They have promised to *see into* the matter for us. 他们已答应为我们调查那件事情。It is about time these irregularities were *seen into*. 现在是必须对这些违规行为进行调查的时候了。I will *see into* this business. 这事我去了解一下。❷(无被动语态形式,用一般时态) understand or have knowledge of (someone or something)理解,明白,知道:I cannot *see into* his full meaning. 我无法完全理解他的意思。Suddenly the teacher *saw into* Linda's strange action. 老师突然弄明白了琳达奇怪的行为。I wish I could be able to *see into* people's hearts as you do. 我希望我也能像你那样看透别人心思。

see off *vt.*【可分性动词短语】❶go with (someone who is beginning a journey) to the airport, railway station, port, etc. that they are leaving from and say goodbye to him or her there (到机场、车站、港口等)与(某人)告别,为(某人)送行: After the inauguration, the Obama couple escorted Bush and his wife Laura to the helicopter and *saw* them *off*. 就职典礼结束后,奥巴马夫妇送布什及其夫人劳拉到直升机旁,并与他们告别。People gathered at the dock to *see off* the sailors. 人们都聚集在码头上为出航者们送行。The Indian guests were *seen off* at the airport by the Pakistan's Foreign Secretary. 巴基斯坦外交部长到机场为印度客人送行。❷(英国英语用法,非正式用语) make (someone or an animal) go away or leave a place, especially by chasing them 赶走(某人或动物): My dog *saw off* the children stealing our apples in the garden. 我的狗赶走了那些正在偷我们园中苹果的孩子们。If they go into my garden again, I'll *see* them *off* with my dogs! 如果他们再进我的园子,我就用狗赶走他们! A cat came into the back garden but our dog soon *saw* it *off*. 一只猫进了后花园,但我们的狗将其赶了出去。❸(英国英语用法) defeat (someone) in a game, fight, etc. 击败(对手);打退(敌人): Our team *saw off* their team by 98 points to 68. 我们队以 98 比 68 的比分战胜了他们队。There is no reason why they cannot *see off* that team. 他们没有任何理由不能击败那个团体。

NOTE **1.** 当本短语的宾语为代词时,该代词须置于本短语的动词和副词中间。

2. 当本短语作"为(某人)送行"解时,同义短语是 send off。

see out *vt.*【可分性动词短语】❶go with (someone who is leaving) to an outer door in order to say goodbye to him 把(某人)送到门口: A polite host *sees* his guest *out* after a party. 有礼貌的主人在

聚会后把客人送到门口。Miss Jones will *see you out* of the building. 琼斯小姐会把你送出楼门口。He was *seen out* by the mistress of the house. 他由这家女主人送到门口。❷(英国英语用法,一般不用被动语态形式,常用一般时态) stay and finish (something) to the end; not quit 把(某事)做完,不放弃: They didn't stay to *see* the play *out*. 他们没坐下去把这部戏看完。Peter's assignment was hard but he *saw* it *out*. 彼得的作业很难,但他还是把它做完了。❸(英国英语用法,用一般时态,不用进行时态)(of someone or something) live or last until the end of (a period of time)(指人)活到;(指物)持续到(某时): I don't think Grandfather will *see out* another month. 我认为祖父不会再活一个月了。"These are good strong shoes and they'll probably *see* me *out*," Grandfather said. "这些鞋子又好又结实,可能够我穿到死了。"爷爷说道。We have enough supplies to *see* the winter *out*. 我们有足够的供应品维持一个冬天。

NOTE 当本短语的宾语为代词时,该代词须置于本短语的动词和副词中间。

see over *vt.* 【不可分性动词短语】(英国英语用法) visit or examine (a place or building, for example a house that is for sale)察看(如供出售的房屋): May we *see over* the house? I understand it is for sale. 我们可以看一看这所房子吗?听说此房供出售。These houses have been *seen over* by many possible buyers. 这些房子已有很多欲购者看过了。

see red *vi.* (非正式用语,用一般时态) become very angry 发火,勃然大怒: Whenever anyone teased Bob about his weight, he *saw red*. 每当有人拿鲍勃的体重开玩笑时,他都会发火。Some Internet customers are *seeing red* as a result of the new virus that slowed the Web traffic. 由于一种新的病毒使网速减慢,一些因特网用户发起火来。

NOTE 本短语的同义短语是 blow one's lid, blow up, flare up 和 lose one's temper;反义短语是 keep one's temper。

see that ⇨ **see to it that**

see through *vt.* ❶(常用一般时态,不用进行时态) recognize or realize (the nature or character of someone or his or her behavior) and not to be tricked by them 看穿,识破(某人或其行径): She tried to set her brother against his old friend, but he *saw through* her. 她想使她弟弟和他的老朋友对立起来,但她弟弟看穿了她。Anybody with common sense can *see through* the attempt of these people. 任何一个有常识的人都会看穿这些人的企图。His double-dealing was *seen through* at once. 他的两面派行径一下子就被识破了。❷(非正式用语,用一般时态,一般不用进行时态) continue doing (something, especially something difficult) until it is finished 坚持把(尤指难做之事)干完: You should never start on a project unless you are prepared to *see* it *through*. 一项工程,如果不准备干完,那就不要开始。I stayed up till deep night and *saw* my essay *through*. 我熬到深夜才完成这篇短文。❸(非正式用语,不用被动语态形式,常用一般时态,不用进行时态) help and encourage (someone) through (trouble or difficulty) 帮助(某人)摆脱(困境): You'll have a difficult time, but I'll *see* you safely *through*. 你将遭遇困难,但我会帮你平安渡过难关。He offered to *see* me *through* college. 他提出帮助我读完大学。❹provide things

S

for, be enough for 提供……,足够……: How much gas do you need? Will five gallons *see* you *through*? 你需要多少汽油?五加仑能解决问题吗? He had just enough money to *see* him *through* a year abroad. 他刚好有足够在国外一年用的钱。

NOTE 当本短语的宾语为代词时,该代词须置于本短语的动词和副词/介词中间。

see to *vt.*【不可分性动词短语】❶(常用一般现在时,一般不用进行时态) deal with, take care of (someone) or attend to (someone, something or doing something) 负责,处理,照料,注意: Who is *seeing to* the arrangements for the next meeting? 谁在负责下一次会议的安排? You ought to have your eyes *seen to* by a doctor. 你应该找医生看一看你的眼睛。Will you *see to* the sick child while we are away? 我们不在时,你能照料一下那生病的孩子吗? ❷ repair; fix; mend 修理,修补: This machine is out of order, get a mechanic to *see to* it. 这部机器出了毛病,找一位技工来修理一下吧。Don't you think your shoes need *seeing to*? 你不认为你的鞋需要修补了吗?

see to it that *vt.* (常用一般现在时,一般不用进行时态) ensure or make sure that (you do something or something is done) 保证……,务必……: "I promise to get everything finished on time." "Good, *see to it that* you do." "我保证按时做完所有的事情。" "好,你务必要做到。" Please *see to it that* these parcels are sent off at once. 请务必把这些包裹立即发出去。

NOTE 本短语的另外一种表达形式是 see that。

see you (again) *s.* (仅用于口语中) (used for saying goodbye to someone you know when you expect to see him or her again soon) goodbye; I'll meet you 再见: *See you* at the station at 7 o'clock. 咱们7点钟车站见。"See you later, Peter." "Yes, *see you again*, John." "彼得,回头见。" "好,再见,约翰。"

NOTE 在英语中,表示告别或说"再见"的词语和短语比较多。最常见的有goodbye,可用于送别或告别的正式和非正式场合; bye-bye 是 goodbye 的简化形式,常用于儿童和妇女中;在熟人之间有时只说 Bye! 但这只能用于非正式场合; bid farewell to 通常在某人长时间或不会再见到某人时使用; see you (again), be seeing you 或 see you (later) 可互换使用,用于朋友和熟人之间; so long 是非正式用语,常用于熟人之间,但在英国一般不用; good night 用作傍晚到将睡时的告别语,其他时间不能使用。

see you (later) *s.* (仅用于口语中) (used for saying goodbye to someone you know when you expect to see him or her again soon, especially later the same day) goodbye (尤其用来指当天)待会儿见,回头见: "*See you later*, Peter." "Yes, *see you*, John." "彼得,回头见。" "好,再见,约翰。"

NOTE 本短语的另外一种表达形式是 catch you later。

seeing as ⇨ **seeing that**

seeing as how ⇨ **seeing that**

seeing is believing *s.* (非正式用语) I'll believe it to exist or be true when I see it with my own eyes 眼见为实,百闻不如一见: "Most people of more than fifty ages are not used to shopping online, because for them, *seeing is believing*," says the board chairman for joyo. com. 卓越网总裁说: "大多数五十岁以上的人不习惯网

上购物,因为对他们来说'眼见才能为实'。" "*Seeing is believing.*" If our friends come to China and see for themselves, they will be able to judge objectively the progress made there in human rights. "百闻不如一见。"只要朋友们到中国亲自看一看,就会对中国在人权方面的进步有客观的评价。

seeing that *conj.* (非正式用语,后接从句)(used for giving the reason why you are saying something) in view of the fact that; considering the fact that; since 鉴于,由于……的缘故,既然: *Seeing that* it is ten o'clock, we will not wait for Mary any longer. 鉴于现在已10点了,我们就不再等玛丽了。*Seeing that* she is legally old enough to get married, I don't see how you can stop her. 既然她已到了法定的结婚年龄,我想象不出你怎么会阻止她。

NOTE 本短语的同义短语 seeing as 和 seeing as how。其中,seeing as 为非正式用语,seeing as how 为非标准用语。例如:

> We may as well go to the concert, *seeing as* we've already paid for the tickets.
> 既然我们已经花钱买了票,我们还是去音乐会吧。

seek after *vt.* (正式用语)【不可分性动词短语】try to get or make a search for (someone or something), as by inner enquiry 企图得到,追求: I will continue to *seek after* the thief who stole my car. 我会一直追查偷走我汽车的那个贼。You shouldn't *seek after* comfort, personal fame and gains. 你不应贪求安逸,追逐名利。We are earnestly *seeking after* the truth. 我们热切追求真理。

seek for *vt.* 【不可分性动词短语】(常为正式用语) try very hard to find (something or someone)竭力找寻,寻求: It's agreed in the international community that to *seek for* a solution to the Korean nuclear issue through political dialogue serves the interests of all the parties. 国际社会一致认为,通过政治对话来寻求朝核问题的解决符合各方利益。Talks have brought the results *for* which we were all *seeking*. 会谈获得了我们都想寻求的结果。She had been *seeking for* a new partner for her business for a long time before at last finding one. 长期以来她一直在寻找一个生意上的新伙伴,最终如愿以偿。

seek out *vt.* 【可分性动词短语】(常为正式用语) keep looking for (something or someone) until you find them 竭力找出,搜寻出: They *sought out* a shady spot where they might sit down and rest. 他们找到了一块可以坐下来休息的阴凉地方。The problem is to *seek out* these people and get them to work as soon as possible. 问题是要找到这些人,并让他们尽早开展工作。They *sought* him *out* in the crowd. 他们在人群中找到了他。

NOTE 当本短语的宾语为代词时,该代词须置于本短语的动词和副词中间。

seep in/through *v.* (常用进行时态)(of a liquid, gas, etc.) make its way gradually through (something such as small openings, usually when this should not happen); flow into or out of something gradually (液体或气体等)逐渐漏出,渗入,渗出: The roof needs mending again, the rain has been *seeping in* recently. 这屋顶需要再修补一下,最近一直在漏雨水。Even when he closed the windows, the noise of the traffic *seeped in*. 即使他把窗户都关

上了,车辆的噪声还能传进来。The rain had *seeped through* his clothes. 雨水浸透了他的衣服。Blood *seeped through* the bandage. 血透过绷带渗了出来。

seize on/onto/upon *vt.* ❶(常用被动语态形式,常用一般时态) take or use (something) in an enthusiastic way in order to gain an advantage 抓住,利用: You have to *seize on* every chance of success as it is not likely repeated. 你必须抓住任何一个时不再来的成功机会。They want to *seize onto* their power in order to do what they like. 他们想抓住权力,为所欲为。The main fear was that both sides may *seize upon* a ceasefire and food aid to rearm. 人们主要担心双方会利用停火和食品援助重整军备。The story was *seized on* by the tabloid press. 这一事件被小报抓住不放。❷accept or adopt(something such as a plan or idea) 接受,采纳(计划或想法等): The board of directors *seized on* my plan to reform. 董事会接受了我的改革计划。I heard his ideas and *seized upon* them very quickly. 听说他的那些想法后,我很快就将其都采纳了。

NOTE 本短语中的 upon 用法比 on 正式,但不及 on 常用。

S

seize up *vi.* (非正式用语)(of something with working action, as machinery) suddenly stop moving or working properly (指运行中的机器等)突然停止运转,出故障: If you don't add oil, the engine will eventually *seize up*. 如果不给加油,发动机最终会停掉。The machine *seized up* this morning. 这部机器今天上午出了故障。I hit two keys at the same time and my computer just *seized up*. 我同时敲击了两个按键,我的电脑就死机了。The snowstorm was so heavy that the city's whole transport and power system *seized up*. 暴风雪大得使整个城市的交通和电力系统都陷于瘫痪。

sell someone down the river ⇨ **sell out**

sell off *vt.* 【可分性动词短语】 sell (something) quickly and for a low price, usually because you need money, or in order to get rid of something (常指因急需资金而)廉价出售,处理(货品): He decided to *sell off* some of the less promising stocks. 他决定廉价出售一部分滞销存货。The store is *selling* these tins of fruit *off* at reduced prices because they're slightly damaged. 商店正在廉价出售这些水果罐头,因为它们都稍有破损。Everything was *sold off* by Frank to pay his debts. 弗兰克为了还债,把所有的东西都廉价卖掉了。

NOTE 本短语可转化为复合词 sell-off,意为"廉价甩卖(货品);(证券等的)跌价,暴跌"。

sell out *v.* ❶(美国英语用法,常与 of 连用)(especially of a shop) sell all that it has so that there is no more available for people to buy (尤指商店)(把……)全部卖光: I went to get some bread, but the shop had *sold out*. 我去买面包,但商店都卖光了。We seem to have *sold out* of your size. 你这个型号的我们好像都卖没了。❷(of tickets) be all sold (指票)售完: The railway tickets from Beijing to Lhasa *sell out* fast. 从北京到拉萨的火车票很快就售完了。I am sorry, all the tickets for tomorrow have been *sold out*. 很抱歉,明天的票已全部售完。❸(非正式用语,贬义用法) stop being loyal or faithful to (someone or something), especially for money or other personal advantage (尤指为了金钱或个人利益而)出卖……: His closest friend *sold* him *out* to the enemy. 他最亲密的朋友把他出卖给了敌人。He was sold out by a traitor and arrested. 他因被叛徒出卖而被捕了。Anyone who would *sell out* his own country for money deserves to go to prison for life. 为钱而出卖祖国者应坐一辈子大牢。❶ accept money to stop following your principles 出卖原则: We hate those whose principles *sell out* to a variety of attractions. 我们憎恨那些经不起各种诱惑而出卖原则的人。He was a good writer, but he *sold out* and now just writes for money. 他曾经是个很好的作家,但他出卖了原则,现在只为金钱而写作。

NOTE 1. 当本短语用作及物性动词短语,所带的宾语为代词时,该代词须置于本短语的动词和副词中间。

2. 当本短语作"出卖……"解时,另外一种表达形式是 sell someone down the river。例如:

> Richard told everything he knew about me, and that *sold me down the river*. 理查德讲出了他所知道的我的一切,就那样把我出卖了。

3. 本短语可转化为复合词 sellout, 意为"背叛;出卖;(商品的)售缺"。

sell up *v.* (主要用于英国英语中) sell (everything you have, such as your house, possessions or your business), usually because you are leaving a place (常指因要离开某处而)(把……)全部卖掉: The news that Sir Cliff is to *sell up* and leave astonished his friends, according to the *Daily Mail*. 据《每日邮报》报道,克利夫爵士要卖掉全部家产然后走人的消息令他的朋友们吃惊。He advised Evens to *sell up* his house and move away to the country. 他建议伊文思卖掉房子,搬到乡村去住。

send away *vt.* 【可分性动词短语】❶ cause (someone) to depart, send (someone or something) to another place 使离去,打发走,送走: I wish you'd got home five minutes earlier. I had to *send* the milkman *away* without paying the money we owe him. 你要是早回家五分钟就好了。欠送奶员的钱我没给就打发他走了。She is going to *send* her son *away* to a university in the United States. 她要把儿子送往美国一所大学里读书。They *sent* the goods *away* immediately. 他们将这些货物立即送走了。❷ order (someone) to leave (a place); dismiss (someone) 赶走,驱逐,解雇(某人): Tom came to see her, but she *sent* him *away*! 汤姆来看望她,可她竟把他赶走了! I soon *sent* the salesman *away*, as I wasn't interested in what he was selling. 我很快就把那个推销员赶走了,因为我对他推销的东西不感兴趣。It was said that the teacher had been *sent away* because of immoral behavior. 据说那位老师因道德行为败坏而被解雇。

NOTE 当本短语的宾语为代词时,该代词须置于本短语的动词和副词中间。

send away/off for *vt.* 【不可分性动词短语】write to a person or organization asking for them to send (goods, etc.) to you 函索(商品等): She *sent away for* a set of bed linen she saw advertised in a magazine. 她写信订购了她在一份杂志广告上看到的一套亚麻布床上用品。When we lived in the country, we had to *send off* to London *for* many things we needed. 我们住在乡下时,不得不往伦敦

S

写信订购我们所需要的许多东西。

NOTE send off for 常用于英国英语中。

send back *vt.*【可分性动词短语】❶return (something) that is not satisfactory 退回(不满意的物品): If you're not happy with it, you can always *send* it *back*. 如果你不满意这件东西,可以随时把它退回来。❷cause (someone or something) to return 使返回,发送回: The teacher beside the lunch line saw Peter cut in, and she *sent* him *back* to wait his turn. 老师在就餐队伍旁看见彼得插队,就让他回到后面去排队。The UN Secretary-General said the UN still needed to assess the security situation carefully before *sending* staff *back* to that country. 联合国秘书长表示,在派遣联合国人员返回该国前还需对那里的安全形势进行评估。The lunar probe has entered the moon's orbit and will soon *send back* images and analyses of the moon's surface. 月球探测卫星已进入月球轨道,并很快会发送回月球表面的图像和分析。

NOTE 当本短语的宾语为代词时,该代词须置于本短语的动词和副词中间。

send down *vt.* &*vi.* (常用一般时态,常与 to 连用) cause (something such as a message or order, or someone) to go down (向楼下等地方)发送通知;把……向下派遣: I'll *send down* to the kitchen for some more coffee. 我来通知厨房再送些咖啡上来。They wanted someone downstairs, so I *sent down* William to help. 因他们楼下需要人手,所以我派威廉下去帮忙。The manager *sent* me *down* to see what had happened here in the workshop. 经理派我下来看看车间里发生了什么事。

—*vt.*【可分性动词短语】❶ cause (something measurable such as temperature or a price) to go down or become lower 使(温度或价格)下降,降低: The strong wind and heavy rain caused by the eighth typhoon of the year, has *sent* the temperature *down* five to ten degrees. 今年第八号台风引起的强风大雨使温度下降了 5～10 度。The oversupply of steel *sent* the prices *down*. 钢材的供过于求使其价格下跌。❷(主要用于英国英语中,常用被动语态形式)(of a student) be ordered to leave a college or university (usually for misconduct)(指大学生)(因不良行为而)被学校开除,被勒令退学: Some students have been *sent down* from Oxford for cheating in examination. 一些学生因考试作弊而被牛津大学开除。Several students were *sent down* after incidents during the visit of a foreign Prime Minister. 几名学生因在外国首相来访期间发生的几起事件而被勒令退学。❸(英国英语用法,非正式用语,常用被动语态形式)(of someone) be convicted and sent to prison (指某人)被判有罪并送进监狱: He was *sent down* for ten years for robbing a bank. 他因抢劫银行而被判入狱服刑十年。The two rapists were *sent down* for life. 那两名强奸犯被判终身监禁。

NOTE 当本短语用作及物性动词短语,所带的宾语为代词时,该代词须置于本短语的动词和副词中间。

send for *vt.*【不可分性动词短语】❶ask for (someone) to come to you 请(某人)来: I think we should *send for* a doctor. 我认为我们应该请医生来。We'd better *send for* a person to repair the TV. 我们最好请人来修理电视机。The police were *sent for* immediately after the disturbance began. 骚乱一开始,警察就

被叫来了。❷arrange for (something) to come to you 安排(某物)到来:He is very ill, you must *send for* an ambulance. 他病得很重,你们必须叫一辆救护车来。❸make a request or order for (something such as goods) to be sent to you by post 索取,订购(商品):I've *sent for* their latest catalogue. 我已向他们索取一份最新的目录。A dozen copies of the dictionary were *sent for*, but only five were received. 这部词典订购了12本,但只收到了5本。

NOTE 本短语与 go for 均表示"去请(某人)"之意。但本短语指派他人去请,而 go for 则是亲自去请。见 go for。

send in *vt.*【可分性动词短语】❶cause (someone) to go to a place 使……进入,派入:*Send in* the next person waiting, nurse. 护士,让下一个待诊的人进来。His doctor *sent* him *in* for more tests at the hospital. 他的医生要他到医院再做几项化验。He has asked the government to *send in* troops to end the riot. 他已请求政府派军队去平定骚乱。❷send (something for official consideration) to a place where it will be dealt with; hand in (something such as a letter or document) to an organization 呈送,提交:Those who have not yet *sent in* applications have to *send* them *in* before this weekend. 那些还没有呈交申请的人须在本周末前交上。Situation reports were *sent in* three times a day. 每日要呈送三次情况报告。Please *send* your letters and suggestions *in* to the BBC. 请把你们的信和建议交到英国广播公司。

NOTE 当本短语的宾语为代词时,该代词须置于本短语的动词和副词中间。

send into *vt.*【可分性动词短语】❶cause (someone or something) to move into (something such as an area)把……送入,派入:The successful Shenzhou-V mission made China the third nation to *send* a man *into* outer space, following the former Soviet Union and the United States. 成功的"神舟"五号飞天使命使中国成了继苏联和美国之后的第三个把人送入太空的国家。More than 100,000 PLA soldiers and armed police were *sent into* the earthquake-hit areas for relief work. 超过10万名解放军和武警官兵被派入地震灾区进行救援工作。❷(常用一般时态)make (someone) to reach (a certain state)使(某人)进入(某种状态):What he said *sent* her *into* a rage. 他说的那番话使她生气。He warned that the world food crisis could *send* millions of people *into* poverty. 他警告说,世界粮食危机会使数百万人处于贫穷状态。The news that scientists had cloned a sheep called Dolly *sent* the public *into* a panic at the prospect that humans might be next. 科学家已经克隆了一只被取名为"多莉"的绵羊的消息引起了公众的恐慌。他们预想,下一个就要轮到人类被克隆了。

send off *vt.*【可分性动词短语】❶post (something such as a letter or parcel) to (someone)给(某人)邮寄(信件或包裹):Why haven't you got my letter? I *sent* it *off* last week. 你怎么还没收到我的信?那封信是我上个星期邮寄的。Have you *sent off* Bill's birthday present? 你把比尔的生日礼物寄走了吗?❷(与 to 连用) arrange (someone) to go somewhere; start (someone) on a journey 打发(某人)去某处;使(某人启程):The mother *sent* her children *off* to the zoo for a whole afternoon. 这位妈妈打发她的孩子们去动物园玩了一个下午。The best way to

S

get rid of a troublesome politician is to *send him off* to a foreign country. 摆脱爱找麻烦的政治家的最佳方法是打发他出国。❸go to the airport, railway station, etc. to say goodbye to (someone who is beginning a journey)(到机场、车站等)为(某人)送行: There was a large crowd to *send* our guests *off*. 有一大群人为我们的客人送行。That hero was warmly *sent off* by a large crowd. 那位英雄受到了一大群人的热烈欢送。❹(英国英语用法,常用被动语态形式)order (a sports player) to leave the playing area during a game as a punishment for seriously breaking the rules 把(严重犯规的运动员)罚出场地: The referee gave the same player three yellow cards before he *sent* him *off*, which has never happened before. 裁判给同一名运动员出示了三次黄牌才把他罚出场地,这是以前从未发生过的事。

NOTE 1. 当本短语的宾语为代词时,该代词须置于本短语的动词和副词中间。

2. 本短语可转化为复合词 send-off,意为"送行,欢送;送葬,葬礼"。sending-off 是本短语的另外一种复合名词形式,意为"(指运动员)被罚出场"。

send out *vt.*【可分性动词短语】❶cause (someone) to go outside 让(某人)出去: Why did you *send* the children *out* to play in this cold weather? 你为什么在这么冷的天气里还让孩子出去玩? He was *sent out* in the morning to buy bread. 早上他被打发去买面包。❷ dispatch; send (someone) on an errand 派遣;派(某人)出去(执行任务): We should *send* more soldiers *out* to the front. 我们应该再往前线派一些士兵。A patrol was *sent out* to search for the attackers, who fled after firing on the American troops from a nearby rooftop. 已派出了一支巡逻队去搜寻那些从附近的屋顶上向美军射击后逃走的袭击者。❸emit; give out (light, heat, signal or sound) 发出(光、热、信号或声音): The sun *sends out* light and heat. 太阳发出光和热。The crew did not send out any distress signal. 机组成员并没有发出任何求救信号。These small animals, like bats, can *send out* sound waves. 这些小动物像蝙蝠一样,能发出声波。❹ allow (a substance such as smoke or chemicals) to escape into the atmosphere 排放出(烟或某种化学物质): A natural gas well blew out, *sending out* a lot of poisonous gas that killed many people. 一天然气井发生井喷,排放出的大量有毒气体造成很多人死亡。❺send (many copies of the same document) to a large number of people at the same time, usually by post (常指通过邮局)(向众多人)发送,邮寄(多份相同文本的材料): The US Department of Homeland Security *sent out* several bulletins to security officials, urging them to be on heightened state of alert during the Christmas period. 美国国土安全部向负责安全保卫的官员发出了数份公告,敦促他们在圣诞节期间都要保持高度戒备状态。How early should I *send* the wedding invitations *out*? Two weeks ahead? 我应该提前多长时间寄出婚礼请柬为好? 提前两周好吗? ❻ (of plants) produce (something such as roots or leaves)(指植物)长出(根、叶等): The trees *send out* new leaves in spring. 树在春天长出新叶。

NOTE 1. 当本短语的宾语为代词时,该代词须置于本短语的动词和副词中间。

2. 本短语可转化为复合词 send(-)out,

意为“输出量”。

send over *vt.*【可分性动词短语】(常与to连用) dispatch; cause (something or someone) to move to a different place 派遣,运送: If you buy more things here we'll *send* them *over* to your house free of charge. 如果你在这里买很多东西,我们会免费送货上门。He was *sent over* to England as the representative of the company. 他作为公司的代表被派往英国。

NOTE 当本短语的宾语为代词时,该代词须置于本短语的动词和副词中间。

send to *vt.*【可分性动词短语】❶cause or order (someone) to go to (a place) to do a particular thing 把(某人)送往(某处);把(某人)派往(某处):I plan to *send* my son (away) *to* school in England. 我计划把我儿子送到英格兰去上学。More soldiers and rescue teams were *sent to* the earthquake-hit areas for relief work. 更多的士兵和救援队被派往地震灾区从事救援工作。❷send (something such as a letter or message) to (someone or a place), especially by post (尤指通过邮寄的方式)把(信件等)寄往(某处);向(某人)发送(信件或信息):Could you *send* a reply *to* them as quickly as possible? 你能尽快寄回信给他们吗? Please *send* your money *to* this address, and you'll get your book. 把款寄往这个地址,你就会收到书。Even though it may appear that these e-mail messages were *sent to* you by Microsoft, they were not. Microsoft does not send junk e-mail. 尽管这些电子邮件信息像是微软公司发送给你的,但不是的。微软公司不发送垃圾邮件。

send up *vt.*【可分性动词短语】❶cause (someone or something) to rise, move upwards, upstairs, etc. 把……送上……;使……上升;把……发射升空;使……上楼: *Sending up* three astronauts into space is a jump both in quantity and quality. 把三名宇航员送上太空,无论是在数量上还是在质量上都是个飞跃。The heavy demand for beef *sent* the price *up* by 20%. 大量的需求使牛肉价格上涨20%。Man-made satellites have been *sent up* into space by many countries. 已有许多国家向太空发射了人造卫星。When the guests arrive, *send* them *up*, will you? 客人来了,就带他们上楼来,好吗? ❷offer (something such as a suggestion) to a higher authority or level (向上级)呈报,提出(建议等):Did you *send up* your report? 你的报告已经交上去了吗? Had Iran failed to agree, the International Atomic Energy Agency could have *sent* the case *up* to the United Nations Security Council for possible action. 如果伊朗拒不同意,国际原子能机构就会将该案提交联合国安理会采取可能的行动。❸(美国英语用法,非正式用语,常用一般时态)send (someone) to prison 把(某人)送进监狱: I'm the one who *sent* him *up*. 是我把他送进了监狱。Did you know that Tom was *sent up* for five years? 你知道汤姆被判入狱服刑五年吗? ❹(主要用于英国英语中,非正式用语) make (someone) seem stupid by imitating him or her in a funny way (用可笑的方式模仿某人以)讽刺,讥笑(某人): In his new play, he *sends* the prime minister *up* brilliantly. 在他新编的剧中,他惟妙惟肖地讽刺了首相。

NOTE 当本短语的宾语为代词时,该代词须置于本短语的动词和副词中间。

sentence to *vt.*【可分性动词短语】(of a

judge or court) declare that (someone) must suffer (something as a punishment) for committing a crime (法官或法庭)判处(某人)徒刑: The judge *sentenced* him *to* 2 years of hard labor. 法官判处他服两年苦役。The court on Thursday *sentenced* the former chairwoman and general manager of the dairy group *to* life in prison for the milk powder scandal. 星期四,法院因奶粉事件判处该奶业集团原董事长兼总经理无期徒刑。

NOTE 本短语中的 to 是介词,但在下面这个句子中的 to 则是动词不定式符号,不要将两者混淆:

> He was *sentenced to* be hanged.
> 他被判处绞刑。

separate from *vt.* 【可分性动词短语】❶(常用一般时态) place (something or someone) apart from (something or someone else)把……与……分开,隔离: Break the eggs and *separate* the whites *from* the yolks. 把鸡蛋打开,然后把蛋清和蛋黄分开来。The child may be *separated from* his mother while she receives treatment. 在他妈妈接受治疗期间,可能得把这孩子他和妈妈分开了。Great Britain is *separated from* the rest of Europe by the English Channel. 英吉利海峡把英国与欧洲其他国家隔离开来。❷(无被动语态形态) move apart from; (cause to) become disconnected with (a group or person)脱离,(使)分离: Once in orbit, the satellite *separated from* its launcher. 一旦进入运行轨道,卫星便脱离其发射器。In the rush to get out of the building, I got *separated from* my mother. 因急于从大楼里撤出来,我和妈妈走散了。❸(无被动语态形态)(of a couple who are married or living together) begin to live apart from (each other)(指婚后同居的夫妻)分居: Since she *separated from* her husband she has led a hard life. 自从她与丈夫分居以来,她生活得一直很苦。

serve as *vt.* (常用一般时态) ❶(of someone) perform official duties as (a civil servant or politician)(指某人)充当,担任: How many years did George Walker Bush *serve as* president? 乔治·沃克·布什当了多少年总统? A man in Chicago has been convicted of *serving as* a long-time spy for another country. 一名芝加哥男子因长期充当某国的间谍而被判有罪。❷(of something) be used for (a particular purpose), often because nothing more satisfactory is available (指某物)被用作: The children used an old sheet to *serve as* a curtain. 孩子们用一条旧床单作窗帘。This small room *serves* Mr Smith *as* a study. 这个小房间是供史密斯先生读书用的。❸(of something) perform a particular function of (指某物)起到……作用: Tourism *serves* gradually *as* an important bridge of cultural exchange, friendship and further exchanges. 旅游活动逐渐起到各国人民交流文化、增进友谊、扩大交往的重要桥梁作用。The decision should *serve as* a warning to companies that pollute the environment. 该决定应对那些污染环境的公司起到警告的作用。

NOTE 当本短语作"充当,担任"解时,同义短语是 work as 和 act as。

serve someone right *vi.* (非正式用语,常用一般现在时)(used for saying that you think someone deserves something unpleasant that happens to him or her) be a suitable punishment for someone (指某

人)罪有应得,自作自受,咎由自取,活该:This punishment *served him right*. 他受到这样的惩罚是罪有应得。Bob said it *served Jane right* when she cut her finger, she had taken his knife without asking him. 鲍勃说,简割破了手指是自作自受,因为她未经他的允许就拿走他的刀。I'm not sorry he hit you, it *serves you right* for starting the fight. 他打了你,但我并不为此感到遗憾。谁让你先动手了,活该。

NOTE 含有本短语的句子常以 it 启首。例如:It *serves you right*! 但在通俗的英语中常常把 it 省略掉,而说成 *Serve you right*!

set about *vt*.【不可分性动词短语】(常用一般时态) ❶(无被动语态形式)begin to do or doing (something), especially in an energetic or purposeful way 着手,开始(某事或做某事):After breakfast Mother *sets about* her household duties. 吃完早饭后,妈妈就动手做家务事了。The government *set about* solving the housing problem by building some new living quarters. 政府着手兴建新的住宅小区以解决住房问题。I don't know how to *set about* it. 我不知道如何开始做此事。I bought a computer, got a book of instructions, and *set about* to learn how to use it. 我买了台电脑,搞了一本说明书,便开始学习怎样使用它。❷(英国英语用法,正式用语,一般不用被动语态形式) attack (someone) (with words, the fists or weapons)(用言词、拳头或武器)抨击,攻击(某人):He *set about* his opponent in strong language. 他以强硬的言辞抨击了他的对手。A gang of boys *set about* a supporter of the other team. 一帮男孩子用拳头打了一名对方球队的支持者。A middle-aged man *set about* her with a knife. 一名中年男子用刀袭击了她。

NOTE 当本短语作"着手,开始(某事或做某事)"解时,同义短语是 go about。

set against *vt*.【可分性动词短语】❶cause (two people or groups) to become enemies or rivals and fight each other although they were in a friendly relationship before 挑拨(某人或某一团体)与(他人或其他团体)相对立:She always *sets* a friend *against* another. 她总是挑拨一个朋友反对另一个朋友。This bitter industrial dispute had *set* workers *against* workers. 这一激烈的劳资争端使工人之间相互对立起来。❷ lessen the bad effect of (something) by treating it as not open to (something else bad)抵消,使得到补偿:He has many virtues to *set against* his faults. 他有许多优点可以弥补他的缺点。❸(常用一般时态) compare (one thing) with (another)把(一物)与(另一物)相对比:The jeweler *set* the diamond *against* a piece of glass. 这位珠宝商把那块钻石和一块玻璃进行了对比。*Setting* the results *against* those of the last election, we can see a clear improvement. 把这次和上次的选举结果进行比较,我们就会看到有明显的改善。This quarter's results have been disappointing *set against* last year's. 本季度的业绩与去年的相比令人失望。

set apart *vt*.【可分性动词短语】❶(常用被动语态形式,常与 from 连用) place (something or someone) separately 分别放置,隔离:The chairs were *set apart* from the others for the special guests. 这些椅子单独放着,供特别宾客坐。During the spread of A/H1N1 influenza, people suffering from the infectious disease were all *set apart*. 在甲型 H1N1 流感流行期间，被感染者通通受到隔离。❷ save (something such as money or time) for a special use or purpose 节省(金钱或时间)：You must *set apart* some money for the future. 你必须省下一些钱以备将来使用。They decided to *set* a day *apart* for the work. 他们决定留出一天的时间来干那项工作。❸ make (someone) be or feel different (from other people), usually better 使(某人)与众不同：Her very appearance *set* her *apart* from her fellow students. 她的外貌就使她在同学中与众不同了。His mastery of colour *sets* him *apart* from other painters of his era. 他在用色方面的技艺使他显得比同时代的画家高出一筹。

NOTE 当本短语的宾语为代词时，该代词须置于本短语的动词和副词中间。

set aside *vt.* 【可分性动词短语】❶ put (something) on one side, especially for a short time 把……(暂时)放在一边：The teacher *set aside* the papers he was marking and reached for his cigarettes and matches. 老师把他正在批阅的试卷放到一旁，去拿香烟和火柴。He *set* the chair *aside*, and sat on the floor. 他把椅子放在一旁，坐在了地板上。❷ not let (a particular belief, feeling, opinion, or principle) influence you, in order to achieve peace 把……搁置起来：The two sides agreed to *set aside* their differences and work together for peace. 双方同意把分歧搁置起来，共同致力于和平。The government has agreed to *set aside* these decrees. 政府已同意把那些法令暂时搁置起来。❸ (常与 for 或动词不定式连用) keep or save (something) in order to use it later for a particular purpose 留出备用，贮藏：Each week she tried to *set aside* some US dollars for use back home. 每周她都留出一些美元好回国花。A sum of money was *set aside* for a new car. 留出一笔款以购买新车。President Shumway asked female students to sort out those clothes that are not appropriate, and *set* them *aside* or throw them away. 沙姆韦校长要求女同学们把那些不合校规的衣物挑出来，或把它们存放起来不再穿用或干脆丢掉。❹ (正式用语，常用一般时态) pay no attention to; disregard; refuse to accept 不顾，拒绝：He *set aside* all objections and granted my request. 他不顾一切反对意见，同意了我的要求。The management *set* our request for more equipment *aside*. 管理部门拒绝了我们增添设备的要求。❺ (正式用语，常用一般时态) (of a judge or court) officially state that a particular legal decision is of no effect (指法官或法庭)驳回(某项法律裁决)：The High Court has *set aside* the lower court's ruling. 高等法院驳回了下一级法院的裁决。

NOTE 当本短语的宾语为代词时，该代词须置于本短语的动词和副词中间。

set back *vt.* 【可分性动词短语】❶ (常用被动语态形式，用一般时态，常与 from 连用) place (something, especially a building) in a position to the back, as away from something 把(尤指建筑物)置于……之后：The house is *set* 15 feet *back* from the road. 这所房子建在距离道路 15 英尺的地方。❷ (常用一般时态) stop the advance or progress of 使退步，倒退，阻碍：Difficulties in raising money have *set back* our building program. 筹集资金方面的困难阻碍了我们的建筑项

目。Most of Israelis opposed giving back the Golan Heights to Syria, Israel-Syria peace effort was *set back*. 大多数以色列人反对把戈兰高地交还给叙利亚,叙以和平的努力受到阻碍。❸(常用一般时态)cause a delay of (something such as a plan or project); delay (someone) from advancing by (an amount of time)推迟,耽搁: The cold weather *set back* the planting by two weeks. 寒冷的天气使播种延迟了两个星期。The accident has *set* the experiment *back* for a long time. 意外事故使实验耽搁了很长时间。It has *set* us *back*, I'm not sure how long it will take for us to catch up. 这事耽搁了我们。我不确定我们得用多长时间才能赶上去。❹(非正式用语,无被动语态形式,常用一般时态) cost (someone) (a particular amount of money, especially a large amount)花费(某人)(一大笔钱): That dinner at the restaurant last night must have *set* you *back*. 昨晚在饭店里吃的那顿饭肯定花了你不少钱。During the war you could take a flight from Amman into Baghdad International Airport, the roundtrip fare would *set* you *back* as much as $1,100. 战争期间,你可以从安曼飞到巴格达国际机场,但往返机票要花掉你1 100美元。

NOTE 1. 当本短语的宾语为代词时,该代词须置于本短语的动词和副词中间。

2. 本短语可转化为复合词 set-back,意为"挫折,失败;倒退;(疾病的)复发"。

set down *vt.*【可分性动词短语】❶cause (someone or oneself) to sit 使(某人或自己)坐下:*Set* the baby *down* here. 把孩子放在这儿坐着。*Set* yourself *down* in this comfortable chair and tell us your story. 坐在这把舒适的椅子上,把你的事情给我们讲讲。❷write down (something) on a piece of paper so that it will not be forgotten and can be looked at later 写下,记下:They asked her to *set down* the facts just as she remembered them. 他们请她根据自己的记忆把这些事实写下来。She *set* all these important events *down* in her diary. 她把所有这些重要的事件都记在了日记中。I have the details set down here in my notebook. 我把详细事项都记在我这记事本上了。❸(与 as 连用) consider (something) in a particular way 认为,把……看作: We *set* it *down* as an impossibility. 我们认为这是不可能的。He *set* the whole plan *down* as a failure. 他认为整个计划是失败的。❹(正式用语,常用被动语态形式,常用一般时态)(of a committee or organization) establish or make (a rule, a principle, etc.) officially 制定(规则,原则等): It's clearly *set down* that you're not allowed to vote twice. 有明确条文规定不许重复投票。These rules were *set down* by the United Nations and must be obeyed. 这些原则是联合国制定的,必须得到遵守。❺(英国英语用法,正式用语)(of a vehicle or its driver) stop and allow (passengers) to get down or out (车辆或其司机)停车让(乘客)下车: The bus stopped to *set down* and pick up passengers. 公共汽车停下来,让乘客上下车。Some passengers asked to be *set down* at the church. 一些乘客要求车到教堂时让他们下车。This bus *sets* the children *down* just outside the school gate. 公共汽车停在了学校门口让孩子们下车。❻(cause to) land (an aircraft) (使)(飞机等)降落: The pilot couldn't *set down* the plane in the heavy fog. 驾驶员无法在大雾中降落飞机。He managed to *set* the glider

down safely in a cornfield. 他把滑翔机安全地降落在了一块玉米地上。

NOTE 1. 当本短语的宾语为代词时,该代词须置于本短语的动词和副词中间。

2. 本短语可转化为复合词 set(-)down,意为"申斥,辱骂"。

set down to *vt.* 【可分性动词短语】(用一般时态) consider (something) to be the result of (something)把……归因于……,把……认为是……的结果: We *set* it *down to* his laziness. 我们将其归因于他的懒惰。The teacher *set down* the boy's poor English *to* his foreign birth. 老师把那名男同学英语不好的原因归于他在国外出生。The failure was *set down to* bad planning. 这次失败被认为是计划不周的结果。

NOTE 本短语的同义短语是 attribute to。

set fire to *vt.* 【不可分性动词短语】(主要用于英国英语中,无被动语态形式) make (something) start burning 放火烧……,使……起火,引燃: The explosion *set fire to* a half-dozen cars parked near the buildings of a police station and municipal offices. 爆炸引燃了停在警察局和市政大楼附近的六辆汽车。Police arrested a 70-year-old man suspected of *setting fire to* the country's top cultural treasure, the 610-year-old Sungnyemun Gate in Seoul. 警方逮捕了一名 70 岁的男子,他被怀疑纵火焚烧首尔市有 610 年历史的国家顶级文化瑰宝崇礼门。

NOTE 本短语与 set on fire 都是及物性动词短语,表示"使……起火燃烧"之意,它们之间的区别是:本短语的宾语只能置于短语之后,而不能置于短语之中,set on fire 的宾语一般置于短语之中(动词 set 之后);本短语的宾语只能是物,而 set on fire 的宾语既可以是物,又可以是人;本短语不能用被动语态形式,而 set on fire 则可以。

set foot on/in *vt.* 【不可分性动词短语】(常用一般时态) go on or into (a place) 踏足于(某地),进入(某处): I firmly believed that no human shape had ever *set foot on* that place. 我坚信,从来没有人涉足过那个地方。Don't *set foot in* my house again! 不要再进入我的家!

set forth (正式用语) *vt.* explain or describe (something) in a clear and detailed way, especially in writing or speech (尤指用文字或在讲话中)(清楚而详细地)解释,陈述,阐明: He *set* the goals for the coming year *forth* in a report. 他在一份报告中陈述了明年的目标。The congress *set forth* the goal of building a well-off society in an all-round way. 大会阐明了全面建设小康社会的目标。Member states must fulfill the obligations *set forth* in the Convention. 成员国必须履行公约中阐明的义务。

—*vi.* (常与 on 连用) start a journey, especially one that is long or difficult 开始(尤指远而艰难的)行程,起程: The troops *set forth* on their twenty-mile hike early. 部队一早就开始了他们 20 英里的徒步行军。What time did he *set forth*? 他是什么时候起程的? *Setting forth* on a journey means a great deal of preparation. 上路旅行意味着要做大量的准备工作。

NOTE 1. 当本短语作"解释,陈述,阐明"解时,同义短语是 set out。

2. 当本短语作"开始(尤指远而艰难的)行程,起程"解时,同义短语是 set off 和 set out。

set forward *vt.* 【可分性动词短语】 ❶offer, suggest or explain (something)

提出,解释:He *set forward* a proposal that would not only improve the quality of the products but also lower the cost. 他提出了一项既能提高产品的质量又能降低成本的建议。The committee's plans are *set forward* in the report. 该委员会的计划在这篇报告中得到了解释。❷make (something) advance 促进,推动:The warm weather has *set* the crops *forward*. 温暖的天气促进了作物的生长。The company was *set forward* by the increase of capital. 该公司通过扩大资本推进了发展。❸move or change (something such as an event) to an earlier time or date 把……提前:We shall have to *set* the meeting *forward*, can you all be present on Tuesday? 我们得把会期提前了,你们星期二都能到会吗? ❹move the hands of (a clock or watch) to a later time 把(钟表的)指针拨快:The clock in the classroom was slow so we *set* it *forward* two minutes. 教室里的钟慢了,所以我们把它拨快了两分钟。I had to *set* my watch *forward* to London time. 我得把手表拨快到伦敦时间。

NOTE 当本短语的宾语为代词时,该代词须置于本短语的动词和副词中间。

set free *vt.* 【可分性动词短语】cause (someone, oneself or an animal) to be free; let go; release 使……自由,释放……:After five years in prison, he was *set free* when the city was liberated. 他在监牢里关了五年,一直到那座城市解放的时候,他才获得自由。A German prisoner managed to *set* himself *free* by hiding in a large box on a mail truck. 一名德国囚犯藏在了邮政卡车上的一个大盒子里,从而使自己得以逃脱。He opened the cage and *set* the eagle *free*. 他打开笼子,把鹰放飞了。

NOTE 当本短语的宾语为代词时,该代词须置于本短语的动词和形容词中间。

set in *vi.* (of a disease, bad weather, etc.) begin and may not stop for a long time (疾病、坏天气等)开始(并有可能持续很久):Now the crop completely failed, owing to a disease that had *set in*. 由于遭受病害,庄稼颗粒无收。Fortunately the wound was treated before infection could *set in*. 很幸运,伤口还没有感染就得到了治疗。Let's get inside, the rain's *set in*. 咱们进来吧。开始下雨了。The sky looks as if a storm may be *setting in*. 看天色,暴风雨可能就要来了。

—*vt.* ❶(常用被动语态形式) fix (something such as a jewel) by placing it carefully in (something) 给……镶嵌上,镶入:Some diamonds were *set in* the gold ring, making it very dear. 这枚金戒指上镶嵌了几颗宝石,使其颇为珍贵。He *set* some diamonds *in* the face of the watch. 他在手表的盘面上镶了几颗宝石。❷cause (a ship) to move towards the shore 使(船)靠岸:The ship from Singapore was *set in*. 来自新加坡的轮船靠岸了。It's time to *set* the ship *in*, we are expected in the harbor in 20 minutes. 船该靠岸了,预计我们 20 分钟就能进港。

NOTE 本短语可转化为复合词 set-in,意为"(冰霜雨雪等的)来临(时节);嵌入物"。

set loose ⇨ **let loose**

set off *vi.* begin a journey or start going in a particular direction 起程,动身,出发:China's first team of peacekeepers to the west African nation of Liberia, composed of five policemen, *set off* on November 30. 中国第一批派往西非国家

S

利比亚的、由五名警察组成的维和小分队于11月30日起程了。I have to *set off* at 7:10 each morning in order to get to the office at eight o'clock. 为了在8点到达办公室,我每天早晨7点10分就得动身。James *set off* for his remote farmhouse in Texas. 詹姆斯起程前往他在得克萨斯州的偏远农庄。They've *set off* on a journey round the world. 他们已出发开始环球旅行。

—*vt.*【可分性动词短语】❶ make (something such as a bomb or firework) explode 使……爆炸,引爆,燃放:Attackers tried, and failed, to *set off* explosive devices at three subway stations and on a double-decker bus. 袭击者们企图在三个地铁车站和一辆双层大巴上引爆爆炸装置,但都没能成功。No one knows how the bomb was made, and who *set* it *off*. 没人知道这枚炸弹是怎么造的,又是谁引爆的。Somebody ignored the government ban and was *setting off* fireworks on the street. 有人不顾政府禁令,正在大街上燃放鞭炮。The children gathered in the garden to *set* the fireworks *off*. 孩子们聚集在庭院中放鞭炮。❷ cause (something such as an alarm) to ring, especially by accident (尤指偶然)触发(警报器):Tom pushed open the front door, which *set off* the alarm. 汤姆推开前门,竟触发了警报器。Somebody *set* the alarm *off* on my car. 不知是谁触发了我车中的警报器。❸(常用一般时态)cause (an event or a series of events) to start happening 引发(某种或某些事件):The arrival of the charity van *set off* minor riots as villagers scrambled for a share of the aid. 载有赈济物品的大篷车的到达引发了一阵阵小的骚乱,村民们都抢着要得到一份救济品。❹(常用被动语态形式,常用一般时态) make (something) more beautiful or attractive to look at by putting near something different 使显得更美丽动人,衬托出:Her features were *set off* by her style of hairdressing. 她的发型把她的容貌衬托得更美丽了。You'd better use blue eye shadow to *set off* your green eyes. 你最好用蓝色眼影衬托你的绿眼睛。

NOTE **1.** 当本短语用作及物性动词短语,所带的宾语为代词时,该代词须置于本短语的动词和副词中间。

2. 本短语与 set out 均有"起程,动身,出发"之意。本短语常用于日常生活中,而 set out 常指为某种目的,为了探险或去较远的地方而出发去某处。

3. 本短语可转化为复合词 setoff,意为"装饰品;陪衬物;(债务的)抵消;用以抵销债务的权利"。

set on/upon *vt.* ❶(常用被动语态形式,常用一般时态)(of a person or animal) attack (someone or something)(指人或动物)袭击……:On her way to the school, two young men *set on* her and had her robbed. 在她去学校的途中,两名青年男子袭击了她并抢走了她的东西。He was *set upon* by an armed robber in a dark alley. 他在一个黑暗的胡同里遭到了武装抢劫者的袭击。Demonstrators began to *set upon* a stopped police car. 示威者开始袭击一辆停下的警车。He was *set upon* by a vicious dog. 他被一条恶犬袭击。❷(英国英语用法)cause (an animal or person) to attack (someone) 让(动物或人)袭击(某人):The soldiers brought two prisoners in and *set* the dog *on* them. 士兵们带进来两名囚犯,并放狗

S

咬他们。If you do that again, I'll *set* my elder brother *on* you! 如果你再干那事，我就让我哥哥揍你。❸(非正式用语) tell (a person) (to do something wrong) 怂恿，唆使(某人)(做错事)：You should not *set on* him to do such a bad thing. 你不应该怂恿他去做这样的坏事。He is held at a jail on a charge of *setting* a boy *on* to commit a crime. 他因被指控教唆一男孩犯罪而入狱。He admitted that he had stolen the apples, but said that he had been *set on* by some older boys. 他承认他偷了苹果，但又说，是一些比他大的男孩子唆使他干的。❹ begin employing (someone) 开始雇用(某人)：Business was so good that the company *set on* more workers. 由于生意不错，公司又雇用了一些工人。Extra hands were *set on* to the job. 额外添加了人手来干这件工作。

set on fire *vt.*【可分性动词短语】cause (something or someone) to start burning 使……燃烧：Stop emptying your pipe into the wastepaper basket, you'll *set* the house *on fire*! 不要再往废纸篓里磕烟灰了，你这样会使房子着火的。During the riot, their clothing store was *set on fire* by rioters and five girl employees were burned to death. 在骚乱中，他们的服装店被骚乱分子放火焚烧，五名女售货员被烧死。

set one's mind on *vt.* (常用一般时态) be determined to have or achieve (something) 下定决心得到(某物)：Once Anna's *set her mind on* something, she will find a way to achieve it. 只要安娜决心得到什么，她就会设法得到它。I've *set my mind on* getting a university degree. 我决心取得一个大学学位。

NOTE 本短语的另外一种表达形式是 have one's mind set on。例如：

> When my wife *has her mind set on* it, there's nothing stopping her.
> 当我妻子决心要得到什么时，什么也无法阻止她。

set out *v.* ❶(常与 for, on 连用) start a journey 出发，起程：The Norwegians *set out* to explore the area of Antarctica with dogs hauling their sleds. 这些挪威人带着狗拉着雪橇动身去南极地区探险。When *setting out* on a long walk, you must wear suitable shoes. 走远路时，你必须穿一双合适的鞋子。❷(后常接动词不定式) begin (to do something) with the intention of achieving a particular aim 打算，试图(做某事)：He *set out* to do a lot of things, but didn't succeed. 他打算做很多事，但都没有做成。China and South Africa *set out* to establish a new type of partnership featuring long-term stability, equality and mutual benefit. 中国和南非意欲建立一种长期稳定、平等互利的新型伙伴关系。They obviously *set out* with the intention of overthrowing the government. 他们很明显要推翻政府。❸(常用被动语态形式) put (something) where it can be seen or used; arrange or display (items) on a table, board, etc. in an attractive or organized way 展示，陈列，摆放：The street traders *set out* their wares on the stalls. 马路上的摊贩把他们的货品都陈列在了摊床上。Put your trash in a garbage bag and *set* it *out* by the curb. 把垃圾放在垃圾袋里，然后将其放到马路旁。The meal was attractively *set out* on a long table. 饭菜都摆在了一张长桌子上，很诱人。❹(正式用语，常用一般时态) explain or

S

describe (a number of facts, reasons, or arguments), especially in writing or speech in a clear, organized way (尤指以文字或在讲演中)陈述,阐明(事实,理由,论点): He has written a letter to *The Times* *setting out* his views. 他已写信给《泰晤士报》陈述了他的观点。The reasons for my decision are *set out* in my report. 我所做决定的理由在我的报告中有说明。

NOTE 1. 当本短语用作及物性动词短语,所带的宾语为代词时,该代词须置于本短语的动词和副词中间。

2. 当本短语作"展示,陈列,摆放"解时,同义短语是 lay out。

3. 本短语可转化为复合词 set-out,意为"开始;开头;布置;设备,装备;(食物、餐具、物品等的)陈列,宴会"。

set right *vt.* 【可分性动词短语】❶(非正式用语) correct (something that was wrong or that was causing problems) to make it the way it should be 改正,纠正: We've discovered what's gone wrong and are going to *set* it *right*. 我们已经发现了错误所在,并准备予以改正。The matter was soon *set right* with the help of a veteran technician. 在一名老技术员的帮助下,问题很快就得到了纠正。If some part of their organization is on the wrong track, managers will try to find out about it and *set* things *right*. 如果该机构的某一部门出错,其管理层就会千方百计地找出原因去矫正。❷ fix or mend (something) 修理(某物): There was something wrong with the motor, please *set* it *right*. 这台发动机有毛病,请你把它修一下。

NOTE 当本短语的宾语为代词时,该代词须置于本短语的动词和形容词中间。

set sail *vi.* (of a ship) leave a port and begin a journey across water (船只)起航: The second fleet of Chinese naval escort ships *set sail* for the Gulf of Aden to replace the first fleet sent there earlier. 中国海军第二批护航舰队前往亚丁湾去接替早些时候被派往那里的第一批护航编队。I was told that the ship would be *setting sail* to London. 我听说这艘船要起航去伦敦。The Snow Dragon carrying a group of Chinese scientists on board *set sail* to discover the South Pole. "雪龙"号载着一些中国科学家出发去南极考察。

set to *vi.* (非正式用语,常用一般时态) ❶ start working or dealing with something busily and energetically 开始做(某事): If we all *set to*, we can finish cleaning the house in an hour. 如果我们大家都努力干,我们就能在一个小时内就把这间房子打扫完。❷begin eating eagerly 大吃起来: The pair of them *set to* and demolished a big pork pie. 他们两个大吃起来,把一个大猪肉饼吃个精光。❸(of two people) start to fight or quarrel (指两个人)打起来,争吵起来: The two boys *set to* as soon as they met each other. 这两个男孩相互一见面就打起来。The two angry housewives *set to* and began to pull each other's hair. 两个愤怒的家庭主妇发生争吵并动手撕扯对方的头发。

NOTE 本短语可转化为复合词 set-to,意为"(短时间的)殴斗,争吵"。

set up *vt.* ❶erect; raise (something) into a fixed position; put upright 竖立,支起,架起: They *set up* a bronze statue to his memory. 他们竖立了一座铜像来纪念他。A volleyball net has been *set up* by the kids. 孩子们支起了排球网。The film production team arrived and began to *set up* the cameras. 影片摄制组到达后便开始把摄影机架了起来。❷start, establish (an organization or institution)建立,设立(组织或机构): We *set up* a command center to guide and coordinate relief work in earthquake-hit areas. 我们设立了一个指挥中心以指导和协调地震灾区的救援工作。By the end of next year, 6 modern agricultural comprehensive development demonstrating zones will be *set up* in the province. 到明年年底,该省将建立六个现代农业综合开发示范区。❸build; assemble; prepare (an instrument, machine, etc.) for use 建造,安装,装配: They *set up* the building only in two months. 这房子他们仅用两个月就建造起来了。My parents bought me a tent, but I had to *set* it *up* myself. 我爸妈给我买了一顶帐篷,但得我得自己安装。Roadblocks were *set up* by the police to catch the escaped prisoner. 警察为抓住逃犯而设置了路障。The mechanic *set* the machine *up* for me. 机械师替我把机器装配起来。❹put forward; propose 提出,建议: Applicants for visas are supposed to call the US consulate to *set up* a face-to-face interview, but many complain of calling the consulate for days on end and only getting a busy tone. 申请签证的人都要给美国领事馆打电话提出面试要求,然而很多人都抱怨连续数日给领事馆打电话,听到的都是忙音。The new theory was *set up* by a young scientist. 这个新理论是一位年轻科学家提出来的。❺arrange or make plans for (something) 安排,计划: Hillary and Linda *set up* a bridal shower for Sunday morning. 希拉里和琳达安排星期日上午举办新娘送礼会。They *set* the all-staff meeting *up* for 2:30 pm tomorrow. 他们计划明天下午 2 点半召开全体员工会议。❻cause; produce 引起,产生: The doctor has no idea how the condition was first *set up*. 医生不知道那病情最先是怎样引起的。Smoking *sets up* an irritation in the throat. 吸烟对咽喉产生刺激。❼establish (a record speed, time, distance, etc.) in a sporting event (在体育项目中)创立(记录): Chinese track athlete Liu Xiang *set up* a new Olympic Games record in the 110-meter hurdle. 中国田径运动员刘翔创立了一项新的奥运会 110 米栏纪录。❽(非正式用语,常用一般时态) make (someone) healthier, stronger, more lively, etc. 使(某人)复原,使(某人)康复: My doctor says that the sea air will *set* me *up*. 我的医生说,海洋的空气能使我恢复健康。A good rest probably *set* you *up* again. 好好地休息一下或许能使你恢复过来。❾begin to shout, etc. loudly 开始大声喊叫: Someone in the crowd *set up* a cry that the police were coming. 人群中有人大喊说警察来了。When the first goal was scored a shout was *set up* by the team's supporters that might have been heard for miles. 当该队首开纪录时,其支持者大声呼叫,几英里外都能听到。❿(常用被动语态形式) provide (with what is necessary or useful, such as money)提供(所需或有用之物): When he was twenty his father *set* him *up* in business as a greengrocer. 他 20 岁那年,他的父亲提供资金让他做蔬菜水果店的生意。We're *set up* with emergency medical supplies. 我们得到了提供的紧急医疗用

品。⓫(无被动语态形式,不用进行时态,用一般时态,常与 as 或 to be 连用) claim (oneself) to be (a certain kind of person)自称为……: He *sets* himself *up* as an authority on French painting, but he really knows very little about it. 他自称为法国绘画作品的权威,但他实际上对其知之甚少。He *set* himself *up* to be a graduate of a medical school, but he was not. 他自称是某医学院校的毕业生,但实际上他不是。I didn't want to *set up* as better than anyone else. 我并不想自称比别人强。

—*vt.* &*vi.* ❶(cause to) start (something such as a business) (使)开始经商,(使)开业: They plan to *set up* an import business in the city. 他们计划在该市经营进口生意。The business was *set up* by the grandfather of the present owner. 这项生意是现任主人的祖父创办的。The Hong Kong-based Bank of East Asia is thinking of *setting up* in Canada. 总部设在香港的东亚银行正考虑在加拿大开行营业。❷(与 as 连用) establish oneself as (a kind of professional worker) 从事(某种职业),当……: John *set* himself *up* as a painter and soon had plenty of work. 约翰干起了油漆工,很快就接了许多活儿。In 2003 he moved to New York, where he *set up* as a school teacher. 他于 2003 年搬到纽约,在那里他当上了教师。

NOTE 1. 当本短语用作及物性动词短语,所带的宾语为代词时,该代词须置于本短语的动词和副词中间。

2. 本短语可转化为复合词 setup,意为"机构,体制;(身体的)姿势,姿态;装置;(机器、设备等的)调整;(工作前的)准备,计划,方案"。

settle down *v.* ❶sit oneself comfortably, as on a soft surface (usually for some quiet, prolonged activity) 舒服地(在……上)坐着: Then we *settled down* to watch TV in the sitting-room. 然后,我们便舒舒服服地坐在客厅里看电视。I *settled down* onto the soft couch, which represented my parents' marriage, my birth, and hundreds of other little events. 我坐在软软的沙发上。这张沙发目睹了我父母的婚姻,我的出生,以及许许多多其他的生活小事。*Settling* himself *down* in his armchair, he resumed his reading of his favorite evening paper. 他坐在他那把手扶椅上,又继续看起他喜欢看的晚报来。❷(cause to) become used to living or staying permanently (in a place) (使)(在某地)定居下来: Many young Chinese have gone to the United States and *settled down* there. 中国有许多年轻人都去了美国并定居在那里。The organization aims to *settle* newcomers *down* in the city. 该组织的目的是使新来者在城中安居下来。❸(of a bird or plane) land and take a firm position (指鸟或飞机)降落: The large bird *settled down* on the branch and folded its wings. 那只大鸟落在树枝上,收起了双翅。The light plane *settled down* in the field. 这架轻型飞机降落在田地里。❹(of people) (cause to) become quiet or calm after being excited, or nervous (使人)(从兴奋或紧张中)安静,镇静: The teacher told her students to *settle down* before she started her lesson. 老师在开始讲课之前让学生们安静下来。The chairman tried to *settle* the audience *down*. 主席设法使听众安静下来。My friend Robert's presence *settled* me *down*. 我朋友罗伯特的出现使我镇定了下来。❺(cause to) fall to the bottom of a container or onto a surface (使)沉淀,落下:When the reaction takes place, the dense white smoke forms and *settles down* into the solution. 当反应发生时,白色烟雾便形成,并沉淀于溶液中。Shaking will *settle* the powder *down*. 摇晃会使那粉末沉淀。

NOTE 当本短语用作及物性动词短语,所带的宾语为代词时,该代词须置于本短语的动词和副词中间。

settle down to *vt.* concentrate on (something such as work, or doing something)专心致志于(工作或做某事): That afternoon it was very difficult for her to *settle down to* her own work. 那天下午,她很难埋头于自己的工作。I can't *settle down to* anything today. It's terrible. 真糟糕,我今天无法专心做任何事情。After trying various pursuits, he has *settled down to* farming. 在尝试过多种职业之后,他已安心务农了。

settle for *vt.* 【不可分性动词短语】(无被动语态形式,常用于否定句中,常用一般时态) accept or agree to (something or doing something less than the best, or less than one had hoped for)(勉强或不称心如意地)接受,满足,同意: I want $5,000 for my car and I won't *settle for* less. 我的汽车要卖5 000美元,少于这个数我不会接受。I could never *settle for* such a quiet life, I want excitement. 我决不能满足这种宁静的生活,我要寻求刺激。She was not prepared to *settle for* staying at home as an ordinary housewife. 当一名普通的家庭妇女待在家里,她是不会甘心的。

settle in *v.* ❶become accustomed to one's new surroundings, job, way of life, etc. 适应于(新环境、新工作、新的生活方式等): It was the first time she had left home, so it took her a while to *settle in*. 这是她第一次离开家,所以过了好一阵她才适应。After three months, she seemed to have *settled in* her new job. 三个月后,她似乎就适应了她的新工作。❷(help or cause to) move comfortably into a new home (帮助或使)迁入新居: The Browns are moving into the new flat tomorrow. Can you go and help *settle* them *in*? 布朗家明天要迁入新居了,你能去帮助他们搬家吗? Please come and see our new house when we've *settled in*. 我们迁入新居后,请来看我们的新房子。

NOTE 当本短语用作及物性动词短语,所带的宾语为代词时,该代词须置于本短语的动词和副词中间。

settle on/upon *vt.* ❶(常用完成时态) make a decision on (something or doing something) after thinking or talking about it 决定,选定: The committee has *settled on* a plan for enlarging the factory. 该委员会决定了一项扩建工厂的计划。They have finally *settled on* the terms of the lease. 他们最后敲定了租赁条件。Have you *settled on* a place to spend your vacation? 你们已选定了度假的地点了吗? Now that the meeting-place has been *settled on*, can we talk about the agenda? 既然会谈地点已经选定,我们能否讨论一下议事日程? ❷land on (something) from above 歇落在,停留在: A beautiful bird *settled on* the branch. 一只美丽的鸟儿落在了树枝上。Look at the dust that has *settled on* the furniture while we've been away! 看,我们不在期间落在家具上的灰尘! ❸(英国英语用法,法律用语) give or leave (someone) (money or property) in a legal and official way, under the terms of a will, etc. (根据遗嘱等)把(钱或财产)留给(某人): Mr Williams in his will *settled upon* his old housekeeper an annuity for life of five hundred dollars. 威廉姆斯先生在他的遗嘱中指定赠给他的老管家终身年金500美元。The greater part of his fortune was *settled upon* his three sons. 他大部分财富都留给了他的三个儿子。The old lady *settled* a sum of money *on* the young man who had helped her. 老妇人留给了那位一直帮助她的年轻人一笔钱。

NOTE 当本短语作"决定,选定"解时,同义短语是 decide on/upon。

settle up *v.* pay all of (an amount of money that you owe) to (a particular person or company)结清(账目),付清(债务等): I'm tired of this hotel, let's *settle up* and go. 我在这家旅馆住腻了。咱们结账走吧。Let's *settle up* the accounts. 让我们结清账目吧。Mary paid the whole restaurant bill and let us *settle up* with her later. 玛丽付了所有的饭款,咱们稍后再和她算账吧。To *settle up* his debts Mr Smith needs $5,000. 史密斯先生需要5 000美元才能付清他的债务。

sew up *vt.*【可分性动词短语】❶join (an opening in someone or something) by sewing it using a needle and thread (用针线)缝合: The surgeon *sewed* the patient *up* and pronounced the operation a success. 外科医生将病人的刀口缝合之后便宣布手术成功。A nurse will come and *sew up* that wound for you soon. 护士一会儿就来为你缝合伤口。Will you *sew up* this hole in my trousers? 你能把我裤子上的这个洞缝补一下吗? This suit was *sewn up* by hand. 这套衣服是手工缝制的。❷(非正式用语,常用被动语态形式) complete or settle (something such as a business) satisfactorily 做完,做成(生意等);解决: It's time to *sew* this *up* and go home. 该把这事做完回家了。It's going to take another week or two to *sew up* this deal. 再有一两个星期,就能做成这笔买卖。We should have the whole deal *sewn up* by the end of the week. 到本周末,我们应该会把这整笔买卖圆满做成。We've got the deal *sewn up* now. 这笔买卖我们已经搞定。He confessed and that *sewed* the whole thing *up*. 他坦白了,于是整个事情就解决了。❸(非正式用语) put into one's control; make sure of winning or gaining 控制,独占;确保: With such a big lead in the opinion polls, they've really got the election *sewn up*. 他们在民意测验中遥遥领先,这次选举他们确实已胜券在握。

NOTE 当本短语的宾语为代词时,该代词须置于本短语的动词和副词中间。

shake hands *v.* hold (someone's right hand) in one's own and move it up and down slightly several times, especially when you meet him/her for the first time or when you make an agreement with him/her (与某人)握手: People customarily *shake hands* with each other when they are introduced. 当被引见时,人们通常相互握手。We *shook hands* after we finalized the deal. 当我们完成了这笔交易之后,我们互相握手。

NOTE **1.** 本短语中的名词 hand 必须用复数形式。

2. 本短语另外的两种形式是 shake someone's hand 和 shake someone by the hand。例如:

> "Nice to meet you," Mr Smith said, *shaking my hand*.
> "很高兴见到你。"史密斯先生握着我的手说道。

> The two leaders *shook* each other *by the hand.*
> 两位领导人相互握了手。

但这两个短语中的 hand 必须用单数形式。

3. 本短语可转化为复合词 shake-hands 和 handshake (均用作单数),均意为“握手”。

shake off *vt.*【可分性动词短语】❶(非正式用语)get rid of or free (oneself) from (something unpleasant such as trouble, illness, or fear)(使自己)摆脱(困境、疾病或恐惧): That is an important way for the peasants to *shake off* poverty. 这是农民摆脱贫困的一条重要途径。I've had a cold for two weeks now, I just can't *shake* it *off*. 我已感冒两周了,就是无法治好它。She couldn't *shake off* her fear of snakes. 她无法摆脱对蛇的恐惧。❷escape from (someone or something that is following or chasing you) 逃脱(……的追踪): We ran into the alley and managed to *shake off* our pursuers. 我们跑进了胡同并设法摆脱了追踪我们的人。He drove through the red lights in an attempt to *shake off* the police car that was chasing him. 他闯过红灯,想以此摆脱追踪他的警车。

NOTE 1. 当本短语的宾语为代词时,该代词须置于本短语的动词和副词或介词中间。

2. 本短语可转化为复合词 shake-off, 意为“摆脱,逃脱”。

shake one's head *vi.* ❶ say "no" or express disagreement or that you don't want or believe something by moving one's head from side to side 摇头(表示拒绝或反对,或不想要某物或不相信某事): My boss *shook his head* and I knew not to ask again. 我的老板摇了摇头,我就知道不能再问了。Asked if she wanted anything to eat, Mother *shook her head*. 当问妈妈是否要吃点什么的时候,她摇头说不。"That's incredible!" he said, *shaking his head* in disbelief. “那难以令人相信。”他怀疑地摇头说道。❷ show you don't understand something by turning your head from side to side 摇头(表示不懂): He just smiled and *shook his head* as they sat and discuss Chinese chess. 当他们坐着谈论中国象棋时,他只是微笑地摇着头表示不懂。

NOTE 世界各地的文化和习俗都不尽相同,本短语所表示的意义在有些国家就恰好相反。例如:

> Unlike most countries, in Bulgaria, when you want to answer with a "yes", *shake your head*. To answer with a "no", nod your head.
> 与大多数国家不同的是,在保加利亚,如果你要回答“是的”就摇头,而要回答“不”时,则点头。

shake up *vt.*【可分性动词短语】❶move (a bottle, etc.) to and fro vigorously in order to mix (something such as liquid) 用力摇动(瓶子等)以摇匀(液体等): *Shake up* the bottle well before drinking the medicine. 在饮用此药之前先用力摇动瓶子。The label should state that you must *shake* it *up* before pouring. 标签上应注明必须摇匀后再将其倒出。The contents in the bottle should be *shaken up* until all the sediment disappears. 瓶内药剂应予以摇动,一直到看不见沉淀物为止。❷(常用一般时态)(of something bad, unexpected, or frightening) make (someone) feel suddenly shocked or surprised (指不好的、出乎意料的或令人

可怕的事情)使(某人)感到震惊：The notice about a cut in pay *shook up* everybody in the office. 减薪的通知使办公室所有的人都大为震惊。The news *shook* him *up* a bit. 那消息使他有点震惊。No one was hurt, but many of the passengers were severely *shaken up* by the collision. 虽然没有人受伤，但许多乘客都因这场撞车事故大受惊吓。❸(非正式用语)(of someone) make big changes in (an organization or a company), especially so as to make it more effective or successful 对(某一组织或公司)重新组合，整顿，改组：That government department needs *shaking up*, it has not been doing its job properly. 那个政府部门一直不能正常地发挥作用，需要整顿。The new manager decided to *shake up* the company. 新上任的经理决定对公司进行改组。

NOTE 1. 当本短语的宾语为代词时，该代词须置于本短语的动词和副词中间。

2. 本短语可转化为复合词 shake-up，意为"摇动；震动；振作；(政策、人员等的)剧变，改组"。

shed light on *vt.* 【不可分性动词短语】explain (something that is difficult to understand) by providing new information; clarify or reveal (something) 解释，阐明，查清，揭示：The latest study could *shed light on* why so many young people have been infected with the new flu. 最新的研究结果会阐明为什么有如此多的年轻人感染了这种新型流感。The police hope that the new evidence will be able to *shed* some *light on* the murder. 警方希望新的证据将有助于查明那起谋杀案。The book *sheds light on* Yao Ming's first year playing in the NBA. 这本书揭示了姚明第一年在 NBA 打球的经历。

NOTE 1. 本短语中的名词 light 要用单数形式。light 前可根据表达需要加形容词来修饰。

2. 本短语的同义短语是 cast light on 和 throw light on。

shelter from *vt.* ❶ (cause to) protect (someone or something) from (bad weather) (使)遮蔽，躲避：This hat can *shelter* your face *from* the strong sunlight. 这顶帽子能遮蔽你的脸部，使其不被强烈的日光所晒。These plants must be *sheltered from* direct sunlight. 这种植物必须遮蔽起来，免受日光的直接照射。In the storm people were *sheltering from* the rain in the doorways of shops. 人们躲在商店门口躲避暴风雨。❷ protect (someone or something) from (something or doing something harmful) 庇护，保护；避免：It's impossible to *shelter* your children *from* the harmful effects of television, unless the broadcasters improve the material. 你无法使你的孩子免受电视节目的不良影响，除非电视台改良节目内容。

shield from *vt.* 【不可分性动词短语】provide shelter for (something or someone) from (something harmful) or save (someone) from harm or danger 遮住，挡住，提供保护(以免受……之害)：She put her hand over her baby's eyes to *shield* them *from* the strong sunlight. 她用手遮住婴儿的双眼，以避免其受到强烈阳光的刺激。He raised his arm to *shield* himself *from* the hard blow. 他举起手臂挡住了向他打来的一记重拳。The man tried to *shield* his friend *from* discovery by the police. 那个人千方百计地保护他的朋友不被警察发现。

S

shoot at *vt.* ❶ fire (a bullet from a weapon such as a gun, or an arrow) at (a person, an animal or something) in order to hit, injure or kill them (用枪或箭)向……射击: The man *shot at* him first, hitting him in the head and back, killing him. 那名男子首先向他开枪,击中了他的头部和背部,致其死亡。The kids were *shooting* arrows *at* a target. 孩子们在向靶子射箭。❷kick or throw (a ball) so as to make a point in a game (体育比赛中)射门,投篮: He missed a great opportunity to *shoot at* goal. 他失去了一次极好的射门机会。In the game he *shot at* the basket 11 times but scored only 10 points. 在比赛中他投篮 11 次,但只得了 10 分。❸(无被动语态形式,常用一般时态) give a look at (someone) very quickly and briefly, often in a way that expresses your feelings 向(某人)投以(表达某种感情的)目光: Mary *shot* a grateful glance *at* the man in the black overcoat. 玛丽向那名身穿黑色大衣的男子投以感激的目光。❹(主要用于英国英语中) ask (someone) (a lot of questions) very quickly, one after the other 向(某人)连续提出(一连串的问题): He *shot* questions *at* me so quickly that I didn't even have time to answer. 他向我连珠炮似的提出了一连串的问题,我都无暇作答。

shoot down *vt.* 【可分性动词短语】❶(常用一般时态) bring down and destroy (a flying object, especially an airplane) by shooting (with gunfire or a missile) (用炮火或导弹)击落(某种飞行物,尤指飞机): The US military successfully *shot down* a damaged spy satellite expected to hit the earth by a SM-3 missile. 美国军方成功地用一枚 SM-3 型导弹将一颗即将撞击地球的受损间谍卫星击落。The plane was carrying troops home on leave when guerrillas *shot* it *down* with a surface-to-air missile. 这架飞机是在运送士兵回国休假时被游击队的一枚地对空导弹击落。Eight soldiers were killed when their Apache helicopter was *shot down* by ground fire. 一架阿帕奇直升机被地面火力击落,机上八名士兵丧生。❷kill (a person, especially an unarmed person) with a gun 枪杀(尤指手无寸铁之人): The government suppressed the riot by *shooting down* the protesters. 政府用枪打死了示威者,平定了那场骚乱。They *shot* him *down* in cold blood. 他们残忍地枪杀了他。❸(非正式用语) criticize (someone or something) very severely; show or claim to be wrong or mistaken 严厉批评,批驳: Why did you shoot him down like that? 你为什么那样严厉地批评他呢? It's my view, you may *shoot* me *down* if you like. 这是我的观点。如果你愿意的话,你可以批驳我。His latest theories have been *shot down* by the experts. 他的最新理论受到了专家们的严厉批评。

NOTE **1.** 当本短语的宾语为代词时,该代词须置于本短语的动词和副词中间。

2. 本短语可转化为复合词 shootdown,意为"击落"。

shoot for *vt.* (主要用于美国英语中,非正式用语) aim at or try to reach; try to achieve (a particular thing); strive for 力争达到(某目标),力图取得……,为……而努力: We are *shooting* this year *for* a goal of a 50% increase in sales. 我们今年力争达到销售额增长 50% 的目标。There is no harm in *shooting for* the

S

directorship, but I think you are too inexperienced for the job. 争取当董事倒没有什么坏处,但我认为你做这个工作经验还太少。When it is achieved there will be other plans to *shoot for*. 这一点实现以后,还要为实现其他计划而努力。

shoot up *vi.* ❶go upwards, arise quickly 迅速上升:As we watched, flames from the roof of the house *shot up* into the air. 我们眼看着火焰从房顶迅速升上天空。❷(非正式用语) increase very quickly (by a large amount or number) 猛增:Petrol prices have *shot up* in the last several months. 在过去的几个月中,汽油价格猛涨。The circulation of the monthly *shot up* to almost 100,000. 该月刊的发行量猛增到近 10 万册。❸(非正式用语)grow taller very quickly 迅速长高:Tommy had always been a small boy, but when he was 15 years old he began to *shoot up*. 汤米一直是一个瘦小的男孩,但到 15 岁时他很快地长高了。After last week's rain, the weeds have *shot up*. 上星期下过雨后,杂草生长得很快。❹appear suddenly 突然出现:There were fast-food restaurants *shooting up* all over town. 全城到处突现了一些快餐馆。

—*vt.* (主要用于美国英语中,非正式用语,常用被动语态形式) shoot at (something) recklessly; damage or wound by shooting 朝……胡乱开枪;击损,击伤: The man got drunk and *shot up* the bar room. 那个人喝醉了酒,朝酒吧间胡乱开枪。His plane had been badly *shot up* by enemy fighters. 他的飞机被敌机严重击损。The castle was badly *shot up* during the war. 这座古堡在战争期间被打得满目疮痍。

short cut *n.* ❶ a path or route that is shorter and more direct than the one usually taken to get somewhere 近路,捷径:It's no thanks to you that we arrived on time; your *short cuts* weren't *short cuts* at all! 我们及时赶到,可你并没有帮上忙,你说的那几条近路一点儿也不近!We were late for school, so we took a *short cut* across the fields. 我们上学要迟到了,所以就穿过田地走了捷径。❷ a method of achieving something more quickly or more easily than if you use the usual methods 快捷简便的方法,做事的捷径: You can do that sum by a *short cut*. 你可以用简便的方法来解那道算术题。There aren't really any *short cuts* to learning English. 学习英语实在没有什么捷径可走。

NOTE 本短语可转化为复合名词 shortcut。但在英国英语中,常分作 short cut 使用。

short for ⇨ **for short**

short of *prep.* ❶ not having enough of (something)缺少……:Our village badly needs a new reservoir but is *short of* money. 我们村非常需要建一座新水库,但没有足够的钱。We shall try to finish the work in time though we are *short of* manpower. 虽然我们缺少人力,但我们仍要尽力按时完成这项任务。This friend of mine is a nice person, but a bit *short of* brains. 我这位朋友是个很好的人,可就是有点缺乏头脑。❷except for; without (a particular thing)除了……外,如果没有……: *Short of* calling a protest meeting I don't know how we can show our opposition. 除了召集抗议大会外,我不知道我们还能怎样表明我们的反对立场。The power plant can be finished on schedule, *short of* an unexpected situation in the engineering. 如果工程中没有预料不到的情况,发电厂可如期完工。❸away from; at a distance from (a place) 远离……: The day's drive still left us a hundred miles *short of* the sea. 开了一天的车,我们距离大海仍有 100 英里之远。He stopped a hundred yards *short of* the building. 他在距离那栋楼 100 码远的地方停了下来。❹not quite reaching; up to but not including 尚未达到……,几乎近于……: The quality of their products comes *short of* the standard set down by us. 他们的产品质量没达到我们规定的标准。We'd tried everything to get our money *short of* actually suing them. 为了讨回我们的钱,我们尝试了各种办法,实际上就差没跟他们打官司了。

NOTE 本短语的第一个义项总是以 be short of 的形式出现和使用的,与 lack for 和 lack in 同义。但本短语比后两者更为常用,而后两者则比本短语正式。见 lack for 和 lack in。

shoulder to shoulder *adv.* ❶ each helping and supporting the other, often by doing something together in order to achieve a common aim (为达到共同目标而)相互帮助地,相互支持地,肩并肩地(同做某事): Chinese experts, doctors, teachers and workers sent to Africa have worked *shoulder to shoulder* with the local people and forged a deep friendship. 被派遣到非洲的中国专家、医生、教师和工人同当地人民并肩工作、友好情深。The two armies fought *shoulder to shoulder* against their common enemy. 两国军队肩并肩地抗击他们共同的敌人。❷side by side; close together and next to each other 并排地,一个紧挨一个地: Bars and restaurants stand *shoulder to shoulder* all along this street. 这条街上,酒吧和餐馆一家挨着一家。The prisoners were packed *shoulder to shoulder* on the truck. 囚犯们被一个紧挨一个地装在了卡车上。

NOTE 1. 本短语是由"身体某部分的名词+介词+身体某部分的名词"构成的副词性短语。同类的短语还有: arm in arm, face to face, hand in hand, side by side 等。

2. 当本短语作"并排地,一个紧挨一个地"解时,同义短语是 side by side。

3. 本短语可以转化为复合副词 shoulder-to-shoulder。例如:

> They fought *shoulder-to-shoulder* against a common enemy.
> 他们肩并肩地抗击他们共同的敌人。

shout at *vt.* speak or say (something) very loudly to (someone); make a loud sound with the voice to (someone) 对(某人)大声喝叫,向(某人)吼叫: I wish you'd stop *shouting at* your students. 我希望你不要再大声向你的学生们吼叫。I *shouted at* him to put the gun down. 我大声喝叫,让他把枪放下。He *shouted* abuse *at* the salesman who had cheated him the other day. 他大声辱骂前几天蒙骗了他的那个推销员。I hated being *shouted at* even when I had been naughty. 即使在我淘气的时候我也不喜欢别人向我吼叫。

shout down *vt.* 【可分性动词短语】 prevent (a speaker or his words) from being heard, (for example at a meeting) by shouting very loudly while he is speaking 大声叫喊以压倒(某人讲话的声音): The angry audience *shouted* the politician *down*. 愤怒的听众大声喊叫压倒了那政客的声音。They *shouted* him *down* when he tried to explain why Zaire needed an interim government. 当他试图解释为什么扎伊尔需要一个过渡政府的原因时,他们大声喊叫压倒了他的声音。Mr Smith suggested that we give our club money to charity, but he was *shouted down*. 史密斯先生建议把俱乐部的钱作慈善之用,但遭到众人的高声反对。

NOTE 当本短语的宾语为代词时,该代词须置于本短语的动词和副词中间。

shout one's head off ⇨ **laugh one's head off**

shout out *vi.* express something loudly; make a loud noise 大声喊叫,发出叫声:I wanted to *shout out* and stop her but she was already gone. 我想大喊一声阻止她,但她已经走了。

—*vt.*【可分性动词短语】say (something) by shouting so that people can hear you clearly 大声说出: She *shouted out* a warning. 她大声发出警告。He *shouted* the news *out*. 他大声讲出那条消息。A few people in the audience *shouted out* questions. 几名听众大声地提出了几个问题。I wanted to *shout* it *out*, and let her know what I had overheard. 我想把我所听到的事情喊出来,让她知道。

S

NOTE 当本短语用作及物性动词短语,所带的宾语为代词时,该代词须置于本短语的动词和副词中间。

show around/round *vt.*【可分性动词短语】lead or conduct (someone) around (a place) for the first time so that he can see all parts of it 带领(某人)参观(或察看): Before you start work, I'll *show* you *around* the building so that you can meet everyone. 在你开始上班之前,我先带你到楼里各处看看,好让你和所有的人见见面。If you are free tomorrow, I shall be delighted to *show* you *around* the Great Wall, one of the world's great wonders. 如果你们明天有时间,我很乐意带你们参观世界奇观之一——长城。They were taken to the house and *shown round*. 他们被带到房里察看了一番。

NOTE 当本短语的宾语为代词时,该代词须置于本短语的动词和副词或介词中间。

show in/into *vt.*【可分性动词短语】lead (someone) in/into (a room) 把(某人)带进(房间): When the visitors arrive, *show* them straight *in*. 当来访者们到达后,请把他们直接领进房间来。The secretary *showed in* the guests one by one. 秘书把客人们一个一个地带了进来。She *showed* me *into* the sitting room and asked me to wait. 她把我领入客厅后,让我稍等。We were *shown into* the living room. 我们被带入起居室。

NOTE 当本短语的宾语为代词时,该代词须置于本短语的动词和副词或介词中间。

show off *vt.* & *vi.* ❶(非正式用语,贬义用法)try to impress people by displaying (oneself, someone or something that one owns) in a very obvious way 卖弄(自己),炫耀,炫示(某人或自己所拥有之物): I'm sick of a man who tries to *show off* in front of strangers. 我讨厌在生人面前卖弄自己的人。He is very rich, but he doesn't like to *show off* himself in the public place. 他很富有,可他从不愿在公开场合炫耀自己。Today, young parents *show off* their newborn babies online and receive congratulations from their relatives and friends right away. 现在,年轻的父母们都在网上展示他们刚出生的宝宝,并能很快得到亲属和朋友们的祝贺。Mary has a very expensive watch and she never misses an opportunity to *show it off*. 玛丽有一块很昂贵的手表，她总是不失时机地向别人炫示它。

—*vt.* ❶ show people (something, especially the skills you are very proud of) so they will admire it 展示(尤指才艺): Young musicians will get the chance to *show off* their musical skills. 年轻的音乐家们将有机会展示他们的音乐才艺。A French student *showed off* his rare mental ability by working out in his head the 13th root of a random 200-digit number in just 72.4 seconds. 一名法国大学生展示了其罕见的心算本领。他在72.4秒内心算出一个随机抽取的200位数的13次方根。❷(常用一般时态) put out (something) nicely for people to see; display; exhibit 陈列，显示(某物): The shopkeeper *shows off* a pair of "lovers' combs", specially designed for the coming Valentine's Day, which falls on February 14. 店主展示了一副专门为即将到来的情人节而设计的"情人梳子"。The girls couldn't wait to *show off* their fine needlework to our guests. 女孩们迫不及待地向我们的客人显示她们精巧的刺绣活。The third version of Nintendo's Game Boy Advance was *shown off* at that year's E3. 任天堂公司的Game Boy Advance第三版游戏机在那一年的E3游戏展会上展出。❸(of something) make (something) look especially attractive 使(某物)显得更加诱人: Her tight-fitting trousers *show off* her fine figure. 她穿的紧身裤更显出她的好身材。

NOTE **1.** 当本短语用作及物性动词短语，所带的宾语为代词时，该代词须置于本短语的动词和副词中间。

2. 本短语可转化为复合词show-off，意为"炫耀，卖弄；爱炫耀的人，爱吹牛的人"。

show over *vt.* 【可分性动词短语】(主要用于英国英语中) lead (someone) around (a place) in order to show him or her how interesting or attractive it is 带(某人)参观(某处): The director *showed* the Prime Minister *over* the new production plant. 厂长陪同首相参观了新的生产车间。She was busy *showing* some important guests *over* the factory. 她正忙于带领一些重要的客人参观工厂。After lunch the VIPs will be *shown over* the new Arts Centre. 午餐后，这些重要客人将被带去参观新艺术中心。

show up *v.* ❶(常用一般时态) (of something) (cause to) be easily seen, especially when previously it has been difficult to see it; reveal clearly 使(某物)显现；显露出: The detective put a chemical on the paper, and the fingerprints *showed up*. 刑侦人员在那页纸上涂上一种化学药剂，指纹便显现了出来。His show-off only serves to *show up* his ignorance. 他的卖弄反而显露出了他的无知。Staying up a whole night *showed up* his wrinkles on his face. 熬了一整夜使他脸上的皱纹显现出来。❷make clear the unpleasant truth about or expose (someone or something) 揭发，揭露: She said she was to *show up* the man for the liar he was. 她说她要揭发那个人是个说谎的骗子。I intend to *show up* this deception. 我打算揭露这一骗局。The impostor has been *shown up*. 那骗子被揭露出来。❸(非正式用语，常用一般时态) (of someone) appear or arrive at a place as expected or arranged (指某人)(按预期或安排)出现，露面，出席，到场: They *showed up* again in Brazil a year later. 他们一年后

又在巴西露面了。More than 80 government leaders from around the world *showed up* at the grand opening ceremony of the Beijing Olympic Games. 有 80 多位来自世界各国的政要出席了北京奥运会盛大开幕式。❹(主要用于英国英语中,非正式用语) cause (someone) to feel embarrassed or ashamed in public 使(某人)感到难堪,使(某人)感到丢脸,出(某人的)洋相: When we go to parties my husband always *shows* me *up* with the rude jokes he tells. 我们去参加聚会时,我丈夫总是说些粗俗的笑话使我感到难堪。She kept saying I ought to try, but I wasn't going to *show* myself *up*. 她总说我应该试一试,但我可不想出洋相。

NOTE 1. 当本短语用作及物性动词短语,所带的宾语为代词时,该代词须置于本短语的动词和副词中间。

2. 当本短语作"(按预期或安排)出现,露面,出席,到场"解时,同义短语是 turn up。

3. 本短语可转化为复合词 show-up,意为"揭发,揭露"。

shrivel up *v.* (of a leaf, skin, etc.)(cause to) become smaller and thinner than usual through dryness or old age (指枝、皮等因干燥或年老等)枯萎,皱缩: The leaves had *shriveled up* in the summer heat. 叶子在暑热中枯萎了。The long drought *shriveled up* this summer's crops. 长期的干旱使今年的夏季作物都枯萎了。

shrug off *vt.* 【可分性动词短语】 ❶remove (clothes) by shaking them off your body 耸肩抖掉穿着的(衣物): He *shrugged* his coat *off* carelessly and let it fall to the floor. 他漫不经心地耸肩抖去上衣,让它滑落在地板上。❷(常用一般时态) treat or regard (something) as unimportant, not worth one's attention; show that something does not worry or upset you 对……不予理睬,对……漠然视之; 不担心……: He had a way of *shrugging off* criticism as though it were beneath his notice. 他对批评不屑一顾,好像那不值得注意。Father cut his finger but he tied a cloth around it and *shrugged* it *off*. 爸爸的手指割破了,但他用一块布把伤指包起来便不再理会了。Please don't *shrug* this *off*. 请不要对此漠然视之。❸(常用一般时态) get rid of (something such as a feeling) 摆脱(某种情绪等): It usually takes me a long time in the morning to *shrug off* sleep. 早晨我常常要花很长时间才能摆脱睡意。

NOTE 当本短语的宾语为代词时,该代词须置于本短语的动词和副词中间。

shut down *v.* ❶(of a school, business or factory)(cause to) close or stop operating, especially for a long time or forever (使)(学校、商业部门或工厂)关闭、停业或停产: The Red Lake High School in the State of Minnesota was *shut down* immediately after the shootings. 明尼苏达州的红湖中学在发生枪击案后马上就被关闭了。Last year, China *shut down* nearly 50,000 internet cafes that were operating without a license. 中国在去年关闭了近 5 万家无照营业的网吧。They have *shut* the shop *down*. 他们已把这家商店关闭了。The factory may *shut down* if supplies cease. 如果供应中断,该工厂就会停产。❷(of a machine or computer)(cause to) stop operating (机器或计算机)停止运转,关闭(机器或计算机): Be sure to *shut down* the computer before you leave. 走前一定要

把计算机关掉。

NOTE 1. 当本短语用作及物性动词短语，所带的宾语为代词时，该代词须置于本短语的动词和副词中间。

2. 当本短语作“关闭、停业或停产”解时，同义短语是 close down。

3. 本短语可转化为复合词 shutdown，意为“(工厂等的)停工，关闭，(机器的)停车”。

shut in *vt.*【可分性动词短语】❶(常用被动语态形式)put(someone or an animal) in a place so that they cannot leave it 把(某人或动物)关在……里：Mrs Smith has been *shut in* for many months now because of her bad leg. 史密斯太太因腿有毛病现已有好几个月不能出门了。Is it kind to *shut* the dog *in* the house while you are away at work? 你上班期间把狗一直关在房里，这仁慈吗？❷ put (yourself) in a place, you stay in there and make sure nobody else can get in 把(自己)关在……里：She *shut* herself *in* the bathroom and wept. 她把自己关在盥洗室里哭泣。Don't *shut* yourself *in* the study all-day, go out for a walk. 别整天把自己关在书房里。出来走一走。❸(常用被动语态形式)enclose; keep out of view 围住，遮住：The school is *shut in* by factories all round. 这所学校被一些工厂所包围。The farmhouse is completely *shut in* by tall trees. 这一农舍完全被高大的树木遮住了。

NOTE 1. 当本短语的宾语为代词时，该代词须置于本短语的动词和副词或介词中间。

2. 本短语可转化为复合词 shut-in，意为“被关在屋里的人，卧病在床的人”

shut off *vt.*【可分性动词短语】❶(常用被动语态形式，与 from 连用) keep (someone or something) separate or away (from people or things)使……与……相隔离，使……脱离……：He has been *shut off* from the outside society ever since he was arrested. 自从被捕以来，他就与外界相隔绝了。She *shut* herself *off* from society. 她使自己与社会相隔绝。It is a great mansion, *shut off* from the road by high walls. 那是一所富丽堂皇的大房子，高高的围墙将其与马路相隔。This village is *shut off* by mountains from the rest of the world. 这个村庄被群山环抱，与世隔绝。❷(of an official organization) stop the flow of (something, usually water or electricity)(指官方机构)切断，停止(尤指水、电等)的供应：He hadn't paid for his water, so the company had *shut* it *off*. 因他没交水费，自来水公司便断了他的水。I haven't had a bath for days, they've *shut off* the hot water supply. 我已经好几天没洗澡了，他们把热水供应给断掉了。The power was *shut off* for several hours while the lines were being checked. 在检查线路期间，电停了数小时。

—*vt.* & *vi.* (of a machine or an electrical item)(cause to) stop working (机器)停止运转；把(机器或电器)关掉：This machine *shuts off* automatically if a certain temperature is reached. 这台机器在到达一定温度时能自动停止运转。They pulled over and *shut off* the engine. 他们把汽车停在路边并关掉了发动机。It's too late. Would you please *shut off* the radio? 天很晚了。请你把收音机关掉，好吗？Will somebody for God's sake *shut* the alarm *off*? 能不能有人看在上帝的面上把闹铃关掉呢？

NOTE 1. 当本短语用作及物性动词短语，所带的宾语为代词时，该代词须置于本短语的动词和副词中间。

2. 本短语可转化为复合词 shutoff，意为"停止，终止"。

shut out *vt.* 【可分性动词短语】❶prevent (someone or something) from getting into a place; keep (someone or something) out by closing the doors, for example 不让……进来，把关……在外面：Ticket-holders who arrive late may find themselves *shut out* of the stadium. 迟到的持票者会发现他们进不去体育场了。We are in duty bound to co-operate with them and have no right to *shut* them *out*. 我们有与他们合作的义务，而没有把他们排斥在外的权利。She closed the door to *shut out* the sound of the rain. 她关上门，不让雨声传进来。He *shut* the dog *out* of the room. 他把狗关在了屋外。❷prevent (something or someone) from being seen; hide (someone or something) from sight 挡住，遮蔽：The trees are very beautiful, but they do *shut out* the light. 这些树非常美，但它们却很挡光。Passing clouds *shut* the sun *out*. 浮云遮蔽了太阳。

NOTE 1. 当本短语的宾语为代词时，该代词须置于本短语的动词和副词中间。

2. 本短语可转化为复合词 shutout，意为"被关在外面的人"。

shut up *vt.*【可分性动词短语】❶close (a house) so that people cannot enter or leave it 关闭(门或窗)：We're going to *shut* the house *up* for the summer while we're away. 我们在夏季外出期间就把房子关闭起来。We got the house *shut up* only minutes before the storm hit. 在暴风雨来临之前几分钟我们才把屋子的门窗关闭起来。❷(英国英语用法，非正式用语)close (a business), either at the end of the working day or for a definite period of time (商店)关门，停业(一段时间)：We got to the store only to find that the owner had *shut up* shop for the weekend. 我们到了商店时才发现，店主已关门度周末去了。The shop has been *shut up*. 这家商店已被关闭。❸confine (someone, something or an animal); put (something) away under lock and key for safe keeping 禁闭……；锁上以保藏(某物)：Peter has been *shut up* with an infectious disease all week. 彼得因患传染病而被禁闭整整一个星期。He *shut* himself *up* in the room, reading and writing everyday. 他每天把自己关在屋子里读书和写作。That dog bites. It should be *shut up*. 那条狗咬人，应该把它关起来。*Shut up* all your valuables in the safe. 把你所有值钱的东西都锁在保险柜里。

—*vt.* & *vi.* (非正式用语，一般用于祈使句中) (cause to) stop talking; be or make quiet (使)住口，闭嘴：You have no right to *shut* me *up*. 你没有权利禁止我说话。I wish she would *shut up* complaining. 我希望她闭嘴别抱怨了。*Shut up*! I'm sick of listening to your complaints. 闭嘴吧！你发的牢骚我都听烦了。

NOTE 1. 当本短语用作及物性动词短语，所带的宾语为代词时，该代词须置于本短语的动词和副词中间。

2. 当本短语作"关闭(门或窗)"解时，宾语要用 house 或 building 等词，而不用 door 或 window。

3. 当本短语作"(使)住口，闭嘴"解时，同义短语是 clam up 和 zip one's lip(s)。

sick and tired *adj.* (非正式用语，常与 of 连用) feeling annoyance, dislike, and impatience from too much of (something or someone) 厌烦……，讨厌……: It makes me *sick and tired* all the time! 此事一直使我厌烦不已。I'm getting *sick and tired* of the same old routine every day. 我对每天一成不变的日常事儿开始厌倦了。To tell you the truth, I'm *sick and tired* of listening to your complaints. 实话对你讲，你发的牢骚我都听烦了。I feel *sick and tired* of a man who tries to show off. 我对自我卖弄的人感到讨厌。

NOTE 1. 本短语的比较级形式是 more sick and tired，最高级形式是 most sick and tired。

2. 本短语的同义短语是 fed up 和 sick to death。

sick to death *adj*. (非正式用语，常与 of 连用) totally disgusted with (something or someone)对……讨厌至极，厌烦……得要命：I've been treated like dirt for two years and I'm *sick to death* of it! 两年来我一直被怠慢，我对此讨厌至极! She's *sick to death* of being blamed for everything that goes wrong. 出什么差错都怪她，真把她烦死了。This reporting about the scandals in the government has me *sick to death*. 我对这则政府中的丑闻报道讨厌至极。I am *sick to death* of one of my buyers! 我的一个买主让我烦得要命!

side by side *adv*. ❶ (of two or more people) sitting or walking next to each other 并排地，肩并肩地：The children sat *side by side* on the sofa watching television. 孩子们都并排坐在沙发上看电视。At the Beijing Olympic Games opening ceremony, a 9-year-old boy from Wenchuan walked ahead of China's 1,099-member delegation, *side by side* with 7-foot-6 basketball star Yao Ming. 在北京奥运会开幕式上，一名来自汶川的 9 岁男孩和身高 7.6 英尺的篮球明星姚明并排走在由 1 099 名成员组成的中国代表团前面。❷ (of people) working close together; beside one another 一道，一起：We have worked *side by side* for many years. 我们一道工作了多年。He expects the strategic partnership between the two countries to continue to grow and become stronger as they fight *side by side* against terrorism. 他希望两国间的战略伙伴关系在共同打击恐怖主义的斗争中不断发展和更加巩固。

side effect *n*. ❶ an effect of a medicine or treatment that is not intended and could be unpleasant, or any additional result that you did not expect or want (某种药物或治疗的)副作用：One significant *side effect* of the drug is headache. 这种药的一个明显副作用是让人头痛。Doctors and patients were asked to look out for *side effects* of the drugs used to treat arthritis. 医生和患者被提请注意用来治疗关节炎的药品的副作用。❷ the unplanned things that happen in addition to the main results or effects that are expected to happen 意外情况，意外后果：The tourist industry is worried about the possible *side effects* of these strict regulations. 旅游业担心这些严厉的规定可能会产生一些意外情况。One *side effect* of the crisis could be that she loses her seat in Parliament. 这场危机的一个意外后果是她失去了她在议会中的席位。

side with *vt*. agree with or support (one person or group) in an argument 偏袒，支持(某人)：Why is it that you always *side* with your father when he and I argue? 在你爸爸和我争论时，你为什么总是向着他？Common citizens *sided with* the central government's handling of the riots. 普通市民都支持中央政府对骚乱事件的处理。

NOTE 本短语的同义短语是 take sides with 和 take the side of。

sign off *vi.* ❶（非正式用语）(of a radio or television station) stop broadcasting, especially at the end of the day（广播电台或电视台）停止（当天的）播出：The broadcasting station usually *signs off* at midnight. 广播电台通常在午夜结束全天的播音。That TV station always *signs off* after a movie. 那家电视台总是在播放一部电影之后结束一天的电视节目。❷ cease employment with a company, etc., by or as by signing a paper（从公司等）签约辞职：After ten years, I at last decided to *sign off* and go into business by myself. 十年后，我终于决定辞职去搞个体经营。❸ quit doing what one has been doing and leave 停止所做之事并离去：I have to *sign off* and get to bed. Good night. 我不干了，睡觉去。晚安。❹ end an informal letter, especially with a signature（尤指以签名）结束（非正式）书信："I'd better *sign off* now, my dear. Love, Jack." "亲爱的，到此停笔。爱你的杰克。"

NOTE 当本短语作"（广播电台或电视台）停止（当天的）播出"和"（从公司等）签约辞职"解时，反义短语是 sign on。

sign on *vi.* ❶ (of a radio or television station) start broadcasting for the day（广播电台或电视台）开始白天的播出：It's time to *sign on* for the day. 现在开始全天的播音。The local TV station is *signing on*. 当地的电视台正在播出节目。Most TV stations *sign on* for the day very early. 大部分电视台很早就开始播出节目。❷ begin work (as with a company, ship or army), by or as by signing a paper 签约受雇（于某一公司、船上或军队）：John *signed on* yesterday and will start work on Monday. 约翰昨天签约受雇，并将从周一开始上班。He *signed on* as a sailor. 他签约受雇为水手。If you join the army you have to *sign on* for at least three years. 如果你参军，你就得在军中服役至少三年。

—*vt.* ❶ employ (someone) to do a job 雇用（某人）：How many workers did our company *sign on*? 我们公司雇用了多少工人？We've *signed on* three new members of staff. 我们又雇用了三名职员。❷ write (your name or a secret word) in order to use a computer（在使用计算机前）登录（户名或密码）：You need your password to *sign on*. 你需要登录你的密码。

sign up *vt.* & *vi.* (cause to) sign one's name when joining an organization, a group, or a course of study（使）报名参加（某一组织或就读某一课程等）：I've *signed up* to take a course at the local college. 我已报名在当地的学院学一门课程。Can you *sign up* any more students to come to our college? 您能否让更多的学生报名来我们学院就读？

—*vt.* ❶（常与介词 for 短语连用）record the agreement of (someone) to participate in something 为（某人）报名参加（某一活动）：Has anyone *signed* you *up* for the school party? 有人给你报名参加学校举行的聚会了吗？Could you please *sign up* Jim for the outing? 能请你给吉姆报个

名参加这次出游吗？❷ cause (someone such as a performer) to sign a contract agreeing to do something 使(演员等)签约受雇：The director was happy to have been able to *sign up* the famous singer for the next concert. 能使那位著名的歌手签约参加下次音乐会的演出，导演十分高兴。The football club has just *signed up* three new foreign players. 该足球俱乐部刚刚与三位外籍新球员签约。

NOTE 当本短语用作及物性动词短语，所带的宾语为代词时，该代词须置于本短语的动词和副词中间。

similar to *adj.* (of two or more things) having a resemblance to 与……相似：Wheat looks similar to barley. 小麦和大麦看上去很相似。My problems are very *similar to* yours. 我的问题与你的差不多。According to the World Health Organization, in humans the symptoms of H1N1 flu are *similar to* those of ordinary. 据世界卫生组织所述，人患了甲型 H1N1 流感的症状与普通流感的那些症状相类似。The bright star HD70642, visible with binoculars, has properties very *similar to* those of our sun. 用双筒望远镜看见的亮星 HD70642 的特性很像我们的太阳。

NOTE 本短语的反义短语是 different from/to。

since then *adv.* from that time up to the moment of speaking or writing 自从那时起：Ever *since then*, I have been longing to meet him face to face. 自从那时起，我就一直渴望与他相见。

NOTE 本短语强调到目前为止一直进行的动作或保持的状态，因此句中谓语动词一般用现在完成时或现在完成进行时。

single out *vt.* 【可分性动词短语】(常与 as 或 for 连用) choose (someone or something) from a group and give them special attention or treatment 选出，挑出：Who would you *single out* as the most promising employee of the year? 你会选谁作为今年最有前途的职员？"We *singled* him *out* as the goodwill ambassador in the campaign against AIDS because of his trustworthy image, and his sense of responsibility," said the Health Minister. 卫生部长说："我们挑选他做防治艾滋病运动的爱心大使是因为他那可信的形象和他的责任感。" Lann was often *singled out* for punishment. 兰恩经常被选作受罚的对象。

NOTE 当本短语的宾语为代词时，该代词须置于本短语的动词和副词中间。

sink into *vt.* ❶ (cause to) be lowered into (something such as water) (使)沉入(水中等)：The ancient merchant boat, named Nanhai Number 1, which *sank into* the South China Sea 800 years ago, was raised from the sea on Friday. 800 多年前沉没于南中国海的被命名为"南海一号"的古代商船在星期五被打捞出水。Our feet *sank into* the mud as we walked. 在我们行走时，我们的脚都陷在泥浆里。❷ (of a liquid or soft substance) enter (something such as material) 渗入：It will take a little time for the rain to *sink into* the dried earth. 雨水很快就会渗到干旱的土壤中去。❸ (无被动语态形式，常用一般时态) reach (a state, usually less conscious or less desirable) 陷入(某种不清醒或不佳的精神状态中)：At last I *sank into* a deep sleep. 我终于沉沉入睡了。Don't allow yourself to *sink into* grief. 不要使自己陷入悲痛之中。She *sank into* a deep depression. 她的情绪极

度消沉。❹put (money, labor, etc.) into (something or doing something) 把(资金、人力等)投入于: They *sank* a lot of money *into* the project. 他们把许多资金都投放在了这一项目上。He's *sunk* all his money *into* buying a new car. 他把所有的钱都花在了购置新车上。

sit about/around *v.* (非正式用语,常为贬义用法) spend time (in a place) doing nothing useful or interesting, especially while waiting or while others are active 无所事事地度时光: Richard isn't the type to *sit about* doing nothing. 理查德不是那种无所事事度时光的人。The foreign correspondents seemed to spend most of their time *sitting around* in bars. 这些外国记者似乎把大部分时间都泡在了酒吧里。

NOTE sit about 为英国英语用法。

sit back *vi.* ❶ take a sitting position leaning backwards or deep in a chair; relax (usually after strenuous activity) 向后靠坐着;(通常在紧张活动之后)放松地休息: He *sat back* in his chair and looked at me. 他向后靠坐在椅子上看着我。*Sit back*, there is no need to be nervous. 放松一点,用不着紧张。At last he *sat back* and enjoyed the results of his hard work. 他终于能坐享其辛勤劳动的成果了。❷(非正式用语) not become involved in something that is happening 不参与,旁观: He is not the sort of person who *sits back* and lets you do it alone. 他不是那种袖手旁观而让你一个人干事的人。You should not *sit* quietly *back* while your classmates are all busy with preparations for the evening party. 你不该在你的同学都忙着为晚会做准备的时候不声不响地袖手旁观。

sit by *vi.* take no proper or necessary action when something wrong or illegal is happening 无动于衷,袖手旁观: We can't just *sit by* while these people break the law. 我们不能无动于衷地眼看着这些人违法。We will not *sit by* and do nothing faced with provocative activities aimed at splitting the motherland. 面对旨在分裂祖国的挑衅活动,我们绝不会袖手旁观、无所作为。

NOTE 本短语与 look on, sit back, stand aside 和 stand by 都表示"旁观"之意。但本短语和 stand by 均指"在不良或违法之事发生时"无动于衷,袖手旁观;而 look on, sit back 和 stand aside 所旁观的则不一定是"不良或违法之事"。

sit down *vt.* & *vi.* (cause to) move your body so that the lower part of it is resting on a seat or on the ground (使)就座,坐下: After entering the room I *sat down* on the sofa next to Robert. 进屋后,我便挨着罗伯特坐在了沙发上。He gave his speech *sitting down*. 他是坐着发表讲演的。They *sat* me *down* and had a very serious talk with me. 他们让我坐下来并和我进行了一次十分严肃的交谈。Why don't you *sit* yourself *down*? We'll do the washing up. 您坐着,我们来洗餐具。

—*vi.* ❶spend time and effort discussing (something) in order to try to achieve something 坐下来商讨(某事): I'm deeply impressed by their willingness to *sit down* and have a constructive dialogue about these issues. 他们愿意坐下来对这些问题进行建设性的对话,给我留下了很深的印象。The parties in the dispute have decided to *sit down* and work out a compromise. 争端各方决定坐下来达成一项妥协。❷sit on the ground to express opposition to something, or refuse to work, etc. 静坐示威：Thousands of people *sat down* in the rain before the presidential building to protest the election result. 成千上万的人在总统府大楼前冒雨静坐，抗议选举结果。

NOTE **1.** 如果让某人“坐下”，通常情况下用“Sit down.”或“Take/Have a seat.”；在非常正式的场合中，用“Be seated”。只有在向狗发出“坐下”的命令时，才用“Sit!”。

2. 当本短语用作及物性动词短语，所带的宾语为代词时，该代词须置于本短语的动词和副词中间。

3. 本短语可转化为复合词 sit-down，意为“坐下；坐的地方；静坐罢工”。

sit for *vt.*【不可分性动词短语】❶(英国英语用法，正式用语) take or enter (an examination)参加(考试)：My friend who had planned to apply for the scholarship from the American Universities *sat for* the TOEFL examination on Saturday. 我朋友计划申请美国大学奖学金，于星期六参加了托福考试。More students than ever before has *sat for* their law examinations this year. 今年，参加法律考试的学生比以往任何一年的都多。He *sat for* a scholarship but failed to win it. 他参加了奖学金考试，但未能获得。❷(无被动语态形式) be a model for (a painter or photographer, etc.)为(画家或摄影家等)当模特：In her youth, she earned a living by *sitting for* art students in a college. 在她年轻时，她曾靠为某学院的艺术系学生当模特谋生。She earns money *sitting for* painters. 她靠为画家当模特赚钱。Linda is looking for someone to *sit for* her so she can develop her skills. 为提高技艺，琳达在找人做她的模特。❸look after children while their parents are out; serve as a babysitter in someone's employ 给……看孩子；为……做保姆：She *sits for* her neighbours when they go out. 当邻居外出时，她就给他们看孩子。I used to *sit for* the Browns. 我曾为布朗家做过保姆。

sit in *v.* ❶(cause to) be in a position in which the lower part of the body is resting on (something)(使)坐在……上：The person *sitting in* the armchair on the right is my father. 坐在右边那个手扶椅上的人是我爸爸。I sometimes *sit* my baby *in* the sofa next to me. 有时，我把我的小宝宝放在沙发上挨着我坐。❷(常与 on 连用) be allowed to attend (something such as a meeting) as a visitor 列席(会议等)：We are having a conference and we'd like you to *sit in*. 我们即将开会，并希望你列席参加。I was invited to *sit in* on the rehearsal. 我应邀出席观看排练。❸be a member of (a group such as a board, committee, or other official groups)担任(理事会、委员会或其他机构的)成员：She was the first journalist to *sit in* parliament. 她是第一位当上议员的记者。❹sit on the ground in, or occupy the building where one is employed, etc. in protest against conditions, the action of authorities (在室内)静坐示威：Some of the students entered the president's office of the college and *sat in* all day. 一些学生进入学院院长的办公室，静坐示威了一整天。

NOTE **1.** 当本短语作“当……的一成员”解时，同义短语是 sit on (第二个义项)，两者可互换使用。

2. 本短语可转化为复合词 sit-in，意为“(室内)静坐抗议，罢工”。

sit in for *vt.*【不可分性动词短语】take (someone else's) usual place, especially in a regular meeting or office job 替换(某人)(主持会议或公务): I will be *sitting in for* the manager at the meeting this afternoon. 我将代替经理参加今天下午的会议。Have you found anyone to *sit in for* you while you are away? 你有没有找一个人在你不在期间替你主持公务?

sit in on *vt.*【不可分性动词短语】attend or be present at (a meeting, a discussion or a lesson while it is taking place) as an observer or visitor 列席(会议或讨论),旁听(课程): We want you to *sit in on* our council meeting tomorrow. 我们希望您列席我们明天的市政会议。Will they permit you to *sit in on* some classes? 他们会允许你旁听一些课程吗?

sit on *vt.* ❶(cause to) be seated on top of (something)(使)坐在……上: There weren't enough chairs so I had to *sit on* the floor. 因为椅子不够,我只好坐在了地板上。The pictures show the plane floating on the water and passengers *sitting on* its wings, awaiting rescue. 照片显示,飞机漂浮在水上,乘客都坐在双翼上等待援救。When you sit on a horse, you *sit on* the house's back. 当你骑马时,你是骑在马背上的。The mother *sat* the baby *on* her knees. 妈妈让宝宝坐在自己的双膝上。❷serve as a member of (a group such as a jury, board, committee, or other official groups)担任(陪审团、理事会、委员会或其他官方组织的)成员: The young man you met this morning *sits on* the jury at the trial. 你今早遇见的那个年轻人在审判中是陪审团成员。She *sits on* the boards of several large companies. 她在几家大公司里任理事会成员。This was only one of the many committees *on* which he had *sat*. 这只是他曾任过委员的许多委员会之中的一个。❸(非正式用语)(of someone) delay dealing with (a request or complaint, etc.) so as to avoid further complications 把(某一要求,投诉等)搁置起来,拖延不处理: The government have been *sitting on* this controversial report. 政府一直把这份有争议的报告搁置着。Are those people still *sitting on* your complaint? It's time you had a reply! 那些人还在拖着不处理你的投诉吗? 你该得到答复了! ❹(常用进行时态) examine or investigate (something such as a case) 审理,调查(案件等): Which judge is *sitting on* this case? 是哪位法官在审理这一案件? The police are *sitting on* the mystery of the stolen jewels. 警方仍在调查那起神秘的珠宝失窃案。❺(主要用于英国英语中) force (someone) to be silent or not to do something 压制(某人): The boss is going to *sit on* him to make sure he says nothing. 他的老板会压制他,肯定不让他说出什么。

sit out *vt.* & *vi.* (at a dance) leave the floor for one dance and sit down with your partner (在舞会中坐下来)不参加跳舞: Let's *sit* this dance *out*, shall we? 这支舞曲我们就坐下来别跳了,好吗? I'm tired, so I think I'll *sit out* the next dance. 我累了,下一支舞曲我不想跳了。If you are tired, let's *sit out*. 如果你累了,我们就坐下别跳了。

—*vt.*【可分性动词短语】❶ not participate in (something) 不参加: I had to *sit* the game *out* because I was sick. 我因病而没能参加比赛。❷(常用一般时态) remain seated until the end of (something, especially something boring or unpleasant)一直坚持坐到……结束：Although we were bored to death by the play, we *sat* it *out* in silence. 虽然我们觉得这出戏无聊得要命，但我们还是静静地坐到终场。I know the meeting is boring, but we're just going to have to *sit* it *out*. 我知道这会议很无聊，但我们还得坚持坐到它结束。

NOTE 当本短语用作及物性动词短语，所带的宾语为代词时，该代词须置于本短语的动词和副词中间。

sit up *v.* ❶(常用一般时态)(cause to)move into a sitting position when you have been leaning back or lying down (使)坐起：*Sit up* and take your medicine. 坐起来把药吃了吧。Finally, I gathered enough strength to *sit up* and looked out my small window into the night. 最终我费了很大的劲儿坐了起来，向小窗外的夜色望去。She *sat* him *up* in bed and made him comfortable. 她扶他从床上坐了起来，让他感到舒服些。❷(英国英语用法) stay awake and do not go to bed although it is very late 熬夜，迟睡：Don't *sit up* for me, you should have a good sleep. 不要为我熬夜了，你应该好好地睡一觉。The mother *sat up* all night with the sick child. 这位母亲守着生病的孩子彻夜未眠。The old man said to his children he would *sit up* to watch the matches. 老人对他的孩子们说，他要熬夜观看比赛。We *sat up* waiting for our daughter to be back. 我们熬夜等女儿回来。❸(非正式用语，用一般时态)(of something) make you suddenly feel interested in, surprised at, or pay attention to what is happening 使(突然)吃惊，觉得有趣：This will make you *sit up*, Jane is going to have a baby! 这件事会使你大感有趣的，简要生小孩儿了! The new crime statistics should make people *sit up* and take notice. 这些新的犯罪统计数字应该使人们感到吃惊并引起注意。

NOTE 1. 当本短语用作及物性动词短语，所带的宾语为代词时，该代词须置于本短语的动词和副词中间。

2. 本短语的同义短语是 stay up 和 wait up。

3. 本短语可转化为复合词 sit-up，意为"坐起；仰卧起坐"。

size up *vt.*【可分性动词短语】(非正式用语) think carefully and form an opinion or judgment about (a person or a situation), so that you can decide how to act 估计，估量，判断：I can't quite *size* him *up*, he's a bit of a mystery to me. 我无法准确地判断他这个人。对我来说，他总是有些神秘兮兮的。He had a feeling that he was being *sized up* by the stranger. 他感到那个陌生人正在琢磨着他。He *sized up* the situation and immediately decided what to do. 他对形势进行了判断后，马上做出了决定。

NOTE 1. 当本短语的宾语为代词时，该代词须置于本短语的动词和副词中间。

2. 本短语可转化为复合词 size-up，意为"估量，估计"。

sketch in *vt.* (常用一般时态) describe (something) roughly with few details; add (something) roughly 概略地叙述，粗略地补充：Let me *sketch in* the main points of our plan. 让我把我们的计划要点概略地叙述一下。We need to *sketch in* a few more details before presenting the plan. 我们需要再补充些细节，然后把它交上去。

sketch out *vt.* (常用一般时态) make a general plan of (something); give a general description or account of (something)草拟……的计划;简述: The general *sketched out* his battle plan to a group of officers, leaving them to organize the details. 将军为军官们草拟出了他的战斗计划,让他们来做出具体的部署。He *sketched* the furniture arrangement *out* to us. 他向我们简述了一下家具的摆法。

skim through *vt.*【不可分性动词短语】(非正式用语) read (a piece of writing) very quickly and not very carefully, simply to get the main idea or general impression of its contents 速读,略读,浏览(文稿): Give me a moment to *skim through* these notes before the meeting. 给我点儿时间在会前看一下这些稿子。This is not the kind of article that can be *skimmed through*, it requires close concentration. 这种文章不能只浏览一下,它需要精心研读。I've *skimmed through* the report but I haven't had time to look at it in detail. 我已浏览了这份报告,但没有时间细读。

sleep in ⇨ **lie in**

sleep on *vt.*【不可分性动词短语】(与代词 it 连用) delay deciding on (a question) until the following day, after you have rested and had more time to think 把(某一问题)拖到第二天再做决定,彻夜思考: There is no need to make a decision now, why don't you go home and *sleep on* it? 不必现在就做决定。你何不回家好好考虑考虑,明天再做决定呢? Let me go home and *sleep on* it and give you an answer tomorrow. 让我回家彻夜思考一下,明天再给你答复。

slide into *vt.* ❶enter (a place) silently 悄悄进入(某处): She had the ability to *slide into* a room without anyone's noticing. 她有潜入屋内而不被人注意的能力。❷pass (something) into (something such as a hand or pocket) secretly 把(某物)偷偷放入(手或口袋)中: He *slid* a note *into* my hand when the teacher was not looking. 他趁老师没注意时把一个纸条偷偷地塞入我的手中。She *slid* the gun *into* her pocket. 她悄悄地把手枪放入口袋中。

NOTE 当本短语作"悄悄进入(某处)"解时,同义短语是 slip into 和 sneak into; 反义短语是 slip off, slip out, sneak away, sneak off 和 sneak out。

slip by *vi.* (of something such as time or an opportunity) pass without being used for your advantage (时间或机会)没得到利用而过去: Two days *slipped by* before I could decide to do something. 我还没决定做什么事,两天就过去了。I had the opportunity to switch jobs, but I let it *slip by*. 我曾有过调换工作的机会,但却失去了。

slip into *vt.* (无被动语态形式) ❶quickly put on (a piece of clothing)匆忙穿上(衣物等): Please give me a moment to *slip into* something more comfortable. 请稍等片刻,我去穿一件更舒服点的衣服。He *slipped into* his shoes and drove home. 他匆忙穿上鞋子,开车回家了。❷(cause to) enter (a place) silently or secretly (使)悄悄进入,溜入(某处): She *slipped into* the room when no one was looking. 她趁无人注意之际悄悄地溜入了房间。The two Palestinians shot dead by Israeli soldiers yesterday might have been trying to *slip into* Israel to seek work. 昨天被以色列士兵开枪打死的两名巴勒斯坦人可

能是试图要潜入以色列去寻找工作。Can you *slip me into* the concert without a ticket? 你能让我无票入场看音乐会吗? ❸put (something) into (something) secretly 把(某物)悄悄放入:I *slipped* a note *into* her hand under the table. 我悄悄地从桌子底下塞给她一张条子。She *slipped* her hand *into* his and fell into step beside him. 她悄悄地拉住他的手并与他同步而行。Last week, a man killed at least 42 people, many of them children, by *slipping* rat poison *into* food. 上星期,一名男子往食物中投放鼠药而毒死了至少42人,其中很多是儿童。

NOTE 当本短语作"匆匆穿上(衣物等)"解时,反义短语是 slip off。

slip off *vt.* ❶(常用一般时态) take (a piece of clothing) off quickly 匆匆脱掉(衣物):She quickly *slipped* her dress *off* and slipped the swimsuit on. 她迅速脱掉连衣裙,换上了泳装。*Slip off* your shoes, they're wet. 快把你的鞋脱下来,它们都湿了。I *slipped off* my woolen gloves. 我脱去了我那副毛织手套。❷slip out of (something) 从……滑落:The soap *slipped off* my hands. 肥皂从我手中滑落了。

—*vi.* leave quietly 悄然离去,溜走:He *slipped off* yesterday to spy out the situation. 他昨天悄悄地离开去秘密调查情况。Mary found the party rather boring, so she *slipped off* while no one was looking. 玛丽觉得聚会十分无聊,便趁没人注意的时候悄悄溜走了。

NOTE 1. 当本短语作"匆匆脱掉(衣物)"解时,另外一种表达形式是 slip out of。

2. 当本短语作"悄然离去,溜走"解时,另外一种表达形式是 slip out。例如:

> The meeting was really dull so I *slipped out*.
> 会议实在是无聊,所以我就悄悄地溜走了。

slip on *vt.*【可分性动词短语】(主要用于英国英语中,无被动语态形式,常用一般时态) put on (a piece of clothing) with ease or speed 轻松或迅速地穿上(衣物等):You'd better *slip* something *on* before you go to the door. 你最好穿件衣服再到门口去。She *slipped on* her shoes and walked out of the room. 她穿上鞋子便走出了房间。

NOTE 1. 本短语与 slip into 的第一个义项在用法上的区别是:本短语是可分性动词短语,而 slip into 是不可分性动词短语。

2. 本短语的反义短语是 slip off。

3. 本短语可转化复合词 slip-on,意为"套领衫,套(穿)裙,无带便鞋"。

slip out ⇨ **slip off**

slip out of ⇨ **slip off**

slow down/up *vt.* & *vi.* ❶(cause to) start to move or happen more slowly (使)减慢,减速:Please *slow down* a little! You are going too fast. I can't keep up with you! 请慢一点! 你们走得太快了,我赶不上你们。The study suggests vitamin D may help to *slow down* the ageing process of DNA, and therefore the ageing process as a whole. 该项研究表明,维生素 D 有助于延缓 DNA 的衰老,从而延缓整个人体的衰老。His bad leg *slows* him *down* a lot. 他的伤腿使他走路很慢。He *slowed* the car *down* as they approached the traffic lights. 当他们接近交通灯时,他减慢了车速。❷(of someone) (cause to) become less active and intensive when he or she has been working very hard or has been very energetic (使)(某人)变得轻松些: For me, holidays are a time to *slow down* and relax. 对我来说,假期就是放松和休息的时间。We should find some way to *slow* him *down*, he is taking on far too much work. 我们要设法使他轻松一点,他承担的工作太重了。The doctor advised him to *slow up* for a time, to give his heart a chance. 医生建议他放松一段时间,给心脏一个休息的机会。

—*vi.* become less busy, especially in business 生意清淡: Business *slows up* at the stores after Christmas. 圣诞节后,商店的生意清淡。

NOTE **1.** 当本短语用作及物性动词短语,宾语为代词时,该代词须置于本短语的动词和副词中间。

2. 当本短语作"(使)减慢,减速"解时,反义短语是 speed up。

3. 本短语可转化为复合词 slowdown 或 slow-up,意为"减速,减退"。

small wonder (that) ⇨ **no wonder (that)**

smell of *vt.* 【不可分性动词短语】(主要用于英国英语中,无被动语态形式,不用进行时态) ❶ have a particular *smell of* (something causing the smell)散发……气味,有……气味: The room *smelt of* smoke. 这个房间散发出一股烟味。Her hands *smelt of* fish. 他手上有鱼腥味。The laboratory *smelled* strongly *of* chemicals. 实验室里有强烈的化学药品味。❷ contain the suggestion of (something usually bad)带有……意味: His offer *smells* strongly *of* shady dealing. 他的报价明显带有不正当交易的意味。If I were you, I should leave his offer alone. It *smells of* a trap. 如果我要是你的话,我就会对他的提议置之不理,因为它带有圈套的味道。

NOTE 本短语中的动词 smell 的过去式和过去分词有两种形式: smelled 和 smelt。在英国英语中常用 smelt,而在美国英语中常用 smelled。

smell out *vt.* 【可分性动词短语】(主要用于英国英语中) ❶ (especially of animals) find (something or someone) by means of the sense of smell (尤指动物)凭嗅觉发现,嗅出: The hounds *smelled out* a hare. 猎狗凭嗅觉发现了一只野兔。At customs, drug dogs are used to *smell out* drugs in passengers' luggage. 海关用缉毒犬查缉旅客行李中的毒品。The police dog *smelt* the criminal *out* and the police captured him. 警犬嗅出了罪犯,警察便将其逮捕。❷ (of someone) discover (something) by careful study or guessing (指人)发现,察觉: A good reporter must be able to *smell out* a new story. 一名优秀的记者必须善于发现新消息。I *smelt out* that she was cheating me. 我察觉出她在欺骗我。

NOTE **1.** 当本短语的宾语为代词时,该代词须置于本短语的动词和副词中间。

2. 本短语与 sniff out 意义和用法相同,两者可互换使用。

smoke break ⇨ **tea break**

smooth away *vt.* 【可分性动词短语】 ❶ cause (something such as a fold or wrinkle) to disappear from a surface by pressing or smoothing 使平滑,除皱: This face cream claims to *smooth away* wrinkles. 这种面霜据说能除皱,使面部平滑。I cannot *smooth* these folds *away*, they keep coming back. 这些皱褶我弄不平,它们还是往回卷。❷ remove or get rid of (problems, difficulties or trouble)

消除(问题、困难或麻烦): Her tender looks seemed to *smooth away* his worry. 她那温柔的神情似乎消除了他的忧虑。There are a few problems to be *smoothed away* before we complete the project. 在我们完成这一工程之前,还有一些问题有待解决。

NOTE 当本短语的宾语为代词时,该代词须置于本短语的动词和副词中间。

smooth down *v.* ❶ move your hand across the surface of (something) until it is flat and even (especially by stroking downwards)把……弄平,捋平: Mary sat there *smoothing* her skirt *down* over her knees. 玛丽坐在那里把她的裙子在膝盖上弄平。The manager straightened his tie, *smoothed down* his hair, and went to welcome the first guest. 经理拉直领带,捋平头发,然后前去迎接第一位客人。❷(cause to) be calmer (使)平静,(使)平息: The sea gradually *smoothed down*. 海面逐渐地平静下来。She is mad. Go and try to *smooth down* her temper. 她要气疯了。去,设法平息她的火气吧。Father's in a bad temper, Mary. Do what you can to *smooth* him *down*. 玛丽,爸爸发脾气了。尽你所能去为他消消火。

NOTE 当本短语用作及物性动词短语,所带的宾语为代词时,该代词须置于本短语的动词和副词中间。

smooth out *vt.* 【可分性动词短语】❶make (something) smooth or smoother 把……弄平: If you *smooth out* the sheets the bed will be more comfortable. 如果你把床单弄平整些,床睡起来就更舒适些。She *smoothed* the wrinkles *out* of the tablecloth with an electric iron. 她用电熨斗把桌布烫平。❷remove (a difference, problem or difficulty, etc.) thus making a situation easier for someone 消除(分歧、问题等): The two countries are working hard to *smooth out* their disagreements. 两国都在致力于消除双方之间的分歧。He is good at *smoothing* the technical problems *out*. 他善于排除技术上的问题。There are some technical problems to be *smoothed out* before we can fly. 在飞行前,有些技术上的问题还需要我们解决。

NOTE 当本短语的宾语为代词时,该代词须置于本短语的动词和副词中间。

smooth over *vt.* 【可分性动词短语】❶rub (a liquid, cream, etc.) gently over or into a surface 轻轻地涂搽(液体、面霜等): She *smoothed* suntan lotion *over* her legs. 她轻轻地把防晒油涂搽在腿上。❷make (a difference, problem, difficulties, etc.) less serious and easier to deal with, especially by talking to the people concerned (通过调停各方)使(分歧、问题等)易于解决;缓解: It'll be difficult for you to *smooth over* their differences after so many years. 经过了这么多年,你要摆平他们之间的分歧谈何容易。They failed to agree on the main issue, and they weren't going to try to *smooth* it *over*. 他们没能就主要问题达成一致,也不想设法将其解决。Perhaps a gift of flowers will help to *smooth* your quarrel *over*. 也许送一些鲜花有助于缓解你们之间的争吵。

NOTE 当本短语的宾语为代词时,该代词须置于本短语的动词和副词或介词中间。

snap up *vt.* 【可分性动词短语】❶(非正式用语) buy or purchase (something) quickly, because the price is low, or because the item is so hard to find, or because it is something you have been searching for 抢购: We put the cheap shirts out for sale this morning and people *snapped* them *up* in only a few minutes. 我们今天上午把廉价的衬衫出架销售，人们在几分钟内就将其抢购一空。The cheapest articles at the sale were quickly *snapped up*. 大减价货物中最便宜的物品很快被抢购一空。As soon as they lower the price we intend to *snap up* the house, it is exactly what we want. 他们一降价我们就打算买下那所房子，那正如我们所愿。❷ believe (something) readily and eagerly 轻信: They are so easily deceived that you can say anything and they'll *snap* it *up*. 他们很容易受骗，你说什么他们就信什么。They will *snap up* anything that sounds good. 听起来不错的事他们都会相信。

NOTE 当本短语的宾语为代词时，该代词须置于本短语的动词和副词或介词中间。

sneak away/off/out *v.* (cause to) leave somewhere quietly or secretly on foot, trying to avoid being seen or heard (使)悄然离去，溜走: As she did not wish anyone to accompany her, she *sneaked away* without telling anyone. 因为她不想要任何人陪伴，所以她谁也没告诉就悄然离去了。She *sneaked* the girl *away*. 她让那姑娘溜走了。While his parents were busy, Joe *sneaked off* to play. 趁父母忙碌之际，乔便溜出去玩。A lot of office workers *snuck out* to watch baseball at coffee shops nearby. 有很多办公室职员溜到附近的咖啡店去看棒球比赛。

NOTE 1. 本短语中的动词 sneak 的过去式和过去分词有两种形式: sneaked 和 snuck。snuck 用于美国英语中。

2. sneak away 常与 from 连用，sneak out 常与 of 连用。例如:

She *sneaked away* from the meeting, but Linda saw her.
她溜出会场，但琳达看到了她。
She *sneaked out* of the meeting, hoping no one would notice.
她悄然离开会场，希望没有人会察觉到。

sneak into *vt.* ❶ enter (a place) quietly and in secret, perhaps without a ticket or permission 秘密进入，偷偷潜入: As it was more difficult to *sneak into* Japan, the snakeheads started to smuggle people to countries in Europe, especially the United Kingdom. 由于进入日本越来越难，蛇头们便开始把人们偷渡到一些欧洲国家，尤其是英国。When I was a child I used to *sneak into* the movie theatre without paying. 我小时候经常不买票而偷偷潜入电影院看电影。❷ take (something) somewhere secretly 把(某物)秘密带入: Let's *sneak* some pizza *into* the cinema. 咱们偷偷地带些比萨饼进电影院吧。

sniff out ⇨ **smell out**

so as to *conj.* (后接原形动词) in order to 为的是，以便: He raised his voice *so as to* be heard. 他提高嗓门，以便让别人听到。I'll have everything ready *so as* not *to* keep you waiting. 我会把一切准备就绪，使你不用等候。

NOTE 1. 本短语是不定式的一种特殊形式，通常表示目的，其否定形式是 so as not to (do something)。

2. 本短语与 in order to 意义相同，但本短语不能用于句首，而 in order to 则可以。见 in order to。

so … as to *conj.* in such a way as to 如此……以至于；以便: Would you be *so* kind *as to* show me how to use this computer?

请您教我怎样使用这台电脑好吗? But the information was not *so* specific *as to* identify a date, time or place for such an attack to be made by al-Qaeda. 然而,并没有详细的情报说明"基地"组织即将发动袭击的日期、时间或地点。Don't work *so* hard *as to* become sick. 不要工作太累,搞坏身体。

NOTE **1.** 本短语的否定形式是 so … as not to。例如:

> Such instruments are *so* well known *as* not *to* require detailed description here.
> 这些仪器是众所熟知的,因此无需在此详述。

2. 本短语中的 so 也可用于修饰动词,多见于科技英语中。例如:

> Any aircraft engine must be *so* designed *as to* keep the weight not too great.
> 任何飞机的发动机都必须设计得重量不能太大。

so be it *s.* (正式用语) ❶(used for saying that you accept a situation in which something has been decided or is necessary, although you are not happy about it) let it be that way 顺其自然吧: "The company will lose money by doing this." "*So be it*." "公司这样做会亏损的。""顺其自然吧。" If you've really decided to quit the business, then *so be it*. 如果你真的决定不干这买卖了,那就算了吧。❷very well; all right 极好,好吧: "He wants to do this work himself." "*So be it*.""他要自己做这件工作。""好吧。"

NOTE **1.** 本短语被认为是 it (should) be so 的倒装形式。

2. 本短语的另外一种表达形式是 be it so。

so far *adv.* ❶(常与现在完成时连用) up until now or until the present stage in a process 到现在为止,迄今: These are the people the President has *so far* picked or proposed to work in his administration. 这些是总统到现在为止已挑选或提名在他政府中任职的人士。❷(非正式用语) only to this or that point 到此程度(范围或距离): Was it wise to push things *so far*? 把事情弄到这种地步明智吗? Now that we've come *so far*, we may as well go all the way. 我们既已来到此地,我们还是走完全程吧。I trust you only *so far* and no further. 我对你的信任只能到这个程度,不能再多。

NOTE **1.** 为了强调,本短语可置于句首,其后加逗号。例如:

> *So far*, the two prime ministers have achieved no concrete results.
> 迄今为止,两位首相还没有取得任何具体的成果。

2. 本短语与 thus far 意义相同,但 thus far 更为正式。

3. 本短语与 as yet 都表示"到现在为止",但用法有所不同。本短语既可用于否定句中,又可用于肯定句中;as yet 一般用于否定句或含有否定词的句子中。

so far as *conj.* to the extent or degree that 到……程度;就……而论: This principle has not been reasoned out, *so far as* we know. 就我们所知,这个原理还没有推导出来。*So far as* the quality of tones is concerned, this radio-set is quite up to standard. 就音质而论,这台收音机已完全达到标准。

NOTE 本短语的同义短语是 in so far as, insofar as 和 in as far as。

So far, so good. *s.* (非正式用语) (used to express satisfaction with the way that a situation or activity is progressing, developing, or happening) until now

S

things have gone well 到目前为止一切都顺利：*So far*, *so good*, 96 per cent of calls have been answered within six seconds. 到目前为止，一切都顺利，在 6 秒钟之内回复了 96％的电话。The first round of talks went well. *So far so good*. The next stage will involve much tougher negotiation. 第一轮会谈，到目前为止，进展良好，一切顺利。下一阶段的谈判将更加艰难。

NOTE 在英国英语中，本短语中的两个组成部分一般不用逗号相隔。

So long. *s.* （美国英语，非正式用语）(used for saying goodbye to someone you know well) goodbye for now 再见：*So long*, we'll see you next week. 再见，我们下周见。If you don't want to see her anymore, would you be able to tell her *so long*? 如果你不愿意再见到她，你能和她说"再见"吗？

so long as *conj.* ❶ provided only that; if; only if 只要；如果：*So long as* electric current flows through a wire, there is a potential difference. 只要有电流通过，导线就有电位差。You can go out this evening *so long as* you promise to be home by midnight. 如果你答应在半夜以前回到家，今晚你就可以出去。❷（常用于句首）since 既然：*So long as* you're driving into town, why not give me a ride? 既然你开车进城，何不让我搭个便车呢？

NOTE 本短语的同义短语是 as long as，两者常可互换使用。

so much as *adv.* （常用于否定句和疑问句中）(used for emphasizing that something did not happen or exist, especially when this is surprising) even; to whatever extent; but rather 竟然；连……也：She left the room without *so much as* a backward glance. 她连头也没回就离开了房间。He didn't *so much as* thank me for returning his money found. 我把捡到的钱还给他，他连说声谢谢都没有。She sold her car without *so much as* taking a ride in it. 她那台车她连开都没开过就卖掉了。Would you *so much as* get me a glass of water? 你愿意替我拿一杯水吗？

so much for *prep.* ❶（主要用于口语中）that is all that can be said about or there is no need to consider (someone or something) 关于……就谈到这里；没有必要再考虑……：*So much for* transmission, and I shall have to say something about television. 有关无线电发射问题就谈到这里，我还要谈谈有关电视的问题。*So much for* past events, let me now move on to speculate about the future. 过去的情况就讲到这儿，现在让我推测一下将来的情况。*So much for* Linda. She just called in sick and can't come to work today. 就别考虑琳达了。她刚刚打来电话说病了，今天不能来上班。❷ (used for expressing disappointment and annoyance at the fact that a situation is not as you thought it was) that is the end of something 完了，结束：A bird hit my windshield, and I thought, *so much for* the bird. 一只鸟撞在了我的汽车挡风玻璃上。我暗想到，这鸟算完了。The car's broken down again. *So much for* our trip to the seaside. 车又坏了。我们去海边的旅途到此结束了。

so much so that *conj.* to that extent of degree so that 到这种程度以至于……：He longed to visit Hawaii, *so much so that* he dreamed about it. 他渴望到夏威夷一游，以至于连做梦都想。The former

S

president was very old, *so much so* he could not stand or walk without help. 这位前总统年事太高,以至于没有帮助就不能站立和行走。*So much so that* in his mind, any mention of Iraq will only remind him of images of destruction. 以至于在他的心目中,一提起伊拉克就会使他想到毁灭的景象。

NOTE 本短语中的 that 往往省略。

so much the better *adv.* (主要用于口语中) still the better 那就更好了:I think he is a suitable person, and if he's a friend of yours, well, *so much the better*. 我认为他是个合适的人选。如果他是你的一个朋友,那就更好了。*So much the better* for you if you obey the rules. 如果你遵守规则,那就更好了。

NOTE 本短语的反义词是 so much the worse。

so much the worse ⇨ **so much the better**

so that *conj.* ❶in order that 以便:He called on all parties to be patient, and continue cooperation *that* the efforts already made will not end in vain. 他呼吁各方保持耐心,继续合作,以避免使迄今所做出的努力前功尽弃。"We need to do all we can *so that* Georgia has normal relations with the neighboring countries and with such a large state as Russia," the Georgian President said. 格鲁吉亚总统说:"我们需要尽力而为,这样,格鲁吉亚才能与邻国,与俄罗斯这样的大国保持正常关系。" ❷with the result or consequence that 所以,因此:All these problems are hard enough, *so that* he cannot solve all of them. 所有这些问题都够难的,所以他无法将它们全部解决。My pencil fell under my desk, *so that* I couldn't see it. 我的铅笔掉在了我的书桌下面,因此我没能看到它。These computations are extremely complicated, *so* it is difficult to work them out without the help of an electronic computer. 这些计算极其复杂,因此没有电子计算机的帮助就很难算出。

NOTE 1. 本短语在句中既能引导目的状语从句,又能引导结果状语从句。从句中多用 can、could、may、will 等情态动词。

2. 在本短语引导的目的状语从句中,so 有时可以省略。而在本短语引导的结果状语从句中,that 有时可以省略。

so … that *conj.* (正式用语) in such a way or to such an extent or degree that 如此……以至于……;所以……:He worked *so* carefully *that* he did not make a single mistake. 他工作非常仔细,所以没有出一点差错。Light travels *so* fast *that* it is difficult for us to imagine its speed. 光速快得令人难以想象。

NOTE 1. 本短语在句中引导结果状语从句。so 之后一般用形容词或副词,但有时也用动词。例如:

> He *so* adores his daughters *that* he keeps buying them expensive toys.
> 他非常疼爱女儿们,经常给她们买些贵重的玩具。

2. "so+形容词"为表语时,为了加强语气可采用主谓倒装形式。例如:

> *So* small are these particles *that* the most powerful microscopes cannot detect them.
> 这些粒子如此之小,连用倍数最高的显微镜也观察不出来。

3. 本短语中的 that 有时可以省略,尤其是在口语中。例如:

> The baby was *so* ill this morning I thought we should lose her.
> 今早,孩子病得很重,我竟认为我们可能要失去她了。

so to say ⇨ **so to speak**

so to speak *adv.* (仅用于口语中) figuratively speaking (when describing or referring to something); as if it were so; as one might say 打个比方说,可以这么说: They were thunderstruck, *so to speak*, on hearing this news. 他们听到这个消息犹如霹雳轰顶一般。I ought not to tell you but I will, since you're in the family, *so to speak*. 我本不该告诉你,但我还是要告诉你,因为可以说你是这个家庭的一个成员。His book is truly the last word on the subject, *so to speak*. 可以说,他的书是有关这一问题的最具权威性的著作。

NOTE 1. 本短语用来引起一个比喻或夸张的说法,位置一般在句尾或句中。

2. 本短语的另外一种表达形式是 so to say。

3. 本短语的同义短语是 in a way, in a manner of speaking, as it were。

So what? *s.* (仅用于口语中,用疑问句形式) (used as an impolite reply to indicate that you think that something someone has said or done is unimportant) who cares?; What does it matter? 那有什么关系: You don't like my drinking? *So what?* 你不喜欢我喝酒? 你不喜欢又怎么样? "She didn't invite us to the party." "*So what?* I don't care." "她没邀请我们去参加聚会。""那有什么关系? 我不在乎。"

NOTE 1. 本短语中的 what 可省略。例如:

—We can't go out together, Bob. Someone will see us.

—*So?*

—鲍勃,我们不能一起出去走。会有人看见我们的。

—那有什么关系?

2. 本短语与 what of it 意义和用法相同。

some day *adv.* at some uncertain time in the future (将来)总有一天,有朝一日: He put away those things, hoping that they may be useful *some day*. 他把那些东西收藏起来,希望总有一天它们会派上用场。She is 40 now, and hopes to get married *some day*. 她现年已 40,希望有朝一日能结婚。

NOTE 本短语可转化为复合词 someday,意为"总有一天,有朝一日"。

something like (非正式用语) Ⅰ *adv.* (used for giving an amount that is not exact or that you are not certain of) about; nearly; almost (用来表示所提供的数字不一定确切,后接用表示数目的词语) 大约,将近: I'm not quite sure of the exact price, but it's *something like* 40—50 pounds. 我说不准确切的价格是多少,大约是 40 到 50 英镑吧。*Something like* 1,000 people were present at the meeting. 大约有 1 000 人出席了会议。It must be *something like* seven o'clock. 一定是 7 点钟左右了。

Ⅱ *prep.* (used for giving a description that is not exact or that you are not certain of) rather like; similar to (用来表示所做的描述不一定确切) 有点像,类似: They say creating a work of art is *something like* giving birth. 他们说创造艺术作品就像生小孩一样(不容易)。This building looked *something like* a church we saw in Toronto. 这个建筑物看起来有点像咱们在多伦多看到的一座教堂。

something of *adv.* (非正式用语) ❶(used for showing that you are not being very definite in the way you are describing someone or something) to a certain extent; to some degree 在某种程度(意义)上;有几分:The soldier found himself *something of* a hero when he returned to his town. 那名士兵回到镇子时,发现自己多少有点儿像凯旋的英雄。There is *something of* uncertainty in it. 那里面有几分含糊性。*Something of* doubt remains. 仍然存在几分怀疑。❷(其后用不定冠词)(used for emphasizing that someone is fairly good at something or has a fairly good knowledge of something) rather a/an (强调某人在某方面有特长、有学问)可以说是一个:He is *something of* an expert on growing vegetables. 他可以说得上是一位种植蔬菜的专家。Jill considers herself to be *something of* a nutritionist. 吉尔以营养学家自居。

sooner or later *adv.* definitely at some time in the future, although you do not know exactly when; if not soon then late; eventually 早晚,迟早:For all difficulties, space travel will come true *sooner or later*. 尽管有种种困难,太空旅行早晚会实现。If you cheat, *sooner or later* you'll be found out. 你如果作弊,迟早会被发现的。*Sooner or later* he will be caught by the police. 早晚他会被警察抓到。

NOTE 本短语是由两个比较级形容词搭配而成的,只能用于一般将来时或表示将来意义的句子里,表达对事物结果的一种预测。

sore about/at *adj.* (主要用于美国英语中,非正式用语)offended or angered with 因……恼怒:I tried to persuade him not to be *sore about* it. 我竭力劝他不要因那事而气恼。Helen was still feeling *sore about* what had happened. 海伦仍在为发生过的事情感到气愤。The result is they are now all feeling very *sore at* you. 结果是他们现在都非常生你的气。

sort of *adv.* (主要用于口语中) slightly; in some way or degree; rather; to some extent 有点儿;在一定程度上:It was *sort of* odd that he didn't come. 他没有来,这有点儿奇怪。I *sort of* thought you might say that. 我有点儿觉得你也许会那么说。He was acting *sort of* crazy. 他的行为有点儿疯狂。People say I look *sort of* like my grandfather when he was young. 人们都说我长得有点儿像我年轻时的祖父。

NOTE 本短语与 kind of 意义和用法相同,两者可互换使用。

sort out *vt.* 【可分性动词短语】❶separate (things) from a mass or group 把(某物)(从一堆或一群中)挑出,拣出:Please *sort* these newspapers *out*, boys. 孩子们,把这些报纸分拣出来。❷ get rid of (things you do not need) and arrange (things that you do need) tidily; divide (things) into classes 整理,分类:I need to *sort out* the mess on my desk. 我需要整理一下我办公桌上的乱东西了。He told me to *sort* the letters *out* and put on his desk. 他让我把信件分类,然后放在他的办公桌上。❸(主要用于英国英语中,非正式用语) solve (a problem or misunderstanding) and find solution to it; deal with or improve (a difficult situation, etc.) successfully 解决(某一问题或误解);处理,改善(某种局面等):We have to talk. We have to *sort* this *out*. 我们得谈一谈,这个问题必须解决。It was just a silly quarrel that's now been *sorted out*. 这只是一场无谓的争吵,现已得到解决。You'd better send somebody over to *sort* the situation *out*. 你最好派一个人去改善一下局面。

NOTE 当本短语的宾语为代词时，该代词须置于本短语的动词和副词中间。

sound the death knell for/of *vt.* ❶foretell the death or destruction of (something)敲响……的丧钟，预告……的毁灭：To resume the ivory trade would *sound the death knell for* the African elephants. 恢复象牙贸易将会敲响非洲象的丧钟。❷cause (something) to end 使……终结：Fresh trade barriers would *sound the death knell for* global growth of economy. 新的贸易壁垒会使世界经济发展停滞不前。The closure of the local car factory *sounded the death knell of* the town. 关闭当地的汽车厂使该城陷于死地。

NOTE 本短语与 toll the death knell for/of 意义和用法相同，两者可互换使用。

speak badly of *vt.* (正式用语，常用一般时态) say unpleasant things about(someone or something) 说……的坏话：You shouldn't *speak badly of* your father. 你不应该说你父亲的坏话。It seems she found it difficult to *speak badly of* anyone. 她似乎发现很难说任何人的坏话。Don't *speak badly of* her behind her back. 不要在背后说她的坏话。"Sour grapes" means the fact that people often *speak badly of* what they cannot get. "酸葡萄"所指的是，人们往往把得不到的东西说得很坏。

S

NOTE 1. 本短语与 speak evil of 意义和用法相同。例如：

> Don't *speak evil of* others behind their backs.
> 不要在背后说别人的坏话。

但其中的 evil 是形容词。

2. 本短语的反义短语是 speak highly of。

speak for *vt.* 【不可分性动词短语】❶(常用一般时态) speak in favor of or make a speech in support of (someone or something) 为……说话；发言支持：He says he will *speak for* us at the committee meeting. 他说他将在委员会会议上为我们说话。At the meeting Peter *spoke for* the change in the rules. 在会议上，彼得发言支持对这些规则进行修改。❷(无被动语态形式) represent the feelings or opinions of (another person or a group of people)代表(某人或某些人)讲话：I know I *speak for* us all when I say how sorry I am for this mistake. 我知道，当我说为这一错误感到遗憾时，我是代表我们大家说的。This is my opinion, and I can only *speak for* myself, not for my colleagues. 这是我的意见，只能代表我自己，不代表我的同事们。❸be a witness of; indicate 证明，表明：His behaviour *speaks for* his willingness to help others. 他的行为证明他乐于帮助他人。

speak for itself/themselves *vi.* (非正式用语，用一般现在时) (of the meaning or quality of something) be so clear and impressive that any further explanation or proof is unnecessary 不言而喻：She said that she was willing to help, but her absence *speaks for itself*. 她说她愿意帮忙，但她没到场就说明问题了。The President of Green Cross International Alexander Likhotal says there is no doubt that such a treaty is needed and the statistics *speak for themselves*. 国际绿色十字会主席亚历山大·利霍塔尔说，不容置疑，这样一个协议是必需的，这些统计数字很说明问题。

speak highly of ⇨ **speak well of**

speak of *vt.* ❶(常用一般时态) mention;

talk about (something or someone) 提及……,谈到……: We have had no rain to *speak of* for the last three weeks. 近三周来的降雨之少,简直不值一提。I have heard him *speak of* it. 我听到他谈到过此事。*Speaking of* books, have you read *Gone With the Wind*? 谈到书,你看过《飘》吗? The international community *spoke* highly *of* China's positive role in resolving the nuclear issue of the Korean Peninsula in a peaceful way. 国际社会高度评价中国在和平解决朝鲜半岛核问题上发挥的积极作用。❷(正式用语,用一般时态) suggest the idea of (something); give proof or evidence of (something)说明……,证明……: Everything at the party *spoke of* their careful planning. 这次聚会上的一切都说明他们做了周密的策划。Her extensive library *spoke of* her love of reading. 她的大量藏书证明她酷爱读书。

NOTE 当本短语作"提及……,谈到……"时,与 talk of(第一个义项)意义和用法相同,两者可互换使用。

speak out *vi.* ❶(常用于祈使句中) talk loudly, so as to be heard 大声地说: *Speak out*, child, I can't hear you. 孩子,大声说,我听不见。He should *speak out* so that those in back can hear him. 他应该大声说,后面的人才能听得到。❷state one's opinions, etc. freely, bravely, and openly, especially after remaining silent for a time (尤指沉默之后)直言表达(意见等): If you don't approve of the idea, why don't you *speak out*? 你要是不赞成这个意见,为什么不直言说出? No one dare to *speak out* against the new law. 没有人敢直言反对这项新法。William *spoke out* for John as club president. 威廉直言支持约翰做俱乐部主席。

NOTE 本短语与 speak up 意义和用法相同,两者可互换使用。

speak to *vt.* 【不可分性动词短语】❶talk to; have conversation with (someone) 对(某人)讲话,与(某人)谈话: *Speaking to* a congress of the United Russia Party Monday, Putin said that he would accept the post of prime minister. 普京星期一在统一俄罗斯党代表大会上讲话并表示,他将接受总理之职。Don't speak until you're *spoken to*! 别人没和你说话你就别讲话! ❷(非正式用语,委婉用法) scold, speak severely to (someone), with a view to changing his or her conduct for the better 训斥,责备(某人): The boy is late again, I'll *speak to* him the minute he gets in. 那个男孩又迟到了。他一进来我就会训斥他一顿的。You must *speak to* the children, John. They never listen to a word I say. 你必须训训这些孩子,约翰。他们从来就不听我一句话。❸(正式用语,常用一般时态) express one's opinion, or make a statement, about (a matter being talked about, as at a meeting of a committee, council, etc.) 对(所谈问题)发表意见,阐述观点: The next item is student accommodation. Mr Smith. Might I ask you to *speak to* this? 下一个讨论项目是学生的膳宿供应问题。史密斯先生,能请您对此发表意见吗?

speak up *vi.* ❶(常用于祈使句中) speak in a loud, clear voice, so that one can be heard 大声地说: You have to *speak up*! The people at the back can't hear you. 你得大点声说! 后面的人听不见你的话。I do wish she'd stop mumbling and learn to *speak up*. 我真希望她不再嘀咕而要学着

大声讲话。❷(常与 against 或 for 连用) give one's opinion freely and clearly 清楚地表明(意见等): It's about time someone *spoke up* for these basic truths. 该是有人清楚地表明这些基本事实的时候了。At the meeting John *spoke up* against letting girls join the club. 在会议上,约翰直言反对让女孩子加入俱乐部。

speak up for *vt.*【不可分性动词短语】say something in support of (someone or something), especially by saying good things about them 替……说话: She has often *spoken up for* working girls. 她经常替女工们说话。Uncle Albert never argued, never *spoke up for* himself. 阿尔伯特叔叔从不与人争论,也从不为自己辩解。The trade union of the factory *spoke up for* better working conditions. 工厂的工会表示支持改善工作条件。

speak volumes *v.* (非正式用语,常用一般时态,不用进行时态) show (something) very clearly or fully in a way other than speaking (不用言语而)十分清楚地表明: He refused to answer their accusation, but his silence *spoke volumes*. 他拒绝回答他们的指控,但他的沉默十分清楚地表明他有罪。Based on my observations, the clothing and the hairstyle of a person *speak volumes* for his personality. 据我的观察,一个人的穿着和发型就能充分地表明他的性格。The present my daughter gave to you *speaks volumes* for how much she loves you. 我女儿送你的礼物十分清楚地表明了她对你爱的程度。

NOTE 本短语中的名词 volume 必须用复数形式。

speak well of *vt.* (正式用语,常用一般时态) express a good opinion of (someone or something) 高度评价,高度赞扬: I've heard a lot of people *speak well of* him. 我听到不少人赞扬他。Mr Jacques Roger, President of the International Olympic Committee, *spoke well of* the opening ceremony of the Beijing Olympic Games. 国际奥委会主席雅克·罗格先生盛赞北京奥运会开幕式。

specialize in *vt.*【不可分性动词短语】(of someone or something) be an expert in (a particular part of a subject or profession), and concentrate a great deal of the time and energy on it 专门研究,专门从事: He *specializes in* computer engineering. 他专门研究计算机工程。Professor James is a scholar in both Chinese and western learning, *specializing in* oriental studies. 詹姆斯教授是一位学贯中西,专攻东方学的学者。After she qualified as a lawyer, she decided to *specialize in* contract law. 取得律师资格后,她决定专门从事合同法的业务。This company *specializes in* handling the software. 这家公司专营软件。

speculate about/on *vt.*【不可分性动词短语】make guesses about (the nature or identity of something), or about (something that might happen in the future) 猜测,推测: The family did not want to *speculate on* the reasons for her suicide. 她的家人不想猜测她自杀的原因。There is little point in *speculating about* the result of the general election. 猜测大选的结果没什么意义。We don't know all the circumstances, so it would be pointless to *speculate on* what will happen. 我们对所有的情况都不了解,因此,对将来要发生的事情妄加推测是毫无意义的。

speed limit *n.* the maximum or top speed at which a vehicle is allowed by law to travel on a particular stretch of road (车

S

辆)(在某一特定路段上的)法定最高速度限制:The police imposed a *speed limit* of 30mph in the downtown area. 警方规定在市区内车辆的最高速度限制为每小时 30 英里。When you drive you must keep within the *speed limit*. 驾车时,你必须保持在最高速度限制之内。The following table lists the *speed limits* for various types of roads in the 50 US states. 下表列示了在美国 50 个州不同类型路段的最高速度限制。

speed up *vi.* (of the speed of something) increase;move or travel faster (速度)加快,加速:You can notice that your breathing has *speeded up* a bit. 你会注意到你呼吸的速度有些快了。Job losses are *speeding up*. 失业的速度在加快。They are ahead of us. Let's *speed up*! 他们在我们前面。咱们加快速度吧。You see drivers *speeding up* when they should be slowing down. 你可以看到这些司机在本应减速的时候却都在加速。

—*vt.*【可分性动词短语】make (something such as a process or activity) go faster or happen faster 加快……速度:The first 20 years of the 21st century represents an important strategic period for China to achieve all-round construction of a better-off society and to *speed up* its socialist modernization. 21 世纪头 20 年,是中国全面建设小康社会,加快推进社会主义现代化的重要战略机遇期。I asked them to *speed* the delivery *up*. 我请他们加快发货速度。Since the advent of jet aircraft, travel has been *speeded up*. 自从喷气式飞机出现以来,旅行的速度加快了。

NOTE 1. 本短语中的动词 speed 的过去式和过去分词有两种形式:sped 和 speeded。在动词短语中,通常使用 speeded。

2. 本短语可转化为复合词 speedup,意为"加速"。

spell out *vt.*【可分性动词短语】❶(常用一般时态)write or say (something such as a word) letter by letter in the correct order 逐个字母地拼出(某一单词等):I never have to *spell out* my first name. 我从不写出我的教名。He *spelt* his full name *out* for me. 他把他的全名逐个字母地给我拼写了出来。If I don't know the word, I ask them to *spell* it *out* for me. 如果我不认识那个单词,就请他们把它为我写出来。❷(非正式用语) explain (something) in a very clear way with details (详细、清晰地)说明,解释:I should have thought it was obvious, but if you want me to *spell* it *out* for you, I'm leaving you. 我本来以为这是显而易见的,但如果你让我向你讲得很清楚,那就是我要离开你。The possible economic benefits of the treaty were *spelt out* in his recent book. 该协定的一些可能的经济利益在他最近出版的那本书中得到了十分清晰的说明。Get a lawyer to *spell out* the contract for you. 请一位律师把这份合同给你详细地解释一下吧。Students have been given a booklet that *spells out* how AIDS is transferred. 发给学生的小册子详细地解释了艾滋病是如何传播的。

NOTE 1. 本短语中的动词 spell 的过去式和过去分词形式都是 spelled。但在英国英语中也使用 spelt 这一形式。

2. 当表达"详细地解释……"时,我们不能说 * spell out ... in (great) detail。*spell out* 本身就是"详细地解释"之意。

3. 当本短语的宾语为代词时,该代词须置于本短语的动词和副词中间。

spend in *vt.*【可分性动词短语】use

(usually time) for (doing something) 耗费(常指时间)做(某事): He's *spent* half his life *in* writing this book. 他花了半辈子时间写了这本书。We *spent* a pleasant hour or two *in* talking with our friends. 我们和朋友交谈,愉快地度过了一两个小时。

NOTE 本短语中的介词 in 可以省略。

spend on *vt.* 【可分性动词短语】use (usually money, time or effort) for (someone or something) 为(某物或某人)而花费(金钱,时间等): How much did you *spend on* your granddaughter for her birthday? 你孙女过生日,你在她身上花了多少钱? How much time do you *spend on* your homework? 你做作业用了多长时间? I don't understand why we have *spent* so much time, money and effort *on* this programmes. 我不明白我们为什么花费这么多时间、金钱和气力搞这个项目。

NOTE 本短语中的介词 on 可以省略。

split into *vt.* (cause to) separate into (smaller parts) (使)分为,分裂成: They *split into* different work groups. 他们分成了不同的工作小组。With a single blow of his axe, he *split* the log *into* two halves. 他一斧子便将那圆木劈成两半。The document said the British Broadcasting Corporation could be *split into* separate entities for England, Wales, Scotland and Northern Ireland. 该文件称,英国广播公司可被拆分为英格兰、威尔士、苏格兰和北爱尔兰四个实体。

split up *v.* ❶cut or divide (something) 切开,劈开,裂开: I'll *split up* the apple so that we can each have a piece. 我把这个苹果切开,咱们好每人都有一块吃。Can you *split up* this piece of wood? 你能把这块木头劈开吗? After having hit the hidden rocks the ship *split up*. 该船触击暗礁之后,船体裂开了。❷(常与 into 连用) (cause to) separate into smaller parts (使)分为,分裂,分开: The committee can *split up* into small groups to talk about the matters in greater detail. 委员会可以分成若干小组,以更加详细地讨论这些问题。I think the article would be easier to read if you *split it up* into sections. 我认为,如果你把这篇文章分成若干部分就比较容易读了。The Chinese delegate warned that the right to national self-determination should not be used as a pretext for *splitting up* sovereign states. 中国代表警告说,民族自决权不应被用来作为分裂主权国家的借口。❸(非正式用语) (of two or more people) (cause to) end a relationship (使)关系分裂: It's a pity when friends *split up* over trifles. 朋友之间因小事而关系分裂是很遗憾的。I was beginning to think that nothing could ever *split* us *up*. 我开始认为,没有什么能把我们分离开。❹(非正式用语) break up a marriage or love affair (夫妻)离婚,(恋人)分手: After four years of separation, Prince Charles and Princess Diana *split up* in August 1996. 经过四年的分居后,查尔斯王子与戴安娜王妃于 1996 年 8 月离婚。I heard that they had *split up* with each other. 我听说他们彼此断了关系。

NOTE **1.** 当本短语用作及物性动词短语,所带的宾语为代词时,该代词须置于本短语的动词和副词中间。

2. 本短语可转化为复合词 split-up,意为"分离,划分;离婚"。

sponge off/on *vt.* (非正式用语,贬义用法) (of someone) ask for (money and other things) from friends or relatives and

S

make no effort to give them anything back or pay for anything in return (指某人)白得,白拿(他人钱财或物品): He should get a job and stop *sponging* money and food *off* his relatives! 他应该找一份工作,不要再白花白吃他的亲属了。She spent her life doing nothing and *sponging on* her parents. 她无所事事,仰仗父母度日。He is always *sponging on* her for meals. 他总是白吃她的。

NOTE 本短语中的动词 sponge 在此表示"吸取(他人的财物等)"之意。

spread out *vt.* 【可分性动词短语】❶open (something) that is folded so that it covers a surface in order that all of it can be seen or used easily 展开,铺开: They took seats opposite me and *spread out* their newspapers. 他们在我对面坐了下来,展开了报纸。She looked at the map that was *spread out* on the floor. 她看着展开在地板上的地图。❷ stretch (your fingers, arms, etc.) out until they are far apart 伸展(手指、胳臂等): He lifted up a hand, the fingers *spread out*. 他举起一只手,把五指伸展开来。You need a bed that's large enough to let you *spread* yourself *out* freely. 你需要一张足能让你自由伸展身体的大床。The big bird *spread out* its wings, throwing a large shadow over the ground. 那只大鸟展开双翅,在地面上投下一个很大的影子。

—*vt.* & *vi* ❶ (cause to) scatter into positions separated by space (使)散开: The line of police *spread out* to search the fields. 一队警察散开来搜索田地。The Kurds are *spread out* across five countries. 库尔德人散居于五个国家。The light is *spread out* by dust particles in the air. 空气中尘埃的粒子使光扩散开。❷(cause to) have effect or influence over a wider area (使)传播,扩散,蔓延: Chinese health officials have warned the SARS labs to strictly obey safety regulations and prevent SARS virus from *spreading out* of laboratories. 中国卫生官员警告"非典"实验室要严格遵守安全规定,避免"非典"病毒扩散出实验室。The fire *spread out* quickly to the other parts of the building. 火势迅速蔓延到大楼的其他部分。This is just a bad rumour *spread out*. 这只不过是一则散布中的恶意谣言而已。

NOTE 当本短语用作及物性动词短语,所带的宾语为代词时,该代词须置于本短语的动词和副词中间。

spread over *v.* ❶place (something wide) so as to cover (something such as a surface); be present in many parts of a large area 覆盖,遍布: We *spread* the blanket *over* the grass and sat down on it. 我们把毯子铺在草地上坐着。His coat was *spread over* the bed. 他的上衣给铺在了床上。The clouds *spread over* the sky. 乌云布满天空。❷extend over a period of time; (cause to) be delayed or take a longer time 延长时间: You can *spread* your payments *over* three or five years. 你可以延期三或五年付款。The grammar lectures *spread over* into the next term. 语法课延续到了下个学期。I'll ask my bank manager if the repayments can be *spread over* two years. 我要向银行经理询问一下需偿付的款项能否延期两年。

NOTE 当本短语用作及物性动词短语,所带的宾语为代词时,该代词须置于本短语的动词和副词、介词中间。

spring up *vi.* (非正式用语) (of something) suddenly appear or come into existence or action quickly or from nothing (指某物)突然出现,冒出: Towards evening a cold wind suddenly *sprang up*. 将近傍晚时分,突然刮起了一阵冷风。Many Japanese inns *sprang up* in the 17th century to accommodate feudal lords traveling along the Tokaido highway to Tokyo. 在17世纪,日本就涌现出大量日式客栈,为当时那些沿东海道公路到东京旅行的封建王族们提供食宿。Towns had *sprung up* in what had been a dry desert. 一些城镇在干旱的沙漠中平地而起。

spy out *vt.* (正式用语) ❶look around an area in order to find (something)寻找: I'm going to *spy out* a suitable place to meet. 我去找一个合适的会面地点。❷try to find out information about (something) secretly 秘密侦察,调查: Some men were trained to *spy out* the opposing party's secret methods. 培训了一些人员去打探对方的秘密方法。We were sent to *spy out* the enemy positions. 我们被派去侦察敌人的阵地。❸notice (someone or something) 注意上……: He quickly *spied out* the waiter. 他很快就注意上了那个侍者。I *spied out* a mistake. 我注意到了一处错误。

squeeze blood from a turnip ⇨ get blood from a stone

squeeze out *vt.* 【可分性动词短语】 ❶get(liquid or soft substance) from (an object) by pressing the object (从某物体中)压出,挤出(液体或软体物质): He *squeezed* the water *out* of the sponge. 他把海绵里的水挤了出来。He *squeezed out* the last bit of toothpaste from the tube. 他把牙膏管里的最后一点牙膏挤了出来。❷(非正式用语) try to get (something such as money) (from someone) by applying pressure of various kinds (for example threats, harsh legislation) 榨取;勒索: If you give in to the blackmailer, he will return to *squeeze out* another thousand later. 如果你对敲诈你的人让步,他以后还会再向你勒索1 000元的。❸(常用被动语态形式) (of someone or something) get or force out, as if by squeezing 挤出: Other directors appeared happy that Mr Smith has been *squeezed out*. 史密斯先生被排挤掉了,其他董事看上去都很高兴。The very aggressive competition *squeezed* the company *out* of the market. 十分激烈的竞争把该公司挤出了市场。

NOTE 当本短语的宾语为代词时,该代词须置于本短语的动词和副词中间。

stain with *vt.* 【可分性动词短语】(常用被动语态形式) ❶mark (something) with (something dirty, dark, or oily) so that the mark cannot be removed easily 玷污,染污: His teeth were *stained with* nicotine from years of smoking. 他的牙齿因多年吸烟而被尼古丁染黄了。Their swords were *stained with* the blood of innocent people. 他们的剑上沾满了无辜人民的鲜血。❷spoil (something) with (something bad) 以……玷污: He has *stained* the good honor of his family *with* the guilt of his crime. 他以其罪行玷污了他家族的良好声誉。❸change (something) in color, especially by darkening with (a dye or chemical substance) 把(某物)染色,着色: I'm going to *stain* the chairs brown *with* wood dye to match the table. 我要将这几把椅子用木材染料染成褐

色，使其与桌子相配。

stamp on/upon *vt.* ❶put your foot down hard and noisily on (usually something), thus crushing it 用脚踩：He doesn't seem able to dance without *stamping on* his partner's feet. 他似乎在跳舞时无法不踩舞伴的脚。In her rage, she threw her things on the floor and *stamped on* them. 愤怒之下，她把自己的东西扔到地板上并用脚在上面踩踏。She *stamped on* the insect and killed it. 她踩死了那只虫子。❷(常用一般时态) put a mark on (something) using ink and a stamp 在……印上：They stamped patterns on cloth. 他们在布料上印上图案。The office *stamps* the date *on* all the incoming letters. 办公室给所有的来信都打印上日期。His name was *stamped on* the briefcase. 他的名字印在了公文包上。The book had the library's name *stamped on* the cover. 这本书的封皮上印有该图书馆的名称。❸stop (something) by taking determined action 坚决禁止：China's Football Association will *stamp on* any violent behavior on the field. 中国足协将坚决制止赛场上的任何暴力行为。❹(非正式用语，常用一般时态) stop (someone) in a very unfair or cruel way from doing something 压制(某人)：They will *stamp on* anyone who gets in their way. 谁要是妨碍他们，他们就会压制谁。Any opposition or disagreement was quickly *stamped on*. 任何反对意见或异议都很快被压制下去了。

NOTE 本短语中的 upon 用法比 on 正式，但不及 on 常用。

stand (a) hope ⇨ **stand (a) chance**

stand against *vt.* 【不可分性动词短语】(英国英语用法) ❶oppose (something or someone), especially in a brave or determined way 坚决反对：I *stand against* all forms of cruelty, especially to children. 我坚决反对各种形式的虐待行为，尤其是对儿童的虐待行为。He had *stood against* her in the party election. 他在党内选举中强烈地反对她。❷resist; withstand 抵抗；对抗：That fence will not *stand against* the wind. 那篱笆抗不住风。Instead of confessing his crimes, the former vice-governor *stood against* the public prosecutors and even continued to seek bribes during the investigation against him. 这位原副省长不但不认罪，反而对抗公诉人，甚至在被调查期间还继续索贿。❸take part in (an election) as a candidate to try to defeat another candidate 作为候选人参加(竞选)对抗另一候选人：The opposition party nominated a former prime minister to *stand against* the present military ruler in the October presidential election. 反对党提名一位前总理在 10 月份的总统选举中对抗现任的军人统治者。

stand aside *vi.* (正式用语，常用于祈使句中) ❶move to one side or move out of the way in order to let someone pass 移步到一边；让开：People were asked to *stand aside* to let the parading procession through. 人们被要求站到一边让游行队伍过去。*Stand aside* and let her pass! 让开，让她过去！❷(英国英语用法，常用一般时态) take no action; not involve oneself in a situation, especially one that you should be trying to prevent 不采取行动；袖手旁观：Don't *stand aside* and let others decide the important issues. 不要坐视让别人决定重要的事宜。Ireland *stood aside* from this conflict. 爱尔兰没有参与到这场冲突中。How can you *stand aside* and watch your colleagues

being treated like that? 你怎么能看着你的同事受到那种对待而无动于衷呢?

stand at ease ⇨ **at ease**

stand back *vi.* ❶ move away (from something or someone) or stand at a distance (from something especially dangerous) 退后,靠后站: The children were told to *stand back* from the fire. 让孩子们靠后些站,离火远一点。*Stand back* and let the doctor through. 靠后站,让医生过去。❷(常用一般时态,与 from 连用) (especially of a building) be situated at a distance, as from a road, etc. (尤指建筑物)坐落于远离道路等的地方: The house *stands back* around twenty yards from the lane. 那所房子坐落在离那条窄路约 20 码的地方。The school *stands* well *back* from a busy street. 该学校位于一处远离繁闹街道的地方。❸(常用一般时态) refuse to take part in or influence something such as an event 不介入;不参加: These were vital discussions from which he could not afford to *stand back*. 这些讨论十分重要,他不能不参与其中。*Stand back* and look objectively at the problem. 不要参与其中,要客观地看待这个问题。

stand behind *vt.* (无被动语态形式,用一般时态) support (someone) 支持(某人): UN Secretary General Ban Ki-moon surveyed one of the towns hit hardest by the earthquake, telling the Chinese Premier that "the whole world *stands behind* you." 联合国秘书长潘基文视察了地震受灾最严重的一个镇,他对中国总理说:"全世界都支持你们。" People say, "*Behind* every successful man *stands* a woman." 常言道:"在每个成功的男人背后,总有一个支持他的女人。"

stand between *vt.* 【不可分性动词短语】(无被动语态形式,常用一般时态) prevent (someone) from gaining or achieving (something); exist as an obstacle between (someone and something he or she wishes to achieve) 阻碍,障碍: Only two men *stood between* him and a coveted place on the board. 仅有两人是他得到董事会中那个令人垂涎的职位的障碍。Mr President, don't *stand between* millions of children and the health care they need. 总统先生,不要为数百万儿童享受他们所需要的卫生保健设置障碍。

stand by *v.* ❶ be present, as standing, near something or someone 在场,站在……旁边: There were several people *standing by* when the accident happened. 事故发生时,有几个人在场。He *stood by* the lathe watching how it was operating. 他站在车床旁边,观看车床怎样运转。❷ do not do anything to stop something bad from happening (对不良之事的发生)袖手旁观: The president has said that he wouldn't *stand by* and let democracy be undermined. 总统表示,他不会袖手旁观让民主受到破坏。We cannot *stand by* and watch while our allies are attacked. 我们不能坐视不管,眼看着我们的盟友挨打。❸(无被动语态形式) continue supporting (someone) even when things are bad 一如既往地支持(某人): We promised to *stand by* him in case of trouble. 我们承诺如果他遇到麻烦,我们也会一如既往地支持他。China and other third world countries would *stand by* and work with each other in international affairs. 中国和其他第三世界国家在国际事务中将一如既往地相互支持和配合。❹(无被动语态形式) keep to; remain faithful to (an early decision, promise, agreement, etc.)信守,遵守(决定、诺言、协议等): The US government will not change its policy and *stand* firmly *by* the one-China policy, the secretary of state of the United States said in Beijing. 美国国务卿在北京表示,美国政府不会改变其政策,将严格遵守"一个中国"的原则。I *stand by* what I said earlier. 我信守前言。❺ be waiting and ready for action, fight, duty, etc. 准备行动;履行职责: Everyone, *stand by* for action! 各位,准备行动!

NOTE 本短语可转化为复合词 standby,意为"可依靠的人(或东西),待命状态";还可转化为复合名词 bystander,意为"(袖手)旁观者"。

stand (a) chance *vi.* (常用于否定句中) have the possibility of being successful 有可能;有希望: I think you *stand* a good *chance* of success. 我认为你很有可能会成功。He doesn't *stand a chance* of winning the tournament. 他不可能赢得这次锦标赛。According to a recent poll, the present president *stands a chance* of being reelected. 根据最近的一项民意调查,现总统有重新当选的可能。I should apply for the post if I were you. I think you *stand* a good *chance*. 如果我是你的话,我一定去申请这个职位,我认为你的希望很大。

NOTE 本短语与 stand (a) hope 意义和用法相同。

stand for *vt.*【不可分性动词短语】❶ rise to one's feet as a mark of respect for (someone or something)起立(以表示对……的敬意): Will all present in court *stand for* the judge. 请到庭所有人员起立向法官表示敬意。At the opening ceremony, the whole crowd *stood for* the national song. 在开幕式上,当奏国歌时,人们全体起立。❷(无被动语态形式,常用一般现在时) be a sign or short form of; represent (something)是……的象征;是……的缩写: The letters NATO *stand for* North Atlantic Treaty Organization. NATO 这四个字母是 North Atlantic Treaty Organization (北大西洋公约组织)的缩写。Every star on the flag of the United States *stands for* a state of the nation. 美国国旗上的每颗星都代表一个州。❸(无被动语态形式,用一般时态) support (particular principles or values) 支持,主张: We *stand for* the complete prohibition and thorough destruction of nuclear weapons. 我们支持全面禁止和彻底销毁核武器。In the world of art and literature, we *stand* firmly *for* the practice of letting a hundred flowers blossom and a hundred schools of thought contend. 在文艺界,我们坚决主张"百花齐放,百家争鸣"。❹(非正式用语,无被动语态形式,常用于否定和疑问句中,用一般时态) be willing to accept or bear (something that someone does) without complaining; tolerate 容忍,忍受(他人之所为): She says she's not going to *stand for* her own children disobeying her. 她说她不能容忍自己的孩子不服从她。"This is unacceptable and we will not *stand for* it," a female protester said when delivering the petition. "这是不可接受的,也是我们不能容忍的。"一位女性抗议者在递交请愿书时说道。I can't *stand for* your rudeness any more. 我再也不能忍受你的粗鲁了。Can you *stand for* always being treated like a child? 你会容忍别人总是把你当小孩子对待吗?

stand guard over ⇨ **keep guard over**

stand hope ⇨ **stand chance**

stand in one's way *vi.* (常用于否定句

S

中) try to stop someone from doing something 妨碍，阻挠：I didn't want to *stand in her way*, so I withdrew my application for the job. 我不想妨碍她，所以我撤回了对这份工作的申请。I won't *stand in your way* if you're really determined. 如果你真的下了决心，我就不阻挡你了。

NOTE 本短语的名词 way 可被 path 替换，两者意义和用法相同。

stand in the way of *vt.*【不可分性动词短语】(常用于否定句中) try to prevent (someone from doing what they want) or prevent (something from happening) 阻止(某人)做(某事)；阻止(某事)发生：You can't *stand in the way of* progress. 你无法阻止进步。Does anything *stand in the way of* the firm accepting this contract? 有什么妨碍公司接受这项合同吗？I never let unimportant details *get in the way of* a good plan. 我绝不会让枝节问题妨碍一个好的计划。

NOTE 本短语的动词 stand 可被 get 替代，两者的意义和用法相同。

stand in with *vt.*【不可分性动词短语】(非正式用语，无被动语态形式) have a friendly relationship with (someone) 与(某人)友好：John *stands in* well *with* all the teachers teaching him. 约翰与所有教他的老师都相处甚好。

S

stand off *vi.* ❶(非正式用语，常用一般时态) stay at a distance; stay apart; keep away from people 保持一定的距离；与人疏远：He *stood off* from an acquaintance. 他避开了一个熟人。At parties, John goes around talking to everyone, but his wife is shy and *stands off*. 在聚会上，约翰四处走动与大家交谈，可他妻子却是羞羞答答，落落寡合。❷(of a ship) remain stationary at a distance from the shore (船)停泊在离岸较远的地方：The ship *stood off* and waited for the order. 船只停泊在离岸较远处待命。

—*vt.* dismiss (workers) (for example during an economic depression), often for a short period of time (在经济萧条期间)临时解雇(工人)：The management had to *stand off* a hundred men this week. 资方本周不得不临时解雇 100 名员工。If the depression continues, more people will be *stood off*. 如果经济萧条持续下去，将有更多的人被解雇。

NOTE 1. 本短语可转化为复合词 standoff，意为“离岸驶去；避开；冷淡；停工；抵消；(比赛等)平局”。

stand on/upon *vt.* ❶(常用一般时态) (cause to) be placed on top of (a surface) (把……)放置在……上面：She *stood* the clock *on* the shelf. 她把时钟放在了搁架上。He *stood* the little girl *on* the wall so that she could see it. 他让小女孩站在墙上，以便她能看得见它。❷(无被动语态形式，用一般时态) act firmly according to (one's principles, rights, etc.) 坚持(原则，权利等)：I *stand on* my rights in this matter, and will take this matter to court if necessary. 在这个问题上，我坚持自己的权利。如有必要，我愿将其提交法庭裁决。

NOTE 本短语中的 upon 用法比 on 正式，但不及 on 常用。

stand on ceremony *vi.* (常与表示否定的助动词连用) follow strict rules of politeness; be very formal with other people 遵从礼节；讲究客套：Do please take your jacket off; we don't *stand on ceremony* in this house. 请你把夹克脱掉吧。在我们家里，是不讲究客套的。

Don't *stand on* the slightest *ceremony* with me. 请一点也不要和我客气。I don't like too much *standing on ceremony* at a simple party like this. 我不喜欢在这么简单的聚会上讲究那么多的礼节。

stand on one's own two feet *vi.* (非正式用语,常用一般时态) depend on yourself; survive without any help; earn your own living; be independent 自立,独立: You're 20 now and should learn how to *stand on your own feet*. 你现在已 20 岁了,该学着如何靠自己生活了。If he doesn't *stand on his own two feet* at his age, he'll lose his self-respect. 在他这个年龄上还不能自立,他就会失去自尊。

NOTE 本短语中的数词 two 可以省略。

stand one's ground ⇨ **hold one's ground**

stand out *vi.* ❶(常用一般时态) be firm in opposition, disagreement, etc., as by refusing to work; refuse to yield (以拒绝工作等方式)坚持反对;拒不屈服: Some of the workers still *stood out* even after the rest had agreed to accept the pay offer. 一些工人仍然坚持其反对意见,尽管其他人已同意接受(资方)提出的工资建议。❷(of something) be very easily seen or noticed because of its colour or shape (指某物因其颜色或形状而)十分显眼: "I'm a daughter of a British man," says Mrs Hassan, whose green eyes and white complexion cause her to *stand out*. "我是一个英国人的女儿。"哈桑太太说道。她绿色的眼睛和白色的肌肤使她十分显眼。The road sign is easy to read, the words *stand out* well. 路标上的字很易认,因为它们都十分显眼。❸(常用一般时态) be much better or much more important than others 突出,杰出: They were all pretty, but she *stood out* among them. 她们都很漂亮,但其中她最为突出。Her talents *stand out* in comparison with the others. 和其他那些人相比,她的才华出众。Among the contemporary writers, he *stands out* as a realist. 在当代作家中,他是个杰出的现实主义者。

NOTE **1.** 当本短语作"十分显眼"解时,同义短语是 stick out。

2. 本短语可转化为复合词 standout,意为"杰出的人(或物);(比赛中)有把握获胜的选手"。outstanding 也是本短语所转化成的复合词,意为"杰出的,显著的"。

stand out against *vt.* (无被动语态形式) oppose (usually something) in a determined way 坚决反对: I'm *standing out against* his idea. 我坚决反对他的意见。They are *standing out against* any change of the law. 他们坚决反对对那项法律做任何改变。The trade unions have continued to *stand out against* the government's wage and price controls. 工会一直反对政府对工资和价格的控制。

stand out for *vt.* refuse to accept less than what you are asking for 坚持要求: The union decided to *stand out for* its original claim. 工会决定坚持其原有的要求。The workers are *standing out for* a fair reward for their hard work. 工人们坚持要求为他们的艰苦工作付合理报酬。

stand over *vi.* postpone; wait or be delayed till a later time 延期,延缓: There is no urgency about this matter; it can *stand over* until next week. 这件事不急,可以延缓到下一个星期再办。

—*vt.* 【不可分性动词短语】 watch (someone at work) closely, usually in order to make sure he or she is doing it

S

correctly 严密监视,监督(正在工作的某人):Don't *stand over* me while I'm cooking, you make me nervous. 我做饭时别盯着我看,你让我好紧张。I hate being *stood over* when I'm doing a job. 我不喜欢在工作时被人监视。My assistant isn't very good, I have to *stand over* him all the time to make sure he does the work well. 我的助手不是太好。为了确保他做好工作,我不得不总是监督着他。

stand up *vt.* & *vi.* (cause to) put your body into an upright position from a sitting or lying position (使)站起:A man at the back *stood up* to ask a question. 后面有个人站起来问了一个问题。No one dared *stand up* as a witness, so I had to give up. 没人敢站出来作证,所以,我不得不放弃。He is drunk, can't you help me to *stand* him *up*? 他喝醉了,你就不能帮我把他扶起来吗?

—*vi.* (常用一般时态) ❶ stay in good condition after testing or hard use, etc.; wear or last well 经得起,经久耐用:Wool *stands up* better than silk. 毛料比丝绸经久耐穿。This old car has already *stood up* well for twenty years. 这台旧汽车已经使用了 20 年。❷ (of something such as a piece of evidence or a claim) be accepted as true or satisfactory after being carefully examined (某一证据或某项主张)为人接受,站得住脚:What we need is a proof that would *stand up* in court. 我们需要的是在法庭上能令人信服的证据。What is false can never *stand up*. 假的东西总是站不住脚的。Your theory will not be able to *stand up* to close examination. 你的理论是经不起仔细推敲的。

—*vt.*【可分性动词短语】(非正式用语,常用一般时态) fail to keep an arrangement to meet (especially someone you are just beginning a romantic or sexual relationship with) 未能按约与人(尤指异性朋友)相会:The mayor *stood up* the visitors because of an emergency city council meeting. 市长因参加紧急市政会议而未能按约会见客人。Where is my boyfriend? If he's *stood* me *up* I'll never speak to him again. 我的男友呢?如果他不按约来见我,我就再也不理他了。He was in a bad mood because he had been *stood up* by his girlfriend. 他因女朋友未能按约与其相会而感沮丧。

NOTE 1. 当本短语用作及物性动词短语,所带的宾语为代词时,该代词须置于本短语的动词和副词中间。

2. 本短语可转化为复合词 standup,意为"坦率正直的;(衣领)直立的;站着的"。

stand up for *vt.*【不可分性动词短语】❶ support or defend (someone or something that is being criticized or attacked) 支持;为……辩护:We *stood up for* her, as she was in the right. 我们支持她,因为她是对的。You should not *stand up for* cops under any circumstances. 你不应该在什么情况下都为警察辩护。❷ demand and make sure that one gets (one's right) 坚决要求,争取(某人的权利):If you don't *stand up for* your rights, no one else is going to fight a battle for you. 如果你不要求自己的权利,别人不会为你争取的。More and more people are beginning to *stand up for* children's rights. 越来越多的人开始争取儿童的权益。

NOTE 本短语与 stick up for 意义和用法相同。

stand up to *vt.*【不可分性动词短语】❶ meet (someone or something) with

S

courage; oppose (usually someone more powerful than you are) without fear 勇敢地面对,无惧地反抗(常指有权势的人): Nobody thought she would be brave enough to *stand up to* her boss. 没人想到她会勇敢地面对自己的老板。❷(用一般时态) (of something) remain in good condition in spite of (long wear, hard use, damage, etc., or doing something harmful) 维持良好状况;经得起: It's not easy for the piano to *stand up to* moving around so often. 这样经常地四处搬动,很难使这台钢琴保持良好的状况。These tyres will *stand up to* the roughest wear and tear. 这些轮胎可经得住最严重的磨损。What we need is metals that *stand* well *up to* high temperature. 我们需要的是能耐高温的金属。

stare at *vt.* 【不可分性动词短语】look at (someone or something) with fixed eyes, usually from interest, surprise, disapproval, or other heightened feeling 凝望着,盯着看: An Italian man was given a sentence of 10 days in prison and a 40-euro fine for *staring* too intensely *at* a woman on the train, according to media reports. 据媒体报道,一名意大利男子因在列车上用眼死盯着一位女士看而被判 10 天监禁,并处罚款 40 欧元。Do you like being *stared at*? 你喜欢被人盯着瞧吗?

start for *vt.* 【不可分性动词短语】(无被动语态形式) leave one place to go to (another) 动身去(某地): It's a long trip, we'll have to start off early and *start* back *for* home in the afternoon. 路程很远,我们得早点出发,下午就动身返回。What time do you *start for* school in the morning? 你早上什么时候去上学? I am on the point of *starting for* Baghdad. 我即将动身去巴格达。

start off *v.* ❶(常用一般时态) begin going in a particular direction; begin a journey 出发,起程: He *started off* for the railway station hurriedly. 他匆匆忙忙地赶往火车站。She *started off* to school at a quarter to seven the next morning. 她第二天早晨 6:45 就动身去学校了。They *started off* on their journey at dawn. 他们在黎明时分便踏上了征途。❷(非正式用语) begin or cause (something) to begin 开始;使(某事)开始: We're to *start off* with a few questions from the audience. 我们还是以听众的提问来开始吧。Let's *start* our meal *off* by eating some soup. 咱们先喝点汤再开始用餐。We don't want to *start off* a riot. 我们不想引发骚乱。❸(无被动语态形式) cause (someone) to begin doing (something) 使(某人)开始做(某事): She had stopped crying, but his remark *started* her *off* again. 她本来已经不哭了,但他的话又使她哭了起来。The slightest bit of dust *starts* me *off* sneezing. 哪怕一点点灰尘也会使我打起喷嚏来。❹(非正式用语,常用一般时态) (cause to) open one's remarks by saying something special at length (使)开始冗长的讲话: It's impossible to stop him talking once he *started off*. 他一打开话匣子就无法住口。Take care what you say or you'll *start* her *off* on that subject. 注意你讲的话,否则你就会使她谈起那个话题没完没了。He *started off* by pointing out the dangers involved in rock climbing. 他开始从在攀岩中所能遇到的危险讲起。

NOTE 1. 当本短语用作及物性动词短语,所带的宾语为代词时,该代词须置于本短

S

语的动词和副词中间。

2. 当本短语作"出发,起程"解时,同义短语是 start out。

3. 当本短语作"开始;使(某事)开始"解时,同义短语是 kick off。

start on *vt.* 【不可分性动词短语】begin doing (a job or a piece of work); start dealing with (something that needs to be done) 开始做(某项工作),着手做(某事):We could have breakfast before we *start on* the painting. 我们可以先吃早餐再开始画画。Will I have time to *start on* digging the garden tonight? 今晚我会有时间给花园翻土吗?

—*vt.* & *vi.* (非正式用语,无被动语态形式) begin to criticize (someone) or complain angrily about (someone or something) with words 用言辞攻击(某人);抱怨(某人或某事): Don't *start on* me! It's not my fault. 别训我! 那不是我的过错! She *started on* at his husband about the way he's looking at other women. 她斥责她丈夫看其他女人的那个样子。She *started on* about this dog barking in the street. 她抱怨这条狗在街上乱叫。

start out *vi.* ❶start to go somewhere 出发,起程(去某地): Tommy *started out* for school on his bicycle. 汤米骑自行车上学去了。❷(常用一般时态) begin with the intention (to do something)开始,打算(做某事): She didn't *start out* to be a model. 她以前并没有当模特的打算。

—*vt.* & *vi.* (cause to) begin one's business or career (使)开始从事(某种职业或生涯): He *started out* as a poor office boy and now he's a millionaire! 他开始是一个很穷的办公室勤杂工,而现在却成了百万富翁。He *started out* as a salesperson before turning to poetry. 他开始做推销员,后来转行写诗歌了。

start over/afresh *vi.* (非正式用语) begin (to do something) again, sometimes in a different way (常指以不同的方式)重新开始:After the fire, they had to *start over* and build the business again from the beginning. 火灾过后,他们不得不重新开始,从头创业。We decided to abandon the first draft of the report and *start afresh*. 我们决定放弃报告的首稿,重新撰写。

NOTE start over 为美国英语用法,而 start afresh 为英国英语用法。

start up *v.* ❶(用一般时态)(of people) rise or stand suddenly, as with a shock (指人)(由于受惊等)突然跳起: He *started up* from his chair when he heard the bell. 他听到铃声便从椅子上跳起来。❷make (something such as an engine) start working; (of an engine, etc.) begin operating 启动(发动机等);(发动机等)发动:It was very cold in the morning and we had some difficulties *starting up* the motor of the car. 早晨很冷,我们启动汽车的发动机都有些困难。Put the key in the ignition and turn it to *start* the car *up*. 把钥匙插入启动开关一转动,就会把车启动了。The machines all *started up* at the same time. 所有的机器都同时启动了。❸begin; resume operation 开始,恢复活动:After Thursday's train explosion occurred, the local government immediately *started up* the rescue work and demanded help from the neighboring areas. 星期四发生火车爆炸事故后,当地政府立即开始了营救工作,并请求邻近地区给予援助。We can't *start* the project *up* until we have more money. 我们在得到资金之前不会开始这一项目。The factory closed since last winter will soon *start up* again. 从去年冬天开始停产的这家工厂将很快恢复生产。❹begin (a business, organization, or project) into existence 开办(企业、机构或项目等): I'm trying to *start up* a swimming club. 我正在设法开办一家游泳俱乐部。It was a brave move to *start up* one's business in wartime. 在战争时期开办企业是勇敢之举。The merchant from New York was thinking of *starting up* in the insurance business. 这位纽约商人正在考虑开办保险业务。

❺come into existence suddenly 突然出现: These young people faced bravely the difficulties that had *started up*. 这些青年人勇敢地应付了突然出现的一些困难。

NOTE 1. 当本短语用作及物性动词短语,所带的宾语为代词时,该代词须置于本短语的动词和副词中间。

2. 本短语可转化为复合词 start-up,意为"(生产或操作的)开始,启动,刚开办的小企业"。

start with *vt.* have (something) at the beginning; cause (something) to begin by having or doing (something)(使)以……开始: His illness *started with* a slight cough. 他的病开始于轻微的咳嗽。I will *start* the press conference *with* a piece of news. 首先我要在这次新闻发布会上发布一条消息。

stay abreast of ⇨ **keep abreast of**

stay at *vt.* 【不可分性动词短语】❶remain behind at (a place) 留在,待在(某处): The women *stayed at* home while the men went to work in the city. 女人们留在家中,而男人都去城里打工。I'll *stay* here *at* the bus stop while you go to find him in the post office. 我留在汽车站这儿,你去邮局找他。❷be a guest at (a place such as a home or hotel) 住在(某人家里或旅馆中): I'll be able to *stay at* my aunt's house while I'm in the town. 我进城时,可以住在我婶婶家。Which hotel are you *staying at*? 你住在哪家旅馆里? The King of Saudi Arabia had been *staying at* Buckingham Palace as a guest of Queen Elizabeth II during his three days in London. 作为女王伊丽莎白二世的客人,沙特阿拉伯国王在伦敦逗留的三天期间一直住在白金汉宫里。

stay away *vi.* (常用一般时态) be absent; remain at a distance (from something or someone) 缺席;远离: If he announces that he will *stay away*, that's all well and good. 如果他宣布他将不出席,那很好。*Stay away* from my daughter, sir! 先生,离我女儿远点儿!

stay clear of ⇨ **remain clear of**

stay in —*vt.* & *vi.* (常用一般时态) remain in position; remain where it is; continue to be present in (a place) 固定(在某一位置);留在原处: I have put the screw in the wood as tightly as I can, but it won't *stay in*. 我尽可能紧地把螺丝拧在了木头上,但就是固定不住。I don't know whether to *stay in* teaching or to try to get another job. 我不知道是该继续教书还是另谋一份工作。My parents *stayed in* my home country when we moved overseas. 我们移居海外,而我的父母却仍留在国内。

vi. ❶remain at home and do not go out, especially during the evening (尤指晚间)待在家里: As a rule, I *stay in* on Friday nights. 星期五晚上我通常待在家里。The doctors advised me to *stay in* for a few days. 医生都建议我在家里休息几天。❷(of a student) be kept in school after others have left, as a punishment (指学生)被罚课后留校: If you go on making such a noise, you'll have to *stay in* after school. 如果你继续搞出这种响动,你就要被罚留校。

—*vt.* (常用一般时态) continue to be in (a state, usually good)保持(尤指好的状态): How has the car *stayed in* such good condition after all those miles of traveling? 这车跑了那么多里数,怎么还保持着这么好的状态呢?

NOTE 1. 当本短语作"(尤指晚间)待在家里"解时,反义短语是 stay out。

2. 当本短语作"(指学生)被罚课后留校"解时,同义短语是 keep in。

stay on *vi.* ❶(常用一般时态) (of something electrical such as a tight) remain in operation; (of fire) keep burning (灯等)继续亮着;(火)继续燃烧着: If the lights of the offices are allowed to *stay on* after people go home at night, the department's electricity bills are certainly going to be high. 如果晚上人都回家了还让办公室的灯亮着,该部门要付的电费当然就会很高。The fire in the bush *stayed on* as there was much wind that day. 由于那天风大,树丛中的火继续烧着。❷remain at a place of study, a job, etc. after others have left, or after the usual time when you were going to leave 继续留在(某处);留级;留任: Are you going to *stay on* at university to do further research? 你打算继续留在大学里从事进一步的研究吗? He becomes a senior student in college as he *stays on* year after year. 由于他年复一年地留级,所以成了学校中的大龄学生。He hopes to *stay on* as Chicago Bulls' coach. 他希望继续留任芝加哥公牛队教练。

stay out *vi.* ❶(常用一般时态) remain away from your home, especially after dark (尤指天黑后)依然离家在外: You *stayed out* after midnight last night. What happened to you? 你昨晚半夜后还没回家,出什么事了? I met some friends and *stayed out* until two o'clock in the morning. 我会了一些朋友,所以在外面一直待到凌晨 2 点才回家。But my mum won't let me *stay out* late. 但是,我妈妈可不让我在外面待得太晚。❷(of workers) remain on strike (指工人)继续罢工: The workers said they were prepared to *stay out* until their demands were met. 工人们说,他们准备继续罢工,直到他们的要求得到满足为止。The electricians at the power stations went on strike and *stayed out* nearly four days. 发电厂的电工们举行了罢工并持续罢工了近四天的时间。

stay out of *vt.* 【不可分性动词短语】(无被动语态形式,常用一般时态) remain at a distance from or have nothing to do with (something such as trouble or other people's affairs)远离(麻烦);不参与(他人之事等): I hope you'll *stay out of* trouble while I' m away. 我不在期间,你不要招惹麻烦。I always try to *stay out of* other people's affairs that don't concern me. 我总是千方百计地不参与和我无关的他人之事。

stay put *vi.* (仅用于口语中,常用一般时态) remain in the same place or position; not leave or move 留在原地;不动: The little girl's father told her to *stay put* until he came back. 小女孩儿的爸爸让她留在原处,等他回来。After Grandmother came home from her trip to visit New York, she said she wanted to *stay put* for a while. 祖母从纽约旅行回来后说,她要在家里住一段时间,哪也不去了。That window keeps rattling; I must make it *stay put*. 那窗户老是发出响动,我必须把它固定住。

stay up *vi.* ❶(常用一般时态)remain awake out of bed, as at night(for example to wait for or accompany someone)晚睡;熬夜: I'll be late home, and please don't *stay up* for me. 我要晚一点才能回家,请不要熬夜等我。Most boy students wanted to *stay up* to watch the World Cup matches. 大多数男同学都想要熬夜看世界杯足球赛。I *stayed up* reading until 1:00 in the morning. 我熬夜看书一直到凌晨1点。❷not fall or sink 不倒,不沉: I'm surprised that these old and shabby houses *stay up* as long as they do. 这些又旧又破的房子久立不倒令我感到惊讶。If you do fall out of the boat, your lifejacket will help you to *stay up* until we can fish you out. 如果你从船上掉下去的话,你穿的救生衣会使你浮而不沉,到时我们就会把你打捞上来。

NOTE 在英国英语的口语中,本短语的另外一种表达方式是 stop up。

steer clear of ⇨ **remain clear of**

stem from *vt.* (无被动语态形式)exist or happen as a result of; have an origin of; be caused by (something or doing something)源于……;由……发生: The two countries have a history of mutual hatred *stemming from* disputes over territory, resources and wartime history. 这两个国家有着相互仇恨的历史,其源于领土、资源和战争历史方面的争端。That error *stemmed from* carelessness. 那一错误是由于粗心大意造成的。His serious illness *stems from* being treated improperly in the early stage. 他的重病是因为早期没有得到适当的治疗所致。

step aside *vi.* ❶(正式用语,常用一般时态) move to one side, as out of the way, to make a space for someone else 往旁边站(以让出路来): *Step aside*, please. The firemen can't get through. 请往旁边站站,消防员过不去。Please *step aside* to make room for the luggage. 请让开一点,腾出地方放行李。❷cease to take part in a competition, as for a position 退出(某职位的)竞选: Party leaders all wanted her to *step aside* for the good of the party. 该党的领导人都希望她为了党的利益而退出竞选。I feel that when there are so many better people for the chairmanship, I should *step aside*. 我感到有那么多优秀的主席人选,我应该退出竞选。❸leave an official position or job, especially so that someone else can take your place 辞职;让位: The manager announced he is *stepping aside*. 经理声明他要辞职。Mr Johnson is unwilling to *step aside* in favor of a younger person. 约翰逊先生不愿把位置让给一个比他年轻的人。

NOTE 当本短语作"辞职;让位"解时,与 step down 意义和用法相同,两者可互换使用。

step by step *adv.* ❶ one step at a time moving slowly 一步步地: *Step by step* she came nearer. 她一步一步地走近前来。They were getting to the top of the mountain *step by step*. 他们一步一步地走上山顶。❷gradually from one stage or level to the next 逐步地,逐渐地: *Step by step* I gained the boy's trust and got the whole story from him. 我逐渐地取得了那个男孩的信任并从他口中了解到了事情的全部经过。*Step by step* I taught the little cat to obey me. 我慢慢地把小猫调教得听我的话了。

NOTE 1. 本短语的另外一种表达形式是 a step at a time。例如:

He wanted to rush through the job, but I asked him to do it *a step at a time*.
他想要匆匆做完这项工作,但我要求他逐步地来做。

2. 本短语可转化为复合词 step-by-step,意为“逐步的,逐渐的”,充当定语来修饰其后的名词。例如:

The conflict can be ended only by *step-by-step* negotiations.
这场冲突只能通过一步一步进行谈判才能解决。

step down *vi.* ❶move to a lower level, as by taking a step 走下来:*Stepping down* from the stage, the star singer took a member of the audience by the hand and led him up the steps. 那位歌星从舞台上走下来,用手拉住一名观众,带他走上台阶。❷resign from an important job or position, often in order to give it to another person 辞职;下台:As you've already heard, I've decided that I will *step down* from my role as Chief Executive Officer. 正像你已经听说的那样,我已决定要辞去首席执行官一职了。

NOTE 1. 本短语可转化为复合词 step-down,意为“下车;下台;(逐渐的)减少,缩小”。

step in *vi.* ❶enter a building or room, often for a short time 走进某处(作短暂的逗留):It was very cold outside, and when the policeman passed, we invited him to *step in* for a cup of hot coffee. 外面很冷,所以当警察路过时我们请他进屋喝一杯热咖啡。❷(常用一般时态) get involved in a difficult situation because you think you can or should help with it (出于帮助之目的而)介入;插手:I asked him why he didn't *step in* and help stop the argument. 我问他为什么他不进行干预,帮助制止这场争论。

step on *vt.* ❶move with the feet on top of (someone or something)踩上,走上,踏上:Ouch! You *stepped on* me! 唉呦!你踩到我了!Mind where you put your feet, you could *step on* some broken glass. 注意脚下,别踩到碎玻璃上。As a developing country, China hopes that the Iraqi people can quickly *step on* the road of stable and peaceful development. 作为一个发展中国家,中国希望伊拉克人民能够尽快走上稳定、和平发展的道路。❷(非正式用语) hurt (someone's feelings)伤害(某人的感情):The manager didn't care whether he *stepped on* anyone or not. 经理不在乎是否伤害了任何人的感情。

step out *vi.* ❶(主要用于美国英语中)walk outside, especially for a short time (尤指短时间地)走出:Mary *stepped out* but she will be back in a few minutes. 玛丽出去了,一会儿就会回来。The two astronauts *stepped out* of the International Space Station at 4:17 pm Thursday and their space-walk was scheduled to last about five hours and 45 minutes. 两名宇航员于星期四下午 4 时 17 分同时走出了国际空间站,进行预计 5 小时 45 分钟的太空行走。❷(常用一般时态) start walking more quickly 快走,加快步伐:Tell the people at the front to *step out*. 告诉前面的人快些走。Come on! If we *step out* we'll be there in half an hour. 加油啊!如果我们加快步伐,半个小时就会赶到那里。

step up *vi.* ❶(常用一般时态) move forwards to a place where an official event is happening 走向前:She *stepped up* to receive her prize. 她走向前去领奖。❷rise to a higher or more important position; be promoted 升迁,提拔:John is now secretary of the club, but I am sure he will *step up* to president next year. 约翰现在是俱乐部的秘书,但我确信他明年会升任主席的。

—*vt.* & *vi.* (非正式用语)(cause to) increase (an amount of something) in size or speed; accelerate (使)增加,加强,加速:Our trade with foreign countries has been *stepping up* recently. 最近以来,我们的对外贸易一直在不断增加。The United States is *stepping up* secret planning for a possible air strike on the country, according to a famous US journalist. 据美国一位著名记者称,美国正在加快制订一项可能对该国实施空袭的秘密计划。When John found he was going to be late, he *stepped up* his pace. 当约翰发现自己要迟到时,便加快了步速。

NOTE 本短语可转化为复合词 step-up,意为"(体积、数量等的)逐渐增加";还可转化为复合形容词 stepped-up,意为"加速的;加强了的"。

stick on *vt.* 【可分性动词短语】❶attach (one thing) to (another) using a sticky substance like paste, glue, etc. (用糨糊等)把(某物)粘在……上:I *stuck* the stamp *on* and ran to the post-box. 我把邮票粘上就朝邮箱跑去。The teacher told her students to *stick* the pictures *on* the wall beside the blackboard. 老师让她的学生把那些图片粘在黑板旁的墙壁上。Don't forget to *stick* it *on* your card. 别忘了把它粘在你的卡上。Pictures of football stars were *stuck on* the wall by her bed. 她床边的墙上贴着一些足球明星的画片。❷ say (that someone is responsible for something bad) 声称(某人应负罪责):Don't try and *stick* the blame *on* me! 别想把罪责归咎于我!

NOTE 1. 当本短语的宾语为代词时,该代词须置于本短语的动词和副词或介词中间。

2. 本短语可转化为复合词 stick-on,意为"粘贴上去的"。

stick out *v.* ❶ be in a position further forward than or away from something; protrude 突出:I could see a pair of feet *sticking out* at the end of the blanket. 我能看到毯子的一头有一双脚突出来。The pot has two handles *sticking out*. 这个罐子有两个突出的把柄。A magazine was *sticking out* of his coat pocket. 一本杂志突出他的上衣口袋。❷(非正式用语)(cause to) project, thrust forward; extend (a part of your body) away from your body 探出,伸出:At the time his head was *sticking out* of the window. 当时,他正把头探出窗外。The naughty girl made a face and *stuck* her tongue *out* at him. 那名顽皮的女生朝他做了个鬼脸,伸了伸舌头。She *stuck out* her foot and tripped him over. 她伸出脚把他绊倒。❸(非正式用语,常用一般时态)(of something) be very clearly seen or noticeable because it is unusual (因异乎寻常或与众不同而)显眼:She has red hair that always *sticks out* in a crowd. 因她长着一头红发,所以她总是在人群中很显眼。Our house is the only brick one on the street. It *sticks out* and you can't miss it. 我们的房子是整条街上唯一的砖房,所以它很显眼。你不会找不到的。What had James done to make him *stick out* from the crowd? 詹姆斯都做什么了使他显得那么出众?❹(非正式用语,常用 stick it out 形式)(of someone) continue (something) until it is done, no matter how long, hard, or unpleasant, rather than give up 坚持到底;忍耐到底:Bill doesn't have a chance of winning the marathon, but he will *stick out* the race even if he finishes last. 比尔没有机会赢得马拉松比赛,但他会坚持跑完全程,即使最后一个到达终点。The miners are determined to *stick* it *out* until they get their demands. 矿工们决心坚持到底,直到他们的要求得到满足为止。

NOTE 当本短语用作及物性动词短语,所带的宾语为代词时,该代词须置于本短语的动词和副词中间。

stick to *vt.* ❶(cause to) be attached to (someone or something) with or as with a sticky substance (使)粘住,附着于……: The adhesive tape *stuck to* me and I couldn't get it off. 胶布粘住我,扯不下来了。Glue has *stuck to* his fingers. 胶水粘住了他的手指头。You just *stick* it *to* the window. 你只要把它贴在窗户上就行了。This paint will *stick to* any surface, whether rough or smooth. 这种油漆能附着于任何粗糙或平滑的表面上。❷(无被动语态形式) continue (doing something), rather than changing to something else; not abandon 坚持(做某事),不放弃: I think we should *stick to* our task until it is finished. 我认为我们应该坚持下去,把任务完成。If you *stick to* practicing the piano everyday, you could become quite a good pianist. 如果你坚持每天都练弹钢琴,你就会成为一名出色的钢琴家。He should have *stuck to* writing. 他本不应放弃写作。❸(无被动语态形式) keep to (something such as a promise, agreement, decision, or principle), rather than changing your mind; persevere in 坚持,遵守(承诺、协议、决定或原则等): We said we'd give her the cash, and we must *stick to* our word. 我们说过要给她这笔现金,我们就必须坚守诺言。We wish the management would *stick to* its wage agreement signed with labour union members last year. 我们希望资方能遵守去年与工会会员签订的工资协议。Officials should *stick to* any decisions they have made. 官员应该坚持他们所做出的任何决定。Programmers must stick *strictly to* the rules of the programming language. 程序编制人员必须严格遵守程序语言规则。❹talk about (one particular subject only) and do not change to something else (在谈话中)不离主题: In a speech to the Duma on Thursday, Russian Premier *stuck* closely *to* economic and social themes. 俄罗斯总理星期四在杜马上的讲话中,紧扣经济和社会的主题。We haven't too much time, so please *stick to* the point. 我们的时间不太多,因此谈话请讲要点。❺keep supporting and trusting (someone), especially when he or she is in a difficult situation; remain loyal or faithful to (something or someone)(在逆境中)坚决支持和信任(某人);忠实于: He will *stick to* his friends whatever happens. 不管发生了什么事,他都将坚决支持和信任他的朋友们。He always *sticks to* his country. 他始终忠实于自己的祖国。❻keep (something, usually illegally)(常指非法)占有: If you lend something to that fellow he'll *stick to* it. 你要是把东西借给那家伙,他就会留住不还。❼stay very close to (someone) and follow them wherever they go 紧跟(某人): *Stick to* me and you won't get lost. 紧跟着我,你就不会迷路的。Moore *stuck* close *to* the race leader until the last lap. 穆尔紧紧地跟在跑在前面的选手,一直到最后一圈。

stick together *vt.* & *vi.* (of two or more things) (cause to) be fixed together, with or as with a sticky substance (指物)粘在一起;(把某物)粘在一起:The pages are *sticking together*, I can't get them apart. 这几页都粘在了一起,分不开了。The cup is broken, can you *stick* the pieces *together*, Dad? 这个杯子打碎了。你能把碎片粘起来吗,爸爸?

—*vi.* (非正式用语) (of two or more people) remain united; stay with each other and support each other (指人)团结一致,相互支持:We ought to *stick together* in time of difficulty. 困难当头,我们应该团结一致。The country's Foreign Minister said that it was very important for small nations to *stick together*. 该国外长指出,小国相互支持是很重要的。

stick up *v.* ❶fasten (something such as a notice) with glue, nails, etc. in a public place 将(通知等)贴(或钉)在……上:The examination results will be *stuck up* on this board tomorrow. 明天,考试的结果就将贴在这块广告板上。Supporters of the government *stuck up* pictures of the Prime Minister on the walls. 政府的支持者们在墙上贴了许多首相的画像。❷(of something) point upwards in an upright position 竖起,翘起:Her hair *stuck up* with fear. 她吓得毛发直竖。Aerials *stick up* above the chimney. 天线高高地竖立在烟囱上方。❸(非正式用语) raise (something, especially your arm or hand) upwards 举起(胳膊或手等):Maggie *stuck up* her hand to answer the question. 马吉举起手要回答问题。His feet *stuck up* in the air as he fell. 他两脚朝天地摔倒了。❹(主要用于美国英语中,非正式用语) rob (someone or a place), usually by using a weapon as a threat (常指持枪)抢劫(某人或某处):When the young lady left the bank, a man jumped out of an alley and *stuck* her *up*. 那位年轻的女士离开银行后,一名男子从胡同里跳出来持枪抢劫了她。Big Jim tried to *stick* the drugstore *up* and got caught. 大个子吉姆企图抢劫药店,但被抓住了。It was reported that a gang of four who had just been freed from prison *stuck up* the bank yesterday. 据报道,一个刚从监狱中释放出来的四人团伙昨天持枪抢劫了那家银行。

NOTE **1.** 当本短语的宾语为代词时,该代词须置于本短语的动词和副词中间。

2. 本短语可转化为复合词 stick-up,意为"粘贴(印刷品),抢劫",还可用作形容词,意为"(供)粘贴的,竖起(或翘起)的"。

stick up for *vt.* 【不可分性动词短语】❶(非正式用语,无被动语态形式) support or defend (someone, yourself, or something such as an idea, belief, or plan), especially when no one else will 支持,辩解,维护(某人、自己、某一思想、信仰或计划):When everyone else was criticizing him she was the only one who *stuck up for* him. 当所有其他的人都在批评他时,她是唯一支持他的人。My son is too young too *stick up for* himself. 我的儿子太小,还不会为自己辩解。More people are beginning to *stick up for* human rights. 更多的人开始维护人权。❷demand and make sure one gets (one's right)要求得到(某种权益):We are determined to *stick up for* our rights. 我们决心争取自己的权益。He has shown a great deal of courage in *sticking up for* democracy and civil rights. 他在争取民主和民权上表现出了极大的勇气。

S

still less *conj.* (正式用语) let alone; and certainly not 更不用说;当然没有:At the age of twenty I had never even been on a train, *still less* an aircraft. 我 20 岁时连火车都没坐过,更不用说飞机了。I did not even see him, *still less* shake hands with him. 我看也没有看见过他,哪里还谈得上同他握手呢? They are not interested in reading poetry, *still less* in writing it. 他们对读诗歌都不感兴趣,何谈写诗歌了。The boy didn't have a girlfriend, *still less* a wife. 这男孩连女朋友都没有,当然没有妻子了。

NOTE 1. 本短语常用于否定句后,其后所接的结构要与前面的相一致。

2. 本短语的同义短语是 even less, much less 和 let alone。

stop by *v.* (主要用于美国英语中,非正式用语,常用一般时态) make a short visit (to a place), before continuing to another place 顺便访问,作短暂的访问:I'll *stop by* to see Robert before going home. 我要在回家前顺便看看罗伯特。Please *stop by* my house when you come this way. 路过这里时,请你顺便到我家来坐坐。

NOTE 本短语的同义短语是 stop in。

stop from *vt.* 【可分性动词短语】prevent (someone) from (doing something) or prevent (something) from (happening) 阻止(某人做某事或某事发生): The American official said Thursday that *stopping* terrorists *from* a new attack on US soil was "the greatest challenge of our day." 这位美国官员星期四说,阻止恐怖分子对美国本土发动新的攻击是"我们当今最大的挑战"。The official said that it might be too late to *stop* that country *from* becoming a nuclear power. 那位官员称,欲阻止该国成为核国家可能为时已晚。

NOTE 本短语与 prevent from 意义和用法相同,但 prevent from 比本短语更正式。

stop in *vi.* (主要用于美国英语中,非正式用语,常用一般时态,常与 at 连用) visit a place briefly 对(某一地点)作短暂的访问:Can you *stop in* at my office for a minute today? 你今天能到我的办公室来坐一会儿吗? She was very glad that I *stopped in* at her office. 她对我到她办公室坐了一会儿感到非常高兴。

stop off *vi.* stop for a short time in the middle of a journey in order to do something (在旅程中)作短暂停留:We *stopped off* at a hotel for the night. 我们在一家旅馆停留过夜。The president *stopped off* in Poland on his way to Munich for the economic summit. 总统在前往慕尼黑出席经济高峰会的途中,在波兰作了短暂停留。I'd like to *stop off* for a few days in the north. 我想在北方停留几天。

NOTE 本短语与 stop over 意义和用法相同。

stop over *vi.* make a short stay (for one night or a few nights) on the way to somewhere else or before returning home (旅途中)作短暂停留:The Azerbaijan cargo liner that crashed on Tuesday shortly after its takeoff from Urumqi had *stopped over* at Taiyuan, capital of China's Shanxi Province. 那架在星期二从乌鲁木齐起飞后不久就坠毁了的阿塞拜疆货机曾在中国山西省的省城太原作短暂停留。After the Brussels meeting he *stopped over* in London. 在布鲁塞尔会议后,他在伦敦作了短暂停留。

NOTE 本短语可转化为复合词 stopover,意为"(旅程)中途停留;中途停留地"。

stop up ⇨ **stay up**

store away *vt.* 【可分性动词短语】❶put or keep (something) in a special or safe place until you need it 把……储存起来:He's *stored away* nearly one ton of potatoes. 他储存了近一吨的土豆。You can *store* these apples *away* in the refrigerator to keep them fresh. 你可以把这些苹果存放在冰箱里保鲜。Be sure that this electronic equipment is safely *stored away*. 一定要把这台电子设备安全地存放起来。❷keep (something such as information) in the mind 记住(信息等):Thank you, I'll *store* that piece of news *away* for a time. 谢谢你,我会把这条消息记一段时间的。

NOTE 当本短语的宾语为代词时,该代词须置于本短语的动词和副词中间。

store up *vt.*【可分性动词短语】❶keep (a lot of something) so that you can use it later 储备,贮藏(大量物品):Mother had *stored up* enough vegetables to last through a long winter. 妈妈储存了足够的蔬菜以在漫长的冬季食用。These small animals are busy *storing up* nuts so they have food in the winter. 这些小动物都在忙着贮存坚果以备冬季食用。❷keep (a strong feeling such as anger) in the mind, often with a later result 怀有(怨恨等):Why don't you tell him instead of *storing up* grudges against him? 你有什么话不好对他直说而要对他怀恨在心呢? You're not doing yourself any good by *storing up* resentment. 怀恨在心对你没有任何好处。

NOTE 当本短语的宾语为代词时,该代词须置于本短语的动词和副词中间。

straight away/off *adv.* immediately and without delay 立即,马上:They can't pay me *straight away*. 他们无法马上付款给我。I knew *straight away* it was a bad injury. 我当即就知道这伤不轻。I told him *straight off* what I thought about the matter. 我立刻向他讲了我对那事的想法。You should have told him *straight off* that we can't go. 你本应当即告诉他,我们去不了。

NOTE straight away 可转化为复合词 straightaway,用作名词意为"(陆路或水陆)上的直段,(赛跑跑道接近终点处的)直线跑道";可用作形容词,意为"立刻的,直线行进的,(作品)通俗易懂的";还可用作副词,意为"立刻,马上"。

straighten up *v.* ❶ stand up straight; (cause to) rise from a bent-over position 挺直身子,直起身来:He *straightened up* and slipped his hands in his pockets. 他挺直身子,把双手插进衣袋里。The old man bent to pick up a piece of paper, and had some difficulty in *straightening up*. 老人弯下腰去拾一张纸,但直起腰时却很困难。❷ put in order; make (something, someone or oneself) neat or tidy 整理;打扮:We hurried to *straighten up* before they arrived. 在他们到来之前,我们赶紧收拾了一番。John had to *straighten up* his room before he could go swimming. 在去游泳之前,约翰把自己的房间收拾利落。He took a few moments to *straighten* himself *up* before entering the meeting room. 在进入会场之前,他用了一点时间把自己打扮了一番。

NOTE 当本短语用作及物性动词短语,所带的宾语为代词时,该代词须置于本短语的动词和副词中间。

stray (away) from *vt.* 【不可分性动词短语】❶wander accidentally away from (the right or proper path or place)走失,迷路:He may belong to those elderly people who *stray from* home. 他可能是那种离家走失的老年人。Some of our sheep have *strayed away from* the flock, and are on the neighboring farmer's field. 我们有些羊走离了群,跑到了附近的农田里。❷leave (a subject, etc.)偏离(主题等):You're *straying from* the subject again, do keep to the point. 你又偏离主题了,要紧扣主题呀。Saudi students in the US *stray away from* their main goal of attaining a university degree, *Arab News* said.《阿拉伯新闻报》称,在美国的沙特留学生偏离了他们取得大学学位的主要目标。

stretch out *v.* ❶make (something soft or elastic) become longer or bigger, as well as thinner, because it is pulled 把(质软、有弹力之物)拉长、拉大,拉细:He *stretched* the elastic band *out* as far as it would go. 他把橡皮带尽量拉长。The elastic band had to be *stretched out* before it would go round the parcel. 橡皮带必须尽量拉长,才能捆住包裹。❷(cause to) hold (a part of your body, such as your hand or arm) out straight (使)伸出(手臂等):He *stretched out* his hand to try and reach the apple. 他伸出一只手设法够到那只苹果。*Stretching out*, the child seized the toy. 那孩子伸出手来,抓住了玩具。This picture shows the Mars Rover Spirit *stretching out* its robotic arm. 这幅图片展示"勇气"号火星车正在伸展机械臂工作。❸lie down, usually in order to relax or sleep 舒展肢体,伸直身子(休息或睡觉):He *stretched* himself *out* on the floor, and fell asleep. 他舒展四肢躺在地板上睡着了。Some people were *stretching out* in the sun outside the window. 一些人在窗外舒展着肢体躺着晒太阳。The cat *stretched out* in front of the fire. 猫在火炉前伸了伸懒腰。❹make (something) sufficient to cover one's needs 使(某物)满足……需要:Will the food *stretch out*? We've got two extra guests for dinner. 吃的东西够吗?我们又多了两位客人用餐。I don't see how I can *stretch out* the housekeeping to the end of the month. 我不知道怎样才能把家庭费用维持到月底。

NOTE 当本短语用作及物性动词短语,所带的宾语为代词时,该代词须置于本短语的动词和副词中间。

string up *vt.*【可分性动词短语】❶hang (something or things) up with or on string 挂起,吊起:They *strung up* coloured lights round the garden. 他们在花园周围挂起了彩灯。The farmer shot two crows and *strung* them *up* on the fence. 农夫打了两只乌鸦并把它们挂在了篱笆上。A notice was *strung up* above the door. 门上方挂着一纸通知。❷(非正式用语) kill (someone) by hanging him or her, as a punishment 绞死(某人),吊死(某人):They *strung up* the robber without a trial. 他们未经审判就绞死了那个强盗。Guards rushed into his cell and *strung* him *up*. 几名看守冲入他的囚室将他绞死。People like that should be *strung up* from a tree. 像那样的人都应该被挂在树上吊死。

NOTE 当本短语的宾语为代词时,该代词须置于本短语的动词和副词中间。

strip of *vt.*【可分性动词短语】❶remove (a layer) from something, especially so that it is completely exposed 从(某物上)剥去(外皮):Deer had *stripped* the tree

S

of its bark. 鹿已把这棵树的树皮啃光了。❷(常用被动语态形式) take away (something of value) from (someone or something); deprive (someone) of (something) 抢去; 盗走; 使失去: The robbers *stripped* him *of* all he possessed. 强盗们抢走了他所有的财物。The thieves *stripped* the house *of* all valuable articles. 盗贼偷走了屋内所有值钱的物品。This preserving process may *strip* food *of* its natural goodness. 这种保藏过程可能会使食物失去自然美味。And among a stream of failed drugs tests during the 2004 Olympic Games in Athens, three Olympic champions were *stripped of* their titles. 在 2004 年雅典奥运赛事中,出现了一批没能通过药检的运动员,其中有三位奥运冠军被剥夺了冠军头衔。

strip off *vt.* 【可分性动词短语】remove (a layer or cover) from (something) little by little 从(某物上)剥去(外皮或外层): The boy was *stripping* the bark *off* the tree. 那男孩在剥树皮。These fruit knives are very good for *stripping* apple skins *off*. 这些水果刀削苹果皮非常好使。Before decorating the room they *stripped off* the old paint from the wall. 他们在装修房间之前,先刮掉了墙壁上的旧漆层。

—*vt.* &*vi.* take off all your clothing; remove (some of your clothes)脱光衣服; 脱去(衣物)(非正式用语) The children *stripped off* and jumped into the pool. 孩子们脱光衣服,跳进了水塘。He *stripped off* his clothes and got into bed. 他脱去衣服上了床。

NOTE 当本短语作"从(某物上)剥去(外皮或外层)"解时,与 strip of 在用法上的区别可以表示为: strip A off B = strip B of A。

strive for *vt.* 【不可分性动词短语】(正式用语) make a lot of effort to achieve (something) 努力争取……: All the countries in the world should respect one another and *strive for* common development through seeking common ground while putting aside differences. 世界各国都应彼此尊重,在求同存异中共同发展。You must understand that and *strive for* balance in your life. 你必须懂得这个道理,并且努力保持生活的平衡。Both countries are *striving for* developing themselves on the most suitable roads. 两国都在致力于走最适合本国国情的发展道路。Some young people today tend to *strive for* what is not real. 现在有些年轻人往往追求一些不实际的东西。

struggle against *vt.* 【不可分性动词短语】oppose (usually something) with difficulty 与……作斗争,反对: We must *struggle against* all difficulties on it. 我们必须同与此有关的一切困难作斗争。The workers have long been *struggling against* bad working conditions. 工人们长期以来一直反对在恶劣的条件下工作。

struggle for *vt.* 【不可分性动词短语】❶try to obtain (something) from someone, with difficulty, as by fighting 从(某人手中)争夺(某物): They were *struggling for* the possession of the money. 他们都争着要得到那笔钱。Different factions in the organization are *struggling for* power. 该组织中的不同派系都在争夺权力。❷try to gain (something) with difficulty 为取得……而斗争: He is *struggling for* a say in decision-making.

S

他在争取决策过程中的表决权。The young writer had to *struggle for* recognition. 那位年轻的作家不得不为了获得认可而奋斗。

stumble across/on/upon *vt.*【不可分性动词短语】(用一般时态) meet (someone) or find (something) by accident 偶然遇到(某人);偶然发现(某物): We *stumbled across* him in the library. 我们在图书馆找到了他。While I was doing my research, I *stumbled on* some fascinating new data. 我在做研究时,偶尔发现了一些有趣的数据。Workmen *stumbled upon* the gold coins while digging foundations for a new building. 施工人员在挖新楼地基时意外地发现了这些金币。

subject to[1] *vt.*【可分性动词短语】❶(常用被动语态形式) make (someone or something) experience, suffer or be affected by (something, usually something unpleasant)遭受,使……受到: A patient will be *subjected to* a great pain when operated without anesthetic. 如果没有麻醉剂,病人接受手术时就会遭受极大痛苦。According to the new law the stocks and shares bought in marriage should be counted as joint property and *subjected to* property division in divorces. 根据这项新法律,婚后购买的股票、债券视为夫妻共同财产,离婚时要进行分割。❷(非正式用语,常用一般时态,与反身代词连用) allow (oneself) to receive and accept (something)使(自己)接受……: No one would willingly *subject* himself *to* such indignities. 没有人愿意使自己蒙受如此的侮辱。

subject to[2] *adj.* ❶likely to be affected by (something, especially something bad); having a tendency towards (something) 易遭受……的;倾向于……: He is too lazy to have physical exercises, so he is in rather poor health and is *subject to* colds. 他太懒,不进行体育锻炼,所以身体相当不好,并且容易感冒。Japan is a country *subject to* earthquakes. 日本是一个常遭地震之害的国家。All train times are *subject to* change in bad weather conditions. 所有列车的运行时间都会因恶劣的天气情况而改变。This motor is *subject to* mechanical wear. 这台马达容易产生机械磨损。❷in a situation where you have to obey a set of rules or laws; under the authority or control of (something or someone)服从于……的;受……控制的: All such gatherings are *subject to* the laws on political meetings. 所有这样的集会都得服从政治集会法的制约。All building firms are *subject to* tight controls. 所有的建筑公司都要受到严格控制。❸depending on (whether something happens)根据……的,取决于……的: You should put on or take off your clothes *subject to* the weather. 你应该根据天气增减衣服。*Subject to* your approval, we'll go ahead. 只要您同意,我们就会继续干下去。

submit to *vt.* ❶formally give (something written, etc.) to (someone or a group) so that they can make a decision about it 向……提出……;把……提交给……: Yesterday he officially *submitted to* the central government his request for resigning from the post as Chief Executive of the special administrative region. 他已于昨日正式向中央政府提出了辞去特区行政长官职务的请求。Have you *submitted* your application *to* the consulate? 你把你的申

S

请交给领事馆了吗？❷give in to or yield to (something), because you are not powerful enough to resist it 屈服于，屈从于：The Iranian President called on his people never to *submit to* foreign threats. 伊朗总统号召伊朗人民绝不要屈服于外来威胁。*To* such threats we have no intention of *submitting*. 我们无意屈从于这些威胁。❸(正式用语，常用一般时态，常与反身代词连用) agree to obey (a rule, a law, or the decision of someone in authority)服从(某项规章、裁决、法律或决定)：They are forced to *submit to* military discipline. 他们被迫服从军规。We will voluntarily *submit* ourselves *to* the court's judgment. 我们将服从法庭的裁决。We should conscientiously *submit to* and support the leadership of the chief executive. 我们都应该自觉服从和支持行政长官的领导。

subscribe to *vt.* ❶pay (money) to (a collection of a charity, or a share in a company)捐(善款)给……；参股于：We *subscribed to* a children and women protection society. 我们为一个妇女儿童保护协会捐了款。China has taken active steps to *subscribe to* shares of the West African Development Bank. 中国在采取积极的步骤参股西非开发银行。❷pay money so that you may regularly receive (copies of a newspaper, magazine, etc.) 订阅(报纸杂志等)：As students majoring in English you should *subscribe to* some newspaper in English. 作为英语专业的学生，你们应该订阅一些英文报纸。We *subscribe to* all the main medical magazines. 主要的医学杂志我们都订阅。❸(正式用语，常用一般时态，常用于疑问句和否定句中) agree with; approve of (an opinion, or an idea)同意，赞同(某种观点等)：More and more members are refusing to *subscribe to* the party leader's point of view. 越来越多的党员不再同意该党领袖的观点。Most people will not *subscribe to* dismissing the student who cursed his teacher in class. 大多数人都不会赞同开除那名在课堂上谩骂老师的学生。

substitute for *vt.* ❶use (something new or different) instead of (what is normally used)用(新的或不同的东西)取代(某种常用的物品)：Nowadays, different types of electronic bank cards are widely used to *substitute for* cash. 当今，不同种类的电子银行卡被广泛用来取代现金。We have now *substituted* transistors *for* electronic tubes in many devices. 现在，在许多仪器中，我们都已经用晶体管代替了电子管。In many places plastics are *substituted for* metals. 在许多地方，塑料都被用来取代金属了。You can *substitute* chicken *for* beef if you don't like red meat. 如果你不愿吃牛肉，你可以用鸡肉来取代它。❷do (someone else's job) for a short period of time (短期)替换，替换(某人)：He *substituted for* the worker who was sick. 他替换了那名患病的工人。Mark will *substitute for* me tomorrow. 马克会在明天替换我。Another actor has been *substituted for* the famous actor. 那位名演员被另一演员代替了。

S

succeed in *vt.*【不可分性动词短语】be successful at (something or doing something) 在……获得成功：There is every chance that he will *succeed in* his career. 他极有可能在事业上取得成功。At last the performer *succeeded in* working his hands free from the ropes. 表演者终于成功地把双手慢慢从绳索中挣脱了出

来。We have to work hard until we *succeed in it*. 我们必须努力,直到取得成功。

such as *conj*. (used for introducing more examples of the type of person or thing that you have just mentioned) of a kind that; for example 诸如,例如:A plan *such as* you proposed will never succeed. 像你提出的这种计划永远不会成功。There are few poets *such as* Keats and Shelley. 像济慈和雪莱那样的诗人现在很少。China's import of American agricultural produce *such as* soybean, wheat and cotton in large quantities provides a huge market for American farmers. 中国从美国进口大量的诸如大豆、小麦和棉花等农产品,为美国农业提供了广阔的市场。The spacewalking astronaut performed tasks *such as* installing equipment and "tightening screws". 进行太空行走的宇航员执行了诸如安装设备和"拧紧螺丝"等任务。"There are a lot of things we can do." "*Such as*?" "我们有很多事情可以做。""比如说?"

NOTE **1.** 本短语在句中用于引出同位语,对前面的事物作举例说明,后多接名词,且常列出两个或两个以上的例子。有时也只接一个名词或代词。例如:

> Large and important projects *such as* this one often take years to finish.
> 像这样大而重要的工程往往需要数年才能完成。
> A career *such as* that is not one that should be thrown up without serious thought.
> 像这样一种职业不应该未经认真考虑就放弃。

2. 不能把所要列举的事物全部罗列于本短语后。例如,不能说: * He can speak four foreign languages, *such as* English, French, Esperanto and Japanese. 正确的表达方式是:

(1)删除 *such as* 之后所列举事物中的1～2个部分。例如:He can speak four foreign languages, *such as* English and French.

(2)用 namely 取代 *such as*。例如:He can speak four foreign languages, namely, English, French, Esperanto and Japanese.

(3)用冒号取代 *such as*。例如:He can speak four foreign languages: English, French, Esperanto and Japanese.

3. 本短语之后无需再加 and so on 或 etc.。例如,不能说: * The Arts Faculty deals only with humanities subjects *such as* history and literature, and so on.

4. 本短语可分开来使用,即 such … as,中间加名词。例如:

> All airlines ban *such* electronic devices *as* portable computers and mobile telephones from being used during takeoff and landing.
> 所有的航空公司都禁止在飞机起飞和降落时使用诸如手提电脑和手机等电子器件。

5. 本短语后不接从句。如后面出现从句,则表示其他的意思。例如:

> *Such* experience *as* I have is useless in this situation.
> 像我所有的这样的经验在这种情况下是没用的。

在本句中, as 是从属连词,而不是介词了。

6. 本短语与 for example 均表示"例如",它们之间的区别是: *such as* 不能作为独立语插入句中,必须与所说明的名词一起使用,而且不能置于句首;而 *for example* 则能单独使用,可修饰整个句子,可以置于句首。

S

suffer from *vt.* 【不可分性动词短语】❶have (a particular illness or physical problem)身患(某种疾病): In spite of negative HIV test results, the patient still insisted that he *suffered from* AIDS. 尽管他的 HIV 检验结果为阴性,可这位患者却依然坚持说他患了艾滋病。"These young students were *suffering from* the'Internet syndrome'—a condition that is endangering the mental health of Internet addicted youngsters," said the medical expert. 这位医学专家指出:"这些年轻的学生患的是'因特网综合征',这种情况危害上网成瘾的年轻人的精神健康。" ❷(一般不用被动语态形式,常用一般时态) experience (something very unpleasant or painful); be afflicted by; be badly affected by (a very difficult or unpleasant situation)遭受,受到: When Saddam was in power, the Iraqi people had *suffered from* several wars and sanctions for many years, the spokesman said. 这位发言人说,萨达姆当政期间,伊拉克人民蒙受数次战争灾难和多年制裁之苦。The Great Wall in China, which receives four million visitors a year, has *suffered* greatly *from* graffiti. 每年接待 400 万游客的中国长城饱受涂鸦之苦。

NOTE 本短语尤指"长期饱受……之苦",其后的宾语多为疾病或长存的痛苦。若指一时的打击或短期的病痛或损害,suffer 之后则不用 from,而直接加宾语。例如:

> CitigroupInc, the largest US bank, said Tuesday it *suffered* losses of nearly 10 billion
> US dollars in the last three months.
> 美国最大银行花旗集团星期二公布,该行在第四季度蒙受巨亏近 10 亿美元。

suit to *vt.* ❶(正式用语,常用被动语态形式) make (something) fit or suitable for (something)使适应: You have to *suit* your spending *to* your income. 你得量入敷出。A gradually improved democratic system *suited to* Hong Kong's reality is an important guarantee for its social and political stability. 逐步完善适合香港实际情况的民主制度,是香港社会政治稳定的重要保障。❷(用被动语态形式) have the right qualities to become (something such as a position)适合于(某种职业): Do you think Smith is *suited to* teaching? 你认为史密斯适合于教学吗?

sum up *v.* ❶ put (something) into a few words; shorten (something) into a brief summery; give the main ideas of (something written or spoken)概括,归纳: The last paragraph should *sum up* the main points of your argument. 最后一段应该概括你的主要论点。I would like to *sum* this lecture *up* by listing the main points. 我把几个要点列出来,作为对这次讲座的总结。*Summing up*, the expert said, "It seems unreasonable to worry about the harmful effects of drinking extra water." 这位专家总结说:"担心多喝水会对身体健康造成损害,似乎是毫无道理的。" To *sum up*, we've got to pay more attention to profitability and cost control. 总而言之,我们必须更加注意赢利能力和成本控制。❷consider and form a judgment or opinion of (someone or a situation) quickly (对某人或某一形势)做出迅速判断: I can't *sum* him *up*, no one knows what he's thinking. 我捉摸不透他,因为没有人了解他的思想。She *summed up* the situation at a glance. 她很快就对形势做出了判断。

NOTE 1. 当本短语用作及物性动词短语，所带的宾语为代词时，该代词须置于本短语的动词和副词中间。

2. 当本短语作"(对某人或某一形势)做出迅速判断"解时，同义短语是 size up。

3. 本短语可转化为复合词 sum-up，意为"总结"。还可转化为另一复合名词 summing-up，意义同 sum-up。

Sunday best *n.* (非正式用语)a person's best and often most formal clothing (在星期日或其他特殊场合穿的)最好的衣服；节日盛装：Everybody says I've got to put on my *Sunday best* if I want to impress that girl. 大家都说，要是我想给那个女孩留下好印象的话，我一定得穿最好的衣服。On the day of welcoming the Olympic torch, we were all wearing in our *Sunday best*. 在迎接奥运火炬的那一天，我们都身着节日盛装。

NOTE 1. 在美国和其他西方国家，根据基督教的传统，人们在星期日去教堂做礼拜的时候，总是穿得非常正式、得体。所以 Sunday best 过去也称为"礼拜服"。本短语亦作 Sunday clothes 和 Sunday-go-to-meeting clothes。

2. 本短语为不可数性名词短语，当被复数性代词修饰时，其形式不变化(见第二个例句)。

S

Sunday school *n.* (常用单数形式) a school organized by a church where Christian children receive religious teaching on Sundays (基督教儿童的)主日学校：A new-style *Sunday school* arose in the town, taught by volunteer teachers and providing a specifically Protestant curriculum. 镇子里出现一所新型的主日学校，讲课的老师都是志愿者，专门讲授新教课程。These are some of the American *Sunday school* books published between 1815 and 1865. 这些是1815至1865年间出版的一些美国主日学校的课本。*Sunday schools* are focused on providing childhood education, but adult Sunday school classes are also widespread in the United States. 主日学校主要提供儿童教育，但在美国，为成人办的主日学校班也很普遍。

superior to *adj.* ❶(of one person) having a higher status or position than (another person)(指人)(地位、职位)高于……：Is a colonel *superior to* a brigadier? 上校比旅长的官衔高吗？Don't think that you are *superior to* others. You are nobody here. 不要认为你高人一等，你在这里无足轻重。❷(of one thing) better than (another thing) in quality, value, etc. (指物)(质量、价值等)优于……：The sound quality is *superior to* that on a regular CD. 这音质比普通光盘的音质好。Of the two dictionaries, I think this one is far *superior to* that one. 我认为这部词典比那部词典好得多。For all babies, breastfeeding is far *superior to* bottle feeding. 对于所有的婴儿来说，母乳喂养要比人工喂养好得多。Synthetic rubbers are in many respects *superior to* natural rubber. 合成橡胶在许多方面优于天然橡胶。

NOTE 1. 不要将本短语误用为 superior than。不能说：* His poetry is *superior than* his brother's.

2. 本短语的反义短语是 inferior to

supply to *vt.* 【可分性动词短语】provide (something) for (someone or something) 为……提供(某物)：Our industry *supplies* a lot of farming machines *to* the farmers. 我们的工业为农民提供大批农业机械。When is power going to be *supplied to* the distant farm? 什么时候

向那家偏远的农场供电? Two huge generators will *supply* power *to* farms in the area. 两台大型发电机将为该地区的农场供电。

supply with *vt.* 【可分性动词短语】provide (someone or something) with (something that they want or need) 向……提供(所需之物): Furthermore, Chinese enterprises *supply* US consumers *with* large quantities of inexpensive and quality consumer goods. 中国企业还给美国消费者提供了大量价廉物美的消费品。He also revealed that they had *supplied* terrorist organizations *with* weapons. 他还揭露说,他们曾为恐怖组织提供过武器。Our friends kept us *supplied with* help. 我们的朋友一直向我们提供帮助。

sure enough *adv.* (常用于连词 and 之后) exactly as was expected 果然,果真: Tom was afraid he had done badly on the test, and *sure enough*, his grade was failing. 汤姆生怕考得不好,果然他的分数不及格。They all said the wall would fall down and *sure enough* it did. 他们都说那堵墙要倒,它果真倒了。

surrender to *vt.* ❶(常用一般时态) place (one's soldiers, oneself, etc.) in the hand of the enemy or someone in authority 向……投降;向……自首: Through the interpreter, the officer tried to persuade us to *surrender to* them. 那位军官通过翻译千方百计地劝我们向他们投降。No country would *surrender to* terrorism in any form. 任何国家都不会向任何形式的恐怖主义投降。❷give control over (a place or person) to (someone who has defeated you) 把(某地或某人)拱手交给……: At last the citizens were forced to *surrender* the town *to* the enemy. 市民们终于被迫献城投降了。They offered to *surrender* the general *to* US troops. 他们愿意将其将军交给美国军队。❸give (something) to (someone in authority) because you have to 把……上交给: The regions refused to *surrender* their powers *to* central government. 这些地区拒绝把权力上交给中央政府。

suspect of *vt.* 【可分性动词短语】(常用一般时态) believe that (someone) may be guilty of (something such as a crime, or doing something bad) 怀疑某人犯有(某种罪行或过错): Which of these people do you *suspect of* the murder? 在这些人当中你怀疑哪个是凶犯? The police *suspect* her *of* murder. 警方怀疑她是凶手。

suspicious of/about *adj.* not trusting (someone or something) 不相信……的,怀疑……的: People are often *suspicious of* strangers. 人们往往都不相信陌生人。I'm *suspicious of* all that they tried to sell me on the cheap. 我对他们极力向我廉价兜售的所有东西表示怀疑。I'm a bit *suspicious about* that package that has been left in the corridor. 我对那个一直放在走廊里的包裹有点怀疑。She's getting *suspicious about* my staying away for so long. 她对我离开这么久开始产生怀疑。

swallow up *vt.* 【可分性动词短语】(常用被动语态形式) ❶eat or gobble up (someone or something) 吞食掉: The wolf *swallowed up* the meat in one bite. 那只狼一口就把肉块吞了进去。The fishermen were *swallowed up* by the whale. 几名渔民被鲸鱼吞食。Then a great fish *swallowed* him *up*. But the fish was soon caught up and brought to the court of King Arthur. 紧接着,一条大鱼把他吞进肚子。恰好那条鱼很快被捕捞上来,并送进亚瑟王的宫廷。❷(常用一般时态) destroy (something) completely and make it disappear; cause (something or someone) to disappear, as if taking (something or someone) in like food 吞没……;使……消失:The waves *swallowed up* the small boat. 波浪吞没了这条小船。The whole building was *swallowed up* by flames. 整个建筑物都被大火所吞没。Tuvalu, a tiny country in the Pacific Ocean, has asked for help as it fears it will be *swallowed up* by the sea. 太平洋上的小国图瓦卢由于担心将被海洋吞噬,发出了求助讯号。She was so embarrassed, she wished the earth would open and *swallow* her *up*. 她困窘得都想有个地缝钻进去。❸ make (something such as a company or country) a part of (a larger or stronger one) 吞并,并吞:Many small businesses have been *swallowed up* by large companies. 许多小企业都已被大公司吞并。❹ exhaust; use up completely 耗尽,用完:The medical costs *swallowed up* all his savings. 医药费耗尽了他的全部积蓄。His reserves of men were soon *swallowed up* in the spring offensive. 他的后备军很快就在春季攻势中消耗殆尽。

S

NOTE 当本短语的宾语为代词时,该代词须置于本短语的动词和副词中间。

swear at *vt.* 【不可分性动词短语】speak curses to (someone); curse (something or doing something) 骂(人),咒骂:She was shouting and *swearing at* everyone. 她在大声叫骂所有的人。He resented being *sworn at*, even if he had made a mistake. 他即使犯了错误也讨厌被别人骂。Why did you *swear at* missing the bus? There'll be another soon. 你干吗诅咒没赶上公共汽车呢? 下一辆马上就来了。She *swore at* the dog when she tripped over it. 她被狗绊了一下,便咒骂起狗来。

swear by *vt.* 【不可分性动词短语】❶(非正式用语) call (someone or something holy) as witness to the truth of what one says or the trustworthiness of one's promise; take an oath upon 对……发誓;凭……发誓:I *swear by* Almighty God that I was elsewhere at the time. 我对着万能的上帝发誓,我当时不在场。A witness *swears by* the Bible that he will tell the truth. 一名证人凭《圣经》发誓说,他一定讲实话。❷ trust in (someone or something) 信任:I would *swear by* Helen any time. She tells the truth. 我任何时候都会信任海伦,她讲实话。For little unbiased reporting, I *swear by The Daily News*. 因少有倾向性的报道,我信任《每日新闻报》。❸(非正式用语,用一般时态,不用进行时态) believe completely in the usefulness or value of (something, especially a certain remedy, etc.)完全相信(尤指某种疗法、药品等):He *swears by* vitamin C pills, and says he hasn't had a cold since he started taking them. 他非常相信维C药片,并说他自从开始服用这种药以来就没患过感冒。He *swears by* his dentist. 他非常信赖他的牙医。She *swears by* hand washing and won't have a machine. 她相信手洗而不肯买洗衣机。

swear in *vt.* 【可分性动词短语】(正式用语) ❶(常用被动语态形式) introduce (a person) into a post or office formally, by making him solemnly promise to fulfill the duties of a new job 使(某人)宣誓就

职：A ceremony to *swear in* the new governor took place yesterday. 新任州长的宣誓就职仪式于昨日举行。Barack Obama, 47, was *sworn in* as the 44th president of the United States on Tuesday, becoming the first African-American president in the country's 233-year history. 47 岁的巴拉克·奥巴马于星期二宣誓就任美国第 44 任总统，成了美国 233 年历史上首位非洲裔总统。The general *swore* himself *in* as new president within an hour of being pronounced victor in the election. 这位将军在宣布选举获胜后不到一小时便宣誓就职为新总统。❷cause (a witness) to take the oath in a court of law 使（证人）在法庭上宣誓：The witness took the stand after the court clerk *swore* her *in*. 法庭书记员令其宣誓后，证人便进入证人席作证。Arrive at the Court House at least an hour before your case is heard, and when your case is called, you, the defendant, and any witnesses must be *sworn in*. 你必须于案件开审前至少 1 小时抵达法庭。当你的案子开审时，你、被告还有所有证人都必须要当庭宣誓。

NOTE 1. 当本短语的宾语为代词时，该代词须置于本短语的动词和副词中间。

2. 本短语可转化为复合词 swearing-in，意为"宣誓就职(仪式)"。

swear oath ⇨ **take oath**

sweep through *vt.* 【不可分性动词短语】❶（无被动语态形式）(of something such as a disease) move or spread quickly among (large numbers of people) or through (an area)（疾病等）在（人群中）迅速流行；在（某一区域）迅速蔓延：This type of influenza can *sweep through* the province in a very short period of time. 这类流感可以在很短的时间内在全省迅速流行。A plague epidemic *swept through* Europe from 1348 through 1351, killing an estimated 25%～60% of Europeans. 从 1348 至 1351 年间，一场瘟疫在欧洲各地迅速流行，据估计有 25%～60%的欧洲人口死亡。❷（主要用于美国英语中，一般不用被动语态形式，常用一般时态）pass (something such as an examination or test) easily 轻易地通过（考试等）：She *swept through* her exams. 她很轻松地通过了各科考试。To my surprise, my son *swept through* his driving test. 令我吃惊的是，我儿子竟轻易地通过了驾驶考试。

switch off *v.* ❶stop (something such as a light or other electrical device) working by turning a *switch off*; (of something such as a light or other electrical device) stop working 关上（……的）开关；切断（……的）电源：*Switch off* when you've finished using the computer. 计算机用完后，要关掉电源。Please *switch off* all the lights when you leave the room to save electricity. 为节约用电，请在离开房间时把灯都关掉。If you *switch off* the electric current, the machine will immediately stop running. 你如果切断电流，机器就会立即停止运转。❷（非正式用语）stop (someone) talking 阻止（某人的）讲话：Once he starts telling you that, it's impossible to *switch* him *off*. 一旦他开始给你讲起那件事，就不可能使他关上话匣子。❸（非正式用语）stop (someone) being interested in (someone or something)（使）（某人）对……不感兴趣：The lecture was so boring I just *switched off* half-way through. 那讲座太枯燥无味，刚听一半我就失去了兴趣。Dull subjects like this are enough to *switch* students *off*. 似这样无聊

S

的主题足以使学生大失兴趣。

NOTE 当本短语用作及物性动词短语,所带的宾语为代词时,该代词须置于本短语的动词和副词中间。

switch on *v.* ❶make (something such as a light or other electrical device) start working by turning a switch on; (of something such as a light or other electrical device) start working 打开(……的)开关,接通(……的)电源: He entered the room, sat before his desk and *switched* the reading lamp *on.* 他进了屋,就坐在书桌前,打开了台灯。She *switched on* the fan to blow away the smoke in the room. 她打开电扇以吹走屋里的烟。The motor will start operating as soon as we *switched* it *on.* 我们一合电闸,电动机就开始运转。The instrument can *switch on* by itself. 本装置可以自动接通电源。❷(非正式用语) (cause to) become interested or excited (使)感兴趣;(使)兴奋: The result of the test didn't *switch* me *on.* 检测的结果并没使我感到兴奋。

NOTE 当本短语用作及物性动词短语,所带的宾语为代词时,该代词须置于本短语的动词和副词中间。

switch over *vt.* & *vi.* ❶(常与 to 连用) (cause to) make a complete change (to something else) (使)彻底转变: He *switched over* from supporting the Conservative Party to supporting the Labour Party. 他从支持保守党彻底转变到支持工党。They have decided to *switch* the factory *over* to bicycle production. 他们决定工厂转产自行车。❷(非正式用语) (cause to) exchange places (使)调换位置: Can we *switch over*? I'd like to sit in the front. 咱们能换一下位置吗? 我想坐在前面。If you *switch* the words *over*, the sentence would sound better. 如果你把这些词调换一下位置,这个句子就会更好些。

—*vi.* (英国英语用法,常与 to 连用) change stations on a radio or change to another channel when watching television 变换(收音机的)电台,变换(电视的)频道: I'm tired of this program, let's *switch over* to Channel 5. 我看腻了这个节目,咱们换到 5 频道吧。

switch to *vt.* ❶change or move by a switch (用开关)转换: *Switch* the freezer *to* the extra cold setting. 把冰柜的冷冻室调到超冷档。It was hot so I *switched* the thermostat from heating *to* cooling. 天太热,所以我把恒温器从制热调到制冷。❷(非正式用语) (cause to) change (from someone or something) to (someone of something else) (使)转(换)到……: In recent years, grain production area has been cut considerably, as farmers have *switched to* more profitable crops, such as fruit and vegetables. 近年来的粮食种植面积锐减,因为农民把土地转产一些更赚钱的作物,如水果和蔬菜。He got tired of teaching and *switched to* writing stories. 他教书教厌了,于是改行写小说了。

S

T t

tailor to *vt.*【可分性动词短语】(常用被动语态形式) form (something such as a plan or system) so as to be suitable for (a particular purpose) by changing the details of it 为(某一特定目的)制定(计划或体制等): We can *tailor* the insurance policy *to* your special needs. 我们可以按你们的特殊需要设计保险单。The school system should be *tailored to* the needs of the children. 学校的体制应根据学生的需要制定。

take a break ⇨ **have a break**

take a chance *v.* try to do something even though it involves risk of danger or failure 冒险做事;碰运气: We'll *take a chance* on the weather and have the party outdoors. 我们将冒着会变天的危险在户外举行这次聚会。They suggested that he *take a chance* on getting there through dark side streets. 他们建议他冒险走黑暗的小路到那里。

NOTE 1. 本短语可根据表达需要变为复数形式使用,即 take chances。

2. 本短语的同义短语是 take a risk。

take a dive *vi.* ❶ fall (in the value of something) (某物的价值)下降: The share price *took a* 30% *dive* last year. 去年,股票的价格下跌了30%。❷(非正式用语) pretend a defeat; pretend to be knocked out (especially of a boxer in a boxing match)(尤指在拳击比赛中)故意输;假装被击倒: I had to *take a dive* when wrestling with my brother. 我和弟弟摔跤时,我不得不假装被摔倒。

NOTE 当本短语作"(某物的价值)下降"解时,其中的不定冠词 a 常可被其他形容词替代。

take a glance at ⇨ **cast a glance at**

take a hand at *vt.* ❶ join a group in (a card game) 参加(纸牌游戏): Please *take a hand at* cards, we're one player short. 请来参加玩牌吧,我们正缺一个人。I *took a hand at* bridge. 我参加了打桥牌的游戏。❷ participate in; have a share in 参加,介入: He has *taken a hand at* the affair. 他已参与了这件事。If we all *take a hand at* digging the garden, it'll soon be done. 如果我们都伸一把手来为花园翻土,活儿很快就会干完。

take a hand in *vt.* ❶(常用一般时态) participate in; be involved in; help with 参加;帮助: I'd like to *take a hand in* planning the party. 我想参与聚会的筹划工作。Louis refused to *take a hand in* the preparations for the evening meal. 路易斯不肯帮助准备晚餐。❷ be partly the cause of or have an effect on (something) 是……的部分原因,对……有影响: The weather *takes a hand in* most of our plans. 天气因素对我们大多数计划都有影响。

take a note *vi.* write something down or

remember it carefully 写下,记下:I'll just *take a note* of your name and address. 我只是把你的姓名和地址写下来。I decide to *take a note* to remember what I did. 我决定把我所做的事情都记下来。

NOTE 1. 不要将本短语与 take note 和 take note of 混淆,三者意义和用法不同。

2. 本短语的同义短语是 take notes 和 make a note。

take a risk *vi.* (常与 of 连用) do something although you know that something unpleasant or dangerous could happen 做危险之事,冒险:You are *taking a* big *risk* showing this to Smith. 你把这给史密斯看,是在做很危险的事。I would rather *take a risk* of losing the opportunity than pay a bribe. 我宁愿冒着失去这次机会的危险也不愿去行贿。You have to *take* a lot of *risks* if you want to succeed in business. 如果你想在生意上取得成功,你就得冒许多风险。

NOTE 1. 本短语是动宾结构,其动词和名词可分开使用。例如:

> This is *a risk* you have to *take*.
> 这是你不得不冒之险。

2. 本短语可根据表达需要变为复数形式使用(如最后一个例句)。

3. 本短语的同义短语是 take a chance。

take a seat *vi.* (正式用语) sit down; become seated 坐下:Hi, come on in, *take a seat*. 你好,里面请。请坐。I *took a seat* at the bar. 我在酒吧里坐了下来。She entered the bus and *took a* front *seat*. 她上了公共汽车,坐在了前排座位上。

NOTE 本短语与 take one's seat 都表示"坐下"之意,但它们的意义并不完全相同,故不能混用。本短语指的是"在任何一个地方,在随便一个座位上坐下",而 take one's seat 则指"在影剧院、会场等中已事先定好或预留的座位上就座"。

take a stand *vi.* state one's opinion clearly or adopt a firm position about an issue (对某一问题)明确表明某人的观点;坚定采取某一立场:The president has not *taken a stand* on this issue. 总统尚未对此问题表明态度。I *take a stand* upon sound precedents. 我按照稳妥的惯例表明我的观点。

NOTE 1. 不要将本短语与 take the stand 混淆。

2. 本短语与 take one's stand 意义和用法相同,两者可互换使用。

take (a) toll *vi.* (常与 of 或 on 连用) cause harm, damage or deaths (to someone or something), especially in a gradual or lasting way (尤指逐渐或长期)(给……)造成损害,损伤(或死亡):The conflict of the last decade has already *taken a* heavy *toll*. 过去十年的冲突已造成了重大损失。Years of hardship and neglect of care had *taken* their *toll* on his health. 多年来的劳累和疏于保健损害了他的健康。The war in Iraq *took a* heavy *toll* of the US armed forces. 这场伊拉克战争使美军伤亡惨重。

NOTE 1. 本短语中的名词 toll,无论其前的物主代词是单数还是复数形式,都必须用单数形式。

2. 本短语中的不定冠词 a 可以根据表达需要替换成 its, their 等。

take aback *vt.*【可分性动词短语】(常用被动语态形式,用一般时态)(especially of something that someone says or does) greatly surprise or shock (someone)(尤指某人所说或做的事情)使(某人)大吃一惊:What the girl had said *took* us all *aback*. 那女孩的话使我们都大吃一惊。We were *taken aback* by the girl's directness. 这女孩说话口无遮拦使我们颇为吃惊。She was *taken aback* when a man answered the phone. 是一个男人接的电话,这使她大吃一惊。

NOTE 1. 当本短语的宾语为代词时,该代词须置于本短语的动词和副词中间。

2. 不要将本短语与 take back 混淆。

take account of *vt.* 【不可分性动词短语】consider (something) when you are trying to make a decision 考虑: Did you *take account of* the number of guests when you were planning the seating for the party? 你在计划聚会的座位时有没有考虑到宾客的人数? *Account* must be *taken of* the worse conditions of air temperature and humidity. 空气温度和湿度方面更恶劣的情况必须予以考虑。He *takes* no *account of* my warning not to do that. 他对我向他提出不要做那件事的警告毫不理会。

NOTE 本短语的同义短语是 allow for, take into account 和 take into consideration。

take action *vi.* begin to do something to solve a particular problem 采取措施,采取行动: Travelers want the airlines to *take action* to make flying safer and more comfortable. 旅客都希望航空公司采取措施,使飞行更加安全、舒适。ASEAN leaders agreed to *take* decisive *actions* to restore market confidence and ensure continued financial stability. 东南亚国家联盟领导人一致同意采取积极果断的措施,重建市场信心,确保金融市场持续稳定。The *actions* we have *taken* will make the world more secure and the world more peaceful in the long run. 我们所采取的行动最终会使这个世界更安全、更安宁。The government says legal action would be *taken against* persons who abandon their parents at their old age. 政府表示,对遗弃老人者将采取法律行动。

take advantage of *vt.* 【不可分性动词短语】❶use (a situation or opportunity) to get what you want 利用(某一条件或机会): We should learn from those advanced countries while *taking advantage of* the economic globalization. 我们应该在利用经济全球化机遇的同时,向那些发达国家学习。He always *takes advantage of* the mistakes made by his rivals. 他总是利用他的对手所犯的错误。China will *take* full *advantage of* the good opportunity of world peace to develop itself and safeguard world peace. 中国将充分利用世界和平的大好时机,努力发展自己,维护世界和平。❷unfairlyget what you want from (someone who is easily persuaded to help you, trust you, or do things for you) (为取得自己的利益而不公平地)利用(某人);占(某人)的便宜: The young man *took advantage of* the old lady's kindness and cheated her out of her money. 那年轻人利用了老妇人的善良,骗走了她的钱。The little children did not know how much to pay for the candy, and the store owner *took advantage of* them. 这些小孩儿不知道买那糖果该付多少钱,于是店主便占了他们的便宜。

NOTE 当本短语作"利用(某一条件或机会)"解时,同义短语是 capitalize on/upon。

take after *vt.* 【不可分性动词短语】❶(无被动语态形式,用一般时态,不用进行时态) resemble (a parent or close relative) in appearance, behavior or character (在外貌、行为或性格上)与(父、母或近亲者)相像: My daughter really *takes after* her mother both in appearance and character. 我的女儿在长相和性格上确

T

实都像她妈妈。Your son does not *take after* you in any way. 你的儿子没有一个地方像你。In sports she *takes after* her father rather than her mother. 在体育运动方面，她很像她的父亲，而不大像她的母亲。❷(美国英语用法，非正式用语) follow (someone) quickly 迅速追赶(某人)：The policemen *took after* the burglars. 警察迅速追赶那几名窃贼。I was afraid that if I started running the man would *take after* me. 我担心，如果我跑的话，那名男子就会追我。

NOTE 本短语与 look like 都表示"与……相像"之意。look like 只是指在外表上看上去像，而 take after 则指不仅在外表上相像，而且在行为或性格等方面也相像。

take aim *vi.* ❶(常与 at 连用) point a gun at something before you shoot, or look at something and decide how to throw or kick in order to hit it 瞄准，看准：I *took* careful *aim* at his head and fired. 我仔细地瞄准他的头部开了火。Before the hunter could *take aim*, the deer jumped out of sight. 猎人还没来得及瞄准，那只鹿就逃得无影无踪。The crash of an army helicopter on Friday reflects a growing threat by insurgents *taking aim* at American aircraft. 一架军用直升机星期五坠毁，这说明武装分子把美国的飞机作为目标的威胁在增大。❷(美国英语用法，与 at 连用) criticize (someone or something) strongly 强烈抨击：In his last speech the President *took aim* at the opposition leader. 总统在他最后一次的讲话中强烈地抨击了反对党领导人。The weekly *took aim* at corrupt officials. 那家周刊把矛头指向了贪官污吏。

take along *vt.* 【可分性动词短语】take (someone or something) with one 携带，带上：May I *take* my girl friend *along* to the party? 我可以带我的女朋友去参加聚会吗？Five hundred years ago Zheng He of the Ming Dynasty led seven maritime expeditions to seek friendly ties with other countries, *taking along* China's fine products, advanced farming and handicraft skills. 五百年前，明朝的郑和带着精美的产品和先进的农业、手工业技术七下西洋，为的是同友邦结好。On long journeys I always *take* my dog *along*. 出远门时我总是带上我的爱犬。

take apart *vt.* 【可分性动词短语】❶separate (something such as a small machine, or clock) into pieces from which it is made 拆开，拆卸：It's easy to *take* a machine *apart* but difficult to put it together. 拆机器容易，但再装起来就难了。My watch stopped, so I *took* it *apart* to see what's wrong with it. 我的表停了，所以我把它拆开，看看它出了什么毛病。The molding box can be *taken apart* to make it easier to remove the pattern. 铸模箱可以拆开，以便更容易地取出模型。❷(非正式用语) criticize (a person or an idea) very severely 严厉批评：If you hand in your work like that, the teacher will *take* you *apart*. 如果你把那样的作业交上去，老师一定会狠狠地批评你的。His first book won praise from the readers, his second was *taken apart*. 他的第一本书赢得了读者的赞扬，但第二本却受到了严厉的批评。❸(非正式用语) beat (someone) very easily in a game or sport 轻易击败(对手)：England were really *taken apart* by Italy's AC Milan in last night's match. 在昨晚的比赛中，英格兰队惨败给意大利 AC 米兰队。He *took* their defence *apart*, scoring three goals in the first twenty minutes. 他轻而易举地打破了他们的防守,在头 20 分钟就进了三个球。

NOTE **1.** 当本短语的宾语为代词时,该代词须置于本短语的动词和副词中间。

2. 本短语与 take down 都表示"拆开,拆卸"之意。本短语指拆开或拆卸小的机械物件(如手表等),而 take down 则指拆开或拆卸大件机器。

take as *vt.* 【可分性动词短语】(常用一般时态) understand or suppose (something) to be (something)把……当作……,把……视为……: In China, more and more people *take* short messages *as* a means of greeting and communication. 在中国,越来越多的人把短信作为致贺和交流的方式。"'*Taking* history *as* a mirror and looking to the future' is the only right attitude to historical issues," he said in Japan. 他在日本表示,"'以史为鉴、面向未来'是对待历史问题的唯一正确态度。" She *took* what he said *as* a compliment. 她把他说的话看作是恭维话。These first two books can be *taken as* a pattern of the whole work. 这前两本书可被视为整个工作的模式。

take away *vt.* 【可分性动词短语】 ❶remove (something) (from especially someone) 将(某物)拿走,拿掉,除去: *Take* your money *away* from me. What do you take me for? 你把钱拿走。你把我当成什么人了? They have a very good reason to *take* them *away*, don't they? 他们有充分的理由把它们拿走,不是吗? We improved the house by *taking* the front porch *away*. 我们拆掉了前门廊以改善房子结构。There are also small amounts of other substances in the iron ore to be *taken away*. 还必须除去铁矿石中的少量其他物质。❷bring (someone) from his or her home (to a place such as a prison or hospital)把(某人从家里)带走(到监狱或医院等地方): Two men claiming to be police officials called at Bob's house and *took* him *away*. 两个自称是警察的男子来到鲍勃的家将其带走。The arrested man was *taken away* in a police car. 被捕的那个男子被押上警车带走了。❸cause (something such as a feeling or sensation) to cease or disappear 使(某种感情或感觉)消失,解除: Put this solution on the burn, and it will *take* the pain *away* at once. 把这药水涂在烧伤处,就可立即止痛。The good news *took away* all his worry and anxiety. 好消息消除了他的一切烦恼和焦虑。❹(用一般时态,常与 from 连用) (in mathematics) remove (one number or amount) (from another) 减去(某一数目): Ten *take away* four leaves six. 10 减去 4 等于 6。*Take away* this number from that, and tell me how much you have left. 把这个数从那个数中减去,告诉我还剩多少。❺(英国英语用法,常用一般时态) buy (cooked food at a restaurant) and carry it away to eat, for example at home (把餐馆里的熟食)买回食用: I'd like three pieces of chicken to *take away*, please. 请给我买三块鸡肉,我要带走。We'll *take away* some pizza, since I am too tired to cook. 咱们买回些比萨饼吧,我累得不能做饭了。

NOTE **1.** 当本短语的宾语为代词时,该代词须置于本短语的动词和副词中间。

2. 本短语可转化为复合词 takeaway,意为"(供带出外吃的)外卖食品,外卖店"。

3. takeaway 是英国英语用词。

take away from *vt.* (用一般时态)

T

❹remove (a smaller number) from (a larger number); reduce (something) 减去(某一数目),减少(某物):What do you get if you *take* 5 *away from* 15? 15 减去 5 得多少? The company will cut jobs because it will not allow anything to *take away from* profits. 公司要裁员了,因为它决不允许任何因素减少利润。❷(无被动语态形式) lessen the effect or value of (something good or desirable)减少(有益或令人满意的事物)的作用,降低价值:The fact that you had help doesn't *take away from* your success. 你有他人的帮助这一事实并无损于你的成功。The gas-saving device does not *take away from* the engine's power. 节油装置不损耗发动机的动力。

take back *vt.* 【可分性动词短语】❶return or cause to return (something) to a place or owner 归还;索回:You should *take* those books *back* to the library. 你应当把那些书还给图书馆了。The general swore to *take back* the fort whatever the cost. 那位将军发誓不惜任何代价要夺回要塞。❷lead or carry (someone) on a return journey 带回,载回:Do you mind *taking* my son *back* in your car? 你能用车把我儿子带回去吗? This bus will *take* you *back* to the city. 这辆公共汽车会把你拉回市里去。❸take (something that you have bought) back to the shops because it is broken or not suitable 退回(所买货品):This shop promises to *take back* any goods that don't satisfy the person who buys them. 该店保证,买主不满意的货物都可以退货。The shop promised to *take* it *back* if it doesn't fit. 如果它不合适,商店承诺给予退货。❹(非正式用语,用一般时态) retract (something that has been said)收回(所说的话):*Take back* what you said about Mary. 把你说玛丽的那些话都收回去。I'm sorry I was rude, I *take* everything I said *back*. 对不起,我失礼了。我收回我所说过的所有的话。❺(用一般时态) cause (someone) to remember or think about(a past time)使(某人)回想起(过去的岁月):These old songs *took* me *back* to my days in the countryside where I worked as an educated young person. 这些老歌使我回想起在农村当知青的日子。Seeing that old film really *took* me *back*! 看了那部老影片的确使我回想起了过去。❻accept (someone, usually a wife or husband) again after they left a relationship and want to return to it 重新接纳(想要恢复关系的丈夫或妻子):Jane *took back* her husband after he stopped drinking. 简在她丈夫不再酗酒以后重新接纳了他。She had an affair with a handsome young man, but her husband *took* her *back*. 她曾与一位漂亮的小伙子有染,但她丈夫还是重新接纳了她。

NOTE 当本短语的宾语为代词时,该代词须置于本短语的动词和副词中间。

take care *vt.* & *vi.* (常用于祈使句中) be careful or watchful 注意,留神:You need to *take* more *care* with your writing. 你需要多注意你的写作。The children must be warned to *take* more *care* of the trains on their way to school. 必须告诫孩子们在上学的路上多加注意火车。You should *take care* not to damage the control unit in operation. 你应注意在操作中不要损坏控制器。*Take care* how you pronounce the word. 注意这个词怎么发音。

T

—*vi*. (仅用于口语中) used for saying goodbye to someone in a friendly way (告别用语)再见: I have to go now, *Take care*! 我现在得走了。再见! "*Take care*, Mary." "Okay. See you later." "再见,玛丽。""好,再见。"

NOTE 1. 当本短语作"再见"解时,为 take care of yourself 的简略形式。这两种表达形式都可用在非正式信件结尾部,来取代 Sincerely 或 Love。例如: *Take care* (*of yourself*), Dad, with love from us both.

2. 当本短语作"再见"解时,与 take (it) easy 意义和用法相同。

take care of *vt*. 【不可分性动词短语】❶do the necessary things for (someone who needs help or protection)照顾(某人): Many migrant workers in this area who lost their children were too busy to *take care of* them. 该地区许多丢失孩子的外来务工人员都是太忙以至于无法照看他们。*Take* good *care of* yourself while I'm away. 我不在的时候你要照顾好自己。The old people are well *taken care of* in the nursing home. 老年人在养老院里都得到很好的照料。❷ treat (something) carefully so that it stays in good condition 照料,照管(某物): Have a good time and don't worry about the business. I'll *take care of* it. 痛痛快快地玩玩吧,不要担心生意,我会负责照料的。As long as the government and residents of Hong Kong could work together, they will surely succeed in *taking* good *care of* Hong Kong. 只要香港政府同广大居民和衷共济,就一定能够成功地把香港管理好。❸(常用一般时态) be careful about or watch out for (something dangerous)注意,警惕(危险之物): The children must be warned to *take* more *care of* the trains as they cross the tracks on their way to school. 必须告诫孩子们在上学的路上横过铁路时多加注意火车。❹(非正式用语,常用一般时态) do what is necessary to deal with (a person or situation)处理,对付: Can you *take care of* this customer, please? 请你处理一下这位顾客的事情,好吗? I will *take care of* these letters. 由我来处理这些信件吧。❺(非正式用语) (used especially when you are offering to pay for someone else) pay for (something) (为他人)付账: She picked up the bill, saying, "Let me *take care of* that." 她拿起账单说道:"我来买单吧。"

NOTE 本短语与 care for 均有"照料"之意,但它们又都有其他不同意义,因此在使用中不能相混。见 care for。

take charge *vi*. begin to lead or control; take control or responsibility; undertake the care or management 负责;管理: When the manager was in the hospital, Mr Jackson was sent to the company to *take charge*. 在经理住院期间,杰克逊先生被派到公司去负责工作。Bob is a natural leader and can *take charge* in an emergency. 鲍勃是个天生的领袖,紧急时能掌管一切。

take charge of *vt*. 【不可分性动词短语】take control and become responsible for (someone or something)负责(人或物): When she was in the hospital, her sister *took charge of* her children. 她住院时,她妹妹负责照料她的孩子。Special organs, staffed with specialists, have been set up in the above-mentioned ministries and commissions to *take charge of* the export control work. 在上述各相关部委中,均

T

设立了负责出口管制的专门机构，并配备了专门的工作人员。

take control of *vt.*【不可分性动词短语】begin to have power over (something or someone such as a group)开始控制：The new government must *take control of* the country as soon as the election results are clear. 新一届政府必须在大选结果揭晓后马上控制国家。He finally *took control of* the company by buying all the shares. 他最终以买下全部股权的方式控制了该公司。It's not an easy task to *take control of* these young children. 要管好这些孩子是不容易的。

take delight in *vt.*【不可分性动词短语】enjoy (something or doing something) very much 特别喜欢；以……为乐：She *takes* much *delight in* singing and dancing. 她非常喜欢唱歌和跳舞。I don't see what *delight* the young people *take in* such loud music. 我不知道年轻人为什么喜欢这么大声音的音乐。It gave me no pleasure to have to tell them they were fired, I *take* no *pleasure in* such things. 我不愿去告诉他们已被解雇，我并不以这样的事为乐。

NOTE 1. 本短语中的名词 delight 前可用不定冠词 a。在美国英语中，尤为常用。例如：

> She *takes* a *delight in* teasing her brother.
> 她喜欢逗弄她的弟弟。

2. 本短语与 take pleasure in 意义和用法相同，两者可互换使用。

take down *vt.*【可分性动词短语】❶get (something) from a higher place 把(某物)取下，放下：That notice has been up for weeks, it's time it was *taken down*. 那个通知已挂了好几周，该摘下来了。Stop, *take down* that shutter before you go. 不要走。先把那百叶窗放下来再走。❷remove (each piece of a temporary structure) into pieces 拆毁(临时建筑物)：Carpenters *took down* the shed, in order to build a house. 木匠拆掉了那棚屋，以便建一所新房。Israel failed to comply with the UN demand to *take down* separation barriers on occupied Palestinian land. 以色列没有按联合国的要求拆毁在巴勒斯坦被占领土上的隔离墙。The platform was *taken down* as soon as the building was completed. 楼房一竣工，那平台就被拆除了。❸write (a piece of information or statement) down 将……写下，记下：We've been trying to contact you, Green, but we think we *took* your number *down* incorrectly. 我们一直在千方百计地联系你，格林。但想必我们把你的电话号码记错了。She *took down* what was being said, careful not to miss a word. 她认真地一字不漏地把所说的话都记了下来。The driver's name and address were *taken down* by the policeman. 警察记下了司机的姓名和地址。

—*vt.* & *vi.* separate (something such as a large machine) to pieces, especially in order to repair or clean it 拆卸(大型机器等)：They are *taking down* a crane. 他们正在拆卸吊车。The machine has been *taken down* for an overhaul. 机器已经拆卸下来进行大修。We'll have to *take* the engine *down* to get to the gearbox. 我们得先拆卸发动机才能接触到变速箱。

NOTE 1. 当本短语用作及物性动词短语，所带的宾语是代词时，该代词须置于本短语的动词和副词中间。

2. 本短语可转化为复合词 takedown，意为"(机械等的)拆卸;失面子,羞辱"。

take easy *vi.* ❶(非正式用语) rest and not do things that will make you tired 休息,放松: You've been working so hard for several months. You must *take* it *easy* and relax over the weekend. 你这样紧张地工作了几个月,周末应该放松点,休息一下。The doctor said that Bob would have to *take* things *easy* for a while after he had his tonsils out. 医生叮嘱鲍勃在切掉扁桃体后要休息一段时间。You'll be much happier if you learn to *take* life *easy*. 如果你学会轻松地生活,你就会更幸福。❷(仅用于口语中)(used for telling someone to be calm when he or she is upset or annoyed)go or act slowly, carefully, and gently; behave in an easy manner 缓慢地走;小心地做事;沉住气: *Take* it *easy*. The roads are icy. 慢点儿走,道路都很滑。He told me to *take* things *easy* and not to worry about getting back to work. 他让我别着急,不要为回来上班发愁。❸(主要用于美国口语中) used for saying goodbye to someone (告别用语)再见: I'm off now. *Take* it *easy*! 我现在就走。再见!

NOTE 本短语的另一种表达形式是 take things easy。

take effect *vi.* ❶(of a new rule or law, policy, etc.)start to be used (新的规定、法律或政策等)开始执行,实施: The new regulation on minimum wage is to *take effect* on March onward. 一项新的最低工资规定将于 3 月起开始执行。The new law will not *take effect* as planned, as it was talked out in the last meeting of the House. 那项新法令将不会如期实施了,因为在上次的议会会议上有人用拖延手法使其未能通过。The official said that the policy of the European Union concerning Belarus hasn't *taken effect* yet. 这位官员称,欧盟对白俄罗斯的政策尚未开始实施。❷(of something) begin to be effective or produce an unexpected or intended result 开始生效,发生作用: Relax for a couple of hours until the pills *take effect*. 休息两个小时后药物才会起作用。It was very clear that his money was *taking effect* in the court. 很明显,他的钱在法庭上起着作用。

NOTE 本短语与 come into effect 意义和用法相同。

take for *vt.*【可分性动词短语】❶regard (someone) as being (something); consider 把(某人)当作……,认为,以为: Everybody here is clever, so don't *take* anyone *for* a fool. 这儿的人都很聪明,因此不要把任何人当傻瓜。❷(用一般时态) believe (someone or something) wrongly to be (someone or something else)把……错当作……,把……误以为是……: I'm sorry, I *took* you *for* your younger brother, you're so much alike. 对不起,我把您错当作您的弟弟了。你们长得太像了。The traveler *took* the house *for* a hotel, and the owner's daughter for a servant. 那个旅行者把这所房子误认为是旅馆,并把房主的女儿误当作是服务员了。I was *taken for* a thief when I was about to break the window to enter my house for my keys I had left inside. 当我要打碎玻璃进屋取我落在里面的钥匙时,人们把我错当成了盗贼。❸(非正式用语)rob or cheat(someone)of (usually a sum of money)抢劫,骗取(常指款项): The old lady was *taken for* all her money. 这位老妇人所有的钱都被骗走了。

NOTE 当本短语作“把……错当作……，把……误以为是……”解时，与 mistake for 意义和用法相同。

take for granted *vt.* ❶ expect (something) always to happen or exist in a particular way without thinking about any possible problems or difficulties 想当然；认为理应如此：He spoke English so well that I *took for granted* he was an American. 他英语讲得那么好，我理所当然地认为他是美国人了。She often told me not to take *things for granted*. 她常常让我不要想当然。All the particulars should be carefully checked, nothing should be *taken for granted*. 每个细节都要仔细检查，什么都不能想当然。❷treat(someone or something) with too little attention or concern 对(某人或某事)不注意，不关心：He is so busy with his business that he *takes* his family *for granted*. 他生意太忙，以致不把家庭放在心上。

NOTE 当本短语作“想当然，认为理应如此”解，接从句时，采用 take it for granted that 的主动或被动形式，其中的 it 为形式宾语，that 从句为实际宾语。例如：

> I *took* it *for granted* that you'll be coming here.
> 我认为你当然会来这里的。
> It may be *taken for granted* that they were honest.
> 可以认为他们是诚实的。

take form *vi.* （正式用语） start to become a particular shape; gradually develop into something that can be recognized 开始成形，逐渐形成：Our plans for 2020 election began to *take form*. 我们2020年的竞选计划开始成形。The patterns of rural society and life styles of rural residents gradually *take form* over a long course of development. 乡村社会的格局和乡民的生活方式是在漫长的发展过程中逐渐形成的。In her body a new life was *taking form*. 在她的身体中，一个新的生命正在逐渐形成。

NOTE 本短语的同义短语是 take shape。

take from *vt.* （常用一般时态）❶remove (one number or quantity) from (another number or quantity)减去，扣除：What do you get If you *take* 3 *from* 10? 10减3等于几？According to the deposit system to curb corruption of civil servants, each month 5 percent is deducted from each civil servant's salary, and the equivalent of 10 percent is *taken from* the department where the person serves. 根据这种公务员廉政金制度，廉政金个人部分按本人每月工资的5%扣取交纳，而相当于10%的数额由其单位交纳。❷remove something from (someone who had it)剥夺，夺走：No government should be allowed to *take* their right *from* the people. 不应允许任何政府剥夺人民的权利。*Take* the knife away *from* her! 把刀从她的手里夺下来！❸(常用被动语态形式) choose or extract(something)from (a book or study from a larger work) 从……选录出：The picture on page 5 is *taken from* a magazine. 第五页上的图片是从一本杂志上剪摘下来的。Our reading today is *taken from* the Bible. 我们今天读的内容是从《圣经》上选录下来的。❹(非正式用语) suffer or receive (something such as a blow)from (usually someone)遭受(常指某人的)打击：I *took* a nasty knock *from* the thief as he ran away. 在盗贼逃跑时，我挨了他重重的一击。He has *taken* more than he can stand *from* these two attackers. 他遭到了那两名袭击者的打击,令他不堪忍受。

take heart *vi.* (常与 from 连用) made to feel encouraged, less worried or more confident (by something), especially in difficult time (尤指在遭遇困难时)受到鼓舞;鼓足信心:The entire world should *take heart* that progress is being made in the effort to eliminate this disease. 根除这种疾病的努力正在取得进展,世人应该为此感到鼓舞。Small business *took heart* from the government's new tax laws. 小型企业深受政府新出台的税法鼓舞。Let them *take heart* from this, but things might have been worse. 让他们通过此事振作起来,尽管情况可能会更糟。

NOTE 本短语的反义短语是 lose heart。

take heed *v.* (正式用语,常用一般时态) watch, give careful attention or listen carefully (especially to someone's advice or warning)当心;听从(尤指他人的劝告或警告):*Take heed* not to spill coffee on the rug. 当心不要把咖啡洒在地毯上。What if the government *takes* no *heed* of the warnings? 要是政府对这些警示不予理睬怎么办? You would be wise to *take heed* of his advice. 听从他的劝告是明智的。

take hold *vi.* ❶ become stronger and difficult to stop 变得猛烈并难以控制:They were fortunate to escape before the fire *took hold*. 在火势变得猛烈并难以控制之前,他们有幸逃了出来。The medical scientist and his research group were determined not to let SARS *take hold* again. 这位医学家和他的研究小组决心不让"非典"再次横行。❷ win recognition; be accepted 获得承认,被接受:This idea does not seem to have *taken hold* very widely. 这一思想似乎没被广泛地接受。And indeed it was only in this period that the Christmas card tradition really *took hold* among US presidents. 事实上,正是在这个时期里,圣诞节寄贺卡的传统为美国总统所接受。

take hold of *vt.* start holding (something or someone)抓住,握住,抱住:*Take hold of* the end of the rope, and we'll pull you up. 抓住绳子的一头,我们把你拉上来。She *took hold of* his hand. 她握住了他的手。They will *take hold of* this good opportunity. 他们会把握住这个好机会的。

NOTE 本短语的同义短语是 catch hold of, have/grab hold of 和 get hold of。

take ill *vt.* &*vi.* (常用被动语态形式,常用一般时态) (cause to) become ill, often suddenly (常指突然)生病,发病:Unfortunately, Father *took ill* just before his birthday. 不幸的是,爸爸在他过生日前突然发病。Shortly after Christmas, Mother was mysteriously *taken ill*. 不知怎的,圣诞节刚过,妈妈就病了。The exhausted Arafat was suddenly *taken ill*, and had to be flown to Paris for treatment. 精疲力竭的阿拉法特突然发病,并不得不用飞机送往巴黎就医。

—*vt.* 【可分性动词短语】(常用一般时态) be hurt or be offended by (something)感到受伤害;恼火:When he heard of his dismissal he *took* the news *ill*. 听到自己被开除的消息,他感到十分伤感。I *take* it *ill* of you to have told my secret. 你把我的秘密讲了出去,我对此很恼火。

NOTE 1. 当本短语作"生病,发病"解时,短语中的 ill 是形容词,这时 ill 可被 sick 替换。但当本短语作"感到受伤害;恼火"解时,短语中的 ill 则是副词,这时的 ill

不可被 sick 替换。

2. 本短语作“突然生病,发病”解时,其同义短语是 fall ill。但两者在用法上有所不同。见 fall ill。

take in *vt.* ❶ lead or carry (someone or something) indoors or into a room 把(某人)带入室内,把(某物)拿进室内:“May I *take* you *in* to dinner?” he asked. “我可以带你进去吃饭吗?”他问道。At least one man was *taken in* on a stretcher, his body covered in blood and a transfusion bottle held above him by an attendant. 至少有一个人是用担架抬进来的。他满身是血,照顾他的人高举着一个输液瓶在他身上。Elizabeth *took in* some cakes for us. 伊丽莎白给我们拿进来了一些点心。*Take* the washing *in*, it's raining! 下雨了,把洗的衣物都收进来。❷ allow (someone) to stay in your house or your country, especially when he or she is homeless or in trouble 收容,接待(尤指无家可归者或遭遇麻烦的人):It is reported that the old couple has *taken in* about ten orphans. 据报道,这对老年夫妇已收容了约十名孤儿。She persuaded her husband to *take* the homeless man *in*. 她劝丈夫收留那个无家可归的人。The farmer and his family warmly *took in* the lost travelers for the night. 那位农民及其家人热情地接待了迷路的旅行者过夜。❸ admit (members) or accept (someone) 吸收(成员),接收(某人):9.75 million people registered to attend 2018 national college entrance exam, while China's higher learning institutions planned to *take in* 7.9 million students. 有 975 万人报名参加 2018 年全国高考,而中国高等院校计划招生 790 万。The firm may *take* you *in* just to please your uncle. 公司可能会接收你,这只是为了讨好你叔叔。❹ accept (something as real or true) 接受(某事为事实):He still hasn't really *taken in* his father's death. 他还没有真正接受他父亲去世的事实。The news came as such a shock that I could not *take* it *in*. 消息来得如此令人震惊,以致我无法接受。❺(非正式用语,常用被动语态形式) trick (someone) into believing something that is not true 欺骗(某人):The newspaper's reports on everything good and nothing bad *take* its readers *in*. 这家报纸只报喜不报忧,尽蒙骗读者。Don't believe him, he'll try to *take* you *in*. 别相信他,他会设法让你上当的。They were completely *taken in* by his story. 他们完全被他的谎言蒙骗了。❻ (of people, animal, or plants) allow (something such as air, drink, or food) to enter their body, usually by breathing or swallowing (指人、动物或植物)吸入,吸收(空气、水分或食物等):The patient certainly needs to *take in* plenty of oxygen and liquid. 这名患者一定要大量吸氧和输液。The roots of the plants *take in* the water and make their food out of it. 植物的根吸收水分并从水中制造植物所需的营养。70 percent of the Chinese drug addicts *take in* heroin, according to statistics of the Ministry of Public Security. 据公安部的统计数字表明,全国 70%的吸毒者吸食海洛因。❼ receive or collect (money, etc.) from sales 收入(钱等):“Fahrenheit 9/11” *took in* $21.8 million in its first three days, becoming the first documentary ever to debut as Hollywood's top weekend film. 《华氏 9·11》上映头三天的票房收入就达到2 180万美元,成为第一部首映即登

上好莱坞周末电影排行榜榜首的纪录片。Senator Conrad added, "There are harmful consequences to spending more money than you *take in*."康拉德参议员又说:"入不敷出有诸多危害后果。"❽(无被动语态形式) include (something or someone)包括,纳入:The tour *takes in* six European capitals. 本次旅游包括六个欧洲国家的首都。This is the total cost of the holiday, *taking* everything *in*. 这是度假的全部费用,一切都包括在内了。The list *takes in* everybody. 名单上包括所有的人。The city now *takes in* parts of several counties. 现在该市把几个县的地方都划入了市区。❾(用一般时态) understand the meaning or importance of (something that you hear or read)理解:They find it easy to *take in* what you taught. 他们觉得你教的课容易理解。They listened to my lecture, but how much did they *take in*, I wonder. 他们听了我的课,但我不知道他们理解了多少。❿(of the police) remove (someone) from his or her home and take him or her to a police station for questioning 把(某人)带到警察局审讯:Detectives on the murder case have *taken in* a new suspect for questioning. 这起谋杀案的办案人员把一名新的嫌疑人带到警察局审讯。We have to *take* you *in* for questioning in connection with the murder of a girl. 我们要带你去警察局就一名女孩的谋杀案接受审问。Two children were found dead in their house, and their parents were *taken in* as murder suspects. 两个孩子被发现死在了家中,因此其父母作为谋杀嫌疑人被带入警察局受审。⓫make (a dress, jacket, or other item of clothing) smaller or tighter by altering its seams so that it fits a thinner person (通过改接缝)把(衣物)改小,改瘦:This dress needs to be *taken in* at the waist. 这件女装腰部需要改小。I'm getting much thinner these days, I'll have *take in* all my clothes. 最近我越加瘦了,我将不得不把我所有的衣服都改小。My dress is a bit loose round the waist, could you *take* it *in* for me? 我这条连衣裙的腰部有点肥,您能把它改瘦吗? ⓬(主要用于美国英语中) see or watch (something such as a movie or performance)观看(电影或表演等):I think we may get something to eat and then *take in* a movie. 我看咱们搞点东西吃,然后去看电影。

NOTE **1.** 当本短语的宾语为代词时,该代词须置于本短语的动词和副词中间。

2. 本短语可转化为复合词 take-in,意为"欺骗,欺诈"。

3. 当本短语作"把(衣物)改小,改瘦"解时,反义短语是 let out。

take (an) interest in *vt.* show that one is interested in (something or someone); be attracted to (someone)对……感兴趣,为(某人)所吸引:The manager was *taking a* keen *interest in* his secretary's affairs. 经理对他秘书的风流韵事颇感兴趣。Jane *takes* no *interest in* her work. 简对自己的工作不感兴趣。He says that decent people do not *take interest in* politics, or elderly people in sport. 他说,正派的人对政治不感兴趣,上了年纪的人对体育运动不感兴趣。

take into account *vt.* 【可分性动词短语】consider (something such as a fact, or situation) when making a judgment or decision 考虑;参考:Both China and the United States should *take into account* each other's concerns and promote the

T

healthy and stable development of bilateral relations. 中美两国都应该考虑对方关心的问题,促进两国关系健康稳定地发展。The regulation on minimum wage rules that the monthly minimum wage should *take* factors such as a worker and his dependents' minimum living cost *into account*.《最低工资规定》中规定:月最低工资标准,应参考诸如就业者及其赡养人口的最低生活费用等因素。The police *took into account* that he was a child and set him free. 警方考虑到他还是个孩子,就把他放了。Time must be *taken into account*. 时间问题必须要考虑进去。

take into consideration *vt.*【可分性动词短语】think about(a particular fact or detail about something) and allow it to have some influence when you are making a decision 考虑到,顾及: It is imperative to *take into consideration* concerns of all sides in a comprehensive and balanced manner and conduct negotiations on all the important items. 重要的是全面、平衡地考虑各方的关注,同时就所有重要议题开展谈判。You should *take* everything *into consideration* before you make any decision. 你做任何决定之前都应该全面考虑。The prisoner's good behavior will be *taken into consideration* when the length of his imprisonment is being decided. 在量刑时,要顾及犯人的良好表现。

T

take it in turn (s)⇨ take turns

take kindly to *vt.* (常用于否定句或疑问句中) like (something or someone); welcome or accept (an idea) easily or willingly 喜欢;接受(某种想法): She didn't *take kindly to* her new responsibilities. 她不喜欢她那些新职责。He did not *take kindly to* being told how to behave. 他不喜欢别人对他的行为指手画脚。It is hard to imagine her *taking kindly to* too much interference. 很难想象她这么爱管别人的事。Will your father *take kindly to* the idea of your leaving college? 你父亲会赞同你退学的打算吗?

take leave of ⇨ take one's leave

take measures *vi.* (正式用语) (of a government or other authority) initiate some action; take the necessary steps, in order to achieve a particular result (指政府或其他机构)采取行动(措施,步骤): It is necessary to *take measures* to control the vehicle exhaust pollution and its harmfulness effect on people's health. 有必要采取措施控制机动车尾气的污染及其对人民健康的有害影响。The World Health Organization urged world governments to *take* adequate precautionary *measures* against influenza H1N1 virus and to prepare for the case of a pandemic. 世卫组织敦促世界各国政府对 H1N1 流感病毒采取充分的预防措施,并为疫情大流行做好准备。

NOTE 1. 本短语中的名词 measure 必须用复数形式。

2. 不要将本短语与 take the measure of someone 混淆。

3. 本短语的同义短语是 take steps。

take note *v.* notice or pay close attention (to something) because you think that it is important or significant 注意,注重: They *took note* that she showed no surprise at the news of the murder. 他们注意到她听到这起谋杀案的消息竟没有吃惊的样子。When the people speak with such passion, government officials should *take* *note*. 人们这样激情地发表言论，政府官员们应该给予重视了。

NOTE 1. 本短语中的名词 note 必须用单数形式。

2. 不要将本短语和 take notes 混淆，两者意义和用法不同。

3. 本短语与 take notice 意义和用法相同，两者可互换使用。

take note of *vt.*【不可分性动词短语】give attention to or notice (something that is important or significant) 注意到，留意到：The committee has *taken* special *note of* the objections. 委员会已特别注意到了那些反对意见。You should *take note of* what he says. 你应该留意他所说的话。

NOTE 本短语中的名词 note 前不能加不定冠词 a，后不能加 s。take a note 与 take notes 均表示"写下，记下"之意。

take notes *vi.* write down details from something such as a lecture or a book, so that you can remember them 记下(讲课或书籍中的详细内容)，记笔记：She *takes notes* of everything that's said at the meeting. 她把会议上的内容都记了下来。Listen to the lecture carefully and *take notes* of what the professor said. 好好听讲，把教授讲的内容都记下来。It'll help you later if you *take notes*. 如果你记笔记，其以后会对你有帮助的。As a student, you are required to *take notes* to help you remember what you are learning. 作为学生，你必须要记笔记以帮助你记住所学内容。

NOTE 本短语中的名词 note 必须用复数形式。

take notice *vi.* pay attention (to something) 注意，关注：Wear what you like, no one seems to *take* any *notice*. 你爱穿什么就穿什么，似乎没人会注意。The recent sudden rise of the price of gasoline made many people *take notice*. 最近汽油价格的突涨引起了许多人的关注。

take notice of *vt.*【不可分性动词短语】❶ give your attention to (someone or something such as a particular fact or situation) 注意(某人)；关注(某一事实或局势等)：Small children will resort to all kinds of tricks to get their elders to *take notice of* them. 小孩们会做各种动作以引起大人对他们的注意。He *took* no *notice of* the spider until it bit him. 他在被蜘蛛咬之前，并没有注意到它。❷(常用于否定句中) listen to (someone or his or her words) with the intention of obeying 听从(某人或某人的话)：Children *take* no *notice of* him in school. 学生在学校里都不听他的。She's a very charming child, but she's never *taken* any *notice of* my words at home. 她是个很可爱的孩子，可就是在家从来不听我的话。What he had said has not been *taken notice of*. 他说的话从没有人听。

take oath *vi.* (of someone) formally promise to tell the truth or to do some task honestly 发誓，宣誓：He *took* an *oath* to give up drinking. 他发誓不再饮酒。My friend *took* his *oath* that he did not steal the mobile phone of his colleague. 我的朋友发誓他没有偷他同事的手机。The new president *take* an *oath* that he would fill the office faithfully. 新任总统宣誓将忠实地履行其职务。

NOTE 1. 本短语与 swear oath 意义和用法相同，两者可互换使用。另外，两个短语里的名词 oath 前均可根据表达需要用 an, the, one's 等词修饰。

take off *v.* ❶ remove (something) (from

something or a place)(从……)拿掉，移去：Let me *take* that piece of thread *off* your skirt, Mary. 玛丽，让我把你裙子上的那根线拿掉吧。Take your feet off the table！把你的两只脚从桌子上挪开！The mountain wind *took off* as much as three inches of snow overnight. 山风一夜之间便刮走了足足三英寸厚的积雪。The drug was found to be dangerous, and was *taken off* the market. 这种药被发现是危险性药品，所以就被从市场上取缔了。❷remove (something, especially a piece of clothing)(from the body)脱掉，脱去，摘掉：The president said he would *take off* his uniform, and he kept his word. 总统表示他将脱掉军服，他履行了诺言。You'd better *take* your coats *off*. 你们最好把外衣脱掉吧。He *took off* his boots before entering the house. 进屋之前他先脱去了靴子。❸(of a plane, etc.) leave the ground and start flying (飞机等)起飞：An amphibious aircraft can *take off* and land both on conventional runways and water, and a seaplane can only *take off* and land on water. 水陆两用飞机能在常规跑道和水上起降，而水上飞机只能在水上起飞和降落。The new generation of carrier rockets, Long March 5, will *take off* from a new space launch center in Hainan, which is expected to be completed in 2012. 新一代的运载火箭“长征五号”将在海南的新航天发射中心升空。该中心预计于 2012 年竣工。❹(非正式用语，常与反身代词连用) (of someone) go away, often suddenly and unexpectedly (某人)突然(或出乎意料地)离开：She *took off* at once without saying goodbye to anyone. 他没和任何人话别就突然走了。He *took* himself *off* to the United States. 他出乎意料地去了美国。❺make (someone) go away with you to a particular place, especially when he or she does not want to go there (尤指强行)带走(某人)：The police stopped her and *took* her *off* to a police station. 警察截住了她，并将她带到警察局。Two foreign engineers were *taken off* by five kidnappers, and one was killed. 两名外国工程师被五名绑架者带走，其中一人被杀害。❻have as a break or a holiday from work on (the stated day) or for (the stated period)(在某日或某段时间)休假；不去上班：Some deputies suggested there should be more public holidays when people can *take* the days *off* to celebrate and have a rest. 一些代表建议增加公共假期，人们可以多休假数日进行庆祝和休息。Mr Green *took* a fortnight *off* in July. 格林先生在 7 月份休假两个星期。I'm *taking* Thursday *off* because I'm moving house. 我星期四不去上班，因为我要搬家。When his wife was sick he *took off* from work. 他在妻子患病期间没去上班。❼reduce a price by (certain amount or rate); remove (part of) a tax 减价；(部分)减税：Can you *take* $5 *off* the price? 你能减价 5 美元吗？They *took off* 25 per cent discount for the goods. 他们给商品打了七五折。It's not known what taxes will be *taken off* in the next Budget. 还不知道在下个预算案中要减哪个税种。❽(常用被动语态形式) remove (a train, bus, plane, etc.) from regular service so that they are no longer available for people to use 取消(某一车次、航班等)：The night flight to New York was *taken off* two months ago. 飞往纽约的夜航班机在两个月前就取消了。They've had to *take* two of the evening buses *off* this route because of a shortage of crews. 由于乘务人员不足,他们不得不取消这条线路的夜班汽车。❾(常用被动语态形式) stop (a television programme, performances of a show, etc.) 停映, 停演: The show was *taken off* because of poor audience figures. 由于上座率差,演出取消了。❿(主要用于英国英语中,非正式用语) imitate or copy (someone and the things he or she does and says), especially for amusement (尤指为取乐而)模仿(某人): At the party, Tom *took off* the headmaster and some of the teachers and made everyone laugh. 在聚会上,汤姆模仿校长和某些老师的样子,逗得人人大笑。She's really good at *taking* famous people *off*. 她很善于模仿名人。⓫(常用一般时态) (of an idea, a product, an activity or someone's career) become popular or very successful (指某种思想、产品、活动或某人的生涯)受欢迎,获得巨大成功: The plan of reform soon *took off* and was accepted by all the directors. 这项改革计划很快得以成功并为所有的董事们所接受。Electronic money has not yet really *taken off* in most of the EU member states. 电子货币在大多数欧盟成员国中还没有真正地受到欢迎。His business has really *taken off*. 他的买卖还真的红火起来了。

NOTE 1. 当本短语用作及物性动词短语,所带的宾语为代词时,该代词须置于本短语的动词和副词中间。

2. 本短语可转化为复合词 takeoff,意为"起飞;起跳(点);出发点;拿走;(嘲弄性的)学样"。

take office *vi.* begin to hold a position of responsibility and power in a government 就职,任职,执政: All the elected officials *took office* after the election. 所有当选的官员都已在选举后就职。It was believed to be the first attack that took place in Pakistan since President Zardari *took office*. 据信,这是自扎尔达里总统就职以来在巴基斯坦发生的第一起袭击事件。With the new generation of leadership *taking office*, a big change has occurred in the government's development policy, which targets at "common wealth" for all. 新一代领导人执政以来,在政府的发展政策上发生的一大变化是实现全体国人"共同富裕"。

take on *vt.* ❶(无被动语态形式,常用一般时态) begin to have or develop (a new appearance, quality, etc.) 开始有(某种新的形状或性质等),呈现出(某种新的面貌): When some metals are combined, the alloy *takes on* new physical properties. 当一些金属化合时,合金就有了新的物理性质。These insects can *take on* the color of their surroundings. 这些昆虫能够呈现出与其周围环境相应的颜色。Thanks to reform and opening-up, our country has *taken on* a completely new look. 由于改革和开放,我们的祖国呈现出崭新的面貌。❷accept or undertake (a particular job or responsibility, especially a difficult one) 接受(尤指困难的工作),承担(尤指难以履行的职责等): "In accordance with the constitution, I will *take on* the responsibilities of the president," he told reporters. 他对记者说:"根据宪法,我要承担起总统的职责。" As a defense lawyer, she earned a reputation for *taking on* cases others dared not touch. 作为一名辩护律师,她因敢于接手别人不敢接触的案子而赢得赞誉。My doctor says I'm too tired and has advised me not to *take* any more work *on*. 医生说我疲劳过度，并建议我不要再承担更多的工作。❸(of a vehicle such as a bus or ship) stop to allow passengers to get on or goods to be loaded on (指车辆或船只)使上客，装货：Buses stopped to *take on* more passengers. 公共汽车停下来让更多的乘客上车。We made a brief stop to *take on* passengers and water. 我们作了短暂的停靠，以让乘客上船并加水。❹ start to employ (someone) to do a job 开始雇用(某人)：We have decided to *take on* a new clerk in the accounts department. 我们已决定在会计部雇用一名新职员。If you like that new job applicant, let's *take* him *on*. 如果你看中了刚来申请工作的那个人，我们就聘用他吧。Some of them were *taken on* for three months' trial. 他们中有些人被录用进入三个月的试用期。❺fight or compete against (someone, especially bigger or more powerful than you are) in a fight or competition 挑战(尤指较强对手)，与……较量：The powerful miners' union *took on* the government by calling a strike and won. 强大的矿工工会通过号召罢工与政府对抗并赢得了胜利。We knew they were bigger and stronger, but we *took* them *on* anyway and beat them. 我们知道他们比我们强壮，但我们挑战并击败了他们。When he issued the challenge he did not expect to be *taken on* by a mere youth. 在他提出挑战时，他没有想到与他较量的仅仅是个年轻人。

—*vi*. ❶(非正式用语，用一般时态) become fashionable or popular 流行，受欢迎：The fashion for leather coats did *take on* for some time in 1970s. 皮衣在20世纪70年代确实流行过一段时间。The idea somehow failed to *take on*. 那种想法不知为何不受欢迎。❷(非正式用语，用一般时态) show great excitement, grief, worry, or anger 激动，焦虑，气愤：Don't *take on* so; there's nothing to worry about. 别这么忧愁，没什么可担心的。At the news of the death of their leader Arafat some Palestinians *took on* like mad people. 当一些巴勒斯坦人听到他们的领袖阿拉法特逝世的消息时，伤心得像发了疯似的。The passengers *took on* terribly about the rudeness of the bus driver. 乘客们对公共汽车司机的无礼行为非常气愤。

NOTE 当本短语用作及物性动词短语，所带的宾语为代词时，该代词须置于本短语的动词和副词中间。

take (it) on/upon oneself *vt*. 【可分性动词短语】(无被动语态形式) accept (a responsibility for doing something) without being asked to 引为己任，亲自负起(某项责任)：He *took it on himself* to see that the children were well looked after. 他负起了照顾好孩子们的责任。She *took upon herself* the responsibility for protecting her children. 她承担起保护孩子的责任。The president decided to *take* the blame *upon himself*. 校长决定自己承担罪责。Is there a reason why the United States should *take upon itself* the role of international policeman? 美国就应该担负起国际警察的角色，这有道理吗？

NOTE 本短语中的 upon 用法比 on 正式，但不及 on 常用。

take one's leave *v*. (正式用语) say goodbye to (someone) and go; go away from (someone or something) 向(某人)告辞，告别：She thanked them for the pleasure of their company and *took her leave*. 她对他们的愉快陪伴表示感谢后便告辞了。Now let me *take leave of* you. 我现在向您告辞了。It saddened me to *take leave of* my home town. 告别我的家乡使我伤悲。

NOTE 1. 本短语中的名词 leave 是不可数名词,其形式不可因前面的物主代词单复数形式的改变而改变。例如:

> She stayed on after other guests had *taken their leave*.
> 她在其他客人都走了以后留了下来。

2. 本短语的另一种表达形式是 take leave of,后者为旧式用法。

take the measure of someone ⇨ **get the measure of someone**

take one's oath ⇨ **take oath**

take one's own way ⇨ **go one's own way**

take one's place *vi.* ❶(of one thing or person) replace the other thing or person 取代,代替,接替:As the warm air rises, cooler air *takes its place*. 当热空气上升时,冷空气便取代其位置。He eventually *took Charlie's place* in a famous band. 他终于取代了查理在一个著名的乐队中的位置。In the United States, if the president dies or resigns, the vice-president *takes his place*. 在美国,如果总统死亡或辞职,副总统便接替他的职位。❷be considered as being 被认为是:This new work will *take its place* among the most important paintings of the century. 这一新作品被认为是本世纪最重要的绘画作品之一。

NOTE 1. 本短语中的名词 place 的形式可根据前面的物主代词单复数形式而变化。例如:

> They will leave Iraq very soon, but it remains unclear who will *take their places*.
> 他们很快就要撤离伊拉克了,但还不清楚谁会接替他们。

2. 当本短语作"取代,代替,接替"解时,另一种表达形式是 take the place of。

take one's seat *vi.* (正式用语) sit down, especially in the place that one has a right to, or has been kept for one (at a theatre, meeting, etc.)(在剧院或会场等)就座:The show is about to start, ladies and gentlemen, so please *take your seats*. 女士们,先生们,演出马上就要开始了,请就座。They *took their seats* in the front row. 他们在前排就座。

take one's side *vi.* support someone in an argument 支持;偏袒某人:My father always *takes my mother's side* when I argue with her. 当我和我妈妈发生争吵时,我爸爸总是偏向她。See, you're *taking her side* again! 瞧,您又在偏袒她!

NOTE 1. 本短语中的名词 side 必须用单数形式。

2. 本短语的同义短语是 take sides。

take one's stand ⇨ **take a stand**

take one's time *vi.* ❶(非正式用语) use as much time as is necessary (to do something); do something slowly or carefully without hurrying 不慌不忙,从容不迫:It is better to *take your time* at this job than to hurry and make mistakes. 这个工作最好慢慢做,不要忙中出错。You can *take your time* to pay the debt you owe me. 你欠我的那笔款可以慢慢还。There is no hurry. You can *take your time* doing these exercises. 不必着急,你可以慢慢地做这些作业。He

took his time and made a careful inquiry. 他从容不迫,进行了细致的调查。❷(贬义用法) take more time than is reasonable to do something; do something too slowly 拖拉地做事,慢吞吞地做事:Paul never works rapidly. He always *takes his time* in everything he does. 保罗干活从来就很慢。无论做什么事,他总是拖拖拉拉的。The workmen seem to be *taking their time* over repairing this road. 这些工人似乎在修路中磨洋工。

take one's turn ⇨ take turns

take out *vt.*【可分性动词短语】❶produce or extract (something) from an inner or enclosed space 从……里拿出,掏出,搬出(某物):He *took out* a packet of cigarettes from his pocket and offered the man one. 他从口袋里掏出一盒香烟,递给那个人一支。The shop owner *took* a gun *out* of a drawer and pointed it at the thief who had wanted to steal his jewels. 店主从抽屉中掏出手枪,逼住了要偷珠宝的贼。All the furniture was *taken out* of the house and left in the road. 所有的家具都从房子里搬了出来,放在了马路上。❷take (someone) to a place like a cinema or a restaurant and usually pay for them; conduct or lead (an animal) outside a room, building, etc. for exercise 把(某人)带出去(娱乐或用餐);把(动物)牵出去(活动):I'm *taking* the children *out* to the theatre tonight. 我今晚要带孩子们去看戏。She's to take her parents out for dinner. 她要带父母出去吃饭。*Take* the dog *out* for a walk, he needs exercise. 把狗带出去遛遛;它需要活动活动了。❸remove (something), as from the material in which it is fixed 去除,拔出,割去:Please help me to *take* this nail *out*. 请帮我把这颗钉子拔出来。She's gone to the dentist to have her bad tooth *taken out*. 她去看牙医,要把她那颗坏牙拔掉。The doctor *took out* the patient's appendix. 医生割去了患者的盲肠。❹take (something such as money or a book) from a place where it is kept 取出(款),拿出(书等):I shall have to go to the bank again and *take* more money *out*. 我还得去一次银行,再取出一些钱来。Some cash was *taken out* of my account without my knowledge. 有人在我不知情的情况下从我的账户中取走了一些现金。Only five books may be *taken out* of our school library at a time. 我们学校图书馆每次只能借五本书。❺(非正式用语) kill (someone), destroy (something), or cause (someone or something) to be ineffective so that they can no longer fight or do anything to harm you 杀死;摧毁;使不起作用:We *took* the factory *out* by bombing it. 我们用轰炸的方式摧毁了那座工厂。❻clean or remove (a mark, dirt, etc.)除去(污迹、灰尘等):He *took out* the pencil marks from his drawing. 他擦去了图画上的铅笔痕迹。Will the usual washing powder *take* this mark *out* of the tablecloth? 普通的洗衣粉能除去桌布上的这块污迹吗? ❼(非正式用语,与 on 连用) make (someone) suffer because you are angry, upset, or tired, even though it is not his or her fault 往(他人身上)发泄(自己的气愤、烦恼或疲劳): Having been defeated in the local elections, the Party leaders *took out* their resentment on one another. 该党的领导人因在当地的选举中落败而相互发泄怨恨。It's not my fault you have had a bad day, don't *take* it *out* on me! 你今天倒霉

又不是我的错，别在我身上撒气！❽(美国英语用法，常用一般时态) take (cooked food) home or outside from a restaurant 把(从餐馆买的)(熟食)带走食用：I'd like three pieces of chicken to *take out*, please. 请给我买三块鸡肉，我要带走。

NOTE 1. 当本短语的宾语为代词时，该代词须置于本短语的动词和副词中间。

2. 本短语可转化为复合词 takeout，意为"取出的东西(或数量)；(供带出外吃的)外卖食品，外卖店"。

take over *vt.*【可分性动词短语】take control or possession of (usually something) 接管：Smith *took over* the farm when his father became seriously ill. 史密斯在父亲病重时接管了农场。An army commander *took over* the government after staging a military coup in the capital Tuesday. 一名军队指挥官于星期二在首都发动军事政变，接管了政府。We are ready to hand over power as soon as there is someone to *take* it *over*. 一有人接管权力，我们就准备将其移交。Gibraltar was *taken over* by Spain in 1462. 直布罗陀是由西班牙于1462年接管的。

—*vt.* & *vi.* accept (a job, duty, or a role) from someone else; take charge 接替，接任：He *took over* the job from the previous headmaster in September. 他于9月份接替了前校长的工作。Mr Smith *took over* the position of chairman from Mr Brown on Thursday. 史密斯先生于星期四接替了布朗先生的主席职务。The governor of New York State resigned over the scandal, and the deputy governor *took over* to become the state's first black governor. 纽约州州长因丑闻而辞职，副州长接任其职并成为该州首任黑人州长。

NOTE 1. 当本短语用作及物性动词短语，所带的宾语为代词时，该代词须置于本短语的动词和副词中间。

2. 本短语可转化为复合词 take-over，意为"接收，接管，接任"。

take part in *vt.*【不可分性动词短语】(无被动语态形式) be involved in (an activity) with other people 参与，参加：The United Nations should play an important role in the reconstruction of Iraq and all countries should *take part in* this process. 联合国应在伊拉克的重建工作中发挥重要作用，所有国家也都应该参与这一进程。Today city dwellers have begun to *take* an active *part in* managing community affairs. 如今，城市居民已开始积极参与社区事务的管理。As an older student, Robert doesn't usually *take part in* any of the class activities. 由于罗伯特是大龄学生，所以他不常参加班级的一些活动。

take pity on *vt.*【不可分性动词短语】feel sympathy or sorry for (someone) and try to help him or her 同情(某人)：How can anyone fail to *take pity on* those children dying of hunger? 怎么能有人对那些即将饿死的儿童毫无同情之心呢？She would bring into the house homeless children *on* whom she had *taken pity*. 她同情那些无家可归的孩子，并会把他们带到家里。We *took pity* on the homeless family and took them into our house. 我们同情这个无家可归的家庭，让他们住进了我们的房子。The tyrant *took* no *pity* on his people who were suffering miserably. 这个暴君毫不同情他遭受痛苦的人民。

NOTE 本短语与 have pity on 的意义和用法相同，两者可互换使用。

take place *vi.* occur; happen, especially by arrangement 发生，举行：Mrs Cooper said her daughter, 17-year-old Mary, called her on a cell phone from the school while the shootings were *taking place*. 库珀夫人说，她 17 岁的女儿玛丽在枪击事件正在发生时还从学校用手机给她打了电话。The Olympics *take place* every four years. 奥运会每四年举办一次。

NOTE **1.** 本短语和另外两个单词 happen, occur 都表示“发生”。经过事先安排或非偶然性事件的发生通常用本短语，而偶然或未能预见的发生的事件则常用 happen，或更正式用 occur。如：

> When will the meeting *take place*?
> 会议什么时候举行？（经过安排的事件的发生）
> When did the explosion *happen/occur*?
> 爆炸什么时候发生的？（偶然的或未能预见的事件的发生）

2. 本短语是不及物性动词短语，后面不能带宾语，也不能用被动语态形式。

take place of ⇨ **take the place of**

take pleasure in ⇨ **take delight in**

take pride in *vt.* 【不可分性动词短语】（常用一般时态）be proud of (someone or what he or she has done) 为……感到骄傲（或自豪）：The old couple *takes* great *pride in* their son, who is now a professor at a famous university. 这老两口为他们在一所名牌大学中当教授的儿子而感到十分自豪。The head coach *took pride in* his team's victory in the Olympic Games. 主教练为其队赢得奥运会比赛的胜利而感到骄傲。Her father is a cripple and he *takes pride in* always being on time for work. 她爸爸是个瘸子，他为自己总能准点到岗而感到自豪。

take revenge on ⇨ **revenge on/upon**

take root *vi.* ❶(of a plant) begin to grow somewhere（植物）扎根生长：Do you think the new rose bush has *taken root*? 你看这些新栽的玫瑰都生根成活了没有？❷(of an idea, custom, belief, or system) become established or fixed and accepted among a group of people（指某种思想、习俗、信仰或体制）被牢固树立，被接受：How did these strange ideas *take root*? 这些怪异的思想怎么这样根深蒂固？Many European customs failed to *take root* in the New World. 许多欧洲习俗在美洲没有被接受。Time would be needed for democracy to *take root* in that country. 在那个国家，让人们普遍接受民主体制尚需时日。

NOTE 本短语中的名词 root 必须用单数形式。

take shape *vi.* start to develop a more clear or certain form; develop into something that can be recognized 开始成形；形成：We watched the vase begin to *take shape* in the potter's hands. 我们眼看着花瓶在制陶工人的手里开始成形。After one year's work, the building began to *take shape*. 经过一年的施工，大楼已见雏形。A comprehensive system of the iron and steel industry has *taken shape* in China. 中国已形成了钢铁工业的综合体系。Before long, a good idea *took shape* in her mind. 不久，一个好主意在她的脑海里形成了。

NOTE 由本短语演化而来的 take the shape of 表示“呈……形状”。例如：

> A liquid *takes the shape of* a container it is in.
> 液体呈现其容器的形状。

take sick ⇨ **take ill**

take sides *vi.* (in an argument or war) support or favor one of the sides against the other (在争论或战争中)支持一方(反对另一方):I never *take sides* when my friends are quarrelling. 当我的朋友们争吵时,我从不偏袒任何一方。Switzerland didn't *take sides* in the last two world wars. 瑞士在前两次世界大战中均保持中立。The International Committee of the Red Cross tries to protect and help war victims worldwide without *taking sides*. 国际红十字会力图在世界范围内为任何一方的战争受害者提供保护和援助。

NOTE 本短语中的名词 side 必须用复数形式。

take sides with *vt.* 【不可分性动词短语】sympathize with (someone) and be on his or her side in a quarrel; support (someone)同情并站在(某人)一边;支持(某人): Why do you always *take sides with* your mother? She is often in the wrong. 你为什么总站在你妈妈一边? 她常常是理亏的。Switzerland refused to *take sides with* any countries in the two world wars. 瑞士在两次世界大战中都拒绝站在任何国家一边。I *take sides with* Group A. 我支持 A 组。

NOTE **1.** 本短语中的名词 side 必须用复数形式。

2. 本短语的同义短语是 side with 和 take the side of。

take someone by surprise *v.* ❶(常用一般时态) cause surprise to (someone); surprise (someone)使某人吃惊: His good examination results have *taken* all the teachers *by surprise*. 他良好的考试成绩使所有的老师都感到惊讶。I was quite *taken by surprise* when he offered me the job. 当他向我提供这份工作时,我感到十分意外。❷happen or appear in front of someone suddenly or unexpectedly (出其不意地)发生,出现:The storm *took* the fishermen completely *by surprise*. 这场风暴来得使渔民猝不及防。The sudden cold weather *took* us all *by surprise*, as if there had never been one before! 突然来临的寒冷天气使我们都猝不及防,好像这在以前从来没有过! The policeman *took* the burglar *by surprise* as he opened the window. 当小偷打开窗子的时候,警察突然出现在他的面前。

NOTE 本短语与 catch someone by surprise 意义和用法相同,但本短语更为常用。

take steps *vi.* (后常接不定式短语) perform an action in order to achieve something 采取行动,采取措施: China hopes that all parties concerned will *take* positive *steps* to solve the nuclear issue peacefully. 中国希望有关各方采取积极措施和平解决核问题。They are *taking steps* to prevent campus shootings. 他们纷纷采取措施以预防校园发生枪击事件。

NOTE **1.** 本短语中的名词 step 必须用复数形式。

2. 本短语本身是动宾结构,动词和名词可分开使用。例如:

> Here are some *steps* you can *take* to improve your children's education.
> 这些是你可以采取的提高孩子教育水平的措施。

T

take the floor *vi.* ❶(主要用于美国英语中,正式用语) start speaking in a discussion, meeting, or debate (在讨论、会议或辩论中)发言:The UN Secretary General *took the floor* at the Security

Council meeting. 联合国秘书长在安理会上做了发言。The minister *took the floor* to denounce the decision by the President. 那位部长发言，谴责总统的决定。The last time you *took the floor*, you talked for more than an hour. 上次你做会议发言，讲了一个多小时。❷stand up and begin to dance at a party, in a dance hall, etc. (在聚会或舞厅)起身参加跳舞：The young couple and their respective parents *took the floor*. 这对年轻的夫妇和他们各自的父母起身跳起舞来。

NOTE 1. 当本短语作"发言"解时，另一种表达方式是 have the floor。

2. 当本短语作"起身参加跳舞"解时，同义短语是 take to the floor。

take the lead *vi.* (常与 in 连用) ❶be in the position ahead of all others (in a race, competition, etc.)(在比赛、竞争等中)处于领先地位：Robert *took the lead* from the very beginning and won the Boston marathon for the third time. 罗伯特一开始就处于领先地位，并第三次赢得了波士顿马拉松长跑冠军。Chinese scientists have been working to find an anti-SARS vaccine and China has *taken the lead* in this field. 中国科学家一直在进行探究抗"非典"疫苗的工作。在这个领域中，中国已处于领先地位。❷do something as an example for others to follow 带头，领先：He always *takes the lead* in response to the government's call. 他总是带头响应政府的号召。China's eastern coastal areas were called for and encouraged to *take the lead* in realizing modernization. 中国要求并鼓励东部沿海地区率先实现现代化。

take the opportunity of/to *vt.* use the chance of (something or doing something); use the chance to do (something) 利用……的机会；利用机会(做某事)：You should *take the opportunity of* every job that's offered to you. 你应该利用每次给你提供的工作机会。May I as chairman *take the opportunity of* thanking you for your interesting talk on international anti-terrorism? 作为大会主席，请允许我借此机会感谢您所作的有关国际反恐的精彩报告。I'd like to *take the opportunity to* thank all of you for coming. 我愿借此机会感谢你们各位的光临。

take the place of *vt.* act or be used instead of (something or someone); replace (something or someone) 代替，取代：Electric trains have now *taken the place of* steam trains in most countries. 在大多数国家中，电气化机车现已取代了蒸汽机车。The recent statistics prove that the Chang Jiang River Delta has *taken the place of* the Pearl River Delta as the most economically up-and-coming area in China. 最近的统计数字证明，长江三角洲已取代了珠江三角洲，成为中国在经济上最有发展的地区。I *took the place of* the former manager, for his "serious problem of discipline violations". 原经理因"有严重违纪问题"而被我取而代之。

NOTE 1. 在日常使用中，本短语中的定冠词 the 有时省略。

2. 本短语另外的表达形式是 take one's *place* 和 take place of。

take (the) roll ⇨ call (the) roll

take the side of *vt.* support or favor (a particular group or person) 站在(某一组织或个人)一边；支持(某一组织或个人)：Please do not *take the side of* the Republican Party. 请不要站在共和党一边。In the time of change, government

T

must take the side of small-business employees and their families. 在变革期间,政府必须偏护小型企业中的雇员以及他们的家属。Why didn't these people *take the side of* Hamas? 这些人为什么没有支持哈马斯?

NOTE 本短语中的名词 side 必须用单数形式。

take the stand *vi.* go to and sit in the witness chair in a courtroom 就位(法庭的)证人席: Will the next witness please *take the stand*? 请下一位证人就位证人席。

take the wheel ⇨ **at/behind the wheel**

take time *vi.* (of something) need a long time (指事物)需要较长时间: Change will come, but it will *take time*. 变革会发生的,但还需要时间。It *takes time* to build intimacy. 建立密切的关系是需要时间的。

NOTE 不要将本短语与 take one's time 混淆,两者的意义不同。take one's time 意为"不慌不忙,从容不迫"。

take to *vt.* ❶move (someone or something) (from one place) to another 把……(从某处)带到(某处),把……送到(某处): *Take* me *to* your manager, I have a complaint to make about your service here! 带我去找你们的经理,我要投诉你们这里的服务! Mankind *took* the Olympic flame *to* the top of the 8844.43-meter summit of Mount Qomolangma for the first time. 人类首次把奥运圣火送上了 8844.43 米高的珠穆朗玛峰峰顶。Three days after the crash of the plane, the second black box, or the flight data recorder, was found and will be *taken to* Beijing for further study. 在飞机坠毁三天后,第二个黑匣子(即飞行数据记录仪)被找到,并将送往北京做进一步的研究。❷(非正式用语,无被动语态形式,用一般时态) begin to like (someone or something), especially after knowing them or thinking about them for only a short time (尤指在短时间内)喜欢上……: Has the baby *taken to* its new baby-sitter? 那孩子喜欢新来的保姆吗? I'm not sure if he'll *take to* the idea. 我拿不准他是否喜欢这个主意。The dog seldom *takes to* strangers. 这狗不大喜欢生人。❸(无被动语态形式,后常接动名词短语) begin to do (something) as a regular habit 开始养成(做某事)的习惯: Tom *took to* drink while he was a sailor. 汤姆在当水手的时候就养成了酗酒的习惯。Some lines are miles long, forcing drivers to wait all day for a turn to fuel, many people have *taken to* spending the night in their cars. 有些队排了数英里长,这迫使驾驶员为加油而整天排队等候。这样,许多人都已习惯在自己的车里过夜。❹(无被动语态形式,常用完成时态) begin (an activity or doing something) 开始(某种活动或做某事): My friend *took to* repairing watches in his spare time. 我朋友在业余时间从事修表的行当。Other factories have *taken to* making children's boots. 其他一些工厂也开始生产儿童皮靴了。❺(无被动语态形式,常用完成时态) go away to (a place), especially to hide, escape, etc. 躲入……;逃到……: Jane *took to* her room and wouldn't come out all weekend. 简躲进她的房里,整个周末都不出来。The criminals have *taken to* the hills to escape from the police. 罪犯们为躲避警察而逃进丛山之中。

take to heart *vt.* 【可分性动词短语】

think about(something such as advice or criticism)seriously 认真考虑(建议或批评等):There is one other piece of advice he should *take to heart*. 还有一点建议他应该认真考虑。I'm glad you have *taken* my advice *to heart* and done as I suggested. 你认真考虑我的劝告并按我的建议行事,我很高兴。I thought the criticism of his behaviour was just. I hope he will *take* it *to heart*. 我认为对他行为的批评是正当的,我希望他能认真考虑。

take to one's bed *vi*. (用一般时态) be forced to stay in bed, especially to recover from an illness (尤指患病后)被迫卧床休息:Father's ill, so he's *taken to his bed*. 爸爸病了,因此他一直在卧床休息。Mother *took to her bed* at the beginning of last spring, and I'm afraid that she may never get up again. 母亲在去年入春时就卧病在床,我担心她可能再也起不来了。

take to the floor *vi*. start dancing at a party, in a dance hall, etc. (在聚会或舞厅)起身参加跳舞:They were the first couple to *take to the floor*. 他们是第一对起身跳舞的夫妇。Everyone was amazed when the girl *took to the floor* with Devil. 当那位姑娘和戴维尔一起跳起舞来的时候,所有的人都感到吃惊。

NOTE 本短语中的介词 to 可省略。

take trouble *vi*. make an additional or special effort or work hard and carefully when doing something 不辞劳苦,不怕麻烦,费心,费力:She *takes* a considerable amount of *trouble* over her appearance. 她在仪表上可谓费尽心机。He has *taken* a lot of *trouble* with this painting. 他在这幅画上花费了许多心力。We must thank you for *taking trouble* to cook for us. 为我们做饭给您添麻烦了,谢谢您。

NOTE 本短语中可以用定冠词。但使用定冠词时,本短语后通常要接不定式短语。如:

> Thank you for *taking the trouble* to reply.
> 谢谢您费心作答。

take turns *vi*. (of two or more people)do something one after the other several times, rather than do it together 轮流:The three men *took turns* with the driving, so one would not be too tired. 三人轮流驾车,所以不至于太疲劳。People from our plant *took turns* to come and help us. 我们厂里的人都轮流来帮助我们。Susan and her sister *take turns* on the swing. 苏珊和她妹妹轮流荡秋千。Since there is only one horse, Mary and Linda have to *take turns* riding. 由于只有一匹马,所以玛丽和琳达只得轮流骑。

NOTE **1.** 本短语中的名词 turn 必须用复数形式。

2. 本短语另外的表达形式是 take it in turn (s)和 take one's turn(s)。take it in turn (s)是英国英语用法。例如:

> Ted and I *took it in turns* to go into hospital and sit with Mary.
> 泰德和我轮流去医院陪玛丽。
> We must *take our turns* at work. Now, please wake Smith up so he can take his turn.
> 我们必须轮流上班。现在请把史密斯叫醒,他好接班。

take up *vt*. ❶ (of something) use (a particular amount of space or time)占用(一定的空间或时间):These boxes of yours *took up* too much space. 你这些箱子占去了太多的地方。It *took up* a whole month to write this report. 写这份报告

整整用了一个月的时间。My time was *taken up* by a lot of trifles. 我的时间都被诸多的琐事占去了。❷begin to work at (a new job, duty, etc.)开始从事(新的工作,职责等):The Foreign Ministry spokesman said he would *take up* the post of ambassador to Afghanistan. 这位外交部发言人说,他即将就任驻阿富汗大使。Russia's First Deputy Prime Minister Medvedev won the country's fifth presidential election and *took up* the duties of presidency. 俄罗斯第一副总理梅德韦杰夫赢得该国第五次总统选举,并担负起了总统的职务。❸become interested in (a subject, habit, or profession) and spend time doing it, either as a hobby or as a career 对……产生兴趣:The man *took up* English at fifty, and now he can use the language freely. 那个人 50 岁开始对学习英语产生兴趣。现在,他能自如地运用这门语言。My brother has just *taken up* playing the guitar. 我弟弟刚刚迷上了弹吉他。Mr Smith *took up* acting while he was at college. 史密斯先生在上大学时就喜欢上了表演这一行。❹(常用一般时态) remove (something) by drawing inside itself 吸收,吸入:Plants and animals *take up* nutrients. 动植物都要吸取营养。 Sponges *take up* water. 海绵能吸水。When the vacuum cleaner bag is full, it will not *take up* dirt from the rug. 当真空吸尘器的尘袋满了的时候,它就不能给地毯吸尘了。❺ raise consideration of (a question or problem) and discuss it further, either agreeing or disagreeing with what has already been said 提出(某一问题)供商讨,讨论(某一问题):I'd like to *take* that *up* again at the meeting. 我想在会上再次提出那个问题。Today the United Nations *takes up* the issue of the conflict between Israel and Lebanon. 今天,联合国提出讨论黎以冲突的问题。We shall *take* the matter *up* with the committee. 我们将把此事向委员会提出。The issue will be *taken up* at the next round of nuclear talks. 这一问题将在下一轮核问题会谈中提出。❻accept (a challenge, an offer or invitation that someone has made)接受(某人提出的挑战、提议或邀请):Our athletes have *taken up* a new challenge. 我们的运动员接受了一项新的挑战。I'd like to *take up* your offer of a ride into town. 我愿接受你骑车进城的提议。My proposal has not been *taken up* so far. 到目前为止,我的建议还没有被采纳。Why didn't you *take* him *up* on his offer of a meal? 他请你吃饭,你为什么不接受邀请呢? ❼(常用一般时态) continue (something such a task or a story) after it has been interrupted or left unfinished 把(未做完的事或未讲完的话)继续下去:After she died her daughter *took up* her cause of women's rights. 她去世后,她的女儿继承了她争取妇女权益的事业。I put the telephone down and *took up* my work again. 我放下电话,又接着干起我的工作。I'll *take up* the story that I left unfinished yesterday. 我将接着把昨天没讲完的故事继续讲下去。❽(常用一般时态) interrupt(someone) in order to show disagreement with what he or she says 打断(某人)的话(以表示异议):"What's the difference?" He *took* me *up* sharply. "那有什么区别?"他猛然打断了我。❾shorten (a piece of clothing, such as a skirt or trousers)剪短(衣物等):The skirt dragged on the floor, so she *took* it *up*. 裙子长得拖地,所以她把

它剪短了。I need to have these trousers *taken up*. 我需要把这几条裤子改短。

NOTE 1. 当本短语所带的宾语是代词时，该代词须置于本短语的动词和副词之间。
2. 本短语可转化为复合词 take-up，意为“吸水；调整；收缩”。

take up arms *vi.* （正式用语，常与 against 连用）(of a group or country) prepare to fight a battle using weapons (against an enemy) 拿起武器准备（与敌人）战斗：Poor peasants *took up arms* to fight against their oppressors. 贫苦的农民纷纷拿起武器与压迫他们的人作斗争。The King called on his people to *take up arms* against the invading forces. 国王号召他的人民准备与侵略军战斗。

NOTE 本短语中的名词 arms 必须用复数形式。

take up on *vt.* 【可分性动词短语】❶（非正式用语）accept (an offer or invitation that someone has made) 接受（某人的提议或邀请）：Since she'd offered to baby-sit, I *took* her *up on* it. 由于她提出要为我看孩子，我便接受了她的提议。❷ask (someone) to explain or justify (something that he or she has just said), because you think that he or she is wrong 让（某人）对（其所言）做出解释：I think I would like to *take* Tony *up on* something that he said. 我想要托尼对他所说的话做出解释。

NOTE 当本短语所带的宾语是代词时，该代词须置于本短语的动词和副词之间。

take up with *vt.* ❶raise consideration of (a matter) with (someone or a group) 向……提出（问题等）：I *took* the matter *up* at once *with* the sales manager, and was informed that he had received no complaint. 我马上向销售经理提出了这个问题，但我被告知说他没收到过任何投诉。As it is a matter of importance, you'd better *take* it *up with* the captain. 因为这是重要的事情，你最好提出来让队长处理。The question of public housing should be *taken up with* the Minister concerned. 应该向有关的部长提出公共住房问题。❷（非正式用语，无被动语态形式，常用一般时态）become friendly or start a relationship with (someone, especially someone who might have a bad influence on you) 开始与（常指不良之人）交往：Her parents were alarmed to find that she had *taken up with* a group of long-haired boys. 她的父母吃惊地发现她与一伙蓄着长发的男孩子们交往。She's *taken up with* a man old enough to be her father. 她一直和一个在年龄上足能做她父亲的男人厮混在一起。❸（用被动语态形式）(of something) keep you busy or fully occupied 使忙于：He can't help, he's too *taken up with* his own problems. 他无法提供帮助，他自己的问题还应付不过来呢。The whole meeting was *taken up with* arguing about the budget. 会议从头至尾都在争论预算问题。

NOTE 当本短语所带的宾语是代词时，该代词须置于本短语的动词和副词之间。

take with *vt.* 【可分性动词短语】lead (someone) or carry (something) together with (one) 随身带着（某人）；随手拿着（某物）：I'd like to *take* my daughter *with* me to the party. 我要带我女儿去参加聚会。Frozen water has been found on Mars, so if people travel there someday in future, they won't have to *take* their own water *with* them from Earth. 已经发现火星上存在冰冻水，这样，如果人类将来有一天去火星旅行，就不必自己从地

球带水了。

talk a donkey's back leg off ⇨ **talk the back leg(s) off a donkey**

talk about *vt.*【不可分性动词短语】❶make an informal speech telling people what you know or think about(someone, something or doing something)谈论,谈到:We were *talking about* you just last night. 我们昨晚还在谈论你。The senator said to *the Washington Post* yesterday that the United States and Iran have plenty to *talk about*. 该参议员昨天对《华盛顿邮报》说,美国和伊朗有很多要讨论的。We're here today to *talk about* doing something that should have been done a long time ago. 我们今天在这里谈谈有关我们很久以前就应该做的事情。❷(常用被动语态形式) discuss (a person)and gossip about him or her in an unfavorable sense 议论(某人),说(某人)闲话:Don't park your car outside my house, you know people are beginning to *talk about* us! 别把你的车停在我家门口,你知道人们开始讲我们的闲话了。They were very often *talked about*. 他们常被人们议论纷纷。❸ consider a possible course of action (though usually without acting in fact)考虑:For years they have been *talking about* moving to the country, getting away from the noisy city life. 几年来他们一直在考虑迁居乡下,以远离喧嚣的城市生活。The most suitable punishment for the boy has been *talked about* for a long time. 给予那男孩最适当的惩处一事已考虑了很长时间。

NOTE 本短语的同义短语是 talk of 和 talk on。

talk back *vi.* (used especially to describe children being rude to their parents)reply quickly and often rudely to something someone says(尤指孩子和父母)顶嘴;反驳:Young people should not *talk back* to their parents. 年轻人不应该跟家长顶嘴。They were arrested after *talking back* to a police officer. 他们顶撞了一位警官后被拘捕了。They spared no efforts to attack him in the newspaper when he couldn't *talk back*. 他们不遗余力地在报纸上攻击他,而他却无法反驳。

talk big *vi.* (非正式用语) talk boastfully; speak with too much pride in yourself, your actions, or possessions 吹牛,说大话:Stop *talking big* or you'll lose all your friends. 不要再吹牛了,否则你就没朋友了。He is always *talking big* about his pitching, but he hasn't won a game. 他总是吹嘘自己的投球技术,但他还从未赢过一场比赛。

talk down *vt.*【可分性动词短语】❶(用于英国英语中) prevent(someone) from speaking by louder, longer and more powerful speech (以高声、滔滔不绝或有说服力的讲话)阻止(某人)讲话:Mr Smith *talked down* all the other members of the committee. 史密斯先生高声舌战驳倒了委员会所有其他成员。I tried to explain, but he just *talked* me *down*. 我试图解释,但他滔滔不绝地讲话不容我开口。❷talk about something in a way that makes it seem less important or less serious than it really is 以言辞贬低:He is doing everything possible to *talk down* my achievements. 他尽其所能地以言辞贬低我的成就。❸guide (a plane or its pilot) safely to the ground, especially when it is impossible to see well, by giving instructions over the radio (尤指在能见度很差时通过无线电通信)引导

T

飞机(或驾驶员)安全着陆:The people on the ground *talked down* the amateur pilot successfully. 地面工作人员成功地引导这位业余飞行员安全着陆。There is a particular need to *talk* aircraft *down* when visibility is poor. 在能见度很差的情况下,就很有必要用无线电通信引导飞机安全着陆。The pilot was *talked down* through the heavy fog. 飞行员靠无线电通讯引导,穿过浓雾着陆。

NOTE 当本短语所带的宾语是代词时,该代词须置于本短语的动词和副词之间。

talk down to *vt.*【不可分性动词短语】(非正式用语) speak to (someone or a group) as if he or she were not very intelligent or not very important 高人一等地对……讲话:It's unwise for a lecturer to *talk down to* his audience. 讲演者用高人一等的口气向听众发表讲演是不明智的。Students do not like to feel that they are being *talked down to*. 学生不喜欢别人用高人一等的口气和他们说话。

talk into *vt.*【可分性动词短语】persuade (someone) into (action or doing something, especially something wrong or stupid) by talking 劝说(某人)做(尤指错事或蠢事):He refused at first, but I managed to *talk* him *into* it. 他开始时拒绝,但我终于设法说服了他去做那件事。He *talked* me *into* marrying him and also *talked* me *into* having a baby. 他劝我嫁给他,还劝我要个孩子。

NOTE 本短语的反义短语是 talk out of。

talk of *vt.*【不可分性动词短语】❶mention or have a conversation about (a subject); speak concerning (someone, something or doing something)提到,谈及:Weren't we *talking of* Jackson just now? 我们刚才是不是谈到了杰克逊? Who is *talking of* failing? This is a success! 谁说这是失败? 这是成功! *Talking of* travel, have you been to Berlin yet? 谈到旅行,你去过柏林吗? ❷(常用进行时态) consider the idea of (usually doing something)考虑(做某事):They are *talking of* going abroad. 他们正在考虑出国。At one stage he *talked of* throwing up his job and going abroad. 有一段时间他曾考虑过放弃他的工作准备出国。

talk on *v.* ❶continue talking 没完没了地说:I had to stop her when she *talked on*. 她没完没了地说个不停,我不得不打断她。How can he *talk on* so long without saying anything useful? 他怎么能把话讲得这么长,又没有一点有用的东西? ❷deliver a speech or talk about(someone or something)谈论,讨论:Today, I will *talk on* Abraham Lincoln, the 16th president of the United States, guiding his country through the Civil War. 今天,我要讲的是带领他的国家走过国内战争的美国第 16 任总统亚伯拉罕·林肯。She will *talk on* the issue she cares about, including education and housing. 她要谈一下她所关心的包括教育和住房在内的问题。

talk one's head off *vi.* (非正式用语) speak at great length, usually loudly (常指高声地)唠叨不休地讲:Here I've been *talking my head off*, and not giving you a chance to tell your news! 你看我,一直说个没完没了而没给你机会讲你的新事! Why does Rosa always *talk her head off*? Doesn't she know she bores people? 罗莎为什么总是唠叨地没完没了? 她就不知道她烦人?

talk out *vt.*【可分性动词短语】❶(常用

被动语态形式) discuss or talk about (something) thoroughly 彻底讨论,把(某事)谈透彻:I think that she *talked out* women's liberation movement at the International Women's Conference. 我认为她在国际妇女大会上把妇女解放运动讲得很透彻。You need to sit down with her and *talk* this *out*. 你需要和她坐下来把这事彻底地讨论一下。I think the whole question has now been *talked out*. 我认为整个问题现已得到彻底的讨论了。❷settle(something such as a quarrel or problem) by discussing or talking about it (通过讨论或商谈)解决(争端或问题):The two countries have *talked out* their differences with the aid of the envoy of the United Nations. 两国在联合国特使的协助下,通过谈判的方式解除了分歧。*Talking* things *out* with someone else can be very helpful. 与他人商讨问题是很有益的。❸(用于英国英语中) prevent(a law, etc.) from being accepted by talking in Parliament until there is no time left for voting (在议会中拖延讨论时间)使(法令等)无时间投票通过:The orator went on and on and at last *talked out* the amendment. 那位演说人滔滔不绝地讲个不停,最后使该修正案无时间投票通过。

NOTE 当本短语所带的宾语是代词时,该代词须置于本短语的动词和副词之间。

talk out of *vt.* 【可分性动词短语】persuade (someone) not to do (something he or she wants or intends to do) 劝阻,劝说:See if you can *talk* her *out of* her foolish idea. 看你能不能劝她放弃她那愚蠢的想法。The policewoman *talked* the young woman *out of* committing suicide by jumping from the bridge into the river. 女警察劝说那名年轻妇女打消从桥上跳入河中自杀的念头。Once he has set his mind on a course of action he is not to be *talked out of* it. 他一旦下定决心要做某件事情,就不可能说服他改变主意。

talk over *vt.* 【可分性动词短语】❶discuss (something) thoroughly and honestly with someone (与他人彻底并富有诚意地)商量,商讨(某事):If you're worried about this change of career, why don't you *talk* it *over* with your family? 如果你对这次改变职业感到担心的话,你为什么不和家人商量一下呢? Chinese and Japanese officials started to *talk over* the poisoned dumplings case. 中日双方的官员开始就毒饺事件进行商讨。Both parties have been *talking over* what should be done immediately. 双方一直在商讨应该立即做些什么。❷persuade (someone) to change his or her opinion 劝说(某人)改变主意:My friend *talked* me *over*. 我的朋友说服了我。He is trying to *talk* the chairman *over* to our side. 他在设法说服主席同意我方看法。

NOTE 当本短语所带的宾语是代词时,该代词须置于本短语的动词和副词之间。

talk round/around *vt.* ❶【可分性动词短语】persuade (someone) to change his or her mind and agree with you or agree to do what you want him or her to do 劝说(某人改变主意或做某事):He tried to *talk round* his friend to sell the bicycle to him very cheaply. 他竭力说服他的朋友把自行车以很便宜的价格卖给他。At first my friend refused to fall in with the scheme we had suggested, but eventually I managed to *talk* him *round*. 开始时我的朋友不同意我们提出的计划,但我终于把他说服了。She resisted to begin with, but we were finally able to *talk* her *around* to our point of view. 她开始时反对，但我们终于服了她接受我们的观点。❷【不可分性动词短语】discuss (something) in a general way and avoid speaking directly about or dealing with the most important issues 兜圈子谈论(问题)，拐弯抹角地说：We don't like *talking round* things without coming to any decision. 我们不喜欢拐弯抹角地谈问题而又不做任何决定。I knew that he was short of money, but he just *talked round* borrowing some from me. 我知道他缺钱，可他兜着圈子提到要向我借点钱。Don't try to put me off this time. I don't want to *talk around* the issue, I want to talk about it. 这次可不要搪塞我了。我不希望拐弯抹角，要直谈问题。

NOTE *talk round* 用于英国英语中。

talk the back leg off a donkey *vi.* (英国英语用法，非正式用语) talk without stopping for a long time 滔滔不绝地讲：You'd better have some excuse to get away from him. If you don't, he'll *talk the back leg off a donkey*. 你最好找个理由走开。否则的话，他会唠唠叨叨地说个不停。Once our neighbor start talking, she will *talk the back leg off a donkey*, so it's as well not to let her get started. 我们那位邻居一旦开口讲话，就滔滔不绝地讲个不停，所以还是别让她开口为好。

NOTE 本短语的另外一种表达形式是 talk a donkey's back leg off。

talk to *vt.* 【不可分性动词短语】❶have a conversation with or speak to (someone) 跟(某人)谈话；对(某人)说话：American visitors to that country are instructed not to *talk to* the locals about politics or economics. 去该国的美国游客都被告诫，不要和当地人谈政治和经济问题。"You don't know who you're *talking to*. You should be careful about who you trust online," she said. "你不知道是在和谁聊天。你应该对在网上相信什么人持谨慎态度。"她说道。*Talking to* a local TV cable network, the Health Minister said human cloning is dangerous, illegal and immoral. 卫生部长对当地的有线电视网说，克隆人是危险的，非法的，也是不道德的。She needs to be *talked to*. 需要和她谈谈。❷(非正式用语) scold (someone) 责备(某人)，训斥(某人)：I'll have to *talk to* my tailor because the suit he made fits very badly. 我得去责备我那位裁缝，他做的这套衣服很不合身。I'll *talk to* some of my students, they have made a lot of careless mistakes in their compositions. 有些学生我得训斥一顿，他们在作文中犯了很多粗心的错误。

talk with *vt.* 【不可分性动词短语】❶have a formal conversation or discussion with (someone), especially in order to do a deal, produce an agreement, or reach a decision 与……交谈；与……讨论：The company *talked with* many potential investors. 公司与许多潜在的投资者进行了交谈。The British Foreign Secretary said in an interview with Reuters in Cairo that *talking with* Hamas is "the right thing to do". 英国外交大臣在开罗接受路透社的采访时表示，与哈马斯对话是"正确的做法"。❷(非正式用语) scold (someone) 责备，斥责(某人)：I shall ask your father to *talk with* you when he comes home. 等你爸爸回家来时我非让他训你一顿不可。

target at/on *vt.* 【可分性动词短语】aim at (a target) 瞄准(某一目标)：Moscow

T

had warned that country that Russia might *target* its missiles *at* it if it joined NATO. 莫斯科已向该国发出警告说,如果其加入北约组织,俄罗斯就会把导弹瞄准该国。The enemy's missiles are *targeted on* our city. 敌方的导弹正在瞄准我们的城市。The European Union wants new international agreement *targeted at* pirates. 欧盟希望新的国际协议能把侵权盗版者作为打击目标。

tea break *n.* (常用单数形式)a short rest from working, usually spent drinking tea, coffee, etc. or eating something (工作期间内的)短暂休息(可在此期间吃茶点等): We had a *tea break* about twelve. 我们吃茶点的休息时间是在 12 点钟左右。In Britain, New Zealand, and Australia, people prefer their *tea breaks* in the mid-morning or mid-afternoon. 在英国、新西兰和澳大利亚,人们喜欢把吃茶点的休息时间安排在上午或下午的中间时段。They have a *tea break* around 3 in the afternoon. 他们的休息时间是在下午 3 点钟左右。The girls in the office *take* two *tea breaks* during the day. 办公室的女职员每天有两次喝咖啡的休息时间。

NOTE 本短语另外的表达形式是 smoke break 和 coffee break。其中, tea break 主要用于英国英语中, coffee break 主要用于美国英语中。

teach (someone) a lesson *vt.* (非正式用语)punish (someone) for something he or she has done so that he or she does not do it again 教训某人: If you go on bullying girls in the class, I'm sure to *teach you a* good *lesson* some day. 如果你再欺负班上的女同学,我总有一天会好好地教训你一番。The bruises they got from fighting each other *taught both of them a good lesson*. 他们相互打得青一块紫一块,这对他们双方来说都是一次沉痛的教训。

tear away *vt.* 【可分性动词短语】(常与 from 连用) ❶remove (something)(from a surface)by pulling roughly and sharply 猛力把……扯掉,拉走: You could *tear away* some of the paneling badly eaten by woodworm with your fingers. 你可以用手指把一些严重遭虫蛀的镶板扯掉。*Tearing* the cover *away*, the child reached into the box to see what his birthday present was. 那孩子把封套扯掉后,把手伸进盒子想知道他那件生日礼物是什么。❷(非正式用语,常与反身代词连用,常与 from 连用)force (oneself or someone else) to leave (someone or a place) or stop doing (an activity)迫使(自己或他人)离开(某人或某种活动): How can I *tear* myself *away* from you? 我怎么能舍得离开你呢? She had to *tear* herself *away* from the party to catch the last bus home. 她不得不依依不舍地离开聚会去赶末班车回家。

NOTE 当本短语所带的宾语是代词时,该代词须置于本短语的动词和副词之间。

tear down *vt.* 【可分性动词短语】❶remove or pull (something) down 撕掉,扯下: The portraits of the former president inside the building had been *torn down* by the soldiers. 楼内前总统的画像都已被士兵扯掉。❷ destroy or remove (something, especially of a building) completely 推倒;彻底拆毁(尤指建筑物): The US President made a speech near the Berlin Wall, challenging the Soviet leader to "*tear down* this wall". 美国总统在柏林墙旁讲演,要苏联领导人"推倒这堵墙"。The new law says

that illegal buildings must be *torn down* and individuals or organizations responsible will be fined. 这项新法规定,违章建筑必须彻底拆毁,责任人或单位将被处以罚款。❸criticize (someone or something) 批评: The boss is always *tearing* Jim *down*. I guess he doesn't like him. 老板总是批评吉姆,我猜想他不喜欢他。

NOTE 1. 当本短语所带的宾语是代词时,该代词须置于本短语的动词和副词之间。
2. 本短语可转化为复合词 teardown,意为"拆卸"。

tear off *vt.* 【可分性动词短语】❶remove (something) by pulling roughly (from something)(从……)撕掉: The boy *tore* the wrapping *off* his birthday present to see what he had received. 那男孩撕掉他生日礼物的包装纸,要看他收到的是什么礼物。Several pages from the book have been *torn off*. 这本书中有几页被撕掉了。Our roof was *torn off* by the hurricane. 我们的屋顶被飓风掀掉了。❷(英国英语用法,非正式用语) write (something) rapidly 匆匆写成: The secretary *tore off* two letters in ten minutes. 秘书用十分钟就赶写出了两封信。Your article reads as if you *tore* it *off* in half an hour. 你这篇文章读起来就好像你用半个小时就把它赶写出来了。

—*vi.* (非正式用语,常用一般时态) leave hurriedly, often in an uncontrolled way 匆匆离去: Suddenly she *tore off* down the road as if a wild animal was chasing her. 她突然抽身沿路而去,就好像有一头野兽在后面追她似的。

NOTE 当本短语用作及物性动词短语,所带的宾语是代词时,该代词须置于本短语的动词和副词之间。

tear up *vt.* 【可分性动词短语】❶destroy (something such as a piece of paper or cloth) by pulling it into pieces 撕碎,扯烂: With trembling hands the old lady *tore up* the letter and threw the pieces into the wastebasket. 老妇人用颤抖的双手把信撕碎扔进了废纸篓。The magician tore up a $100 note and then made it whole again. 魔术师把一张 100 元美钞撕碎,然后又使其恢复原样。❷(常用一般时态) refuse to accept (something such as an agreement) or be controlled by it any more 撕毁(协议等): I believe the government intends to *tear up* its agreement with the unions. 我看政府打算撕毁它和工会达成的协议。We will *tear up* the whole treaty rather than accept this clause. 我们宁可撕毁整个条约也不接受这一条款。The other side clearly doesn't regard such contracts as binding, they can be *torn up* at will. 对方显然认为这样的合同没有约束力,它们可以被任意撕毁。❸ dig a hole in or remove the surface of (something)挖开,掀起(某物的表面): The city *tore up* the street to lay a new water pipe. 该市挖开路面以铺设新的输水管道。The workers *tore* the street *up* to repair a sewer. 为修下水道,工人们挖开了路面。Mother *tore up* the old rug in the living room and had a new one put in. 妈妈把客厅的旧地毯掀走,铺上了一块新的。❹damage or destroy (something) by attacking it violently 毁坏: Several trees were *torn up* in last night's storm. 在昨夜的暴风雨中,好几棵树被刮倒。Dozens of miles of railway track have been *torn up* by the heavy floods. 几十英里的铁路线都已被大水冲毁。❺make (someone) feel very unhappy or upset 使(某人)感到悲伤,不安:It *tears* me *up* to leave you. 要离开你,我很难过。

NOTE 当本短语所带的宾语是代词时,该代词须置于本短语的动词和副词之间。

tell apart *vt.* 【可分性动词短语】(常用一般时态) recognize or distinguish (the difference between two people or things that are very similar)辨认出,区别出(相似的人或物): Even their teacher has trouble *telling* the twin brothers *apart*. 就是他们的老师也难以辨别出这对双胞胎兄弟。The two women are so similar that only their husbands can *tell* them *apart*. 这两位女士长得如此相像,以致只有她们的丈夫才能辨认出她们。Special gravity is a very useful way of *telling* different things *apart*. 比重是区别不同物体的很有用的方法。

NOTE 当本短语所带的宾语是代词时,该代词须置于本短语的动词和副词之间。

tell from *vt.* 【可分性动词短语】(常用一般时态)recognize the difference between (one person or thing and another)区分,辨别出……与……之间的不同: The twin sisters look so much alike that I can never *tell* one *from* the other. 这对孪生姐妹长得如此相像,以致我无法分辨出她们谁是谁。Can you *tell* butter *from* margarine? 你能区分出奶油和人造黄油吗? We should *tell* a genuine product *from* its reproduction. 我们应该能区分产品的真伪。

tell of *vt.* ❶(正式用语)give (someone) information such as a story, concerning (someone, something or doing something)把(某事)告诉(某人): Have you *told* your mother *of* your real intention? 你有没有把你的真实目的告诉给你妈妈? He *told* us *of* having found a perfect place for the camp. 他告诉我们说,他找到了一处绝佳的露营地点。❷(正式用语) mention or talk about (something)提到,讲述: Most women interviewed *told of* at least one family member killed and tortured by their tribe leader. 大多数受访的妇女都提到她们至少有一名家庭成员被他们的部族首领所杀害或折磨。The film *The Warlords* is a martial arts drama, *telling of* three brothers who turn against one another over a beautiful woman.《投名状》是一部武打影片,讲述了三位结拜兄弟因一美貌女子反目成仇的故事。❸(非正式用语,无被动语态形式)(especially among schoolchildren) inform against (someone) (尤指在学生之间)告发(某人): Tom, I'll *tell of* you if you don't stop damaging the desk! 汤姆,如果你还继续损坏这课桌,我就去告发你! I was *told of* by my best friend, and it was a long time before I could forgive her. 我被我最好的朋友告发了,过了很久我才原谅了她。

tell on *vt.* (非正式用语,无被动语态形式) (especially among schoolchildren) report or give information about (someone or his bad behavior)(尤指学生之间)告发(某人或某人的不良行为): I'm going to *tell* your father *on* you if you do that again! 如果你再做那事,我就告诉你爸爸。My brother *told on* me when I didn't go to school. 我没有去上学,我弟弟就告发了我。

ten to one *adv.* (非正式用语,常用将来时态) (used for saying that something is very likely) almost certainly; nearly sure to be true; very likely to happen 几乎一定,十有八九,很有可能发生: He will, *ten to one*, succeed in doing the experiment. 他十有八九会取得实验的成功。*Ten to one* they will fulfill the task ahead of time. 他们很可能提前完成任务。It is *ten to one* that they miss the train. 他们很可能赶不上火车。

tend to[1] *v.* (后接原形动词)have a tendency or be likely to (do or be something)有……倾向;易于……: It *tends to* rain here a lot in the spring. 这里春天往往雨水很多。The girl *tends to* get very angry if you disagree with her. 你如果不顺着那姑娘,她就会大发脾气。Matter, which is in motion, *tends to* keep on moving. 运动着的物质倾向于持续运动。

tend to[2] *vt.* 【不可分性动词短语】❶(无被动语态形式,用一般时态)be likely to have, do, or think (something such as a quality); have a tendency of 趋向: Modern camera design *tends to* simplicity. 现代照相机的设计趋于简单化。His family have always *tended to* overweight. 他的家人都有身体肥胖的倾向。❷take care of (someone or something)照料,护理:I have to *tend to* the children before I go out. 我得先照顾好孩子才能出去。The nurse *tended to* the soldier's wounds. 护士为那名士兵的伤口做了护理。

thank for *vt.* 【可分性动词短语】❶tell (someone) that you are grateful for (something he or she has done or given to you)因……向(某人)表示感谢: I'd like to take this opportunity to *thank* you very much *for* all the work you have done for the conference. 我愿借此机会十分感谢你们为大会所做的一切工作。The former prime minister *thanked* the nation *for* supporting him during his time in office and apologizing for his mistakes. 前首相感谢国人在他执政时对他的支持,并为其错误而表示道歉。❷hold (someone or something) responsible for (something unpleasant that happened) 认为……应对……负责: You can *thank* John *for* the trouble we're in. 你可以认为,约翰应对我们现在身处困境负责任。We can *thank* the parade *for* this traffic jam. 我们可以认为,这交通堵塞是游行造成的。

NOTE 当本短语作"因……向(某人)表示感谢"解时,另外一种常用表达形式是 be grateful (to someone) for (something)。例如:

> I'm very *grateful* to my teacher *for* her help.
> 我十分感谢我的老师给予的帮助。

thanks to *prep.* ❶(used for saying that someone or something is responsible for something good that happened) owing to or because of (用以指好事发生的原因)幸亏,由于: *Thanks to* my good friend James, I found this great apartment. 多亏了我的好友詹姆斯,我才找到这套上好的公寓。It's *thanks to* Rogers that I heard about the job. 幸亏罗杰斯,我才听说了这份工作。The official said that corruption cases in China had declined on the whole, *thanks to* the improvement of legal system and the nation's anti-corruption efforts. 这位官员表示,中国的腐败案件总体下降是由于法律体系的完善和全国反腐斗争的结果。❷(used for saying that you blame someone or something for something bad that happened) because of (用于指坏事发生的原因)因为,由于: *Thanks to* his laziness, he ended up achieving nothing. 由于懒惰,他最终一事无成。It was *thanks to* your fault that we lost the game. 是因为你的失误,我们才输掉了这场比赛。❸ with the help of 在……的帮助下:*Thanks to* a good teacher, Tom passed the examination. 在一位好老师的帮助下,汤姆通过了考试。I finished washing the dishes, no *thanks to* you. 没有你的帮助,我也把那些盘子洗完了。

NOTE 1. 本短语中的名词 thanks 必须用复数形式。

2. 不要将本短语与 give thanks to 混淆, give thanks to 意为"感谢某人"。例如:

> I'd like to *give* my special *thanks to* the organizers of the conference.
> 我想特别地感谢大会的组织者。

that (all) depends ⇨ **it (all) depends**

that goes without saying ⇨ **it goes without saying**

that is *adv.* (used when explaining more clearly or precisely what you have just said) in other words; that means; namely (用以更准确地解释所述内容)换句话说,就是说: Literal translation, *that is*, word-for-word translation, is not to be encouraged. 直译,换句话说,逐字地翻译,不应提倡。Arabic is written in the opposite direction to English, *that is*, from right to left. 阿拉伯文的书写方向与英文的相反,即从右向左写。

NOTE 1. 在书面语中,本短语常被 i. e. (拉丁语 id est 的缩略形式)所代替。例如:

> The cinema is only open to adults, *i. e.* people over 18.
> 本影院只对成人,即 18 岁以上人士开放。

2. 本短语独立使用时,不能缩略成 that's 的形式。

3. 本短语是 that is to say 的简略形式。见 that is to say。

4. 本短语的同义短语是 in other words。

that is all *s.* (仅用于口语中,常置于句尾) (used for saying that there is nothing more involved than what you have mentioned) there is no alternative; nothing more happens; that is all that can be said or done 没别的办法,仅此而已,再没什么可说(或做)的了: If all the seats are booked, we shall have to stay at home, *that is all*. 如果座位都已预定光了,我们只有待在家里,再也没有其他办法了。I wasn't interfering. I was just trying to make suggestions; *that is all*. 我不是干预,只是提些建议,仅此而已。If there are no more questions, *that is all* for today's press conference, the spokesperson said finally. 发言人最后说,如果没有其他问题,今天的记者招待会就到这里。

that is to say *adv.* (正式用语)(used for explaining something you have just said in a more exact way) in other words; namely; that means (用以更准确地解释前面所述内容)换句话说,即: Speed is the rate of motion, *that's to say*, the rate of change of position. 速度就是运动的速率,即位置变更的速率。Our friends, *that is to say* our son's friends, will meet us at the railway station. 我们的朋友,确切地说是我儿子的朋友,会在火车站接我们的。*That's to say*, China has promulgated laws and regulations on export control in such fields as nuclear, biological, chemical weapons and missiles. 也就是说,中国在核、生物、化学武器和导弹等领域已颁布了出口控制法规。

NOTE 本短语的简略形式为 that is。

That will do. *s.* ❶ that is enough or is suitable for a particular purpose 够了,那正好:"I suppose we ought to tip the

T

waiter, but I've only got 2 dollars left." "*That'll do.*""我想,咱们应该给这位侍者一点小费,但我只剩 2 美元了。""那就够了。" "Will $500 do?" "*That'll do* nicely." "500 美元够吗?""那足够了。" ❷used to order someone to stop doing or saying something (让某人)不要再做(某事): *That will do*, Tommy! There's to be no running near the pool. 停下,汤米!别再往池塘跟前跑了。*That'll do*, children, you're getting far too noisy. 别说话了,孩子们。你们太吵啦。

the clock around/round ⇨ **round/around the clock**

the final straw ⇨ **the last straw**

the last straw *n.* the last in a series of bad events that makes you angry and you will not tolerate it any longer 使人不能忍受的最后一件事情: He'd been unhappy at work for a long time but *the last straw* came when he was refused promotion. 很长时间以来,他工作就不舒心;但使他更不能忍受的是他晋职也被拒绝了。The hotel was expensive, the food poor, and the bad weather was *the last straw*. 这家旅馆要价昂贵,饮食糟糕,而且这儿恶劣的天气更不能使人忍受。

NOTE 1. 本短语是 the straw that breaks the camel's back 的简化形式。

2. 本短语为不可数性名词短语。

3. 本短语与 the final straw 意义和用法相同,两者可互换使用。

the least bit ⇨ **in the least**

the minute (that) *conj.* (used for emphasizing that something happens immediately after the other thing) as soon as or at the first moment when (you do something) 一……就……: *The minute* the mother saw her son, who returned home safely after having been kidnapped in Iraq for days, she could not conceal her feeling. 妈妈一看到在伊拉克被绑架数日后平安地回到家的儿子便掩饰不住自己的感情。He was caught by the police *the minute* he arrived at the airport. 他刚一抵达机场,便被警方逮捕了。*The minute* I saw this, it appealed to me. 我一看到这东西,就喜欢上了。He rushed to the spot *the minute that* he heard of the accident. 他一听说发生了事故,就立即跑到了现场。*The minute* the button is pressed the machine will start. 一按电钮,机器就会启动。

NOTE 1. 由本短语引出的时间状语从句可置于主句之后或之前。

2. 本短语中的名词 minute 可被 moment, instant 替换,构成的短语与本短语意义和用法相同。

the other day *adv.* (非正式用语) on a recent day; a few days ago 前几天 :*The other day*, as I walked up to town, I saw a strange sight. 几天前,在进城的路上,我见到了一种奇异的景象。I was glad to see him *the other day*. 前几天我见到了他,真是很高兴。*The other day* I had a long talk with an old friend of mine whom I hadn't met for 10 years. 前几天,我和一位十年未曾谋面的老朋友谈了许久。I saw Richard at the club *the other day*. 我前几天在俱乐部见过理查德。

NOTE 本短语中的名词 day, 可被 afternoon, evening, night 等替换,分别表示前几天的下午、晚上、夜里等。

the straw that breaks the camel's back *n.* the last in a series of unpleasant events which finally makes you feel that you cannot continue to accept a bad situation 使人不能忍受的最后一件事情：She's always been very rude to me, but it was *the straw that broke the camel's back* when she started insulting my mother. 她对我总是很粗鲁，但她开始侮辱我的母亲使我不能忍受。You broke a lot of rules and we tried to ignore it. But stealing money from us was *the straw that broke the camel's back*. 你违犯了许多纪律，我们就尽量不去追究了。可你偷我们的钱是令人不能容忍的。

NOTE **1.** 本短语源自阿拉伯谚语，原意是：即使是负重再大的沙漠之舟——骆驼，要是它背上装载东西已达到其所能承受的负重量，哪怕再多加一根稻草也会它承受不住而被压垮。

2. 本短语的简化形式是 the final straw 和 the last straw，三者均为不可数性名词短语。

then and there *adv.* （非正式用语）immediately at that moment and in that place 当即，立即：They wanted me to make a decision *then and there*. 他们让我当即做出决定。I took one look at the car and offered to buy it *there and then*. 我看了一眼那辆汽车，便立即出价把它买了下来。

NOTE **1.** 本短语的另一种表达方式是 there and then。then 表示“当时”，there 表示“当场”。需要强调时间时，用 then and there，而要强调地点时则用 there and then。

2. 本短语一般用于表示过去发生的事，若表示现在发生的事，则使用 now and here 或 here and now。

there and then ⇨ **then and there**

thick and thin ⇨ **through thick and thin**

think about *vt.* 【不可分性动词短语】❶（常用进行时态）have thoughts concerning (something or someone); have (something or someone) in the mind 想着，思考：I had so many things to *think about* at the time. 当时我有很多事情在想。He walked to and fro *thinking about* his experiment. 他来回地走动着，思考着他的实验。I often *thought about* what you said last time I saw you. 我常常思考上次见到你时你所说的话。❷carefully consider (something or doing something) in order to understand something, make a decision, or solve a problem 仔细考虑：“Dad, will you buy me a new bike?” “I don't know, I'll have to *think about* it.” “爸爸，您能给我买一台新自行车吗?” “不知道。我得好好考虑考虑。” “We have to *think about* where the students will continue their class since all houses were destroyed during the quake,” the dean of a primary school said. 一位小学校的主任说：“我们得考虑学生在哪里继续上课的问题，因为学校的房屋在地震中全部倒塌了。” Next time you have a problem, *think about* how you can improve the situation instead of dwelling on all the negative aspects. 下次再遇到问题时，要考虑如何改善局面，而不是只想消极的方面。This matter needs to be *thought about* most carefully before committing ourselves. 这件事我们要认真考虑后再决定是否同意。❸（无被动语态形式，用一般时态，不用进行时态）have a particular opinion about (something or someone) 对……有……看法：What do you *think about* the government's latest offer to the teachers? 你对政府最近提出的教师待遇方案有什么看法？What do you *think about* John? 你对约翰有何看

T

法? ❹remember (someone or something); recall 想起，记得，回想: She *thought about* him and decided to call. 她想起了他，便决定给他打电话。She is *thinking about* her childhood days. 她在回想她的童年时代。

think again *vi.* (非正式用语，常用一般时态) reconsider; think more carefully about something; carefully consider whether what you are planning to do is a good idea 重新考虑；谨慎思量: I'd like to *think again* about the contract before signing it. 我想把这份合同再谨慎考虑一下然后签字。I'd *think again* before buying that car if I were you. 如果我要是你的话，在买那辆车前我要谨慎地考虑一下。The United Nations Anti-Corruption Agreement is sure to make life harder for corrupt Chinese officials on the run and make would-be criminals *think again* before they act.《联合国反腐败公约》不仅让外逃的中国贪官日子没那么好过，还会让试图犯罪的官员们三思而后行。

NOTE 本短语与 think twice 意义和用法相同，两者可互换使用。

think of *vt.*【不可分性动词短语】❶have thoughts concerning (something or someone); have (something or someone) in one's mind 想着: He was *thinking of* the time he spent in the army. 他在想着他在部队里度过的那些时日。He is *thinking* all the time *of* how he can do more for the country. 他一直在想着怎样为国家多做一点贡献。❷consider or take into account(someone, something or doing something)考虑: Nobody seriously *thought of* him as a candidate for the job. 没有人认真地考虑过他作为该项工作的候选人。I was *thinking of* how to fulfill our task. 我在考虑如何完成我们的任务。Considering that there are as many as 670,000 chemical bombs abandoned by Japanese troops in this area of China, we are *thinking of* using automatic excavators to do excavations. 鉴于日本军队在这一地区遗弃的化学炸弹有 67 万枚，我们正考虑使用自动挖掘机来挖掘。❸(常用一般时态) suggest; invent, or have the idea of (something or doing something)提出，想到: Can you *think of* a good person to become the next chairman? 你能提出一个合适的人选做下届主席吗? I've got to *think of* a way to earn more money. 我得想出一个多赚钱的路子。Whenever he *thinks of* China, two things pop up in a French tourist's mind, chopsticks and bicycles. 每当这个法国游客想到中国，他就会想到两种东西：筷子和自行车。He has never *thought of* letting his daughter marry a fellow like you. 他从未想到过让他的女儿嫁给你这样的人。❹(无被动语态形式，常用一般时态，用于 can 或 could 之后) remember (something or someone)想起，记得 I tried to *think of* her phone number, but I just couldn't remember it. 我竭力地想她的电话号码，可怎么也想不起来。I couldn't *think of* his address at the moment. 我一时想不起他的地址了。Will you *think of* me after I've left? 我走了以后，你还会记得我吗? ❺(用一般时态) have a particular opinion about (something or someone)对……有……看法: What do you *think of* Mary's new husband? 你们对玛丽的新丈夫看法如何? Everyone there seems to *think* very highly *of* him. 那里的人都对他有很好的看法。❻show consideration for (someone or something) and pay attention to their needs 为……着想:We mustn't just think of ourselves, but should *think of* other people first. 我们绝不能只为自己着想,而应首先想到他人。We should have the interest of 300, 000 customers to *think of*. 我们应该为30 万客户的利益着想。❼(常用一般时态,常与 as 连用) regard (someone or something)(as or for something)把……看作……: We all *thought of* her as a mother. 我们都把她看作妈妈。You mustn't *think of* him as being irresponsible. 你千万不要把他看作是一个不负责任的人。During the spread of SARS, going out without a mask would have been *thought of* as daring and even irresponsible. "非典"流行期间,在拥有 1 300 万人口的北京城里不带口罩外出会被视为鲁莽,甚至不负责任的做法。

think out *vt.*【可分性动词短语】❶consider carefully (all the important facts and details in a situation) before doing anything or making a decision 认真全面地考虑:*Think* it *out* properly before you make a decision. 在做出决定前,你要适当地做全面性的考虑。I don't think the government has really *thought out* all the consequences of this decision. 我认为政府没有对这项决定将产生的后果考虑周全。This plan was well *thought out*. 这一计划是经过全面考虑的。❷work out or plan (something) in the mind through careful thinking (通过仔细考虑)想出;设计出:All this prompted us to *think out* various ways to overcome the difficulties. 这一切都促使我们想出各种办法来克服困难。Like any of other sciences, nobody sat down and *thought out* computer science all at once. 像任何其他科学门类一样,计算机科学也不是某个人坐在那里一下子就想出来的。

NOTE 1. 当本短语所带的宾语是代词时,该代词须置于本短语的动词和副词之间。
2. 当本短语作"认真全面地考虑"解时,同义短语是 think over 和 think through。

think over *vt.*【可分性动词短语】❶consider (an idea or plan) carefully before making a decision 认真思考(或考虑):After *thinking* things *over* she at length succeeded in letting reason prevailed over her prejudices. 经过认真思考后,她终于以理智战胜了偏见。Please *think over* what I've said. 请仔细地考虑一下我所说的话。Your offer is very attractive, but I need to *think* it *over* before I can let you know my decision. 你的提议很有吸引力,但我需要全面地考虑一下,再把决定告诉你。❷reconsider (something), often with a change of opinion 重新考虑(之后常常改变主意):I've *thought* the plan *over* and decided not to join it. 我重新考虑了这项计划并决定不参与了。

NOTE 当本短语所带的宾语是代词时,该代词须置于本短语的动词和副词之间。

think through *vt.*【可分性动词短语】consider (something) carefully and in detail; reach a decision about (something) after much careful thought 仔细考虑:Have you had time to *think* things *through*? 你有没有时间仔细地考虑这些事情? It was the first time she'd had a chance to *think* it *through*. 她第一次有机会仔细考虑那一问题。

NOTE 当本短语所带的宾语是代词时,该代词须置于本短语的动词和副词之间。

think twice ⇨ **think again**

thirst for/after *vt.*【不可分性动词短

T

语】(正式用语,常用一般时态) want or need (something) very much 渴望,热望: On these dry days, you soon *thirst for* a cool drink. 在这些干旱的日子里,你不久就会渴望喝点清凉的东西。These activities were planned to appeal to young people *thirsting for* adventure. 这些活动是为迎合年轻人冒险的热望而设计的。When I was young I studied hard and *thirsted after* knowledge. 我年轻的时候,学习努力,渴求知识。

NOTE thirst after 的语气比 thirst for 强,但不及 thirst for 常用。

thirsty for *adj.* (正式用语,常用一般时态) having a strong desire for (something); wanting (something) very much 渴望,极需: The politician was *thirsty for* more power. 这位政客渴求更多的权力。Citizens seem *thirsty for* any kind of reform. 国民似乎很需要任何方式的改革。Young people should be *thirsty for* knowledge. 青年人应该渴求知识。The fields are *thirsty for* rain. 田地极需雨水。

thrill at/to *vt.* 【不可分性动词短语】(正式用语,无被动语态形式,常用一般时态) feel very excited and pleased because of (usually something) 因……激动,因……兴奋: She *thrilled at* the sound of his footsteps on the stairs. 听到他在楼梯上的脚步声,她激动不已。We *thrilled to* his tales of the North Sea adventure. 我们在听他讲述北海历险的故事时都感到很兴奋。

T

through lack of ⇨ rom lack of

through thick and thin *adv.* in all situations; through both good times and bad times 在(好和坏)任何情况下: I'll stand by James *through thick and thin*. 在任何情况下,我都会支持詹姆斯。The old couple has been together *through thick and thin* for more than 50 years. 这对老年夫妇在一起同甘苦共患难了50年。

NOTE 本短语的另外一种表达形式是 thick and thin。

throw a glance at ⇨ cast a glance at

throw at *vt.* 【可分性动词短语】❶direct (something) towards (someone or something) with a sharp movement of the hand or arm, especially so as to harm 把(某物)投向……: In Arab culture, *throwing* shoes *at* someone is considered an especially serious insult. 在阿拉伯文化中,向某人扔鞋子被认为是一种特别严重的侮辱行为。He had a brick *thrown at* him at that gathering. 在那次集会上,有人向他投掷砖块。❷aim (a look, smile, etc.) towards (someone) 向(某人)投以(某种眼色、微笑等): Mark *threw* an angry glance *at* her. 马克向她投以愤怒的目光。

throw away *vt.* 【可分性动词短语】❶get rid of (something that you do not want any more) 扔掉;淘汰: So when are you going to *throw away* those old magazines of yours? 那你什么时候扔掉你那些旧杂志? Let's *throw* the old television set *away*, we should get a new one. 咱们把这台旧电视机淘汰了吧;我们应该买一台新的了。Over 800,000 metric tonnes of clothing and shoes were *thrown away* in the UK last year. 去年,英国有80万吨的衣服和鞋子被扔掉了。❷fail to make use of or waste (something such as an opportunity or advantage) 没能利用,浪费掉(机会或优势): She *threw away* a good chance for a better job. 她丧失了一个得到更好工作的良机。This could be the best chance you'll ever have, don't *throw* it *away*. 这很可能是你能得到的最好机会，别白白浪费掉。

NOTE 1. 当本短语所带的宾语是代词时，该代词须置于本短语的动词和副词之间。

2. 当本短语作“扔掉，淘汰”解时，同义短语是 chuck out 和 throw out。

3. 本短语可转化为复合词 throwaway，意为“免费散发的传单（或小册子、报纸等）”。

throw cold water on ⇨ **pour cold water on**

throw into *vt.*【可分性动词短语】❶direct (something or someone) with some force, as with the hand, inside or into (something) 把……扔进……：I just *throw* all the clothes *into* the washing machine. 我索性把衣服都扔进了洗衣机。The Chinese girls *threw* their head coach *into* the air after they won the first volleyball World Cup title in 18 years. 在18年来首次赢得世界杯冠军称号后，中国女排的姑娘们把她们的主教练抛向空中。❷（常用被动语态形式）force (someone) to go to (prison), often in a brutal way 将（某人）强行投入（监狱）：In fact we had *thrown* them *into* prison for a night. 实际上我们已经把他们关进监狱里一个晚上了。Some Chinese forced to work in Japan as slave laborers between 1937 and 1945 were *thrown into* a Nagasaki jail. 一些在1937年至1945年期间被迫到日本当劳工的中国人被投入了长崎监狱。❸（常用一般时态）put (someone or something) into an unpleasant situation or a bad state 使……处于（某种不良状态）：Your remarks have *thrown* her *into* a temper. 你的那些话使她发了脾气。This unexpected change of situation *threw* us all *into* confusion. 形势的突然变化使我们所有的人都不知所措。A single computer problem can *throw* the whole office *into* chaos. 哪怕电脑出现一点问题，都会搞乱整个办公室的工作。❹（常用一般时态，与反身代词连用）start giving all your energy or attention to doing (a job or an activity) 集中精力于；投身于（某种活动）之中：They *threw* themselves wholeheartedly *into* the task. 他们全心全意地投身于那项任务之中。It was said that the old senator was preparing to *throw* himself *into* the presidential election. 据说，这位老年议员曾准备投身到总统竞选中。She *threw* herself *into* a modelling career. 她投身于模特生涯。

throw light on *vt.*【不可分性动词短语】（非正式用语，常用一般时态）provide information that helps people understand (something) more clearly; make (something) clearer, or easier to understand 提供线索；说明：I wonder if this new clue will *throw* any further *light on* the mystery. 我不知道这个新线索能否使该疑案真相大白。The research report has *thrown light on* the occurrence of short-circuit. 这篇研究报告说明了短路发生的原因。New *light* may be *thrown on* the cause of cancer by research that is now in progress. 现在正在进行着的研究可能会明确癌症的起因。The summit meeting in Oslo in October *threw* some new *light on* how to settle the question of Palestine. 10月份在奥斯陆举行的高峰会谈提供了解决巴勒斯坦问题的新思路。

NOTE 1. 本短语中的名词 light 必须用单数

形式。但前面可用形容词来修饰。

2. 本短语的同义短语是 shed light on 和 cast light on。

throw off *vt.*【可分性动词短语】❶quickly remove (a piece of clothing)迅速脱掉(衣物):He *threw off* his shirt and trousers and plunged into the river. 他迅速脱下衬衣和裤子，跳进河水中。He briskly *threw* his shoes *off*. 他很快地脱掉了鞋子。❷(常用一般时态) get rid of (something unwanted or something that makes you unhappy)摆脱(不需要或令人不快之物)：They tried to *throw off* the chains of tradition. 他们设法摆脱传统的束缚。Generally speaking, it will take you a week to *throw* off your cold. 一般来说，如果你患了感冒，一个星期后才会好。I can't *throw off* this feeling of sadness. 我无法摆脱这种悲痛的心情。What he had said made her very sad, and wherever she went she could not *throw* it *off*. 他那一番话使她非常难过。不管走到哪里她都无法忘掉它。❸escape from (someone who is chasing you or trying to find you)逃脱(追赶之人)：In order to *throw off* the photographers on motorcycles, Princess Diana allowed the driver to drive fast thus leading to the deadly accident. 为了摆脱那些骑摩托车的摄影记者，戴安娜王妃让司机加快车速，于是导致了致命的车祸。We finally succeeded in *throwing off* our pursuers. 我们终于摆脱了追赶我们的那些人。If we run fast we might be able to *throw* them *off*. 如果我们快跑，就能甩掉他们。❹ write (something) quickly and without apparent effort 很快写出：They sat down and *threw off* a few songs for the concert. 他们坐下来，很快就为音乐会写了几首歌。It shouldn't take me more than an afternoon to *throw* this article *off*. 应该用不了一个下午我就会写完这篇文章。

NOTE 当本短语所带的宾语是代词时，该代词须置于本短语的动词和副词之间。

throw out *vt.*【可分性动词短语】❶get rid of (something), for example by putting it in a dustbin, because it is no longer useful 扔掉，丢掉：You really should *throw out* that filthy old sofa and get a new one. 你真的该把那件又脏又旧的沙发扔掉，再买件新的。It's time we *threw* that old chair *out* , it's completely broken. 咱们该把那把旧椅子扔掉了，它都散架了。The broken cooking pots were *thrown out*. 那些破锅都被扔掉了。❷(非正式用语，常用一般时态) force (someone) to leave (a place, house, college, school or organization)撵出；开除(某人)：The noisy fellow with a cigarette in his mouth was *thrown out* of the meeting hall. 那个嘴里叼着香烟吵吵嚷嚷的人被撵出了会议大厅。At least five students have been *thrown out* of school for cheating on exams. 至少有五名学生因考试作弊而被开除。If you keep breaking the club rules you'll get *thrown out*. 如果你继续违反俱乐部的规章制度，就会被开除。❸(常用一般时态) (of someone in authority) refuse to accept (a plan, proposal, etc.); reject (something such as a law case)(指有权力者)拒绝接受(计划、建议等)；驳回(诉讼等)：As a manager he should not *throw out* any suggestions of his employees easily. 作为经理，他不应轻易拒绝接受其雇员的任何建议。The bill was *thrown out* by the House of Lords. 该法案被上院否决。

T

The defense asked the judge to *throw out* the case. 被告方要求法官驳回诉案。The judge *threw* the lawsuit *out* because it was silly. 法官因该诉讼荒唐而将其驳回。❹(常用一般时态)offer or produce (something such as a suggestion, a hint) 提出(建议、暗示等): Let me just *throw* these ideas *out* to you and see if you like them. 让我把这些想法给你们提出来,看你们是否喜欢。I *threw out* some hints, but unfortunately he failed to catch on. 我给他提了一些暗示,可惜他没能领会。Several suggestions for possible examination questions were *thrown out* by the teacher. 老师就考题范围给了几点提示。❺produce (something such as heat, light, smoke, or smell)发出(光、热、烟或气味等): My torch *threw out* enough light to see the path. 我的手电筒能发出足够的光看清路面。His new heater is very effective, it *throws out* a lot of heat. 他新买的加热器效率很高,供热量很大。In winter time the chimneys in the city were *throwing out* huge plumes of thick smoke. 在冬季,市里的一座座烟囱都冒着滚滚的浓烟。When this material burns, it *throws out* a nasty smell. 这种材料燃烧时散发出难闻的味道。❻(主要用于英国英语中,常用一般时态) say (something) carelessly or without considering the result 随口说出: The teacher *threw out* a few ideas and asked the students to write an essay. 老师随口说了几个想法,要求学生写出一篇短文。❼(主要用于英国英语中,常用一般时态)confuse (someone); make a mistake in (something); cause mistakes in (something)使(某人)不知所措,(使)在……中出错: His sudden resignation completely *threw* all of us *out*. 他的突然辞职使我们所有的人一时不知所措。Keep quiet for a while or you'll *throw* me *out* in my calculations. 安静一会儿,不然你会使我在计算中出错。

NOTE **1.** 当本短语所带的宾语是代词时,该代词须置于本短语的动词和副词之间。

2. 当本短语作"撵出;开除(某人)"解时,同义短语是 chuck out。

3. 本短语可转化为复合词 throw-out,意为"被遗弃的人;被抛弃的东西"。

throw over *vt.* 【可分性动词短语】(非正式用语,常与 for 连用) end a relationship with (someone, usually of a different sex) and start one with another person 中断与(常指异性者)的关系: Her mother scolded her angrily because she *threw over* her longstanding boy friend for a richer man. 她妈妈气愤地责骂了她,因为她把相处了很久的男友抛弃而开始与一个富人交往了。Bob *threw* Mary *over* for a new girlfriend. 鲍勃因又有了新的女友而抛弃了玛丽。

NOTE 当本短语所带的宾语是代词时,该代词须置于本短语的动词和副词之间。

throw up *vt.* 【可分性动词短语】❶(主要用于英国英语中,常用一般时态)produce or bring (a particular person or thing) into existence 出(人才),产生: Our town *threw up* a lot of famous artists. 我们的镇子里出了许多著名的艺术家。Political struggles have *thrown up* some outstanding leaders. 政治斗争催生了一些杰出的领导人。The discussion has *thrown up* a lot of interesting ideas. 在这次讨论会上大家提出了不少有趣的想法。❷ build (something such as a house) very quickly, usually so that it is not of very good quality 匆忙建造: They *threw up*

T

some temporary sheds to hold the new equipment. 他们赶建了一些临时性简易棚来存放新设备。They *threw* that house *up* in only a few weeks. 他们仅用几个星期的时间就把那房子匆匆建了起来。Makeshift dwellings were *thrown up* almost overnight. 几乎是一夜之间一些临时住房建起了。❸(非正式用语)give up (something such as a job)放弃(工作等): At one stage he talked of *throwing up* his job in advertising, but nothing much came of it. 有一段时间他曾说过要放弃他在广告业方面的工作,但后来并没什么结果。A career such as that is not one that should be *thrown up* without serious thought. 像这样一种职业未经认真考虑就放弃,是不应该的。❹(常用被动语态形式)mention (something harmful to someone)提到(对某人不利的事): His father *threw up* Tom's laziness and wastefulness to his teacher. 汤姆的爸爸向汤姆的老师提及了他的懒惰和浪费。That's the third time this week you have *thrown* that mistake *up* to me. 这是你这个星期第三次向我提起那个错误了。

—*vt.* & *vi.* (非正式用语)(of food and drink) come back up from your stomach and out of your mouth; vomit(something such as food)呕吐,吐出(食物等): I felt some nausea, but I didn't *throw up* anything. 我感到恶心,但没吐出什么来。The treatment consisted of making him *throw up* what was in his stomach. 治疗方法包括使他吐出胃中之物。He took the medicine but *threw* it *up* a minute later. 他虽然把药吃了,但一分钟后就吐了出来。

NOTE 1. 当本短语用作及物性动词短语,所带的宾语为代词时,该代词须置于本短语的动词和副词之间。

2. 当本短语作"呕吐,吐出(食物等)"解时,同义短语是 bring up。

thrust into *vt.* 【可分性动词短语】❶(常用一般时态)push or move (something or someone) forcefully into (something such as a space or container)塞入,插入,推入: He *thrust* the gun *into* his pocket and went out of the room. 他把手枪塞进衣袋里便走出了房间。With a shout, he *thrust* his sword *into* his enemy's body. 他大吼一声,将剑刺入敌人的身体之中。The thieves *thrust* him *into* the back room and tied him up on a chair. 盗贼把他推进里间,捆绑在一把椅子上。❷move (yourself or your way) with a lot of force into (something or a crowd)用力挤入: They *thrust* themselves *into* the bus. 他们用力挤入公共汽车。She *thrust* her way *into* the crowd. 她奋力挤入人群之中。

thrust on *vt.* 【可分性动词短语】(常用一般时态,常用被动语态形式) force (someone) to deal with or accept (something)迫使(某人)做……,迫使(某人)接受……;把……强加给(某人): She had more responsibility *thrust on* her. 她有很多事务要承担。I've three of the neighbors' children *thrust on* me for the afternoon! 下午我得照看邻居们的三个孩子! The actress said she had been perfectly happy until fame was *thrust on* her. 那位女演员说,在她身不由己地成名之前她一直过得很快活。

thumb a lift *vi.* (非正式用语)stand near the edge of a road and make a signal with your thumb to passing drivers to ask them to stop and take you somewhere (伸出手并竖起拇指向过路的司机)请求

免费搭车：I *thumbed a lift* to Birmingham. 我向过路的司机请求免费搭车去伯明翰。He was hoping to *thumb a lift* to the stadium. 他想请求免费搭车上体育馆。Sometimes it's dangerous to *thumb a lift* with a stranger. 搭陌生人的车，有时是危险的。I've no car, can I *thumb a lift* home with you? 我没有车，我能不能搭您的车回家？

NOTE 1. 本短语的另外一种表达形式是 thumb a ride。本短语是英国英语用法，thumb a ride 是美国英语用法。

2. 本短语的动词 thumb 可被 hitch 替换，两者的意义和用法相同。

thumbs down ⇨ **thumbs up**

thumbs up *n.* ❶a gesture represented by a closed fist held with the thumb extended upward in approval 赞许的手势：He smiled and gave a big *thumbs up*. 他微笑着给我打了一个十分赞许的手势。❷(非正式用语，常用于动词 get, give 之后)an official approval of something, such as an idea or plan 同意，批准：The manager has given our plan the *thumbs up*. 经理同意了我们的计划。The administration's plan got a *thumbs up* in Congress. 政府的计划在国会中被同意了。Their proposals were finally given the *thumbs up*. 他们的提议最终被同意了。

NOTE 1. 本短语中的名词 thumb 必须用复数形式。

2. 本短语的反义短语是 thumbs down，两者的用法相同。

thus far ⇨ **so far**

tick away/by *vi.* (常用进行时态)(of a machine, especially a clock)beat time with a quiet noise, continuously showing the passing of (minutes, seconds, etc.)(钟表)以滴答声表示时间过去：The time bomb has been *ticking away* for over an hour now, and we are all getting nervous about when it will explode. 这枚定时炸弹现已滴滴答答地响了一个多小时了，我们都很紧张，不知道它何时会爆炸。As the hours *ticked away* we waited anxiously for news about the President's health condition. 几个钟头过去了，我们都焦急地等待着有关总统健康状况的消息。

tick off *vt.* 【可分性动词短语】❶(英国英语用法)put the symbol "√" next to (something)on a list to show that you have examined or dealt with it 在……上画对号，用对号勾出：He *ticked off* my name on a piece of paper. 他在一张纸上的我的名字旁画了个对号。The teacher *ticked* the children's names *off* as they entered. 老师在学生入场的时候，在学生的名单上一一画了对号。Those jobs can be *ticked off*. I've already done them. 这些工作可以用对号勾出来，我已经把它们做完了。*Tick* it *off* in the box. 在方框里画上钩。❷(英国英语用法，非正式用语)speak angrily to and criticize (someone who has done something wrong)训斥(某人)，责骂(某人)：If I'm late again, I'll be *ticked off* by my boss. 如果我再迟到就会遭到老板的训斥。I *ticked* the rude fellow *off* for speaking to me in that way. 那个粗野的家伙以那种方式和我说话，所以我把他骂了。His mum *ticked* him *off* at home. 他妈妈在家里责骂了他。❸(美国英语用法，非正式用语)make (someone) angry or annoyed 使(某人)感到气愤，使(某人)感到烦恼：It really *ticks* me *off* when she doesn't keep her promises. 她不遵守承诺令我感到十分气愤。Constant delays *ticked* me *off*. 持续的延误使我感到烦恼。

NOTE 当本短语所带的宾语是代词时，该代

词须置于本短语的动词和副词之间。

tick over *vi.* (英国英语用法,常用进行时态) ❶(of a motor engine) continue working at a low speed or rate, for example before the gears are engaged and the vehicle moves off (汽车发动机)慢转,空转: If you stay in the car with the engine *ticking over*, the police cannot charge you with unlawful parking. 如果你待在车里,让发动机慢慢地转着,警察就不会指控你违章停车。If an engine *ticks over* too slowly or too fast, an adjustment must be made to the carburetor. 如果汽车发动机空转的速度过慢或过快,就必须要调整汽化器。❷(非正式用语)(especially of a business) operate steadily but not very well (尤指生意)平稳运营但状况不佳: During the summer months the company just *ticks over*. 在夏季的几个月里,公司的运营状况不太好。The market is at least *ticking over*. 市场至少是在平稳运营。

tide over *vt.* 【可分性动词短语】(非正式用语,常用一般时态,一般不用被动语态形式) help (someone) to get through a difficult period of time, especially by lending money until he or she can get some more (尤指通过贷款)帮助(某人)度过(困难时期): Can you lend me some money to *tide* me *over* till the payday? 你能借我点钱帮助我熬到发薪日吗? The Chinese President called on the international community to join hands to *tide over* the current global financial crisis at the G20 financial summit in London. 中国国家主席在伦敦二十国集团金融峰会上呼吁国际社会携手合作、共同渡过当前的全球性经济危机。

NOTE 当本短语所带的宾语是代词时,该代词须置于本短语的动词和副词之间。

tidy up *vt.* & *vi.* put things back in their correct places so that everything is neat; make (a room) look better by putting things back in their proper places; put (a room) in order 收拾,使(房间)整洁: I really must *tidy up*, not wanting the guests to see the mess. 我真得收拾一下,别让客人看到这乱糟糟的东西。When are you going to *tidy* your room *up*, Tom? 汤姆,你打算什么时候收拾自己的房间呀? I must *tidy up* my resume before the interview tomorrow. 我在明天去面试之前必须把简历整理一下。

—*vt.* 【可分性动词短语】make (yourself) look better by washing your face, brushing your hair, etc. 梳洗(自己): I ought to have found a wash-room and *tidied* myself *up*. 我本应找个盥洗室梳理一下。

NOTE 当本短语用作及物性动词短语,所带的宾语是代词时,该代词须置于本短语的动词和副词之间。

tie down *vt.* 【可分性动词短语】(常用被动语态形式) ❶(非正式用语,用一般时态) stop (someone) from being free to do what he or she wants; restrict or limit (someone's freedom of action or movement) 限制,束缚(某人行动的自由): I don't want to *tie* you *down*, feel free to do it by using your own ideas. 我不想限制你,这事随便以你自己的主意去做吧。Having an old sick relative to look after really *ties* you *down*. 照顾一位年老有病的亲戚确实会使你无法脱身。He refused to be *tied down* by petty restrictions. 他不愿受琐细的规章所束缚。He was *tied down* by his work. 工作使他不得自由。❷ keep (usually an enemy) in one place 牵制(常指敌人): A small rebel force is *tying down* thousands of government troops. 一小股叛军牵制了数

千之众的政府军。The navy *tied* the enemy *down* with big gun fire while the marines landed on the beach. 海军用炮火牵制住了敌人,陆战队趁机抢滩登陆。Armour coming up in support was *tied down* by air strikes. 前来增援的装甲部队被来自空中的打击牵制住了。

NOTE 当本短语所带的宾语是代词时,该代词须置于本短语的动词和副词之间。

tie the knot *vi.* (非正式用语,常与 with 连用) get married 结婚: Many young Chinese chose to *tie the knot* on the day of the three eights, that is, 8/8/2008, when Beijing Olympic Games opened. 许多中国的年轻人都选择了在有三个"8"的这个日子结婚,即 2008 年 8 月 8 日北京奥运会开幕这一天。He *tied the knot* with the model less than three months after they first met. 他与那个模特在相识不到三个月后便结婚了。

NOTE 1. 本短语的名词 knot 前可使用 marriage,意义不变。

2. 本短语的反义短语是 untie the knot。例如:

> Now that divorce is easier, *untying the knot* is no longer such a problem.
> 现在离婚很容易,要解除婚姻关系不再是个难题了。

tie up *vt.* 【可分性动词短语】❶tie (the ends of something) together 系住,包扎: *Tie up* your shoelaces before you run. 在跑前,你要把鞋带系好。He *tied up* the bag and took it outside. 他把袋子捆好后搬到了外面。He *tied* the package *up* and put a label on it. 他把包裹捆好,然后往上放了个标签。Make sure the parcel is securely *tied up* before you post it. 包裹在寄出之前务必要包扎好。❷ fasten ropes or string, etc. around (someone) so that he or she cannot move or escape 捆绑(某人): The thieves *tied* the owner of the jewels *up* and locked him in the cupboard. 盗贼们把珠宝的主人捆绑起来锁到了柜橱里。The three robbers thrust him into the back room and *tied* him *up*. 三名劫匪将他推入后房并把他捆绑了起来。He was *tied up* to the bed by the burglars. 他被入室窃贼们绑在了床上。❸fasten (an animal such as a horse or a dog) to (something such as a post) so that it cannot wander off 把(马或狗等动物)拴在……上: This is where you *tie up* your horse. 这是你拴马的地方。Would you go and *tie* your horse *up* please? 请你去把你的马拴上,好吗? ❹(非正式用语,常用被动语态形式,用一般时态) complete (the arrangements or organization of something); finish (something) 安排妥当;完成(某事): I like to get all the arrangements for a holiday *tied up* a month in advance. 我要提前一个月把度假的安排全部搞定。I've just *tied up* arrangements for a bank loan. 我已为银行的贷款做好了一切安排。I'd like to *tie* the project *up* before I leave. 在我离职前,我要把这个项目做完。❺(非正式用语,常用被动语态形式,用一般时态) keep (someone) very busy or occupied 使(某人)繁忙不堪;占用: I'm sure this work will *tie* me *up* for the next two weeks. 这项工作肯定会使我下两周繁忙不堪了。This project *tied up* a great deal of manpower. 这项工程占用了大量的人力。I can't come out tonight , I'm *tied up* at work. 今晚我出不来了,我有工作脱不开身。She has been *tying up* the phone lines for hours now. 她现已占用电话线数小时。❻(非正式用语,常用被动

语态形式，与 in 连用）place (money) in an account, business, etc. where free use is limited 把（资金等）用于某一用途（而不能随意动用）: Her money is *tied up* in a trust fund and she can't take it out. 她的钱存入了信托基金，所以提不出来。All his money is *tied up* in stocks. 他所有的资金都套在了股票上，因而无法动用。❼ (cause to) stop working; delay（使）停顿；阻碍：The stalled bus *tied* the traffic *up* for over an hour. 抛锚的公共汽车使交通停顿了一个多小时。The traffic in the center of the city was *tied up* by the parade. 游行队伍使市区中心的交通停顿。The strike tied up production for a week. 这次罢工造成停产一周。

—*vt* & *vi*. (of a ship or boat) be fastened to something, or fasten (a boat) to something（舰船）停泊，系泊：The big battle cruisers *tie up* at the island's western end. 几艘巨大的战舰都停泊在海岛的西端。This is the proper way to *tie up* your boat. 这才是船只系泊的正确方法。

NOTE 当本短语用作及物性动词短语，所带的宾语是代词时，该代词须置于本短语的动词和副词之间。

tie up with *vt*.【可分性动词短语】（非正式用语，常用被动语态形式，用一般时态）connect (something) with (something else) 把……与……联系起来：The police are trying to *tie up* his escape from prison *with* the murder. 警方试图把他越狱逃跑与那起谋杀联系起来。The future of the island is *tied up with* the fortunes of the ruling power. 该岛的前途与统治集团的命运紧密相连。

time after time *adv*. many times, usually so often that you become annoyed; again and again; repeatedly 屡次，反复地，再三地：I have told him *time after time* not to park the car there. 我曾屡次跟他说过，叫他不要把车停在那里。*Time after time*, I hear the stories of missing children on the news. 我多次从新闻中听到儿童失踪的事。You've made the same error *time after time*! Please try to be more careful! 同样的错误你一犯再犯！请你尽量多注意！

time and time again *adv*. many times; on many occasions, usually so often that you become annoyed 反复地，多次地，经常不断地：However, our endeavor for peace has *time and again* been challenged by the opposite forces. 但是，我们的和平努力一再受到"反对"势力的挑战。*Time and time again* we warned him not to do it, but he just wouldn't listen. 我们一再警告他不要做那件事，可他就是不听。

time zone *n*. one of the areas that the world is divided into for measuring time 时区：The world is divided into a number of standard *time zones*. 世界被划分成一些不同的标准时区。If you go from New York to London, you cross five *time zones*. 如果你从纽约去伦敦，要跨越五个时区。

tip over *v*. (cause to) fall over or turn over（使）翻倒，翻转：Who knocked the bottle over? It couldn't have *tipped over* by itself. 是谁把瓶子弄倒的？它不会自己翻倒的。She *tipped over* the chair and collapsed. 她弄翻了椅子并摔倒了。He *tipped* the table *over* in front of him. 他把他前面的桌子弄倒了。I fell against the man beside me and *tipped* him *over*. 我倒在了我身边的那个人身上，并把他弄倒了。

NOTE 当本短语用作及物性动词短语，所带的宾语是代词时，该代词须置于本短语的动词和副词之间。

tip up *v.* (cause to) turn upwards around a hinge or pivot (使)(围绕铰链或枢轴)向上翻起：The seats in this cinema *tip up* so that you can get past the other people in the row. 这家影院中的座位都可以翻起来，这样你就可以从同排的其他观众前走过去。Many theatres and cinemas have seats that can be *tipped up*. 很多影剧院都装有可以翻起来的座位。

NOTE 本短语可转化为复合词 tip-up，意为"翻起来的；折叠的"。

tire of *vt.* 【不可分性动词短语】(无被动语态形式) grow weary of (someone or something); no longer be interested in or become bored with (someone, something) 失去兴趣；厌烦：She soon *tired of* doing the same thing everyday. 她很快就对每天做同样的事情失去了兴趣。He was *tired of* people telling him what to do. 他讨厌向他发号施令的人。The things *of* which he never *tires* are gardening and music. 从事园艺和听音乐是他百做不厌的事情。

tire out *vt.* 【可分性动词短语】❶(常用被动语态形式) exhaust or tire (someone, oneself or an animal) completely 使……疲劳不堪：The long journey *tired* us all *out*. 这次长途旅行把我们都累坏了。He shouldn't *tire* himself *out* like that. 他不应该把自己搞得那样疲劳不堪。Too much work will *tire out* the horses. 过多的活儿会累坏马匹的。❷ become exhausted 疲劳不堪：He's worried that our team is going to *tire out*. 他担心我们队会疲劳不堪。When I had the flu, I found that I *tired out* easily. 我发现我在患流感时很容易疲倦。

NOTE 1. 当本短语所带的宾语是代词时，该代词须置于本短语的动词和副词之间。

2. 本短语不能与表示程度的副词如 completely, entirely, extremely, thoroughly 和 utterly 等连用。

tired of *adj.* no longer wanting something or wanting to do something because you are bored with it or annoyed by it 厌烦，讨厌：A Japanese man who said he was *tired of* life killed seven people and wounded more than a dozen with a knife on Sunday in a Tokyo shopping street. 一名自称厌倦生活的日本男子于星期日在东京的一条商业街上持刀刺死七人，刺伤十多人。I am *tired of* watching television, let's go for a walk. 我看腻了电视，咱们去散步吧。She's growing *tired of* going into that office every day. 她为每天都要去那间办公室而感到厌倦了。I'm *tired of* you telling me what to do all the time. 我讨厌你总是对我指手画脚。

tired out *adj.* exhausted or extremely tired 筋疲力尽，疲劳不堪的：I must sit down and have a rest, I'm *tired out*. 我得坐下来休息一下了，我太累了。She looked *tired out* after her long journey. 长途旅行过后，她看上去疲劳不堪了。

tit for tat *n.* (非正式用语) something unpleasant done in return for something unpleasant one has suffered; something you do to harm someone because he or she has harmed you 针锋相对，一报还一报：I didn't invite her to my party because she didn't invite me to hers. It was just *tit for tat*. 我没有请她参加我的聚会，因为她上次举行聚会时没邀请我。这就叫一报还一报。I told him if he did me any harm I would return *tit for tat*. 我告诉他,如果他加害于我,我就要以牙还牙。If you hit me, I'll hit you back, *tit for tat*. 如果你打我,我就还击。一报还一报嘛。

NOTE 1. 本短语通常以单数形式使用,复数形式是 tit for tats。例如:

> Cristina and Chris Brown go *tit for tats*.
> 克里斯蒂娜和克里斯・布朗两人针锋相对。

2. 本短语可转换为复合词 tit-for-tat,意为"针锋相对的,报复的"。例如:

> Their *tit-for-tat* trade disputes finally led to an all-out trade war.
> 他们针锋相对的贸易争端终于导致全面的贸易战。

to a certain degree *adv.* partly but not entirely 在一定程度上,在某种程度上:I think that's true *to a certain degree*, but the situation is not quite so simple. 我认为那有几分正确,但情况并不那么简单。He is, *to a certain degree*, disinclined to believe me. 他有点不愿相信我。To increase exchanges and understanding between different cultures so as to promote peace will, *to a certain degree*, have a bearing on the fate of mankind in the 21st century. 增进不同文化之间的互相理解和交流而促进和平将在一定程度上影响 21 世纪人类的命运。I can tell you that I've solved this problem *to a certain degree*. 我可以告诉你,在某种程度上,我已经解决了这个问题。

NOTE 1. 本短语一般用于句尾或句中。但如果强调,也可置于句首。例如:

> *To a certain degree*, the pedestrian was responsible for the traffic accident.
> 在一定程度上,这名行人在这起交通事故中负有责任。

2. 本短语另外的表达形式是 to a certain extent, to some degree 和 to some extent.

3. 本短语的同义短语是 in a sense 和 in a way。

to a certain extent ⇨ **to a certain degree**

to a day ⇨ **to the day**

to a great degree *adv.* to a great extent 非常地,极度地,在很大程度上:In some things she must have been stupid *to a great degree*. 在有些事情上,她肯定是非常愚蠢的。She's untidy *to a great degree*, her papers are all over the floor! 她这个人极不整洁,文件扔得满地都是! *To a great degree* parents should take the blame. 在很大程度上,家长应该负责任。

NOTE 本短语的形容词 great 可被 high, large 等替换,构成的短语与本短语意义和用法相同。

to/for all intents and purposes *adv.* in almost every way; exactly; virtually 几乎在各个方面,事实上,实际上:Escape from that prison was, *for all intents and purposes*, impossible. 从那座监狱里逃出去,几乎是不可能的。The "revised edition" is *to all intents and purposes* a new book. 这部"修订版"几乎就是一部新书。*For all intents and purposes* the matter is settled. 这件事实际上已经得到了解决。

NOTE 1. to all intents and purposes 是英国英语用法,for all intents and purposes 是美国英语用法。

2. 本短语的同义短语是 in effect, in essence 和 in practice。

to and fro *adv.* in one direction and then back again; backwards and forwards 来回地,往复地:The pendulum swung *to* *and fro*. 钟摆来回地摆动。Trucks full of sugar cane are rushing *to and fro* between sugar farm and sugar refinery mill. 满载着甘蔗的卡车往复穿梭于甘蔗园和制糖厂之间。

NOTE 1. 本短语的同义短语是 back and forth 和 backwards and forwards。

2. 本短语可转化为复合词 to (-) and (-) fro,意为"来来往往的,往复的";还可用作名词,意为"来来往往,往复,动摇"。

to be sure *adv.* (used for admitting that something is true, before you say something that seems to be the opposite of this) without a doubt; certainly; surely 毫无疑问,的确: *To be sure*, most people are law-abiding, but crime remains a problem. 毫无疑问,大多数的人都安分守法,但犯罪仍然是个问题。She is not pretty, *to be sure*, but she is very intelligent. 她的确不漂亮,可她非常聪明。

to begin with *adv.* ❶(常用于口语中)(used for introducing the first thing in a list of things you are going to say) in the first place; first of all 首先,第一: The meeting, *to begin with*, recalled the latest advances of biochemistry all over the world. 会议首先回顾了世界生物化学的最新进展。I'm not going. *To begin with* I haven't got a ticket, and secondly I don't like the play. 我不去。一是我没有票,二是我不喜欢这出戏。❷ at the beginning of a process, event or situation; initially 起初,开始时: Why didn't you get involved *to begin with*? 你为什么一开始没有参与呢? *To begin with*, things went quite well, but later on we ran into trouble. 起初事情进展得十分顺利,但后来我们就遇到了麻烦。She resisted *to begin with*, but we were finally able to talk her around to our point of view. 她开始时反对,但我们终于说服她接受了我们的观点。

NOTE 1. 本短语是插入语,在句中作状语。当本短语作"首先,第一"解,用来表示顺序时,通常与 secondly(其次), thirdly(再次)等词连用。而当本短语作"起初,开始时"解,用来表示时间的先后时,通常与 later (on)(后来), finally (最终)等词连用。

2. 不要将本短语与 begin with 混淆,两者的意义和用法不同。见 begin with。

3. 本短语与 to start with 意义和用法相同。

to date *adv.* (正式用语) up to now; until the present time 迄今,到目前为止: *To date*, Project Hope has received more than 3 billion yuan of domestic and overseas donations, said the founder of the project. 希望工程的发起人称:迄今,希望工程已收到的国内外捐款已超过30亿元。Contributions *to date* are encouraging, but far short of needs. 目前的捐赠数量令人鼓舞,但仍远不能满足需要。

NOTE 1. 作为副词性短语,本短语一般在句中作状语,但也可作后置定语。

2. 本短语的比较级形式是 more to date, 最高级形式是 most to date。

to one's credit *adv.* ❶ deserving praise or respect 值得赞扬,值得尊敬: *To his great credit*, Jackson never told anyone exactly what had happened. 杰克逊从没告诉过任何人到底发生了什么,这点十分值得赞扬。Jane, *to her credit*, did not believe his story. 简没有相信他编造的故事,值得赞扬。It was greatly *to her credit* that she managed to stay calm. 她保持了冷静,值得大为称赞。❷ in someone's name; belonging to or done by someone

在某人的名下；由某人所作：He has over 20 books and 15 academic papers *to his credit*. 他已写了 20 多本书和 15 篇学术论文。

to one's heart's content *adv.* to your complete satisfaction, without limitation; as much or as often as you like 尽情地，痛快地：I was delighted to be able to eat my favorite dishes *to my heart's content*. 我很高兴能尽情地吃我喜欢的那些菜肴。It's the weekend, so you can listen to the music *to your heart's content*. 是周末了，你可以痛痛快快地欣赏音乐了。

to one's knowledge *adv.* as far as one knows 就某人所知：I am not quite sure, but *to my knowledge* his story is true. 我不能太肯定，但就我所知，他说的情况是真实的。*To my knowledge*, the peace-keeping operations in Liberia were not discussed during the consultations between the vice ministers of defense of the two countries. 据我了解，利比里亚的维和问题并未在两国国防部副部长级磋商中讨论。"Has she arrived?" "Not *to my knowledge*." "她到了吗？""据我所知，还没有。"

NOTE 本短语可扩展为 to the best of one's knowledge 的形式。例如：

> He has been there several times, *to the best of my knowledge*.
> 据我所确知，他已去过那里数次。

to one's liking *adv.* & *adj.* to one's taste, interests or wishes; suited to one's ideas or needs 合某人口味地(的)；合某人意愿地(的)：I have had the office decorated *to my liking*. 我已按自己的口味把办公室装饰了一番。The dishes here in the south are not *to my liking*. 南方这儿的菜肴都不合我的口味。Let's see if we can find something *to her liking*. 咱们看看能不能找到合她意的东西。Did they find the temperature there *to their liking*? 那里的温度适合于他们吗？

NOTE 本短语的同义短语是 to one's taste。

to one's mind *adv.* (用于口语中)(used for emphasizing that one is expressing his own opinion) according to what one thinks; to one's way of thinking 照某人的看法，据某人的意见：*To my mind*, it's all a lot of nonsense! 照我看，这全是一派胡言！*To my mind*, she's quite wrong. 据我看来，她是完全错的。The professor made a comment about her appearance that, *to her mind*, was not appropriate. 教授对她的外表作了一番评论，但她认为评论不妥。

NOTE 1. 本短语常以 to my mind 的形式使用。

2. 本短语一般用于句首。

3. 不要将本短语与 in one's mind 混淆。in one's mind 意为"在某人的头脑中"。例如：

> I wonder what's going on *in her mind*.
> 我不知道她在想什么。

4. 本短语与 in one's opinion 意义和用法相同，两者可互换使用。见 in one's opinion。

to one's surprise *adv.* to one's (great) astonishment 使某人(甚感)吃惊：*To our surprise*, by the time we got there all were gone. 令我们吃惊的是，等我们赶到那里时，所有的人都不见了。Much *to my surprise*, they offered me the job. 使我甚为吃惊的是，他们竟给了我这份工作。

NOTE 在一般情况下，本短语置于句首使用，并用逗号与其后的具有完整结构的句子分开。

to one's taste *adj.* &*adv.* to one's liking; in a way that one likes 合某人口味(的), 合某人意愿(的):The dish you cooked is *to my taste*. 你做的菜合我的口味。Their house has not been decorated *to my taste*, but it's very luxurious. 他们的房子装修得不合我的品味,但是非常豪华。

NOTE 不要将本短语与 to taste 混淆。to taste 意为"随个人的口味"。例如:

> Add salt and pepper *to taste*.
> 随个人口味加盐和胡椒。

to perfection *adv.* in a way that could not be better; extremely well; perfectly 极好,完美地:The beef was cooked *to perfection*. 这牛肉烧得好极了。I cooked my steak *to perfection* and both my husband and I enjoyed it. 我做的牛排好极了,我丈夫和我都喜欢吃。The dress fitted her *to perfection*. 这件连衣裙她穿太合适了。He imitates people *to perfection*. 他模仿别人,惟妙惟肖。

to say nothing of *prep.* (used for adding extra information to what you have just said)in addition to; without ever needing to say about (用来强调所述内容)除了……以外,更不必说:My sister takes singing and dancing lessons, *to say nothing of* swimming and tennis lessons. 我妹妹除了游泳和网球课以外,还修歌舞课程。Their house is worth at least a million, *to say nothing of* their other assets. 光他们的房子就值至少 100 万,更不必说他们的其他财产了。

to some degree ⇨ **to a certain degree**

to some extent ⇨ **to a certain degree**

to start with *adv.* ❶at the beginning; initially 起初,开始时:"*To start with*, the 'Internet syndrome' sufferers turn to the virtual world for comfort and gradually become more reluctant to face life," said the medical expert. "起初,这些患有'因特网综合征'的人求助于虚拟世界寻求安慰,后来逐渐地越来越不愿面对生活。"这位医学专家说道。I was a bit nervous *to start with*, but I soon got used to it. 我开始时有点紧张,但很快就适应了。❷(used before the first in a list of facts, reasons, etc.)in the first place; first and foremost (用于所列举的一系列事实、理由等之前)首先,第一:There are many reasons why she shouldn't get the job. *To start with*, she isn't qualified. 她不应该获得这份工作的原因有很多。首先,她不具备资格。It won't work: *to start with*, it would take too long, and secondly it would cost too much. 这行不通。第一,它用时太长。第二,它花费太大。

NOTE 1. 本短语是插入语,在句中作状语。

2. 不要将本短语与 start with 混淆,两者的意义和用法不同。start with 是一个动词性短语,意为"(使)以……开始"。

to taste ⇨ **to one's taste**

to tell the truth *adv.* (used for admitting something, or for saying what you really think about something)if I am to tell the truth; really; actually 实话讲,老实说:*To tell* you *the truth*, I'm bored with my present job. 实话对你讲,我对我现在这份工作不感兴趣。*To tell the truth*, I don't care. 老实说,我并不在乎。*To tell the truth* I forgot it was Mother's birthday last Friday. 我真的忘记了上周五是妈妈的生日。

NOTE 本短语用于表达个人对某事的真实想法或承认某事等。在使用本短语时,一般要将其置于句首,后用逗号,再接

T

"主语+动词"的句子。

to the best of one's knowledge ⇨ **to one's knowledge**

to the contrary *adj.* & *adv.* to the opposite effect; different(ly)相反的(地),完全不同的(地): You may be right, there is no evidence *to the contrary*. 你也许是对的,因为没有相反的证据证明你不对。I asked him to behave himself, but the boy did everything *to the contrary*. 我要他规矩点,可这个男孩却反其道而行之。He also said that imposing sanctions or restrictions will not help solve the problem, but *to the contrary* it will hurt the interests of both sides. 他还指出,实行制裁或限制不但无助于问题的解决,相反会损害双方的利益。

to the core *adv.* (used for emphasizing the character of someone or something) thoroughly; completely; in every part (用于强调某人或某物的特点)地道地;十足地:He is honest *to the core*. 他这个人真是诚实到家了。I was shocked *to the core*. 我感到极为震惊。She's a feminist *to the core*. 她是个十足的女权主义者。The apple is rotten *to the core*. 这个苹果烂透了。

to the day *adv.* (英国英语用法)(used for saying that something happened on the same day in a different year)exactly; to a degree of accuracy measured in units of days 恰好,一天也不差: It is now five years *to the day*. 到现在恰好是五年。Her father died ten years ago *to the day*. 她的父亲去世已十年整。It is now 22 years *to the day* since the Berlin Wall fell in November 1989. 自 1989 年 11 月柏林墙被推倒到现在整整 22 年了。

NOTE 1. 本短语的另外一种表达形式是 *to a day*. 但本短语更为常用。

2. 不要将本短语与 to date 混淆。to date 虽也是一副词性短语,但它的意思是"到目前为止","迄今"。

to the fore *adv.* (常与动词 bring 或 come 连用)(of something or someone) into a noticeable or leading position 进入显著位置,崭露头角: The issue of taxation has once again come *to the fore*. 税收再次成为显著的问题。The new film brings the director and the leading actress *to the fore*. 这部新影片使该片的导演和女主演崭露头角。

to the full *adv.* to the greatest degree or extent; completely or entirely; very much; fully 非常充分: The children enjoyed their trip *to the full*. 孩子们非常喜欢他们的旅行。We appreciated *to the full* the teacher's help. 我们十分感激老师的帮助。My aim is to enjoy life *to the full*. 我的目的是充分享受人生。

NOTE 本短语的比较级形式是 more to the full,最高级形式是 to the fullest。

to the letter *adv.* (正式用语)exactly; to the fullest degree 确实地;不折不扣地: I expect my instructions to be carried out *to the letter*. 我希望我的指示能得到确实地执行。You must obey my orders *to the letter*. Otherwise, you'll lose your job. 你必须不折不扣地服从我的命令。否则,就会丢掉你的工作。

to the point *adj.* & *adv.* relevant(ly) to the subject under discussion 中肯(地),切题(地): His remarks are short and quite *to the point*. 他的言语简洁且十分中肯。Please be concise and *to the point*. 务请简明扼要。In spite of all his talk he never seems to come *to the point*. 他虽然

说了那么多话,但似乎从没谈及正题。We haven't got more time, so please get *to the point*. 我们没有更多的时间,所以请直谈正题。

to the tune of *prep.* (非正式用语)(used for emphasizing how large an amount is) to the amount/sum of 达到……数量: They're running Simpson's story *to the tune of* five pages an installment. 他们连续刊载辛普森的故事每期长达五页。The company is in debt *to the tune of* $2 billion. 该公司负债达 20 亿美元。

together with *prep.* in the company of; along with; in addition to 和……一起,连同: He said that we should work *together with* other countries to tide over the crisis. 他说,我们应该与其他国家共同努力,渡过危机。*Together with* our African brothers, we are ready to do whatever is helpful to peace and development in Africa. 凡是有利于非洲和平与发展的,我们都愿意同非洲的兄弟国家一道去做。Private Lynch, 20, *together with* six other US soldiers, was captured by the Iraqi troops near the city of Nasiriya . 二十岁的二等兵林奇连同其他六名美军士兵一起在纳西里耶附近被伊军俘虏。

NOTE 1. 本短语作为介词性短语,在句中是附加成分,不影响句中谓语动词的单复数形式。例如:

> The woman, *together with* her three children, has come.
> 那名妇女和她的三个孩子已经来了。

与本短语用法相同的还有 accompanied by, along with, in company with 等。

2. 本短语与 along with 稍有不同。前者只表示“与……一道”,而后者还含有“配合”“协调”之意。

toll the death knell for/of ⇨ **sound the death knell for/of**

too … to … *conj.* so much (of a particular quality) that something is not possible; that cannot 太……以致不能……: After the powerful earthquake, residents spent the night outdoors, *too* afraid of aftershocks *to* sleep indoors. 强烈地震后,市民们害怕余震而不敢在室内睡觉,都在户外过夜。It's *too* early for us *to* go yet. 我们现在就去有点太早。He is *too* much of a coward *to* fight. 他太懦弱,不敢抗争。It is *too* good *to* be true. 这件事太好了,好像不是真的。

NOTE 1. 在本短语中,too 是程度副词,修饰其后所接的形容词或副词;而 to 是不定式符号,后接原形动词,作结果状语。

2. 本短语本身表示否定意义。但是当 too 前面有 all, but, never, not, only 时,本短语则不再表示否定。例如:

> They are all *too* satisfied *to* follow others suit without the pain of thought for themselves.
> 他们十分满足于依样学样,而不肯自己花力气、动脑筋。
> He knew but *too* well *to* hold his tongue on that occasion.
> 他深知在那种场合少说为妙。
> One is never *too* old *to* learn.
> 活到老,学到老。
> Swimming is not *too* difficult *to* learn.
> 游泳并不十分难学。
> She will be only *too* pleased *to* help me master the new skill.
> 她很愿意帮助我掌握那门新的技艺。

另外,当 to 前面用否定词 not 时,本短语则表示“太……不会不……”,具有肯定意义。如:

T

He is *too* careful not *to* have noticed it. 他那么小心,一定会注意到这一点的。

touch down *vi.* (of something such as a plane or spacecraft) land; reach the ground (飞机或宇航器等)降落,着陆: The plane carrying the Olympic flame *touched down* at a military airbase in Pakistan and was welcomed by many people. 运送奥运圣火的专机降落在巴基斯坦的一个空军基地并受到了很多人的欢迎。The Phoenix Mars Lander *touched down* safely on the surface of the red planet on May 25, NASA mission controllers said. 美国国家航空航天局飞行控制人员宣布,"凤凰"号火星着陆探测器已于5月25日安全地在那颗红色星球的表面上着陆。In Florida, tornadoes *touched down* in at least three counties yesterday. 昨天,龙卷风至少在佛罗里达州的三个郡登陆。

NOTE 本短语可转化为复合词 touchdown, 意为"(飞机等的)降落,降落时间;(橄榄球的)底线得分"。

touch on/upon *vt.* ❶ feel (someone) on (a part of the body)接触,触碰(某人身体的某一部位): Suddenly I felt someone *touching* me *on* the arm to attract my attention. 我突然感觉到有人碰了一下我的胳膊以吸引我的注意力。❷(常用一般时态) mention (something such as a subject or problem) briefly when you are talking or writing 谈及,涉及,提到(某一主题或问题等): During the interview, we only *touched on* how much I would be paid. 在面试中,我们只谈论了我的报酬多少。The report also *touched upon* the serious economic problems that would crop up. 报告还提到了可能出现的严重经济问题。It is briefly *touched upon* in her article. 在他的文章中,这事只是略略地提了一下。❸(无被动语态形式,常用一般时态) relate to or show some connection with (a subject)与……有关: How does your story *touch on* this case? 你的陈述与此案有什么关系呢? He is reading all the current publications *touching on* his field of research. 所有最近出版的涉及他研究范围的出版物,他都在读。He likes to read all the books that *touch upon* computer science. 凡是与计算机科学有关的书籍他都喜欢读。❹(用一般时态) come very near or be much like (something)接近,近乎: His manner was very inconsiderate, *touching on* rudeness. 他的态度十分轻率,近乎于粗野。

NOTE 本短语中的 upon 用法比 on 正式,但不及 on 常用。

touch up *v.* ❶ make (a surface) look better with small improvements 对(……的表面)稍加修饰: It's only a little scratch. I can *touch* it *up* easily. 这只是一处小小的划痕。我会很容易把它修整好。He *touched up* the scratches with a little paint. 他用一点油漆把几处划痕修整好。Do not worry about the scratches on the wall, they can easily be *touched up*. 不用担心墙上的那些划痕,很容易修整好的。❷ improve (a painting, photograph, or writing, etc.)by making small changes or additions 润色,改进(图画、照片或文稿等): This is the original painting, without being *touched up* in any way. 这是一件油画的原作,没有做过任何方式的润色。He *touched up* the painting so it looked as good as new. 他把这幅画又修饰了一番,因此它看上去就和新的一样好。I want to spend a few days to *touch*

T

the thesis *up* before I send it to the professor. 我想花几天时间把论文修改一下,再把它交给教授。On the whole, the article is very well written, but the last part needs *touching up*. 总体来说,这篇文章写得不错,只是最后一部分需要再改进一下。

NOTE 当本短语所带的宾语是代词时,该代词须置于本短语的动词和副词之间。

toy with *vt.*【不可分性动词短语】❶ keep touching or moving (an object) with your fingers, especially while you are thinking about something or feeling nervous(在思考问题或感到紧张时)不断摆弄(某物): He sat in his chair, his feet on the desk, *toying with* a glass paperweight. 他坐在椅子里,把双脚放在办公桌上,手中摆弄着一块玻璃压纸器。The new employee *toyed with* a button on his jacket as he spoke with his boss. 这名新雇员和老板说话时手里不断地摆弄着上衣的一颗纽扣。❷ treat (something or someone) inconsiderably, or not seriously; deal lightly with (someone's emotions)轻率地对待;玩弄(某人的感情): You shouldn't *toy with* great issues. 你不应拿重大问题当儿戏。He makes a great show of being fond of her in front of other people, but he's only *toying with* her really. 他当着别人的面极力表现出他喜欢她,但实际上他只是在玩弄她而已。❸ consider (an idea), but not in a very serious way, and without making a decision 不认真地考虑(某种想法): He *toyed with* the idea of becoming an actor. 他没很认真地考虑过当演员。The idea has been *toyed with*. 这一想法没被认真地考虑过。

trace back to *vt.*【可分性动词短语】(常用一般时态) ❶ discover the source or cause of (something) by going back over a series of events, etc. 追溯……的起源: The custom of celebrating the moon can be *traced back to* the Xia and Shang dynasties of ancient China. 中秋赏月的习俗可以追溯到中国远古时代的夏朝和殷商时期。We can *trace* most forms of energy *back to* the sun directly or indirectly. 我们能将大多数形式的能量直接或间接地归因于太阳。❷ find the origin of (something such as your family) or how it developed (especially by going back in time)(家世)溯源于: His father claims to be able to *trace* the family *back to* the time of the Norman Conquest. 他父亲声称他的家世可追溯到诺曼人征服英国的时代。

NOTE 当本短语作"追溯……的起源"解时,同义短语是 date back to/from。

track down *vt.*【可分性动词短语】find (something or someone) after a difficult or long search or hunting, especially by following signs or clues that show you where they are 找到;追查: I finally managed to *track* him *down* in Manchester. 我终于在曼彻斯特找到了他。After the Sunday bomb attack, the government vowed to *track down* those responsible for the bombing. 星期日的炸弹袭击事件发生后,政府誓言要追查到这起爆炸事件的责任者。We must try to *track* these terrorists *down*. 我们一定要千方百计地追捕到这些恐怖分子。

NOTE 当本短语所带的宾语是代词时,该代词须置于本短语的动词和副词之间。

trade for *vt.*【可分性动词短语】(主要用于美国英语中) agree to exchange (something or someone) for (usually the other thing or someone else) 用……换取……: I *traded* my radio *for* a typewriter. 我用自

己的收音机换得了一台打字机。He was able to ransom the infant by *trading* a horse *for* him. 他用一匹马才赎回了婴孩。

trade in *vt.* ❶(常与 for, on 连用) give (an old car or appliance) as part of the payment for (something new)用(旧车或器件)折价换取(新物): Will the dealer allow us to *trade in* the car for the latest model? 经销商允许我们以这辆汽车折价贴换最新型的车吗? My friend recently *traded* his old Ford *in* for a new Honda. 我朋友最近把他的旧福特轿车折价换购了一辆新本田车。Richard refused to *trade in* his old Canon camera. 理查德不肯折价换掉他那台旧佳能相机。❷(of people, firms, or countries) sell (a certain kind of goods)出售(某种商品): He has been *trading in* furniture for 15 years. 15 年来,他一直销售家具。They became rich by *trading in* palm oil, cocoa and rubber in West Africa. 他们通过在西非销售棕榈油、可可粉和橡胶而发了财。Some shops *trade in* iron and steel products. 一些商店经销钢铁产品。

NOTE 当本短语作"出售(某种商品)"解时,同义短语是 deal in。

trade on *vt.* 【不可分性动词短语】(无被动语态形式,常用一般时态) get (your own advantage) by making use of (something), often in an unfair way (常指不公平地)利用……得到(某种好处): He *traded on* his brother's kindness to get more money from him. 他利用他弟弟的善良,从他那儿弄到了更多的钱。I don't deny that he suffers from poor health, but I think he is *trading on* it in order to get out of as much work as possible. 我不否认他的身体不好,但我认为他正利用这个原因尽可能地少做工作。They are *trading on* their reputation. 他们在利用自己的名声捞取利益。

trail away/off *vi.* (of someone's voice or words) gradually become weak or silent (指某人的声音或话语)变弱,逐渐消失: When he found someone had entered the room, his voice *trailed off* in fear. 当他发现有人进了屋子时,声音便因恐惧而变小了。Her voice *trailed off* as she realized he wasn't listening. 当她意识到他根本没听时,便不再讲了。

transfer to *vt.* ❶(常用被动语态形式) (of someone) move from one job, office, or department to (another within the same company or organization)调转: After five years working in the department, I was *transferred to* another one. 在该部门工作了五年后,我被调到了另外一个部门。Helen was *transferred* from marketing *to* sales. 海伦从市场部调到了销售部。❷move (something or someone) from one place to (another)把……从……转移到……: Wait until the cakes cool before *transferring* them *to* a plate. 等这些蛋糕凉了以后再把它们移放到盘中。*The New York Times* said the 544 Guantanamo detainees have been *transferred to* 39 countries. 据《纽约时报》报道,544 名关塔那摩囚犯已被转移到了 39 个国家。❸give the ownership of (property, etc.) to (another person)把(财产等的)所有权转让给(他人): The present owner will *transfer* the rights in the property *to* your family. 现主人将把这些财产的所有权转让给你家。He has already *transferred* ownership of most of the works *to* a foundation. 他已把大部分作品的所有权转给了一个基金会。❹(cause to) move from one bus, vehicle, plane, or boat to (another) as part of a longer journey (使)中途换乘(汽车、火车等): At this point, passengers will *transfer to* a special bus. 乘客将在这个地方换乘专列巴士。At London we *transferred* from the train *to* a bus. 我们在伦敦由火车换乘了公共汽车。We're being *transferred to* another plane in Amsterdam. 我们要在阿姆斯特丹换乘另外一个航班。❺(of a student) stop studying at one school or university and go to (another)(指学生)转校: The children will *transfer to* a new school in September. 孩子们将在 9 月份转入新学校。❻(主要用于英国英语中) (especially of a football player) stop playing for a club and start playing for (another club)(尤指足球运动员)转会:Some very high-profile British players have *transferred to* clubs abroad. 一些受人高度关注的英国运动员纷纷转会国外。He was *transferred* from Crystal Palace *to* Arsenal for £2. 5 million. 他以 250 万英镑的身价从水晶宫队转会到阿森纳队。❼move (money) from one account or bank to (another)把(资金)从一个账户转移到(另一账户):I need to *transfer* $5,000 *to* my daughter's account. 我需要把 5 000 美元转到我女儿的账户上。More than 70 billion yuan was *transferred* from savings accounts *to* stock trading accounts in the first four months of this year, the bank estimated on Saturday. 该银行星期六估测,今年前四个月,有 700 多亿元的存款转移到了股票的交易账户中。❽copy (a recorded material, etc.) onto (a different medium)把(录音材料等)转录到……:Callas's original recording has been *transferred to* compact disc. 卡拉斯的原始录音已转刻到光盘上。

transform into *vt.*【可分性动词短语】change (something or someone) into (something or someone else)把……变成……: We can *transform* electric energy *into* light energy as well as into heat energy. 我们不仅能把电能变为光能,还能将其变为热能。In only a few years, Shenzhen, a small fishing village, was *transformed into* a big and prosperous city with tall buildings. 仅在几年的时间里,深圳这样一个小渔村就被建设成了一个高楼林立的繁荣大城市。The man was *transformed* from a hard-drinking womanizer by his wife *into* a responsible husband and father. 那位男士被他的妻子从一个酗酒成性、追求女色的人改造成了一个负责任的丈夫和父亲。

translate into *vt.*【可分性动词短语】❶change (spoken or written words) into (another language)把……翻译成……: In the 17th and 18th centuries foreign missionaries *translated* Chinese classics *into* European languages and introduced them to Europe. 在 17 和 18 世纪,外国传教士把中国的文化典籍翻译成西文传到了欧洲。*The Bible* has been *translated into* more than 100 languages.《圣经》已有 100 多种语言的译本了。❷change (something) into (a different form) or express (something) in a different way (for example in action)把……转换成(另外一种形式);把……转化为(行动):We can *translate* this substance *into* concrete application of alloy to the chemical industry. 我们可以把这种物质转换为合金在化学工业中应用。The past years since Hong Kong's return to the motherland saw "one country, two systems" being

T

translated from a scientific concept *into* a vivid reality. 香港回归祖国数年来，见证了"一国两制"由科学构想变为生动现实。

NOTE 当本短语作"把……翻译成……"解时，动词 translate 通常指文字翻译。若表示口语翻译时，则用 interpret。

transmit to *vt.*【不可分性动词短语】(常用被动语态形式) ❶ send out (electrical signals, messages, news, etc.) by radio, etc. (用无线电等)发射；播出(电子信号、消息等)：On board the ship, telephone messages may be *transmitted to* the shore by radio. 在船上，可用无线电把电话信息传递到岸上。Data of the picture taken by the lunar probe satellite has now been *transmitted* back *to* Earth, the China National Space Administration said. 中国国家宇航局宣布，探月卫星所拍摄的图片数据现已传回地面。The final was *transmitted* via satellite *to* over 20 countries. 决赛通过卫星在 20 多个国家直播。❷ pass (something such as a disease or quality) to (someone else) 传播，传染，传给：It is believed that this infection is *transmitted* by certain animals *to* people. 据信，这种传染病是由某些动物传播给人的。Experts fear that bird flu might combine with the human influenza virus to create a new strain that could be easily *transmitted to* humans. 专家们担心，禽流感病毒可能会与人流感病毒相结合成新的变种，那就很容易传染给人了。Your panic and fear may *transmit* itself *to* the horse that you're riding. 你的惊恐会传给你胯下所骑的马匹。None of his fine qualities seem to have been *transmitted to* his son. 他的优秀品质似乎一点儿也没有传给他的儿子。

trip on/over *vt.*【不可分性动词短语】hit your foot on (something) when you are walking and lose your balance so that you fall or nearly fall 被……绊倒：He *tripped on* a cable and broke his ankle. 他绊在了一根电缆上，摔断了踝骨。The cables are all in bright yellow to prevent you from *tripping over* them. 电缆线都呈鲜黄色以避免人们绊到它们。He *tripped over* someone's foot in the dark cinema and almost fell. 他在黑暗的电影院里绊在了一个人的脚上，几乎摔倒。

triumph over *vt.*【不可分性动词短语】(正式用语，常用一般时态) gain victory or success, especially in dealing with (a very difficult situation, something bad or opponent, etc.) 克服(困难等)，战胜(敌人或对手等)：Common sense and friendliness *triumphed over* their problems. 普通常识和友谊解决了他们的问题。Advancing culture is bound to *triumph over* declining culture. 先进的文化必然战胜没落的文化。The Romans *triumphed over* their enemies. 罗马人战胜了他们的敌人。

try it on(with someone) (with someone) *vi.* (英国和澳大利亚英语用法，非正式用语，常用进行时态) behave badly or to try to deceive people, especially in order to make them do something for you 行为粗野；耍弄花招：She slapped his face because he *tried it on with her*. 她因他对她行为粗野而打了他耳光。Don't believe all his sweet talk, he's *trying it on with you*. 不要相信他的甜言蜜语，他是在和你耍花招。

NOTE 不要将本短语与 try it on 混淆。try it on 表示"试穿(衣物)"。例如：

> What a lovely dress! Why don't you *try it on* for size?
> 多可爱的连衣裙！你为什么不试穿下？

try on *vt.* 【可分性动词短语】❶put on (a garment, hat, shoes, etc.) to see if it fits, looks well, etc. 试穿，试戴：*Try* this white shirt *on*. 试试这件白色衬衫吧。She *tried on* several hats before she found one she really liked. 她试了几顶帽子后才找到一顶自己真正喜欢的。It's silly to buy expensive shoes without *trying* them *on*. 不经过试穿就买下昂贵的鞋子是愚蠢的。❷(英国和澳大利亚英语用法，非正式用语，无被动语态形式，常与 with 连用) attempt (something such as a trick)耍弄花招：The policeman warned the man not to *try* anything *on* with him. 警察警告那名男子不要和他耍花招。

NOTE 1. 当本短语所带的宾语是代词时，该代词须置于本短语的动词和副词之间。
2. 本短语可转化为复合词 try-on，意为"试穿，试用；耍花招，欺骗"。

try one's best *vi.* try as hard as you can in order to achieve something 竭尽(某人)所能，尽力：We should *try our best* to help her. 我们应该尽最大努力帮助她。The premier stressed the military forces should *try their best* to open up roads to the epicenter and at the same time to air-drop food and medicine to the areas. 总理强调，部队指战员要全力以赴打通通往震中灾区的道路，同时要将食品和药品空投到灾区。He will *try his best* to help them by means of his conventional medical knowledge. 他会尽力用他所知道的传统医疗知识来帮助他们。

NOTE 本短语的同义短语是 try one's utmost 和 do one's best。

try one's utmost ⇨ **try one's best**

try out *vt.* 【可分性动词短语】❶use, handle or test (something) in order to see if it function well or if you like it 试用，试验(某物)：Let's *try out* the computer before we finally decide to buy it. 在最后决定买下这台电脑之前，咱们先试用一下。Before I purchase that car, I'd like to *try* it *out*. 在买那辆汽车之前我想要试开一下。The idea sounds fine, but we need to *try* it *out* in practice. 这个主意听起来不错，但我们要在实践中试行一下。The idea seems good but it needs to be *tried out*. 这个想法似乎不错，但需要试一下。❷test (someone) to see what he or she is like or whether he or she is suitable or effective 试用，考查(某人)：The director wanted to *try out* several of the new singers for the part. 导演想试用几名新歌手来扮演那一角色。He has got the right person and wants to *try* him *out* on the job. 他已找到了合适的人选，并想在实际工作中考查他一下。

NOTE 1. 当本短语的宾语为代词时，该代词须置于本短语的动词和副词之间。
2. 本短语可转化为复合词 tryout，意为"试用，考察；试演，选拔表演"。

try out for *vt.* 【不可分性动词短语】(主要用于美国英语中) try to become a member of a sports team or get a part in a play or film by showing someone how well you can play or perform 参加(运动员或演员的)选拔：Are you going to *try out for* the college football team? 你要参加入校足球队的选拔吗？Mary is *trying out for* the female lead in the school play. 玛丽在参加一部校园话剧中女主角的选拔。

tuck away *vt.* ❶store or hide (something or someone) somewhere 贮藏；隐藏：(非正式用语，常用被动语态形式) Grandfather *tucked* many old bottles *away* in the cellar. 爷爷把许多旧瓶子收藏在地下室里。*Tuck* this *away* where you can find it later. 把这藏在一个你以后能找到它的地方。I was *tucked away* in a secluded corner of the room. 我被藏在房间的一个隐秘角落里。❷(常用被动语态形式，常与动词 get, have, keep 连用) put (money) in a safe place so that you can use it later 把(钱)存放于安全之处：She's had a lot of money *tucked away*. 她把许多钱存了起来。I bet Grandpa's kept quite a bit *tucked away*. 我敢打赌，爷爷肯定存了好多钱。❸(主要用于英国英语中，非正式用语) eat (great quantities of food) quickly, because you like it or because you are hungry 很快吃掉(大量食物)：The child *tucked away* a small Christmas pudding and a plate of pies. 这孩子很快就吃掉了一份圣诞布丁和一盘馅饼。

NOTE 当本短语所带的宾语是代词时，该代词须置于本短语的动词和副词之间。

tune in *v.* ❶listen to or watch (a particular program broadcast on the radio or television) 收听，收看(某一电台或电视台的节目)：Which station are you *tuning in* to? 你在收听哪个电台？Please *tune in* again tomorrow to hear "How English is Taught in China". 请明天继续收听《英语教学在中国》这一节目。Will you *tune in* to Channel 6 to watch the film *Spider Man II*? 把电视调到 6 频道，看影片《蜘蛛人》第二部吧，好吗？Billions of people all over the world *tuned in* for the wedding ceremony of Prince Charles and Camilla Parker. 全球数十亿人收看了查尔斯王子和卡米拉·帕克的婚礼庆典。❷(非正式用语，用被动语态形式，与 to 连用) understand (something such as a subject or other people's feelings) 了解(某一主题或他人之情感等)：You're more *tuned in* to the subject than most people. 你比大多数人了解这一主题。He is such a politician who's *tuned in* to popular feeling on this issue. 他就是这样一位了解公众对这一问题的想法的政治家。

turn a blind eye (to) *v.* (非正式用语) pretend not to see or notice (someone or something usually bad or illegal), so that you will not have to do anything about it 假装看不见(……)，(对……)熟视无睹：US military officials complained that Pakistani military personnel stationed at border outposts often *turned a blind eye to* Taliban fighters. 美军官员曾抱怨说，驻扎在边境哨所的巴基斯坦军人对塔利班武装分子往往视而不见。Sometimes a store might sell stolen goods because the owner has *turned a blind eye to* where they come from. 有时，商店会出售一些被盗的物品，因为店主不理会这些物品的来源。We should not *turn a blind eye to* terrorism, which is a global threat that has to be dealt with jointly by the international community. 我们不应对恐怖主义熟视无睹，它是国际社会必须共同应对的一个全球性威胁。

NOTE 1. 本短语本身是动宾结构，动词和名词可分开使用。例如：

> *A blind eye* has been *turned to* these irregularities long enough, we shall have to do something about them.
> 相当长时期内，我们对这些违规行为熟视无睹，我们得对它们采取些行动了。

2. 本短语与 turn a deaf ear 意义和用法相同,其中的名词 eye 和 ear 必须用单数形式。

turn a deaf ear (to) *v.* (非正式用语,一般不用被动语态形式)pretend or refuse to listen (to a request, a warning, or an attempt to change your attitude); ignore someone when he or she complains or asks for something 假装听不到(……),(对……)不听,(对……)置若罔闻: Mary *turned a deaf ear to* Liza's asking to ride her bicycle. 莉莎要借骑玛丽的自行车,可玛丽却假装没有听到。I told her not to go, but she *turned a deaf ear to* my warning and got lost. 我告诉她不要去,可她对我的警告却置若罔闻,结果走失了。He has *turned a deaf ear to* what his parents said. 他对父母的话置之不理。The local government continues to *turn a deaf ear* and refuses to protect the rare animals. 当地政府仍然置若罔闻,不去保护那些珍稀动物。

turn against *vt.* (cause to) stop liking or supporting (someone or something) and start opposing them (使)不再喜欢,不再支持;反目: Even those who were once his supporters *turned against* him. 连那些原来支持他的人也不再支持他了。He claims that his ex-wife has tried to *turn* the children *against* him. 他声称他的前妻一直设法使孩子们与他作对。They were very good friends, but with the changes of their political views, they *turned against* each other. 他们曾是最要好的朋友,但随着他们政治观点的变化,他们反目为敌。The weapons with which the bourgeoisie felled feudalism to the ground are now *turned against* the bourgeoisie itself. 资产阶级用来推翻封建制度的武器,现在却对准资产阶级自己了。

turn around/round *v.* ❶(cause to) make a complete turn in order to face in the opposite direction (使)转身,(使)转向: *Turn around* and let me see your profile. 转过身去,让我看看你的侧面。She *turned* her car *round* and drove off the opposite direction. 她把汽车掉过头来,朝相反的方向开去。A cargo plane was hit by a SAM-7 surface to air missile, but it *turned around* and came back to the airport where it safely landed. 一架货机被一枚萨姆-7 型地对空导弹击中,但其调头返回机场并平安着陆。❷(of trade or business) (cause to) stop being unsuccessful and start being successful (使)(经济或贸易状况)好转: Do you think our housing sales will *turn round* during this year? 你认为我们的住房销售在今年中会好转吗? We've hired a new director who we hope will *turn around* the failing company. 我们雇用了一位新董事。我们希望他能使衰退中的公司兴隆起来。The £400 million loan will help *turn* the Russian economy *around*. 4 亿英镑的贷款将有助于俄罗斯的经济好转。❸change one's opinion or argument 改变(意见或论点): The chairman seems to have quite *turned round*. 主席的意见似乎大有改变。It was your idea, so don't *turn around* and say you're too busy. 这可是你的主意,所以你不要改口说你太忙。

NOTE 1. turn round 主要用于美国英语中,而 turn around 则主要用于英国英语中。
2. 本短语可转化为复合词 turnaround 或 turn (-)round,意为"回车场,回车道;(立场、方针等的)改变"。

turn away *vt.* &*vi.* (cause to) change the position of your body or head so that you are facing in a different direction (使)(身或脸)转过去: Mary glared at the other man for a while and then *turned away*. 玛丽盯着另外那个男人看了一会儿,然后才转过身去。She *turned away* in horror at the sight of so much blood. 看到这么多的血,她吓得把脸扭向了一边。She *turned* her head *away* so that they could not see her tears. 她把头转了过去,好不让他们看到她的眼泪。

—*vt.*【可分性动词短语】❶ refuse to allow (someone) to enter a place 拒绝让(某人)入内: The theatre *turned* us *away* at the entrance because we hadn't got tickets. 因为我们没有票,所以剧院拒绝我们入场。Hundreds of tourists holding tickets gathered outside Disneyland demanding for entry after they were *turned away*. 数百名被拒之门外的手持入场券的游客集聚在迪斯尼乐园外要求入园。❷ cause (someone or an animal) to avoid moving toward something 不让(某人或动物)靠近某物: The police officer *turned* the pedestrians *away* from the scene of the accident. 警察不让行人靠近事故现场。With such a ban, Madrid's fashion week had to *turn away* overly thin models. 由于这一禁令,马德里时装周不得不拒绝让过瘦的模特上台表演。❸ refuse one's sympathy or support (for someone) 不同情(某人);拒绝帮助(某人): He never *turned away* anyone who asked for his help. 任何人来找他帮忙,他是从来不拒绝的。

NOTE 当本短语用作及物性动词短语,所带的宾语是代词时,该代词须置于本短语的动词和副词之间。

turn away from *vt.*【不可分性动词短语】refuse to accept or use (something) any longer 不再接受,不再使用(某物): Many consumers *turned away* from products that were not environmentally friendly. 许多消费者都不再接受非环保产品。More and more teenagers in South Korea have *turned away* from E-mail. "E-mail is an old and formal communication means," they say. 越来越多的韩国青少年已不再使用电子邮件。他们说:"电子邮件是一种陈旧而拘谨的通信工具。"

turn back *v.* ❶ (cause to) return the same way that you came instead of continuing on your journey (使)返回,遣返: Shall we *turn back*? The snow is getting heavier. 咱们是不是往回返? 雪越下越大了。The police *turned* them *back*. 警察把他们挡了回来。When the refugees reached the border they were *turned back*. 难民们到达边境后,都被遣返回来。❷ fold the edge of (a sheet of the paper, etc.) 折叠(纸张等): If you *turn back* the page where you stop reading, it will be easy for you to find it next time. 如果你看到哪页把它折起来,下次就容易找到。Don't *turn back* the corner of the page to mark your place. 不要把书页折角做读到什么地方的标记。

NOTE 当本短语所带的宾语是代词时,该代词须置于本短语的动词和副词之间。

turn down *vt.*【可分性动词短语】❶ reduce (the amount of sound, heat, or light produced by a piece of equipment) by pressing a button, moving a switch or adjusting the controls 把(音量、热度或亮度等)调小,调低: Please *turn* that radio *down* at once. It's too loud! 请马上把那收音机的音量调低。它的声太大了! Do you mind *turning down* the radio? 请你把收音机的音量关小一点好吗? Would you *turn down* the heater? It's rather hot in here. 你能把加热器调小吗? 这里太热了。If you feel hot you can *turn* the heating *down*. 如果你感到热,你可以把暖气调低。❷ refuse to accept (something such as a proposal or request, or the person who makes it) 拒绝接受……Tehran has *turned down* Washington's latest request that it stop its nuclear programme immediately. 德黑兰已拒绝接受华盛顿提出的要其立即停止核项目的要求。It was told that some foreign journalists' requests to visit those areas were *turned down*. 据说,有些外国记者申请去那些地区采访被拒绝了。He asked Helen to marry him but she *turned* him *down*. 他要求海伦嫁给他,但遭到了她的拒绝。

—*vi.* (especially of finance) become weaker; decline; decrease (尤指财政状况)疲软,衰退,下降: The economy was *turning down* at that time. 那时,经济正日趋衰退。The divorce rate *turned down* last year. 去年的离婚率下降了。

NOTE 1. 当本短语用作及物性动词短语,所带的宾语是代词时,该代词须置于本短语的动词和副词之间。

2. 当本短语作"把(音量、热度或亮度等)调小,调低"解时,反义短语是 turn up。

3. 当本短语作"拒绝接受……"解时,反义短语是 take up。

turn in *vt.*【可分性动词短语】❶(主要用于美国英语中) give back (something no longer needed) to the proper or original owner; return 退回,归还: Tickets may be *turned in* at the box office. 票可以在售票处退掉。The policeman had to *turn in* his pistol, for he was dismissed for serious mistakes. 该警员因错误严重而被开除,所以他必须将手枪上缴。When the football season was over we *turned in* our uniforms. 足球赛季结束后,我们交还了队服。❷(非正式用语,常用一般时态,常与 to 连用) tell the police about (someone), or take (him or her) to the police, because he or she has committed a crime; give (yourself) to the police 向警方告发(某人),把(某人)交给警方;自首: His own brother *turned* him *in*. 他的亲兄弟告发了他。The man was in two minds whether to *turn* the thief *in* to the police or let him go. 是把那小偷交给警方还是放他走,那个人犹豫不决。The third suspect in the murder of a French woman was *turned in* by his parents Thursday night. 第三名谋杀一法国女子的嫌犯被其家长于星期四夜里交给了警方。You should *turn* yourself *in* as soon as possible. 你应该尽快去自首。❸(主要用于美国英语中) give (a completed piece of work, especially written work) to the person who has officially asked for it or who is in charge 交上: *Turn in* your homework, please, children. 孩子们,把你们的作业都交上来。Our papers have to be *turned* in one week before the examination. 我们的论文必须在考试前一个星期交上去。I want everybody to *turn* a report *in* before Friday. 我要你们每个人在星期五之前都交上一份报告。Mr Smith *turned in* his resignation to the manager. 史密斯先生向经理提交了辞呈。❹(主要用于美国英语中) return (something) to the person it belongs to or to a person in charge, especially something that was lost 把(尤指拾到的物品)交

(还)给……: You'd better *turn in* the money that you found on the bus to the police. 你最好把在公共汽车上拾到的钱交给警察。"I found an expensive diamond ring in the restroom this morning." "If I were you, I would *turn* it *in* to the security office." "我今早在厕所拣到一枚很值钱的钻石戒指。""我要是你的话,就把它交到保安室去。"

—*vi.* (非正式用语)go to bed at night 就寝: He *turned in* at 11∶30 and slept till 7 the next morning. 他 11 点半就寝,一觉睡到第二天早上 7 点钟。Would you like some tea before you *turn in*? 在睡前你要喝点茶吗? It's time I was *turning in*. 我该去睡觉了。

NOTE 1. 当本短语用作及物性动词短语,所带的宾语是代词时,该代词须置于本短语的动词和副词之间。

2. 当本短语作"交上"和"把(尤指拾到的物品)交(还)给……"解时,同义短语是 hand in。

turn inside out *vt.* 【可分性动词短语】❶ make (the inside of something) face outwards 把……向外翻: Are you sure you haven't got the key on you? *Turn* your pockets *inside out*. 你确信钥匙没带在你身上? 把你的衣袋都向外翻一下。The wind *turned* my umbrella *inside out*. 风把我的伞吹得翻了过来。He *turned* his sleeping bag *inside out* and shook it. 他把睡袋内侧翻过来抖了抖。❷ search (a place) very thoroughly (with the result that things are in disorder) 翻乱(某处): If you don't give us the evidence we want, we'll *turn* your room *inside out*. 如果你不把我们需要的证据交出来,我们就要把你的房间翻个底朝上。The police *turned* the place *inside out* looking for the stolen money. 警察把这个地方进行了彻底的翻查,搜寻被盗款。

turn into *vt.* make (something or someone) change or develop into (something different) (使)变为,变成: Water *turns into* ice when it freezes. 水冻结后便成冰。The success of China's first lunar exploration mission *turns* the Chinese nation's 1,000-year-old dream of flying to the moon *into* a reality. 中国首次探使命的成功,使中华民族千年的奔月梦想变为现实。After the royal family's exit, the palace would be *turned into* a museum, the Nepal's new government said. 尼泊尔新政府宣布,王室迁出王宫后,王宫将变身为一座博物馆。The witch *turned* the prince *into* a frog. 女巫把王子变成了青蛙。

NOTE 本短语的同义短语是 make into。

turn loose ⇨ let loose

turn off *v.* ❶ stop using (a piece of equipment) by pressing a button or moving a switch 把(某种电器)关掉: Make sure to *turn off* the radio before you go out. 出去之前一定要把收音机关掉。In order to save electricity, *turn* all the lights *off* when you are out. 为了节电,出外时,要把灯全部关掉。Before he left the room, he made sure that all the lights were *turned off*. 他确信所有的灯都关掉了才离开房间。Shall I *turn* the electric oven *off*? 我把电烤炉关掉好吗? ❷(用一般时态)stop using (a supply of water or gas) by turning a tap, pressing a button, or moving a switch 关掉;把(自来水、煤气等的供应)关掉: The tap won't *turn off*, and there's water all over the floor. 这水龙头关不上,地板上都是水了。*Turn* the tap *off* before the

T

bath overflows. 把水龙头关上，要不浴缸里的水就溢出来了。Water will start flowing in the Diana Memorial Fountain on Thursday, three weeks after it was *turned off* because of safety fears. 戴安娜纪念泉将于本周四重新喷珠泻玉。三周前，出于担心安全问题，喷泉一度被关闭。He *turned* the gas *off*. 他关掉了煤气。The emergency crew has *turned off* gas supplies. 抢修队已切断煤气的供应。❸（无被动语态形式）leave the road you are traveling along in order to go along another one that leads away from it 从一条路转入另一条路，离开（某一条路）转入岔道：*We turned off* the freeway at Detroit. 我们在底特律下了高速公路。The car *turned off* the main road and found a quieter one. 小轿车驶离了干道，找了一条僻静的路走。You go along the road till you see the Grand Hotel, and then you *turn off* there. 你沿这条路走，看到大酒店时就转到另一条路上去。❹（英国英语用法，非正式用语）stop employing (someone) 解雇（某人）：During the recession they had to *turn* the workers *off* for three months. 在经济衰退时期，他们不得不解雇工人三个月。The servant was *turned off* for being lazy. 这仆人因懒惰而被解雇。❺（非正式用语）(of something) make (someone) feel bored or no longer interested in (a particular subject or activity); cease to like (someone or something)（使）（某人）对……感到厌烦，对……失去兴趣：I *turned off* when they started talking about computers. 当他们开始讨论起电脑时，我就失去了兴趣。This sort of talk could *turn* a lot of voters *off*. 这种讲话会使许多选民失去热情。Such poor teaching always *turns* students *off*. 这样糟糕的教学总会使学生感到厌烦。It really *turns* me *off* to see you biting your nails. 我实在讨厌看到你咬指甲。

NOTE **1.** 当本短语的宾语是代词时，该代词须置于本短语的动词和副词之间或介词之后。

2. 本短语可转化为复合词 turnoff，意为“岔开，避开；岔道，支路；成品”。

turn on *v.* ❶ start using (a piece of equipment) by pressing a button or moving a switch（通过按电钮或滑动开关）打开（某种电器）：I laid aside my book and *turned on* the radio to listen to the Special English program on VOA. 我把书本放在一边，打开收音机收听《美国之音》的“特别英语”节目。*Turn* the television *on*, please. 请把电视机打开。Please *turn* all the lights *on*, this room is dark. 请把所有的电灯都打开吧，这房间太暗了。Is your computer *turned on*? 你的电脑打开了吗？❷（用一般时态）start using (a supply of water or gas) by turning a tap, pressing a button, or moving a switch 打开（自来水、煤气等）：If you want to have a shower, you may *turn on* the hot water faucet. 如果你想洗淋浴，可拧开热水龙头。The cook walked into the kitchen and *turned* the water *on*. 厨师走进厨房，打开了水龙头。You should light the gas as soon as it is *turned on*. 煤气一打开，就应马上点火。❸（常用一般时态）make a sudden and unexpected attack on (someone) using violence or very angry words（突然以暴力或言辞）攻击，抨击（某人）：The young man who *turned on* the president's motorcade was arrested by the police. 袭击总统车队的那个年轻人被警方抓了起

T

来。I did not expect to be *turned on* by a person whom I had befriended. 我没想到受到我以朋友相待的人的攻击。The two presidential candidates *turned on* one another over their own positions on the war in Iraq. 这两位总统候选人针对伊拉克战争问题各持立场，相互抨击。Why did she *turn on* me like that? 她为什么那样抨击我呢？❹(英国英语用法，无被动语态形式，用一般时态) depend on (something) 取决于，有赖于：The success of a party *turns on* the guests invited. 聚会的成功与否取决于应邀而来的客人。The success of the negotiations *turns on* getting the agreement of the Iranian delegation. 谈判的成功与否有赖于取得与伊朗代表团的一致意见。The success of the talks *turns on* whether both sides are willing to make some concessions. 会谈的成功与否取决于双方是否愿意做出某些让步。❺(非正式用语，常与 to 连用) make (someone) become interested in (something) 使(某人)对(某物)感兴趣：Mozart's music always *turns* me *on*. 我对莫扎特的音乐总是百听不厌。That book really *turned* me *on* to astronomy. 那本书着实地使我迷上了天文学。❻(非正式用语，常与 to 连用) (cause to) take an illegal drug, especially for the first time (使)吸毒，(尤指勾引某人)吸毒：He *turned* her *on* to cocaine. 他勾引她吸食可卡因。

NOTE 当本短语用作及物性动词短语，所带的宾语是代词时，该代词须置于本短语的动词和副词之间或介词之后。

turn out *v.* ❶stop using (something such as a light) by pressing a button or moving a switch 关掉(电灯等)：When you leave the classroom, remember to *turn out* all the lights. 离开教室时，别忘了把所有的灯都关掉。*Turn* the light *out*, please. I'm trying to sleep. 请把电灯关掉。我要睡觉。Don't forget to *turn out* the heater before you go to bed. 别忘了在就寝前把电热器关掉。❷(用一般时态) prove (to be) in the result; be discovered (to be); happen to be in the end 证明(是)，原来(是)，结果成为：As it has *turned out* that the process of learning to program is an excellent opportunity to practice problem-solving skills. 正如事实所证明，学习编程序的过程是一个非常好的练习解决问题能力的机会。Some predictions made by famous people *turned out* to be wrong. 名人所做出的一些预言都被证明是错的。The president of Iran *turns out* to be a blogger, who has been keeping the web log for more than a year and promises to spend 15 minutes a week updating it. 伊朗总统原来也是位博客作者。他一年多以来一直撰写博文，并承诺每星期用 15 分钟来更新其博文。Things *turned out* contrary to what we had expected. 结果事情与我们所预料的相反。❸(非正式用语) (of a crowd) come out or get together in order to be present at an event or take part in an activity (众多的人)出来，集结：The whole town *turned out* when she performed here last month. 上个月她在这里演出时，全镇子的人都到场观看。The whole city *turned out* to welcome the distinguished guests from Britain. 全城的人都出来欢迎来自英国的贵宾。❹produce or make (something), often quickly or in large numbers (常指迅速或大量地)制造，生产：The company plans to *turn out* 2,000 small planes a year. 该

公司计划每年制造2 000架小型飞机。The factory is *turning* the bicycles *out* as fast as it can. 该厂在以最快的速度生产这种自行车。66 ships were *turned out* here during August. They exceeded all previous records for monthly production. 8 月份,这里造了 66 艘轮船。这个数字超过了所有以前单月产量的记录。❺(主要用于美国英语中) train or produce (someone with certain skills or talents)培养(具有某种技艺或才能的人员): The state's law schools *turns* lawyers *out* by the dozen. 该州的法学院校培养出大量的律师。He accused the medical college of *turning out* too many veterinarians. 他谴责这家医学院培养的兽医太多。❻(常用一般时态) force (someone) to leave a particular place, especially the place where he or she has been living 迫使(某人)离开(尤指其居所): The landlord *turned* them *out* because they couldn't pay the rent. 房东把他们赶出去,因为他们交不起房租。If you don't behave yourself, you will be *turned out* of the hotel. 如果你不守规矩,就会被赶出旅馆。❼(英国英语用法) remove (something) from a container by turning it upside down 从(容器中)倒出(某物): We *turned out* all the drawers and found things we hadn't seen for years. 我们把所有的抽屉都倒空后发现了一些我们多年未见的物品。We shall probably find the missing articles when that cupboard is *turned out*. 把这柜子腾空后,我们就可能找到那几件不见之物了。*Turn* the flowers *out* of the pots. 把这些花都从花盆中倒出来。❽(英国英语用法) empty (everything) by removing them from your pockets or a bag 把(口袋或包中的所有东西)翻出来: But you must have the tickets on you somewhere. *Turn out* your pockets again. 票肯定在你身上的什么地方。再把你衣袋里的东西都倒出来找找。

NOTE 1. 当本短语用作及物性动词短语,所带的宾语是代词时,该代词须置于本短语的动词和副词之间。

2. 本短语可转化为复合词 turnout,意为"出动;集会的人群;罢工,罢工的工人"。

turn over *v.* ❶(cause to) be moved so that the top part is facing downwards (使)翻转,把……翻过来: A bus *turned over* on a highway, killing 26 people and injuring another 24 on board. 一辆公共汽车在公路上翻车,造成车上 26 人死亡,另有 24 人受伤。That record is finished. *Turn* it *over* to play the other side. 唱片的这面已放完,翻过来听另一面吧。They helped to *turn* the rock *over*. 他们帮着把石头翻了过来。The soil must be thoroughly *turned over* before planting. 在种植之前,土壤必须要彻底翻一下。❷(cause to) move your body in the bed so that you are lying in a different position (使)在床上翻身: My sister *turned over* in her bed as though she was as light as a leaf. 我妹妹在床上轻如树叶般地翻了个身。The nurses *turned* the patient *over* so they could give her some medicine. 几名护士给病人翻了个身,这样她们就能给她喂药了。❸(与 to 连用) deliver (something) into the possession or control of someone else 把……交给, The father *turned* his business *over* to his two children. 父亲把生意交给了他的两个孩子经营。The corrupt official's illegal income of 2.68 million yuan has been *turned over* to the national treasury. 这个

贪官的非法所得 268 万元已上缴国库。❹(与 to 连用)take (a criminal) to the police or other authority 把(犯罪分子)移交给……：As soon as Thomas came home his parents *turned* him *over* to the police. 托马斯一到家，他父母就把他交给了警方。The local police *turned* him *over* to the FBI. 当地警方把他移交给了联邦调查局。❺turn (a page in a book or a sheet of paper) so that the other side is towards you 翻(书或纸页)：*Turn* the page *over* very carefully, there is a surprise on the next page! 非常小心地把这页翻过来，在下一页上有意想不到的东西！You may *turn over* your exam papers now. 你们现在可以开考卷了。❻think carefully about (all the details of something) 仔细地考虑(某事的所有细节)：I began to *turn over* in my head all I had learned from this article. 我开始把我从这篇文章中读到的东西在脑中思考了一番。She *turned* the problem *over* in her mind. 她在心里仔细地考虑了那个问题。❼do business or sell goods worth (a sum of money) 做(多少钱的)生意，营业额为……：This store is currently *turning over* more than ＄5,000 a week. 这家商店现在每星期的营业额达 5 000 美元。❽(英国英语用法，常与 to 连用) stop watching one television station and start watching another 换看(其他电视台节目)：Let's *turn over* to another channel, this is really boring. 咱们换个台看吧。这个台的节目实在无聊。These programmes are not interesting ,shall we *turn over* to Phoenix Television? 这些节目都没意思，咱们换看凤凰卫视吧？❾(英国英语用法，非正式用语) (of someone) steal (a lot of things) from a place, especially in an organized way (尤指有组织地)盗窃(大量物品)：Half the class is on probation for *turning over* a supermarket. 该班有一半的学生因偷超市里的东西而被监外察看。We got back to find the flat had been *turned over*. 我们回到公寓时发现被盗了。

NOTE **1.** 当本短语用作及物性动词短语，所带的宾语是代词时，该代词须置于本短语的动词和副词之间。

2. 本短语可转化为复合词 turnover，意为“翻转(物)；倒转；营业额，成交量；流动，流通；人员调整”。

turn to *v.* ❶(非正式用语，常用一般时态) begin working with much energy; act vigorously 着手工作；积极地做起来：The workers soon *turned to* and got the task done quickly. 工人们立刻动手并很快就完成了任务。It's time we *turned to* our work. 是我们开始工作的时候了。❷(常用一般时态) (cause to) change the position of (someone or something) to face (someone or something) (使)转体朝向……：Maria *turned to* the reporters and said,“I'm innocent.” 玛丽亚转过身来对记者们说道：“我是无辜的。”The nurse *turned* the patient *to* the sun so she could get some sunlight on her back. 护士使病人转身朝向太阳，这样阳光就能晒到她的背上了。He *turned* the plant *to* the light. 他把植物转向阳光。❸open (a particular page) in a book, magazine, etc. 把(书、杂志等)翻到：*Turn to* page 10 for our prices. 要了解我们的价格，请翻到第 10 页。The opening of Hong Kong Disneyland on September 12, 2005 is thought to *turn to* a new page of Hong Kong tourism. 人们认为，香港迪斯尼乐园于 2005 年 9 月 12 日的开园翻开了香

T

港旅游业的新篇章。❹go to (someone) or start to use (something) in an attempt to help yourself when you are having difficulty dealing with a situation 求助于(某人);借助于(某物): I can't tell my parents about it, I don't know who to *turn to*. 这事我不能和我的父母说,我不知道该求助于谁。The Hyundai Motor Company *turned to* Microsoft for help in developing a new generation of music and information system. 现代汽车公司求助于微软公司开发新一代车载音乐和信息系统。More and more British women *turn to* man's best friends, dogs and cats, for comfort when they are stressed. 越来越多的英国妇女在有压力时借助于人类的最好朋友狗和猫来寻求慰藉。❺(cause to) become (usually the same thing in a different form)(使)变成(相同之物的另一种形式): Water *turns to* ice at 0℃. 水在零摄氏度时变成冰。His San Diego home had *turned to* ash in the biggest wildfire in California history. 他在圣地亚哥的房子在加利福尼亚州历史上最大的山火中化为灰烬。People's shock at the so-called mistake bombing quickly *turned to* anger. 大家对所谓"误炸"表现出的震惊很快就变成了愤怒。After seven days of rain countryroads were *turned to* mud. 下了七天雨后,乡村的道路变得泥泞不堪。❻(用一般时态) lead in (a certain direction) by changing direction 转向: Here the road *turns* sharply *to* the right. 路在这里向右急转。❼ direct (your attention, thoughts, etc.) towards (something) 把(注意力、思路等)转到……上: We *turned* our attention *to* extending the area of our pastures. 我们把注意力转到了扩大我们的牧场面积上。It is time he *turned* his mind *to* more serious problems. 他该把思路转到重要的问题上了。❽direct (something such as an ability or efforts) towards (a purpose or doing something) 致力于: He *turned to* the study and practice of medicine at twenty. 他20岁起就致力于医学的研究与实践。

turn up *v.* ❶(用一般时态)(cause to) face or point upwards (使)翻起,卷起,翘起: I *turned up* the collar of my coat against the cold wind. 我把外套的领子翻了起来,以遮挡寒风。You should *turn* your sleeves *up* before you wash the dishes. 在洗盘子前把袖子卷起来。The foreigner *turned up* his thumb and said in Chinese, "Tai bang le". 那名外国人跷起大拇指,用中国话说:"太棒了。"❷increase (the amount of sound, heat, or light produced by a piece of equipment) by pressing a button, moving a switch or adjusting the controls 把(音量、热量或光度)调高,调大: *Turn up* the radio please, I can't hear it clearly. 请把收音机的音量调高一点,我听不清。*Turn* the volume control *up*. 把音量控制调高。She drew the curtain close and turned the light up. 她把窗帘拉上,把灯光旋大。*Turn up* the fire, please. I need some boiling water. 请把火开大一点,我需要点儿开水。❸ find or discover (something hidden, or unknown) by thoroughly looking for it (通过彻底搜索)发现,找到(隐藏或未知之物): American investigators in Iraq have not *turned up* any chemical or biological weapons or prohibited weapons so far. 美国在伊拉克的调查人员至今还没找到任何生化武器或其他违禁武器。The police have *turned up* some new evidence about the murder. 警方又找到

T

了一些有关那起谋杀案的新证据。Our first look at the records did not *turn* anything *up*. 我们第一次查阅这些记录时并没有发现任何情况。Once the evidence is *turned up*, you may criticize the presuppositions. 一旦找到证据,你就会批判那些先前的假设。❹(非正式用语,常用一般时态)be found, especially by accident, after being lost or not known about (尤指意外地)被找到: The missing bag *turned up*, completely empty, in the lake. 丢失的手提包在湖里被找到了,包内空无一物。The book she lost has *turned up*. 她丢失的书已经找到了。❺(非正式用语,常用一般时态)make one's appearance; arrive, often unexpectedly or after you have been waiting for a long time 出现,到来: Guess who *turned up* at my door this morning? 你猜,今天早上谁出现在了我家门口? The deputy headmistress of the Baghdad Middle School for Girls said only about a fifth of her 750 pupils had *turned up*. 巴格达女子中学副校长说,该校 750 名学生中仅有 1/5 的人到课。She failed to *turn up* for work on Monday. 星期一她没来上班。❻(非正式用语,常用一般时态)happen unexpectedly or fortunately (意外地)发生;出现转机: She seems very worried. Something must have *turned up*. 她好像很忧虑,一定是发生了什么事。Those words will *turn up* in your reading! 那些词将会在你的阅读中出现。Don't worry, something's sure to *turn up*. 别担心,事态会有好转的。❼(英国英语用法)make (a piece of cloth or clothing such as a skirt or trousers) shorter by folding and sewing it up along the bottom edge 把(裙、裤等)折起底边,把(裙、裤等)改短: Can you *turn* my skirt *up* for me? 您能把我的裙子改短吗? One leg of the trousers is longer than the other, ask someone to *turn* it *up* for you. 这裤子的一条裤腿比另一条长,请人把它改短一点吧。

NOTE **1.** 当本短语用作及物性动词短语,所带的宾语是代词时,该代词须置于本短语的动词和副词之间。

2. 当本短语作"把(裙、裤等)折起底边,把(裙、裤等)改短"解时,反义短语是 let down。

3. 本短语可转化为复合词 turn-up,意为"翻起物;衣物的卷起部分;吵架,打闹"。

turn upside down *vt.*【可分性动词短语】❶turn (something or someone) the other way up 把……颠倒,把……倒置: Don't *turn* the bottle of phosphorus *upside down*. 不要把装有磷的瓶子倒置。The child loves being *turned upside down*. 这孩子喜欢被倒立起来。❷(非正式用语)make (a place, especially a room) very untidy while you are searching for something 把(某个地方,尤指房间)翻得乱七八糟: The police came and *turned* the place *upside down*. 警察来了,把这个地方翻得乱七八糟。Everything in the room was *turned upside down*. 室内的一切东西都搞得乱七八糟。❸(非正式用语)cause disorder and confusion in (something)把(某事)搞乱,搞混淆: Do you have to *turn* our arrangement *upside down*? 你非得把我们的安排打乱吗? The truth of history has been *turned upside down* by these historians. 历史的真相被这些历史学家们颠倒了。

two of a kind ⇨ **of a kind**

U u

unable to *adj*. not having or lacking the necessary physical or mental skill, power, know-how, time, or other qualities to do something 没有能力做某事;不能做某事:A little baby is *unable to* walk or talk. 婴儿既不会走路也不会说话。The interruption of electricity made us *unable to* do anything. 电力的中断让我们什么也不能做。Despite its best efforts, including raising its bid by roughly $5 billion, Microsoft was still *unable to* buy Yahoo. 虽然尽了最大的努力,包括将收购价格提高了大约50亿美元,微软仍没能够收购雅虎。

NOTE 本短语的反义短语是 able to。

unaware of *adj*. not knowing about or conscious of (something)不知道,没意识到:She was completely *unaware of* the whole affair. 她对此事一无所知。Some of the Congo hospitals keep AIDS patients *unaware of* their conditions because the deadly disease remains a taboo in the country. 刚果的一些医院不让艾滋病患者知道他(她)们的病情是因为这一致命性疾病在该国依然是一大禁忌。He seemed to be *unaware of* the trouble he was causing. 他似乎还没有察觉到自己惹出来的麻烦。

NOTE 本短语的反义短语是 aware of。

under a cloud *adj*. ❶(非正式用语) regarded with distrust; under suspicion; in doubt 不受信任,受到怀疑: Mary has been *under a cloud* since her roommate's mobile phone and purse disappeared all together. 自从她室友的手机和钱包一道不翼而飞之后,玛丽就一直受到怀疑。Several people at my company have suddenly left *under a cloud* and are being investigated by the police. 我们公司的几个人突然受到怀疑并被警方调查。❷(非正式用语) with your reputation damaged because you may have done something wrong (因做错事而)名誉扫地,声名狼藉: I was already *under a cloud* at the office. 我在办公室里已搞得声名狼藉。❸ sad, depressed; discouraged 痛苦,抑郁,沮丧: Little Tom has been *under a cloud* since his dog died. 自从他的狗死后,小汤姆一直很痛苦。

under age *adj*. not legally old enough (to do something)未达法定年龄的:Jane was not allowed to take the Life Saving Course because she was *under age*. 简未被允许学习救生课程,因为她还没成年。The boy was just one month *under age*, but still they wouldn't give him a license to drive. 这男孩只差一个月就到法定年龄了,但他们还是不发给他驾驶执照。It's against the law to sell liquor and cigarettes to anyone *under age*. 向未成年人销售烟酒是违法的。

NOTE 本短语的反义短语是 of age, come of age 和 over age。

under arrest *adj*. having been caught by the police and not allowed to go free 被逮捕: Twenty-one people have been *under arrest* in connection with a plot to blow up aircraft flying from Britain to the United States. 已有 21 名与一起企图炸毁英国飞往美国航班阴谋有关的嫌犯被逮捕。The three men were seen breaking into the apartment building and soon found themselves *under arrest*. 有人看到有三名男子闯入公寓大楼内行窃，不久他们就被逮捕了。The man believed to have robbed the bank was placed *under arrest*. 被确信为抢劫银行的那个男子被逮捕了。

under consideration *adj*. being thought about or under discussion 在考虑中，在讨论中，在研究中: The proposals are currently *under consideration*. 目前，这些建议正在考虑之中。What countries have been *under consideration* for becoming part of NAFTA besides USA, Canada and Mexico? 除了美国、加拿大和墨西哥以外，还有哪些国家在考虑成为北美自由贸易协定成员国? It has nothing to do with the matter *under consideration*. 这与所讨论的事情无关。

NOTE 本短语的同义短语是 in hand 和 in question。

under control *adj*. having the power to make all the important decisions, especially in a dangerous or confused state; controlled in the correct way 在控制之下: The Philippines President lifted the alert status on Friday, saying the situation was *under control*. 菲律宾总统星期五解除了紧急状态，她说局势已经得到了控制。A fire in London's world famous Camden Market area has been brought *under control*. 世界著名的伦敦卡姆登市场区发生的大火已经得到控制。The official of the World Health Organization also said that having a vaccine is only one element in the fight to get the flu *under control*. 世卫组织的这位官员还表示，研究出疫苗仅仅是控制这种流感的一个组成部分。The firemen soon had the fire *under control*. 消防队员很快就把火势控制住了。

NOTE 1. 本短语中的名词 control 前可加名词，形容词和代词等修饰词。如:

> After Turkey's air-strikes on Sunday the Iraqi official said, "The Americans are responsible because the Iraqi sky is *under* their full *control*."
> 在星期日土耳其的空袭之后，这位伊拉克官员说:"美国人要负责任，因为伊拉克的领空完全由他们控制。"

2. 本短语中的名词 control 前不能加任何冠词。如果加定冠词，则必须使用 under the control of 的形式。如:

> The government has been overthrown and the country is now *under the control of* the military.
> 政府已被推翻，国家现处于军方的控制之下。

3. 本短语的比较级形式是 more under control，最高级形式是 most under control。

4 本短语的同义短语是 in hand。

under (the) cover of *prep.* ❶hidden or concealed by 趁着……: The prisoners escaped *under* (*the*) cover of darkness. 囚犯们趁着黑夜逃跑了。They planned to attack *under cover of* night. 他们计划趁夜间发动袭击。❷pretending to be (someone else); under the pretence of 冒充(某人);以……为借口: The thieves entered the apartment building *under cover of* repairmen. 盗贼们冒充修理工进入了公寓大楼。He tried to get rid of his political rivals *under the cover of* fighting corruption. 他企图打着“反腐”的幌子除掉自己的政敌。

under fire *adj.* ❶ subjected to enemy attack 受到敌方的攻击: The report said that the convoy came *under fire* but did not provide details. 该报道说,车队曾受到攻击,但并未提供细节。❷ being criticized for something you have done 受到批评或抨击: Williams came *under fire* in the office after he wrote a very critical article in the company magazine. 威廉姆斯在公司的杂志上写了一篇很有批评性的文章后,在办公室受到了严厉的批评。The government's decision is *under* heavy *fire*. 政府的决定受到了猛烈的抨击。Finding himself *under fire*, he had no alternative but to abandon his scheme for the time being. 在受到批评的情况下,他别无选择,只好暂时放弃自己的计划。

under no circumstances *adv.* (used for emphasizing that something cannot be allowed to happen) in no case; never 决不,无论如何都不: *Under no circumstances* can customers' money be refunded, he said. 他说,在任何情况下都不能给顾客退款。*Under no circumstances* must a soldier leave his post. 士兵无论如何都不能擅离岗位。China will *under no circumstances* be the first to use nuclear weapons. 中国在任何情况下都不会首先使用核武器。We should *under no circumstances* give transfusion without knowing the blood type. 不知道血型,我们决不能进行输血。

NOTE 1. 当表示否定意义的本短语用于句首时,句中的主谓结构一定要构成倒装。但是,当本短语置于句中较后的部分时,句中的主谓结构则不倒装。

2. 本短语中的名词 circumstance 必须用复数形式。

3. 本短语与 in no circumstances 意义和用法相同。后者主要用于英国英语中。

4. 本短语的另外一种表达形式是 not under any circumstances。例如:

> “Can I talk you into serving as a teacher again?” “No! *Not under any circumstances*!”
> “我能不能说服你再去当老师?”“不!绝不能的!”

under one's breath *adv.* (非正式用语) in a low voice or a whisper, often because you do not want other people to hear what you are saying 低声地,小声地: The teacher heard the boy say something *under his breath* and she asked him to repeat it aloud. 老师听到那男孩在低声地讲着什么,于是就让他大声地再把它讲一遍。Speaking *under her breath*, she told me the secret. 她小声地把那个秘密告诉了我。

under/in the circumstances *adv.* considering the condition at a particular time 在这种(或那种)情况下:*Under the circumstances* Smith had better stay away. 在这种情况下,史密斯最好不在场。There was a snowstorm and, *under the circumstances* they decided to stay at home. 暴风雪来临了,在这种情况下,他们决定留在家里。The result was the best that could be expected *in the circumstances*. 这是在那种情况下可以期待的最佳结果了。

NOTE 1. 本短语中的名词 circumstance 必须用复数形式。

2. 本短语中的定冠词 the 可被指示代词 these 或 those 替换。例如:

> *Under these/those* circumstances we must be very cautious.
> 在这些/那些情况下,我们必须非常小心。

本短语中的定冠词 the 还可被不定代词 some 或 certain 替换。例如:

> *Under some/certain circumstances* air conducts electricity.
> 在某些情况下,空气能导电。

under repair *adj.* being mended or repaired 正在维修之中:This section of the road will be *under repair* until July. 这个路段在 7 月份之前将一直处于维修之中。The offices are still *under repair*. 办公室还都在修缮中。A vacant house *under repair* on a hill slope suddenly collapsed Wednesday afternoon. 山坡上一所正在维修之中的空房于星期三下午突然倒塌。

under siege *adj.* ❶ in a state of being surrounded; in a siege 被包围:The town was *under siege* for six months. 该城被围困了六个月之久。Supplies were continuously sent to the city *under siege*. 被围困的城市得到了源源不绝的物品供应。❷(主要用于新闻英语中) being criticized or attacked by a lot of different people at the same time 同时受到各方人士的批评;受到围攻:The industry is currently *under siege* from the press. 该行业现正在遭受新闻界的围攻。

under someone's (very) nose(s) *adj.* (非正式用语)(used about something bad which happens in an obvious way but in a way that you do not notice or cannot prevent) right in front of someone; quite openly 就在某人眼前,公然:Do you want to read the book? It's right *under your nose*. 你想看那本书吗? 它就在你的眼前。The thieves stole the jewels *under the guides' noses*. 盗贼们在数名警卫的眼皮底下盗走了珠宝。

NOTE 1. 在英国英语中,本短语前常用介词 from。在美国英语中则常用 out from。例如:

> She stole the ring *from/out from* right *under the assistant's nose*.
> 她竟在售货员的眼皮底下偷走了戒指。

2. 本短语的另外一种表达形式是 under the nose(s) of someone。例如:

> The action was taken *under the* very *noses of the enemy*.
> 行动就在敌人的眼皮底下采取。

under the influence ⇨ **under the weather**

under the nose(s) of someone ⇨ **under someone's (very) nose(s)**

under the weather *adj.* ❶(非正式用语)not healthy; feeling slightly ill; not feeling well 身体欠佳,不舒服: She has been *under the weather* recently. 她最近一直身体欠佳。I'm feeling a little of *under the weather* today , I think I've caught a cold. 我今天感觉不太舒服。我想,我是感冒了。You look a bit *under the weather*. 你看上去有点不舒服。❷(主要用于美国英语中) intoxicated; drunk 醉酒的: Daddy's had a few beers and is a bit *under the weather* again. 爸爸喝了几瓶啤酒,又有点醉了。Many accidents are caused by drivers who are *under the weather*. 很多事故都是因驾驶员醉酒引起的。In the town of Wood, about twenty drivers were caught *under the weather* on the rainy night. 在伍德镇,大约有 20 名驾驶员在雨夜中因醉酒驾车而被抓。

NOTE 当本短语作"醉酒的"解时,另外一种表达形式是 under the influence。例如:

> My brother was caught driving while *under the influence*.
> 我弟弟因酒醉驾车而被抓。

under way *adj*. (of an activity or plan) in operation; in progress (指某种活动或计划)在进行中: An investigation was *under way* into the cause of the crash of a rescue helicopter transferring injured local residents. 一架运送当地伤员的救援直升机坠毁,原因正在调查之中。Preparations are *under way* for a wedding. 婚礼的准备工作正在进行中。Now I'd like to draw your attention again to the project *under way*. 我想再次提请您注意正在进行中的那一项目。The boss gave his consent for the project to get *under way*. 老板同意将该方案付诸于实施。

NOTE 1. 本短语中的名词 way 之前不可加任何冠词。

2. 本短语可转化为复合词 underway,意为"在进行中的"。例如:

> Our project is now well *underway*.
> 我们的计划现正在顺利地进行着。

until now ⇨ **up to now**

up and down Ⅰ *adv*. ❶moving upwards and downwards alternately 上下地,时上时下地,起伏地: The children were jumping *up and down* with excitement. 孩子们兴奋地上上下下地蹦跳着。She looked at me *up and down*, but I couldn't tell whether she approved of my appearance or not. 她上上下下地打量了我一番,但我不知道她相没相中我的长相。The float went *up and down* on the water. 漂浮物在水面上时上时下地浮动。❷moving backwards and forwards along a given course 前前后后地,来回地: He kept pacing *up and down* in his office, as if in deep thought. 他在办公室里若有所思地来回踱着步子。I could hear him in his bedroom walking *up and down*. 我可以听到他在卧室里来回地走动。❸(of one's health or relationship with someone) sometimes well or good, and sometimes ill or bad(指身体或与他人的关系)时好时坏:"How is your father?" "Rather *up and down*." "你父亲怎么样?""还不是时好时坏。" My relationship with him was *up and down*. 我与他的关系时好时坏。❶everywhere 到处: Early in August, rumors were whispered *up and down* in London. 8 月初,谣言已在伦敦各处传开了。

Ⅱ *n.* (用复数形式,常与 have 连用) a variety of situations and experiences that are sometimes good and sometimes bad 时好时坏的情势,好坏交替的经历: The relationship between the two countries has a lot of *ups and downs*. 两国关系经历了多次起落。This couple had their *ups and downs*, but they stayed married for more than 60 years. 这对夫妇的婚姻历经曲折,但却一直维持了 60 多年。Life is full of *ups and downs*. 生活充满了苦与乐。

NOTE 本短语可转化为复合词 up-and-down,意为"上下的,起伏的;不平坦的;时好时坏的"。

up in the air *adj.* (非正式用语)(of a plan, etc.) not yet decided, or finished; uncertain (指计划等)尚未决定的;还未完成的:Plans for next meeting have been left *up in the air* until Mary feels better. 在玛丽身体情况好转之前,还不能确定下次会议的计划。The plan to build a golf course next to the airport is still *up in the air*. 在机场旁建高尔夫球场的计划尚无定论。Let's leave this question *up in the air* until next week. 这个问题咱们下星期再定吧。"Will a strike take place?" "That's *up in the air*." "会发生罢工吗?""这可说不定。"

NOTE 本短语中的 up 往往可以省略。例如:

> Plans for the picnic are still *in the air* since we can't decide where to go.
> 关于出去野餐的计划还悬而未决,因为去哪儿我们还不能定下来。

up to *prep.* ❶ (used for stating the most an amount can be, or what level it can reach) to and including 达到(某一最多的数量或最大的程度):The children were forced to work *up to* 14 hours a day, 7 days a week in the clothing factory. 在这家制衣厂里,童工们被迫每天工作 14 个小时,每周工作 7 天。Taiwan decided to launch direct weekend flights from July and allow *up to* 3,000 mainland tourists in per day. 台湾决定自 7 月份开通周末直航包机,允许每天多达 3 000 名大陆游客入台。Before long, the water was *up to* their knees, and they began to get worried. 水很快就到达了他们的膝部,于是他们开始担忧了。❷ until (something) 直到: Read *up to* Page 35. 一直读到 35 页。*Up to* now he's been very quiet. 直到现在,他还是那么沉默寡言。❸ (常用否定形式) (used for stating a particular standard something can reach) equal to (someone or something) in standard 赶得上,达到(某一标准): He is not *up to* his father as a scholar. 作为学者,他赶不上他父亲。The new book of Green's isn't *up to* his last one. 格林的这本新书不及他的上一本。Employees face dismissal if they fail to match *up to* the standards set by the company. 未能达到公司所定标准的雇员将面临解雇。❹ (常用在动词 be, leave 之后) decided by (someone) 由(某人)来决定,取决于(某人): It's *up to* you to decide whether we go or stay. It's not *up to* me. 我们去还是留由你决定,而不是由我决定。It's *up to* you whether to get the black one or the blue one. 要黑色的还是蓝色的由你定。I leave it *up to* you. 我让你自己决定。❺ (常用在 it's 后) being the duty or responsibility of (someone)是(某人)的义务,是(某人)的责任: It's *up to* the travel companies to warn customers of any possible dangers. 向游客提出任何潜在危险的警告是旅游公司的责任。"But I think that the direct conversation with those forces is *up to* the government," the UN Secretary General told reporters in Colombia. 联合国秘书长在哥伦比亚对记者说:"但我认为政府有责任同那些武装力量进行直接对话。"❻well enough, strong enough, or good enough to do something 合适于,胜任:She's supposed to leave the hospital tomorrow, but I don't think she's *up to* it. 她期待着明天出院,但我认为她还不适合出院。This old car is not *up to* a long journey. 这辆旧汽车不适于长途旅行。I don't think I'm *up to* doing a five-mile walk. 我想,五英里的路我走不动。My German isn't *up to* translating that article. 我的德语还不行,翻译不了那篇文章。❼(非正式用语)(of someone) doing (something)(指某人)做(某事): What are you *up to* in there? Open the door! 你在那里做什么呢? 开门! The children are so quiet, I wonder what they're*up to*! 孩子们都这么安静,我不知道他们在搞什么名堂!

up to date Ⅰ *adj*. modern and using the latest ideas or knowledge 新式的,时行的: Not all the existing equipment is *up to date*. 现有的设备并不都是新式的。I've been away for a long time, you'll have to bring me *up to date* with the news. 我很长时间一直在外,你得把最新的消息告诉我。Keep your boss *up to date* on your progress. 让你的老板随时了解你的最新进展。Throw away your old clothes, keep *up to date*! 把你的旧衣服扔掉,跟上时尚吧!

Ⅱ *adv*. up to the present time; to this time 到现在为止,直到现在: I haven't received any letter from him *up to date*. 直到现在我还没有接到他的信。

NOTE 1. 当本短语用作形容词性短语时,比较级形式是 more up to date,最高级形式是 most up to date。

2. 当本短语用作副词性短语时,为 to date 的语气加强形式。

3. 当本短语用作形容词性短语时,可转化为复合词 up-to-date,意为"新式的,时行的"。例如:

> This factory used the most *up-to-date* methods.
> 这家工厂使用最新的生产方法。

up to no good *adj*. (非正式用语)(of someone) doing (something bad or illegal), usually secretly (常指秘密地)做(坏事或违法之事): "The children are so quiet, I wonder what they're getting up to!" "I believe that they are *up to no good*." "孩子们都这么安静,我不知道他们在搞什么!""我相信,他们没在做好事。" This person seems like an angel on the surface, but he's *up to no good*. 这个人表面看上去像个天使,但他不做什么好事。

NOTE 本短语与 up to something 意义和用法相同,两者可以互换使用。

up to now *adv*. (常用完成时态,常用于否定句中) until now; until the present time 迄今为止,直到现在: I know nothing about it *up to now*. 直到现在我对此事还一无所知。We have not got any news from him *up to the present*. 直到现在我们还没得到他的任何消息。

NOTE 1. 本短语与 until now 意义和用法相同,两者可以互换使用。如:

> *Until now* we've had no problems.
> 直到现在为止,我们没有遇到任何问题。

2. 本短语的另一种表达形式是 up to the present。

up to the present ⇨ **up to now**

up to something ⇨ **up to no good**

upside down *adv.* ❶with the top part at the bottom or lower than the bottom part 倒置地,颠倒地:The car landed *upside down* in the ditch. 那部汽车底朝上地翻在了沟里。The man was holding his newspaper *upside down*. 那名男子倒拿着报纸。You've got the picture *upside down*. 你把那幅照片给装倒了。❷ into confusion or in disorder 混乱地,乱七八糟地: The office is being decorated so everything's *upside down*. 办公室正在装修,因此所有东西都混乱不堪。The police came and turned the room *upside down*. 警察来了,把房间翻得乱七八糟。

NOTE 1. 本短语可转化为复合词 upside-down,意为"颠倒的,乱七八糟的"。

2. 本短语的比较级形式是 more upside down,最高级形式是 most upside down。

U

use as *vt.* 【可分性动词短语】employ (something or someone) to serve the purpose of (something) 把……用作……: He *used* the bad weather *as* an excuse for not coming. 他拿天气不好作不来的借口。Sunshine can be *used as* a source of energy. 阳光可作为能源使用。I hate being *used as* a servant here. 我不愿在这儿被当作仆人使用。

use for *vt.* 【可分性动词短语】❶employ (usually something) for (a particular purpose or doing something) 把……用于: Don't *use* the silver spoon *for* opening a tin. 不要用这把银匙开罐头。Psychological tests are sometimes *used for* selection purposes. 心理测试有时用于选拔之目的。During the war the castle was *used for* keeping prisoners in. 战争期间该城堡被用来监禁囚犯。❷take unfair advantage of (someone) 利用(某人): He's just *using* you *for* his own ends. 他只是为达到自己的目的在利用你而已。

use up *vt.* 【可分性动词短语】❶use all of a supply of (something) 用完,耗尽(某物):He has *used up* all his strength. 他已用尽了自己的体力。I have *used* all my paper *up*. I will have to get some more. 我的纸都用完了,我要再弄些来。He got two weeks of vacation but he *used* it *up* in the first half of the year. 他有两个星期的休假,上半年他就把它休完了。The resources of the area have been *used up*. 该地区的资源已经耗尽。❷(非正式用语) exhaust; tire out 筋疲力尽: I'm totally *used up* from digging that hole. 挖那个坑累得我筋疲力尽。

NOTE 1. 本短语中的副词 up 表示"光,尽,完"之意。类似形式的动词性短语还有: burn up (烧光), buy up (买光), eat up (吃光), finish up (吃光,喝尽,用完), pay up(还清)等。

2. 当本短语所带的宾语是代词时,该代词须置于本短语的动词和副词中间。

used to[1] *v.* (后接原形动词) (used for

saying what happened regularly in the past, especially when you want to emphasize that this is not true or does not happen now) did formerly; did in the past 以前习惯做(某事): I don't play golf now, but I *used to*. 我现在不玩高尔夫球了,但我过去玩。People *used to* think that the Chinese are not as healthy and fit as the people in the west, but I find that's far from the case. 过去人们认为中国人没有西方人健康,但我发现情况绝非如此。Tour guides' practice of taking tips *used to* be considered as illegal, yet it has been an open secret that all tour guides receive tips. 导游收小费曾被认为是违法的,然而所有的导游都收小费早已是一个公开的秘密。You work harder than you *used to* do. 你比以前工作努力多了。

NOTE 1. 本短语的否定形式不止一种。例如:

> I didn't *use to* like him, but now we're good friends.
> 我过去并不喜欢他,但现在我们是好朋友。
> He never *used to* allow the shop to be open on Sundays.
> 他过去不让商店周日开门营业。
> When we were younger, we *used* not *to* be allowed to drink coffee.
> 我们年轻时是不允许喝咖啡的。

didn't use to 是广泛使用的一种否定形式。英国英语正式文体中,否定形式是 used not to。

2. 本短语的疑问形式也不止一种。例如:

> Did you *use to* work here?
> 你以前在这儿工作吗?
> *Used* there *to* be a hotel on that corner?
> 以前在那个角落有一家饭店吗?
> *Used* you *to* live in the same house? (或 Did you *used to* live in the same house?)
> 过去你们是不是住在同一所房子里?
> What method *used* you *to* employ to engage in calculation?
> 你们过去用什么方法进行计算?

Did/ Didn't he use to …? 是广泛使用的一种疑问形式。英国英语正式文体中,使用 used you to …? 这种形式。

3. 本短语不能用来表示某事发生的次数或时间的长短。例如,我们不能说: * He *used to live* in London for 20 years.

used to[2] *adj*. (后接名词或动名词短语) familiar with or accustomed to (someone or something or doing something) because you have often experienced it before, so it no longer seems difficult or strange 熟悉,习惯于: I am *used to* the doctor I have and I don't want to change. 我已熟悉了我现在这位医生,所以就不想换别的医生了。I haven't got *used to* the new system yet. 我对这套新的体制还不熟悉。People in the northern part of the country are *used to* cold weather. 该国的北方人习惯于寒冷的气候。I never got *used to* going to bed so late. 我始终没能习惯这么晚上床睡觉。

NOTE 1. 本短语中的 to 是介词,而不是动词不定式符号。

2. 本短语的比较级形式是 more used to, 最高级形式是 most used to。

3. 本短语的同义短语是 accustom to, adapt to 和 adjust to。

used to be *v.* (used for saying what was true in the past, especially when you want to emphasize that this is not true now) formerly or once was 以前是,曾经是: He isn't what he *used to be*. 他不再是原来的他。Over the past three years the Dead Sea has decreased by three meters and the whole area is currently one third less than it *used to be* in the 1960s, experts said. 专家称,在过去三年中,死海的水位已经下降了 3 米。目前整个死海水域的水量已经不足 20 世纪 60 年代时的三分之一。

usher in *vt.* ❶ help (someone) to get into a place, especially by showing them the way 迎入(某人): They *ushered in* the visitors. 他们把客人迎了进去。He opened the door wide and *ushered* them *in*. 他将门大开,把他们迎了进去。I was *ushered in* to the palace, and stood before the king. 迎宾员把我带入宫殿,站在了国王的面前。❷(正式用语,常用一般时态)(of one thing) indicate that the other thing is about to begin; signal the start of (something about to come) 预示……的来临: The first snowfall *ushers in* the winter. 第一场雪预示着冬季的来临。The Viennese held a concert of music by Strauss to *usher in* the new year. 维也纳人举行施特劳斯音乐会迎接新年。

NOTE 当本短语所带的宾语是代词时,该代词须置于本短语的动词和副词之间。

usher into *vt.* 【可分性动词短语】 lead (a person, a group, or something) into (a place) 把……引领入(某处): She *ushered* me *into* the living room, which served as her office. 她把我引入客厅,这也是她的办公室。Staff members, please *usher* leaders *into* the VIP Room for a short break. 请工作人员把各位领导引领到贵宾厅稍作休息。They were quickly *ushered into* the office. 他们很快被带进了办公室。

usher out *vt.* 【可分性动词短语】 show (someone) or out a room or building 把(某人)带出……: The secretary *ushered out* the guest. 秘书把客人带了出去。I will ask my secretary to *usher* you *out* of the building. 我会让我的秘书把你们送出楼的。We were asked to leave and *ushered out* of the door. 我们被要求离开并被带出门外。

V v

vaccinate against *vt.* (常用被动语态形式) treat (a person or an animal) with a vaccine to protect them against (a certain disease)(给人或动物)接种疫苗预防(某种疾病): They had to *vaccinate* us *against* the influenza. 他们不得不给我们接种了抗这种流感的疫苗。Have you been *vaccinated against* TB? 你接种预防肺结核的疫苗了吗? Have you had your children *vaccinated against* whooping cough? 你给你的孩子们接种百日咳疫苗了没有? All the chickens on the farm have been *vaccinated against* bird flu. 鸡场所有的鸡只都已接种了抗禽流感疫苗。

value at *vt.* 【可分性动词短语】(用一般时态) calculate the value, price, or worth of (something)计算(某物)的价值为……: We *value* the house *at* 30,000 dollars. 我们计算这所房子的价值为 3 万美元。The seized smuggled goods was *valued at* about 500,000 pounds. 被截获的走私品价值约 50 万英镑。

vary from … to … *vt.* (用一般时态) change or be different from (one thing) to (another) in size, amount, or degree 从……变化到……,从……到……不同: The weather here *varied from* very cold *to* quite mild. 这里的天气变化很大,会从很冷变得相当温暖。The number of the new-generation TOEFL test questions may *vary from* one test administration *to* another, but there will never be fewer than 140 questions. 新一代托福考试每次考题的题目数量可能不尽相同,但都绝不会少于 140 个。Today's prices of color television sets *vary from* 100 dollars *to* 1,000 dollars. 如今的彩电价格从 100 美元到 1 000 美元不等。

verge on/upon *vt.* 【不可分性动词短语】❶(用一般时态) be near or close to (something)接近,靠近: The village *verges on* forests. 那村庄靠近森林。That street *verges on* Times Square. 那条街靠近泰晤士广场。❷be near or close to (the stated quality or condition); be very much like (something) 近乎,濒于: Her strange behavior sometimes *verges on* madness. 有时她的古怪行为近乎疯狂。The young man had taken over an old firm *verging on* liquidation. 这位年轻人接管了一家濒于破产的旧商号。The test was so difficult it was *verging on* the ridiculous. 这次的考试难得近于荒唐的地步。

NOTE 本短语中的 upon 用法比 on 正式,但不及 on 常用。

vice versa *adv.* (前常用连词 and 或 or) (used to indicate that the reverse of what you have said is also true) the other way around; conversely 反过来也是如此;反之亦然: Students should learn from teachers and *vice versa*. 学生应向教师学习,教师也应向学生学习。The brighter the light, the higher the current, and *vice versa*. 灯越亮,电流就越高;而灯越暗,电流就越低。John dislikes Mary and *vice versa*. 约翰不喜欢玛丽,玛丽也不喜欢约翰。Should I come to your house or *vice versa*? 是我去你家,还是你来我家?

NOTE 本短语来自拉丁语,虽然意为"反过来也是如此,反之亦然",但在翻译时往往不可简单地按字面翻译,而是要把它表示的意义比较具体地表达出来。

vie for *vt.*【不可分性动词短语】compete for (something) 竞争: Five candidates were currently *vying for* the Democratic presidential nomination. 目前有 5 名候选人在争夺民主党总统候选人的提名。The movie earned the actor a chance to *vie for* best male lead at the Film Independent Spirit Awards. 该影片为这位演员赢得了角逐电影独立精神奖最佳男主角的机会。There are seven teams *vying for* the prize. 有 7 个队在竞争这一奖项。

vie with *vt.*【不可分性动词短语】compete with (someone)与(某人)竞争: China will not *vie with* other countries in any form in space, the expert said. 这位专家表示,中国不会以任何方式与其他国家进行太空竞争。The shipping companies *vied with* each other to make the fastest Atlantic crossing. 船运公司相互竞争,欲以最快的速度跨越大西洋。

view as *vt.*【可分性动词短语】consider (someone or something) to be (something or doing something)把……认为是……: All of us *view* him *as* our strong competitor. 我们都认为他是我们强劲的竞争者。He told the BBC that "I don't *view* the Olympics *as* a political event. I view it as a sporting event." 他对英国广播公司说:"奥运会在我看来不是一个政治事件,我把它看作体育事件。" Don't *view* things *as* static and isolated. 不要把事物看成是静止的和孤立的。They admitted that the coalition forces were *viewed* by many Iraqis *as* an occupying force. 他们承认,许多伊拉克人都把联军视为占领军。

NOTE 本短语的同义短语是 see as 和 regard as,三者中 regard as 最为常用。

vote against *vt.*【不可分性动词短语】oppose (someone, something or doing something) in an election or vote (在选举或表决中)投票反对: Yet even then, I would still refuse to *vote against* him. 然而,甚至到了那个时候,我还是不肯投票反对他。Two Republican Senators from Arizona and Rhode Island joined 31 Democrats in *voting against* the bill. 来自亚利桑那和罗德岛的两名共和党议员同 31 名民主党议员一道投票反对该议案。At the meeting many people in the union *voted against* striking. 在会议上,许多工会成员投票反对罢工。

NOTE 本短语的反义短语是 vote for。

vote down *vt.*【可分性动词短语】defeat or reject(a person or his proposal)by voting 投票击败,投票否决: If he demands too much, the committee will *vote* him *down*. 如果他的要求过分,委员会就会投票否决。The Congress *voted down* a motion to change the department's structure. 国会否决了一项改革该部门结构的动议。Someone proposed that the proceedings of the meeting should be recorded on tape, but the suggestion was *voted down*. 有人

建议会议讨论情况应该录音，但这项建议被投票否决了。

NOTE 当本短语所带的宾语是代词时，该代词须置于本短语的动词和副词中间。

vote for *vt.*【不可分性动词短语】support (someone or something) in an election or vote (在选举或表决中)投票支持(某人)，投票赞成(某事)：I shall *vote for* Kevin because I think he's the better man. 我将投票支持凯文，因为我认为他是个好人。Over 60% of members *voted* in *for* the motion. 60%的成员投票赞成这一动议。

NOTE 本短语与 vote in favor of 的意义和用法相同，两者可互换使用。

vote in *vt.*【可分性动词短语】elect (a particular person or political party) to (a position of authority) by voting 投票选出(某人或某一政党)：(常用被动语态形式) The members of the national assembly will *vote in* a prime minister by a simple majority. 国民议会的议员以简单多数的选票就能选出总理。I never thought he would keep secrets about the matter from the people who *voted* him *in* as president. 我从未想到他会向投票选举他为总统的人们隐瞒此事。The 44-year-old opposition leader was *voted in* as Thailand's 27th prime minister. 这位 44 岁的反对党领导人当选为泰国第 27 任总理。

NOTE **1.** 当本短语所带的宾语是代词时，该代词须置于本短语的动词和副词中间。

2. 本短语的反义短语是 vote out。

vote in favor of ⇨ **vote for**

vote on/upon *vt.*【不可分性动词短语】make a decision about (a matter) by one's vote 投票对……进行表决：As we can't agree on this matter, let's *vote on* it. 既然我们在这个问题上不能达成一致，就投票表决吧。The National Assembly delayed *voting on* the bill due to strong opposition of the lawmakers. 由于一些议员的强烈反对，国民大会推迟了对该议案的投票表决。Berliners are to *vote upon* religious education. 柏林市民将就宗教教育问题进行投票表决。

NOTE 本短语中的 upon 用法比 on 正式，但不及 on 常用。

vote out ⇨ **vote in**

W w

wade in *vi.* (英国英语用法,非正式用语) ❶become involved in someone else's discussion, argument, or fight in a confident way that may not be very welcome 参与争论;参与战斗: It wasn't his affair, but he *waded in* with his opinion. 这本来不关他的事,但他却要参与进来发表意见。I *waded in* to help, but got kicked to the ground. 我上前助战,但被踢倒在地上。She just *waded in* and hit the kid smack in the face. 她参与进来,打了那个孩子一记耳光。❷start doing (something) in a determination way 坚定地开始做(某事): Let's *wade in* immediately because the job has to be done as soon as possible. 这项工作必须尽早完成,咱们马上开始干吧。

wade into *vt.* 【不可分性动词短语】❶(非正式用语) begin an attack of (someone or something) forcefully and with determination 抨击,攻击: He *waded into* his critics with his opening remarks. 他发表公开评论反击他的批评者。Tom *waded into* the boys with his fists flying. 汤姆挥着拳头痛击这些男孩。❷(非正式用语) intervene in (something) in a determined and a forceful way, often without thinking enough about the sequences (常指不计后果地)参与到(某事)中: She *waded into* the negotiation and the deal failed. 她参与到了谈判之中,结果这笔买卖砸锅了。He *waded into* the discussion without thinking. 他毫不犹豫地参与到了这场讨论中去。

wade through *vt.* 【不可分性动词短语】(非正式用语) spend a lot of time and efforts reading (a lot of information or correspondence); go through, or complete (something long, unpleasant, or uninteresting) with an effort 辛苦地阅读(大量资料或信件);艰难地完成(长而乏味之事): I've got all this correspondence to *wade through* before I can go home. 我得看完所有这些信件才能回家。A research worker has to *wade through* piles of data. 研究工作者必须要研读一堆堆的数据。

wait for *vt.* ❶stay in one place expecting or hoping (that someone or something will arrive) 等候,等待: At Hong Kong Airport government officials along with local people *waited* enthusiastically *for* the astronauts to arrive. 政府官员与香港人民一道在香港机场热情地等候着宇航员们的到来。We *waited*20 minutes *for* the bus. 我们等了 20 分钟的公共汽车。The airport was full of anxious relatives, *waiting* nervously *for* news of the missing plane. 机场里挤满了心急如焚的乘客亲属,他们都在等待着失踪客机的消息。❷hope or expect (that something will happen) 期待(某事的发生): There's no *point waiting for* her to change her mind. 期望她改变主意是徒劳的。We're *waiting for* the rain to stop before we go out. 我们等雨停了才能出去。❸(of something) be ready for (someone to take, have or use)(某物)等候(某人来领取、拥有或使用): There's a package *waiting for* you in the office. 办公室里有你的包裹待取。More than 3,000 flats at the outer edge of the city are *waiting for* buyers. 城边地区仍有 3 000 多套住房待售。There is a car *waiting for* you. 有一辆小轿车在等你。❹(主要用于美国英语中,非正式用语)delay the beginning of (a meal) until (someone) arrives 等(某人)到后再用餐: Don't *wait* dinner *for* me, I will be back very late. 别等我吃饭,我要很晚才会回来。

wait on/upon *vt.* &*vi.* (英国英语用法,非正式用语,常用于祈使句中) await; wait for me; wait a minute 等待,等一会儿: I'm not going to *wait on* you any longer. 我不再等你了。*Wait on*, will you? I'm just coming. 等一会儿,好吗? 我这就来。—*vt.*【不可分性动词短语】❶(常用一般时态) attend (someone) with everything he or she needs or wants as a servant, helper, etc. 服侍,伺候(某人): The nurses *waited upon* the wounded soldiers from morning till night. 护士们从早到晚地服侍伤员。He seems to expect me to *wait upon* him hand and foot. 他似乎要我必须无微不至地伺候他。Confined to bed, she needed to be *waited on* in everything. 她卧病在床,事事都需要别人侍候。❷(美国英语用法) sell goods in a store 在商店售货: She *waited on* customers all day at the department store. 她整天在百货商店售货。❸(主要用于美国英语中,正式用语) serve (someone) with food and drink, especially to customers in a restaurant (尤指在餐馆里)招待(顾客)进餐: The boy *waited on* us at the table. 那名男服务员在桌旁招待我们用餐。The waitress asked, "Have you been *waited on* yet?" "已经有人招待您了吗?"女服务员问道。❹(主要用于美国英语中,正式用语) wait for (a particular thing) to happen, before you do or decide anything 等待(某事)的发生: The foreign investors are *waiting on* election results there. 外国的投资者在等待着那里的选举结果。We cannot *wait on* the government to make changes at its own pace. 我们不能等政府按其速度进行改革。❺(正式用语,常用一般时态) make a formal visit to (someone) 正式拜访(某人): They *waited on* the ambassador yesterday. 他们昨天拜访了大使。We will *wait upon* you at your office tomorrow. 我们明天到你的办公室去拜访你。We *waited upon* the widow out of respect for her husband. 我们拜访那位寡妇太太是出于对她丈夫的尊敬。❻(用一般时态) follow 随着……而产生: Success *waits on* hard work. 成功是努力的结果。

NOTE 1. 本短语中的 upon 用法比 on 正式,但不及 on 常用。

2. 当本短语作"服侍,伺候(某人)"解时,第二个例句中的 wait upon someone hand and foot 已成为固定短语,意为"无微不至地伺候(某人)"。

3. 当本短语作"服侍,伺候(某人)"解时,同义短语是 attend on/upon 和 attend to。

wait out *vt.* (主要用于美国英语中) stay

where you are until something ends, usually something bad (原地)等待……结束: We *waited out* the storm all night, and made our way into the harbour in the morning. 我们等了一夜,风暴才停息,上午我们才进港。Let's go into the store and *wait out* the heavy rain. 咱们进到商店里去,等到大雨停吧。Don't interfere when they're like this. Let's *wait* it *out*. 当他们都这个样子的时候就不要去干预。等他们都过了这个劲后再说吧。

NOTE 当本短语所带的宾语是代词时,该代词须置于本短语的动词和副词中间。

wait up *vi.* ❶(非正式用语)not go to sleep or stay awake at night waiting for someone tore 熬夜等候(某人回家): The parents *waited up* for their daughter until she got home safe and sound. 父母熬夜等候他们的女儿,一直等到她平安地回到家才睡。I shan't be back till after midnight, so don't bother to *wait up*. 我得后半夜才能回来,所以不要熬夜等我。❷(仅用于美国英语的口语中,用于祈使句中,用一般时态)ask someone to stop so you can walk with him or speak to him (让别人停下来)等候(自己): Don't go so fast! *Wait up* for me! I need to talk to you. 别走得那么快! 停下来等我一下! 我要和你谈谈。I was running down the hill shouting, "Richard, Richard, *wait up*." 我跑下山,喊着:"理查德,理查德,等一等。"

wake up *v.* ❶(cause to) become awake after being asleep 醒来,唤醒: I *wake up* at the same time every morning without having to use an alarm clock. 我每天早晨不用闹表就能在同一时间醒来。Has she *woken up* yet? 她已经醒了吗? Mary always *wakes up* feeling hungry. 玛丽总是醒来就感觉饿。At six I *woke* him *up* and said we were leaving. 六点钟,我叫醒了他,并告诉他我们要走了。"We were all *waked up* by the explosion." said Ms Kalin, who worked in the American Embassy in Saudi Arabia's capital, Riyadh. "我们都被爆炸声惊醒了。"在美国驻沙特阿拉伯首都利雅德大使馆中工作的卡琳女士说道。❷(非正式用语,常用于祈使句中) start to pay more attention (to something), or make people pay more attention (to something)(使人们)注意: *Wake up* at the back! 后面的要多注意! It takes time to *wake* people *up*. 让人们都引起重视还需要时间。

NOTE 当本短语的宾语为代词时,该代词须置于本短语的动词和副词中间。

wake up to *vt.* 【不可分性动词短语】(常用一般时态) start to realize (something such as a situation or problem) 认识到(某种形势、问题等): The west began to *wake up to* the danger it faced. 西方开始认识到所面临的危险。People *woke up* at last *to* this threat. 人们终于认识到了这一威胁。Having *woken up to* the issue, the government is working hard to protect the rights and interests of rural workers by helping them solve various problems. 政府认识到了这个问题后,便努力去帮助农民工解决各种问题,保护他们的权益。

walk about/around/round *v.* (cause to) walk in a place or around (something), usually with no particular goal (使)四处走动,绕着……走动: Mark was tired of *walking about* on his own. 马克讨厌一个人四处转悠。After the race, *walk* the horse *around* for a time. 比赛过后，要把马遛一会儿。Mary often *walked around* the block to clear her head. 玛丽经常绕着大楼漫步以清理她的思绪。The old lady *walked* slowly *round* the garden. 老太太绕着花园慢慢地行走着。

walk away *vi.* leave a place, situation, or person on foot 走开，离开：Tom turned and *walked away*, then stopped. 汤姆转身走开了，然后又停住了脚步。No one knows you're a part of it. You can just *walk away*. 没人知道你参与其中，你可以一走了之了。

NOTE 本短语可转化为复合词 walk-away，意为"轻易取胜(的比赛)，轻易完成的事情"。

walk away from *vt.*【不可分性动词短语】❶ leave (something or someone) on foot 从……离开，从……走开：When I was *walking away from* my office, the telephone rang. 当我正要离开办公室时，电话铃响了。She was so angry that she *walked away from* him without a word. 她非常生气，连句话也没说就从他身边走开了。❷ abandon (something) 放弃：He decided to *walk away from* his job after quarreling with his boss. 和老板发生争吵后，他决定辞职。❸(非正式用语，无被动语态形式) defeat (a competitor) with little difficulty 轻而易举地战胜(竞争对手)：I'm sure that with Yao Ming and Wang Zhizhi playing in the team, our team will *walk away from* the other team. 我相信，队里有姚明和王治郅参战，我们队将能轻取对手。My horse just *walked away from* all the others in that race. 我的马在那场比赛中轻而易举地胜过了所有其他的马。

walk away with *vt.*【不可分性动词短语】(非正式用语) ❶ win or obtain (something such as a competition or a prize) very easily 轻而易举地赢得(比赛或奖品等)：The Labour Party candidate *walked away with* the election. 工党候选人轻松地赢得了选举。Our team should *walk away with* the cricket competition. 我们队应该会轻而易举地赢得这场板球赛的。Mary *walked away with* two first prizes. 玛丽轻松地赢得了两项头等奖。❷ steal and take away (something) 盗走(某物)：Someone *walked away with* my purse! 有人偷走了我的钱包！How can a thief *walk away with* a safe in broad daylight? 小偷怎么能够在光天化日之下把保险箱偷走呢?

NOTE 当本短语作"盗走(某物)"解时，同义短语是 make away with, run away with 和 walk off with。

walk into *vt.*【不可分性动词短语】❶ enter (a place) on foot 走进：On an early October morning in 1909, President Taft became the first US President to *walk into* the oval office. 1909 年 10 月的一个清晨，塔夫特总统成了第一位进入椭圆形办公室的美国总统。I saw her getting out of the car and *walking into* a bar. 我看见她下了汽车走进一家酒吧。❷(非正式用语) accidentally hit a part of your body against (something) when you are walking (在走路时)无意撞到(某物)：I *walked into* a table and bruised my right foot. 我在走路时无意中撞到了一张桌

子,使右脚皮肉青肿。❸(非正式用语,用一般时态,常与 straight 连用)succeed in getting (a job) very easily 轻而易举地得到(一份工作): She *walked* straight *into* a job at the bank as soon as she graduated. 她刚一毕业就轻而易举地在银行得到了一份工作。❹become caught in (something), especially because you were not sensible or careful enough to avoid it (尤指由于疏忽而)陷入……中: Mind you don't *walk into* a trap. 你要注意别落入圈套之中。They set a trap for him and he *walked* right *into* it. 他们给他设了一个圈套,而他正好中计。

walk of life *n.* (正式用语)a group consisting of all types of people with different backgrounds, jobs, etc. (由具有各种不同背景、职业等人员构成的)界,阶层;行业: The Chinese president hoped the Hong Kong Special Administrative Region government would continue its efforts to improve communications with all *walks of life* in Hong Kong, and be close to the general public. 中国国家主席希望香港特区政府继续加强与社会各界的沟通,贴近民众。Such a thing happens in all different *walks of life*. 这样的事在各个不同阶层都有发生。It is a fact that people from every *walk of life* enjoy television. 各行各业的人都爱看电视,这是个事实。

NOTE 本短语的复数形式是 walks of life。本短语的构成形式是"名词+介词+名词"。这类名词性短语复数形式的变化,一般都发生在第一个名词上。与此形式相同的名词性短语还有: brother in law (大/小叔子或大/小舅子), commander in chief (总司令), head of state (国家元首), point of view (观点), prisoner of war (战俘), way of life (生活方式),等等。

walk off *vi.* leave somewhere on foot, usually without telling people that you are going to leave 走开,不辞而别: Don't *walk off* yet, I haven't finished my story. 别走啊,我的事还没讲完呢。He turned and *walked off* without a word. 他一句话也没说,就转身离去了。

—*vt.* reduce or get rid of (something unwanted) by going for a walk 用走路来消除(无益之物): I'll have to go out into the country more, and *walk off* some of this fat. 我得多到乡下去走走,把我身上这些脂肪减下去。He tried to *walk off* his depressed mood. 他试图靠走路来消除其沮丧的情绪。

walk off with *vt.* 【不可分性动词短语】(非正式用语) ❶take (something that does not belong to him) without permission; steal (something)(不经允许)拿走(他人之物); 偷走(某物): I'll bet you *walked off* with my mobile phone. 你肯定把我的手机拿走了。Don't leave your suitcases there unguarded, somebody may *walk off* with them. 你们不要把手提箱放在那儿无人看管,可能会有人把它们偷走。❷(常用于新闻英语中) win or achieve (something) very easily 轻而易举地赢得(某物),轻易得到(某物): He *walked off* with the title in men's 60 meter hurdles at the World Indoor Championships. 他在世界室内田径锦标赛男子 60 米栏决赛中轻松夺冠。Maybe she'll *walk off* with the first prize! 她也许会轻而易举地拿到一等奖呢!

walk on *vi.* ❶continue walking in one's

intended direction 继续走下去：She *walked on without a backward glance.* 她连头也没回，继续走了下去。❷ have a small part or appear briefly, in a play or film 在戏剧或电影中担当不重要角色：Tom was happy just to be able to *walk on*, to play the policeman. 汤姆在戏中能扮演个跑龙套的警察就心满意足了。

NOTE 本短语可转化为复合词 walk-on，意为"（在戏剧或电影中担任的）小角色"。

walk out *vi.* ❶ go outside on foot 走出去：The astronauts *walked out* of the re-entry capsule of the spaceship, smiling and waving to the recovery team. 宇航员们面带微笑地走出航天飞船返回舱，并向回收人员挥手致意。❷（非正式用语，常用一般时态）(especially of workers) go on strike（尤指工人）罢工：All the workers *walked out* on Friday morning. 所有的工人们都在星期五上午罢工了。French diplomats *walked out* on December 1 to protest the government's planned budget cuts. 法国外交官 12 月 1 日举行了罢工，以抗议政府计划削减财政预算。❸（常用一般时态，常与 of 连用）leave (a meeting, performance, or an unpleasant situation) suddenly, especially as an expression of one's disapproval（尤指表示抗议而）退席，退场：Both teams of negotiators had *walked out* of the peace talks. 双方的谈判代表都曾从和平会谈中退席过。It was such a bad movie that I felt like *walking out* in the first fifteen minutes. 电影很不好看，开演 15 分钟时我就想退场了。Shortly after the start of the third session, the defense team *walked out* of the court in protest. 在第三次开庭后不久，辩护律师团愤然退出了法庭以示抗议。❹（非正式用语，常与 with 连用）(of a man and woman) form a serious relationship, usually leading to marriage（男女间）建立恋爱关系，谈恋爱：He understood that this was an invitation from her. She was prepared to *walk out* with him. 他明白这是她的邀请。她准备与他谈恋爱了。

NOTE 本短语可转化为复合词 walkout，意为"罢工（者），罢课（者）；（表示抗议的）退席"。

walk out on *vt.*【不可分性动词短语】（非正式用语，常用一般时态）❶ suddenly leave and end your relationship with (usually someone who needs you or depends on you) 突然离开（常指需要或依靠你的人）：She *walked out on* her boyfriend. 她突然离开了她的男友。Her husband had *walked out on* her and their children a year before. 她的丈夫在一年前就遗弃了她和孩子们。❷ stop doing (something) before it is completed 放弃做（某事）：So you are *walking out on* the job, aren't you? 那么，这份工作你就不打算干下去了？

walk over *vt.* & *vi.*（非正式用语）win without difficulty (against someone) 轻易地取胜（某人）：（常用一般时态）The horse *walked over* in the third race. 这匹马在第三场竞赛中轻而易举地获胜了。Our team just *walked over* the opposition. 我们队轻取了对手。

—*vt.*【不可分性动词短语】treat (someone) badly or inconsiderately 欺负；轻率地对待（某人）：You'd better not *walk over* the little girl. 你最好不要欺负这位小姑娘。Don't let your husband *walk* all

over you like that. 不要让你的丈夫那样虐待你。Time and time again the weak have been *walked over* by the strong. 常常有这种情况,弱者遭受强者随意欺凌。I'm not about to let them *walk over* me. 我不会让他们轻率地对待我。

NOTE 本短语可转化为复合词 walkover,意为"轻易取得的胜利"。

wander about/around *v.* walk around (an area or place) in a casual way, often without intending to go in any particular direction 漫步,徘徊: Look at that little boy *wandering about*, perhaps he's lost his mother. 看那个四处徘徊的小男孩,他可能是找不到妈妈了。My sister likes *wandering around* the city at night. 我的妹妹喜欢晚上在城里逛逛。

want for *vt.* (正式用语,无被动语态形式,主要用于否定句中,用一般时态)(of a person) lack (something you really need, especially food, clothing, shelter, money, love, etc.)(指人)缺少: We make sure that our children don't *want for* anything. 我们保证让我们的孩子什么都不缺。She's never *wanted for* money or possessions. 她从不缺钱财。I have always tried to make sure that my children *want for* nothing. 我一直努力保证我的孩子们要什么有什么。

NOTE 本短语最后一个例句中的 want for nothing 已成为固定短语,意为"应有尽有"。

want in *vi.* (非正式用语,用一般时态) ❶(of a person or an animal) wish to enter (a place)(指人或动物)想要进入(某处): The visitor *wants in*. 来访者想要进来。Open the door. The dog *wants in*. 把门打开,狗要进来。❷want to be involved in (something such as a plan or an activity)想要参与(某项计划或活动): This is the last time I'm asking you, do you *want in* or not? 我问你最后一次,你想不想参与进来?

NOTE 本短语的反义短语是 *want out*。

want out *vi.* (非正式用语,用一般时态,常与 of 连用) ❶(of a person or an animal) wish to leave (a place)(指人或动物)想要出去: She *wanted out* of the jail cell so badly she started to scream. 她极想从囚室里出去,所以她就叫了起来。The dog scratches on the door when he *wants out*. 那狗想要出去时就用爪子挠门。❷(of a person) wish to leave a situation or relationship and no longer be involved in it (指人)想离开;想摆脱某种处境: He couldn't stand that job any longer, so he *wanted out*! 他忍受不了那种工作,所以他不想干了! Don't imagine that you can depend on his support any longer, he *wants out*. 别以为你可以依靠他的支持,他还想摆脱目前的处境呢。Mary is fed up with her husband, she *wants out* of the marriage. 玛丽讨厌她的丈夫,便想与他脱离婚姻关系。

ward off *vt.* ❶do (something) to prevent (someone or something) from harming you 防止: Brushing your teeth regularly helps to *ward off* tooth decay. 按时刷牙有助于防止蛀牙。The findings prove that a "positive emotional style" can help *ward off* the common cold and other illnesses. 研究结果证明,"积极的情绪"有助于预防普通感冒和其他疾病。It is no easy job to *ward off* a cultural invasion. 防止文化侵入并非易事。❷keep (a person or an animal) away or at a distance 避开：She was so beautiful that she had difficulty in *warding off* all the men who wanted to marry her. 她长得太漂亮了，以致她很难避开所有想要娶她的男士。They have built a fence to *ward off* dogs. 他们筑起了围栏来拦挡狗。

warm up *vt.*【可分性动词短语】❶make (something or someone) warm 加热，使……变暖：I'll *warm up* some soup for lunch. 我要热点汤，午餐时喝。The remainder of Sunday's joint was *warmed up* for lunch on Monday. 星期日吃剩下的大块肉热了一下充当了星期一的午餐。Mr Smith was so late that his dinner got cold, his wife had to *warm* it *up*. 史密斯先生回家太晚，饭菜都凉了，他的太太不得不把饭菜热一下。Have a cup of coffee to *warm* you *up*. 喝杯咖啡，暖暖身子吧。

—*vi.* get warmer 变暖：Why is it this room always takes so long to *warm up*? 这个房间怎么总是用这么长时间才变暖呢？Drink this and you'll soon *warm up*. 把这喝下去，你很快就会暖和起来。When spring comes, it will *warm up* soon. 春天一到，天气很快就会暖和起来。

—*vt.* & *vi.* ❶(cause to) prepare for a race, by doing exercises or by practicing just before it starts(使)(在比赛前)做准备活动：On Saturday morning I arrived at the stadium a little earlier than my friend and jogged to *warm up* for the baseball practice. 星期六上午，我比我的朋友稍早到达体育馆，并慢跑为棒球练习热身。Do some stretching exercises to *warm up* your muscles. 做一些伸展运动好好活动一下肌肉。This is a good exercise for *warming* you *up*. 这是一种很好的热身练习。❷(of a machine or engine)(cause to) become ready for use a little while after being switched on or started (给)(机器或发动机)预热：He is going to *warm up* the engine, because we'll start soon. 他要去预热发动机，因为我们很快就将出发了。Don't forget to *warm* the car *up* for a few minutes before you go. 别忘了先把车预热几分钟再起车。The instrument should be *warmed up* before it is used. 这种仪器在使用之前应预热。In cold weather it takes longer for the car to *warm up*. 在寒冷的天气里，汽车需要较长的预热时间。❸(especially of a comedian or speaker) make (the audience) become more excited or enthusiastic (使)(观众或听众)变得更兴奋，变得更活跃：The comedian told jokes to *warm up* the crowd. 滑稽演员讲了些笑话使观众活跃了起来。The class is so boring, let's *warm* it *up*. 课堂气氛太沉闷了，让我们活跃起来吧。By midnight the party had really *warmed up*. 到了午夜，聚会才真的热闹起来了。

NOTE **1.** 当本短语用作及物性动词短语，所带的宾语是代词时，该代词须置于本短语的动词和副词中间。

2. 本短语可转化为复合词 warm-up，意为"(在体育活动或比赛前的)热身，准备动作；(发电机、收音机等的)预热"。

warn about/of *vt.*【可分性动词短语】make (someone) conscious of (a possible problem or danger) so he or she will not

W

be hurt 使(某人)意识到(可能发生的问题或危险);警告;Why didn't you *warn* me *about* his quick temper? 你为什么没警示过我他爱发脾气呢? The American Embassy to Saudi Arabia *warned about* such a terrorist attack on Friday. 美国驻沙特阿拉伯大使馆曾在星期五对这一恐怖袭击发出过警告。She was *warned of* the danger of being cheated by that guy, but she insisted on doing things her own way. 她被警告过有被那小子欺骗的危险,但她却坚持自行其是。The Defense Secretary *warned* the government *of* dealing with the next generation of terrorists. 国防部长告诫政府要应对新一代恐怖分子。

warn against/off *vt.* advise (someone) to avoid (someone, something or doing something) 警告(某人)不要……: The government *warned* its citizens on Saturday *against* traveling to the central Asian state. 政府星期六警告其公民不要去那个中亚国家旅行。I've been *warned against* that company, so I'll find a job somewhere else. 因有人警告我不要去那家公司工作,所以我便到别处谋职。Recent studies *warn off* drinking too much caffeine. 最近的研究结果警示人们不要喝过多含咖啡因的饮料。

NOTE warn off 常用于英国英语中。

wash away *vi.* wash continuously 不断地洗:That machine *washes away* automatically. 那台机器能自动地连续洗涤。

—*vt.*【可分性动词短语】❶(of something such as rain or floods) destroy (something) and carry it away by the force of the water (雨水或洪水)冲毁,冲走(某物): Heavy rains caused by the typhoon have *washed away* many houses. 台风所造成的强降雨冲毁了许多房屋。The stone bridge was *washed away* by the flood. 那座石桥被洪水冲毁。The water is muddy because it *washes away* soil from the hill slopes. 水流里含有泥土,那是因为它冲走了山坡上的土壤。When running down the hill slopes, the water *washes* soil *away*. 水从山坡往下流时便冲走了土壤。❷remove (something) by or as if by washing 洗去,洗刷:The nurse *washed away* the blood. 护士洗去了血迹。Her tears had *washed* the paint *away* from her face. 泪水把她脸上的胭脂都冲掉了。Prayers can *wash away* your sins. 祈祷能洗刷你的罪过。

NOTE 当本短语用作及物性动词短语,所带的宾语是代词时,该代词须置于本短语的动词和副词中间。

wash down *vt.*【可分性动词短语】❶wash the whole surface of (something) with a lot of water (用大量的水)冲洗(某物的)表面: Use hot water and detergent to *wash down* the kitchen worktables. 要用热水和清洁剂来冲洗厨房工作台。They earn their living by *washing* people's cars *down*. 他们靠为人冲洗汽车生活。❷drink (something such as water) after putting food or medicine in your mouth, especially to make them easier to swallow 用(水等)吞送(食物或药物): He swallowed some coffee to *wash down* the remainder of the toast in his mouth. 他大口喝了些咖啡,把留在口中的烤面包咽了下去。At the meal the two first ladies *washed* their meal *down* with soft drinks. 用餐

时，两位第一夫人都喝无酒精饮料下饭。He took two tablets immediately and *washed* them *down* with a cup of water. 他很快地拿了两片药，用一杯水把它们吞服下去。

NOTE 当本短语所带的宾语是代词时，该代词须置于本短语的动词和副词中间。

wash off *v.* (常用一般时态)(cause to) be removed by washing (把……)洗掉：Don't worry about the dirty marks. They'll *wash off* easily. 不用担心那些污迹。它们很容易洗掉的。I let some ink fall on the tablecloth, and I don't know whether I can *wash* it *off*. 我在桌布上洒了一些墨水，我不知道能不能把它洗掉。

NOTE 当本短语用作及物性动词短语，所带的宾语是代词时，该代词须置于本短语的动词和副词中间。

wash one's hands of *vt.* (非正式用语，常用一般现在时) intentionally stop being involved with (someone or something) and not to take any responsibility for them 与……断绝关系；不再参与……：I've decided to *wash my hands of* her. 我已决定与她断绝关系。The government had *washed their hands of* the affair. 政府已不再插手那项事务。He seems to have *washed his hands of* the job. 他好像已经不干那件工作了。

NOTE 本短语中的名词 hand 必须用复数形式。

wash out *v.* ❶(常用一般时态)(cause to) be removed by washing (把……)洗掉：Thick ink like that doesn't usually *wash out*. 像那样浓的墨迹一般是洗不掉的。It's hard to wash out the spot from the coat. 那件上衣的污点很难洗掉。I don't think you can *wash* the mark *out*. 我想你洗不掉那块污迹。❷wash (something) thoroughly and quickly, especially the inside of a container 把(尤指容器内部)彻底、洗净：Don't you ever *wash out* your coffee cups? 你就不彻底地洗一洗自己的咖啡杯子？We must *wash* the tubes *out* after the experiment. 做完实验后，我们必须要彻底清洗试管。❸(常用一般时态) destroy or make (something such as a bridge, road) impossible to use by the action of a lot of water 冲毁，冲垮(道路、桥梁等)：Heavy rain *washed out* three important roads overnight. 一夜的工夫大雨就冲毁了三条主要的道路。The old stone bridge was *washed out* yesterday morning. 昨天上午，那座旧石桥被冲垮了。❹(常用一般时态)(of rain) prevent (a sports match or an outdoor event) from continuing (雨)使(体育比赛或某种户外活动)中断：Heavy rain *washed out* five of the seven games. 大雨使七场比赛中的五场中断。The cricket match was *washed out* by rain. 这场板球赛因下雨而被迫中断。I'm afraid this rain will *wash* our garden party *out* again. 恐怕这场雨又要使我们的游园会泡汤了。❺(of dye, etc.) be removed by washing; fade (染料等)因洗涤而褪色，褪色：Permanent dyes won't *wash out*. 耐久性染料不会因洗涤而褪色。All the color has *washed* out of these old curtains. 这些旧窗帘的颜色全都给洗掉了。The cloth was gradually *washed out*. 这块布已洗得逐渐褪了颜色。❻(非正式用语，用被动语态形式) feel or look very tired 感到疲倦，看上去疲倦：After a

day' work in the garden, Tom looked *washed out*. 在园子里干了一整天的活，汤姆看上去十分疲倦。The flu really *washed* me *out*. 这场流感着实把我搞得精疲力竭。

NOTE **1.** 当本短语作"冲毁,冲垮(道路桥梁等)"解时,可用主动形式表被动意义。例如:

> The old stone bridge had *washed out*.
> 那座桥已被冲垮。

2. 当本短语用作及物性动词短语,所带的宾语是代词时,该代词须置于本短语的动词和副词中间。

3. 本短语可转化为复合词 washout,意为"(道路或铁路)被冲坏的部分;大败,破产;失败者"。

wash up *v.* ❶(英国英语用法)wash (the plates, pans, glasses, cups, knives, forks, and other things which have been used in cooking and eating a meal)洗(用过的餐具):I can help you to cook and *wash up*. 我可以帮你做饭和洗盘子。It's my turn to *wash up* the plates and dishes. 该我洗盘子和碟子了。The breakfast things haven't been *washed up* yet. 早餐用的餐具还都没有洗。❷(美国英语用法)clean (yourself) with soap and water, especially your hands and face 洗手,洗脸,洗澡:After crying so much, she had to *wash up* before coming downstairs. 大哭一场后,她不得不把脸洗了洗才下楼去。I'll go *wash up* for dinner. 要吃饭了,我去洗洗手和脸。She *washed up* and then went to bed. 她洗完澡后就上床睡觉了。❸(常用被动语态形式)(of a river or sea) carry (something) onto a piece of land and leave it there (河水或海水)将……冲上岸:Some of the oil has *washed up* on a neighboring island. 一些油污已冲上了附近的一个岛屿上。The incoming tide *washed up* the body of the drowned sailor. 上涨的潮水把溺死水手的尸体冲上了岸。A lot of dead fish were *washed up* on the beach. 有许多死鱼被冲上了海滩。❹(常用被动语态形式) bring about the end of; finish 结束,使完蛋:Ever since the investment scandal, Mr Smith's career has been *washed up*. 自从出了投资丑闻,史密斯先生的职业生涯就被断送掉了。This error is going to *wash* me *up*. 这一失误将把我断送掉。❺(非正式用语,用被动语态形式)(of a relation) be ruined; be no longer happily married (指关系)被毁;婚姻破裂:Smith and I aren't husband and wife any more. We are *washed up*. 史密斯和我已不再是夫妻,我们的婚姻关系已破裂。

NOTE 当本短语用作及物性动词短语,所带的宾语是代词时,该代词须置于本短语的动词和副词中间。

waste away *vi.* (especially of a person) gradually become thinner and weaker or lose weight, strength and health, etc. over a period of time, because he or she is ill or not eating properly (尤指人)变瘦,虚弱:Since my aunt's operation, she has simply been *wasting away* and may not last long. 我姑姑自手术以来就日益消瘦,也许活不了多久了。They *wasted away* for lack of food. 由于吃不饱,他们越来越虚弱了。He has *wasted away* to skin and bones. 他已瘦得皮包骨了。

waste one's breath *vi.* (主要用于口语中) have no effect with what you say;

talk in vain; talk without making any impression (of someone) 枉费唇舌，白说：Don't *waste your breath* reporting it to the police , they never care about stolen bicycles. 别枉费唇舌去报案了，警察从来不理会自行车被盗的事。The tone of her voice told him that he was *wasting his breath*. 她说话的语调告诉他，他在浪费口水。

NOTE 1. 本短语常以 don't waste your breath 的形式使用。

2. 本短语的另外一种表达形式是 waste one's words。例如：

> Please don't *waste your words* speaking to her, she never listens.
> 请你不要和她白费口舌了。她从来就不听话。

3. 本短语的名词性短语形式是 a waste of breath。例如：

> I could try and persuade her to stay, but it would probably be *a waste of breath*.
> 我可以试着劝她留下来，但可能是枉费唇舌。

watch dog *n.* ❶ a dog who provides protection by watching for or guarding a house or property against intruders 看门狗：A *watch dog* guards the house against thieves. 看门狗看家防盗。*Watch dogs* bark to alert their owners of an intruder's presence. 看门狗吠叫是向主人报警：有人闯进来了。❷(一般用 watchdog 形式) a person or an organization that tries to guard against stealing, wasteful use of public money, understandable practices, etc. 监督者，监督机构：She is a *watch dog* of public morals. 她是公共道德的监督者。China's discipline *watch dog* sent an inspection team to Sichuan to ensure the proper use of relief funds and materials. 中国的纪律监察机构向四川派出了一个检查组以确保救灾资金和物资的适当使用。The International Atomic Energy Agency (IAEA) is UN's nuclear *watchdog* agency established on 29 July, 1957. 1957年7月29日成立的国际原子能机构是联合国的核监督机构。

NOTE 当本短语作"看门狗"解时，另外一动表达形式是 guard dog，其为美国英语用法。

watch for *vt.* pay attention so that you notice or see (something) when it arrives or happens 关注，等着观看：We'll be *watching for* any developments. 我们将关注事态的任何发展。We'd better *watch for* a better chance to do that. 我们最好找个更好的机会去做那件事。The boy *watched for* dolphins jumping on the horizon. 男孩翘首等着看海豚跃出水面。

watch out *vi.* (非正式用语，常用一般时态，常用于祈使句中) (used to warn someone) be careful, because something unpleasant might happen to him or her (用来警示某人)留神，注意：You have to *watch out* because there are land mines everywhere. 你们必须留神，因为到处都有地雷。You could have a nasty accident if you don't *watch out*. 你要是不注意，就会出大事故。*Watch out*! Those mushrooms could be poisonous! 注意！那些蘑菇可能有毒！

NOTE 本短语与 look out 的第二个义项意义和用法相同，两者可互换使用。

watch out for *vt.*【不可分性动词短语】(常用于祈使句中) ❶(常用一般时态)be careful of or look out for (someone or something) in order to avoid a problem 注意,提防,当心:*Watch out for* that man who wears dark glasses. 要提防那个戴墨镜的人。You must *watch out for* the traffic here. 你一定要当心这儿的车辆。❷ be aware of (someone or something) 注意,留意(某人或某物):*Watch out for* this girl. She's going to be a great tennis player one day. 注意这个女孩子,她将来有一天会成为一个了不起的网球运动员。*Watch out for* big discounts and clearance sales at the time of the year. 留意点今年这个时候的大减价和清仓大甩卖。

watch over *vt.*【不可分性动词短语】(正式用语) guard, protect or take care of (someone or something) to make sure that nothing bad happens to them 护卫,警戒,看守:The prince has two bodyguards *watching over* him every hour of the day. 王子有两名保镖全天候护卫。He was watched over by a policeman. 他由一名警察看守着。Engineers and workmen *watched over* the dikes day and night during the flood. 洪灾期间,工程师和工人们日夜看守着堤堰。

wave aside *vt.*【可分性动词短语】(常用一般时态) ignore (someone's ideas, feelings, or opinions) because you don't think they are important enough to consider seriously 对……置之不理,对……不屑一顾:Whenever we mention finance, he just *waves aside* our concerns. 每当我们提出资金问题时,他都对我们所关注的事置之不理。Their criticisms were *waved aside*. 他们提出的批评意见没人理睬。The manager *waved* their protests *aside*. 经理对他们的抗议不屑一顾。

NOTE 当本短语所带的宾语是代词时,该代词须置于本短语的动词和副词中间。

wave at *vt.*【可分性动词短语】move (something such as your hands) smoothly and gently from side to side at (someone) 朝(某人)挥动(手等):She *waved at* her parents as the bus pulled away. 当公共汽车开动时,她向父母挥手告别。Is that woman *waving* her hand *at* me? I don't know her. 那位女士是在向我挥手吗?我并不认识她呀。He *waved* his fists *at* the other man in a threatening manner. 他威胁地朝另一名男子挥舞着双拳。

wave down *vt.*【可分性动词短语】make (a vehicle) stop by waving your arm or hand as a signal at the driver 挥手以示意(车辆)停下:She went out of the building and *waved down* a taxi. 她走出大楼,挥手叫了一辆出租车。If a taxi comes along, *wave* it *down*. 如果有出租车过来,挥手让它停下。When I was driving along quite happily when a policeman *wave* me *down*. 我正十分快活地驾车行驶时,一名警察招手让我停车。

NOTE 当本短语所带的宾语是代词时,该代词须置于本短语的动词和副词中间。

wave to *vt.* move the hand and arm as a greeting to (someone) 挥手向(某人)致意:The Queen *waved to* the people who stood along the street welcoming her. 女王向沿路站立欢迎她的人群挥手致意。The children are *waving to* you, please wave back. 孩子们在向你招手,请你也向他们招招手。

way of life *n.* a pattern in which people in a particular place live in 生活方式：Now you have stayed in London for 3 years. Do you like the British *way of life*? 你已在伦敦住了三年，你喜欢英国的生活方式吗？A modern society should accept a variety of different *ways of life*. 一个现代社会应该接受各种不同的生活方式。

wear away *v.* ❶(cause to) become thin and disappear because it has been used or rubbed a lot; be reduced gradually (使)磨薄，逐渐磨损：The footsteps of thousands of visitors have *worn away* the steps. 成千上万游客的脚步已把台阶磨损了。The inscription on the ring had almost *worn away*. 戒指上刻的文字几乎都磨没了。In the course of centuries, the wind has *worn* the rocks *away*. 经过几个世纪，这些岩石已被风化掉。❷(常用被动语态形式)(cause to) weaken (使)虚弱，削弱：The illness *wore away* her strength. 疾病使她体力虚弱。My aunt has been *worn away* by her recent illness. 最近一场疾病使我的姑妈身体很虚弱。❸(of a feeling) gradually disappear (指某种情感)逐渐消失：At last my patience *wore away*. 我终于慢慢地失去了耐性。Her patience is almost *worn away* by his endless complaints. 她的耐心几乎被他没完没了的怨言消磨殆尽。❹(常用一般过去时)(of time)(cause to) pass slowly (指时间)慢慢地消逝，消磨(时间)：The year was *wearing away*, and Christmas would soon be here. 一年慢慢地过去，圣诞节很快就要到来了。If you don't study or work hard, you'll *wear away* your youth. 如果你不努力学习或工作，你将虚度青春。We *wore* the afternoon *away* in arguing. 整个下午我们都在争论中度过。

wear down *vt.* & *vi.* (cause to) gradually disappear or become thinner by using or rubbing it (使)逐渐磨掉，磨薄：The synthetic rubber tyre has *worn down* badly. We should fit a new one. 那只合成橡胶的轮胎已磨损得很严重，我们得换新的了。The feet of countless visitors *wore down* the threshold of the old building. 无数游客的脚步磨损了这座古老建筑物的门槛。The stone steps had been *worn down* by many years of use. 由于多年的使用，这些石阶已被磨得很薄了。

—*vt.* make (someone) gradually lose his or her energy or patience 使(某人)筋疲力尽，感到厌倦：Looking after high-spirited children can soon *wear* a person *down*. 照管这些活泼好动的孩子很快就会使人筋疲力尽。Months of illness *wore* her mother *down*. 患病数月使她母亲精疲力竭。The monotony of his voice *wore* the listeners *down*. 他那单调乏味的声音使听众不胜厌烦。He believed that he could *wear* her *down* if he asked many questions. 他相信，如果问她许多问题就能使她感到厌烦。

NOTE 当本短语用作及物性动词短语，所带的宾语为代词时，该代词须置于本短语的动词和副词中间。

wear off *vt.* & *vi.* (usually of a surface) (cause to) be reduced, as by rubbing (使)(常指表面)磨损，磨掉：I bought those new plates cheaply, and the pretty rose pattern has *worn off* already. 我买的那些新盘子都很便宜,但上面漂亮的玫瑰花图案都已磨损。Heavy traffic has *worn off* the rough surfaces of the stone-paved streets in that small town. 繁忙的交通磨损了那小镇粗糙的石头路面。

—*vi.* ❶ gradually disappear 逐渐消失: The smell of the new paint will *wear off* in about a week. 新刷油漆的味儿大约一个星期之后就会消失。The effect of the painkilling drug did not *wear off* for several hours. 止痛药的效力持续了数小时后才消失。❷ (of something such as a sensation or emotion) pass away gradually (感觉或情感)逐渐消逝: The pain in her shoulder was starting to *wear off*. 她肩部的疼痛感觉已开始慢慢地消失了。I got bored with the job once the novelty *wore off*. 当新奇感消失后,我对这件工作就失去了兴趣。

wear on *vi.* (用一般时态)(of time) pass gradually or slowly; (of a meeting, etc.) last long in an uninteresting manner (时间)缓慢地过去: As the evening *wore on*, my headache grew worse. 随着夜晚慢慢地过去,我的头痛加剧了。The meeting *wore on* all afternoon. 会议一直开了一个下午。

—*vt.*【不可分性动词短语】(of something) annoy (someone) 使人厌烦: Your constant complaining is really *wearing on* me. 你没完没了的抱怨真让我厌烦。

wear out *vt.* & *vi.* ❶ use (something) a lot so that it no longer works, or can no longer be used 把(某物)用坏,损坏: The rear tyres of the car had *worn out*. 汽车的后轮胎都磨损了。The children have all *worn out* their shoes. 孩子们都把鞋穿坏了。That child can *wear* a pair of shoes *out* in a month. 那孩子一个月就能穿坏一双鞋。I must buy a new suit. This one is *worn out*. 我要买一套新衣服。这套已穿坏了。❷ (常用被动语态形式) make (someone or oneself) very tired or exhausted 使(某人或自己)筋疲力尽: The game *wore* him *out*. 比赛使他筋疲力尽。You need a holiday or you'll *wear* yourself *out*. 你需要休假了,要不就会把自己搞得精疲力竭。She was *worn out* from looking after her elderly mother. 照顾年迈的母亲使她疲惫不堪。

—*vt.*【可分性动词短语】cause to be used up 使用尽,耗尽: After about an hour, my patience was *worn out*. 大约一个小时以后,我耐不住性子了。Little Tom got a toy car that would run on a battery, and he used it so much that he soon *wore* it *out*. 小汤姆得到了一台靠电池驱动的玩具汽车。由于他玩的时间太长,很快就把电池的电耗尽了。

NOTE 当本短语用作及物性动词短语,所带的宾语为代词时,该代词须置于本短语的动词和副词中间。

wear thin *vt.* & *vi.* (cause to) become thin from much use, wearing, or the passing of time (使)变薄: My trousers have *worn thin* at the knees. 我裤子的膝部都磨薄了。These old silver coins have *worn* very *thin*. 这些古老的银币都用得很薄了。I've *worn* the seat of this skirt *thin*. 我都把这条裙子的臀部磨薄了。

—*vi.* ❶ (非正式用语,常用进行时态) (of a joke, an excuse, or an explanation) become less interesting or effective because it has been used too much (笑话、借口或解释由于使用过多而)变得无趣,变得不起作用: The joke began to *wear thin* when you heard it too many times. 笑话听太多遍就没有意思了。This excuse about not having enough staff to run the trains is *wearing thin*. 没有足够的人手开火车的这个借口站不住脚了。❷(常用进行时态)(of patience) become less and less (指耐性)慢慢失去: I've warned you several times about being late and my patience is *wearing thin*. 就你迟到的事,我已经警告了你几次。我都要失去耐性了。The teacher's patience began to *wear thin* when he saw that no one knew the lesson. 老师发觉大家对功课一无所知,就开始不耐烦起来。

wed to *vt.* (正式用语,用被动语态形式) strongly support (an idea, opinion, etc.) or enjoy (doing something) very much 固守(某种观念、见解等);倾心于(做某事): The minister is very much *wedded to* the idea of free trade. 这位部长坚守自由贸易的思想。His firm is still *wedded to* old-fashioned methods, and is sure to fail. 他的公司还按老一套方式经营,这注定会失败的。

weep about/for/over *vt.* (正式用语) cry because of (something or someone); cry (tears) because of (something or someone) 因……而哭,为……而流泪: What is that woman *weeping about* now? 那名妇女为什么在哭? She needed to *weep for* the loss of her husband. 她失去了丈夫当然要哭。She's *weeping* bitter tears *over* her lost son. 她为失去的儿子而痛哭。

weigh down *vt.* 【可分性动词短语】(常用被动语态形式) ❶(正式用语) make (someone) heavy and unable to move easily with heavy load 使(某人)负重,不堪重负: If you *weigh* yourself *down* you'll get very tired. 如果你身负重物,你就会很疲劳。I was *weighed down* with the shopping on my back. 我背着购买的货物,腰都给压弯了。Get the bundle off my back, it's really *weighing* me *down*. 把我背上的包裹拿下来,它要把我压趴下了。She was *weighed down* by the extra work and the burden of the family. 额外的工作和家庭负担把她压得喘不过气来。❷make (someone) feel worried because of problems, responsibilities, and duties (由于某些问题、责任或义务)使(某人)担忧: All the news of murder and famine is *weighing* me *down*. 所有这些谋杀和饥荒的消息都令我担忧。Wall Street has been *weighed down* by economic uncertainty. 经济形势的不确定性使华尔街感到忧虑。She looked older, *weighed down* by all her new responsibilities. 由于被新的责任所困扰,她看上去比以前老了。

NOTE 当本短语所带的宾语是代词时,该代词须置于本短语的动词和副词中间。

weigh in *v.* ❶(cause to) be weighted; be of a particular weight (使)称重量,重量为: Who is responsible for *weighing* these men *in*? 谁负责称这几名男选手的体重? Because it was such a small plane, the passengers and their luggage had to *weigh in* before takeoff. 因为这架飞机很小,所以在起飞前乘客及其行李的重量都要称一下。The world heavyweight champion boxer Tyson *weighed in* at 245 lbs. 世界

重量级拳击冠军泰森的体重为245磅。❷(非正式用语,常与with或动词不定式短语连用)join in a discussion or conversation by saying something important 参与讨论,参与谈话:Several experts *weighed in* with some opinions. 几位专家参与讨论并提出了一些意见。One angry woman *weighed in* to remind us that a lot of what we'd read was not true. 一名愤怒的妇女插话,提醒我们说,我们所看到的很多内容都不真实。

weigh on/upon *vt.*【不可分性动词短语】(无被动语态形式) cause problems or worry to (someone or someone's mind); be burdensome to 使苦恼;成为……的负担:The decision to leave her has been *weighing* heavily *on* Tom's mind. 离她而去的决定使汤姆十分苦恼。John's wrong doing *weighed upon* his conscience. 约翰的错误行为使他深感内疚。The high price of property *weighs* heavily *on* many businesses. 房地产价格的居高不下成了许多企业的沉重负担。

NOTE 本短语中的upon用法比on正式,但不及on常用。

weigh up *vt.*【可分性动词短语】(主要用于英国英语中) ❶(非正式用语)judge or form an opinion about (something or someone)估量,评价:The judges carefully *weighed up* all the evidence. 法官们仔细地推敲了所有的证据。She's a strange person, I can't quite *weigh* her *up*. 她是个怪人,我无法对她做出充分的评价。She looked at me, *weighing* me *up* when I first walked into her office. 当我第一次步入她的办公室时,她边看边琢磨着我。❷consider (the good and bad aspects of something) in order to reach a decision about it(在做决定之前)考虑;权衡:Before buying something *weigh up* the advantages and disadvantages of it. 在购物之前,要考虑一下其优缺点。*Weighing up* the pros and cons, we think the Renminbi's exchange rate should not appreciate too much at present, but should remain basically stable. 权衡利弊,我们认为人民币的汇率目前不应增值太多,而应保持基本稳定。I am *weighing up* whether to go or not. 我正在考虑去还是不去。

NOTE 当本短语所带的宾语是代词时,该代词须置于本短语的动词和副词中间。

well off *adj.* ❶(非正式用语)rich, or having enough money to live well 富裕的,小康的:They worked long hours and became quite *well off*. 他们加班加点地工作,这使他们变得相当富裕。It's hard to believe he can be *well off* working for his father. 他给他父亲打工竟也能这么富有,真是令人难以相信。❷(英国英语用法,与for连用) having a lot of (something)有很多的:We're *well off* for jobs around here. 我们这里的工作机会很多。Our city is *well off* for parks and gardens. 我们市有很多公园和花园。❸(非正式用语,与for连用)in a good situation, or very lucky 处于顺境的,十分幸运的:We're fairly *well off* for cinemas where we live. 我们很幸运,因为在我们住的地方看电影方便。

NOTE 1. 本短语后可接现在分词(短语)作补语。例如:

> The laid-off worker is *well off* running a grocery store.
> 这位下岗工人经营一间杂货店,生活过得不错。

W

2. 本短语的比较级形式是 better off 或 more well off,最高级形式是 best off 或 most well off。见 better off。

3. 本短语的反义短语是 badly off。

4. 本短语可转化为复合词 well-off,意为"富裕的,很多的;供应充足的;处于有利地位的"。

well out *vi.* (与 from, of 连用)(of a lot of liquid) come to the surface and begin to flow (大量液体)流出: Blood *welled out* from the cut. 血从切口中涌出。Water was *welling out* of the ground. 水从地下源源流出。

well to do *adj.* (正式用语) having or making enough money to live comfortably; rich; prosperous; rich 小康的,富裕的: He came from a *well to do* family. 他出身小康之家。John's father owns a company and his family is very *well to do*. 约翰的爸爸拥有一家公司,所以他家非常富裕。

NOTE 本短语可转化为复合词 well-to-do。well-to-do 可用来表示一类人,前面也要加定冠词。如:

> This is the part of town where the *well-to-do* live.
> 这个城区是富人居住区。

well up *vi.* ❶(常与 in, out of 连用)(of a liquid) come to the surface and begin to flow (某种液体)流出,涌出,喷出: She was so angry that tears *welled up* in her eyes. 她气得热泪都流出来了。American scientists announced that Mars rover Spirit discovered signs that small amounts of water once *welled up* in the soil where the rover landed. 美国科学家宣布,"勇气"号火星车在它着陆地点的土壤中发现曾有小股水流出的迹象。Oil *welled up* out of the ground. 石油从地下喷出。❷(与 in 或 inside 连用)(of an emotion) rise or suddenly become stronger, to the point where you have to express it(某种感情)产生;突然变得很强烈: A sense of hurt *welled up* in her heart. 一种受伤害的感觉从她内心油然而生。He could feel the anger *welling up* inside him. 他能感觉到怒气在涌上心头。When he walked offstage to the sound of enthusiastic applause, he felt a triumphant joy *welling up* inside. 当他在热情的掌声中走下舞台时,内心里感有一种胜利的喜悦。

What about …? *s.* (仅用于口语中,用于句首) ❶(used in making a suggestion or request) would you like (something or to do something); what do you think of (something or doing something)(用于提出建议、要求或征求意见)……怎么样: *What about* a cup of coffee? 喝杯咖啡怎么样? "When and where shall we meet next time?" "*What about* Thursday afternoon at Frank's?" "我们下次什么时候、在哪儿见面?""星期四下午在弗兰克家怎么样?" *What about* selling me the car? 把车卖给我怎么样? *What about* Linda, should we invite her? 琳达我们该不该请? ❷(used in inquiring for information) what news or plans have you concerning (someone or something)(用于打听消息)……怎么样?: *What about* Robert? What happened to him? 那罗伯特怎么样? 他出什么事了吗? We are all ready. *What about* you? 我们都准备好了,你呢? "*What about* transport?" "That's all arranged." "交通怎么样?""都安排妥当了。" You're talking to yourself. Well, *what about* it? 你在自言自语地说什么?

what for *n.* (主要用于英国英语中,仅用于口语中,常与动词 get 或 give 连用) a scolding, or other punishment 责骂,处罚: Tom got *what for* from his father for answering him rudely. 汤姆因与爸爸顶嘴而受到了爸爸的责骂。If I catch that boy in my garden again, I'll give him *what for*. 如果我再在我的花园里抓到那个男孩子的话,看我将怎么惩罚他。

NOTE 1. 本短语为不可数性名词短语。

2. 本短语常以 what-for 形式使用。

What (…) for? *s.* (仅用于口语中)(used for asking the reason for something) for what purpose or reason; why 为什么?: "I need to have your name and address." "*What for*?" "我需要你的姓名和地址。" "做什么用?" Jim's mother told him to wear his hat. "*What for*?" he asked. 吉姆的妈妈让他戴帽子。吉姆问道,"为什么?" *What* did you do that *for*? 你为什么做那事呢?

what have you *n.* (仅用于口语中,常与 and 或 or 连用)(used for showing that you could also mention other things of the same kind) and other similar things; and so on 同一类东西,等等: The abandoned office was full of documents, books, and *what have you*. 这间不再使用的办公室里到处是文件、书籍等这类东西。So many things are unsafe theses days, water, milk, medicine, or *what have you*. 现在,不安全的东西太多了,水、牛奶、药品等等。She has to deal with the various taxes and *what have you*. 她不得不应付各种税费等等。

NOTE 1. 本短语为不可数性名词短语。

2. 本短语与 what not 意义和用法相同,两者可互换使用。what not 常以其连体形式 whatnot 使用。

what if *conj.* (主要用于口语中,用于句首)(used when asking about the consequences of something happening, especially something undesirable) what will or would happen if … 如果……怎么办: *What if* you don't pass your exams? 如果你考试不及格怎么办? *What if* it rains while we are a long way from a shelter? 如果天下了雨而我们离避雨的地方又很远,那该怎么办? "*What if* students really pay more attention to good-looking teachers and learn more?" they asked. "如果学生们真的更注意长相漂亮的教师并且能够学到更多的东西,那怎么办呢?" 他们问道。

NOTE 本短语用于询问事情发生的后果,其后通常接令人不快或不受欢迎的事情。

What's cooking? *s.* (非正式用语)(used to ask about what is happening) what's the matter; what'sha ; what's going on 发生了什么事: *What's cooking*? Why is the crowd in the street? 发生什么事了?为什么街上有这么多人? I just saw the police arrive, *what's cooking*? 我刚才看到警察来了。出了什么事? *What's cooking* at the office these days? 办公室里这些天都发生了什么事?

NOTE 1. 本短语为旧式英语用法,现已较少使用。

2. 本短语的同义短语是 What's the matter? 和 What's up? 的第一个义项。

what is more *adv.* (主要用于口语中,常与 and 连用)(used for introducing an additional statement that supports what you have already said) moreover; in addition; and more importantly 而且,更重要的是: *What is more*, 35 pairs of provinces or states and 145 pairs of cities from China and the United States have forged friendly ties. 而且中美两国已缔结了35对友好省州和145对姊妹城市。Roses are such beautiful flowers, and *what's more* they are very easy to grow. 玫瑰是一种十分漂亮的花，而且还很容易种植。He came home after midnight, and *what's more* he was drunk. 他半夜之后才回家。更有甚者，他还喝醉了。

NOTE 本短语的同义短语是 in addition。

What's the matter? *s.* (仅用于口语中，常与 with 连用)(used to ask or talk about why someone seems worried, unhappy, or ill, why something about a situation seems wrong, or why a machine seems not to be working properly) what's wrong; what's the problem; what's happening 怎么了？发生了什么事?：“*What's the matter* with you?” “I'm ill. I have a headache and a stomachache.” “你怎么了?”“我生病了。我头痛，胃也痛。” Why are you crying? *What's the matter*, son? 你为什么哭？发生了什么事了，儿子？*What* on earth *was the matter* with her? 她到底出了什么事?

what's up *s.* ❶(仅用于口语中，常与 with 连用)(used to express suspicion or curiosity) what's happening; what's the matter (用于表示怀疑或惊奇) 发生了什么事：Why are you crying? *What's up*? 你为什么哭？出了什么事？*What's up* with David? Is he drunk or something? 戴维怎么了？他是喝醉了，还是怎么回事？*What's up* with this bill? I don't owe you any money. 这账单是怎么回事？我不欠你钱呀。❷(非正式用语)(a greeting used when meeting someone you know) how are you; nice to meet you (见到熟人时用的问候语) 你好：“*What's up* (with you), Robert?” “你好吗，罗伯特?”

NOTE 当本短语作“你好”解时，相近的致候语还有：How are things (with you)? / How's it going? / How are you doing? / How goes it? / How are things?

what is what *n.* (仅用于口语中，常用于动词 know 或 learn 之后) the real facts about a situation that are important to know 要熟悉的真实情况：He's worked in the insurance business all his life, so he knows *what's what*. 他在保险业干了一辈子，对那一行十分熟悉。When Tom started his new job, it took him several weeks to learn *what was what*. 当汤姆开始从事他的新工作时，用了好几周的时间熟悉情况。It's high time you told him *what's what*. 你该告诉他事情的真相了。

what not ⇨ **what have you**

What of it? *s.* (仅用于口语中)(used to rudely say that you think a particular fact someone has mentioned is not important) why should I care; what does it matter; why is that important 这有什么可在乎的，那有什么关系的：“She didn't invite us to the party.” “*What of it*? I don't care.” “她没邀请我们参加聚会。”“这有什么？我才不在乎呢。”“Tom missed the first bus.” “*What of it*?” “汤姆没赶上头班车。”“那有什么要紧的?”

What time do you make it? *s.* (英国英语用法)(used to ask someone with a watch what time it is) what time is it (用于询问时间) 几点了?：*What time do you make it* now, Robert? 现在几点了，罗伯特?

NOTE 在英语中,用于询问时间的表达法有很多。较常用的有:*What is the time*? / *What time is it*? /*What time you got*? / *What time do you have*? (美国英语用法)/*Have you got the time*? (英国英语用法)/*Do you have the time*? (美国英语用法)/*Do you know the time*? 等。

when necessary ⇨ **if necessary**

whether (…)or … *conj*. used to show a choice of things, or that different things are possible 是……还是……: *Whether* there is peace *or* war on the peninsula is difficult to say. 半岛上是和还是战还很难说。Someone's got to tell her, *whether* it's you *or* me. 不管是你还是我,总得有人告诉她。She doesn't even know *whether* her daughter is dead *or* alive. 她甚至不知道她的女儿死了还是活着。I am weighing up *whether* to go or not. 我正在考虑去还是不去。

NOTE 本短语可用来引导主语从句、宾语从句、表语从句、同位语从句和让步状语从句。

while away *vt*. 【可分性动词短语】spend (time)pleasantly in a relaxed way, because you have nothing else to do (以轻松愉快的方式)消磨,打发(时间): He *whiled* his time *away* by playing cards with others. 他以与他人玩牌来消磨时间。She *whiled away* the hours on the train by reading newspapers. 坐火车时,她以看报纸来打发时间。The evenings were *whiled away* in endless games of cards. 晚上的时间都在没完没了的牌戏中消磨掉了。

whistle in the dark *vi*. (主要用于美国英语中,非正式用语,常用进行时态) pretend to be calm or brave when in fact you feel afraid or worried 故作镇静,装作勇敢: Tom said he could fight the bully with one hand, but we knew that he was just *whistling in the dark*. 汤姆说他只用一只手就可以打败那个暴徒,但我们知道他只是在说大话壮胆子。

NOTE 本短语的原意是,人在黑暗中走路,边走边吹口哨,以给自己壮胆,并显示自己不害怕。与此相同的短语还有 whistle past the graveyard。

white lie *n*. a small or unimportant lie told to spare feelings or from politeness (为避免伤害他人感情或出于礼貌的)谎言:"I saw Mary yesterday and told her that her baby was lovely." "Well, we both know her baby isn't. But a *white lie* isn't going to hurt anyone." "我昨天遇见玛丽,并跟她说她的小宝宝很可爱。""嗯,我们都知道她的小宝宝并不可爱。不过善意的谎言不会伤害任何人。" Here's why we sometimes tell *white lies*. First, white lies hide painful truths. They help avoid suffering. 这是我们有时善意说谎的原因:首先,善意的谎言能隐瞒令人痛苦的事实,有助于避免痛苦。

NOTE 本短语中的 white 意为"无害的"。

willing to *adj*. (后接原形动词) ready to (do something) 愿意做(某事): Bush expressed deep concerns over the strong quake in Sichuan province, and was *willing to* provide any possible assistance for disaster relief. 布什对四川省发生的强烈地震深表关切,并愿意为救灾提供一切可能的帮助。Is your father *willing to* help? 你爸爸愿意帮忙吗? He is not *willing to* accept advice. 我不愿接受劝告。

NOTE 本短语的比较级形式是 more willing

to,最高级形式是 most willing to。

win back *vt.*【可分性动词短语】get back (something or someone that you have lost)赢回,重新得到:We hope to *win back* the trophy we lost last year. 我们希望赢回去年失去的奖杯。How can I *win back* your trust? 我怎么才能重新得到你的信任呢? What can I do to *win* my wife *back*? 我怎样才能使我妻子重新回到我的身边?

NOTE 当本短语所带的宾语是代词时,该代词须置于本短语的动词和副词中间。

win out/through *vi.* (非正式用语,用一般时态) succeed, especially after great difficulty or struggle(尤指经历巨大困难后)最终成功,获胜:Half way through the race Tom was last, but in the end he *won out*. 赛跑的前半程汤姆落后,但最终他却赢得了胜利。It was a struggle, but truth *won out* in the end. 这是一场斗争,但真理最终取得了胜利。I know that you are sure to *win through* in spite of difficulties. 我知道你肯定会克服重重困难,取得成功的。

win over/around/round *vt.*【可分性动词短语】❶persuade (someone) to agree with you or support you, often when he or she was opposed to you before (通过说服而)赢得(常指以前不同意或反对你的人)支持:He disagrees at the moment, but we can finally *win* him *around* to our point of view. 虽然他现在不赞同,但我们最终能赢得他对我们所持观点的赞同。Bush's visit to Britain was designed to *win over* Europeans who strongly opposed the US-led war against Iraq, reports said. 报道称,布什对英国的访问旨在争取强烈反对以美国为首发动的对伊战争的欧洲人。She wanted to marry, but her mother could never be *won over*. 她想结婚,但总是无法赢得母亲的支持。We still hope to *win* her *round*. 我们仍然希望把她争取过来。❷gain a victory over (something or someone)取得对……的胜利:They had *won over* a lot of difficulties before accomplishing the task. 他们战胜了许多困难才圆满地完成了那项任务。The Chinese *won over* his US rival Johnson at the International Athletics Association All-Star Tournament. 这名中国选手在国际田径协会全明星锦标赛上战胜了他的美国对手约翰逊。

NOTE 当本短语所带的宾语是代词时,该代词须置于本短语的动词和副词中间。

win the day *vi.* be successful (in dealing with opposition or an opponent)成功,取胜:To *win the day* in the highly competitive society is easier said than done. But she has made it. 在竞争激烈的社会里获得成功说起来容易做起来难,但是她已经做到了。It was Foster's bowling that finally *won the day* for England. 福斯特的投球最终为英格兰队赢得了胜利。Few in Westminster doubt that the government will *win the day*. 英国议会中没几个人怀疑政府会取胜。

NOTE 本短语中的动词 win 可被 carry 替换,两者的意义和用法相同。

wind down *vt.*【可分性动词短语】❶(英国英语用法,常用一般时态)make (the window of a vehicle) move downwards, usually by turning a handle 把(汽车车窗)摇下:If a stranger stops you, just *wind* the car window *down* a fraction. 如果有生人拦住你的车,你只能把车窗摇下一个小缝。He stopped next to her and

winded down his window. 他把车停在她身边，并摇下车窗。❷(of a business) gradually reduce (the amount of work that it does) before closing down completely (指企业在关闭之前)逐渐减少(产量)：The factory will *wind down* production before closing next year. 该厂在明年关闭之前将逐渐减少产量。

—*vt.* & *vi.* end or finish (something) gradually 结束，逐渐完成(某事)：The party started to *wind down* around 2:00 am. 聚会于凌晨两点左右才结束。The UN has decided to *wind down* the peace-keeping mission in the region. 联合国决定逐步结束在该地区的维和使命。The government intends to *wind* the project *down* in early summer. 政府计划今年初夏完成该项目。

—*vi.* (非正式用语)(of a person) relax and become calmer or less active, especially after work or excitement (尤指人在工作或兴奋之后)放松，平静下来：Television is very useful for *winding down* before going to bed. 睡前看看电视很有助于精神放松。I often have a cup of cold drink to *wind down*. 我经常喝杯冷饮料使自己平静下来。

NOTE 当本短语作"把(汽车车窗)摇下"和"放松，平静下来"解时，反义短语是 wind up。

wind up *vt.* 【可分性动词短语】❶(英国英语用法，常用一般时态) make (the window of a vehicle) move upwards, usually by turning a handle, etc. 把(汽车车窗)摇上去：The car windows don't *wind up* very easily. 这些车窗都很不容易摇上去。He *wound up* all the car windows and drove along. 他摇上了所有车窗便驱车前行。She started *winding* the window *up* but I grabbed the door and opened it. 她开始把车窗往上摇，但我紧紧抓住并打开了车门。Are all the windows *wound up*? 所有的车窗都摇上去了吗？❷ tighten (the spring of a clock, watch, etc.), usually by turning a key, to make it work or run 上紧(钟、表等的)发条：If you forget to *wind up* your watch it will stop. 如果你忘记给手表上弦，它就会停掉。I forgot to *wind* my watch *up*. What time is it? 我忘记了给手表上发条。几点啦？The clock's stopped, you'd better *wind* it *up*. 钟停了，你最好给它上一下发条。Mary *wound up* the toy car and let it run across the room. 玛丽把玩具汽车的发条上紧，让它在房间里跑。❸(英国英语用法，常用一般时态) stop running (a business company or other organizations) and close them down completely 使(公司或其他机构)停止运营：The Bank of England was determined to *wind up* the company. 英格兰银行决心停止该公司的运营。The company is losing a lot of money, so it's being *wound up*. 该公司亏损大量资金，所以其将停止运营。❹(英国英语用法，非正式用语，常用被动语态形式) cause (someone) to become excited or angry 使(某人)振奋；使(某人)生气：The football game always *wound* the fans *up* into a high pitch of excitement. 足球比赛总是令球迷们极度兴奋。Mary got *wound up* about the matter and talked for two hours. 玛丽对那件事颇感振奋，她一直讲了两个小时。Please don't *wind* him *up*, he causes me enough trouble. 请别惹他生气了，他给我制造的麻烦够多的了。

—*vt.* &*vi.* (非正式用语,用一般时态) finish, end or stop doing (something such as an activity) (使)结束:The meeting finally *wound up* in the early hours of the morning. 会议终于在次日凌晨结束了。After Putin *wound up* his second term of presidency, he served as a premier. 普京在结束其第二个总统任期后,担任了总理职务。I wish they would *wind* this meeting *up*, so I could go home. 我希望他们结束会议,这样我就可以回家了。

NOTE 当本短语用作及物性动词短语,所带的宾语是代词时,该代词须置于本短语的动词和副词中间。

wink at *vt.* 【不可分性动词短语】❶quickly close and open one eye, usually as a signal or an informal greeting to (someone)向(某人)使眼色,向(某人)眨眼示意:Mark *winked at* me knowingly. 马克会意地朝我眨了眨眼。❷(非正式用语,常用一般时态) pretend that one does not know about(something bad or illegal) in a way that suggests approval (对不好或违法之事)佯装不知,睁一只眼闭一只眼:The *mother winked at* her son's bad habit. 那位妈妈对她儿子的坏习惯佯作不知。I don't know why the government *winks at* corruption. 我不知道为什么政府对腐败现象视而不见。His wife's extravagance is usually *winked at*. 他对妻子的铺张通常睁一只眼闭一只眼。

wipe off *vt.* 【可分性动词短语】❶remove (dirt or liquid) (from something), for example by using a cloth or your hand 把……擦去:She applied a little lipstick and *wiped* it *off*. 她抹了一点口红,可又把它擦掉了。Paint can't be *wiped off*. 油漆是擦不掉的。❷(常用一般时态) put an end to (something such as a debt)免除(债务):Generously he agreed to *wipe off* their small debt to him as a mark of respect for their dead father. 出于对他们死去的父亲的尊敬,他慷慨地同意免除他们所欠的一小笔债务。

NOTE 当本短语所带的宾语是代词时,该代词须置于本短语的动词和副词或介词中间。

wipe out *vt.* 【可分性动词短语】❶clean (the inside of a container) after use, with a cloth (用抹布)把(某种容器的内部)擦干净:Just *wipe out* the fridge with a dump cloth. 用湿抹布把冰柜里面擦干净。We always *wipe* the bottles *out* before returning them to the milkman. 在把奶瓶退还给送奶员之前,我们总是把瓶内擦洗干净。Make sure the inside of the coffee pot is thoroughly *wiped out*. 咖啡壶的里面一定要彻底擦干净。❷(常用一般时态)remove or get rid of (something) completely 彻底消除,去掉:We want to *wipe out* our world hunger in twenty years. 我们想要在二十年之内在我们这个世界上彻底消除饥饿。Scientists throughout the world are searching for a cure that will *wipe out* cancer. 全世界的科学家们都在寻求能根除癌症的疗法。❸(非正式用语,常用被动语态形式) completely destroy (something) or kill (a group of people or animals)彻底摧毁,消灭:The floods *wiped* the whole town *out*. 洪水把整个城镇冲毁。The Indians *wiped out* the soldiers who were sent to stop their attacks. 印第安人将派来阻止他们攻击

的士兵全部歼灭。The entire population on the island was *wiped out* by the terrible disease. 岛上所有的居民都被那场可怕的疾病夺去了生命。❹(非正式用语)make (someone) extremely tired 使(某人)疲劳不堪: The early-morning meetings really *wipe* me *out*. 一大早就开了几个会议,真搞得我疲劳不堪。

NOTE 1. 当本短语所带的宾语是代词时,该代词须置于本短语的动词和副词中间。

2. 本短语可转化为复合词 wipeout,意为"失败,丢丑"。

wipe (up) the floor with ⇨ **mop (up) the floor with**

wish for the moon ⇨ **cry for the moon**

with a light heart *adv.* feeling happy 心情愉快地: I accepted her invitation *with a light heart*. 我愉快地接受了她的邀请。He went to meet her *with a light heart*. 他满身轻松地去见她。

NOTE 本短语里的形容词 light 可被 heavy 所替换,构成短语 with a heavy heart,意为"心情沉重地"。

with a view to *prep.* ❶(正式用语,后接动名词短语) with the hope of (doing something) in the future; with the aim or intention of (doing something) 希望,目的在于: *With a view to* improving his ability to speak French, he spends most of his holidays in France. 为了提高讲法语的能力,他的大部分假期都在法国度过。He has bought a piece of land *with a view to* building a house. 他买了块地皮,目的是要建一所房子。❷considering 考虑到,鉴于: This subject is one that should be handled *with a view to* the long-range interests of the country. 这是一个应从国家的长远利益来考虑的问题。

NOTE 当本短语作"希望,为了,目的在于"解时,另外一种表达形式是 with an eye to。例如:

> The company took these measures *with an eye to* increasing its profits.
> 公司采取这些措施的目的是增加利润。

with all one's heart and soul *adv.* (used for emphasizing that a feeling is very strong) with one's whole heart; in earnest; sincerely (用于强调某种强烈的感情)全心全意地,真诚地: Who do you love *with all your heart and soul*? 你全心全意地爱着谁? She wished *with all her heart and soul* that he would come. 她诚心诚意地希望他能来。I thank you *with* all *my heart and soul*. 我向你表示真诚的感谢。

NOTE 1. 本短语中的 and soul 可以省略。

2. 本短语的同义短语是 from the (bottom of one's) heart。

with all one's might and main *adv.* (正式用语) by using all your strength, energy or complete effort 竭尽全力,不遗余力地: Tom was tugging the rope *with all his might and main*. 汤姆竭尽全力地拉拽着绳子。John tried *with all his might and main* to solve the problem. 约翰不遗余力地去解决那一问题。She pushed and pulled *by all her might and main*, but the door remained firmly closed. 她拼命地又推又拉,可是门仍然紧紧地关着。

NOTE 1. 本短语中的 and main 可以省略。

2. 本短语的另外一种表达形式是 by all

one's might and main,但已不常用。

with an eye for ⇨ **have an eye for**

with an eye to ⇨ **with a view to**

with confidence ⇨ **in confidence**

with ease *adv.* easily; without much effort 容易地,不费劲地:Young children seem to master computer games *with* great *ease.* 儿童们似乎很容易就能掌握如何玩电脑游戏。We completed the work *with* relative *ease.* 我们比较容易地做完了那项工作。The advantage of electric energy is that it can be controlled *with ease*. 电能的优点是其易于控制。

with … in mind *prep.* with something as one's aim or as the reason or basis for one's action 出于……目的,出于……原因:He is old. *With* this *in mind* he always drives slowly. 他上了年纪,他因此一贯开慢车。

with one accord *adv.* (正式用语) with everyone expressing their agreement at the same time, either in words or in action (在语言或行动上)一齐地,一致地:All the faces turned our way *with one accord*. 所有的人都一起转过脸朝我们这边看来。They protested *with one accord* that they had not done it. 他们一致抗议说他们没有干那件事。

with regard(s) to *prep.* concerning; about(a particular subject)关于,至于:(正式用语) He knew nothing with regard to the case. 关于这个案子他一无所知。*With regards to* whether that company is in breach of the contract, it is essential to point out the following. 至于那家公司是否违反了合同,有必要指出下面几点。What advice do you have *with regards to* sharing the house with them? 对于同他们合住这套房子,你有何高见?

NOTE 1. with regard to 为标准用法,且较为常用,而 with regards to 则为非标准用法。

2. 本短语的同义短语是:in regard(s) to, in respect of, with respect to 和 with reference to。

with/in respect to *prep.* (正式用语) concerning; about(a subject)关于,至于:*With respect to* the purchase of combat aircrafts, the Government has not taken any decision. 关于购买战斗机的事宜,政府还没有做出任何决定。"We have the same position *with respect to* this problem, the same as the six previous Administrations," said the American ambassador to China. 美国驻华大使表示:"对于这一问题,我们与前六届政府的立场是相同的。"

NOTE in respect to 常用于美国英语中。

with that *adv.* and then, or after saying or doing that 接着就,随即:"Good luck!" he said, and *with that* he walked off into the darkness. "祝你好运!"他说着便移步消失在黑暗中。"*With that*, I'm happy to take your questions," the Foreign Ministry Spokesperson said after having made two announcements at the regular press conference. 外交部发言人在例行的记者招待会上发布了两则通告后接着说:"下面,我很高兴回答大家的提问。"

with the exception of *prep.* (used for saying that a person or thing is not included in what you are saying) except; not included in; apart from 除……之外:The players should all be fit for Sunday's game, *with the exception of* Tom. 除了汤姆之外,应该说所有的运动员都适于

参加星期日那场比赛。I know nothing *with the exception of* what I read in the newspapers. 除了在报纸上看到的之外，我一无所知。*With the exception of* the earth, none of the planets is inhabited. 除了地球之外，其他星球上都没有居民。

NOTE 本短语的同义短语是 except for。

with the hope(s) of ⇨ **in the hope(s) of**

with the intent of *prep.* (正式用语) intending 意欲，打算：He put too many sleeping tablets in her drink *with the intent of* murder. 他往她的饮料里投放了大量的安眠药片，其目的在于谋杀。He broke into the house *with the intent of* stealing. 他闯入房中企图偷窃。In some places it has become common among young women to get married *with the intent of* divorce. 年轻女子结婚的目的就是为了离婚，这在有些地方已司空见惯。No one goes to college *with the intent of* failing each exam. 没有一个上大学的人想每次考试都不及格。

NOTE 本短语中的名词 intent 可被 intention 替换，两者的意义和用法相同。

withdraw from *vt.* ❶(cause to)leave or move away (使)撤出，撤走：Most Iraqis want the US-led occupation forces to *withdraw from* Iraq as early as possible. 大多数伊拉克人都希望以美国为首的占领军尽早撤离伊拉克。Our forces should be *withdrawn from* the dangerous country to avoid further loss. 我们的军队应该撤那个危险的国家，以避免进一步的损失。We must *withdraw* our children *from* that unsuitable school. 我们一定得让我们的孩子从那所不合适的学校退学。❷(cause to) not take part in an activity (使)退出，(使)不参加：So far, more than 500 liberal candidates have *withdrawn from* legislative elections, the Interior Ministry said. 内务部称，迄今为止已有500多名自由派候选人退出了议会选举。Why are you *withdrawing from* the race? 你为什么要退出比赛？He *withdrew* his horse *from* the race. 他拉马退出了比赛。❸take(money) out of (a bank account, etc.)从(银行账户等)提取(款项)：She *withdrew* $5,000 *from* her bank account. 她从银行账户中提取了5 000美元。

within an ace of *prep.* (英国英语用法，非正式用语) very close to; within a narrow margin of (doing something) 几乎，差一点儿就(做成某事)：He was *within an ace of* success. 他几乎就要成功了。My friend came *within an ace of* winning the game. 我的朋友差一点儿就赢得了那场比赛。He was *within an ace of* falling into the pond, when I managed to catch hold of his coat. 他差一点儿就掉进池塘里，幸亏我一把抓住他的大衣。I came *within an ace of* death in Iraq. 我几乎把命丢在了伊拉克。

NOTE 1. 本短语后一般接表示危险之事的名词或动名词(短语)。

2. 本短语与 within an inch of 意义和用法相同，两者可互换使用。

within an inch of ⇨ **within an ace of**

within/in (one's) reach *adj.* being able to touch by stretching, or to have or do something because they have enough money or skill 伸手可及，买得起，做得到：I like to have my reference books *within my reach*. 我喜欢把参考书放在我伸手可及的地方。Reduced ticket prices put the best seats

W

within everyone's reach. 减低的票价使所有的人都能买得起最好的座位。Don't price this item too high, it should be *within reach* of the average customer. 本品不要定价太高,应该让普通的顾客都能买得起。

without delay *adv.* without waiting; immediately; at once 立即,马上,迅速: Do it *without* any *delay*! 立即去做,不得延误! We are calling on rich nations to honor their debt reduction promises *without* further *delay*. 我们呼吁富裕国家加速兑现减债的承诺。

without (a) doubt *adv.* (used for emphasis) beyond all doubt; very definitely (用于强调)毫无疑问,一定,不容置疑: *Without doubt*, investigation will lead us to correct conclusions. 毫无疑问,调查会使我们得出正确的结论。The UN chief said the past year was *without doubt* "a difficult year" for the world. 联合国秘书长称,过去的一年对这个世界来说,无疑是"困难的一年"。The refugees, *without a doubt*, are the most vulnerable. 这些难民无疑是最弱势群体。"Are you going to watch the final of the World Cup tonight? It's Italy to France." "*Without (a) doubt*!" "你今晚看不看世界杯决赛? 是意大利队对法国队。""肯定要看啦!"

NOTE 1. 本短语的强调形式是 without a shadow of a doubt。例如:

> This is *without a shadow of a doubt* the best film I have seen all year.
> 这部电影,无可置疑,是我全年中所看到的最好的电影。

2. 本短语与 no doubt 意义和用法相同,但 no doubt 不及本短语的语气强烈。

without fail *adv.* ❶(used to emphasize that something always happens) definitely or certainly (用于强调某事经常发生)肯定,一定: He calls me every Sunday night *without fail*. 他每周日晚上都肯定给我打电话。In the afternoon he would *without fail* take a nap lasting from 2 to 3 hours. 每天下午他一定得睡上两三个小时的觉。❷(used to emphasize that something will definitely happen) certainly (用于强调某事即将发生)一定: I want to see you here at 12 o'clock *without fail*. 我一定要在12点钟在这个地方见你。I shall kill you, *without fail*, if you ever mention my visit here. 如果你说出我来过这里的话,我一定杀了你。The chief criminal shall be punished *without fail*. 首恶者必办。

NOTE 本短语用于修饰句中动词,通常置于句尾。

wolf in sheep's clothing *n.* ❶a person who seems to be harmless or friendly, but is in fact dangerous or evil 披着羊皮的狼,伪装善良的险恶之人: I want you to stay away from that man. He's a *wolf in sheep's clothing*. 我要你离那个男人远一点。他是一只披着羊皮的狼。I do not trust the salespeople at that store. They are all *wolves in sheep's clothing*. 我不相信那家商店里那些卖货的,他们都是些表面好心里坏的家伙。❷something that seems good at first but is in fact harmful 初看上去好但实际上有害的东西: We believed that their proposal was a *wolf in sheep's clothing*. 我们相信,他们的建议包藏祸心。

wonder about *vt.*【不可分性动词短语】❶think about (someone or something) because you have doubts or are worried about them 对……表示怀疑;担心:"He claims to be her father," said James. "We've *wondered about* him." "他声称是她的父亲,"詹姆斯说道。"我们曾对他表示过怀疑。" Mrs White *wondered about* her husband's remark. 怀特太太对她丈夫的话感到怀疑。Linda's in hospital! I was *wondering about* her. 琳达住院了！我对她感到担心。❷ think about what (something or someone) might be; think about (something or someone) that one wishes to know; consider 想……是什么样；希望知道……；考虑：I'm *wondering about* the place where we are to have the holiday. 我在想我们要去度假的地方是什么样子。I often *wonder about* why she treated me like that. 我总在纳闷她为什么那样对待我。Now that we've finished the project, I am *wondering about* our next move. 我们已完成了这项工程，我想知道下一步要做什么。"Have you decided where you're going this summer?" "I've been *wondering about* going to Florida." "你决定今年夏天去哪儿了吗?" "我一直在考虑去佛罗里达。"

NOTE 不要将本短语与 wander about 混淆，两者的意义和用法不同。

wonder at *vt.* 【不可分性动词短语】(非正式用语，常用一般时态) feel surprised and amazed about (something) 对……感到诧异，对……好奇：When he was a little boy he liked to sit there and *wonder at* all that had happened. 他小时候喜欢坐在那里对所发生的一切都感到好奇。So she's finally left him? I don't *wonder at* it. 她终于离他而去了？我对此并不感到奇怪。The fact that she left home is not to be wondered at. 他离家出走并不令人为奇。

word for word *adv.* in exactly the same words as someone else wrote or said 一字不变地，逐字地：Bob copied Mary's composition *word for word*. 鲍勃一字不变地照抄了玛丽的作文。He repeated what I have said *word for word*. 他把我说的话一字不变地重复了一遍。I don't try to memorize the speech *word for word*. 我可不费力去逐字地记忆那篇讲演稿。

NOTE 本短语可转化为复合词 word-for-word 或 wordforword，意为"逐字的，一字不变的"。

work as *vt.* 【不可分性动词短语】do the job of (a particular kind of person); serve as (a kind of worker); work in the capacity of (something) 充当，担任，做……：From 1990, Putin *worked as* an assistant to the president of the Leningrad State University. 自1990年起，普京就担任彼得格勒国立大学校长助理。Four Chinese forced to *work as* slave laborers by Japanese invaders between 1937 and 1945 flew to Japan Thursday to sue the Japanese Government. 四名在1937—1945年期间被日本侵略者胁迫当劳工的中国人星期四飞往日本起诉日本政府。Nowadays, a cell phone can also *work as* a camera, remote control, and tour guide. 如今，手机还可以充当照相机、遥控器和旅行向导。

work at *vt.* 【不可分性动词短语】❶ have one's job in (a place) 在(某处)工作：How long have you been *working at* the bank? 你在这家银行工作有多久了？Soon after the rescuers arrived they started to *work at* the site of the plane crash. 救援人员赶到坠毁现场后不久就开始了工作。❷put effort into (something or doing something); try hard to develop or improve (something)从事于,致力于: He was trained as a carpenter but he seldom *works at* it. 他学的是木工,但很少干木工活。Many scientists are *working at* the problem. 许多科学家都在从事这一问题的研究。If she *works at* improving her game, she could be a champion. 如果她致力于改善其比赛策略,她就能夺冠。

work for *vt.* 【不可分性动词短语】❶be employed by (a person or an organization) 为(某人或某一机构)工作: My boss is not kind to his employees, so I decided not to *work for* him any longer. 我的老板对待雇员很不好,所以我决定不再为他工作了。Following graduation from the university, he began to *work for* the Federal Bureau of Investigation. 大学毕业后,他就开始为美国联邦调查局工作。❷do one's job so as to gain (money or a purpose)为了(赚钱或到达某一目的)而工作: Those people used to *work* in a match factory *for* only a few pennies a day. 这些人曾为了每天挣几个便士而在那家火柴厂里工作。The former president is still *working* hard *for* world peace. 这位前总统仍在为世界和平而努力地工作着。❸apply to 适用于: The results of the investigation *work for* the Spanish-speaking countries of Latin America. 本项调查结果适用于拉丁美洲说西班牙语的国家。The regulations of safe driving *work for* every driver. 安全驾驶的法规适用于所有的驾驶员。

work in/into *vt.* (常用一般时态) add or include (something)(in or into another) 加进……,把……加入……: The speaker *worked in* a few jokes in his speech. 讲演者在他的讲话中插进了几则笑话。I'll try to *work in* a mention of the help you gave to us. 我会想办法提及您给予我们的帮助。He *worked* a mention of her *in* his speech. 他在讲话中巧妙地提到了她。They *work* a lot of Brazilian rhythms *into* their music. 他们在其音乐中融入了很多巴西韵律。

work in with *vt.* (无被动语态形式) (cause to) be able to join in work with (other people or idea)(使)能与……配合,合作: A difficult task can be made easier if people will *work in with* one another. 如果大家能相互配合,再难的工作也会变得容易。I'll try to *work* my timetable *in with* yours. 我将尽量使我的时间表能与你们的合拍。

work off *vt.* & *vi.* ❶(cause to) become loose and fall off by gradual movement (使)脱落: The nut has *worked off*. 螺帽已经脱落了。Can you *work* this lid *off*, it seems to be stuck? 你能把这个盖子拧下来吗? 它好像卡住了。

—*vt.* ❶(常与 by, with 连用) get rid of (something such as a feeling or some unwanted weight) by doing something that involves a lot of physical activity 通过做体力活动来消除(某种感觉、情感或体重): You can *work off* the stiffness with some exercise. 你可以通过做一些运动来消除这种僵直的感觉。She generally *works off* her anger by going for a run. 她一般通过跑步来消除怒气。John *worked off* a few pounds by exercising every morning. 约翰每天早晨运动,减轻了几磅的体重。❷ finish

(something) by work 做完(某事)：I hope to *work off* these urgent letters by tomorrow. 我希望在明天之前把这些紧急信件写完。❸(常与 on 连用) get rid of (an unpleasant feeling such as anger) (at someone else's expense)(在他人身上)发泄(怒气等)：There's no need for you to *work* your anger *off* on your wife. 你没必要把你的怒气发泄在你老婆身上。On that occasion there was no one on whom his temper could be *worked off*. 在那种场合，没有一个他能借以撒气的人。❹ repay (someone something you owe him, for example a debt) by doing a job for him instead of giving him money 以工作偿还(欠某人的债务)：The report proposes that students be allowed to *work off* their debts through community service. 该报告提议应允许大学生通过为社区服务来偿还贷款。Two thousand pounds of the loan is still outstanding, but I shall have *worked* that *off* by the end of the year. 2 000 英镑的借款还没偿还，但年底前我会以做工抵债还清它。

work on/upon *vi.* work continuously 继续工作：I'll have to stay in the office and *work on* until the report for tomorrow's meeting is ready. 我得留在办公室继续工作，把明天开会用的报告准备出来。Our goal is to push forward the talks and the peace process, for which we stand ready to *work on*. 我们的目标是推进会谈与和平进程，我们愿意为此而继续工作下去。

—*vt.*【不可分性动词短语】❶ spend one's time and give one's attention to doing or trying to do (something) 从事于，致力于：Professor Green is *working on* his new book about commercial bank management. 格林教授正在从事他那部有关商业银行管理的新书写作。The medical experts are *working on* the ways of curing bird flu. 医学专家们仍在致力于寻找治疗禽流感的办法。Israel and Palestine have been *working on* arranging a meeting between their prime ministers. 以巴一直致力于安排双方总理之间的会谈。❷(非正式用语，无被动语态形式，常用一般时态) try to influence or persuade (someone)竭力影响(某人)；做(某人)工作：He might accept our suggestion if someone *works on* him properly. 如果有人适当地对他做些工作，他也许会接受我们的建议。I'm *working on* my brother to get him to take me to the airport. 我准备说服我弟弟送我去机场。❸ have an effect on (someone or someone's feelings, etc.)对(某人的情感或感觉等)产生作用，作用于：Will the high figure for unemployment *work on* the conscience of the government officials? 庞大的失业数字会使政府官员的良心不安吗？The sight *worked on* our hearts so that we were filled with pity. 此情此景打动了我们的心，使我们都充满了同情。Some pills *work* well *upon* the nerves and make people feel more relaxed. 有些药丸能很好地作用于神经，使人感觉更轻松。

NOTE 本短语中的 upon 用法比 on 正式，但不及 on 常用。

work out *vt.* & *vi.* ❶ devise, plan or arrange (something) by thinking or talking about it (通过思量或商议)设计，制订，安排：We have finished *working out* an overall plan for carrying out the second phase of the moon program. 我们已为第二阶段的探月工程制订出了一个全面的

计划。Emergency plans for the occurrence of the new flu must be *worked out* as soon as possible. 必须尽快制订出预防新型流感发生的应急计划。❷solve (a problem) by doing a calculation 通过计算解决(难题),算出:Let me give you some time to *work* this difficulty problem *out*. 我给你一些时间来解这个难题。My father was born in 1925. Can you *work out* his age? 我父亲是 1925 年出生的。你能算出他老人家多大年纪吗? Can you *work out* how much your holiday journey will cost? 你能不能算出你假日旅行要花多少钱? This sum won't *work out*. 这个总数就是算不出来。❸(主要用于英国英语中) find (a satisfactory way of doing something) by thinking 想出(令人满意的办法等):The scientists *worked out* a way of sending men to the moon. 科学家们想出了一个把人送上月球的办法。I can't *work out* what to do. 我可想不出该怎么办好。❹(主要用于英国英语中,常用一般时态) think about (something) and manage to understand it 理解,明白:I can't *work out* the meaning of this poem. 我理解不了这首诗的意义。I haven't really *worked* it *out* in my own mind yet. 我至今还没把它真正想明白。There will be a full investigation to *work out* what caused the accident. 将进行全面调查以查明事故的原因。❺(非正式用语,用于否定句中) understand (someone) 了解(某人):I have never been able to *work* him *out*. 我一直无法了解他。❻(常用被动语态形式) complete the use of (a mine); (of someone) exhaust through working (指矿井)采掘完;(指人)(由于劳作而)筋疲力尽:That mine was *worked out* years ago. 该矿在几年前就已被开采完了。He was *worked out*, having sat at his task for twelve hours without ceasing. 他连续不停地坐在那里干了 12 个小时,已经筋疲力尽了。

—*vi*. ❶ be successful or to end in a particular way; result in a good conclusion; progress in a satisfactory way; develop well 取得成功,结果良好,发展良好:The situation *worked out* quite well. 事态发展良好。Things did not *work out* as we had expected. 事情发展得并不像我们所预期的那样。❷(常与 at, to 连用) (of something) be calculated to be (a particular amount) (通过计算)得出(某一数目):These figures *work out* differently each time I add them. 这些数字我每次加起来得数都不同。The mortgage on my house *works out* at about $200 a month. 我的房贷算起来是每月大约 200 美元。The cost *works out* to £30 per person. 费用算下来是每人 30 英镑。❸(of someone) do physical exercises as a way of keeping fit (为保持身体健康而)进行身体锻炼:She *works out* at the gym three times a week. 她每周三次在健身房里锻炼身体。The middle-aged professor keeps fit by *working out* for an hour in the local gym every day. 这位中年教授每天都在当地的健身房锻炼一个小时以保持身体健康。

NOTE **1.** 当本短语用作及物性动词短语,所带的宾语是代词时,该代词须置于本短语的动词和副词中间。

2. 本短语可转化为复合词 workout,意为"(体育)锻炼;(工作)能力测验;(市场)疲软的"。

work over *vt*.【可分性动词短语】❶(主

要用于美国英语中) do (something such as work) for a second time; redo; rework 重做(某项工作等),重新加工: I shall have to *work* the report *over* if it's not satisfactory. 如果这篇报告不令人满意的话,我还得重写。The old story was *worked over* for television. 那个古老的传说被重新加工成了电视剧。❷(非正式用语) beat or hit (someone) very severely or violently 狠揍,猛击(某人): The gang *worked* me *over* in a quieter corner. 那帮坏蛋在一个僻静的街角处把我痛打了一顿。The young lovers were robbed and *worked over* by several people with masks at a dark corner in the park. 这对年轻的恋人在公园的一个黑暗角落被几个戴面罩的人抢劫之后还遭到了殴打。

NOTE 当本短语所带的宾语是代词时,该代词须置于本短语的动词和副词中间。

work up *v.* ❶(非正式用语) rise or move to a higher position by one's own efforts (靠自己的努力)升迁: He *worked up* to the presidency. 他步步高升到了总统的职位。The manager of the company claims to have *worked* his way *up* from deliver boy. 该公司的经理声称他是从一个送货员逐步干上去的。❷(of someone) start to have (enthusiasm or an appetite) (指某人)开始具有(某种热情或食欲): I'm afraid I can't *work up* much enthusiasm for this scheme. 恐怕我不会对这计划有什么热情。I've *worked up* quite a thirst playing tennis. 我对打网球开始有了瘾。We went for a long walk to *work up* an appetite. 为了产生食欲,我们还走了很长的路。❸(cause to) develop or increase gradually (使)逐渐发展,(使)逐渐增加: It took Mr Smith some years to *work up* a market for his products. 史密斯先生用了好几年时间才使其产品逐渐打开了市场。He has *worked* the firm *up* from almost nothing. 他几乎白手起家把这个公司慢慢地发展起来。The wind is *working up*. 风力在逐渐加大。❹(常与反身代词连用) excite (the feeling of oneself or others) 激起,鼓起(自己或他人的情绪): She *works* herself *up* about the most trivial things. 一点点小事都会使她情绪激动。The politician *worked* the crowd *up* until they were shouting and cheering. 那位政客煽动起了听众的情绪,使他们又是喊叫又是喝彩。He'd *worked* himself *up* into a terrible state about the coming exam. 面对即将来临的考试,他把自己搞得紧张不堪。Tom *worked up* the nerve to ask the boss for help. 汤姆鼓足勇气去请老板帮忙。

NOTE 当本短语所带的宾语是代词时,该代词须置于本短语的动词和副词中间。

work up into *vt.* 【可分性动词短语】 develop (written material) into (a full form) 把(文字材料)整理成(整体作品): You may *work* these facts *up into* an article for a weekly journal. 你可以把这些事实加工成一篇文章在某一周刊上发表。I'm hoping to *work up* these notes *into* a book. 我希望把这些笔记整理成一本书。

work up to *vt.* 【不可分性动词短语】 ❶prepare yourself to do something difficult or to try to prepare someone for bad news (使自己)准备好(做困难之事); (使他人)准备好(听到不好的消息): Are you *working up to* telling me that you can't pay? 你是不是准备告诉我你付不起这笔钱? ❷(无被动语态形式,常用进

行时态)develop or increase and reach a particular level 发展到,增加到,达到(某种程度或水平): Things are *working up to* a climax. 事态发展到了顶点。Soon the engine was *working up to* its top speed. 发动机很快就达到了最高速度。

worry about/over *vt.* have (something or someone) as the cause or object of deep concern 为……担心,为……发愁: There's nothing to *worry about*, Dad. 爸爸,没什么可担心的。I wouldn't *worry about* it, if I were you. 如果我是你,我就不会担心。Most young people who were born in the 1980s are *worried about* getting well paid jobs. 大多数"80后"担心的是如何找到一份收入较高的工作。However, quake victims are still *worried about* how to spend the time before they have their own homes again. 然而,地震灾区群众依然忧虑着如何度过重有家园前的这段时间。Once upon a time, you could leave your doors unlocked at night and not *worry about* someone breaking in. 以前,你的房门夜里不上锁都不必担心有人会进来偷东西。

worse off *adj.* having less money than other people or than you had before; in a worse situation than you were before, or than someone else is now 更拮据的,更贫穷的: They were *worse off* now than when they started the business. 他们现在比刚开业那时更拮据。There is always somebody who is *worse off* than you. 总是有人比你更贫穷。

NOTE 1. 本短语是 badly off 和 bad off 的比较级形式。

2. 本短语的反义短语是 better off。

worthy of *adj.* (正式用语,常用作表语) deserving respect, admiration or praise; deserving to be given attention, notice, etc. 值得……的,应得……的: Such a brave man like Yang Liwei is *worthy of* our respect, admiration and reward. 像杨利伟这样勇敢的人值得我们尊敬、敬佩和奖励。This man is *worthy of* praise, he has done quite well. 此人应受表扬,他干得相当不错。Two points in this report are especially *worthy of* notice. 这份报告中有两点特别值得注意。This phenomenon is *worthy of* being studied. 这种现象值得研究。

NOTE 本短语的比较级形式是 worthier of,最高级形式是 worthiest of。

would be better *v.* (英国英语用法,仅用于口语中) used for saying that someone should do something else rather than what he or she is in fact doing 应该,最好(做某事): Why does he waste his time studying poetry? He'*d be better* getting some practical experience of business. 他为什么浪费时间学习诗歌呢? 他应该习得一些做生意的实践经验。"Do you think I should fly directly to New Zealand or break my journey in Sydney?" "You'*d be better* to spend a few days in Sydney. There're so many things to see there." "你认为我应该直接飞往新西兰,还是中途在悉尼停留一下?""你最好在悉尼停留几日,那儿可看的东西太多啦。"

NOTE 1. 本短语在使用中常常略为 'd be better。不要将其与 'd better (= had better)混淆。

2. 本短语与 had better 之间在用法上不同是:(1)本短语后可接动名词(短语)和动词不定式(短语),而 had better 后只能

接原形动词。(2)在比较两种行为过程时,要使用本短语,而不用 had better。

would rather *v.* (would 常被略写为 'd) (used for expressing a choice) prefer to do something or prefer that something happened 宁可,宁愿:He doesn't want to learn, he'*d rather* stay at home and play computer games. 他不想学习,他宁可待在家里玩电脑游戏。Which *would* you *rather* do, go to the cinema or stay at home? 你是愿意去看电影还是待在家里? As a man of unyielding character, he *would rather* break than bend. 作为一个具有不屈不挠性格的人,他宁折不弯。I shall certainly not write if you *would rather* that I didn't. 你若不愿我写信给你,我当然不会写的。I *would rather* you posted the letter right away. 我希望你马上把这封信寄出去。

NOTE 1. 当本短语后接原形动词与 than 连用时,than 的后面也必须接原形动词。但当 than 后所用的动词与 would rather 后的动词相同时,则在 than 的后面省略该动词。例如:I'd rather deal with a man than with a woman.

2. 当本短语后接省去 that 的从句时,表示一种"让他人做或不做某事"的愿望。因此,从句中的谓语动词要用过去式或过去完成式表示虚拟。

3. 本短语与 had rather 意义和用法相同,后者现已较少使用。

wrap around/round *vt.*【可分性动词短语】❶(常用一般时态) put(something such as a piece of cloth)so as to surround (something or someone)用……把……包上,缠上:Each box has a bright red ribbon *wrapped round* it. 每个盒子都用一条鲜艳的红丝带包扎着。She *wrapped* a towel *around* her waist. 她用一条浴巾缠在自己的腰上。❷put (your arms, fingers, or legs) firmly around (someone or something) 抱住,夹住:He *wrapped* his arms *around* her. 他用双臂抱住她。

NOTE wrap around 是美国英语用法,wrap round 是英国英语用法。

wrap in *vt.* ❶cover (something or someone) in (usually paper or cloth)用……把……包上,穿上:I put the book in a box and *wrapped* it up *in* brown paper before I posted it. 寄书之前,我先把书装在盒子里,再用牛皮纸把它包好。It was cold outside, so we decided to *wrap* our little dog up *in* a thick blanket. 外面很冷,所以我们决定用一条厚毛毯把我们的小狗包起来。The baby was *wrapped in* wool clothes and was far too hot on such a hot day! 这么热的天还给孩子穿毛衣,也太热了! ❷(常用被动语态形式) surround (something) with (something such as clouds or fog)(so that nothing is visible) (云或雾)笼罩……:The signposts along the road were *wrapped in* fog. 沿路的标志牌都被雾遮住而看不见了。

wrap up *v.* ❶cover (something or someone) by putting something such as paper or cloth round it or him 把……包起来:We've just finished *wrapping up* Tom's birthday present. 我们刚刚把给汤姆的生日礼物包完毕。*Wrap* yourself *up* in your blanket if you are cold. 如果冷,你就用毯子把身子裹起来。❷(cause to) wear warm clothing; put warm clothes on (someone, especially a child)(使)穿上保暖的衣服:It is wise to *wrap up* well in such cold weather. 这么冷的天,多穿

些保暖的衣物才是明智的。I could hear mother telling me to *wrap up* warm. 我能听到妈妈要我穿得暖和些。Keep the child well *wrapped up* in the early morning. 清早时要给孩子多穿点保暖的衣服。❸(非正式用语) complete (something) in a satisfactory way (圆满)结束,完成: US Secretary of State Hillary Clinton concluded a three-day visit to China, *wrapping up* her four-nation Asian tour. 美国国务卿希拉里·克林顿结束了对中国为期三天的访问,从而圆满结束了她的亚洲四国之行。Each meeting is *wrapped up* with a speech from the manager. 每次的会议都以经理的一番讲话结束。It's late and I have to go home, so let's *wrap* it *up* as soon as we can. 天晚了,我还要回家,所以咱们尽快把它搞完吧。❹(非正式用语,用一般时态,常用于祈使句中) (used to tell someone to stop talking in a rather rude way) be quiet; shut up (以粗鲁的方式让他人)安静点,住口: *Wrap up*, will you? Stop ringing those bells! 你们安静点儿,好吗? 不要再摇那些铃了! *Wrap* it *up*, we've heard enough of your complaints. 住嘴吧。你的牢骚我们已经听够了!

NOTE 当本短语用作及物性动词短语,所带的宾语是代词时,该代词须置于本短语的动词和副词中间。

wrap up in *vt.* 【不可分性动词短语】(用被动语态形式) give all one's love or attention to (someone or something)倾心爱慕(某人);全神贯注于(某事): She's so *wrapped up in* him she can't see his faults. 她倾心爱他,以至于看不到他的毛病。He is so *wrapped up in* himself that he rarely calls me. 他如此专注于自己的事情,以至于很少给我打电话。It's no use trying to talk to father when he's *wrapped up in* his work. 当父亲全神贯注于他的工作时,你怎么和他说话都没有用。

write about *vt.* have (something or someone) as the subject of (one's) writing 写关于……的事: He traveled around Mexico and *wrote about* his experiences. 他周游了墨西哥,并写下了他所经历的事情。This is an event *about* which many newspapers articles have been *written*. 这是一个许多家报纸都曾为之泼墨的事件。People like to *write about* what they know, and what interests them. 人们都喜欢写他们知道并感兴趣的事情。

write back *vi.* (常与 to 连用) reply (to someone) in writing (给某人)回信: Sam *wrote back* saying that he could certainly help. 山姆回信说他当然会帮忙。I *wrote back* to Jim at once, thanking him for his invitation. 我立即给吉姆写了回信,感谢他的邀请。

write down *vt.* 【可分性动词短语】❶record (something) on a piece of paper using a pen, etc. 写下,记下: The teacher asked his students to *write down* ten words to describe what they felt about the story. 老师让他的学生写 10 个单词来描述他们对那篇故事的感觉。If you have any questions, please *write* them *down*. 如果你们有什么问题的话,请把它们写下来。*Write down* everything he says at the meeting. 把他在会议上所说的一切都记下来。Yet it will finally depend on further consultation among various parties to get the results *written down*. 但最终能否得出一个书面的成果还取决于各方的进一

W

步协商。❷depreciate by writing 写文章贬低：The reporter *wrote* the play *down* as he had not liked it. 该记者写文章贬低了这出戏剧，因为他不喜欢它。

NOTE 1. 当本短语所带的宾语是代词时，该代词须置于本短语的动词和副词中间。

2. 当本短语作"写文章贬低"解时，反义短语是 write up。

write in *vi.* (常与介词 to 连用，后接动词不定式或动名词短语) write a letter or email (to an organization, a newspaper, a radio or TV program), to state an opinion or ask something (给某一机构、报纸等)写信(或电子邮件)：Many listeners have *written in* to the BBC to express their opinions. 许多听众给英国广播公司写信表达了他们的观点。Some tourists *wrote in* to complain about the quality and customer service on the local tour. 一些游客写信投诉本地游的质量和服务。Hundreds of people have *written in* to the TV program asking for more details. 成百上千的观众给该电视节目写信，询问更详细的情况。

—*vt.* ❶add (words, numbers, etc. that are missing from something) in writing 把(漏掉的文字、数字等)加写进去：*Write in* the letter that is missing from each word. 把每个单词中丢掉的字母都加写进去。You'd better *write in* another example to make the meaning of this passage quite clear. 你最好再加进去一个例子，使这段的意思更明了。❷ write (the name of someone) in a special place on a ballot, indicating a vote for the person 把(某人的名字)写在选票上：Let us *write* her name *in* her name on the ballot. 咱们都把她的名字写在选票上。

write into *vt.* 【可分性动词短语】(常用被动语态形式) include (a particular rule or detail) in (something written such as an official document) 把(某一规定或细节)写入(某种正式文件)：The provision that "private property obtained legally shall not be violated" was *written into* China's Constitution. "公民合法的私有财产不受侵犯"这一条款写入了中国的宪法中。The right to withdraw is *written into* the agreement. 退股权被写入协议中。The President has opposed *writing* it *into* law. 总统反对将此写入法律中。

write off *vi.* (常与 to, for 连用) send a letter (to an organization), usually asking for some information about something or asking it to send you one of its products (给某一机构)写信询问，发信函购：She *wrote off* to the New Zealand Government for the information about emigration to New Zealand. 她立即给新西兰政府写信询问有关移民新西兰的信息。Why don't you *write off* for more details? 你为何不立即写信询问更多的详情呢？You'd better *write off* to check your financial situation. 你最好立即写信查一下你们的财政状况。She *wrote off* for the book because the local shop didn't have it. 当地书店没有这本书，她就写信去外地函购。

—*vt.* 【可分性动词短语】❶(常用一般时态) write (something) quickly and easily 迅速写出：He *wrote off* an account of the sports meet in a few minutes. 他几分钟就写好了一篇运动会的报告。She *wrote* the letter *off* on the spur of the moment. 她马上就写出了那封信。❷(非正式用语，常用一般时态) cancel; regard (something or someone) as unimportant or useless, and they are not worth further serious attention 取消；认为(某物或某人)无用：We'll just have to *write* the plans *off* if we can't raise enough fund for them. 如果我们筹措不到足够的资金，我们只好取消这些计划了。This year about nine hundred volumes have been *written off*. 今年，大约有 900 册图书已被注销。A lot of companies seem to *write* people *off* if they're over 50. 许多公司似乎认为人过 50 岁就没用了。He hates those people *writing* him *off* because of his age. 他恨那些因他的年龄而认为他没有用的人。❸(常用一般时态) remove (a debt owed by someone or a country) from the records or amounts (从记录或账目中)勾销(某人或某一国家的债务)：It's no use carrying the debt forward, we might as well *write* it *off*. 这笔欠账不必再往下转了，我们不妨把它一笔勾销。Nearly a thousand pounds worth of bad debts have been *written off* as irrecoverable. 近千英镑的坏账因无法收回而被一笔勾销。❹(英国英语用法) (of someone) damage (especially a vehicle) so badly that it is not worth repairing 报废(尤指车辆)：He's *written off* two cars this year. 他今年报废了两辆汽车。One of Peter's friends *wrote* his car *off* there. 彼得的一个朋友在那儿报废了他的汽车。His car was completely *written off* in the accident. 他的汽车在那起事故中彻底报废了。

NOTE **1.** 当本短语用作及物性动词短语，所带的宾语是代词时，该代词须置于本短语的动词和副词中间。

2. 本短语可转化为复合词 write-off，意为“销账，删除账面值；被勾销的项目”。

write on/upon *vt.* 【可分性动词短语】 have (usually something) as the subject of writing; write (a quantity or form) on the subject of (usually something) 以……为写作主题，写关于……的东西：*Write* an essay of 300 words *on* the subject given below. 就下面给出的题目用 300 个词写出一篇短文。He is an expert on breeding dogs, he's *written* several books *on* the subject. 他是位育狗专家，他已写了好几本有关这一主题的书籍。

NOTE 本短语中的 upon 用法比 on 正式，但不及 on 常用。

write out *vt.* 【可分性动词短语】 ❶write (something) in full or in its final form 完整写出：Could you *write out* exactly what you need me to do? 你能不能确切地写一下你都需要我做些什么？He was busily engaged in *writing out* his new play. 他正忙于写他的新剧本。The teacher asked all his students to *write out* the complete answer. 老师要求他所有的学生都要写出完整的答案。Do it in rough before you *write* it *out* properly. 在写出正稿之前，先打个草稿。❷complete (an official document such as a cheque, receipt, or prescription) by writing information on it and usually sign it 写出，开出(支票、收据、处方等)：We went straight to the estate agent and *wrote out* a cheque. 我们直接到了房地产中介开出一张支票。Shall I *write* you *out* a recipe, sir? 先生，要我给你开一张收据吗？It only takes a minute to *write out* a prescription. 只需一分钟就能开出一个处方来。I went into my office to *write out* the death certificate. 我走进办公室，开出一份死亡证书。

❸(非正式用语,常用被动语态形式,常与 of 连用) take out(a character in a drama series on television or radio)取消(电视或广播连续剧中的某一角色): The actor was alarmed to hear that his part is being *written out* of the script. 那名演员听说他的角色要从剧本中取消颇为吃惊。When the actor died, the character he played in the soap opera had to be *written out*. 那名男演员去世后,他在那部肥皂剧中所扮演的角色只好被取消了。Maybe soon the scriptwriters will have to *write* her *out* of the series. 剧本作者可能很快就得取消她在连续剧中的角色。

NOTE 1. 当本短语所带的宾语是代词时,该代词须置于本短语的动词和副词中间。

2. 当本短语作"写出,开出(支票、收据、处方等)"解时,同义短语是 make out。

write up *vt.*【可分性动词短语】❶make a full written record of (someone or something that has been done or said)详细描写,详细记述: A reporter *wrote* me *up* for the *Sunday* newspaper. 一名记者在《星期日报》上对我还详细地描写了一番。He *wrote up* his visit in a report of over 500 pages. 他写了一份 500 多页的报告,详细地描写了他的访问历程。Mr Simpson conducted the interviews, and his girlfriend *wrote* them *up*. 辛普森先生进行采访,他的女朋友则将那些采访内容做了详细记录。❷write a review of (a play, book, film, etc.) (usually for a newspaper)(尤指为报纸)写(戏剧、书籍、电影等的)评论: Has anyone *written up* last night's concert? 有没有人为昨天晚上的音乐会作评? ❸write about(something) in an exciting way so as to increase its effect, or give it a good judgment 泼墨渲染;撰文赞扬: The account of the murder was *written up* to attract more readers. 对谋杀情节的渲染是为了吸引更多的读者。They've *written* our new play *up* in the local newspaper. 他们在当地的报纸上撰文赞扬了我们的新剧。

NOTE 1. 当本短语所带的宾语是代词时,该代词须置于本短语的动词和副词中间。

2. 本短语可转化为复合词 write-up,意为"捧场文章"。

Y y

year after year *adv.* (of something happening) regularly and continuously for several years; one year after another (指事情定期或不断地发生)年复一年地,逐年: The American envoy accused the country of having deceived the international community about their nuclear issues *year after year*. 美国特使指责该国年复一年地在其核问题上欺骗国际社会。The number of mainland compatriots traveling to Taiwan for sightseeing or exchanges of various kinds has also increased *year after year*. 大陆同胞赴台旅游或进行各种交流的人数也逐年增多。

NOTE 与本短语结构相同的短语有 day after day, week after week, month after month。

year by year *adv.* (of something changing) as time passes; as years go by (指事物在变化着)随着时间的过去,一年年地: The department has been shrinking *year by year* because of budget cuts. 由于预算的削减,该部门的规模一年年地在缩小。Our university gets bigger *year by year*. 我们学校的规模一年比一年大。

NOTE 与本短语结构相同的短语有 day by day, week by week, month by month。

year in, (and) year out *adv.* (of something happening regularly) every year, without ever changing, especially in a way that seems boring (指事情一成不变地发生)年复一年地,年年如此: *Year in, year out*, nothing changes. 年复一年,没有任何改变。They go to the same campsite *year in, and year out*. 他们年年都到同一个营地野营。

NOTE 与本短语结构相同的短语有 day in, (and) day out, week in week out。

yearn for *vt.* 【不可分性动词短语】(正式用语) want (something or someone, especially that you know you may not be able to have) very much 渴望得到: He *yearned for* her love. 他渴望得到她的爱。Influenced by their fathers, the children of migrant workers *yearn for* the city life. 在他们父辈的影响下,这些农民工的子女都向往城市生活。He *yearned for* her return. 他盼望她回来。They were *yearning for* another baby. 他们渴望再有一个小孩儿。

NOTE 本短语的同义短语是 long for。两者之间的区别是:本短语所表示"渴望得到"的物或人往往是难以得到的,而 long for 则不如此。见 long for。

yell out *v.* (非正式用语,常用一般时态) cry or shout (something) very loudly, especially in fear, anger, pain, or excitement, or to draw attention (尤指因恐惧、愤怒等)大声叫喊,大声喊出: Don't touch his arm, it makes him *yell out* in pain. 别碰他的胳膊,他会疼得大声喊叫的。She *yelled out* for help, but no one came. 她大声呼救,但无人前来。He

yelled out orders at everyone. 他向所有的人大声发号施令。

yes man *n.* (非正式用语,贬义用法) a person who always agrees with everything his or her employer, superior, etc. says, in order to please them and gain favor 对上司唯命是从者,唯唯诺诺的人: "Why does the boss love Smith so much?" "Because he is a *yes man*. He agrees with everything the boss says!" "老板为什么那么喜欢史密斯?""因为他是个对上司唯命是从的人。老板说什么,他就附和什么!" "I don't want any *yes men* around me. I want everybody to tell me the truth," said the manager. "我不想我周围都是些唯唯诺诺之人。我要让所有的人都和我说实话。"这位经理说道。

NOTE 1. 本短语可连写为 yes-man。例如: He denies that he's simply a *yes-man*.
2. yes woman (复数形式是 yes-women) 用来表示女性中的"对上可唯命是从者,唯唯诺诺之人"。

yield to *vt.* ❶agree to do something that you do not want to do or should do; give up (something) under pressure (由于压力而)屈从于,屈服于: Our view that we should not *yield to* terrorism will not change as a result of the attack, said the official. 这位官员表示:我们不会因这次袭击而改变我们决不屈服于恐怖主义的立场。We will determine our stand and policy without *yielding to* any outside pressure. 我们将决定自己的立场和政策,而不会屈从于任何外来压力。❷(正式用语) surrender to; bend one's will to (something or someone)向……投降,向……让步: We shall never *yield to* our enemy. 我们决不向敌人投降。Mrs Brown *yielded to* her daughter's request. 布朗夫人对她女儿的要求让步了。After months of refusing Mary *yielded to* Robert and agreed to marry him. 玛丽拒绝几个月之后向罗伯特作了让步,并同意和他结婚。❸give (something) to (someone else)把某物交给(他人),把(某物)让与(他人): At last the citizens were forced to *yield* the town *to* the enemy. 最终,市民们被迫把城池让给了敌人。The following year, control of the industry was *yielded to* the government. 第二年,该产业的控制权便交与政府。❹(美国英语用法) allow (another vehicle) to go before you when you are driving (在行车时)让(另一车辆)先行: You must *yield to* traffic from the left. 你必须让左侧驶来的车辆先行。

yield up *vt.* 【不可分性动词短语】(正式用语,常用一般时态,常与 to 连用) hand (usually something) (to usually an enemy) in admission of defeat; give (something) (to someone)把(某物)交给(常指敌人),把(某物)让与(某人): We had to *yield up* our position to the enemy. 我们不得不放弃阵地,把它让给敌人。The city would only be *yielded up* when ammunition and food supplies were exhausted. 在弹尽粮绝的情况下只能献城投降。It is polite to *yield up* your seat on the bus to the old. 在汽车上,给老年人让座位是礼貌的。

You are welcome. *s.* (主要用于美国英语中) (said as a polite answer after someone has thanked you for doing something) no thanks are needed 不用谢,别客气,没什么: "Thanks for picking me up." "*You're welcome.*""谢谢您来接我。""不用谢。"

NOTE 1. 本短语的同义短语是 Don't mention it. ,No at all. 和 No problem. 。

Z z

zero hour *n.* ❶(亦称 H-hour) the time at which something such as a military operation is planned to begin 军事行动开始时间：*Zero hour* is fixed for midnight. 军事行动的时间定在午夜。They were told that their *zero hour* was 4 am. 他们奉命于凌晨 4 点开始行动。❷ the time when an important decision or change is supposed to come 做出重要决定的时间：On the day of the game, as the *zero hour* came near, the players grew nervous. 在比赛那天，当决定胜负的赛事即将开始时，运动员们都很紧张。Both sides are working hard to get every vote before the *zero hour* at nine o'clock tomorrow morning when the final voting will start. 因为明天上午 9 点开始决定性的最后一轮投票，所以双方在关键时刻前夕都在努力争取每一张选票。

NOTE 本短语为不可数性名词短语。

zero in (on) *vt.* 【不可分性动词短语】❶(常用一般时态) adjust(especially a gun) so it will hit(an exact target location); aim precisely at(someone or something) 调整(尤指枪、炮的瞄准器)；瞄准……：The soldier *zeroed in* a machine gun at 200 meters. 士兵把机枪的瞄准器调整到 200 米的距离上。Modern military planes use computers to help them to *zero in on* their targets. 现代军机都使用电脑来帮助锁定目标。Linda raised the binoculars again and *zeroed in on* her husband. 琳达再次拿起望远镜对准了她丈夫罗伯特。❷(非正式用语) direct one's attention to (someone or something); concentrate or focus attention on (a problem or subject) 把注意力集中在……，集中精力于(某一问题或主题)：The police have *zeroed in on* the man they suspected to be responsible for the bombing. 警方已把注意力集中在了那名涉嫌搞爆炸的男子身上。The Senate *zeroed in on* the Latin-American problems. 参议院集中精力应对拉丁美洲的问题。Critics have *zeroed in on* his plan to raise the tax rate and electricity prices. 批评家们把批评的焦点集中在他提高税率和电价的计划上。

zip code *n.* a group of numbers, or letters and numbers, that you write at the end of a person's address to help the post office to sort the mail 邮政编码：Germany was the first country to introduce a *zip code* system, in 1941. The United followed in 1959 and the Unite in 1963. 德国是最先采用邮政编码系统的国家，那是在 1941 年。接着是英国(1959 年)和美国(1963 年)。

NOTE 本短语为美国英语用法，在英国和加拿大英语中使用 postal code 或 post code (亦连写为 postcode)。

zip on/up *vt.* 【可分性动词短语】close (something that has a zip); close (a zip

Z

on a piece of clothing) for someone 拉上(有拉链之物),给(某人的衣物)拉上拉链:She *zipped up* her dress. 她把连衣裙的拉链拉上了。Please help me to *zip* my dress *on*, the fastener's at the back and I can't reach it. 请帮我把衣服的拉链拉上。拉链在后边,我够不着。Do you want me to *zip* your coat *up*? 你想让我帮你把你上衣的拉链拉上吗?

—*vi.* be closed by means of a zip 用拉链拉上:My jeans wouldn't *zip up*. 我工装裤的拉链拉不上了。This dress *zips up* at the back. 这件连衣裙在后面拉拉链。

NOTE 当本短语用作及物性动词短语,所带的宾语是代词时,该代词须置于本短语的动词和副词中间。

zip one's lip(s) *vi.* keep something secret; promise not to tell what has just been said; shut up 保守秘密,闭嘴:"What I told you is really important, so *zip your lip*!" he said. "我告诉你的事真的很重要,因此你要守口如瓶。"他说道。*Zip your lip* on any politically sensitive issues during your visit there. 在那里访问期间,不得谈论任何政治敏感问题。It would be useless to ask them to *zip their lips*, I think. 我认为,让他们缄口不言可能没用。Why don't you just *zip your lip*? I'm tired of listening to you! 你为什么还不闭嘴? 你的话我都听烦啦!

zone off *vt.* 【可分性动词短语】(常用被动语态形式) make a separate zone of (for example where traffic is restricted) especially in a town or city 把……划为独立专区:The commercial center has now been *zoned off*, private cars are prohibited. 商业中心已划为专门区域,私家车禁止进入该区域。The city government *zoned off* the land for a park. 市政府把这块地划为公园区。

zoom over/past *v.* move very quickly above or past (someone or something) with a loud noise (从……)呼啸而过:Just then, a military plane *zoomed over* the house. 正在那时,一架军用飞机从房顶呼啸而过。A few large birds *zoomed over* the mountain climbers. 几只大鸟在登山者头上掠过。Tom went *zooming past* in his new car. 汤姆开着他的新车飞驰而过。Our train *zoomed past* town after town. 我们所乘坐的列车风驰电掣地驶过一个又一个城镇。

zoom up *vi.* ❶(of a plane) rise quickly (飞机)飞起:With the skilled pilot at its controls, the plane *zoomed up* into the sky, and soon out of sight. 那架飞机在一名技术娴熟的飞行员的操纵下冲上天空,一会儿就不见了踪影。❷(非正式用语) suddenly increase in price, quantity, or size (价格、数量或体积)迅速上涨,迅速增加: The price started at forty pounds, then *zoomed up* to a hundred. 起初的价格是 40 英镑,后来竟猛涨到 100 英镑。China's car exports *zoom up* in the first half of the year. 中国的汽车出口量在今年上半年增长迅速。

新版国际音标发音表

	发 音	例 词
单元音	[iː]	tea three piece receive
	[ɪ]	six picture decide
	[e]	any lesson head bread
	[æ]	hand happy
	[ʌ]	bus come blood trouble
	[ɜː]	girl turn work learn
	[ə]	China today teacher doctor dollar
	[uː]	do food room blue
	[ʊ]	put look foot should
	[ɔː]	small autumn short warm four
	[ɒ]	hot watch
	[ɑː]	car garden class plant
双元音	[eɪ]	name play great rain they
	[aɪ]	bike night my
	[ɔɪ]	boy soil voice
	[əʊ]	go know boat
	[aʊ]	house flower
	[ɪə]	beer near here fierce idea
	[eə]	bear chair there care
	[ʊə]	tour poor sure
半元音	[w]	when window
	[j]	your yellow
舌侧音	[l]	long world